To start, download the free BouncePages app on your smartphone or tablet. Simply search for the BouncePages app in your mobile app store. The app is available for Android and IOS (iPhone®/iPad®).

## Activate your digital course video directly from the page.

To launch the videos look for this icon.

1.  **AIM** the camera so that the page is easily viewable on your screen.
2.  **TAP** the screen to scan the page.
3.  **Bounce** the page to life by clicking the Bounce icon.

ISBN-13: 978-0-328-92512-4
ISBN-10:   0-328-92512-8
19   23

# Miller & Levine Biology

**SAVVAS**

LEARNING COMPANY

## About the Authors

**Kenneth R. Miller** grew up in Rahway, New Jersey, attended the local public schools, and graduated from Rahway High School in 1966. Miller attended Brown University on a scholarship and graduated with honors. He was awarded a National Defense Education Act fellowship for graduate study, and earned his Ph.D. in Biology at the University of Colorado. Miller is professor of Biology at Brown University in Providence, Rhode Island, where he teaches courses in general biology and cell biology. Miller's research specialty is the structure of biological membranes. He has published more than 70 research papers in journals such as *Cell*, *Nature*, and *Scientific American*. He has also written the popular trade books *Finding Darwin's God* and *Only a Theory*. His honors include the Public Service Award from the American Society for Cell Biology, the Distinguished Service Award from the National Association of Biology Teachers, the AAAS Award for Public Engagement with Science, the Stephen Jay Gould Prize from the Society for the Study of Evolution, and the Laetare Medal from Notre Dame University.

Miller lives with his wife, Jody, on a small farm in Rehoboth, Massachusetts. He is the father of two daughters, one a wildlife biologist and the other a high-school history teacher. He swims competitively in the masters' swimming program and umpires high school and NCAA softball.

**Joseph S. Levine** was born in Mount Vernon, New York, attended public schools, and graduated from Mount Vernon High School. He studied at Tufts University, and earned his Ph.D. in biology working between Harvard University and the Marine Biological Laboratory in Woods Hole. His research has been published in scientific journals ranging from *Science* to *Scientific American*, and in several academic books, and his popular scientific writing has appeared in trade books, in magazines such as *Smithsonian* and *Natural History*, and on the web. He has taught lecture and field courses at Boston College and Boston University, and currently teaches Inquiry in Rain Forests, a field-based, graduate-level professional development course for biology teachers through the Organization for Tropical Studies.

Following a fellowship at WGBH-TV, he served as science correspondent for National Public Radio, and as scientific advisor to NOVA for programs including *Judgment Day*, for OMNI-MAX films including *Coral Reef Adventure*, and for the PBS series *The Secret of Life* and *The Evolution Project*. He has designed exhibit programs for state aquaria in Texas, New Jersey, and Florida, and has led seminars and professional development workshops for teachers across the United States, Mexico, Puerto Rico, the US. Virgin Islands, Indonesia, and Malaysia, as well as Singapore—where he served as "Outstanding Educator in Residence" for the Ministry of Education. He serves on the MBL Council at the Marine Biological Laboratory in Woods Hole, on the Board of Visitors of the Organization for Tropical Studies, and on the Board of Directors of the Museum Institute for Teaching Science.

Levine and his family live in Concord, Massachusetts, a short distance from the Old North Bridge, where the first shots of the American Revolution were fired, and only slightly farther from Thoreau's Walden Pond.

## Carol Baker

### Science Curriculum

Dr. Carol K. Baker is superintendent for Lyons Elementary K-8 School District in Lyons, Illinois. Prior to this, she was Director of Curriculum for Science and Music in Oak Lawn, Illinois. Before this she taught Physics and Earth Science for 18 years. In the recent past, Dr. Baker also wrote assessment questions for ACT (EXPLORE and PLAN), was elected president of the Illinois Science Teachers Association from 2011–2013 and served as a member of the Museum of Science and Industry in Chicago advisory boards. Dr. Baker received her BS in Physics and a science teaching certification. She completed her masters of Educational Administration (K-12) and earned her doctorate in Educational Leadership.

## Jim Cummins

### ELL

Dr. Cummins's research focuses on literacy development in multilingual schools and the role technology plays in learning across the curriculum. *Miller Levine Biology* incorporates research-based principles for integrating language with the teaching of academic content based on Dr. Cummins's work.

## Elfrieda Hiebert

### Literacy

Dr. Hiebert is the President and CEO of TextProject, a non-profit aimed at providing open-access resources for instruction of beginning and struggling readers, and a former primary school teacher. She is also a research associate at the University of California Santa Cruz. Her research addresses how fluency, vocabulary, and knowledge can be fostered through appropriate texts, and her contributions have been recognized through awards such as the Oscar Causey Award for Outstanding Contributions to Reading Research (Literacy Research Association, 2015), Research to Practice award (American Educational Research Association, 2013), and the William S. Gray Citation of Merit Award for Outstanding Contributions to Reading Research (International Reading Association, 2008).

## Content Reviewers

**J. David Archibald, PhD**
Professor Emeritus of Biology
College of Sciences
San Diego State University
San Diego, CA

**Darleen A. DeMason, PhD**
Professor Emerita of Botany
Department of Botany and
Sciences
University of California,
Riverside
Riverside, CA

**Elizabeth A. De Stasio PhD**
Raymond H. Herzog Professor
of Science
Biology Department
Lawrence University
Appleton, WI

**Katherine Glew, PhD**
Curatorial Associate, Lichen
Collection
Herbarium Department
University of Washington
Seattle, WA

**Donald C. Jackson**
Professor Emeritus of
Medical Science, Adjunct
Professor of Molecular
Pharmacology, Physiology,
and Biotechnology
Department of Molecular
Pharmacology, Physiology,
and Biotechnology
Brown University
Providence, RI

**Jeremiah N. Jarret, PhD**
Professor of Biology
Biology Department
Central Conneticut State
University
New Britain, CT

**Janet Lanza, PhD**
Professor Emeritus of Biology
Biology Department
University of Arkansas, Little
Rock
Little Rock, AR

**David E. Lemke, PhD**
Professor of Biology
Biology Department
Southwest Texas State
University
San Marcos, TX

**Martha Newsome, PhD**
Adjunct Instructor of Biology
Biology Department
Lone Star College
Tomball, TX

**Martin K. Nickels, PhD**
Adjunct Professor of
Anthropology
Department of Sociology and
Anthropology
Illinois State University
Bloomington, IL

**Jan Pechenick, PhD**
Professor of Invertebrate
Zoology and Marine Biology
Biology Department
Tufts University
Medford, MA

**Edward J. Zalisko, PhD**
Professor of Biology
Biology Department
Blackburn College
Carlinville, IL

## Lab Testers

**Dr. Jack Breazeale**
Adjunct Professor of Chemistry
College of Charleston
Charleston, SC

**Ruth Hathaway**
Cape Girardeau, MO

**Andria McElvain**
High School Science Teacher
Blue Eagle Academy
Clover, SC

**Henry Ramsey**
Adjunct Instructor
Lamar State College—Orange
Orange, TX

## High-School Reviewers

**Alaaddin Akgu**
Mandarin Campus Principal
River City Science Academy
Jacksonville, FL

**Erica Everett**
Science Department Chair
Science Department
Manchester-Essex Regional
High School
Manchester, MA

**Noreen Fiske**
Biology and Honors
Biology Teacher
Science Department
Lead Teacher
Nature Coast Technical
High School
Brooksville, FL

**Heather M. Gannon**
Biology Teacher
Science Department
Elisabeth Ann Johnson High
School
Grand Blanc, MI

**Virginia Glassock**
Science Department Chair/
Teacher
Science Department
California High School
Whittier, CA

**Ruth Gleicher**
Biology Teacher
Science Department
Niles West High School
Skokie, IL

**Lance Goodlock**
Science Department Chair/
Teacher
Science Department
Sturgis High School
Sturgis, MI

**Lisa Keen**
Science Department Chair/
Teacher
Science Department
Harpeth Hall School
Nashville, TN

**David Kerins**
Biology Teacher/Academic
Facilitator
Science Department
Gateway High School
Westminster, MD

**Michelle L. Odierna**
Biology Teacher
Science Department
Hopkinton High School
Hopkinton, MA

**Nicole Perkins**
Science Teacher
Queen Creek High School
Queen Creek, AZ

**Cynthia L. Perouty**
Biology Teacher
Science Department
Century High School
Sykesville, MD

**Jennifer T. Perry**
Biology Teacher
Upper School Science
Harpeth Hall School
Nashville, TN

**Tina Rowe**
Biology Teacher
Science Department
Westminster High School
Westminster, MD

**Kim Saltsburg**
Biology Teacher
Science Department
Westminster High School
Westminster, MD

**Gary Schott**
Biology Teacher
Science Department
Harpeth Hall School
Nashville, TN

**Stephen David Wright**
Biology Teacher
Science Department
Sherwood High School
Sand Springs, MD

# Explore Your World

Biology is all around you. In *Miller & Levine Biology*, you are directly engaged in real-world problem solving, analysis, and critical thinking. **Authentic Case Studies** drive inquiry-based learning. Dig into interesting biology phenomena and understand core scientific concepts as you learn about real-life issues in your community—just as scientists do every day.

## Identify Real Problems

**CASE STUDY**

## What's to blame for the bloom?

Green slime. Toxic muck. Tourist-repelling, fish-killing scum. Guacamole-thick sludg These are just a few of the more polite words that Florida residents were speaking ing the summer of 2016. They were describing a huge algal bloom that spread acr the waters of the state. An algal bloom is a sudden, rapid growth of algae in a bod water. In severe blooms, the surface of the water may look like an ugly green carp worse, some blooms release poison into the water.

The Florida bloom of 2016 started in Lake Okeechobee in the southern part of the state. Then the bloom spread both eastward and westward along rivers and into coastal areas. The thick, poisonous floating mats of algae were so large that they could be seen from space. They fouled beaches and marinas, and they killed fish.

Mild algal blooms occur naturally in lakes, Some small

In the same year when Florida wa: a huge algal bloom spread along the of China. One year earlier, the west c the United States suffered the bigges widespread algal bloom ever recorde bloom stretched from the Channel Isl California, north to Oregon and Wash and all the way to the Alaska Peninsul event shut down the fish and shellfish tries, causing losses of millions of doll Algal blooms are also striking Lak a year. In 2016

An authentic **Case Study** begins each chapter to:

- Provide an example of biology in the real world
- Connect to chapter concepts
- Make biology relevant

The **Case Study** is revisited throughout the chapter to:

- Connect related activities, visual features, and labs together for greater comprehension
- Include concept assessment in lesson review
- Unify biology concepts around a single story, making them easier to understand

**CASE STUDY**  Analyzing Data

### Trace Elements

Just four elements: oxygen, carbon, hydrogen, and nitrogen make up 96 percent of living things. The table shows the percentages of some other elements.

1. **Construct an Explanation** Is the importance of an element in the body related to its percentage of body weight? Cite the evidence in the table to support your explanation.
2. **Evaluate Claims** A student claims that the four types of macromolecules make up all of the important compounds of the human body. Provide evidence and reasoning to support or refute this claim.

| Element | Percentage of Body Weight | Uses |
|---|---|---|
| Phosphorus | 1.0 | Bones, nucleic acids |
| Potassium | 0.25 | Regulating nerve function |
| Sulfur | 0.25 | Two amino acids |
| Sodium | 0.15 | Regulating nerve function, blood levels |
| Chlorine | 0.15 | Fluid balance |
| Magnesium | 0.05 | Bone and muscle function |
| Iron | 0.006 | Carrying oxygen in the blood |

Other trace elements include fluorine, copper, zinc, and iodine.

# Understand Evidence

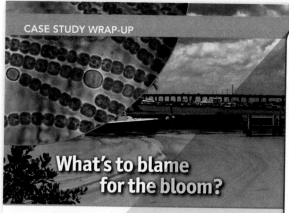

**CASE STUDY WRAP-UP**

## What's to blame for the bloom?

Several factors are causing rapidly-spreading, severe algal blooms. Global climate change is one of the factors.

### Make Your Case

As you have read, algal blooms form when excess nitrogen enters the water. Yet changes in Earth's climate are affecting how and when blooms form. In 2016, Florida experienced unusually heavy winter rains. Runoff washed fertilizer from farms into Lake Okeechobee. When the lake water swelled and threatened surrounding lands, engineers diverted the fertilizer-rich water into rivers. As for the bloom that occurred on the U.S. west coast that year, it likely was caused by unusually warm temperatures in the eastern Pacific Ocean.

### Develop a Solution

1. Construct an Explanation How can human activities contribute to algal blooms? Use the algal blooms of 2016 as an example.
2. Engage in Argument What actions could be taken in Florida, California, or elsewhere to prevent severe algal blooms? Would the benefits of these actions be worth the costs? Conduct research and cite evidence to help support your argument.

### Make Your Case

As you have read, algal blooms form when excess nitrogen enters the water. Yet changes in Earth's climate are affecting how and when blooms form. In 2016, Florida experienced unusually heavy winter rains. Runoff washed fertilizer from farms into Lake Okeechobee. When the lake water swelled and threatened surrounding lands, engineers diverted the fertilizer-rich water into rivers. As for the bloom that occurred on the U.S. west coast that year, it likely was caused by unusually warm temperatures in the eastern Pacific Ocean.

### Develop a Solution

1. Construct an Explanation How can human activities contribute to algal blooms? Use the algal blooms of 2016 as an example.
2. Engage in Argument What actions could be taken in Florida, California, or elsewhere to prevent severe algal blooms? Would the benefits of these actions be worth the costs? Conduct research and cite evidence to help support your argument.

The **Make Your Case** feature lets you:

- Conduct investigations around the case as you progress throughout the chapter
- Analyze evidence and present data to support your claim
- Construct solutions to solve the problem

# Go Beyond the Classroom

## Technology on the Case

### Turning Waste Into a Solution

Thick, brown sludge. Clogged pipes. If you t͟ that's a problem, you would be correct. But turns out it can also be a solution.

Wastewater from homes, businesses, and even farms often ends up in wastewater trea͟ ment plants. These plants process wastewa͟ so that the water can be returned safely to ͟ environment. Wastewater contains much m͟ than just water, including food, feces, dirt, soaps, and industrial chemicals.

One of the challenges of treating wastew͟ ter is to remove the limiting nutrients, such ͟ phosphorus and nitrogen. If the nutrients ar͟ not removed, then they may end up in our l͟ and streams. One way that scientists and e͟ neers are working to make wastewater treat͟ plants more efficient at removing phosphor͟ by harnessing a chemical called struvite. St͟ itself is a problem for wastewater treatment͟ plants because it accumulates on the walls ͟

## Careers on the Case

### Work Towards a Solution

Algal blooms are only one way that bodies of water can be harmed. People in many careers help keep aquatic ecosystems healthy and the water safe for human use.

### Water Quality Technician

Bodies of water can be fouled by tiny living things, like bacteria and algae. The water can also contain toxic elements or other harmful chemicals. The job of the water quality technician is to test water supplies to make sure they meet environmental standards.

▶ **VIDEO**

Watch this video to learn about other careers in biology.

The **College and Careers** features enable you to:

- Experience first-hand accounts from biology professionals in the field in the Scientists at Work Career Videos
- Learn about science-related career paths
- Discover how scientists use technology to make an impact

# Build Your Success

Everyone studies differently. *Miller & Levine Biology* lets you "experience" science and master biology class. **Visuals, interactivity,** and **built-in point-of-use support** helps you unpack information, ask the right questions, build understanding, and stay interested.

## Get the Big Picture

**Reading Support**

The Biology Foundations: Reading and Study Guide Workbook

- Helps build science literacy and improve your abilities to read complex scientific text
- Includes interactive learning experiences with exercises to reinforce topics
- Improve skills at reading scientific charts, tables, and graphs

**KEY QUESTIONS**

**READING CHECK**

**Margin Support**
- **Key Questions** identify core topics
- **Reading Checks** ensure you understand concepts before you move on
- Highlighted **vocabulary** and in-text definitions make content easier to digest.

**The Nucleus** In the same way that the main office controls a large factory, the nucleus is the control center of the cell. ⚷ The *nucleus contains nearly all the cell's DNA and, with it, the coded instructions for making proteins and other important molecules.* Only eukaryotic cells have a nucleus. In prokaryotic cells, DNA is found in the cytoplasm.

The nucleus, shown in **Figure 8-7**, is surrounded by a nuclear _____. The nuclear envelope is _____

Visual Analogy
Figure 8-6
**The Cell as a Factory**

Specialized machines enable a factory to function. Similarly, specialized structures in a cell enable a cell to carry out the processes of life.

**Visual Analogies**

- Use familiar real-world issues to maximize understanding
- Provide a different perspective to enhance lesson content
- Include dynamic photos, engaging illustrations, and clearly constructed tables and graphs

# Prepare for Quizzes and Tests

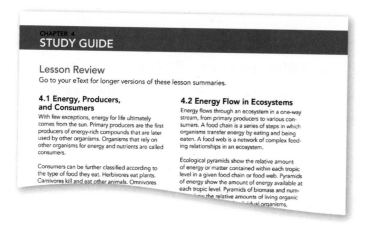

CHAPTER 4
STUDY GUIDE

Lesson Review
Go to your eText for longer versions of these lesson summaries.

4.1 Energy, Producers, and Consumers
With few exceptions, energy for life ultimately comes from the sun. Primary producers are the first producers of energy-rich compounds that are later used by other organisms. Organisms that rely on other organisms for energy and nutrients are called consumers.

Consumers can be further classified according to the type of food they eat. Herbivores eat plants. Carnivores kill and eat other animals. Omnivores

4.2 Energy Flow in Ecosystems
Energy flows through an ecosystem in a one-way stream, from primary producers to various consumers. A food chain is a series of steps in which organisms transfer energy by eating and being eaten. A food web is a network of complex feeding relationships in an ecosystem.

Ecological pyramids show the relative amount of energy or matter contained within each trophic level in a given food chain or food web. Pyramids of energy show the amount of energy available at each trophic level. Pyramids of biomass and num-

## Study Guide

- Includes lesson summaries, vocabulary, and visual support
- Enables you to study the relationships between chapter concepts using graphic organizers
- Receive additional study support online in Savvas Realize™

## Performance-Based Assessments

- Demonstrate mastery of the chapter concepts with authentic assessments of STEM learning
- Practice scientific inquiry by evaluating solutions, constructing arguments and analyzing data
- STEM, Science, or Engineering focus ties into new standards

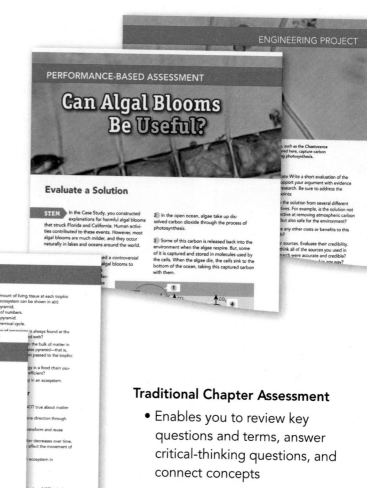

ENGINEERING PROJECT

PERFORMANCE-BASED ASSESSMENT

## Can Algal Blooms Be Useful?

### Evaluate a Solution

**STEM** In the Case Study, you constructed explanations for harmful algal blooms that struck Florida and California. Human activities contributed to these events. However, most algal blooms are much milder, and they occur naturally in lakes and oceans around the world.

2. In the open ocean, algae take up dissolved carbon dioxide through the process of photosynthesis.

3. Some of this carbon is released back into the environment when the algae respire. But, some of it is captured and stored in molecules used by the cells. When the algae die, the cells sink to the bottom of the ocean, taking this captured carbon with them.

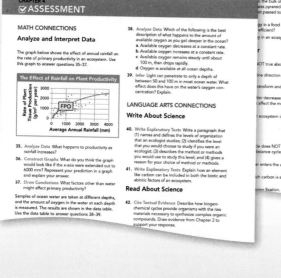

CHAPTER 4
ASSESSMENT

KEY QUESTIONS AND TERMS

4.1 Energy, Producers, and Consumers

1. Primary producers are organisms that

7. The total amount of living tissue at each trophic level in an ecosystem can be shown in a(n)
a. energy pyramid.
b. pyramid of numbers.
c. biomass pyramid.
d. biogeochemical cycle.

CHAPTER 4
ASSESSMENT

MATH CONNECTIONS

Analyze and Interpret Data

The graph below shows the effect of annual rainfall on the rate of primary productivity in an ecosystem. Use this graph to answer questions 35-37.

The Effect of Rainfall on Plant Productivity

Rate of Plant Tissue Production (g/m² per year)
3000
2000
1000
FPO
0
0   1000  2000  3000  4000
Average Annual Rainfall (mm)

35. Analyze Data What happens to productivity as rainfall increases?

36. Construct Graphs What do you think the graph would look like if the x-axis were extended out to 6000 mm? Represent your prediction in a graph and explain your answer.

37. Draw Conclusions What factors other than water might affect primary productivity?

Samples of ocean water are taken at different depths, and the amount of oxygen in the water at each depth is measured. The results are shown in the data table. Use the data table to answer questions 38-39.

38. Analyze Data Which of the following is the best description of what happens to the amount of available oxygen as you get deeper in the ocean?
a. Available oxygen decreases at a constant rate.
b. Available oxygen increases at a constant rate.
c. Available oxygen remains steady until about 100 m, then drops rapidly.
d. Oxygen is available at all ocean depths.

39. Infer Light can penetrate to only a depth of between 50 and 100 m in most ocean water. What effect does this have on the water's oxygen concentration? Explain.

LANGUAGE ARTS CONNECTIONS

Write About Science

40. Write Explanatory Texts Write a paragraph that (1) names and defines the levels of organization that an ecologist studies; (2) identifies the level that you would choose to study if you were an ecologist; (3) describes the method or methods you would use to study this level; and (4) gives a reason for your choice of method or methods.

41. Write Explanatory Texts Explain how an element like carbon can be included in both the biotic and abiotic factors of an ecosystem.

Read About Science

42. Cite Textual Evidence Describe how biogeochemical cycles provide organisms with the raw materials necessary to synthesize complex organic compounds. Draw evidence from Chapter 2 to support your response.

## Traditional Chapter Assessment

- Enables you to review key questions and terms, answer critical-thinking questions, and connect concepts
- Features **interdisciplinary Math and ELA sections**
- Includes **Standardized Test Prep**

# Experience Science Phenomena

Biology extends beyond the textbook. Your *Miller and Levine Biology* program features tools that allow you to experience science first hand. Immerse yourself in an active learning environment with hands-on and virtual labs, STEM activities, research projects, and more!

## Problem-Based Learning

**Problem-based learning (PBL)** poses a complex challenge that requires asking questions, making choices, and finding resources. The Problem-Based Learning Strand introduced in the unit opener is just one way this program engages you in the practice and language of science. Throughout the unit you will:

- Complete a path of activities, STEM projects, labs, authentic readings, and scientific research to develop a solution to the problem
- Record and evaluate findings in your *Digital Explorer's Journal: Problem Based Learning Workbook*
- Hone your Science and Engineering skills throughout the unit as you solve the problem

**Digital Explorer's Journal**
The Explorer's Journal: Problem-Based Learning Workbook is the ultimate tool for navigating the Problem-Based Learning activities.

- Take notes, answer questions, track your progress, and evaluate your work
- Answer prompts and questions to help extract the information you need from each activity in the path
- Record data and develop your own conclusion

# Inquiry-Focused Labs

Labs that are Guided, Open-Ended, or Argument-Driven enhance your biology course.

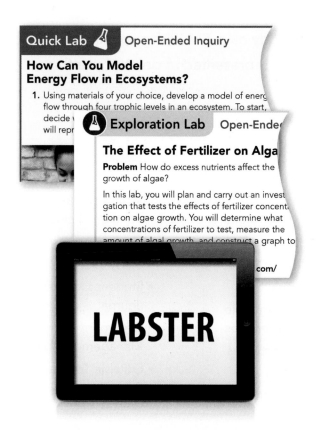

## Quick Labs

- Interact with chapter concepts
- Focus on science and engineering practices
- Complete in a short period of time

## Chapter Labs

- Conduct in-depth laboratory investigations
- Make models, study local science issues, and complete experiments while strengthening inquiry skills
- Customize labs to fit every classroom

## Virtual Labs

- Simulate the classroom lab experience in an enhanced environment
- Labs are based on real-life case stories and equipment to highlight the connection between science and the real-world
- Render safety concerns and cleanup obsolete

# Science and Engineering Activities

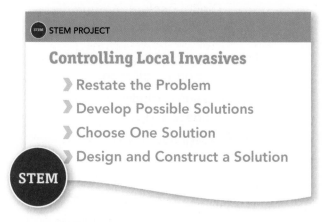

## STEM Projects

- Support Active Learning
- Mimic actions of real-world scientists
- Feature integrated science and engineering practices

## Analyzing Data

- Uses real data, often featuring graphs and tables
- Hones science and engineering skills
- Connects science to your math classes

# Online Support Enhances the Learning Experience

*Miller and Levine Biology* combines the best biology narrative with a robust online program. Throughout the lessons, digital support is presented at point of use to enhance your learning experience.

## Online Resources

**Savvas Realize™** is your biology class online. This robust digital learning environment includes:

- Student eText
- Teacher Edition eText
- Virtual Labs
- Customizable Chapter Labs
- Interactivities
- Videos
- Animations
- Flexible Assessments
- Study tools
- Student Explorer's Journal
- Classroom Management Tools
- Editable Teacher Resources

## Digital Features

- ▶ VIDEO
- ◀)) AUDIO
- 👆 INTERACTIVITY
- 📖 ETEXT
- 👁 ANIMATION
- VIRTUAL LABS
- ☑ ASSESSMENT

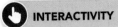

**INTERACTIVITY**

Watch an interactive video on the cycling of matter and flow of energy in ecosystems.

**Interactivity**

- Online assets require student interactions through prompts or question
- Variety of options including digital art, art review, videos and vocabulary cards
- Located throughout the narrative to enhance explanations

Keep an eye out for these **icons** which show you different ways your textbook is enhanced online.

**Student Components List:**

- Student Edition
- Student Edition eText
- Biology Foundations: Reading and Study Guide Workbook
- Digital Explorer's Journal: Problem-Based Learning Workbook
- Savvas Realize™

# UNIT 2 Ecology

Go Online to access your digital course.

Go Online to access your digital course.

Go Online to access your digital course.

>> **PROBLEM-BASED LEARNING** Power From Pond Scum

Go Online to access your digital course.

Go Online to access your digital course.

**PROBLEM-BASED LEARNING** Genetic Modification of Animals

Go Online to access your digital course.

Go Online to access your digital course.

Go Online to access your digital course.

Go Online to access your digital course.

Go Online to access your digital course.

>> **PROBLEM-BASED LEARNING** Fossilized Evidence of Life Long Ago

Go Online to access your digital course.

Go Online to access your digital course.

Go Online to access your
digital course.

Go Online to access your
digital course.

# Diversity of Life

Go Online to access your digital course.

Go Online to access your digital course.

# LABS AND ACTIVITIES

**Chapter Labs**

# Standards at a Glance

The *Miller and Levine Biology* program provides comprehensive coverage and assessment of the Next Generation Science Standards. As you read through the chapters and complete the activities and assessment you will see code references to these standards. Each standard is written as a performance expectation that integrates three dimensions: science and engineering practices (SEP), disciplinary core ideas (DCI), and crosscutting concepts (CCC). This blending of practices for *doing* science, content for *knowing* science, and themes for *connecting* science is what makes the Next Generation Science Standards a unique shift in science education.

## Life Science

| Code | Performance Expectation |
|------|-------------------------|
| **HS-LS1 From Molecules to Organisms: Structure and Processes** | |
| HS-LS1-1 | Construct an explanation based on evidence for how the structure of DNA determines the structure of proteins which carry out the essential functions of life through systems of specialized cells. |
| HS-LS1-2 | Develop and use a model to illustrate the hierarchical organization of interacting systems that provide specific functions within multicellular organisms. |
| HS-LS1-3 | Plan and conduct an investigation to provide evidence that feedback mechanisms maintain homeostasis. |
| HS-LS1-4 | Use a model to illustrate the role of cellular division (mitosis) and differentiation in producing and maintaining complex organisms. |
| HS-LS1-5 | Use a model to illustrate how photosynthesis transforms light energy into stored chemical energy. |
| HS-LS1-6 | Construct and revise an explanation based on evidence for how carbon, hydrogen, and oxygen from sugar molecules may combine with other elements to form amino acids and/or other large carbon-based molecules. |
| HS-LS1-7 | Use a model to illustrate that cellular respiration is a chemical process whereby the bonds of food molecules and oxygen molecules are broken and the bonds in new compounds are formed resulting in a net transfer of energy. |
| **HS-LS2 Ecosystems: Interactions, Energy, and Dynamics** | |
| HS-LS2-1 | Use mathematical and/or computational representations to support explanations of factors that affect carrying capacity of ecosystems at different scales. |
| HS-LS2-2 | Use mathematical representations to support and revise explanations based on evidence about factors affecting biodiversity and populations in ecosystems of different scales. |

| HS-LS2-3 | Construct and revise an explanation based on evidence for the cycling of matter and flow of energy in aerobic and anaerobic conditions. |
|---|---|
| HS-LS2-4 | Use mathematical representations to support claims for the cycling of matter and flow of energy among organisms in an ecosystem. |
| HS-LS2-5 | Develop a model to illustrate the role of photosynthesis and cellular respiration in the cycling of carbon among the biosphere, atmosphere, hydrosphere, and geosphere. |
| HS-LS2-6 | Evaluate the claims, evidence, and reasoning that the complex interactions in ecosystems maintain relatively consistent numbers and types of organisms in stable conditions, but changing conditions may result in a new ecosystem. |
| HS-LS2-7 | Design, evaluate, and refine a solution for reducing the impacts of human activities on the environment and biodiversity.* |
| HS-LS2-8 | Evaluate the evidence for the role of group behavior on individual and species' chances to survive and reproduce. |

## HS-LS3 Heredity: Inheritance and Variation

| HS-LS3-1 | Ask questions to clarify relationships about the role of DNA and chromosomes in coding the instructions for characteristic traits passed from parents to offspring. |
|---|---|
| HS-LS3-2 | Make and defend a claim based on evidence that inheritable genetic variations may result from: (1) new genetic combinations through meiosis, (2) viable errors occurring during replication, and/or (3) mutations caused by environmental factors. |
| HS-LS3-3 | Apply concepts of statistics and probability to explain the variation and distribution of expressed traits in a population. |

## HS-LS4 Biological Evolution: Unity and Diversity

| HS-LS4-1 | Communicate scientific information that common ancestry and biological evolution are supported by multiple lines of empirical evidence. |
|---|---|
| HS-LS4-2 | Construct an explanation based on evidence that the process of evolution primarily results from four factors: (1) the potential for a species to increase in number, (2) the heritable genetic variation of individuals in a species due to mutation and sexual reproduction, (3) competition for limited resources, and (4) the proliferation of those organisms that are better able to survive and reproduce in the environment. |
| HS-LS4-3 | Apply concepts of statistics and probability to support explanations that organisms with an advantageous heritable trait tend to increase in proportion to organisms lacking this trait. |
| HS-LS4-4 | Construct an explanation based on evidence for how natural selection leads to adaptation of populations. |
| HS-LS4-5 | Evaluate the evidence supporting claims that changes in environmental conditions may result in: (1) increases in the number of individuals of some species, (2) the emergence of new species over time, and (3) the extinction of other species. |
| HS-LS4-6 | Create or revise a simulation to test a solution to mitigate adverse impacts of human activity on biodiversity.* |

## Engineering Design

| Code | Performance Expectation |
|---|---|
| HS-ETS1-1 | Analyze a major global challenge to specify qualitative and quantitative criteria and constraints for solutions that account for societal needs and wants. |
| HS-ETS1-2 | Design a solution to a complex real-world problem by breaking it down into smaller, more manageable problems that can be solved through engineering. |
| HS-ETS1-3 | Evaluate a solution to a complex real-world problem based on prioritized criteria and trade-offs that account for a range of constraints, including cost, safety, reliability, and aesthetics, as well as possible social, cultural, and environmental impacts. |
| HS-ETS1-4 | Use a computer simulation to model the impact of proposed solutions to a complex real-world problem with numerous criteria and constraints on interactions within and between systems relevant to the problem. |

## Earth Science

| Code | Performance Expectation |
|---|---|
| HS-ESS2-4 | Use a model to describe how variations in the flow of energy into and out of Earth's systems result in changes in climate. |
| HS-ESS2-6 | Develop a quantitative model to describe the cycling of carbon among the hydrosphere, atmosphere, geosphere, and biosphere. |
| HS-ESS3-3 | Create a computational simulation to illustrate the relationships among management of natural resources, the sustainability of human populations, and biodiversity. |
| HS-ESS3-4 | Evaluate or refine a technological solution that reduces impacts of human activities on natural systems.* |
| HS-ESS3-5 | Analyze geoscience data and the results from global climate models to make an evidence-based forecast of the current rate of global or regional climate change and associated future impacts to Earth systems. |
| HS-ESS3-6 | Use a computational representation to illustrate the relationships among Earth systems and how those relationships are being modified due to human activity. |

Dear Student,

Biology is one of the subjects you're going to study this year, but I hope you'll realize from the very first pages of this book that biology is a lot more than just a "subject." Biology is what makes an eagle fly, a flower bloom, or a caterpillar turn into a butterfly. It's the study of ourselves—of how our bodies grow and change and respond to the outside world, and it's the study of our planet, a world transformed by the actions of living things. Of course, you might have known some of this already. But there's something more—you might call it a "secret" that makes biology unique.

That secret is that you've come along at just the right time. In all of human history, there has never been a moment like the present, a time when we stood so close to the threshold of answering the most fundamental questions about the nature of life. You belong to the first generation of students who can read the human genome almost as your parents might have read a book or a newspaper. You are the first students who will grow up in a world that has a chance to use that information for the benefit of humanity, and you are the very first to bear the burden of using that knowledge wisely.

If all of this seems like heavy stuff, it is. But there is another reason why we wrote this book, and we hope that is not a secret at all. Science is fun! Biologists aren't a bunch of serious, grim-faced, middle-aged folks in lab coats who think of nothing but work. In fact, most of the people we know in science would tell you honestly, with broad grins on their faces, that they have the best jobs in the world. They would say there's nothing that compares to the excitement of doing scientific work, and that the beauty and variety of life make every day a new adventure.

We agree, and we hope that you'll keep something in mind as you begin the study of biology. You don't need a lab coat or a degree or a laboratory to be a scientist. What you do need is an inquiring mind, the patience to look at nature carefully, and the willingness to figure things out. We've filled this book with some of the latest and most important discoveries about living things, but we hope we've also filled it with something else: our wonder, our amazement, and our sheer delight in the variety of life itself. Come on in, and enjoy the journey!

Sincerely,

Ken Miller

Dear Student,

"NO! I won't get the flu shot!"

The words screamed at me from my computer screen. I'd been web surfing for information on influenza vaccinations, and many hits led to anti-vaccination rants from public figures and "celebrities."

I was shocked, because I know how profoundly vaccines have improved our lives. Ken and I are (just) old enough to remember life before the polio vaccine. A cousin of mine, just a few years my senior, limped all his life because of childhood polio. And he was a "lucky" polio patient. Thousands suffered body-wide paralysis, and many died. Then, the development and widespread use of polio vaccine virtually eliminated the disease. Waves of wonder and relief swept over our generation. You and your parents never needed to worry about it.

And that's just one success story. Biomedical research, including development of new vaccines, is just one reason biology is more exciting, and more important to daily life today than it has ever been. And it's only going to get more important to you and to society during your lifetime. That's why it is important to study biology. It is important to learn the information that can protect personal and public health. But at a deeper level, it is important to understand what science is, how it works, and how you can use scientific information in making personal decisions.

Ken and I wrote this book because we love biology … in part because, properly applied, it helps improve the human condition. We want you to really understand biology—which means more than just memorizing "facts." We don't deny that this book contains lots of specific information. But we've worked hard to put that information together in ways that will help you understand why that information is important. We hope that no matter where you start off in your knowledge of biology, this book will open your eyes to an exciting, fascinating, and important world—our world, your world, of life.

Sincerely,

*Joe Levine*

# UNIT 1 The Nature of Life

## CHAPTER 1
The Science
of Biology

## CHAPTER 2
The Chemistry
of Life

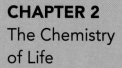

**❯❯ Crosscutting Concepts** Science is humanity's most important way to gather information about the natural world, analyze that information, and apply it to inform the way we live with each other, with other living things, and with the planet that is home to us all. Scientific methodology includes a rich and varied set of tools and approaches that can be adapted for different areas of study. In both the living and nonliving parts of our world, energy and matter interact in predictable ways that help us understand how life works.

**BOUNCE TO ACTIVATE**

▶ **VIDEO**

Author Joe Levine talks about seeing the world as a scientist by asking questions.

# SOLVING LOCAL AND GLOBAL
# Water Scarcity

## For many people, getting

clean, fresh water to drink is not as easy as turning on the faucet. In fact, more than 40 percent of humans are affected by water scarcity, or the lack of clean, fresh water to meet their needs. So, how do we solve this problem? Scientists are investigating many options, such as figuring out how to efficiently remove the salt from sea water. But, on a small, local level, one solution that may help is a solar still. A solar still uses the energy of sunlight to distill clean water from salty or polluted water. Although the energy source is free, many solar stills are costly and inefficient. In this activity, you will design and build your own solar still.

**PROBLEM LAUNCH**
Conduct research on global water scarcity and potential solutions.

▶ **VIDEO**

ⓑ **BOUNCE TO ACTIVATE**

Watch a video about water scarcity and what technologies could help with this problem.

## PROBLEM: How can you make fresh water from salt water?

➤➤ **TO SOLVE THIS PROBLEM, perform these activities as they come up in the unit, and record your findings in your 📓 Explorer's Journal.**

## AUTHENTIC READING

Read about scientists who have designed a new, inexpensive technology that can distill water.

## STEM PROJECT

Design and build a solar still using the engineering design process. You will define the problem, identify criteria and constraints, choose your materials, and then build a working still.

## INTERACTIVITY

Manipulate variables to optimize the output of a solar still.

## STEM PROJECT LAB

Test the efficacy of your solar still by measuring output as well as the salinity of the distillate.

## PROBLEM WRAP-UP

Present your solar still design as well as the data on its efficacy.

**1.1**
What Is Science?

**1.2**
Science in Context

**1.3**
Patterns of Life

**Go Online to
access your
digital course.**

▶ **VIDEO**

🔊 **AUDIO**

👆 **INTERACTIVITY**

📖 **eTEXT**

👁 **ANIMATION**

🧪 **VIRTUAL LAB**

☑ **ASSESSMENT**

Hydroponic plants
on the International
Space Station

**HS-ETS1-2, HS-ETS1-3, HS-ESS3-4**

Cucumber
*Cucumis sativus*

# Biology and technology solve problems

Biology is the science of life, the study of everything from molecules within living cells to the effects of human activity on our planet. Biological knowledge can be combined with technology to solve challenges, such as supplying fresh greens, fruits, and vegetables to researchers in the Antarctic in the dead of the long, dark frozen winter.

The continent of Antarctica has an average annual temperature of −57°C (−70.6°F), and no sunlight at all for months. During winter, weather is so extreme that researchers must be completely self-sufficient for at least 4 months—because no supply flights dare to reach the station except in life-or-death emergencies. In most places, any soil that might exist is buried beneath thick layers of ice and snow. And visitors must be careful not to introduce diseases or insects into the biologically pristine environment.

Yet, for nutritional reasons, scientists stationed at those stations need at least some fresh produce in their diet. For psychological reasons, it's also helpful to have a little light and warmth in their lives. How might biological knowledge and technology work together under these conditions? The answer is hydroponics.

As you probably know, most edible plants normally grow in soil where roots anchor the plants, and take up water and nutrients. During the 1600s, scientists began trying to grow plants in water. They soon learned that plants grow better in water from natural sources, such as ponds or rivers, than in pure water. Later, they identified specific minerals that plants need to thrive. And by the early twentieth century, researchers successfully raised crop plants in tanks of water enriched with those nutrients.

Today, advanced hydroponic techniques, including use of intense artificial light, enable the crews of Antarctic research stations to grow their own fresh fruits and vegetables. Much of the research that developed those techniques was sponsored by NASA (National Aeronautics and Space Agency), because hydroponics could provide fresh food for astronauts on space missions, or for colonists on Mars. In a more down-to-earth context, some produce you buy in supermarkets—including some lettuce and tomatoes—is already grown hydroponically!

In theory, all you need to grow hydroponic plants is a container of water with the right nutrients, along with light and warm temperatures. But during the long Antarctic winter, there is virtually no sunlight available at all! So providing the right kind and intensity of artificial light is essential—as it would be in space.

What steps did biologists and engineers take to develop modern hydroponic techniques? What other examples can you think of where biology and technology were used to solve a problem?

**Throughout this chapter, look for connections to the CASE STUDY to help you answer these questions.**

# What Is Science?

## VOCABULARY

observation
inference
hypothesis
controlled experiment
independent variable
dependent variable
control group
data
theory

### READING TOOL

List in order the parts of a typical experiment that uses scientific methodology. Use the headings in your text as a guide to fill in the chart in your  Biology Foundations Workbook.

Humans have wondered about their place in the cosmos since the earliest time. How do we fit into the grand scheme of nature? How much power do we hold over nature? What are the limits to our abilities? These and other questions are more relevant today than ever before. This chapter begins our effort to show you how science tries to answer those questions.

## What Science Is and Is Not

This book will help you understand how biologists try to make sense of nature. These pages are filled with many scientific "facts" and ideas. But one of the first things you should understand is that scientific knowledge is always changing. Some "facts" and ideas you'll find here may have changed since this text was written, and others will change soon. Why? Because scientists are constantly testing, debating, and revising scientific explanations of events in the natural world. That constant testing and revising helps explain why scientists don't "believe" in scientific facts or ideas. Scientists either understand and accept a particular scientific explanation of the natural world, or they reject that explanation. But if science is not a list of unchanging facts and beliefs, what is it?

**The Nature of Science** The term *science* is usually defined as the use of evidence to construct testable explanations and predictions of natural phenomena, as well as the knowledge generated through this process. Most importantly, science is a process—an organized way of observing and asking questions about the natural world, developing those questions into testable explanations, and gathering and analyzing data that support or reject those explanations. The word *science* can also refer to the constantly growing and changing body of knowledge that the process of science generates.

How is science different from other ways of explaining how the world works? First, science deals only with the natural world. Scientific research never concerns, in any way, supernatural phenomena of any kind. Second, scientists collect and organize information in an orderly way, looking at events for patterns and connections of cause and effect. Third, scientists propose explanations based on evidence and understanding, not belief. Some ways that scientists study the natural world are shown in **Figure 1-1**.

**The Goals of Science** Science is based on the view that the physical universe is composed of interacting parts and processes. From a scientific perspective, all objects in the universe, and all interactions among those objects, are governed by universal natural laws. The same natural laws apply whether the objects and events are large (like a hurricane) or small (like the cells in your body).

Greek philosophers were among the first to try to explain the natural world in terms of events and processes they could observe. Modern scientists continue that tradition. ✎ *One goal of science is to provide natural and testable explanations for events in the natural world. Science also aims to use explanations supported by data to understand patterns in nature, and to make useful predictions about natural events.*

▶ **VIDEO**

Discover how scientists use scientific processes to discover the wide diversity of insects that live in people's homes.

☞ **INTERACTIVITY**

**CASE STUDY**

**Figure 1-1**

**Studying the Natural World**

How do chimpanzees interact with one another? What is the ideal temperature for basil plants in a hydroponics system? What kinds of fish live in the Colorado River? Researchers can use science to answer these questions and many others.

**Science, Change, and Uncertainty** Scientists have gathered lots of important information that helps cure and prevent disease, grow food, and link the world electronically. Yet much of nature remains a mystery. Almost every scientific discovery raises more questions than it answers. Often, research yields surprises that point future studies in new and unexpected directions. This constant change doesn't mean science has failed. On the contrary, it shows that science continues to advance.

That's why studying science means more than just memorizing what we know. It also means understanding what we don't know. You may be surprised to hear this, but science rarely "proves" anything. Scientists aim for the best understanding of the natural world that current methods can reveal. Uncertainty is always part of the scientific process, and is part of what makes science exciting!

We hope to show you that understanding science isn't just about learning "facts." We hope you'll gain some understanding of the spirit of scientific inquiry, of the way scientists think, and of both the process and excitement of discovery. Don't just memorize today's scientific facts and ideas. And please don't believe them, just because they are in a textbook! Instead, try to understand how scientists developed those ideas. Pose the kinds of questions scientists ask. Try to see the thinking behind the experiments we describe.

☑ **READING CHECK** **Construct an Explanation** How is scientific knowledge different from other types of knowledge?

# Scientific Methodology

Is science a mysterious process that only scientists do under special circumstances? Nope! You use scientific thinking all the time! Suppose your family's car won't start. What do you do? You use what you know about cars to ask questions. Is the battery dead? You test that idea by turning the key in the ignition. If the starter motor works but the engine doesn't start, you reject the dead battery idea. Is the car out of gas? A glance at the fuel gauge tests that idea. Again and again, you apply scientific thinking until the problem is solved—or until you run out of ideas and call a mechanic!

Scientists work in pretty much the same way. There isn't a single, cut-and-dried "scientific method." But there is a general style of investigation we call scientific methodology, which is a fancy way of saying "the way science works." ⚲ *Scientific methodology involves observing and asking questions, forming hypotheses, conducting controlled experiments, collecting and analyzing data, and drawing conclusions.* **Figure 1-2** shows how one research team used scientific methodology in its study of one particular species of marsh grass in a New England salt marsh.

**INTERACTIVITY**

Discover the power of scientific methodology.

## Figure 1-2
## Salt Marsh Experiment

Salt marshes are coastal environments often found where rivers meet the sea. Researchers made an interesting observation about the way a particular species of marsh grass grows. They then applied scientific methodology to answer questions that arose from their observation.

### 1. OBSERVING AND ASKING QUESTIONS

**Location A**  **Location B**

Researchers observed that marsh grass grows taller in some places than others. This observation led to a question: *Why do marsh grasses grow to different heights in different places?*

### 2. INFERRING AND HYPOTHESIZING

More nitrogen?

The researchers inferred that something limits grass growth in some places. It could be any environmental factor—temperature, sunlight, water, or nutrients. Based on their knowledge of salt marshes, they proposed a hypothesis: *Marsh grass growth is limited by available nitrogen.*

### 3. DESIGNING CONTROLLED EXPERIMENTS

The researchers selected similar plots of marsh grass. All plots had similar plant density, soil type, input of freshwater, and height above average tide level. The plots were divided into control and experimental groups.

**Control Group**      **Experimental Group**

No nitrogen added      Nitrogen added

The researchers added nitrogen fertilizer (the independent variable) to the experimental plots. They then observed the growth of marsh grass (the dependent variable) in both experimental and control plots.

### 4. COLLECTING DATA

**Control Group**      **Experimental Group**

The researchers sampled all the plots throughout the growing season. They measured growth rates and plant sizes, and analyzed the chemical composition of living leaves.

### 5. ANALYZING CONCLUSIONS

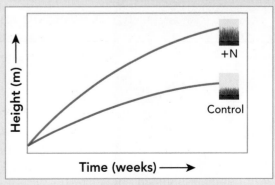

Data from all plots were compared and evaluated by statistical tests. Data analysis confirmed that marsh grasses in experimental plots with additional nitrogen did, in fact, grow taller and larger than controls. The hypothesis and its predictions were supported.

**READING TOOL**

Make a chart that lists and describes the different steps of scientific methodology.

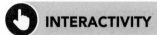

**INTERACTIVITY**

Try your hand at a simulation of a scientific investigation.

## Figure 1-3
## Collecting Data

This scientist is collecting data on a coral reef in Indonesia.

**Observing and Asking Questions** Scientific investigations begin with **observation**, the act of noticing and describing events or processes in a careful, orderly way. Of course, scientific observation involves more than just "looking." The right kind of observation leads to asking questions that no one has asked (or answered) before.

**Inferring and Forming a Hypothesis** After posing questions, scientists use further observations to make inferences. An **inference** is a logical interpretation based on what scientists already know. Inference, combined with a creative imagination, can lead to a hypothesis. A **hypothesis** is a tentative scientific explanation that can be tested by further observation or by experimentation. Scientific hypotheses must then be tested by gathering data that can either support or reject them.

**Designing Controlled Experiments** Testing hypotheses often involves designing experiments that measure factors that can change. These changeable factors are called variables. Some possible variables include temperature, light, time, and availability of nutrients. Ideally, a hypothesis should be tested by an experiment in which only one variable is changed. All other variables should be kept unchanged, or controlled. This is called a **controlled experiment**.

*Controlling Variables* It is important to control variables because if several variables are changed, researchers can't easily tell which variable is responsible for any results they observe. The variable deliberately changed is called the **independent variable**. The variable that is observed and that changes in response to the independent variable is called the **dependent variable**.

*Control and Experimental Groups* Typically, experiments are divided into control and experimental groups. A **control group** is exposed to the same conditions as the experimental group except for changes in the independent variable. Scientists always try to reproduce or replicate their observations by setting up several control and experimental groups, rather than just a single pair.

**Collecting and Analyzing Data** Scientists observe their experiments, gathering two main types of **data**. *Quantitative data* are numbers obtained by counting or measuring. In the marsh grass experiment, quantitative data could include the number of plants per plot; the length, width, and weight of each blade of grass; and so on. *Qualitative data* are descriptive and involve characteristics that cannot usually be measured. Qualitative data in the marsh grass experiment might include notes about whether the grass was growing upright or sideways, or whether one or another plot was disturbed by clam diggers.

*Selecting Equipment and Technology* Scientists collect and analyze data using tools that range from simple meter sticks to complex hardware that measures leaf nitrogen content. Data are often gathered directly by hardware controlled by computers running software that organizes and analyzes results. Statistical analysis helps determine if an experimental treatment is significantly different from controls.

*Sources of Error* Researchers must avoid errors in data collection and analysis. Tools used to measure the size and mass of marsh grasses, for example, have limited accuracy. Data analysis and sample size must be chosen carefully. The larger the sample size, the more reliably researchers can analyze variation within each group, and evaluate differences between experimentals and controls.

## Interpreting Data and Drawing Conclusions
Data analysis may lead to conclusions that support or refute the hypothesis being tested. Often, new data indicate that a hypothesis is on the right track, but is off-base about a few details. New questions lead to new and revised hypotheses, which are tested with new experiments that involve better control of variables or other changes in experimental design.

## When Experiments Aren't Possible
Not all hypotheses can be tested by experiments. Animal behavior researchers, for example, might propose hypotheses about how groups of animals interact in nature. These hypotheses are tested by field observations designed to disturb natural behavior as little as possible. Analysis of data from these observations may lead to new hypotheses that can be tested in different ways. If investigations suggest, for example, that members of a group are related to one another, genetic tests can gather data that support or reject that hypothesis.

Sometimes ethics prevent certain types of experiments. For example, in medical research, when a chemical is suspected as a cause of cancer, researchers do not purposely expose volunteers to the chemical. They study people who have already been exposed, using those who have not as the control group.

**✓ READING CHECK Describe** What is the difference between quantitative data and qualitative data?

---

**Analyzing Data**

### What's in a Diet?

The circle graph shows the diet of the siamang gibbon, a type of ape found in the rain forests of Southeast Asia.

1. **Analyze Graphs** According to the circle graph, which plant parts do siamangs rely on most as a food source?

2. **Form a Hypothesis** How would siamangs be affected if the rain forests they live in produced less fruit? Explain your reasoning.

Flowers, buds, and insects: 13%

Leaves: 38%

Fruits: 49%

# Scientific Theories

Researchers hope that data from many individual experiments add up to something bigger—a larger and more useful understanding of how the world works. That's where we encounter an important scientific term: **theory**. Many other terms you'll learn this year will be new to you, because they are used only in science. But the word *theory* is also often used in everyday life. That causes problems, because nonscientists use the word *theory* in a very different way than scientists do. When most people say, "I have a theory," they mean, "I have a hunch" or "I have a guess." When a friend says, "That's just a theory," she may mean, "People aren't too certain about that idea." Scientists would never use the word *theory* in that way. In those situations, a scientist would use the common words "guess" or "hunch" or a scientific term we've already discussed: *hypothesis*.

When scientists refer to gravitational theory or evolutionary theory, they do not mean "a hunch about gravity" or "a guess about evolution." *In science, the word theory applies to a tested, highly-reliable scientific explanation of events in the natural world that unifies many repeated observations and incorporates durable, well-supported hypotheses that enable scientists to make accurate predictions.* Charles Darwin developed lots of hypotheses over many years. It took a long time for him to assemble his thoughts and hypotheses into his theory of evolution by natural selection. Since then, evolutionary theory has predicted things Darwin couldn't have imagined, such as the evolution of bacteria that resist antibiotics and insects that are immune to pesticides. Today, evolutionary theory is the central organizing principle of all biological science.

Once a theory has been thoroughly tested and supported by many lines of evidence, it may become the dominant scientific view. But remember that no theory is absolute truth. Science is always changing; as new evidence is uncovered, a theory may be revised or replaced by a more useful explanation.

## BUILD VOCABULARY

**ACADEMIC WORDS** A scientific **theory** describes a well-tested explanation for a range of phenomena. Scientific theories are different from scientific laws, and it is important to understand that theories do not become laws. Laws, such as ideal gas laws in chemistry or Newton's laws of motion, are concise, specific descriptions of how some aspects of the natural world are expected to behave in a certain situation. In contrast, scientific theories, such as cell theory or the theory of evolution, are more dynamic and complex. Scientific theories encompass a greater number of ideas and hypotheses than laws, and are constantly fined-tuned through the process of science.

## ☑ LESSON 1.1 Review

### ⚲ KEY IDEAS

1. In your own words, define the term *science*.

2. Why are hypotheses so important to controlled experiments?

3. How does a theory differ from a hypothesis?

### CRITICAL THINKING

4. **Form a Hypothesis** You observe mold growing on one side of a slice of bread, but not on the other side. Form a hypothesis to explain this difference in mold growth.

5. **Plan an Investigation** Design a controlled experiment to test the effect of water temperature on goldfish. Be sure to include your hypothesis, independent variable, and dependent variable, as well as the experimental and control groups in your experiment.

# Science in Context

## KEY QUESTIONS

- *What attitudes and experiences generate new ideas?*
- *Why is peer review important?*
- *What is the relationship between science and society?*
- *What practices are shared by science and engineering?*

The testing of ideas is the heart of science and engineering. In their quest for understanding, scientists engage in many different activities: They ask questions, make observations, seek evidence, share ideas, and analyze data. These activities are all part of the dynamic process of science.

The process of science typically consists of the components shown in **Figure 1-4**. Notice that the parts of the process do not proceed in a linear fashion. Real science usually involves many activities that loop back on themselves, building up knowledge as they proceed. In fact, science is at its heart a creative endeavor. Scientists take many different paths through the process depending on the questions they are investigating and the resources available to them.

**VOCABULARY**
bias

**READING TOOL**

Before you read, study **Figure 1-4**. As you read, list examples of each of the different aspects of science in the table in your 📕 **Biology Foundations Notebook.** Then use **Figure 1-9** to add examples for engineering.

Exploration and Discovery

Testing Ideas

Benefits and Outcomes

Community Analysis and Feedback

Adapted from *Understanding Science*, UC Berkeley, Museum of Paleontology

 **INTERACTIVITY**

Figure 1-4

**The Process of Science**

As the arrows indicate, the different aspects of science are interconnected—making the process of science dynamic, flexible, and unpredictable.

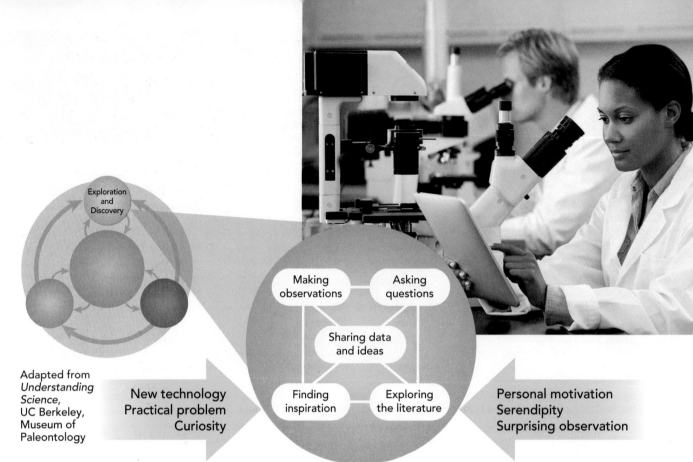

Adapted from *Understanding Science*, UC Berkeley, Museum of Paleontology

**Figure 1-5**

**Exploration and Discovery**

Ideas in science can arise in many ways—from simple curiosity or from the need to solve a particular problem. Scientists often begin investigating by making observations, asking questions, talking with colleagues, and reading about previous experiments.

# Exploration and Discovery

Usually, the testing of ideas begins with observations and questions. Those observations and questions come from a variety of different sources, as shown in **Figure 1-5**.

**Scientific Attitudes** Good scientists share scientific attitudes, or habits of mind, that lead them to exploration and discovery. 🔑 *Curiosity, skepticism, open-mindedness, and creativity help scientists and engineers ask new questions and define new problems.*

**Curiosity** A scientist may look at a salt marsh and ask, "What's that plant? Why is it growing here?" Previous studies can spark curiosity and lead to new questions. Engineering problems often arise from practical issues involving humans and health or environmental issues.

**Skepticism** Scientists and engineers should be skeptics who question existing ideas and hypotheses, and refuse to accept explanations without evidence. Scientists often design new experiments to test hypotheses proposed by other scientists. Engineers work to solve problems in the physical world using scientific thinking.

**Open-Mindedness** Scientists and engineers should be open-minded, meaning that they are willing to accept different ideas that may not agree with their hypotheses.

**Creativity** Creativity and critical thinking are essential for asking questions, defining problems, proposing hypotheses, and designing experiments that yield accurate data.

**Practical Problems** Ideas for scientific investigations often arise from practical problems involving humans and health or environmental issues. Salt marshes, for example, are vital nurseries for commercially important fish and shellfish. Yet salt marshes are under intense pressure from agriculture and from development. An engineer might wonder, "How would nearby construction affect the marsh and how can that impact be minimized?"

**New Technology** New technology often opens new ways of asking questions for both scientists and engineers. For example, portable, remote data-collecting equipment enables field researchers to monitor environmental conditions around the clock, in several different locations at once. This information allows researchers to pose and test new hypotheses.

> ☑ **READING CHECK** **Describe** Describe a "fact" that you have heard or read that made you skeptical. Explain your reasons for doubt.

## Community Analysis and Feedback

Scientists often collaborate in groups and communicate with other research groups. In order for research to be accepted, however, it must be officially shared with the scientific community. The communication must follow a variety of rules that ensure it is scientifically appropriate. Some of the steps that scientists use when communicating their results are shown in **Figure 1-6**.

Scientists also share their work with the general public, especially when the results or information could benefit society. This communication is less formal, and can take the form of a newspaper or magazine article, television program, or blog post.

▶ **VIDEO**

Listen to scientists discussing their work in extreme environments.

**Figure 1-6**

**Community Analysis and Feedback**

Communication is an important part of science. Scientists review and evaluate one another's work to ensure accuracy. Results from one study may lead to new ideas and further studies.

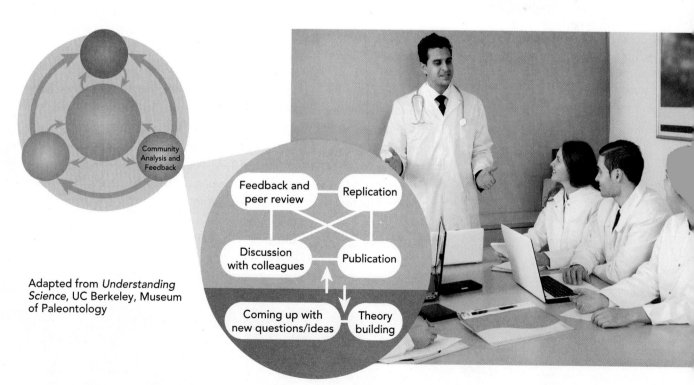

Adapted from *Understanding Science*, UC Berkeley, Museum of Paleontology

Community Analysis and Feedback

Feedback and peer review — Replication

Discussion with colleagues — Publication

Coming up with new questions/ideas — Theory building

## Replicating Procedures

1. Working with a partner, assemble ten blocks into an unusual structure. Write directions that others can use to replicate that structure without seeing it.

2. Exchange directions with another team. Replicate the team's structure by following their directions.

3. Compare each replicated structure to the original. Identify which parts of the directions were clear and accurate, and which were unclear or misleading.

### ANALYZE AND CONCLUDE

1. **Evaluate** How could you have written better directions?

2. **Construct an Explanation** Based on what you have learned in this investigation, explain why it is important that scientists write procedures that can be replicated.

**Figure 1-7**

## Mangrove Swamp

In tropical areas, mangrove swamps serve as the ecological equivalents of temperate salt marshes. The results of the salt marsh experiment suggest that nitrogen might be a limiting nutrient for mangroves and other plants in these similar habitats.

**Peer Review** Scientists share findings with other scientists by publishing their hypotheses, experimental methods, results, and analysis in scientific journals. Papers submitted to these journals are reviewed by anonymous, independent reviewers who work in the same field. Reviewers look carefully for mistakes, oversights, unfair influences, or fraud, in techniques and analysis. Their goal is to ensure that articles meet the highest standards of quality. This process is called peer review. *Publishing articles in peer-reviewed scientific journals allows researchers to share ideas. It also allows other scientists to evaluate and test the data and analysis.* Peer review does not guarantee that a piece of work is correct, but it does certify that the work meets standards set by the scientific community.

**Sharing Knowledge and New Ideas** After research has been published, it enters the dynamic marketplace of scientific ideas. How do new data fit into existing scientific understanding? For example, the finding that growth of salt marsh grasses is limited by available nitrogen sparks more questions: Is the growth of other plants in the same habitat also limited by nitrogen? What about the growth of different plants in similar environments, such as the mangrove swamp shown in **Figure 1-7**? These logical and important questions leads to new hypotheses that must be independently supported or rejected by controlled experiments.

☑ **READING CHECK** **Explain** Why is it necessary for other scientists to evaluate the findings of scientists in their field?

# Benefits and Outcomes

Scientists, engineers, and scientific information interact constantly with our society, our economy, our laws, and our moral principles, as shown in **Figure 1-8**. Think of medical issues relevant to your life and the lives of others close to you. That list may include effect of drugs and alcohol, high blood pressure, diabetes, AIDS, cancer, and heart disease. Science and engineering also play an important role in guiding decisions about health, social, and environmental issues. Should communities produce electricity using fossil fuels, nuclear power, solar power, wind power, or hydroelectric dams? How should chemical wastes be disposed of?

As journalist Dan Rather wrote in a *Scientific American* blog: "In the end, science is about hope; it's about expanding our horizons, and endeavoring to understand more. It is an instinct so deeply human, and an instinct we need now more than ever." (Copyright Scientific American, A Division of Nature America, Inc.)

### Science, Ethics, and Morality

Useful answers to these questions require scientific information. But science alone is often not enough. In most cases, science and engineering can only tell us what is technically possible, or what we *could* do. Science and engineering alone can almost never tell us whether we *should or should not* do something. 🔍 *Applying scientific information involves understanding the role of science context in society and its limitations.*

Science by itself does not automatically include ethical or moral viewpoints. When scientists explain "why" something happens, their explanation involves only natural phenomena. For example, biologists try to explain in scientific terms what life is, how life operates, and how life has changed over time. But science cannot answer questions about the meaning of life or why life exists.

**CASE STUDY**

👆 **INTERACTIVITY**

Design a solar still using the engineering design process as it relates to science.

**CASE STUDY**

**Figure 1-8**

## Benefits and Outcomes

Science both influences society and is influenced by society.

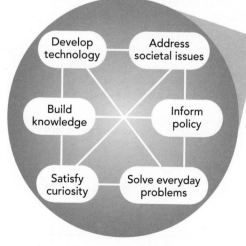

- Develop technology
- Address societal issues
- Build knowledge
- Inform policy
- Satisfy curiosity
- Solve everyday problems

Benefits and Outcomes

Adapted from *Understanding Science*, UC Berkeley, Museum of Paleontology

**INTERACTIVITY**

Learn how the science and engineering practices are similar.

**Avoiding Bias** Scientists aim to be objective, but they have likes, dislikes, and biases. A **bias** is a personal, rather than scientific, point of view for, or against, something. Examples of biases include preferences for, or against, certain kinds of people or activities.

Given this background, it is no surprise that scientific data can be interpreted in different ways by scientists with different personal perspectives. Recommendations from scientists with personal biases may or may not be in the public interest. But if enough of us understand science, we can help make certain that science is applied in ways that benefit individuals and society.

☑ **READING CHECK** **Explain** What might happen if a scientist were biased?

# Science and Engineering Practices

In contrast to scientists, engineers design, and build machines and structures. Although this book focuses on the science of biology, many of the methods and practices—the things that scientists and engineers actually do—are very similar. As a result, when you practice and master science skills, you also are learning skills that are useful in engineering. For additional information about these skills, see the Science and Engineering Handbook.

If you wonder how the "testing ideas" part of science compares to the kinds of things that engineers do, look at **Figure 1-9**. ✎ *Athough some of the specifics vary, the steps in scientific inquiry and engineering design are basically the same.* Not surprisingly, engineers are trained in basic science as well as the principles of their profession.

**Figure 1-9**

**Experimental Methodology**

The experimental methodology used in scientific inquiry and engineering design are adaptations of the same approach to scientific research.

| Scientific Inquiry | Engineering Design |
|---|---|
| Planned or chance observations, and/or personal or outside motivation generate a question | Colleagues and/or clients present a need to be solved through engineering design |
| Define/refine the question with colleagues/collaborators | Define/refine a design problem that addresses the need with colleagues and clients |
| Research how others may have answered the same question | Research how others may have solved the same design problem |
| Brainstorm hypotheses and choose one | Brainstorm design solutions and choose one |
| Design and conduct pilot experiment to test hypothesis; gather and analyze data | Design and create a prototype/model; test it to gather and evaluate performance data |
| Modify hypothesis and/or experimental protocol as needed based on analysis of data | Redesign prototype based on performance data |
| Conduct revised experiment; gather and analyze data | Test revised prototype; gather and evaluate performance data |
| Draw conclusion, write paper | Finalize design, make drawings |
| Submit paper for peer review; respond to consecutive feedback | Present best available solution to client; respond to client feedback |
| Publish the paper! | Build the project! |

**Developing and Using Models** Both scientists and engineers use models, such as those shown in **Figure 1-10**. When you hear the word *model*, you may think of model trains or other representations of much larger objects. But there are many different kinds of models. Mathematical representations and computer simulations are examples, as are two-dimensional drawings, diagrams, and maps. In fact, the flowcharts used throughout this lesson are models. Models help visualize and summarize ideas and communicate ideas to others.

## Using Mathematics and Computational Thinking

Mathematics and computational thinking (the process of mathematical calculation) are also important tools. The relationships between variables are essential to the understanding of scientific phenomena. Ratios, rates, percentages, and unit conversions are used to analyze and interpret data. A mathematical representation can represent and model data; it can also support claims and explanations.

## Constructing Explanations and Designing Solutions

Scientists aim to construct explanations for events in the natural world that caused them to ask a question. After a scientist collects data, analyzes and interprets that data, and finds that it supports the hypothesis, the next step is to construct an explanation. An explanation describes how variables relate to one another, and it is supported by evidence. In engineering, the goal is to design a solution to a problem within certain constraints.

**Engaging in Argument From Evidence** In science, an argument is a reason or set of reasons used to persuade others that an idea is right or wrong. Once a scientist has constructed an explanation, the next step is to use evidence (analyzed and interpreted data) to persuade others that the explanation is correct. Part of this process is receiving critiques and responding thoughtfully. Engineers defend claims that a design solution is effective or evaluate competing design solutions.

**Figure 1-10**

## Models

Models can be elaborate pictures that a computer generates (top), physical models, (middle), or illustrations (bottom). All three of these models show DNA, a molecule essential for life.

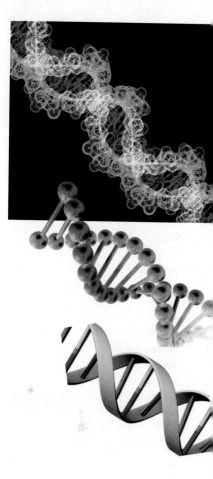

---

### ☑ LESSON 1.2 Review

#### 🔍 KEY QUESTIONS

1. How are both curiosity and skepticism useful in science?

2. How can peer review help scientists improve their work?

3. How is the use of science related to its context in society?

4. Why is testing ideas an important part of all science and engineering practices?

#### CRITICAL THINKING

5. Apply Concepts An advertisement claims that studies of a new sports drink show it boosts energy. You discover that none of the study results have been peer-reviewed. What would you tell consumers who are considering buying this product?

6. Apply Concepts A study shows that a new pesticide is safe for use on food crops. The researcher who conducted the study works for the pesticide company. What potential biases may have affected the study?

# Patterns of Life

## KEY QUESTIONS

- What characteristics do all living things share?
- What are the crosscutting concepts of biology?
- How do fields of biology differ in their approaches?
- How is the metric system important to science?

**VOCABULARY**

biology
sexual reproduction
asexual reproduction
DNA
metabolism
stimulus
homeostasis
evolve

**READING TOOL**

Complete the chart in your *Biology Foundations Workbook* by writing the main idea and details from this lesson on the characteristics of life.

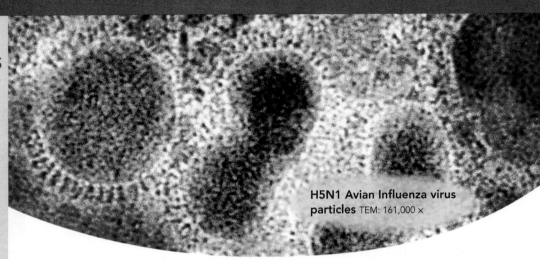

**H5N1 Avian Influenza virus particles** TEM: 161,000 ×

Think about some of the important and exciting news stories you've read or heard about recently. Bird flu spreads around the world, killing thousands of birds and threatening a human epidemic. Users of certain illegal drugs experience permanent damage to their brains and other parts of their nervous systems. Reports surface about the use of cloned human cells to grow new organs to replace those lost to disease or injury. These and many other stories involve **biology**—the science that employs scientific methodology to study living things. (The Greek word *bios* means "life," and *-logy* means "study of.")

## Characteristics of Living Things

Biology is the study of life. But what is life? What distinguishes living things from nonliving matter? Surprisingly, it isn't as simple as you might think to describe what makes something alive. No single characteristic is enough to describe a living thing. Also, some nonliving things share one or more traits with organisms. For example, a firefly and a fire both give off light, and each moves in its own way. Mechanical toys, automobiles, and clouds (none of which are alive) move around, while mushrooms and trees (which are alive) stay in one spot. To make matters more complicated, some things, such as viruses, exist at the border between living and nonliving things.

Despite these difficulties, we can list characteristics that most living things have in common. *Living things are made up of basic units called cells, reproduce, are based on a universal genetic code, grow and develop, obtain and use materials and energy, respond to their environment, maintain a stable internal environment, and evolve, changing over time.*

**Made Up of Cells** Living things, or organisms, are made up of small, self-contained units called cells. Cells are the smallest units of an organism that can be considered alive. Cells can grow, respond to their surroundings, and reproduce. Despite their small size, cells are complex and highly organized.

**Reproduction** All organisms produce new organisms through a process called reproduction. There are two basic kinds of reproduction: sexual and asexual. The vast majority of multicellular organisms reproduce sexually. In **sexual reproduction**, cells from two different parents unite to produce the first cell of the new organism. In **asexual reproduction**, the new organism has a single parent.

### Based on a Universal Genetic Code

Offspring usually resemble their parents. With asexual reproduction, offspring and their parents have the same traits. With sexual reproduction, offspring differ from their parents in some ways. Explaining how organisms inherit traits is one of the greatest achievements of modern biology. Biologists now know that the directions for inheritance are carried by a molecule called **DNA**. This genetic code, with a few minor variations, determines the inherited traits of every organism on Earth.

DNA helix

**Growth and Development** All living things grow during at least part of their lives. For some single-celled organisms, such as bacteria, growth is mostly a simple increase in size. Multicellular organisms, like this monarch butterfly, typically go through a process called development. During development, a single fertilized egg cell divides again and again to produce the many cells of mature organisms. As those cells divide, they change in shape and structure. This process is called differentiation, because it forms cells that look different from one another and perform different functions.

**VIDEO**

Learn about the characteristics of life and what it means to be alive.

## Need for Materials and Energy

Think of what an organism needs as it grows and develops. Just as a building grows taller because workers use energy to assemble new materials, an organism uses energy and a constantly supply of materials to grow, develop, and reproduce. Organisms also need materials and energy just to stay alive. The combination of chemical reactions as it carries out its life processes is called **metabolism**.

## Response to the Environment

Organisms detect and respond to stimuli from their environment. A **stimulus** is a signal to which an organism responds. External stimuli, which come from the environment outside an organism, include factors such as light and temperature. In contrast, internal stimuli come from within an organism. This field of sunflowers is responding the the stimulus of sunlight.

### Maintaining Internal Balance

Even though conditions in the external environment may vary widely, most organisms must keep internal conditions, such as temperature and water content, fairly constant to survive. The relatively constant set of conditions is called **homeostasis**. Often internal stimuli help maintain homeostasis. For example, when your body needs more water to maintain homeostasis, internal stimuli make you feel thirsty.

### Evolution

Although individual organisms experience many changes during their lives, the basic traits they inherited from their parents usually do not change. As a group, however, any given kind of organism can **evolve**, or change over time.

Over a few generations, the changes in a group may not seem significant. But over hundreds of thousands or even millions of years, the changes can be dramatic. The ability of a group of organisms to change over time is invaluable for survival in a world that is always changing.

### What About Viruses?

Viruses are particles made up of proteins, nucleic acids, and sometimes lipids. Viruses depend entirely upon other living organisms for their existence, making them parasites. After infecting living things, viruses can reproduce, regulate gene expression, and evolve.

✅ **READING CHECK** Explain Why is it important for organisms to maintain homeostasis?

# Crosscutting Concepts in Biology

The units of this book seem to cover different subjects, but all biological sciences are tied together by themes and methods of study that cut across disciplines. These concepts overlap and interlock, and crop up throughout the book. You'll also notice that several of these concepts overlap with the characteristics of life or the nature of science.

🔍 *The study of biology revolves around several crosscutting concepts: cause and effect; systems and system models; stability and change; patterns; scale, proportion, and quantity; energy and matter: flows, cycles, and conservation; and structure and function.*

**Cause and Effect: Mechanism and Explanation** Science is not a list of facts, but "a way of knowing." The job of science is to use observations, questions, and experiments to explain the natural world in terms of natural forces and events, or cause and effect. Successful scientific research reveals rules and patterns that can explain and predict at least some events in nature. Science enables us to take actions that affect events in the world around us.

**Systems and System Models** Within the biosphere, all of the different parts of the system work together and interact with one another. Predation, competition, and symbiosis within an ecological community are examples of interactions that occur within a biological system. The regulation of blood pressure in the human body can be studied as interactions among the nervous, endocrine, excretory, and circulatory systems.

**Stability and Change** Living things maintain a relatively stable internal environment, a process known as homeostasis. For most organisms, any breakdown of homeostasis may have serious or even fatal consequences.

**Patterns** You can compare similar patterns among all sorts of objects in nature, such as those shown in **Figure 1-11**. Patterns can be either linear or cyclical. Linear patterns include the tendency for organ systems to become more complex as you move through vertebrates from fishes to mammals. Cyclical patterns include seasonal migrations of animals or movement of materials such as carbon and nitrogen through the environment.

**Scale, Proportion, and Quantity** Just about everything, from atoms to rocks to organisms, can be described in terms of structure. How something's structure is studied and described depends on the scale on which it is being studied. On a molecular scale, a scientist might study a human in terms of proteins in the body. On a global scale, a scientist might study humans in terms of their impact on the ozone layer.

**Figure 1-11**

**Patterns in Nature**

Throughout nature you will find patterns. Similar patterns can be in structures ranging from an unrolling fern frond to a shell to a pine cone.

## Energy and Matter: Flows, Cycles, and Conservation

Living things obtain and use material and energy. Life requires matter that serves as nutrients to build body structures, and energy that fuels life's processes. Some organisms, such as plants, obtain energy from sunlight and take up nutrients from air, water, and soil. Other organisms, including most animals, eat plants or other animals to obtain both nutrients and energy. The need for matter and energy link all living things on Earth in a web of interdependent relationships.

**Structure and Function** Each major group of organisms has evolved its own particular body part "tool kit," a collection of structures that have evolved in ways that make particular functions possible. From capturing food to digesting it, and from reproducing to breathing, organisms use structures that have evolved into different forms as species have adapted to life in different environments.

✔ **READING CHECK** **Apply Concepts** Give an example of a cause-and-effect relationship.

# Fields of Biology

Living systems range from groups of molecules that make up cells to collections of organisms that make up the biosphere. ⚲ *Biology includes many overlapping fields that use different tools to study life from the molecular level to the planetary level.* Here's a peek into a few of the largest and smallest branches of biology, some of which are shown in **Figure 1-12**.

*Global Ecology* Life on Earth is shaped by weather patterns and processes in the atmosphere so large that we are just beginning to understand them. We are also learning that activities of living organisms—including humans—profoundly affect both the atmosphere and climate. Humans now move more matter and use more energy than any other species on Earth. Global ecological studies, aided by satellite technology and supercomputers, are enabling us to learn about our global impact, which affects all life on Earth.

*Biotechnology* This field, created by the molecular revolution, is based on our ability to "edit" and rewrite the genetic code—in a sense, redesigning the living world to order. We may soon learn to correct or replace damaged genes that cause inherited diseases. Other research seeks to genetically engineer bacteria to clean up toxic wastes. Biotechnology also raises enormous ethical, legal, and social questions. Should we tamper with the fundamental biological information that makes us human?

**Building the Tree of Life** Biologists have discovered and identified roughly 1.8 million different kinds of living organisms. That may seem like an incredible number, but researchers estimate that somewhere between 2 and 100 million more forms of life are waiting to be discovered around the globe—from caves deep beneath the surface, to tropical rain forests, to coral reefs and the depths of the sea. Identifying and cataloguing all these life-forms is enough work by itself, but biologists aim to do much more. They want to combine the latest genetic information with computer technology to organize all living things into a single universal "Tree of All Life."

**Ecology and Evolution of Infectious Diseases** HIV, bird flu, and drug-resistant bacteria may seem to have appeared out of nowhere, but the science behind their stories shows that relationships between hosts and pathogens are dynamic and constantly changing. Organisms that cause human disease have their own ecology, which involves our bodies, medicines we take, and our interactions with each other and the environment. Over time, disease-causing organisms engage in an "evolutionary arms race" with humans that creates constant challenges for public health around the world. Understanding these interactions is crucial to safeguarding our future.

**Genomics and Molecular Biology** These fields focus on studies of DNA and other molecules inside cells. The "molecular revolution" of the 1980s created the field of genomics, which is now looking at the entire sets of DNA code contained in a wide range of organisms. Ever more powerful computer analyses enable researchers to compare vast databases of genetic information in a fascinating search for keys to the mysteries of growth, development, aging, disease, cancer, and the history of life on Earth.

☑**READING CHECK** **Evaluate** Which of these fields of biology is of the greatest interest to you? Cite your reasons.

**Figure 1-12**
**Fields of Biology**

Biologists work in fields that include, from left to right, global ecology, biotechnology, ecology of infectious diseases, and molecular biology.

 **INTERACTIVITY**

Discover the different branches of life science in this activity.

# Performing Biological Investigations

You will soon have the opportunity to perform scientific investigations. Biologists, like other scientists, rely on a common system of measurement and practice safety procedures when conducting studies. As you study and perform experiments, you will become familiar with scientific measurement and safety procedures.

**Scientific Measurement** Because researchers need to replicate one another's experiments, and because many experiments involve gathering quantitative data, scientists need a common system of measurement. ⚲ *Scientists use the metric system when collecting data and performing experiments.* The metric system is a decimal system of measurement whose units are based on certain physical standards and are scaled on multiples of 10. A revised version of the original metric system is called the International System of Units, or SI. The abbreviation *SI* comes from the French *Le Système International d'Unités.*

Because the metric system is based on multiples of 10, it is easy to use. Notice in **Figure 1-13** how the basic unit of length, the meter, can be multiplied or divided to measure objects and distances much larger or smaller than a meter. The same process can be used when measuring volume and mass. You can learn more about the metric system in the Lab Skills Handbook.

**BUILD VOCABULARY**

**Prefixes** The SI prefix *milli-* means "thousandth." Therefore, 1 millimeter is one-thousandth of a meter, and 1 milligram is one-thousandth of a gram.

| Common Metric Units | |
|---|---|
| **Length** | **Mass** |
| 1 meter (m) = 100 centimeters (cm)<br>1 meter = 1000 millimeters (mm)<br>1000 meters = 1 kilometer (km) | 1 kilogram (kg) = 1000 grams (g)<br>1 gram = 1000 milligrams (mg)<br>1000 kilograms = 1 metric ton (t) |
| **Volume** | **Temperature** |
| 1 liter (L) = 1000 milliliters (mL)<br>1 liter = 1000 cubic centimeters (cm$^3$) | 0°C = freezing point of water<br>100°C = boiling point of water |

**Figure 1-13**

## The Metric System

Scientists usually use the metric system in their work. This system is easy to use because it is based on multiples of ten. This scientist is measuring the tortoise while its neck is stretched.

## ⚗ Develop a Solution Lab  Open-ended Inquiry

### Algae in the Water

**Problem** What are the ideal growth conditions for algae?

In this lab, you will plan and conduct an experiment to determine the effects of a variable, such as temperature or sunlight, on algae growth. Then you will propose ideas for a system for raising algae.

You can find this lab in your digital course.

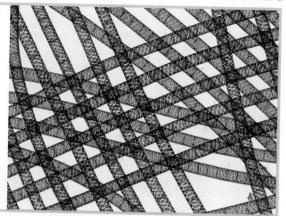

**Safety** Scientists, such as those shown in **Figure 1-14**, are trained to use safety procedures, such as wearing protective glasses and gloves. Laboratory work may involve flames or heating elements, electricity, chemicals, hot liquids, sharp instruments, or breakable glassware. Laboratory work and fieldwork may involve contact with living or dead organisms—not just potentially poisonous plants and venomous animals but also disease-carrying organisms and substances contaminated with dangerous microorganisms.

Whenever you work in your biology laboratory, you must follow safe practices. Careful preparation is the key to staying safe. Before performing any activity in this course, study the safety rules in the Lab Skills Handbook. Before you start each activity, read all the steps and make sure you understand them, including safety precautions.

The single most important safety rule is to always follow your teacher's instructions and directions in this textbook. Anytime you are in doubt, ask your teacher for an explanation. And because you may come in contact with organisms you cannot see, it is essential that you wash your hands thoroughly with soap and warm water after every scientific activity. Remember that you are responsible for your own safety and that of your teacher and classmates. If you are handling live animals, you are responsible for their safety, too.

**Figure 1-14**

**Safety in the Laboratory**

These scientists are wearing protective glasses and gloves in keeping with the safety protocols in their lab.

## ☑ LESSON 1.3 Review

### 🔍 KEY QUESTIONS

1. How do living things differ from nonliving things?
2. How do crosscutting concepts help unite the study of biology?
3. How can biology be studied at different scales, or levels?
4. Why do scientists use a common system of measurement?

### CRITICAL THINKING

5. **Identify Patterns** To analyze the characteristics of life, why is it useful to identify patterns at the level of molecules and cells?
6. **Calculate** In an experiment, you need 250 grams of potting soil for each of 10 plant samples. How many kilograms of soil in total do you need?

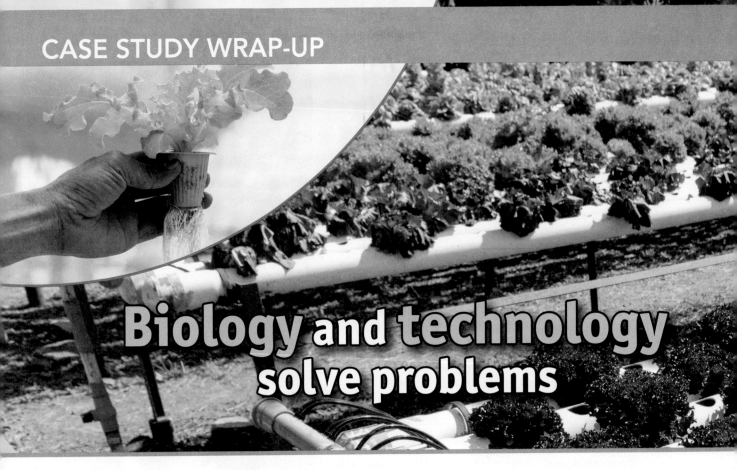

# Biology and technology solve problems

**Growers apply science and engineering practices to hydroponics, designing systems to grow food in new ways, and in new places.**

HS-ETS1-2, CCSS.ELA-LITERACY.WHST.9-10.2

## Make Your Case

As the field of hydroponics has matured over time, biology, engineering, and computer science have worked together to develop new techniques and approaches to grow food in many different environments: Antarctica, deserts, abandoned city lots, urban rooftops. The many faces of hydroponics offer solutions to the challenge of growing food under difficult conditions. What are some ways you can think of to adapt hydroponics or related technology to raising food?

## Develop a Solution

1. **Identify a Problem** Think of a challenge related to providing the right kind and intensity of light to hydroponically grow a particular crop, or in a hydroponic installation in a particular place.

2. **Develop Possible Solutions** With a partner or small group, research different ways of generating light in hydroponic setups. What color should the light be? How much heat do various kinds of grow-lamps generate? Then pick one particular hydroponic installation and discuss possible solutions or improvements.

3. **Communicate** Present your solution in an oral report or computer presentation to classmates.

## Technology on the Case

### Feeding the World

For most of history, farming techniques changed slowly. Then, during the middle of the twentieth century, a series of breakthroughs in biology and technology transformed agriculture, during what was called the Green Revolution. Intensive plant breeding produced new strains of crops that could adapt to local growing conditions, better resist diseases, and produce higher yields. Technological breakthroughs in fertilizer and pesticide manufacture and advances in irrigation technology enormously increased world food production and helped prevent famine in parts of the world.

As important as Green Revolution technology has been to humanity, its broad application has produced environmental challenges we will discuss in detail in the next unit. Careless pesticide use has introduced poisons into soil and water. Overuse of fertilizer use has disrupted many aquatic environments. These issues remain, even as global human population continues to increase, and demand for food continues to grow.

Scientists continue to research new ways to raise crops and improve yields. Can hydroponic culture conserve water and decrease use of pesticides and fertilizers? Can genetic engineering help develop new and better crop varieties? These questions challenge both science and society. Finding the best answers requires a deep understanding of how science provides information about the world we all share.

## Careers on the Case

### Work Toward a Solution

How can we improve the way farm crops are raised? Scientists from many fields may contribute ideas that help answer this question.

### Agronomist

Plants are raised for food, fuel, fabrics, and construction materials such as wood. The job of an agronomist is to develop new kinds of plants and new ways to raise plants, and to help farms and greenhouses run as efficiently as possible. Agronomists often work outdoors, where they study crops in the field. More often, though, they conduct experiments on plants in the laboratory.

 **VIDEO**

Watch this video to learn about other careers in biology.

hhmi | BioInteractive

# Lesson Review

Go to your Biology Foundations Workbook for longer versions of these lesson summaries.

## 1.1 What Is Science?

Science is a process—an organized way of observing and asking questions about the natural world. The goal of science is to provide natural and testable explanations for events in the natural world. Science also aims to use these explanations to make useful predictions about natural events.

Scientific methodology involves observing and asking questions, forming hypotheses, conducting controlled experiments, collecting and analyzing data, and drawing conclusions.

In science, the word *theory* applies to a tested, highly-reliable scientific explanation of events in the natural world that unifies many repeated observations and incorporates durable, well-supported hypotheses that enable scientists to make accurate predictions.

- observation
- inference
- hypothesis
- controlled experiment
- independent variable
- dependent variable
- control group
- data
- theory

Nitrogen added | No nitrogen added

☑ **Interpret Visuals** An experiment tests the hypothesis that nitrogen compounds cause grass to grow faster. Which of these pictures shows the control group for this experiment? Explain.

## 1.2 Science in Context

Often the testing of ideas in science begins with observations and questions. Curiosity, skepticism, open-mindedness, and creativity help scientists and engineers ask new questions and define new problems.

Once ideas are identified, scientists often work in groups to collaborate and communicate. Publishing articles in peer-reviewed scientific journals allows researchers to share ideas. It also allows other scientists to evaluate and test the data and analysis.

Scientists, engineers, and scientific information interact with society, economy, laws, and moral principles. Applying scientific information involves understanding the role of science context in society and its limitations.

Although some of the specifics vary, the steps in scientific inquiry and engineering design are basically the same.

- bias

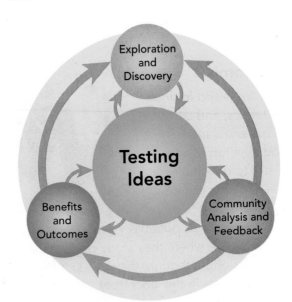

Adapted from *Understanding Science*, UC Berkeley, Museum of Paleontology

☑ **Form an Opinion** How does this illustration relate to the process of science?

## 1.3 Patterns of Life

Living things are made up of basic units called cells, are based on a universal genetic code, obtain and use materials and energy, grow and develop, reproduce, respond to their environment, maintain a stable internal environment, and change over time.

The study of biology revolves around several crosscutting concepts: cause and effect; systems and system models; stability and change; patterns; scale, proportion, and quantity; energy and matter; and structure and function.

Biology includes many overlapping fields that use different tools to study life from the molecular level to the planetary level.

Scientists use the metric system when collecting data and performing experiments.

- biology
- sexual reproduction
- asexual reproduction
- DNA
- metabolism
- stimulus
- homeostasis
- evolve

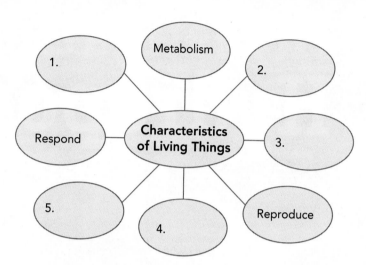

☑ **Summarize** What characteristics are common among all living things? Complete the concept map, and then explain in your own words.

## Organize Information

Fill in this KWL chart with information about biology, the science of life.

| What I Know | What I Want to Learn | What I Learned |
|---|---|---|
| Biology is the study of life. | What is the goal of science? | 1. |
| | What are benefits and outcomes for the study of biology? | 2. |
| | What are the characteristics of living things? | 3. |

# Investigating Hydroponics

## Design a Solution

HS-ETS1-2, HS-ETS1-3, HS-ESS3-4, CCSS.ELA-LITERACY.WHST.9-10.7

**STEM** Modern hydroponics systems use a variety of methods to bring water and nutrients to plants. In many of these methods, the plant roots do not dangle in the water. Instead they are held in place by a growth medium, such as fine rocks or pellets. Pumps and hoses bring water into the growth medium.

A greenhouse might use elaborate and costly materials to raise plants with hydroponics. On a smaller scale, however, simpler hydroponics systems can work just as well. The diagram shows an example of a type of hydroponics called a water culture. The materials include an ordinary aquarium, plastic cups to hold the plants, and a foam platform to hold the cups above the water.

In this activity, you will design your own hydroponics system. Your design plan should explain the problem you aim to solve, the factors that guide your decision making, details about the materials, and the cost.

1. **Conduct Research** Do some research in order to help you gather information that will help in the design of your hydroponics system.

2. **Ask Questions** With your classmates, brainstorm ways to build your own hydroponics system.

3. **Specify Design Criteria** Your hydroponics system must meet certain performance requirements in order to successfully solve the problem. These requirements are your design criteria. You also must specify the constraints that limit the scope of your design solution.

4. **Develop Models** Create sketches or a scale model of the systems you think will work for your hydroponics system.

5. **Evaluate Models** Have your classmates evaluate your groups' model or drawings of the hydroponic system you developed.

6. **Redesign and Retest the Solution** Use your classmates' feedback to help you further modify and refine your hydroponics system design. Explain how your revised design optimizes the achievement of your design criteria.

7. **Communicate Information** Communicate your final design to your class. Include detailed sketches, computer simulations, and written descriptions. Provide evidence that was collected when the prototype was tested. This evidence might include mathematical representations, such as graphs and data tables that support your choice for a final design.

## ⚲ KEY QUESTIONS AND TERMS

### 1.1 What Is Science?

1. By measuring the height of the tortoise, this scientist is gathering

   a. independent variables.
   b. dependent variables.
   c. quantitative data.
   d. qualitative data.

2. The statement "The worm is 2 centimeters long" is a(n)
   a. observation.
   b. theory.
   c. inference.
   d. hypothesis.

3. An inference is
   a. the same as an observation.
   b. a logical interpretation of an observation.
   c. a statement involving numbers.
   d. a way to avoid bias.

4. To be useful in science, a hypothesis must be
   a. measurable.
   b. observable.
   c. testable.
   d. correct.

5. Which of the following statements about a controlled experiment is accurate?
   a. All the variables must be kept the same.
   b. Only one variable is tested at a time.
   c. Everything can be studied by setting up a controlled experiment.
   d. Controlled experiments cannot be performed on living things.

6. A scientific theory is
   a. the same as a hypothesis.
   b. a well-tested explanation that unifies a broad range of observations.
   c. the same as the conclusion of an experiment.
   d. the first step in a controlled experiment.

7. What are the goals of science?

8. How does an observation about an object differ from an inference about that object?

9. How does a hypothesis help scientists understand the natural world?

10. Why does it make sense for scientists to test just one variable at a time in an experiment?

11. Distinguish between an experimental group and a control group.

12. What steps are involved in drawing a conclusion?

13. How can a graph of data be more informative than a table of the same data? (*Hint:* You may wish to refer to the Science and Engineering Handbook for help answering this question.)

14. Why are scientific theories useful?

15. Why aren't theories considered absolute truths?

### 1.2 Science in Context

16. A skeptical attitude in science
   a. prevents scientists from accepting new ideas.
   b. encourages scientists to readily accept new ideas.
   c. means a new idea will only be accepted if it is backed by evidence.
   d. is unimportant.

17. The purpose of peer review in science is to ensure that
   a. all scientific research is funded.
   b. the results of experiments are correct.
   c. all scientific results are published.
   d. published results meet standards set by the scientific community.

18. What does it mean to describe a scientist as skeptical? Why is skepticism an important quality in a scientist?

## 1.3 Patterns of Life

19. The process in which two cells from different parents unite to produce the first cell of a new organism is called
    a. homeostasis.
    b. development.
    c. asexual reproduction.
    d. sexual reproduction.

20. The relatively stable set of internal conditions that organisms maintain is called
    a. metabolism.
    b. a genome.
    c. evolution.
    d. homeostasis.

21. How are unicellular and multicellular organisms alike? How are they different?

22. Give an example of changes that take place as cells in a multicellular organism differentiate.

23. List three examples of stimuli that a bird responds to.

## CRITICAL THINKING

24. **Engage in Argument** Provide evidence to support the claim that viruses fall on the border between living and nonliving.

25. **Plan an Investigation** Suggest an experiment that would show whether one food is better than another at speeding an animal's growth.

26. **Identify Variables** Explain why you cannot draw a conclusion about the effect of one variable in an investigation when the other key variables are not controlled.

27. **Evaluate** Why is it misleading to describe science as a collection of facts?

28. **Develop Possible Solutions** How would having a scientific attitude help you in everyday activities, for example, in trying to learn a new skill?

29. **Conduct Peer Review** If you were one of the anonymous reviewers of a paper submitted for publication, what criteria would you use to determine whether or not the paper should be published?

30. **Evaluate Information** A classmate suggests a new hypothesis for researchers to test: Taller salt marsh grasses are prettier than shorter marsh grasses. Explain why this hypothesis is not scientific.

31. **Apply Concepts** Scientists often describe science as "self-correcting." Explain what this means regarding some theories as new areas of science and new technologies are developed.

32. **Define** Typical dictionaries have many definitions for the word *theory*. One definition is "a speculation, an assumption, or a belief." Provide the scientific definition of *theory*, and explain why the common definition given here is in many ways the opposite of a *scientific theory*.

A researcher studied two groups of fruit flies. Population A was kept in a 0.5-L container. Population B was kept in a 1-L container. In other respects, both groups were treated similarly. The graph shows the changes to both populations over time. Use the graph to answer questions 33–35.

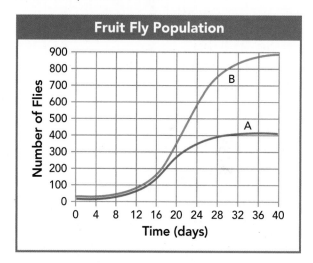

33. **Identify Variables** What is the independent variable in the experiment? What is the dependent variable?

34. **Draw Conclusions** What conclusion is supported by the data in the graph?

35. **Predict** A researcher puts a third group of fruit flies, labeled Population C, into a 2-L container. Predict the change in this population of fruit flies over time. Assume that the population is treated similarly to Populations A and B.

## CROSSCUTTING CONCEPTS

**36.** Patterns How do the traits of cells, proteins, and the genetic code form a pattern among living things?

**37.** Scale, Proportion, and Quanitity Why does mastery of biology depend on studies at different scales, from the small to the very large?

## MATH CONNECTIONS

### Analyze and Interpret Data

CCSS.MATH.CONTENT.HSN.Q.A.1

The following graphs show the size of four different populations over a period of time. Use the graphs to answer questions 38–40.

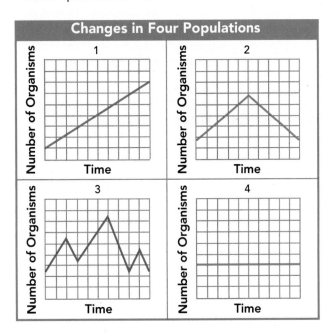

**38.** Interpret Graphs Write a sentence to describe the trend in population shown in each graph.

**39.** Reason Quantitatively Before any of the graphs could be used to make direct comparisons among the populations, what additional information would be necessary?

**40.** Compare and Contrast Graphs of completely different events can have the same appearance. Select one of the graphs and explain how the shape of the graph could apply to a different set of events.

## LANGUAGE ARTS CONNECTION

### Write About Science

CCSS.ELA-LITERACY.WHST.9-10.2

**41.** Write Procedures Suppose you have a pet cat and want to determine which type of cat food it prefers. Write an explanation of how you could use scientific methodology to determine the answer. (*Hint:* Before you start writing, list the steps you might take. Then, arrange them in order, beginning with the first step, to link the ideas together cohesively.)

### Read About Science

CCSS.ELA-LITERACY.RST.9-10.2

**42.** Summarize Text Why does studying biology involve more than memorizing facts about organisms and how they live?

## Questions 1–2.

Valerie designed and conducted an experiment on pothos plants, which are common houseplants. Her hypothesis is that the direction of light will affect the growth pattern of a pothos plant. To test the hypothesis, she sets up two test groups of pothos plants and observes them three weeks later. The table summarizes the test groups and observations.

| Test Group | Growth Conditions | Observations |
|---|---|---|
| 1 | Light source is only on the side of the plant | Stems and leaves are bent toward the light |
| 2 | Light source comes from all directions | Stems and leaves are not bent |

1. What are the roles of the two test groups in this investigation?
   A. Both are experimental groups, and each individually shows the effect of the direction of light.
   B. One is the experimental group and one is the control group, and together they show the effect of the direction of light.
   C. Both are control groups, but only Test Group 1 shows the effect of the direction of light.
   D. Both are experimental groups, but only Test Group 1 shows the effect of the direction of light.
   E. Both are experimental groups, but only Test Group 2 shows the effect of the direction of light.

2. After analyzing the results of the experiment, Valerie asks if her hypothesis should be classified as a theory. Which is the **best** response to Valerie's question?
   A. Yes, because her data support the hypothesis.
   B. Yes, but only if additional experiments show similar results.
   C. No, because the experiment did not provide enough data to support the hypothesis.
   D. No, because a theory is a highly reliable explanation that incorporates many well-tested hypotheses.
   E. No, because a theory and a hypothesis do not relate to one another.

3. Evolutionary theory has become the central organizing principle of biological science. Could this scientific theory ever become a scientific law?
   A. Yes, if scientists decide that enough evidence supports the theory.
   B. Yes, if the theory is shown to predict future events.
   C. No, because a theory is a complex explanation that does not become a law.
   D. No, because a theory can be proven correct while a law cannot be proven.
   E. No, because a theory cannot be proven correct while a law can be proven.

4. A griffin is a mythical creature that appears in many stories. It has the head of an eagle and the body of a lion. What role, if any, could the griffin have in the science of biology?
   A. The griffin could be the subject of an investigation of animals.
   B. The griffin could be cited as evidence to evaluate a hypothesis or theory.
   C. The griffin could be used to test new ideas about animal structures or behaviors.
   D. The griffin could provide data for an investigation of real animals.
   E. The griffin has no role in biology, because it is not real.

5. In her report of an investigation, Shira states that the height of a bush is 0.65 meters. Nathaniel states that the height of the same bush is 65 centimeters. How do the statements of the two students compare?
   A. Shira stated a greater height.
   B. Nathaniel stated a greater height.
   C. The students used different metric units to state the same height.
   D. The students used different units, only one of which is metric, to state the same height.
   E. Shira stated the height more accurately.

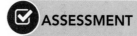 ASSESSMENT

For additional assessment practice, go online to access your digital course.

## If You Have Trouble With...

| Question | 1 | 2 | 3 | 4 | 5 |
|---|---|---|---|---|---|
| See Lesson | 1.1 | 1.1 | 1.1 | 1.1 | 1.3 |

**2.1**
The Nature
of Matter

**2.2**
Properties
of Water

**2.3**
Carbon
Compounds

**2.4**
Chemical
Reactions
and Enzymes

**Go Online to
access your
digital course.**

▶ **VIDEO**

🔊 **AUDIO**

👆 **INTERACTIVITY**

📖 **eTEXT**

👁 **ANIMATION**

📱 **VIRTUAL LAB**

☑ **ASSESSMENT**

HS-LS1-6, HS-ETS1-1, HS-ESS2-5

# Something is missing. But what?

Life goes on slowly in the rural village of Daxin, much as it has for centuries. Daxin is located in the landlocked province of Henan in central China. Chinese health workers once spoke of Daxin with a sense of dread, knowing that many of its people suffered from serious intellectual disabilities. They remember how small people with curious, childlike faces would peer out from the doorways of houses and the shadows of buildings.

Sadly, these were not the faces of children. The faces belonged to adults with cretinism, a condition of severely stunted growth—both physically and mentally.

Cretinism becomes apparent in infancy. Generally, the damage to the brain and body is permanent. People with cretinism grow up stunted, both physically and intellectually. In China, the disorder has been common in inland farming villages like Daxin. In some years, as many as 25 percent of the school-children in the Henan province were affected. However, cretinism seems confined to the inland provinces. It is effectively absent in the coastal regions of China.

The disorder occurs worldwide, and was once known as Alpine cretinism, named after inland regions in the Alps mountain range in Switzerland. The word "cretin" comes from *crestin*, a word in an Alpine French dialect that means "a fellow human being." The term was a reminder to treat people afflicted with mental or physical disorders with care and compassion. Just as in China, the disorder is confined to inland regions, and is rarely found among people living along the seacoast.

Goiter is another condition that is common in places where cretinism occurs. Goiter is a condition in which the neck and throat swell up. Goiter is produced when a gland known as the thyroid, increases in size so much that it causes a large bulge to appear at the base of the neck, where it is located. Unlike cretinism, goiter, which occurs in adulthood, can be treated and reversed.

Some possible explanations for these disorders have proved false. Neither is inherited. Children born to families that had moved out of the affected regions develop normally, without any signs of cretinism. This is true even if a parent has the disorder. Neither cretinism nor goiter are caused by pollution or toxic chemicals, and they do not spread from person to person, like a communicable disease. Rather, the cause of both disorders is not something present in places like Daxin, but rather something that is missing. Can you figure out what that might be?

**Throughout this chapter, look for connections to the CASE STUDY to help you answer these questions.**

Surface tension allows this double-crested basilisk to "run" across the water.

# 2.1 LESSON

# The Nature of Matter

## ⚘ KEY QUESTIONS

- *What three subatomic particles make up atoms?*
- *How are all of the isotopes of an element similar?*
- *In what ways does a compound differ from its component elements?*
- *What are the main types of chemical bonds?*

## VOCABULARY

atom
nucleus
electron
element
isotope
compound
ionic bond
ion
covalent bond
molecule
van der Waals forces

## READING TOOL

As you read your textbook, outline the headings and sub-headings throughout this lesson. Fill in the table in your 📖 **Biology Foundations Workbook.**

What are you made of? Just as buildings are made from bricks, steel, and wood, all forms of life are made from chemical compounds. When you breathe, eat, or drink, your body uses the substances in air, food, and water to carry out chemical reactions that keep you alive.

## Atoms

The study of chemistry begins with the basic unit of matter, the **atom**. The concept of the atom came first from the Greek philosopher Democritus, nearly 2500 years ago. Democritus called the smallest fragment of any substance an atom, from the Greek word *atomos*, which means "unable to be cut."

Atoms are incredibly small. Placed side by side, 100 million sulfur atoms would make a row only about 1 centimeter long—about the width of your little finger! Despite its extremely small size, an atom contains subatomic particles that are even smaller. **Figure 2-1** shows the subatomic particles in a carbon atom. ⚘ *The subatomic particles that make up atoms are protons, neutrons, and electrons.*

**Protons and Neutrons** Protons and neutrons have about the same mass. However, protons are positively charged particles (+), and neutrons carry no charge at all. Strong forces bind protons and neutrons together to form the **nucleus**, at the center of the atom.

**Electrons** The **electron** is a negatively charged particle (−) with only 1/1840 the mass of a proton. Electrons are in constant motion in the space surrounding the nucleus. They are arranged in a series of shells or orbitals. The first shell can contain no more than two electrons, and the second shell, no more than eight. Atoms have equal numbers of electrons and protons, and are electrically neutral because the opposite charges cancel out.

# Elements and Isotopes

A chemical **element** is a pure substance that consists entirely of one type of atom. Elements are represented by one- or two-letter symbols. C, for example, stands for carbon, H for hydrogen, Na for sodium, and I for iodine. The number of protons in the nucleus of an element is called its atomic number. Carbon's atomic number is 6, meaning that each atom of carbon has six protons and, consequently, six electrons.

Although there are nearly a hundred naturally occurring chemical elements on Earth (see the Periodic Table in Appendix D), fewer than 20 of them are commonly found in living organisms. About 99 percent of the mass of living things is composed of just six elements: calcium, carbon, hydrogen, oxygen, nitrogen, and phosphorus. However, the remaining 1 percent, or trace elements, are also essential. In fact, a lack of trace elements can stunt plant growth or damage the developing organs in unborn animals.

If all atoms are made of the same three elementary particles, then why do different elements have such different properties? Part of the answer is found in their electron shells. When two atoms interact, their shells overlap and may even swap electrons with each other. This affects how they can interact with other atoms and even how they may participate in chemical reactions. You might say that the number of electrons in that outer shell is the "face" that a particular atom shows to its neighbors.

**Isotopes** Atoms of an element may have different numbers of neutrons. For example, look at **Figure 2-2**. Although all atoms of carbon have six protons, they may have different numbers of neutrons. Carbon-14, for example, has 8 neutrons. Atoms of the same element that differ in the number of neutrons they contain are known as **isotopes**.

The total number of protons and neutrons in the nucleus of an atom is called its mass number. Isotopes are identified by their mass numbers. The weighted average of the masses of an element's isotopes is called its atomic mass. "Weighted" means that the abundance of each isotope in nature is considered when the average mass is calculated.

Although neutrons affect the atomic mass of an isotope, they do not affect its chemical properties. *Isotopes have different masses, but their chemical properties are the same.*

| Isotopes of Carbon | | | |
|---|---|---|---|
| Isotope | Number of Protons | Number of Electrons | Number of Neutrons |
| Carbon–12 (nonradioactive) | 6 | 6 | 6 |
| Carbon–13 (nonradioactive) | 6 | 6 | 7 |
| Carbon–14 (radioactive) | 6 | 6 | 8 |

## Figure 2-1
## A Carbon Atom

All atoms have a nucleus of protons and neutrons. Electrons move around the nucleus.

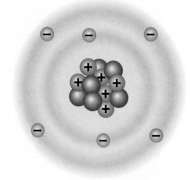

+ Proton
Neutron
– Electron

**INTERACTIVITY**

Explore an interactive periodic table to discover the properties of the elements.

## Figure 2-2
## Carbon Isotopes

Isotopes of carbon all have 6 protons but different numbers of neutrons—6, 7, or 8. Isotopes are identified by the total number of protons and neutrons in the nucleus: carbon-12, carbon-13, and carbon-14. ✓**Interpret Tables** Which isotope of carbon is radioactive?

**Radioactive Isotopes** Some isotopes are radioactive, meaning that their nuclei are unstable and break down at a constant rate over time. The radiation these isotopes give off can be dangerous, but radioactive isotopes have a number of important scientific and practical uses. Geologists can determine the ages of rocks and fossils by analyzing the isotopes found in them. Radiation from certain isotopes can be used to detect cancer and to kill bacteria that cause food to spoil. Radioactive isotopes can also be used as labels or "tracers" to follow the movements of substances within organisms. For example, if the radioactive isotope of iodine, $^{131}$I, is injected into the body, in just a few minutes nearly all of the radioactivity is found in just one place—a gland in the front of the neck called the thyroid (See **Figure 2-3**).

✓ **READING CHECK** **Define** What is an isotope?

**CASE STUDY**

**Figure 2-3**

**Radioactive Imaging of the Thyroid**

A radioactive scan reveals the location of the thyroid gland at the base of the neck. Iodine, including the radioactive isotope $^{131}$I, is concentrated in the thyroid.

# Chemical Compounds

In nature, most elements are found combined with other elements in compounds. A chemical **compound** is a substance formed by the chemical combination of two or more elements in definite proportions. Scientists show the composition of compounds by a kind of shorthand known as a chemical formula. Water, which contains two atoms of hydrogen for each atom of oxygen, has the chemical formula $H_2O$. The formula for table salt, NaCl, indicates that the elements that make up table salt—sodium and chlorine—combine in a 1:1 ratio.

✎ *The physical and chemical properties of a compound are usually very different from those of the elements from which it is formed.* For example, hydrogen and oxygen, which are gases at room temperature, can combine explosively and form liquid water. Sodium is a silver-colored metal that is soft enough to cut with a knife. It reacts explosively with water. Chlorine is very reactive, too. It is a poisonous, yellow-green gas that was used as a weapon in World War I. But the compound sodium chloride, more commonly known as table salt, shown in **Figure 2-4**, is a white solid that dissolves easily in water. As you know, sodium chloride is not poisonous. In fact, it is essential for the survival of most living things.

**Figure 2-4**

**Sodium Chloride**

Sodium (left) is a silvery metal. Chlorine (middle) is a poisonous yellow-green gas. Yet, the compound made from sodium and chlorine is sodium chloride—common table salt (right).

# Chemical Bonds

The atoms in compounds are held together by chemical bonds. Much of chemistry is devoted to understanding how and when chemical bonds form. Bond formation involves the electrons that surround each atomic nucleus. The electrons in an atom's outer shell that are available to form bonds are called valence electrons. 🔍 *The main types of chemical bonds are ionic bonds and covalent bonds.*

**Ionic Bonds** An **ionic bond** is formed when one or more electrons are transferred from one atom to another. Recall that atoms are electrically neutral when they have equal numbers of protons and electrons. A neutral atom that loses electrons becomes positively charged. A neutral atom that gains electrons has a negative charge. These positively and negatively charged atoms are known as **ions**.

**Figure 2-5**

**Ionic Bonding**

The compound sodium chloride forms when sodium loses its valence electron to chlorine.

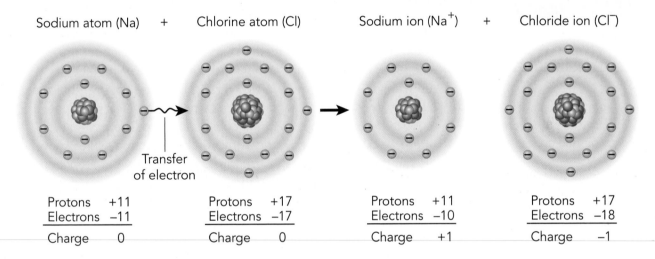

| Sodium atom (Na) | + | Chlorine atom (Cl) | | Sodium ion (Na⁺) | + | Chloride ion (Cl⁻) |
|---|---|---|---|---|---|---|

Transfer of electron

| | | | | | | |
|---|---|---|---|---|---|---|
| Protons +11 | | Protons +17 | | Protons +11 | | Protons +17 |
| Electrons −11 | | Electrons −17 | | Electrons −10 | | Electrons −18 |
| Charge 0 | | Charge 0 | | Charge +1 | | Charge −1 |

**Figure 2-5** shows how ionic bonds form between sodium and chlorine in table salt. A sodium atom loses its one electron from its outer shell to become a sodium ion (Na⁺). A chlorine atom gains an electron and becomes a chloride ion (Cl⁻). In a salt crystal, there are trillions of sodium and chloride ions. These oppositely charged ions have a strong attraction for each other, forming an ionic bond.

**Covalent Bonds** Sometimes electrons are shared by atoms instead of being transferred. What does it mean to share electrons? It means that the moving electrons actually travel about the nuclei of both atoms, forming a **covalent bond**. When the atoms share one electron from each atom, a single covalent bond is formed. Sometimes the atoms share four electrons to form a double bond. In other cases, atoms can share six electrons, forming a triple bond. The structure that results when atoms are joined together by covalent bonds is called a **molecule**, as shown by the diagram of a water molecule in **Figure 2-6**. The molecule is the smallest unit of most compounds.

☑ **READING CHECK** **Compare** How are ionic and covalent bonds alike? How are they different?

**Figure 2-6**

**Covalent Bonding**

In a water molecule, each hydrogen atom shares two electrons with the oxygen atom.

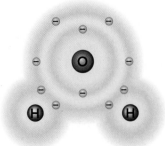

Water molecule ($H_2O$)

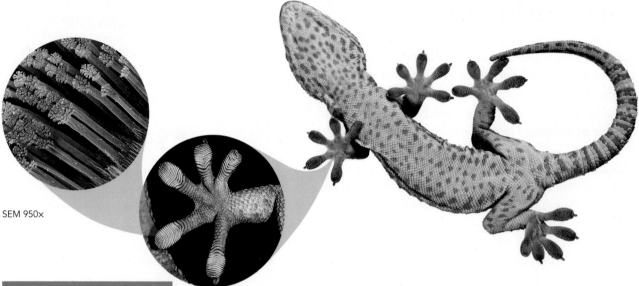

SEM 950x

**Up Close**

**Figure 2-7**

**Van der Waals Forces**

The underside of each foot of this gecko is covered by millions of tiny hairlike projections. The projections themselves are made of even finer fibers, creating more surface area for "sticking" to surfaces at the molecular level. This allows geckos to scurry up walls and across ceilings.

**BUILD VOCABULARY**

**Academic Words** The noun interaction means "a shared action or influence." The interactions between molecules due to van der Waals forces can hold them together.

**Weak Interactions** While the strongest chemical bonds are ionic or covalent, one of the most interesting things about the chemistry of living things is the importance of weak interactions between atoms and molecules. Within a living cell, many molecules interact only briefly to send signals, carry out chemical reactions, or copy information from one molecule to another. One example of these weak interactions is the attraction between molecules known as **van der Waals forces**. These forces produce a slight attraction between the molecules when they are very close together. If two molecules have shapes that match so they can fit against each other with very little space between them, these forces may be strong enough to hold the molecules together. The combined van der Waals forces along the feet of a gecko are strong enough to hold the gecko to a wall, as shown in **Figure 2-7**.

Hydrogen bonds are another form of weak interaction. These bonds form between a hydrogen atom of one molecule and an oxygen or nitrogen atom of a neighboring molecule. Because hydrogen bonds are essential to understanding the special properties of water, they will be considered in detail in the next lesson.

# ✓ LESSON 2.1 Review

## ⚘ KEY QUESTIONS

1. Describe the major subatomic particles that make up an atom.

2. Explain why isotopes of an element have the same chemical properties.

3. Compare the physical and chemical properties of a compound to those of the elements of which it is composed.

4. What are the differences between ionic bonds and covalent bonds?

## CRITICAL THINKING

5. **Use Models** How could you use red, blue, and yellow marbles to model a carbon atom?

6. **Evaluate Models** Evaluate the model you described in question 5. Describe its usefulness and its limitations.

7. **Synthesize Information** A calcium atom tends to lose two electrons to become a calcium ion, while a chlorine atom tends to gain one electron to become a chloride ion. Given this information, write out the chemical formula for the compound calcium chloride.

# Properties of Water

## KEY QUESTIONS

• *How does the structure of water contribute to its unique properties?*

• *How does water's polarity influence its properties as a solvent?*

• *Why is it important for cells to buffer solutions against rapid changes in pH?*

**HS-ESS2-5:** Plan and conduct an investigation of the properties of water and its effects on Earth materials and surface processes.

Looking back at our planet, an astronaut in space once said that if other beings have seen the Earth, they must surely call it "the blue planet." He referred, of course, to the oceans of water that cover nearly three fourths of Earth's surface. The very presence of liquid water tells a scientist that life may be present on such a planet. Why should life itself be connected so strongly to something so ordinary that we often take it for granted? The answer is that there is something very special about water and the role it plays in living things.

## VOCABULARY

**hydrogen bond • cohesion adhesion • mixture solution • solute • solvent suspension • pH scale acid • base • buffer**

## The Water Molecule

Water is one of the few compounds found in a liquid state over most of Earth's surface. Water ($H_2O$) looks like an ordinary molecule. However, there is more to the story.

## READING TOOL

As you read the section of the lesson under The Water Molecule, use the table in your 📖 **Biology Foundations Workbook** to list the causes and effects of the properties of water.

**Polarity** With 8 protons, water's oxygen nucleus attracts electrons more strongly than the single protons of water's two hydrogen nuclei. As a result, water's shared electrons are more likely to be found near the oxygen nucleus. So, water has a partial negative charge on one end and a partial positive charge on the other. A molecule in which the charges are unevenly distributed is said to be polar, because the molecule is a bit like a magnet with two poles.

Because of their partial charges, polar molecules such as water can attract each other. The attraction between a hydrogen atom with a partial positive charge and another atom with a partial negative charge is known as a **hydrogen bond**, which is shown in **Figure 2-8**.

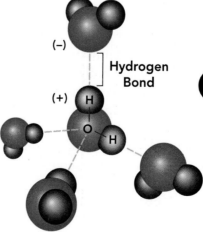

(−)

Hydrogen Bond

(+)

H

O

H

## 👆 INTERACTIVITY

**Figure 2-8**

**Hydrogen Bonding**

Each molecule of water can form multiple hydrogen bonds with other water molecules.

**INTERACTIVITY**

Explore the properties of water that make it so important to life on Earth.

**Special Properties of Water** Hydrogen bonds are not as strong as covalent or ionic bonds, but they give one of life's most important molecules many of its unique characteristics. 🔍 *Because water is a polar molecule, it is able to form multiple hydrogen bonds, which account for many of water's special properties.* These include the fact that water expands slightly upon freezing, making ice less dense than liquid water. Hydrogen bonding also explains water's ability to dissolve so many other substances, a property essential in living cells.

*Cohesion* The attraction between molecules of the same substance is called **cohesion**. Because a single water molecule may be involved in as many as four hydrogen bonds at the same time, water is extremely cohesive. Cohesion causes water molecules to be drawn together, which is why drops of water form beads on a smooth surface. Cohesion also produces surface tension, explaining why some insects and spiders can walk on a pond's surface.

*Adhesion* The attraction between molecules of different substances is called **adhesion**. Have you ever been asked to read the volume in a graduated cylinder at eye level? If so, you may have noticed that the surface of the water in the graduated cylinder dips slightly in the center. This is because the adhesion between water molecules and glass molecules is stronger than the cohesion between water molecules. Adhesion between water and glass also causes water to rise in a narrow tube against the force of gravity. This effect is called capillary action. Capillary action is one of the forces that draws water out of the roots of a plant and up into its stems and leaves. Cohesion holds the column of water together as it rises.

*Heat Capacity* Because of hydrogen bonding, water's heat capacity is relatively high. A substance's heat capacity is the amount of energy needed to raise its temperature by making its molecules move faster. This allows bodies of water, such as oceans and lakes, to absorb large amounts of heat with only small changes in temperature. The organisms living in the water are thus protected from drastic changes in temperature.

*Water in Living Things* Living things are composed mostly of water. Water accounts for approximately 60 percent of the mass of the human body. As a result, the chemical reactions that take place within living things do so in a water environment. Nearly everything that cells do—from growth and development to movement—takes place by means of chemical reactions in a water environment. That's why all living things, even those found in the driest places on Earth, depend upon a source of water.

✅ **READING CHECK** Compare and Contrast How are cohesion and adhesion similar? How are they different?

# Solutions and Suspensions

Water is often found as part of a mixture. A **mixture** is a material composed of two or more elements or compounds that are physically mixed together but not chemically combined. Earth's atmosphere is a mixture of nitrogen, oxygen, carbon dioxide, and other gases. Living things are in part composed of mixtures involving water. Two types of mixtures that can be made with water are solutions and suspensions.

**Solutions** If a crystal of table salt is placed in a glass of warm water, sodium and chloride ions on the surface of the crystal are attracted to the polar water molecules. Ions break away from the crystal and are surrounded by water molecules, as illustrated in **Figure 2-9**. The ions gradually become dispersed in the water, forming a type of mixture called a **solution**. All the components of a solution are evenly distributed throughout the solution. In a saltwater solution, table salt is the **solute**—the substance that is dissolved. Water is the **solvent**—the substance in which the solute dissolves.

🔍 *Water's polarity gives it the ability to dissolve both ionic compounds and other polar molecules.* Water easily dissolves salts, sugars, minerals, gases, and even other solvents such as alcohol. Without exaggeration, water is life's most important solvent. But even water has limits. When a given amount of water has dissolved all of the solute it can, the solution is said to be saturated.

**Suspensions** Some materials do not dissolve when placed in water but separate into pieces so small that they do not settle out. The movement of water molecules keeps the small particles suspended. Such mixtures of water and nondissolved material are known as **suspensions**. Some of the most important biological fluids are both solutions and suspensions. The blood that circulates through your body is mostly water. The water in the blood contains many dissolved compounds. However, blood also contains cells and other undissolved particles that remain in suspension as the blood moves through the body.

✅ **READING CHECK** **Classify** In a cup of tea, what is the solvent? What is the solute?

**READING TOOL**

Complete a T-chart to compare and contrast solutions and suspensions. Be sure to include examples of each type of mixture.

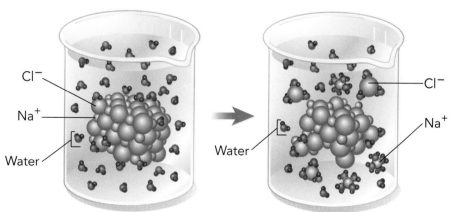

**Figure 2-9**

**A Salt Solution**

When an ionic compound such as sodium chloride is placed in water, water molecules surround and separate the positive and negative ions.
✅ **Interpret Diagrams** What happens to the sodium ions and chloride ions in the solution?

## Figure 2-10

### The pH Scale

The concentration of H⁺ ions determines whether solutions are acidic or basic. The most basic material on this scale is oven cleaner. The most acidic material on this pH scale is stomach acid.

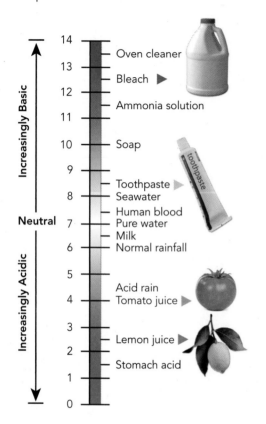

Increasingly Basic

Neutral

Increasingly Acidic

14 — Oven cleaner
13 — Bleach ▶
12 — Ammonia solution
11
10 — Soap
9
8 — Toothpaste ▶
   — Seawater
   — Human blood
7 — Pure water
   — Milk
6 — Normal rainfall
5
4 — Acid rain
   — Tomato juice ▶
3
2 — Lemon juice ▶
   — Stomach acid
1
0

# Acids, Bases, and pH

Water molecules sometimes split apart to form ions. This reaction can be summarized by a chemical equation in which double arrows are used to show that the reaction can occur in either direction.

$$H_2O \rightleftharpoons H^+ + OH^-$$
water ⇌ hydrogen ion + hydroxide ion

How often does this happen? In pure water, about 1 water molecule in 550 million splits to form ions in this way. Because the number of positive hydrogen ions produced is equal to the number of negative hydroxide ions produced, pure water is electrically neutral.

**The pH Scale** Chemists have devised a measurement system called the **pH scale** to indicate the concentration of H⁺ ions in solution. As **Figure 2-10** shows, the pH scale ranges from 0 to 14. At a pH of 7, the concentration of H⁺ ions and OH⁻ ions is equal. Pure water has a pH of 7. Solutions with a pH below 7 are called acidic because they have more H⁺ ions than OH⁻ ions. The lower the pH, the greater the acidity. Solutions with a pH above 7 are called basic because they have more OH⁻ ions than H⁺ ions. The higher the pH, the more basic the solution. Each step on the pH scale represents a factor of 10. For example, a liter of a solution with a pH of 4 has 10 times as many H⁺ ions as a liter of a solution with a pH of 5.

---

## Quick Lab | Guided Inquiry

### Acidic and Basic Foods

1. Construct a data table. Include spaces for food samples to be tested, predicted pH, and actual pH.

2. Predict whether the food samples provided are acidic or basic.

3. Tear off a 2-inch piece of pH paper for each sample you will test.

4. Test each food sample and record your observations in your data table. Touch the cut surface of each sample to a square of pH paper. Use a dropper pipette to place a drop of any liquid sample on a square of pH paper. Record the pH of each sample in your data table.

### ANALYZE AND CONCLUDE

1. **Analyze Data** Use the pH measurements to classify the foods as acidic and basic. Was your prediction correct?

2. **Construct an Explanation** Based on your observations, are you able to classify the foods according to pH? For example, what pH group would you generalize most fruits to to be in? Explain your response using the data you collected.

**Acids** Where do all those extra H⁺ ions in a low-pH solution come from? They come from acids. An **acid** is any compound that releases H⁺ ions into solution. Acidic solutions contain higher concentrations of H⁺ ions than pure water and have pH values below 7. The hydrochloric acid (HCl) produced by the stomach to help digest food is a strong acid with a pH of 1.5 to 3.0.

**Bases** A **base** is a compound that produces hydroxide (OH⁻) ions in solution. Basic, or alkaline, solutions contain lower concentrations of H⁺ ions than pure water and have pH values above 7. Strong bases, such as the lye (commonly NaOH) used in soapmaking, tend to have pH values ranging from 11 to 14.

**Buffers** The internal pH of most cells in the human body must generally be kept between 6.5 and 7.5. If the pH is lower or higher, it will affect the chemical reactions that take place within the cells. Thus, controlling pH is important for maintaining homeostasis. One of the ways that organisms control pH is through dissolved compounds called buffers. **Buffers** are weak acids or bases that can react with strong acids or bases to prevent sharp, sudden changes in pH. You can see one example of how buffers work in **Figure 2-11**. Blood, for example, has a normal pH of 7.4. Sudden changes in blood pH are usually prevented by a number of chemical buffers, such as bicarbonate and phosphate ions. ⚲ *Buffers dissolved in life's fluids play an important role in maintaining homeostasis.*

**INTERACTIVITY**

Explore how buffers help stabilize the pH of the blood during exercise.

**Figure 2-11**

## Buffers

Buffers help prevent drastic changes in pH. Adding acid to an unbuffered solution causes the pH of the unbuffered solution to decrease. If the solution contains a buffer, however, adding the acid will cause only a slight change in pH.

HS-ESS2-5

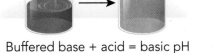

Base          Neutral          Acid

Unbuffered base + acid = acidic pH          Buffered base + acid = basic pH

## ✔ LESSON 2.2 Review

### ⚲ KEY QUESTIONS

1. What does it mean when a molecule is said to be "polar"?

2. Why is water such a good solvent?

3. What is a buffer? Why is it useful to cells?

### CRITICAL THINKING

4. Classify Identify some beverages that are mixtures. Classify them as solutions, suspensions, or neither. Explain your classifications.

5. Cite Evidence Describe two observations of water that provide evidence that water molecules are attracted to one another.

6. Integrate Information Discuss how the properties of water help Earth support life.

# Carbon Compounds

**KEY QUESTIONS**

- *What elements does carbon bond with to make up life's molecules?*

- *What are the functions of each of the four groups of macromolecules?*

**HS-LS1-6:** Construct and revise an explanation based on evidence for how carbon, hydrogen, and oxygen from sugar molecules may combine with other elements to form amino acids and/or other large carbon-based molecules.

**VOCABULARY**

**monomer • polymer**
**carbohydrate**
**lipid • nucleotide**
**nucleic acid • protein**
**amino acid**

**READING TOOL**

As you read, identify the similarities and differences between the different groups of macromolecules. Take notes in your *Biology Foundations Workbook.*

A fern fossil made of carbon

Chemists once called the compounds in living things "organic," believing they were different from nonliving compounds. Today we understand that living things obey the same chemical principles as nonliving. But the term "organic chemistry" is still around, referring today to the chemistry of carbon.

## The Chemistry of Carbon

What's the big deal about carbon? Why is it so interesting that it has its own branch of chemistry? There are two reasons for this. First, carbon atoms have four valence electrons, allowing them to form strong covalent bonds with many other elements. *Carbon can bond with many elements—including hydrogen, oxygen, phosphorus, sulfur, and nitrogen—to form compounds with many different chemical properties.* Living organisms depend upon these compounds.

Even more important, one carbon atom can bond to another, which gives carbon the ability to form chains that are almost unlimited in length. As shown in **Figure 2-12**, these carbon-carbon bonds can be single, double, or triple covalent bonds. Chains of carbon atoms can even close up on themselves to form rings, as shown by the structure of benzene. No other element matches carbon's versatility or the size of molecules that carbon can build.

**Figure 2-12**

## Carbon Structure

Carbon can form single, double, or triple bonds with other atoms. Each line between atoms in a molecular drawing represents one covalent bond.

**Methane**     **Acetylene**     **Butadiene**     **Benzene**

# Macromolecules

The large organic molecules found in living things are known as macromolecules, literally—"giant molecules"—because of their size. Most macromolecules are produced by a process known as polymerization (pah lih mur ih ZAY shun), in which larger compounds are built by joining smaller ones together. The smaller units, or **monomers**, are joined together to form **polymers**. The monomers in a polymer may be identical, like the links on a metal watchband, or different, like the beads in a multicolored necklace. **Figure 2-13** illustrates the process of polymerization.

Four major groups of macromolecules are found in living things: carbohydrates, lipids, nucleic acids, and proteins. As you read about these molecules, compare their structures and functions.

**Carbohydrates** Examples of carbohydrates include sugar, starch, and cellulose. **Carbohydrates** are made up of carbon, hydrogen, and oxygen atoms, usually in a ratio of 1 : 2 : 1. 🔎 *Organisms use carbohydrates to store and release energy, as well as for structural support and protection.* The breakdown of sugars, such as glucose, supplies immediate energy for cell activities. Many organisms store extra sugar as complex carbohydrates known as starches. The monomers in starch polymers are sugar molecules.

**Simple Sugars** Single sugar molecules are also known as monosaccharides (mahn oh SAK uh rydz). Besides glucose, which is shown in **Figure 2-14**, monosaccharides include galactose, which is a component of milk, and fructose, which is found in many fruits. Ordinary table sugar, sucrose, is a disaccharide, a compound made by joining together two simple sugars, fructose and glucose.

**Complex Carbohydrates** The macromolecules formed by joining many monosaccharides together are known as polysaccharides. Many animals store excess sugar in a polysaccharide called glycogen. When the level of glucose in your blood runs low, glycogen is broken down into glucose, which is then released into the blood. The glycogen stored in your muscles supplies the energy for muscle contraction and, thus, for movement.

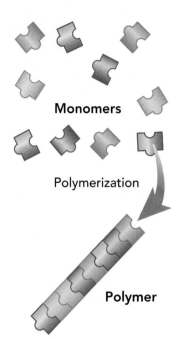

**Figure 2-13**

## Polymerization

When monomers join together, they form polymers.

**BUILD VOCABULARY**

**Prefixes** The prefix *mono-* means one, the prefix *di-* means "two," and the prefix *poly-* means "many."

▶ **Video**

Discover the stinky chemicals in the durian fruit.

**Figure 2-14**

## Carbohydrates

Starches form when sugar molecules join together in a long chain. Potatoes are made up mostly of starches, as are foods like bread and pasta.

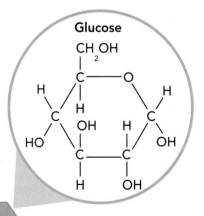

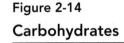

## Trace Elements

Just four elements—oxygen, carbon, hydrogen, and nitrogen—make up 96 percent of living things. The table shows the percentages of some other elements.

1. **Construct an Explanation** Is the importance of an element in the body related to its percentage of body weight? Cite the evidence in the table to support your explanation.

2. **Evaluate Claims** A student claims that the four types of macromolecules make up all of the important compounds of the human body. Provide evidence and reasoning to support or refute this claim.

| Element | Percentage of Body Weight | Uses |
|---|---|---|
| Phosphorus | 1.0 | Formation of bones and teeth |
| Potassium | 0.25 | Regulation of nerve function |
| Sulfur | 0.25 | Present in two amino acids |
| Sodium | 0.15 | Regulation of nerve function, blood levels |
| Chlorine | 0.15 | Fluid balance |
| Magnesium | 0.05 | Bone and muscle function |
| Iron | 0.006 | Carrying oxygen in the blood |

Other trace elements include fluorine, copper, zinc, and iodine.

 **INTERACTIVITY**

Explore how dietary fat affects blood cholesterol levels.

**Figure 2-15**

### Lipids

Lipid molecules, like this triglyceride, are built from fatty acids and glycerol. Olive oil, which contains mainly unsaturated fatty acids, is liquid at room temperature.

***Starches and Cellulose*** Plants use a slightly different polysaccharide, called starch, to store excess sugar. Plants also make an important polysaccharide called cellulose. Tough, flexible cellulose fibers give plants much of their strength and rigidity. Cellulose is the major component of both wood and paper, so you may actually be looking at cellulose if you are reading these words on a printed page.

**Lipids** Lipids are a large and varied group of macromolecules that are generally not soluble in water. **Lipids** are made mostly from carbon and hydrogen atoms, as shown in **Figure 2-15**. Lipids include the compounds we call fats, oils, and waxes. 🔍 *Lipids can be used to store energy, and they form important parts of biological membranes and waterproof coverings.* Many lipids, such as steroid hormones, function as chemical messengers.

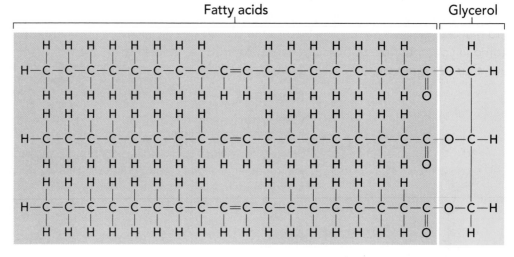

Many lipids are formed when a glycerol molecule combines with compounds called fatty acids. If each carbon atom in these fatty acid chains is joined to another carbon atom by a single bond, the lipid is said to be saturated because the fatty acids contain the maximum possible number of hydrogen atoms. If there is at least one carbon-carbon double bond in a fatty acid, the fatty acid is said to be unsaturated. Lipids whose fatty acids contain more than one double bond are said to be polyunsaturated. If the terms *saturated* and *polyunsaturated* seem familiar, you have probably seen them on food package labels. Lipids that contain unsaturated fatty acids, such as olive oil, tend to be liquids at room temperature. Other cooking oils, such as corn oil, sesame oil, canola oil, and peanut oil, contain polyunsaturated lipids.

✓ **READING CHECK** **Compare** How are saturated fats different from unsaturated fats?

**Nucleic Acids** As shown in **Figure 2-16**, **nucleotides** are monomers that consist of three components: a 5-carbon sugar, a phosphate group ($-PO_4$), and a nitrogenous base. **Nucleic acids** are polymers assembled from nucleotides. Some nucleotides, including the compound known as adenosine triphosphate (ATP), have important functions in capturing and transferring chemical energy. Individual nucleotides can be joined by covalent bonds to form a polynucleotide, or nucleic acid.

There are two kinds of nucleic acids: ribonucleic acid (RNA) and deoxyribonucleic acid (DNA). As their names indicate, RNA contains the sugar ribose while DNA contains the sugar deoxyribose. The sequence of bases in both DNA and RNA contains information used by the cell to build other molecules such as proteins. 🔍 *Nucleic acids store and transmit hereditary, or genetic, information.*

**Proteins** **Proteins** are macromolecules containing nitrogen as well as carbon, hydrogen, and oxygen. Proteins are polymers of molecules called amino acids. **Amino acids** are compounds with an amino group ($-NH_2$) on one end and a carboxyl group ($-COOH$) on the other end. In addition to serving as the building blocks of proteins, many amino acids serve other purposes. The amino acid tyrosine, shown in **Figure 2-17**, is used to produce a hormone, or chemical messenger, known as thyroxine. Thyroxine is produced in the thyroid gland from tyrosine and as many as four atoms of iodine.

**INTERACTIVITY**

Explore how the body breaks down sugar molecules in order to build other types of macromolecules needed by the body.

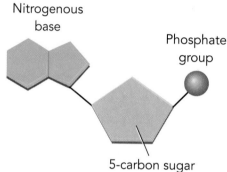

**Figure 2-16**

**A Nucleotide**

The monomers that make up a nucleic acid are nucleotides. Each nucleotide has a 5-carbon sugar, a phosphate group, and a nitrogenous base.

**CASE STUDY**

**Figure 2-17**

**Amino Acids**

All amino acids have the same basic structure. Only the R group differs among them. Amino acids join together to form proteins or may help form compounds like thyroxine.

**General Structure of Amino Acids**

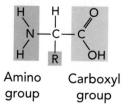

Amino group     Carboxyl group

**Tyrosine**

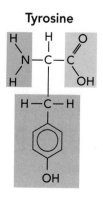

## Figure 2-18

## Peptide Bonding

Peptide bonds are formed between the amino group of one amino acid and the carboxyl group of another amino acid. In this diagram, the amino groups are shaded in green, the carboxyl groups are shaded in blue, and the R-groups are shaded in purple.

**Formation of Peptide Bond**

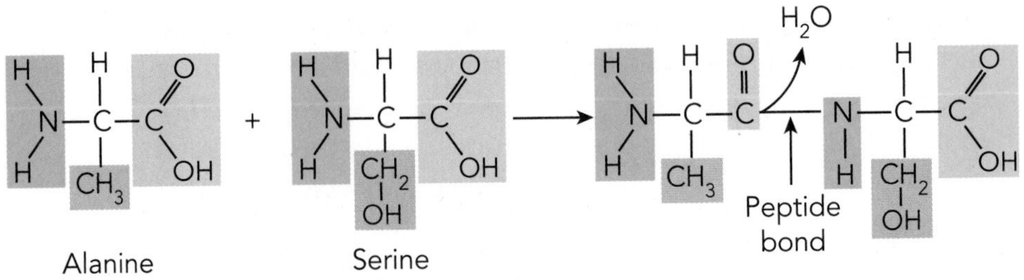

Alanine          Serine

Peptide bond

## Figure 2-19

## Protein

Hair and nails are made of a tough protein called keratin.

**Peptide Bonding** Covalent bonds called peptide bonds link amino acids together to form a polypeptide. As shown in **Figure 2-18**, the amino group ($-NH_2$) of one amino acid links to the carboxyl group ($-COOH$) of another amino acid. When the two groups react, they release a water molecule ($H_2O$) as the peptide bond forms.

**Function** A protein is a functional molecule built from one or more polypeptides. Proteins can have a variety of shapes and sizes, and they serve a variety of purposes as well. 🔍 *Some proteins function to control the rate of reactions and regulate cell processes. Others form important cellular structures, while still others transport substances into or out of cells or help to fight disease.* Hair (shown in **Figure 2-19**) and nails are made of protein.

Proteins enable the cells of the body to communicate and interact. Many cells have proteins exposed on their surfaces that act as receptors to certain compounds. When a receptor encounters such a compound, it transmits a chemical signal into the cell, setting off a response. The result may be an increase or decrease in cellular activity, the production of a new protein, or a change in the cell's pattern of growth and development.

For example, thyroxine binds to cells with a specific receptor protein on their surfaces. That binding increases cell activity. In this way, the thyroid gland can send chemical signals throughout the body that control the activities of millions of cells. If thyroxine levels are too low, especially during childhood, development of the brain and nervous system can be affected.

**Structure** More than 20 different amino acids are found in nature. All amino acids are identical in the regions where they may be joined together by covalent bonds. This uniformity allows any amino acid to be joined to any other amino acid by linking an amino group to a carboxyl group.

Proteins are among the most diverse macromolecules. The reason is that amino acids differ from each other in a side chain called the R-group, which can have a range of different properties. Some R-groups are acidic and some are basic. Some are polar, some are non-polar, and some even contain large ring structures. Two of the amino acids—methionine and cysteine—contain sulfur in their R-groups.

***Levels of Organization*** Amino acids are assembled into polypeptide chains according to instructions coded in DNA. However, proteins do not take on a linear shape. Instead, the polypeptides bend and twist into three-dimensional shapes.

To help understand these large molecules, scientists describe proteins as having four levels of structure. A protein's primary structure is the sequence of its amino acids. Secondary structure is the folding or coiling of the polypeptide chain. Tertiary structure is the complete three-dimensional arrangement of a polypeptide chain. Proteins with more than one chain are said to have a fourth level of structure, describing the way in which the different polypeptides are arranged with respect to each other. **Figure 2-20** shows the structure of hemoglobin, a protein found in red blood cells that transports oxygen in the bloodstream.

The shape of a protein is maintained by a variety of forces, including ionic and covalent bonds, as well as van der Waals forces and hydrogen bonds. In the next lesson, you will learn why a protein's shape is so important.

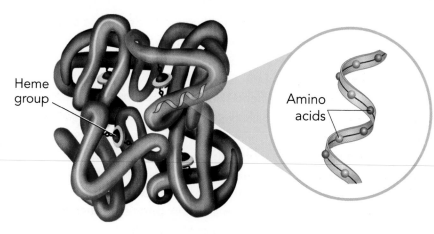

Heme group

Amino acids

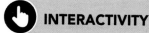

**INTERACTIVITY**

Figure 2-20

**Protein Structure**

The protein hemoglobin consists of four subunits. The iron-containing heme group in the center of each subunit gives hemoglobin its red color. An oxygen molecule binds tightly to each heme group.

HS-LS1-6

# ✓ LESSON 2.3 Review

## 🔍 KEY QUESTIONS

1. What properties of carbon explain carbon's ability to form different large and complex structures?

2. What are the four major categories of macromolecules? Describe the basic structures and the primary functions of each.

## CRITICAL THINKING

3. **Compare and Contrast** What three elements do all macromolecules share? Explain how the chemical properties of lipids, nucleic acids, and proteins differ from carbohydrates.

4. **Construct an Explanation** How does the structure of an amino acid relate to its function in cellular processes? Use the role of amino acids in the structure of proteins as supportive evidence.

5. **Integrate Information** What elements differentiate the amino acids of a protein from the sugars of a carbohydrate?

## KEY QUESTIONS

- What happens to chemical bonds during chemical reactions?

- How do energy changes affect whether a chemical reaction will occur?

- What role do enzymes play in living things, and what affects their function?

HS-LS1-6: Construct and revise an explanation based on evidence for how carbon, hydrogen, and oxygen from sugar molecules may combine with other elements to form amino acids and/or other large carbon-based molecules.

## VOCABULARY

chemical reaction
reactant
product
activation energy
catalyst
enzyme
substrate

### READING TOOL

As you read the lesson, complete the concept map in your 📘 Biology Foundations Workbook that shows the relationship between vocabulary terms.

Living things are made up of chemical compounds—some simple and some complex. But chemistry isn't just what life is made of— chemistry is also what life does. Everything that happens in an organism—its growth, its interaction with the environment, its reproduction, and even its movement—is based on chemical reactions. Even the twinkle of a firefly's body comes from a chemical reaction.

## Chemical Reactions

A **chemical reaction** is a process that changes, or transforms, one set of compounds into another. An important scientific principle is that mass and energy are conserved during chemical transformations. This is also true for chemical reactions that occur in living organisms. Some chemical reactions occur slowly, such as the combination of iron and oxygen to form an iron oxide called rust. Other reactions occur quickly. The elements or compounds that engage in a chemical reaction are known as **reactants**. The elements or compounds produced by a chemical reaction are known as **products**. ⚲ *Chemical reactions involve changes in the chemical bonds that join atoms in compounds.*

## Energy in Reactions

Energy is released or absorbed whenever chemical bonds are formed or broken. This means that chemical reactions also involve changes in energy. Some chemical reactions release energy, and other reactions absorb energy. Energy changes are one of the most important factors in determining whether a chemical reaction will occur. ⚲ *Chemical reactions that release energy often occur on their own, or spontaneously. Chemical reactions that absorb energy require a source of energy.*

An example of an energy-releasing reaction is the burning of hydrogen gas, in which hydrogen reacts with oxygen to produce water vapor.

$$2H_2 + O_2 \rightarrow 2H_2O$$

The energy is released in the form of heat, and sometimes—when hydrogen gas explodes—as light and sound.

The reverse reaction, in which water is changed into hydrogen and oxygen gas, absorbs so much energy that it generally doesn't occur by itself. In fact, the only practical way to reverse the reaction is to pass an electrical current through water. Thus, in one direction the reaction releases energy, and in the other direction the reaction requires energy.

**Energy Sources** In order to stay alive, organisms need to carry out reactions that require energy. Because matter and energy are conserved in chemical reactions, every organism must have a source of energy to carry out chemical reactions. Plants get that energy by trapping and storing the energy from sunlight in energy-rich compounds. Animals consume plants or other animals for food. Then chemical reactions break apart the food and capture its energy.

**Activation Energy** Chemical reactions that release energy do not always occur spontaneously. Otherwise, the pages of a book might burst into flames without warning. The cellulose in paper burns only if you light it with a flame, which supplies enough energy to get the reaction started. The energy that is needed to get a reaction started is called its **activation energy**. As **Figure 2-22** shows, activation energy is involved in chemical reactions regardless of whether the overall chemical reaction releases energy or absorbs energy.

**☑ READING CHECK** **Interpret Graphs** Look at **Figure 2-22**. How does the energy of the reactants and products differ between an energy-absorbing reaction and an energy-releasing reaction?

**Figure 2-21**
## Chemical Reactions

Burning is a type of chemical reaction that releases energy. When wood burns it releases energy in the form of heat and light.

**Figure 2-22**
## Activation Energy

The peak of each graph represents the energy needed for the reaction to go forward. The difference between this required energy and the energy of the reactants is the activation energy.

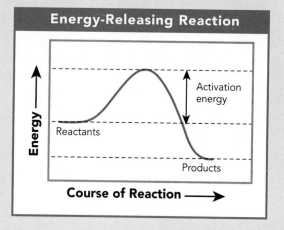

Energy-Absorbing Reaction

Products

Activation energy

Energy

Reactants

Course of Reaction ⟶

Energy-Releasing Reaction

Activation energy

Energy

Reactants

Products

Course of Reaction ⟶

## Figure 2-23
## Effect of Enzymes

Notice how the addition of an enzyme lowers the activation energy in this reaction. The enzyme speeds up the reaction.

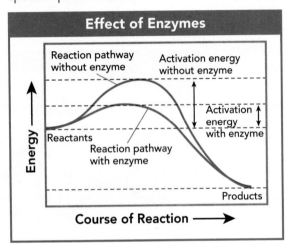

**Effect of Enzymes**

Reaction pathway without enzyme

Activation energy without enzyme

Activation energy with enzyme

Reactants

Reaction pathway with enzyme

Products

Energy →

Course of Reaction →

**ANIMATION**

## Figure 2-24
## An Enzyme-Catalyzed Reaction

Carbonic anhydrase binds both substrates: carbon dioxide and water. The substrates react to form carbonic acid.

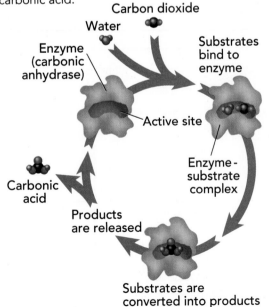

Carbon dioxide

Water

Enzyme (carbonic anhydrase)

Substrates bind to enzyme

Active site

Enzyme-substrate complex

Carbonic acid

Products are released

Substrates are converted into products

# Enzymes

Some chemical reactions that are essential to life would happen so slowly or require such high activation energies that they could never take place on their own. These chemical reactions are made possible by a process that would make any chemist proud—by catalysts made by living cells. A **catalyst** is a substance that speeds up the rate of a chemical reaction without being consumed by the reaction. Catalysts work by lowering a reaction's activation energy.

**Nature's Catalysts** **Enzymes** are biological catalysts, and most enzymes are proteins. ⚲ *The role of enzymes is to speed up chemical reactions that take place in cells.* Like other catalysts, enzymes act by lowering activation energies, as illustrated by the graph in **Figure 2-23**. Lowering the activation energy has a dramatic effect on how quickly the reaction is completed. How big an effect does it have? Consider the reaction in which carbon dioxide combines with water to produce carbonic acid, as shown in **Figure 2-24**.

Left to itself, this reaction is so slow that carbon dioxide might build up in the body faster than the bloodstream could remove it. Fortunately, the bloodstream contains an enzyme called carbonic anhydrase that speeds up the reaction by a factor of 10 million. With carbonic anhydrase, the reaction takes place immediately and carbon dioxide is removed from the blood quickly.

Enzymes are very specific, generally catalyzing only one chemical reaction. For this reason, part of an enzyme's name is usually derived from the reaction it catalyzes. Carbonic anhydrase gets its name because it also catalyzes the reverse reaction, which removes water from carbonic acid.

**The Enzyme-Substrate Complex** How do enzymes do their jobs? For a chemical reaction to occur, the reactants must collide with each other with sufficient energy that existing bonds will be broken and new bonds will be formed. If the reactants do not have enough energy, they will be unchanged after the collision.

Enzymes provide a site where reactants can be brought together, reducing the energy needed for the reaction. The reactants of enzyme-catalyzed reactions are known as **substrates**. In the reaction catalyzed by carbonic anhydrase, the substrates are water and carbon dioxide.

**Exploration Lab**   Open-Ended Inquiry

## Temperature and Enzymes

**Problem** How does temperature affect the rate of an enzyme-catalyzed reaction?

Cells must regulate their content of hydrogen peroxide ($H_2O_2$), a chemical that helps fight infections but can be harmful in high concentrations. Catalase is the enzyme that catalyzes the breakup of hydrogen peroxide into water and oxygen. In this lab, you will investigate how temperature affects the function of catalase.

You can find this lab in your digital course.

The substrates bind to a site on the enzyme called the active site. The active site and the substrates have complementary shapes, and they may be held together by weak interactions such as hydrogen bonds and van der Waals forces. The fit is so precise that the active site and substrates are often compared to a lock and key. You can even think of the catalyst as being the key that turns on a chemical reaction machine, allowing products to be created much faster than they would be without the catalyst.

**Regulation of Enzyme Activity** Enzymes play essential roles in chemical pathways, making materials that cells need, releasing energy, and transferring information. Because the activity of an enzyme depends upon the structure of its active site, conditions that tend to change protein structure can affect enzyme activity. These conditions include high temperature and extreme pH, which may weaken hydrogen bonds, causing proteins to unfold and disrupting active site structure.

Not surprisingly, the enzymes produced by human cells generally work best at temperatures close to 37°C, the normal temperature of the human body. Similarly, the stomach enzyme pepsin, which acts on food in the stomach, works best under acidic conditions. In addition, the activities of most enzymes are regulated by molecules that carry chemical signals within cells, switching enzymes "on" or "off" as needed.

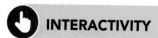 **INTERACTIVITY**

Explore enzymes and the variables that affect them.

## ☑ LESSON 2.4 Review

### ⚲ KEY QUESTIONS

1. What changes occur to chemical bonds during a chemical reaction?

2. How does the change in energy of a chemical reaction predict whether or not the reaction will occur?

3. Explain the role of enzymes and how they affect the chemical reactions of living things.

### CRITICAL THINKING

4. **Use Models** Explain why a key that fits into a lock is a useful model for the function of enzymes.

5. **Construct an Explanation** Explain how consuming an acid-neutralizing antacid might affect protein digestion. Apply the concept of activation energy to support your explanation.

6. **Plan an Investigation** Predict which temperature—20°C, 39°C, or 50°C—you would expect a human enzyme to function best. Plan a simple investigation to test your hypothesis.

# Something is missing.
## But what?

The element iodine makes up a small fraction of the human body. Nevertheless, a steady supply of iodine is very important for good health.

## Make Your Case

The human diet requires certain trace elements. A key trace element was missing from the diets of children and adults in Daxin, China. Try to identify the missing element, and then to connect it with both cretinism and goiter.

## Communicate Information

1. **Conduct Research** Using library or Internet resources, identify the missing element, and describe why it is important to human health. Explain why the lack of this element causes cretinism in children and goiter in adults. Explain why goiter is reversible, but cretinism is not.

2. **Communicate Information** Explain why these disorders are usually found in landlocked regions far from the coast. Are there ways in which the diets of people in places like Daxin could be supplemented to prevent both disorders?

## Careers on the Case

### Work Toward a Solution

Diet is the key to preventing many health problems, including iodine deficiency. Food scientists work to make sure that the food people eat is healthy and safe.

### Food Scientist

Food scientists study ways to make food healthier, to keep food fresh, and to produce food more efficiently. They may work in laboratories or packaging plants.

▶ **Video**

Watch this video to learn about other careers in biology.

hhmi | **BioInteractive**

## Society on the Case

### Fukushima and Thyroid Cancer

In March 2011, a tsunami overwhelmed a coastal nuclear power station in Fukushima, Japan. A cooling system failed, leading to a meltdown of its radioactive core, an explosion, and the release of radioactive material. Knowing that one radioactive isotope in particular may cause thyroid cancer, authorities debated whether to distribute tablets of non-radioactive potassium iodide (KI). Potassium iodide helps block radioactive iodine from being absorbed by the thyroid gland.

Fearing that some people might panic and take too much potassium iodide, which can be toxic, the authorities decided not to widely distribute the tablets, although employees of the power company and their families did take the tablets. A 2014 survey after the accident found 75 cases of thyroid cancer among evacuated children, a rate much higher than the pre-accident incidence of 1 case per million.

Some people think that authorities made the right decision in balancing the potential risks and benefits of widespread distribution of KI tablets. Others disagree. What would you recommend if a similar emergency occurred in your community today?

Issues involving science, technology, and society require that members of the community study the issues and engage in informed discussion. People need to understand the goals, costs, constraints, and trade-offs to make wise decisions for themselves and their communities.

# Lesson Reviews
Go to your Biology Foundations Workbook for longer versions of these lesson summaries.

## 2.1 The Nature of Matter
Atoms are extremely small, and they are made of even smaller particles called protons, neutrons, and electrons.

A chemical element is a pure substance made of one type of atom. Of the more than 100 elements, only about two dozen are common in living things. However, other elements are important to life in small amounts.

Atoms of different elements join together to form compounds. Chemical bonds hold atoms together in a compound. The two main types of chemical bonds are covalent and ionic.

- atom
- nucleus
- electron
- element
- isotope
- compound
- ionic bond
- ion
- covalent bond
- molecule
- van der Waals forces

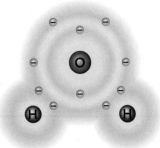

Water molecule ($H_2O$)

☑ **Classify** What kind of bonds are shown in this diagram?

## 2.2 Properties of Water
All living things depend on water. A water molecule ($H_2O$) is polar, which means one of its ends has a slight positive charge and another end has a slight negative charge.

Hydrogen bonds form between the relatively positive and relatively negative ends of adjacent molecules. These bonds account for water's special properties, including its ability to dissolve many other substances.

Water solutions may be acidic or basic, which is measured by pH. In blood and similar fluids, compounds called buffers help keep pH within tolerable limits.

- hydrogen bond
- cohesion
- adhesion
- mixture
- solution
- solute
- solvent
- suspension
- pH scale
- acid
- base
- buffer

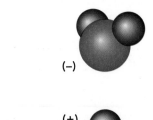

(−)

(+)

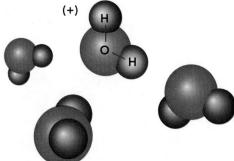

☑ **Use Models** Add dotted lines to show the hydrogen bonds in this diagram of water molecules.

## 2.3 Carbon Compounds

Carbon atoms are able to form long chains that may include many other elements. As a result, the molecules of carbon compounds can be long, varied, and stable. Living things contain four types of macromolecules, based on carbon. These are carbohydrates, lipids, nucleic acids, and proteins.

Carbohydrates include sugars and starches. They store and release energy. Lipids include fats, oils, and waxes. Some lipids function as chemical messengers. Nucleic acids carry genetic information. Proteins have many roles: they may control chemical reactions, form cell structures, or carry substances in and out of cells.

- monomer
- polymer
- carbohydrate
- lipid
- nucleotide
- nucleic acid
- protein
- amino acid

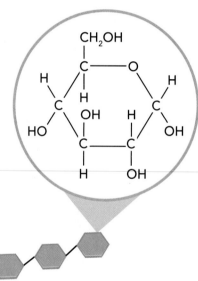

☑ **Classify** Identify the monomers and polymer in this example of a macromolecule.

## 2.4 Chemical Reactions and Enzymes

Chemical reactions always involve changes in the chemical bonds that join atoms in compounds.

Chemical reactions that release energy often occur on their own, or spontaneously. Other reactions depend on an input of energy.

Living things make and use enzymes, which act as catalysts to speed up a reaction. Enzymes depend on many conditions, including temperature and pH, to function properly.

- chemical reaction
- reactant
- product
- activation energy
- catalyst
- enzyme
- substrate

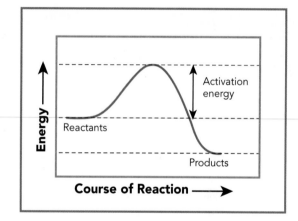

☑ **Interpret Graphs** Does the reaction described by this graph absorb or release energy? Explain your reasoning.

# Organize Information

Complete the main idea table to review the chapter.

| Main Idea | Details |
|---|---|
| All living things are made up of compounds. | 1. |
| All living things depend on liquid water. | 2. |
| All living things depend on compounds of carbon. | 3. |
| The chemical compounds of living things are constantly changing. | 4. |

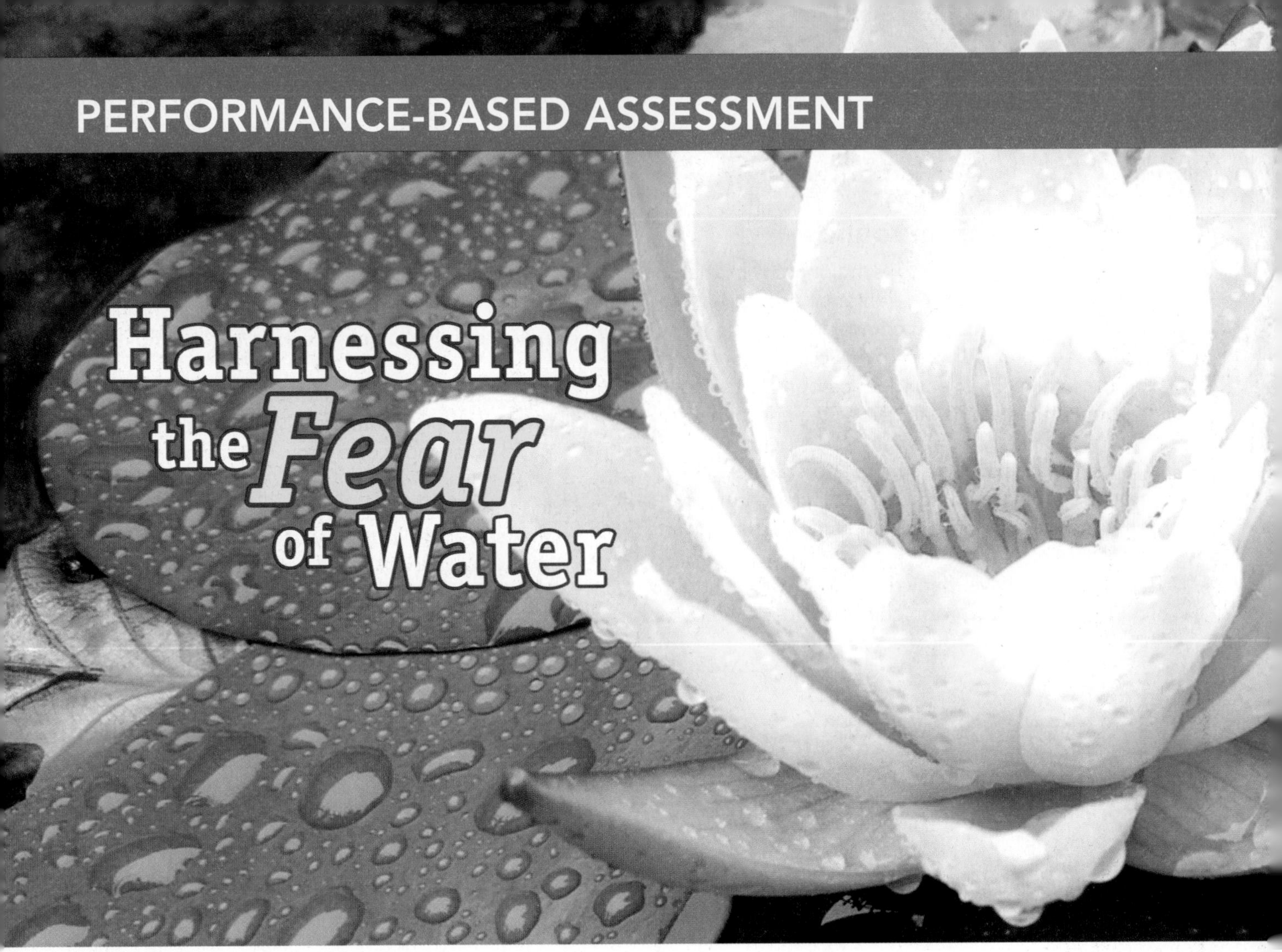

# Harnessing the *Fear* of Water

## Design a Solution

HS-ETS1-1, CCSS.ELA-LITERACY.RST.9-10.3, CCSS.ELA-LITERACY.WHST.9-10.2

**STEM** If you've ever been caught in a rainstorm, you know how quickly your clothes can get drenched with water. Most of your everyday clothes are made of materials that absorb water. But some of your clothes—think of your raincoat or your windbreaker—are made of materials that are waterproof.

The leaves of plants are naturally waterproof. The top and bottom surfaces of leaves are covered with a thin, waxy layer that acts as a protective barrier. Some leaves are more waterproof than others. In fact, some are so waterproof that scientists call them hydrophobic, or "water fearing."

The leaves of the lotus flower are a well-known example. Water on a lotus leaf immediately beads up and rolls off the leaf surface, almost as if the leaf itself were pushing the water away. Try doing a video search for "lotus effect" and "hydrophobic effect," and you can see for yourself.

What makes a hydrophobic substance "fear" water? Now that you know about some of the special properties of water, investigate the phenomenon of hydrophobicity on your own or with a partner. Find out what causes the lotus effect, and discuss the technological innovations that have been inspired by it.

1. **Obtain Information** Search for and watch an online video clip that shows the lotus effect. What do you think causes this phenomenon? Discuss possible answers with your classmates. Then do your own research to deepen your understanding of what you observed.

2. **Construct an Explanation** Write a scientific explanation of the lotus effect. Your explanation should include descriptions of the microscopic structure of the leaf surface and the physical properties of the materials involved. You should also identify the function that the lotus effect provides to the plant. What problem or need does it solve?

3. **Develop Models** Draw a diagram or build a model that illustrates the main points of your explanation. Ask your classmates to identify any gaps or weaknesses in your diagram or model. Then refine your work based on the feedback.

4. **Construct Explanations** Hydrophobic phenomena in the natural world have inspired inventions in the fields of materials science and nanotechnology. Identify a product that uses hydrophobic technology, and specify the problem or need that it solves. What claims have been made about the product's effectiveness? Explain how you could scientifically test the validity of such claims and how the data generated from your procedure would be used.

5. **Design a Solution** Think of a problem or need in your own world that could be solved by hydrophobic technology. What are the criteria for a successful solution to this problem? Discuss ideas for possible solutions, and then write a proposal outlining how you would design a solution to the problem.

## 🔍 KEY QUESTIONS AND TERMS

## 2.1 The Nature of Matter

1. In the atom, which particles are in constant motion around the nucleus?
   a. protons
   b. protons and neutrons
   c. neutrons
   d. electrons

2. How do the properties of sodium chloride (NaCl) compare with the properties of its component elements, sodium (Na) and chlorine (Cl)?

3. How do the isotopes of an element differ?

4. Describe the electric charges of the three main subatomic particles.

5. When might van der Waals forces be strong enough to hold two molecules together?

6. How does the behavior of an electron change when it forms a covalent bond?

## 2.2 Properties of Water

### HS-ESS2-5

7. What are produced when a base is mixed with water?
   a. hydrogen ions
   b. hydroxide ions
   c. oxygen atoms
   d. oxygen ions

8. Which type of bonds hold two or more water molecules together, as shown?
   a. covalent bonds
   b. van der Waals forces
   c. hydrogen bonds
   d. ionic bonds

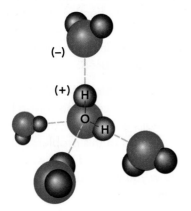

9. What is the function of a buffer, such as bicarbonate ions in the blood?

10. What does the pH scale measure?

11. What property of water molecules allows water to dissolve many substances?

12. What is the difference between the solute and solvent? Give an example.

13. Why is water essential to all living things?

## 2.3 Carbon Compounds

### HS-LS1-6

14. Carbohydrates may form larger carbon-based macromolecules by combining with which elements?
   a. sodium, potassium, nitrogen
   b. nitrogen, sulfur, phosphorus
   c. potassium, sodium, sulfur
   d. silicon, phosphorus, sodium

15. Which type of macromolecule stores genetic information?
   a. carbohydrates
   b. proteins
   c. lipids
   d. nucleic acids

16. Which type of macromolecule regulates cell processes or transports material into and out of cells?
   a. carbohydrates
   b. proteins
   c. lipids
   d. nucleic acids

17. What is the relationship between monomers and a polymer?

18. What are three major roles of proteins?

19. What is the general structure of an amino acid?

20. Describe the parts of a nucleotide.

## 2.4 Chemical Reactions and Enzymes

HS-LS1-6

21. Which are the catalysts of reactions in living things?
    a. enzymes
    b. lipids
    c. carbohydrates
    d. substrates

22. What changes during a chemical reaction between two compounds?
    a. number of atoms
    b. chemical bonds
    c. total mass
    d. total energy

23. Which type of chemical reaction tends to occur on its own, or spontaneously?

24. What is the name for the amount of energy that a reaction needs to get started?

25. How do enzymes act as catalysts in a chemical reaction?

26. What changes to the environment can affect the activity of enzymes?

## CRITICAL THINKING

HS-LS1-6

27. Integrate Information An oxygen atom has eight protons. From this information, can you determine numbers of neutrons and electrons in an oxygen atom? Explain.

28. Interpret Visuals Describe the process shown in this diagram. What will the outcome of the process be?

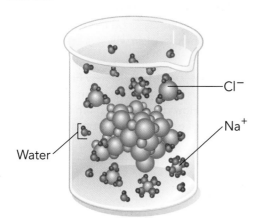

29. Apply Scientific Reasoning By identifying the properties of water ($H_2O$), can you predict or infer the properties of its component elements, hydrogen and oxygen? Explain why or why not.

30. Communicate Information Describe the basic molecular structures and primary functions of the four major categories of biological macromolecules.

31. Design an Experiment Suggest one or two simple experiments to determine whether a solid white substance is a lipid or a carbohydrate. What evidence would you need to support each hypothesis?

32. Synthesize Information In a multistep process, cells can combine the reactants glucose ($C_6H_{12}O_6$) and oxygen ($O_2$) to form the products carbon dioxide ($CO_2$) and water ($H_2O$). Some cells can also perform the reverse of this process. Must one, both, or neither of the processes release energy? Explain.

33. Construct an Explanation The temperature of the interior of the human body is about 37°C (98.6°F), regardless of the air temperature. Explain the importance of a constant body temperature given the role of enzymes as catalysts in the body.

34. Integrate Information In a series of chemical reactions, sugar molecules are combined with other reactants to form a protein. What elements must be included in the reactants? Explain your reasoning.

35. Plan an Investigation Like other enzymes, carbonic anhydrase is affected by the pH of the solution surrounding it. Describe the steps of an investigation to identify the ideal pH for the enzyme.

36. Construct an Explanation Changing the temperature or pH can change an enzyme's shape. Explain how changing the temperature or pH might affect the function of an enzyme.

37. Construct an Explanation How does the high heat capacity of water contribute to the ability of a river, lake, or ocean to support life?

38. Integrate Information How does water's versatility as a solvent help living things survive?

# ☑ASSESSMENT

## CROSSCUTTING CONCEPTS

**39. Energy and Matter** A burning log releases energy in the form of heat and light. Describe the changes to matter at the level of atoms and molecules that cause this energy to be released.

**40. Cause and Effect** As part of the digestive process, the human stomach produces hydrochloric acid, HCl. Sometimes excess acid causes discomfort. In such a case, a person might take an antacid such as magnesium hydroxide, $Mg(OH)_2$. Explain how this substance can reduce the amount of acid in the stomach.

## MATH CONNECTIONS

## Analyze and Interpret Data

CCSS.MATH.CONTENT.MP2, CCSS.MATH.CONTENT.MP4, CCSS.MATH.CONTENT.HSN.Q.A.1

The half-life is a unit of time that measures the stability of an isotope. During the time span of one half-life, half of a supply of the isotope has decayed into other isotopes or elements. The least stable isotopes have half-lives that are fractions of a second.

The table below shows half-lives and other properties of six isotopes of carbon. Use this table to answer questions 41–43.

| Isotope | Number of Protons | Number of Neutrons | Abundance (percentage of all carbon atoms) | Half-life |
|---|---|---|---|---|
| Carbon-10 | 6 | 4 | 0 | 19.29 seconds |
| Carbon-11 | 6 | 5 | 0 | 20.33 minutes |
| Carbon-12 | 6 | 6 | 98.9 | (stable) |
| Carbon-13 | 6 | 7 | 1.1 | (stable) |
| Carbon-14 | 6 | 8 | Less than 0.1 | 5730 years |
| Carbon-15 | 6 | 9 | 0 | 2.45 seconds |

**41. Identify Patterns** Describe the pattern in half-lives and abundance shown by the data.

**42. Apply Scientific Reasoning** Among the six isotopes shown in the table, which would be most useful for labeling, or tracing, a carbon compound through an organism? Explain.

**43. Reason Quantitatively** A molecule of a complex carbohydrate is made of 12 carbon atoms. Assuming that carbon and other atoms combine in the expected ratio, calculate the numbers of hydrogen and oxygen atoms in the molecule.

**44. Model With Mathematics** A hydrogen atom has 1 proton and 1 electron, while an oxygen atom has 8 protons and 8 electrons. Construct a table to show the changes in protons and electrons when a water molecule ($H_2O$) splits apart to form a hydrogen ion ($H^+$) and a hydroxide ion ($OH^-$).

## LANGUAGE ARTS CONNECTIONS

## Write About Science

CCSS.ELA-LITERACY.WHST.9-10.2, CCSS.ELA-LITERACY.WHST.9-10.4

**45. Write Explanatory Texts** The four main types of macromolecules are carbohydrates, lipids, nucleic acids, and proteins. Write a method for classifying a macromolecule based on its chemical composition.

**46. Write Informative Texts** Write a paragraph that explains the role of enzymes in biological systems. Focus on a specific reaction, such as the combining of carbon dioxide and water to form carbonic acid. Note the importance of the shapes of the enzyme active site and substrate in the reaction.

## Read About Science

CCSS.ELA-LITERACY.RST.9-10.2, CCSS.ELA-LITERACY.RST.9-10.7

**47. Summarize Text** Describe three properties of water that help explain why it is essential to all living things.

**48. Integrate With Visuals** Review **Figure 2-13**, which shows how monomers combine to form polymers. How does the diagram help explain the formation of each type of macromolecule?

# END-OF-COURSE TEST PRACTICE

## Questions 1–2

The diagram shows the structure of glucose, a molecule that organisms make and use.

**Glucose**

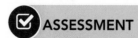

1. Which of these statements describes how organisms could use molecules of glucose?
   - I. Several glucose molecules could be assembled into a larger molecule.
   - II. Glucose molecules could be broken apart to form smaller molecules.
   - III. The atoms of glucose molecules could be combined with other elements to form a different molecule.
   - **A.** I only
   - **B.** III only
   - **C.** I and II only
   - **D.** I and III only
   - **E.** I, II, and III

2. What structural feature does glucose share with larger organic molecules, including DNA and proteins?
   - **A.** A basic structure, or backbone, formed by chains of carbon atoms
   - **B.** A ratio of 1 carbon atom to 2 hydrogen atoms to 1 oxygen atom
   - **C.** The presence of double covalent bonds between carbon atoms
   - **D.** Strong bonds between carbon atoms that cannot be broken
   - **E.** Ionic bonds between carbon atoms and oxygen atoms

3. Roger is comparing a model of a sugar molecule to a model of an amino acid. Which of the following evidence statements would be supported by the two models?
   - **A.** Sugars and amino acids are made of exactly the same elements.
   - **B.** Sugars and amino acids have the same structure.
   - **C.** Sugars and animo acids are made of the same elements but amino acids also contain nitrogen.
   - **D.** Sugars and amino acids are made of the same elements but sugars also contain phosphorus.
   - **E.** Sugars and amino acids are both polymers.

4. Lisa is investigating a chemical reaction involving carbon compounds. Which of these results could NOT occur, according to scientific laws about chemical reactions, matter, and energy?
   - **A.** The reaction releases energy to the environment.
   - **B.** The reaction absorbs energy from the environment.
   - **C.** The mass of carbon in the products is greater than the mass of carbon in the reactants.
   - **D.** The mass of carbon in the products is equal to the mass of carbon in the reactants.
   - **E.** The reaction occurs faster in the presence of a certain protein.

5. Two students are developing a computer simulation of a chemical reaction that forms amino acids. Their simulation uses colored spheres to represent atoms of different elements. It uses lines connecting the spheres to represent chemical bonds. For the simulation to be accurate, which of these features should be included?
   - **A.** Lines that break and reform between the spheres
   - **B.** Spheres that break apart into small pieces
   - **C.** Spheres that disappear during the simulation of the reaction
   - **D.** Spheres that appear during the simulation of the reaction
   - **E.** Lines that never break once they are placed

☑ **ASSESSMENT**

For additional assessment practice, go online to access your digital course.

## If You Have Trouble With...

| Question | 1 | 2 | 3 | 4 | 5 |
|---|---|---|---|---|---|
| See Lesson | 2.3 | 2.3 | 2.3 | 2.4 | 2.4 |
| Performance Expectation | HS-LS1-6 | HS-LS1-6 | HS-LS1-6 | HS-LS1-6 | HS-LS1-6 |

# UNIT 2 Ecology

American crocodile, Everglades National Park, Florida

**Crosscutting Concepts** Ecology
deals with life at all scales, from microscopic to planetary. Organisms interact
with each other and with their environments, forming global systems driven by
energy. Those systems are rarely stable;
causes of global change produce measurable effects on all living things, including
humans.

**BOUNCE TO ACTIVATE**

**▶ VIDEO**

Author Joe Levine
talks about
stability and
change, using
succession as an
example.

# Invasives
## IN YOUR NEIGHBORHOOD

## It was just a little snake

when you bought it. But, a year later, your Burmese python was as long as you are tall and weighed more than you do. This was not the kind of pet you had in mind. Unfortunately, some Burmese python owners have reached the same conclusion and have abandoned their enormous pets in Florida's Everglades National Park. These pythons have flourished in their new home and are causing large declines in small mammal populations in the Everglades. Burmese pythons are an invasive species . . . and they are not alone. In fact, invasives are all around us.

**PROBLEM LAUNCH**
Choose an invasive species in your local ecosystem to focus on.

▶ VIDEO

**BOUNCE TO ACTIVATE**

Watch a video about Australia's battle with the poisonous cane toad.

# PROBLEM: How can you reduce the impact of an invasive species on your local ecosystem?

» **TO SOLVE THIS PROBLEM,** perform these activities as they come up in the unit and record your findings in your 📖 Explorer's Journal.

## INTERACTIVITY

Investigate how invasive species can disrupt a native food web.

## INTERACTIVITY

Conduct a virtual investigation to see the effect of the introduced Burmese pythons on the Everglades ecosystem.

## STEM PROJECT

Design a solution to help control the population of the local invasive species you chose.

## AUTHENTIC READING

Read about how an invasive species is changing hemlock forests in the Smoky Mountains.

## INTERACTIVITY

Virtually test different strategies for controlling an invasive frog in the American southwest.

## PROBLEM WRAP-UP

Present your findings, and propose a solution for reducing the impact of a local invasive species.

| 3.1 | 3.2 | 3.3 |
|---|---|---|
| Introduction to Global Systems | Climate, Weather, and Life | Biomes and Aquatic Ecosystems |

Biosphere 2

**Go Online to access your digital course.**

- ▶ VIDEO
- 🔊 AUDIO
- 👆 INTERACTIVITY
- 📖 eTEXT
- 👁 ANIMATION
- ⚗ VIRTUAL LAB
- ☑ ASSESSMENT

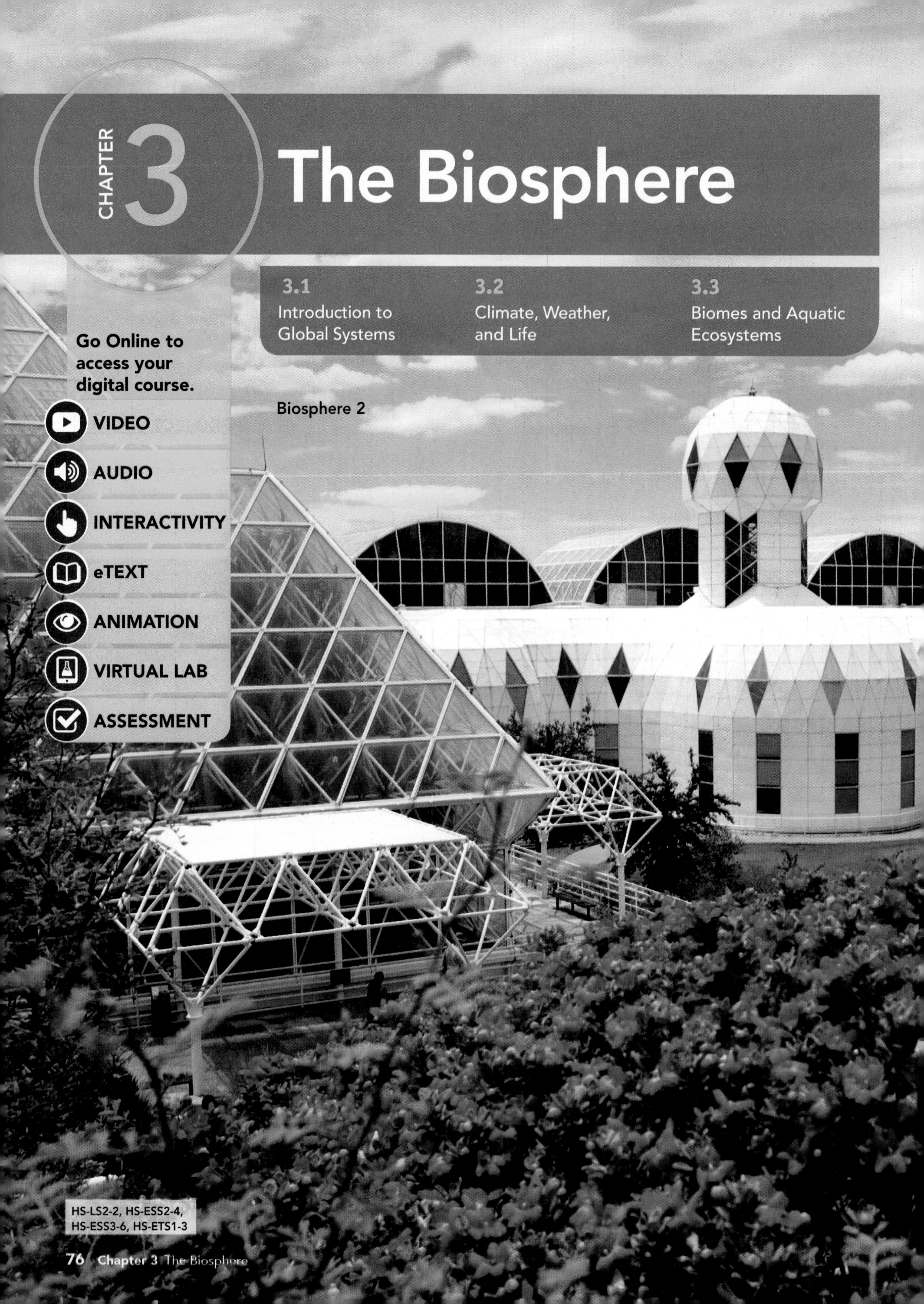

HS-LS2-2, HS-ESS2-4,
HS-ESS3-6, HS-ETS1-3

# Can we make a working model of our living planet?

Rising like a mirage in the desert 30 miles north of Tucson, Arizona, a huge greenhouse shaped like an Aztec pyramid towers over smaller greenhouses, domes, and oddly-shaped buildings. It would be easy to think that this place was built as a set for a science fiction movie on Mars. As it turns out, that impression wouldn't be far from the truth.

This is "Biosphere 2"—built in the late 1980s in hopes of providing a model for human space colonies. Its builders knew that colonists would need to produce food to eat, oxygen to breathe, and clean water to drink. Recycling waste products was essential. But how could they mange all this?

"Biosphere 1" is Earth, whose living and physical global systems support life through complex processes that we only partly understand. So a team of biologists and engineers set out to design and build a "biosphere in miniature" that could support human life sealed off from the outside world. Biosphere 2 included three acres of greenhouses in which to grow food, and, in miniature, a tropical rain forest, an ocean with a coral reef, a desert, a grassland, and a mangrove forest. These artificial environments contained roughly 3000 documented species, and many species of undocumented microorganisms. A crew of eight "biosphereans" sealed themselves inside.

Was Biosphere 2 a success? That depends on how you define "success." Almost as soon as Biosphere 2 was sealed, the composition of its atmosphere started changing. Oxygen concentrations dropped so dramatically that supplemental oxygen had to be piped in.

Meanwhile, carbon dioxide levels rose steadily. Many desirable plant and animal species died—including all pollinating insects. Nuisance insects and weeds grew exponentially.

Mass media were quick to label the entire $150 million project a complete failure. But was it? In science, few experiments are total failures, because even flawed designs usually produce useful data. Biosphere 2 showed that its living and physical systems used more oxygen than they produced, and produced more carbon dioxide than they could absorb. In fact, Biosphere 2's "ocean" produced the first evidence that increased atmospheric carbon dioxide concentrations can cause ocean acidification. Today, the facility is run by the University of Arizona as one of the only places where certain types of large-scale experiments can be conducted.

What can we learn from Biosphere 2 about how Earth's much larger systems work? What are the natural subsystems that operate on a global scale? How can studying small parts of the biosphere help us understand the planet-sized picture?

**Throughout this chapter, look for connections to the** CASE STUDY **to help you answer these questions.**

# Introduction to Global Systems

## 🔍 KEY QUESTIONS

- *Why is ecology important?*
- *What methods are used in ecological studies?*
- *What are biotic and abiotic factors?*
- *How can we model global systems?*

### VOCABULARY

biosphere
ecology
species
population
community
ecosystem
biotic factor
abiotic factor
atmosphere
hydrosphere
geosphere

### READING TOOL

As you read, use the lesson headings and subheadings to help you organize this lesson into the table in your 📖 **Biology Foundations Workbook.**

 **VIDEO**

Watch this video to learn about various sampling techniques.

In the early days of space travel, astronauts made lots of scientific discoveries about the moon and space. That was expected. But they also made some unexpected emotional discoveries when they saw our planet suspended in lifeless space. "We came all this way," Astronaut William Anders wrote, "to study the moon, and the most important thing is that we discovered the Earth." Scott Carpenter added, "It's small. It's isolated, and there is no resupply." Wally Schirra summed it up: "I left Earth three times and found no other place to go. Please take care of Spaceship Earth." How might we care for Spaceship Earth? A good start would be to understand the global systems that shape our planet.

## Ecology: Studying Our Living Planet

Astronauts were impressed with Earth's beauty, and with their understanding that our planet is covered with a thin skin of life that biologists call the biosphere. The biosphere includes all life on Earth, from bacteria underground, to trees in rain forests, fishes in the oceans, mold spores floating in the air … and humans. Because all forms of life are tightly connected with their surroundings, the **biosphere** includes all parts of Earth in which life exists.

**The Science of Ecology** All forms of life interact with each other and with their environments. 🔍 *Ecology is the scientific study of interactions among organisms, populations, and communities and their interactions with their environment.* The root of the word *ecology* is the Greek word *oikos*, meaning "house." **Ecology** is the study of nature's "houses," organisms that live in those houses, and interactions based on energy and nutrients. *Oikos* is also the root of the word *economics*. Economics studies human "houses" and interactions based on money or trade, energy, and nutrients.

**Why Study Ecology?** Although economics studies human economy, and ecology studies the economy of nature, those two fields developed independently. For much of history, that wasn't a global problem. Human populations were small and scattered. Our environmental impacts were local. In many cases, human economies could function more or less independently from nature's economy … or so people thought.

Recently we've learned (sometimes the hard way) that economics and ecology are actually tightly linked. As human populations have grown, and as the power of our technology have increased, our impact on local and global environments has also grown. The world is changing around us. As you will learn later in this unit, much of that change is caused by human activity. In the midst of this change in both local and global environments, some economists are discovering what biologists have known for years: Human economies depend on healthy ecological systems for essential needs such as drinkable water and fertile soil.

We need to understand ecology so that we can design human economies that are sustainable—which means that they can function without constantly degrading the environment. We also need to learn to design our economies in ways that offer resilience, which means that they can adapt and continue to function as global ecology changes around us.

**Levels of Ecological Organization** Ecologists study organisms and their environments on several levels. These levels of organization are shown in **Figure 3-1**. Some ecologists study individual organisms. Others study communities, ecosystems, or the entire biosphere. Ecological studies on a global scale are vital to charting a sustainable course for humanity.

**✓ READING CHECK** **Summarize** What is the difference between a population and a community?

**Figure 3-1**

## Levels of Organization

The kinds of questions that ecologists may ask about the living environment can vary, depending on the level at which the ecologist works.

**Individual Organism**
A **species** is a group of similar organisms that can breed and produce fertile offspring.

A **population** is a group of individuals that belong to the same species and live in the same area.

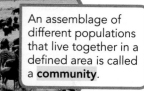

An assemblage of different populations that live together in a defined area is called a **community**.

All the organisms that live in a place, together with their physical environment, are known as an **ecosystem**.

A biome is a group of ecosystems that share similar climates and typical organisms.

Our entire planet, with all its organisms and physical environments, is known as the biosphere.

# Gathering Ecological Data

Given the wide range of systems and levels of organization that ecologists study, it isn't surprising that their studies may use a wide range of approaches and tools. ⚲ *Ecologists generally rely on three main approaches, all of which are part of scientific methodology: observation, experimentation, and modeling. Many studies involve all three approaches, with ecologists using tools ranging from DNA analysis to data gathered from satellites.*

**Observation** Observation is often the first step in asking ecological questions. Some observations are simple, such as: Which species live here? How many individuals of each species are there in a community? Other observations are more complex: What happens if a particular species is removed from a community? How will organisms respond to climate changes? If these questions are asked properly, they can lead to the development of testable scientific hypotheses.

**Experimentation** Experiments are designed to test hypotheses by gathering data that support or reject those hypotheses. Some ecological experiments, such as the one shown in **Figure 3-2**, carefully monitor conditions in selected parts of natural environments. This can be difficult to do, because some variables, such as weather, cannot be controlled.

Alternatively, ecologists may design artificial environments, like Biosphere 2. Experiments in artificial environments show how plants, bacteria, animals, or artificial communities react to changes such as temperature, lighting, or carbon dioxide concentration.

**Modeling** Many ecological processes, such as climate change, occur over long periods of time or occur over areas as large as our entire planet. Ecologists often make models to help them understand these phenomena. Many ecological models consist of mathematical formulas based on data that have been collected through observation and experimentation. Useful models make predictions that lead to the development of additional hypotheses. Those hypotheses, in turn, may lead to the design of new experiments to test them. Additional data may also lead to changes in models that improve their ability to make useful predictions.

☑️ **READING CHECK** Apply Concepts When have you used the skills of observation, experimentation, or modeling? Describe an example of how you have used this skill.

# Biotic and Abiotic Factors

When we talk about an organisms's environment, we are referring to all the conditions, or factors, around the organism that affect it in any way. Traditionally, these factors have been divided into biotic factors and abiotic factors.

**Figure 3-2**

**Studying Environmental Conditions**

Scientists gather ecological data in many ways. In this particular experiment, scientists are studying the effects of elevated levels of carbon dioxide on plant growth. Data collected in experiments such as this, can be used to model, make inferences, or apply to larger-scale experiments.

**Biotic Factors** Living things affect one another, and are therefore parts of each others' environment. ✎ *A biotic factor is any living part of the environment with which an organism might interact.* **Biotic factors** important to the heron, for example, might include the fish it eats, predators that eat herons, and other species that compete with them for food or space.

**Abiotic Factors** Physical factors also affect organisms. ✎ *An abiotic factor is any nonliving part of the environment, such as sunlight, heat, precipitation, humidity, wind or water currents, and soil type.* For example, a heron could be affected by **abiotic factors** such as water availability and quality, temperature, and humidity.

**Biotic and Abiotic Factors Together** The difference between biotic and abiotic factors may seem clear. But many so-called abiotic factors are strongly influenced by organisms, which means that they aren't entirely abiotic. Bullfrogs, for example, often hang out in soft "muck" along the shores of ponds. You might think that muck is a strictly abiotic factor, because it contains nonliving particles of sand and mud. But typical pond muck also contains decomposing plant material from trees and other plants around the pond. Muck is also home to bacteria and fungi that decompose the remains of other organisms while using them as "food." That's a lot of "biotic" mixed in with "abiotic"!

**READING TOOL**

Use **Figure 3-3** to create a Venn diagram listing the biotic and abiotic factors in the pond ecosystem shown.

**INTERACTIVITY**

Measure how various abiotic factors affect organisms in a pond.

Figure 3-3

**Biotic and Abiotic Factors**

Like all ecosystems, this pond is affected by a combination of biotic and abiotic factors. Some environmental factors are a mix of biotic and abiotic components. Biotic and abiotic factors are dynamic, meaning that they constantly affect each other.

Biotic Factors

Environment (Biotic and Abiotic)

Abiotic Factors

"Abiotic" conditions around a pond's mucky shore are also shaped by organisms. Trees and shrubs around the pond provide shade from strong sun, affecting the amount of sunlight and the range of temperatures the muck experiences. Those plants can also provide protection from dry winds, affecting the humidity of air above the muck. Plant roots determine how much soil washes into the pond during heavy rains. If pine trees grow nearby, decomposing needles make the soil acidic. Decomposing oak leaves, on the other hand, make soil more alkaline.

☑ **READING CHECK** **Explain** Give two examples of how abiotic factors are influenced by biotic factors.

# Modeling Global Systems

A dynamic mix of biotic and abiotic factors shapes all ecosystems—from ponds to global systems. So understanding global ecology is tough! Yet that understanding is vital to humanity's future. How can we handle this challenge? 🔍 *One way to understand global systems is to develop a model that shows those systems, the processes that operate within in each system, and ways those systems and processes interact.* One model, shown in **Figure 3-4** begins by identifying four major global spheres—the biosphere, the atmosphere, the hydrosphere, and the geosphere.

**INTERACTIVITY**

Figure 3-4
**Model of Earth Systems**

Earth's four global systems are constantly interacting. ☑ **Infer** What are some ways that the biosphere interacts with the other three systems?

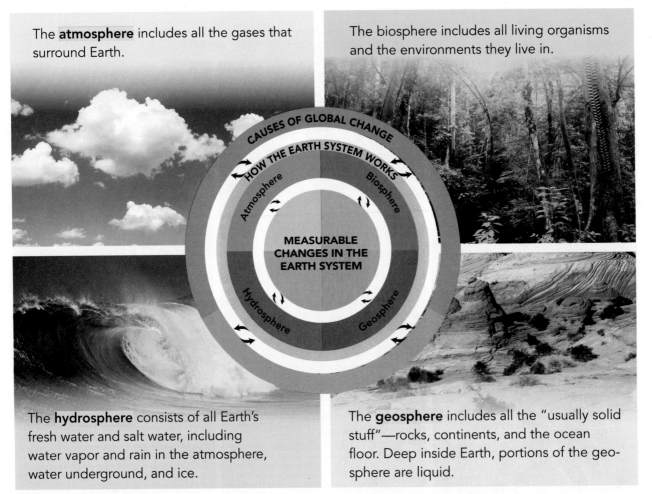

The **atmosphere** includes all the gases that surround Earth.

The biosphere includes all living organisms and the environments they live in.

CAUSES OF GLOBAL CHANGE

HOW THE EARTH SYSTEM WORKS

Atmosphere

Biosphere

**MEASURABLE CHANGES IN THE EARTH SYSTEM**

Hydrosphere

Geosphere

The **hydrosphere** consists of all Earth's fresh water and salt water, including water vapor and rain in the atmosphere, water underground, and ice.

The **geosphere** includes all the "usually solid stuff"—rocks, continents, and the ocean floor. Deep inside Earth, portions of the geosphere are liquid.

**Global Systems and Change** Our model has three main parts, each of which represents a category of ecological concepts and processes. You will see this model referred to throughout this unit.

The model's outer ring, labeled "Causes of Global Change," represents a combination of human activities and nonhuman events and processes that can drive changes in Earth's global systems. In this chapter, we will discuss several nonhuman causes of global change. Human causes of global change will be discussed in Chapter 7.

The model's middle ring, labeled "How the Earth System Works," represents events, processes, and cycles within the biosphere, atmosphere, geosphere, and hydrosphere. This part of the model includes some phenomena we discuss in this chapter, including the global climate system. It also includes cycles of matter, energy flow, and interactions among organisms that we will discuss in later chapters.

The model's inner circle, "Measurable Changes in the Earth System," contains the kinds of changes in global systems that scientists can measure. These include changes in climate, sea level, air and water quality, and so on. We emphasize "measurable changes" to emphasize that these represent data, not hypotheses.

This model, like most models, can't describe everything as accurately as we might like. For example, the hydrosphere includes water that is physically located in the atmosphere and the geosphere. The biosphere as we defined it earlier includes parts of the atmosphere, hydrosphere, and geosphere. Still, as we develop this model, you will see that it provides a useful framework for organizing information, demonstrating cause and effect, arguing from evidence, and examining connections among ecological events and processes. The model includes changes in global systems that scientists can measure, and the effects those changes have on ecological systems, including human society.

**BUILD VOCABULARY**

**Multiple Meanings** In geometry, a *sphere* is the shape of a round ball. In terms such as *biosphere* and *atmosphere*, it is a region or area.

**INTERACTIVITY**

Explore a tundra to learn about the levels of organization, Earth systems, and abiotic and biotic factors that make up this biome.

## In Your Neighborhood Lab  Open-Ended Inquiry

### Abiotic Factors and Plant Selection

**Problem** What plants will grow well in a garden near you?

For plants to grow, they need the right combination of biotic and abiotic factors. In this lab, you will collect data about abiotic factors in your region. Then, you will plan a garden by selecting the plants that can grow successfully in your area.

You can find this lab online in your digital course.

Visual Analogy

**Figure 3-5**

### The Earth Systems Model as a Jigsaw Puzzle

The earth systems model is similar to a jigsaw puzzle. Each piece of the puzzle represents a different process within the biosphere. As you work through this unit, you will see references to the model and the icons that represent the processes.

**Building and Using The Model** Where do we go from here in building the model, and how will it be useful? To answer those questions, let's start by saying that you will be learning about a lot of events, processes, and interactions in this unit. If that was all you learned, you would be left with a long list of facts to memorize, without a clear way to understand how those individual pieces of information relate to the way the world works. You would have no way to relate those facts to one another.

In a sense, you would have what you could think of as lots of separate pieces of a very complicated jigsaw puzzle ...without a clear idea of how those pieces fit together to form a picture of global systems. It would also be difficult for you to relate individual events and processes to important crosscutting concepts in biology.

That's where the Understanding Global Change model comes in. The model serves as a kind of "information organizer." Whenever we discuss important ecological events and processes, each of them will be assigned a visual icon, like those shown in **Figure 3-5**. Some icons represent processes in Earth's systems. Other icons represent causes of global change. Still other icons represent measurable effects of change. As we learn about these events and processes, we will add their icons to the model in much the same way that you would assemble a puzzle.

As we build the model across the unit, it will help you create concept maps that show how, for example, different aspects of weather and climate influence organisms, and how various causes of global change can affect climate. As you build the model, you can use it to explore connections among causes and effects in global change.

## LESSON 3.1 Review

### KEY QUESTIONS

1. What is the definition of *ecology*?
2. Describe the three basic methods of ecological research.
3. How are biotic and abiotic factors related? What is the difference between them?
4. Describe an approach for understanding global systems and the changes they undergo.

### CRITICAL THINKING

5. CASE STUDY Which approach to ecological investigations is illustrated by Biosphere 2? Defend your classification.
6. **Systems and System Models** In creating a model of our living planet, scientists need to consider four major Earth systems. Briefly describe these four systems, and then explain why it is difficult to study these systems individually.

# Climate, Weather, and Life

## KEY QUESTIONS

- *What is the difference between weather and climate?*
- *How are Earth's climate and average temperature determined?*
- *What causes ocean currents?*
- *What factors shape regional climate?*
- *What does climate change involve?*

HS-LS2-2: Use mathematical representations to support and revise explanations based on evidence about factors affecting biodiversity and populations in ecosystems of different scales.

HS-ESS2-4: Use a model to describe how variations in the flow of energy into and out of Earth's systems result in changes in climate.

People always talk about the weather. Storms like Hurricane Katrina or superstorm Sandy can cause widespread damage and loss of life. A summer may be uncomfortably hot, or a winter bitterly cold. Weather and climate are two terms we use to describe variations and averages in environmental factors that affect our lives.

## Climate and Weather

Weather and climate are important parts of local and national conversations these days, so it is worth looking at them closely. *Climate is defined by patterns and averages of temperature, precipitation, clouds, and wind over many years.* **Climate** also includes the frequency of extreme weather events such as heat waves, droughts, and floods, as shown in **Figure 3-6**. *Weather consists of short-term changes in temperature, precipitation, clouds, and wind from day to day, or minute to minute.* **Weather** can change rapidly, and can be tough to predict. It may be sunny in the morning but rainy in the afternoon. Climate is usually more predictable, so you wouldn't be surprised if you heard that it is hot today in Miami, Florida, but cool in Seattle, Washington.

Either short-term weather changes (such as droughts) or long-term climate changes (such as the frequency of droughts) can make the difference between success and failure of crops. Weather and climate also shape natural populations, communities, and ecosystems.

### VOCABULARY
climate
weather
greenhouse effect

### READING TOOL

As you read, identify the cause and effect relationships that the text describes. Fill in the table in your 📖 Biology Foundations Workbook.

**Figure 3-6**

**Climate**

Climate includes long-term averages of wind, clouds, precipitation, temperature, and extreme weather events such as droughts, floods, and heat waves.

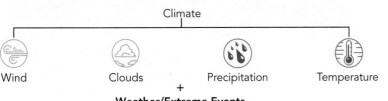

Climate

Wind  Clouds  Precipitation  Temperature
+
**Weather/Extreme Events**

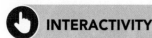
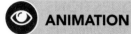
**Visual Analogy**

Figure 3-7

## The Greenhouse Effect

Greenhouse gases in the atmosphere allow solar radiation to enter the biosphere but slow down the loss of reradiated heat to space.

# The Global Climate System

Climate and weather are produced by a global climate system composed of winds and ocean currents. ✐ *The global climate system is powered and shaped by the total amount of solar energy retained in the biosphere as heat, and by the unequal distribution of that heat between the equator and the poles.*

**Solar Energy and the Greenhouse Effect**  The main force that shapes climate is solar energy that arrives as sunlight striking Earth's surface. Some of that energy is reflected into space, and some is absorbed and converted into heat. Some heat, in turn, is re-radiated into space, and some is trapped within the atmosphere. ✐ *Earth's average temperature is determined by the balance between the amount of heat that stays in the atmosphere and the amount of heat that is lost to space.*

This balance is largely controlled by the concentrations of three gases in the atmosphere—carbon dioxide, methane, and water vapor. These gases, called greenhouse gases, act like glass in a greenhouse. The gases allow visible light to enter but trap heat, as shown in **Figure 3-7**. This phenomenon is called the **greenhouse effect**. Without the greenhouse effect, Earth would be about 30 degrees Celsius cooler than it is today. Note that these three gases enter and leave the atmosphere as part of global cycles of matter. Their concentration in the atmosphere can therefore be affected by changes in those cycles driven by both nonhuman causes and by human activities. If changes in these cycles increase the greenhouse gas concentrations, the atmosphere retains more heat, and Earth warms. If changes decrease greenhouse gas concentrations, more heat escapes, and Earth cools.

**Sunlight**

Light reflected by earth's surface

Heat lost to space

Heat reradiated

Greenhouse gases in atmosphere

Some solar energy reflected, some absorbed, and some reradiated as heat

Heat absorbed and reradiated by greenhouse gases and retained in the earth system

86

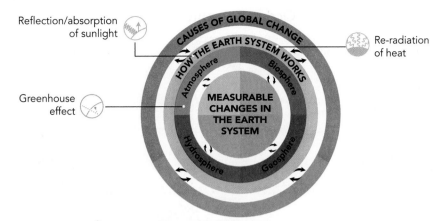

Figure 3-8

## Global Change And The Greenhouse Effect

The amount of sunlight that is reflected or absorbed, the amount of heat that is re-radiated in the Earth system, and the intensity of the greenhouse effect influences Earth's energy balance.

**Latitude and Solar Energy** Because Earth is curved and tilted on its axis, solar radiation strikes the surface at angles that vary from place to place and at different times of the year. Earth's curvature causes the same amount of solar energy to spread out over a larger area near the poles than near the equator, as **Figure 3-9** shows. Near the equator, the sun is directly overhead at noon, and day length varies little over the year. North and south of the equator, the sun drops lower in the sky during winter as tilted Earth revolves in orbit, and days become shorter. For both these reasons, more solar energy per unit area, and therefore more heat, arrives each year near the equator than near the poles.

The difference in heat received at the poles compared to the equator creates three main climate zones: tropical, temperate, and polar. The tropical zone is located between 23.5° north and 23.5° south latitudes near the equator. Here temperatures near sea level are warm or hot all year. Two temperate zones are located between 23.5° and 66.5° north and south latitudes. Here, summers may be quite hot, and winters can be very cold. The polar zones lie beyond the temperate zones, between 66.5° and 90° north and south latitudes. Here, winters are bitterly cold, and summers barely get warm.

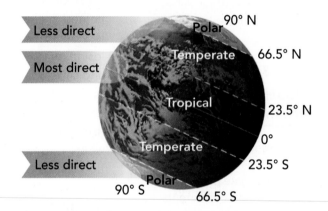

Figure 3-9

## Climate Zones

Earth's climate zones are produced by unequal distribution of the solar energy across Earths' surface. The tilt of Earth's axis causes this distribution to change over the course of a year, resulting in seasons.

HS-ESS2-4

---

## Quick Lab · Guided Inquiry

### Why Do Different Earth Surfaces Have Different Temperatures?

1. Review the procedure. Prepare a data table to record the temperature measurements.

2. Half fill each of three cups: one cup with gravel, a second cup with soil, and a third cup with water.

3. Place a thermometer inside each cup. Record the temperatures.

4. Place each cup under the heat lamp. Wait 30 minutes and then record the temperatures again.

### ANALYZE AND CONCLUDE

1. **Use Models** How do the materials you used in the model represent Earth's surface?

2. **Draw Conclusions** Use the data in your data table as evidence to draw a conclusion about the way Earth's surface is heated by sunlight.

3. **Form a Hypothesis** What if you turned off the heat lamp, and then measured the temperatures of the three cups over time? Form a hypothesis, and then test it with your teacher's approval.

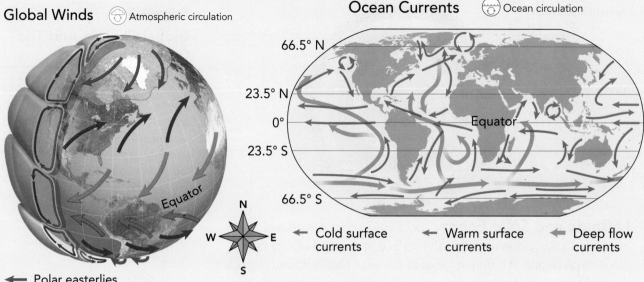

## Global Winds · Atmospheric circulation

## Ocean Currents · Ocean circulation

66.5° N
23.5° N
0°
23.5° S
66.5° S

Equator

← Cold surface currents     ← Warm surface currents     ← Deep flow currents

← Polar easterlies
← Westerlies
← Northeast trade winds
← Southeast trade winds
▨ Polar front

**Figure 3-10**

**Global Winds and Ocean Currents**

Earth's winds (left) and ocean currents (right) interact to help produce climate patterns. The paths of winds and currents are the result of heating and cooling, Earth's rotation, and geographic features.

**Differential Heating and Global Winds** This unequal distribution of heat creates winds and ocean currents. Air that is heated in a warm area, such as near the equator, expands, becomes less dense, and rises. As the air rises, it spreads north and south, losing heat along the way. As that air cools, it becomes more dense and sinks. Meanwhile, cold air over the poles also sinks. This pattern of rising and sinking air creates circulating cells of air that rise, travel north or south, sink towards Earth's surface, warm, and then rise again. As that air travels from places where it sinks to places where it rises, it creates winds, as shown in **Figure 3-10**. Earth's rotation causes winds to blow from west to east over both land and sea in the temperate zones, and from east to west over the tropics and the poles.

✓ **READING CHECK Synthesize Information** How does wind form?

## Ocean Currents

An oceanographer might say that ocean currents would flow around the world in much the way global winds do … but continents get in their way! ⚲ *Ocean currents are driven and shaped by patterns of warming and cooling, by winds, and by the locations of continents.*

**Winds and Surface Currents** Prevailing winds blowing over the ocean create surface currents that profoundly affect weather and climate in coastal areas. The warm Gulf Stream, for example, travels north along the east coast of North America, carrying heat from the Caribbean and Gulf of Mexico. Air passing over the Gulf Stream picks up moisture and heat, moderating winter temperatures in coastal areas. Along the West coast, the cool California Current carries cold water southwards, cooling the Pacific Northwest and the California coast. These interactions between atmosphere and hydrosphere shape weather and climate in coastal areas around the world. These interactions also influence water temperature and salinity that affect marine organisms and communities.

**Deep Ocean Currents** Cold ocean water near the poles sinks and flows along the ocean floor. This bottom water rises to the surface in some places, through a process called upwelling. Upwelling usually occurs where prevailing winds push surface water away from a continent. Cold water from the bottom rises to take the place of that surface water. One of the best-known upwellings in the Western Hemisphere occurs in the eastern Pacific Ocean off the coast of Peru. Increases and decreases in the strength of this upwelling are part of a phenomenon called El Niño. El Niño affects weather patterns from the southwestern United States all the way across the Pacific to Australia and Indonesia.

# Regional Climate

Washington State and Montana are located at similar latitudes, and are affected by the same prevailing winds that blow from west to east. Yet Montana has a very different climate than coastal Washington. Why? Because of mountains. 🔑 *Regional climates are shaped by latitude, by the transport of heat and moisture by winds and ocean currents, and by geographic features such as mountain ranges, large bodies of water, and ocean currents.*

The states of Oregon and Washington border the northern Pacific Ocean, where cold surface currents cool and humidify the prevailing winds that blow over them from west to east. That moist air hits the Cascade Mountains, is pushed upwards, and cools, causing moisture to condense and form clouds. Those clouds drop rain or snow, mainly on the western side of the mountains that faces the winds, as seen in **Figure 3-11**. For that reason, coastal climate in these states is cool and wet, and it supports a temperate rain forest. East of the Cascades, that same air sinks to lower altitudes, warms, and dries out. As a result, eastern Washington and Montana are drier and much warmer in summer, and can get much colder in winter.

✅ **READING CHECK** **Cause and Effect** What causes more rain to fall on one side of a mountain than the other side?

**READING TOOL**

Identify the effects of winds, ocean currents, and mountains on climate. Take notes in your notebook.

 **VIDEO**

Learn about El Niño and its effects on weather and climate.

**Figure 3-11**

## The Effect of Coastal Mountains

As moist ocean air rises over the upwind side of coastal mountains, it condenses, cools, and drops precipitation. With depleted moisture, the sinking air warms and becomes drier.

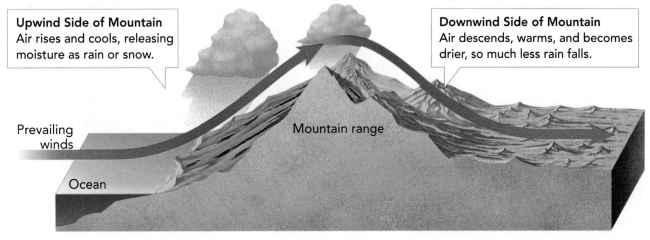

**Upwind Side of Mountain**
Air rises and cools, releasing moisture as rain or snow.

**Downwind Side of Mountain**
Air descends, warms, and becomes drier, so much less rain falls.

Prevailing winds

Mountain range

Ocean

# Changes in Climate

Earth's climate has remained pretty stable during recorded human history. The patterns of clouds, deserts, and vegetative areas as shown in **Figure 3-12** could be taken from any typical day over the last several thousand years. But global climate has changed dramatically over the far longer history of life. Earth's average temperature has increased and decreased over periods ranging from tens of thousands to millions of years. Those changes in temperature affected both the structure and the function of the global climate system. Recall that climate involves a lot more than just temperature. It also includes winds, precipitation, clouds, and extreme weather events. Climate change, therefore, involves more than global warming or cooling. ⚛ *Climate change involves changes in temperature, clouds, winds, patterns and amounts of precipitation, and the frequency and severity of extreme weather events.* **Figure 3-13** shows climate change in the "Measurable changes" portion of our global change model.

**Figure 3-12**

## Global Climate

In this computer-generated map of Earth, the white regions show a typical example of cloud cover.
☑ **Predict** How could changes to the global winds and ocean currents affect climate on land?

**Figure 3-13**

## Climate Change

Climate includes wind, clouds, precipitation, and temperature. Climate change involves changes in all of those factors and impacts both the atmosphere and hydrosphere.

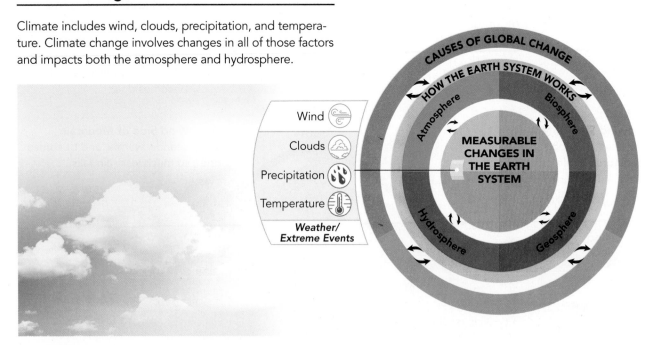

**Nonhuman Causes of Climate Change** Several factors have caused long-term changes in regional and global climate. As shown in **Figure 3-14**, these factors include: changes in solar energy, variations in Earth's orbit, meteorite impacts, changes in the distributions of continents and oceans, mountain building, volcanic activity, and meteorite impact.

The sun's output of solar energy varies over time. Changes in Earth's orbit and the tilt of its axis vary, in cycles of about 100,000 years. Once in a while, a giant meteorite hits Earth—like the one that led to the extinction of dinosaurs around 65 million years ago. The positions of Earth's continents change over millions of years, in ways that affect patterns of both winds and ocean currents. Episodes of mountain building can cause dramatic changes in regional climate, by affecting temperatures and patterns of precipitation. Major changes in the amount of volcanic activity worldwide can cause changes in the concentrations of greenhouse gases in the atmosphere.

## Results of Past Changes in Global Climate

These factors have caused both warm and cold periods over long periods of time. The most recent cold cycle caused the last major glacial period, which ended about 10,000 years ago. The global climate system creates regional climates that govern which plants, animals, and other organisms can survive in different places. Some changes in global climate have occurred slowly enough that most life on Earth could adapt and survive. But five times in Earth's history, climate change happened too fast for many organisms to survive, and vast numbers of species of all kinds died off. Those episodes are known as mass extinctions. In the Evolution unit, we will discuss mass extinctions driven by these nonhuman causes of global change. And in the last chapter of this unit, we will discuss whether human causes of global change are driving another mass extinction right now.

### Figure 3-14

### Nonhuman Causes of Climate Change

Geological and astronomical systems, processes, and events have caused major changes to global systems over the history of life on Earth. However, most of these nonhuman causes of global change act over extremely long time scales, ranging from thousands to millions of years.

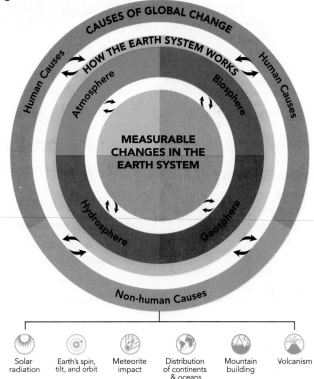

HS-LS2-2, HS-ESS2-4

## ✅ LESSON 3.2 Review

### 🔍 KEY QUESTIONS

1. Explain how *weather* and *climate* differ.

2. How does solar energy and the greenhouse effect impact Earth's global climate system?

3. Describe the factors that affect ocean currents.

4. What are the factors that result in different climates in different parts of the world?

5. Describe the different causes of climate change.

### CRITICAL THINKING

6. Apply Scientific Reasoning How might the speed of climate change affect the ability of life on Earth to adapt and survive?

7. CASE STUDY For Biosphere 2 to meet its goal, why was it necessary for it to replicate a variety of climates?

# Biomes and Aquatic Ecosystems

Golden lion tamarin, adult and baby

The factors that create regional climates establish conditions that govern which plants, animals, and other organisms can survive in particular geographic areas. These areas are described in this lesson.

## Life on Land: Natural Biomes

Ecologists typically classify the homes of organisms into roughly ten different regional climate communities called **biomes**. 🔍 *Biomes are described in terms of abiotic factors such as climate and soil type, and biotic factors such as plant and animal life.* Each biome is associated with seasonal patterns of temperature and precipitation that can be summarized in a graph called a climate diagram, like the one in **Figure 3-15**. The distribution of major biomes is shown in **Figure 3-16**. Note that even within a defined biome, there is often considerable variation among plant and animal communities. These variations can be caused by differences in exposure, elevation, or local soil conditions. Local conditions also can change over time.

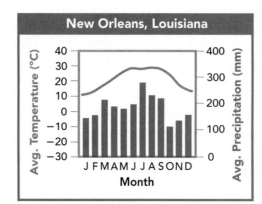

### Figure 3-15

### Climate Diagram

A climate diagram shows the average temperature and precipitation of a given location during each month of the year. In this graph, and those to follow, temperature is plotted as a red line, and precipitation is shown as vertical blue bars.

**Figure 3-16**

# Biomes

This map shows the locations of the world's major biomes. Each biome has a characteristic climate and community of organisms.

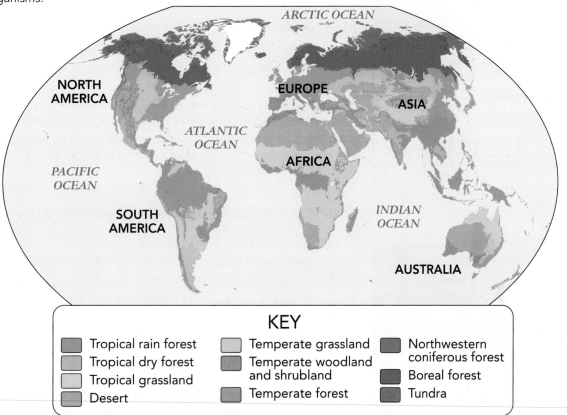

## KEY

- Tropical rain forest
- Tropical dry forest
- Tropical grassland
- Desert
- Temperate grassland
- Temperate woodland and shrubland
- Temperate forest
- Northwestern coniferous forest
- Boreal forest
- Tundra

## TROPICAL RAIN FOREST

Tropical rain forests have more species than all of the other biomes combined. Tropical rain forests typically get at least 2 meters of rain annually. Tall trees form a dense, leafy covering called a **canopy** from 50 to 80 meters above the forest floor. In the shade below, shorter trees and vines form a layer called the **understory**. Organic matter on the forest floor is recycled and reused so quickly that the soil in most tropical rain forests is not very rich in nutrients.

**Abiotic factors:** warm and wet year-round; thin, nutrient-poor soils subject to erosion

**Biotic factors**

*Plant life:* Understory plants compete for sunlight, so many have large leaves to capture light. Tall trees growing in shallow soil often have buttress roots, which act like props for support. Epiphytic plants grow on the branches of tall plants, taking advantage of available sunlight.

*Animal life:* Animals are active all year. Many use camouflage to hide from predators; some can change color to match their surroundings. Animals in the canopy have adaptations for climbing, jumping, and flight.

**Belem, Brazil**

## TROPICAL DRY FOREST

Tropical dry forests grow where rainy seasons alternate with dry seasons. In most places, a period of rain is followed by a prolonged period of drought.

**Abiotic factors:** warm year-round; alternating wet and dry seasons; rich soils subject to erosion

**Biotic factors**

*Plant life:* Many plants here lose their leaves during the dry season. Some leaves have an extra thick waxy layer to reduce water loss. Others store water in their tissues.

*Animal life:* Many animals reduce their need for water by entering long periods of inactivity similar to hibernation, but typically taking place during a dry season. Other animals, including many birds and primates, move to areas where water is available during the dry season.

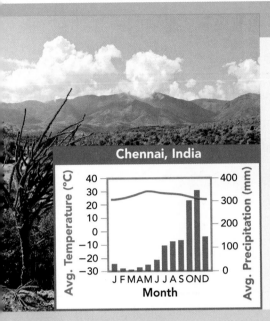

## TROPICAL GRASSLAND/SAVANNA/SHRUBLAND

This biome receives more seasonal rainfall than deserts but less than tropical dry forests. Grassy areas are spotted with isolated trees and small groves of trees and shrubs.

**Abiotic factors:** warm; seasonal rainfall; compact soils; frequent fires set by lightning

**Biotic factors**

*Plant life:* Plant adaptations are similar to those in the tropical dry forest, including waxy leaf coverings and seasonal leaf loss. Some grasses have a high silica content that makes them less appetizing to grazing herbivores. Also, grasses have adaptations that enable them to continue to grow after being grazed.

*Animal life:* Many animals migrate in search of water during the dry season, while some smaller animals burrow and remain dormant.

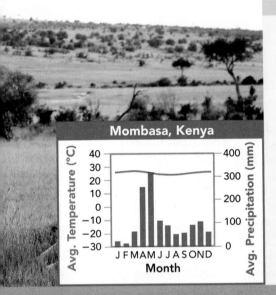

## DESERT

Deserts receive less than 25 centimeters of precipitation annually, but vary greatly depending on elevation and latitude. Many deserts undergo extreme daily temperature changes between hot and cold.

**Abiotic factors:** low precipitation; variable temperatures; soils rich in minerals but poor in organic material

**Biotic factors**

*Plant life:* Many plants, including cacti, store water in their tissues, and minimize leaf surface area to cut down on water loss. Cactus spines are actually modified leaves.

*Animal life:* Many desert animals get the water they need from their food. To avoid the heat of the day, many are active only at night. Blood vessels near the skin help animals lose body heat.

## TEMPERATE GRASSLAND

Plains and prairies with fertile soils once covered much of the Midwestern and central United States, land that is now used for farms. Periodic fires and heavy grazing by herbivores maintained the plant communities dominated by grasses.

**Abiotic factors:** warm to hot summers; cold winters; moderately seasonal precipitation; fertile soils; occasional fires

### Biotic factors

*Plant life:* Grassland plants, especially grasses, are resistant to grazing and fire. Dispersal of seeds by wind is common. The root structure of native grassland plants helps establish and retain deep, rich, fertile topsoil.

*Animal life:* These open, exposed environments make predation a constant threat for smaller animals. Camouflage and burrowing are common protective adaptations.

**Dallas, Texas**

## TEMPERATE WOODLAND AND SHRUBLAND

Here, large areas of grasses and wildflowers such as poppies are interspersed with oak and other trees. Communities that are more shrubland than forest are known as chaparral. Dense, low plants that contain flammable oils make fire a constant threat.

**Abiotic factors:** warm, dry summers; cool, moist winters; thin, nutrient-poor soils; periodic fires

### Biotic factors

*Plant life:* Woody chaparral plants have tough waxy leaves that resist water loss. Fire resistance is important, although the seeds of some plants need fire to germinate.

*Animal life:* Animals tend to eat varied diets of grasses, leaves, shrubs, and other vegetation. In exposed shrubland, camouflage is common.

**Los Angeles, California**

## TEMPERATE FOREST

Temperate forests have cold winters and warm summers. Coniferous trees produce seed-bearing cones. In autumn, deciduous trees shed their leaves. Fertile soils are often rich in **humus**, a material formed from decaying leaves and other organic matter.

**Abiotic factors:** cold to moderate winters; warm summers; year-round precipitation; fertile soils

### Biotic factors

*Plant life:* Deciduous trees drop their leaves and go into a state of dormancy in winter. Conifers have needlelike leaves that minimize water loss in dry winter air.

*Animal life:* Animals may cope with changing weather by hibernating or migrating to warmer climates. Other animals may be camouflaged to escape predation in the winter when bare trees leave them more exposed.

**Philadelphia, Pennsylvania**

## NORTHWESTERN CONIFEROUS FOREST

Mild, moist air and abundant rainfall nurture many tall conifers, from giant redwoods to spruce, fir, and hemlock, along with flowering trees and shrubs. Moss often covers tree trunks and the forest floor. This biome is sometimes called a "temperate rain forest."

**Abiotic factors:** mild temperatures; abundant precipitation in fall, winter, and spring; cool, dry summers; rocky, acidic soils

### Biotic factors

*Plant life:* Seasonal temperature variation means that there is less diversity here than in tropical rain forests. However, ample water and nutrients support lush, dense plant growth.

*Animal life:* Camouflage helps insects and ground-dwelling mammals avoid predation. Many animals are browsers—they eat a varied diet—an advantage in an environment where vegetation changes seasonally.

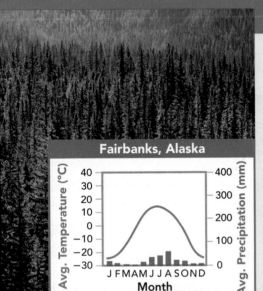

## BOREAL FOREST/TAIGA

The word *boreal* comes from the Greek word for "north." Dense forests of coniferous evergreens along the northern edge of the temperate zone are called boreal forests, or **taiga** (TY guh). Winters are bitterly cold, but summers are mild and long enough to allow the ground to thaw.

**Abiotic factors:** long, cold winters; short, mild summers; moderate precipitation; high humidity; acidic, nutrient-poor soils

### Biotic factors

*Plant life:* Conifers' shape and wax-covered needlelike leaves shed snow, and prevent excess water loss.

*Animal life:* Staying warm is the major challenge. Most have small extremities and extra insulation in the form of fat or downy feathers. Some migrate to warmer areas in winter.

## TUNDRA

The tundra is characterized by **permafrost**, a layer of permanently frozen subsoil. During the short, cool summer, the ground thaws to a depth of a few centimeters and becomes soggy. This cycle of thawing and freezing rips and crushes plant roots, which is one reason that tundra plants are small and stunted. Cold temperatures, high winds, a short growing season, and humus-poor soils also limit plant height.

**Abiotic factors:** strong winds; low precipitation; short and soggy summers; long, cold, dark winters; thin soils

### Biotic factors

*Plant life:* Ground-hugging mosses and other low-growing plants avoid damage from frequent strong winds. Seed dispersal by wind is common.

*Animal life:* Many animals migrate to avoid winters. Year-round residents display adaptations, including natural antifreeze, small extremities that limit heat loss, and a varied diet.

**Polar Regions** Polar regions border the tundra and are cold year-round. Plants are few, though some algae grow on snow and ice. Where rocks and ground are exposed seasonally, mosses and lichens may grow. Marine mammals, insects, and mites are the typical animals. In the north, where polar bears live, the Arctic Ocean is covered with sea ice, although more and more ice is melting each summer. In the south, the continent of Antarctica, inhabited by many species of penguins, is covered by ice nearly 5 kilometers thick in places.

**Biomes Today** There's just one problem with the traditional concept of biomes: There aren't many natural communities left. In our modern world, humans have altered nearly 75 percent of all land outside the steepest mountain slopes, the coldest polar regions, and the driest deserts. If you go outside your school or home, the overwhelming odds are that there won't be one shred of an original, untouched biome anywhere near you.

The concept of biomes, however, remains useful for describing large regions in which natural biological systems contain certain organisms and function in certain ways. Those regions differ from one another in terms of climate and other environmental factors in ways that are useful to understand, even if the original ecosystem is no longer there. And, as you will learn later in this unit, areas that have been modified by humans are still influenced by the same factors that shaped the ecosystems before our species came along.

**INTERACTIVITY**

Study three organisms to determine what biomes they are best suited for.

HS-LS2-2

## Analyzing Data

### Which Biome?

An ecologist collected climate data from two locations. The graph shows the monthly average temperatures in the two locations. In Location A, the total yearly precipitation is 273 cm. In Location B, the total yearly precipitation is 11 cm.

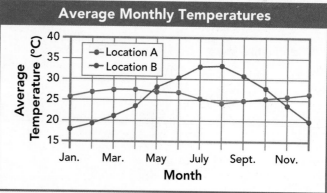

1. **Analyze Graphs** What specific question is this graph addressing?

2. **Analyze Graphs** Use the graph as evidence to draw a conclusion about the temperature over the course of the year in Location A and Location B.

3. **Apply Scientific Reasoning** In which biome would you expect to find each location, given the precipitation and temperature data? Use scientific reasoning to explain your answer.

4. **Construct Graphs** Look up the average monthly temperature last year for your community. Construct a graph and plot the data. Then, research the monthly rainfall for your city, and plot those data on your graph. Based on your results, which biome do you live in? Did the data predict the biome correctly?

# Marine Ecosystems

Similar to organisms living on land, underwater organisms are affected by external environmental factors. ✎ *Aquatic ecosystems are described primarily by salinity, depth, temperature, flow rate, and concentrations of dissolved nutrients.* There are three main groups of aquatic ecosystems: marine ecosystems, freshwater ecosystems, and estuaries.

Just as biomes typically occupy certain latitudes and longitudes, marine ecosystems typically occupy specific areas within the ocean. Ecologists usually divide the ocean into zones based on depth and distance from shore, as shown in **Figure 3-17**.

Water depth influences aquatic life because sunlight doesn't penetrate far in water. The sunlit region near the surface in which photosynthesis can occur is known as the **photic zone**. The photic zone may be as deep as 200 meters in tropical seas, but just a few meters deep or less in rivers and swamps. Below the photic zone is the dark **aphotic zone**, where photosynthesis cannot occur.

Food chains in many aquatic ecosystems are based on **plankton**, a term that includes floating algae—called phytoplankton—and small, free-swimming animals called zooplankton. Phytoplankton need enough light for photosynthesis, so they can grow only in the photic zone. Zooplankton, many of which feed on phytoplankton, may swim up and down, in and out of the photic zone.

## BUILD VOCABULARY

**Prefixes** The prefix *photo-* refers to light. A photic zone is well-lit, and photosynthesis uses the energy of light.

## Figure 3-17

### Ocean Zones

The ocean can be divided vertically into zones based on light penetration and depth, and horizontally into zones based on distance from shore.

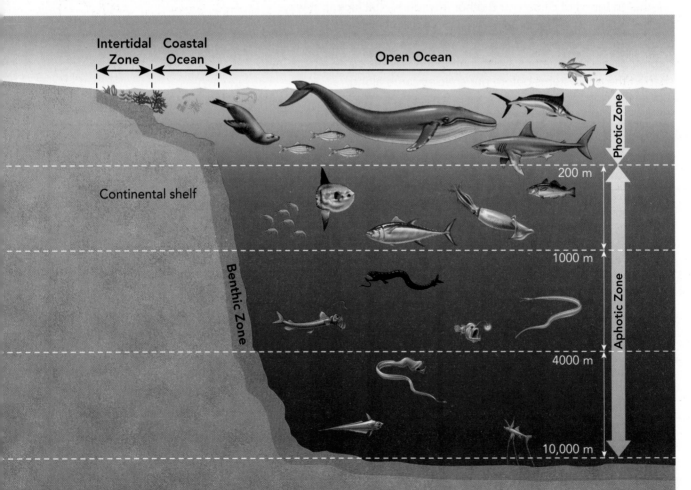

**Intertidal Zone** Organisms in the intertidal zone are submerged in seawater at high tide and exposed to air and sunlight at low tide. These organisms experience regular and extreme changes in temperature, and are often battered by waves and currents. There are many different types of intertidal communities. A typical rocky intertidal community exists in temperate regions where exposed rocks line the shore. There, barnacles and seaweed permanently attach themselves to the rocks.

**Coastal Ocean** The coastal ocean extends from the low-tide mark to the outer edge of the continental shelf—the relatively shallow border that surrounds the continents. Water here is brightly lit, and is often supplied with nutrients by freshwater runoff from land. As a result, coastal oceans tend to be highly productive. Kelp forests and coral reefs are two important coastal communities. A coral reef is shown in **Figure 3-18**.

**Open Ocean** The open ocean begins at the edge of the continental shelf and extends outward. More than 90 percent of the world's ocean area is open ocean. Depth ranges from about 500 meters along continental slopes to more than 10,000 meters in deep ocean trenches. The open ocean can be divided into two main zones according to light penetration: the photic zone and the aphotic zone.

**Figure 3-18**

**Coastal Ocean: Coral Reef**

Tropical coral reefs are among the most diverse and productive communities on Earth.

*Open Ocean Photic Zone* The open ocean typically has low nutrient levels and supports only the smallest species of phytoplankton. Still, the sunlit top 100 meters of the open ocean cover much of Earth's surface. So, most photosynthesis occurs here—and not in rain forests or other terrestrial environments.

*Open Ocean Aphotic Zone* The permanently dark aphotic zone includes the deepest parts of the ocean, where no photosynthesis can occur. Deep ocean organisms are exposed to high pressure, frigid temperatures, and total darkness. The deep ocean floor was once thought to be nearly devoid of life but is now known to have islands of high productivity. Deep-sea vents, where superheated water boils out of cracks on the ocean floor, support entire ecosystems based on chemical energy.

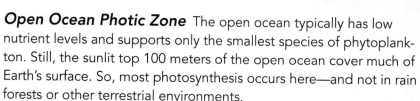 **READING CHECK Compare** How does the coastal ocean zone compare with the open ocean zone?

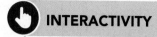 **INTERACTIVITY**

Learn about how factors such as chemistry, light, salinity, and temperature are influenced at different depths.

# Freshwater Ecosystems

Only 3 percent of Earth's surface water is fresh water, but that small percentage provides terrestrial organisms with drinking water, food, and transportation. Often, a chain of streams, lakes, and rivers begins in the interior of a continent and flows through several biomes to the sea. 🔍 *Freshwater ecosystems can be divided into three main categories: rivers and streams, lakes and ponds, and freshwater wetlands.*

## RIVERS AND STREAMS

Rivers, streams, creeks, and brooks often originate from underground water sources in mountains or hills. Near a source, water has plenty of dissolved oxygen but little plant life. Downstream, sediments build up and plants establish themselves. Still farther downstream, water may meander slowly through flat areas. Animals in many rivers and streams depend on terrestrial plants and animals that live along their banks. Often, a chain of streams and rivers begins in the interior of a continent and flows through several biomes to the sea.

## LAKES AND PONDS

Much of the life in lakes and ponds depends on a combination of plankton and attached algae and plants. Water typically flows in and out of lakes and ponds, often through rivers or streams. Water also circulates between the surface and the bottom during at least some seasons. This circulation distributes heat, oxygen, and nutrients. During a cold winter, thick ice might cover the lake for many months. Fish and other animals still live in the liquid water beneath.

👆 INTERACTIVITY

## FRESHWATER WETLANDS

A **wetland** is an ecosystem in which water either covers the soil or is present at or near the surface for at least part of the year. Water may flow through freshwater wetlands or stay in place. Wetlands are often nutrient-rich and highly productive, and they serve as breeding grounds for many organisms. Freshwater wetlands have important environmental functions: they purify water by filtering pollutants and help to prevent flooding by absorbing large amounts of water and releasing it slowly. Three main types of freshwater wetlands are freshwater bogs, freshwater marshes, and freshwater swamps.

# Estuaries

An **estuary** (ES tyoo er ee) is a wetland formed where a river meets the sea. Fresh water and salt water often mix here, rising and falling with ocean tides. ⚲ *Estuaries serve as spawning and nursery grounds for many ecologically and commercially important fish and shell-fish.* The species include bluefish, striped bass, shrimp, and crabs.

Salt marshes are temperate estuaries characterized by salt-tolerant grasses above the low-tide line and seagrasses below water. One of the largest salt marshes in the United States surrounds the Chesapeake Bay in Maryland.

Mangrove swamps are tropical estuaries characterized by several species of salt-tolerant trees, collectively called mangroves. The largest mangrove area in America is part of Florida's Everglades National Park, shown in **Figure 3-19**.

**Figure 3-19**

## Mangrove Swamps

Mangroves have several adaptations for growing in salty water. Roots that grow down from branches, called prop roots, help stabilize the plant in the damp soil.

HS-LS2-2

# ☑ LESSON 3.3 Review

### ⚲ KEY QUESTIONS

1. What abiotic and biotic factors describe a biome? Give examples for a specific biome.

2. What factors define aquatic ecosystems?

3. Why are wetlands important?

4. Where are estuaries found?

### CRITICAL THINKING

5. **Connect to Society** Many years ago, a wetland area was filled in to build a baseball field and playground. Now the town proposes to restore the area to become a shallow pond surrounded by a marsh. What do you think are the strongest arguments for and against this plan? What information would help people decide whether or not to support the plan?

6. **Critique** Shrublands are often referred to as *scrub* or *scrubland*. Why do you think the authors decided to use the term *shrubland* instead? Do you agree or disagree with their choice?

# Can we make a working model of our living planet?

**Biosphere 2, a habitat designed to model a life-sustaining space colony, didn't make the grade. But its "failure" taught us a lot.**

HS-LS2-2, HS-ESS2-4, HS-ETS1-2, HS-ETS1-3

## Make Your Case

Engineers and ecologists thought they'd designed a system that could sustain eight people sealed off from the outside world. But unexpected things happened. Some problems involved chemical reactions with parts of the project's structure. Others arose when organisms that were stocked in the system—and some that got in on their own—interacted in unexpected ways. Research the detailed history of Biosphere 2, along with more recent efforts to design self-sustaining systems.

## Developing and Using Models

1. **Evaluate Models** Biosphere 2 was intended to be a small-scale model of Biosphere 1. From your research, discuss the limitations of this model.

2. **Evaluate and Revise** If you were an engineer designing a new artificial biosphere, what approach would you use? How could your design attempt to avoid the problems faced by Biosphere 2? Can you find any papers published by current projects using this facility to support your explanation with evidence?

## Technology on the Case

### Eyes Above the Sky

Biosphereans could easily measure changes in their habitat's mini-ecosystems using simple tools. They could see which species were doing well, and which were dying. They could easily record population changes in weedy plants and insect pests. But many natural systems are far too large to be studied using standard methods. New technology offers a solution to this problem.

For years, scientists have been using satellites and airplanes to carry devices sensitive to short-wave ultraviolet (UV) and long-wave infrared (IR) light. These tools can distinguish forests, grasslands, and farms. Now, an amazing improvement is being developed at the Carnegie Institute for Science. Spectranomics, as it is called, can identify individual tree species in a forest, and even record their height.

How does it work? New technology precisely measures light reflected by plants across a very broad spectrum. The data make it possible to pinpoint individual trees and shrubs. Meanwhile, researchers on the ground take samples of plant leaves, record which wavelengths those leaves absorb and reflect, and identify the species to which each type of leaf belongs. When data gathered by the airborne instruments are analyzed together with the information that connects plant leaf characteristics with species names, they identify plant species!

## Careers on the Case

### Work Toward a Solution

Organizing data for useful analysis is the job of a data scientist.

### Data Scientist

Data scientists are experts at selecting the most useful way to display complex data. Then they design and construct their displays, often with the aid of computers. Some data

scientists work to display data on climate or populations. Others work for engineers, financial institutions, and other businesses.

▶ **VIDEO**

Watch this video to learn about other careers in biology.

hhmi | BioInteractive

## Lesson Review
Go to your Biology Foundations Workbook for longer versions of these lesson summaries.

### 3.1 Introduction to Global Systems
Ecology is the scientific study of interactions among organisms, populations, and communities and their interactions with their environment.

Ecologists generally rely on three main approaches, all of which are part of scientific methodology: observation, experimentation, and modeling. Ecologists may use tools ranging from DNA analysis to data gathered from satellites.

A biotic factor is any living part of the environment with which an organism might interact, including animals, plants, mushrooms, and bacteria. An abiotic factor is any nonliving part of the environment, such as sunlight, heat, precipitation, humidity, wind or water currents, and soil type.

The model of global systems has three major components: causes of global change, Earth's global system processes (how the Earth system works), and the measurable changes in the Earth system that scientists can monitor. Processes in the atmosphere, hydrosphere, geosphere, and biosphere interact to shape global ecosystems and climate.

- biosphere
- ecology
- species
- population
- community
- ecosystem
- biotic factor

- abiotic factor
- atmosphere
- hydrosphere
- geosphere

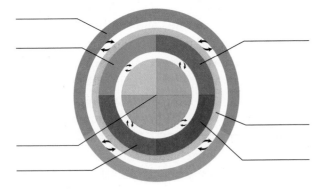

☑**Use Models** Identify the three main parts of the model, and the four spheres that are used to organize concepts in two of these parts.

### 3.2 Climate, Weather, and Life
Climate is defined by patterns and averages of temperature, precipitation, clouds, and wind over many years. Weather consists of short-term changes in temperature, precipitation, clouds, and wind from day to day, or minute to minute.

The global climate system is powered and shaped by the total amount of solar energy retained in the biosphere as heat, and by the unequal distribution of that heat between the equator and the poles. Earth's average temperature is determined by the balance between the amount of heat that stays in the atmosphere and the amount of heat that is lost to space.

Ocean currents are driven and shaped by patterns of warming and cooling, by winds, and by the locations of continents.

Regional climates are shaped by latitude, the transport of heat and moisture by winds and ocean currents, and by geographic features such as mountain ranges, large bodies of water, and ocean currents.

Climate change involves changes in temperature, clouds, winds, patterns and amounts of precipitation, and the frequency and severity of extreme weather events.

- climate
- weather
- greenhouse effect

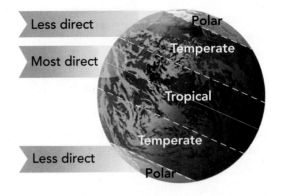

☑**Observe** Which climate zone gets the least amount of direct sunlight? The most direct sunlight?

## 3.3 Biomes and Aquatic Ecosystems

Biomes are described in terms of abiotic factors such as climate and soil type, and biotic factors such as plant and animal life.

Aquatic ecosystems are described primarily by salinity, depth, temperature, flow rate, and concentrations of dissolved nutrients.

Freshwater ecosystems can be divided into three main categories: rivers and streams, lakes and ponds, and freshwater wetlands.

Estuaries serve as spawning and nursery grounds for many ecologically and commercially important fish and shellfish.

- biome
- canopy
- understory
- humus
- taiga
- permafrost
- photic zone
- aphotic zone
- plankton
- wetland
- estuary

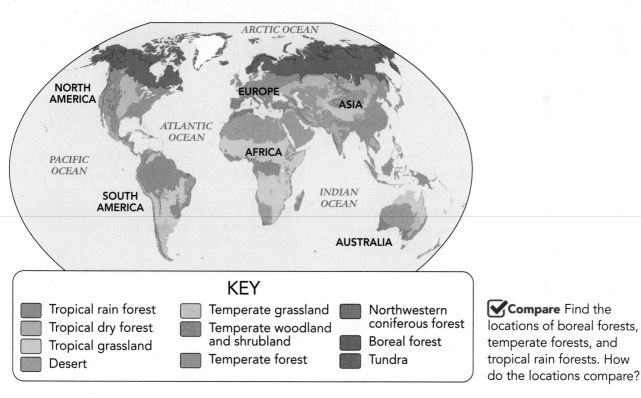

### KEY

Tropical rain forest
Tropical dry forest
Tropical grassland
Desert

Temperate grassland
Temperate woodland and shrubland
Temperate forest

Northwestern coniferous forest
Boreal forest
Tundra

☑**Compare** Find the locations of boreal forests, temperate forests, and tropical rain forests. How do the locations compare?

# Organize Information

Complete the table. For each cause, identify an effect and describe an example.

| Cause | → | Effect | Example |
|---|---|---|---|
| Greenhouse gases | → | warms the atmosphere. | 1. |
| Wind currents | → | 2. | 3. |
| Ocean currents | → | 4. | El Niño |

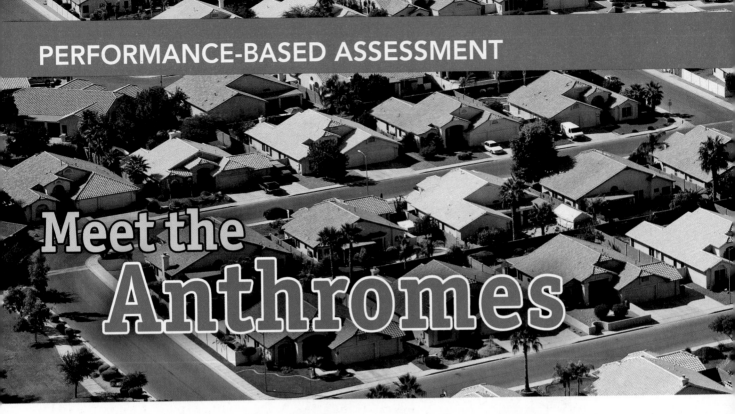

# Meet the Anthromes

## Construct an Argument

HS-ESS3-6, CCSS.ELA-LITERACY.WHST.9-10.8,
CCSS.ELA-LITERACY.WHST.9-10.9

Mosses and lichens grow on the tundra, lions hunt zebras on grasslands, and tall pine trees cover the taiga. However, do these classifications of biomes apply to the place where you live? Probably not. Scientists use the term *anthropogenic biome*, or *anthrome*, to describe biomes that humans have altered. Examples include dense urban areas. Here, buildings and pavement may cover nearly all of the land, with only small areas put aside for parks or stands of trees. Other anthromes consist of land used for farm crops and livestock. In these anthromes, human-selected plants and animals have replaced native species.

The map shows the major anthromes of the world. Compare it to the map of the natural biomes shown in **Figure 3-16**.

1. **Classify** Describe the properties of the place where you live. Then, use the information in the map to classify the anthrome you live in.

2. **Synthesize Information** How does the distribution of anthromes across the world compare to the distribution of biomes?

3. **Use Evidence to Construct an Argument** How do you think the world's natural biomes and anthromes will change in the future? Conduct research to help you construct your argument. Look for data and opinions from different sources, such as these.

   - nonprofit organizations devoted to conservation and wildlife

   - government agencies

   - economists and business groups

4. **Communicate** Write a short essay to present your argument about the future of Earth's natural biomes and anthromes. Support your argument with evidence from this chapter and from your research. Address the following criteria in your essay:

   - Predict which natural biomes or anthromes will expand, which will shrink, and which will stay the same size.

   - Include data, scientific reasoning, or expert opinions to support your predictions.

   - Cite your sources and evaluate their credibility. If you find reliable sources that provide conflicting information or opinions, discuss your evaluation of them.

In suburbs, pavement and houses have replaced the natural biome.

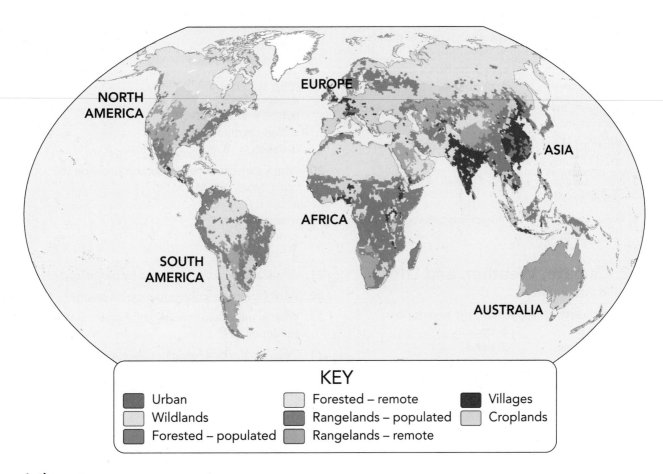

**KEY**

- Urban
- Wildlands
- Forested – populated
- Forested – remote
- Rangelands – populated
- Rangelands – remote
- Villages
- Croplands

**Anthromes**

This map shows the locations of major anthropogenic biomes of the world.

# ☑ASSESSMENT

## 🔑 KEY QUESTIONS AND TERMS

### 3.1 Introduction to Global Systems

1. The study of the complex system of interactions that sustain life on the planet is
   a. zoology.
   b. ecology.
   c. chemistry.
   d. economics.

2. Which photo represents the geosphere?

3. Nonliving factors of an environment are
   a. biotic.
   b. bacteria.
   c. abiotic.
   d. plankton.

4. The global system that contains most of the life on Earth is the
   a. atmosphere.
   b. geosphere.
   c. hydrosphere.
   d. biosphere.

5. Compare the terms *population*, *community*, and *ecosystem*.

6. What are the three general approaches that are used to study ecology?

7. What are the properties of a useful model of global systems?

8. Describe one of the interactions between the four major Earth systems.

### 3.2 Climate, Weather, and Life

**HS-LS2-2, HS-ESS2-4**

9. The climate zone closest to the equator is
   a. polar.
   b. temperate.
   c. tropical.
   d. torrid.

10. Average temperatures, precipitation, and wind patterns in an area define its
    a. geosphere.
    b. climate.
    c. weather.
    d. atmosphere.

11. The concentrations of gases in the atmosphere that trap heat produce
    a. radiation.
    b. solar energy.
    c. the greenhouse effect.
    d. the hydrosphere.

12. How is climate different from weather?

13. What accounts for the unequal distribution of heat between the equator and the poles?

14. What causes wind?

15. What factors affect the path of an ocean current?

16. How do mountain ranges affect climate?

17. What are some of the long-term, natural causes of climate change?

### 3.3 Biomes and Aquatic Ecosystems

**HS-LS2-2**

18. The biome that supports more species than all other biomes is the
    a. savannah.
    b. temperate grassland.
    c. boreal forest.
    d. tropical rain forest.

19. Taiga is a synonym for the
    a. boreal forest.
    b. temperate woodland.
    c. tropical dry forest.
    d. desert.

20. Which variable do scientists use to divide the open ocean into two zones?
    a. salinity
    b. latitude
    c. depth
    d. oxygen

21. Which biome is characterized by permafrost?

22. What factors describe aquatic ecosystems?

23. What is the ocean zone in which photosynthesis cannot occur?

24. Describe the difference between a wetland and an estuary.

25. Where does the most photosynthesis on Earth occur?

# CRITICAL THINKING

HS-LS2-2, HS-ESS2-4

26. **Compare and Contrast** How are aquatic ecosystems similar to ecosystems on land? How are they different?

27. **Plan Your Investigation** Ecologists have discovered that the seeds of many plants that grow in forests cannot germinate unless they have been exposed to fire. Design an experiment to test whether a particular plant has seeds with this requirement. Include your hypothesis statement, a description of both the control and experimental groups, and an outline of your procedure.

28. **Use Models** Give an example of a model biologists use to better understand ecological phenomena. How does the model help?

29. **Construct an Argument** One friend says biotic factors are more important than abiotic factors to ecology. Another friend says abiotic factors are more important than biotic factors. What do you think? Defend your position using examples from a specific biome of your choice.

30. **Construct an Explanation** A plant grower has a greenhouse where she grows plants in the winter. The greenhouse is exposed to direct sunlight and often gets too hot for the plants. She paints the inside of the glass with a chalky white paint, and the temperature drops to comfortable levels. Explain why this solution works.

31. **Integrate Information** Although the amount of precipitation is low, most parts of the tundra are very wet during the summer. How would you explain this apparent contradiction?

32. **Identify Patterns** Consider these two biomes: (1) the temperate grassland and (2) the temperate woodland and shrubland. Coyotes live in both biomes. Describe two adaptations that might enable coyotes to tolerate conditions in both biomes.

33. **Construct an Explanation** How does the greenhouse effect help to explain Earth's climate?

34. **Form a Hypothesis** The deep ocean lies within the aphotic zone and is very cold. Suggest some of the unique characteristics that enable animals to live in the deep ocean.

35. **Communicate Information** A developer has proposed filling in a salt marsh to create a coastal resort. What positive and negative effects do you think this proposal would have on wildlife and local residents? Would you support the proposal?

Use the Understanding Global Change model to answer questions 36 and 37.

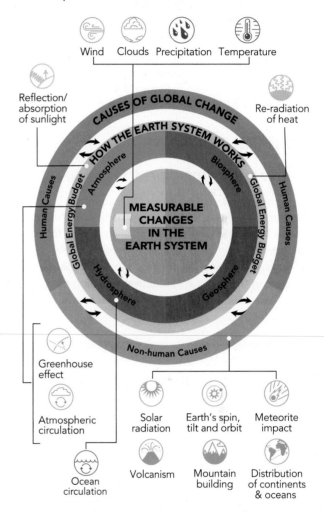

36. **Use Models** How are processes in the How the Earth System Works category related to Measurable Changes in the Earth System? Describe at least one relationship between two topics shown in the model.

37. **Evaluate Models** What does the model communicate about how processes and phenomena shape global systems? What have you learned about these topics that is not explained in the model?

## CROSSCUTTING CONCEPTS

**38. Structure and Function** Deciduous trees in tropical dry forests lose water through their leaves every day. During summers with adequate rain, the leaves remain on the trees. During the cold dry season, the trees drop their leaves. In an especially dry summer, how might the adaptation of dropping leaves enable a tree to tolerate the drought?

**39. Systems and System Models** Review the models in **Figure 3-1** and **Figure 3-4**. How are these two models similar or different? Are all of the components of the model in **Figure 3-1** represented in **Figure 3-4**? Explain why or why not.

## MATH CONNECTIONS

### Analyze and Interpret Data

CCSS.MATH.CONTENT.HSN.Q.A.2,
CCSS.MATH.CONTENT.HSS.IC.B.6

The graph below summarizes the changes in the total volume of ice in all the world's glaciers since 1960. (Volume is calculated from measurements of glacier surface area and depth.) Note that the volume changes on the y-axis are negative, meaning an overall loss of volume. Use the graph to answer questions 40–42.

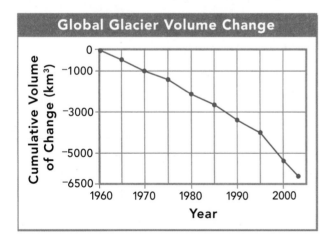

**40. Analyze Graphs** In which ten-year span was the greatest volume of glacial ice lost? What was the total loss of volume over that timespan?

**41. Calculate** Suppose a particular glacier covers 100 km², and it loses 30 cm of depth in a decade. Approximately what volume (km³) is lost? Show your work.

**42. Conduct Research** Investigate the most reasonable explanation for the loss of global glacier mass since 1960. Summarize your findings in a short paragraph.

## LANGUAGE ARTS CONNECTIONS

### Write About Science

CCSS.ELA-LITERACY.WHST.9-10.2

**43. Write Explanatory Texts** Choose one of the major biomes, and write an overview of its characteristics. Explain how abiotic factors and common plants and wildlife are interrelated. Support your explanation with specific examples.

### Read About Science

CCSS.ELA-LITERACY.RST.9-10.2

**44. Central Ideas** Review Lesson 3.2 to summarize generally how heat (or lack of heat) affects the vertical movements of large masses of air and large volumes of water. Then summarize the effects of other factors that influence wind and ocean currents and regional climate patterns.

1. Kara uses a model that shows slight changes to Earth's motion through space over many thousands of years. This model helps her explain long-term climate change due to what variable?
   A. volcanic activity
   B. meteor or asteroid strikes
   C. ocean circulation
   D. carbon dioxide levels in the atmosphere
   E. input of solar energy

2. Lionel uses a model that includes the atmosphere and sunlight to predict Earth's temperatures. In this model, why does increasing the levels of carbon dioxide in the atmosphere cause temperatures to increase?
   A. Sunlight passes through carbon dioxide.
   B. Sunlight is absorbed by carbon dioxide.
   C. Heat is trapped by carbon dioxide.
   D. Carbon dioxide generates heat.
   E. Carbon dioxide reacts with water to release heat.

3. Scientists have concluded that human activities are affecting the atmosphere and causing rapid climate change on a global scale. Which statement provides the strongest evidence that these changes to global climate are NOT the result of natural causes, such as variations in Earth's orbit?
   A. Until recently, Earth's climate had remained relatively constant.
   B. Variations in Earth's orbit cannot be measured precisely.
   C. Variations in Earth's orbit would affect climate only minimally.
   D. Earth's climate depends mostly on the output of the sun.
   E. Variations in Earth's orbit occur gradually over 100,000 years.

## Questions 4 and 5

This climate diagram shows the average temperature (line graph) and precipitation (bar graph) during each month of the year.

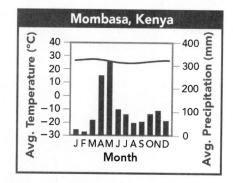

4. Plants that thrive in this type of climate are most likely adapted to which of these conditions?
   A. seasonal variations in temperature
   B. seasonal variations in precipitation
   C. year-long cold temperatures
   D. dense, competitive growth
   E. rich, fertile soil

5. Which plant feature would MOST LIKELY be common in this type of climate?
   A. leaves with waxy coverings
   B. tall, woody trunks
   C. broad, flat leaves
   D. watery fruits
   E. roots that dangle in the air

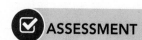 **ASSESSMENT**

For additional assessment practice, go online to access your digital course.

## If You Have Trouble With...

| Question | 1 | 2 | 3 | 4 | 5 |
| --- | --- | --- | --- | --- | --- |
| See Lesson | 3.2 | 3.2 | 3.3 | 3.3 | 3.3 |
| Performance Expectation | HS-ESS2-4 | HS-ESS2-4 | HS-ESS3-6 | HS-LS2-2 | HS-LS2-2 |

| 4.1 | 4.2 | 4.3 |
|---|---|---|
| Energy, Producers, and Consumers | Energy Flow in Ecosystems | Cycles of Matter |

**Go Online to access your digital course.**

- ▶ VIDEO
- ◀ AUDIO
- 👆 INTERACTIVITY
- 📖 eTEXT
- 👁 ANIMATION
- ⚗ VIRTUAL LAB
- ☑ ASSESSMENT

A Common Kingfisher captures its meal

HS-LS2-2, HS-LS2-3, HS-LS2-4, HS-LS2-5, HS-LS4-5, HS-LS4-6, HS-ESS2-6, HS-ETS1-3

# What's to blame for the bloom?

Green slime. Toxic muck. Tourist-repelling, fish-killing scum. Guacamole-thick sludge. These are just a few of the more polite words used to describe an ugly green "living carpet" that spread across bodies of water in and around Florida during the summer of 2016. That "carpet" was an algal bloom— an out-of-control growth of algae. Often, either algae themselves, or bacteria that grow on dead algae, release poisonous and often foul-smelling compounds that can kill aquatic animals and affect human health.

Natural blooms of aquatic algae can appear in freshwater and salt-water ecosystems at certain times of year. Usually natural blooms provide some extra input into the food chain, and color the water green for a while. But not-so-natural blooms produced by the effects of human activity, can cause serious problems. The giant 2016 bloom in Florida, for example, started in Lake Okeechobee. From there, thick, floating mats of algae spread along rivers and into coastal areas along both the Atlantic and Gulf Coasts. These poisonous mats, so large that they could be seen from space, fouled beaches and marinas and killed fish.

Unfortunately, this is not an isolated event. Toxic algal blooms are happening more frequently and in more places, growing larger, and lasting longer. In 2015, the biggest algal bloom ever recorded on the United States West Coast stretched all the way from California's Channel Islands to the Alaskan Peninsula. That bloom forced closures of fish and shellfish industries in California, Oregon, and Washington for months, causing losses of millions of dollars. Freshwater algal blooms also occur in small lakes and streams, and can cover many square kilometers in both Lake Erie and Lake Michigan.

What's going on? Some algal blooms—usually mild ones—occur naturally in freshwater and salt-water ecosystems when available nutrients combine with favorable temperatures and other environmental factors. In lakes, natural blooms often occur in springtime. In coastal oceans, they often occur in summer. But around the world, in fresh and salt water alike, bigger and more frequent blooms seem to result from several factors involved in global change.

Researchers hypothesize that the Florida bloom—which involved both freshwater and salt-water ecosystems—was triggered by unusually heavy rains. The West Coast bloom seems to have been caused by unusually warm water in the Pacific.

Why would heavy rains trigger a bloom in Florida? And why would higher temperatures cause one off the coast of California? Despite their different causes, did those blooms have anything in common? Do we know enough to act in ways that could head off future blooms?

**Throughout this chapter, look for connections to the** CASE STUDY **to help you answer these questions.**

# Energy, Producers, and Consumers

**HS-LS2-3:** Construct and revise an explanation based on evidence for the cycling of matter and flow of energy in aerobic and anaerobic conditions.

## KEY QUESTIONS

- *What are primary producers?*
- *How do consumers obtain energy and nutrients?*

## VOCABULARY

**autotroph**
**primary producer**
**photosynthesis**
**chemosynthesis**
**heterotroph**
**consumer**
**detritus**

## READING TOOL

As you read, make a concept map to show the relationships between different types of organisms. Complete the concept map in your 📘 **Biology Foundations Workbook.**

All living things need energy. You think about energy and its relationship to your life all the time, whether you realize it or not, and not just when you grab an "energy bar" on your way to exercise. To control your weight, you need to balance energy you take in, energy your body uses at rest, energy you "spend" during exercise, and energy your body stores. When we burn "fossil fuels" we release energy captured and stored by ancient organisms! But where does all that energy come from?

## Primary Producers

No living thing can *create* energy, but organisms called **autotrophs** can capture energy from nonliving sources and convert it into forms living cells can use. Autotrophs also store energy in ways that make it available to other organisms, which is why they are also called **primary producers**. *Primary producers are the first producers of energy-rich compounds that can be used later by other organisms.* All life depends on primary producers.

**Energy From the Sun** The energy that powers most life on Earth comes from sunlight. Algae and plants harness solar energy to build living tissues through **photosynthesis**, using that energy to convert carbon dioxide and water into oxygen and energy-rich carbohydrates such as sugars and starches. Photosynthetic primary producers also add oxygen to the atmosphere and remove carbon dioxide. Plants are the main primary producers on land. Algae and plants share that role in freshwater ecosystems, and algae do most of the heavy lifting in sunlit parts of the ocean. Certain bacteria also harness sunlight, but use a different kind of photosynthesis. These

**Life Without Light** In 1979, biologists discovered thriving eco-systems inhabited by strange animals around volcanic vents spewing superheated water in the pitch-black depths of the Pacific Ocean. Where did the energy that powers life in these ecosystems come from? It turns out that the water gushing from those vents is rich in energy-rich inorganic compounds. Some bacteria can not only tolerate high temperatures near the vent, but can also harness chemical energy from inorganic molecules such as hydrogen sulfide. These bacteria use a process called **chemosynthesis** (kee moh SIN thuh sis) in which chemical energy is used to produce carbohydrates as shown on the right in **Figure 4-1**. Around the vents, many chemosynthetic bacteria live inside the tissues of certain types of worms and large clams. The bacteria pass some of the carbohydrates they produce to their animal partners.

This astonishing discovery opened researchers' eyes to the eco-logical importance of chemosynthesis. Thanks to studies that were inspired by this work, we now know that chemosynthetic primary producers are a lot more common, and live in many more environments, than anyone expected. Recent studies have shown that chemosynthetic bacteria thrive deep within Earth's crust, in total darkness and exposed to extremely high temperatures. They are also found closer to the surface in underground streams and caves previously thought to be lifeless. Still other chemosynthetic bacteria live buried in the mud of tidal flats all over the world. We have a great deal more to learn about these lightless ecosystems—all of it fascinating.

> ✓ **READING CHECK** **Compare and Contrast** How are photosynthesis and chemosynthesis similar? How are they different?

**BUILD VOCABULARY**

**Prefixes** The prefix *chemo-* means "chemical," or "chemistry." The process of chemosynthesis uses chemical energy to produce organic compounds in an organism.

 **VIDEO**

Watch an interactive video that compares the flow of energy and the roles of producers and consumers in two ecosystems: a kelp forest and a hydrothermal vent.

**Figure 4-1**

## Photosynthesis and Chemosynthesis

Plants use the energy from sunlight to carry out the process of photosynthesis. Other autotrophs, such as sulfur bacteria, use the energy stored in chemical bonds in a process called chemosynthesis. In both cases, energy-rich carbohydrates are produced.

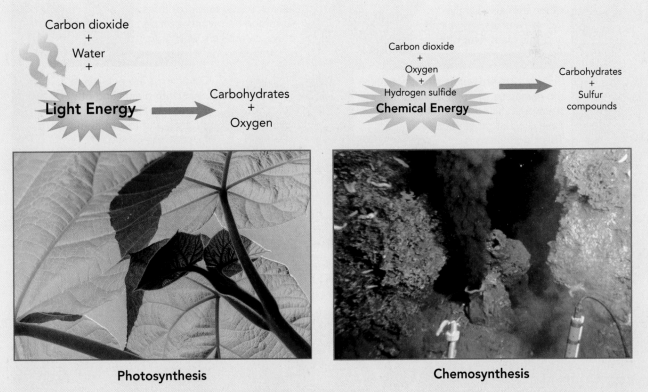

Carbon dioxide + Water + **Light Energy** → Carbohydrates + Oxygen

**Photosynthesis**

Carbon dioxide + Oxygen + Hydrogen sulfide + **Chemical Energy** → Carbohydrates + Sulfur compounds

**Chemosynthesis**

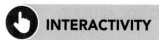
# Consumers

Animals, fungi, and many bacteria cannot harness energy directly
from the environment as primary producers do. These organisms,
known as **heterotrophs**, must acquire energy from other organisms,
usually by eating them. Heterotrophs are also called **consumers**.
🔍 *Consumers are organisms that rely on other organisms for
energy and nutrients.*

**Types of Consumers** Consumers are classified by the way
they acquire energy and nutrients from other organisms. Some examples of the different types of consumers are shown in **Figure 4-2**.

**Beyond Consumer Categories** Many organisms do not
fit neatly inside the tidy categories ecologists try to place them in.
For example, some animals usually described as carnivores, such as
hyenas, will scavenge if they get a chance. Many aquatic animals eat
a mixture of algae, bits of animal carcasses, and tiny bits of organic
matter—including the feces of other animals! Toucans use their razor-
sharp bills to cut up fruit, but they also can swallow frogs, small mammals, and even baby monkeys! Consumers often lumped together
may also differ from one another in more subtle ways. Herbivores
may select different parts of the plants they eat. That's important
because different plant parts often contain very different amounts of
available energy.

**Figure 4-2**

**Consumers**

Consumers rely on other
organisms for energy and
nutrients. The Amazon
rain forest shelters examples
of each type of consumer, as
shown here.

**Carnivores** kill and eat
other animals. Carnivores
include snakes, dogs, cats,
and this giant river otter.

**Herbivores** like this military
macaw obtain energy and
nutrients by eating plant
leaves, roots, seeds, or fruits.
Common herbivores include
cows, caterpillars, and deer.

**Scavengers** are animals that consume
the carcasses of other animals that
have been killed by predators or
have died of other causes.
This king vulture is
a scavenger.

**Omnivores** are animals that
eat both plants and other
animals. Humans, bears,
pigs, and this white-nosed
coati are omnivores.

**Decomposers** "feed" by chemically breaking
down organic matter. This process produces
**detritus**, or small pieces of dead and
decaying plant and animal
remains. Bacteria and fungi,
like these mushrooms,
are decomposers.

**Detritivores**
such as this giant
earthworm chew or grind detritus
particles into smaller pieces. Many
types of mites, snails, shrimp, and crabs
are detritivores. They commonly digest
decomposers that live on, and in,
detritus particles.

Fruits, such as berries are easy to digest, and are usually rich in energy and nutrients. So it isn't surprising that many birds and mammals feed on these types of foods. The world's human population also gets much of its energy from the seeds of grasses: rice, corn, wheat, oats, and barley.

Leaves are plentiful in many ecosystems, but are low in energy and tough to digest. Why? Leaves are composed largely of cellulose. No multicellular organism can manufacture an enzyme to break down cellulose molecules. Only fungi and certain single-celled organisms manufacture those enzymes. So how can many animals eat leaves? Animals that eat leaves have microorganisms inside their guts that digest cellulose for them!

Cattle and many other grazing animals spend a long time chewing their food into a pulp. When they swallow this pulp, it enters a complex digestive tract, part of which supports microorganisms that can break down cellulose. Many grazers periodically regurgitate the mixture of food and bacteria, which is called cud. Then they chew the cud and reswallow it. Even with all this extra work, grazers can extract relatively little energy from each mouthful of leaves. They therefore spend a lot of their time eating. What's more, the kind of digestive system needed to extract energy and nutrients from leaves is very heavy. That's why only a handful of birds eat leaves.

## Analyzing Data

### Ocean Water and Oxygen Concentration

Samples of ocean water are taken at different depths, and the amount of oxygen in the water at each depth is measured. The results are shown in the data table.

1. **Analyze Data** Describe what happens to the amount of available oxygen as you get deeper in the ocean.

2. **Infer** Light can penetrate to only a depth of between 50 and 100 m in most ocean water. What effect does this have on the water's oxygen concentration? Explain.

| Concentration of Oxygen | |
|---|---|
| Depth of Sample (m) | Oxygen Concentration (ppm) |
| 0 | 7.5 |
| 50 | 7.4 |
| 100 | 7.4 |
| 150 | 4.5 |
| 200 | 3.2 |
| 250 | 3.1 |
| 300 | 2.9 |

HS-LS2-3

## ✓ LESSON 4.1 Review

### ⚲ KEY QUESTIONS

1. What are the two primary sources of energy that power living systems?

2. How do consumers obtain energy?

### CRITICAL THINKING

3. **Develop Models** Draw a model to illustrate the flow of energy from a nonliving source to an herbivore.

4. **Construct an Explanation** Termites are insects that feed on wood, which contains cellulose. Scientists have observed that some termite species prefer wood that has been attacked by fungi. Construct an explanation for this observation.

LESSON 4.2

# Energy Flow in Ecosystems

**KEY QUESTIONS**

- *How does energy flow through ecosystems?*
- *How do ecological pyramids help analyze energy flow through trophic levels?*

**HS-LS2-4:** Use mathematical representations to support claims for the cycling of matter and flow of energy among organisms in an ecosystem.

**VOCABULARY**
**food chain**
**phytoplankton**
**food web**
**trophic level**
**ecological pyramid**
**biomass**

**READING TOOL**

As you read, identify the main idea and supporting details under each heading. Take notes in your **Biology Foundations Workbook.**

When one organism eats another, energy moves from the "eaten" to the "eater." That sounds simple, but you would be surprised at how complicated ecological studies of "Who eats whom?" can be!

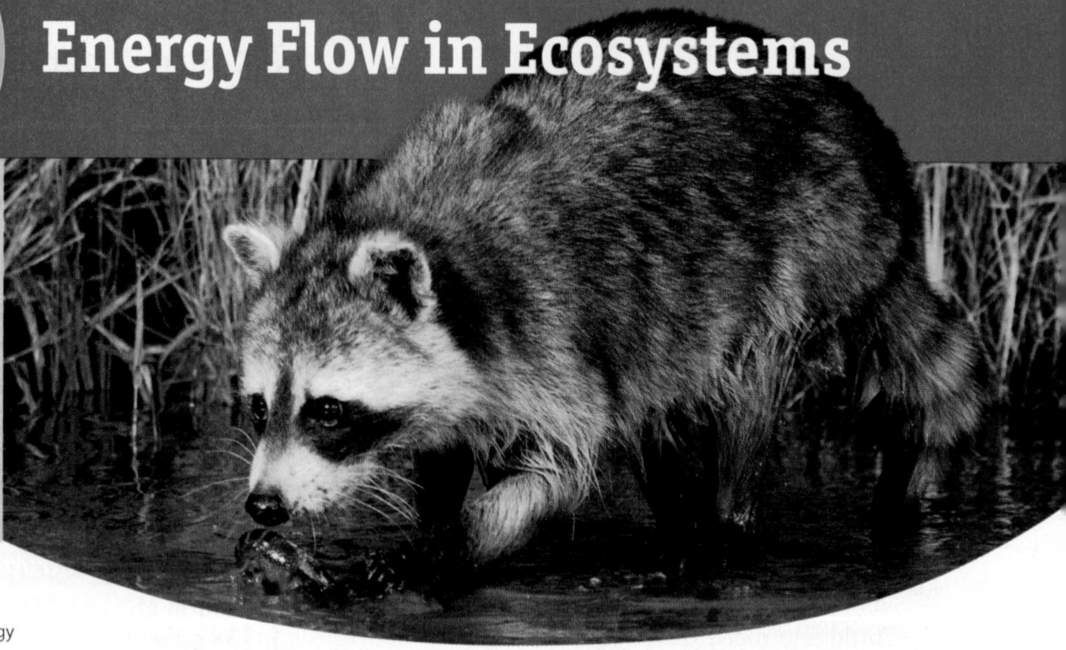

## Food Chains and Food Webs

In every ecosystem, primary producers and consumers are linked through feeding relationships. Details of those relationships vary a lot among ecosystems, but energy always flows in similar ways. ***Energy flows through an ecosystem in a one-way stream, from primary producers through various consumers.***

**Food Chains** The simplest way to think of energy moving through an ecosystem is to imagine it flowing along a food chain. A **food chain** is a series of organisms in which energy is transferred from one organism to another. Some food chains are very short. In Gorongosa National Park in Mozambique, an antelope feeds on grass, a primary producer. A lion feeds upon the antelope, making the lion two steps removed from the primary producer.

In the open ocean, food chains can be much longer. There, primary producers are usually tiny floating algae called **phytoplankton**, which are mostly eaten by small animal plankton. There are typically two or three more steps in this food chain to larger fish like tuna, which are four or five steps from primary producers.

**Food Webs** In most ecosystems, energy and matter move through feeding relationships that are much more complicated than a simple chain. Why? Many animals eat more than one kind of food. For example, in many salt marshes along the coast of Florida and other Gulf states, raccoons and moorhens eat several species of plants, as shown in **Figure 4-3**. Several predators, such as alligators and panthers, in turn, often prey upon these animals. Ecologists call this network of feeding interactions, through which both energy and matter move, a **food web**.

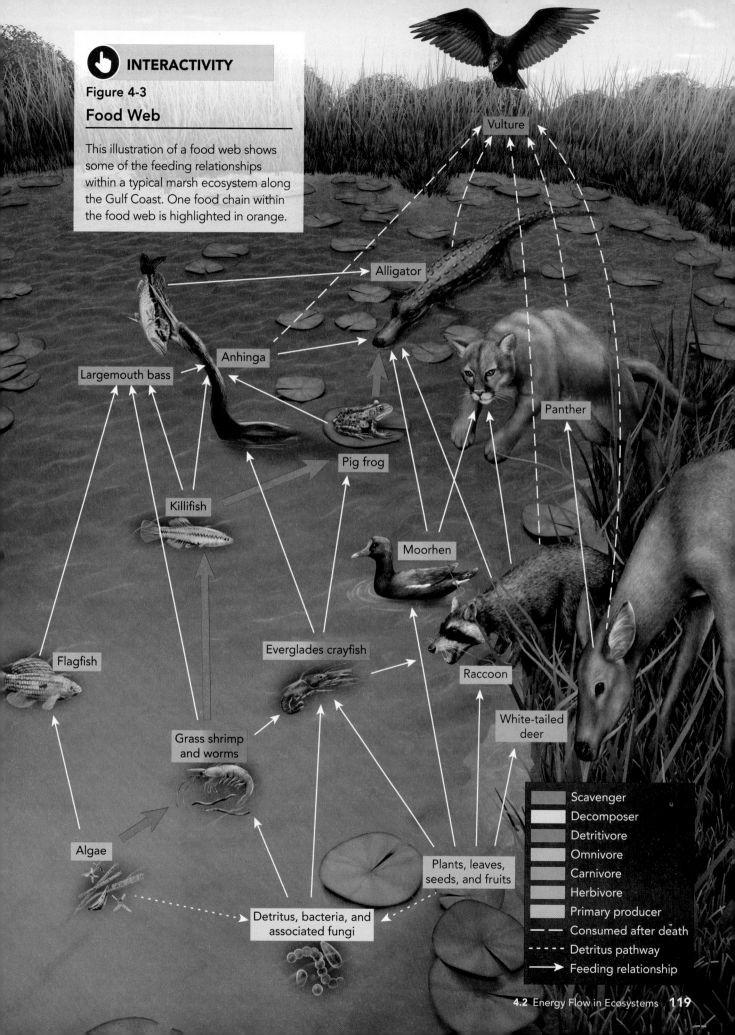

This illustration of a food web shows some of the feeding relationships within a typical marsh ecosystem along the Gulf Coast. One food chain within the food web is highlighted in orange.

Vulture

Alligator

Anhinga

Largemouth bass

Pig frog

Panther

Killifish

Moorhen

Flagfish

Everglades crayfish

Raccoon

White-tailed deer

Grass shrimp and worms

Algae

Plants, leaves, seeds, and fruits

Detritus, bacteria, and associated fungi

Scavenger
Decomposer
Detritivore
Omnivore
Carnivore
Herbivore
Primary producer
– – – Consumed after death
· · · · Detritus pathway
——► Feeding relationship

## INTERACTIVITY

Use the interactive food web activity to explore the effects of invasive species on food webs.

## BUILD VOCABULARY

**Academic Words** The word <u>convert</u> means "to change from one form to another." Decomposers convert, or change, uneaten dead plant matter into detritus.

## Visual Analogy

**Figure 4-4**

### Earth's Recycling Center

Decomposers break down dead and decaying matter and release nutrients that can be reused by primary producers.
☑ **Use Analogies** How are decomposers like a city's recycling center?

*Food Chains Within Food Webs* Look back at **Figure 4-3**. Starting with a primary producer, see how many different routes, or food chains, you can take to reach the vulture, panther, or alligator. One path, from the algae to the alligator, is highlighted in orange. A food web, therefore, is a network that includes all the food chains in an ecosystem. Note that this is a highly simplified representation of this food web, in which many species have been left out. Now, you can appreciate how complicated food webs are!

*Decomposers and Detritivores in Food Webs* Decomposers and detritivores have vital roles in the movement of energy and matter through food webs. Look again at the food web. Although white-tailed deer, raccoons, shrimp, and flagfish feed at least partly on primary producers, most producers die without being eaten. In the detritus pathway, decomposers <u>convert</u> that dead material to detritus, which is eaten by detritivores, such as shrimp and crayfish. Decomposition also releases matter in the form of nutrients that can be used by primary producers as shown in **Figure 4-4**. Without decomposers, nutrients would remain locked within dead organisms.

**Food Webs and Disturbance** Food webs are complex, so it is difficult to predict exactly how they will respond to an environmental change. Look again at **Figure 4-3**. Think about questions an ecologist might ask about changes following a disturbance. What if an oil spill caused a serious decline in the number of the bacteria and fungi that break down detritus? What effect do you think that might have on populations of shrimp and crayfish? Do you think those populations would decline? If they did, how might pig frogs change their feeding behavior? How might changes in frog behavior affect other species?

Because food webs contain so many different interactions among so many different organisms, you might expect that answers to these questions would not be simple or easy to predict—and you'd be right! Sometimes the effects of disturbances are minor. Other times a disturbance can have dramatic effects throughout the web.

☑ **READING CHECK** **Explain** How are food chains and food webs related?

**Decomposers**　　　　　**Primary Producers**

# Ecological Pyramids

Each step in a food chain or food web is called a **trophic level**. Primary producers make up the first trophic level. Various consumers occupy other levels. One way to illustrate trophic levels in an ecosystem is with a model called an ecological pyramid. **Ecological pyramids** are models that show the relative amount of energy or matter contained within each trophic level in a food chain or food web.

**Pyramids of Energy** Theoretically, there is no limit to the number of trophic levels in a food web, or the number of organisms on each level. But there's a catch. Only a small portion of the energy stored in any trophic level is available to organisms at the next level. This is because organisms use up much of the energy they acquire on life processes, such as respiration, movement, growth, and reproduction. Most of the remaining energy is released into the environment as heat—a byproduct of these activities. ✎ *Pyramids of energy show the relative amount of energy available at each trophic level of a food chain or food web.*

The shape of a pyramid of energy depends on the efficiency of energy transfer from one trophic level to the next. On average, about 10 percent of the energy available within one trophic level is transferred to the next trophic level, as shown in **Figure 4-5**. For instance, one tenth of the solar energy captured and stored in the leaves of grasses ends up stored in the tissues of cows and other grazers. One tenth of that energy—10 percent of 10 percent, or 1 percent of the original amount—gets stored in the tissues of humans who eat cows.

**READING TOOL**

Refer to the Pyramid of Energy visual. Draw a concept map that shows how the terms are related.

Figure 4-5

## Pyramid of Energy

Pyramids of energy show the amount of energy available at each trophic level. An ecosystem requires a constant supply of energy from photosynthetic or chemosynthetic producers.

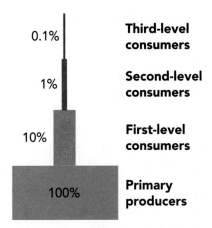

0.1%  **Third-level consumers**

1%  **Second-level consumers**

10%  **First-level consumers**

100%  **Primary producers**

HS-LS2-4

---

## Quick Lab 🧪 Open-Ended Inquiry

### How Can You Model Energy Flow in Ecosystems?

1. Using materials of your choice, develop a mathematical model of energy flow through four trophic levels in an ecosystem. To start, decide what will represent one energy unit. Then, decide what will represent the trophic levels.

2. Model the amount of available energy in the first trophic level. Set up a data table to record the number of energy units available in your model.

3. Next, model how this energy transfers to the second, third, and fourth trophic levels. Record your data in your data table.

### ANALYZE AND CONCLUDE

1. **Use Models** About how much energy is transferred from one trophic level to the next? How does your model show this flow of energy?

2. **Evaluate Claims** A classmate claims that energy is conserved as it flows through an ecosystem. Use your model and scientific reasoning to support or refute this claim.

3. **Support Claims** Support the claim that matter is conserved when one organism eats another.

**Figure 4-6**

**Pyramids of Biomass and Numbers**

With each step to a higher trophic level, biomass and numbers decrease. The pyramid shape shows this relationship.

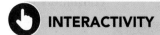

**INTERACTIVITY**

Learn more about how energy flows through ecosystems by interacting with ecological pyramids.

**Pyramids of Biomass and Numbers** The total amount of living tissue within a given trophic level is called its **biomass**. Biomass is usually measured in grams of organic matter per unit area. The amount of biomass a given trophic level can support is determined, in part, by the amount of energy available to the organisms in that trophic level. 🔍 *A pyramid of biomass is a model that illustrates the relative amount of living organic matter in each trophic level of an ecosystem.*

Ecologists interested in the number of organisms at each trophic level often use a pyramid of numbers. 🔍 *A pyramid of numbers is a model that shows the relative number of individual organisms at each trophic level in an ecosystem.* In most ecosystems, the pyramid of numbers is similar in shape to the pyramid of biomass. The numbers of individuals on each level decrease from the level below it. To understand this point more clearly, imagine that an ecologist marked off a large field, and then weighed and counted every organism in that area. The result might look something like the pyramid in **Figure 4-6**.

In some cases, however, consumers are much smaller in size and mass than the organisms they feed upon. Thousands of insects may graze on a single tree, for example. In such cases, the normal pyramid of numbers may be turned upside down, but the pyramid of biomass usually has the normal orientation. Even a single tree has a lot more biomass than the insects that feed on it!

HS-LS2-4

# ✅ LESSON 4.2 Review

## 🔍 KEY QUESTIONS

1. Energy is said to flow in a "one-way" stream through an ecosystem. In your own words, describe what that means.

2. What are the three types of ecological pyramids? Explain how each type of pyramid models energy and matter in ecosystems.

## CRITICAL THINKING

3. **Construct an Explanation** Suppose there was a sudden decrease in the number of crayfish in the food web shown in **Figure 4-3**. Construct an explanation to explain how this change may affect the food web.

4. **Calculate** Imagine you have a five-step food chain. If 100 percent of the energy is available at the first trophic level, what percentage of energy is available at the highest trophic level?

5. **Use Models** Choose one of the food chains shown within the food web in **Figure 4-3**. Write a paragraph describing the feeding relationships among the organisms in the food chain. **Hint:** Use the terms *producers*, *consumers*, and *decomposers* in your description.

6. **Construct an Explanation** Why are decomposers and detritivores essential parts of all food webs?

# Cycles of Matter

## 🔍 KEY QUESTIONS

- *How does matter flow between trophic levels and among ecosystems?*
- *How does water cycle globally?*
- *What is the importance of the main nutrient cycles?*
- *How does nutrient availability affect primary productivity?*

All organisms are composed of compounds that act as the building blocks of living tissue: water, carbohydrates, lipids, nucleic acids, and proteins. Those compounds are mainly made up of elements often called *essential nutrients*. Six of these elements—oxygen, hydrogen, carbon, nitrogen, phosphorus, and potassium—are required in relatively large amounts. But organisms can't manufacture these elements and they never get "used up." So, where do essential nutrients come from? How does their availability affect ecosystems?

## Recycling in Nature

You might think that matter would flow through ecosystems as energy does. But there's a big difference. As nutrients move through ecosystems, the compounds they form are often transformed. But matter is never created or destroyed. 🔍 *Matter flows from one trophic level to another, and elements are recycled within and among ecosystems.* These cycles, called **biogeochemical cycles**, are powered by the flow of energy as shown in **Figure 4-7**.

**HS-LS2-3:** Construct and revise an explanation based on evidence for the cycling of matter and flow of energy in aerobic and anaerobic conditions.

**HS-LS2-4:** Use mathematical representations to support claims for the cycling of matter and flow of energy among organisms in an ecosystem.

**HS-LS2-5:** Develop a model to illustrate the role of photosynthesis and cellular respiration in the cycling of carbon among the biosphere, atmosphere, hydrosphere, and geosphere.

**HS-ESS2-6:** Develop a quantitative model to describe the cycling of carbon among the hydrosphere, atmosphere, geosphere, and biosphere.

### VOCABULARY
biogeochemical cycle
nutrient
nitrogen fixation
denitrification
limiting nutrient

### READING TOOL
Before you read, preview and compare each of the cycle diagrams. Take notes in your 📕 **Biology Foundations Workbook.**

### Visual Analogy

**Figure 4-7**

### The Matter Mill

Nutrients are recycled through biogeochemical cycles. These cycles are powered by the one-way flow of energy through the biosphere, similar to water powering a mill's water wheel.

The processes that drive these cycles can be classified as biological processes, geological processes, physical and chemical processes, and processes driven by human activity, as shown in **Figure 4-8**. This cycling continues indefinitely, because matter is never created or destroyed.

*Biological Processes* Biological processes consist of any activities performed by living organisms. These include photosynthesis, eating, "burning" food (respiration), and eliminating waste products. These processes occur mainly in the biosphere, but affect the other three spheres as well.

*Geological Processes* Geological processes include volcanic eruptions, formation and breakdown of rock, and major movements of matter within and below Earth's surface. These processes occur mainly in the geosphere, but also affect the other three spheres.

*Physical and Chemical Processes* Physical and chemical processes include cloud formation and precipitation, the flow of running water, and the action of lightning. These processes occur primarily in the hydrosphere, atmosphere, and geosphere, but also affect the biosphere.

*Human Activities* Human activities that affect these cycles on a global scale include mining and burning of fossil fuels, clearing land for building and farming, cutting or burning and replanting of forests, and manufacture and use of fertilizers. Human causes of global change are found in the outermost ring of our global change model. Humans can change system processes in the four spheres leading to measurable changes in the system.

## BIOLOGICAL PROCESSES

## GEOLOGICAL PROCESSES

## PHYSICAL AND CHEMICAL PROCESSES

## HUMAN ACTIVITIES

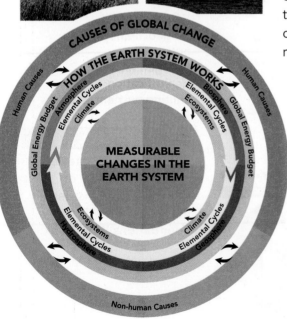

### Figure 4-8

## Global Processes and Global Systems

Biological, geological, physical, and chemical processes, as well as human activities, cycle atoms like carbon and nitrogen, through the biosphere, atmosphere, hydrosphere, and geosphere. These processes and the Elemental Cycles are represented in the Understanding Global Change model. Human activities are located in the model's outer ring, labeled "Causes of Global Change." Human activities can affect the global system processes located within the model's middle ring, and result in "Measurable Changes in The Earth System."

# The Water Cycle

Every time you see rain or snow, or watch a river flow, you are witnessing part of the water cycle. ⚲ *Water cycles among the hydrosphere, the atmosphere, and the geosphere—sometimes outside the biosphere and sometimes within it.* As **Figure 4-9** shows, water molecules typically enter the atmosphere as water vapor, a gas, when they evaporate from the ocean or other parts of the hydrosphere. Water can also enter the atmosphere from the biosphere by evaporating from leaves of plants in the process of transpiration. This cycle is represented in the Understanding Global Change diagram within the hydrosphere.

Water vapor may be transported through the atmosphere over great distances by winds. If the air carrying the water vapor cools, the water condenses into tiny droplets that form clouds. When the droplets become large enough, they fall as rain, snow, sleet, or hail. On land, some precipitation flows along the surface in what scientists call runoff, until it enters a river or stream that carries it to an ocean or lake.

Water can also be absorbed into the soil and is then called groundwater. Groundwater can enter plants through their roots, or flow into rivers, streams, lakes, or oceans. Some groundwater penetrates deeply enough into the ground to become part of underground reservoirs. Water that reenters the atmosphere through transpiration or evaporation begins the cycle anew. So the water cycle, like other cycles of matter, can be shown as passing through the atmosphere, hydrosphere, geosphere, and biosphere.

**ANIMATION**

hhmi | **BioInteractive**

**Figure 4-9**

## The Water Cycle

This diagram shows the main processes involved in the water cycle. Scientists estimate that it can take a single water molecule as long as 4000 years to complete one cycle.

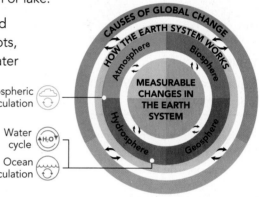

Atmospheric circulation

Water cycle

Ocean circulation

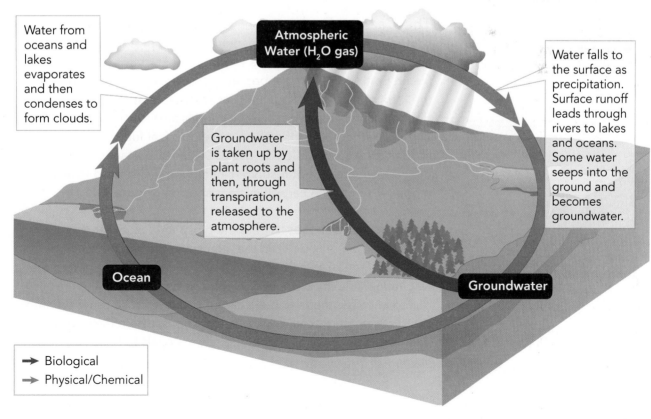

Water from oceans and lakes evaporates and then condenses to form clouds.

**Atmospheric Water (H₂O gas)**

Water falls to the surface as precipitation. Surface runoff leads through rivers to lakes and oceans. Some water seeps into the ground and becomes groundwater.

Groundwater is taken up by plant roots and then, through transpiration, released to the atmosphere.

**Ocean**

**Groundwater**

→ Biological
➜ Physical/Chemical

**Figure 4-10**

**Rainforests Have Many Benefits**

Rainforest trees return water to the atmosphere through transpiration. The trees also absorb excess carbon dioxide from the atmosphere.

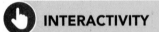

**INTERACTIVITY**

Apply your engineering skills to design a wetland ecosystem.

**READING TOOL**

As you read about a process, locate it in the corresponding cycle diagrams to help you understand the text.

In the past, many people viewed the water cycle as a physical phenomenon that affects life but is itself little affected by life. But we now know that water cycles locally through the biosphere, and that rainfall patterns can be strongly affected by living organisms. For example, rainforest trees (**Figure 4-10**) return a great deal of water to the atmosphere through transpiration from their leaves. That moisture feeds heavy local rainstorms. Cutting down large tracts of rainforests can interrupt this cycle, and can cause long-lasting local climate change. As you will see in subsequent chapters, other human-caused changes in the biosphere may also affect the global water cycle.

**READING CHECK** **Interpret Visuals** What are the two primary ways that precipitation passes through the water cycle?

# Nutrient Cycles

**Nutrients** are elements that an organism needs to sustain life. *Every organism needs nutrients to build tissues and carry out life functions. Like water, nutrients pass through organisms and the environment through biogeochemical cycles. The cycles that carry carbon, nitrogen, and phosphorus through the biosphere are especially vital for life.*

Note that oxygen participates in parts of the carbon, nitrogen, and phosphorus cycles by combining with these elements and cycling with them through parts of their journeys. Oxygen gas in the atmosphere is released by one of the most important of all biological activities: photosynthesis. Oxygen is also used in cellular respiration by all multicellular forms of life, and many single-celled organisms.

**The Carbon Cycle** Carbon is a major component of organic compounds, including carbohydrates, lipids, proteins, and nucleic acids. In fact, carbon is such a key ingredient of living tissue that life on Earth is often described as "carbon-based life." Carbon in the form of calcium carbonate ($CaCO_3$) is an essential part of many different kinds of animal skeletons and is also found in several kinds of rocks. Other forms of carbon make up fossil fuels. Carbon and oxygen form carbon dioxide gas ($CO_2$), an important component of the atmosphere. Major reservoirs of carbon are located in all four global systems. The carbon cycle is shown in **Figure 4-11**.

**Biological Processes** Across the biosphere, plants and algae remove carbon dioxide from the atmosphere through photosynthesis, and return some carbon dioxide to the atmosphere through respiration. Primary producers use the carbon dioxide taken in during photosynthesis to build carbohydrates. Those carbohydrates pass from primary producers to heterotrophs, where they are used as energy sources or as part of the raw materials to build proteins, lipids, and nucleic acids.

When organisms die, decomposers usually break down their bodies, releasing carbon (and other nutrients). But sometimes, primary producers are buried before they decompose. Million of years ago, remains of many land plants were buried, and transformed, over time, into coal deposits. Similarly, buried remains of marine algae were transformed into oil or natural gas. Over geologic time, this process removed carbon from the atmosphere and stored it in the geosphere. That's why coal, oil, and natural gas are called fossil fuels. They are, in fact, "fossilized" organic carbon!

## Figure 4-11
## The Carbon Cycle

Carbon is found in several large reservoirs. In the atmosphere, it can be found as carbon dioxide gas ($CO_2$); in the hydrosphere, as dissolved carbon dioxide; in the geosphere, in rocks and soil, and underground, as coal and petroleum, and calcium carbonate; and in the biosphere as organic matter.

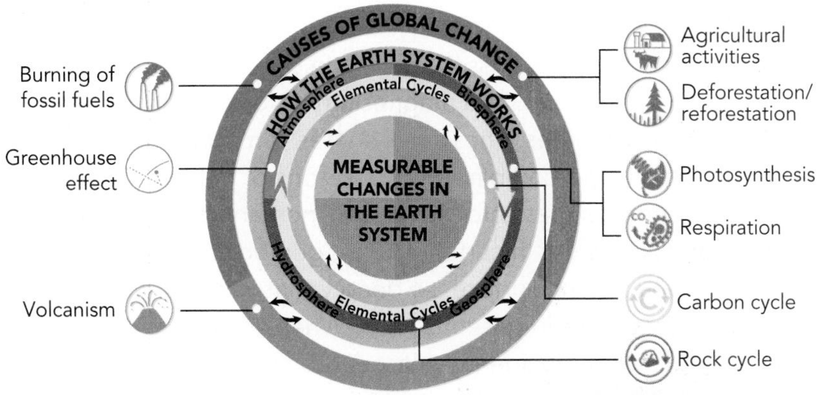

Burning of fossil fuels

Greenhouse effect

Volcanism

CAUSES OF GLOBAL CHANGE
HOW THE EARTH SYSTEM WORKS
Atmosphere   Biosphere
Elemental Cycles

MEASURABLE CHANGES IN THE EARTH SYSTEM

Hydrosphere   Geosphere
Elemental Cycles

Agricultural activities

Deforestation/reforestation

Photosynthesis

Respiration

Carbon cycle

Rock cycle

→ Biological
→ Human
→ Geological
→ Physical/Chemical

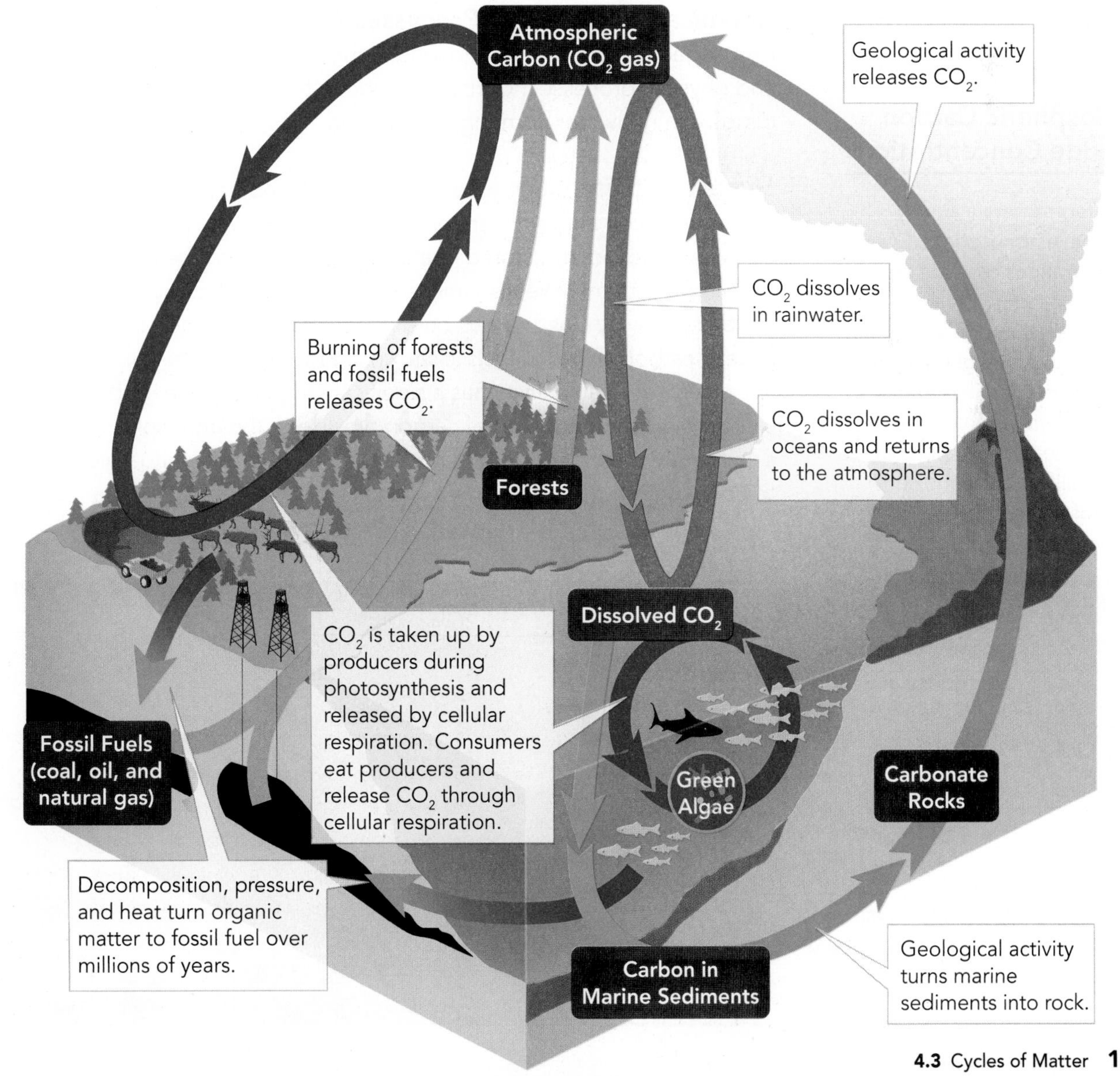

Atmospheric Carbon ($CO_2$ gas)

Geological activity releases $CO_2$.

Burning of forests and fossil fuels releases $CO_2$.

$CO_2$ dissolves in rainwater.

$CO_2$ dissolves in oceans and returns to the atmosphere.

Forests

Dissolved $CO_2$

$CO_2$ is taken up by producers during photosynthesis and released by cellular respiration. Consumers eat producers and release $CO_2$ through cellular respiration.

Fossil Fuels (coal, oil, and natural gas)

Green Algae

Carbonate Rocks

Decomposition, pressure, and heat turn organic matter to fossil fuel over millions of years.

Carbon in Marine Sediments

Geological activity turns marine sediments into rock.

**INTERACTIVITY**

Examine the effects of human activities on the water, carbon, and nitrogen cycles.

Amazingly, we can measure the effects of photosynthesis, respiration, and decomposition on the atmosphere! During our northern temperate zone summer, primary producers photosynthesize actively, removing carbon dioxide from the air. In winter, photosynthesis slows down, but respiration and decomposition continue, returning carbon dioxide to the air. These biological processes cause enough of a change in atmospheric carbon dioxide concentration to show up in measurements taken at a research station in Hawaii, as shown in **Figure 4-12**.

***Geological Processes*** Dissolved carbon dioxide in the oceans may combine with calcium and magnesium to form insoluble compounds called carbonates. These carbonates can accumulate on the ocean bottom and combine with skeletons of marine organisms to form vast deposits that harden into sedimentary rocks such as limestone and dolomite. In certain places, geological activity forces those rocks beneath the surface, so deeply that intense heat drives the carbon dioxide out in gaseous form. When volcanoes erupt, this underground carbon dioxide is released into the atmosphere.

***Chemical and Physical Processes*** Carbon dioxide is constantly exchanged between the atmosphere and oceans through chemical and physical processes. Carbon dioxide in the atmosphere can also dissolve in rainwater, forming a weak acid.

***Human Activity*** When we extract coal, oil, and natural gas from the carbon reservoir in the geosphere and burn them, we return carbon that was removed and stored over millions of years to the atmosphere in a very short time. We also release carbon from the carbon reserve in the biosphere by clearing and burning forests. The change in atmospheric carbon dioxide levels is shown in **Figure 4-12**. The carbon released by human activity has a significant impact on the global carbon cycle. Our addition of carbon dioxide to the atmosphere is significantly adding to the greenhouse effect, raising average global temperature and driving climate change.

**Figure 4-12**

## Atmospheric Carbon Dioxide Concentrations

The graph shows a steady increase in atmospheric $CO_2$ concentrations over the last several decades. Seasonal variations—the regular ups and downs in the graph—are due to variations in photosynthesis between summer and winter. The green regions of the satellite map (right) show areas of active photosynthesis in summer.

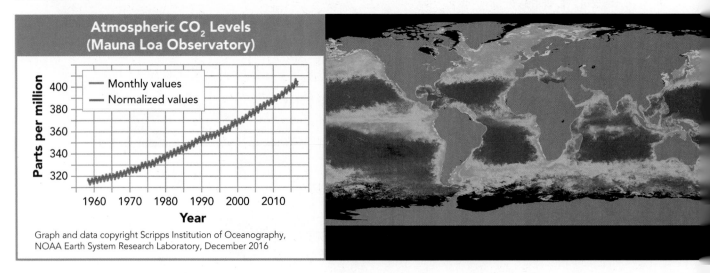

**Atmospheric CO₂ Levels (Mauna Loa Observatory)**

— Monthly values
— Normalized values

Parts per million: 400, 380, 360, 340, 320

Year: 1960, 1970, 1980, 1990, 2000, 2010

Graph and data copyright Scripps Institution of Oceanography, NOAA Earth System Research Laboratory, December 2016

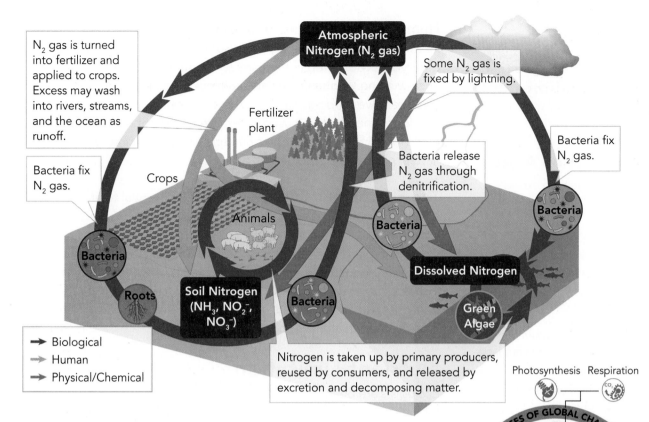

N₂ gas is turned into fertilizer and applied to crops. Excess may wash into rivers, streams, and the ocean as runoff.

Some N₂ gas is fixed by lightning.

Bacteria fix N₂ gas.

Bacteria release N₂ gas through denitrification.

Bacteria fix N₂ gas.

Atmospheric Nitrogen ($N_2$ gas)

Fertilizer plant

Crops

Animals

Bacteria

Bacteria

Roots

Soil Nitrogen ($NH_3$, $NO_2^-$, $NO_3^-$)

Bacteria

Dissolved Nitrogen

Green Algae

→ Biological
→ Human
→ Physical/Chemical

Nitrogen is taken up by primary producers, reused by consumers, and released by excretion and decomposing matter.

Photosynthesis   Respiration

CAUSES OF GLOBAL CHANGE
HOW THE EARTH SYSTEM WORKS
Atmosphere   Elemental Cycles   Biosphere
Human Causes
MEASURABLE CHANGES IN THE EARTH SYSTEM
Human Causes
Hydrosphere   Elemental Cycles   Geosphere
Global Energy Budget
Non-human Causes

Nitrogen & phosphorus cycles

Agricultural activities

## The Nitrogen Cycle

All organisms require nitrogen to make amino acids, which combine to form proteins, and nucleic acids such as DNA and RNA. Many different forms of nitrogen occur naturally. The largest reservoir of nitrogen is in the atmosphere, where nitrogen gas ($N_2$) makes up 78 percent of the air we breathe. Nitrogen reservoirs in the biosphere and geosphere include nitrogen-containing substances such as ammonia ($NH_3$), nitrate ions ($NO_3^-$), and nitrite ions ($NO_2^-$), which are found in soil, in wastes produced by many organisms, and in dead and decaying organic matter. There is also a large reservoir of dissolved nitrogen in the hydrosphere. **Figure 4-13** shows how different forms of nitrogen cycle through the biosphere.

*Natural Processes* Nitrogen gas is abundant, but most organisms can't use it. Among living organisms, only certain types of bacteria can convert nitrogen gas into ammonia, a process known as **nitrogen fixation**. Some nitrogen-fixing bacteria live in soil and on the roots of plants such as peanuts and peas. Lightning can fix small amounts of nitrogen in a process called atmospheric nitrogen fixation.

Other bacteria convert ammonia into nitrite and nitrate, which can be used by primary producers. When consumers eat producers, those nitrogen compounds are reused. The bacteria and fungi that act as decomposers are also vital parts of the nitrogen cycle. Decomposers release nitrogen compounds from animal wastes and dead organisms that producers may take up again. Some bacteria obtain energy by converting nitrates into nitrogen gas, which is released into the atmosphere in a process called **denitrification**.

**CASE STUDY**

Figure 4-13

**The Nitrogen Cycle**

The atmosphere is the largest reservoir of nitrogen. Nitrogen also cycles through the biosphere, geosphere, and hydrosphere.

## Exploration Lab

### Guided Inquiry
### The Effect of Fertilizer on Algae

**Problem** How do excess nutrients affect the growth of algae?

In this lab, you will plan and carry out an investigation that tests the effects of fertilizer concentration on algae growth. You will select nutrient amounts and compare the growth of algae when nutrients are limited and when nutrients are abundant.

You can find this lab in your digital course.

**Figure 4-14**

## The Phosphorus Cycle

Phosphorus in the biosphere cycles among the land, ocean sediments, and living organisms.

***Human Activities*** Humans have used various forms of organic matter as fertilizer for a long time. But our involvement in the nitrogen cycle skyrocketed in the early twentieth century after two Nobel Prize-winning German chemists developed an industrial process that could remove nitrogen gas from the atmosphere and transform it into forms that could be used in fertilizer. Today, the use of this process around the world enables humans to fix more nitrogen than all natural processes combined.

**The Phosphorus Cycle** Phosphorus is essential to life because it is part of molecules such as DNA and RNA. Unlike carbon, oxygen, and nitrogen, phosphorus does not cycle through the atmosphere. One reservoir of inorganic phosphorus is found in the geosphere in the form of phosphate rock and soil minerals. Another reservoir is located in the hydrosphere, in the form of dissolved phosphate and phosphate sediments in both freshwater and marine environments. The phosphorus cycle is shown in **Figure 4-14**.

## Nutrient Limitation

Ecologists are often interested in an ecosystem's primary productivity—the rate at which primary producers create new organic material. 🔍 *If ample sunlight and water are available, the primary productivity of an ecosystem may be limited by the availability of nutrients.* If even a single essential nutrient is in short supply, primary productivity will be limited. All nutrient cycles work together like the gears in **Figure 4-15**. If any nutrient is in short supply—if any wheel "sticks"—the productivity of the entire food web can be limited. Any nutrient whose supply limits productivity is called a **limiting nutrient**.

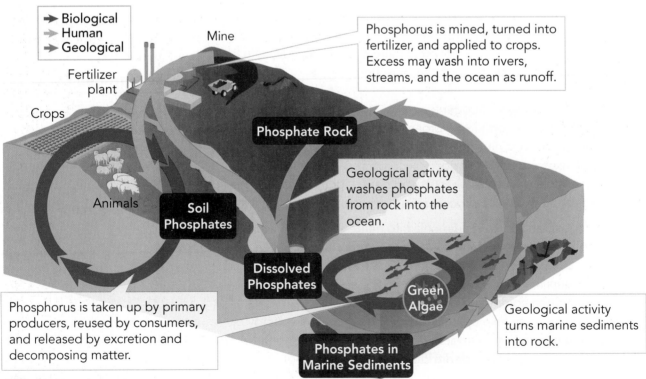

Biological
Human
Geological

Mine

Phosphorus is mined, turned into fertilizer, and applied to crops. Excess may wash into rivers, streams, and the ocean as runoff.

Fertilizer plant

Crops

Phosphate Rock

Geological activity washes phosphates from rock into the ocean.

Animals

Soil Phosphates

Dissolved Phosphates

Green Algae

Geological activity turns marine sediments into rock.

Phosphorus is taken up by primary producers, reused by consumers, and released by excretion and decomposing matter.

Phosphates in Marine Sediments

## Nutrient Limitation in Soil

In all but the richest soil, plant growth can be limited by a short supply of one or more nutrients. Nutrient limitation is the reason farmers use fertilizers to maximize crop growth. Most fertilizers contain nitrogen, phosphorus, and potassium, all of which help plants grow better in poor soil. Micronutrients such as calcium, magnesium, sulfur, iron, and manganese are sometimes included in small amounts. Carbon is not included in fertilizers because plants absorb carbon dioxide from the atmosphere. Applying too much fertilizer to soil near streams and rivers, however, can disrupt natural nutrient cycles, with serious consequences.

## Nutrient Limitation in Aquatic Ecosystems

In the ocean, nitrogen is often the limiting nutrient. Seawater typically contains only 0.00005 percent nitrogen, or 1/10,000 of the amount often found in soil. In streams, lakes, and freshwater environments, on the other hand, phosphorus is often the limiting nutrient.

Sometimes, runoff from heavy rains carries large amounts of a limiting nutrient from heavily fertilized fields into aquatic ecosystems. This fertilizer runoff delivers abnormally high concentrations of limiting nutrients such as nitrogen and phosphorus into bodies of water. These nutrients stimulate primary producers such as algae to grow and reproduce far beyond their normal rates, causing what is called an algal bloom. Severe algal blooms can cover the water's surface and disrupt the functioning of an entire ecosystem. In the ocean, excess nitrogen is often the cause of an algal bloom. In freshwater environments, excess phosphorus is usually the cause.

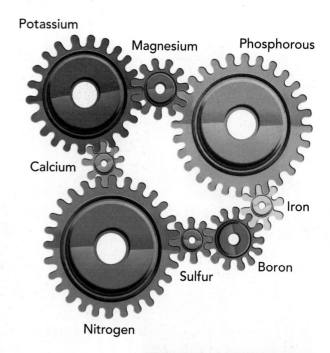

Potassium
Magnesium
Phosphorous
Calcium
Iron
Sulfur
Boron
Nitrogen

**Visual Analogy**

### Figure 4-15

### Interlocking Nutrients

The movement of each nutrient through ecosystems depends on the movements of all the others, because all are needed for living systems to function.

HS-LS2-3, HS-LS2-4, HS-LS2-5, HS-ESS2-6

## ✓ LESSON 4.3 Review

### 🔍 KEY QUESTIONS

1. How does the way that matter cycles through an ecosystem differ from the way that energy flows?

2. What two processes cycle water from the land to the atmosphere?

3. Why do living organisms need nutrients?

4. Explain how a nutrient can be a limiting factor in an ecosystem.

### CRITICAL THINKING

5. **Analyze Data** Based on your knowledge of the carbon cycle and the graph in **Figure 4-12**, predict what will happen if humans continue to clear and burn vast areas of forests for farming.

6. **Construct an Explanation** Describe one way in which water from the ocean may make one complete cycle through the atmosphere and back to the ocean. Include the names of each process involved in your cycle.

7. **Develop Models** Although oxygen does not have an independent cycle, it moves through the biosphere as part of the carbon cycle. Develop a model to illustrate how oxygen fits into the carbon cycle. Include the various forms that oxygen takes in your model.

8. **CASE STUDY** Review the nitrogen and phosphorus cycles. How is fertilizer runoff related to algal blooms?

# What's to blame for the bloom?

## Global change is causing rapidly-spreading, severe algal blooms.

HS-LS2-2, HS-LS4-5, HS-LS4-6

## Make Your Case

You've learned that algal blooms can form when limiting nutrients are present, and that other environmental factors help drive rapid algal growth. Often, global climate change plays a major role. In 2016, winter rains in Florida were unusually heavy. And water in the eastern Pacific Ocean was unusually warm. But heavy rains and warmer water alone couldn't have caused blooms. What other factors were involved? In Florida, rains washed fertilizer containing both nitrogen and phosphorus into Lake Okeechobee. The lake reached flood stage, so that nutrient-rich water had to be diverted into rivers that flowed to both coasts, driving blooms in both freshwater and salt water. Might similar factors have fuelled the West Coast bloom?

## Communicating Information

1. **Ask Questions** How could human activities have contributed to both blooms in different ways? Examine limiting factors for algal growth as you gather evidence to support your argument.

2. **Construct a Solution** What actions could be taken in Florida to help prevent the same situation from occurring again? Conduct research and cite evidence to support your solution. (**Hint:** Through what ecosystem did overflow from Lake Okeechobee pass before people changed the drainage pattern?)

# Technology on the Case

## Turning Waste Into a Solution

Thick, brown sludge. Clogged pipes. If you think that's a problem, you would be correct. But it turns out it can also be a solution.

Wastewater from homes, businesses, and even farms often ends up in wastewater treatment plants. These plants process wastewater so that the water can be returned safely to the environment. Wastewater contains much more than just water, including food, feces, dirt, soaps, and industrial chemicals.

One of the challenges of treating wastewater is removing the limiting nutrients, such as phosphorus and nitrogen. If the nutrients are not removed, they may end up in our lakes and streams. One way that scientists and engineers are working to make wastewater treatment plants more efficient at removing phosphorus is by harnessing a chemical called struvite. Struvite itself is a problem for wastewater treatment plants because it accumulates on the walls of pipes, eventually leading to clogged pipes. However, water treatment plants are now being designed to intentionally make struvite. Why? Because struvite can be used as a fertilizer.

Struvite crystals contain phosphorus, nitrogen, and magnesium. Producing and collecting struvite results in less phosphorus entering our waterways. In addition, selling struvite as a fertilizer allows the facilities to offset the costs of wastewater treatment. Another benefit of struvite is that the struvite crystals slowly release nitrogen and phosphate. This slow release decreases the runoff of limiting nutrients.

# Careers on the Case

## Work Toward a Solution

People in many careers help keep aquatic ecosystems healthy and the water safe for human use.

## Water Quality Technician

Bodies of water can be fouled by living things, such as bacteria and algae. The water can also contain toxic elements or other harmful chemicals. The job of the water quality technician is to test water supplies to make sure they meet environmental standards.

## ▶ VIDEO

Watch this video to learn about other careers in biology.

**hhmi | BioInteractive**

# Lesson Review

Go to your Biology Foundations Workbook for longer versions of these lesson summaries.

## 4.1 Energy, Producers, and Consumers

With few exceptions, energy for life ultimately comes from the sun. Primary producers are the first producers of energy-rich compounds that are later used by other organisms. Primary producers are also called autotrophs.

Organisms that rely on other organisms for energy and nutrients are called heterotrophs, or consumers. Consumers can be further classified according to the type of food they eat. Herbivores eat plants. Carnivores kill and eat other animals. Omnivores eat both plant and animal matter. Scavengers eat the carcasses of dead animals. Decomposers chemically break down organic matter, producing detritus. Detritivores eat detritus.

- autotroph
- primary producer
- photosynthesis
- chemosynthesis
- heterotroph
- consumer
- detritus

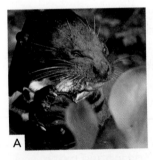

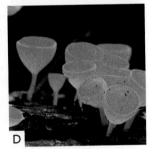

✓ **Identify** Is each organism shown a producer, an herbivore, a carnivore, or a decomposer?

## 4.2 Energy Flow in Ecosystems

Energy flows through an ecosystem in a one-way stream, from primary producers to various consumers. A food chain is a series of steps in which organisms transfer energy by eating and being eaten. A food web is a network of complex feeding relationships in an ecosystem.

Ecological pyramids show the relative amount of energy or matter contained within each trophic level in a given food chain or food web. Pyramids of energy show the amount of energy available at each trophic level. Pyramids of biomass and numbers show the relative amounts of living organic matter and relative numbers of individual organisms, respectively, at each trophic level.

- food chain
- phytoplankton
- food web
- trophic level
- ecological pyramid
- biomass

## 4.3 Cycles of Matter

Matter is recycled within and among ecosystems, unlike the one-way flow of energy. Matter cycles through organisms and the environment through biogeochemical cycles. The flow of matter can involve biological processes, geological processes, chemical and physical processes, and human activity. These global processes cycle matter through global systems.

Water cycles among the oceans, atmosphere, and land. The water cycle affects life and is affected by living organisms.

Every organism needs nutrients to survive. The carbon, nitrogen, and phosphorus cycles are especially important for life. The availability of nutrients can influence the long-term survival of organisms. If ample sunlight and water are available, the primary productivity of an ecosystem may still be limited by the availability of nutrients.

- biogeochemical cycle
- nutrient
- nitrogen fixation
- denitrification
- limiting nutrient

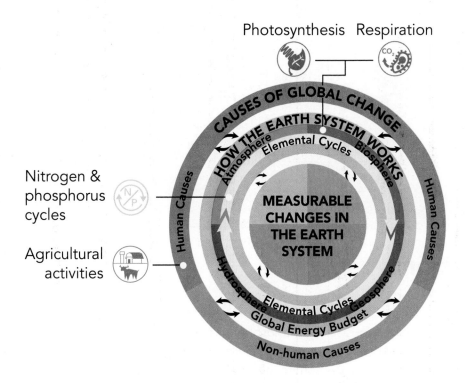

Photosynthesis    Respiration

CAUSES OF GLOBAL CHANGE
HOW THE EARTH SYSTEM WORKS
Elemental Cycles
Atmosphere        Biosphere

Human Causes                    Human Causes

**MEASURABLE CHANGES IN THE EARTH SYSTEM**

Nitrogen & phosphorus cycles

Agricultural activities

Hydrosphere        Geosphere
Elemental Cycles
Global Energy Budget

Non-human Causes

☑ **Evaluate Models** Through which spheres does nitrogen cycle? Describe how photosynthesis, respiration, and agricultural activities influence the nitrogen cycle.

# Organize Information

Cite evidence for each statement from the text, investigations, and other activities you have completed. Then, draw a model to support each statement.

| Statement | Evidence | Model |
|---|---|---|
| Consumers are dependent on producers. | 1. | 2. |
| The amount of available energy is reduced at each successive trophic level. | 3. | 4. |
| Water cycles through ecosystems. | 5. | 6. |

# Can Algal Blooms Be Useful?

## Evaluate a Solution

HS-LS2-5, HS-ETS1-3, CCSS.ELA-LITERACY.RST.9-10.1

**STEM** A significant amount of primary production occurs in the sea, as marine algae take in carbon dioxide to build living tissue. Studies had shown that surface water in parts of the ocean contains high enough concentrations of nitrogen and phosphorus to support higher rates of primary production than naturally occur there. What's missing? A vital micronutrient: iron.

So it seemed reasonable, back in the 1990's, when scientists trying to avoid human-caused climate change proposed to stimulate algal growth by adding iron to the ocean. They hoped that this increased marine primary productivity would remove carbon dioxide from the atmosphere and store it at the bottom of the sea. Here is the system that researchers hypothesized (and hoped!) they could tweak, using iron fertilization, to accomplish that goal.

**1** Iron, a micronutrient essential to algal growth, is added to parts of the ocean where the lack of iron limits phytoplankton growth.

**2** Atmospheric $CO_2$ can dissolve in the ocean, or can be released from the ocean into the atmosphere, depending on its relative concentrations in air and water. When atmospheric carbon dioxide concentrations rise, or when dissolved $CO_2$ concentrations drop, more dissolves in the ocean.

**3** Algae take up dissolved carbon dioxide during photosynthesis (3a). Some of this carbon is released when the algae respire (3b), and some is stored in cell structures.

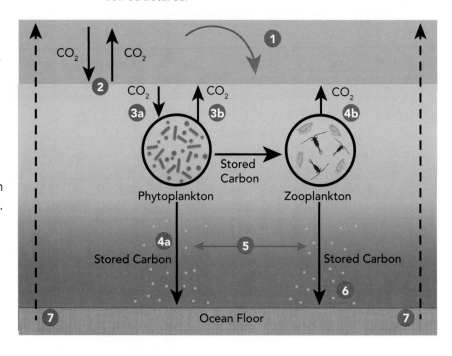

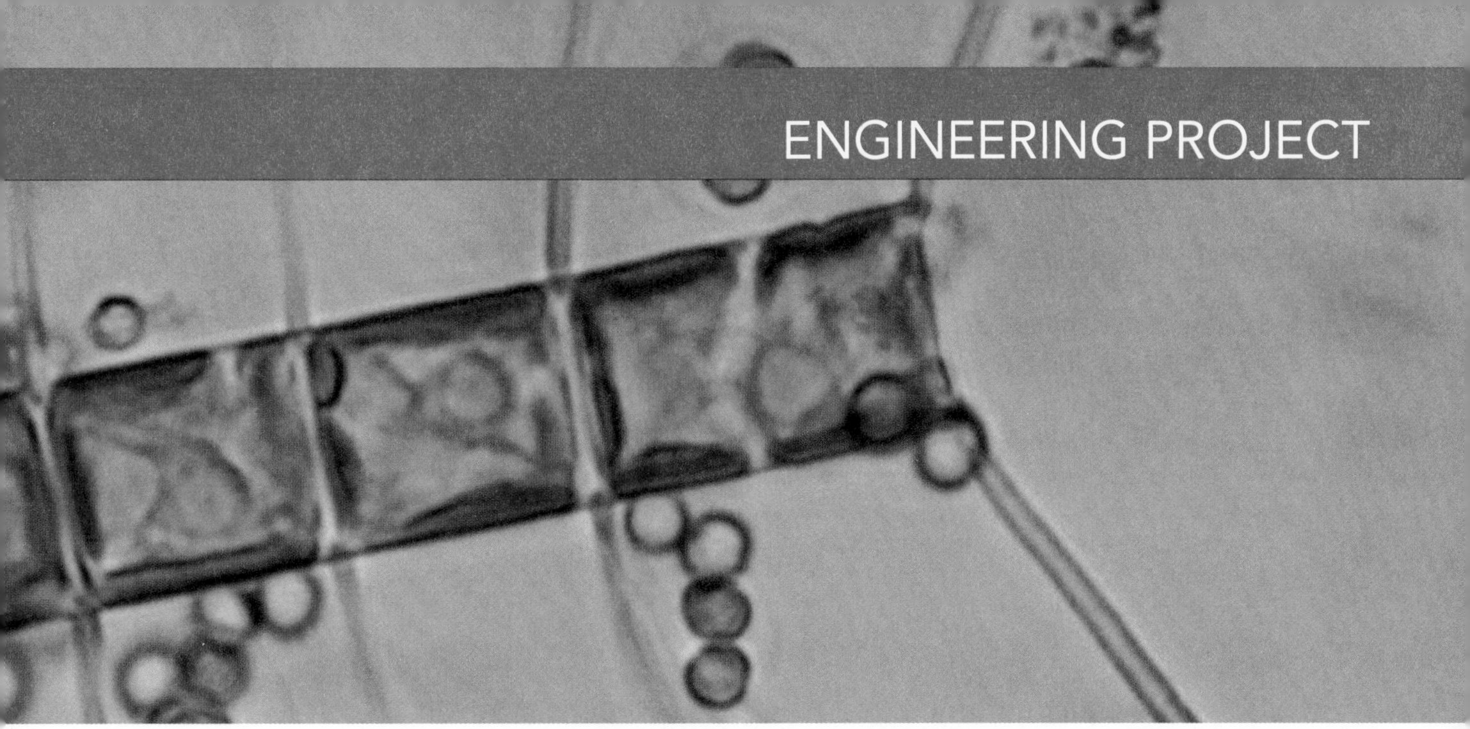

Floating algae are important primary producers in the sea. Could they be useful in removing large amounts of excess carbon dioxide from the atmosphere? Or is the ocean's role in the carbon cycle more complicated than it appears?

**4** Some algae are eaten by zooplankton and other consumers. These organisms store some of that carbon, and release some when they respire.

**5** If algae die without being eaten, they may sink to the bottom of the ocean, taking captured carbon with them. Other organisms that also die and sink to the bottom, along with their solid wastes, also carry stored carbon with them.

**6** If the remains of those organisms, along with solid wastes of consumers, are buried rapidly, this captured carbon can be stored on the ocean floor.

**7** Dead organisms on and near the ocean floor could decompose, returning carbon to the sea, and, ultimately to the atmosphere.

1. **Develop Models** Using **Figure 4-11**, the Understanding Global Change model, and your own research, develop a model that focuses on carbon cycle pathways in the ocean. Be certain to include any step whose rate could affect where carbon ends up!

2. **Construct an Argument** Closely examine each step in your model to see which pathways store carbon, and which end up releasing it back into the atmosphere. What assumptions about the rate of processes in each step are necessary in order to hypothesize that iron fertilization would reduce atmospheric carbon dioxide concentrations?

3. **Conduct Research** In the years since ocean iron fertilization was proposed, researchers gathered data to test those assumptions and hypotheses. Search for information about those experiments. What is the current scientific consensus on whether or not ocean iron fertilization could help to limit climate change? Do current data support or reject the hypothesis that this solution would work? Why or why not?

4. **Communicate** Write an evaluation of the ocean iron fertilization solution to climate change. Support your argument with evidence from your research and the model you developed.

## 🔍 KEY QUESTIONS AND TERMS

### 4.1 Energy, Producers, and Consumers
HS-LS2-3

1. Primary producers are organisms that
   a. rely on other organisms for their energy and food supply.
   b. consume plant and animal remains and other dead matter.
   c. use energy they take in from the environment to convert inorganic molecules into complex organic molecules.
   d. obtain energy by eating only plants.

2. Which of the following organisms is a carnivore?

a.

b.

c.

d.

3. How are detritivores different from decomposers? Provide an example of each.

4. Classify each of the following as an herbivore, a carnivore, an omnivore, or a detritivore.
   a. an earthworm that eats the decaying remains of plants and animals
   b. a bear that feeds on plants and animals
   c. a cow that feeds only on plants
   d. a snail that feeds on plants, algae, and fungi
   e. an owl that feeds only on animals
   f. a human that feeds on plants and animals

5. What are the two basic processes in which energy from nonliving sources is captured and stored in molecules that can be used by living things? How are they similar? How are they different?

### 4.2 Energy Flow in Ecosystems
HS-LS2-4

6. The series of steps in which a large fish eats a small fish that has eaten algae is a
   a. food web.
   b. food chain.
   c. pyramid of numbers.
   d. pyramid of biomass.

7. The total amount of living tissue at each trophic level in an ecosystem can be shown in a(n)
   a. pyramid of energy.
   b. pyramid of numbers.
   c. pyramid of biomass.
   d. biogeochemical cycle.

8. Which group of organisms is always found at the base of a food chain or food web?

9. What ultimately happens to the bulk of matter in any trophic level of a pyramid of biomass—that is, the matter that does not get passed to the trophic level above?

10. Why is the transfer of energy in a food chain usually only about 10 percent efficient?

11. Describe the flow of energy in an ecosystem.

### 4.3 Cycles of Matter
HS-LS2-3, HS-LS2-4, HS-LS2-5, HS-ESS2-6

12. Which of the following is NOT true about matter in the biosphere?
    a. Matter is transferred in one direction through the biosphere.
    b. Biogeochemical cycles transform and reuse molecules.
    c. The total amount of matter decreases over time.
    d. Human activity does not affect the movement of matter.

13. Nutrients move through an ecosystem in
    a. biogeochemical cycles.
    b. water cycles.
    c. pyramids of energy.
    d. ecological pyramids.

14. Which biogeochemical cycle does NOT include a major path in which the substance cycles through the atmosphere?

15. List two ways in which water enters the atmosphere in the water cycle.

16. Describe three ways in which carbon is stored in the biosphere.

17. Explain the process of nitrogen fixation.

18. What is meant by "nutrient limitation"?

19. How do changes in nutrient levels affect the structure of aquatic food webs?

20. Construct a table with a row for each of the following cycles of matter (water, carbon, and nitrogen) and a column for each process (physical/chemical, biological, geological, and human). Fill in the table with examples of each process, using the text and figures in Lesson 4.3.

# CRITICAL THINKING

HS-LS2-3, HS-LS2-4, HS-LS2-5

21. **Develop Models** Give an example of an ecological phenomenon that could be studied by modeling. Explain why modeling would be useful.

22. **Ask Questions** You live near a pond that you have observed for years. One year you notice the water is choked with a massive overgrowth of green algae. What are some of the questions you might have about this unusual growth?

23. **Use Models** Study the food web shown.
    a. Use the food web to identify and distinguish the producers and consumers.
    b. Identify examples of decomposers that could be added to the food web. How are decomposers distinguished from producers and consumers?
    c. Identify and draw two different food chains from the food web: one food chain that ends with a second-level consumer and one that ends with a third-level consumer.
    d. Using the two food chains, compare the energy available to the second-level consumer with the energy available to the third-level consumer. Assume that the amount of energy supplied by producers is the same in all food chains.

24. **Form a Hypothesis** People who explore caves where there is running water but no sunlight often find them populated with unique types of fishes and insects. What testable hypothesis can you develop to explain the ultimate source of energy for these organisms?

25. **Analyze Text Structure** Using the text from Lessons 4.2 and 4.3, analyze the relationships among the key terms *food chain*, *food web*, *nutrient*, and *biogeochemical cycle*.

26. **Construct an Explanation** Why are normally unseen members of the food web, such as soil microorganisms, essential to the nitrogen cycle? Use a model to support your answer.

27. **Cite Evidence** Ecologists discovered that larger-than-normal numbers of trout were dying in a stream that ran through some farmland. A local scientist claimed nitrogen fertilizer that was used on the crops caused the deaths. Explain the types of evidence that would support the scientist's claim.

28. **Use Models** Using a flowchart, trace the flow of energy in a simple marine food chain. Then, show where nitrogen is cycled through the chain when the top-level carnivore dies and is decomposed.

29. **Construct an Explanation** Explain the role of photosynthesis in the carbon cycle.

30. **Evaluate a Solution** Phosphate detergents are effective for cleaning laundry and dirty dishes. However, these phosphorus-laden products have been banned in Australia, the European Union, Canada, and some states in the United States. Why do you think the detergents were banned? How might you evaluate the effectiveness of this solution?

31. **Construct an Explanation** Explain why available energy is reduced as energy transfers through the trophic levels of an ecosystem.

# ☑ASSESSMENT

## CROSSCUTTING CONCEPTS

**32. Energy and Matter** The cycling of matter is dependent on the flow of energy. Using the carbon cycle, explain how this flow of energy drives the cycling of carbon through the environment.

**33. Systems and System Models** Think about the connections and interactions among processes and phenomena in the Understanding Global Change model.

**a.** Select at least one topic from each of the three categories in the Understanding Global Change model (Causes of Global Change, How the Earth System Works, and Measurable Changes in the Earth System) and explain if and how these processes or phenomena are related.

**b.** For each of your chosen topics, use words and arrows to describe how these phenomena or processes are related to three additional concepts discussed in Chapter 4.

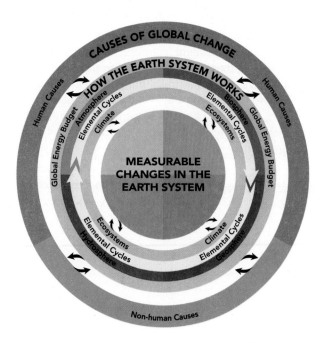

## MATH CONNECTIONS

### Analyze and Interpret Data

CCSS.MATH.CONTENT.HSN.Q.A.1

The graph below shows the effect of annual rainfall on the rate of primary productivity in an ecosystem. Use this graph to answer questions 34–36.

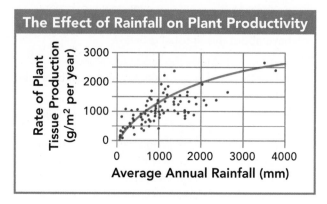

**34. Analyze Data** What happens to productivity as rainfall increases?

**35. Construct Graphs** What do you think the graph would look like if the x-axis were extended out to 6000 mm? Represent your prediction in a graph and explain your answer.

**36. Draw Conclusions** What factors other than water might affect primary productivity?

## LANGUAGE ARTS CONNECTIONS

### Write About Science

CCSS-ELA-LITERACY.WHST.9-10.2

**37. Conduct Research Projects** Sustainable agriculture is a method of growing and raising food by taking advantage of natural biogeochemical cycles without disrupting them. Write down a question you have about sustainable agriculture and conduct a research project to answer your question. Use multiple sources to gather your information.

### Read About Science

CCSS-ELA-LITERACY.RST.9-10.1

**38. Cite Textual Evidence** Describe how biogeochemical cycles provide organisms with the raw materials necessary to synthesize complex organic compounds. Cite textual evidence from Chapter 2 to support your response.

# END-OF-COURSE TEST PRACTICE

1. A carnivore obtains energy by eating other animals. Which of the following shows the process by which energy flows to a carnivorous animal?
   A. light energy → plant → carnivore
   B. plant → light energy → carnivore
   C. light energy → herbivore → carnivore
   D. light energy → plant → herbivore → carnivore
   E. light energy → plant → decomposer → herbivore → carnivore

2. The diagram is a pyramid of biomass for a meadow ecosystem. The triangular shape of the diagram is useful for explaining which relationship among the trophic levels in this ecosystem?

   A. The amount of living organic matter is equal at all trophic levels in this ecosystem.
   B. Third-level consumers in this ecosystem have the greatest amount of living organic matter.
   C. With each step to a higher trophic level in this ecosystem, the amount of living organic matter increases.
   D. Third-level consumers in this ecosystem provide living organic matter to producers and other consumers.
   E. The amount of living organic matter decreases at each trophic level in this ecosystem.

3. The ecological pyramid models energy flow in a particular ecosystem.

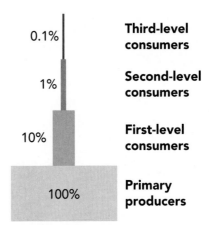

0.1% — **Third-level consumers**
1% — **Second-level consumers**
10% — **First-level consumers**
100% — **Primary producers**

   If the primary producers produce 5000 energy units, about how much of this energy is available to the secondary consumers?
   A. 5 energy units
   B. 50 energy units
   C. 1000 energy units
   D. 5000 energy units
   E. 5,000,000 energy units

4. Which of the following explains the role of plants in the carbon cycle?
   A. Plants transfer carbon in the atmosphere to carbohydrates in the biosphere.
   B. Plants transport carbon dioxide in the atmosphere to groundwater.
   C. Plants transfer oxygen and carbon in the biosphere to carbon dioxide in the atmosphere.
   D. Plants transfer oxygen in the atmosphere to fossil fuels.
   E. Plants transfer carbon in the groundwater to carbohydrates in the biosphere.

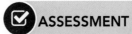 **ASSESSMENT**

For additional assessment practice, go online to access your digital course.

## If You Have Trouble With...

| Question | 1 | 2 | 3 | 4 |
| --- | --- | --- | --- | --- |
| See Lesson | 4.1 | 4.2 | 4.2 | 4.3 |
| Performance Expectation | HS-LS2-3 | HS-LS2-4 | HS-LS2-4 | HS-LS2-5 |

CHAPTER

# 5

# Populations

**5.1**
How Populations Grow

**5.2**
Limits to Growth

**5.3**
Human Population Growth

**Go Online to access your digital course.**

▶ **VIDEO**

🔊 **AUDIO**

👆 **INTERACTIVITY**

📖 **eTEXT**

👁 **ANIMATION**

🧪 **VIRTUAL LAB**

☑ **ASSESSMENT**

HS-LS2-1, HS-LS2-2, HS-LS2-6,
HS-LS2-7, HS-LS4-5, HS-ETS1-1, HS-ESS3-1

# What can we learn from China?

China has had a sophisticated culture and a productive economy for much of its history. The country's abundant natural resources and use of technology have long supported a large, and growing, population. Between 1650 and 1800, China's population doubled from 150 million to 300 million. By the late 1800s, it reached 450 million … and the country started running out of farmland. By then, the government was struggling to cope with China's population explosion.

In the years since, China's population generally kept increasing despite many internal struggles, battles with Western powers, and civil war. One exception occurred between 1958 and 1962. China's leader, Mao Zedong, enforced a program of agricultural policies called "The Great Leap Forward." The result was one of the worst catastrophes in Chinese history. Farmers were not able to supply the food that the large population needed. As a result, as many as 45 million people died. To justify his approach, Mao made an extraordinary statement: "When there is not enough to eat, people starve to death. It is better to let half of the people die so that the other half can eat their fill."

But almost immediately after that disaster ended, population growth resumed. On average, Chinese women were bearing close to six children each. By 1970, China's population had grown to 790 million. The needs of that growing population caused serious social and ecological problems. In response, the government enacted a program to control population growth. They tried to encourage people to marry when they were older and have fewer children. The birthrate fell, but not far enough to meet the government's goals.

In 1979, the government set up a "one child" policy. It rewarded families that had only a single child with better access to schools, medical care, housing, and government jobs. Couples with more than one child were heavily fined. This policy has been reworked several times, and has had several unintended results. In 2005, there were 32 million more males under the age of 20 than females. (In traditional Chinese society, sons are preferred because they provide support for aging parents.)

In 2016, the government relaxed the policy and allowed families to have two children. Yet the one-child policy definitely slowed population growth, and it is still affecting the country. Today, most women have fewer than two children on average. This puts China in a better position as it tries to handle its major economic and environmental problems.

Many other countries, and the world as a whole, face the challenge of large and rapidly growing populations. Are there lessons to be learned from China's experience? What can we learn from nature that can help us understand human populations? How does the environment affect the growth of populations in general? How do populations affect their environment?

**Throughout this chapter, look for connections to the CASE STUDY to help you answer these questions.**

Students taking an exam in the Shaanxi province of China

# LESSON 5.1 How Populations Grow

## 🔍 KEY QUESTIONS

- *How do ecologists study populations?*
- *What factors affect population growth?*
- *What happens during exponential growth?*
- *What happens during logistic growth?*

**HS-LS2-1:** Use mathematical and/or computational representations to support explanations of factors that affect carrying capacity of ecosystems at different scales.

**HS-LS2-2:** Use mathematical representations to support and revise explanations based on evidence about factors affecting biodiversity and populations in ecosystems of different scales.

### VOCABULARY

**population density**
**population distribution**
**age structure**
**immigration**
**emigration**
**exponential growth**
**logistic growth**
**carrying capacity**

### READING TOOL

As you read this lesson, use the graphic organizer in your 📖 **Biology Foundations Workbook** to take notes on how both types of population growth occur.

Off the coast of California, southern sea otters are making a comeback. These mammals, along with the closely-related northern sea otters, once lived in an area that stretched from Baja California all the way up to Alaska. They were nearly wiped out by fur hunters during the eighteenth century. However, in 1911, otters were protected by international treaty, and their numbers began increasing. But southern sea otters are still endangered because they live only along a short stretch of the California coastline. A single large oil spill could wipe them out. Otters are important to the health of kelp forests because they feed on sea urchins and other invertebrates that eat the kelp. Without the otters, the kelp forests were disappearing.

Meanwhile, divers off the coast of North Carolina couldn't believe their eyes. They were certain they'd seen a lionfish. Why was that surprising? Because lionfish are native to the Pacific Ocean, not the East Coast of the United States! Recently, more and more lionfish have been reported around Florida, throughout the Caribbean, and all around the Gulf of Mexico, and they are still spreading. Fisheries and biologists are worried, because lionfish are predators that eat at least 70 species of native fishes. How did they get here? Why are their numbers increasing so rapidly? Can we control them?

## Describing Populations

Imagine that you're investigating an aggressively spreading species like lionfish, or an endangered species like sea otters. Some of the first questions you ask might be "How many individuals of this species live here?" "Where else do they live?" or "Are those populations stable, increasing, or decreasing?" Welcome to population biology! 🔍 *Ecologists study populations by examining their geographic range, growth rate, density and distribution, and age structure.*

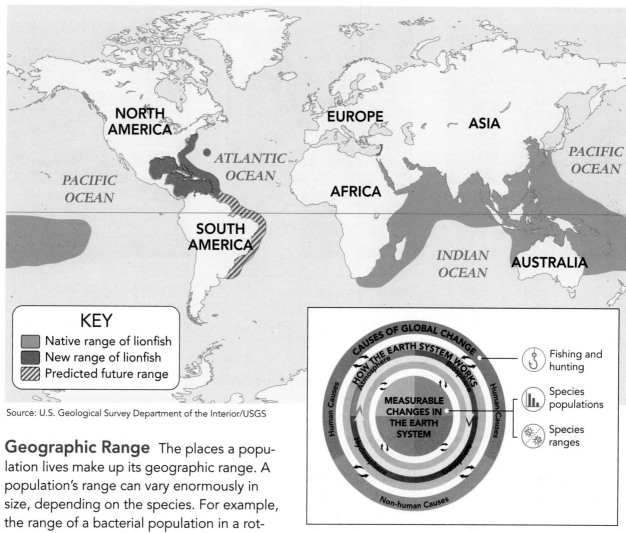

KEY
- Native range of lionfish
- New range of lionfish
- Predicted future range

Source: U.S. Geological Survey Department of the Interior/USGS

## Causes of Global Change
- Fishing and hunting
- Species populations
- Species ranges

**Geographic Range** The places a population lives make up its geographic range. A population's range can vary enormously in size, depending on the species. For example, the range of a bacterial population in a rotting pumpkin is smaller than a cubic meter. The natural range of lionfish, on the other hand, stretches thousands of kilometers across the Pacific and Indian Oceans, as shown in **Figure 5-1**. The range of the invading lionfish population, shown in red, now stretches from as far north as Boston to at least as far south as Venezuela.

The range of sea otters, on the other hand, has been changing in the opposite direction, and for other reasons. Their range decreased during the time they were hunted, and has only partly recovered over the last century. Ranges of both northern and southern sea otters today are still only a fraction of the sizes they once were. Knowing an organism's range today, as well as its historic range, is important in understanding its relationships with other species in its habitat.

**Growth Rate** Will the size of a population stay the same, increase, or decrease? The answer to that question depends on the population's growth rate. Lionfish populations in their native habitats stay pretty much the same size over time, so their growth rate is about zero. By contrast, lionfish populations in the Atlantic, Caribbean, and Gulf of Mexico have very high growth rates, so those populations are increasing rapidly. Populations can also have negative growth rates, meaning that their numbers decrease. That was the case for otters in the Pacific before hunting was banned.

**Figure 5-1**

## Geographic Range of Lionfish

The geographic range of the lionfish is increasing from the green areas in the Pacific and Indian Oceans, where it is native, to the Atlantic and Caribbean, where it is an introduced invasive species.

Random

In a random population, individuals are spaced unevenly. These trees shown a random population distribution.

Uniform

In a uniform population, such as this king penguin population, individuals are spaced evenly from one another.

Clumped

In a clumped population, such as these striped catfish, several individuals are packed closely together.

**Figure 5-2**

## Patterns of Distribution

The dots in the inset illustrations represent individual members of a population. ✔ **Compare** How do the three types of distribution differ from one another?

### 👆 INTERACTIVITY

Learn about the ways populations may be described.

**Density and Distribution** The number of individuals that can be found per unit area is called an area's **population density**. Different species can have very different densities, even in the same environment. A population of ducks in a pond may have a very low density, while algae that cover the pond surface have a high density. Why does population density matter? A few, widely spaced lionfish entering a new environment might not disturb existing communities very much. But these invaders can reach densities of over 200 adults per acre. And at that density, they can eat more than 460,000 other fish each year! In some places, lionfish have already devoured as much as 90 percent of the local species they eat!

**Population distribution** describes the way individuals are spaced out across their range. **Figure 5-2** shows three main distribution patterns: random, uniform, and clumped. Some patterns serve a purpose. Clumping, for example, can help animals avoid predators. Uniform distribution can result when individuals compete with one another for space or other resources. A random distribution occurs when the location of an individual in a population is independent of other individuals.

**Age Structure** To fully understand a plant or an animal population, researchers need to know more than just the number of individuals it contains. They also need to know the ages of those individuals, and how many of them are male, and how many are female. Those data describe the **age structure** of the population. Why is that information important? Because most plants and animals cannot reproduce until they reach a certain age. Also, among animals, only females can produce offspring.

✔ **READING CHECK** **Summarize** What is the difference between population density and population distribution?

# Population Growth

What determines whether a population increases, decreases, or stays the same size? A population will increase or decrease in size depending on how many individuals are added to it or removed from it, as shown in **Figure 5-3**. 🔍 *Birthrate, death rate, and the rate at which individuals enter or leave a population all affect population growth.*

**Birthrate and Death Rate** Populations can increase if more individuals are born in any period of time than die during that same period. In other words, a population can increase when its birthrate is higher than its death rate. Note that *birth* means different things in different species, and that species vary wildly in the amount of young they produce. Sea otters are born much like humans are born, usually one at a time. Lionfish, on the other hand, release as many as 15,000 eggs at once!

If the birthrate equals the death rate, the population may stay the same size. But if the death rate is greater than the birthrate, the population will decrease. That's what happened to sea otters. Otters breed once every year or two, and usually give birth to only one pup each time. Intensive hunting during the eighteenth century raised the otter death rate so high that births couldn't keep up.

Lionfish, by contrast, appear to have no predators or other natural enemies in the Atlantic. In the Atlantic, the lionfish death rate is lower than in their native range, and their "birth" rate is very high. Many dive groups have launched campaigns to hunt the invading fish, trying to increase their death rate and cause the population to decrease. Lionfish, it so happens, are quite tasty, and several chefs have produced a "Lionfish Cookbook" in an effort to encourage divers to hunt these invasive animals. But with a birthrate as high as lionfish have, human hunting can barely put a dent in their population.

**CASE STUDY**

Figure 5-3

### Factors That Affect Population Growth

The numbers of individuals that are born, that die, or that enter or leave a population affect the growth of a population. ✅ **Use Models** How would you expand this model to include the effects of fishing on this population?

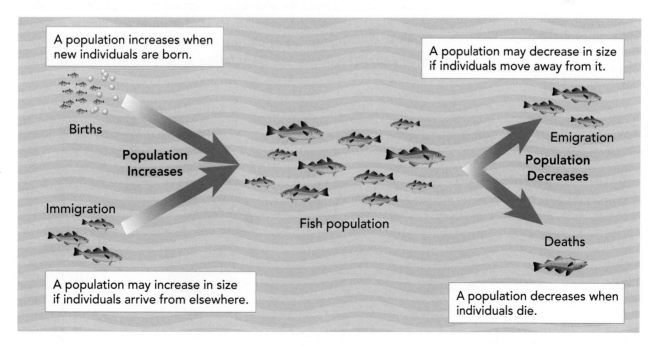

A population increases when new individuals are born.

Births

**Population Increases**

Immigration

A population may increase in size if individuals arrive from elsewhere.

Fish population

A population may decrease in size if individuals move away from it.

Emigration

**Population Decreases**

Deaths

A population decreases when individuals die.

**Immigration and Emigration** A population may increase if individuals move into its range from elsewhere, a process called **immigration**. Suppose, for example, that an oak grove in a forest produces a bumper crop of acorns one year. The squirrel population in that grove may increase as squirrels from nearby areas immigrate in search of food. On the other hand, a population may decrease in size if individuals move out of the population's range, a process called **emigration**. A local food shortage or a lack of another limiting resource can cause emigration. Young animals may emigrate from the area where they were born to find mates or establish new territories.

How quickly organisms immigrate and emigrate depends, in part, on how far they travel, how quickly they move, and whether or not human activity moves them around. Sea otters, for example, don't migrate or travel very far from their home turf. Lionfish, on the other hand, live for several weeks as larvae that float wherever currents take them. That's one reason lionfish are showing up as far north as Boston, because their larvae are carried north from Florida by the Gulf Stream. Lionfish didn't immigrate into the Atlantic on their own, but were released into the wild by home aquarium keepers who had bought them as pets.

# Exponential Growth

If you provide a population with all the food and space it needs, protect it from predators and disease, and remove its waste products, the population will increase. Why? Because members of the population will survive and produce offspring. Later, those offspring will produce their own offspring. Then, the offspring of *those* offspring will reproduce.

Although the birthrate may be more or less constant, the rate of population growth changes. Why? Because each generation contains more individuals than the generation before it! The population increases rapidly as more and more offspring are produced in a situation called **exponential growth**. ⚲ *Under ideal conditions with unlimited resources, a population will increase exponentially. This means that the larger the population gets, the faster it grows.*

HS-LS2-1

## 🧪 Argument-Based Inquiry   Guided Inquiry

### Estimating Population Size

**Problem** How can you estimate the size of a large population of plants, animals, or other living things?

In this lab, you will estimate the size of various populations in a model ecosystem. Then you will use mathematical representations to explain the factors that affect the carrying capacity of the model ecosystem for the species.

Find this lab online in your digital course.

## Organisms That Reproduce Rapidly

Let's say that we begin a hypothetical experiment with a single bacterium that divides to produce two cells every 20 minutes. We supply it with ideal conditions—and watch. After 20 minutes, the bacterium divides to produce two bacteria. After another 20 minutes, those two bacteria divide to produce four cells. At the end of the first hour, those four bacteria divide to produce eight cells.

Do you see what is happening? After three 20-minute periods, we have $2 \times 2 \times 2$, or 8, cells. Another way to say this is to use an exponent: $2^3$ cells. In another hour (six 20-minute periods), there will be $2^6$, or 64, bacteria. In just one more hour, there will be $2^9$, or 512. In one day, this bacterial population will grow to an astounding 4720 quintillion individuals (A quintillion is written as the digit "1" followed by 18 zeroes!) What would happen if this growth continued without slowing down? In a few days, this bacterial population would cover the planet!

If you plot the size of this population on a graph over time, you get a curve shaped like the letter "J." This J-shaped curve rises slowly at first, and then rises faster and faster, as shown in **Figure 5-4**. If nothing interferes with this exponential growth, the population will become larger and larger, faster and faster.

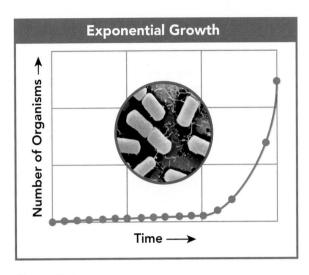

**Exponential Growth**

Number of Organisms →

Time →

**Figure 5-4**

## Exponential Growth

In the presence of unlimited resources and in the absence of predation and disease, populations will increase exponentially. The characteristic J-shape of the graph shows exponential growth.

## Organisms That Reproduce Slowly

Of course, many organisms grow and reproduce much more slowly than bacteria. For example, a female elephant can produce a single offspring only every two to four years. Newborn elephants take about ten years to mature. But, if exponential growth continued indefinitely, the result would still be impossible. In the unlikely event that all descendants of a single elephant pair survived and reproduced, after 750 years there would be nearly 20 million elephants!

## Organisms in New Environments

Sometimes, when an organism migrates or is moved to a new environment, its population grows exponentially for a time. That's happening with lionfish in the Atlantic. It also happened when a few European gypsy moths were accidentally released from a laboratory near Boston. Within a few years, these plant-eating pests had spread across the northeastern United States. In peak years, gypsy moth caterpillars devour the leaves of thousands of acres of forest. In some places, they form a living blanket that covers the ground, sidewalks, and cars!

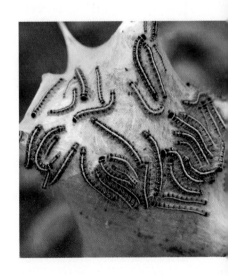

**READING CHECK** **Calculate** How many bacteria will there be after four hours from a single bacterium that divides to produce two cells every 15 minutes?

# Logistic Growth

If you think about it, the ability of populations to grow exponentially presents a pretty clear puzzle. Obviously, bacteria, lionfish, and gypsy moths don't cover Earth or fill the oceans! This means that natural populations don't grow exponentially for long. Sooner or later, something—or several "somethings"—stop exponential growth. What happens?

**Phases of Growth** One way to begin answering this question is to watch how populations behave in nature. **Figure 5-5** traces the phases of growth that a population goes through after a few individuals are introduced into a real-world environment.

**Phase 1: Population Grows Rapidly** After a short time, the population begins to grow exponentially. During this phase, resources are unlimited, so individuals grow and reproduce rapidly. Few individuals die, and many offspring are produced, so both the population size and the rate of growth increase more and more rapidly.

**Phase 2: Growth Slows Down** In real-world populations, exponential growth does not continue for long. At some point, the rate of population growth begins to slow down. This growth slow down is due to a variety of limiting factors such as competition for resources. This does not mean that the population size decreases. The population still increases, but the rate of growth slows down, so the population size increases more slowly.

**Phase 3: Growth Stops** At some point, the rate of population growth drops to zero. This means that the size of the population levels off. Under some conditions, the population will remain at or near this size indefinitely.

**INTERACTIVITY**

**Figure 5-5**

**Logistic Growth**

Real-world populations show the characteristic S-shaped curve of logistic growth. As resources become limited, population growth slows or stops, leveling off at the carrying capacity.

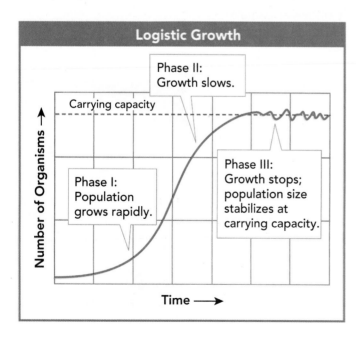

**The Logistic Growth Curve** The curve in **Figure 5-5** has a shape like the letter "S." This S-shaped curve represents what is called **logistic growth**. 🔎 *Logistic growth occurs when a population's growth slows and then stops, following a period of exponential growth.* Many familiar plant and animal populations follow a logistic growth curve.

What changes in a population's growth rate produce a logistic curve? Remember that a population increases when more organisms are added to it, such as by birth, than leave the population, such as by dying. Thus, population growth may slow for several reasons. Growth may slow if the birthrate decreases.

Growth may also slow if the death rate increases—as it did for otters when they were hunted. Rates of immigration and emigration also affect population growth.

**Carrying Capacity** A population will stop growing when a population's birthrate and death rate are the same, and when immigration equals emigration. The population size may still rise and fall somewhat, but the ups and downs average out around a certain population size.

Look again at **Figure 5-5**. You will see a jagged, horizontal line through the region of the graph where population growth levels off. The point at which that line intersects the y-axis represents what ecologists call the carrying capacity. **Carrying capacity** is the maximum number of individuals of a particular species that a particular environment can support. Once a population reaches the carrying capacity of its environment, a variety of biotic and abiotic external factors affect the population in ways that stabilize it at that size. In **Figure 5-6**, you can see the effect of seasonal changes on migration patterns of wildebeests.

**Figure 5-6**

**Carrying Capacity and Seasonal Changes**

Seasonal changes in food availability in different parts of the species range cause seasonal changes in the carrying capacity of certain environments for wildebeests and other African ungulates. These seasonal changes in carrying capacity drive Africa's extraordinary migrations.

HS-LS2-1, HS-LS2-2

# ✓ LESSON 5.1 Review

## ९ KEY QUESTIONS

1. What characteristics do ecologists study to learn about populations?

2. What factors determine the rate at which a population is increasing or decreasing?

3. What happens to the growth of a population when resources are unlimited?

4. How does logistic growth occur?

## CRITICAL THINKING

5. **Develop Models** A scientist is using a computer model to predict changes to a population of rabbits in a meadow. Identify the information about the rabbit population that should be included in the computer model.

6. **Identify Variables** A population of 5000 longhorn beetles lives in a tract of forest. What variables would affect the rate at which the population increases or decreases?

### 🔍 KEY QUESTIONS

- *What factors determine carrying capacity?*
- *What limiting factors depend on population density?*
- *What limiting factors do not typically depend on population density?*
- *What is the relationship between limiting factors and extinction?*

**HS-LS2-1:** Use mathematical and/or computational representations to support explanations of factors that affect carrying capacity of ecosystems at different scales.

**HS-LS2-2:** Use mathematical representations to support and revise explanations based on evidence about factors affecting biodiversity and populations in ecosystems of different scales.

**HS-LS2-6:** Evaluate the claims, evidence, and reasoning that the complex interactions in ecosystems maintain relatively consistent numbers and types of organisms in stable conditions, but changing conditions may result in a new ecosystem.

**HS-LS4-5:** Evaluate the evidence supporting claims that changes in environmental conditions may result in: (1) increases in the number of individuals of some species, (2) the emergence of new species over time, and (3) the extinction of other species.

### VOCABULARY

**limiting factor**
**density-dependent limiting factor**
**density-independent limiting factor**

### READING TOOL

As you read, compare and contrast density-dependent limiting factors and density-independent limiting factors. Complete the Venn diagram in your 📘 **Biology Foundations Workbook.**

If populations are theoretically able to grow exponentially, why do they often show logistic growth in the real world? One reason is predation. One factor that limits warthog populations in part of Africa is predation by lions. Now, think about lionfish. In their native Pacific habitats, lionfish populations increase in size until they reach carrying capacity. Then population growth stops because some combination of factors limits their population size. In the Atlantic and Caribbean, however, lionfish populations are growing out of control. Why does a species that is "well-behaved" in one environment become a pest in another?

## Limiting Factors

Recall that growth of primary producers can be controlled by a limiting nutrient. A limiting nutrient is a specific example of a more general ecological concept called a limiting factor. A **limiting factor** is any factor that controls the growth of a population. Limiting factors are either biotic or abiotic environmental factors that affect members of the population. The strength of some interactions depends on the density of the population. Other interactions act in more or less the same way regardless of population density. 🔍 *Acting separately or together, limiting factors determine the carrying capacity of an environment for a species.* Often, although not always, limiting factors keep most populations in their natural habitat at a population size somewhere between extinction and overrunning the ecosystem.

Charles Darwin recognized that long-term population growth and species survival are often dependent on limiting factors. Ecological limiting factors produce the pressures of natural selection that stand at the heart of Darwin's evolutionary theory.

✅ **READING CHECK** **Stability and Change** How do limiting factors affect the population of a species?

# Density-Dependent Limiting Factors

Limiting factors that operate strongly when the number of organisms per unit area, or population density, reaches a certain level are called **density-dependent limiting factors**. These factors do not strongly affect small, scattered populations. ✎ *Density-dependent limiting factors include competition, stress from overcrowding, parasitism, disease, predation, and herbivory.* Note that some of these involve abiotic factors, and others involve biotic factors.

**Competition** When populations become crowded, individuals compete for food, water, space, sunlight, and other potentially limiting resources. Some individuals obtain enough resources to survive and reproduce. Others may obtain enough to survive but not enough to raise offspring. Still others may starve or die from lack of shelter. Thus, competition for limiting resources can decrease birthrates, increase death rates, or both.

Competition is a density-dependent limiting factor, because the more individuals that are present in an area, the sooner they use up the available resources. Many animals compete for the territory they use to find food, to make a home, and to breed. Small animals might compete for a very specific territory. Individuals that can't establish and defend a territory cannot breed.

Competition can also occur among members of different species. In many cases, members of different species attempt to use similar or overlapping resources that are limited. This type of competition is a major force behind evolutionary change.

**Parasitism and Disease** When parasites and disease-causing organisms feed, they weaken their hosts and cause stress or even death. Parasitism and disease are density-dependent effects because the denser the host population, the more easily parasites can spread from one host to another.

**Stress From Overcrowding** Some species fight amongst themselves if overcrowded. In some species, such as chimpanzees, the winner in a fight may kill his opponent. In other cases, constant fighting can cause stress, which weakens the body's ability to resist disease. Overcrowding can have other effects, too. In some species, overcrowding stress can cause females to neglect, kill, or even eat their own offspring. Thus, overcrowding can lower birthrates, raise death rates, or both. Stress can also increase rates of emigration.

**Figure 5-7**

## Competition

Species interactions, such as competition, parasitism, disease, stress from overcrowding, predation, and herbivory, can result in changes in species populations, leading to changes in species ranges or biodiversity.

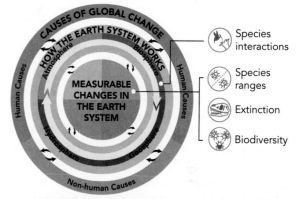

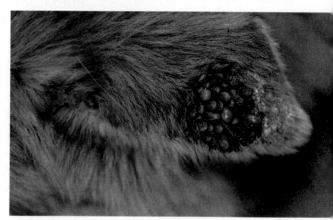

**Figure 5-8**

## Parasitism

The ticks in this dog's ear are parasites but also often carry disease-causing organisms.

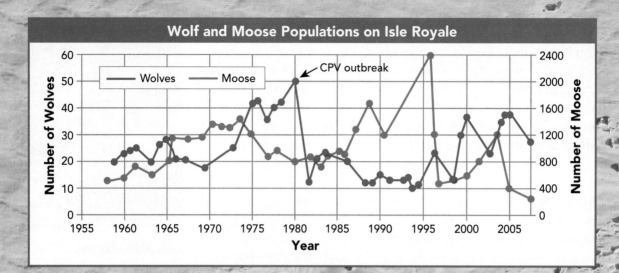

**Wolf and Moose Populations on Isle Royale**

*Figure 5-9*

**Moose-Wolf Populations on Isle Royale**

These data showing changes in moose and wolf populations on Isle Royale illustrate how predators (wolves) affect prey populations (moose), and how availability of prey affects predator populations. The moose population was also affected by a change in their food supply (plants). At one point, the wolf population decreased due to a canine parvovirus (CPV). ☑ **Interpret Graphs** How do differences between the peaks and valleys of the two graphs demonstrate interactions between these populations?

**BUILD VOCABULARY**

**Academic Words** The verb fluctuate means "to rise and fall as if in waves." A population that fluctuates is unstable. Its numbers go up and down rapidly.

 **INTERACTIVITY**

Learn about the effects of limiting factors on a population.

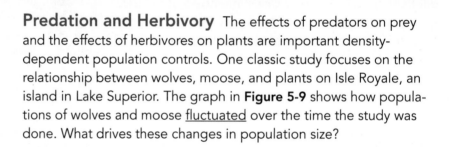

**Predation and Herbivory** The effects of predators on prey and the effects of herbivores on plants are important density-dependent population controls. One classic study focuses on the relationship between wolves, moose, and plants on Isle Royale, an island in Lake Superior. The graph in **Figure 5-9** shows how populations of wolves and moose <u>fluctuated</u> over the time the study was done. What drives these changes in population size?

*Predator-Prey Relationships* Populations of predators and prey may rise and fall over time. Sometimes, the moose population on Isle Royale increases enough that moose become easy prey for wolves. When wolves have plenty to eat, their population increases. As the wolf population increases, wolves begin to kill more moose than are born. This causes the moose death rate to rise higher than the birthrate, so the moose population decreases. As the moose population decreases, wolves begin to starve. Starvation raises the wolves' death rate and lowers their birthrate, so the wolf population also decreases. When only a few predators are left, the moose death rate drops, and the cycle may repeat.

Notice that the graph in **Figure 5-9** shows a dramatic drop in the wolf population after 1980. At that time, a virus accidentally introduced to the island killed all but 14 wolves—and all but three females. This drop in the wolf population enabled moose populations to skyrocket to 2400. Those densely packed moose then became infested with winter ticks that caused hair loss and weakness.

**Herbivore Effects** Herbivory can also contribute to changes in population size. From a plant's perspective, herbivores are predators. So it isn't surprising that populations of herbivores and plants cycle up and down, just like populations of predators and prey. On parts of Isle Royale, large, dense moose populations can eat so much balsam fir that the population of these favorite food plants drops. When this happens, moose may suffer from lack of food.

**Humans as Predators** In some situations, human activity limits populations. For example, eighteenth-century hunters killed many otters, greatly increasing the population death rate. Otters' birthrate of just one or two pups every year or two just couldn't keep up. As a result, the otter populations decreased. Since the beginning of the twentieth century, otter populations have been recovering, because hunting stopped. If hunting otters significantly decreased their population size, could hunting lionfish do the same? That's theoretically possible, but lionfish are hard to catch using hook and line or big nets. And it is unlikely that hunting them one at a time with hand nets could make any difference, given that females can produce thousands of eggs at a time!

✓ **READING CHECK Describe** How does competition affect a population?

**READING TOOL**

Make a two-column chart. List examples of density-dependent limiting factors you have read about in this text and note their effects on populations.

Figure 5-10

**Plant-Herbivore Interactions**

Plants are the "prey" of herbivores. Interactions between herbivore populations and plant populations can experience the same kinds of fluctuations that occur between predators and prey.

HS-LS2-2

## Analyzing Data

### Monarchs in Decline

Every year, monarch butterflies migrate between their summer homes in the north and their winter homes in tropical regions, such as Mexico. The line graph shows the changing winter population of monarchs in Mexico. Data from other monarch homes confirm a similar trend.

1. **Analyze Graphs** What trend in the monarch population does the graph show?

2. **Evaluate Claims** A student claims that the monarch population increases and decreases in a cycle, similar to the pattern of predator-prey populations like wolves and moose. Use the data to evaluate this claim.

3. **Ask Questions** What questions would you ask to identify the limiting factors that are affecting the monarch population?

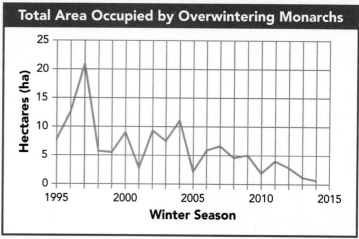

**Total Area Occupied by Overwintering Monarchs**

Source: Monarchwatch.org

# Density-Independent Limiting Factors

**Density-independent limiting factors** affect all populations regardless of population size and density. 🔍 *Environmental extremes— including weather extremes such as hurricanes, droughts, or floods, and natural disasters such as wildfires—can act as density-independent limiting factors.* In response to such factors, a population may "crash." After the crash, the population may build up again quickly, or it may stay low for some time.

Storms can nearly extinguish local populations of some species. For example, aphids, and other leaf-eating insects can be washed out by a heavy rainstorm. Waves whipped up by hurricanes can devastate coral reefs. Extremes of cold or hot weather can also take their toll, no matter how sparse or dense a population is. More prolonged environmental changes include severe drought, shown in **Figure 5-11**. These changes can cause severe declines in population sizes. If affected populations do not recover, these kinds of environmental changes can affect ecosystem stability. California's long-term drought, along with human-caused environmental change, is affecting populations of plants, insects, and birds.

**True Density Independence?** Sometimes, effects of so-called density-independent factors actually vary with population density. On Isle Royale, for example, the moose population grew exponentially for a time after the wolf population crashed. Then, a bitterly cold winter with very heavy snowfall covered the plants that moose feed on, making it difficult for all those moose to move around to find food. Because emigration wasn't possible for this island population, many moose died from starvation.

The effects of bad weather on this large, dense population were greater than they would have been on a small population. In a smaller population, there would have been less competition, so individual moose would have had more food available. This situation shows that it is sometimes difficult to say that a limiting factor acts only in a density-independent way.

**Controlling Introduced Species** What kinds of limiting factors might help control lionfish populations? Artificial density-independent control measures—such as hunting—offer only temporary solutions and are very expensive. When European rabbits were introduced to Australia, for example, the original introduced population soon multiplied wildly out of control. Soon, the two dozen rabbits, intentionally released for hunting, grew into a population estimated at 600 million individuals! This living carpet of rabbits ate its way across the Australian landscape, threatening native plants and herbivores with extinction. Intensive hunting and trapping removed many thousands of rabbits.

**INTERACTIVITY**

Figure 5-11

**Density-Independent Limiting Factors**

Kern Valley Wildlife Refuge in California is an important nesting ground for migrating birds and waterfowl. As a result of four years of drought, the lake bed dried up and the migrating birds have nowhere to go.

**Figure 5-12**

## Overrun by Rabbits

Rabbits breed very quickly. Overly large populations of rabbits have had devastating effects on island ecosystems—including islands the size of Australia. Even extensive hunting could not control the rabbits in Australia.

But these density-independent efforts at population control couldn't stop the invasion, as shown in **Figure 5-12**. Finally, in 1950, after careful experimentation, a lethal virus that causes a rabbit disease called myxomatosis was introduced into the rabbit population. That density-dependent control effort was originally very successful. But over time, rabbits evolved resistance to the disease, and less deadly viral strains also evolved. Not surprisingly, efforts to control lionfish populations in the Caribbean have had very limited success. Ecologists are trying to identify density-dependent limiting factors that control lionfish in their natural habitats. So far … no luck.

## Limiting Factors and Extinction

Limiting factors do not always stay the same over time. Temperature and rainfall, for example, are limiting factors for some organisms in certain environments. Both temperature extremes and rainfall patterns can change if climate changes. Available space for feeding and other activities can also be a limiting factor for many animals. So when human activities divide natural environments into small pieces, the carrying capacity of those pieces of habitat for those species can be much smaller. *If carrying capacity falls low enough, populations can be wiped out, leading to species extinction.*

**INTERACTIVITY**

Conduct an experiment to see how the introduction of a non-native species affects a native population.

HS-LS2-1, HS-LS2-2, HS-LS2-6, HS-LS4-5

## ☑ LESSON 5.2 Review

### KEY QUESTIONS

1. What is a limiting factor?
2. Why are competition, predation, herbivory, parasitism, disease, and stress from overcrowding density-dependent limiting factors?
3. What happens to a population in response to a density-independent limiting factor?
4. What may cause a species to become extinct?

### CRITICAL THINKING

5. **Apply Scientific Reasoning** How could a change to an ecosystem increase the carrying capacity for one species and decrease it for another? Include an example in your answer.
6. **Synthesize Information** In a dense forest, trees compete with one another for space to grow and for sunlight. Although all trees need water, why is water not generally a limiting factor in the forest?

# 5.3 Human Population Growth

Human populations—locally and globally—increase, remain the same, or decrease because of the same factors that affect the population growth of other species. How quickly is global human population growing today? In the United States and other developed countries, population growth has slowed. But in some developing countries, the population is still growing rapidly. Worldwide, four humans are born every second. With this birthrate, the human population is on its way to reaching 9 billion during your lifetime. What do the present and future of human population growth mean for our species and its interactions with the rest of the biosphere?

## Historical Overview

*Human populations, like other populations, tend to increase, and the rate of those increases has changed over time.* For most of human existence, our population grew slowly. Food was hard to find. Predators and diseases were common and life-threatening. These limiting factors caused high death rates. Until a few decades ago, only half the children in the world survived to adulthood. With death rates so high, families had many children, just to make sure that some would survive.

**Exponential Human Population Growth** As countries became more developed, food supplies became more reliable, and the global human population began to grow more rapidly. That trend continued through the Industrial Revolution in the 1800s. In addition to improved nutrition, improvements in sanitation, medicine, and public health dramatically reduced death rates. Yet, birthrates in much of the world remained high. The combination of lower death rates and high birthrates led to exponential growth. It took 123 years for the human population to double from 1 billion in 1804 to 2 billion in 1927. Then it took just 33 years for it to grow by another billion.

The time it took for the population to increase each additional billion continued to fall until 1999, when it began, very slowly, to rise.

## The Predictions of Malthus
As you've learned, exponential growth cannot continue forever. Two centuries ago, this problem troubled English economist Thomas Malthus, who argued that survival of human populations is dependent on limited resources. Malthus suggested that only war, famine, and disease could limit human population growth. Can you see what Malthus was suggesting in biological terms? He thought that human populations would be regulated by competition (war), limited resources (famine), parasitism (disease), and other density-dependent factors. This aspect of Malthus's work was vitally important in shaping Charles Darwin's thinking about natural selection.

## World Population Growth Slows
Exponential growth of the global human population continued until the second half of the twentieth century. The global human population growth rate reached a peak around 1959. That growth rate then decreased sharply for a couple of years before rising again. Since the mid 1960s the growth rate of our global population has been slowly decreasing. Note that we are talking about increases and decreases in the rate of growth, not of the total population. Global human population has continued to increase over this entire period, as shown in **Figure 5-13**. The decrease in growth rate just means that our population is growing more slowly now than it did during most of the twentieth century.

## INTERACTIVITY

Explore human population growth and compare population growth with population growth rate.

## CASE STUDY

**Figure 5-13**

## World Population Growth

The world's human population has increased because of improved nutrition and innovations such as sanitation and medicine, reducing death rates while birthrates remained high. However, the rate of growth has been decreasing. The future will likely bring moderate growth or a steady population size.

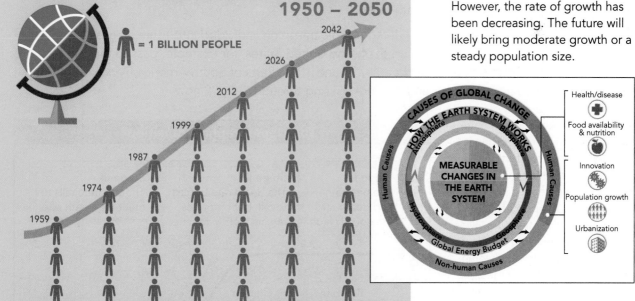

Source: U.S. Census Bureau, International Data Base, August 2016 Update.

Quick Lab 🧪 Open-Ended Inquiry

## Modeling Population Changes

1. Use counters to model a population. Prepare a data table to record the changes to population size.

2. Choose a birthrate and death rate to model. Then, add and remove counters to represent the rates for one year. Record the new population size. Repeat to model the changing population over several years.

3. Repeat the procedure to model other combinations of birthrates and death rates.

### ANALYZE AND CONCLUDE

1. **Use Models** When did the model show the greatest population increase? When did it show the greatest population decrease?

2. **Revise Models** How could you revise the model to show age structure?

# Patterns of Human Population Growth

The scientific study of human populations is called **demography**. Demography examines characteristics of human populations and attempts to explain how those populations will change over time. Scientists have identified several social and economic factors that affect human population growth. 🔍 *Birthrates, death rates, and the age structure of a population help predict why some countries have high growth rates while other countries' populations increase more slowly.*

### BUILD VOCABULARY

**Prefixes** The prefix *demo-* means "people" or "population." A **demographic transition** is a change in a population.

### Figure 5-14

## Demographic Transition

Human birthrates and death rates were high for most of history (Stage 1). Advances in nutrition, sanitation, and medicine led to lower death rates. Birthrates remained high for a time, so births greatly exceeded deaths (Stage 2), and the population increased exponentially. As levels of education and living standards rose, families had fewer children, and the birthrate fell (Stage 3), and population growth slowed. The demographic transition is complete when the birthrate meets the death rate, and population growth stops.

**The Demographic Transition** Human societies had equally high birthrates and death rates during most of history. But during the past century, population growth in the United States, Japan, and much of Europe slowed dramatically. Demographers developed a hypothesis to explain this shift. According to this hypothesis, these countries have completed the **demographic transition**, a dramatic change from high birthrates and death rates to low birthrates and death rates.

The demographic transition is divided into three stages, as shown in **Figure 5-14**. The United States, for example, passed through Stage 2 between 1790 and 1910. Parts of South America, Africa, and Asia are passing through Stage 2 now.

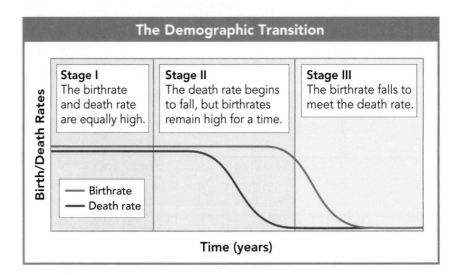

**The Demographic Transition**

| Stage I | Stage II | Stage III |
|---|---|---|
| The birthrate and death rate are equally high. | The death rate begins to fall, but birthrates remain high for a time. | The birthrate falls to meet the death rate. |

Birth/Death Rates

— Birthrate
— Death rate

**Time (years)**

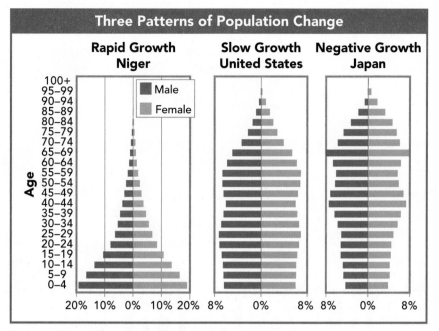

**Three Patterns of Population Change**

Rapid Growth
Niger

Slow Growth
United States

Negative Growth
Japan

Male
Female

Age

100+
95–99
90–94
85–89
80–84
75–79
70–74
65–69
60–64
55–59
50–54
45–49
40–44
35–39
30–34
25–29
20–24
15–19
10–14
5–9
0–4

20% 10% 0% 10% 20%    8%  0%  8%    8%  0%  8%

Source: United Nations, World Population Prospects

 **INTERACTIVITY**

Figure 5-15

**Population Age Structure**

The age structure of a population reveals how fast a population is growing. ☑ **Interpret Graphs** How can you tell that Japan has a negative growth rate?

A large part of ongoing human population growth is happening in only ten countries, with India, China, and sub-Saharan Africa in the lead. Our J-shaped exponential growth curve may be changing into a logistic growth curve, but in the meantime, global human population is still growing.

**Age Structure and Population Growth** Age structure diagrams, such as those in **Figure 5-15**, compare the number of people in different age categories. The age structure of a population reveals how fast a population is growing—a greater percentage of young people indicate a growing population, and a greater percentage of older people indicate a shrinking population. In the United States, there are nearly equal numbers of people in each age group, indicating that our population is growing slowly. The population of Niger is increasing, while the population of Japan is decreasing slightly.

Demographers consider many factors to predict human population growth. The factors include the age structure, the effects of deadly diseases such as AIDS, malnutrition, and death rates. Current projections suggest that by 2050 the world population will reach 9 billion people.

**INTERACTIVITY**

Investigate four different countries and the factors that determine their population growth.

HS-LS2-1, HS-LS2-2

☑ **LESSON 5.3** Review

**🔍 KEY QUESTIONS**

1. How has the human population size changed throughout history?

2. What factors help explain the differences in human population growth in different countries?

**CRITICAL THINKING**

3. **Ask Questions** What questions should you ask to determine whether a population has passed through a demographic transition?

4. **Analyze Graphs** Review the age structure graphs shown in **Figure 5-15**. How do patterns in the graphs indicate the rate at which a population is increasing or decreasing?

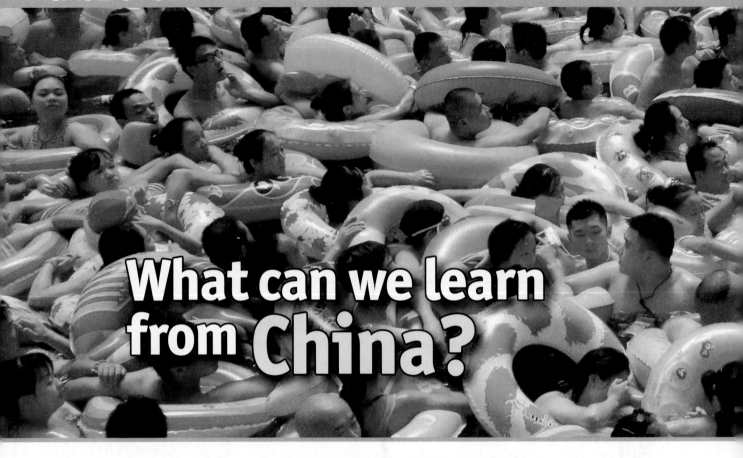

# What can we learn from China?

China is home to about 1.4 billion people, making it the most populous country in the world. Efforts of the Chinese government to control population growth are worth studying.

HS-LS2-2, HS-LS2-7, HS-ETS1-1

## Make Your Case

For almost 40 years, the Chinese government used a one-child policy to curb a large and rapidly growing population. Many Chinese families complied with the policy, but others resisted. Violators often were punished, sometimes cruelly. Data suggest that the policy helped keep the population in check. Are there lessons here for the rest of the world?

## Develop a Solution

1. **Define the Problem**  Do you think issues resulting from the world's growing human population could affect global society? Conduct research to define issues and challenges, and evaluate their severity.

2. **Evaluate a Solution**  Do you think China's one-child policy was justified? What alternatives, if any, do you think would have been preferable? Did the policy reduce the impacts of human activity on the environment, and if so, how? Could a similar policy be implemented elsewhere? Research China's policy and its long-term effects. Cite data, evidence, and other information you learn to support your evaluation.

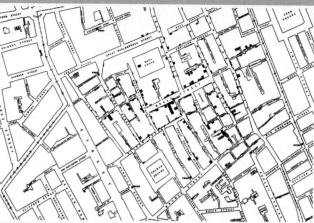

## Society on the Case

### A Deadly Lesson

For much of history, people wandered in groups or lived in small communities. Then agriculture and other technologies fueled the growth of cities. Cities were vital in the development of great civilizations. But their high population densities meant that city dwellers were more vulnerable to density-dependent population limiting factors, including disease.

Some diseases were chronic problems. One of the worst was a deadly intestinal disease called cholera, which first appeared in India centuries ago. During the Industrial Revolution, cholera spread around the world, appearing in England in 1831. Over the next 20 years, cholera epidemics claimed thousands of lives worldwide. Physicians could do nothing to stop it. There was no cure, and no one understood how it spread. (The discovery that microscopic organisms could cause disease hadn't happened yet.)

Finally, in 1854, English physician John Snow hypothesized that cholera was somehow spread through contaminated water. By carefully examining public records and data from hospitals, Snow identified a single water pump as the source of the outbreak. As it turned out, sewage had mixed into the water drawn from that pump. Years later, scientists identified the bacteria that causes cholera, which is spread by sewage.

Snow is often called the father of epidemiology, the study of public health. His work showed that when population density increases, health risks can increase as well.

## Careers on the Case

### Work Toward a Solution

The scientists who study populations often rely on others to gather or generate data, as well as to organize data properly. Statistics is the science of learning from data.

### Statistician

Statisticians may work in teams with scientists from other fields. They may also work for businesses, government agencies, or the military. Many statisticians work to improve public health, protect the environment, or manage populations of wildlife.

▶ **VIDEO**

Watch this video to learn about other careers in biology.

# Lesson Review

Go to your Biology Foundations Workbook for longer versions of these lesson summaries.

## 5.1 How Populations Grow

Ecologists study populations by examining their geographic range, growth rate, density and distribution, and age structure. For a population to increase, the number of births needs to exceed the number of deaths. Other factors affecting population growth are immigration and emigration.

A population will grow exponentially under ideal conditions with unlimited resources. Over time, though, this exponential growth will slow and eventually stop. The logistic S-shaped growth curve reflects this pattern. The maximum number of individuals of a particular species that a particular environment can support is its carrying capacity.

- population density
- population distribution
- age structure
- immigration
- emigration
- exponential growth
- logistic growth
- carrying capacity

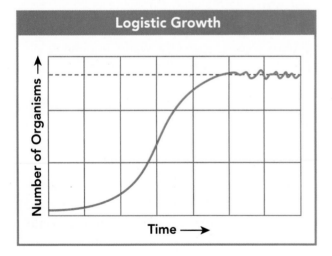

**Logistic Growth**

Number of Organisms →

Time →

☑**Analyze Graphs** At what point has this population reached its carrying capacity? How do you know?

## 5.2 Limits to Growth

The carrying capacity of a species in an environment is determined by limiting factors, which can be density dependent or density independent. Density-dependent limiting factors operate strongly when the population density reaches a certain level. The factors include competition, predation, herbivory, parasitism, disease, and stress from overcrowding.

Density-independent limiting factors affect all population sizes and densities. Density-independent factors including weather extremes such as hurricanes, droughts, or floods, and natural disasters such as wildfires may cause populations to crash. Human activities such as hunting and environmental degradation can also stress populations, sometimes leading to their extinction.

- limiting factor
- density-dependent limiting factor
- density-independent limiting factor

 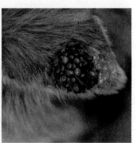

☑**Classify** Describe how each photo illustrates an example of a density-dependent or density-independent factor.

## 5.3 Human Population Growth

Human populations, like other populations, tend to increase. The rate of human population increases has changed over time. For most of human existence, our population grew slowly. Improvements in nutrition, sanitation, medicine, and public health in the 1800s led to a period of exponential growth, which continued into the mid-twentieth century. Although the growth rate has been slowly decreasing since then, the global population continues to grow.

Demography is the study of human populations and attempts to explain how those populations will change over time. Some countries have high growth rates, while others increase more slowly. Birthrates, death rates, and the age structure of a population can be used to make predictions about population growth rates. Some countries have reached a demographic transition, a dramatic change from high birthrates and death rates to low birthrates and death rates.

- demography
- demographic transition

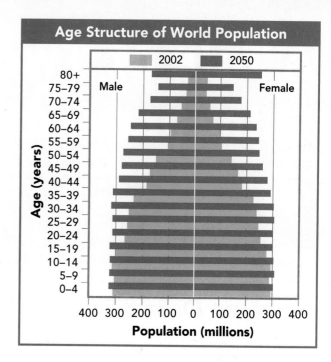

**Age Structure of World Population**

**Analyze Graphs** Describe the changes in human population growth predicted by this figure. How do you think those changes will affect society?

........

## Organize Information

List key details that support the main idea in each column.

| What supports population growth? | What limits population growth? |
|---|---|
| 1. | Competition |
| Immigration from other areas | 2. |
| 3. | 4. |
| 5. | 6. |

# A Tale of Two Countries
## China and India

## Analyze Data

HS-LS2-2, HS-LS2-7, CCSS.ELA-LITERACY.RST.9-10.3, CCSS.ELA-LITERACY.RST.9-10.7, CCSS.MATH.CONTENT.HSN.Q.A.1

**STEM** The line graph shows the birthrates and death rates in China from 1950 onward. The difference between the two rates shows how the population has changed each year. China's policies have had other effects, too. The age distribution of the population is very unusual, as shown by the age structure diagram on the next page. The shape reflects the changes in birthrates and death rates over time.

Another example to consider is India, which is the world's second most populous country after China. In fact, experts predict that India's population will overtake China by 2100. Unlike China, the government of India has not legislated laws to limit the size of families. Nevertheless, India faces problems that are similar to China's problems. Both countries have limited land for farming. If ocean levels rise due to global climate change, then much of the coastal farmland will be lost.

1. **Interpret Graphs** Use the line graph to determine the trend in China's population from 1950 onward.

2. **Conduct Research** Identify the factors that affect the human populations of China and India. Then, predict how these factors could affect their populations in the future.

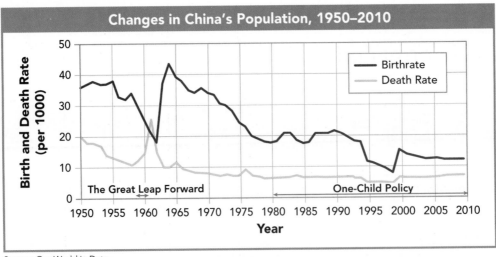

Source: Our World in Data

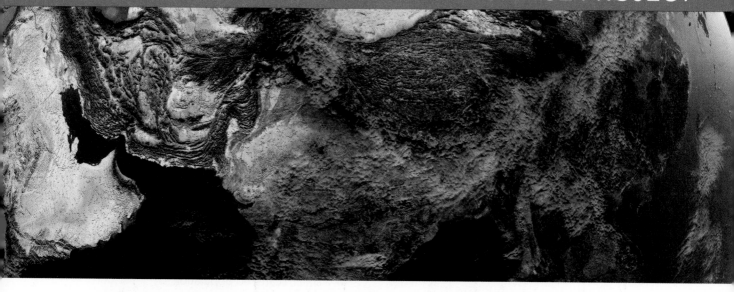

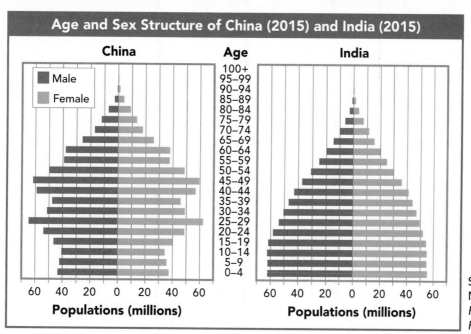

Age and Sex Structure of China (2015) and India (2015)

Source: United Nations, *World Population Prospects*, 2006

3. **Construct an Explanation** Compare the age distributions of the populations of China and India. How do the government policies of the two countries help explain the differences you observe? Use evidence and logical reasoning to support the explanation you construct.

4. **Conduct Research** Choose one of the world's most populous countries, such as China, India, Nigeria, or the United States. Research how experts predict the population of the country will change over the next 50 to 100 years, and how people's lives will change as a result. Evaluate your sources for reliability, and cite the sources that provide the information you think is useful and accurate.

5. **Communicate** Organize and present your findings in the form of a poster, computer slide show, or written essay. Share your presentation with the class. Include these features:

- A line graph or bar graph that shows the size of the population over time, including predictions for the future

- An explanation for the predicted change in population

- Likely effects of the change in population, including global effects

# ☑ASSESSMENT

## 🔍 KEY QUESTIONS AND TERMS

## 5.1 How Populations Grow

**HS-LS2-1, HS-LS2-2**

1. The primary factors affecting population growth include birthrate, death rate, immigration, and
   a. density.
   b. geographic range.
   c. emigration.
   d. demography.

2. Which factor might NOT contribute to an exponential growth rate in a given population?
   a. lower death rates
   b. higher birthrates
   c. less competition
   d. reduced resources

3. The graph shows a model of the growth of a bacterial population. Which of the following correctly describes the growth curve?
   a. demographic
   b. logistic
   c. limiting
   d. exponential

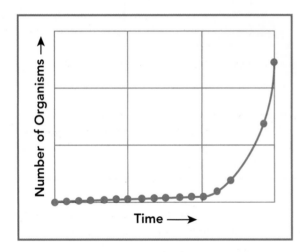

4. The maximum number of individuals of a particular species that a particular environment can support is its
   a. logistic growth.
   b. carrying capacity.
   c. age structure.
   d. population.

5. What are the phases of logistic growth?

6. What is the difference between immigration and emigration?

7. What is population density?

8. What are some examples of geographic range?

## 5.2 Limits to Growth

**HS-LS2-1, HS-LS2-2, HS-LS2-6, HS-LS4-5**

9. If a population grows larger than the carrying capacity of its environment, the
   a. death rate may rise.
   b. birthrate may rise.
   c. death rate must fall.
   d. birthrate must fall.

10. Which would be least likely to be affected by a density-dependent limiting factor?
    a. a small, scattered population
    b. a population with a high birthrate
    c. a large, dense population
    d. a population with a high immigration rate

11. Which of the following is a density-independent limiting factor?
    a. a struggle for food, water, space, or sunlight
    b. predator/prey relationships
    c. flood damage from a hurricane
    d. parasitism and disease

12. How might increasing the amount of a limiting nutrient in a pond affect the carrying capacity of the pond?

13. What are some limiting factors that contribute to a species' extinction?

14. Why is the rise-and-fall cycle of a predator-prey relationship an example of a density-dependent limiting factor?

15. What are some consequences of stress from overcrowding?

16. What human activities are examples of density-independent limiting factors?

## 5.3 Human Population Growth

**HS-LS2-1, HS-LS2-2, HS-ESS3-1**

17. The scientific study of human populations is called
    a. ecology.
    b. demography.
    c. natural selection.
    d. transition.

18. Since the Industrial Revolution, human populations have
    a. decreased.
    b. reached carrying capacity.
    c. grown more rapidly.
    d. leveled off.

19. Demographic transition refers to a shift from
    a. high birthrates and death rates to low birthrates and death rates.
    b. immigration to emigration.
    c. population decrease to population increase.
    d. logistic growth to exponential growth.

20. Much of the world's human population is growing exponentially because
    a. human populations have not reached their exponential curve.
    b. most countries have not yet completed the demographic transition.
    c. human populations do not conform to the logistic model.
    d. the food supply is limitless.

21. What were the limiting factors that Malthus identified as controls to human population increase?

22. How do age-structure diagrams predict the growth of a population?

23. How does population growth in the United States compare with that in Niger? (You may wish to refer to **Figure 5-15**.)

# CRITICAL THINKING

HS-LS2-1, HS-LS2-2

24. **Integrate Information** A scientist is studying a population of endangered Florida panthers. Why is the age structure of the population important to include in the study?

25. **Construct an Explanation** Asian carp were introduced to the lakes and rivers in the midwestern United States. They have no natural enemies there, and their population continues to increase. Use the concepts of birthrate and death rate to explain this population increase.

26. **Use Math** How can the size of a population continue to increase even as its rate of growth is decreasing? Assume that the increase in population is not due to immigration.

In this chapter, we have discussed how populations change over time. Use the diagram below to answer questions 27 and 28.

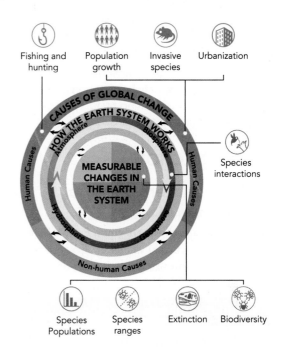

27. **Interpret Diagrams** Choose one human cause of global change. What Earth system processes and measurable changes are connected to that human activity? Explain at least three connections.

28. **Evaluate** How has hunting changed sea otter populations? How might changes in sea otter populations affect the kelp forest ecosystem? Make connections among the Understanding Global Change topics in your explanation. (*Hint:* Look back at the diagrams in Chapters 3 and 4, as well as the diagrams in this chapter.)

29. **Use Models** An aquarium is used to represent the population of fishes in a large lake. Describe one of the limiting factors that affects the fishes in the lake. Then, describe how the aquarium could model this factor.

30. **Classify** A fungus that attacks ears of corn can ruin a corn crop. Is the fungus an example of a density-dependent or density-independent limiting factor? Cite your reasoning in your answer.

31. **Apply Scientific Reasoning** Over the past 150 years, the world's human population has increased from 1 billion to more than 7 billion. Will this rate of increase continue over the next 150 years? Include evidence to support your answer.

# ☑ ASSESSMENT

## CROSSCUTTING CONCEPTS

**32.** **Systems and System Models** Suppose all the wolves were removed from Isle Royale, leaving the moose with no natural predators. What would a graph of the moose population versus time look like? Explain your reasoning.

**33.** **Stability and Change** Why does exponential growth continue for only brief periods of time? Use the concepts of limiting factors and carrying capacity to construct your answer.

## MATH CONNECTIONS

## Analyze and Interpret Data

CCSS.MATH.CONTENT.HSN.Q.A.2

The data table shows the years when Earth's human population reached certain values. It also shows predictions for population size in the future. Use the data to answer questions 34–36.

| World Population Milestones | | |
|---|---|---|
| Population (billion) | Year | Time Interval (year) |
| 1 | 1804 | — |
| 2 | 1927 | 123 |
| 3 | 1960 | 33 |
| 4 | 1974 | 14 |
| 5 | 1987 | 13 |
| 6 | 1999 | 12 |
| 7 | 2012 | 13 |
| 8 | 2027 | 15 |
| 8.9 | 2050 | 23 |

**34.** **Identify Patterns** Describe the pattern in world population growth shown by the data.

**35.** **Construct an Explanation** Based on your knowledge of human history and population science, propose an explanation for the pattern in the data you identified.

**36.** **Apply Scientific Reasoning** Do you think it is likely that the human population will ever increase at the same rate as it did from 1974 to 2012? Cite evidence and use logical reasoning to support your answer.

The graph shows the changing rabbit population in South Australia over many years. The points at which various population control measures were introduced are indicated. Use the graph to answer questions 37–39.

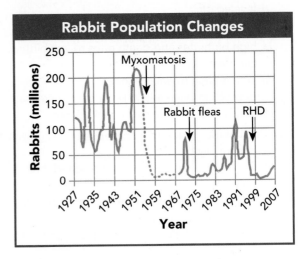

**37.** **Interpret Graphs** Describe the changes to the rabbit population shown by the graph.

**38.** **Evaluate Data** How successful were each of the three measures used to control the rabbit population? Explain how the graph supports your answer.

**39.** **Predict** Assume that in 2020, myxomatosis is again introduced to the rabbit population. How do you predict the rabbit population will change as a result?

## LANGUAGE ARTS CONNECTION

## Write About Science

CCSS.ELA-LITERACY.WHST.9-10.2

**40.** **Write Informative Texts** Write a paragraph to explain the concept of the demographic transition, and to identify its three stages. Include references to **Figure 5-14** to illustrate your paragraph.

**41.** **Write Procedures** A science student is studying the growth of algae in a beaker of pond water. Write a procedure for the student to follow to investigate the limiting factors for the growth of the algae.

## Read About Science

CCSS.ELA-LITERACY.RST.9-10.2

**42.** **Determine Central Ideas** How do factors that affect all plant and animal populations help explain the history of the human population? How do they help predict future changes?

1. Green lacewings are used to control aphids, which are pests of many crops. A population of 1000 green lacewings is released into a farmer's field. The graph shows the change in the population over time.

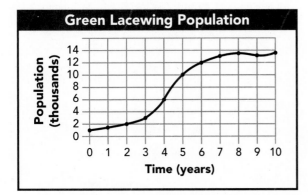

**Green Lacewing Population**

What is the most likely explanation for the approximately constant population of the lacewings after the eighth year?
A. The lacewings had eaten all of the aphids in the field.
B. The lacewing population had reached the carrying capacity of the field.
C. New predators of lacewings had arrived in the field.
D. The birthrate of lacewings had increased, while the death rate remained constant.
E. The death rate of lacewings had increased, while the birthrate remained constant.

2. About 800 ash trees live in a tract of conservation land. Which of these events would have the LEAST effect on the land's carrying capacity for ash trees?
A. Maple trees are introduced to the land, where they grow well.
B. Human activities drain about half of the water that the land generally receives.
C. A beetle that infects ash trees is introduced to the land.
D. About one third of the ash trees are cut down and hauled away.
E. About one third of the land is cleared of all trees and used for new houses.

3. A lake is home to many native fishes and aquatic plants. Which of these events is most likely to threaten the biodiversity of the lake ecosystem?
A. A 20 percent increase in the population of one of the native fish species.
B. The arrival of migrating birds that prey on the native fishes.
C. The introduction of a nonnative fish species that has no natural enemies in the lake.
D. A storm that swells the lake and floods the surrounding land.
E. The arrival of winter weather that causes the water to freeze.

4. For many years in the 1800s, human hunters on the U.S. Great Plains hunted bison almost to extinction. Which statement, if true, best explains why the hunters were such a threat to the bison population?
A. The death rate from hunting was greater than the birthrate of the bison.
B. The death rate from hunting was greater than the natural death rate of the bison.
C. The hunting removed individuals of all ages, including very young bison.
D. Human hunters replaced the natural predators of the bison.
E. The hunting removed both male and female bison equally.

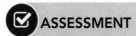

## ASSESSMENT

For additional assessment practice, go online to access your digital course.

| If You Have Trouble With... | | | | |
|---|---|---|---|---|
| **Question** | 1 | 2 | 3 | 4 |
| **See Lesson** | 5.1 | 5.2 | 5.2 | 5.2 |
| **Performance Expectation** | HS-LS2-1 | HS-LS2-1 | HS-LS2-2 | HS-LS2-2 |

# Communities and Ecosystem Dynamics

**6.1**
Habitats, Niches, and Species Interactions

**6.2**
Succession

**6.3**
Biodiversity, Ecosystems, and Resilience

**Go Online to access your digital course.**

▶ VIDEO

◀)) AUDIO

👆 INTERACTIVITY

📖 eTEXT

👁 ANIMATION

🧪 VIRTUAL LAB

☑ ASSESSMENT

Beavers build dams that shape river ecosystems.

HS-LS2-2, HS-LS2-6, HS-LS2-7,
HS-LS4-6, HS-ETS1-4

# How do species interactions shape ecosystems?

As dusk falls over Yellowstone National Park, elk emerge from dense woods to browse on tender willows along a stream. Suddenly, they freeze. An instant later, wolves dash from the forest, aiming for a kill. The elk react in the nick of time, bolting out of reach. This hunt, like most, has failed. But those elk have been attacked here before. Will they now decide to graze elsewhere?

This dramatic encounter offers a window into community ecology, the study of interactions among species in a food web. As it turns out, human disturbance of this web set the stage for experiments that have improved our understanding of both wild ecosystems and those affected by human activity.

The story began during the 1800s, as ranchers started shooting and poisoning wolves that preyed on livestock. By the 1920s, they had eliminated all wolves in the region. Elk populations boomed, and they overgrazed willows along streambeds.

The overgrazing affected beavers, which eat willows and also use them to build dams that create ponds. Those dams create marshy areas, keeping the water table close to the surface and providing good growing conditions for willows. Streams with dams and willows also offer homes to fishes and birds.

By the 1950s, elk overgrazing caused beaver populations to collapse. Dams and marshy areas disappeared. Streams flowed faster, carving deeper channels. The water table fell. Fishes and birds suffered. These changes, all resulting from removal of one key predator, are called a trophic cascade. In this cascade, wolf removal reshaped both the biological community and its physical environment.

In an effort to restore these habitats, biologists reintroduced wolves in the late 1990s, and have been monitoring the situation ever since. After so many changes spread through the ecosystem, could returning wolves to the system "reboot" it?

In some places, the answer seems to be yes. As wolf populations grew, elk populations fell, and willows grew back. Beavers returned and built dams, and the ecosystem was restored. But elsewhere, willows didn't recover after elk populations dropped. Beavers didn't return. The system seemed stuck in an altered state.

It turns out that this complex community is hard to understand and rebuild. Yellowstone is home to more than 60 other mammal species, some of which prey on elk, while others are alternate prey for wolves. Also, in some parts of Yellowstone, the loss of beavers changed stream structure in ways that couldn't easily be reversed.

This case raises many questions. How do predators and prey affect each other? How do community structure and complexity affect species diversity? Why is this diversity important? What factors change an ecosystem? What do those changes look like? Can they be reversed?

**Throughout this chapter, look for connections to the CASE STUDY to help you answer these questions.**

# Habitats, Niches, and Species Interactions

Moray eels hide in rocky crevices and coral reefs.

If you ask someone where they live, he or she might answer "the Caribbean" or "the West Coast." That kind of answer doesn't tell you very much. To learn more about a person, you need more data. Answers like "Miami" or "the Bay Area" still don't tell you all you'd like to know. Where in those cities? Miami Beach or downtown? San Francisco or Oakland? What street address? Is there an apartment number? What does he or she do for a living? That's the kind of specific information ecologists seek about species and ecosystems.

## Habitat and Niche

Biomes, as you learned in Chapter 3, are large areas with broadly similar environmental conditions that can house a variety of different ecosystems. Within those ecosystems, the actual place an organism lives is called its **habitat**. 🔑 *A habitat can be described as an area with a particular combination of physical and biological environmental factors that affect which organisms can live within it.* You can think of a habitat as an organism's ecological "address."

Knowing the habitat an organism lives in, however, doesn't provide much more information than knowing the city a person lives in. Think about habitats like the Everglades, or a redwood forest, or a coral reef. Large animals, such as Florida panthers, black bears, or sharks, might roam through large parts of those habitats, and might also spend time in other habitats nearby. We can understand that situation, because we easily recognize the kinds of environmental conditions that affect organisms our own size. But what about smaller animals, such as insects, birds, or eels? They might be found only in certain parts of their habitats. To understand why, we need to look closely.

**Microhabitats** Many small organisms live only in very small parts of the larger habitats we humans see. To understand where these organisms live and why, we must examine environmental conditions on the much smaller scale that matters to those organisms. Look under leaves on a forest floor, or under the bark of a rotting log, and you will discover many different smaller *microenvironments* or *microhabitats*.

Many different microhabitats can exist within short distances of each other, as shown in **Figure 6-1**. From worm tunnels in the ground, to beetle burrows under tree bark, each microhabitat has its own set of environmental conditions called its *microclimate*. For example, fungi that live on tree roots are affected mainly by the microclimatic conditions within a few millimeters of their location.

**Figure 6-1**

## Microenvironments

Each part of a tree, including fallen branches, provides various microhabitats with microclimates. The microhabitat of moths is dry and exposed to the sun, whereas the salamander lives in moist, sheltered spaces. What other microhabitats do you see?

Moth and its caterpillar

Emerald ash borer

Bird louse

Termites

Biofilm

Beetle

Spider

Shelf fungi

Salamander

Bacteria

Millipede

Earthworm

Fungal hyphae

**Microbiomes** The discovery of microbial communities called *microbiomes* has dramatically changed our understanding of ecology. These communities inhabit places never before considered "habitats," and perform more important functions than anyone imagined. For example, in addition to decomposing organic matter, soil microbiomes, like the ones shown in **Figure 6-1**, also affect plant health, and the ability of roots to absorb water and nutrients. Some members of the microbiome transfer carbon from plants to fungi, and from one plant to another. Others carry "messages" between plants. Many ecological interactions, including several discussed in this chapter, are regulated by microbiomes. Even your mouth, gut, and skin are home to microbiomes whose inhabitants outnumber your own cells and powerfully influence your health!

**Tolerance** Every species has its own range of **tolerance**, the variety of environmental conditions within which it can survive and reproduce, as shown in **Figure 6-2**. Within a species' optimum range, environmental conditions enable individuals to find enough energy and nutrients to maintain homeostasis, to grow and reproduce.

**Figure 6-2**

**Tolerance**

The graph shows the response of a hypothetical organism to a single environmental variable, such as sunlight or temperature. ☑ **Interpret Graphs** Why is the same graph useful for many different environmental factors?

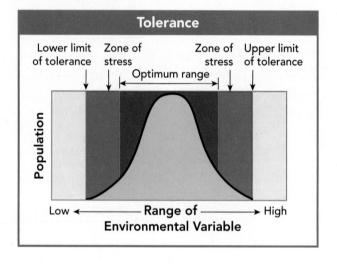

If one or more environmental conditions, such as temperature, rise above or fall below that optimum range, then individuals experience stress. Why? Organisms under stress must expend more energy to maintain homeostasis, and that leaves less energy for growth and reproduction. Individuals may survive and reproduce under slightly stressful conditions, but they will typically produce fewer offspring, and fewer of those offspring will survive. In more stressful conditions that are beyond a species' tolerance limits, individuals may survive but not reproduce. Without reproducing, the species can't survive.

☑ **READING CHECK** **Infer** What are the possible consequences to an organism when the temperature becomes colder than the optimum range for a species?

**The Niche** The habitat of a species, or its ecological address, only tells part of its story. Ecologists also study a species' ecological occupation, or how it stays alive. A **niche** (nich) describes where an organism lives and what it does "for a living," including the way it interacts with biotic and abiotic factors. ✎ *A species' niche includes the range of physical and biological conditions in which it can survive and reproduce, as well as the way it obtains resources it needs.*

**Resources and the Niche** The term **resource** can refer to any necessity of life. For plants, necessary resources include sunlight, water, and soil nutrients. For animals, resources can include nesting space, shelter, types of food, and places to feed.

**Physical Aspects of the Niche** A species' niche includes all the physical, or abiotic, factors to which it is adapted. Most amphibians, for example, absorb and lose water through their skin, so they must live in moist places. If an area is too hot and dry for too long, most amphibians cannot survive. In contrast, plants such as cacti, which are adapted to deserts, will die if their roots stay wet for too long.

**Biological Aspects of the Niche** A species' niche also involves the biological, or biotic, factors it requires for survival. Examples of biological factors include the food an organism eats, the way it obtains that food, and when and how it reproduces. Communities of seabirds on a remote island, for example, may all nest in the same habitat. But each species may prey on fish of different sizes and hunt in different places. Thus, each species occupies a distinct niche. The warblers shown in **Figure 6-3** each rely on different physical spaces and biotic factors, and therefore occupy distinct niches.

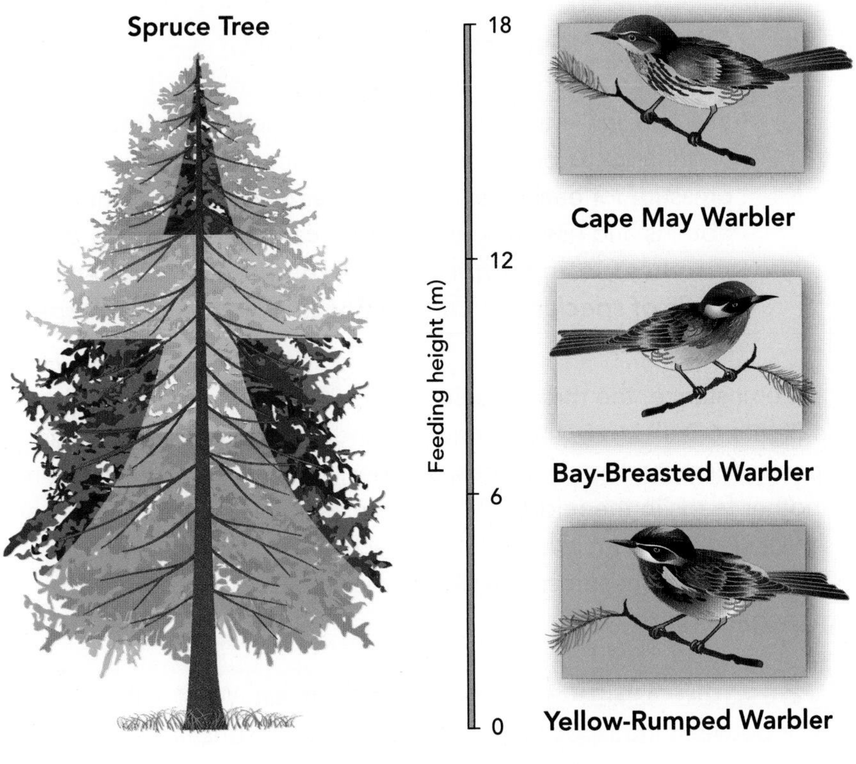

**READING TOOL**

Make a concept map to help understand an organism's niche. Use the terms *abiotic, biotic, ecological address, food, habitat, light, niche, reproduction, resources, temperature,* and *water.*

Spruce Tree

Feeding height (m)

Cape May Warbler

Bay-Breasted Warbler

Yellow-Rumped Warbler

**Figure 6-3**

**Resource Sharing**

Each of these warbler species has a different niche in its spruce tree habitat. By feeding in different areas of the tree, the birds avoid competing directly with one another for food. ☑ **Infer** What would happen if two of the warbler species tried to occupy the same niche in the same tree at the same time?

# Competition

If you look at any community, you will probably find more than one kind of organism attempting to use the same resources. When more than one organism attempts to use the same limited ecological resource in the same place at the same time, competition occurs. In a forest, for example, plant roots compete for water and nutrients in the soil. Animals compete for resources such as food, mates, and places to live and raise their young. Competition among members of the same species is known as *intraspecific competition*. Competition between members of different species is known as *interspecific competition*.

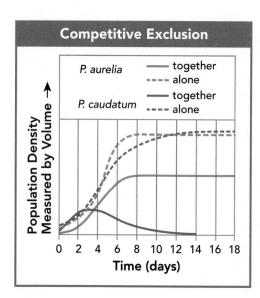

**Figure 6-4**

**Competitive Exclusion**

The two species of paramecia *P. aurelia* and *P. caudatum* have similar requirements. When grown in cultures separately (dashed lines), both populations grow quickly and then level off. When grown together under certain conditions (solid lines), however, *P. aurelia* outcompetes *P. caudatum* and drives it to extinction.

**Competitive Exclusion Principle** Direct competition between species almost always produces a winner and a loser—and the losing species dies out. One series of experiments demonstrated this using two species of single-celled organisms. The results of the experiment are summarized in the graph in **Figure 6-4**. When each species was grown in a separate culture under the same conditions, each successfully survived. But when both species were grown together in the same culture, one species outcompeted the other. The less competitive species did not survive.

Experiments like this one, along with observations in nature, led to the recognition of an important ecological rule. The **competitive exclusion principle** states that no two species can occupy exactly the same niche in exactly the same habitat at exactly the same time. If two species attempt to do so, one species will be better at competing for limited resources and will eventually exclude the other species.

**Dividing Resources** The competitive exclusion principle explains the observation that we rarely find more than one species in a habitat occupying exactly the same niche. That happens because competition for resources creates pressure for each species to specialize in the way that it obtains and uses resources. ✑ *By causing species to divide resources, competition helps determine the numbers and kinds of species in a community and the niche each species occupies.*

For instance, the three species of North American warblers shown in **Figure 6-3** all live in the same trees and feed on insects. But one species feeds on high branches, another feeds on low branches, and another feeds in the middle. The resources used by these species are similar, but not identical. Therefore, each species has its own niche. This division of resources was likely brought about by competition among the birds.

**☑ READING CHECK** **Compare and Contrast** What is the difference between intraspecific competition and interspecific competition?

# Predation and Herbivory

Recall that food webs involve numerous producers and many consumers on several trophic levels. The lynx shown in **Figure 6-5** will feed on the snowshoe hare—if it catches it. However, organisms interact in ways that are much more dynamic than you might guess from looking at food web diagrams. Remember also that populations of predators and prey, and of herbivores and plants, powerfully influence each other, and often cycle up and down over time. We review these interactions because they are important in shaping communities. Any natural or human-caused environmental change that affects a population of a key species can dramatically change the structure of an ecosystem.

**Predator-Prey Relationships** In Lesson 5.2, you learned about predator-prey cycles, and the ways those populations affect each other. Now suppose that predators catch prey more easily in some parts of a habitat than in other parts. Over time, those predators can affect where prey spend most of their time. For example, if wolves catch elk more often in open space, elk might spend more time hiding in the woods.

**Herbivore-Plant Relationships** Herbivores and plants have the same sort of relationship as predators and prey—except that plants can't move! 🔍 *Herbivores affect the size and distribution of plant populations in a community, and determine the places that certain plants can survive and grow.* For example, if elk spend a lot of time grazing in certain areas, they almost wipe out local willow populations in those areas.

## Figure 6-5

## Predator and Prey

Hares are the main prey of lynx. ☑ **Infer** How do the populations of predator and prey affect each other?

 **INTERACTIVITY**

Analyze the population dynamics in a coral reef environment.

HS-LS2-2

---

**CASE STUDY** Analyzing Data

### Predator-Prey Dynamics

The relationships between predator and prey are often tightly intertwined, particularly in an environment in which each prey species has a single predator and vice versa. The graph here shows an idealized computer model of changes in predator and prey populations over time.

1. **Use Computational Models** Suppose a bacterial infection kills off most of the prey at point B on the graph. How would this affect the predator and prey growth curves on this computer model at point C? At point D?

2. **Analyze Graphs** Suppose a sudden extended cold spell destroys almost the entire predator population at point F on the graph. Predict how the next cycle of the prey population would appear on the graph.

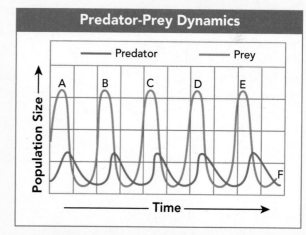

3. **Develop Possible Solutions** Suppose a viral infection kills all the prey at point D. What effect would this have on the predator and prey curves at point E? What will happen in future years to the predator population? What solution could ecologists develop to ensure the continued survival of the predators?

**READING TOOL**

Read actively! Look for in-text definitions of any unfamiliar terms or concepts.

# Keystone Species

Sometimes, a single species has such a powerful influence on community structure that changes in its population size can dramatically change the structure of an entire ecosystem. As described in **Figure 6-6**, sea otters along the Pacific coast of North America are a prime example. Along much of that coast, giant algae called kelp can grow abundantly, creating complex ecosystems called kelp forests. Kelp's main "enemies" are herbivorous sea urchins. When this community is in balance, sea otters eat enough urchins to control their population, and kelp grow thickly.

A century ago, hunters nearly eliminated otters across much of their range. After that, kelp forests up and down the coast vanished. What had happened? Without otters preying on sea urchins, urchin populations skyrocketed. Armies of urchins devoured kelp. Without kelp forests as habitats, fishes, seabirds, and many other species disappeared.

In this community, otters function as what is called a **keystone species**. ⚲ *A keystone species plays a vital and unique role in maintaining structure, stability, and diversity in an ecosytem.* When otters were protected from hunting, their populations recovered. Urchin populations dropped, and kelp forests began to thrive again. But there are other species in that ecosystem. Recently, otter populations have fallen again, possibly because of increased predation by killer whales. Note that once an ecosystem has been changed by the removal of a keystone species, it may or may not be possible to restore the original community by simply putting the keystone species back.

**CASE STUDY**

**Visual Analogy**

**Figure 6-6**

**Keystone Species**

A keystone is the stone at the top of an arch that holds the other stones in place. Similarly, a keystone species provides structure and stability in an ecosystem. Sea otters are a keystone species on the Pacific coast of North America.

KEYSTONE SPECIES

# Symbioses

A particularly close, interdependent relationship between two species is called **symbiosis** (sim by OH sis), which means "living together." 🔍 *Three main types of symbiotic relationships are mutualism, commensalism, and parasitism.*

## Commensalism

A relationship in which one organism benefits and the other is neither helped nor harmed is called **commensalism** (kuh MEN sul iz um). For example, small marine animals called barnacles often attach themselves to whales. The barnacles benefit from the movement of water full of food particles past their swimming hosts. Although barnacles perform no known service to whales, they don't harm them either. Many members of microbiomes have commensal relationships with each other and with larger organisms.

## Mutualism

A relationship between two species in which both species benefit is called **mutualism**. Sea anemones, for example, use stinging tentacles to protect themselves from predators and to capture prey. Despite those weapons, certain fishes still manage to snack on anemone tentacles. Some anemone species, however, have mutualistic partners called clownfishes, which are immune to anemone stings. When a clownfish is threatened by a fish-eating predator, it seeks shelter by snuggling deep into tentacles that would kill or paralyze most other fish, as shown in **Figure 6-7**. But if an anemone-eating species tries to attack their living home, the spunky clownfish dart out and fiercely chase away fish many times their size. Mutualism is also very common in microbiomes, including both soil and human microbiomes. Many members of human gut microbiota, for example, help keep disease-causing microorganisms under control through competition and other interactions.

## Parasitism

A relationship in which one organism lives inside or on another organism and harms it is called **parasitism.** The parasite obtains all or part of its nutritional needs from the host organism. Generally, parasites weaken but do not kill their host. Tapeworms, for example, live in the intestines of mammals, where they absorb large amounts of their hosts' partially-digested food. Fleas, ticks, lice, and leeches live on the skin or hair of many animals.

**INTERACTIVITY**

**Figure 6-7**

**Symbiosis**

Mutualism is one type of symbiosis. Clownfish living among the sea anemone tentacles are protected from predators, and the clownfish chase away predators of the sea anemone. Recently, scientists have discovered that anemones with clownfish partners are healthier. The movement of the fish through the anemone's tentacles improves water circulation.

**INTERACTIVITY**

Analyze the types of symbiotic relationships.

HS-LS2-2, HS-LS2-6

# ☑ LESSON 6.1 Review

## 🔍 KEY QUESTIONS

1. How can you describe the habitat in which an organism lives?

2. Explain why no two species can occupy the same niche at the same time.

3. Why are predator-prey and herbivore-plant relationships important in shaping communities?

4. List and describe the three main types of symbiotic relationships.

## CRITICAL THINKING

5. **Evaluate Claims** In a forest ecosystem, both owls and hawks prey on small, ground-dwelling animals. A student claims that because the two birds prey on the same animals, they occupy the same niche. Evaluate this claim, and include an explanation to either support or refute it.

6. **Evaluate Models** What are the limitations of using a model of a very small biome, or microbiome, to study the habitats of bacteria and other microorganisms?

## KEY QUESTIONS
- *How do communities change over time?*
- *How do communities recover after a disturbance?*

**HS-LS2-2:** Use mathematical representations to support and revise explanations based on evidence about factors affecting biodiversity and populations in ecosystems of different scales.

**HS-LS2-6:** Evaluate the claims, evidence, and reasoning that the complex interactions in ecosystems maintain relatively consistent numbers and types of organisms in stable conditions, but changing conditions may result in a new ecosystem.

### VOCABULARY
**ecological succession**
**primary succession**
**pioneer species**
**secondary succession**

### READING TOOL

In your 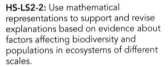 Biology Foundations Workbook, identify the effects of the major elements from this lesson. The causes are already filled in the table for you.

In 1883, the volcanic island of Krakatau in the Indian Ocean was destroyed by an eruption. The tiny island that remained was completely barren. Within two years, however, grasses were growing. Fourteen years later, there were 49 plant species, along with lizards, birds, bats, and insects. By 1929, a forest containing 300 plant species had grown. Today, the island is blanketed by mature rain forest. What events and processes changed the island's populations and species diversity so dramatically?

## Primary and Secondary Succession

The story of Krakatau after the eruption is just one example of **ecological succession**, a series of somewhat predictable events that occur in a community over time. **⚲ *Ecosystems change over time, especially after disturbances, as new species move in, populations change, and some species die out.*** As the history of Krakatau shows, species diversity typically increases over the course of succession.

**Primary Succession**  Volcanic explosions, such as the ones that destroyed Krakatau and blew the top off Mount Saint Helens in Washington State a century later, can create new land or sterilize existing areas. Retreating glaciers can have the same effect, leaving only exposed bare rock behind them. Succession that begins on newly formed rock or other areas that have no remnants of an older community is called **primary succession**, as shown in **Figure 6-8A**.

   **Pioneer species** are the first species to colonize barren areas. The term is named after rugged human pioneers who first settle wilderness areas. Human pioneers create the first settlements, and do the ground breaking work that makes an area habitable for subsequent settlers.

In ecological succession, pioneer species have broad ranges of tolerance for environmental factors. That's how they manage to survive on bare rock, or in soil that lacks nutrients and a mature microbiome.

One ecological pioneer that grows on bare rock is lichen—a symbiosis between a multicellular fungus, a yeast, and a photosynthetic organism. Mosses and certain grasses, like those that first colonized on Krakatau, are also pioneer species. Pioneer species break down rock, synthesize organic material, and begin to form soil.

**Secondary Succession** When a disturbance affects an existing community but doesn't completely destroy it, a process of **secondary succession** occurs. Secondary succession proceeds faster than primary succession, in part because bits of the old community survive and can regrow rapidly. Secondary succession is shown in **Figure 6-8B**. On land, secondary succession often follows a wildfire, a hurricane, or another natural disturbance. We think of these events as disasters, but many species are adapted to them. Although forest fires kill some trees, for example, other trees are spared, and fire can stimulate their seeds to germinate. Secondary succession can also follow human activities like logging and farming.

**BUILD VOCABULARY**

**Word Origins** The origin of the word *succession* is the Latin word *succedre*, meaning "to come after." Ecological succession involves changes that occur one after the other as species move into and out of a community.

**ANIMATION**

**Figure 6-8**

**Primary and Secondary Succession**

In both types of succession, one group of species replaces another group.

— Time —

15 years          35 years          80 years          115+ years

**A. Primary succession** occurs on newly exposed surfaces. In Glacier Bay, Alaska, a retreating glacier exposed barren rock. Over the course of 100 years, a series of changes has led to the hemlock and spruce forest.

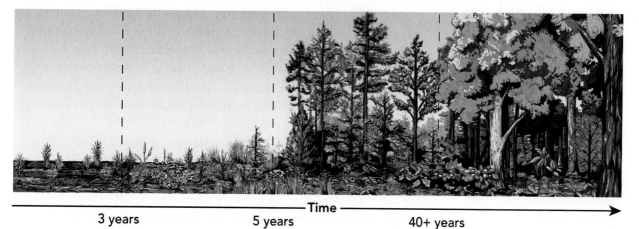

— Time —

3 years          5 years          40+ years

**B. Secondary succession** occurs in disturbed areas where remnants of previous ecosystems remain. In both examples, changes will continue for years to come.

## Quick Lab | Guided Inquiry

### How Does Succession Occur?

**Procedure**

1. Place a handful of dried plant material into a clean jar.

2. Fill the jar with boiled pond water (that has cooled) or sterile spring water. Determine the initial pH of the water with pH paper.

3. Cover the jar and place it in an area that receives indirect light.

4. Examine the jar every day for the next few days.

5. When the water in the jar appears cloudy, prepare microscope slides of water from various levels of the jar. Use a pipette to collect the samples.

6. Look at the slides under the low-power objective lens of a microscope and record your observations.

### ANALYZE AND INTERPRET DATA

1. **Evaluate Your Plan** Why did you use boiled or sterile water in this investigation?

2. **Draw Conclusions** Where did the organisms you observe come from?

3. **Support Your Explanation with Evidence** Was ecological succession occurring? Cite evidence from this investigation to support your answer.

4. **Evaluate Evidence** Check your results against those of your classmates. Do they agree? How do you explain any differences?

**INTERACTIVITY**

Compare and contrast primary succession and secondary succession.

## Why Succession Happens

Succession can happen in different environments for several reasons. In most cases, each species alters its environment in ways that make it easier for other species to compete for resources and survive. For example, as lichens add organic matter and form soil, mosses and other small plants can colonize and grow. When trees arrive, their branches and leaves shade and protect the ground, and provide shelter and food for animals. These processes increase the complexity of the environment, enabling more plant and animal species to find homes and food. As succession continues, species diversity usually increases.

**READING CHECK** Apply Concepts How is primary succession different from secondary succession?

# Climax Communities

Years ago, ecologists thought that succession in a given area would always proceed through the same stages to produce a specific, uniform, and stable *climax community* like the spruce/hemlock forest developing in Glacier Bay. But recent studies have shown that succession doesn't always follow the same path, and that climax communities are often not uniform and stable.

## Succession After Natural Disturbances

Many communities regularly experience natural events that disturb areas of varying sizes. Healthy temperate forests and grasslands recover from wildfires. The photos in **Figure 6-9** show how a shoreline in Indonesia recovered from a tsunami. ✎ *When natural disturbances happen in healthy ecosystems, the events and processes that occur during secondary succession often, but not always, reproduce the original climax community.* Powerful waves during storms can damage portions of a coral reef. Windstorms can knock over rain-forest trees, creating sunny breaks in the canopy. Fires can kill trees in parts of a forest. Once the disturbance is over, each of these patches undergoes succession. So different patches within the larger community may be in a different stage of secondary succession at the same time. Some climax communities are disturbed so often that they look like ecological "patchwork quilts" and can't really be called either uniform or stable.

Figure 6-9

**Recovery From a Natural Disaster**

These photos show the coastline of Banda Aceh, Indonesia, immediately following a tsunami in December, 2004 (left), and then again in December, 2014 (right). ☑ **Interpret Photos** What kind of succession occurred in this region? How do you know?

**Succession After Human-Caused Disturbances** In North America, land cleared for farming and then abandoned often passes through succession that eventually produces a community that may or may not resemble the original climax community. Ecosystems may or may not recover from extensive human-caused disturbances. *Secondary succession can take different paths, and produce different communities, depending on the kind of disturbance, the season in which the disturbance occurs, and other factors.* Clearing and farming of tropical rain forests, for example, can change the physical structure of soil and the soil microbiome in ways that prevent regrowth of the original community.

**Studying Patterns of Succession** Ecologists study succession by comparing different cases and looking for similarities and differences. For example, they learned that at both Mount Saint Helens and Krakatau, primary succession proceeded through stages. Pioneer species arrived via seeds, spores, or adult stages that traveled over long distances.

The pioneer species are important because they help stabilize loose volcanic debris. This allowed later species to take hold. Historical studies in Krakatau and ongoing studies on Mount Saint Helens confirm that early stages of primary succession are slow, and that chance can play a large role in determining which species colonize at different times.

**INTERACTIVITY**

Learn about disturbances by studying populations of native animals and non-native animals.

HS-LS2-2, HS-LS2-6

## ☑ LESSON 6.2 Review

### ⚘ KEY QUESTIONS

1. Explain why ecological succession occurs.
2. Describe the factors that affect the paths of secondary succession.

### CRITICAL THINKING

3. **Construct an Explanation** Provide evidence to support the claim that secondary succession tends to occur faster than primary succession.

4. **Define the Problem** After taking antibiotics for several weeks, a patient develops a severe bacterial infection in his intestines. The doctor claims the antibiotics changed the microbiome of the patient's gut, allowing the infection to develop. What evidence would the doctor need to support the claim? Explain how competition and succession played a role in developing the bacterial infection.

5. **Synthesize Information** A section of tropical rain forest is cleared for a farm. Why might the forest community never return to its original form, even if the farm is abandoned?

# Biodiversity, Ecosystems, and Resilience

🔍 **KEY QUESTIONS**
- *What kinds of biodiversity exist?*
- *What are the benefits of biodiversity?*
- *What are some important ecosystem services?*

**HS-LS2-6:** Evaluate the claims, evidence, and reasoning that the complex interactions in ecosystems maintain relatively consistent numbers and types of organisms in stable conditions, but changing conditions may result in a new ecosystem.

**HS-LS2-7:** Design, evaluate, and refine a solution for reducing the impacts of human activities on the environment and biodiversity.

**HS-LS4-6:** Create or revise a simulation to test a solution to mitigate adverse impacts of human activity on biodiversity.

**VOCABULARY**
biodiversity
ecosystem diversity
species diversity
genetic diversity
resilience
ecosystem services

**READING TOOL**

As you read, list the many benefits that are gained when there is rich biodiversity within an ecosystem. Fill in the table in your 📖 **Biology Foundations Workbook.**

 **INTERACTIVITY**

Learn about the importance of biodiversity by examining several ecosystems.

From multicolored coral reefs to moss-draped forests, variety is the spice of life. But variety in the biosphere gives us more than interesting things to look at. Our well-being is closely tied to the health of ecosystems, which in turn depends on community interactions among different organisms.

## Types of Biodiversity

Biological diversity, or **biodiversity**, is the total of all genetically-based variation in all organisms in the biosphere. 🔍 *Biodiversity can be defined as the variety and variability of animals, plants, and microorganisms, including ecosystem diversity, species diversity, and genetic diversity.*

**Community/Ecosystem Biodiversity** Ecosystem diversity refers to the variety of habitats, communities, and ecological processes in the biosphere.

**Species Diversity** The number of different species in the biosphere, or in a particular area, is called **species diversity**. To date, biologists have identified and named more than 1.2 million eukaryotic species, and they estimate that at least 9 million more are yet to be discovered—and that estimate doesn't include microbiomes! Much more diversity exists among single-celled organisms.

**Genetic Diversity** The term **genetic diversity** usually refers to the total of all different forms of genes present in a particular species. Genetic diversity can be invisible, but is responsible for within-species variations among organisms, both in individual ecosystems and among different ecosystems. Genetic diversity is the raw material that enables organisms to adapt to changing external factors.

# Biodiversity Benefits

You might not think of biodiversity as a natural resource, but it is a great treasure. ⚲ *Biodiversity's benefits include offering invaluable contributions to medicine and agriculture, and enabling organisms and ecosystems to adapt to environmental change.*

**Biodiversity and Medicine** Many medicines, including painkillers like aspirin and antibiotics like penicillin, were first discovered in wild species. Other plant compounds from wild species are used to treat diseases like depression and cancer.

**Biodiversity and Agriculture** Most crop plants have wild relatives, like the potatoes in **Figure 6-10**. These wild plants may carry genes that promote disease resistance, pest resistance, or other useful traits. These genes could be transferred to crop plants through plant breeding or genetic engineering.

**Biodiversity and Ecosystem Resilience** The biological diversity of an ecosystem can affect that ecosystem's structure, stability, and function. Recall that the presence of a keystone species can increase community biodiversity. The removal of a keystone species can decrease biodiversity and stability.

In addition, several ecological models suggest that a decrease in an ecosystem's species diversity can affect its resilience. **Resilience** describes a natural or human system's ability to recover after a disturbance. Resilient ecosystems also have some ability to adapt over time to changes in their surroundings. How could biodiversity fit into a resilience model? The more species that are present in an ecosystem, the more likely that some of those species have different tolerance ranges for environmental conditions, such as temperature and rainfall. And if that is the case, populations of those species can rise and fall under different conditions, as modeled in **Figure 6-11**.

### Figure 6-10
### Potato Diversity

The genetic diversity of wild potatoes in South America can be seen in the colorful varieties shown here. The International Potato Center, based in Peru, houses a "library" of more than 4500 tuber varieties.

**BUILD VOCABULARY**

**Related Words** The noun **resilience** is the ability to recover after a change. The adjective *resilient* describes something that is able to adjust easily to change.

|  | Average Year | Wet Year | Dry Year |
|---|---|---|---|
| Diverse Ecosystem | | | |
| Ecosystem dominated by "red" species | | | |
| Ecosystem dominated by "gold" species | | | |

**Time**

### Figure 6-11
### Resilience to Climate

In this model, the "red" species better tolerate wet weather, while the "yellow" species better tolerate dry weather. Ecosystems containing just one of those species change more dramatically than an ecosystem containing both species. ☑ **Use Models** What does this model suggest about biodiversity and ecosystem resilience?

Adapted from: Cleland, E. E. (2011) Biodiversity and Ecosystem Stability. *Nature Education Knowledge* 3(10):14.

**In Your Neighborhood** Guided Inquiry

### Biodiversity on the Forest Floor

**Problem** How does biodiversity help leaves decompose?

In this lab, you will investigate the microorganisms that break apart dead leaves on the forest floor, and evaluate their role in maintaining a healthy forest ecosystem.

You can find this lab in your digital course.

---

**READING TOOL**

Use the key idea sentence to help you predict the information that follows it.

 **INTERACTIVITY**

Put your engineering skills to the test as you design a rainwater capture system.

# Ecosystem Services and Biodiversity

Human society depends on healthy ecosystems in a number of ways, although many people don't think much about that dependence. **Ecosystem services** are the benefits provided by ecosystems to humans as shown in **Figure 6-12**. *Important ecosystem services include producing food, cycling nutrients, purifying water, storing carbon, regulating pests, pollinating crops, and buffering the effects of extreme weather events.*

**Food Production** Diverse ecosystems, such as prairies, can provide a resilient mix of food for livestock. Wild species can preserve genes that may improve related crops or livestock.

**Nutrient Cycling and Soil Structure** Both carbon and nitrogen cycles depend, in part, on the activities of the soil microbiome. A resilient soil microbiome helps maintain soil fertility and structure under changing conditions.

**Purifying Water** Soil microbiomes, along with algae and plants, play vital roles in filtering and purifying fresh water.

**Storing Carbon** Healthy and actively growing terrestrial and marine ecosystems with high primary productivity remove carbon dioxide from the atmosphere and store the carbon. Biodiverse ecosystems are generally more resilient and can provide this function under a wider range of environmental conditions.

**Regulating Pests and Pollinating Crops** Biologically diverse and resilient ecosystems include predators that feed on herbivores that might attack crop plants. Diverse terrestrial ecosystems offer food and shelter to vital pollinating insects.

**Buffering Effects of Extreme Weather Events** Diverse and resilient coastal wetlands protect against erosion and shield shorelines against storms. Forests can protect mountainsides against erosion and landslides.

**READING CHECK Review** How do predators provide ecosystem services?

## Services Provided and Examples

### Purifying water

Wetlands and intact forests along rivers and around reservoirs filter and clean groundwater. Preserving buffer zones that perform these natural processes is significantly cheaper than building water-purification plants.

### Buffering effects of weather

Mangrove forests protect tropical shorelines from erosion by storm waves and runoff. Dune grasses and salt marsh grasses do the same in temperate regions.

### Pollinating

Bees, flies, and butterflies pollinate crop plants, including fruit trees and vegetables. Beetles, bats, and hummingbirds pollinate many other important plants.

### Regulating pests

Many species of birds and bats eat insects like mosquitoes that can spread disease. These and other predators also eat crop-damaging insects.

### Food production

Highly productive ocean areas provide large fishes, such as tuna, with food and space to thrive. Many wild plants may also produce food for humans.

### Nutrient cycling

Healthy, actively growing forests remove carbon dioxide from the atmosphere. Bacteria and fungi also take up nitrogen and fix it into organic compounds.

### Maintaining soil structure

Detritivores and other soil organisms aerate soil and prevent it from becoming too compacted. Bacteria and fungi in soil as well as leaf litter microbiomes produce humus.

 **INTERACTIVITY**

**Figure 6-12**

## Ecosystem Services

Healthy ecosystems provide many benefits to human society. The benefits are called ecosystem services.

HS-LS2-6, HS-LS2-7, HS-LS4-6

## ☑ LESSON 6.3 Review

### 🔍 KEY QUESTIONS

1. Describe three different types of biodiversity.

2. Explain how biodiversity benefits medicine and agriculture.

3. Explain how biodiversity affects ecosystem services.

### CRITICAL THINKING

4. **CASE STUDY** Apply Scientific Reasoning Why does the biodiversity of an ecosystem affect its resilience?

5. **Construct an Argument** A farmer decides to use a pesticide on a cherry orchard. The pesticide would kill nearly all insects, including those that feed on cherries. Construct arguments both in support of and against the farmer's decision. Research the use of pesticides in orchards to help you construct the arguments.

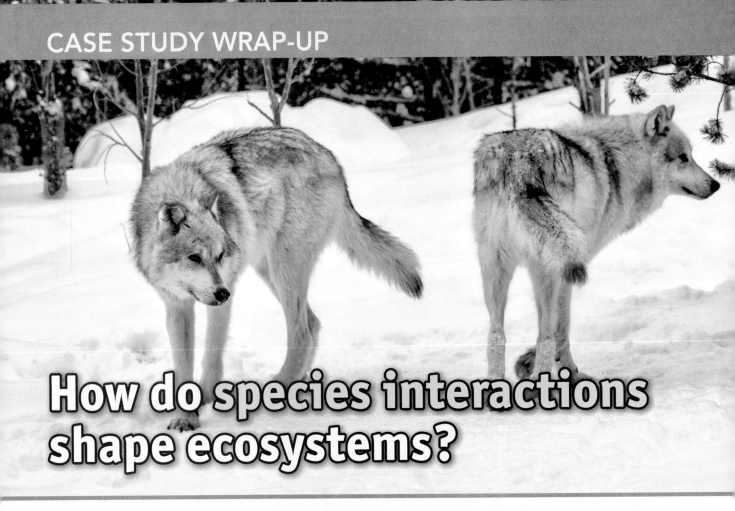

# How do species interactions shape ecosystems?

In some places, wolf populations are small and endangered. Yellowstone's wolf packs are healthy—for now.

HS-LS2-1, HS-LS2-6, CCSS.ELA-LITERACY.WHST.9-10.1

## Make Your Case

Scientists and park rangers agree that reintroducing wolves to Yellowstone was a well-informed decision. Happily, the wolves helped reverse many of the changes in parts of Yellowstone, restoring biodiversity in certain areas. However, wolves weren't the only cause of the improvements, and wolf reintroduction didn't restore all areas.

## Apply Scientific Reasoning

1. **Conduct Research** Compare the Yellowstone wolf story with a situation in your region where human activity that affected one species, or a couple of species, resulted in a trophic cascade. Which aspects are similar to the Yellowstone story, and which are different? Have researchers offered and tested hypotheses to explain the changes?

2. **Engage in Argument** Develop an argument, supported by evidence, about ways to protect or restore the ecosystem that you researched. Do you think your solution will work throughout the ecosystem, or just in certain parts of it? Compare and contrast your chosen system with Yellowstone.

## Technology on the Case

### Follow that Wolf!

How can researchers figure out where wolves spend their time? And how can rangers track wolves in a park as vast as Yellowstone? Technology provides the answers.

Data about which animals live in certain places can be gathered by hidden cameras. If animals are active at night, infrared light and special sensors allow pictures to be taken in the dark.

Researchers also attach tracking devices onto animals. Some tracking devices are simple radio transmitters. Researchers locate these animals using receivers equipped with directional antennae to home in on the signal. Other devices use satellite-based global positioning systems (GPS)—the same sort of technology used in cars and smart phones.

These devices must withstand outdoor conditions, and should not interfere with subjects' natural behavior. Devices used to track elephants must stand up to being rubbed against tree trunks! Migratory birds can be tracked using much smaller and more lightweight devices. Still other tracking tools are so tiny and light that they can be carried by bumblebees!

In Yellowstone, scientists have been placing radio collars on 25 to 30 wolves every year. These collars enable researchers to gather data on the sizes of wolf home ranges, and on how their movements change from one season to another. Sometimes, a collar will reveal bad news about the individual wearing it. When the signal comes from the same place for several days, the tagged animal has probably died.

## Careers on the Case

### Work Toward a Solution

National parks help preserve biodiversity, and they can provide useful evidence about the way ecosystems function. Park rangers work with scientists and government officials to help manage these parks.

### Park Ranger

The U.S. National Park System covers more than 84 million acres. Rangers help educate visitors, protect park land and wildlife, and enforce laws. Many rangers are experts in specific fields of science, such as forestry, geology, and wildlife management.

▶ **VIDEO**

Learn more about park rangers and other related careers.

## Lesson Review

Go to your Biology Foundations Workbook for longer versions of these lesson summaries.

### 6.1 Habitats, Niches, and Species Interactions

A habitat refers to the physical and biological environmental factors of an ecosystem that affect the organisms living there. Every species in a habitat has its own range of tolerance, which are the environmental conditions in which it can survive and reproduce. Within a habitat, a species occupies a niche, which includes the range of physical and biological conditions in which it can survive and reproduce.

Competition within and among species helps determine the numbers and kinds of species in a community and the niche each species occupies. Populations of predators and prey, and of herbivores and plants, powerfully influence each other, and often cycle up and down over time.

Symbiosis describes the interdependent relationship between two species. In commensalism, one organism benefits and the other is neither helped nor harmed. In mutualism, both species benefit. A parasitic relationship is one in which one organism lives inside or on another organism.

- habitat
- tolerance
- niche
- resource
- competitive exclusion principle
- keystone species
- symbiosis
- commensalism
- mutualism
- parasitism

☑ **Apply Concepts** What role does a keystone species have in its ecosystem?

### 6.2 Succession

Ecological succession is a series of somewhat predictable changes over time in a community. Primary succession occurs on bare rock, where there are no remnants of an older community. The first species to colonize a barren area are called pioneer species. Secondary succession occurs when some members of the older community remain. It often occurs after human activities like farming and logging. In both types of succession, a series of new communities replace older ones.

When a natural disturbance occurs in a healthy ecosystem, secondary succession often, but not always, reproduces the original climax community. However, secondary succession can also take different paths and produce different communities.

- ecological succession
- primary succession
- pioneer species
- secondary succession

### 6.3 Biodiversity, Ecosystems, and Resilience

Biodiversity is the total of all genetically-based variation in all organisms in the biosphere. Biodiversity includes ecosystem diversity, species diversity, and genetic diversity. Ecosystem diversity refers to the variety of habitats, communities, and ecological processes. Species diversity refers to the number of different species. Genetic diversity refers to the total of all different forms of genes present in a species.

Biodiversity is one of Earth's greatest resources. Biodiversity contributes to medicine and agriculture and enables organisms and ecosystems to adapt to change. The more diverse an ecosystem is, the higher its resilience to natural and human disturbances.

Ecosystem services refer to the benefits provided to humans by ecosystems. Food production, cycling of nutrients, water purification, carbon storage, pest regulation, crop pollination, and buffering effects of extreme weather events are all important ecosystem services.

- biodiversity
- ecosystem diversity
- species diversity
- genetic diversity
- resilience
- ecosystem services

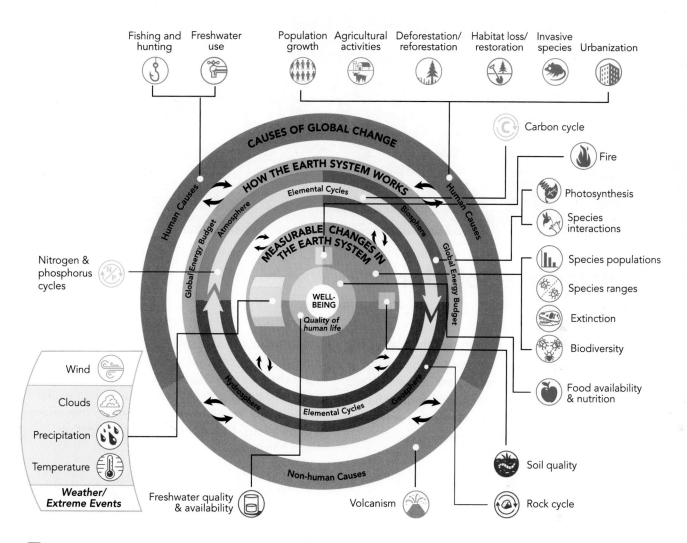

Fishing and hunting • Freshwater use • Population growth • Agricultural activities • Deforestation/reforestation • Habitat loss/restoration • Invasive species • Urbanization • Carbon cycle • Fire • Photosynthesis • Species interactions • Species populations • Species ranges • Extinction • Biodiversity • Food availability & nutrition • Soil quality • Rock cycle • Volcanism • Freshwater quality & availability • Nitrogen & phosphorus cycles • Wind • Clouds • Precipitation • Temperature • Weather/Extreme Events

CAUSES OF GLOBAL CHANGE • HOW THE EARTH SYSTEM WORKS • MEASURABLE CHANGES IN THE EARTH SYSTEM • Human Causes • Elemental Cycles • Atmosphere • Biosphere • Global Energy Budget • Global Energy Budget • Hydrosphere • Geosphere • Elemental Cycles • Non-human Causes • WELL-BEING Quality of human life

☑ **Use Models** How do humans affect species interactions? What measurable changes can result from changing species interactions in ecosystems? Use arrows and words to connect the processes and phenomena that are shown in the Understanding Global Change model. How are these measurable changes related to these three key concepts: keystone species, biodiversity, and resilience.

# Organize Information

Cite evidence for each statement from the text, investigations, and other activities you have completed.

| Statement | Evidence |
|---|---|
| Each species has tolerances for environmental factors. | 1. |
| Lichen can act as a pioneer species. | 2. |
| Biodiversity can be valuable medically. | 3. |

# The Populations of Yellowstone

## Construct a Solution

HS-ETS1-4, HS-LS2-2, HS-LS2-7, HS-LS4-6

**STEM** As you have read in this chapter's Case Study, wolves were reintroduced to Yellowstone National Park in the 1990s. Ever since, scientists have been monitoring the populations of wolves and other species in the park. The graphs show some of their data.

As you analyze the data, remember that many factors affect the Yellowstone ecosystem. Wolves prey on elk, but so do other Yellowstone predators, such as coyotes and bobcats. Elk graze on a variety of trees that grow in Yellowstone, but other factors that affect the trees include climate, diseases, and other herbivores.

In some parts of Yellowstone, wolf reintroduction allowed willows to regrow, and significantly restored stream communities. In other places within the park, reintroduction did not have that full effect. Research studies both in Yellowstone and in Banff National Park in Canada have provided data for scientists to propose hypotheses to explain these differences.

1. **Analyze Graphs** Describe the trends in each of the four populations shown in the graphs. What data do the graphs provide? Describe any trends in the data that you observe.

2. **Construct an Explanation** Using the evidence in the graph, construct an explanation for how the changes in wolf population might have affected other populations. Support your explanation with your knowledge of factors that affect populations, such as competition, predation, and herbivory.

3. **Identify Variables** What factors other than the wolf population could explain the trends in the data? Consider biotic factors, such as other species that live in Yellowstone, as well as abiotic factors, such as climate.

4. **Construct a Simulation** Work in a small group to plan, develop, and construct a simulation of the reintroduction of wolves to Yellowstone. The simulation should model changes in the populations of other species upon the reintroduction of wolves into the ecosystem. You may choose to construct a physical simulation, in which students model wolves and other species. Or, if possible, prepare a computer simulation.

Follow these steps:

- Conduct additional research on factors that affect the populations of these species.

- Identify the initial conditions, which are the sizes of the populations before the wolves were reintroduced.

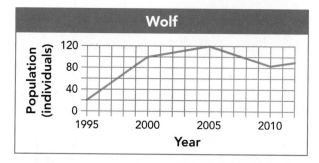

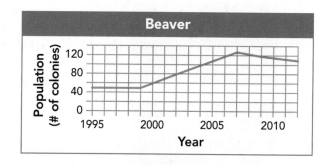

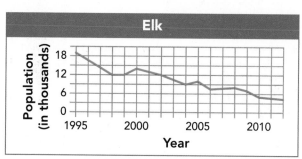

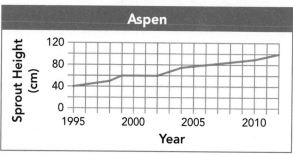

Credit, all graphs: National Park Service. U.S. Department of the Interior

- Identify how the initial conditions changed from year to year, which are the rates that the populations increase or decrease.

- Begin the simulation by modeling the initial conditions. Then model the changing conditions, as well as the events—such as wolves preying on elk—that help explain these changes.

- Use the simulation to help predict the effects of possible changes to the Yellowstone ecosystem. For example, simulate the effect of a rapid decrease in the population of trees, or a rapid increase in the elk population.

- Discuss the limitations of your simulation. Explain why any simulation may not accurately predict the changes in a real ecosystem, such as Yellowstone.

# ☑ASSESSMENT

## 🔍 KEY QUESTIONS AND TERMS

### 6.1 Habitats, Niches, and Species Interactions

HS-LS2-2, HS-LS2-6

1. Which species directly affects the size and distribution of the plant population in its community?

a.

b.

c.

d.

2. What of the following is most likely to occur if an organism's environment is outside the organism's range of tolerance?
   a. The growth of the organisms increases.
   b. The organisms fail to reproduce.
   c. The organisms produce more offspring to increase the chance of survival.
   d. The organisms develop mutualistic relationships.

3. What is the difference between an organism's habitat and its niche?

4. How can different species of insect-eating birds live in the same tree?

5. How is commensalism different from mutualism?

6. What is the competitive exclusion principle?

7. How is parasitism different from other types of symbiosis?

### 6.2 Succession

HS-LS2-2, HS-LS2-6, HS-LS2-7

8. Place these stages of succession in order from earliest to latest.

a.

b.

c.

d.

9. The first organisms to repopulate an area affected by a volcanic eruption are called
   a. keystone species.
   b. climax species.
   c. primary producers.
   d. pioneer species.

10. What determines whether ecological succession is classified as primary succession or secondary succession?

11. What is often the end result of secondary succession?

12. What is the meaning of the word "pioneer" in the term *pioneer species*?

13. Describe the two major types of ecological succession.

### 6.3 Biodiversity, Ecosystems, and Resilience

HS-LS2-6, HS-LS2-7, HS-LS4-6

14. Which term describes the variety of species in a certain area?
    a. succession          c. biodiversity
    b. ecosystem          d. genetic diversity

**15.** A salt marsh that helps prevent flooding of a coastal town is an example of what ecosystem service?
   **a.** nutrient cycling
   **b.** buffering
   **c.** carbon storage
   **d.** pest regulation

**16.** How is species diversity different from genetic diversity?

**17.** What is an ecosystem service? List three examples.

**18.** What describes the resilience of an ecosystem? Include an example of resilience.

## CRITICAL THINKING

HS-LS2-2, HS-LS2-6, HS-LS2-7, HS-LS4-6

**19.** Draw Conclusions A polar bear and a grizzly bear live in very different biomes. Based on this information, can you conclude that the microbiomes inside their intestines are also very different from each other? Explain your reasoning.

**20.** Analyze Text Structure Using the text from this chapter, analyze the relationships among the key terms *habitat*, *niche*, *resource*, and *competitive exclusion principle*.

**21.** Construct Graphs Banana plants are native to tropical climates. In an experiment, a scientist raises two groups of banana plants. One group is kept at a temperature of 30°C (85°F). In the second group, the scientist decreases the temperature from 30°C by one 1°C every day. Predict the results of this experiment. Construct a graph to illustrate your prediction.

**22.** Plan an Investigation A scientist discovers a colony of bacteria growing on the roots of a peanut plant. The scientist wonders if the bacteria are a parasite of the plant, or if they live in a mutualistic relationship. Outline the steps of an investigation that could provide evidence to answer this question.

**23.** Design a Solution There is growing concern over the decline in the U.S. honeybee population due to the use of pesticides. How could a reduced honeybee population affect biodiversity and ecosystem services? Design a solution for this problem.

**24.** Predict A developer plans to build a resort with golf courses, a shopping mall, and lots of paved parking lots on the shrubland and sand dunes beside a beach. Predict how this development will affect ecosystem services in the area.

**25.** Construct an Explanation Years after a forest burns, the land is covered in tall grasses and some young trees. Will the tall grasses eventually die off? Explain why or why not.

**26.** Construct an Argument Choose an ecosystem near you, or another familiar ecosystem. Why is biodiversity important to the health of the ecosystem, or to the ecosystem services it provides? Support your argument with specific examples.

The table describes the niches of wildebeests and zebras. Use the table to answer questions 27–29.

### Wildebeest and Zebra

| Habitat | Grassy plains and open woodlands of Africa |
| --- | --- |
| Diet | Both graze on grasses. Wildebeests prefer short grass with new growth. |
| Predators | Lion, cheetah, hyena, wild dog |
| Behavior | Both migrate in large herds. Wildebeests tend to follow zebras from one area to the next. |

**27.** Summarize Describe and compare the niches of the zebras and wildebeests.

**28.** Apply Scientific Reasoning Why must the zebras and wildebeests fill different niches on the open plains and woodlands of Africa? Use your knowledge of niches and the information in the table to justify your answer.

**29.** Gather Evidence What evidence would you need to distinguish the niches of the zebras and wildebeests?

**30.** Summarize What type of events can lead to a loss of biodiversity? After the event, how does biodiversity recover?

**31.** Construct an Explanation Describe the events that occur in an ecosystem after a catastrophic event.

## CROSSCUTTING CONCEPTS

**32. Scale, Proportion, and Quantity** Why is it useful to describe the soil of a forest as a microbiome, and separate from the forest biome above it?

**33. Stability and Change** After a climax community is disturbed, such as by a fire or flood, will it always return to its original condition? Explain why or why not.

## MATH CONNECTIONS

## Analyze and Interpret Data

CCSS.MATH.CONTENT.MP4, CCSS.MATH.CONTENT.HSS.IC.A.1

Scientists at Oregon State University developed a computer model to analyze the carbon storage of a developing forest. The graph below describes the carbon storage of a forest during primary succession. Use the graph to answer questions 34–36.

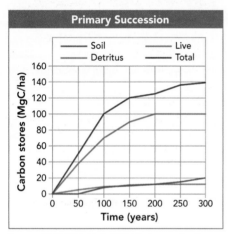

Source: HARMON, M. E. 2001. Carbon cycling in forests: simple simulation models. H. J. Andrews Research Report Number 2

**34. Interpret Graphs** According to the model, how does the rate of carbon storage change during the first 300 years of primary succession?

**35. Construct an Explanation** The graph shows when live plants, detritus, and soil each begin storing carbon during primary succession. Explain why they begin storing carbon at different times.

**36. Develop Models** A student writes a quadratic equation to represent the curve in the graph for total carbon storage shown. The equation has the form $C = -at^2 + bt$, in which $C$ represents total carbon storage, $t$ is time, and $a$ and $b$ are constants. How well does this equation model the curve?

**37. Analyze Data** The graph shows the tolerance of a species to environmental variables. Draw a graph that shows a species with greater tolerance to the same variables. Draw a graph that shows a species with lesser tolerance.

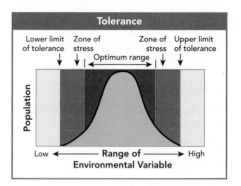

## LANGUAGE ARTS CONNECTION

## Write About Science

CCSS.ELA-LITERACY.WHST.9-10.2

**38. Write Explanatory Texts** The diagram below shows the changes to a plot of land over time. Write a paragraph or a list of numbered captions that describes these changes. Be sure to use the appropriate vocabulary terms from the chapter.

**39. Write Procedures** Science students are observing a population of pheasants in a wilderness area. Write a procedure for the students to follow to help them identify the niche of the pheasants.

## Read About Science

CCSS.ELA-LITERACY.RST.9-10.1

**40. Cite Textual Evidence** Review the list of ecosystem services presented at the end of Lesson 6.3. Is biodiversity necessary for ecosystems to supply all of these services? Include statements from the text to support your answer.

1. From 1970 to 2016, scientists were regularly observing the Joshua County Nature Reserve. Their data show that a community of grasses and other small plants was gradually replaced by a pine forest. Which claim or set of claims about the history of the nature reserve could be supported by the data and logical reasoning?

   I. Several years before 1970, a forest fire burned down a pine forest.

   II. For several years until 1970, a pine forest was gradually replaced by grasses and other small plants.

   III. The land was used for farming or ranching before 1970, but was then abandoned.

   **A.** I only   **B.** II only   **C.** III only

   **D.** I and III only   **E.** I, II, and II.

2. Modern farming practices often act to reduce biodiversity, such as when genetically-identical crops are raised in large fields. Which of the following proposed solutions would most likely improve the genetic diversity of a field of potato plants and increase the value of the potato crop?

   **A.** Raise a variety of wild potatoes in the field

   **B.** Reduce the use of pesticides and fertilizer

   **C.** Increase the use of pesticides and fertilizer

   **D.** Transfer useful genes from wild potato plants to the crop plants

   **E.** Allow some potatoes to remain in the field over winter

3. Which of these events is MOST LIKELY to be followed by primary succession in the area where the event occurs?

   **A.** A fire burns most of the trees of a forest.

   **B.** Floodwaters cover and then drain away from a valley.

   **C.** A volcanic eruption covers a mountainside with molten rock.

   **D.** A farmer stops raising crops on a field.

   **E.** Snow covers a meadow during the winter.

4. A community is concerned about the effect of a proposed housing development on the biodiversity of a local pond. To mitigate the effect of the houses, the community is considering a ban on lawn fertilizer. A computer simulation was used to predict the outcome of the ban. The results are shown in the table.

| | Number of Species | | |
|---|---|---|---|
| Year | No development | Development unregulated | Development, with a fertilizer ban |
| 0 | 100 | 100 | 100 |
| 5 | 95 | 90 | 90 |
| 10 | 102 | 77 | 83 |
| 15 | 98 | 60 | 78 |
| 20 | 103 | 51 | 74 |
| 25 | 99 | 50 | 75 |

   If the community decides to allow the housing development, what is the strongest argument for banning the use of fertilizer that is supported by the results of the simulation?

   **A.** Biodiversity would be 50 percent greater with a fertilizer ban than without a fertilizer ban.

   **B.** Compared to initial conditions, banning lawn fertilizer decreases species diversity by 25 percent after 25 years.

   **C.** Compared to no housing development, banning lawn fertilizer decreases species diversity by 25 percent after 25 years.

   **D.** With no regulations, species diversity decreases from year to year.

   **E.** Without the housing development, species diversity remains about the same from year to year.

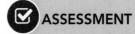 **ASSESSMENT**

For additional assessment practice, go online to access your digital course.

| If You Have Trouble With... | | | | |
|---|---|---|---|---|
| **Question** | 1 | 2 | 3 | 4 |
| **See Lesson** | 6.2 | 6.3 | 6.2 | 6.3 |
| **Performance Expectation** | HS-LS2-6 | HS-LS2-7 | HS-LS2-6 | HS-LS4-6 |

CHAPTER 7

# Humans and Global Change

7.1 Ecological Footprints

7.2 Causes and Effects of Global Change

7.3 Measuring and Responding to Change

7.4 Sustainability

Go Online to access your digital course.

- VIDEO
- AUDIO
- INTERACTIVITY
- eTEXT
- ANIMATION
- VIRTUAL LAB
- ASSESSMENT

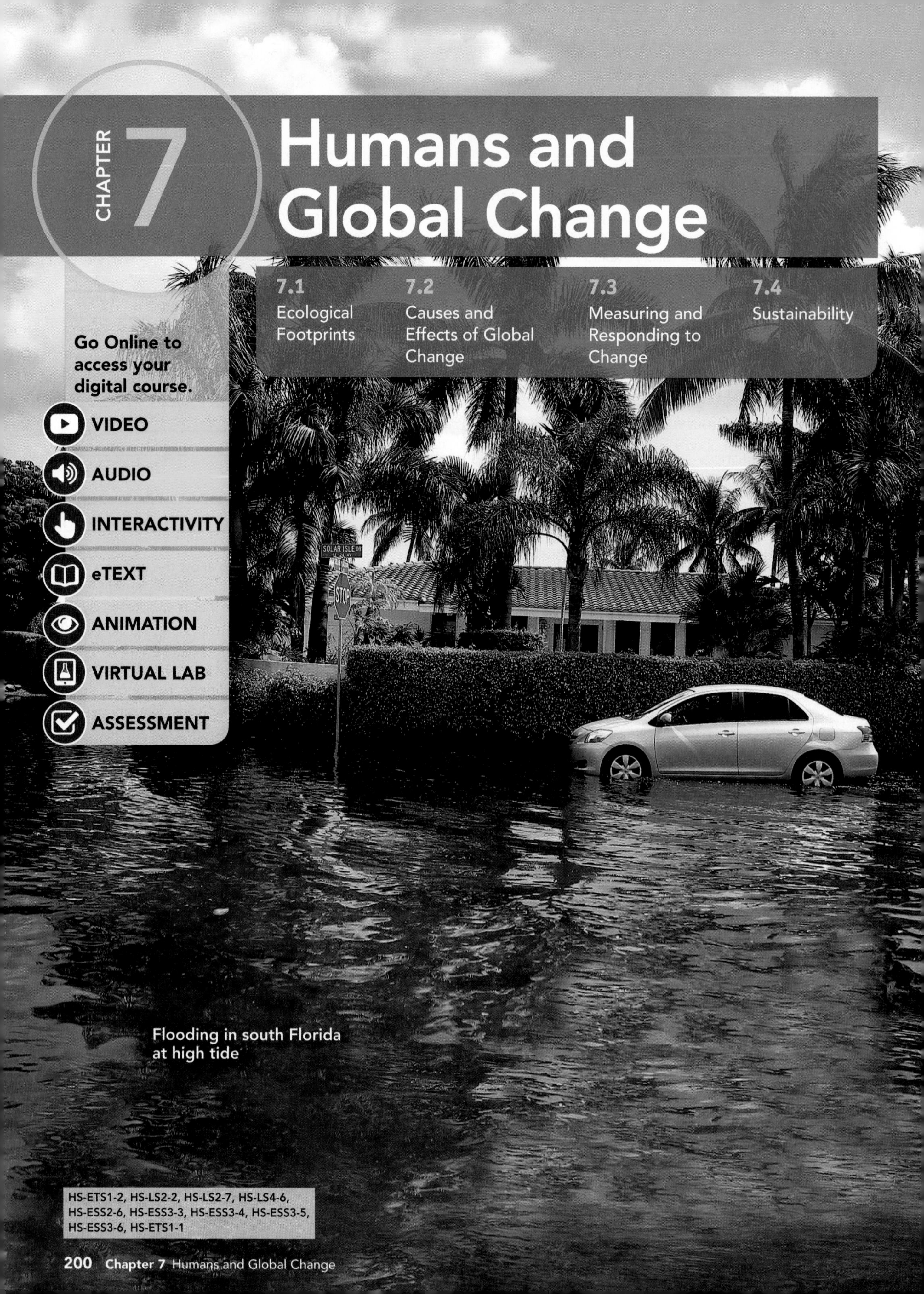

Flooding in south Florida at high tide

HS-ETS1-2, HS-LS2-2, HS-LS2-7, HS-LS4-6, HS-ESS2-6, HS-ESS3-3, HS-ESS3-4, HS-ESS3-5, HS-ESS3-6, HS-ETS1-1

# How can a rising tide be stopped?

An octopus thrashing around on the floor of a parking garage? Storm drains that flow backward for a few days every month? Flooded streets during a week of dry, sunny, windless weather? Welcome to southern Florida in the twenty-first century.

Southern Florida—surrounded by the Atlantic Ocean, the Gulf of Florida, and the Gulf of Mexico—has always been tied to the sea. From its "discovery" by European sailors to maritime trade and fishing to the tourist industry, it's hard to imagine the Sunshine State without its beaches and waterways.

But the oceans around Florida are changing. Sea level is rising. Rapidly. Why? Because of changes in Earth systems. As human activity releases greenhouse gases into the atmosphere, the planet warms. Ice in glaciers and on continents like Greenland and Antarctica melts. As ocean water warms, it expands slightly. And climate change affects powerful ocean currents like the Gulf Stream, too, which causes changes in the way tides rise and fall.

The situation might not be serious if Miami and other beach cities in southern Florida had been built on solid rock. But southern Florida is mostly porous limestone, whose consistency geologists compare to Swiss cheese. Florida is also really flat. Most land in and around Miami is less than 2 meters above sea level, and the highest places are only about 4 meters above sea level. Under these conditions, porous limestone and low-lying land make for problems.

Miami Beach has endured frequent ocean flooding of streets, yards, and businesses. Some low-lying areas flood regularly at high tides, while other places flood any time the sun, Earth, and the moon align to produce the highest high tides. Salt water also penetrates through porous limestone to contaminate drinking water. Rising seawater mixes into coastal soil, killing trees and producing "ghost forests."

Facing this threat, Palm Beach, Broward, Miami-Dade, and Monroe counties joined to form the Southeast Florida Climate Compact, whose motto is "Pioneering climate resilience through regional action." Miami Beach has already invested $400 million to build new seawalls, raise street levels, and install powerful drainage pumps. At the time of this writing, those actions seem to be working, but the long-term outlook is still grim.

In some low-lying nations, such as the Netherlands, engineers designed and built dikes and elaborate barriers to close harbors from the open sea when necessary. Those approaches have limited value in Miami, however, because of that limestone "Swiss cheese" beneath the sand. Build a seawall, and sooner or later water will percolate under it.

Is there anything we can do about rising seas? If we can't stop them, can we reduce their harmful effects? What are the most useful actions to take or policies to enact?

**Throughout this chapter, look for connections to the** CASE STUDY **to help you answer these questions.**

## KEY QUESTIONS

- *How do ecological footprints of typical Americans compare to the global average?*
- *What is the Anthropocene?*

**HS-LS2-7:** Design, evaluate, and refine a solution for reducing the impacts of human activities on the environment and biodiversity.

### VOCABULARY

ecological footprint
anthrome

### READING TOOL

Review Figure 7-1 in your text to determine what makes up an individual's ecological footprint. For each term listed in your ▱ **Biology Foundations Workbook,** list two ways you can reduce the impact you make on the planet.

### Visual Analogy

**Figure 7-1**

### Ecological Footprint

Your ecological footprint includes all of the resources you use.

Remember Earth as astronauts saw it, an island of life in the void of space. What they couldn't see is that our planet's human population is climbing toward 9 billion. Our species has triumphed. We've transformed Earth to house and feed ourselves. Yet our success has caused major changes in local and global environments. Human-caused changes in Earth's global systems are affecting Earth's atmosphere, oceans, and climate.

## Our Changing Ecological Footprints

How can we wrap our heads around the reality that human activities are affecting global systems? It's hard to conceive of anything powerful enough to change our entire planet. An asteroid impact, maybe. Or a giant solar storm. But people? That's one reason that understanding, controlling, and adapting to human-caused global change are the greatest scientific challenges of this century. The view of global systems and the model of global change we've been building in this unit will help. But to begin, we need to understand how and why each of us as individuals impacts the environment.

**Ecological Footprints** Let's start with what ecologists call your **ecological footprint.** Your ecological footprint is the total area of healthy land and water ecosystems needed to provide the resources you use. As shown in **Figure 7-1,** ecological footprints include your use of resources such as energy, food, water, and shelter, and your production of wastes, such as sewage, trash, and greenhouse gases.

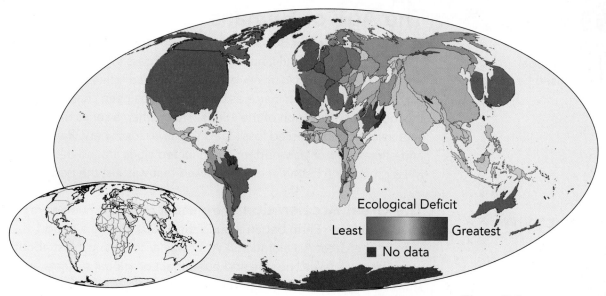

Ecological Deficit
Least ▬▬▬▬ Greatest
■ No data

**Figure 7-2**

## National Footprints

The countries in red have ecological footprints that are disproportionately large.

**National and Global Ecological Footprints** There is no universally accepted formula for calculating ecological footprints. Still, we can make useful comparisons among footprints of people in different countries, as shown in **Figure 7-2**. To determine a country's ecological footprint, researchers calculate the footprint of a typical citizen and multiply that by the size of the population.  *According to some calculations, the average American has an ecological footprint more than four times larger than the global average.* An average American uses almost twice the resources of an average person in England, more than twice the resources used by an average person in Japan, and almost six times the resources used by an average person in China. Now think, not just about your footprint, but about nearly 9 billion footprints. That incredible amount of human activity drives changes in global systems that affect environments worldwide.

▶ **VIDEO**

Learn about the origins and activities of Earth Day.

✔ **READING CHECK** **Describe** What is one way to calculate the ecological footprint of a country?

HS-LS2-7, HS-ETS1-1

 **Argument-Based Inquiry**   Guided Inquiry

### Calculating Ecological Footprint

**Problem** How can you calculate your use of natural resources?

In this lab, you will determine what your ecological footprint is regarding three types of natural resources: water, land, and fossil fuels. Then, you will explore ways to effectively reduce your ecological footprint in one of these areas.

You can find this lab in your digital course.

As you read, note the order of the global changes caused by human activities.

Investigate the causes and effects of The Great Acceleration.

Figure 7-3

**The Great Acceleration**

Starting around the 1950s, the pace at which human activity affected Earth's resources skyrocketed.

# The Age of Humans

Back in 1969, inventor Buckminster Fuller coined the term "spaceship Earth." Until recently, humans were only passengers on this ship. Although we affected local environments, we had little impact on global systems. But our status as passengers has been changing since the Industrial Revolution of the 1800s. That's when a series of brilliant inventions harnessed fossil fuels to power machinery. Railroads and other forms of transportation connected cities around the globe. Mass production began and spread. And that was just the beginning.

**The Great Acceleration** The greatest change in humanity's relationship with Earth began around the 1950s, during a period called "The Great Acceleration." What was accelerating? Just about everything related to people and our impact on global systems, as shown in **Figure 7-3**. We burned more fossil fuels. We farmed more land enriched with fertilizers, and we caught more fish, so we could feed more people. Medical discoveries saved millions of lives. Within a single lifetime, the well-being of millions of people improved dramatically. Death rates fell worldwide. Birth rates stayed high, so the global population grew rapidly. Advancing technology was used by more people, multiplying our impact on local and global systems.

**The Anthropocene** Today, human activities drive global change. We move more sediment and rock every year than is moved by erosion and all the world's rivers. We have altered roughly three quarters of all land outside polar regions and mountain ranges. We fix and distribute vast quantities of nitrogen for fertilizer, dramatically altering the global nitrogen cycle. We've increased greenhouse gas levels to a concentration higher than the planet has seen for more than a million years. Many scientists feel that we are causing so many planet-wide changes, so quickly, that we should use a new name for the time period we're living in.

**SOCIO-ECONOMIC TRENDS**

Fertilizer Consumption (million tons)

Primary Energy Use (EJ)

Water Use (thousand $km^3$)

World Population (billions)

**EARTH SYSTEM TRENDS**

Coastal Nitrogen (Mtons/year)

Marine Fish Capture (million tons)

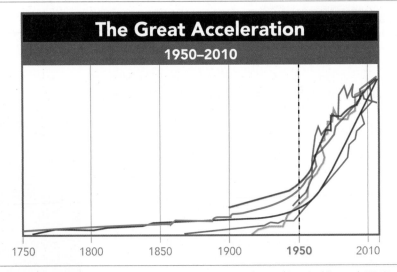

**The Great Acceleration**
1950–2010

Sources: (1) Olivier Rousseau, IFA; IFA database. (2) A Grubler, International Institute for Applied Systems Analysis (IIASA); Grubler et al. (2012). (3) M Flörke, Centre for Environmental Systems Research, University of Kassel; Flörke et al. (2013); aus der Beek et al. (2010); Alcamo et al. (2003). (4) HYDE database; Klein Goldewijk et al. (2010). (5) Mackenzie et al. (2002). (6) Data are from the FAO Fisheries and Aquaculture Department online database (Food and Agriculture Organization-FIGIS (FAO-FIGIS), 2013).

Figure 7-4

## Anthromes

The continental United States' human-altered biomes or anthromes, are shown on this map.

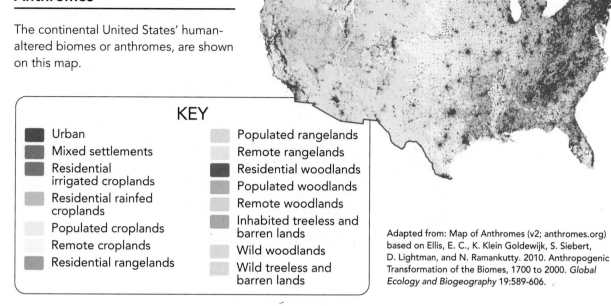

### KEY

| | | | |
|---|---|---|---|
| ■ Urban | | ☐ Populated rangelands |
| ■ Mixed settlements | | ☐ Remote rangelands |
| ■ Residential irrigated croplands | | ■ Residential woodlands |
| ☐ Residential rainfed croplands | | ■ Populated woodlands |
| ☐ Populated croplands | | ☐ Remote woodlands |
| ☐ Remote croplands | | ■ Inhabited treeless and barren lands |
| ■ Residential rangelands | | ☐ Wild woodlands |
| | | ☐ Wild treeless and barren lands |

Adapted from: Map of Anthromes (v2; anthromes.org) based on Ellis, E. C., K. Klein Goldewijk, S. Siebert, D. Lightman, and N. Ramankutty. 2010. Anthropogenic Transformation of the Biomes, 1700 to 2000. *Global Ecology and Biogeography* 19:589-606.

*The Anthropocene, or "age of humans," is the period during which human activity has become the major cause of global change.* For this reason, as we discuss causes of global change in the twenty-first century, you will see that human causes of change occupy a larger portion of our global change model's outer ring than non-human causes.

**INTERACTIVITY**

Learn about habitat restoration and how it can increase biodiversity.

### Anthromes: Human-Altered Biomes

Recall that classic biomes no longer cover most land areas. What's in all those places now? Human-altered biomes that ecologists refer to as anthromes, or anthropogenic biomes. **Anthromes**, shown in **Figure 7-4,** are globally significant ecological patterns created by long-term interactions between humans and ecosystems. Examples of anthromes include cities, villages, croplands, and rangelands. Chances are that wherever you live, you are surrounded by anthromes rather than biomes. That doesn't mean that anthromes are "bad" or ugly. It does mean that there isn't a lot of untouched nature left.

HS-LS2-7

## ☑ LESSON 7.1 Review

### ⚲ KEY QUESTIONS

1. What kinds of resources make up your ecological footprint?

2. Why are some scientists using the name *Anthropocene* to describe the current time period?

### CRITICAL THINKING

3. **Cite Evidence** What evidence supports the argument that human activities are causing major changes to global systems?

4. **Use an Analogy** Buckminster Fuller compared Earth to a spaceship. During the period called the Great Acceleration, what changes affected the spaceship analogy?

5. **Design a Solution** Which part of your ecological footprint do you think could be reduced most significantly? Describe a method for reducing it.

# Causes and Effects of Global Change

Most vehicles on the road today burn fossil fuels.

## 🔍 KEY QUESTIONS

- *How do human activities change the atmosphere and climate?*

- *How do changes in the atmosphere drive climate change and other changes in global systems?*

- *How do the ways we use land drive change in global systems?*

- *What kinds of pollutants are drivers of global change?*

**HS-LS2-2:** Use mathematical representations to support and revise explanations based on evidence about factors affecting biodiversity and populations in ecosystems of different scales. **HS-LS2-7**: Design, evaluate, and refine a solution for reducing the impacts of human activities on the environment and biodiversity. **HS-LS4-6:** Create or revise a simulation to test a solution to mitigate adverse impacts of human activity on biodiversity. **HS-ESS2-6:** Develop a quantitative model to describe the cycling of carbon among the hydrosphere, atmosphere, geosphere, and biosphere. **HS-ESS3-6:** Use a computational representation to illustrate the relationships among Earth systems and how those relationships are being modified due to human activity.

## VOCABULARY

**climate change**
**global warming**
**deforestation • monoculture**
**invasive species • pollutant**
**ozone layer • smog**
**biological magnification**

## READING TOOL

For each heading in the lesson, explain the main idea in the table in your 📖 **Biology Foundations Workbook.** Then, list details that support and explain the main idea.

The Great Acceleration "promoted" us from spaceship Earth's passengers to crew. There's just one problem. This spaceship didn't come with an operating manual! We must understand how Earth systems work, and how our actions are changing them, in order to write that manual ourselves.

## Human Causes of Global Change

Throughout this unit, we've been building our Understanding Global Change (UGC) model, shown in **Figure 7-5**. We began with global systems, shown in the model's middle ring. We also discussed non-human causes of global change, shown in the lower portion of the model's outer ring. Ecological interactions and processes we discussed are in the model's "biosphere" section.

We will now focus on the human causes of global change, which occupy most of our model's outer ring. Why do they occupy so much space? Because all human activities combined are now more powerful drivers of change in global systems than non-human causes of change. 🔍 *Human activities affect global systems by changing the atmosphere in ways that change climate, changing the way we use land, over-harvesting some species, introducing species to new environments, and producing plastics and other pollutants.* All these actions together create stress on organisms and ecosystems in ways that threaten biodiversity and ecosystem services. Note that the combined action of these human activities is more powerful than the effect of any single action alone. Note also that a single human activity, such as converting land to agriculture or burning fossil fuels, can affect several global systems in several ways. As we discuss each of these human activities in detail, keep referring back to Figure 7-5 to see how the activity fits into the Understanding Global Change model.

**Figure 7-5**

## Understanding Global Change

Processes and phenomena in the atmosphere, biosphere, geosphere, and hydrosphere interact to shape the Earth system. Both non-human factors and human activities affect the Earth system, resulting in measurable changes.

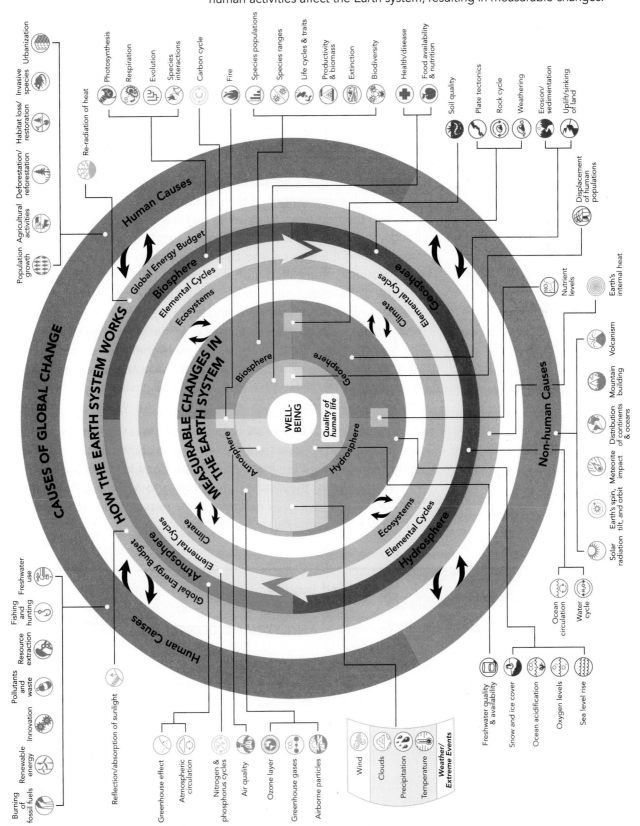

Adapted from the *Understanding Global Change Infographic,* © University of California Museum of Paleontology, Berkeley.

**VIDEO**

Learn about a disturbing area of the ocean that is saturated with trash.

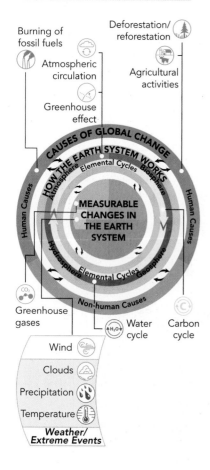

Burning of fossil fuels

Atmospheric circulation

Greenhouse effect

Deforestation/ reforestation

Agricultural activities

CAUSES OF GLOBAL CHANGE

HOW THE EARTH SYSTEM WORKS

Atmosphere Elemental Cycles Biosphere

Human Causes

MEASURABLE CHANGES IN THE EARTH SYSTEM

Human Causes

Hydrosphere Elemental Cycles Geosphere

Non-human Causes

Greenhouse gases

Water cycle

Carbon cycle

Wind

Clouds

Precipitation

Temperature

**Weather/ Extreme Events**

# Changing Atmosphere and Climate

We are currently subjecting Earth to an uncontrolled experiment in atmospheric chemistry. Human activity is changing Earth's atmosphere faster than it has changed during the entire history of life. Some activities raise concentrations of greenhouse gases, driving climate change. Other activities release different gases into the atmosphere, causing a variety of effects on global systems.

**Fossil Fuels and the Atmosphere** Quantitative data gathered over decades confirm two scientific facts. First, one data set confirms that atmospheric carbon dioxide concentrations have been rising since the Industrial Revolution. Second, other data show that most of that carbon dioxide is released by burning fossil fuels.

***Climate Change*** **Climate change** is defined as measurable long-term changes in averages of temperature, clouds, winds, precipitation, and the frequency of extreme weather events such as droughts, floods, major storms, and heat waves. Climate change as we are experiencing it now is caused by the increase in average global temperatures often called **global warming**. Recall from Chapter 3 that the global climate system is powered by the total amount of heat retained within the atmosphere, and is shaped by the distribution of heat between the equator and the poles. That's why the strength of the greenhouse effect is so important. *Higher concentrations of greenhouse gases, such as carbon dioxide and methane, trap more heat in the biosphere and cause global warming, which drives climate change.*

Climate change is a threat to biodiversity and ecosystem stability. Organisms have specific tolerance ranges to abiotic factors. *If climate change alters environmental conditions beyond organisms' tolerance ranges, they must adapt, move to a more suitable location, or face extinction. For those same reasons, climate change can have major impacts on agriculture.*

HS-LS2-2

**CASE STUDY** Quick Lab  Guided Inquiry

## How Does Acid Affect Shells?

Vinegar is a solution of acetic acid. Mix vinegar and water in 5 beakers. Put only water in one beaker, only vinegar in another beaker, and mixtures of varying concentrations in the other beakers. Label each beaker with its contents and the concentration of vinegar (if appropriate).

1. Place 6 to 10 crushed pieces of egg shells in each beaker.

2. Wait one day. Then pour out the liquid from each beaker, and place the egg shell pieces on a paper towel. Examine the egg shell pieces.

### ANALYZE AND CONCLUDE

1. Observe How did vinegar affect the egg shell pieces? Make a chart to record your observations.

2. Draw Conclusions Egg shells are made of calcium carbonate. How could ocean acidification affect corals, lobsters, snails, and other marine organisms that also have skeletons or shells made of calcium carbonate?

3. Construct an Argument How could ocean acidification become a severe problem? Use evidence and logical reasoning to support your answer.

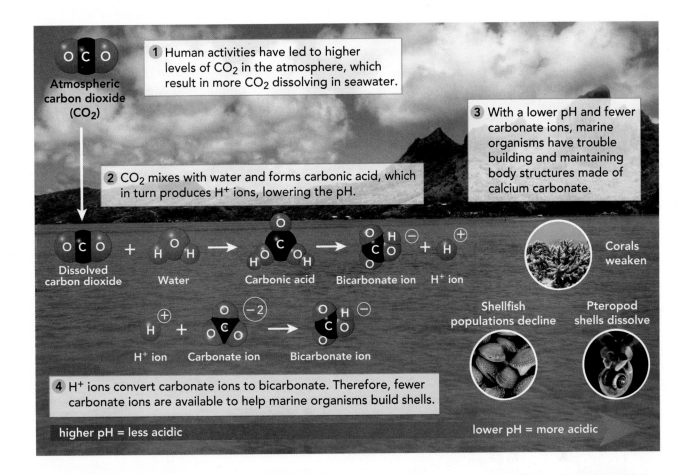

**1** Human activities have led to higher levels of $CO_2$ in the atmosphere, which result in more $CO_2$ dissolving in seawater.

Atmospheric carbon dioxide ($CO_2$)

**2** $CO_2$ mixes with water and forms carbonic acid, which in turn produces $H^+$ ions, lowering the pH.

**3** With a lower pH and fewer carbonate ions, marine organisms have trouble building and maintaining body structures made of calcium carbonate.

Dissolved carbon dioxide + Water → Carbonic acid → Bicarbonate ion + $H^+$ ion

Corals weaken

$H^+$ ion + Carbonate ion → Bicarbonate ion

Shellfish populations decline

Pteropod shells dissolve

**4** $H^+$ ions convert carbonate ions to bicarbonate. Therefore, fewer carbonate ions are available to help marine organisms build shells.

higher pH = less acidic

lower pH = more acidic

**Acid Rain** Burning fossil fuels also releases sulfur dioxide and nitrous oxides that dissolve in fog or raindrops to form sulfuric acid and nitric acid. This creates acid rain, fog, and snow that affect nutrient cycling. Acid rain damages plant leaves and harms roots by releasing aluminum and other metals from some soils. Soil acidification can interfere with bacterial decay. The acidification of fresh water kills aquatic organisms from algae to fishes.

**Ocean Acidification** A significant amount of carbon dioxide released by burning fossil fuels dissolves in seawater, where it drives a chemical reaction that produces an acid, as shown in **Figure 7-6**. This process, called ocean acidification, poses serious problems for marine life. Many marine organisms, from plankton to corals and shellfish, build skeletons from calcium carbonate that they remove from seawater. When seawater is more acidic, these organisms must expend more energy to build their skeletons. So ocean acidification stresses many marine organisms and ecosystems.

**Nitrogen Enrichment From Fossil Fuels** Nitrogen released by burning fossil fuels travels through the air in dry form as tiny particles, or dissolved in water droplets. This nitrogen may therefore fall far from its source. Because nitrogen is a limiting nutrient for primary producers, nitrogen enrichment from burning fossil fuels can cause algal blooms.

**CASE STUDY**

**Figure 7-6**

**Ocean Acidification**

Many marine organisms—such as plankton, coral, pteropods, and shellfish—build skeletons from calcium carbonate. Carbon dioxide dissolves in seawater to form carbonic acid. Both the decrease in pH and the consumption of carbonate ions harm marine life.

**Agriculture and the Atmosphere** Agriculture is a widespread human activity because it provides a dependable food supply. Certain agricultural practices release methane, an even more powerful greenhouse gas than carbon dioxide. Methane is produced and released through cattle farming and the cultivation of rice in flooded paddies. Methane contributes to global warming and other changes in Earth's climate system.

# Changes in Land Use

It takes a lot of land to provide housing, food, and energy for people! Human activity has already transformed roughly three quarters of Earth's land surface in several ways and for several reasons.

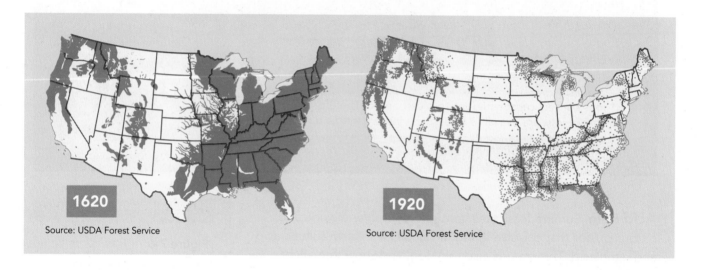

1620
Source: USDA Forest Service

1920
Source: USDA Forest Service

**Figure 7-7**

**Primary Forest**

Between 1620 and 1920, roughly 90 percent of the primary forests that once covered the United States were cut for lumber, farming, or both.

**Deforestation/Reforestation** Healthy forests hold soil in place, protecting the quality of freshwater supplies, absorbing carbon dioxide, and moderating local climate. When forests are lost, those ecosystem services disappear.

**Deforestation** The cutting of forests for lumber or farming, or **deforestation**, has altered natural environments. Most of us live in places that haven't been in a natural state for a long time, as **Figure 7-7** shows. *Deforestation can affect water quality in streams and rivers. In mountainous areas, deforestation increases soil erosion, which can cause landslides.*

**Natural Regrowth Through Succession** Most forests east of the Mississippi River are secondary forests that grew back after primary forests were cut. In some places, logged areas can undergo secondary succession, so forests can regrow. In tropical rain forests, on the other hand, topsoil is thin, and organic matter decomposes rapidly. If small areas of tropical rain forests are cleared and left alone, secondary succession can occur and restore biodiversity. If large tropical forest areas are cleared, natural regrowth may not be possible.

**Reforestation** Scientifically guided reforestation, or replanting of forests, can replace trees that have been cut for lumber, fuel, or agriculture. Reforestation efforts by local communities around the world are bringing back forests and restoring ecosystem services. One of the most important ecosystem services that reforestation can restore is the provision of dependable, clean drinking water. **Figure 7-8** shows reforestation work by a local Mayan community in Totonicapán, Guatemala, where deforestation had caused local streams and springs to dry up. Those water sources are now returning.

## Figure 7-8
## Reforestation

Scientifically-informed, grassroots reforestation, guided by long-term partnership between local communities and the non-governmental organization EcoLogic Development Fund, is restoring the integrity of local watersheds in Totonicapán, Guatemala.

**Agriculture** During the Great Acceleration, agriculture provided food for our growing population using a mixture of agricultural practices called the "Green Revolution." Today, agricultural activities cover more of Earth's land surface than any other human activity.

**Monoculture** The Green Revolution was based on a strategy called **monoculture**, which involves planting large areas with a single highly productive crop year after year. Monoculture enables efficient sowing, tending, and harvesting. However, most large-scale monocultures require lots of artificial fertilizers and pesticides. ⚲ *When large areas are used for grazing, or to grow monocultures for long periods, fertilizers and pesticides can change soil structure and microbiomes in ways that degrade soil and prevent secondary succession.*

**Figure 7-9**

# Toxic Algal Bloom

In July 2015, an enormous algal bloom stretched from California to Alaska. One of the algae involved in the bloom was the marine diatom *Pseudo-nitzschia*, shown in the inset. This algae produces a toxin that builds up in the food chain and can poison fish, seabirds, marine mammals, and humans.

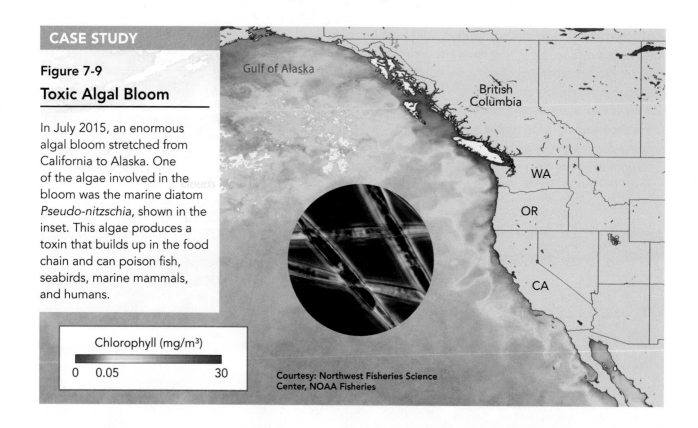

Chlorophyll (mg/m³)

0    0.05                    30

Courtesy: Northwest Fisheries Science Center, NOAA Fisheries

**Figure 7-10**

# Cities

Large cities such as Chicago produce huge amounts of waste that must be removed every day.

***Nitrogen Enrichment From Agriculture*** Humans use industrial processes to fix atmospheric nitrogen to make fertilizer. This added nitrogen fueled the Green Revolution and helped avoid global famine by dramatically increasing food production. Today, fertilizer manufacture and application has more than doubled the amount of biologically active nitrogen cycling through the biosphere, dramatically changing the natural nitrogen cycle. A lot of that nitrogen "leaks" out of agriculture, usually in soil water runoff. Too much nitrogen in streams and rivers can upset the balance in freshwater and marine ecosystems, as shown in **Figure 7-9**.

## Development/Urbanization
As modern societies develop, many people move to cities like the one in **Figure 7-10**, and to suburbs around those cities. Suburban development consumes farmland and divides natural habitats into fragments. Roughly two thirds of Americans live in urban areas today, and migration to cities is increasing in developing countries around the world. These dense human communities produce large amounts of wastes. If these wastes are not disposed of properly, they affect air, water, and soil resources.

One result of urbanization has been an increase in the production of sewage, which includes everything you flush down the toilet or the drain. In some cities, sewage includes runoff from roofs, sidewalks, and streets. Sewage isn't poisonous, but it does contain lots of nitrogen and phosphorus. Reasonable amounts of these nutrients can be processed and absorbed by healthy ecosystems. Large amounts of sewage can disrupt nutrient cycles and stimulate the growth of toxic or ecologically damaging blooms of bacteria and algae. Raw sewage also contains microorganisms that can spread disease.

### Habitat Loss, Fragmentation, and Restoration

Human-caused changes in natural habitats can occur in a number of ways and for several reasons. These include habitat loss, habitat fragmentation, and habitat restoration.

**Habitat Loss** When natural habitats are completely changed, species that once lived in that area either emigrate or disappear. Habitats can be lost to urban, suburban, or industrial development, as well as to logging or agriculture.

**Habitat Fragmentation** Habitats don't need to be completely destroyed to put species at risk. Development and agriculture can split ecosystems into pieces, a process called habitat fragmentation. You can think of ecosystem fragments as habitat "islands." You probably think all islands are land surrounded by water. But a biological island can be any patch of habitat surrounded by a different habitat, as shown in **Figure 7-11**. The smaller a habitat <u>fragment</u> is, the smaller the number of species that can live there, and the smaller the populations the fragment can support. ⚡ *Habitat fragmentation causes biodiversity loss and makes ecosystems more vulnerable to other disturbances.*

**Habitat Restoration** Under some conditions, and with a great deal of work, damaged habitats can be repaired. Ecological restoration aims to recreate, in a degraded area, conditions that resemble as closely as possible the ecosystem that existed before it was disturbed. Wetlands may be restored by removing material originally used to fill them. Degraded estuaries may be improved by dredging to increase tidal flow, or to reestablish the natural flow of rivers feeding the estuary.

✅ **READING CHECK** **Identify** What is the relationship between habitat size and the number of species that can live there?

**Figure 7-11**
## Biological Islands

A cattle pasture now surrounds this remnant of forest, making the forest a biological island.

## Figure 7-12
## Human Activity and Global Change

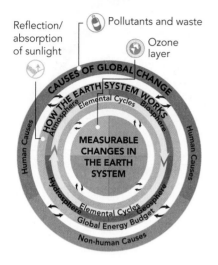

Reflection/absorption of sunlight

Pollutants and waste

Ozone layer

**CAUSES OF GLOBAL CHANGE**

HOW THE EARTH SYSTEM WORKS

Atmosphere · Elemental Cycles · Biosphere

Human Causes

Human Causes

**MEASURABLE CHANGES IN THE EARTH SYSTEM**

Hydrosphere · Elemental Cycles · Geosphere

Global Energy Budget

Non-human Causes

### Hunting and Fishing

Many animals are hunted and fished for food or are hunted for hides, feathers, body parts believed to have medicinal properties. Humans have hunted species to extinction for thousands of years. Illegal hunting of animals threatens many species, including gorillas and elephants. Elephants are often hunted for the ivory in their tusks.

Overfishing has caused declines in fish populations around the world. In the United States, endangered species are protected from hunting. The Convention on International Trade in Endangered Species (CITES) bans international trade in products from endangered species, but it's difficult to enforce laws in remote wilderness areas.

### Invasive Species

Recall that organisms introduced to new habitats can sometimes experience exponential population growth and become invasive species because they lack predators and parasites in their new homes. If these organisms are **invasive species**, they can cause tremendous harm. An invasive species is any nonnative species whose introduction causes, or is likely to cause, economic harm, environmental harm, or harm to human health. Ecological disruption caused by invasive species can drive native species to extinction. Most invasive species are carried to new habitats by human trade and travel. Ecological problems caused by invasive species around the world have grown to the point where they are included as drivers of global change. There are roughly 3000 invasive species in the United States alone. The purple loosestrife in **Figure 7-13** is just one example of an invasive species.

## Pollution

A **pollutant** is any harmful material created as a result of human activity and released into the environment. Many pollutants threaten biodiversity. Certain kinds of air pollution are local concerns, but others act globally. And some pollutants once considered "local problems" are now known to have global effects. *Common forms of air pollution include smog, greenhouse gases, heavy metals, and aerosols. The primary sources of water pollution are industrial and agricultural chemicals, residential sewage, and nonpoint sources.*

### INTERACTIVITY

Investigate the impact humans have on ecosystems through pollution, farming, hunting, building, and overfishing.

### Figure 7-13
### Invasive Species

Purple loosestrife is growing in dense stands, displacing the native plants that wetland animals use for food and nesting grounds.

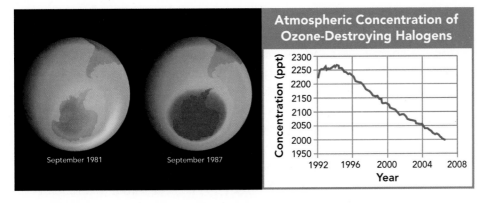

**Atmospheric Concentration of Ozone-Destroying Halogens**

Figure 7-14

## Ozone Hole

In these satellite images, the size and intensity of the blue region increased from 1981 to 1999, indicating a thinning of the ozone layer over Antarctica. The graph shows how the levels of atmospheric halogens have decreased since legislation was passed to ban CFCs.

**CFCs and Stratospheric Ozone** Chlorofluorocarbons (CFCs) are industrially produced gases. They once were widely used as propellants in aerosol cans and fire extinguishers, as coolants in refrigerators and air conditioners, and in the production of plastic foams. A few decades ago, the use of CFCs was tied to the destruction of ozone in a section of the upper atmosphere called the stratosphere. This high-level ozone, called the **ozone layer**, absorbs ultraviolet light, acting like a global sunscreen. Beginning in the 1970s, satellite data revealed that the ozone concentration over Antarctica was decreasing, as shown in **Figure 7-14**. The area of lower ozone concentration was called an "ozone hole." For several years after the hole was discovered, ozone concentrations continued to drop, and the hole grew larger and lasted longer every year.

No one could explain this phenomenon until three researchers made a breakthrough that earned them a Nobel Prize. In 1974, researchers demonstrated that CFCs act as catalysts to destroy ozone molecules under conditions in the upper atmosphere. This research led to hypotheses that were tested in several ways. Research flights over the poles gathered data demonstrating that CFCs combine with ice crystals in frigid air in a way that allows sunlight to destroy ozone. Once this research was published and accepted by the scientific community, the rest was up to policymakers and industry—as you will learn in the next lesson.

**Ground-Level Ozone** Ozone in the upper atmosphere is a good thing, but ozone at ground level is not. If you live in a large city, you've probably seen **smog**, a gray-brown haze formed by chemical reactions among pollutants released by industrial processes and automobile exhaust. Ozone is one product of these reactions. Ozone and other pollutants at ground level threaten human health, especially for people with respiratory conditions. Many athletes in the 2008 Summer Olympics in Beijing, China, expressed concern that the intense smog, seen in **Figure 7-15**, would affect their health and performance. In the United States, automobile emission standards and clean-air regulations have improved air quality in many cities.

**Figure 7-15**

## Smog

Despite closing factories and restricting vehicle access to the city, Beijing remained under a dense blanket of smog just days before the 2008 Summer Olympics.

**Industrial and Agricultural Pollution** Industry, science, and technology provide us with the conveniences of modern life—and require energy. We produce most of this energy by burning fossil fuels that release greenhouse gases and other pollutants. Since the Industrial Revolution, many industries have discarded wastes from manufacturing and energy production into air, water, and soil. Large-scale monoculture increased the use of pesticides and insecticides. These chemicals can enter the water supply in the form of runoff after heavy rains, or they can seep directly into groundwater. This type of pollution is called nonpoint source pollution.

## Figure 7-16
## Biological Magnification

In the process of biological magnification, the concentration of a pollutant like DDT—represented by the orange dots—is multiplied as it passes up the food chain from producers to consumers.

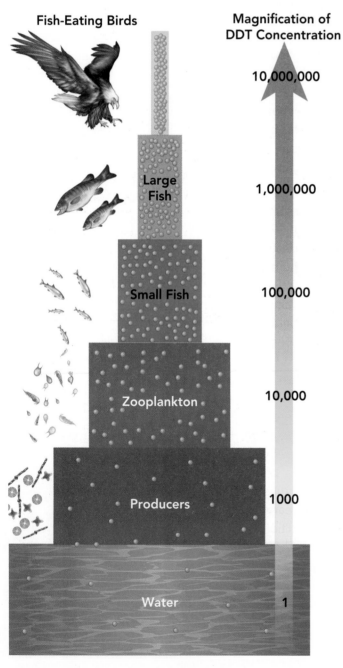

Fish-Eating Birds

Large Fish

Small Fish

Zooplankton

Producers

Water

Magnification of DDT Concentration

10,000,000

1,000,000

100,000

10,000

1000

1

*Biological Magnification* When certain pollutants are picked up by organisms, the pollutants are not broken down or eliminated. Instead, they collect in body tissues. Primary producers can absorb pollutants, even if those pollutants are present in the environment in very low concentrations. Herbivores that eat those producers store the pollutant and concentrate it further. When carnivores eat herbivores, pollutants are further concentrated. In the highest trophic levels, pollutant concentrations may reach 10 million times their original concentration in the environment, as shown in **Figure 7-16**. The process in which pollutants are concentrated as they pass through trophic levels is called **biological magnification**. These high concentrations can cause serious problems for wildlife and humans.

*DDT* One of the first widely used pesticides, DDT, is cheap, long lasting, and effective at controlling agricultural pests and disease-carrying mosquitoes. But when DDT gets into a water supply, it is concentrated by biological magnification and can have disastrous effects. Widespread DDT use in the 1950s threatened fish-eating birds like pelicans, osprey, falcons, and bald eagles. It caused females to lay eggs with thin, fragile shells, reducing hatching rates and causing a drop in bird populations. Since DDT was banned in the 1970s, bird populations have been recovering.

**PCBs** One industrial water pollutant is a class of toxic organic chemicals called PCBs (polychlorinated biphenyls), which were widely used in industry until the 1970s. PCBs have been banned, but they persist in the environment and accumulate in food webs through biological magnification. Mud and sand in parts of the Great Lakes and some coastal areas are still polluted with PCBs today.

**Heavy Metals** Other harmful industrial pollutants are heavy metals like cadmium, lead, mercury, and zinc. Heavy metals also accumulate in food webs and pose health threats. Mercury, for example, accumulates in certain marine fishes such as tuna and swordfish. Even at low concentrations, mercury and lead can cause neurological problems in young children and adults.

Although the country's lead levels still need to improve, the current situation demonstrates the positive effects of scientifically informed environmental legislation. At one time, all gasoline was enriched with lead. But as leaded gasoline burned, lead was released in exhaust fumes and washed onto land and into rivers and streams. U.S. efforts to phase out leaded gasoline started in 1973 and were completed in 1996, when the sale of leaded gasoline was banned. Now that unleaded gasoline is used widely, lead levels in soils, rivers, and streams around the country have dropped significantly, as shown in **Figure 7-17**.

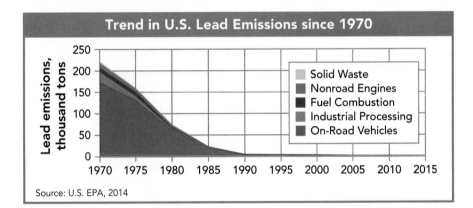

**Trend in U.S. Lead Emissions since 1970**

Source: U.S. EPA, 2014

**Figure 7-17**

**Get the Lead Out**

The lead from car exhaust proved a dangerous pollutant. Transitioning from leaded to unleaded gasoline has resulted in a decline of lead emissions in the United States.

HS-LS2-2, HS-LS2-7, HS-LS4-6, HS-ESS2-6, HS-ESS3-6

# ✓ LESSON 7.2 Review

## ⚲ KEY QUESTIONS

1. Why do human causes of global change occupy a larger portion of the global change model than nonhuman causes?

2. What is the relationship between global warming and global climate change?

3. Explain one way that land use by humans affects nutrient cycles.

4. What kinds of harmful changes can pollution cause?

## CRITICAL THINKING

5. **Use Models** Explain three cause and effect relationships between the human activities and the measurable changes in the Earth system represented in the Understanding Global Change model.

6. **Design a Solution** What is a possible solution for preventing the loss of biodiversity by habitat fragmentation?

7. **Analyze** Food production is an ecosystem service. Explain how human activities are affecting this ecosystem service.

8. **CASE STUDY** How is ocean water becoming more acidic?

# Measuring and Responding to Change

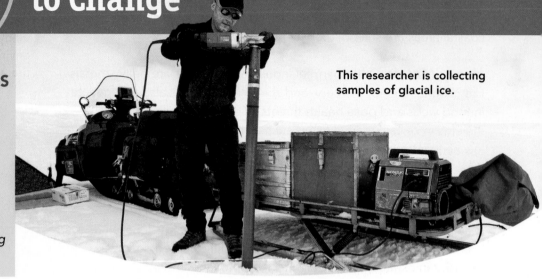

This researcher is collecting samples of glacial ice.

## 🔍 KEY QUESTIONS

- *What evidence supports the claims that the climate is changing?*
- *What are some impacts of climate change?*
- *What is the role of science in responding to global change?*

**HS-LS2-7:** Design, evaluate, and refine a solution for reducing the impacts of human activities on the environment and biodiversity.

**HS-ETS1-1:** Analyze a major global challenge to specify qualitative and quantitative criteria and constraints for solutions that account for societal needs and wants.

**HS-ESS3-4:** Evaluate or refine a technological solution that reduces impacts of human activities on natural systems.

**HS-ESS3-5:** Analyze geoscience data and the results from global climate models to make an evidence-based forecast of the current rate of global or regional climate change and associated future impacts to Earth systems.

**HS-ESS3-6:** Use a computational representation to illustrate the relationships among Earth systems and how those relationships are being modified due to human activity.

### READING TOOL

Complete the graphic organizer in your 📖 **Biology Foundations Workbook** with the possible effects and solutions of climate change.

In recent years, bodies of ancient humans have been emerging from melting glaciers. One of the first, nicknamed Ötzi and found in the Italian Alps, died 5300 years ago. Ötzi stayed frozen until rising temperatures melted the ice above him.

## Climate Change: The Data

Ötzi's emergence from the ice led Worldwatch Institute to suggest that "Our ancestors are emerging from the ice with a message for us: Earth is getting warmer." That dramatic announcement got public attention. But scientists need data.

**IPCC Climate Data** The most reliable climate data come from the Intergovernmental Panel on Climate Change (IPCC). The IPCC is an international organization established to provide the best possible scientific information on climate change. IPCC reports contain data and analyses that have been agreed upon and accepted by more than 2500 international climate scientists and all governments participating in the study. The most recent IPCC report from 2014 makes a strong case that global climate is changing and that human activity influences climate.

**Climate Changes** Data indicate that Earth is warming, and that the warming is greater than anything in recorded history. 🔍 *Data show that both the atmosphere and the oceans have been warming; that sea levels are rising; and that Arctic sea ice, glaciers, and snow cover are all decreasing.* Data on sea ice, sea level, and $CO_2$ emissions are shown in **Figure 7-18**. The greatest changes are occurring in and near the Arctic Circle. Average temperatures in Alaska, for example, increased 2.4 degrees Celsius over the last 50 years.

**Human Activity Influences Climate** The latest IPCC report states firmly that "Human influence on the climate system is clear, and recent anthropogenic emissions of greenhouse gases are the highest in history."

**Modeling With Data** Researchers use data to construct computer models to predict future climate trends. The most widely accepted models predict that average global temperatures will increase somewhere between 0.3 and 1.7 degrees Celsius above their year 2000 level by the end of the twenty-first century if all the world's countries agree on very strong measures to curb greenhouse gas emissions. If emissions continue increasing as they have been in recent years, the global temperature could increase somewhere between 2.6 and 4.8 degrees Celsius by the year 2100.

CASE STUDY

**Figure 7-18   IPCC Data**

These diagrams represent just a small part of the data from the 2014 report from the Intergovernmental Panel on Climate Change. Human activities are altering global climate. Recent anthropogenic emissions of greenhouse gases are the highest in history.

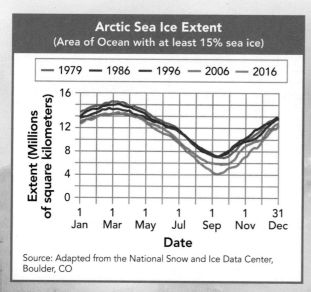

**Arctic Sea Ice Extent**
(Area of Ocean with at least 15% sea ice)

Source: Adapted from the National Snow and Ice Data Center, Boulder, CO

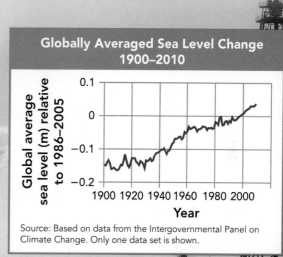

**Globally Averaged Sea Level Change 1900–2010**

Source: Based on data from the Intergovernmental Panel on Climate Change. Only one data set is shown.

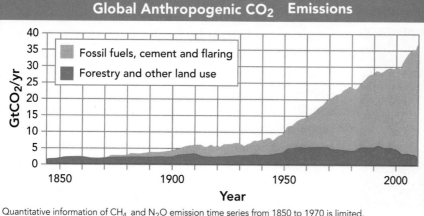

**Global Anthropogenic $CO_2$ Emissions**

Quantitative information of $CH_4$ and $N_2O$ emission time series from 1850 to 1970 is limited.
Source: Adapted from Intergovernmental Panel on Climate Change.

**INTERACTIVITY**

Identify the impacts of climate change.

# Climate Change Impacts

The IPCC report concludes: "… changes in climate have caused impacts on natural and human systems on all continents and across oceans." As you learned earlier, climate change includes much more than just the direct effects of warming. 🔍 *Total precipitation and seasonal distribution of precipitation are changing. Heat waves are expected to become longer and more intense. Many areas will experience more episodes of extreme heat and storms.*

One reason for those changes is that temperatures are increasing faster in the Arctic than they are in the temperate zone and tropics, as you can see by the red areas in the map in **Figure 7-19**. Recall that the global climate system is powered and shaped both by the total amount of heat retained by the atmosphere and by the difference in temperatures between the polar regions and warmer areas. As the poles warm more than the temperate zone, that difference in temperature decreases. This affects both the speed and the behavior of major winds such as the jet stream.

**Figure 7-19**

## Increasing Temperatures

Higher-than-normal temperatures are shown in yellow and red. The highest above-normal temperatures (red) are concentrated in the Arctic region.

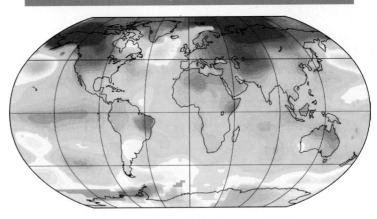

**Global Mean Surface Temperature (GISS) January–June 2016**

Temperature Anomaly in Degrees Celsius

-4   -3   -2   -1   0   1   2   3   4

Source: NASA/GISS

**Figure 7-20**
## Ecological Impacts on Organisms

Hummingbirds are arriving in their breeding grounds earlier every year.

**Ecological Impacts** Small changes in climate can affect organisms and ecosystems. Remember that each organism's geographic range is determined by its tolerance to ranges in temperature, humidity, and rainfall. If conditions change beyond an organism's tolerance, the organism must adapt, move to a more suitable location, or face extinction. For example, if the temperature rises, organisms move away from the equator toward cooler places. They also move from warm lowlands to cooler, higher altitudes.

## CASE STUDY  Analyzing Data

### Evidence in Ice

Since 2002, NASA has used satellites to measure the mass of ice on Antarctica. The data is shown in the line graph.

1. **Interpret Graphs** What is the overall trend in the mass of ice on Antarctica?

2. **Evaluate Evidence** How do the data support the conclusion that Earth's climate is warming?

3. **Predict** How do you think the mass of Antarctic ice will change in the future? Cite evidence and use logical reasoning to support your prediction.

4. **Connect to Society** Explain why it is important for scientists to collect and monitor Antarctic ice data.

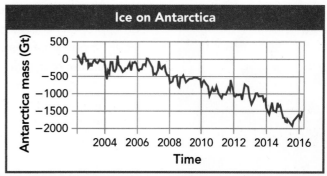

Source: NASA

Life cycles of many plants and animals are cued by seasonal changes in temperature. Plant flowering and animal breeding are sensitive to both daytime and nighttime temperatures. If warming is occurring, researchers hypothesize that organisms should respond as though spring were beginning earlier. Data from studies covering more than 1700 plant and animal species confirm that those organisms' life cycles are shifting as though they were experiencing rising temperatures. For example, hummingbirds like the one shown in **Figure 7-20** are changing the timing of their migration, arriving in their summer breeding grounds earlier every year. Globally, climate change alone threatens a great many species with extinction. Add climate change to all the other human-caused changes in global systems, and the result is that many more organisms—and entire ecosystems—are at risk.

**Impacts on Human Systems** Changes in temperature and precipitation have already begun to negatively affect crop yields of corn and wheat in some places. Water availability is changing in many agricultural areas, and is expected to affect farming in years to come. For example, the average winter snowpack in the western mountains of the United States is decreasing and is melting earlier in the spring. Farmers depend on water stored in this snowpack and the timing of its summer melt. Several areas in the western and southwestern United States are experiencing more droughts during the summer growing season.

**Sea Level Rise** Global warming also affects sea level. Sea level has risen, on average, at a rate of 1.8 millimeters every year since 1961. This increase has two causes. Melting ice from glaciers and polar ice caps add water to the oceans. In addition, a lot of the extra heat retained by the atmosphere is absorbed by the oceans. As oceans warm, their water expands slightly. Although this expansion might not seem like much, when you think of ocean basins a mile or more deep, even a small amount of <u>expansion</u> affects sea level.

### BUILD VOCABULARY

**Academic Words** The noun <u>expansion</u> means "the action of becoming larger." The expansion of water when it warms ultimately leads to an increase in its volume. This, in turn, contributes to rising sea levels.

INTERACTIVITY

**Figure 7-21**

**Success Story**

The giant panda was removed from the endangered species list in September 2016.

INTERACTIVITY

Investigate carbon sequestration by planning an urban tree planting.

# Designing Solutions

The goal of science is to help us understand the natural world and to apply that knowledge to improve the human condition. Scientific data, properly collected, analyzed, and applied, can help us make vitally important decisions to positively affect the future of humanity. *Scientific research can have a positive impact on the global environment by (1) recognizing a problem in the environment, whether from human or other causes, (2) gathering data to document and analyze that problem and identify its cause, and then (3) guiding changes in our behavior based on scientific understanding.*

**Environmental Successes** Several examples we've discussed show how research can guide us toward positive results for humanity and the biosphere. Take, for example, the presence of lead in streams in the U.S. The first step was to recognize that lead in water supplies was partly due to pollution from car exhaust. Then, industrial research figured out how to enable cars to run efficiently on unleaded fuel, and leaded gasoline was phased out. The successful global response to ozone depletion offers a model for international action based on scientific information. Once research connecting CFCs with ozone depletion was published, replicated, and accepted by the scientific community, the rest was up to policymakers and industry. Following scientific recommendations, 191 countries signed the Montreal Protocol, an agreement banning most uses of CFCs. Then, manufacturers developed alternatives to CFCs that work in most applications. Stratospheric ozone is now recovering!

**Climate Change Challenge** Of all the ecological challenges humanity has faced, climate change is the most complicated and difficult to fix. The world still depends heavily on fossil fuels and agriculture that produces methane. It will take a lot of effort to find solutions that work. Hopefully, governments around the world will let science inform their decisions on this globally important issue.

HS-LS2-2, HS-LS2-7, HS-ETS1-1, HS-ESS3-4, HS-ESS3-5, HS-ESS3-6

## ✓ LESSON 7.3 Review

### ⚲ KEY QUESTIONS

1. How does the climate change that scientists are observing now compare with climate change in the past?

2. How has climate change affected plant and animal species on Earth?

3. What actions have scientists already taken to help society address global climate change? What actions should be taken next?

### CRITICAL THINKING

4. **Use Models** According to the climate models that scientists have developed, what variable will most affect the average increase in global temperature this century?

5. **Construct an Explanation** How can increasing temperatures in polar regions affect climate all across Earth?

6. **Evaluate Claims** Scientists claim that changes to global climate will affect both natural ecosystems and human systems, such as farms and ranches. Cite evidence and logical reasoning to evaluate this claim.

# Sustainability

## KEY QUESTIONS

- What criteria can be used to evaluate whether development is sustainable?
- Why are innovation and resilience important?

**HS-LS2-7:** Design, evaluate, and refine a solution for reducing the impacts of human activities on the environment and biodiversity.

**HS-LS4-6:** Create or revise a simulation to test a solution to mitigate adverse impacts of human activity on biodiversity.

**HS-ETS1-1:** Analyze a major global challenge to specify qualitative and quantitative criteria and constraints for solutions that account for societal needs and wants.

**HS-ESS3-4:** Evaluate or refine a technological solution that reduces impacts of human activities on natural systems.

**HS-ESS3-5:** Analyze geoscience data and the results from global climate models to make an evidence-based forecast of the current rate of global or regional climate change and associated future impacts to Earth systems.

Ecological science can help guide us to provide for human needs without causing long-term environmental harm. That guidance requires understanding everything you've learned in this unit—and more. Science alone isn't enough. Global planning requires input from economics, sociology, and other disciplines beyond the realm of this book. Here we will discuss only the scientific aspects of ecological planning for the future.

## Sustainable Development

Using resources in ways that preserve ecosystem services is called **sustainable development**. Sustainable development recognizes the links between ecology and economics. You can think of sustainable development as three nested spheres: Earth's life support system (the environment), society, and the economy, as shown in **Figure 7-22**. This diagram symbolizes that our economy operates within society, and both operate within Earth's life support system.

**VOCABULARY**

**sustainable development**
**renewable resource**
**nonrenewable resource**
**resilience**

**READING TOOL**

For each section of this lesson, take notes in your 📘 **Biology Foundations Workbook** about sustainable development and how it can be achieved.

▶ **VIDEO**

Learn how the human taste for seafood is affecting the world's oceans.

## Figure 7-22

### Sustainable Development

This diagram symbolizes that the economy operates within society, which in turn operates within Earth's life support system.

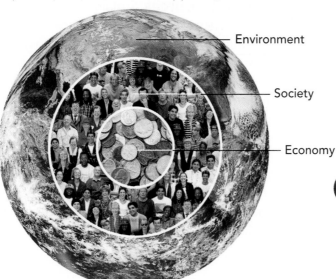

- Environment
- Society
- Economy

**Figure 7-23**

**United Nations Sustainable Development Goals**

The United Nations has set 17 goals for sustainable development. In 2015, the organization promoted the goals on its headquarters building in New York City.

**INTERACTIVITY**

Investigate sustainable development.

**READING TOOL**

Identify details in the text that support sustainable development goals.

**United Nations Sustainable Development Goals** What should sustainable development aim for? 🔍 *Sustainable development should provide for human needs while preserving ecosystem services. It should cause no long-term harm to soil, water, and climate. It should consume as little energy and material as possible. Finally, sustainable development must take into account human needs and economic systems.* It must do more than just enable people to survive. It must help them improve their situation. The United Nations has set and promoted Sustainable Development Goals, as shown in **Figure 7-23**.

**Renewable Resources** Sustainable development focuses on careful use of renewable ecosystem services. A **renewable resource** can be produced or replaced by a healthy ecosystem. A single southern white pine is one example of a renewable resource because a new tree can grow in place of an old tree that dies or is cut down. Another example is drinkable water. In many places, drinking water is provided naturally by streams, rivers, and lakes, and it is filtered by forest soils and wetlands. But if human-caused environmental changes impact ecosystem function, water quality may fall. If that happens, cities and towns must pay for mechanical or chemical treatment to provide safe drinking water. Electricity generated from wind farms, like the one shown in **Figure 7-24**, or solar power is also a renewable resource.

**Nonrenewable Resources** If natural processes cannot replenish resources within a reasonable time, they are considered to be **nonrenewable resources**. Fossil fuels such as coal, oil, and natural gas are nonrenewable resources formed from buried organic materials over millions of years. When existing deposits are depleted, they are gone.

# Innovation and Resilience

Human intelligence and creativity related to science have gotten us out of a lot of scrapes! Still, technology won't automatically solve our problems, unless it is guided by sustainable goals. We need constant innovation—new ideas and new engineering solutions that provide a necessary service at a reasonable cost. Solar generation of electricity, for example, was technically possible more than twenty years ago. Back then, however, solar panels were much too expensive for individual consumers to afford them. But a steady stream of engineering and manufacturing innovations has dramatically lowered the price of this technology. Now, solar panels are mass-market products that are widely installed on both commercial buildings and private homes.

Ecologists and many government agencies—including the U.S. military—recognize that life in the Anthropocene involves unpredictability. Some of that unpredictability involves loss of ecosystem services from biodiversity loss. More unpredictability will result from increased frequency of droughts in some places. And even more unpredictability will result from increasing frequency of other extreme weather events, such as hurricanes and floods.

That's why sustainable development must include **resilience,** which is the ability to deal with change and move on.  *Sustainable development must be flexible enough to survive environmental stresses like droughts, floods, storms, and heat waves or cold snaps.* When hurricanes hit the United States, for example, they can cause some loss of life and significant loss of property. But our cities are resilient enough (or at least they have been so far) to deal with the damage and rebuild. When serious hurricanes hit places like Haiti or Honduras, for example, those much less resilient countries experience major loss of life and widespread destruction that is difficult to handle on their own.

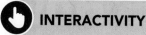

**INTERACTIVITY**

**Figure 7-24**

**Renewable Energy**

The electricity produced by these wind turbines is considered a renewable resource. The wind energy that turns the turbines cannot be used up.

**INTERACTIVITY**

Investigate how biogas is made from the breakdown of wastes.

HS-LS2-7, HS-LS4-6 HS-ETS1-1, HS-ESS3-4, HS-ESS3-5

# ✓ LESSON 7.4 Review

## ⚘ KEY QUESTIONS

1. How are resources used in sustainable development?

2. Why is resilience important for sustainable development?

## CRITICAL THINKING

3. Identify Variables City planners are deciding where to build a new stadium. Choices include the city center, an old farm just outside the city, and wetlands by a river. To make a decision that promotes sustainable development, what variables should the planners identify?

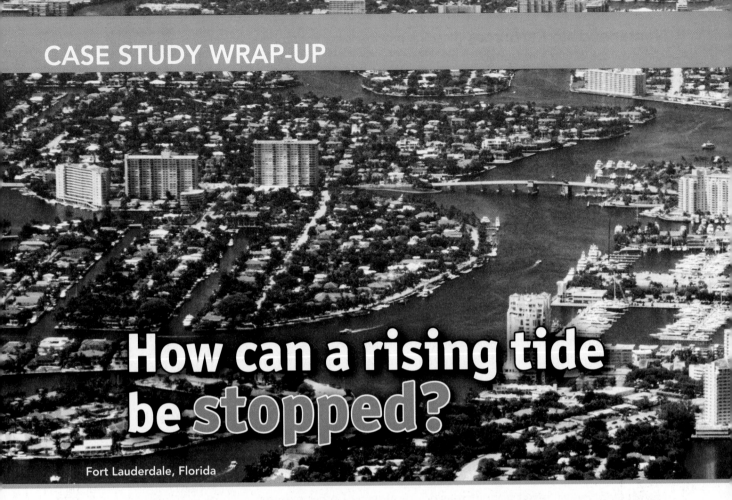

# How can a rising tide be stopped?

Fort Lauderdale, Florida

**Rising seas threaten coastal areas around the world. Southern Florida is uniquely at risk because three quarters of its population lives densely packed along its low-lying coasts.**

HS-ETS1-1, CCSS.MATH.HS.MP.2, CCSS.ELA-LITERACY.RST.9-10.1, CCSS.ELA-LITERACY.RST.9-10.2, CCSS.ELA-LITERACY.WHST.9-10.1, CCSS.ELA-LITERACY.WHST.9-10.2, CCSS.ELA-LITERACY.WHST.9-10.7, CCSS.ELA-LITERACY.WHST.9-10.8

## Make Your Case

Human-caused global change creates a wide variety of challenges for people everywhere. Some challenges can be addressed at a local level, but others require international cooperation on a global scale.

## Develop a Solution

1. **Conduct Research** Explore the goals, accomplishments, and limitations of a regional group, such as the Southeast Florida Climate Compact, the Will Steger Foundation's Climate Generation, or the Totonicapán reforestation project guided by EcoLogic Development fund. Your research should include verifiable scientific facts and expert scientific opinions.

2. **Construct an Argument** Evaluate successes and challenges you perceive in the work of your chosen organization. Apply that information as you develop and propose a course of action to address related issues in your local area. What are the costs and benefits of action compared with those of inaction? Write a persuasive, evidence-based argument in support of your ideas.

# Society on the Case

## Flooded Lands

Changes in global systems have many causes and many effects. Scientists and governments are struggling to understand global change and what it means to humanity everywhere.

The effects of sea level rise are among the easiest to see today and to predict. Americans are learning about challenges faced by Miami, New Orleans, and parts of North Carolina. As real and as serious as those problems are, they pale in comparison to threats faced by many millions of people in low-lying parts of Asia. The coastal city of Shanghai, China, currently home to 24 million people, is built on a low, flat river delta. During this century, between 18 and 40 million people in that city alone could be displaced by rising seas! Bangladesh could lose not only equivalent parts of coastal cities, but millions of hectares of fertile farmland as well.

In addition, fresh water for drinking and irrigation is threatened in many places. In some regions, such as southern Florida, salt water from rising seas is already affecting drinking water supplies. In parts of the southwestern United States, southern California, and much of Mexico's Central Valley, a mix of climate change, population growth, and increased irrigation is causing more frequent and more severe water shortages. Rising to these challenges will require data from the best available science, inputs from economists and engineers, and responsible government action.

# Careers on the Case

## Work Toward a Solution

Scientists and engineers are working on ways to cope with global change. Jobs in many fields are being created by rising seas, more variable weather, and changes in precipitation.

### Aquaculture Farmer

For hundreds of years, people have harvested fish and other seafood directly from the sea. Today, farmers are also raising marine animals like other livestock. This type of farming is called aquaculture. Natural stocks of commercial fish species might decline sharply due to global climate change, overfishing, or other causes. Aquaculture could help replace them.

> **▶ VIDEO**
>
> Watch this video to learn about other careers in biology.

# Lesson Review

Go to your Biology Foundations Workbook for longer versions of these lesson summaries.

## 7.1 Ecological Footprints

Humanity's ecological footprint—which includes the use of resources such as energy, food, water, and shelter, and the production of wastes such as sewage and greenhouse gases—is measurable. By some calculations, the average American has an ecological footprint four times larger than the global average.

The Age of Humans, or the Anthropocene, began with the onset of the Industrial Revolution in the 1800s and accelerated beginning in the 1950s with technological developments in mining, farming, and medicine. Today, human activities are the single most powerful force for global change. People live in anthromes, or anthropogenic biomes, of their own creation.

- ecological footprint
- anthrome

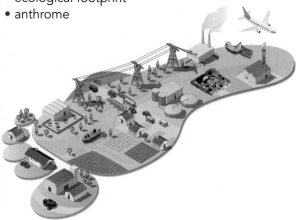

☑ **Interpret Visuals** Add labels to the different parts of the visual and explain how they describe an ecological footprint. Some labels may be used more than once.

**Labels:** agriculture, housing, cars, garbage, cattle, cropland, sewage treatment, electricity, coal-burning power plant, travel, fishing, agricultural runoff

## 7.2 Causes and Effects of Global Change

Human activities affect global environments and systems through pollution, land use, and interaction with other species.

Pollutants, harmful materials created as a result of human activity and released into the environment, drive global changes in air quality and temperature averages. Burning fossil fuels increases concentrations of greenhouse gases, which contribute to global warming. This warming leads to climate change.

Biological magnification of pollutants such as lead, mercury, PCBs, and DDT has produced serious toxic effects on human and animal populations. Other harmful practices, such as deforestation and habitat fragmentation, have contributed to the loss of biodiversity of animal and plant populations.

- climate change
- global warming
- deforestation
- monoculture
- invasive species
- pollutant
- ozone layer
- smog
- biological magnification

1620

Source: USDA Forest Service

1920

Source: USDA Forest Service

☑ **Compare** How did the area covered by primary forest in the continental United States changed over 300 years?

## 7.3 Measuring and Responding to Change

Scientific research can have a positive impact on the global environment by recognizing a problem, researching the problem to determine its cause, and then guiding changes. Correcting the damage to the ozone layer from the use of chlorofluorocarbons is a case in point.

The problem of climate change is a complicated issue, but data have been gathered, analyzed, and reviewed, indicating that Earth is warming faster than at any time in recorded history. Shifts in temperate zones and rising sea levels are among the effects that must be addressed. Changing patterns of precipitation in agricultural areas has immediate consequences on food production, as well as long-term effects on entire ecosystems.

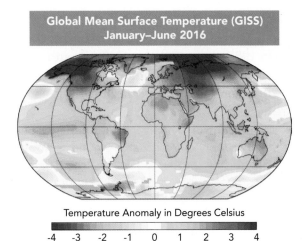

**Global Mean Surface Temperature (GISS) January–June 2016**

Temperature Anomaly in Degrees Celsius

-4  -3  -2  -1  0  1  2  3  4

Source: NASA/GISS

☑ **Interpret Data** What patterns are observed in these data?

## 7.4 Sustainability

Using resources in a way that preserves environmental resources is called sustainable development. Scientific, economic, and political action must intertwine to support the needs of sustainability. The focus is on careful use of renewable resources in innovative ways to replace older technologies based on the consumption of nonrenewable resources. Addressing unpredictable events, such as devastation from fires or floods, requires flexibility and resilience.

- sustainable development
- renewable resource
- nonrenewable resource
- resilience

☑ **Connect to Society** Describe two examples of how innovations, guided by sustainable development goals, are being used to decrease the effects of human activity on the Earth system. Identify and explain which system processes and phenomena in the UGC model are affected by these innovations.

## Organize Information

Complete the T-chart by giving a brief explanation of the problems associated with each issue

| Issue | Problem |
|---|---|
| Acid rain | 1. |
| Nitrogen enrichment | 2. |
| Ocean acidification | 3. |
| Ozone layer | 4. |
| DDT | 5. |

Burmese python

# Biodiversity in the Everglades

## Design a Solution

HS-LS2-7, HS-ETS1-2, HS-ESS3-3, HS-ESS3-4, HS-ESS3-6

**STEM** Florida residents once dismissed the value of the Everglades, the marshy wetlands that covered much of the southern half of the state. Ideas began changing in 1947, when Marjory Stoneman Douglas published the book *The Everglades: River of Grass*. Douglas described the rich biodiversity of the Everglades, as well as the role of the wetlands in providing clean water for the region.

The Everglades once covered almost 3 million acres of southern Florida. Now it has shrunk to about a third of that size. Much of the Everglades is part of a national park, where human activities are limited and wildlife is protected. However, more than 20 Everglades species are classified as endangered, and many more are threatened. Dense urban areas and commercial farms sur-round the Everglades on all sides—and they have proven to be disruptive neighbors.

The following bullet points list some of the ways that human activities have threatened the Everglades environment and its biodiversity. As you read the list, relate each entry to the rapid increase in Florida's human population. One hun-dred years ago, Florida was home to about

1 million people, most of whom lived far away from the Everglades in the northern part of the state. In 1980, the population shifted south and had grown to 10 million. Today, the population is over 20 million—and still increasing.

- **Water Control** The Everglades depends on a steady supply of fresh water that flows slowly from north to south. Today, canals and dams divert water for human uses and to prevent flooding. Much of the original Everglades has already been drained for new farms and housing developments.

- **Fertilizer** Runoff from farms has been adding fertilizer to the Everglades water supply. The fertilizer supports the growth of plants such as cattails and duckweed that otherwise would not grow in the Everglades. The fertilizer also supports harmful algal blooms.

- **Invasive Species** Through carelessness or ignorance, human actions have introduced all sorts of new species into the Everglades, some of which have proved invasive. The Burmese python is now competing with the alligator to be the top predator of the Everglades. Invasive plants, such as the Brazilian pepper and Australian pine, are now displacing native species.

Fields of crops, such as the sugar cane shown here, now take up much of Florida's land.

In this assessment, you will design, evaluate, and refine a solution for reducing the impact of human activities on the Everglades environment and its biodiversity.

**1. Conduct Research** Find out more about the biodiversity of the Everglades ecosystem and the threats to it. Also research how government agencies, private organizations, and individual citizens have been working to protect the Everglades, and what the results of these actions are.

**2. Define the Problem** In your own words, define one or more of the problems in the Everglades ecosystem that human activities have caused.

**3. Design Possible Solutions** Work in a small group. With your group members, propose ideas for solutions to one or more of the problems that you identified. Your ideas might include new laws to regulate water use, volunteer brigades to combat invasive species, or research into new farming practices that reduce fertilizer in runoff.

**4. Evaluate a Solution** Choose one of the potential solutions to develop further. Identify criteria for evaluating the solution, such as its potential effectiveness in improving the Everglades and protecting biodiversity. Also identify the costs and other constraints of the solution. Conduct additional research to evaluate the solution according to these criteria and constraints.

**5. Refine a Solution** Based on your research, refine your original proposal. Present your solution in a written or oral report, or as a computer presentation. Your report should include the following information:

- a change to the Everglades or its biodiversity, and an explanation of the problems that this change could cause or is causing

- the details of your proposed solution to the problems

- an evaluation of the benefits and drawbacks of the solution

Share your report with classmates.

## 🔍 KEY QUESTIONS AND TERMS

## 7.1 Ecological Footprints

HS-LS2-7

1. The total area of land and water ecosystems an individual needs to obtain food, shelter, home heating, travel, and waste absorption is called
   a. a land-management plan.
   b. an environmental problem.
   c. an ecological footprint.
   d. a measure of diversity.

2. The Anthropocene is said to have begun
   a. with the American Revolution.
   b. with the Industrial Revolution.
   c. in the 1950s.
   d. at the end of the twentieth century.

3. Which of the following would have the LEAST adverse effect on the environment?
   a. clearing a forested area outside of a city to build houses
   b. building apartments at the site of an abandoned factory in the city
   c. building a neighborhood in a meadow at the edge of the city
   d. filling a wetland area and building oceanfront condominiums

4. How does an anthrome differ from a biome?

5. How does the average American's environmental footprint compare with the global average?

6. Why is the current era called the Anthropocene?

## 7.2 Causes and Effects of Global Change

HS-LS2-2, HS-LS2-7, HS-LS4-6, HS-ESS2-6, HS-ESS3-6

7. What term describes measurable long-term changes in averages of temperature, clouds, winds, precipitation, and the frequency of extreme weather events?
   a. climate change
   b. global warming
   c. monoculture
   d. biological magnification

8. All of the following cause global change EXCEPT
   a. biological magnification of toxic compounds.
   b. habitat preservation.
   c. habitat fragmentation.
   d. deforestation.

9. Introducing an exotic species to an environment can
   a. improve soil fertility.
   b. cause biological magnification.
   c. cause native species to die out.
   d. increase crop yields.

10. DDT was banned for use in the United States because over the long run it is
    a. a deadly insecticide.
    b. toxic to herbivores.
    c. subject to biological magnification.
    d. poisonous to soil bacteria.

11. Which pollutant is the major cause of global change?

12. What are the advantages and disadvantages of monoculture farming?

13. What steps can be taken to reduce the problem of smog in urban areas?

## 7.3 Measuring and Responding to Change

HS-LS2-7, HS-ETS1-1, HS-ESS3-4, HS-ESS3-5, HS-ESS3-6

14. Study the following graph:

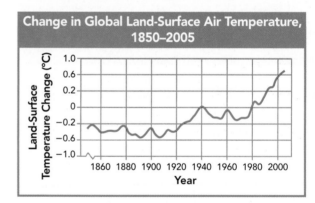

What problem did ecologists identify as a result of studying graphs like this one?
a. habitat fragmentation
b. the hole in the ozone layer
c. deforestation
d. global warming

15. The major cause of global warming is
    a. sun flare pollution.
    b. biological magnification.
    c. monoculture farming.
    d. burning fossil fuels.

16. Air and water pollution have been reduced by
    a. using fossil fuels in factories.
    b. raising more cattle for food.
    c. using only unleaded gasoline.
    d. increasing biological magnification.

17. What was the effect on the environment of banning chlorofluorocarbons?

18. In what ways does global warming affect food production?

19. Identify some areas most likely to be impacted by the effects of global warming.

## 7.4 Sustainability

**HS-LS2-7, HS-LS4-6, HS-ETS1-1, HS-ESS3-4, HS-ESS3-5**

20. Which of the following is a renewable resource?
    a. coal          c. oil
    b. trees         d. natural gas

21. Using resources in ways that do not cause long-term environmental degradation is called
    a. sustainable development.
    b. monoculture.
    c. resilience.
    d. deforestation.

22. The ability of a city to rebuild after a natural disaster such as a hurricane is called
    a. reforestation.     c. resilience.
    b. recycling.          d. resourcing.

23. How can solar energy contribute to a sustainable development program?

24. What is the scientific importance of the United Nations Sustainable Development Goals?

25. How does resilience complement sustainability?

## CRITICAL THINKING

**HS-LS2-2, HS-LS2-7, HS-LS4-6, HS-ETS1-1, HS-ESS3-3, HS-ESS3-4, HS-ESS3-5, HS-ESS3-6**

26. **Evaluate a Solution** The Montreal Protocol banning the use of CFCs was put into force in 1989. Explain the long-term goals of the Montreal Protocol.

27. **Analyze** How have human activities led to changes in biodiversity?

28. **Construct an Explanation** Recall that purifying water is an ecosystem service. How can human activities disrupt this service?

29. **Use Models** Throughout the last five chapters, we have added Earth system processes and phenomena to the Understanding Global Change model. Choose two topics from the Causes of Global Change category in this model. Using words and arrows, explain how these Causes of Change affect processes in the How the Earth System Works and Measurable Changes in the Earth System.

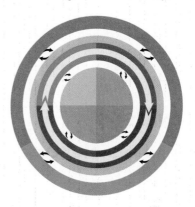

30. **Use Visuals** The photo shows purple loosestrife, a nonnative species that grows in marshes and other wetlands. Describe how purple loosestrife can result in the loss of biodiversity. Propose a solution to mitigate the adverse effects of loosestrife on the environment.

31. **Use Computational Models** What trends in average global temperature do computational models predict if greenhouse gas emissions continue to increase as they have in recent years? Propose a solution to decrease the rise in average global temperature. Identify criteria and constraints for your solution.

32. **Evaluate Claims** Scientists have come to a consensus that Earth's climate is changing. Cite evidence to support this claim, and explain how this change in climate affects populations.

33. **Evaluate a Solution** How would decreasing the burning of fossil fuels help reduce acid rain?

## CROSSCUTTING CONCEPTS

**34. Cause and Effect** How has the burning of fossil fuels contributed to global climate change?

**35. System and System Models** Why is it important to include oceans, the atmosphere, and human activities when developing a useful model of ocean acidification?

**36. Stability and Change** How could decisions that people make today determine whether global systems will change or remain stable in the future? Cite evidence and a specific example to support your answer.

## MATH CONNECTIONS

## Analyze and Interpret Data

CCSS.MATH.CONTENT.MP2, CCSS.MATH.CONTENT.MP4, CCSS.MATH.CONTENT.HSS.IC.B.6

Use the graph to answer questions 37–39.

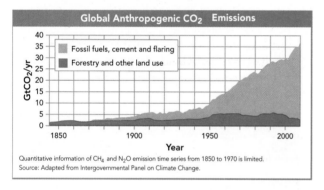

Global Anthropogenic $CO_2$ Emissions

Fossil fuels, cement and flaring
Forestry and other land use

Quantitative information of $CH_4$ and $N_2O$ emission time series from 1850 to 1970 is limited.
Source: Adapted from Intergovernmental Panel on Climate Change.

**37. Interpret Graphs** How have global anthropogenic (human-caused) $CO_2$ emissions changed since 1850? What is the main cause of this change?

**38. Evaluate Solutions** If humans reduce $CO_2$ emissions in the future and reverse the trend shown in the graph, does this solve the problem of global warming?

**39. Design a Possible Solution** What actions or policies do you recommend to reverse global $CO_2$ emissions? Describe the value of your recommendations.

The following circle graph describes the sources of greenhouse gases from the United States. Use the circle graph to answer questions 40–43.

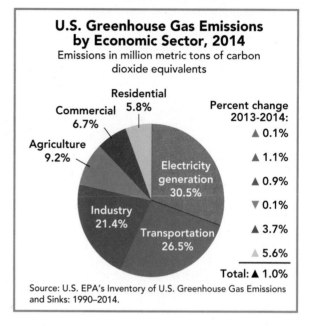

**U.S. Greenhouse Gas Emissions by Economic Sector, 2014**
Emissions in million metric tons of carbon dioxide equivalents

Residential 5.8%
Commercial 6.7%
Agriculture 9.2%
Electricity generation 30.5%
Industry 21.4%
Transportation 26.5%

Percent change 2013-2014:
▲ 0.1%
▲ 1.1%
▲ 0.9%
▼ 0.1%
▲ 3.7%
▲ 5.6%
Total: ▲ 1.0%

Source: U.S. EPA's Inventory of U.S. Greenhouse Gas Emissions and Sinks: 1990–2014.

**40. Analyze Graphs** Identify the three main sources of greenhouse gas emissions.

**41. Analyze Data** Either directly or indirectly, do you contribute to each of the sources of greenhouse gas emissions shown in the graph? Explain.

**42. Infer** From 2013 to 2014, which sector had the greatest percentage increase in greenhouse gas emissions? Propose a possible explanation.

**43. Design a Solution** Suppose you are asked to propose a plan to reduce the emissions of greenhouse gases. On which form of transportation would you concentrate your efforts, and why?

## LANGUAGE ARTS CONNECTION

## Write About Science

CCSS.ELA-LITERACY.WHST.9-10.2, CCSS.ELA-LITERACY.WHST.9-10.4

**44. Produce Clear Writing** Write a paragraph that defines your ecological footprint.

## Read About Science

CCSS.ELA-LITERACY.RST.9-10.7

**45. Integrate With Visuals** Choose one of the line graphs from the chapter and review the text passage that accompanies it. How does the graph illustrate the process discussed in the passage?

1. Evaluate the following activities. Which activity is MOST LIKELY to have the smallest impact on environmental systems?
   A. using more land to grow corn that is used to produce fuel
   B. using land to create a national park
   C. building a dam for energy production
   D. building new housing in an area far from a city
   E. building new highways so automobiles can travel faster

2. Legislation was introduced in 1987 to ban the use of compounds that were depleting the ozone layer. The graph below shows the levels of halogens in the atmosphere for several years after the legislation was passed.

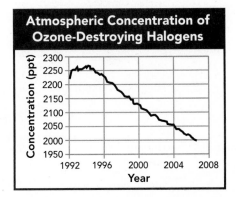

**Atmospheric Concentration of Ozone-Destroying Halogens**

What conclusion can you draw from this graph?
   A. The size of the ozone layer decreased during this time period.

   B. The concentration of ozone in the upper atmosphere increased during this time period.

   C. The concentration of halogens in the atmosphere decreased during this time period.

   D. The size of Antarctica below the ozone layer decreased during this time period.

   E. The concentration of heavy metals in the atmosphere decreased during this time period.

3. Which of the following could be a solution to help reverse a loss of biodiversity?
   A. habitat fragmentation
   B. reducing the size of the ozone layer
   C. increased use of monocultures
   D. reforestation
   E. invasive species

4. Fossil fuels are commonly used as an energy source for transportation vehicles. Burning fossil fuels has led to more carbon dioxide in the atmosphere and dissolved in seawater. Which of the following describes how burning fossil fuels is MOST LIKELY to impact marine organisms?
   A. Increased levels of carbon dioxide in seawater would increase the rate of photosynthesis in marine plants.
   B. Dissolved carbon dioxide in seawater would cause an increase in shellfish populations due to strengthened skeletons.
   C. Increased levels of carbon dioxide in seawater would cause ocean acidification and weaken corals.
   D. Dissolved carbon dioxide in seawater would cause invasive species to out-compete native species.

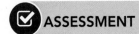 **ASSESSMENT**

For additional assessment practice, go online to access your digital course.

| If You Have Trouble With... | | | | |
|---|---|---|---|---|
| **Question** | 1 | 2 | 3 | 4 |
| **See Lesson** | 7.1 | 7.2 | 7.2 | 7.2 |
| **Performance Expectation** | HS-LS2-7 | HS-LS2-7 | HS-ESS3-4 | HS-ESS3-6 |

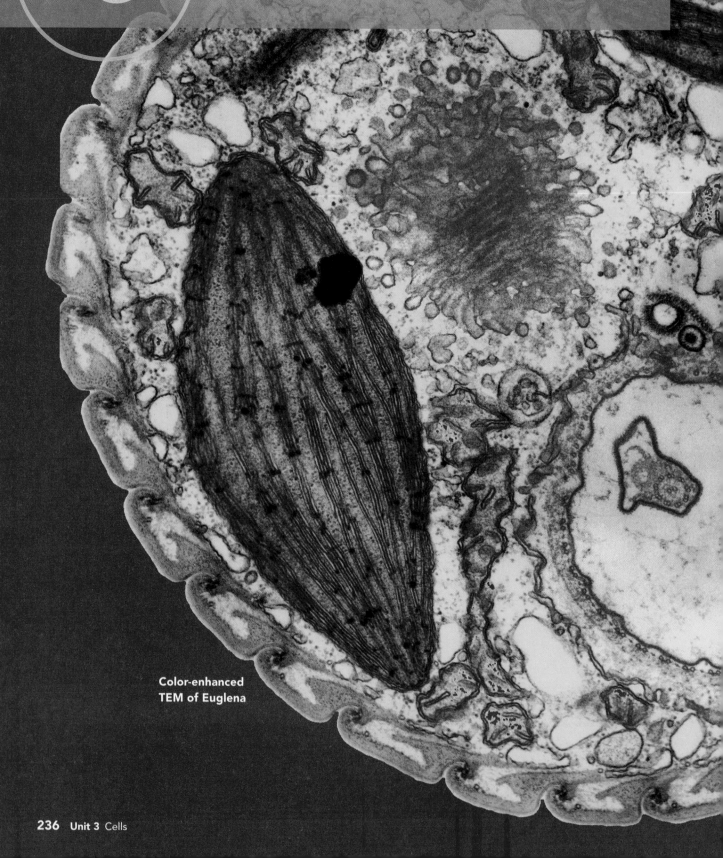

Color-enhanced
TEM of Euglena

> **Crosscutting Concepts** Cells are the basic units of life. Every cell is a living system that can grow and reproduce, capture and transform energy, and pass along genetic information. The unity of life at the cellular level allows us to use organisms like bacteria, fruit flies, and even worms as model systems to learn how cells interact to produce the remarkable properties shared by all living things, including ourselves.

**BOUNCE TO ACTIVATE** ▶ **VIDEO**

Author Ken Miller explains how a leaf uses solar energy to produce food.

# POWER FROM
# Pond Scum

## Fuel comes in many forms.

If you have burned wood logs in a campfire or a fireplace, then you have used biofuels. A biofuel is a fuel made from living matter. Unlike fossil fuels, such as coal and oil, a biofuel is renewable, meaning it can be replaced in a relatively short time. Today, engineers are looking at algae as a source of biofuel. Why algae? One of the reasons is that they are easy to raise. All they need is water, a few nutrients, and sunlight.

**PROBLEM LAUNCH**
Conduct research on algae as a biofuel. Report on different methods to maximize algal growth.

▶ **VIDEO**

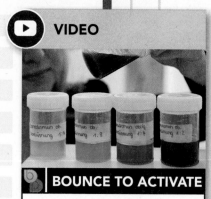

**BOUNCE TO ACTIVATE**

Watch a video about nonrenewable energy—where it comes from and is there a way to use a renewable source for fuel.

# PROBLEM: What is the best way to grow algae for biofuel?

**TO SOLVE THIS PROBLEM, perform these activities as they come up in the unit and record your findings in your 📘 Explorer's Journal.**

## LAB INVESTIGATION

Observe algal cells and classify cell structures. Discuss how algae live and grow.

## AUTHENTIC READING

Read an article describing how companies plan to use algae to create biofuels in the future.

## STEM PROJECT

Design an experiment to raise algae efficiently and effectively. Then evaluate your technique for large-scale production.

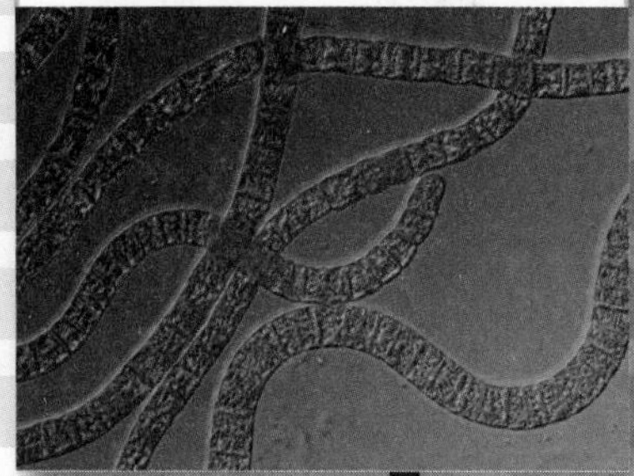

## INTERACTIVITY

Investigate the processes of photosynthesis and respiration in algae.

## INTERACTIVITY

Explore cell division and reproduction of algal cells.

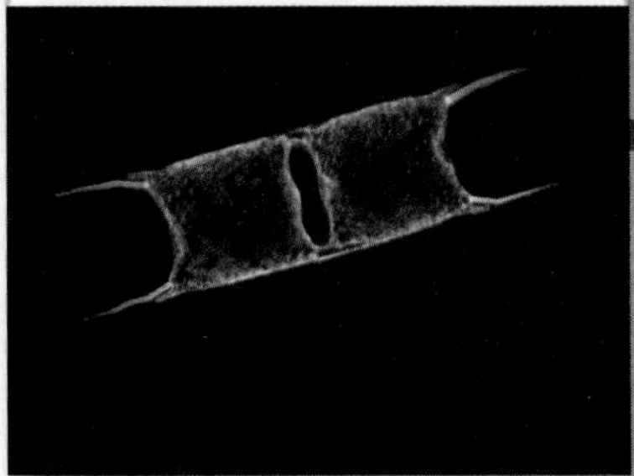

## PROBLEM WRAP-UP

Present your findings, and prepare a report to a transportation company convincing them to use a biofuel made from algae for their vehicles.

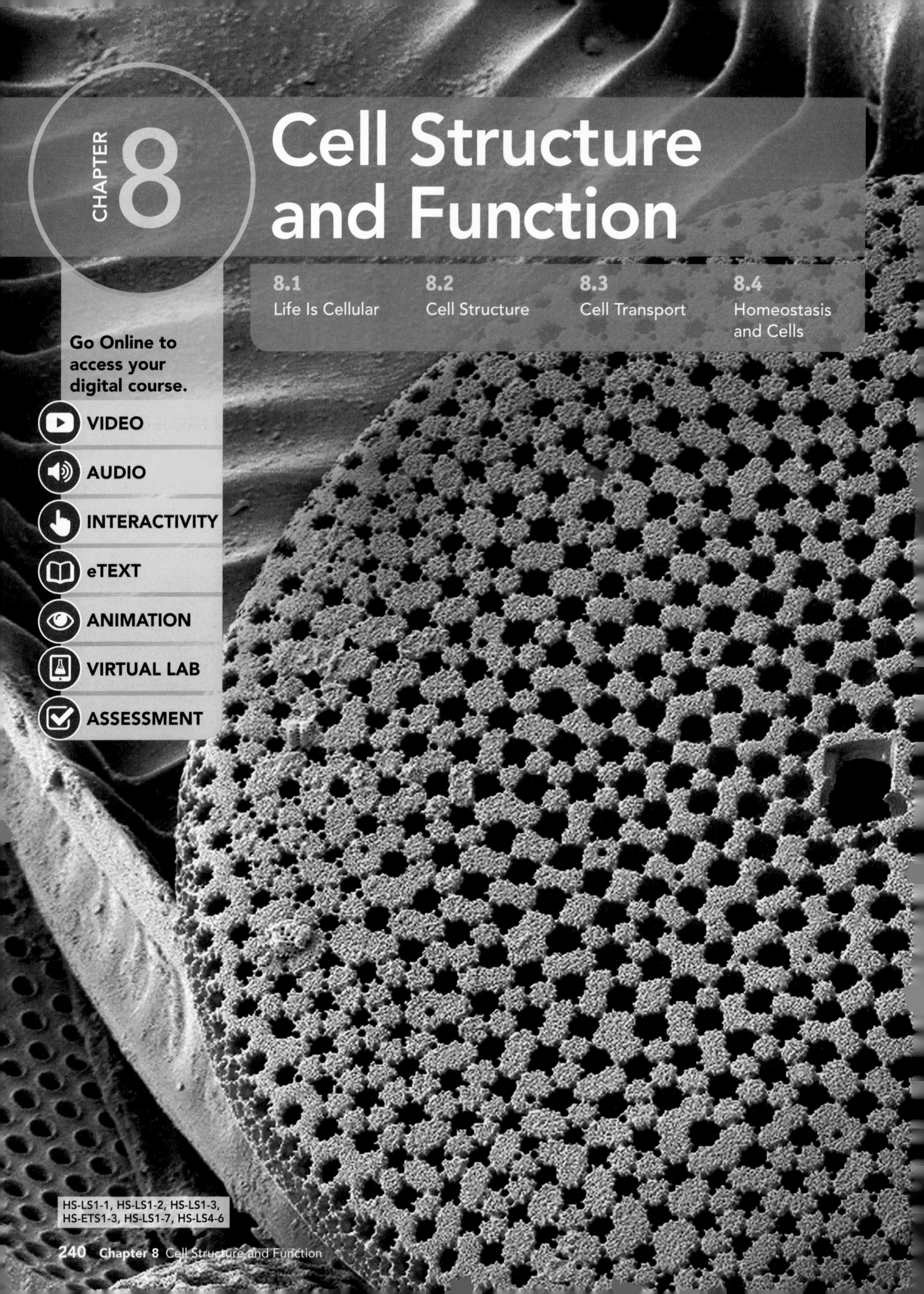

# Cell Structure and Function

**Go Online to access your digital course.**

▶ VIDEO

🔊 AUDIO

👆 INTERACTIVITY

📖 eTEXT

👁 ANIMATION

📱 VIRTUAL LAB

☑ ASSESSMENT

HS-LS1-1, HS-LS1-2, HS-LS1-3, HS-ETS1-3, HS-LS1-7, HS-LS4-6

# What's happening to me?

David was in his second year of college when it took him by surprise. At first, he had a little trouble seeing words on a page. Vision through his left eye was a little blurry, but he wasn't concerned. Then, a few days later, things went downhill. When he awoke in the morning, he had lost all of the vision in his left eye. The doctor in the college infirmary sent him to a specialist. To David's dismay, the specialist discovered that the vision in his right eye was failing, too. What was going on?

When he called home, David's mother told him that her brother had suffered vision problems as well. Her brother had died of heart problems at a young age. Once the eye doctor heard this news, he drew a blood sample to test David's DNA. A week later David received the bad news. He listened numbly to the doctor's somber, quiet voice. "I'm very sorry," said the doctor. "You have an inherited disease called Leber's hereditary optic neuropathy (LHON). There is no cure or useful treatment." The doctor went on to explain more, and then spoke about specialists, social workers, and support groups. David was shocked and frightened.

About one hundred people are diagnosed with this disease in the United States every year. Although vision is recovered occasionally, most of the time the loss is permanent. LHON causes the death of optic nerve cells, which carry visual information from the eye to the brain.

The cause of LHON is a change in the mitochondria. Mitochondria are some of the tiny components, or organelles, inside cells. This change causes these organelles to work just a little bit less efficiently than they should. In David's case, the optic nerve had broken down as a result. Both males and females can inherit a tendency to develop the disease, but only females can pass it along to their children. Sometimes it affects the heart muscle as well, which explained David's uncle's heart problems.

What do mitochondria do in healthy cells, and why had defective mitochondria caused David to lose his vision? Where do mitochondria come from, why are they inside our cells, and what can medical science do to fix them when they are faulty?

**Throughout this chapter, look for connections to the CASE STUDY to help you answer these questions.**

Diatoms (shown in this false color image) are a diverse group of aquatic unicellular organisms that form the base of many food chains (SEM 2200×).

# Life Is Cellular

Drawings by Anton van Leeuwenhoek

What's the smallest part of any living thing that still counts as being "alive"? Is a leaf alive? How about your big toe? What about a drop of blood? Can we just keep dividing living things into smaller and smaller parts, or is there a point at which what's left is no longer alive? As you will discover, there is such a limit: The smallest living unit of any organism is a cell.

## The Discovery of the Cell

"Seeing is believing" goes an old saying. It would be hard to find a better example of this than the discovery of the cell. Without the instruments to make them visible, cells remained unknown for most of human history. All of this changed with a dramatic advance in technology—the invention of the microscope.

**Early Microscopes** In the late 1500s, eyeglass makers in Europe discovered that using several glass lenses in combination could magnify even the smallest objects. Before long, they had built the first true microscopes from these lenses, opening the door to the study of biology as we know it today.

In 1665, Robert Hooke, an Englishman, used an early microscope to look at a nonliving thin slice of cork, a plant material. Under the microscope, cork seemed to be made of thousands of tiny empty chambers, as shown in **Figure 8-1**. Hooke called the chambers "cells," because they reminded him of a monastery's tiny rooms. That term, *cell*, is used in biology to this day.

In Holland around the same time, Anton van Leeuwenhoek used a single-lens microscope to observe pond water and other things. To his amazement, the microscope revealed a fantastic world of tiny living organisms that seemed to be everywhere—in the water that he and his neighbors drank, and even in his own mouth.

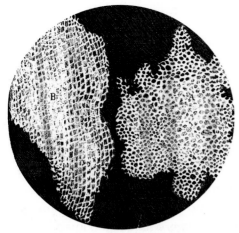

Hooke's observations

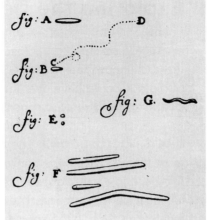

Leeuwenhoek's observations

**Figure 8-1**

## Early Microscope Images

Robert Hooke used a microscope to observe dead cells in thin sections of cork. Using a simple microscope, Anton van Leeuwenhoek was the first to observe living microorganisms. These drawings show some of the bacteria he found in his own mouth.

**The Cell Theory** Before long, it became clear that **cells** are the basic units of all living things. In 1838, German botanist Matthias Schleiden concluded that all plants are made of cells. The next year, German biologist Theodor Schwann stated that all animals are made of cells. In 1855, German physician Rudolf Virchow published the idea that new cells can be produced only from the division of existing cells. These discoveries, confirmed by many biologists, are summarized in the **cell theory**, a fundamental concept of biology.

 *The cell theory states:*

- *All living things are made up of cells.*
- *Cells are the basic units of structure and function in living things.*
- *New cells are produced from existing cells.*

☑ **READING CHECK** **Summarize** How were cells discovered?

---

**Quick Lab** 🔬 **Guided Inquiry** 📋

### What Is a Cell?

1. Observe one prepared slide under the low-power lens of the microscope and then under the high-power lens. Sketch the structures you observe under both lenses.

2. Repeat step 1 with the other prepared slides. With your partner, discuss and ask questions about your observations.

### ANALYZE AND CONCLUDE

1. **Compare and Contrast** What features do the cells you observed have in common? How are they different from one another?

2. **Use Models** Study Figure 8-5, which shows different types of cells and some of their structures. Which of these cells or structures do you think you observed and sketched?

3. **Classify** Review your sketches, and then classify the slides of cells into two or three groups. Explain your classification scheme.

4. **Ask Questions** Pose questions based on your observations that would help you better classify and identify the cells you studied.

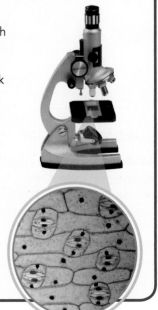

# Exploring the Cell

Following in the footsteps of Hooke, Virchow, and others, modern biologists still use microscopes to explore the cell. But today's researchers use technology that is more powerful than the pioneers of biology could have ever imagined. 🔑 *Microscopes work by using beams of light or electrons to produce magnified images.*

**Light Microscopes** The type of microscope you are probably most familiar with is the compound light microscope. A typical light microscope allows light to pass through a specimen and uses two lenses to form an image. The first lens, called the objective lens, is located just above the specimen. This lens enlarges the image of the specimen. The second lens, called the ocular lens, magnifies this image still further. Unfortunately, light itself limits the detail, or resolution, of images in a microscope. Like all forms of radiation, light waves are diffracted, or scattered, as they pass through matter. Because of this, light microscopes can produce clear images of objects only to a magnification of about 1000 times.

Since most living cells are nearly transparent, chemical stains or dyes are used to help make cells and their parts visible. Many of the slides you'll examine in your biology class laboratory will be stained this way. A powerful variation on these staining techniques uses dyes that give off light of a particular color when viewed under specific wavelengths of light, a property called fluorescence. Fluorescent labels of different colors, shown in **Figure 8-2**, can be attached to certain molecules within the cell. These labels make it possible to locate and even watch molecules move around in a living cell.

**Electron Microscopes** Light microscopes can be used to see cells and cell structures as small as 1 millionth of a meter—certainly pretty small! But what if scientists want to study something smaller than that, such as a virus or a DNA molecule? For that, they need electron microscopes. Instead of using light, electron microscopes use beams of electrons focused by magnetic fields. Electron microscopes offer much higher resolution than light microscopes. Some types of electron microscopes can be used to study cellular structures that are 1 billionth of a meter in size.

Electrons are easily scattered by molecules in the air, which means samples must be placed in a vacuum to be studied with an electron microscope. As a result, researchers must chemically preserve their samples. This means that electron microscopy, despite its higher resolution, can be used to examine only nonliving cells and tissues. The two major types of electron microscopes are transmission and scanning.

## Figure 8-2

## Fluorescent Dyes

By treating cells with stains or dyes, a scientist can clearly identify large molecules and cell parts. Fluorescent dyes are especially useful for contrasting one cell part from another such as in these skin cells.

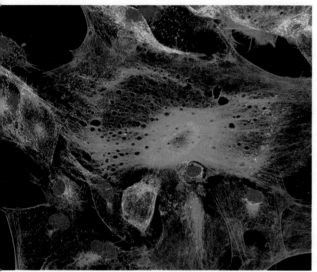

LM 500×

***Transmission Electron Microscopes*** These microscopes make it possible to explore cell structures and large protein molecules. Beams of electrons can only pass through thin samples, so cells and tissues must be cut into extremely thin slices before they can be examined. This is the reason that such images often appear flat and two dimensional.

***Scanning Electron Microscopes*** In these microscopes, a pencil-like beam of electrons is scanned over the surface of a specimen. Because the image is formed at the specimen's surface, samples do not have to be cut into thin slices to be seen. The scanning electron microscope produces stunning three-dimensional images of the specimen's surface.

Look at **Figure 8-3**, which shows yeast cells as they look under a light microscope, a transmission electron microscope, and a scanning electron microscope. You may wonder why the cells appear to be different colors in each micrograph. (A micrograph is a photo of an object seen through a microscope.) The colors in light micrographs come from the cells themselves or from the stains and dyes used to highlight them. Electron micrographs, however, are actually black and white. Electrons, unlike light, don't come in colors. So scientists often use computer techniques to add "false color" to make certain structures stand out.

**VIDEO**

Learn about the advantages and disadvantages of a light microscope, a SEM, a TEM, and a stimulated emission depletion.

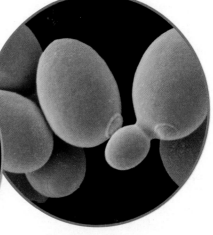

**Scanning electron micrograph (SEM)**

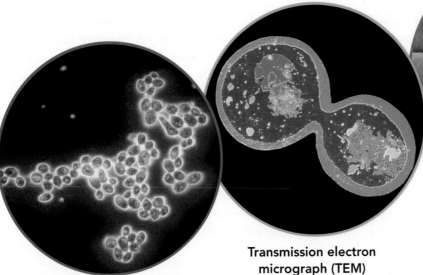

**Transmission electron micrograph (TEM)**

**Light micrograph (LM)**

**INTERACTIVITY**

**Figure 8-3**

## Micrographs

Different types of microscopes can be used to examine cells. Here, yeast cells are shown in a light micrograph (LM 500x), a transmission electron micrograph (TEM 4375x), and a scanning electron micrograph (SEM 3750x).

In the past decade, new microscopes have been developed that use precise, computer controlled laser beams to scan across samples and gather very high resolution information. These instruments and techniques are making it possible to study living cells at a level of detail never possible before, opening up even more opportunities for research.

☑ **READING CHECK** **Infer** If scientists were studying a structure found on the surface of yeast, which kind of microscope would they likely use?

# Prokaryotes and Eukaryotes

Cells come in an amazing variety of shapes and sizes, some of which are shown in **Figure 8-4**. Typical cells range from 5 to 50 micrometers (μm) in diameter. The smallest *Mycoplasma* bacteria, which are only 0.2 micrometer across, are so small they are difficult to see with even the best light microscope. In contrast, the giant amoeba *Chaos chaos* can be 1000 micrometers (1 millimeter) in diameter, large enough to see with the unaided eye as a tiny speck in pond water. Despite their differences, all cells, at some point in their lives, contain DNA, the molecule that carries biological information. In addition, all cells are surrounded by a thin flexible barrier called a **cell membrane**. (The cell membrane is sometimes called the *plasma membrane*, because many cells in the body are in direct contact with the fluid portion of the blood—the plasma.) There are other similarities as well, as you will learn in the next lesson.

Cells fall into two broad categories, depending on whether they contain a nucleus. The **nucleus** (plural: nuclei) is a large membrane-enclosed structure that contains genetic material in the form of DNA. DNA controls many of the cell's activities. **Eukaryotes** (yoo KAR ee ohts) are cells that enclose their DNA in nuclei. In contrast, **prokaryotes** (pro KAR ee ohts) are cells that do not enclose DNA in nuclei. **Figure 8-5** shows a typical prokaryotic cell and two typical eukaryotic cells.

**Prokaryotes** Prokaryotic cells are generally smaller and simpler when compared with eukaryotic cells, although there are many exceptions to this rule. The organisms we commonly call bacteria are prokaryotes. ⚲ *Prokaryotic cells do not enclose their genetic material within a nucleus.* Despite their simplicity, prokaryotes carry out every activity associated with living things. They grow, reproduce, and respond to the environment.

Prokaryotes perform very important roles in the environment. In fact, the very first photosynthetic organisms to appear on Earth, nearly 3 billion years ago, were cyanobacteria. The oxygen these prokaryotes released into the atmosphere forever changed Earth's environment, making possible plant and animal life as we know it.

**Figure 8-4**

**Cell Size Is Relative**

The human eye can see objects larger than about 0.5 mm. Most of what interests cell biologists, however, is much smaller than that. Microscopes make seeing the cellular and subcellular world possible.

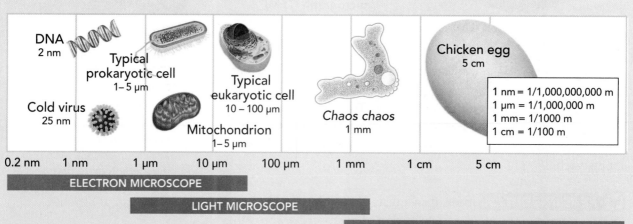

**Figure 8-5**

## Prokaryotic and Eukaryotic Cells

In general, eukaryotic cells are larger and more complex than prokaryotic cells. Eukaryotic organisms include plants, animals, fungi, and many unicellular organisms.

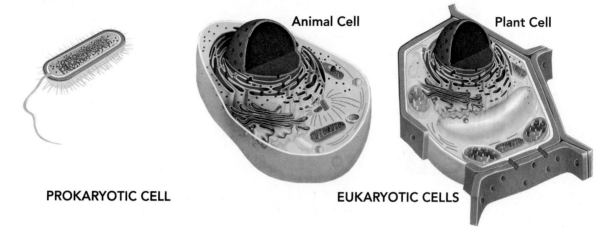

**Animal Cell**          **Plant Cell**

**PROKARYOTIC CELL**          **EUKARYOTIC CELLS**

**Eukaryotes** Eukaryotic cells are generally larger and more complex than prokaryotic cells. Most eukaryotic cells contain dozens of structures and internal membranes, and many are highly specialized. ✎ *In eukaryotic cells, the nucleus separates the genetic material from the rest of the cell.* Eukaryotes display great variety. Some, like the ones commonly called "protists," live solitary lives as unicellular organisms; others form large, multicellular organisms—plants, animals, and fungi.

In multicellular organisms, cells are specialized for specific tasks, such as support, communication, movement, or the production of proteins or other cell products. As a general rule, the cells of multicellular organisms cannot survive individually. They work together to complete the tasks of life.

> **INTERACTIVITY**
>
> Compare and contrast prokaryotes and eukaryotes, including their different DNA structures.

HS-LS1-2

## ☑ LESSON 8.1 Review

### ✎ KEY QUESTIONS

1. How did Hooke's work contribute to the cell theory?

2. What does it mean if a micrograph is "false-colored?"

3. What is the defining characteristic of eukaryotic cells? What types of organisms have eukaryotic cells?

### CRITICAL THINKING

4. **Construct a Counter-Argument** A classmate argues that Schwann and Schleiden are responsible for the cell theory. How do you respond? Cite facts and use logical reasoning to support your argument.

5. **Ask Questions** You observe a tiny structure under a microscope. What question would you ask, and then investigate, to determine whether the structure was part of a living thing?

6. **Integrate Information** Review the micrographs of cells shown in **Figure 8-3**. What information about cells do these micrographs show? What information might the micrographs suggest, which might not be accurate?

# Cell Structure

**HS-LS1-1:** Construct an explanation based on evidence for how the structure of DNA determines the structure of proteins which carry out the essential functions of life through systems of specialized cells.

**HS-LS1-2:** Develop and use a model to illustrate the hierarchical organization of interacting systems that provide specific functions within multicellular organisms.

## 🔍 KEY QUESTIONS

- *What is the role of the cell nucleus?*
- *What organelles help make and transport proteins and other macromolecules?*
- *What are the functions of vacuoles, lysosomes, and the cytoskeleton?*
- *What are the functions of chloroplasts and mitochondria?*
- *What is the function of the cell membrane?*

## VOCABULARY

**cytoplasm • organelle
ribosome
endoplasmic reticulum
Golgi apparatus
vacuole • lysosome
cytoskeleton • chloroplast
mitochondrion
cell wall • lipid bilayer
selectively permeable**

### READING TOOL

Use the figures in this lesson to help you identify and describe each part of the cell. Fill in the graphic organizer in your 📘 **Biology Foundations Workbook.**

If you've ever visited or worked in a factory, you know it can be a puzzling place. Machines buzz and clatter; people move quickly in different directions. So much activity can be confusing. However, if you take the time to watch carefully, what might at first seem like chaos begins to make sense. The same is true for the living cell.

## Cell Organization

A eukaryotic cell is a complex and busy place. But if you look closely at eukaryotic cells, patterns begin to emerge. For example, it's easy to divide each cell into two major parts: the nucleus and the cytoplasm. The **cytoplasm** is the portion of the cell outside the nucleus. Both the nucleus and the cytoplasm work together in the business of life. The interior of a prokaryotic cell, which lacks a nucleus, is also referred to as the cytoplasm.

In our discussion of cell structure, we will consider each major component of plant and animal eukaryotic cells—some of which are also found in prokaryotic cells—one by one. Because many of these structures act like specialized organs, they are known as **organelles**, literally "little organs." Understanding what each organelle does helps us understand the cell as a whole. A summary of cell structures and functions can be found at the end of this lesson.

**Comparing the Cell to a Factory** In some respects, the eukaryotic cell is much like a living version of a modern factory, as shown in **Figure 8-6.** The different organelles of the cell can be compared to the specialized machines and assembly lines of a factory. In addition, cell parts, like people and machines in factories, follow instructions and produce products. As you read about the organization of the cell, you'll find many places in which the comparison works so well that it will help you understand how cells function.

## The Nucleus

In the same way that the main office controls a large factory, the nucleus is the control center of the cell. 🔍 *The nucleus contains nearly all the cell's DNA and, with it, the coded instructions for making proteins and other important molecules.* Only eukaryotic cells have a nucleus. In prokaryotic cells, DNA is found in the cytoplasm.

The nucleus, shown in **Figure 8-7**, is surrounded by a nuclear envelope composed of two membranes. The nuclear envelope is dotted with thousands of nuclear pores, which allow material to move into and out of the nucleus. Like messages, instructions, and blueprints moving in and out of a factory's main office, a steady stream of proteins, the nucleic acid RNA, and other molecules move through the nuclear pores to and from the rest of the cell.

Chromosomes, which carry the cell's genetic information, are also found in the nucleus. Most of the time, the threadlike chromosomes are spread throughout the nucleus in the form of chromatin—a complex of DNA bound to proteins. When a cell divides, its chromosomes condense and can be seen under a microscope. Most nuclei also contain a small dense region known as the nucleolus (noo klee OH lus), where the assembly of ribosomes begins.

✔ **READING CHECK** **Use an Analogy** How is a cell's cytoplasm like a factory floor?

**Visual Analogy**

Figure 8-6

### The Cell as a Factory

Specialized machines enable a factory to function. Similarly, specialized structures in a cell enable a cell to carry out the processes of life.

**READING TOOL**

Using Figure 8-6 and the cell-as-a-factory analogy, predict the function of each of the organelles. If you cannot identify the organelle by name, use its color in your description.

Figure 8-7

### Nucleus

Both plant and animal cells have a nucleus. Like a factory's computing cloud or server room, the nucleus contains the information needed for a cell to function. A cell's information is in the form of DNA.

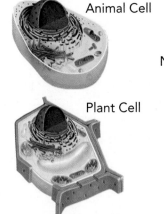

Animal Cell

Plant Cell

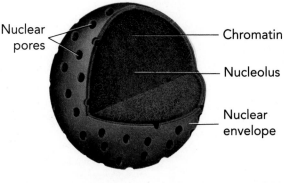

Nuclear pores

Chromatin

Nucleolus

Nuclear envelope

# Organelles That Build Proteins

Life is a dynamic process, and living things are always at work synthesizing new molecules. Because proteins carry out so many of the essential functions of living things, including the synthesis of other macromolecules such as lipids and carbohydrates, a big part of the cell is devoted to their production and distribution. The process of making proteins is summarized in **Figure 8-8**.

**Ribosomes** One of the most important jobs carried out in the cellular "factory" is making proteins. ⚡ *Proteins are assembled on ribosomes.* **Ribosomes** are small particles of RNA and protein found throughout the cytoplasm in both eukaryotes and prokaryotes. Ribosomes produce proteins by following coded instructions that come from DNA. Each ribosome, in its own way, is like a small machine in a factory, turning out proteins on orders that come from its DNA "boss." Cells that are especially active in protein synthesis often contain large numbers of ribosomes.

**Endoplasmic Reticulum** Eukaryotic cells contain an internal membrane system known as the **endoplasmic reticulum** (en doh PLAZ mik reh TIK yoo lum), or ER. The endoplasmic reticulum is where lipids, including those needed for the cell membrane, are synthesized, along with proteins and other materials that are exported from the cell.

The portion of the ER involved in the synthesis of proteins is called rough endoplasmic reticulum, or rough ER. It is given this name because of the ribosomes found on its surface. Newly made proteins leave these ribosomes and enter the rough ER, where they may be chemically modified.

**Figure 8-8**

## Making Proteins

Together, ribosomes, the endoplasmic reticulum, and the Golgi apparatus synthesize, modify, package, and ship proteins.

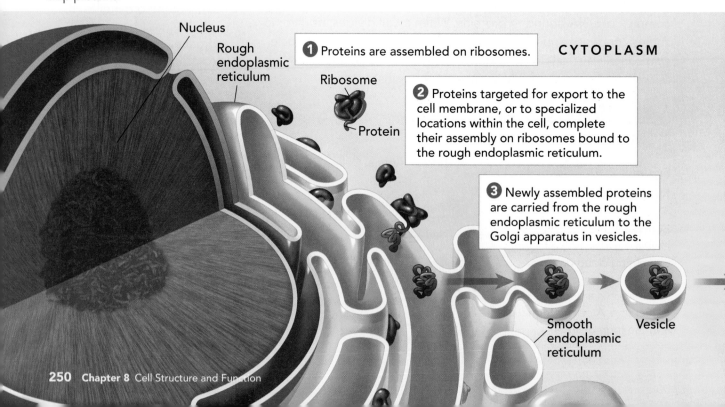

Nucleus

Rough endoplasmic reticulum

Ribosome

Protein

**CYTOPLASM**

❶ Proteins are assembled on ribosomes.

❷ Proteins targeted for export to the cell membrane, or to specialized locations within the cell, complete their assembly on ribosomes bound to the rough endoplasmic reticulum.

❸ Newly assembled proteins are carried from the rough endoplasmic reticulum to the Golgi apparatus in vesicles.

Smooth endoplasmic reticulum

Vesicle

🔍 *Proteins made on the rough ER include those that will be released, or secreted, from the cell; many membrane proteins; and proteins destined for other specialized locations within the cell.* Rough ER is abundant in cells that produce large amounts of protein for export. Other cellular proteins are made on "free" ribosomes, which are not attached to membranes.

The other portion of the ER is known as smooth endoplasmic reticulum (smooth ER) because ribosomes are not found on its surface. In many cells, the smooth ER contains collections of enzymes that perform specialized tasks, including the synthesis of lipids and the detoxification of drugs. Smooth ER also plays an important role in the synthesis of carbohydrates.

**Golgi Apparatus** In eukaryotic cells, proteins produced in the rough ER move next into an organelle called the **Golgi apparatus**, which appears as a stack of flattened membranes. As proteins leave the rough ER, molecular "address tags" get them to the right destinations. As these tags are "read" by the cell, the proteins are bundled into tiny membrane-enclosed structures called vesicles that bud from the ER and carry the proteins to the Golgi apparatus. 🔍 *The Golgi apparatus modifies, sorts, and packages proteins and other materials from the endoplasmic reticulum for storage in the cell or release from the cell.* The Golgi apparatus is somewhat like a customization shop, where the finishing touches are put on proteins before they are ready to leave the "factory." From the Golgi apparatus, proteins are "shipped" to their final destinations inside or outside the cell.

☑️ **READING CHECK** **Identify** Does the rough ER or the smooth ER send proteins on to the Golgi apparatus?

👆 **INTERACTIVITY**

Build a cell and look at specialized cells under a microscope.

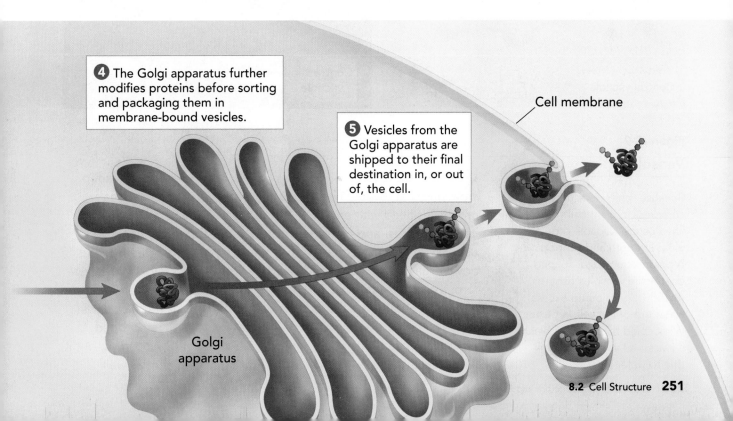

**4** The Golgi apparatus further modifies proteins before sorting and packaging them in membrane-bound vesicles.

**5** Vesicles from the Golgi apparatus are shipped to their final destination in, or out of, the cell.

Cell membrane

Golgi apparatus

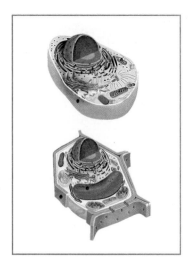

# Organelles That Store, Clean Up, and Support

Cells have many functions to perform other than building and transporting proteins. Structures such as vacuoles, vesicles, lysosomes, and the cytoskeleton represent the cellular factory's storage space, cleanup crew, and support structures.

**Vacuoles and Vesicles** Every factory needs a place to store things, and so does every cell. Many cells contain **vacuoles**, which are large saclike, membrane-enclosed structures. *Vacuoles store materials like water, salts, proteins, and carbohydrates.* In many plant cells, there is a single large central vacuole filled with liquid. The pressure of the central vacuole in these cells increases their rigidity, making it possible for plants to support heavy structures, such as leaves and flowers. **Figure 8-9** shows a typical plant cell's central vacuole.

Vacuoles are found in many eukaryotic cells. The paramecium in Figure 8-9 contains an organelle called a contractile vacuole, which pumps excess water out of the cell.

In addition, nearly all eukaryotic cells contain smaller membrane-enclosed structures called vesicles. Vesicles store and move materials between cell organelles, as well as to and from the cell surface.

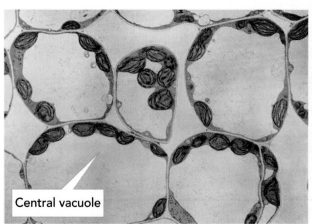

Central vacuole

TEM 7000×

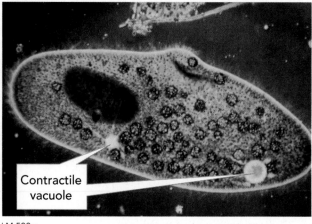

Contractile vacuole

LM 500×

**Figure 8-9**

**Vacuoles**

Because water does not compress, a plant cell's fluid-filled central vacuole provides strength and support. A paramecium's star-shaped contractile vacuoles contract rhythmically to pump excess water out of the cell. ☑ **Infer** What could happen to a plant if its central vacuoles shrunk due to water loss?

**Lysosomes** Even the neatest, cleanest factory needs a cleanup crew, and that's where lysosomes come in. **Lysosomes** are small organelles filled with enzymes. *Lysosomes break down lipids, carbohydrates, and proteins into small molecules that can be used by the rest of the cell.* They are also involved in breaking down organelles that have outlived their usefulness. Lysosomes perform the vital function of removing "junk" that might otherwise accumulate and clutter up the cell. A number of rare but serious human diseases can be traced to lysosomes that fail to function properly. Biologists once thought only animal cells contained lysosomes, but it is now clear that a few types of plant cells contain them as well.

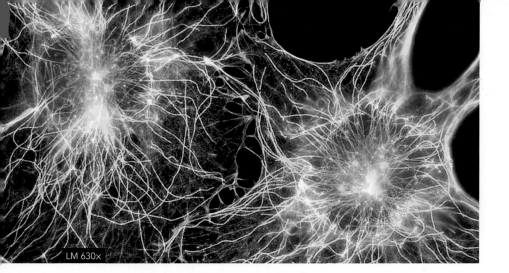

**Figure 8-10**

## Cytoskeleton

The cytoskeleton supports and gives shape to the cell and is involved in many forms of cell movement. These connective tissue fibroblast cells have been treated with fluorescent labels that bind to certain proteins. Microfilaments are pale purple, microtubules are yellow, and the nuclei are green.

**The Cytoskeleton** A factory building is supported by steel or cement beams and by columns that hold up its walls and roof. Eukaryotic cells are given their shape and internal organization by a network of protein filaments known as the **cytoskeleton**. Certain parts of the cytoskeleton also help transport materials between different parts of the cell, much like the conveyor belts that carry materials from one part of a factory to another. Cytoskeletal components may also be involved in moving the entire cell, as in cell flagella and cilia. ⚲ *The cytoskeleton helps the cell maintain its shape and is also involved in movement.* Fluorescence imaging, as seen in **Figure 8-10**, clearly shows the complexity of a cell's cytoskeletal network. Microfilaments (pale purple) and microtubules (yellow) are two of the principal protein filaments that make up the cytoskeleton.

**BUILD VOCABULARY**

**Prefixes** The prefix *cyto-* refers to cells. The cytoskeleton acts like a skeleton for the cell.

*Microfilaments* Microfilaments are threadlike structures made up of a protein called actin. They form extensive networks in some cells and produce a tough, flexible framework that supports the cell. Microfilaments also help cells move. Microfilament assembly and disassembly are responsible for the cytoplasmic movements that allow amoebas and other cells to crawl along surfaces.

*Microtubules* Microtubules are hollow structures made up of proteins known as tubulins. In many cells, they play critical roles in maintaining cell shape. Microtubules are also important in cell division, where they form a structure known as the mitotic spindle, which helps to separate chromosomes. In animal cells, organelles called centrioles are also formed from tubulins. Centrioles are located near the nucleus and help organize cell division. Centrioles are not found in plant cells.

Microtubules also help build projections from the cell surface—known as cilia (singular: cilium) and flagella (singular: flagellum)—that enable cells to swim rapidly through liquid. The microtubules in cilia and flagella are arranged in a "9 + 2" pattern, as shown in **Figure 8-11**. Small cross-bridges between the microtubules in these organelles use chemical energy to pull on, or slide along, the microtubules, producing controlled movements.

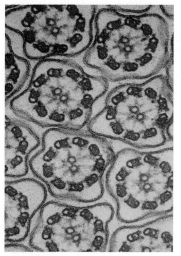

TEM 75,000×

**Figure 8-11**

## The "9 + 2" Pattern of Microtubules

The microtubules in eukaryotic cilia and flagella are arranged in a "9 + 2" pattern. In this micrograph showing the cross section of a group of cilia, you can clearly see the 9 + 2 arrangement of the microtubules.

✔ **READING CHECK** **Use an Analogy** How is a cell's cytoskeleton like the girders and beams of a warehouse?

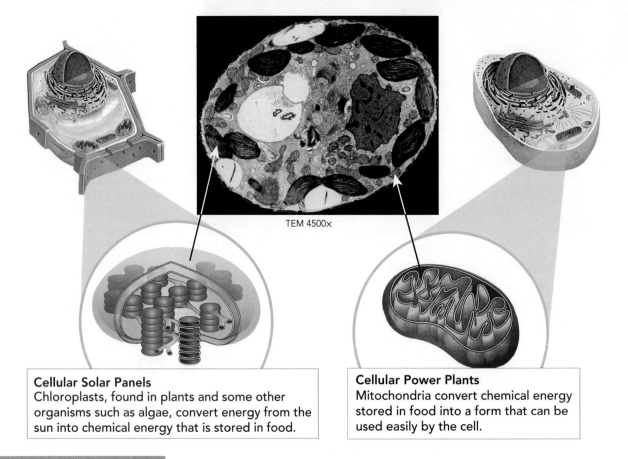

TEM 4500×

**Cellular Solar Panels**
Chloroplasts, found in plants and some other organisms such as algae, convert energy from the sun into chemical energy that is stored in food.

**Cellular Power Plants**
Mitochondria convert chemical energy stored in food into a form that can be used easily by the cell.

# Organelles That Capture and Release Energy

All living things require a source of energy. That makes energy conversion one of the most important processes in the cell. Factories are hooked up to the local power company, but how do cells get their energy? Most cells are powered by food molecules that are built using energy that ultimately comes from sunlight.

**Chloroplasts** Plants and some other organisms contain chloroplasts (KLAWR uh plasts). **Chloroplasts** are the biological equivalents of solar power plants. 🔍 *Chloroplasts capture the energy from sunlight and convert it into chemical energy stored in food during photosynthesis.* Two membranes surround chloroplasts. Inside the organelle are large stacks of other membranes, which contain the green pigment chlorophyll.

**Mitochondria** Nearly all eukaryotic cells, including plants, contain mitochondria (myt oh KAHN dree uh; singular: mitochondrion). **Mitochondria** are the power plants of the cell. 🔍 *Mitochondria convert the chemical energy stored in food molecules into compounds that are more convenient for the cell to use.* Like chloroplasts, two membranes—an outer membrane and an inner membrane—enclose mitochondria. The inner membrane is folded up inside the organelle, as shown in **Figure 8-12**.

**Figure 8-13**

**Lynn Margulis (1938–2011)**

Lynn Margulis hypothesized that chloroplasts and mitochondria are descended from free-living prokaryotes that were engulfed by ancestral eukaryotes.

One of the most interesting aspects of mitochondria is the way in which they are inherited. In humans, all or nearly all of our mitochondria originate from the cytoplasm of the ovum, or egg cell. This means that when your relatives are discussing which side of the family should take credit for your best characteristics, you can tell them that you got your mitochondria from Mom!

Another interesting point: Chloroplasts and mitochondria contain some of their own genetic information in the form of small DNA molecules. This observation led biologist Lynn Margulis, shown in **Figure 8-13**, to suggest that both organelles are descended from prokaryotic cells that once lived independently. Her idea, known as the endosymbiotic theory, is that ancient bacteria and photosynthetic cyanobacteria took up residence inside the earliest eukaryotes. This means that both chloroplasts and our own mitochondria owe their existence to the mutualistic relationship established between these cells more than a billion years ago. It also means that genetic changes in human mitochondria can affect the health of our cells and our bodies. One such change in mitochondrial DNA is responsible for LHON, the disorder described in this chapter's Case Study.

✓ **READING CHECK** **Use an Analogy** How are chloroplasts like solar panels? How are mitochondria like electric power plants?

## Quick Lab

### Open-Ended Inquiry

## How Can You Make a Model of a Cell?

1. Work together as a class to make a room-sized model of a plant cell. Begin by reviewing the structure of the plant cell shown in **Figure 8-16**. With a partner or a small group, choose a cell part or an organelle to model.

2. Using materials of your choice, make a three-dimensional model of the cell part or organelle.

3. Label an index card with the name of your cell structure or organelle. List its main features and functions, including how it interacts with other organelles. Attach the card to your model.

4. Attach your model to an appropriate place in the room. If possible, attach your model to another related cell part or organelle.

### ANALYZE AND CONCLUDE

1. **Calculate** Assume that a typical plant cell is 50 micrometers wide ($50 \times 10^{-6}$ m). Calculate the scale of your classroom cell model. (**Hint:** Divide the width of the classroom by the width of a cell, making sure to use the same units.)

2. **Specify Design Constraints** How is your model cell part or organelle similar to the real cell part or organelle? Describe any design constraints that caused your model cell part or organelle to be different from the real cell part or organelle.

3. **Evaluate Models** Exchange models with another group. Evaluate the strengths and limitations of the model. Use the evaluation to suggest improvements for your model.

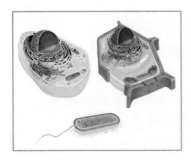

# Cellular Boundaries

A working factory needs walls and a roof to protect it from the environment outside and also to serve as a barrier that keeps its products safe and secure until they are ready to be shipped out. Cells have similar needs, and they meet them in a similar way. As you have learned, all cells are surrounded by a barrier known as the cell membrane. Many cells, including most prokaryotes, also produce a strong supporting layer around the membrane known as a **cell wall**.

**Cell Walls** Many organisms have cell walls that lie just outside their cell membranes. The main function of the cell wall is to support, shape, and protect the cell. Most prokaryotes and many eukaryotes, including plants and fungi, have cell walls, although animal cells do not. Most cell walls are porous enough to allow water, oxygen, carbon dioxide, and certain other substances to pass through easily.

Cell walls provide much of the strength needed for plants to stand against the force of gravity. In trees and other large plants, nearly all of the tissue we call wood is made up of cell walls. The cellulose fiber used for paper as well as the lumber used for building comes from these walls. So if you are reading these words from a sheet of paper in a book resting on a wooden desk, you've got cell walls all around you.

**Cell Membranes** All cells contain cell membranes, generally made up of a double-layered sheet called a lipid bilayer, as shown in **Figure 8-14**. The **lipid bilayer** gives cell membranes a flexible structure that forms a strong barrier between the cell and its surroundings. ✎ *The cell membrane regulates what enters and leaves the cell and also protects and supports the cell.*

**INTERACTIVITY**

Compare and contrast structures in animal and plant cells.

**Figure 8-14**

## Cell Membrane

Every cell has a membrane that regulates the movement of materials. Nearly all cell membranes are made up of a lipid bilayer in which proteins and carbohydrates are embedded.

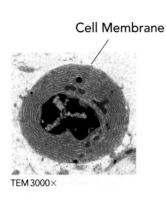

Cell Membrane

TEM 3000×

TEM 1400×

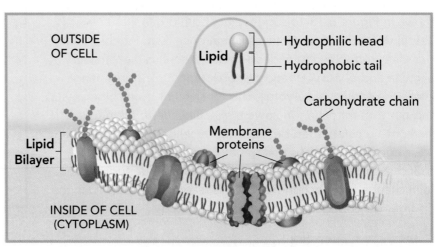

**The Properties of Lipids** The layered structure of cell membranes reflects the chemical properties of the lipids that make them up. You may recall that many lipids have oily fatty acid chains attached to chemical groups that interact strongly with water. In the language of a chemist, the fatty acid portions of this kind of lipid are hydrophobic (hy druh FOH bik), or "water-hating," while the opposite end of the molecule is hydrophilic (hy druh FIL ik), or "water-loving." When these lipids, which are common in cell membranes, are mixed with water, their hydrophobic fatty acid "tails" cluster together, while their hydrophilic "heads" are attracted to water. A lipid bilayer is the result. As you can see in Figure 8-14, the head groups of lipids are exposed on both sides of the membrane, while the fatty acid tails form an oily layer inside the membrane that keeps water from passing across it.

Although many substances can cross cell membranes, some are too large or too strongly charged to cross the lipid bilayer. If a substance is able to cross a membrane, the membrane is said to be permeable to it. A membrane is impermeable to substances that cannot pass across it. Most cell membranes are **selectively permeable**, meaning that some substances can pass across them and others cannot. Selectively permeable membranes are also called semipermeable membranes.

**The Fluid Mosaic Model** Protein molecules are embedded in the lipid bilayer of most cell membranes. Carbohydrate molecules are attached to many of these proteins. Because the proteins embedded in the lipid bilayer can move around and "float" among the lipids, and because so many different kinds of molecules make up the cell membrane, scientists describe the cell membrane as a "fluid mosaic." (A mosaic is a kind of art, such as the example shown in **Figure 8-15**, that involves putting bits and pieces of different colors or materials together.) Some of these proteins form channels and pumps that help to move material across the cell membrane. Many of the carbohydrate molecules act like chemical identification cards, allowing individual cells to identify one another. Some proteins attach directly to the cytoskeleton, enabling cells to respond to their environment by using their membranes to help move or change shape.

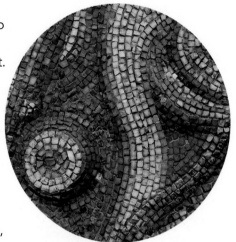

**Figure 8-15**

**Mosaic**

Mosaics are made by assembling small pieces of different colors and types of materials. Similarly, cell membranes are made up of different kinds of molecules.

HS-LS1-1, HS-LS1-2

# ✓ LESSON 8.2 Review

## ⚲ KEY QUESTIONS

1. What are the two major parts of a eukaryotic cell?

2. Describe the steps in making, packaging, and exporting a protein from a cell.

3. Compare the role of vacuoles and lysosomes in a cell.

4. Explain why plant cells require both chloroplasts and mitochondria to meet their energy needs.

5. Explain how the structure of a cell's membrane is related to its function.

## CRITICAL THINKING

6. **Develop a Model** Using Figure 8-16 on the next page as a guide, draw your own models of a prokaryotic cell, a plant cell, and an animal cell. Then use each of the vocabulary words from this lesson to label your cells. Describe any differences between the models in Figure 8-16 and your models.

7. **Cite Evidence** What evidence supports the argument that ancestors of mitochondria and chloroplasts once lived as independent organisms?

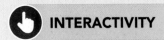
## Visual Summary

**Figure 8-16**

# Comparing Typical Cells

Eukaryotic cells have many different kinds of organelles. Some of these organelles are also found in prokaryotic cells. The table on the facing page compares prokaryotic cells, animal cells, and plant cells.

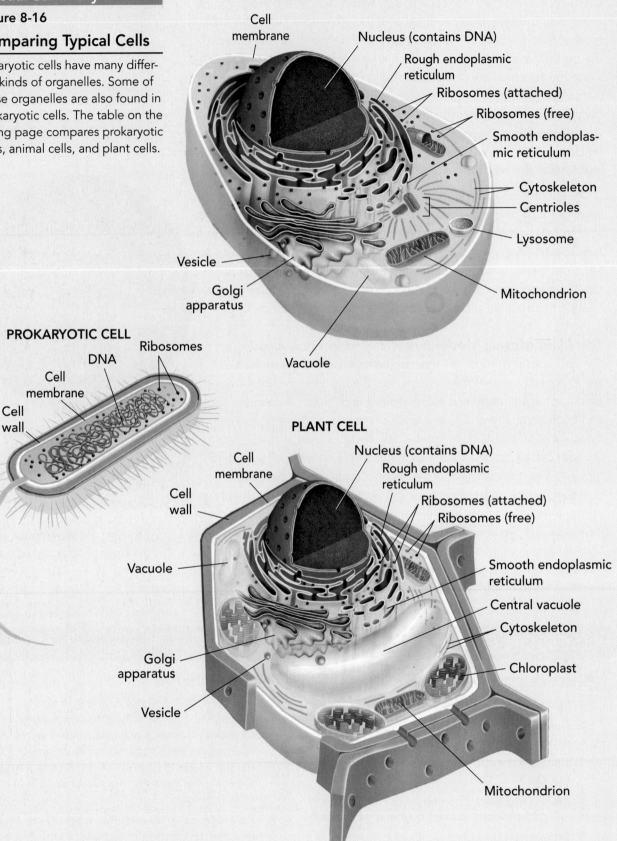

ANIMAL CELL

Cell membrane

Nucleus (contains DNA)

Rough endoplasmic reticulum

Ribosomes (attached)

Ribosomes (free)

Smooth endoplasmic reticulum

Cytoskeleton

Centrioles

Lysosome

Vesicle

Golgi apparatus

Mitochondrion

Vacuole

PROKARYOTIC CELL

DNA

Ribosomes

Cell membrane

Cell wall

PLANT CELL

Cell membrane

Cell wall

Vacuole

Golgi apparatus

Vesicle

Nucleus (contains DNA)

Rough endoplasmic reticulum

Ribosomes (attached)

Ribosomes (free)

Smooth endoplasmic reticulum

Central vacuole

Cytoskeleton

Chloroplast

Mitochondrion

| | Structure | Function | Prokaryote | Eukaryote: | |
|---|---|---|---|---|---|
| | | | | Animal | Plant |
| Cellular Control Center | Nucleus | Contains DNA | Prokaryote DNA is found in cytoplasm. | ✓ | ✓ |
| Organelles That Build Proteins | Ribosomes | Synthesize proteins | ✓ | ✓ | ✓ |
| | Endoplasmic reticulum | Assembles proteins and lipids | | ✓ | ✓ |
| | Golgi apparatus | Modifies, sorts, and packages proteins and lipids for storage or transport out of the cell | | ✓ | ✓ |
| Organelles That Store, Clean-Up, and Support | Vacuoles and vesicles | Store materials | ✓ | ✓ | ✓ |
| | Lysosomes | Break down and recycle macromolecules | | ✓ | ✓ (Rare) |
| | Cytoskeleton | Maintains cell shape; moves cell parts; helps cells move | Prokaryotic cells have protein filaments similar to actin and tubulin | ✓ | ✓ |
| | Centrioles | Organize cell division | | ✓ | |
| Organelles That Capture and Release Energy | Chloroplasts | Convert solar energy to chemical energy stored in food | In some prokaryotic cells, photosynthesis occurs in association with internal photosynthetic membranes. | | ✓ |
| | Mitochondria | Convert chemical energy in food to usable compounds | Prokaryotes carry out these reactions in the cytoplasm rather than in specialized organelles. | ✓ | ✓ |
| Cellular Boundaries | Cell wall | Shapes, supports, and protects the cell | ✓ | | ✓ |
| | Cell membrane | Regulates materials entering and leaving cell; protects and supports cell | ✓ | ✓ | ✓ |

# Cell Transport

🔍 **KEY QUESTIONS**
- *How does passive transport work?*
- *How does active transport work?*

**HS-LS1-2:** Develop and use a model to illustrate the hierarchical organization of interacting systems that provide specific functions within multicellular organisms.

**HS-LS1-3:** Plan and conduct an investigation to provide evidence that feedback mechanisms maintain homeostasis.

## VOCABULARY

**homeostasis**
**diffusion**
**facilitated diffusion**
**aquaporin**
**osmosis**
**isotonic**
**hypertonic**
**hypotonic**
**osmotic pressure**

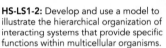

### READING TOOL

As you read, compare and contrast passive and active transport. Complete the Venn Diagram in your 📖 **Biology Foundations Workbook.**

In the previous lesson, we compared cell walls and cell membranes to the roof and walls of a factory. When you think about how cells move materials in and out, it might be more helpful to think of a cell as a nation. The boundaries of a nation are its borders, and nearly every nation tries to regulate and control the goods that move across its borders, like the shipping containers seen here entering and leaving a seaport. Each cell has its own border, which separates the cell from its surroundings and also determines what comes in and what goes out. How can a cell separate itself from its environment and still allow materials to enter and leave? That's where the transport of molecules across its border, the cell membrane, comes in.

## Passive Transport

Every living cell exists in a liquid environment. One of the most important processes carried out by the cell membrane is to keep a cell in homeostasis. **Homeostasis** is a state of relatively constant internal physical and chemical conditions. It does this by regulating the movement of molecules and other substances from one side of the membrane to the other side.

**Diffusion** The cytoplasm consists of many different substances dissolved in water. In any solution, solute particles move constantly. They collide with one another and tend to spread out randomly. As a result, the particles tend to move from an area where they are more concentrated to an area where they are less concentrated. When you add sugar to coffee or tea, for example, the sugar molecules move away from their original positions in the sugar crystals and disperse throughout the hot liquid. The process by which particles move from an area of higher concentration to an area of lower concentration is known as **diffusion** (dih FYOO zhun). Diffusion is the driving force behind the movement of many substances across the cell membrane.

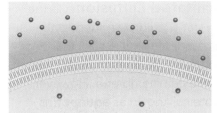

There is a higher concentration of solute on one side of the membrane than on the other.

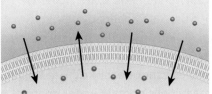

Diffusion causes a net movement of solute particles from the side of the membrane with the higher solute concentration to the side with the lower solute concentration.

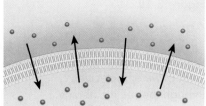

Once equilibrium is reached, solute particles continue to diffuse across the membrane in both directions but at approximately equal rates, so there is no net change in solute concentration.

**Figure 8-17** shows a substance that can cross the cell membrane. Its molecules will tend to move toward the area where it is less concentrated until it is evenly distributed. Equilibrium is reached when the concentration of the substance on both sides of the cell membrane is the same. Even at equilibrium, molecules continue to move across the membrane in both directions. However, there is no further net change in the concentration on either side.

Diffusion depends on random molecular movements. Therefore, substances diffuse across membranes without requiring the cell to use additional energy. ✎ *The movement of molecules across the cell membrane without using cellular energy is called passive transport.*

**Facilitated Diffusion** Since cell membranes are built around lipid bilayers, the molecules that pass through them most easily are small and uncharged. These properties allow them to dissolve in the membrane's lipid environment. But many charged ions, like Cl⁻, and large molecules, like the sugar glucose, seem to pass through cell membranes very quickly, as if they have a shortcut.

How does this happen? Proteins in the cell membrane act as carriers, or channels, making it easy for certain molecules to cross. Red blood cells, for example, have protein carriers that allow the sugar glucose to pass through them in either direction. These channels facilitate, or help, the diffusion of glucose across the membrane. In **facilitated diffusion**, molecules that cannot directly diffuse across the membrane pass through special protein channels. Hundreds of different proteins allow substances to cross cell membranes. Although facilitated diffusion is fast and specific to certain molecules, it is still diffusion, so it does not require any use of the cell's energy.

**✓ READING CHECK Compare** What is the difference between diffusion and facilitated diffusion?

**Figure 8-17**
## Diffusion

Diffusion is the process by which molecules move from an area of higher concentration to an area of lower concentration. The cell does not use energy during this process.

HS-LS1-3

 **Exploration Lab**

### Open-ended Inquiry
## Detecting Diffusion

**Problem** How can you model the diffusion of solutes across a cell membrane?

In this lab, you will use dialysis tubing to model a cell membrane. You will use the model to determine the role of cellular transport in maintaining homeostasis.

You can find this lab in your digital course.

## Figure 8-18
## Aquaporins

Aquaporins assist the movement of water molecules through the cell membrane.

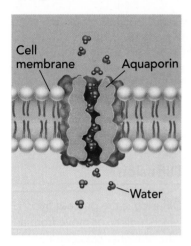

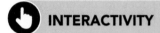

**INTERACTIVITY**

Investigate the movement of water during osmosis.

## Figure 8-19
## Osmosis

Osmosis is a form of facilitated diffusion. **A.** In a laboratory experiment, water moves through a selectively permeable barrier from lower to higher solute concentration. **B.** In the cell, water passes by osmosis through aquaporins embedded in the cell membrane.

## Osmosis: An Example of Facilitated Diffusion

In the 1990s, researchers discovered that water should be added to the list of molecules that enter cells by facilitated diffusion. Recall that the inside of a cell's lipid bilayer is hydrophobic. As a result, water molecules cannot easily diffuse through the cell membrane. However, many cells contain water channel proteins, known as **aquaporins** (ak wuh PAW rinz), that allow water to pass right through them, as shown in **Figure 8-18**. The movement of water through cell membranes by facilitated diffusion plays a role in an extremely important biological process—the process of osmosis.

**Osmosis** is the diffusion of water through a selectively permeable membrane. In osmosis, as in other forms of diffusion, molecules move from an area of higher concentration to an area of lower concentration. The only difference is that the molecules moving in the case of osmosis are water molecules, not solute molecules.

*How Osmosis Works* Look at the experimental setup in **Figure 8-19A**. The barrier is permeable to water but not to sugar. This means that water can cross the barrier in both directions, but sugar cannot. To start, there are more sugar molecules on the right side of the barrier than on the left side. Therefore, the concentration of water is lower on the right, where more of the solution is made of sugar. Although water molecules move in both directions across the membrane, there is a net transport of water toward the concentrated sugar solution. Water will tend to move across the membrane until equilibrium is reached. At that point, the concentrations of water and sugar will be the same on both sides of the membrane. When this happens, the two solutions will be **isotonic**, which means "same strength." Note that "strength" refers to the amount of solute, not water. When the experiment began, the more concentrated sugar solution on the right side of the tube was **hypertonic**, or "above strength," compared to the left side. So the dilute sugar solution was **hypotonic**, or "below strength." **Figure 8-19B** shows how osmosis works across a cell membrane.

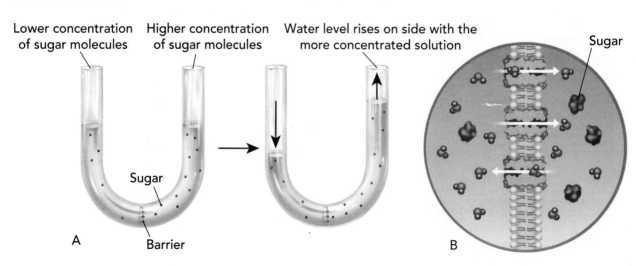

Lower concentration of sugar molecules

Higher concentration of sugar molecules

Water level rises on side with the more concentrated solution

Sugar

Sugar

A

Barrier

B

*Osmotic Pressure* Driven by differences in solute concentration, the net movement of water out of or into a cell produces a force known as **osmotic pressure**. As shown in **Figure 8-20**, osmotic pressure can cause an animal cell in a hypertonic solution to shrink and one in a hypotonic solution to swell. Because cells contain salts, sugars, proteins, and other dissolved molecules, they are almost always hypertonic to fresh water. As a result, water tends to move quickly into a cell surrounded by fresh water, causing it to swell. Eventually, the cell may burst like an overinflated balloon. In plant cells, osmotic <u>pressure</u> can cause changes in the size of the central vacuole, which shrinks or swells as water moves into or out of the cell.

Fortunately, cells in large organisms are not in danger of bursting, because most of them do not come in contact with fresh water. Instead, the cells are bathed in blood or other isotonic fluids. The concentrations of dissolved materials in these isotonic fluids are roughly equal to those in the cells themselves.

What happens when cells do come in contact with fresh water? Some, like the eggs laid in fresh water by fish and frogs, lack water channels. As a result, water moves into them so slowly that osmotic pressure is not a problem. Others, including bacteria and plant cells, are surrounded by tough walls. The cell walls prevent the cells from expanding, even under tremendous osmotic pressure. Notice how the plant cell in Figure 8-20 holds its shape in both hypertonic and hypotonic solutions, but the animal red blood cell does not. However, increased osmotic pressure does make plant cells extremely vulnerable to cell wall injuries.

**READING CHECK Summarize** In your own words, explain why osmosis is really just a special case of facilitated diffusion.

**INTERACTIVITY**

Discover how cell transport occurs in plants when they are exposed to different conditions.

**Figure 8-20**

**Osmotic Pressure**

Different solute concentrations inside and outside of the cell can lead to a net loss or net gain of water.

| | The Effects of Osmosis on Cells | | |
|---|---|---|---|
| **Solution** | **Isotonic:** The concentration of solutes is the same inside and outside the cell. Water molecules move equally in both directions. | **Hypertonic:** The solution has a higher solute concentration than the cell. A net movement of water molecules out of the cell causes it to shrink. | **Hypotonic:** The solution has a lower solute concentration than the cell. A net movement of water molecules into the cell causes it to swell. |
| **Animal Cell** | Water in and out | Water out | Water in |
| **Plant Cell** | Cell membrane / Cell wall / Central vacuole — Water in and out | Water out | Water in |

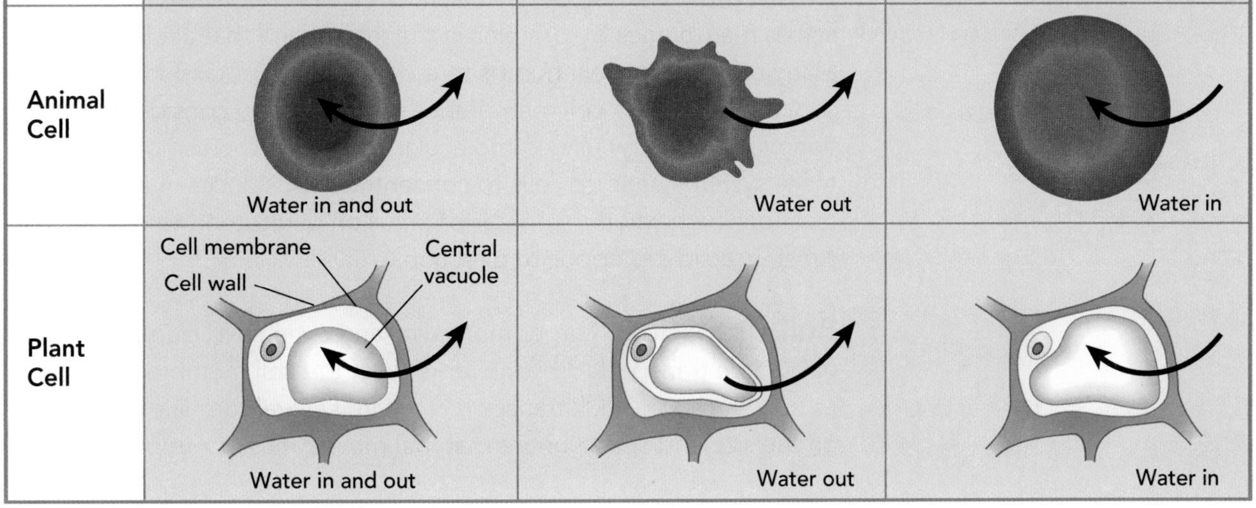

**Protein Pumps**
Energy from ATP is used to pump small molecules and ions across the cell membrane. Active transport proteins change shape during the process, binding substances on one side of the membrane, and releasing them on the other.

**Endocytosis**
The membrane forms a pocket around a particle. The pocket then breaks loose from the cell membrane and forms a vesicle within the cytoplasm.

**Exocytosis**
The membrane of a vesicle surrounds the material then fuses with the cell membrane. The contents are forced out of the cell.

CYTOPLASM

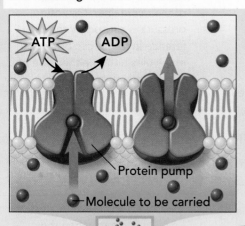
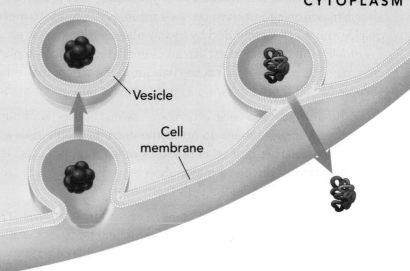

Vesicle

Cell membrane

**ANIMATION**

**Visual Summary**

**Figure 8-21**

**Active Transport**

Energy from the cell is needed to move substances against a concentration difference.

☑ **Compare and Contrast** What are the similarities and differences between facilitated diffusion and active transport by a protein pump?

# Active Transport

Although diffusion is useful, cells sometimes must transport materials against a concentration difference. ⚭ *The movement of materials against a concentration difference is known as active transport, and it requires energy.* The active transport of small molecules or ions across a cell membrane is generally carried out by transport proteins—protein pumps—that are found in the membrane. Larger molecules and clumps of material can also be actively transported across the cell membrane by processes known as endocytosis and exocytosis. The transport of these larger materials sometimes involves changes in the shape of the cell membrane. The major types of active transport are shown in **Figure 8-21**.

**Molecular Transport** Small molecules and ions are carried across membranes by proteins in the membrane that act like pumps. Many cells use protein pumps to move calcium, potassium, and sodium ions across cell membranes. Cells spend a considerable portion of their energy use on molecular transport. The use of energy in these systems enables cells to concentrate substances in a particular location, even when the forces of diffusion might tend to move these substances in the opposite direction.

**Bulk Transport** Larger molecules and even solid clumps of material can be transported by movements of the cell membrane known as bulk transport. Bulk transport can take several forms, depending on the size and shape of the material moved into or out of the cell.

**Endocytosis** Endocytosis (en doh sy TOH sis) is the process of taking material into the cell by means of infoldings, or pockets, of the cell membrane. Figure 8-21 shows how the pocket that results breaks loose from the cell membrane and forms a vesicle or vacuole within the cytoplasm. Large molecules, clumps of food, and even whole cells can be taken up in this way.

Phagocytosis (fag oh sy TOH sis) is a type of endocytosis in which extensions of cytoplasm surround a particle and package it within a food vacuole. The cell then engulfs it. White blood cells use phagocytosis to remove damaged or foreign cells and destroy them. Amoebas use this method for taking in food, as shown in **Figure 8-22**. Engulfing material in this way requires a considerable amount of energy and is considered a form of active transport.

Many cells take up liquid from the surrounding environment in a process similar to phagocytosis. During a type of endocytosis called pinocytosis (py nuh sy TOH sis), tiny pockets form along the cell membrane, fill with liquid, and pinch off to form vacuoles.

**Exocytosis** Many cells also release large amounts of material, a process known as exocytosis (ek soh sy TOH sis). During exocytosis, the membrane of the vesicle or vacuole surrounding the material fuses with the cell membrane, forcing the contents out of the cell. The removal of water by means of a contractile vacuole is one example of this kind of active transport.

From its simple beginnings, life has spread to every corner of our planet, penetrating deep below Earth's surface and far beneath the surface of the seas. The diversity of life is so great that you might have to remind yourself that all living things are composed of cells, have the same basic chemical makeup, and even contain the same kinds of organelles. This does not mean that all living things are the same. As you'll discover in Lesson 8.4, differences arise from the ways in which cells are specialized and the ways in which cells associate with one another to form multicellular organisms.

## Figure 8-22
## Phagocytosis

An amoeba (blue) is consuming an algal cell using phagocytosis. The amoeba will surround the algal cell. Then chemicals inside the amoeba will break down the algal cell for nutrients and energy.

TEM 3000x

**READING TOOL**

Without using the word *endocytosis*, summarize how a white blood cell would engulf a damaged cell.

HS-LS1-2, HS-LS1-3

# ✓ LESSON 8.3 Review

### 🔍 KEY QUESTIONS

1. Describe how molecules enter and leave a cell without the use of the cell's energy.

2. Describe the two major types of active transport.

### CRITICAL THINKING

3. **Construct an Explanation** Water molecules diffuse through the cell membrane through aquaporins. How are these proteins helpful in osmosis?

4. **Apply Scientific Reasoning** How are the transport problems of a freshwater organism different from those of a saltwater organism?

5. **Develop Models** A student draws a fence with several gates as part of a model of cellular transport. Explain what the fence and the gates represent, relating their structures to their functions. Explain how the model could represent both active transport using protein pumps and facilitated diffusion.

# Homeostasis and Cells

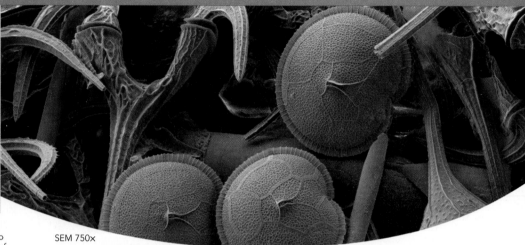

SEM 750×

Cells are the basic living units of all organisms, but sometimes a single cell actually is the organism. In fact, in terms of their numbers, unicellular organisms dominate life on Earth. This false-color micrograph shows a type of plankton (in blue). Plankton are unicellular marine organisms that do everything you would expect a living thing to do.

## The Cell as an Organism

Just like other living things, unicellular organisms must maintain homeostasis, relatively constant internal physical and chemical conditions. 🔍 *To maintain homeostasis, unicellular organisms grow, respond to the environment, transform energy, and reproduce.*

Unicellular organisms include both prokaryotes and eukaryotes. Prokaryotes, especially bacteria, are remarkably adaptable. Bacteria live almost everywhere—in the soil, on leaves, in the ocean, in the air, even within the human body.

Many eukaryotes, like amoebas and many algae, also live as single cells. Yeasts, or unicellular fungi, are common worldwide. Yeasts play an important role in breaking down complex nutrients, making them available for other organisms. People use yeasts to make bread and other foods.

Prokaryote or eukaryote, homeostasis is still an issue for each unicellular organism. A tiny cell in a pond or on the surface of your pencil still needs to find sources of energy or food, to keep concentrations of water and minerals within certain levels, and to respond quickly to changes in its environment. The microscopic world around us is filled with unicellular organisms that successfully maintain homeostatic balance.

# Multicellular Life

Unlike most unicellular organisms, the cells of humans and other multicellular organisms do not live on their own. They are interdependent. Like the members of a baseball team, they work together. In baseball, each player occupies a particular position: pitcher, catcher, infielder, outfielder. To play the game effectively, players and coaches communicate with one another by sending and receiving signals. Cells in a multicellular organism work the same way. ⚲ *The cells of multicellular organisms become specialized for particular tasks and communicate with one another to maintain homeostasis.*

**Cell Specialization** Although we each began life as a single cell, that cell grew and divided to give rise to many other cells. The new cells became specialized, with different cell types playing different roles. Some cells became specialized to move. Other cells react to the environment. Still other cells produce substances needed by the rest of the body. No matter what its role, each specialized cell contributes to homeostasis in a multicellular organism.

☑ **READING CHECK** **Compare** How does homeostasis compare between unicellular and multicellular organisms?

**INTERACTIVITY**

Learn about cell differentiation and cell specialization.

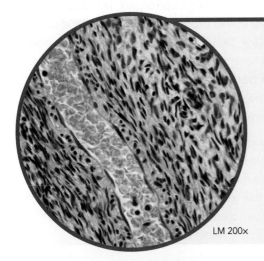

LM 200x

***Specialized Animal Cells*** All of your cells need oxygen, and they release carbon dioxide as waste. Carrying gases to and from the body is the job of red blood cells, which are shown in pink in the micrograph. These cells flow through blood vessels of varying lengths and widths. In this micrograph, the cells in the wall of the blood vessel and surrounding tissue are stained purple. Notice that the vessel is wide enough for many red blood cells to pass together. The path through the narrowest vessels, called capillaries, is only as wide as a single red blood cell.

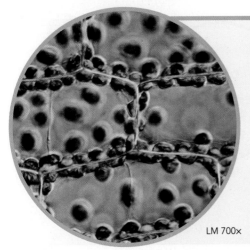

LM 700x

***Specialized Plant Cells*** This micrograph shows plant cells that contain many green, oval-shaped structures. These structures are chloroplasts, the organelles where photosynthesis occurs. Specialized cells with numerous chloroplasts typically make up the leaves of most plants. Cells in other plant parts have few if any chloroplasts, and are specialized for other purposes. Root cells have tiny hairs on their outer layer, which help take in water. In some flowers, certain cells are specialized for making sweet-smelling nectar, which attracts animal pollinators.

## CASE STUDY  Analyzing Data

### Mitochondria in a Mouse

Some cells have more mitochondria than others. Scientists isolated the mitochondria from mouse cells and then calculated the percentage of the cell that mitochondria would fill by volume. The greater the percentage, the more mitochondria in the cell. The bar graph shows the results.

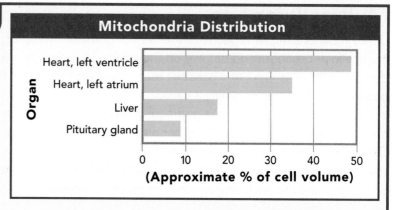

**Mitochondria Distribution**

Organ: Heart, left ventricle; Heart, left atrium; Liver; Pituitary gland

(Approximate % of cell volume) — 0, 10, 20, 30, 40, 50

1. **Interpret Graphs**  Compare the distribution of mitochondria in the four organs, or organ parts, shown in the graph.

2. **Draw Conclusions**  How is it useful for organisms to have an uneven distribution of mitochondria among their cells?

3. **Infer**  Which of these tissues would be most vulnerable to problems caused by defective mitochondria? Explain.

---

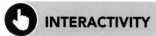

**READING TOOL**

Draw a concept map to model the levels of organization. Use the model to illustrate the interactions between cells, tissues, organs, and an organ system.

**👆 INTERACTIVITY**

**Figure 8-23**

**Levels of Organization**

Nerve cells, or neurons, make up nerve tissue. Tissues combine to make up organs, such as the brain. The brain, spinal cord, and nerves make up the nervous system.

**Levels of Organization**  The specialized cells of multicellular organisms are organized into tissues, then into organs, and finally into organ systems, as shown in **Figure 8-23**. A **tissue** is a group of similar cells that perform a particular function. Many tasks in the body are too complicated to be carried out by just one type of tissue. In these cases, many groups of tissues work together as an **organ**. For example, the brain is an individual organ. It is made of nerve tissue, as well as fat tissue and blood vessels. Each type of tissue performs an essential task to help the organ function. In most cases, an organ completes a series of specialized tasks. A group of organs that work together to perform a specific function is called an **organ system**. For example, the brain, spinal cord, and nerves throughout the body work together as the nervous system.

The organization of the body's cells into tissues, organs, and organ systems creates a division of labor among those cells that allows the organism to maintain homeostasis. Specialization and interdependence are two of the remarkable attributes of living things. Appreciating these characteristics is an important step in understanding the nature of living things.

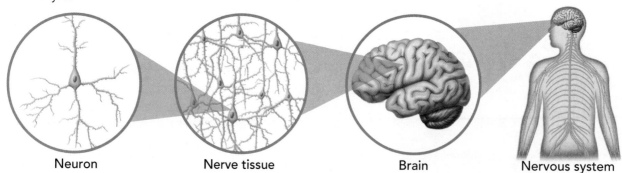

Neuron      Nerve tissue      Brain      Nervous system

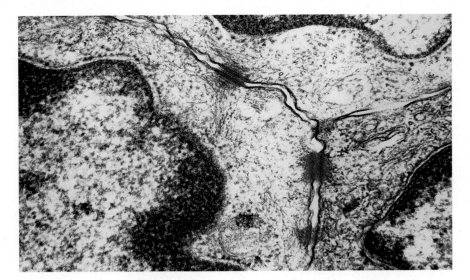

**Figure 8-24**

**Cellular Junctions**

Some cellular junctions hold cells together in tight formations. This micrograph shows junctions between epithelial cells in the human body. (TEM 47,500×).

**Cellular Communication** Cells in a large organism communicate by means of chemical signals that are passed from one cell to another. These cellular signals can speed up or slow down the activities of the cells that receive them and can even cause a cell to change what it is doing in a most dramatic way.

Certain cells in the heart, the liver, and other organs form connections, or cellular junctions, to neighboring cells. Some of these junctions, such as those shown in **Figure 8-24**, hold cells together firmly. Others allow small molecules carrying chemical messages or signals to pass directly from one cell to the next. To respond to one of these chemical signals, a cell must have a **receptor** to which the signaling molecule can bind. Some receptors are on the cell membrane. Receptors for other types of signals are inside the cytoplasm.

In many animals, impulses carried by nerve cells, or neurons, carry messages rapidly from one part of the body to another. An example is the optic nerve, which carries visual information from the eye to the brain. A steady supply of energy, produced by mitochondria, is necessary to keep neurons functioning. Without enough energy, neurons may fail to function and even die. This is what happens as a result of the defective mitochondria caused by LHON.

▶ **VIDEO**

Explore how cystic fibrosis starts as a problem with cell transport that leads to problems with homeostasis at the organism level.

**BUILD VOCABULARY**

**Related Words** The term **receptor** is related to the verb *receive*, which means "to accept or take." A receptor accepts and responds to molecular signals.

HS-LS1-2, HS-LS1-3

## ☑ LESSON 8.4 Review

### ⚗ KEY QUESTIONS

1. In what ways do single-celled organisms maintain homeostasis?

2. What are two ways the cells of multicellular organisms enable the organism to maintain homeostasis?

### CRITICAL THINKING

3. **Construct an Argument** Give three reasons supported by the text that "specialization and interdependence" could be considered the keys to homeostasis in a multicellular organism.

4. **Evaluate a Model** Review Figure 8-23. How well does the diagram represent the levels of organization of multicellular organisms? How could the model be improved?

5. **Use Analogies** Think of an example from your own life such as school, sports, or an extracurricular activity. Develop an analogy to explain why specialization and communication are as important to that activity as they are to a cell.

6. **CASE STUDY** Explain the relationship among homeostasis, defective mitochondria, and the symptoms caused by LHON.

# What's happening to me?

**LHON is an inherited mitochondrial disorder. How could a mitochondrial defect be related to vision and heart problems?**

HS-LS1-1, CCSS.ELA-LITERACY.RST.9-10.1, CCSS.ELA-LITERACY.RST.9-10.7

## Make Your Case

Mitochondria are organelles in cells throughout the body. LHON is caused by a defect in mitochondrial DNA that affects their function as energy-generating organelles. How might this be linked to the symptoms of LHON? And how might it be possible to prevent this disorder from being passed from parent to child?

## Construct an Explanation

1. **Cite Evidence** Although the genes that cause LHON are found in cells throughout the body, LHON especially affects specific cells in the eyes and heart. Why do you think that tissues with these cells are among the first to fail as a result of defective mitochondria? Cite evidence from the text to support your claim.

2. **Construct an Explanation** Draw an illustration that explains the procedure described in Technology on the Case. Then, using your illustration and evidence from the text, construct an explanation for how this procedure prevents the transmission of LHON from one generation to the next.

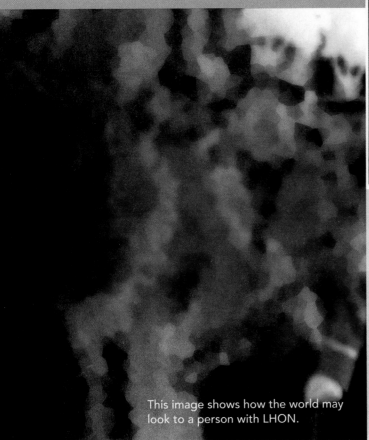

This image shows how the world may look to a person with LHON.

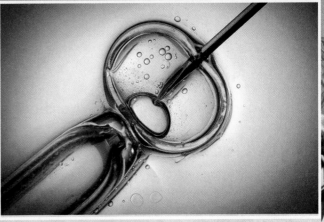

## Technology on the Case

### Stopping LHON Before It Starts

In vitro fertilization (IVF) is a technique many couples have used to help them have children. Sperm from the father are mixed with an egg cell from the mother in the laboratory. If fertilization is successful, the growing cluster of cells is implanted into the mother's uterus, where it develops into a baby. Scientists have used this technique to develop a way to prevent mitochondrial diseases from being passed from mother to child.

The method involves removing the nucleus from an egg cell and transferring it to the cytoplasm of an egg cell from a third parent: a female donor with healthy mitochondria. That egg cell is then fertilized with sperm from the father, and implanted back into the mother who provided the egg nucleus as it develops.

If the procedure is successful, the child that results will inherit nearly all of his or her genes from the mother and father, but the mitochondrial DNA (0.2% of all DNA) will come from the cytoplasm donor. In 2016, the first baby was born who was the result of this technique.

The United Kingdom has approved this technique to help women at risk of passing mitochondrial disorders to their offspring. While this practice might indeed help to eliminate such disorders, it also raises moral and ethical issues. The technique allows physicians to make permanent, heritable changes to human beings.

## Careers on the Case

### Work Toward a Solution

New technologies sometimes raise complex societal issues. Many careers combine both knowledge and understanding of cells and ethics.

### Bioethicist

As medical technology develops, serious ethical and moral issues often arise. Bioethicists are trained to deal with issues involving biology, philosophy, and moral reasoning. They advise medical institutions and government agencies on questions of ethics.

 **VIDEO**

Learn more about careers in bioethics and related fields.

# Lesson Review
Go to your Biology Foundations Workbook for longer versions of these lesson summaries.

## 8.1 Life Is Cellular

The smallest living unit of any organism is the cell. Most cells can be seen only with the aid of a microscope. The cell theory states that all living things are made up of cells; cells are the basic units of structure and function in living things; and new cells are produced from existing cells.

Cells were discovered in the 1600s. As microscopes were improved, scientists learned about the parts of the cell and how cells function. Today, electron microscopes can show cell structures as small as 1 billionth of a meter wide.

All cells contain DNA at some point and are surrounded by a cell membrane. Eukaryotic cells are usually larger and more complex than prokaryotic cells. In eukaryotic cells, the nucleus separates the genetic material from the rest of the cell. Prokaryotic cells do not have a nucleus.

- cell
- cell theory
- cell membrane
- nucleus
- eukaryote
- prokaryote

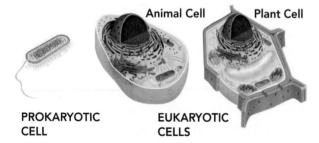

Animal Cell      Plant Cell

PROKARYOTIC CELL      EUKARYOTIC CELLS

☑ **Compare and Contrast** How are the three types of cells shown here alike? How are they different?

## 8.2 Cell Structure

All cells have specialized structures called organelles. Eukaryotic cells have a nucleus, which contains nearly all the cell's DNA and is the control center of the cell. Proteins are assembled on the ribosomes. Cell membrane proteins and lipids are made in association with the endoplasmic reticulum. The Golgi apparatus sorts and packages proteins and other materials from the endoplasmic reticulum for use inside or outside the cell.

Vacuoles store water, salts, proteins, and carbohydrates. Lysosomes contain enzymes to break down these nutrients in the cell. The cytoskeleton maintains shape in eukaryotic cells and is involved in movement.

In plant cells, chloroplasts use sunlight to produce energy rich compounds. Mitochondria convert chemical energy into compounds the cell can use.

Cell walls surround cell membranes and support and protect plant, fungal, and prokaryotic cells. Cell membranes, which regulate the substances that enter and leave the cell, are made up of a flexible lipid bilayer and are selectively permeable.

- cytoplasm
- organelle
- ribosome
- endoplasmic reticulum
- Golgi apparatus
- vacuole
- lysosome
- cytoskeleton
- chloroplast
- mitochondrion
- cell wall
- lipid bilayer
- selectively permeable

☑ **Use Visuals** Write a caption to accompany this art piece. The caption should include the ultimate product produced by these three structures and their individual functions.

## 8.3 Cell Transport

Homeostasis refers to the relatively constant internal physical and chemical conditions of an organism. The cell membrane regulates substances that move across it. The movement of molecules across the cell membrane without the use of energy is called passive transport. During diffusion, substances move from an area of higher concentration to an area of lower concentration. During facilitated diffusion, molecules move through protein channels in the cell membrane.

Water moves through channels called aquaporins during osmosis. When the solutions on either side of a membrane are the same in concentration, they are isotonic. A more concentrated solution is hypertonic; a more dilute solution is hypotonic.

The movement of material against a concentration difference requires energy and is called active transport. Molecular transport of small molecules is carried out by proteins in the cell membrane. Larger molecules enter the cell by endocytosis and exit the cell by exocytosis.

- homeostasis
- diffusion
- facilitated diffusion
- aquaporin
- osmosis
- isotonic
- hypertonic
- hypotonic
- osmotic pressure

☑**Identify Patterns** What do all forms of active transport have in common?

## 8.4 Homeostasis and Cells

Like other living things, unicellular organisms must maintain homeostasis. To do so, they grow, respond to the environment, use energy, and reproduce. There are both prokaryotic and eukaryotic unicellular organisms. Unicellular eukaryotes include protists, some algae, and some fungi.

In multicellular organisms, such as plants and animals, cells become specialized to perform specific tasks. The different cells communicate and work with each other to maintain homeostasis.

Specialized cells are organized into tissues, organs, and organ systems. A tissue is a group of similar cells that perform a function. An organ is made up of many groups of tissues that work together. An organ system is composed of a group of organs that work together to carry out a task.

- tissue
- organ
- organ system
- receptor

☑**Synthesize Information** How is the pumping action of contractile vacuoles an example of how a cell maintains homeostasis?

# Organize Information

Complete the concept map by listing the cell structures that are involved in each function.

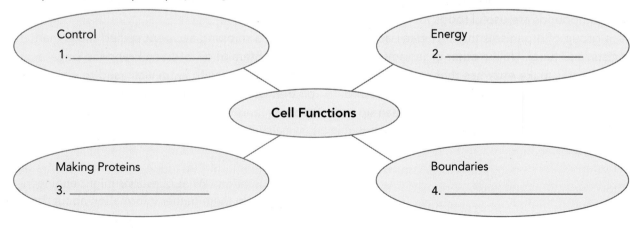

Control
1. _____

Energy
2. _____

**Cell Functions**

Making Proteins
3. _____

Boundaries
4. _____

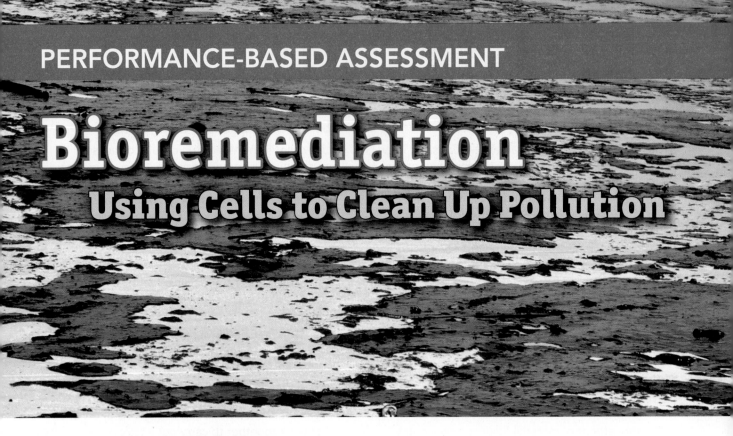

# Bioremediation
## Using Cells to Clean Up Pollution

## Evaluate a Solution

HS-ETS1-3, HS-LS1-7, HS-LS4-6, CCSS.ELA-LITERACY.WHST.9-10.4, CCSS.ELA-LITERACY.WHST.9-10.8

**STEM** As you read in this chapter, all cells break apart food molecules to gain energy. Have you ever wondered which molecules are useful as food, and which molecules are not useful? For many cells, useful foods come in a wider variety than you might guess.

Consider cellulose and lignin, two compounds that provide the toughness in wood, leaves, and other plant parts. Humans and most other animals lack the enzymes to break apart cellulose and lignin, which is why you cannot live on a diet of paper scraps and wood shavings. However, both compounds are useful foods for decomposers, a group of organisms that includes bacteria, protists, and fungi. Unlike other organisms, the decomposers make enzymes that can break apart the chemical bonds that hold cellulose and lignin together. Their actions serve to clean up dead wood, fallen leaves, and other discarded plant parts.

Today, scientists and engineers are finding new uses for the "clean up" abilities of bacteria, protists, and fungi. One of these uses is the cleaning up of pollutants and toxic wastes! The term *bioremediation* is used to describe any clean-up process that involves living things. Some bacteria can remove heavy metals, such as lead, from a contaminated area. Fungi are useful for bioremediation because of the powerful enzymes they release. The enzymes can break apart pesticides, dyes, and toxic byproducts from paper-making and other industrial processes. Some fungi can be used to absorb oil from an oil spill.

In 2007, a shipping accident spilled more than 190,000 liters of oil into San Francisco Bay. Bioremediation with fungi was used to clean up oil that washed ashore. Study the steps of the process, and then answer the questions.

1. **Define the Problem** What problem is this solution addressing?

2. **Ask Questions** What questions might engineers ask to help them gather information about the problem and any potential solution?

How can hair and oyster mushrooms be used to clean up this beach?

## BIOREMEDIATION WITH OYSTER MUSHROOMS

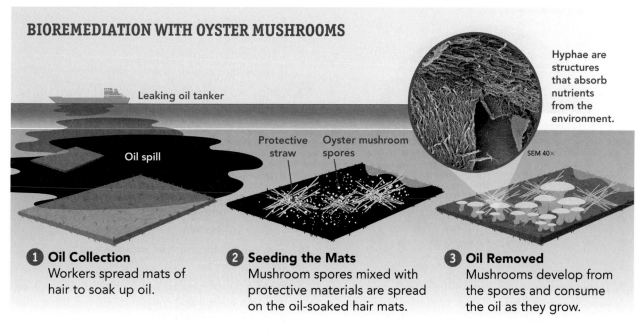

Leaking oil tanker

Oil spill

Protective straw

Oyster mushroom spores

Hyphae are structures that absorb nutrients from the environment.

SEM 40×

**1 Oil Collection**
Workers spread mats of hair to soak up oil.

**2 Seeding the Mats**
Mushroom spores mixed with protective materials are spread on the oil-soaked hair mats.

**3 Oil Removed**
Mushrooms develop from the spores and consume the oil as they grow.

3. **Conduct Research** Look online for more information about the use of bioremediation, either to clean up oil spills or for other purposes. Compare the benefits and drawbacks of a bioremediation solution with those of other types of solutions that engineers proposed or considered.

4. **Communicate** Write a one-page essay or develop a computer presentation to share your findings. Address the following questions, as well as other questions that you researched.

- How well do you think bioremediation achieves the goal of cleaning up pollution?

- What are the costs and benefits of the bioremediation solution that you researched?

- Scientists have used genetic technology to develop strains of bacteria that are especially suited for cleaning up oil spills. How would you evaluate the use of this technology for this purpose?

# ☑ASSESSMENT

## ✍ KEY QUESTIONS AND TERMS

### 8.1 Life Is Cellular

HS-LS1-2

1. Despite differences in size and shape, at some point all cells have DNA and a
   a. cell wall.      c. mitochondrion.
   b. cell membrane.      d. nucleus.

2. German scientists Schleiden and Schwann determined that the basic unit of structure and function in living things is the
   a. atom.      c. cell.
   b. molecule.      d. nucleus.

3. What basic concept of biology includes the idea that new cells can be produced only by the division of existing cells?

4. How does a light microscope work?

5. Why are microscopes useful tools in biology?

6. Identify evidence that this micrograph is from a scanning electron microscope.

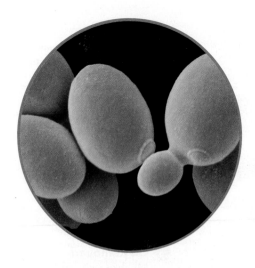

7. If you wanted to observe a living organism—an amoeba for example—which type of microscope would you use?

8. In what important way are prokaryotic cells and eukaryotic cells different?

## 8.2 Cell Structure

HS-LS1-1, HS-LS1-2

9. The portion of the cell outside the nucleus is called the
   a. organelle.      c. nucleolus.
   b. cytoplasm.      d. ribosome.

10. Proteins are assembled on
    a. ribosomes.      c. lysosomes.
    b. vacuoles.      d. centrioles.

11. Which of the following structures convert light energy into chemical energy stored in food?

    a.       c.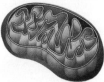

    b.       d.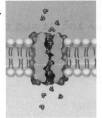

12. Which organelles are known as the "power plants" of the cell because they transfer chemical energy from food to compounds the cell can use?
    a. mitochondria
    b. ribosomes
    c. lysosomes
    d. vacuoles

13. Which two organelles are involved in the movement of a cell in its environment?
    a. microtubules and centrioles
    b. flagella and cilia
    c. centrioles and the cell wall
    d. cytoskeleton and lysosomes

14. Identify the structural and functional differences between the rough endoplasmic reticulum and the smooth endoplasmic reticulum.

15. How are the functions of vacuoles and lysosomes different?

16. What is the process by which chloroplasts capture the sun's energy and convert it into food that contains chemical energy?

17. What is the function of the Golgi apparatus?

18. What is the function of the cytoskeleton?

19. Describe the structure of the cell membrane.

20. For each of the following, indicate if the structure is found only in eukaryotes, or if it is found in eukaryotes and prokaryotes: cell membrane, mitochondria, ribosome, Golgi apparatus, nucleus, cytoplasm, and DNA.

## 8.3 Cell Transport

HS-LS1-2, HS-LS1-3

**21.** The relatively constant internal physical and chemical conditions that all organisms must maintain to survive is known as

**a.** osmosis.      **c.** homeostasis.
**b.** endocytosis.      **d.** exocytosis.

**22.** Solute particles move from an area of higher concentration to an area of lower concentration in a process called

**a.** osmosis.      **c.** diffusion.
**b.** transport.      **d.** equilibrium.

**23.** Large molecules such as glucose move across cell membranes through special protein channels during

**a.** active transport.
**b.** facilitated diffusion.
**c.** osmosis.
**d.** bulk transport.

**24.** What is the term that describes the diffusion of water through a selectively permeable membrane?

**25.** Explain why cells are almost always hypertonic to fresh water.

**26.** What is the main difference between passive transport and active transport of materials across a cell membrane?

**27.** What are the two types of active transport, and how do they differ?

## 8.4 Homeostasis and Cells

HS-LS1-2, HS-LS1-3

**28.** Which type of organism consists of specialized cells?

**a.** unicellular prokaryotes
**b.** multicellular prokaryotes
**c.** unicellular eukaryotes
**d.** multicellular eukaryotes

**29.** All unicellular organisms

**a.** are prokaryotes.
**b.** are bacteria.
**c.** reproduce.
**d.** have a nucleus.

**30.** In what way does specialization of cells contribute to maintaining homeostasis in multicellular organisms?

**31.** Describe the levels of organization in a multicellular organism.

**32.** In general, how do cells in a multicellular organism communicate?

## CRITICAL THINKING

HS-LS1-1, HS-LS1-2, HS-LS1-3

**33.** **Evaluate Models** Cells are often compared to factories. How is a factory a useful model for explaining the cell?

**34.** **Evaluate Reasoning** A student is asked to classify examples of cells based on prepared microscope slides. The student classifies the cells according to their most prominent color. Evaluate the student's classification scheme.

**35.** **Construct an Explanation** In a multicellular organism, the DNA in every cell is essentially the same. How does the cell theory help explain this?

**36.** **Apply Scientific Reasoning** The beaker shown here has a membrane that separates two solutions. Water can pass through the membrane, but starch cannot pass through it. How will the fluid levels change over time? Explain your prediction.

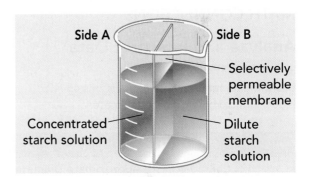

**37.** **Critique** In constructing a model of a plant cell, a student surrounds the model with plastic bricks. The bricks represent the cell wall. How could the model be improved to represent the cell wall more accurately?

**38.** **Synthesize Information** Why is intercellular communication essential for a multicellular organism to function properly?

**39.** **Infer** Pacemakers are devices that help keep heart muscles contracting at a steady rate. If a person needs a pacemaker, what does that suggest about his or her heart cells' ability to send and receive messages?

**40.** **Plan an Investigation** You want to know how temperature affects the rate of diffusion. Describe an investigation that would provide evidence to support a conclusion. Include simple materials such as water and food coloring.

## CROSSCUTTING CONCEPTS

**41. Connect to Nature of Science** What are the statements of the cell theory? Based on what you learned in Chapter 1, describe how the history of its development is typical of the process of science.

**42. Systems and System Models** The nucleus of the cell is often compared to the control center or main office of a factory. How is this model accurate? What are its limitations?

**43. Structure and Function** Why are cell walls useful in plant cells but not animal cells?

**44. Scale, Proportion, and Quantity** Review Figure 8-23, which shows the levels of organization in the human body. Use your own words to define levels of organization in a way that applies to all multicellular organisms.

## MATH CONNECTIONS

## Analyze and Interpret Data

CCSS.MATH.CONTENT.HSN.Q.A.1

Use the data table to answer questions 45–47.

**Note:** 1 micrometer (µm) = $10^{-6}$ meter

| Cell Sizes | |
|---|---|
| **Cell** | **Approximate Diameter** |
| *Escherichia coli* (bacterium) | 0.5–0.8 µm |
| Human erythrocyte (red blood cell) | 6–8 µm |
| Human ovum (egg cell) | 100 µm |
| *Saccharomyces cerevisiae* (yeast) | 5–10 µm |
| *Streptococcus pneumoniae* (bacterium) | 0.5–1.3 µm |

**45. Interpret Data** Classify each of the cells listed in the table as either prokaryotic or eukaryotic.

**46. Calculate** The width of a human hair is about 17 micrometers. How many human erythrocytes could fit across the width of a hair? How many *E. coli* bacteria could fit?

**47. Infer** *Chlamydomonas reinhardtii* is a single-celled organism with an approximate diameter of 10 µm. Is the organism more likely to be a prokaryote or a eukaryote? Explain.

Most materials entering the cell pass across the cell membrane by diffusion. In general, the larger the molecule, the slower the molecule diffuses across the membrane. The graph shows the sizes of several molecules that can diffuse across a lipid bilayer. Use the graph to answer questions 48 and 49.

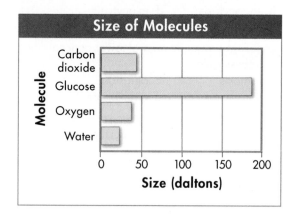

**48. Calculate** By approximately what percentage is a molecule of carbon dioxide smaller than a molecule of glucose?

**49. Predict** Which of the following is a logical prediction based on the graph shown? Explain.
   **a.** Cells contain more glucose than oxygen.
   **b.** Glucose molecules must cross the cell membrane by active transport.
   **c.** Carbon dioxide crosses the cell membrane faster than glucose.

## LANGUAGE ARTS CONNECTIONS

## Write About Science

CCSS.ELA-LITERACY.WHST.9-10.2

**50. Produce Clear Writing** Write a paragraph that defines and describes the cell theory. Include a familiar organism, such as a tree or a cat, as an example to illustrate the theory.

**51. Write Informative Texts** Write a paragraph that describes how cell parts work together to assemble proteins.

## Read About Science

CCSS.ELA-LITERACY.RST.9-10.7

**52. Integrate With Visuals** Choose one of the cell diagrams from the chapter and its accompanying passage. How does the diagram illustrate the structures and functions described in the passage? How does the diagram support other information in the chapter?

1. A student is developing a model that shows the steps of protein synthesis. The model should include activities in which three structures?
   A. ribosomes, rough endoplasmic reticulum, Golgi apparatus
   B. nucleus, Golgi apparatus, mitochondria
   C. mitochondria, rough endoplasmic reticulum, nucleus
   D. Golgi apparatus, nucleus, lysosome
   E. nucleus, cytoskeleton, cell membrane

2. This model of a plant cell shows the structures that are likely to be observed in a typical plant cell. Cells from actual plants may differ from the model if the cells are specialized for specific functions.

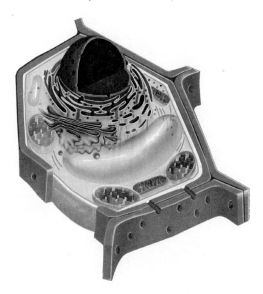

   How could this model be changed to best represent a specialized leaf cell?
   A. Remove the cell wall because only cells in plant stems have cell walls.
   B. Remove the mitochondria because leaf cells don't need much energy.
   C. Add tiny hairs because leaf cells need to take in water.
   D. Add chloroplasts because leaves are where photosynthesis occurs.
   E. Remove the cell membrane because a leaf cell has a cell wall instead of a cell membrane.

3. Which of the following processes is directly controlled by the cell nucleus?
   A. Osmosis because the nucleus has nuclear pores that allow water to move in and out.
   B. Energy production because the nucleus contains mitochondria.
   C. Cell membrane assembly because the cell membrane is made from the nuclear envelope.
   D. Waste removal because a steady stream of molecules moves out of the nucleus.
   E. Protein synthesis because DNA in the nucleus contains the instructions for making proteins.

4. In an investigation, plant cells are placed in water that has been tinted blue. The investigators observe the color of the cells changing to blue. What additional observation would be evidence that the cells maintain homeostasis in response to this change?
   A. The cells burst apart.
   B. The cell membranes shrinks away from the cell walls.
   C. The central vacuole in the cells increases in size.
   D. The cells pumps out water by endocytosis.
   E. The cells pump in additional water until they burst apart.

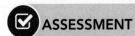 ASSESSMENT

For additional assessment practice, go online to access your digital course.

| If You Have Trouble With... | | | | |
|---|---|---|---|---|
| Question | 1 | 2 | 3 | 4 |
| See Lesson | 8.2 | 8.4 | 8.2 | 8.3, 8.4 |
| Performance Expectation | HS-LS1-2 | HS-LS1-2 | HS-LS1-1 | HS-LS1-3 |

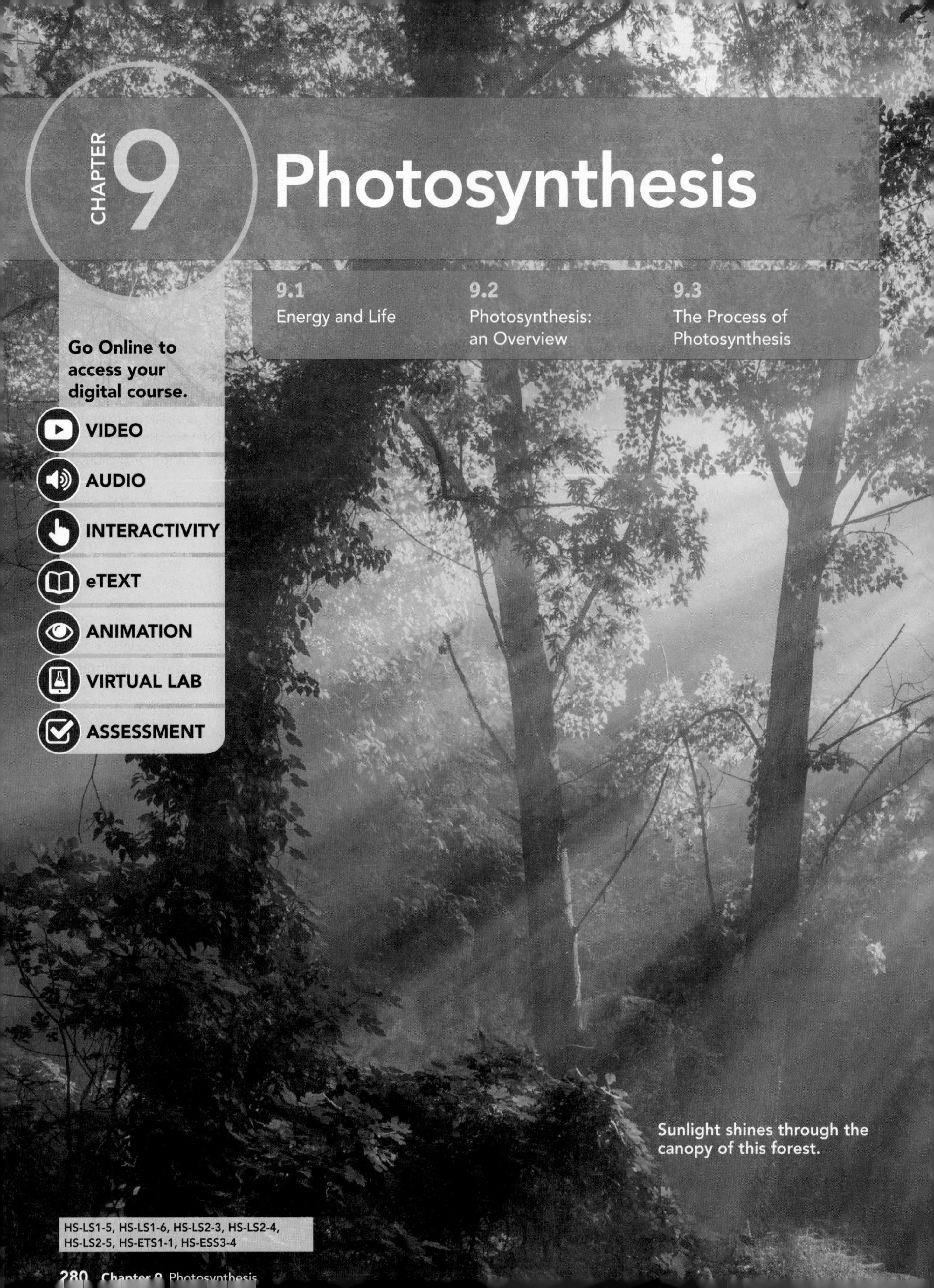

CHAPTER 9

# Photosynthesis

9.1 Energy and Life

9.2 Photosynthesis: an Overview

9.3 The Process of Photosynthesis

**Go Online to access your digital course.**

- VIDEO
- AUDIO
- INTERACTIVITY
- eTEXT
- ANIMATION
- VIRTUAL LAB
- ASSESSMENT

Sunlight shines through the canopy of this forest.

HS-LS1-5, HS-LS1-6, HS-LS2-3, HS-LS2-4, HS-LS2-5, HS-ETS1-1, HS-ESS3-4

# What would it take to make an artificial leaf?

Have you seen solar panels around your city or town? Conventional solar panels use the energy from sunlight to produce an electric current, which can then be used to power a home or factory. The electricity can also feed into the wires of the electrical grid. But storing that electricity is difficult and expensive. Most panels capture only a fraction of the energy in the sunlight that hits them.

Solar panels are wonderful for converting sunlight to electricity. However, they're not so great in places that are not sunny. Even in places where solar panels can supply the electrical needs of an entire building during the summer, energy-independence is lost during the winter, when the days are shorter and snow periodically covers the panels.

What if solar panels could capture energy from the sun and convert it into stable, energy-containing substances that could be used as fuel? In other words, what if a solar panel acted more like, well . . . a leaf?

Green plants don't produce an electric current that can be run through a wire. However, they do harness the energy from sunlight very efficiently. The process is called photosynthesis. Plants store that energy in chemical form as sugars, oils, and complex carbohydrates. Might it be possible to design and build an artificial leaf, a device that captures sunlight like a plant and uses that energy to build stable, energy-containing substances that can be used for fuel?

For decades, researchers around the world have been trying to learn from nature and mimic the way in which plants carry out photosynthesis. As you will see in this chapter, the energy plants absorb from sunlight is used to raise the energy level of electrons taken from water to a point where these high-energy electrons can do useful chemical work.

An artificial photosynthetic system would do much the same thing. If energy from the sun could be used to make a chemical fuel that was easy to store and transport, this would solve many of the problems associated with solar energy.

But what sort of fuel should an artificial leaf produce? Sugars, like plants do? Or something else? The possibilities are intriguing. Perhaps we can make a fuel that burns more cleanly than fossil fuels. Or a fuel that is carbon-neutral. A carbon-neutral fuel does not produce carbon-based waste products like carbon dioxide when it is broken down to release energy. Hydrogen gas ($H_2$) is one example of a carbon-neutral fuel. It burns with oxygen gas ($O_2$) in the air to produce only one product, water vapor ($H_2O$). Carbon-neutral fuels do not produce greenhouse gases and therefore do not contribute to climate change.

Is it possible to build a cost-effective artificial leaf? What are the other constraints on designing this solution to an urgent real-world problem? What criteria should be used when evaluating competing solutions?

**Throughout this chapter, look for connections to the** CASE STUDY **to help you answer these questions.**

**HS-LS1-5:** Use a model to illustrate how photosynthesis transforms light energy into stored chemical energy.

**HS-LS2-3:** Construct and revise an explanation based on evidence for the cycling of matter and flow of energy in aerobic and anaerobic conditions.

## VOCABULARY

ATP
photosynthesis

## READING TOOL

As you read the lesson, complete the main idea table for each heading. Fill out the table in your 📖 **Biology Foundations Workbook.**

## BUILD VOCABULARY

**Apply Prior Knowledge** Your previous experience of the prefix *tri-* (three) in words like *triangle* and *tricycle* can help you remember that there are three phosphate groups in ATP.

Homeostasis is hard work. Just to stay alive, organisms and the cells within them have to grow and develop, move materials around, build new molecules, and respond to environmental changes. Plenty of energy is needed to accomplish all this work, to be sure, but where does it come from?

## Chemical Energy and ATP

Energy is the ability to do work. Without energy, lights, appliances, and computers stop working. Living things depend on energy, too. Even when you are sleeping, your cells are busy using energy to synthesize new molecules, contract muscles, and carry out active transport. Simply put, without the ability to obtain and use energy by converting from one form to another, life would cease to exist.

Energy comes in many forms, including light, heat, and electricity. Energy can be stored in chemical compounds, too. For example, when you light a candle, the wax melts, soaks into the wick, and is burned. As the candle burns, chemical bonds between carbon and hydrogen atoms in the wax are broken. New bonds then form between these atoms and oxygen, producing $CO_2$ and $H_2O$ (carbon dioxide and water). These new bonds are at a lower energy state than the original chemical bonds in the wax. The energy lost is released as heat and light in the glow of the candle's flame.

**Storing Energy** Whether they get energy from food or from sunlight, all living cells store energy in the chemical bonds of certain compounds. One of the most important compounds is adenosine triphosphate (uh DEN us seen try FAHS fayt), abbreviated **ATP**. As shown in **Figure 9-1**, ATP consists of adenine, a 5-carbon sugar called ribose, and three phosphate groups. Those phosphate groups are the key to ATP's ability to store and release energy.

Adenosine diphosphate (ADP) is a compound that looks almost like ATP, except that it has two phosphate groups instead of three. This difference is the key to the way in which living things store energy. When a cell has energy available, it can store small amounts of it by adding phosphate groups to ADP to produce ATP.

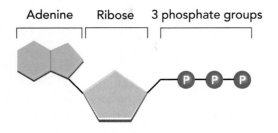

Adenine  Ribose  3 phosphate groups

**Figure 9-1**

**Adenosine Triphosphate (ATP)**

All cells use a small molecule called ATP to store and release energy.

**Releasing Energy** Cells can release the energy stored in ATP by the controlled breaking of the chemical bonds between atoms in the second and third phosphate groups. As **Figure 9-2** shows, this means that ATP functions a little bit like a rechargeable battery.

Because energy is used to add a phosphate group to ADP to generate ATP, and energy is released when a phosphate group on ATP is split off and released, ATP serves the cell as a way of storing and releasing energy as needed. *ATP can release and store energy by breaking and re-forming the bonds between its phosphate groups. This characteristic of ATP makes it exceptionally useful as a basic energy source for all cells.*

**INTERACTIVITY**

Visual Analogy

**Figure 9-2**

**ATP and Batteries**

ATP is like a fully-charged battery, and ADP is like a partially-charged battery. When a phosphate group combines with ADP, they form energy-rich ATP. When ATP loses the phosphate group, it releases energy and becomes ADP again.

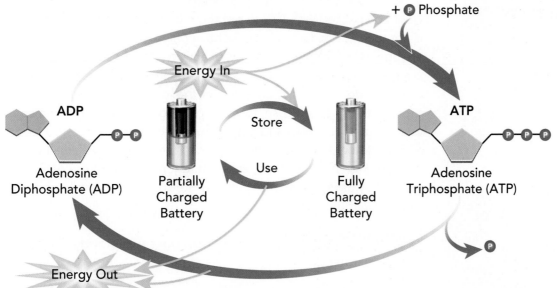

+ P Phosphate

Energy In

ADP

Adenosine Diphosphate (ADP)

Partially Charged Battery

Store

Use

Fully Charged Battery

ATP

Adenosine Triphosphate (ATP)

P

Energy Out

## How Do Organisms Capture and Use Energy?

1. Your teacher will provide you with two test tubes wrapped in foil. The test tubes contain colonies of *Euglena*, which are photosynthetic microorganisms. Find the hole in the foil around one of the test tubes.

2. Where do you predict *Euglena* will be found in each test tube? Record your prediction.

3. Carefully remove the foil from each test tube. Make sure not to shake or disturb their contents. Observe the locations of *Euglena* in the test tubes, and record your observations.

### ANALYZE AND CONCLUDE

1. **Identify Patterns** What pattern do you observe in the distribution of *Euglena* in the two test tubes?

2. **Construct an Explanation** How could the pattern you observed in *Euglena* behavior be useful or beneficial to the organism? Propose a logical explanation.

3. **Apply Scientific Reasoning** *Euglena* can also live heterotrophically. If you repeated the experiment with test tubes of *Euglena* that also contained a food source, do you think the results of your experiment would be the same? Explain your reasoning.

### READING TOOL

Write down the main idea of this section of text. As you read, list details about how cells use ATP to store and release energy.

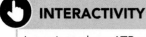

### INTERACTIVITY

Investigate how ATP powers the chemical reactions within a cell.

**How Cells Use ATP** What do cells use ATP for? One way cells use the energy provided by ATP is for carrying out active transport. Many cell membranes contain sodium-potassium pumps, membrane proteins that pump sodium ions ($Na^+$) out of the cell and potassium ions ($K^+$) into it. ATP provides the energy that keeps this pump working, maintaining a carefully regulated balance of ions on both sides of the cell membrane. The energy stored in ATP also enables cells to move, providing power for motor proteins that contract muscle and power the wavelike movement of cilia and flagella.

Energy from ATP can be transferred to other molecules in the cell to power processes such as protein synthesis and responses to chemical signals at the cell surface. The chemical energy from ATP can even be converted to light. In fact, the blink of a firefly on a summer night comes from an enzyme that is powered by ATP!

ATP is such a useful source of energy that you might think cells would be packed with ATP to get them through the day—but this is not the case. In fact, most cells have only a small amount of ATP, enough to last for a few seconds of activity. Why? Even though ATP is a great molecule for transferring energy, it is not a good one for storing large amounts of energy over the long term. A single molecule of the sugar glucose, for example, stores more than 90 times the energy required to add a phosphate group to ADP to produce ATP. Therefore, it is more efficient for cells to keep only a small supply of ATP on hand. Instead, cells can regenerate ATP from ADP as needed by using the energy in foods like sugar. As you will see, that's exactly what they do.

**READING CHECK** **Describe** How does ATP provide the energy cells need?

# Heterotrophs and Autotrophs

Cells have to produce ATP constantly because it gets used up quickly in an active cell. So, where do living things get the energy they use to produce ATP? There are several ways. Most animals obtain the chemical energy they need from food. Organisms that obtain food by consuming other living things are known as heterotrophs. Some heterotrophs get their food by eating plants such as grasses. Other heterotrophs, such as the heron in **Figure 9-3**, obtain food from plants indirectly by feeding on other animals. Still other heterotrophs obtain food by absorbing nutrients from decomposing organisms in the environment. Mushrooms obtain food this way.

Originally, however, the energy in food comes from the sun. Plants, algae, and some bacteria are able to use energy from sunlight to synthesize food molecules. Organisms that make their own food are called autotrophs. Ultimately, nearly all life on Earth depends on the ability of autotrophs to capture and convert the energy from sunlight to synthesize high-energy carbohydrates—sugars and starches—that can be used as food. This process is known as **photosynthesis**. The word *photosynthesis* comes from the Greek words *photo*, meaning "light," and *synthesis*, meaning "putting together." Therefore, *photosynthesis* means "using light to put something together." *In the process of photosynthesis, plants convert the energy of sunlight into chemical energy stored in the bonds of carbohydrates.* In the rest of this chapter, you will learn how this process works.

## Figure 9-3
## The Lives of Heterotrophs

Herons are heterotrophs that get their energy by eating other organisms, such as fish.

☑ **Compare and Contrast** How are heterotrophs and autotrophs similar? How are they different?

 **VIDEO**

Learn how autotrophs use photosynthesis to their advantage.

HS-LS1-5, HS-LS2-3

## ☑ LESSON 9.1 Review

### ⚲ KEY IDEAS

1. How do molecules of ATP store and provide energy for the cell?

2. Describe the transformation of energy that occurs during photosynthesis.

### CRITICAL THINKING

3. Use Models Explain how a rechargeable battery can be used as a model of ADP and ATP.

4. Develop Models Develop a model to illustrate the role of photosynthesis in transforming energy. Include the terms *photosynthesis*, *sun*, *light energy*, *chemical energy*, *carbohydrates*, and *bonds*.

5. CASE STUDY Solar cells can provide the energy to run calculators, outdoor lights, and other devices. How does the conversion of light energy into stored chemical energy by solar cells compare to the process of photosynthesis?

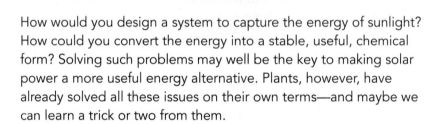

# Photosynthesis: An Overview

## KEY QUESTIONS

- What role do pigments play in the process of photosynthesis?
- What are electron carrier molecules?
- What are the reactants and products of photosynthesis?

HS-LS1-5: Use a model to illustrate how photosynthesis transforms light energy into stored chemical energy.

HS-LS2-5: Develop a model to illustrate the role of photosynthesis and cellular respiration in the cycling of carbon among the biosphere, atmosphere, hydrosphere, and geosphere.

## VOCABULARY

**pigment**
**chlorophyll**
**thylakoid**
**stroma**
**NADP+**
**light-dependent reactions**
**light-independent reactions**

### READING TOOL

Fill in the concept map in your 📖 **Biology Foundations Workbook** to show the organization of a chloroplast.

### BUILD VOCABULARY

**Prefixes** The prefix *chloro-* refers to the color green. Chlorophyll and chloroplasts are green in color.

How would you design a system to capture the energy of sunlight? How could you convert the energy into a stable, useful, chemical form? Solving such problems may well be the key to making solar power a more useful energy alternative. Plants, however, have already solved all these issues on their own terms—and maybe we can learn a trick or two from them.

## Chlorophyll and Chloroplasts

Our lives, and the lives of nearly every living thing on the surface of Earth, are made possible by the sun and the process of photosynthesis. In order for photosynthesis to occur, light energy from the sun must somehow be captured.

**Light** Energy from the sun travels to Earth in the form of light. Sunlight, which our eyes perceive as "white" light, is actually a mixture of different wavelengths. Many of these wavelengths are visible to our eyes and make up what is known as the visible spectrum. Our eyes see the different wavelengths of the visible spectrum as different colors: shades of red, orange, yellow, green, blue, indigo, and violet.

**Pigments** Light-absorbing compounds, whether they are found on a painter's brush or in a living cell, are known as **pigments**. ⚲ *Photosynthetic organisms use pigments to capture the energy in sunlight.* The principal pigment of green plants is known as **chlorophyll** (KLAWR uh fil). The two types of chlorophyll found in plants, chlorophyll *a* and chlorophyll *b*, absorb light very well in the blue-violet and red regions of the visible spectrum. However, chlorophyll does not absorb light well in the green region of the spectrum, but instead reflects it. That's why most leaves are green.

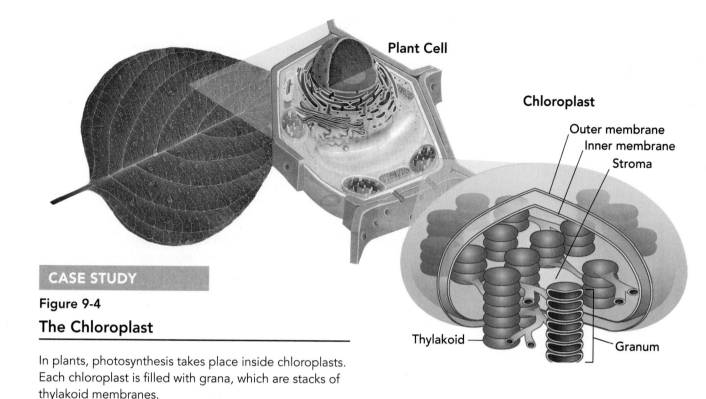

**Plant Cell**

**Chloroplast**

Outer membrane
Inner membrane
Stroma

Thylakoid

Granum

**Figure 9-4**

## The Chloroplast

In plants, photosynthesis takes place inside chloroplasts. Each chloroplast is filled with grana, which are stacks of thylakoid membranes.

Plants also contain red and orange pigments such as carotene that absorb light in other regions of the spectrum. Most of the time, the intense green color of chlorophyll overwhelms these accessory pigments, so we don't notice them. As temperatures drop late in the year, however, chlorophyll molecules break down first, leaving the reds and oranges of the accessory pigments for all to see. The beautiful colors of fall in some parts of the country are the result of this process.

**Chloroplasts** Recall from Chapter 8 that in plants and other photosynthetic eukaryotes, photosynthesis takes place inside organelles called chloroplasts. Chloroplasts are surrounded by two envelope membranes, and they are filled with saclike chlorophyll-containing membranes called **thylakoids** (THY luh koydz). These thylakoids are interconnected and arranged in stacks known as grana (singular: granum). The fluid portion of the chloroplast, outside of the thylakoids, is known as the **stroma**. The structure of a typical chloroplast is shown in **Figure 9-4**.

**Energy Collection** What's so special about chlorophyll that makes it essential for photosynthesis? Chlorophyll absorbs light very efficiently, transferring light energy to its own electrons. These high-energy electrons are then available to do chemical work, such as the building of sugar molecules from low-energy compounds like carbon dioxide and water. This is what makes photosynthesis work.

☑ **READING CHECK** **Cause and Effect** How does photosynthesis depend on chlorophyll?

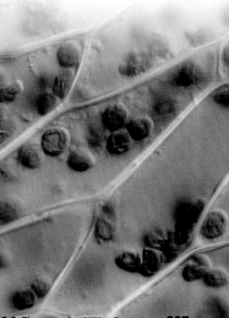

# High-Energy Electrons

In a chemical sense, the high-energy electrons produced by chlorophyll are highly reactive and require a special "carrier." Think of a high-energy electron as being similar to a red-hot coal from a fireplace or campfire. If you wanted to move the coal from one place to another, you wouldn't pick it up in your hands. You would use a pan or bucket—a carrier—to transport it, as shown in **Figure 9-5**.

Plant cells treat these high-energy electrons in much the same way. Instead of a pan, however, they use electron carriers to transport high-energy electrons from chlorophyll to other molecules. 🔍 *An electron carrier is a compound that can accept a pair of high-energy electrons and transfer them, along with most of their energy, to another molecule.*

One of these carrier molecules is a compound known as **NADP$^+$** (nicotinamide adenine dinucleotide phosphate). The name is complicated, but the job that NADP$^+$ does is simple. NADP$^+$ accepts and holds two high-energy electrons, along with a hydrogen ion (H$^+$). This converts the NADP$^+$ into NADPH. The conversion of NADP$^+$ into NADPH is one way in which some of the energy of sunlight can be trapped in chemical form. The NADPH can carry the high-energy electrons that were produced by light absorption in chlorophyll to chemical reactions elsewhere in the chloroplast. Those high-energy electrons can then be used to help build sugars like glucose from nothing more than carbon dioxide and water.

☑ **READING CHECK Define** What is NADP$^+$?

**Visual Analogy**

**Figure 9-5**

## Carrying Electrons

Like a pan being used to carry hot coals, NADP$^+$ carries pairs of electrons and an H$^+$ ion from place to place.

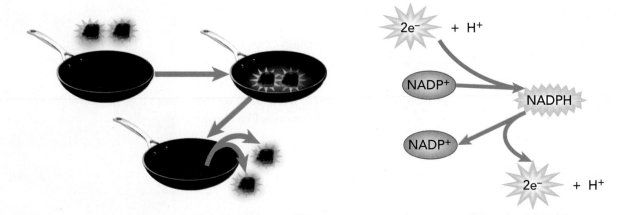

## Plant Pigments and Photosynthesis

**Problem** Which wavelengths of light support plant growth?

In this lab, you will investigate the wavelengths of light that are used in photosynthesis, and construct an explanation for how light wavelength affects plant growth. You will use *Elodea*, a type of aquatic vegetation, as a test subject.

You can find this lab in your digital course.

# An Overview of Photosynthesis

Many steps are involved in the process of photosynthesis. However, the overall process of photosynthesis can be summarized in one sentence. 🔍 *Photosynthesis uses the energy of sunlight to convert water and carbon dioxide (low-energy reactants) into high-energy sugars and oxygen (products).* Plants use these sugars to produce complex carbohydrates such as starches, and to provide energy for the synthesis of other compounds, including proteins and lipids.

Because photosynthesis usually produces 6-carbon sugars ($C_6H_{12}O_6$) as the final product, the overall reaction for photosynthesis can be shown as follows:

**In Symbols:**

$$6CO_2 + 6H_2O \xrightarrow{\text{Light}} C_6H_{12}O_6 + 6O_2$$

**In Words:**

$$\text{Carbon dioxide} + \text{Water} \xrightarrow{\text{Light}} \text{Sugars} + \text{Oxygen}$$

**Light-Dependent Reactions** Although the equation for photosynthesis looks simple, there are many steps to get from the reactants to the final products. In fact, photosynthesis actually involves two sets of reactions. The first set of reactions is known as the **light-dependent reactions** because they require the direct involvement of light and light-absorbing pigments. The light-dependent reactions take place in thylakoid membranes and use energy from sunlight to add a third phosphate to ADP to make ATP.

The light-dependent reactions also do something truly remarkable, which is to take low-energy electrons from water molecules, and use solar energy to raise them to a much higher energy level. These high-energy electrons are then transferred to the electron carrier, NADP⁺, which is converted to NADPH as shown in **Figure 9-5**. NADPH is used in other chemical reactions. What happens to water after a pair of electrons is taken away from it? That's pretty remarkable, too. The oxygen atoms left over are released to the atmosphere as the oxygen gas we and all other animals breathe.

**READING TOOL**

Create a two-column table to describe and compare the light-dependent and light-independent reactions of photosynthesis.

 **INTERACTIVITY**

Conduct a virtual experiment to examine how the distance from a light source can affect the rate of photosynthesis.

Figure 9-6

## Stages of Photosynthesis

There are two stages of photosynthesis: the light-dependent reactions and the light-independent reactions. Light-dependent reactions depend on sunlight, while light-independent reactions may occur in the dark.

**Light-Independent Reactions** Plants absorb carbon dioxide from the atmosphere and complete the process of photosynthesis by producing carbon-containing sugars and other carbohydrates. During the **light-independent reactions**, the ATP and NADPH molecules produced in the light-dependent reactions are used to build high-energy sugars from carbon dioxide. As the name implies, no light is required to power the light-independent reactions, which take place outside the thylakoids, in the stroma of the chloroplast.

The interdependent relationship between the light-dependent and light-independent reactions is shown in **Figure 9-6**. As you can see, the two sets of reactions work together to capture the energy of sunlight and transform it into energy-rich compounds such as carbohydrates.

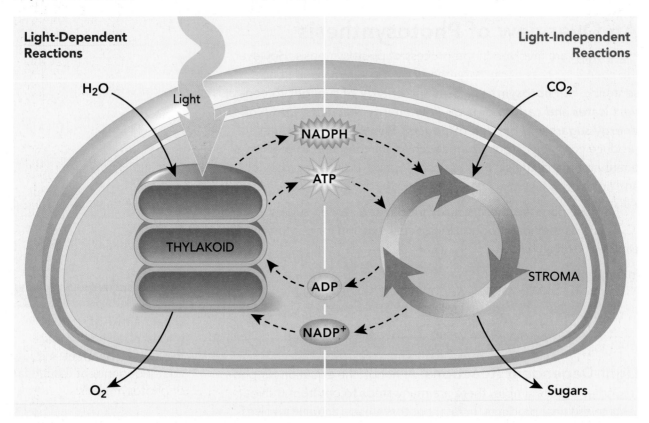

HS-LS1-5, HS-LS2-5

## ☑ LESSON 9.2 Review

### ⚗ KEY IDEAS

1. What is chlorophyll? What is its role in photosynthesis?

2. $NADP^+$ is an example of an electron carrier. Describe its function in photosynthesis.

3. Identify the reactants, products, and basic functions of photosynthesis.

### CRITICAL THINKING

4. Develop Models Draw a model to show how the process of photosynthesis impacts both the flow of energy and the cycling of carbon through the atmosphere and biosphere.

5. Summarize What roles do ADP and ATP play in the light-dependent and light-independent reactions?

6. Use Models Use **Figure 9-6** as a model to describe how the light-dependent and light-independent reactions transform light energy into stored chemical energy.

# The Process of Photosynthesis

*Lithops lesliei* plants have thick, water-storing leaves and thrive in intense sunlight.

🔍 **KEY QUESTIONS**

- *What happens during the light-dependent reactions?*
- *What happens during the light-independent reactions?*
- *What factors affect photosynthesis?*

**HS-LS1-5:** Use a model to illustrate how photosynthesis transforms light energy into stored chemical energy.

**HS-LS1-6:** Construct and revise an explanation based on evidence for how carbon, hydrogen, and oxygen from sugar molecules may combine with other elements to form amino acids and/or other large carbon-based molecules.

**HS-LS2-5:** Develop a model to illustrate the role of photosynthesis and cellular respiration in the cycling of carbon among the biosphere, atmosphere, hydrosphere, and geosphere.

Why are chloroplasts so full of membranes? Is there something about the thylakoid membranes in chloroplasts that makes them absolutely essential for the process of photosynthesis? As you'll see, there is. Membranes are barriers, and the thylakoids of chloroplasts keep positive and negative charges generated by light absorption on opposite sides of the membrane. This is the key to how the light-dependent reactions trap the energy of sunlight in chemical form.

## The Light-Dependent Reactions: Generating ATP and NADPH

Recall that the process of photosynthesis involves two primary sets of reactions: the light-dependent and the light-independent reactions. The light-dependent reactions include the steps of photosynthesis that directly involve sunlight. These reactions explain why plants need light to grow. 🔍 *The light-dependent reactions use energy from sunlight to convert ADP and NADP$^+$ into the energy and electron carriers ATP and NADPH. These reactions also produce oxygen ($O_2$) as a by-product.*

The light-dependent reactions occur in the thylakoids of chloroplasts. Recall that thylakoids are saclike membranes. They contain most of the machinery needed to carry out photosynthesis, including clusters of chlorophyll and proteins known as **photosystems**. These photosystems are surrounded by accessory pigments and are essential to the light-dependent reactions. Photosystems absorb sunlight and generate high-energy electrons that are then passed to a series of electron carriers embedded in the membrane. Light absorption by chlorophyll molecules in the photosystems is the beginning of this important process.

**VOCABULARY**

**photosystem**
**electron transport chain**
**ATP synthase**
**Calvin cycle**

**READING TOOL**

As you read the lesson, complete the main idea table for the primary headings in your 📖 **Biology Foundations Workbook.**

**Figure 9-7**

**Changing Colors**

The green color of most leaves is caused by the reflection of green light by the pigment chlorophyll. Other pigments are revealed in autumn, when the chlorophyll breaks down.

**Photosystem II** The light-dependent reactions begin in photosystem II. This first photosystem is called photosystem II simply because it was discovered after photosystem I. As shown in **Figure 9-8,** chlorophyll molecules in photosystem II absorb light. This absorption of light raises electrons in chlorophyll to a higher energy level, and these high-energy electrons ($e^-$) are passed from chlorophyll to the electron transport chain. An **electron transport chain** is a series of electron carrier proteins that shuttle high-energy electrons during ATP-generating reactions.

As light continues to shine, more and more high-energy electrons are passed to the electron transport chain. Does this mean that chlorophyll eventually runs out of electrons? No, the thylakoid membrane contains a system that provides new electrons to chlorophyll to replace the ones it has lost. These new electrons come from water molecules ($H_2O$).

Enzymes on the inner surface of the thylakoid pull apart each water molecule into two electrons, two hydrogen ions $H^+$, and one oxygen atom (O). Because the negatively-charged electrons move to the outside of the membrane while the positively-charged $H^+$ ions are released inside, a charge separation is built up across the membrane.

These two electrons from water replace the high-energy electrons that chlorophyll lost to the electron transport chain. As electrons are taken from water, oxygen gas ($O_2$) is left behind and is released into the air. This is the source of nearly all of the oxygen in Earth's atmosphere, and it is another way in which photosynthesis makes our lives possible.

**Electron Transport Chain** What happens to the electrons as they move along the electron transport chain? Energy from the electrons is used by the proteins in the chain to pump still more $H^+$ ions from the stroma inside the thylakoid sac. At the end of the electron transport chain, the electrons themselves pass to a second photosystem called photosystem I.

**Photosystem I** Because some energy has been used to pump $H^+$ ions across the thylakoid membrane, electrons do not contain as much energy as they used to when they reach photosystem I. Pigments in photosystem I use energy from light to reenergize these electrons and pass them to other carriers and eventually to the electron carrier $NADP^+$. At the end of a short second electron transport chain, $NADP^+$ in the stroma picks up the high-energy electrons, along with $H^+$ ions, at the outer surface of the thylakoid membrane, to become NADPH. This NADPH becomes very important, as you will see, in the light-independent reactions of photosynthesis.

**☑ READING CHECK** **Explain** Why do organisms that perform photosynthesis require water and sunlight?

**Hydrogen Ion Movement and ATP Formation** Recall that in photosystem II, hydrogen ions began to accumulate within the thylakoid space. Some were left behind from the splitting of water at the end of the electron transport chain. Other hydrogen ions were "pumped" in from the stroma. The buildup of hydrogen ions makes the space within the thylakoids strongly positive with respect to the stroma on the other surface of the membrane. This gradient, the difference in both charge and $H^+$ ion concentration across the membrane, provides the energy to make ATP.

$H^+$ ions cannot cross the membrane directly. However, the thylakoid membrane contains a protein complex called **ATP synthase** that spans the membrane and allows $H^+$ ions to pass through it. Powered by the $H^+$ concentration difference, $H^+$ ions pass through ATP synthase and force it to rotate, almost like a turbine being spun by water in a hydroelectric power plant. As it rotates, ATP synthase binds ADP and a phosphate group together to produce ATP. This process enables light-dependent electron transport to synthesize not only NADPH (at the end of the electron transport chain), but ATP as well.

## ANIMATION

### Up Close

**Figure 9-8**

## The Light-Dependent Reactions

The light-dependent reactions occur inside the thylakoids of a chloroplast. They use energy from sunlight to produce ATP and NADPH. Oxygen is released in the process.

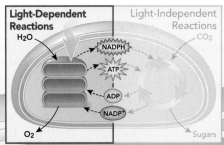

**CYTOPLASM**

$$2H^+ + 2\ \text{NADP}^+ + 4e^- \longrightarrow 2\ \text{NADPH}$$ ➤ To Light-Independent Reactions

$H^+$

**ATP** ➤ To Light-Independent Reactions

**ADP** + $P$

**STROMA**

Light

$H^+$

$H^+$

$H^+$

Light

$H^+$

**Electron carriers**

**Thylakoid membrane**

**Photosystem I**

**ATP synthase**

**Photosystem II**

$4e^-$

$H^+$

**THYLAKOID SPACE**

$H^+$

$H^+$

$H^+$

$H^+$

$H^+$

$2\ H_2O$    $4H^+$    $O_2$

**Photosystem II**
Light energy absorbed by photosystem II produces high-energy electrons. Water molecules are split to replace those electrons, releasing $H^+$ ions and oxygen.

**Electron Transport**
High-energy electrons move down the electron transport chain, to photosystem I. Energy generated is used to pump $H^+$ ions across the thylakoid membrane and into the thylakoid space.

**Photosystem I**
Electrons are reenergized in photosystem I. A second electron transport chain then transfers these electrons to NADP$^+$, producing NADPH.

**Hydrogen Ion Movement and ATP Formation**
As the thylakoid space fills up with positively-charged $H^+$ ions, the inside of the thylakoid membrane becomes positively charged relative to the outside of the membrane. $H^+$ ions pass back across the thylakoid membrane through ATP synthase. As the ions pass through, the ATP synthase molecule rotates and the energy produced is used to convert ADP to ATP.

**Summary of Light-Dependent Reactions** The light-dependent reactions of photosythesis use light energy and water to produce oxygen gas and convert ADP and $NADP^+$ into the energy carriers ATP and NADPH. What good are these compounds? As you will see, they have an important role to play in the cell: They provide the energy needed to build high-energy sugars from low-energy carbon dioxide.

✅ **READING CHECK Describe** What is the role of ATP synthase in photosynthesis?

**READING TOOL**

Draw a flowchart to show the sequence of events in the Calvin cycle. Be sure to include the inputs and outputs into the cycle.

# The Light-Independent Reactions: Producing Sugars

The ATP and NADPH formed by the light-dependent reactions contain plenty of chemical energy, but they are not stable enough to store that energy for more than a few minutes. ⚗ *During the light-independent reactions, ATP and NADPH from the light-dependent reactions are used to synthesize high-energy sugars.* The light-independent reactions are commonly referred to as the Calvin Cycle. The Calvin cycle is named after the American scientist Melvin Calvin, who worked out the details of this remarkable cycle. Follow **Figure 9-9** to see each step in this set of reactions.

**Carbon Dioxide Enters the Cycle** Carbon dioxide molecules ($CO_2$) enter the Calvin cycle from the atmosphere. An enzyme in the stroma of the chloroplast combines these carbon dioxide molecules with 5-carbon compounds already present in the organelle, producing 3-carbon compounds that continue into the cycle. For every six carbon dioxide molecules that enter the cycle, a total of twelve 3-carbon compounds are produced. Other enzymes in the chloroplast then convert these compounds into higher energy forms in the rest of the cycle. The energy for these conversions comes from ATP and high-energy electrons from NADPH.

**Sugar Production** At midcycle, two of the twelve 3-carbon molecules are removed from the cycle. This is a very special step because these molecules become the building blocks that the plant cell uses to synthesize sugars, lipids, amino acids, and other compounds. In other words, this step in the Calvin cycle contributes to all of the products needed for plant metabolism and growth.

The remaining ten 3-carbon molecules are converted back into six 5-carbon molecules. These molecules combine with six new carbon dioxide molecules to begin the next cycle. As the cycle continues, more and more carbon dioxide is removed from the air and converted into the compounds the plant needs for growth and development.

👆 **INTERACTIVITY**

Explore more details of the light-dependent and light-independent reactions to gain a deeper understanding of photosynthesis.

## Summary of the Calvin Cycle

The Calvin cycle uses six molecules of carbon dioxide to produce a single 6-carbon sugar molecule. The energy for the reactions is supplied by compounds produced in the light-dependent reactions. As photosynthesis proceeds, the Calvin cycle removes carbon dioxide from the atmosphere and turns out energy-rich sugars. The plant uses the sugars to meet its energy needs and to synthesize macromolecules needed for growth and development, including lipids, proteins, and complex carbohydrates such as cellulose. When other organisms eat plants, they, too, can use the energy and raw materials stored in these compounds.

## The End Results

The two sets of photosynthetic reactions work together—the light-dependent reactions trap the energy of sunlight in chemical form, and the light-independent reactions use that chemical energy to synthesize stable, high-energy sugars from carbon dioxide and water. In the process, animals, including ourselves, get plenty of food and an atmosphere filled with oxygen. Not a bad deal at all!

### Up Close

**Figure 9-9**

## The Light-Independent Reactions

The light-independent reactions occur in the stroma of the chloroplast, which is the region outside the thylakoids. ATP and NADPH from the light-dependent reactions provide the energy for glucose to be assembled. ☑ **Interpret Visuals** How many molecules of ATP are needed for each "turn" of the Calvin cycle?

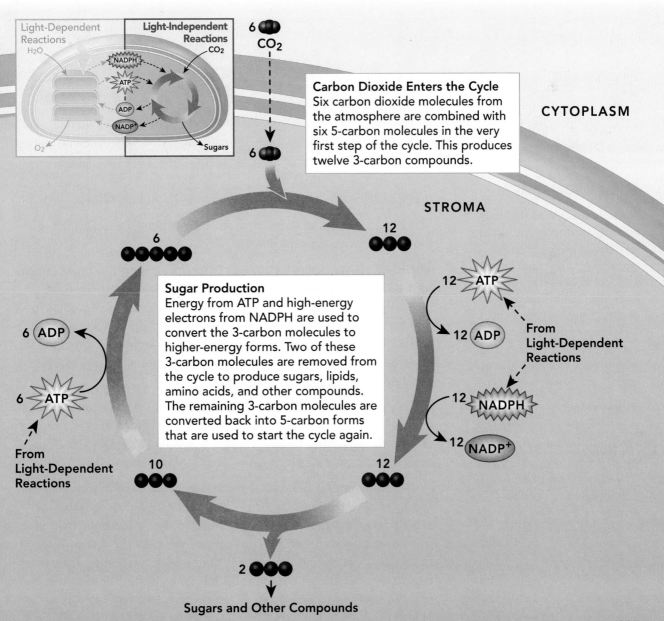

**Carbon Dioxide Enters the Cycle**
Six carbon dioxide molecules from the atmosphere are combined with six 5-carbon molecules in the very first step of the cycle. This produces twelve 3-carbon compounds.

CYTOPLASM

STROMA

**Sugar Production**
Energy from ATP and high-energy electrons from NADPH are used to convert the 3-carbon molecules to higher-energy forms. Two of these 3-carbon molecules are removed from the cycle to produce sugars, lipids, amino acids, and other compounds. The remaining 3-carbon molecules are converted back into 5-carbon forms that are used to start the cycle again.

From Light-Dependent Reactions

From Light-Dependent Reactions

**Sugars and Other Compounds**

## Analyzing Data

### Rates of Photosynthesis

Different plants perform photosynthesis at different rates. The rates may change in response to several factors, including temperature, available water, and light intensity. The graph shows how the rates of photosynthesis vary with light intensity for two groups of plants: plants that thrive in direct sunlight, and plants that thrive in the shade.

1. **Analyze Graphs** When light intensity is below 200 μmol photons/m²/s, do sun plants or shade plants have a higher rate of photosynthesis?

2. **Analyze Data** Light intensity in the Sonoran Desert averages about 400 μmol photons/m²/s. What is the approximate rate of photosynthesis for sun plants that grow in this environment?

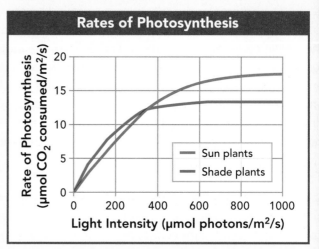

**Rates of Photosynthesis**

3. **Draw Conclusions** As the rate of photosynthesis increases, what do you think happens to the rate at which sugars are produced by the plant?

# Factors Affecting Photosynthesis

Many factors affect the rate of chemical reactions, including those that occur during photosynthesis.

**Temperature, Light, and Water** ✎ *Among the most important factors that affect photosynthesis are temperature, light intensity, and the availability of water.* The reactions of photosynthesis are made possible by enzymes that function best between 0°C and 35°C. Temperatures above or below this range may affect those enzymes, slowing down the rate of photosynthesis. At very low temperatures, photosynthesis may stop entirely.

The intensity of light also affects the rate at which photosynthesis occurs. As you might expect, high light intensity increases the rate of photosynthesis. After the light intensity reaches a certain level, however, the plant reaches its maximum rate of photosynthesis.

Because water is one of the raw materials of photosynthesis, a shortage of water can slow or even stop photosynthesis. Water loss can also damage plant tissues. To deal with these dangers, plants (such as desert plants and conifers) that live in dry conditions often have waxy coatings on their leaves that reduce water loss. They may also have biochemical adaptations that make photosynthesis more efficient under dry conditions.

**Photosynthesis Under Extreme Conditions** In order to conserve water, most plants under bright, hot conditions (of the sorts often found in the tropics) close the small openings in their leaves that normally admit carbon dioxide. While this closure keeps the plants from drying out, it also causes carbon dioxide within the leaves to fall to very low levels. When this happens to most plants, photosynthesis slows down or even stops. However, some plants have adapted to extremely bright, hot conditions. There are two major groups of these specialized plants: C4 plants and CAM plants. C4 and CAM plants have biochemical adaptations that minimize water loss while still allowing photosynthesis to take place in intense sunlight.

*C4 Plants* C4 plants have a specialized chemical pathway that allows them to capture very low levels of carbon dioxide and pass it to the Calvin cycle. The name "C4 plant" comes from the fact that the first compound formed in this pathway contains four carbon atoms instead of three. The C4 pathway enables photosynthesis to keep working under intense light and high temperatures, but it requires extra energy in the form of ATP to function. C4 organisms include important crop plants like corn, sugar cane, and sorghum.

*CAM Plants* Other plants adapted to dry climates use a different strategy in which carbon dioxide becomes incorporated into organic acids during photosynthesis. The process is called Crassulacean Acid Metabolism (CAM) because it was first observed in members of the family Crassulacea. CAM plants admit air into their leaves only at night. In the cool darkness, carbon dioxide is combined with existing molecules to produce organic acids, "trapping" the carbon within the leaves. During the daytime, when leaves are tightly sealed to prevent the loss of water, these compounds release carbon dioxide inside the leaf, enabling carbohydrate production. CAM plants include pineapple, many desert cacti, and the fleshy "ice plant" shown in **Figure 9-10**. Ice plants are often planted near freeways along the California coast to lessen brush fires and prevent erosion.

**Figure 9-10**

**CAM Plants**

This ice plant is an example of a CAM plant. It survives in very dry conditions because air enters its leaves only at night, minimizing water loss.

HS-LS1-5, HS-LS1-6, HS-LS2-5

# ☑ LESSON 9.3 Review

## ⚲ KEY IDEAS

1. Describe three chemical changes that occur during the light-dependent reactions.

2. What do plants do with the high-energy sugar molecules they produce during the Calvin cycle?

3. Assuming there is enough light and water for photosynthesis to occur, explain why a temperature between 0°C and 35°C is still important.

## CRITICAL THINKING

4. Develop Models Draw a model that shows how the six carbon atoms that enter the Calvin cycle as carbon dioxide flow through the cycle.

5. Construct an Explanation In a laboratory experiment, a plant receives sunlight and water, but not carbon dioxide. Predict what happens to the plant and construct an explanation for your prediction using what you know about the light-dependent and light-independent reactions.

6. Plan an Investigation How would you investigate the effect of temperature on photosynthesis? Outline the steps of a practical investigation.

7. Develop Models Draw a model to illustrate how high-energy sugar molecules produced during the Calvin cycle move through the carbon cycle.

# What would it take to make an artificial leaf?

Scientists have used their knowledge of photosynthesis to make an artificial leaf. The next step is to improve artificial leaves and develop practical, cost-efficient ways of using the technology.

HS-LS1-5, HS-ETS1-1, HS-ESS3-4

## Make Your Case

Scientists are developing a variety of new technologies for artificial leaves. None of them involve duplicating all of the steps and reactions of photosynthesis. However, these artificial leaves are able to use sunlight to assemble energy-rich molecules, such as hydrogen ($H_2$) and methane ($CH_4$). Research the latest developments in this technology, as well as the potential benefits and drawbacks.

## Evaluate a Solution

1. **Define the Problem** What problems could an artificial leaf help solve?
2. **Identify Constraints** How well do you think an artificial leaf could solve one or more of the problems you identified? Describe the costs, constraints, and reliability of the solution, as well as its impact on the environment.

Daniel Nocera

## Technology on the Case

### Chemistry and the Leaf

A leaf is like a miniature chemistry factory. The raw materials are water, carbon dioxide, and sunlight, and the products are glucose and oxygen. To develop a useful artificial leaf, chemist Daniel Nocera adapted a well-known chemical process that also involves an energy input. The process is called electrolysis. Two electrodes are placed in water, and a strong electric current is passed through them. The electricity pulls the water molecules apart. Oxygen gas ($O_2$) bubbles out at the positive electrode, and hydrogen gas ($H_2$) bubbles out at the negative electrode.

In Nocera's artificial leaf, light energy powers electrolysis inside a thin wafer. The device uses the energy to distribute positive and negative charges to opposite sides of the wafer. On each surface, catalysts make use of the charge separation to split water molecules. This releases a stream of tiny bubbles, some of which contain hydrogen gas and some oxygen. Hydrogen gas can be compressed and used as a fuel to power engines and other devices.

More recently, Nocera and other researchers have taken their invention a step further. They have paired their original artificial leaves with bacteria that absorb the hydrogen molecules. The bacteria combine the hydrogen with carbon dioxide from the atmosphere. The products are alcohols that can be burned as fuels.

## Careers on the Case

### Work Toward a Solution

Applying chemical processes in nature to develop new technologies requires efforts from many professionals, including chemical engineers.

### Chemical Engineer

After a new chemical process has been developed in the laboratory, chemical engineers research ways to adapt the process for large-scale production. The result of their efforts may be a new medicine, or food, or a new kind of plastic or some other material. Sometimes, their work allows an existing product to be produced much more easily—and at a lower cost.

 **VIDEO**

Watch this video to learn about other careers in biology.

# Lesson Review

Go to your Biology Foundations Workbook for longer versions of these lesson summaries.

## 9.1 Energy and Life

All living things need energy to stay alive and carry out their life processes. Cells can store energy in the bonds of chemical compounds. One of the most important of these compounds is ATP (adenosine triphosphate). A cell can store a small amount of energy by adding a phosphate group to ADP to make ATP. When a cell needs energy, it can release it by breaking the chemical bond between the second and third phosphate groups of ATP.

Most life on Earth depends on the ability of autotrophs (plants and algae) to capture the energy from sunlight and convert it into the chemical energy stored in carbohydrates. This process is known as photosynthesis.

- ATP
- photosynthesis

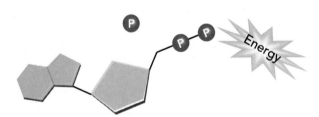

**☑ Use An Analogy** Describe how ADP and ATP act like a rechargeable battery to store and release energy.

## 9.2 Photosynthesis: An Overview

Nearly every living thing on Earth depends on photosynthesis. Photosynthetic organisms capture energy from sunlight with pigments.

Plant cells use compounds called electron carriers to accept and transfer pairs of high-energy electrons from the chlorophyll to other molecules. One of these carrier compounds is $NADP^+$ (nicotinamide adenine dinucleotide phosphate).

Photosynthesis uses light energy to convert water and carbon dioxide into high-energy sugars and oxygen. Photosynthesis involves two sets of reactions: light-dependent and light-independent. The light-dependent reactions take place in the thylakoid membranes. The light-independent reactions take place in the stroma.

- pigment
- chlorophyll
- thylakoid
- stroma
- $NADP^+$
- light-dependent reactions
- light-independent reactions

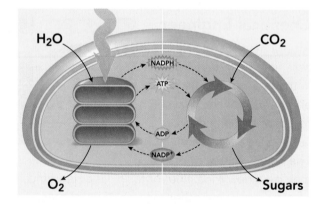

**☑ Interpret Diagrams** Label each side of the diagram. Then, write a caption to describe each process.

## 9.3 The Process of Photosynthesis

The light-dependent reactions of photosynthesis use light energy to produce oxygen and convert ADP and NADP$^+$ into ATP and NADPH.

The light-independent reactions of photosynthesis are also known as the Calvin cycle. The Calvin cycle uses the ATP and NADPH synthesized during the light-dependent reactions and carbon dioxide to make high-energy sugars.

Although many factors affect the rate of photosynthesis, the most important are temperature, light intensity, and the availability of water.

- photosystem
- electron transport chain
- ATP synthase
- Calvin cycle

☑ **Apply Concepts** Explain why temperature, light intensity, and water availability affect the rate of photosynthesis.

## Organize Information

Complete the table to summarize the processes described in this chapter.

| Process | Occurs in | Inputs | Outputs |
|---|---|---|---|
| 1. | 2. | $CO_2$, $H_2O$, sunlight | $O_2$, high-energy sugars |
| Calvin cycle | 3. | NADPH, ATP, $CO_2$ | 6-carbon sugar, ADP, NADP$^+$ |
| 4. | thylakoids | 5. | NADPH, ATP, $O_2$ |
| Electron transport chain | 6. | 7. | low-energy electrons, energy to pump H$^+$ ions from the stroma inside the thylakoid sac |
| | Photosystem II | 8. | 9. |
| | Photosystem I | 10. | 11. |
| | ATP synthase | 12. | 13. |

# Data From the Corn Field

## Design a Solution

HS-LS1-5, HS-LS1-6, HS-LS2-4, HS-LS2-5, CCSS.ELA-LITERACY.RST.9-10.1, CCSS.ELA-LITERACY.WHST.9-10.1, CCSS.ELA-LITERACY.WHST.9-10.7, CCSS.MATH.CONTENT.HSN.Q.A.1, CCSS.MATH.CONTENT.HSS.IC.B.6

Matter is constantly moving in and out of the biosphere, which is the part of Earth in which all life exists. For example, consider the gain in mass that might be shown by a typical field of corn in the American Midwest.

On a warm morning in late spring, a farmer plants his fields with row after row of corn seeds. After a week or so, tiny seedlings begin poking out of the ground. Then the seedlings grow taller. Over the next few weeks they develop new roots and leaves, and then corn ears. After only three or four months, the fields are covered in tall, green corn plants, the ears ready to harvest. This process and these changes are repeated year after year across the United States, especially in a band of land that stretches from Ohio to Nebraska.

A typical acre can yield more than 3800 kilograms of corn. This yield includes only the corn itself. More than half the mass of the corn plant is not harvested, but is plowed under to enrich the soil for the next growing season. What is the source of the mass of these plants? It cannot be the soil. The soil remains thick and fertile year after year. Water is part of the source of the mass, but not all of it. Only about one fourth of the mass of a corn plant is water. A corn plant is about 40 percent carbon by mass. Where does all that carbon come from?

The table describes the significant inputs and outputs of a one-acre corn field. The inputs are things that are added to the field, either by the farmer or naturally. The outputs are the products that the field produces.

| Typical Inputs and Outputs of a One-Acre Corn Field | | |
|---|---|---|
| **Component** | **Role** | **Weight** |
| Corn | Output | 3800 kg (8400 lb) |
| Seeds | Input | 5 kg (11 lb) |
| Fertilizer | Input | 23 kg (50 lb) |
| Water (56 cm of rain) | Input | 2.3 million kg (5 million lb) |

1. **Construct an Explanation** What are the sources of the mass of corn plants? How does photosynthesis contribute to the mass of corn plants?

2. **Calculate** Use the data provided to calculate, as precisely as you can, the amount of carbon dioxide removed from the atmosphere by one acre of corn.

3. **Design a Solution** Is it reasonable to expect that Earth's plants can take up the extra carbon that human activities are adding to the atmosphere? Would some plants be better than others?

   • Research the productivity of different types of plants, including agricultural crops as well as forests. Include plants from different climates. You also may wish to research carbon sequestration in soil.

   • Identify other criteria that should be considered—for example, uses of the plants, water consumption, and cold hardiness.

   • Choose 2–3 plants that could be the most effective at removing carbon from the atmosphere. Write a proposal, citing evidence from your research. Include a model of how your solution depends on plants, photosynthesis, and the carbon cycle.

## 🔍 KEY QUESTIONS AND TERMS

## 9.1 Energy and Life

HS-LS1-5, HS-LS2-3

1. Energy is defined as the ability to
   a. communicate.
   b. reproduce.
   c. grow.
   d. do work.

2. Which of the following is NOT a form of energy?
   a. light
   b. oxygen
   c. heat
   d. electricity

3. Which of the following is used by cells to store and release the energy needed to power cellular processes?
   a. ATP.
   b. RNA.
   c. DNA.
   d. NADP+.

4. How do heterotrophs and autotrophs differ in the way they obtain energy?

5. Compare the amounts of energy stored by ATP and glucose. Which compound is used by a cell as an immediate source of energy?

6. Describe how ATP can release and store energy for the cell.

7. How do plants synthesize high-energy carbohydrates?

## 9.2 Photosynthesis: An Overview

HS-LS1-5, HS-LS2-5

8. Plants use the green pigment chlorophyll to
   a. absorb sunlight.
   b. store sunlight.
   c. reflect sunlight.
   d. change light to heat.

9. High-energy electrons are transported from chlorophyll to other molecules in the chloroplast by
   a. the thylakoid membranes.
   b. pigments such as carotene.
   c. electron carriers such as NADP+.
   d. the protein ATP synthase.

10. Identify and describe the two main parts of a chloroplast where photosynthesis occurs.

11. Write the basic equation for photosynthesis using the names of the starting and final substances of the process.

## 9.3 The Process of Photosynthesis

HS-LS1-5, HS-LS1-6, HS-LS2-5

12. The clusters of chlorophyll and proteins that absorb sunlight and generate high-energy electrons in the chloroplasts are called
    a. carrier proteins.
    b. transport chains.
    c. photosystems.
    d. synthase proteins.

13. In photosystem II, as high-energy electrons are passed to the electron transport chain, the chlorophyll gains new electrons from
    a. oxygen atoms.
    b. water molecules.
    c. hydrogen ions.
    d. carbon dioxide.

14. The light-independent reactions of photosynthesis are also known as the
    a. Calvin cycle.
    b. sugar cycle.
    c. carbon cycle.
    d. ATP cycle.

15. What is the function of the electrons as they move along the electron transport chain?

16. What occurs as $H^+$ ions pass through ATP synthase in the thylakoid membrane, and what is this process called?

17. Why is it important that carbon dioxide molecules from the atmosphere enter the Calvin cycle?

18. Name three important factors that can affect the rate of photosynthesis.

19. Crabgrass is an example of a C4 plant. In addition to biochemical adaptations seen in C4 and CAM plants, what is another way that plants can protect themselves from dry, hot conditions?

**20.** How does a cow use the sugar molecules stored in the grass it eats?

**21.** Summarize the events of the Calvin cycle.

# CRITICAL THINKING

HS-LS1-5, HS-LS1-6, HS-LS2-5

**22. Use Models** Photosynthesis usually produces glucose ($C_6H_{12}O_6$) as a final product. What are the sources of the carbon atoms and hydrogen atoms in glucose? Use a symbolic equation as a model to support your explanation.

**23. Develop Models** Draw a diagram to use as a model of photosynthesis. The model should show the flow of matter and the transformation of light energy into chemical energy.

**24. Summarize** Explain the role of $NADP^+$ as an energy carrier in photosynthesis.

**25. Analyze Text Structure** Using the text from this chapter, analyze the relationships among the key terms *ATP*, *NADP^+*, and *ATP synthase*.

**26. Construct an Explanation** How does photosynthesis benefit both the organism that undergoes it and many other organisms? Include in your explanation how carbon, hydrogen, and oxygen atoms from the reactants of photosynthesis recombine to form compounds that are useful to the organisms.

**27. Use Models** The diagram shows a model of ATP. How would you revise the diagram to illustrate how ATP provides energy for the cell?

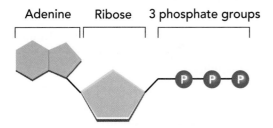

Adenine    Ribose    3 phosphate groups

**28. Defend Your Claim** Could heterotrophs survive without autotrophs? Could autotrophs survive without heterotrophs? Make a claim, and then cite evidence from the text and use logical reasoning to defend it.

**29. Ask Questions** You are observing a species of single-celled algae in a well-lit aquarium. What questions could you ask, and then investigate, to help explain the role of photosynthesis in the algae?

**30. Evaluate** A student plans to isolate chlorophyll, mix it in a solution of carbon dioxide and water, and then shine light on the mixture. Do you predict glucose will be produced inside the mixture? Evaluate this investigation and explain your reasoning.

**31. Construct an Explanation** During photosynthesis, water molecules ($H_2O$) split to produce $H^+$ ions. Use this information, and what you know about the reactions involved in photosynthesis, to explain why water is necessary for photosynthesis to occur.

**32. Energy and Matter** Review the diagram that summarizes the light-independent reactions (Calvin cycle) shown.

  **a.** Why are the light-independent reactions shown as a cycle? What are the inputs and outputs of the cycle?

  **b.** How many carbon atoms enter the Calvin cycle to produce one molecule of glucose? What is the source of these carbon atoms?

  **c.** Why do the light-independent reactions depend on the light-dependent reactions?

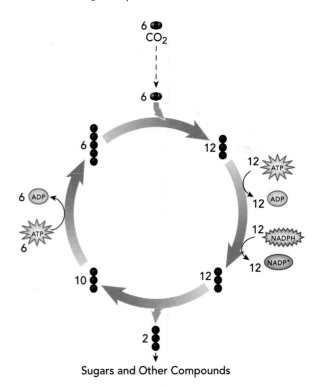

Sugars and Other Compounds

## CROSSCUTTING CONCEPTS

**33. Systems and System Models** A student uses a marble track, like the one shown below, as a model to demonstrate part of the process of photosynthesis. The marbles represent electrons. What process of photosynthesis does the model demonstrate? Describe a way that the model could be improved.

**34. Energy and Matter** Explain how the process of photosynthesis can be used as evidence that energy flows through an ecosystem while matter cycles through an ecosystem.

## MATH CONNECTIONS

### Analyze and Interpret Data

CCSS.MATH.CONTENT.MP2, CCSS.MATH.CONTENT.HSF.BF.A.1, CCSS.MATH.CONTENT.HSS.ID.A.1

Consider the chemical equation that describes the flow of matter in the process of photosynthesis. Use the equation to answer questions 35–37.

$$6CO_2 + 6H_2O \rightarrow C_6H_{12}O_6 + 6O_2$$

**35. Draw Conclusions** What is the source of the hydrogen atoms in glucose ($C_6H_{12}O_6$), one of the products of the reaction?

**36. Infer** When a carbon dioxide molecule ($CO_2$) enters the reaction, do all three of its atoms become part of a glucose molecule ($C_6H_{12}O_6$)? Explain your reasoning.

**37. Reason Quantitatively** Over time, a leaf converts 264 grams of carbon dioxide into 180 grams of glucose. How do you account for the difference in mass of 84 grams?

An aquatic plant emits bubbles of oxygen when placed under a bright light. The table shows the results of an experiment to show the effect of light intensity on bubble production. Use the data in the table to answer questions 38–40.

| Oxygen Production | |
| --- | --- |
| Distance From Light (cm) | Bubbles Produced per Minute |
| 10 | 39 |
| 20 | 22 |
| 30 | 8 |
| 40 | 5 |

**38. Create an Equation** Write a linear equation that fits the data approximately. To determine the equation, plot the points and draw a line that passes near the points.

**39. Interpret Graphs** Describe the trend in the data. Use the linear equation you constructed to predict the number of bubbles that would appear when the light source is 5, 25, and 50 cm away.

**40. Draw Conclusions** What conclusion about photosynthesis is supported by the evidence from this experiment? Explain your reasoning.

## LANGUAGE ARTS CONNECTIONS

### Write About Science

HS-LS1-5, CCSS.ELA-LITERACY.WHST.9-10.2

**41. Write Informative Texts** Write a paragraph that describes how the light-dependent and light-independent reactions work together to perform photosynthesis.

**42. Write Explanatory Texts** Write a paragraph that explains how the flow of matter and energy into a cell results in the transfer from light energy to stored chemical energy in photosynthesis.

### Read About Science

CCSS.ELA-LITERACY.RST.9-10.5

**43. Analyze Text Structure** Explain the relationship among these parts or systems of photosynthesis: photosystem I, photosystem II, ATP, NADP+, light-dependent reactions, and light-independent reactions. Use the organization and headings of Lesson 9.2 to help you construct your response.

# END-OF-COURSE TEST PRACTICE

1. A student is making a model to illustrate the functions of ADP and ATP in photosynthesis. Which model best illustrates the role of ATP in photosynthesis?
   A. A power plant that generates energy
   B. A rechargeable battery that stores and releases energy
   C. A pigment that receives the energy of sunlight
   D. A pan that carries coal
   E. A hammer that helps break apart water molecules

**Questions 2 and 3.**
The diagram is a model of the process of photosynthesis.

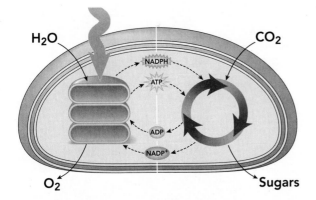

2. During photosynthesis, how is the light energy that strikes the cell transformed into the chemical energy stored in sugars?
   A. Energy is transferred directly to sugars, with no intermediates.
   B. Energy is transferred to sugars through intermediates such as $H_2O$, $O_2$, and $CO_2$.
   C. Energy is transferred to sugars through intermediates, such as ATP and NADPH.
   D. Energy is transferred to sugars through intermediates, such as chloroplasts.
   E. Energy is transferred to sugars through light-dependent reactions.

3. Which statement accurately describes the role of the light-independent reactions?
   A. Transforming light energy into chemical energy
   B. Transferring chemical energy to high-energy sugars
   C. Returning chemical energy to light energy
   D. Transferring light energy among different compounds
   E. Performing chemical reactions without an energy source

4. Which of the following describe the role of photosynthesis in the carbon cycle?
   A. Storage of carbon in the atmosphere
   B. Storage of carbon in the geosphere
   C. Transfer of carbon from the hydrosphere to the atmosphere
   D. Transfer of carbon from the atmosphere to the hydrosphere
   E. Transfer of carbon from the atmosphere to the biosphere

5. Plants use the sugars produced by photosynthesis to synthesize which of the following types of macromolecules?
   I. complex carbohydrates
   II. amino acids
   III. lipids
   A. I only
   B. II only
   C. III only
   D. I and II only
   E. I, II, and III

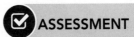 **ASSESSMENT**

For additional assessment practice, go online to access your digital course.

| If You Have Trouble With... | | | | | |
|---|---|---|---|---|---|
| **Question** | 1 | 2 | 3 | 4 | 5 |
| **See Lesson** | 9.1 | 9.2 | 9.3 | 9.2 | 9.3 |
| **Performance Expectation** | HS-LS1-5 | HS-LS1-5 | HS-LS1-5 | HS-LS2-5 | HS-LS1-6 |

CHAPTER 10

# Cellular Respiration



Go Online to access your digital course.

- VIDEO
- AUDIO
- INTERACTIVITY
- eTEXT
- ANIMATION
- VIRTUAL LAB
- ASSESSMENT

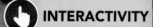

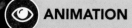

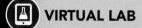

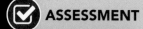

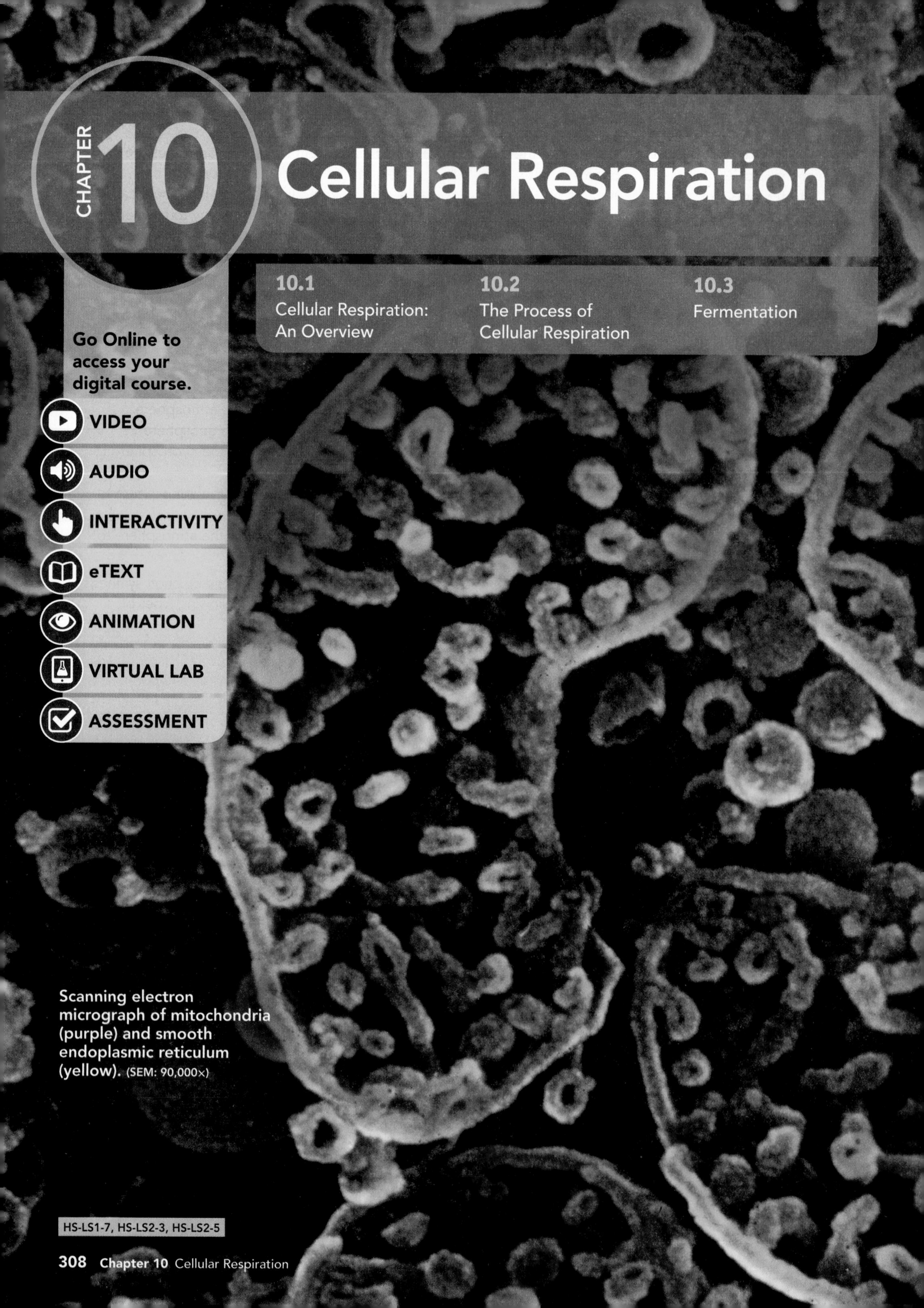

Scanning electron micrograph of mitochondria (purple) and smooth endoplasmic reticulum (yellow). (SEM: 90,000×)

HS-LS1-7, HS-LS2-3, HS-LS2-5

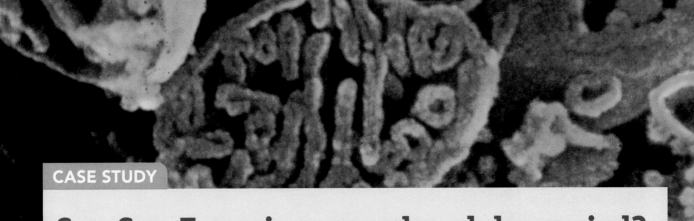

# Can San Francisco sourdough be copied?

The city of San Francisco is famous for many things, including its sourdough bread. The bread has a distinctive chewy texture and tangy acidic taste, making it one of the city's favorite treats.

Breads that are not sourdough are made by combining flour with a mixture of water, baker's yeast, and sometimes a little sugar. After the ingredients are thoroughly mixed, the moist dough is left to rise as the yeast does its work. Then the dough is formed into a loaf and baked. Sourdough is different in several ways. Instead of baker's yeast, sourdough relies on "wild" yeast from the environment. Bacteria also contribute to the bread-making process. The yeast and bacteria are captured and then kept alive in a sourdough starter.

Making sourdough starter from scratch is a mysterious and hotly debated process. Many people use nothing but flour and water. Some people say all-purpose white flour is fine, but others insist on using rye or whole wheat flour or a mixture of different flours. Some starter recipes call for additional ingredients, such as active dry yeast, milk, buttermilk, yogurt, whey, or even crushed grapes.

The ingredients, whatever they may be, are mixed together and allowed to remain at room temperature. Within a day or so, the mixture begins to bubble. More flour and water are stirred in, and some of the mixture is discarded. Feeding the starter with fresh water and flour is done every day. After a few days, if all goes well, the would-be baker has a beige, bubbly lump that smells sour but is not spoiled. Some of this starter can be baked into bread, and some of it can be saved to make more starter.

In San Francisco, most of the bakeries captured their yeast and bacteria many years ago. One bakery claims that their sourdough starter was established in 1849 and has been growing ever since! The bakers maintain the starter by adding fresh flour and water, which keeps their microscopic friends alive and healthy. Then, for every batch of bread, they mix some of that starter with fresh dough. The yeast and bacteria grow rapidly, and they produce tiny bubbles that cause the dough to rise. The bacteria also produce compounds such as lactic acid and acetic acid, which provide the bread with its distinctive taste.

Bakeries in other cities have tried to duplicate San Francisco sourdough. Some have taken samples of the best sourdough starters and tried to maintain them. These bakeries have made some very good bread. However, try as they might, they have not been able to match the best loaves from San Francisco.

Why is the San Francisco sourdough so distinctive? Why has it been so hard to match this taste in other places around the country?

**Throughout this chapter, look for connections to the** CASE STUDY **to help you answer these questions.**

# Cellular Respiration: An Overview

**HS-LS1-7:** Use a model to illustrate that cellular respiration is a chemical process whereby the bonds of food molecules and oxygen molecules are broken and the bonds in new compounds are formed resulting in a net transfer of energy.

**HS-LS2-3:** Construct and revise an explanation based on evidence for the cycling of matter and flow of energy in aerobic and anaerobic conditions.

**HS-LS2-5:** Develop a model to illustrate the role of photosynthesis and cellular respiration in the cycling of carbon among the biosphere, atmosphere, hydrosphere, and geosphere.

### VOCABULARY

**calorie**
**cellular respiration**
**aerobic**
**anaerobic**

### READING TOOL

As you read, record the key ideas from each heading in your 📖 **Biology Foundations Workbook.**

When you are hungry, how do you feel? If you are like most of us, you might feel sluggish, a little dizzy, and—above all—weak. You feel weak when you are hungry because food serves as a source of energy. This is your body's way of telling you that your energy supplies are low. How does food get converted into a usable form of energy? Do our bodies burn food the way a car burns gasoline, or is there something more to it?

## Chemical Energy and Food

Food provides living things with the chemical building blocks needed to grow and reproduce. Food molecules contain chemical energy that is released when their chemical bonds are broken. 🔍 *Organisms get the energy they need from food.*

How much energy is actually present in food? Quite a lot, although it varies with the type of food. Energy that is stored in food is expressed in units of calories. A **calorie** is the amount of energy needed to raise the temperature of 1 gram of water 1 degree Celsius. The Calorie (capital *C*) that is used on food labels is actually a kilocalorie, or 1000 calories. Cells can use all sorts of molecules for food, including fats, proteins, and carbohydrates. The energy stored in each of these macromolecules (also called biomolecules) varies because their chemical structures, and therefore their energy-storing bonds, differ. For example, 1 gram of the sugar glucose releases 3811 calories of heat energy when it is burned. By contrast, 1 gram of the fat found in beef releases 8893 calories of heat energy. In general, carbohydrates and proteins contain approximately 4000 calories (4 Calories) of energy per gram, whereas fats contain approximately 9000 calories (9 Calories) per gram.

Of course, cells don't simply burn food and release energy as heat. Instead, they break down food molecules gradually, capturing a little bit of chemical energy every step along the way. This enables cells to use the energy stored in foods like glucose to synthesize compounds such as ATP that directly power the activities of the cell.

**☑ READING CHECK** **Compare** What is the difference between the calorie (lowercase *c*) and the Calorie (capital *C*)?

# Overview of Cellular Respiration

If oxygen is available, organisms can obtain energy from food by **cellular respiration**. 🔍 *Cellular respiration is a process of energy conversion that releases energy from food in the presence of oxygen.* Although cellular respiration involves dozens of separate reactions, an overall chemical summary of the process is remarkably simple:

**In Symbols:**

$$6O_2 + C_6H_{12}O_6 \rightarrow 6CO_2 + 6H_2O + \text{Energy}$$

**In Words:**

$$\text{Oxygen} + \text{Glucose} \rightarrow \text{Carbon dioxide} + \text{Water} + \text{Energy}$$

As you can see, cellular respiration requires oxygen and a food molecule such as glucose, and it gives off carbon dioxide, water, and energy. Do not be misled, however, by the simplicity of this equation. If cellular respiration took place in just one step, all of the energy from glucose would be released at once, and most of it would be lost in the form of light and heat. Clearly, a living cell has to control that energy. It can't simply start a fire—the cell has to release the explosive chemical energy in food molecules a little bit at a time, trapping the energy in the form of ATP.

 **INTERACTIVITY**

Explore what happens during the different stages of cellular respiration.

---

**CASE STUDY** Analyzing Data

## You Are What You Eat

The table shows the amount of proteins, carbohydrates, and fats for several different foods.

1. **Interpret Data** Per serving, which of the foods included in the table has the most protein? Which has the most carbohydrates? Which has the most fat?

2. **Reason Quantitatively** Approximately how many more Calories are there in 2 slices of bacon than there are in 3 slices of roasted turkey? Why is there a difference?

3. **Compare** Use the table to compare nutrients in a slice of sourdough bread with other foods.

| Composition of Some Common Foods | | | |
|---|---|---|---|
| Food | Protein (g) | Carbohydrate (g) | Fat (g) |
| Apple, 1 medium | 0 | 22 | 0 |
| Bacon, 2 slices | 5 | 0 | 6 |
| Chocolate, 1 bar | 3 | 23 | 13 |
| Eggs, 2 whole | 12 | 0 | 9 |
| 2% milk, 1 cup | 8 | 12 | 5 |
| Potato chips, 15 chips | 2 | 14 | 10 |
| Sourdough bread, 2 slices | 8 | 36 | 1 |
| Skinless roasted turkey, 3 slices | 11 | 3 | 1 |

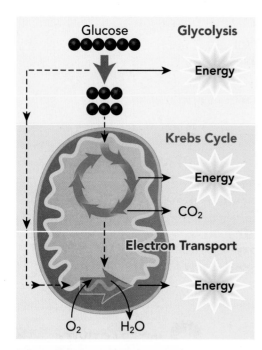

Glucose    Glycolysis

Energy

Krebs Cycle

Energy

$CO_2$

Electron Transport

Energy

$O_2$    $H_2O$

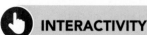

## INTERACTIVITY

**Figure 10-1**

## The Stages of Cellular Respiration

There are three stages to cellular respiration: glycolysis, the Krebs cycle, and the electron transport chain.

## BUILD VOCABULARY

**Using Prefixes** The prefix *an-* in *anaerobic* means "not" or "without." Anaerobic processes do not use oxygen, so they are not aerobic.

**Stages of Cellular Respiration** Cellular respiration captures the energy from food in three main stages—glycolysis, the Krebs cycle, and electron transport. Although cells can use just about any food molecule for energy, we will concentrate on just one as an example—the simple sugar glucose.

Glucose first enters a chemical pathway known as glycolysis. Only about 10 percent of its energy is captured to produce ATP during this stage. In fact, at the end of glycolysis, about 90 percent of the chemical energy that was available in glucose is still unused, locked in the chemical bonds of a molecule called pyruvic acid.

How does the cell extract the rest of that energy? First, pyruvic acid enters the second stage of cellular respiration, the Krebs cycle, where a little more energy is captured. The bulk of the energy, however, comes from the final stage of cellular respiration, the electron transport chain. This stage requires reactants from the other two stages of the process, as shown by dashed lines in **Figure 10-1**. How does the electron transport chain extract so much energy from these reactants? It uses one of the world's most powerful electron acceptors—oxygen.

**Oxygen and Energy** Oxygen is required at the very end of the electron transport chain. Any time a cell's demand for energy increases, its use of oxygen increases, too. The double meaning of respiration points out a crucial connection between cells and organisms: Most of the energy-releasing pathways within cells require oxygen, and that is the reason we need to breathe, or respire.

Pathways of cellular respiration that require oxygen are said to be **aerobic** ("in air"). The Krebs cycle and the electron transport chain are both aerobic processes. Even though the Krebs cycle does not *directly* require oxygen, it is classified as an aerobic process because it cannot run without the oxygen-requiring electron transport chain. Glycolysis, however, does not directly require oxygen, nor does it rely on an oxygen-requiring process to run. Glycolysis is therefore said to be **anaerobic** ("without air"). Even though glycolysis is anaerobic, it is considered part of cellular respiration because its final products are key reactants for the aerobic stages.

Glycolysis occurs in the cytoplasm. In contrast, the Krebs cycle and electron transport chain, which generate the majority of ATP during cellular respiration, take place inside the mitochondria. If oxygen is not present, another anaerobic pathway, known as fermentation, makes it possible for the cell to keep glycolysis running, generating ATP to power cellular activity. You will learn more about fermentation later in this chapter.

✓ **READING CHECK** **Summarize** What stages of cellular respiration are considered aerobic?

# Comparing Photosynthesis and Cellular Respiration

If nearly all organisms break down food by the process of cellular respiration, why doesn't Earth run out of oxygen? As it happens, cellular respiration is balanced by another process: photosynthesis. The energy flows in photosynthesis and cellular respiration take place in completely opposite directions. Look at **Figure 10-2**, and then think of the chemical energy as part of Earth's savings account. Photosynthesis is the process that "deposits" energy. Cellular respiration is the process that "withdraws" energy. As you might expect, the equations for photosynthesis and cellular respiration are the reverse of each other.

Chemically, the process of photosynthesis uses water and carbon dioxide as the raw materials to synthesize carbohydrates. Cellular respiration does the opposite, using carbohydrates as sources of chemical energy while releasing water and carbon dioxide. ⌕ *Photosynthesis removes carbon dioxide from the atmosphere, and cellular respiration puts it back. Photosynthesis releases oxygen into the atmosphere, and cellular respiration uses that oxygen to release energy from food.*

The global balance between cellular respiration and photosynthesis is essential to maintain Earth as a living planet. Another necessity is a constant input of energy into the system. This input comes from the sun. You can trace the flow of energy from the sun to organisms that perform photosynthesis and then to a series of organisms that perform cellular respiration.

**INTERACTIVITY**

Investigate how algae can be used to create biofuels by conducting a virtual experiment.

**Figure 10-2**

## A Global Balance

Photosynthesis and respiration can be thought of as opposite processes because the products of one are the reactants of the other. Note that plants perform both processes.

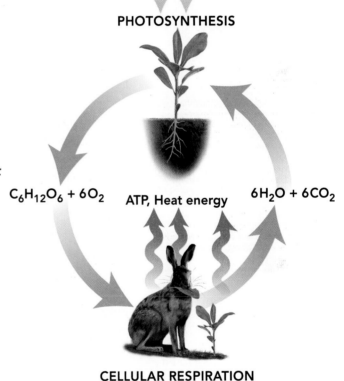

Light energy

**PHOTOSYNTHESIS**

$C_6H_{12}O_6 + 6O_2$     ATP, Heat energy     $6H_2O + 6CO_2$

**CELLULAR RESPIRATION**

HS-LS1-7, HS-LS2-3, HS-LS2-5

---

## ✓ LESSON 10.1 Review

### ⌕ KEY QUESTIONS

1. Why do all organisms need food?
2. Write the overall reaction for cellular respiration.
3. "Photosynthesis and cellular respiration have opposite effects on gases in the atmosphere." Explain this statement.

### CRITICAL THINKING

4. **Identify** Breathing is required for cellular respiration. Use the reactants, products, and stages of cellular respiration to explain why breathing is required.

5. **Construct an Explanation** Compare the chemical equations for photosynthesis and cellular respiration. Explain how the two processes are interrelated.

# The Process of Cellular Respiration

## KEY QUESTIONS
- *What happens during the process of glycolysis?*
- *What happens during the Krebs cycle?*
- *How does the electron transport chain use high-energy electrons from glycolysis and the Krebs cycle?*
- *How much ATP does cellular respiration generate?*

**HS-LS1-7:** Use a model to illustrate that cellular respiration is a chemical process whereby the bonds of food molecules and oxygen molecules are broken and the bonds in new compounds are formed resulting in a net transfer of energy.

**HS-LS2-3:** Construct and revise an explanation based on evidence for the cycling of matter and flow of energy in aerobic and anaerobic conditions.

**HS-LS2-5:** Develop a model to illustrate the role of photosynthesis and cellular respiration in the cycling of carbon among the biosphere, atmosphere, hydrosphere, and geosphere.

## VOCABULARY

glycolysis
NAD$^+$
Krebs cycle
matrix

## READING TOOL

As you read, take note of the sequence of events in cellular respiration. Fill in the graphic organizer in your ▨ **Biology Foundations Workbook.**

Food burns! It's true that many common foods (think of apples, bananas, and ground beef) have too much water in them to actually light with a match, but foods with little water (think of sugar, flour, and cooking oil) will burn. In fact, wheat grain, which contains both carbohydrates and protein, is so flammable that it has caused many fires, including the one seen here at a grain elevator in North Dakota. So, plenty of energy is available in food, but how does a living cell extract that energy without catching fire or blowing itself up? The trick is to release and capture that energy a little bit at a time.

## Glycolysis

The first set of reactions in cellular respiration is known as **glycolysis**, which literally means "sugar-breaking." ⚲ *During glycolysis, 1 molecule of glucose, a 6-carbon compound, is transformed into 2 molecules of the 3-carbon compound pyruvic acid.* As the bonds in glucose are broken and rearranged, small amounts of energy are released and captured in other molecules. The process of glycolysis is shown in **Figure 10-3**.

**ATP Production**  Even though glycolysis is an energy-releasing process, the cell needs to put in a little energy to get things going. At the pathway's beginning, 2 ATP molecules are used up. Earlier in this chapter, photosynthesis and cellular respiration were compared, respectively, to a deposit to and a withdrawal from a savings account. Similarly, the 2 ATP molecules used at the onset of glycolysis are like an investment that pays back interest. Although the cell puts 2 ATP molecules into its "account" to get glycolysis going, glycolysis produces 4 ATP molecules. This gives the cell a net gain of 2 ATP molecules for each molecule of glucose that enters glycolysis.

**NADH Production** One of the reactions of glycolysis removes 4 electrons, now in a high-energy state, and passes them to an electron carrier called **NAD⁺**, or nicotinamide adenine dinucleotide. Like NADP⁺ in photosynthesis, each NAD⁺ molecule accepts a pair of high-energy electrons and a hydrogen ion. This molecule, now known as NADH, holds the electrons until they can be transferred to other molecules. As you will see, in the presence of oxygen, these high-energy electrons can be used to produce even more ATP molecules.

## The Advantages of Glycolysis

In the process of glycolysis, 4 ATP molecules are synthesized from 4 ADP molecules. Given that 2 ATP molecules are used to start the process, there is a net gain of just 2 ATP molecules. Although the energy yield from glycolysis is small, the process is so fast that cells can produce thousands of ATP molecules in just a few milliseconds. The speed of glycolysis can be a big advantage when the energy demands of a cell suddenly increase.

Besides speed, another advantage of glycolysis is that the process itself does not require oxygen. This means that glycolysis can quickly supply chemical energy to cells when oxygen is not available. When oxygen is available, however, the pyruvic acid and NADH "outputs" generated during glycolysis become the "inputs" for the other processes of cellular respiration.

✓ **READING CHECK** **Use Analogies** How is the ATP produced in glycolysis like earning a return on an investment?

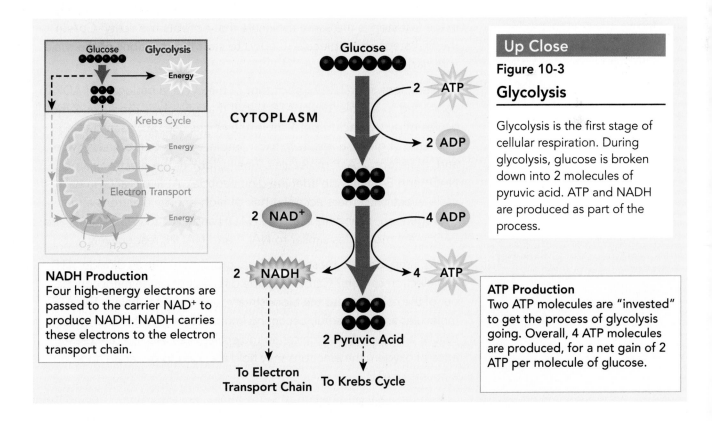

**Glucose** **Glycolysis**
**Energy**
**Krebs Cycle**
**Energy**
CO₂
**Electron Transport**
**Energy**
O₂ H₂O

**NADH Production**
Four high-energy electrons are passed to the carrier NAD⁺ to produce NADH. NADH carries these electrons to the electron transport chain.

**Glucose**

**CYTOPLASM**

2 **ATP**
2 **ADP**

2 **NAD⁺**
4 **ADP**

2 **NADH**
4 **ATP**

2 **Pyruvic Acid**

**To Electron Transport Chain**
**To Krebs Cycle**

**Up Close**

**Figure 10-3**

**Glycolysis**

Glycolysis is the first stage of cellular respiration. During glycolysis, glucose is broken down into 2 molecules of pyruvic acid. ATP and NADH are produced as part of the process.

**ATP Production**
Two ATP molecules are "invested" to get the process of glycolysis going. Overall, 4 ATP molecules are produced, for a net gain of 2 ATP per molecule of glucose.

**READING TOOL**

Make a T-chart for the three stages of cellular respiration. Write down the inputs in one column and the outputs in the other.

# The Krebs Cycle

In the presence of oxygen, the pyruvic acid produced in glycolysis passes to the second stage of cellular respiration, the **Krebs cycle**. The Krebs cycle is named for Hans Krebs, the British biochemist who demonstrated its existence in 1937. ✎ *During the Krebs cycle, pyruvic acid is broken down into carbon dioxide in a series of energy-extracting reactions.* Because citric acid is the first compound formed in this series of reactions, the Krebs cycle is also known as the citric acid cycle.

**Citric Acid Production**  The Krebs cycle begins when pyruvic acid produced by glycolysis passes through the two membranes of the mitochondrion and into the matrix. The **matrix** is the innermost compartment of the mitochondrion and the site of the Krebs cycle reactions. Once inside the matrix, 1 carbon atom from pyruvic acid is split off to produce carbon dioxide, which is eventually released into the air. The other 2 carbon atoms from pyruvic acid rearrange to form acetic acid, which is joined to a compound called coenzyme A. The resulting molecule is called acetyl-CoA. As the Krebs cycle begins, acetyl-CoA hands off that 2-carbon acetyl group to a 4-carbon molecule already present in the cycle, producing a 6-carbon molecule called citric acid.

**Energy Extraction**  Follow the reactions in **Figure 10-4** to see how the cycle continues. First, look at the 6 carbon atoms in citric acid. One is removed, and then another is removed, releasing 2 molecules of carbon dioxide and leaving a 4-carbon molecule. Why is the Krebs cycle a "cycle"? Because the 4-carbon molecule produced in the last step is the same molecule that accepts the acetyl-CoA in the first step. The molecule needed to start the reactions of the cycle is remade with every "turn."

Next, look for ATP. For each turn of the cycle, a molecule of ADP is converted to a molecule of ATP. Recall that glycolysis produces 2 molecules of pyruvic acid from 1 molecule of glucose. So, each starting molecule of glucose results in two complete turns of the Krebs cycle and, therefore, 2 ATP molecules. Finally, look at the electron carriers, $NAD^+$ and FAD (flavine adenine dinucleotide). At five places in each cycle, electron carriers accept a pair of high-energy electrons and a hydrogen ion, changing $NAD^+$ to NADH and FAD to $FADH_2$. FAD and $FADH_2$ are molecules similar to $NAD^+$ and NADH, respectively.

What happens to these Krebs cycle products—carbon dioxide, ATP, and electron carriers? Carbon dioxide diffuses out of the mitochondria, out of the cell, and into the bloodstream, and then is exhaled. The ATP molecules are *very* useful, becoming immediately available to power cellular activities. As for the carrier molecules like NADH, in the presence of oxygen, the electrons they hold are used to generate huge amounts of ATP.

☑ **READING CHECK** List  Make a list of the energy carriers involved in the Krebs cycle. Include their names before and after they accept the electrons.

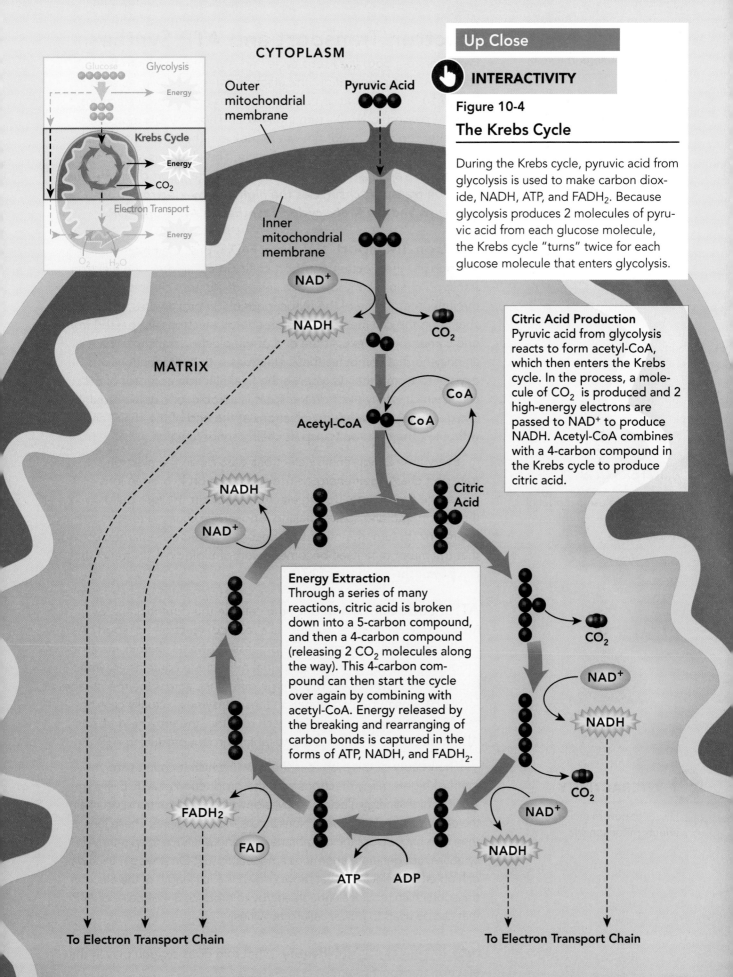

CYTOPLASM

Outer mitochondrial membrane

Inner mitochondrial membrane

Pyruvic Acid

MATRIX

NAD+

NADH

$CO_2$

CoA

Acetyl-CoA — CoA

NADH

NAD+

Citric Acid

$CO_2$

NAD+

NADH

$CO_2$

NAD+

NADH

FADH₂

FAD

ATP   ADP

To Electron Transport Chain

To Electron Transport Chain

Figure 10-4

### The Krebs Cycle

During the Krebs cycle, pyruvic acid from glycolysis is used to make carbon dioxide, NADH, ATP, and FADH₂. Because glycolysis produces 2 molecules of pyruvic acid from each glucose molecule, the Krebs cycle "turns" twice for each glucose molecule that enters glycolysis.

**Citric Acid Production**
Pyruvic acid from glycolysis reacts to form acetyl-CoA, which then enters the Krebs cycle. In the process, a molecule of $CO_2$ is produced and 2 high-energy electrons are passed to NAD+ to produce NADH. Acetyl-CoA combines with a 4-carbon compound in the Krebs cycle to produce citric acid.

**Energy Extraction**
Through a series of many reactions, citric acid is broken down into a 5-carbon compound, and then a 4-carbon compound (releasing 2 $CO_2$ molecules along the way). This 4-carbon compound can then start the cycle over again by combining with acetyl-CoA. Energy released by the breaking and rearranging of carbon bonds is captured in the forms of ATP, NADH, and FADH₂.

Glucose   Glycolysis

Energy

Krebs Cycle

Energy

$CO_2$

Electron Transport

Energy

$O_2$   $H_2O$

# Electron Transport and ATP Synthesis

Products from both the Krebs cycle and glycolysis feed into the last stage of cellular respiration, the electron transport chain, as seen in **Figure 10-5**. Recall that glycolysis generates high-energy electrons that are passed to $NAD^+$, forming NADH. Those NADH molecules can enter the mitochondrion, where they join the NADH and $FADH_2$ molecules generated by the Krebs cycle. The electrons are then passed from all those carriers to the electron transport chain. ⚡ *The electron transport chain uses the high-energy electrons from glycolysis and the Krebs cycle to synthesize ATP from ADP.*

**Electron Transport** NADH and $FADH_2$ pass their high-energy electrons to the electron transport chain. In eukaryotes, the electron transport chain is composed of a series of electron carriers located in the inner membrane of the mitochondrion. In prokaryotes, the same chain is in the cell membrane. High-energy electrons are passed from one carrier to the next. At the end of the electron transport chain is an enzyme that combines these electrons with hydrogen ions and oxygen to form water. Oxygen is the final electron acceptor of the chain, which is why electron transport is aerobic, or oxygen-requiring. Oxygen accepts low energy electrons at the end of the chain, and without it, the electron transport chain cannot function.

Every time 2 high-energy electrons pass down the electron transport chain, their energy is used to transport hydrogen ions ($H^+$) across the membrane. During electron transport, $H^+$ ions build up in the intermembrane space, making it positively charged relative to the matrix. In turn, the other side becomes negatively charged so that the membrane itself becomes a sort of biological "battery" that can power the synthesis of ATP.

**ATP Production** How does the cell use the potential energy from charge differences built up as a result of electron transport? As in photosynthesis, the cell uses a process known as chemiosmosis to produce ATP. The inner mitochondrial membrane contains enzymes known as ATP synthases. The charge difference across the membrane forces $H^+$ ions through channels in these enzymes, actually causing the ATP synthases to spin. With each rotation, the enzyme grabs an ADP molecule and attaches a phosphate group, producing ATP.

The beauty of this system is the way in which it couples the movement of high-energy electrons with the production of ATP. Every time a pair of high-energy electrons moves down the electron transport chain, the energy is used to move $H^+$ ions across the membrane. These ions then rush back across the membrane with enough force to spin the ATP synthase and generate enormous amounts of ATP. On average, each pair of high-energy electrons that moves down the full length of the electron transport chain provides enough energy to produce 3 molecules of ATP that can be used to power cellular activities.

**INTERACTIVITY**

Develop and use a model of the three stages of cellular respiration.

**INTERACTIVITY**

Discover how exercise affects mitochondria.

✓ **READING CHECK** **Identify** What role does oxygen play in the electron transport chain?

# The Electron Transport Chain and ATP Synthesis

The electron transport chain uses high-energy electrons transported by the carrier molecules NADH from both the Krebs cycle and glycolysis, and $FADH_2$ from the Krebs cycle, to convert ADP into ATP.

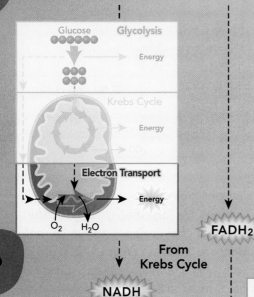

**Electron Transport**

**From Krebs Cycle**

**FADH₂**

**MATRIX**

**NADH**

**From Glycolysis**

**NADH**

**ATP Production**
H⁺ ions pass back across the mitochondrial membrane through ATP synthase, causing the base of the synthase molecule to rotate. With each rotation, driven by the movement of an H⁺ ion, ATP synthase generates ATP from ADP.

**Electron Transport**
High-energy electrons from NADH and $FADH_2$ are passed from carrier to carrier, down the electron transport chain. Water is formed when oxygen accepts the electrons in combination with hydrogen ions. Energy generated by the electron transport chain is used to move H⁺ ions across the inner mitochondrial membrane and into the intermembrane space.

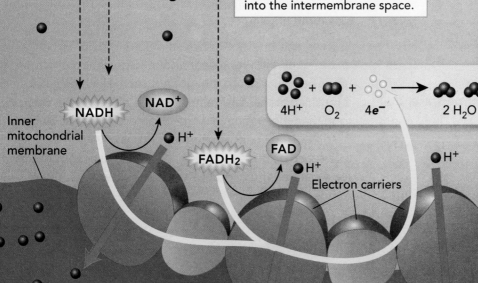

$$4H^+ + O_2 + 4e^- \longrightarrow 2\,H_2O$$

Inner mitochondrial membrane

NADH    NAD⁺

H⁺

FADH₂    FAD

H⁺

Electron carriers

H⁺

H⁺

ATP

ADP

H⁺    H⁺    H⁺

**INTERMEMBRANE SPACE**

Outer mitochondrial membrane

**CYTOPLASM**

## Modeling Lab  Open-ended Inquiry

### Making a Model of Cellular Respiration

**Problem** How can you create a model of cellular respiration?

In this lab, you will plan and construct a model of cellular respiration. You will use the model to demonstrate how matter and energy flow in and out of the cell. Then you will evaluate the model and the models made by classmates.

You can find this lab in your digital course.

## The Totals

Glycolysis nets just 2 ATP molecules per molecule of glucose. In the presence of oxygen, everything changes. *Together, glycolysis, the Krebs cycle, and the electron transport chain release about 36 molecules of ATP per molecule of glucose.* Notice in **Figure 10-6** that under aerobic conditions, these pathways enable the cell to produce 18 times as much energy as can be generated by anaerobic glycolysis alone. This is roughly 36 ATP molecules per glucose molecule versus just 2 ATP molecules in glycolysis.

Our diets contain much more than just glucose, of course, but that's no problem for the cell. Complex carbohydrates are broken down to simple sugars like glucose. Lipids and proteins can be broken down into molecules that enter the Krebs cycle or glycolysis at one of several places. Like a furnace that can burn oil, gas, or wood, the cell can generate chemical energy in the form of ATP from just about any source.

How efficient is cellular respiration? The 36 ATP molecules generated represent about 36 percent of the total energy of glucose. That might not seem like much, but it means that the cell is actually more efficient at using food than the engine of a typical automobile is at burning gasoline. What happens to the remaining 64 percent? It is released as heat, which is one of the reasons your body feels warmer after vigorous exercise and why your body temperature remains a steady 37°C day and night.

### Figure 10-6
### Energy Totals

The complete breakdown of glucose through cellular respiration results in the production of 36 molecules of ATP.

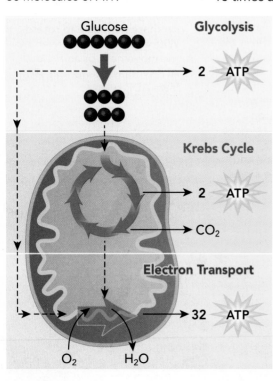

HS-LS1-7, HS-LS2-3, HS-LS2-5

## ☑ LESSON 10.2 Review

### 🔍 KEY QUESTIONS

1. What are the products of glycolysis?

2. What happens to pyruvic acid in the Krebs cycle?

3. How does the electron transport chain use the high-energy electrons from glycolysis and the Krebs cycle?

4. How many molecules of ATP may be produced from glucose?

### CRITICAL THINKING

5. **Integrate Information** How does the presence of oxygen affect the chemical pathways used to extract energy from glucose?

6. **Construct an Explanation** How are hydrogen ions (H⁺) essential for the production of ATP?

7. **Use Models** Create a model to show the bonds that are broken and formed in cellular respiration.

# Fermentation

### KEY QUESTIONS

- *How do organisms generate energy when oxygen is not available?*
- *How does the body produce ATP during different stages of exercise?*

HS-LS1-7: Use a model to illustrate that cellular respiration is a chemical process whereby the bonds of food molecules and oxygen molecules are broken and the bonds in new compounds are formed resulting in a net transfer of energy.
HS-LS2-3: Construct and revise an explanation based on evidence for the cycling of matter and flow of energy in aerobic and anaerobic conditions.

We are air-breathing organisms who use oxygen to release chemical energy from the foods we eat. What happens if oxygen is not available? What happens when you hold your breath and dive underwater like a dolphin, or use up oxygen so quickly that you cannot replace it fast enough? Do your cells simply stop working? Microorganisms in places where oxygen is not available, like the middle of a mound of moist bread dough, face the same problem. Is there a pathway that allows cells to extract energy from food in the absence of oxygen?

## Fermentation

Recall from earlier in this chapter that two benefits of glycolysis are that it can produce ATP quickly and that it does not require oxygen. This means that in the absence of oxygen, many cells can use glycolysis alone to generate all the ATP they need. However, when a cell begins to generate large amounts of ATP this way, it runs into a problem. In just a few seconds, all of the cell's available $NAD^+$ molecules are filled up with electrons. Without oxygen, the electron transport chain does not run, so there is nowhere for the NADH molecules to deposit their electrons. Thus, NADH does not get converted back to $NAD^+$. Without $NAD^+$, the cell cannot keep glycolysis going, and ATP production stops. That's where a process called fermentation comes in.

When oxygen is not present, glycolysis is kept going by a pathway that makes it possible to continue to produce ATP without oxygen. The combined process of this pathway and glycolysis is called **fermentation**. 🔍 *In the absence of oxygen, fermentation releases energy from food molecules by producing ATP.*

**VOCABULARY**
**fermentation**

**READING TOOL**

As you read the text, compare and contrast cellular respiration and fermentation. Fill in the Venn Diagram in your 📘 Biology Foundations Workbook.

**BUILD VOCABULARY**

**Word Origins** The word **fermentation** comes from the Latin word *fermentum*, which means "yeast".

During fermentation, cells convert NADH to NAD$^+$ by passing high-energy electrons back to pyruvic acid. This action converts NADH back into the electron carrier NAD$^+$, allowing glycolysis to keep going and to produce a steady supply of ATP. Fermentation is an anaerobic process that occurs in the cytoplasm of cells. Sometimes, glycolysis and fermentation are together referred to as anaerobic respiration. There are two slightly different forms of the process—alcoholic fermentation and lactic acid fermentation, which are summarized in **Figure 10-7**.

**Alcoholic Fermentation** Alcoholic fermentation is carried out by yeast, producing ethyl alcohol and carbon dioxide. A summary of alcoholic fermentation after glycolysis is written below.

$$\text{Pyruvic acid} + \text{NADH} \rightarrow \text{Alcohol} + CO_2 + \text{NAD}^+$$

Alcoholic fermentation is used to produce beer, wine, and other alcoholic beverages. It is also the process that causes bread dough to rise. Since the yeast very quickly use up any oxygen dissolved in the dough, they switch over to fermentation, giving off tiny bubbles of carbon dioxide. These bubbles form the air spaces you see in a slice of bread. The small amount of alcohol produced in the dough evaporates when the bread is baked.

**Lactic Acid Fermentation** Other organisms carry out fermentation using a chemical reaction that converts pyruvic acid to lactic acid. Unlike alcoholic fermentation, lactic acid fermentation does not give off carbon dioxide. However, like alcoholic fermentation, lactic acid fermentation also regenerates NAD$^+$ so that glycolysis can continue. Lactic acid fermentation after glycolysis is summarized here.

$$\text{Pyruvic acid} + \text{NADH} \rightarrow \text{Lactic acid} + \text{NAD}^+$$

### Figure 10-7
### Fermentation

In alcoholic fermentation, pyruvic acid produced by glycolysis is converted into alcohol and carbon dioxide. Lactic acid fermentation converts the pyruvic acid to lactic acid.

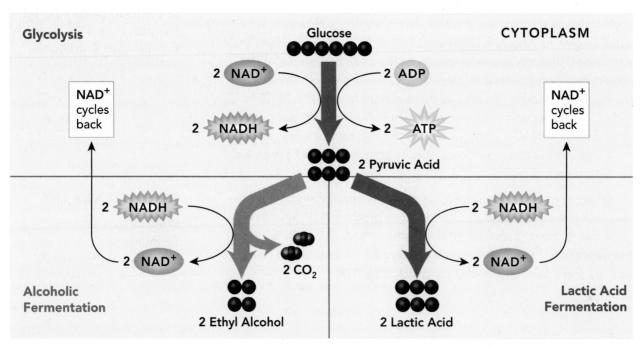

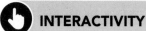
**Figure 10-8**

**Evidence of Fermentation**

The foods in this photograph are all produced using lactic acid fermentation.

Certain bacteria that produce lactic acid as a waste product during fermentation are important to the food industry. Fermentation by these bacteria help to produce cheese, yogurt, buttermilk, and sour cream—to which the acid contributes the familiar sour taste. Pickles, sauerkraut, and kimchi, which are shown in **Figure 10-8**, are also produced using lactic acid fermentation. Lactic acid fermenting bacteria are also found in sourdough starters, and the acids they produce contribute to the taste and texture of sourdough bread.

Humans are also lactic acid fermenters. During brief periods without enough oxygen, many of the cells in our bodies produce ATP by lactic acid fermentation. The cells best adapted to doing that are muscle cells, which often need very large supplies of ATP for rapid bursts of activity.

✓ **READING CHECK** **Identify** In what part of the cell does fermentation occur?

---

**CASE STUDY** **Quick Lab** **Guided Inquiry**

### Rise Up

1. Obtain three balloons and three plastic bottles or flasks. Stretch the balloons by pulling on them and then blowing them up once or twice. Label the bottles #1, #2, and #3. Fill each plastic bottle about half full with very warm water.

2. To each bottle, add the following, and then gently swirl to dissolve the contents.

   Bottle #1: packet of yeast (7 g)
   Bottle #2: 60 mL of sugar
   Bottle #3: packet of yeast and 30 mL of sugar

3. Record your observations, and then carefully stretch a balloon over the mouth of each bottle.

4. Every 5 minutes for 30 minutes, use string to measure the widest circumference of each balloon. Record your measurements.

**ANALYZE AND CONCLUDE**

1. **Communicate Information** How did the results for the three bottles differ?

2. **Draw Conclusions** What caused this difference? Explain.

3. **Design an Experiment** Write a procedure for testing another factor that could affect the rate of fermentation in yeast.

## READING TOOL

Create a cause-and-effect diagram to summarize what happens in cells during a sprint and a long-distance race.

**VIDEO**

Discover how athletes can use lactic acid fermentation to their advantage.

# Energy and Exercise

Bang! The starter's pistol goes off. The swimmers dive from their blocks and sprint furiously through the water toward the other end of the pool, 50 meters away. The race takes a little more than 20 seconds, and many of the swimmers don't even take a single breath once they hit the water. When they reach the wall, some of the swimmers are thrilled and others are disappointed, but all of them are out of breath. For nearly a minute, much longer than the race itself, they huff and puff to recover from the effort. Most of them aren't breathing normally until several minutes afterward. What's going on? How did they manage to swim such a fast race without breathing? Why does it take so long to recover, even for the best athletes in the world?

To figure out why it takes so long for the swimmers to recover, think of the pathways the body uses to provide the chemical energy needed to power these swimmers through 50 meters of water. As they begin the race, the competitors have only enough ATP in their muscle cells to power them for a few seconds. To keep going, they must immediately generate new ATPs by cellular respiration or by lactic acid fermentation.

**Quick Energy** If the swimmers in **Figure 10-9** had entered the pool for a leisurely swim, they'd be able to produce all the ATP they needed using the process of cellular respiration. The oxygen they breathed in and passed along to their muscles via the bloodstream would be more than enough to keep aerobic respiration going. But this is not a leisurely swim or a walk in the park. These athletes are depending on their muscles to produce their absolute maximum effort and to sustain it for the length of the pool. The oxidative pathways of aerobic respiration simply cannot supply the ATP they need quickly enough to keep them going at top speed. They need to flood their muscles with ATP, and they need to do it quickly.

The solution is lactic acid fermentation. As we've seen, the fermentation pathway doesn't involve the Krebs cycle, the electron transport chain, or oxygen. As a result, it works much more rapidly, supplying all the ATP a well-trained athlete needs to support maximum effort for 30 to 40 seconds. Sprinters, whether swimming or running, rely on this pathway for bursts of quick energy that make the difference between winning or losing a race.

**Figure 10-9**

**Exercise and Energy**

During a 50-meter race, swimmers rely on the energy supplied by ATP to make it to the finish line.

This process, of course, produces lactic acid as a byproduct, which quickly builds up in the muscles and bloodstream of the athletes. When the race is over, the only way to get rid of this lactic acid is by means of another chemical pathway that requires extra oxygen. For that reason, you can think of a quick sprint as building up an "oxygen debt" that the swimmers have to repay with plenty of heavy breathing after the race. That's why just 20 seconds of swimming may produce an oxygen debt that requires several minutes of huffing and puffing to clear. ⚭ *For short, quick bursts of energy, the body uses ATP already in muscles as well as ATP made by lactic acid fermentation.*

**INTERACTIVITY**

Explore the differences between cellular respiration and fermentation.

**Long-Term Energy** What happens if the race is longer? How does your body generate the ATP it needs to swim or run for thousands of meters or to engage in a soccer game that lasts more than an hour? ⚭ *For exercise longer than about 90 seconds, cellular respiration is the only way to continue generating a supply of ATP.* Cellular respiration releases energy more slowly than fermentation does, which is why even well-conditioned athletes have to pace themselves during a long race or over the course of a game.

Your body stores energy in muscle cells and other tissues in the form of the carbohydrate glycogen. These stores of glycogen are usually enough to last for 15 or 20 minutes of activity. After that, your body begins to break down other stored molecules, including fats, for energy. This is one reason that aerobic forms of exercise—such as running, dancing, and swimming—are so beneficial for weight control. Athletes competing in long-distance events, like the marathon in **Figure 10-10**, depend upon the efficiency of their respiratory and circulatory systems to supply oxygen to their muscles to support aerobic respiration for long periods of time.

**Figure 10-10**

**Marathon Runners**

Runners need well-conditioned circulatory and respiratory systems to maintain aerobic respiration in their muscles to go the distance.

HS-LS1-7, HS-LS2-3

# ☑ LESSON 10.3 Review

## ⚭ KEY QUESTIONS

1. Name the two main types of fermentation.

2. Why do runners breathe heavily after a sprint race?

## CRITICAL THINKING

3. **Infer** Why is lactic acid fermentation useful for short bursts of energy but not for meeting a long-term energy demand, such as running a marathon?

4. **Construct an Explanation** Pyruvic acid is the final product of glycolysis, which is the first stage of cellular respiration. Why is pyruvic acid never the end product of fermentation?

5. **Apply Scientific Reasoning** An Olympic sprinter has just broken the world record for the 100-meter dash. Which process will her body likely use to recover from her "oxygen debt"? Explain.

# Can San Francisco sourdough be copied?

San Francisco sourdough bread has a unique taste. To begin explaining this taste, scientists investigated the microorganisms that contribute to the sourdough.

HS-LS2-3

## Make Your Case

Many years ago, San Francisco bakers realized that their sourdough starters contained two very special microorganisms: a useful "wild" yeast and a type of bacteria called *Lactobacillus*. After scientists studied the bacteria closely, they realized they had discovered a new species. The bacteria are now called *Lactobacillus sanfranciscensis* in honor of the city in which they were discovered.

## Develop a Solution

1. **Conduct Research** Why is the taste of San Francisco sourdough so distinctive and difficult to match? Research facts and opinions to construct an answer.

2. **Design a Solution** Describe steps you could take to develop an effective method for copying San Francisco sourdough bread. Assume that you have access to sourdough starter and all the ingredients and equipment you need.

## Technology on the Case

### Like Bread Dough in a Vat?

The photo shows an example of a bioreactor. Like bread dough, a bioreactor holds growing colonies of bacteria or other organisms, generally in a liquid mixture. Over time, the products of biochemical reactions build up in the mixture. Bioreactors are used to produce ingredients for many drugs and medicines. Other bioreactors produce fermented beverages or foods like sour cream and yogurt. A Korean dish called kimchi is made from fermented vegetables. In one traditional method, the fermentation takes place in a sealed pot that is kept underground.

Modern bioreactors are designed so that conditions can be tightly controlled. Variables such as temperature, light, oxygen levels, and acidity of the solution can all affect the growth of microorganisms, which in turn affects the products they release. Bioreactors are also designed to prevent contamination. If unwanted bacteria or yeast cells enter the bioreactor, they could reduce the yield of the desired product or ruin the product completely.

Scientists and engineers have been investigating a new way to use bioreactors, by sending them into space! On Earth, the pull of gravity can make it difficult to produce a delicate drug or gather a cell culture. In space, the effects of gravity are minimal.

Whether in space or here on Earth, all bioreactors take advantage of the chemical reactions of living organisms. For that reason, they really are like bread dough in a vat!

## Careers on the Case

Bread bakers and people in many other careers need to know about fermentation and its effects.

### Baker

Bread depends on the products of fermentation, as do many beverages, cheeses, and other foods. In other cases, though, fermentation can ruin or spoil foods. Understanding fermentation and the actions of microorganisms is essential for bakers, chefs, and anyone who prepares food or helps keep food safe to eat.

 **VIDEO**

Watch this video to learn about other careers in biology.

## Lesson Review

Go to your Biology Foundations Workbook for longer versions of these lesson summaries.

### 10.1 Cellular Respiration: An Overview

Organisms get the energy they need from food. Cellular respiration is the process that releases energy from food in the presence of oxygen. There are three stages of cellular respiration: glycolysis, the Krebs cycle, and the electron transport chain.

Photosynthesis removes carbon dioxide from the atmosphere, and cellular respiration puts it back. Photosynthesis releases oxygen into the atmosphere, and cellular respiration uses that oxygen to release energy from food.

- calorie
- cellular respiration
- aerobic
- anaerobic

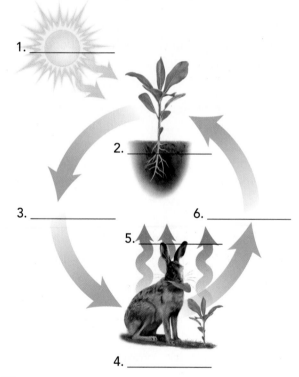

1. _____
2. _____
3. _____
5. _____
6. _____
4. _____

☑️**Summarize** Complete this diagram by filling in numbers 1 through 6.

### 10.2 The Process of Cellular Respiration

During glycolysis, 1 molecule of glucose is transformed into 2 molecules of pyruvic acid.

During the Krebs cycle, pyruvic acid is broken down into carbon dioxide in a series of energy-extracting reactions.

The electron transport chain uses the high-energy electrons from glycolysis and the Krebs cycle to convert ADP into ATP.

Together, glycolysis, the Krebs cycle, and the electron transport chain release about 36 molecules of ATP per molecule of glucose.

- glycolysis
- $NAD^+$
- Krebs cycle
- matrix

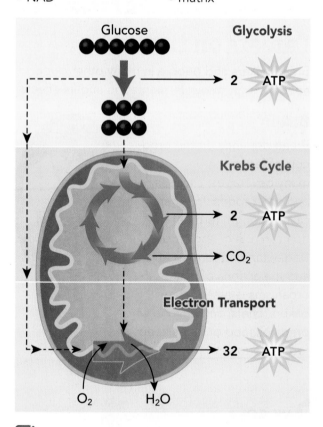

☑️**Use Visuals** How many times more energy is produced by all three stages of cellular respiration than by glycolysis alone?

## 10.3 Fermentation

In the absence of oxygen, glycolysis is kept going by the pathway of fermentation, which releases energy from food molecules by producing ATP. There are two slightly different forms of the process: alcoholic fermentation and lactic acid fermentation.

For short, quick bursts of energy, the body uses ATP already in muscles as well as ATP made by lactic acid fermentation. For exercise longer than about 90 seconds, cellular respiration is the only way to continue generating a supply of ATP.

• fermentation

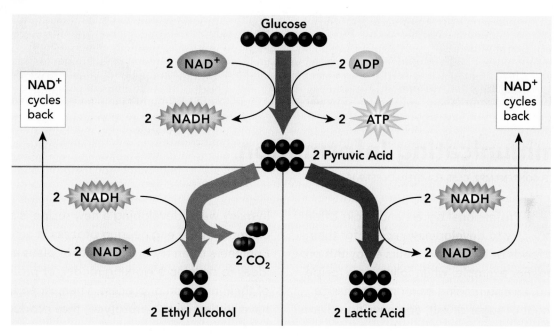

**Compare and Contrast** How are alcoholic fermentation and lactic acid fermentation similar? How are they different?

# Organize Information

Complete the flowchart to show the stages of cellular respiration and fermentation.

**Cellular Respiration and Fermentation**

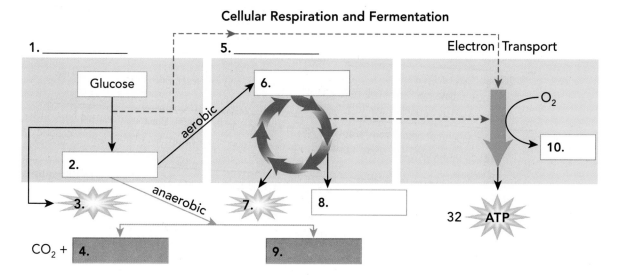

# Making a Better Bread
## Mastering Fermentation

## Communicating Information

CCSS.MATH.CONTENT.MP2, CCSS.ELA-LITERACY.RST.9-10.3

**STEM** Professional bakers and cooks often try to develop new recipes for their favorite foods or dishes. Amateurs enjoy this process, too. For example, when following a recipe for bread, an enterprising baker might change the amount of sugar or salt, add new ingredients like raisins or sesame seeds, or change the timing of the different steps.

In many ways, developing a new recipe is an example of the engineering process in action. Engineers often try out a variety of plans and ideas to develop a working model, or prototype, of their invention or process. Then, when they have settled on the prototype, they produce it full size or in large amounts.

Read the recipe for sourdough bread shown here, and then answer these questions.

### Sourdough Bread

**Ingredients:** 4 cups bread flour, 3 tablespoons sugar, 2 tablespoons salt, 1/4 ounce dry yeast, 1 cup warm milk, 2 tablespoons margarine, 1 1/2 cups sourdough starter

**Steps**

1. In a large bowl, combine 1 cup flour and the sugar, salt, and dry yeast. Add milk and margarine. Stir in starter. Gradually mix in 3 cups flour.

2. Turn dough out onto a floured surface and knead for 8 to 10 minutes. Place in a greased bowl, turn once to oil surface, and cover. Let the dough rise at room temperature for 1 hour or until doubled in volume.

3. Punch down, and let rest 15 minutes. Shape into 2 or 3 small loaves. Place on a greased baking pan. Allow to rise for 1 hour or until doubled.

4. Bake at 375°F (190°C) for 30 minutes.

1. **Construct an Explanation** How is fermentation important in the baking of sourdough bread? During which step does fermentation occur? To construct your answer, apply your knowledge of fermentation and scientific reasoning.

2. **Conduct Research** A sourdough starter is essential to making sourdough bread. Research how to make and maintain your own sourdough starter.

3. **Predict** Consider the following changes to the recipe. Predict the result of each change, and explain your reasoning. Assume that each change occurs individually, without enacting any of the other changes.

   a. Step 2 is eliminated.

   b. Before step 3, the dough is rolled into very thin sheets.

   c. In step 3, the dough rises for only 30 minutes.

   d. In step 2, the dough rises inside a refrigerator.

4. **Conduct Research** Bakers might follow many recipes or procedures for baking bread or related products. Select a recipe from a cookbook or the Internet, and research how it relies on fermentation.

5. **Communicate Information** Write a brief report to share your research findings and conclusions. Be sure to address the following points:

   - Describe the steps that are followed to produce the food. Explain how fermentation is used.

   - Which organisms are used to perform the fermentation process? Why are the organisms useful for the food?

   - How does the food-making process compare with the processes used for other foods that depend on fermentation?

Swiss cheese gets its unique flavor from lactic acid fermentation and the effects of bacteria on lactic acid. The holes in the cheese come from pockets of carbon dioxide gas that fermentation releases.

🔍 **KEY QUESTIONS AND TERMS**

## 10.1 Cellular Respiration: An Overview
HS-LS1-7, HS-LS2-3, HS-LS2-5

1. Cells use the energy available in food to make a final energy-rich compound called
   **a.** water.
   **c.** ATP.
   **b.** glucose.
   **d.** ADP.

2. Each gram of glucose contains approximately how much energy?
   **a.** 9 calories
   **c.** 4 calories
   **b.** 9 Calories
   **d.** 4 Calories

3. The process that releases energy from food in the presence of oxygen is
   **a.** synthesis.
   **b.** cellular respiration.
   **c.** ATP synthase.
   **d.** photosynthesis.

4. The first step in releasing the energy of glucose in a cell is known as
   **a.** fermentation.
   **b.** glycolysis.
   **c.** the Krebs cycle.
   **d.** electron transport.

5. What is a calorie? Briefly explain how cells use a high-calorie molecule such as glucose.

6. Write a chemical equation for cellular respiration. Label the molecules involved.

7. What percentage of the energy contained in a molecule of glucose is captured in the bonds of ATP at the end of glycolysis?

8. What does it mean if a process is "anaerobic"? Which part of cellular respiration is anaerobic?

## 10.2 The Process of Cellular Respiration
HS-LS1-7, HS-LS2-3, HS-LS2-5

9. The net gain of energy in glycolysis from one molecule of glucose is
   **a.** 4 ATP molecules.
   **b.** 2 ATP molecules.
   **c.** 8 ADP molecules.
   **d.** 3 pyruvic acid molecules.

10. In eukaryotes, the Krebs cycle takes place within the
    **a.** chloroplast.
    **c.** mitochondrion.
    **b.** nucleus.
    **d.** cytoplasm.

11. The electron transport chain uses the high-energy electrons from the Krebs cycle to
    **a.** produce glucose.
    **b.** move $H^+$ ions across the inner mitochondrial membrane.
    **c.** convert acetyl-CoA to citric acid.
    **d.** convert glucose to pyruvic acid.

12. How is glucose changed during glycolysis?

13. What is $NAD^+$? Why is it important?

14. Summarize what happens during the Krebs cycle. What happens to high-energy electrons generated during the Krebs cycle?

15. How is ATP synthase involved in making energy available to the cell?

## 10.3 Fermentation
HS-LS1-7, HS-LS2-3

16. Because fermentation takes place in the absence of oxygen, it is said to be
    **a.** aerobic.
    **b.** anaerobic.
    **c.** cyclic.
    **d.** oxygen-rich.

17. Most of the time, the process carried out by yeast that causes bread dough to rise is
    **a.** alcoholic fermentation.
    **b.** lactic acid fermentation.
    **c.** cellular respiration.
    **d.** mitosis.

18. During heavy exercise, the buildup of lactic acid in muscle cells results in
    **a.** cellular respiration.
    **b.** oxygen debt.
    **c.** fermentation.
    **d.** the Krebs cycle.

19. How are fermentation and cellular respiration similar?

20. Write equations to show how lactic acid fermentation compares with alcoholic fermentation. Which reactant(s) do they have in common?

# CRITICAL THINKING

HS-LS1-7, HS-LS2-5

21. **Construct an Explanation** Explain how cellular respiration and photosynthesis can be considered both opposite and interrelated processes.

The diagram shown is a model summarizing the stages of cellular respiration. Use the diagram to answer questions 22 and 23.

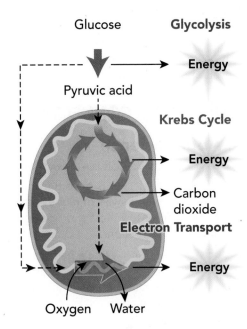

Glucose          **Glycolysis**

Energy

Pyruvic acid

**Krebs Cycle**

Energy

Carbon dioxide

**Electron Transport**

Energy

Oxygen     Water

22. **Use Models** Suppose a chemical in a cell were to inhibit the function of mitochondria. Predict how the model would be affected, and explain why.

23. **Evaluate Models** The model shows the same image for energy during each stage. Explain how you could improve the model to better represent the energy released during each stage.

24. **Identify** What are the reactants of anaerobic cellular respiration? What are the products?

25. **Identify** What are the reactants of aerobic cellular respiration? What are the products?

26. **Compare and Contrast** How is the function of $NAD^+$ in cellular respiration similar to that of $NADP^+$ in photosynthesis?

27. **Use Analogies** Why is comparing cellular respiration to a burning fire a poor analogy?

28. **Compare and Contrast** Where is the electron transport chain found in a eukaryotic cell? Where is it found in a prokaryotic cell?

29. **Use Models** Explain how the products of glycolysis and the Krebs cycle are related to the electron transport chain. Draw a flowchart that shows the relationships between these products and the electron transport chain.

30. **Use Models** Draw and label a mitochondrion surrounded by cytoplasm. Indicate where glycolysis, the Krebs cycle, and the electron transport chain occur in a eukaryotic cell.

31. **Infer** Certain types of bacteria thrive in conditions that lack oxygen. What does that fact indicate about the way they obtain energy?

32. **Design an Investigation** Would individuals who carry out regular aerobic exercise suffer less muscle discomfort during intense exercise than other individuals? Outline an experiment that could answer this question.

33. **Apply Scientific Reasoning** To function properly, heart muscle cells require a steady supply of oxygen. After a heart attack, small amounts of lactic acid are present. What does this evidence suggest about the nature of a heart attack?

34. **Form a Hypothesis** In certain cases, regular exercise causes an increase in the number of mitochondria in muscle cells. How might that change improve an individual's ability to perform activities that require great amounts of energy?

35. **Predict** Yeast cells can carry out both fermentation and cellular respiration, depending on whether oxygen is present. In which case would you expect yeast cells to grow more rapidly? Explain.

36. **Explain** Explain how a sprinter gets energy during a 30-second race. Is the process aerobic or anaerobic? How does it compare to a long-distance runner getting energy during a 5-kilometer race?

## CROSSCUTTING CONCEPTS

**37.** **Energy and Matter** Energy cannot be created or destroyed. Explain how energy is conserved in cellular respiration. Include in your explanation how energy is transferred and converted at the levels of a single cell and of an organism.

**38.** **Systems and System Models** Edie uses snap beads to model cellular respiration. She uses red beads for oxygen atoms, black beads for carbon atoms, and white beads for hydrogen atoms. How can she describe this reaction? What is one limitation of the model?

## MATH CONNECTIONS

## Analyze and Interpret Data

CCSS.MATH.CONTENT.MP2

Use the graph to answer questions 39 and 40. The graph shows data collected by a scientist who compared the volume of oxygen breathed per minute to the difficulty level of exercise, measured in watts.

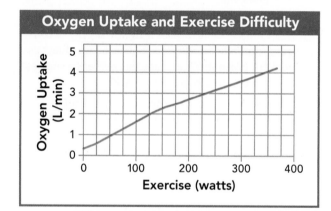

**Oxygen Uptake and Exercise Difficulty**

**39.** **Interpret Graphs** Based on the graph, which increase in exercise difficulty level resulted in an increase in oxygen uptake of approximately 2 L/min?

**40.** **Draw Conclusions** Which of the following is a valid hypothesis for the trend shown on the graph? Evaluate the choices, and then explain why you selected the answer you did. Identify the criteria you used to select the answer, and describe how the other choices failed to meet your criteria.

**a.** As exercise becomes more difficult, the body relies more and more on lactic acid fermentation.

**b.** Exercise below a level of 100 watts does not require increased oxygen uptake.

**c.** Difficult exercise requires additional oxygen intake in order to generate extra ATP for muscle cells.

**d.** The human body cannot maintain exercise levels above 500 watts.

## LANGUAGE ARTS CONNECTIONS

## Write About Science

CCSS.ELA-LITERACY.WHST.9-10.2, CCSS.ELA-LITERACY.WHST.9-10.4

**41.** **Write Explanatory Texts** Expand the analogy of deposits and withdrawals of money that was used in the chapter to write a short paragraph to explain cellular respiration.

**42.** **Produce Clear Writing** Write a paragraph that explains the conditions under which fermentation occurs and differentiates between alcoholic and lactic acid fermentation.

## Read About Science

CCSS.ELA-LITERACY.RST.9-10.1, CCSS.ELA-LITERACY.RST.9-10.10

**43.** **Cite Textual Evidence** Carbon monoxide (CO) molecules bring the electron transport chain in a mitochondrion to a stop by binding to an electron carrier. Use this information and cite additional information from the text to explain why carbon monoxide gas kills aerobic organisms.

**44.** **Read and Comprehend** Review **Figure 10-5** and the text that accompanies it. How does the diagram illustrate the process described in the passage? How does the diagram relate to the information presented about the other stages of cellular respiration?

1. In a model summarizing cellular respiration, which of the following must be represented as raw materials, or the reactants of the process?
   A. glucose and carbon dioxide
   B. glucose and oxygen
   C. carbon dioxide and oxygen
   D. oxygen and lactic acid
   E. water and oxygen

2. Which statement best describes an event represented in the model that contributes to the production of ATP?
   A. A net gain of 6 ATP molecules is achieved.
   B. Oxygen molecules are broken down and converted into pyruvic acid.
   C. High-energy electrons are passed to $NAD^+$ forming NADH.
   D. Carbon atoms in glucose are transformed into energy in the form of ATP.
   E. Pyruvic acid is broken down to form carbon dioxide.

The diagram shows a model of glycolysis. Use the diagram to answer question 3.

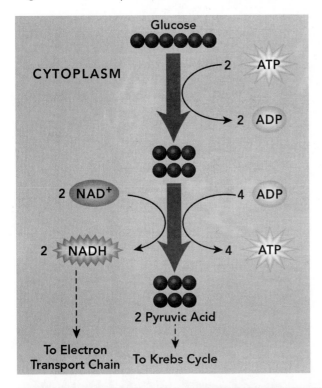

3. During glycolysis, what is the source of the chemical energy that is captured in ATP?
   A. the chemical bonds in pyruvic acid
   B. the chemical bonds in glucose
   C. the nuclei of atoms in glucose
   D. high-energy electrons in the cytoplasm
   E. high-energy electrons in mitochondria

4. What best describes the role of molecular oxygen ($O_2$) in cellular respiration?
   A. It is accepts electrons when reacting to form water.
   B. It combines with carbon and hydrogen to form glucose.
   C. It is released when water breaks apart.
   D. It is released when glucose breaks apart.
   E. It reacts to form carbon dioxide and water.

5. Which is a role of cellular respiration in cycling materials between the atmosphere and biosphere?
   A. It transfers carbon to the atmosphere as carbon dioxide.
   B. It transfers carbon to the biosphere as glucose.
   C. It transfers oxygen gas to the atmosphere.
   D. It transfers water from the atmosphere to the biosphere.
   E. It transfers carbon to the atmosphere as pyruvic acid.

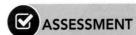 **ASSESSMENT**

For additional assessment practice, go online to access your digital course.

| If You Have Trouble With... | | | | | |
| --- | --- | --- | --- | --- | --- |
| **Question** | 1 | 2 | 3 | 4 | 5 |
| **See Lesson** | 10.1 | 10.2 | 10.2 | 10.2 | 10.1 |
| **Performance Expectation** | HS-LS1-7 | HS-LS1-7 | HS-LS1-7 | HS-LS1-7 | HS-LS2-5 |

# CHAPTER 11 Cell Growth and Division

11.1 Cell Growth, Division, and Reproduction

11.2 The Process of Cell Division

11.3 Regulating the Cell Cycle

11.4 Cell Differentiation

**Go Online to access your digital course.**

- VIDEO
- AUDIO
- INTERACTIVITY
- eTEXT
- ANIMATION
- VIRTUAL LAB
- ASSESSMENT

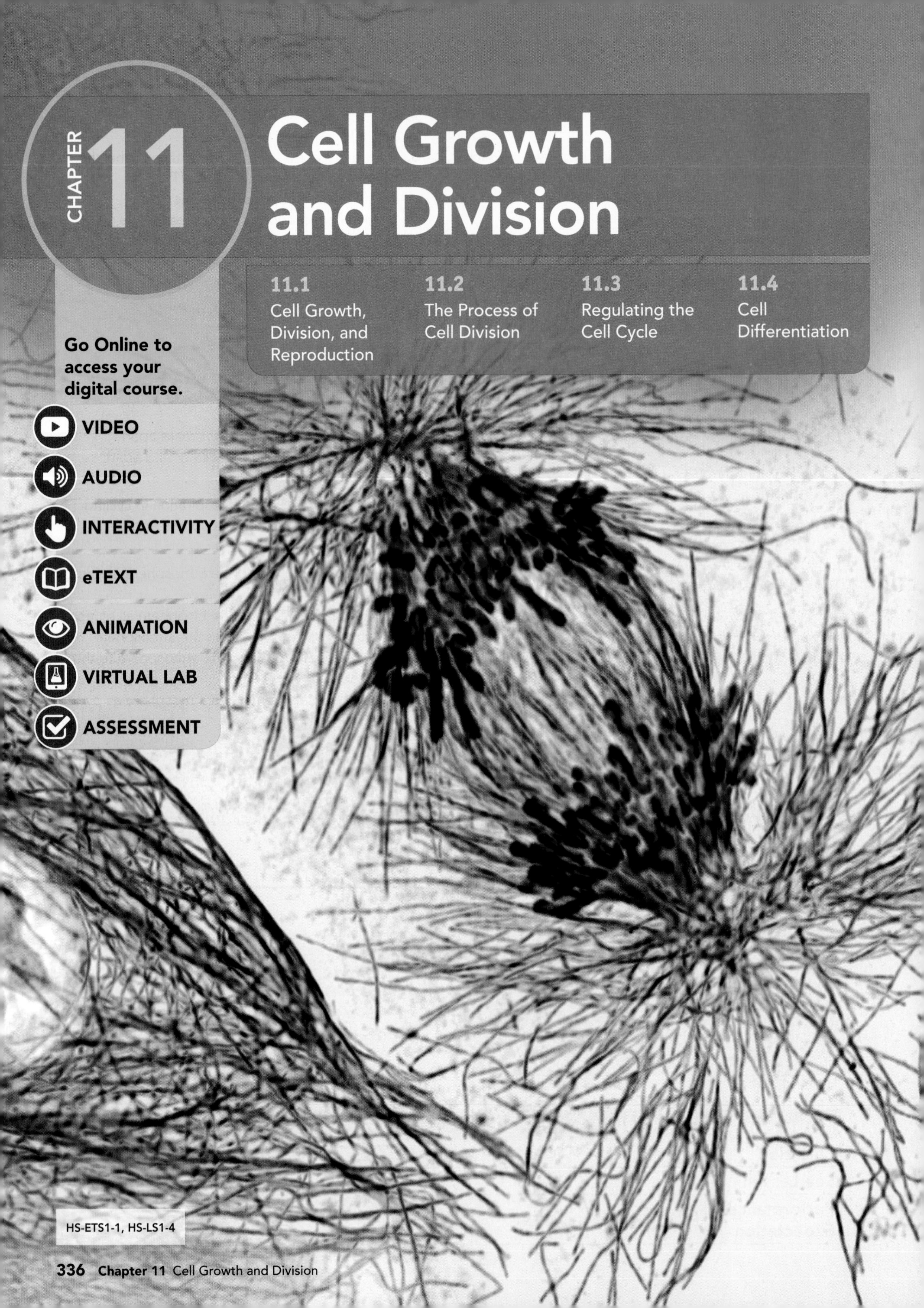

HS-ETS1-1, HS-LS1-4

# Will stem cells change the future of healing?

> More than 50 years ago, a young British scientist named John Gurdon carried out a revolutionary experiment. He transferred the nucleus from an adult frog cell into the cytoplasm of a frog egg cell. The result was that the cytoplasm "reprogrammed" the nucleus. The transformed cell developed first into an embryo and then into a fully functional tadpole.

Most cells in an adult organism are specialized to carry out specific tasks, such as carrying oxygen, producing digestive enzymes, or fighting disease. Gurdon's work showed that even adult cells could be changed back into the unspecialized embryonic "stem cells" that have the potential to grow into nearly any cell type.

Today, many physicians are beginning to apply the biological principle that Gurdon demonstrated in order to replace cells damaged by injury or disease. In so doing, they have begun to establish a new field called regenerative medicine. They hope that transplants of stem cells taken from embryos, from adult tissues like bone marrow, or from reprogrammed adult cells will make it possible to treat patients with failing eyesight, arthritic joints, or diseased livers. In the future, stem cells could also be used to treat heart attacks and strokes. If stem cells could repair an injured spinal cord, a paralyzed person might walk again.

Experts agree on the many potential benefits of stem cell therapies. However, there also are dangers. Injected stem cells may not develop into the cell types they are intended to replace. They also might damage neighboring tissues or produce tumors. In many cancerous tumors, the cells are undifferentiated and resemble stem cells in some ways. The Food and Drug Administration (FDA) and other government agencies are considering whether stem cell clinics should go through an approval and regulatory process, such as that required for medicines and drugs.

Physicians, researchers, and patients are faced with many questions about stem cells. Are the benefits of stem cell therapies worth the costs or the risks? How closely should the therapies be regulated? Who should make the important decisions?

**Throughout this chapter, look for connections to the CASE STUDY to help you answer these questions.**

**Cell division in an animal cell.**
(False-color LM: 9000×)

Eaglets will grow into adult eagles.

HS-LS1-4: Use a model to illustrate the role of cellular division (mitosis) and differentiation in producing and maintaining complex organisms.

## KEY QUESTIONS

- What are some of the difficulties a cell faces as it increases in size?
- How do asexual and sexual reproduction compare?

## VOCABULARY

cell division
asexual reproduction
sexual reproduction

## READING TOOL

As you read, identify the similarities and differences between sexual and asexual reproduction. Include the advantages and disadvantages of each in the Venn diagram in your 📖 **Biology Foundations Workbook.**

When a living thing grows, what happens to its cells? Does an organism get larger because each cell increases in size or because it produces more cells? In most cases, living things grow by producing more cells. What is there about growth that requires cells to divide and produce more of themselves?

## Limits to Cell Size

Each of us begins life as a single cell. By the time we are adults, however, that single cell has grown and divided so many times that the average human body contains nearly 40 trillion cells. To impress your math teacher, you might want to calculate how many rounds of cell division would be required to go from one cell to 40 trillion ($40 \times 10^{12}$). The answer might surprise you!

Cells can grow by increasing in size, but eventually, most cells divide after growing to a certain point. There are two main reasons that cells divide rather than continuing to grow. 🔑 *The larger a cell becomes, the less efficient it is in moving nutrients and waste materials across its cell membrane. In addition, as a cell grows, it places increasing demands on its own DNA.*

**A Problem of Size** All cells are connected to the outside world through their cell membranes. To stay alive, a cell must allow food, oxygen, and water to enter through its cell membrane. Waste products have to leave the cell in the same way. The rate at which this exchange takes place depends on the surface area of the cell, which is the total area of its cell membrane. The rate at which food and oxygen are used up and wastes are produced depends on a cell's volume. As a cell gets larger, these rates increase, as does its surface area. However, volume and surface area do not increase at the same rate, and this is a key reason that cells must eventually divide rather than continue to grow without limit.

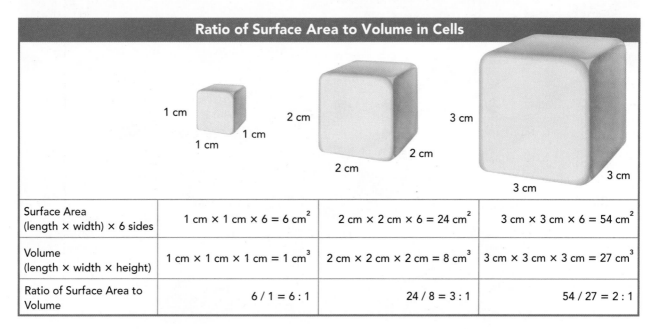

**Ratio of Surface Area to Volume in Cells**

| | 1 cm | 2 cm | 3 cm |
|---|---|---|---|
| Surface Area (length × width) × 6 sides | 1 cm × 1 cm × 6 = 6 cm$^2$ | 2 cm × 2 cm × 6 = 24 cm$^2$ | 3 cm × 3 cm × 6 = 54 cm$^2$ |
| Volume (length × width × height) | 1 cm × 1 cm × 1 cm = 1 cm$^3$ | 2 cm × 2 cm × 2 cm = 8 cm$^3$ | 3 cm × 3 cm × 3 cm = 27 cm$^3$ |
| Ratio of Surface Area to Volume | 6 / 1 = 6 : 1 | 24 / 8 = 3 : 1 | 54 / 27 = 2 : 1 |

***Ratio of Surface Area to Volume*** Imagine a cell that is shaped like a cube. The formula for area (*l* × *w*) is used to calculate the surface area. The formula for volume (*l* × *w* × *h*) is used to calculate the amount of space inside. By using a ratio of surface area to volume, you can see how the size of the cell's surface area grows compared to its volume.

Notice that for a cell with sides that measure 1 cm in length, the ratio of surface area to volume is 6/1 or 6 : 1. Increase the length of the cell's sides to 3 cm, and the ratio becomes 54/27 or 2 : 1. As you can see from the calculations shown in **Figure 11-1**, surface area does not increase as fast as volume does. For a growing cell, this decrease in the relative amount of cell membrane available creates serious problems. The largest cells, such as the one shown in **Figure 11-2**, use unusual shapes or structures to maintain the ratio.

☑ **READING CHECK** **Infer** If a cell keeps growing, why must it eventually divide?

**Figure 11-1**

**Ratio of Surface Area to Volume**

As the length of the sides of the cube increases, the cube's volume increases more than its surface area.

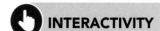 **INTERACTIVITY**

Investigate how and why cells are limited in how large they can grow.

**Figure 11-2**

**A Long Cell**

Most single-celled organisms are too small to see without a microscope. However, the cell that makes up *Caulerpa taxifolia*, a type of algae, can grow up to 30 cm (12 in.). The cells of *Caulerpa taxifolia* are the largest known living cells of any organism!

**Visual Analogy**

**Figure 11-3**

## Growing Pains

Lots of growth can mean lots of trouble—both in a town and in a cell. ☑ **Use Analogies** How could cell growth create a problem that is similar to a traffic jam?

**READING TOOL**

Relate cause and effect to explain why cell size is limited.

*Traffic Problems* Compare a growing cell to a small town with a two-lane main street running through it, such as the one shown in **Figure 11-3**. As the town grows, more and more traffic begins to clog the main street. Moving materials in and out of town becomes increasingly difficult. Businesses cannot get the goods they need and trash piles up because garbage trucks are stuck in traffic jams. In the same way, if a cell were to get too large, it would be more difficult to get sufficient amounts of oxygen and nutrients in and waste products out.

*Information Overload* Many cells face another problem as they grow. Living cells store critical information in a molecule known as DNA. As a cell grows, that information is used to build the molecules needed for cell growth. But as a cell increases in size, its "library" of information in DNA remains the same. If a cell were to grow too large, an "information crisis" might occur. A growing town with an overused library that no longer serves its needs might decide to build a new library. In the case of a cell, it might be time to make a duplicate copy of that DNA and divide it between two new cells.

## Cell Division

The process by which a cell divides into two new daughter cells is called **cell division**. Before cell division can occur, its DNA must be copied, or replicated. DNA replication solves the problem of information overload because each daughter cell gets one complete copy of genetic information. Cell division also solves the problem of increasing size by reducing cell volume. This results in an increase in the ratio of surface area to volume for each daughter cell, allowing for a more efficient exchange of materials between the cell and its environment.

☑ **READING CHECK Summarize** What potential problems of a cell are solved by cell division?

# Cell Division and Reproduction

All living things must be able to reproduce by forming new individuals. For an organism composed of just one cell, cell division itself can serve as a perfectly good form of reproduction. You don't have to meet someone else, conduct a courtship, or deal with rivals. All you have to do is to divide, and *presto*—there are two of you!

**Asexual Reproduction**   For many single-celled organisms, such as the bacterium in **Figure 11-4**, cell division is their only form of reproduction. The process can be relatively simple, efficient, and effective, enabling populations to increase in number very quickly. In most cases, the two cells produced by cell division are genetically identical to the cell that produced them. This kind of reproduction is called **asexual reproduction**. *The production of genetically identical offspring from a single parent is known as asexual reproduction.*

Asexual reproduction also occurs in many multicellular organisms—even in such organisms as plants that can reproduce sexually. The small bud growing off the hydra will eventually break off and become an independent organism, an example of asexual reproduction in an animal. Each of the small shoots or plantlets on the tip of the kalanchoe leaf may also grow into a new plant.

**Sexual Reproduction**   Unlike asexual reproduction, in which cells separate to form a new individual, **sexual reproduction** involves the fusion of two reproductive cells formed by each of two parents. *Offspring produced by sexual reproduction inherit some of their genetic information from each parent.* Most animals and plants reproduce sexually, as do many single-celled organisms. You will learn more about the special form of cell division that produces these reproductive cells in Chapter 12.

**INTERACTIVITY**

Explore the reproductive strategies of algae.

**BUILD VOCABULARY**

**Prefixes** The prefix *a-* in **asexual** means "without." Asexual reproduction is reproduction without the fusion of reproductive cells.

**Figure 11-4**

**Asexual Reproduction**

Cell division leads to reproduction in single-celled organisms and some multicellular organisms.

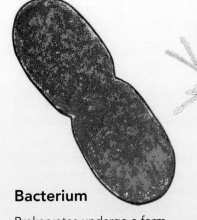

**Bacterium**

Prokaryotes undergo a form of asexual reproduction known as binary fission, in which the cell splits in two after the chromosome replicates.

(False-color TEM: 34,000x)

**Hydra**

Hydras reproduce by budding. An offspring starts off as a lump on its parent. This bud grows, develops tentacles, and eventually separates from its parent.  (LM: 16x)

**Kalanchoe**

Plants reproduce asexually through vegetative propagation. The plantlets at the edge of this kalanchoe leaf will eventually drop off and grow on their own.

## Asexual and Sexual Reproduction

The runners, or plantlets, growing off this strawberry plant are the result of asexual reproduction. The strawberries, which form from the flowers, are the result of sexual reproduction.

**Comparing Asexual and Sexual Reproduction** Each type of reproduction has its own advantages and disadvantages in terms of survival strategies. For many single-celled organisms, asexual reproduction provides clear advantages. When conditions are right, these organisms can reproduce quickly, enabling them to compete successfully with other organisms. However, a lack of genetic diversity can become a disadvantage when conditions change in ways that do not fit the characteristics of an organism.

Sexual reproduction involves finding a mate and then allowing for the growth and development of offspring. This may require more time than asexual reproduction. However, this can be an advantage for species that live in environments where seasonal changes affect weather conditions and food availability. Sexual reproduction produces genetic diversity. If an environment changes, genetic diversity in a species may help to ensure that the population contains the right combination of characteristics needed to survive.

Some organisms, such as the strawberry plant shown in **Figure 11-5**, reproduce both sexually and asexually. The different advantages of each type of reproduction may help to explain why the living world includes organisms that reproduce sexually, those that reproduce asexually, and many organisms that do both.

HS-LS1-4

## ✓ LESSON 11.1 Review

### 🔍 KEY QUESTIONS

1. What factors limit the size of a cell?

2. What are the advantages and disadvantages of both asexual and sexual reproduction?

### CRITICAL THINKING

3. **Calculate** The volume of a sphere increases with the cube of its radius. If the radius of a sphere increases from 2 cm to 6 cm, by what factor does its volume increase?

4. **Use Models** Compare a cell that has grown too large to be efficient with a wireless network that has too many users. Explain how both have the same two problems noted for the city shown in **Figure 11.3**. Illustrate how "division" helps in both cases.

5. **Synthesize Information** Aphids are a type of insect. They reproduce asexually in the spring and summer. They reproduce sexually in the fall. How might this pattern improve the species' chances of survival?

# The Process of Cell Division

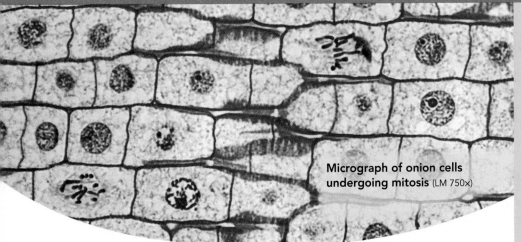

**Micrograph of onion cells undergoing mitosis** (LM 750x)

## 🔍 KEY QUESTIONS

- *What is the role of chromosomes in cell division?*
- *What are the main events of the cell cycle?*
- *What happens during the phases of mitosis?*
- *How do daughter cells split apart after mitosis?*

**HS-LS1-4:** Use a model to illustrate the role of cellular division (mitosis) and differentiation in producing and maintaining complex organisms.

**VOCABULARY**

chromosome • chromatin
cell cycle • interphase
mitosis • cytokinesis
prophase • chromatid
centromere • centriole
metaphase • anaphase
telophase

**READING TOOL**

In the cell cycle diagram in your 📖 **Biology Foundations Workbook,** each section represents the time the cell spends in each stage. Write the stages of the cell cycle into the diagram.

What role does cell division play in your life? You know that small children grow bigger every year. This growth depends on the production of new cells through cell division. But what happens when you are finished growing? Does cell division simply stop? Now, think about what must be happening when your body heals a cut or a broken bone. Where do the cells come from that heal a cut in your skin or seal together the fractured ends of a bone? Next, think about the daily wear and tear on your skin and on the cells of your digestive system. How about red blood cells that live for only about four months in your circulatory system? Where do the cells that replace them come from? The more you think about it, the more you will realize that cell division doesn't stop when we stop growing. In fact, cell division takes place all the time, keeping us healthy by replacing worn cells and regenerating the tissue we lose to injury or disease.

## Chromosomes

What would happen if a cell were simply to split in two, without any advance preparation? The results might be disastrous, especially if some of the cell's essential genetic information wound up in one of the daughter cells but not in the other. In order to make sure this doesn't happen, cells first make a complete copy of their genetic information before cell division begins.

Even a small cell like the bacterium *E. coli* has a tremendous amount of genetic information in the form of DNA. In fact, the total length of this bacterium's DNA molecule is 1.6 mm, roughly 1000 times longer than the cell itself. In terms of scale, imagine a 300-meter rope stuffed into a school backpack. Cells can handle such large molecules only by careful packaging. Genetic information is bundled into packages of DNA known as **chromosomes**.

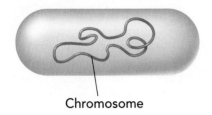

Chromosome

**Figure 11-6**

## Prokaryotic Chromosome

In most prokaryotes, a single chromosome holds most of the organism's DNA.

**Figure 11-7**

## Eukaryotic Chromosome

As a eukaryotic cell prepares for division, each chromosome coils more and more tightly to form a compact structure.

**Prokaryotic Chromosomes** Prokaryotic cells lack membrane-bound nuclei and many of the organelles found in eukaryotes. The DNA molecules of prokaryotic cells are found in the cytoplasm, along with most of the other contents of the cell. Most prokaryotes contain a single circular DNA chromosome, as you can see in **Figure 11-6**. That circular DNA contains all, or nearly all, of the cell's genetic information.

**Eukaryotic Chromosomes** Eukaryotic cells generally have much more DNA than prokaryotes have, and therefore they contain multiple chromosomes. Fruit flies, for example, have 8 chromosomes per cell, carrot cells have 18, and human cells have 46. The chromosomes in eukaryotic cells contain DNA tightly bound to proteins known as histones. This complex of DNA and protein is referred to as **chromatin**. DNA tightly coils around the histones, and together, the DNA and histone molecules form beadlike structures called nucleosomes. Nucleosomes pack together to form thick fibers, which condense even further during cell division. The X-like chromosome shape you often see drawn in textbooks is actually a duplicated chromosome with supercoiled chromatin, as shown in **Figure 11-7**.

Why do cells go to such lengths to package their DNA into chromosomes? One of the principal reasons is to ensure equal division of DNA when a cell divides. ⚷ *Chromosomes are precisely separated into two daughter cells during cell division.*

✅ **READING CHECK** **Compare** How are the chromosomes in eukaryotic cells different from those in prokaryotic cells?

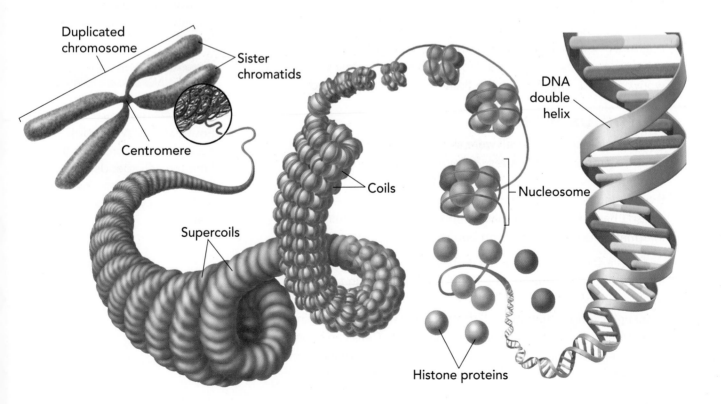

Duplicated chromosome

Sister chromatids

Centromere

Coils

Supercoils

DNA double helix

Nucleosome

Histone proteins

# The Cell Cycle

Cells go through a series of events known as the **cell cycle** as they grow and divide. ✎ *During the cell cycle, a cell grows, prepares for division, and then divides to form two daughter cells.* Each daughter cell then moves into a new cell cycle of activity, growth, and division.

**The Prokaryotic Cell Cycle** The prokaryotic cell cycle is a regular pattern of growth, DNA replication, and cell division that can take place very rapidly under ideal conditions. Researchers are just beginning to understand how the cycle works in prokaryotes, and relatively little is known about its details. It is known that most prokaryotic cells begin to replicate, or copy, their DNA chromosomes once they have grown to a certain size. When DNA replication is complete, or nearly complete, the cell begins to divide.

The process of cell division in prokaryotes is a form of asexual reproduction known as binary fission. Once the chromosome has been replicated, the two DNA molecules attach to different regions of the cell membrane. A network of fibers forms between them, stretching from one side of the cell to the other. These fibers constrict and the cell is pinched inward, dividing the cytoplasm and chromosomes between two newly formed cells. Binary fission results in the production of two genetically identical cells.

**The Eukaryotic Cell Cycle** In contrast to prokaryotes, much more is known about the eukaryotic cell cycle. As you can see in **Figure 11-8**, the eukaryotic cell cycle consists of four stages: $G_1$, S, $G_2$, and M. The length of each stage of the cell cycle—and the length of the entire cell cycle—varies depending on the type of cell.

At one time, biologists described the life of a cell as one cell division after another separated by an "in-between" period of growth called **interphase**. We now appreciate that a great deal happens in the time between cell divisions, so interphase is now divided into three phases: $G_1$, S, and $G_2$.

***$G_1$: Cell Growth*** Cells do most of their growing during the $G_1$ phase. In this phase, cells increase in size and synthesize new proteins and organelles. The G in $G_1$ and $G_2$ stands for "gap," but the $G_1$ and $G_2$ phases are actually periods of intense growth and activity.

***S: DNA Replication*** The $G_1$ phase is followed by the S phase. The S stands for "synthesis." During the S phase, new DNA is synthesized as the chromosomes are replicated. By the end of the S phase, the cell contains twice as much DNA as it did at the beginning of the phase.

**READING TOOL**

As you read, create a timeline of the sequence of events of the cell cycle. Include details for each event.

**INTERACTIVITY**

Learn about the various stages of the cell cycle.

**Figure 11-8**

## The Cell Cycle

During the cell cycle, a cell grows, prepares for division, and divides to form two daughter cells. The cell cycle includes four phases—$G_1$, S, $G_2$, and M.

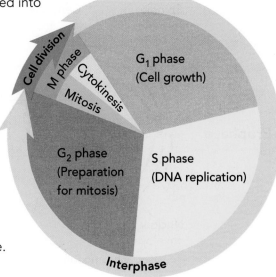

*G₂: Preparing for Cell Division* When DNA replication is completed, the cell enters the $G_2$ phase. $G_2$ is usually the shortest of the three phases. During the $G_2$ phase, many of the organelles and molecules required for cell division are produced. When the events of the $G_2$ phase are completed, the cell is ready to enter the M phase and begin the process of cell division.

*M Phase: Cell Division* The M phase of the cell cycle, which follows interphase, produces two daughter cells. The M phase takes its name from the process of mitosis. During the normal cell cycle, interphase can be quite long. In contrast, the process of cell division usually takes place quickly.

In eukaryotes, cell division occurs in two main stages. The first stage of the process, the division of the cell nucleus, is called **mitosis**. The second stage, the division of the cytoplasm, is called **cytokinesis**. In many cells, the two stages may overlap, so that cytokinesis begins while mitosis is still taking place.

**READING CHECK** Define What events occur during interphase?

# Mitosis

Biologists divide the events of mitosis into four phases: prophase, metaphase, anaphase, and telophase. Depending on the type of cell, mitosis may last anywhere from a few minutes to several days.

**Prophase** The first phase of mitosis, **prophase**, is usually the longest and may take up to half of the total time required to complete mitosis. ✍ *During prophase, the genetic material inside the nucleus condenses and the duplicated chromosomes become visible.* Outside the nucleus, a spindle starts to form.

During prophase, each duplicated chromosome condenses to appear as two thick strands known as sister **chromatids** (KROH muh tids), attached at a point called the **centromere**. When the process of mitosis is complete, the sister chromatids will have separated, one to each of the daughter cells. Also during prophase, the cell starts to build a spindle, a fanlike system of microtubules that will help to separate the duplicated chromosomes. Spindle fibers extend from a region called the centrosome, where tiny paired structures called **centrioles** are located. Early in prophase, the centrioles move toward opposite ends, or poles, of the cell. Plant cells lack centrioles, and organize spindles directly from their centrosome regions.

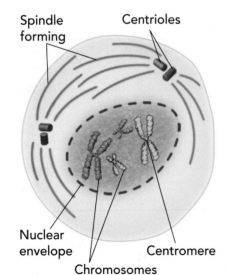

Spindle forming

Centrioles

Prophase

Nuclear envelope

Chromosomes

Centromere

🧪 **Open-Ended Inquiry**

## Make a Model of Mitosis

1. With your partner, discuss a plan for modeling the stages of mitosis. Choose available materials, such as yarn, chenille stems, or candy pieces, to represent the chromosomes. Then describe how to use the materials to demonstrate each stage.

2. Carry out your plan. Make sketches or take photographs of each stage.

3. Organize the sketches or photos to show all the stages of mitosis in the proper order. Add labels or captions to create a flip book, slide show, or video presentation.

### ANALYZE AND CONCLUDE

1. **Use Models** How many chromosomes did you include in your model?

2. **Evaluate Models** How accurately does your model show an original cell and the two daughter cells that are produced after mitosis? Compare your model with other representations of mitosis, such as those shown in the lesson. How could you improve your model?

3. **Use Models** Use your model to explain the function of mitosis to your classmates.

---

**Metaphase** The second phase of mitosis, **metaphase**, is generally the shortest. 🔍 *During metaphase, the centromeres of the duplicated chromosomes line up across the center of the cell.* Spindle fibers connect the centromere of each chromosome to the two poles of the spindle. The cell is now ready to separate those sister chromatids.

**Anaphase** The third phase of mitosis, **anaphase**, begins when sister chromatids suddenly separate and begin to move apart. Once anaphase begins, each sister chromatid is now considered an individual chromosome. 🔍 *During anaphase, the chromosomes separate and move along spindle fibers to opposite ends of the cell.* Anaphase movement requires the rapid disassembly of microtubules as chromosomes move toward the poles of the mitotic spindle. Anaphase comes to an end when this movement stops and the chromosomes are completely separated into two groups. The microtubules that once made up the mitotic spindle have almost completely disassembled by the end of anaphase.

**Telophase** Following anaphase is **telophase**, the final phase of mitosis. 🔍 *During telophase, the chromosomes, which were distinct and condensed, begin to spread out into a tangle of chromatin.* A nuclear envelope re-forms around each cluster of chromosomes, and gradually a nucleolus becomes visible in each daughter nucleus. Mitosis is complete, but the process of cell division has one more step.

✅ **READING CHECK** **Review** What structures are responsible for the movement of chromosomes to the center of the cell in metaphase and their separation in anaphase?

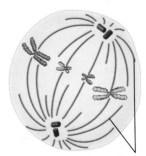

Spindle
**Metaphase**

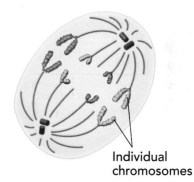

Individual chromosomes
**Anaphase**

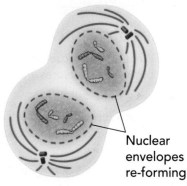

Nuclear envelopes re-forming
**Telophase**

# Cytokinesis

As a result of mitosis, two nuclei—each with a duplicate set of chromosomes—are formed. All that remains to complete the M phase of the cycle is cytokinesis, the division of the cytoplasm to form two separate cells. Cytokinesis usually occurs at the same time as telophase. ⚲ *Cytokinesis completes the process of cell division by dividing one cell into two.* The process of cytokinesis differs in animal and plant cells, as shown in **Figure 11-9**.

**Cytokinesis in Animal Cells** During cytokinesis in most animal cells, the cell membrane is drawn inward until the cytoplasm is pinched into two nearly equal parts. Each part contains its own nucleus and cytoplasmic organelles.

**Cytokinesis in Plant Cells** Cytokinesis in plant cells proceeds differently. The cell membrane is not flexible enough to draw inward because of the rigid cell wall that surrounds it. Instead, a structure known as the cell plate forms halfway between the divided nuclei. The cell plate gradually develops into cell membranes that separate the two daughter cells. A cell wall then forms in between the two new membranes, completing the process.

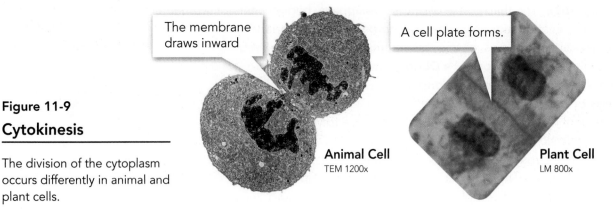

**Figure 11-9**

**Cytokinesis**

The division of the cytoplasm occurs differently in animal and plant cells.

The membrane draws inward

A cell plate forms.

**Animal Cell**
TEM 1200x

**Plant Cell**
LM 800x

HS-LS1-4

## ✓ LESSON 11.2 Review

### ⚲ KEY QUESTIONS

1. What are chromosomes? How are they different between prokaryotes and eukaryotes?

2. What is the cell cycle?

3. What happens during each of the four phases of mitosis? Write one or two sentences for each phase.

4. What happens during cytokinesis?

### CRITICAL THINKING

5. **Construct an Explanation** Explain how mitosis maintains the chromosome number of the original cells when forming new cells.

6. **Construct an Explanation** Describe the role of microtubules in mitosis. Why must microtubules both assemble and disassemble for mitosis to occur properly?

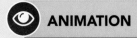
**Figure 11-10**

# Mitosis

The phases of mitosis shown here are typical of animal cells. These light micrographs are from a developing whitefish embryo (LM 415x).

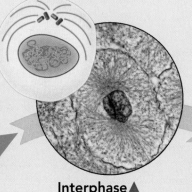

**Interphase▲**
The cell grows and replicates its DNA and centrioles.

**◄ Cytokinesis**
The cytoplasm pinches in half. Each daughter cell has an identical set of duplicate chromosomes.

**Prophase▶**
The chromatin condenses into chromosomes. The centrioles separate, and a spindle begins to form. The nuclear envelope breaks down.

**▼ Telophase**
The chromosomes gather at opposite ends of the cell and lose their distinct shapes. Two new nuclear envelopes will form.

**Metaphase▼**
The chromosomes line up across the center of the cell. Each chromosome is connected to spindle fibers at its centromere.

**Anaphase ▼**
The sister chromatids separate into individual chromosomes and are moved apart.

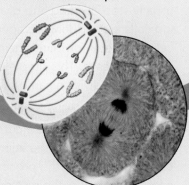

# Regulating the Cell Cycle

## KEY QUESTIONS
- *How is the cell cycle regulated?*
- *How do cancer cells differ from other cells?*

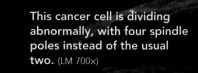

This cancer cell is dividing abnormally, with four spindle poles instead of the usual **two.** (LM 700×)

**VOCABULARY**
growth factor
cyclin
apoptosis
cancer
tumor

### READING TOOL

As you read, fill in the graphic organizer in your **Biology Foundations Workbook** with the key words from this lesson.

How do cells know when it is time to divide? One striking fact about cells in multicellular organisms is how carefully cell growth and cell division are controlled. Think of what might happen, for example, if the cells in one of your internal organs were to suddenly start growing while the other parts of the body did not. That's why careful control of the cell cycle is essential for orderly growth and development. If something goes wrong with that control, serious diseases such as cancer sometimes result. In the human body, for example, most muscle cells and nerve cells do not divide at all once they have developed. In contrast, blood-producing cells in the bone marrow, as well as cells of the skin and digestive tract, grow and divide regularly throughout life. In this way they produce new cells to replace those that wear out or break down.

## Controls on Cell Division

When scientists grow cells in the laboratory, most cells will divide until they come into contact with one another. Once they do, they usually stop dividing and growing. What happens if those neighboring cells are suddenly scraped off the culture dish? The remaining cells will begin dividing again until they once again make contact with other cells. This simple experiment shows that controls on cell growth and division can be turned on and off.

Something similar happens inside the body. Look at **Figure 11-11.** When an injury such as a cut in the skin or a break in a bone occurs, cells at the edges of the injury are stimulated to divide rapidly. New cells form, starting the process of healing. When the healing process nears completion, the rate of cell division slows, controls on growth are restored, and normal activities return.

## INTERACTIVITY

Explore how cell growth is regulated.

**Regulatory Proteins** For many years, biologists searched for a signal that might <u>regulate</u> the cell cycle—something that would "tell" the cell when it was time to divide, duplicate its chromosomes, or enter another phase of the cell cycle. They found out that there is not just one signal, but many. Scientists have identified dozens of proteins that help to regulate the cell cycle. 🔍 *The cell cycle is controlled by regulatory proteins both inside and outside the cell.*

**Internal Regulators** One group of internal regulatory proteins responds to events inside the cell. These proteins act as checkpoints, allowing the cell cycle to proceed only when certain events have taken place. For example, one set of checkpoint proteins makes sure a cell does not enter mitosis until its chromosomes have replicated. Another checkpoint prevents a cell from entering anaphase until spindle fibers have attached to each of the chromosomes.

**External Regulators** Proteins that respond to events outside the cell are called external regulatory proteins. External regulatory proteins direct cells to speed up or slow down the cell cycle. One important group of external regulatory proteins is the group made up of growth factors. **Growth factors** stimulate the growth and division of cells. These proteins are especially important during embryonic development and wound healing. Other external regulatory proteins on the surface of neighboring cells often have the opposite effect. These regulatory proteins cause cells to slow down or stop their cell cycles. This prevents excessive cell growth and keeps body tissues from disrupting one another.

✓ **READING CHECK Summarize** Why must multicellular organisms tightly control the cell cycle?

**Up Close**

**Figure 11-11**

# Cell Growth and Healing

When a person breaks a bone, cells at the edges of the injury are stimulated to divide rapidly. The new cells that form begin to heal the break. As the bone heals, the cells stop dividing and growing.

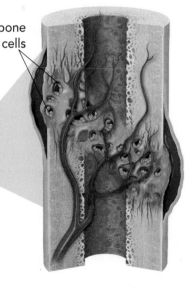

New bone cells

**Cyclins** Biologists had been searching for years for the signal that regulates the cell cycle because they realized that it could help them treat diseases. Learning that there is not just one signal but many has made that job more complicated.

Scientists discovered the first regulatory protein in the early 1980s. When they injected this protein into a nondividing cell, a mitotic spindle would form. They named this protein **cyclin** because it seemed to regulate the cell cycle. Investigators have since discovered a family of proteins known as cyclins that regulate the timing of the cell cycle in eukaryotic cells. Cyclins rise and fall in a pattern, as shown in **Figure 11-12**.

**Figure 11-12**

**Cyclin Levels**

Cyclin binds with an enzyme to produce mitosis-promoting factor (MPF). The levels of MPF Cyclin rise and fall to control the cell cycle.

**Mitosis Factor**

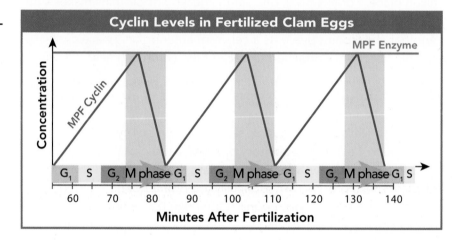

Cyclin Levels in Fertilized Clam Eggs

**READING TOOL**

Review the timeline you created for Lesson 2, which showed the events of the cell cycle. Create a similar timeline for apoptosis.

**Apoptosis** Just as new cells are produced every day in a multicellular organism, many other cells die. A cell may die by accident due to damage or injury, or a cell may actually be "programmed" to die. **Apoptosis** (ayp up TOH sis) is a process of programmed cell death. Once apoptosis is triggered, a cell undergoes a series of controlled steps leading to its self-destruction. First, the cell and its chromatin shrink, and then parts of the cell's membranes break off. Neighboring cells then quickly clean up the cell's remains.

Apoptosis plays a key role in growth and development by shaping the structure of tissues and organs. When apoptosis does not occur as it should in humans, a number of diseases can result. For example, the cell loss seen in AIDS and Parkinson's disease can result if too much apoptosis occurs.

---

**Analyzing Data**

## The Rise and Fall of Cyclins

Scientists measured cyclin levels in clam embryonic cells as the cells went through their first mitotic divisions after fertilization. The data are shown in the graph in **Figure 11-12**.

Cyclins are continually produced and destroyed within cells. Cyclin production signals cells to enter mitosis, whereas cyclin destruction signals cells to stop dividing and to enter interphase.

### ANALYZE AND CONCLUDE

1. **Analyze Graphs** How long does cyclin production last during a typical cell cycle in embryonic clam cells?

2. **Apply Scientific Reasoning** During which part of the cell cycle does cyclin production begin? How quickly is cyclin destroyed?

3. **Form a Hypothesis** Suppose that the regulators that control cyclin production are no longer produced. Hypothesize two possible outcomes.

# Cancer: Uncontrolled Cell Growth

Why is cell growth regulated so carefully? The principal reason may be that the consequences of uncontrolled cell growth in a multicellular organism are very severe. **Cancer**, a disorder in which body cells lose the ability to control growth, is one such example.

🔑 *Cancer cells do not respond to the signals that regulate the growth of most cells. As a result, the cell cycle is disrupted, and cells grow and divide uncontrollably.* Cancer cells form a mass of cells called a **tumor**. However, not all tumors are cancerous. Some are benign, or noncancerous. A benign tumor does not spread to surrounding healthy tissue or to other parts of the body. Cancerous tumors, such as the one shown in **Figure 11-13**, are malignant. Malignant tumors invade and destroy surrounding healthy tissue.

As the cancer cells spread to surrounding healthy tissue, they absorb the nutrients needed by other cells, block nerve connections, and prevent the organs they invade from functioning properly. Soon, the delicate balances that exist in the body are disrupted, and life-threatening illness results.

**What Causes Cancer?** Cancers are caused by defects in the genes that regulate cell growth and division. There are several sources of such defects, including smoking or chewing tobacco, radiation exposure, and even viral infection. All cancers, however, have one thing in common: The control over the cell cycle has broken down. Some cancer cells will no longer respond to external growth regulators, while others fail to produce the internal regulators that ensure orderly growth.

An astonishing number of cancer cells have a defect in a gene for a checkpoint protein known as p53, which normally halts the cell cycle until all chromosomes have been properly replicated. Damaged or defective p53 genes cause cells to lose the information needed to respond to signals that normally control their growth.

✓ **READING CHECK** **Make Generalizations** Why is the presence of cancer cells so harmful to the body?

**ANIMATION**

hhmi | **BioInteractive**

Figure 11-13

## Growth of Cancer Cells

Normal cells grow and divide in a carefully controlled fashion. Cells that are cancerous lose this control and continue to grow and divide, producing tumors.

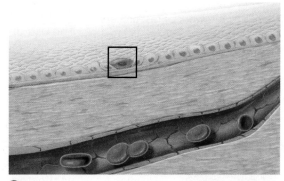

❶ A cell begins to divide abnormally.

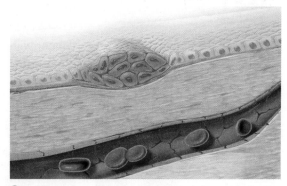

❷ The cancer cells produce a tumor, which begins to displace normal cells and tissues.

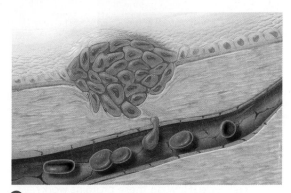

❸ Cancer cells are particularly dangerous because of their tendency to spread once they enter the bloodstream or lymph vessels. The cancer then moves into other parts of the body and forms secondary tumors, a process called metastasis.

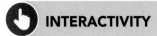

**INTERACTIVITY**

Investigate how the cell cycle is regulated and what happens when things go wrong.

**Figure 11-14**

## Cancer Research

Thanks to the work of researchers around the world, cancer can be treated more effectively than it was in the past. The false-colored micrograph shows a small cancerous tumor (blue) in the air sacs of the lungs.

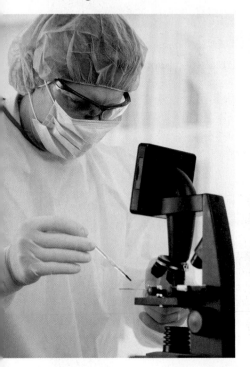

**Treatments for Cancer** When a cancerous tumor is localized, it can often be removed by surgery. Skin cancer, one of the most common forms of the disease, can usually be treated this way. Melanomas, the most serious form of skin cancer, can be removed surgically, but only if spotted very early.

As shown in **Figure 11-14**, cancerous tumors tend to grow more rapidly than normal cells. For this reason, they need to copy their DNA relatively quickly. This makes them especially vulnerable to damage from high-energy radiation. As a result, many tumors can be effectively treated with carefully targeted beams of radiation.

Medical researchers have worked for years to develop chemical compounds that would kill cancer cells, or at least slow their growth. The use of such compounds against cancer is known as chemotherapy. Great advances in chemotherapy have taken place in recent years and have even made it possible to cure some forms of cancer. However, because most chemotherapy compounds target rapidly dividing cells, they also interfere with cell division in normal, healthy cells. This produces serious side effects in many patients, which is why researchers are trying to find highly specific ways in which cancer cells can be targeted for destruction while leaving healthy cells unaffected.

Cancer is a serious disease. Understanding and combating cancer remains a major scientific challenge, but scientists at least know where to start. Cancer is a disease of the cell cycle, and conquering cancer will require an even deeper understanding of the processes that control cell division.

(SEM: 240×)

## ✓ LESSON 11.3 Review

### ⚘ KEY QUESTIONS

1. Name the two types of proteins that regulate the cell cycle. How do these proteins work?

2. Why is cancer considered a disease of the cell cycle?

### CRITICAL THINKING

3. Translate Scientific Information How did experimental results show the effect of cyclins on the cell cycle?

4. Construct an Explanation How might a drug that alters events in mitosis or the cell cycle be useful for treating cancer?

# Cell Differentiation

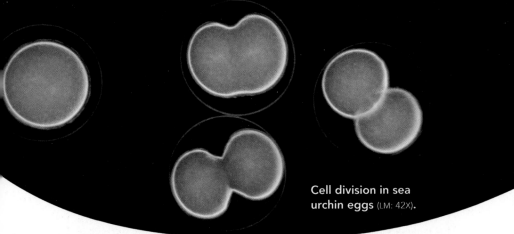

Cell division in sea urchin eggs (LM: 42X).

🔍 **KEY QUESTIONS**

- *How do cells become specialized for different functions?*
- *What are stem cells?*
- *What are some possible benefits and issues associated with stem cell research?*

HS-LS1-4: Use a model to illustrate the role of cellular division (mitosis) and differentiation in producing and maintaining complex organisms.

**VOCABULARY**
embryo
differentiation
totipotent
blastocyst
pluripotent
stem cell
multipotent

**READING TOOL**

In the chart in your 📖 **Biology Foundations Workbook,** fill in the details that support the main ideas from this lesson.

Each of us started life as just one cell. So, for that matter, did your pet dog, a sea urchin, and the petunia on a windowsill. Cell division explains how one cell could produce millions or even billions of cells in each of these organisms, but it leaves one critical question unanswered: Why do some cells turn into muscle cells, some into nerve cells, and others into bone and skin cells? Plainly stated, how do cells become so different from one another?

## From One Cell to Many

Animals and higher plants pass through a developmental stage called an **embryo**, from which the adult organism is gradually produced. During the developmental process, cells become more and more different from one another and specialized for particular functions. **Figure 11-15** shows some of the specialized cells found in the parts of a plant.

**Figure 11-15**
### Specialized Plant Cells

The first cell of a plant forms inside a reproductive structure, such as a flower. After many cell divisions, the new plant develops the specialized tissues it needs to survive as a multicellular organism.

▶ **VIDEO**

Learn how meat can be grown in a lab using stem cells.

Leaf tissue
(LM: 255X)

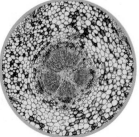

Root tissues
(LM: 46X)

Cross-section of a stem (LM: 27X)

**Defining Differentiation** The process by which cells become specialized is known as **differentiation** (dif ur en shee AY shun). 🔍 *During the development of an organism, cells differentiate into many distinct cell types.* A differentiated cell has become, quite literally, different from the embryonic cell that produced it and specialized to perform certain tasks, such as contraction, photosynthesis, or protection. Our bodies, and the bodies of all multicellular organisms, contain highly differentiated cells that carry out the jobs we need to perform to stay alive.

**Mapping Differentiation** The process of differentiation determines a cell's ultimate identity, such as whether it will spend its life as a nerve cell or a muscle cell. In some organisms, a cell's role is rigidly determined at a specific point in the course of development. In the microscopic worm *Caenorhabditis elegans*, for example, biologists have mapped the outcome of each and every cell division from fertilized egg to adult.

The process of cell differentiation in *C. elegans* begins with the very first division and continues throughout embryonic development. **Figure 11-16** shows when some of the cells found in the adult begin to differentiate during development. Every time a new worm develops, the process is the same, resulting in exactly 959 cells with precisely determined functions.

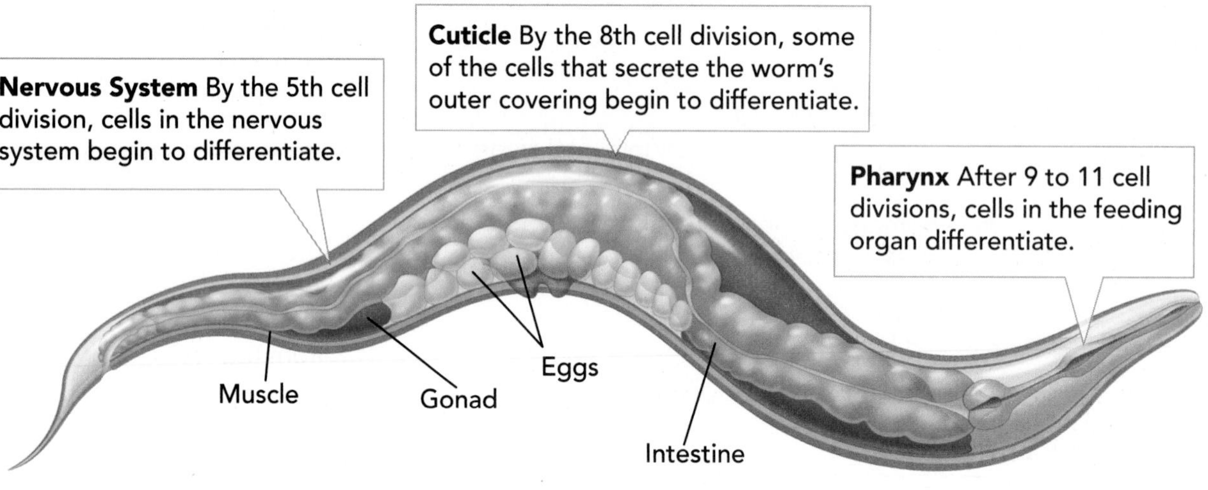

**INTERACTIVITY**

**Figure 11-16**

**Differentiation in C. elegans**

A fertilized egg develops into an adult worm after many cell divisions. Daughter cells from each cell division follow a specific path toward a role as a particular kind of cell.

**Nervous System** By the 5th cell division, cells in the nervous system begin to differentiate.

**Cuticle** By the 8th cell division, some of the cells that secrete the worm's outer covering begin to differentiate.

**Pharynx** After 9 to 11 cell divisions, cells in the feeding organ differentiate.

Muscle

Gonad

Eggs

Intestine

**Differentiation in Mammals** Other organisms, including mammals, go through a more flexible process in which cell differentiation is controlled by a number of interacting factors in the embryo, many of which are still not well understood. What is known, however, is that adult cells generally do reach a point at which their differentiation is complete—when they can no longer turn into other types of cells.

✅ **READING CHECK** **Identify** How does a single fertilized egg cell develop into so many different types of specialized cells?

# Stem Cells and Development

One of the most important questions in biology is how all of the specialized, differentiated cell types in the body are formed from just a single cell, the fertilized egg, called a zygote. Biologists say that the zygote is **totipotent** (toh TIP uh tunt)—literally, able to do everything, to develop into any type of cell in the body (including the cells that make up the extra-embryonic membranes and placenta). Only the fertilized egg and the cells produced by the first few cell divisions of embryonic development are truly totipotent. If there is a "secret" by which cells start the process of differentiation, these are the cells that know that secret.

**Human Development** After about four days of development, a human embryo forms into a **blastocyst**, a hollow ball of cells with a cluster of cells inside known as the inner cell mass. Even at this early stage, the cells of the blastocyst have begun to specialize. The outer cells form tissues that will attach the embryo to its mother, while the inner cell mass becomes the embryo itself. The cells of the inner cell mass are said to be pluripotent (plu ri POH tunt). **Pluripotent** cells can develop into any of the body's cell types, although they generally cannot form the tissues surrounding the embryo.

**Stem Cells** As the name implies, **stem cells** sit at the base of a branching "stem" of development from which different cell types form. ✎ *Stem cells are the unspecialized cells from which differentiated cells develop.* Stem cells are found in the early embryo, of course, but they are also found in many places in the adult body.

*Adult Stem Cells* Cells in some tissues, like blood and skin, have a limited life span and must be constantly replaced. Pools of adult stem cells, found in various locations throughout the body, produce the new cells needed for these tissues. New blood cells differentiate from stem cells found in the bone marrow, and many skin stem cells are found in hair follicles. Small clusters of adult stem cells are even found in the brain, in the heart, and in skeletal muscle. These adult cells are referred to as **multipotent** (muhl TIP uh tunt) stem cells, because the types of differentiated cells they can form are usually limited to replacing cells in the tissues where they are found.

## INTERACTIVITY

Explore stem cells and differentiated cells.

## Exploration Lab    Open-ended Inquiry

### Regeneration in Planaria

**Problem** Are planarian cells multipotent or totipotent?

In this lab, you will design an experiment to determine whether planarian stem cells are multipotent or totipotent. Then you will share your results with the rest of the class. From these combined results, you will infer where multipotent or totipotent stem cells are found in a planarian's body.

You can find this lab in your digital course.

**Embryonic Stem Cells** Pluripotent embryonic stem cells are more versatile than adult stem cells, since they are capable of producing every cell type in the body, as shown in **Figure 11-17**. In laboratory experiments, scientists have managed to coax embryonic stem cells to differentiate into nerve cells, muscle cells, and even sperm and egg cells. In 1998, researchers at the University of Wisconsin found a way to grow human embryonic stem cells in culture, making it possible to explore the potential of these remarkable cells.

✓ **READING CHECK** **Compare and Contrast** How are pluripotent and multipotent cells similar? How are they different?

## Figure 11-17
## Embryonic Stem Cells

After fertilization, the human embryo develops into a hollow ball of cells known as a blastocyst. The actual body of the embryo develops from the inner cell mass, a cluster of cells inside the blastocyst. Because of their ability to differentiate into each of the body's many cell types, the cells are known as embryonic stem cells.

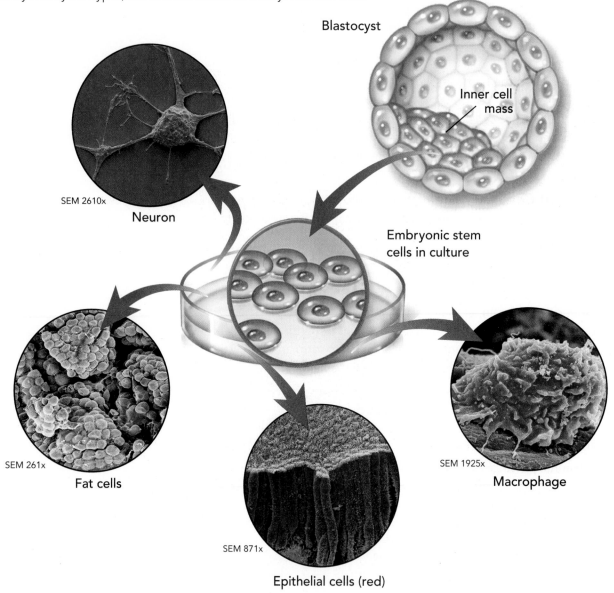

Blastocyst

Inner cell mass

SEM 2610x

Neuron

Embryonic stem cells in culture

SEM 261x

Fat cells

SEM 871x

Epithelial cells (red)

SEM 1925x

Macrophage

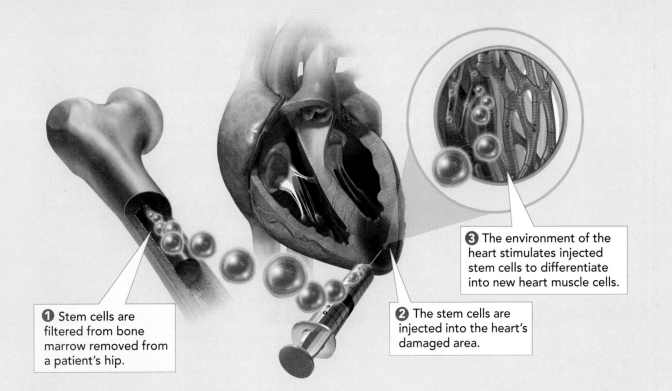

**①** Stem cells are filtered from bone marrow removed from a patient's hip.

**②** The stem cells are injected into the heart's damaged area.

**③** The environment of the heart stimulates injected stem cells to differentiate into new heart muscle cells.

# Frontiers in Stem Cell Research

Basic research on stem cells takes on a special urgency in light of the importance it might have for human health. Heart attacks destroy cells in the heart muscle, strokes injure brain cells, and spinal cord injuries cause paralysis by breaking connections between nerve cells. Not surprisingly, the prospect of using stem cells to repair such cellular damage has excited medical researchers.

**Figure 11-18** shows how stem cells might be used in the future to repair the damage caused by a heart attack. During a heart attack, the blood supply to part of the heart muscle is cut off, causing the cells to die. This damages the heart and prevents it from functioning properly. Stem cells harvested from the bone marrow might be cultured and then injected into the damaged portion of the heart. Once in place, the stem cells would "learn" what kind of cells they needed to be from the surviving cells around them. The stem cells would differentiate to become heart muscle cells.

**Ethical Issues**  Because adult stem cells can be harvested from a willing donor, research with these cells has raised few ethical questions. This is not the case with embryonic stem cells, which are generally obtained in ways that cause the destruction of an embryo. For this reason, individuals who seek to protect human embryonic life oppose such research as unethical. Other groups support such research as essential for saving human lives and argue that it would be unethical to restrict research. 🔍 *Human embryonic stem cell research is controversial because the arguments for it and against it both involve ethical issues of life and death.* However, new developments in research may help to address these concerns.

**CASE STUDY**

Figure 11-18

**Future Treatment for Heart Disease?**

Stem cell research may lead to new ways to reverse the damage caused by a severe heart attack. The diagram shows one method currently being investigated.

**READING TOOL**

Make a two-column chart to list the benefits and issues related to stem cell research. Fill in the chart as you read.

**Induced Pluripotent Stem Cells** A fundamental breakthrough took place in 2007 when Shinya Yamanaka of Kyoto University in Japan was able to convert human fibroblasts into cells that closely resembled embryonic stem cells. His work is summarized in **Figure 11-19**. These induced pluripotent stem cells (iPS cells), as they are known, are now widely used in research. Under certain conditions, iPS cells may be able to replace embryonic stem cells.

In a sense, what Yamanaka and his lab achieved was to take the work of John Gurdon in cloning frogs to its logical conclusion. Gurdon had shown that the nucleus of an adult cell could be reprogrammed to develop into an embryo by unknown factors in the cytoplasm of an egg cell. To produce iPS cells, Yamanaka found a set of precise conditions that could reprogram an entire cell to put it back into an embryonic state. For these two discoveries, more than 50 years apart, Gurdon and Yamanaka shared the Nobel Prize in Physiology or Medicine in 2012. Today, it seems clear that this work has the potential to solve the ethical problems that can make embryonic stem cell research highly controversial.

**CASE STUDY**

**Figure 11-19**

## Shinya Yamanaka

Dr. Shinya Yamanaka's breakthrough research on induced pluripotent stem cells has made a huge impact on the field of regenerative medicine. Study the diagram to see how specialized cells can become stem cells.

# Induced Pluripotent Stem Cells

**1 Genes are added to adult cells**

Dr. Yamanaka introduced four transcription factor genes into mouse skin fibroblasts.

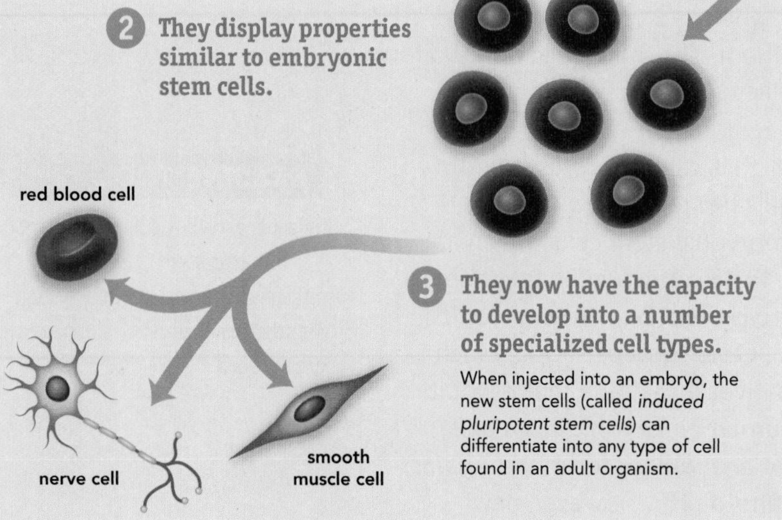

**2 They display properties similar to embryonic stem cells.**

red blood cell

nerve cell

smooth muscle cell

**3 They now have the capacity to develop into a number of specialized cell types.**

When injected into an embryo, the new stem cells (called *induced pluripotent stem cells*) can differentiate into any type of cell found in an adult organism.

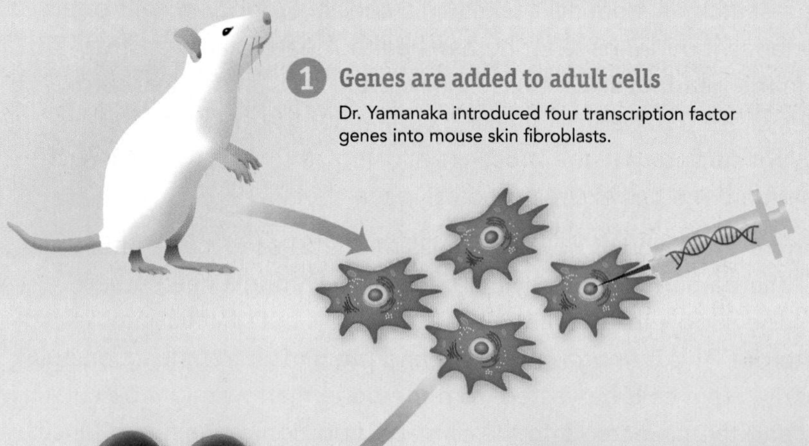

**Regenerative Medicine** Work on many types of stem cells, including adult stem cells and iPS cells, has now opened up an entirely new field of medicine. Regenerative medicine makes use of stem cells to repair or replace damaged cells and tissues. By studying what happens when stem cells differentiate, researchers have now developed laboratory "recipes" that can remake cells into certain other cell types. These differentiated cells may then be used to repair or replace damaged or diseased cells, tissues, and even whole organs.

One promising treatment, now in clinical trials, uses stem cells to treat a form of macular degeneration. This condition affects the most sensitive part of the retina, the light-sensing layer of cells within the eye. When these cells break down, the result is a loss of vision. Experimental treatments have taken cells from a patient's own body and converted them into iPS cells. These cells were then stimulated to differentiate into cells that could be transplanted directly into the eye. In at least a few cases, this treatment seems to have reversed the process of macular degeneration.

Such research is not without risk, of course, since the transplanted cells may behave in unpredictable ways. They could differentiate into unwanted cell types, spread beyond the site of the transplant, or even grow uncontrollably into a tumor. This means that there are good reasons to proceed cautiously before putting these techniques into wide use. However, given its potential to alleviate human pain and suffering, it seems that the age of regenerative medicine is now upon us.

As researchers also know, some organisms do an excellent job of regenerating lost body parts. For example, if a sea star loses one or more of its arms, the central part of its body is capable of growing back the lost parts. Scientists continue to study the steps of this process. The research may lead to a method of replicating the steps in the human body.

 **VIDEO**

Discover how animals regenerate lost body parts.

HS-LS1-4

## ☑ LESSON 11.4 Review

### ⚲ KEY QUESTIONS

1. What happens during differentiation?

2. What are stem cells? How are embryonic stem cells different from adult stem cells?

3. What do the arguments for and against the use of stem cells in medical research share?

### CRITICAL THINKING

4. **Construct an Explanation** Why is cell differentiation essential for every complex multicellular organism?

5. **Communicate Information** Use what you learned in this lesson to discuss how cells become specialized for different functions. Include an explanation of how the potential for specialization varies with cell type and how it varies over the life span of an organism.

# Will stem cells change the future of healing?

Scientists are able to reprogram certain differentiated cells to make them act like stem cells. However, stem cell technology involves both benefits and risks.

HS-ETS1-1

## Make Your Case

Different people may analyze new technologies in different ways. Even when observers understand the technology and agree on the evidence, they may draw different conclusions about whether the benefits outweigh the drawbacks. As you research stem cell therapies, you will likely find conflicting opinions and judgments about them. Be sure to evaluate the reliability of your sources as you form your opinion.

## Construct an Argument

1. **Conduct Research** Research stem cell technology. Find out about both sides of the issue, including scientific and ethical considerations. The United States Food and Drug Administration (FDA) is one useful source.

2. **Engage in Argument From Evidence** Based on your research, pick one side of the debate. Construct a useful set of guidelines for regulating stem cell therapies. Your guidelines should account for constraints such as costs, reliability, and safety, as well as social impacts.

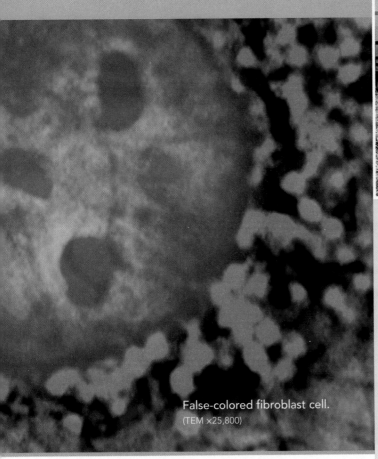

False-colored fibroblast cell.
(TEM ×25,800)

# Careers on the Case

## Work Toward a Solution

Researching and writing about stem cells and other scientific findings includes the coordination of many different types of careers.

### Science Journalist

Science journalists are required to have a knowledge of science as well as communication skills. Newspapers, television networks, and online media all employ journalists to report on developments in science, technology, and engineering.

▶ **VIDEO**

Watch this video to learn about other careers in biology.

# Technology on the Case

## Here Come the Clones

A clone is an exact genetic duplicate of a cell or an organism. John Gurdon created the first cloned frog when he transferred a nucleus from an adult frog cell into an egg cell. The result was a new frog, or clone, that had the same genes as the adult.

Cloning technology has advanced greatly since Gurdon's original experiments. In the 1990s, researchers in Scotland welcomed Dolly the sheep, the first cloned mammal. Today, more than 20 different kinds of animals have been cloned, including cattle, horses, and pigs. The technique is generally the same as Gurdon pioneered: An adult cell nucleus is transferred into the cytoplasm of an egg cell.

Cloning provides many benefits. Ranchers are expanding their herds by cloning their strongest, healthiest animals. Then the clones can be used as breeding stock. Government agencies, including the Federal Drug Administration (FDA), have confirmed the safety of milk and meat products from animal clones and their offspring.

Could cloning be used for human reproduction? It might be possible, but the practice raises many serious ethical issues. Many countries now prohibit human cloning. In other countries, including the United States, bans have been proposed but not yet enacted.

# STUDY GUIDE

Go to your Biology Foundations Workbook for longer versions of these lesson summaries.

## 11.1 Cell Growth, Division, and Reproduction

The larger a cell becomes, the more demands the cell places on its DNA. In addition, a larger cell is less efficient in moving nutrients and waste materials across the cell membrane. The process of cell division solves this problem.

Asexual reproduction is the production of genetically identical offspring from a single parent. Offspring produced by sexual reproduction inherit some of their genetic information from each parent. Sexual reproduction produces genetic diversity and may help a species to survive in a changing environment.

- cell division
- asexual reproduction
- sexual reproduction

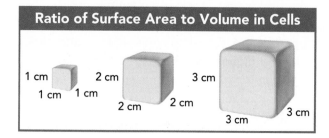

**Ratio of Surface Area to Volume in Cells**

1 cm  1 cm  1 cm
2 cm  2 cm  2 cm
3 cm  3 cm  3 cm

☑ **Cause and Effect** What changes occur to the ratio of surface area to volume as a cell grows?

## 11.2 The Process of Cell Division

Genetic information is bundled into packages of DNA known as chromosomes. Prokaryotic cells have a single circular chromosome. Eukaryotic cells have multiple chromosomes enclosed in the nucleus.

Cell division in prokaryotes is a form of asexual reproduction known as binary fission. The eukaryotic cell cycle consists of four stages: cell growth, DNA replication, preparing for cell division, and cell division.

Mitosis is the division of the cell nucleus. During mitosis, chromosomes duplicate and condense into sister chromatids, which line up and then separate. In the final phase of mitosis, the separated chromosomes cluster and form duplicate nuclei. After mitosis, cytoplasm divides in the process known as cytokinesis, forming two daughter cells.

- chromosome
- chromatin
- cell cycle
- interphase
- mitosis
- cytokinesis
- prophase
- chromatid
- centromere
- centriole
- metaphase
- anaphase
- telophase

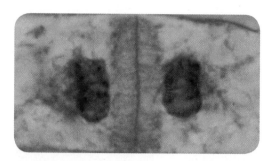

☑ **Classify** What type of cell is undergoing cytokinesis in the photo? How do you know?

## 11.3 Regulating the Cell Cycle

Cell cycles are regulated by internal proteins such as cyclin and external proteins such as growth factors. Other external regulatory proteins cause cells to slow down or stop their cell cycles. Apoptosis is a process of programmed cell death, which shapes the structure of tissues and organs.

Cancer results in uncontrolled cell growth and division. Cancer cells form tumors, which invade and destroy surrounding healthy tissue. Rapidly growing cancer cells can be targeted by radiation or chemotherapy or by surgically removing the tumor.

- growth factor
- cyclin
- apoptosis
- cancer
- tumor

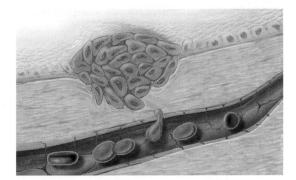

☑**Interpret Diagrams** Write a caption to describe the events shown in the illustration.

## 11.4 Cell Differentiation

Differentiation is the process by which cells become specialized. The differentiation process can be mapped in simple organisms but the process is more complicated in more complex organisms.

A zygote, the fertilized egg, is totipotent, in that it will develop into any type of cell for the organism, including cells that make up the extra-embryonic membranes and placenta. Embryonic stem cells are pluripotent, which means they are able to produce every type of cell. Adult stem cells are multipotent, so they are capable of replacing cells in the tissues where they are found.

The use of embryonic stem cells for research raises many ethical concerns, but stem cell research has made promising advances in repairing or replacing damaged cells and tissues.

- embryo
- differentiation
- totipotent
- blastocyst
- pluripotent
- stem cell
- multipotent

 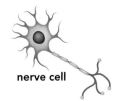 

nerve cell        red blood cell        smooth muscle cell

☑**Compare** How is a differentiated cell different from a stem cell?

# Organize Information

Describe the events that occur in each stage of mitosis and cytokinesis.

| Prophase | Metaphase | Anaphase | Telophase | Cytokinesis |
|----------|-----------|----------|-----------|-------------|
| 1. | 2. | 3. | 4. | 5. |

# Taxol
## A Drug, a Poison, or Both?

# Construct an Explanation

HS-LS1-4, HS-ETS1-1, CCSS.ELA-LITERACY.RST.9-10.7,
CCSS.ELA-LITERACY.RST.9-10.10

**STEM** As you read in this chapter, cell division is an essential process in the life of a multicellular organism. Repeated rounds of cell division allowed you to develop from a single cell into the fully functioning, inquisitive science student that you are today! Proper cell division is also essential to allow your body to recover from injury, and to replace damaged or diseased cells.

Generally, cell division is a tightly controlled and regulated process. But sometimes something goes wrong and that control is lost. The result may be cancer, a disease in which rapidly dividing cells form clusters known as tumors and invade tissues throughout the body.

The drug taxol has become widely used to treat many kinds of cancer, especially breast cancer. The drug works by acting on microtubules. As you read in this chapter, during prophase and metaphase of mitosis, microtubules attach to the chromosomes and move them to the center of the cell. Then, during anaphase, microtubules disassemble, separating the chromosomes into two daughter cells.

Taxol works by binding to microtubule proteins, and preventing their disassembly. The result is that the cell is "stuck" in metaphase, cannot complete mitosis, and may undergo spontaneous cell death. Cancer cells divide especially rapidly, so taxol harms them more than it harms normal cells.

If you think that a drug that stops mitosis is acting like a poison, you may be correct. Taxol acts on normal cells and cancer cells alike. As a result, it has many side effects, including hair loss and reduced blood cell counts. Doctors try to prescribe taxol in just the right dosages to fight cancerous tumors while minimizing the damage it causes.

The drug Taxol is used to treat cancer. It is derived from the bark of the Pacific Yew, the tree shown here.

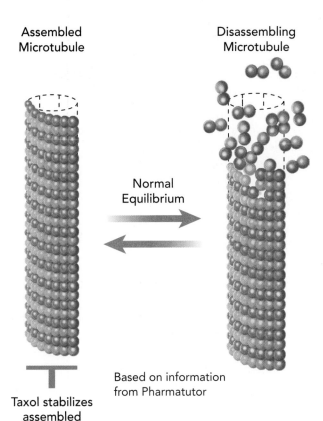

Assembled Microtubule

Disassembling Microtubule

Normal Equilibrium

Taxol stabilizes assembled microtubules

Based on information from Pharmatutor

1. **Interpret Visuals** Use the diagram to explain, in your own words, how taxol acts on microtubules.

2. **Defend Your Claim** Is it accurate to describe taxol as both a drug and a poison? Use logical reasoning to defend or support your answer.

3. **Construct an Explanation** Why is taxol useful for fighting cancer? (**Hint:** Review Lesson 3 for the definition of *cancer* and the examples of malignant tumors.)

4. **Conduct Research** What additional questions do you have about cancer and the drugs that fight this disease? Record your questions, and then conduct research to learn the answers or to find more information.

5. **Develop a Model** Choose one of the cancer drugs that you have researched. Draw a diagram or make a flowchart to show how the drug works and why it is useful. Share your model with your classmates.

## 🔍 KEY QUESTIONS AND TERMS

### 11.1 Cell Growth, Division, and Reproduction
HS-LS1-4

1. The rate at which materials enter and leave the cell depends on the cell's
   a. volume.
   b. weight.
   c. speciation.
   d. surface area.

2. In order for a cell to divide successfully, the cell must first
   a. duplicate its genetic information.
   b. decrease its volume.
   c. increase its number of chromosomes.
   d. decrease its number of organelles.

3. The process that increases genetic diversity within a population is
   a. asexual reproduction.
   b. sexual reproduction.
   c. cell division.
   d. binary fission.

4. Describe what is meant by each of the following terms: *cell volume, cell surface area, ratio of surface area to volume.*

5. Describe asexual and sexual reproduction as survival strategies.

### 11.2 The Process of Cell Division
HS-LS1-4

6. Sister chromatids are attached to each other at an area called the
   a. centriole.
   b. centromere.
   c. spindle.
   d. chromosome.

7. If a cell has 12 chromosomes, how many chromosomes will each of its daughter cells have after mitosis and cytokinesis?
   a. 4            c. 12
   b. 6            d. 24

8. In plant cells, what forms midway between the divided nuclei during cytokinesis?
   a. nuclear membrane
   b. centromere
   c. cell membrane
   d. cell plate

9. Describe how a eukaryotic cell's chromosomes change as a cell prepares to divide.

10. What is the relationship between interphase and cell division?

11. List the following stages of mitosis in the correct sequence, and describe what happens during each stage: anaphase, metaphase, prophase, and telophase.

12. Identify the stage of mitosis shown here. Describe the events that occur in this stage.

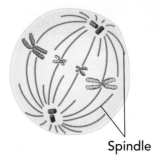

Spindle

### 11.3 Regulating the Cell Cycle

13. The timing in the cell cycle in eukaryotic cells is believed to be controlled by a group of closely related proteins known as
    a. chromatids.
    b. centromeres.
    c. cyclins.
    d. centrioles.

14. Which statement does NOT describe external regulatory proteins?
    a. They respond to events occurring inside a cell.
    b. Growth factors are one group of external regulatory proteins.
    c. They can speed up or slow down the cell cycle.
    d. Some can cause cells to slow down or stop their cell cycles.

15. How do cancer cells differ from noncancerous cells? How are they similar?

**16.** When some cells are removed from the center of a tissue culture, will new cells replace the cells that were removed? Explain.

**17.** Describe the role of cyclins.

# 11.4 Cell Differentiation

HS-LS1-4

**18.** Bone marrow cells that produce blood cells are best categorized as
   **a.** embryonic stem cells.
   **b.** adult stem cells.
   **c.** pluripotent cells.
   **d.** totipotent cells.

**19.** Which type of cell has the potential to develop into the widest variety of differentiated cells?
   **a.** totipotent
   **b.** pluripotent
   **c.** multipotent
   **d.** differentiated

**20.** What is a blastocyst?

**21.** What is cell differentiation? Make a drawing that illustrates the process.

**22.** Describe two ways that technology may address the ethical concerns related to stem cell research.

## CRITICAL THINKING

HS-LS1-4

**23.** **Use Models** Two objects modeling cellular shapes are shown. All of the sides in Shape A are equal in size.

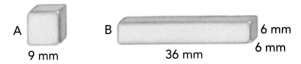

A    9 mm

B    36 mm    6 mm    6 mm

Compare the ratio of surface area to volume for the two objects. Then use your results to explain how the long, flattened shapes of some organisms, such as single-celled paramecia, help them survive.

**24.** **Predict** A cell will usually undergo apoptosis if the cell experiences DNA damage that could lead to a tumor. Predict what may happen if a gene that controls apoptosis is damaged.

**25.** **Form a Hypothesis** A particular environment undergoes frequent changes. Which organisms are more likely to have an advantage in that environment—those that reproduce asexually or those that reproduce sexually? Explain your reasoning.

**26.** **Summarize** Create a flowchart that relates the following terms: *prophase, metaphase, anaphase, telophase,* and *cytokinesis.* Be sure to describe each phase and identify the relationships among them.

**27.** **Compare and Contrast** Differentiate between DNA replication in prokaryotes and DNA replication in eukaryotes.

**28.** **Use Models** The model shows a phase of mitosis.

   **a.** Determine whether this model represents a plant or an animal cell.
   **b.** The four chromosomes in the center of this cell each have two connected strands. Explain how the two strands on the same chromosome compare with regard to the genetic information they carry. Why is this important to the cell?

**29.** **Use Evidence to Construct an Argument** A researcher observes that some cells in a sample have several nuclei within their cytoplasm. Considering the events in a typical cell cycle, propose an argument to explain what could have occurred in these cells.

**30.** **Draw Conclusions** A scientist is developing a new cancer treatment. She is investigating a chemical that prevents DNA synthesis.

   **a.** In which stage of mitosis does the chemical act?
   **b.** Why would the chemical affect cancer cells more than normal cells?

## CROSSCUTTING CONCEPTS

**31. Cause and Effect** The nerve cells in the human nervous system seldom undergo mitosis. How might this affect the recovery of an injury to the nervous system?

**32. Systems and System Models** Different models, such as that of a growing town, may be used to describe the relationship between the surface area of a cell and its volume. Develop a new model you could use to describe the cell system, and explain why the size of a cell is limited.

**33. Cause and Effect** Researchers discovered how to make skin stem cells pluripotent. Describe how this discovery affected research involving treatments for heart attack patients.

## MATH CONNECTIONS

### Analyze and Interpret Data

A scientist performed an experiment to determine the effect of temperature on the length of the cell cycle in onion cells. These data are summarized in the table. Use the data table to answer questions 34–36.

| Effect of Temperature on Length of Onion Cell Cycle | |
|---|---|
| **Temperature (°C)** | **Length of Cell Cycle (hours)** |
| 10 | 54.6 |
| 15 | 29.8 |
| 20 | 18.8 |
| 25 | 13.3 |

**34. Analyze Data** On the basis of the data in the table, how long would you expect the cell cycle to take at 5°C?
a. less than 13.3 hours
b. more than 54.6 hours
c. between 29.8 and 54.6 hours
d. about 20 hours

**35. Construct Graphs** Construct a line graph of the data in the table. Describe the shape of the graph.

**36. Interpret Tables** Given this set of data, what is one valid conclusion the scientist could state?

Use the diagram model of the cell cycle to answer questions 37–39.

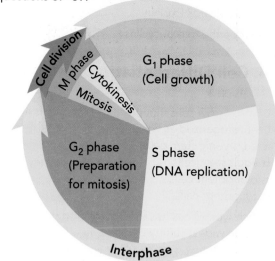

**37. Use Models** Explain how the model represents the cell cycle. Discuss the circular shape of the model and the relative sizes of the regions for the phases.

**38. Revise Models** How could you revise the model to show the stages of mitosis?

**39. Calculate** A human cell has 46 chromosomes. After a cell passes through three rounds of the cell cycle, how many cells are formed? How many copies of chromosomes are in these cells? Assume that each cell divides to form two new daughter cells.

## LANGUAGE ARTS CONNECTION

### Write About Science
CCSS.ELA-LITERACY.WHST.9-10.2, CCSS.ELA-LITERACY.WHST.9-10.4

**40. Write Explanatory Texts** Write a paragraph explaining the cell cycle and its importance in living organisms.

**41. Produce Clear Writing** Differentiation is essential to multicellular organisms. Clearly describe a model that would illustrate differentiation.

### Read About Science
CCSS.ELA-LITERACY.RST.9-10.5, CCSS.ELA-LITERACY.RST.9-10.10

**42. Summarize Text** Reread the text under the heading Stem Cells and Development. In a brief paragraph, summarize the information you learned from reading this text.

**43. Analyze Text Structure** Review the content about the cell cycle and mitosis. Describe how the use of headings of different sizes and colors are used to make the content easier to understand.

# END-OF-COURSE TEST PRACTICE

1. A cow has 60 chromosomes in each of its body cells. How does mitosis function to maintain this number of chromosomes?
   A. Chromosomes are replicated in interphase and separated in anaphase.
   B. Chromosomes are replicated in prophase and separated in telophase.
   C. Chromosomes are separated in anaphase and replicated in telophase.
   D. Chromosomes are replicated and separated into daughter cells during mitosis.
   E. Chromosomes are replicated during asexual reproduction and separated during sexual reproduction.

2. Cell division occurs in animal cells and plant cells. The illustration below shows an animal cell and a plant cell during the same phase of cell division.

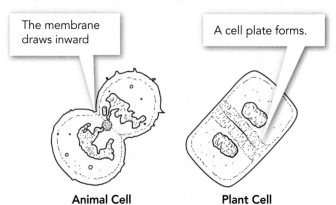

The membrane draws inward

A cell plate forms.

**Animal Cell**     **Plant Cell**

Which of the following **best** describes this phase of cell division?
   A. The cells are completing the growth phase and entering prophase.
   B. The chromosomes in each cell have just replicated and the cells are entering mitosis.
   C. Mitosis has just begun and the chromosomes are condensing into chromatids.
   D. Mitosis is complete and the plant cell is forming a cell plate because plants have cell walls.
   E. The cells are in metaphase and the animal cell is drawing inward where chromosomes will line up for separation.

3. Cells from a plant leaf, root, and stem have different characteristics that can be observed when viewed under a microscope. How can cells from a single plant have different characteristics?
   A. The cells have a different number of chromosomes.
   B. The cells have differentiated to produce different cell types.
   C. The cells are in different phases of mitosis.
   D. The cells are produced by sexual reproduction.
   E. The cells divide into prokaryotes and eukaryotes.

4. Why is cell division a necessary process for cells to function?
   A. If cells don't divide then cells won't have enough DNA.
   B. Cell division is necessary for prokaryotic cells to differentiate into eukaryotic cells.
   C. If cells don't divide then the volume of the cells will be too small compared to the surface area of the cells.
   D. Cell division is necessary for sexual reproduction to produce genetically identical offspring.
   E. If cells continue to grow without dividing they won't be able to efficiently move nutrients across the cell membrane.

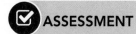 **ASSESSMENT**

For additional assessment practice, go online to access your digital course.

| If You Have Trouble With... | | | | |
|---|---|---|---|---|
| **Question** | 1 | 2 | 3 | 4 |
| **See Lesson** | 11.2 | 11.2 | 11.3 | 11.1 |
| **Performance Expectation** | HS-LS1-4 | HS-LS1-4 | HS-LS1-4 | HS-LS1-4 |

Island

rcation

idge ending

Fingerprint
identification system

>> **Crosscutting Concepts** Cells are built from molecules, and none are more essential to life than DNA. The science of heredity began with experiments in a garden, and now touches every aspect of our lives, from the food we eat to medical care to personal identification. As a result, historians of the future may well call ours the golden age of biology.

**BOUNCE**
**TO ACTIVATE**

**VIDEO**

Author Ken Miller talks about how studying patterns of inheritance can help explain how genes work.

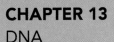

# Genetic Modification
## OF ANIMALS

**Humans have a long history** of breeding animals. Breeders choose parents that have useful traits, such as sheep with thick wool, or chickens that lay large eggs. Our familiar farm animals are the result of these efforts repeated over many generations. Now, however, scientists can use genetic technology to modify animals. New technologies can directly change the DNA of an animal, often by introducing genes from another organism. The technology raises ethical questions that are not easy to answer.

**PROBLEM LAUNCH**
Conduct research on a current or proposed genetically modified animal.

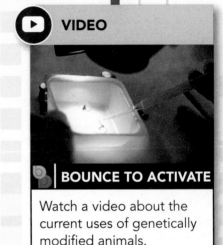

▶ **VIDEO**

**BOUNCE TO ACTIVATE**

Watch a video about the current uses of genetically modified animals.

# PROBLEM: For what purposes should humans genetically modify animals?

» **TO SOLVE THIS PROBLEM,** perform these activities as they come up in the unit, and record your findings in your 📒 Explorer's Journal.

## LAB INVESTIGATION

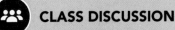

Model the inheritance of genetically modified traits from parents to offspring.

## CLASS DISCUSSION

Discuss the structure of DNA and how it is similar and different among organisms.

## INTERACTIVITY

Investigate the science behind genetically modifying insect populations to help control the spread of disease.

## INTERACTIVITY

Complete the steps to isolate, splice, and transfer a gene to genetically modify an animal.

## AUTHENTIC READING

Read about scientists that are studying the mouse genome to better understand human diseases.

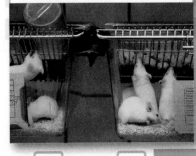

## STEM PROJECT

Create a survey to gauge the opinions of your classmates or community members on specific uses of genetically modified animals.

## PROBLEM WRAP-UP

Organize the results of your survey to create an opinion piece for the use of genetically modified animals.

**12.1**
The Work of
Gregor Mendel

**12.2**
Applying Mendel's
Principles

**12.3**
Other Patterns
of Inheritance

**12.4**
Meiosis

**Go Online to
access your
digital course.**

▶ VIDEO

◀) AUDIO

👆 INTERACTIVITY

📖 eTEXT

👁 ANIMATION

⏱ VIRTUAL LAB

☑ ASSESSMENT

HS-LS3-1, HS-LS3-2, HS-LS3-3

# Genetic disorders: understanding the odds

It should have been a perfect morning. There was excitement on the ranch over the birth of a new foal the night before. Both of his parents were champion paint horses bearing distinctive *frame overo* markings.

The overo coat pattern is beautiful, and highly valued. Overo horses look as if some-one has splashed white paint on a solid-colored horse. In *frame overo* horses, it looks like the white spots have been framed by the horse's dark back and legs and the dark mark-ings on the sides that separate the spots.

But when the veterinarian saw the white foal with blue eyes, she frowned. Her concern was not that the foal had failed to inherit his parents' pretty overo pattern. White horses with blue eyes can be perfectly healthy—but not when their parents are both *frame overos*.

The little colt's stark white color and blue eyes indicated he had been born with overo lethal white syndrome (OLWS). In foals with OLWS, the digestive system has failed to form properly. There is no way to treat this, and affected foals will die within a few days of being born.

Because their death is painful and unavoidable, foals with OLWS need to be euthanized. In fact, dying from OLWS is so painful that owners and veterinarians once euthanized any foals suspected of having OLWS.

This colt was actually the third foal from this mare and stallion pairing, and their first two offspring had been perfectly healthy. Why had this one been born with such a serious problem?

Should the mare's owner try again to breed the mare with the same stallion? If so, what would be the odds of producing another foal with OLWS?

Meanwhile, a couple held their day-old baby girl in the soft fluorescent light of a local hospital ward. They were waiting for the results of a blood test that had been per-formed the day before. Even though both parents were healthy, their family histories had led their physician to suggest they be tested for a potentially lethal genetic disorder known as cystic fibrosis (CF). Sure enough, they both carried a gene that might put their child at risk of the disorder, and were told their baby's chances of having CF would be one in four. Today they would learn the results of the baby's blood test.

Their pediatrician opened the door with the test report tucked under his arm. They held their breath. The doctor told them that their baby did not have cystic fibrosis. However, he cautioned them that any future children would still be at risk.

What causes disorders like OLWS and CF? How are they passed from parent to child? And how can an adult be perfectly healthy and still have a child with an inherited disorder?

**Throughout this chapter, look for connections to the CASE STUDY to help you answer these questions.**

# The Work of Gregor Mendel

Gregor Mendel and a pea plant

HS-LS3-3: Apply concepts of statistics and probability to explain the variation and distribution of expressed traits in a population.

## KEY QUESTIONS

- Where does an organism get its unique characteristics?

- How are different forms of a gene distributed to offspring?

## VOCABULARY

genetics
fertilization
trait
hybrid
gene
allele
principle of dominance
segregation
gamete

## READING TOOL

Identify the sequence of events that influenced Mendel's conclusions about genetics. Fill in the graphic organizer in your 📘 Biology Foundations Workbook.

What is an inheritance? It might be money or property left by relatives who have passed away. That kind of inheritance matters, of course, but there is another kind that matters even more. It is something we each receive from our parents—a contribution that determines our blood type, the color of our eyes and hair, and so much more. This is the biological form of inheritance we call genetics.

## Mendel's Experiments

Every living thing—plant or animal, microbe or human being—has a set of characteristics inherited from its parent or parents. Since the beginning of recorded history, people have wanted to understand how inheritance is passed from generation to generation. The scientific study of biological inheritance is called **genetics**.

The modern science of genetics began with the work of an Austrian scientist and priest named Gregor Mendel, who is shown above. Mendel was born in 1822 in what is now the Czech Republic. After studying science and mathematics at the University of Vienna, he spent the next 14 years working in a monastery and teaching local students. In addition to his teaching duties, Mendel was in charge of the monastery garden. In this simple garden, he was to do the work that changed biology forever.

Mendel carried out his work with ordinary garden peas, partly because peas are small, easy to grow, and can produce hundreds of offspring. Today, we would say that Mendel used peas as a "model system," an organism that is convenient to study and may help us learn about other species, including humans. By using peas, Mendel was able to carry out, in just one or two growing seasons, experiments that would have been impossible to do with humans and would have taken years—if not decades—with other organisms.

## The Role of Fertilization

Mendel knew that part of each flower produces pollen grains containing the male reproductive cells, or sperm. Similarly, he knew that the female portion of each flower produces reproductive cells called eggs. During sexual reproduction, male and female reproductive cells join in a process known as **fertilization** to produce a new cell. In peas, this new cell develops into a tiny embryo encased within a seed.

Pea flowers are normally mostly self-pollinating, which means that sperm fertilize egg cells from within the same flower. A plant grown from a seed produced by self-pollination inherits all of its characteristics from the single plant that bore it; it has a single parent.

Mendel's monastery garden had several stocks of pea plants. These plants were "true breeding," meaning that they were self-pollinating, and produced offspring with traits identical to themselves. A **trait** is a specific characteristic, like seed color or plant height. One stock of Mendel's seeds produced only tall plants, while another produced only short ones. One produced only green seeds, another produced only yellow seeds.

To learn how these traits were determined, Mendel decided to "cross" his stocks of true-breeding plants—that is, he caused one plant to reproduce with another plant. To do this, he prevented self-pollination by cutting away the pollen-bearing male parts of a flower. He then dusted pollen from a different plant onto the female part of that flower, as shown in **Figure 12-1**. This process, known as cross-pollination, allowed Mendel to cross plants with different traits and then study the results.

Mendel examined seven different traits of pea plants. Each of these seven traits had two contrasting characteristics, such as green or yellow pod color. Mendel crossed plants with each of the seven contrasting characteristics and then studied their offspring. The offspring of crosses between parents with different contrasting characteristics are called **hybrids**.

### Self-Pollination

### Cross-Pollination

Female part

Male parts

Pollen

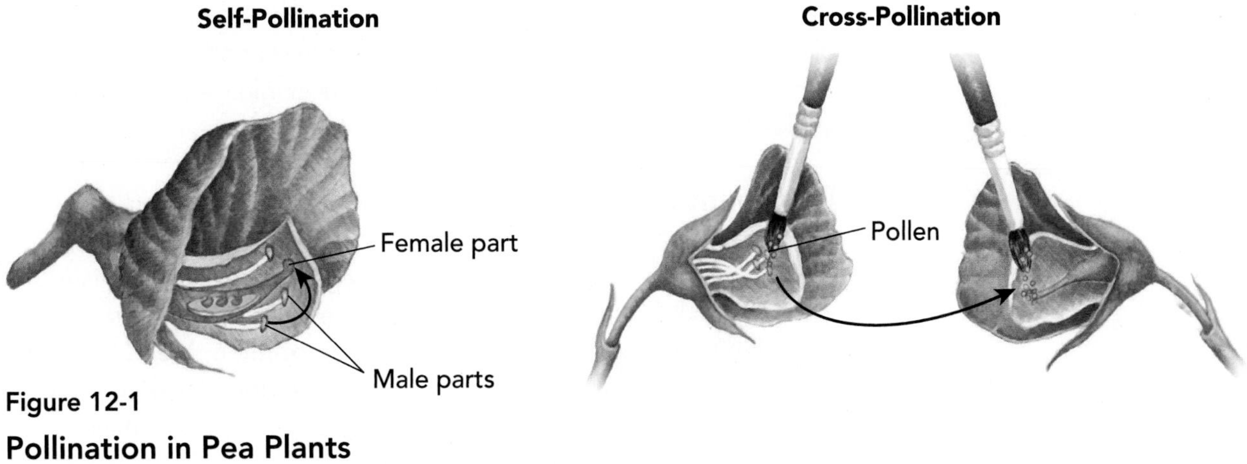

**Figure 12-1**

## Pollination in Pea Plants

Pea plants are usually self-pollinating, which means that the sperm cells fertilize the egg cells within the same flower. To cross-pollinate pea plants, Mendel cut off the male parts of one flower and then dusted the female part with the pollen from another flower.

| Mendel's Seven F₁ Crosses on Pea Plants | | | | | | |
|---|---|---|---|---|---|---|
| | Seed Shape | Seed Color | Flower Color | Pod Shape | Pod Color | Flower Position | Plant Height |
| **P** | Round × Wrinkled | Yellow × Green | Purple × White | Smooth × Constricted | Green × Yellow | Axial × Terminal | Tall × Short |
| **F₁** | Round | Yellow | Purple | Smooth | Green | Axial | Tall |

**Figure 12-2**

## Mendel's F₁ Crosses

When Mendel crossed plants with contrasting traits, the resulting hybrids had the traits of only one of the parents.

**INTERACTIVITY**

Explore Mendel's experiments on pea plants and the conclusions he reached.

**Genes and Alleles** When doing genetic crosses, we call the original pair of plants the P, or parental, generation. Their offspring are called the F₁, or first filial, generation. (*Filius* and *filia* are the Latin words for "son" and "daughter.")

What were Mendel's F₁ hybrid plants like? To his surprise, for each trait studied, the offspring had the characteristics of only one of its parents, as shown in **Figure 12-2**. In each cross, the nature of the other parent, with regard to each trait, seemed to have disappeared. From these results, Mendel drew two conclusions. His first conclusion formed the basis of our current understanding of inheritance. 🔑 *An individual's characteristics are determined by factors that are passed from one parental generation to the next.* Today we call these factors **genes**.

Each of the traits Mendel studied was controlled by a single gene that occurred in two contrasting varieties. These variations produced different expressions, or forms, of each trait. For example, one form of the gene for height produced tall plants and another form produced short plants. The different forms of a single gene are called **alleles** (uh LEELZ).

**Dominant and Recessive Alleles** Mendel's second conclusion is called the **principle of dominance**. This principle states that some alleles are dominant and others are recessive. An organism with both a dominant allele and a recessive allele for a particular trait will exhibit the dominant characteristic. For example, Mendel found that the allele for tall plants was dominant over the recessive allele for short plants. Likewise, the allele for green pods was dominant over the recessive allele for yellow pods.

✅ **READING CHECK Explain** How did the results of the F₁ crosses influence Mendel's thinking?

# Segregation

Mendel didn't just stop after crossing the parent plants, because he had another question: Had the recessive alleles simply disappeared, or were they still present in the new plants? To find out, he allowed all seven kinds of $F_1$ hybrids to self-pollinate. In effect, Mendel crossed the $F_1$ generation with itself to produce a $F_2$ (second filial) generation, as shown in **Figure 12-3**.

**The $F_1$ Cross** When Mendel examined the $F_2$ plants, he made a remarkable discovery: Traits produced by the recessive alleles reappeared in the second generation. Roughly one fourth of the $F_2$ plants showed the trait controlled by the recessive allele. Why, then, did the recessive alleles seem to disappear in the $F_1$ generation, only to reappear in the $F_2$ generation?

**Explaining the $F_1$ Cross** To begin with, Mendel assumed that a dominant allele had masked the corresponding recessive allele in the $F_1$ generation. However, the trait controlled by the recessive allele did show up in some of the $F_2$ plants. This reappearance indicated that, at some point, the allele for yellow pods had separated from the allele for green pods. How did this separation, or **segregation**, of alleles occur? Mendel suggested that the alleles for green pods and yellow pods in the $F_1$ plants must have segregated from each other during the formation of the reproductive cells, or **gametes** (GAM eetz). Did that suggestion make sense?

**The Formation of Gametes** Let's assume, as Mendel might have, that all the $F_1$ plants inherited an allele for green pods from the green parent and one for yellow pods from the yellow parent. Because the allele for green pods is dominant, all the $F_1$ plants have green pods. ✎ *During gamete formation, the alleles for each gene segregate from each other, so that each gamete carries only one allele for each gene.* Thus, each $F_1$ plant produces two kinds of gametes— those with the green pod allele and those with the yellow pod allele.

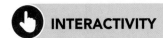

**INTERACTIVITY**

Discover how Mendel's ideas apply to the genetics of flies.

**READING TOOL**

As you read this section, identify the observation Mendel made about recessive traits. Then, describe the experimental results that explained his observation.

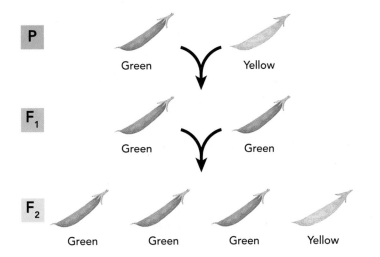

| P | Green | Yellow |

| $F_1$ | Green | Green |

| $F_2$ | Green | Green | Green | Yellow |

**CASE STUDY**

**Figure 12-3**

**Results of the $F_1$ Cross**

When Mendel allowed the $F_1$ plants to reproduce by self-pollination, the traits controlled by recessive alleles reappeared in about one fourth of the $F_2$ plants in each cross. ✓ **Infer** The allele responsible for cystic fibrosis is recessive. How are the inheritances of yellow pod color in peas and cystic fibrosis in humans similar to each other?

## Quick Lab  Guided Inquiry

### Simulating Segregation

1. Create a data table with the column headings Trial Number, Results, and Phenotype.

2. With a partner, obtain one cup of beans labeled Parent 1 and one cup of beans labeled Parent 2. Each person will be responsible for one parental cup. Each cup contains a total of 30 beans: 15 red (*R*) and 15 white (*r*). The beans represent gametes.

3. At the same time as your partner, and without looking, pull out one bean from your cup. Record the gamete pulled from each cup (*R* or *r*) in your data table.

4. Return the beans to their original cups and repeat Step 2 of this procedure 14 times.

### ANALYZE AND INTERPRET DATA

1. **Use Models** Determine whether each offspring is white or red. Then, calculate the percentage of offspring for each color. Assume red color is dominant.

2. **Refine Your Plan** How would you revise this investigation to simulate the crossing of two genes, each with two alleles?

### INTERACTIVITY

**Figure 12-4**

### Segregation

During gamete formation, alleles segregate from each other so that each gamete carries only a single copy of each gene.

Look at **Figure 12-4** to see how alleles separate during gamete formation and then pair up again in the $F_2$ generation. A capital letter represents a dominant allele. A lowercase letter represents a recessive allele. Now we can see why the recessive trait for yellow pods, *g*, reappeared in Mendel's $F_2$ generation. Each $F_1$ plant in Mendel's cross produced two kinds of gametes—those with the allele for green pods and those with the allele for yellow pods. Whenever a gamete that carried the *g* allele paired with another gamete with the *g* allele to produce an $F_2$ plant, that plant had yellow pods. Every time one or both gametes of the pairing carried the *G* allele, a plant with green pods was produced. The genes of the $F_1$ plants had been reshuffled to produce new combinations of alleles.

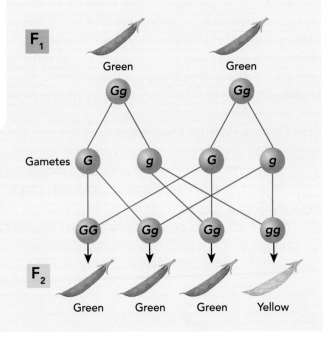

## ✓ LESSON 12.1 Review

### ⚘ KEY QUESTIONS

1. What did Mendel conclude determines biological inheritance?

2. What is segregation?

### CRITICAL THINKING

3. **Compare and Contrast** How is self-pollination similar to cross-pollination? How is it different?

4. **Infer** What evidence did Mendel use to explain how segregation occurs?

5. **Construct an Argument** In pea plants, the allele for tallness (*T*) is dominant over the allele for shortness (*t*). If two tall pea plants are crossed, can you predict the height of the offspring? Use logical reasoning to support your answer.

## KEY QUESTIONS

- *How can we use probability to predict traits?*
- *How do alleles segregate when more than one gene is involved?*
- *What did Mendel contribute to our understanding of genetics?*

*Nothing in life is certain.* There's a great deal of wisdom in that old saying, and genetics is a fine example. If a parent carries two different alleles for a certain gene, we can't be sure which of those alleles will be inherited by any one of the parent's offspring. However, think carefully about the nature of inheritance and you'll see that even if we can't predict the exact future, we can do something almost as useful—we can figure out the odds.

## Probability and Heredity

Whenever Mendel performed a cross with pea plants, he carefully categorized and counted the offspring. Consequently, he had plenty of data to analyze. For example, whenever he crossed two plants that were hybrids for pod color (*Gg*), about three fourths of the resulting plants had green pods and about one fourth had yellow pods.

Upon analyzing his data, Mendel realized that the principles of probability could be used to explain the results of his genetic crosses. **Probability** is the likelihood that a particular event will occur. As an example, consider an ordinary event, such as flipping a coin. There are two possible outcomes of this event: The coin may land either heads up or tails up. The chance, or probability, of either outcome is equal. Therefore, the probability that a single coin flip will land heads up is 1 chance in 2. This amounts to $\frac{1}{2}$, or 50 percent.

If you flip a coin three times in a row, what is the probability that it will land heads up every time? Each coin flip is an independent event with a $\frac{1}{2}$ probability of landing heads up. Therefore, the probability of flipping three heads in a row is:

$$\frac{1}{2} \times \frac{1}{2} \times \frac{1}{2} = \frac{1}{8}$$

**HS-LS3-3:** Apply concepts of statistics and probability to explain the variation and distribution of expressed traits in a population.

**VOCABULARY**
probability
homozygous
heterozygous
phenotype
genotype
Punnett square
independent assortment

**READING TOOL**

Before you read, preview **Figure 12-7** and try to infer the purpose of this diagram. After you read, revise your inference and answer the questions about punnett squares in your 📖 **Biology Foundations Workbook.**

## Segregation and Probability

In this cross, the *GG* and *Gg* allele combinations produced three plants with green pods, while the *gg* allele combination produced one plant with yellow pods. These quantities follow the laws of probability. ☑ **Reason Quantitatively** What is the probability that an offspring from a hybrid cross has the recessive phenotype?

$F_1$ Green × Green

Both $F_1$ plants have the same set of alleles (*Gg*) and have green pods.

Gametes

The probability of each gamete acquiring the green (*G*) allele is $\frac{1}{2}$. Similarly, the probability of acquiring the yellow (*g*) is also $\frac{1}{2}$.

$F_2$ Green Green Green Yellow

homozygous heterozygous homozygous

When the alleles pair up in the $F_2$ generation, the probability of offspring with green pods (*GG* or *Gg*) is $\frac{1}{4} + \frac{1}{4} + \frac{1}{4}$, or $\frac{3}{4}$. The probability that the offspring will have yellow pods (*gg*) is $\frac{1}{4}$.

### Using Segregation to Predict Outcomes

The way in which alleles segregate during gamete formation is every bit as random as a coin flip. Therefore, the principles of probability can be used to predict the outcomes of genetic crosses.

Look again at Mendel's $F_1$ cross, shown in **Figure 12-5**. This cross produced a mixture of plants with green and yellow pods. Each $F_1$ plant had one green pod allele and one yellow pod allele (*Gg*), so $\frac{1}{2}$ of the gametes produced by the plants would carry the yellow allele (*g*). Because the *g* allele is recessive, the only way to produce a plant with yellow pods (*gg*) is for two gametes, each carrying the *g* allele, to combine.

Like the coin toss, each $F_2$ gamete has a one in two, or $\frac{1}{2}$, chance of carrying the *g* allele. There are two gametes, so the probability of both gametes carrying the *g* allele is $\frac{1}{2} \times \frac{1}{2} = \frac{1}{4}$. In other words, roughly one fourth of the $F_2$ offspring should have yellow pods, and the remaining three fourths should have green pods. This predicted ratio—3 offspring exhibiting the dominant trait to 1 offspring exhibiting the recessive trait—showed up consistently in Mendel's experiments. For each of his seven crosses, about $\frac{3}{4}$ of the plants showed the trait controlled by the dominant allele. About $\frac{1}{4}$ showed the trait controlled by the recessive allele. Segregation did occur according to Mendel's model.

As you can see in the $F_2$ generation, not all organisms with the same characteristics have the same alleles. Both the *GG* and *Gg* allele combinations resulted in green pea pods. Organisms that have two identical alleles for a particular gene—*GG* or *gg* in this example—are **homozygous**. Organisms that have two different alleles for the same gene—such as *Gg*—are **heterozygous**.

### BUILD VOCABULARY

**Prefixes** The prefix *homo-* means "the same." The prefix *hetero-* means "different." The term **homozygous** refers to identical alleles for the same gene. The term **heterozygous** refers to two different alleles for the same gene.

**Probabilities Predict Averages** Probabilities predict the average outcome of a large number of events. If you flip a coin twice, you are likely to get one heads and one tails. However, you might also get two heads or two tails. To get the expected 50:50 ratio, you might have to flip the coin many times. The same is true of genetics. Think, for example, of two horses each of which carries a dominant allele for normal coat color along with the recessive allele for overo lethal white syndrome. The odds are that three out of four of their foals will be healthy. But there is one chance in four they will produce a foal with the OLWS, the lethal syndrome, and this could occur in their very first birth.

Statistically, the larger the number of offspring, the closer the results will be to the predicted values. If an $F_2$ generation contains just three or four offspring, it may not match Mendel's ratios. When an $F_2$ generation contains hundreds or thousands of individuals, the ratios usually come very close to matching predictions.

### Genotype and Phenotype

One of Mendel's most revolutionary insights followed directly from his observations of $F_1$ crosses: Every organism has a genetic makeup as well as a set of observable characteristics. All of the pea plants with green pods had the same **phenotype**, or physical traits. They did not, however, have the same **genotype**, or genetic makeup. Look again at **Figure 12-5**. There are three different genotypes among the $F_2$ plants: *GG*, *Gg*, and *gg*. Plants with *GG* or *Gg* combinations of alleles have different genotypes, but the same phenotype—they have green pods. Now look at the pea plant in **Figure 12-6**. Can you tell its phenotype and genotype for flower color?

### Using Punnett Squares

One of the best ways to predict the outcome of a genetic cross is with a diagram known as a **Punnett square**. ⚲ *Punnett squares use mathematical probability to help predict the genotype and phenotype combinations in genetic crosses.* Constructing a Punnett square is fairly easy. You begin with a square. Then, following the principle of segregation, all possible combinations of alleles in the gametes produced by one parent are written along the top edge of the square. The other parent's alleles are then segregated along the left edge. Next, every possible genotype is written inside the boxes within the square, just as they might appear in the $F_2$ generation. **Figure 12-7** describes how to construct Punnett squares.

✔ **READING CHECK** **Define** In your own words, define the terms *genotype* and *phenotype*.

**INTERACTIVITY**

Explore the genetics behind the fur color, coat type, and eye color of guinea pigs.

**Figure 12-6**

### Genotype and Phenotype

Phenotype is the physical trait of an organism, such as the purple flower color of this pea plant. Genotype is the genetic makeup, which is hidden inside it.

# Constructing a Punnett Square

By drawing a Punnett square, you can determine the allele combinations that might result from a genetic cross.

| **One-Factor Cross** | | **Two-Factor Cross** |
|---|---|---|

Write the genotypes of the two organisms that will serve as parents in a cross. In this example we will cross a male and female osprey, or fish eagle, that are heterozygous for large beaks. They each have genotypes of *Bb*.

**① Start With the Parents**

In this example we will cross two pea plants that are heterozygous for size (tall and short alleles) and pod color (green and yellow alleles). The genotypes of the two parents are *TtGg* and *TtGg*.

**Bb and Bb**

**TtGg and TtGg**

Determine what alleles would be found in all of the possible gametes that each parent could produce.

**② Figure Out the Gametes**

Determine what alleles would be found in all of the possible gametes that each parent could produce.

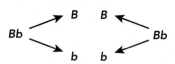

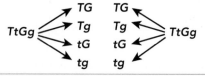

Draw a table with enough squares for each pair of gametes from each parent. In this case, each parent can make two different types of gametes, *B* and *b*. Enter the genotypes of the gametes produced by both parents on the top and left sides of the table.

**③ Line Them Up**

In this case, each parent can make 4 different types of gametes, so the table needs to be 4 rows by 4 columns, or 16 squares.

|  | TG | tG | Tg | tg |
|---|---|---|---|---|
| **TG** |  |  |  |  |
| **tG** |  |  |  |  |
| **Tg** |  |  |  |  |
| **tg** |  |  |  |  |

Fill in the table by combining the gametes' genotypes.

**④ Write Out the New Genotypes**

Fill in the table by combining the gametes' genotypes.

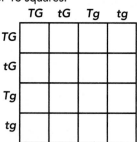

|  | TG | tG | Tg | tg |
|---|---|---|---|---|
| **TG** | TTGG | TtGG | TTGg | TtGg |
| **tG** | TtGG | ttGG | TtGg | ttGg |
| **Tg** | TTGg | TtGg | TTgg | Ttgg |
| **tg** | TtGg | ttGg | Ttgg | ttgg |

Determine the genotype and phenotype of each offspring. Calculate the percentage of each. In this example, $\frac{3}{4}$ of the chicks will have large beaks, but only $\frac{1}{2}$ will be heterozygous for this trait (*Bb*).

**⑤ Figure Out the Results**

In this example, the color of the squares represents pod color. Alleles written in black indicate short plants, while alleles written in red indicate tall plants.

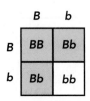

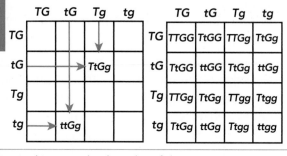

# Independent Assortment

After showing that alleles segregate during the formation of gametes, Mendel wondered if the segregation of one pair of alleles affects another pair. For example, does the gene that determines the shape of a seed affect the gene for seed color? To find out, Mendel followed two different genes as they passed from one generation to the next. Because it involves two different genes, Mendel's experiment is known as a two-factor, or dihybrid, cross. Single-gene crosses are monohybrid crosses.

## The Two-Factor Cross: F₁

First, Mendel crossed true-breeding plants that produced only round yellow peas with plants that produced only wrinkled green peas. The round yellow peas had the genotype *RRYY*, and the wrinkled green peas had the genotype *rryy*. All of the F₁ offspring produced round yellow peas. These results showed that the alleles for yellow and round peas are dominant. As **Figure 12-8** shows, the genotype in each of these F₁ plants is *RrYy*. In other words, the F₁ plants were all heterozygous for both seed shape and seed color.

## The Two-Factor Cross: F₂

Next, Mendel crossed the F₁ plants to produce F₂ offspring. Remember, each F₁ plant was formed by the fusion of a gamete carrying the dominant *RY* alleles with another gamete carrying the recessive *ry* alleles. Would the two dominant alleles always stay together, or would they segregate independently, so that any combination of alleles was possible?

In Mendel's experiment, the F₂ plants produced 556 seeds. Mendel noted that 315 of the seeds were round and yellow, while another 32 seeds were wrinkled and green—the two parental phenotypes. However, 209 seeds had combinations of phenotypes—and, therefore, combinations of alleles—that were not found in either parent. This clearly meant that the alleles for seed shape segregated independently of those for seed color. Put another way, genes that segregate independently (such as the genes for seed shape and seed color in pea plants) do not influence each other's inheritance.

Mendel's experimental results were very close to the 9 : 3 : 3 : 1 ratio that the Punnett square shown in **Figure 12-9** predicts. Mendel had discovered the principle of **independent assortment**. 🔍 *The principle of independent assortment states that genes for different traits can segregate independently during the formation of gametes.* Independent assortment helps account for the many genetic variations observed in plants, animals, and other organisms—even when they have the same parents.

✓ **READING CHECK** **Review** How did Mendel's experiments provide evidence for the principle of independent assortment?

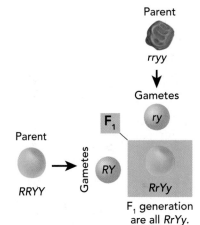

### Figure 12-8

### Two-Factor Cross: F₁

Mendel crossed plants that were homozygous dominant for round yellow peas (*RRYY*) with plants that were homozygous recessive (*rryy*) for wrinkled green peas. All of the F₁ offspring were heterozygous dominant for round yellow peas.

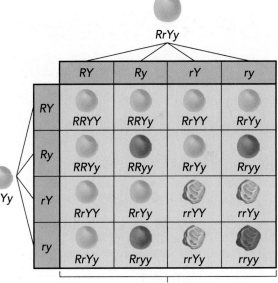

F₂ Generation

 **INTERACTIVITY**

### Figure 12-9

### Two-Factor Cross: F₂

Mendel's F₂ plants produced seeds with four different phenotypes.

# A Summary of Mendel's Principles

As you have seen, Mendel's principles of segregation and independent assortment can be observed through one- and two-factor crosses. 🔍 *Mendel's principles of heredity, observed through patterns of inheritance, form the basis of modern genetics.* These principles of heredity are as follows:

- The inheritance of biological characteristics is determined by individual units called genes, which are passed from parents to offspring.

- Where two or more forms (alleles) of the gene for a single trait exist, some alleles may be dominant and others may be recessive.

- In most sexually reproducing organisms, each adult has two copies of each gene—one from each parent. These genes segregate from each other when gametes are formed.

- Alleles for different genes usually segregate independently of each other.

Mendel's principles don't apply only to plants. At the beginning of the 1900s, the American geneticist Thomas Hunt Morgan wanted to use a model organism of another kind to advance the study of genetics. He decided to work on a tiny insect that kept showing up, uninvited, in his laboratory. The insect was the common fruit fly, *Drosophila melanogaster*, shown in **Figure 12-10**.

*Drosophila* can produce many offspring—a single pair can produce hundreds of young. Before long, Morgan and other biologists had tested all of Mendel's principles and learned that they applied to flies and other organisms as well. In fact, Mendel's basic principles of inheritance can even be used to study the inheritance of human traits and genetic disorders such as cystic fibrosis.

**Figure 12-10**

## Modeling Genetics

The common fruit fly is an ideal organism for genetic research. Traits that are commonly studied by geneticists include eye color, body color, and wing shape.

Long, flat wings

Red eyes

Golden body

HS-LS3-3

### 🔍 KEY QUESTIONS

1. What is probability?

2. How does the principle of independent assortment help explain Mendel's results?

3. Describe Gregor Mendel's contribution to our understanding of inherited traits.

### CRITICAL THINKING

4. **Use Models** Draw a Punnett square to represent the cross of two pea plants, each heterozygous for tallness (*Tt*). Use the Punnett square to identify the probability of an offspring that is short.

5. **Synthesize Information** In pea plants, the allele for yellow seeds (*Y*) is dominant over the allele for green seeds (*y*). Describe the genotypes and phenotypes of pea plants that are homozygous dominant, homozygous recessive, and heterozygous for this trait.

6. **CASE STUDY** A man and woman are deciding whether to have a child. The genotype of the man includes a recessive allele for an inherited disease. The genotype of the woman does not include this allele. Both parents have a normal phenotype. Could the child inherit the disease? Explain your reasoning.

# Other Patterns of Inheritance

Feather color in parakeets is controlled by multiple genes.

## KEY QUESTIONS
- What are some exceptions to Mendel's principles?
- How does the environment play a role in how genes determine traits?

HS-LS3-3: Apply concepts of statistics and probability to explain the variation and distribution of expressed traits in a population.

## VOCABULARY
**incomplete dominance**
**codominance**
**multiple alleles**
**polygenic trait**

## READING TOOL

As you read, identify the different types of non-traditional inheritance. Fill in the graphic organizer in your 📕 Biology Foundations Workbook.

Mendel's principles offer a tidy set of rules with which to predict various patterns of inheritance. Unfortunately, biology is not a tidy science, and there are exceptions to every rule, including Mendel's.

## Beyond Dominant and Recessive Alleles

Most genes do not behave quite so neatly as the two-allele pattern of simple dominance shown by Mendel's peas. Many genes are quite a bit more complicated.

**Incomplete Dominance** A cross between two four o'clock (*Mirabilis jalapa*) plants shows a common exception to Mendel's principles. 🔑 *Some alleles are neither completely dominant nor recessive.* As shown in **Figure 12-11**, the F₁ generation produced by a cross between red-flowered (*RR*) and white-flowered (*rr*) *Mirabilis* plants consists of pink-colored flowers (*Rr*). Which allele is dominant in this case? Neither one. Cases in which one allele is not completely dominant over another are called **incomplete dominance**. In incomplete dominance, the heterozygous phenotype lies somewhere between the two homozygous phenotypes.

## Figure 12-11

### Incomplete Dominance

In four o'clock plants, the alleles for red and white flowers show incomplete dominance. Heterozygous (*Rr*) plants have pink flowers—a mix of red and white coloring.

*RR*

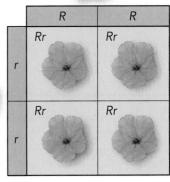

*rr*

|  | R | R |
|---|---|---|
| r | *Rr* | *Rr* |
| r | *Rr* | *Rr* |

INTERACTIVITY

**Figure 12-12**

## Other Patterns of Inheritance

Codominance is one type of inheritance that does not follow the simple dominance Mendel observed. Codominant white and black alleles result in a mixture of white and black feathers.

**Codominance** A similar situation arises from **codominance**. ⚲ *Codominance is a situation in which the phenotypes produced by both alleles are clearly expressed.* For example, in certain varieties of chickens, the allele for black feathers is codominant with the allele for white feathers. Heterozygous chickens have a color described as "erminette," speckled with black and white feathers, as shown in **Figure 12-12**. Unlike the blending of red and white colors in heterozygous four o'clock flowers, black and white colors appear separately in chickens. Many human genes, including one for a protein that controls cholesterol levels in the blood, show codominance, too. People with the heterozygous form of this gene produce two different forms of the protein, each with a different effect on cholesterol levels.

**Multiple Alleles** So far, our examples have described genes for which there are only two alleles, such as $a$ and $A$. In nature, such genes are the exception rather than the rule. ⚲ *Many genes exist in several different forms and are therefore said to have multiple alleles.* A gene with more than two alleles is said to have **multiple alleles**. An individual, of course, usually has only two copies of each gene, but many different alleles are often found within a population. One of the best-known examples is coat color in rabbits. A rabbit's coat color is determined by a single gene that has at least four different alleles as shown in **Figure 12-13**. The four known alleles display a pattern of simple dominance that can produce four coat colors. Many other genes have multiple alleles, including the human genes for blood type.

**Figure 12-13**

## Multiple Alleles

Coat color in rabbits is determined by a single gene that has at least four different alleles. Different combinations of alleles result in the four colors you see here.

Full color: $CC$, $Cc^{ch}$, $Cc^h$, or $Cc$

Chinchilla: $c^{ch}c^h$, $c^{ch}c^{ch}$, or $c^{ch}c$

Himalayan: $c^h c$ or $c^h c^h$

Albino: $cc$

$C$ = full color; dominant to all other alleles
$c^{ch}$ = chinchilla; partial defect in pigmentation; dominant to $c^h$ and $c$ alleles
$c^h$ = Himalayan; color in certain parts of the body; dominant to $c$ allele
$c$ = albino; no color; recessive to all other alleles

## Polygenic Traits
 *Many traits are produced by the interaction of several genes.* Traits controlled by two or more genes are said to be **polygenic traits**, meaning "many genes." At least two and as many as a dozen genes are responsible for the many different shades of human eye color. As you might expect, polygenic traits often show a wide range of phenotypes.

## Non-Mendelian Inheritance
Nearly one hundred years ago, botanists realized that some traits did not follow the patterns of inheritance described by Mendel. One example is leaf color in the morning glory, which is determined solely by the color of petal tissue in the maternal parent. This pattern, known as *maternal inheritance*, would not be predicted from Mendel's principles. *Some traits follow non-Mendelian patterns of inheritance.*

What causes maternal inheritance? Chloroplasts and mitochondria contain genes of their own on small DNA molecules within both organelles. Chloroplasts in the morning glory plant are inherited from the egg cell, and these determine the leaf colors of the offspring. Similarly, human mitochondria are inherited from the mother's egg cell. As a result, genetic disorders in human mitochondrial DNA also follow a pattern of maternal inheritance.

Another source of non-Mendelian inheritance is caused by chemical modification of certain genes, a process known as genetic imprinting. In mice, for example, a gene regulating body size is imprinted in a way that silences it in the next generation whenever it is carried by a female. Mice inheriting the gene from their mothers may suffer from dwarfism. However, mice inheriting the very same gene from their fathers do not. Genetic imprinting occurs in many human genes as well.

**INTERACTIVITY**

Use Punnett squares to predict the results of crosses in examples of non-Mendelian inheritance.

---

## Analyzing Data

### Human Blood Types
Red blood cells carry antigens, molecules that can trigger an immune reaction, on their surfaces. Human blood type A carries an A antigen, type B has a B antigen, type AB has both antigens, and type O carries neither antigen. The gene for these antigens has three alleles: A, B, and O.

For a blood transfusion to succeed, it must not introduce a new antigen into the body of the recipient. So, a person with type A blood may receive type O, but not vice versa.

| Blood Transfusions | | | | |
|---|---|---|---|---|
| **Blood Type of Donor** | **Blood Type of Recipient** | | | |
| | A | B | AB | O |
| A | √ | X | √ | X |
| B | X | √ | √ | X |
| AB | X | X | √ | X |
| O | √ | √ | √ | √ |

X = Unsuccessful transfusion   √ = Successful transfusion

### ANALYZE AND INTERPRET DATA

1. **Draw Conclusions** Which blood type is sometimes referred to as the "universal donor"? Which is known as the "universal recipient"?

2. **Analyze Data** In a transfusion involving the A and O blood types, does it make a difference which blood type belongs to the recipient and which to the donor?

3. **Apply Concepts** Write a brief explanation for the results in the table using information about phenotypes and genotypes in blood group genes.

| Environmental Temperature and Butterfly Needs | | |
|---|---|---|
| Temp. Needed for Flight | Average Spring Temp. | Average Summer Temp. |
| 28–40°C | 26.5°C | 34.8°C |

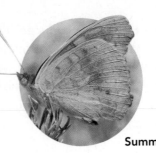

Summer

Autumn

**Figure 12-14**

**Temperature and Wing Color**

The buckeye butterflies shown in the photographs are darker in the autumn than they are in the summer. Similarly, western white butterflies that hatch in the spring have darker wing patterns than those that hatch in the summer. The dark wing color helps increase their body heat. This trait is important because the butterflies need to reach a certain temperature in order to fly (see table).

# Genes and the Environment

The characteristics of any organism—whether plant, fruit fly, or human being—are not determined solely by the genes that the organism inherits. Genes provide a plan for development, but how that plan unfolds also depends on the environment. In other words, the phenotype of an organism is only partly determined by its genotype.

Consider the buckeye butterfly, *Precis coenia*, shown in **Figure 12-14**. It is found throughout North America. Butterfly enthusiasts had noted for years that buckeyes hatching in the summer had different color patterns on their wings than those hatching in the fall. Scientific studies suggested a reason—butterflies hatching in the shorter days of autumn had greater levels of pigment in their wings, making their markings appear darker than those hatching in the longer days of summer. In other words, the environment in which the butterflies develop influences the expression of their genes for wing coloration. *Environmental conditions can affect gene expression and influence genetically determined traits.* An individual's actual phenotype is influenced by its environment as well as its genes.

Studies on another species, the western white butterfly, have shown the importance of changes in wing pigmentation. In order to fly effectively, the body temperature of the butterfly must be 28°C–40°C (about 84°F–104°F). Since the spring months are cooler in the West, greater pigmentation helps them reach the body temperature needed for flight. Similarly, in the hot summer months, less pigmentation enables the butterflies to avoid overheating.

**INTERACTIVITY**

Use a simulation to explore genetics in lilies.

HS-LS3-3

# ✓ LESSON 12.3 Review

### ⚴ KEY QUESTIONS

1. Why is incomplete dominance considered an exception to Mendel's principles of inheritance?

2. What is the relationship between the environment and phenotype?

### CRITICAL THINKING

3. Construct an Explanation The iris of the human eye can have many colors, including brown, blue, green, and hazel. How does polygenic inheritance explain why many iris colors are possible?

4. Plan an Investigation Based on observational evidence, variations in the color of flamingos appears to be determined by their diet, and not their genes. Describe the steps of an investigation to provide evidence to support or refute this hypothesis.

5. Develop a Model Petal color in roses is an example of incomplete dominance. Draw a Punnett square to show the results of a cross between two pink roses (Rr). Use the model to predict the petal colors of the offspring.

# Meiosis

These mallard ducks have 78 chromosomes in their cells, almost double the number found in human cells.

**KEY QUESTIONS**

- *How many sets of genes are found in most adult organisms?*
- *What events occur during each phase of meiosis?*
- *How is meiosis different from mitosis?*
- *How can two alleles from different genes be inherited together?*

**HS-LS3-1:** Ask questions to clarify relationships about the role of DNA and chromosomes in coding the instructions for characteristic traits passed from parents to offspring.

**HS-LS3-2:** Make and defend a claim based on evidence that inheritable genetic variations may result from: (1) new genetic combinations through meiosis, (2) viable errors occurring during replication, and/or (3) mutations caused by environmental factors.

**VOCABULARY**
homologous
diploid
haploid
meiosis
tetrad
crossing-over

**READING TOOL**

Identify the sequence of events of meiosis and fill in the diagram in your *Biology Foundations Workbook*.

As geneticists in the early 1900s applied Mendel's principles, they wondered where genes might be located. They expected genes to be carried on structures inside the cell, but *which* structures? What cellular processes could account for segregation and independent assortment as Mendel had described?

## Chromosome Number

In order to hold true, Mendel's principles require at least two events to occur. First, an organism with two parents must inherit a single copy of every gene from each parent. Second, when that organism produces gametes, those two sets of genes must be separated so that each gamete contains just one set of genes. As it turns out, chromosomes —those strands of DNA and protein inside the cell nucleus—fit that description perfectly. Genes are located on chromosomes.

**Diploid Cells** Each cell of the fruit fly, *Drosophila*, has eight chromosomes. Four of these chromosomes came from its male parent, and four came from its female parent. These two sets of chromosomes are **homologous**, meaning that each of the four chromosomes from the male parent has a corresponding chromosome from the female parent. A cell with two sets of homologous chromosomes is said to be **diploid**, meaning "double." *The diploid cells of most adult organisms contain two complete sets of inherited chromosomes and two complete sets of genes*. The diploid number of chromosomes is sometimes represented by the symbol 2N. Thus, for *Drosophila*, the diploid number is 8, or 2N = 8, where *N* represents the single set of chromosomes found in a sperm or egg cell.

## Figure 12-15
## Fruit Fly Chromosomes

These chromosomes are from a fruit fly. Each of the fruit fly's body cells is diploid, containing eight chromosomes. The gametes of the fruit fly are haploid, containing four chromosomes.

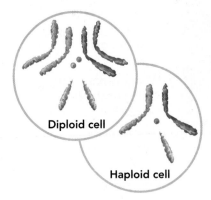

Diploid cell

Haploid cell

## Figure 12-16
## Crossing-Over

Crossing-over occurs during Prophase I, when pieces of homologous chromosomes sometimes swap positions.

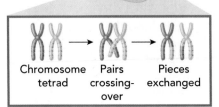

Chromosome tetrad → Pairs crossing-over → Pieces exchanged

### BUILD VOCABULARY

**Prefixes** The prefix *tetra-* means "four." A **tetrad** contains four chromatids.

**Haploid Cells** Some cells have a single set of chromosomes and, therefore, a single set of genes. Such cells are **haploid**, meaning "single." The gametes of sexually reproducing organisms, including fruit flies and peas, are haploid. Compare the diploid and haploid cells of *Drosophila* in **Figure 12-15.**

☑ **READING CHECK Calculate** The diploid number for most human cells is 46. What is the haploid number in human gametes?

# Phases of Meiosis

How do sexually-reproducing organisms produce haploid (N) gamete cells from diploid (2N) cells? That's where meiosis (my OH sis) comes in. **Meiosis** is a process in which the number of chromosomes per cell is cut in half through the separation of homologous chromosomes in a diploid cell. Meiosis usually involves two distinct divisions called meiosis I and meiosis II. By the end of meiosis, a single diploid cell has produced four haploid cells.

**Meiosis I** Just prior to meiosis I, the cell undergoes a round of chromosome replication during interphase. Each replicated chromosome from the male and the female consists of two identical chromatids joined at the center.

**Prophase I** After interphase I, the cell begins to divide, and the chromosomes pair up. 🔍 *In prophase I of meiosis, each replicated chromosome pairs with its corresponding homologous chromosome.* This pairing forms a structure called a **tetrad**, which contains four chromatids. As the chromosomes pair, they sometimes undergo a process called **crossing-over** in which bits and pieces of the homologous chromosomes are exchanged. As shown in **Figure 12-16,** crossing-over produces new combinations of alleles on each chromosome.

**Metaphase I and Anaphase I** As prophase I ends, a spindle forms and attaches to each tetrad. 🔍 *During metaphase I of meiosis, paired homologous chromosomes line up across the center of the cell.* As the cell moves into anaphase I, the homologous pairs of chromosomes separate. 🔍 *During anaphase I, spindle fibers pull each homologous chromosome pair toward opposite ends of the cell.*

**Telophase I and Cytokinesis** When anaphase I is complete, the separated chromosomes cluster at opposite ends of the cell. 🔍 *The next phase is telophase I, in which a nuclear membrane forms around each cluster of chromosomes. Cytokinesis follows, forming two new cells.*

Meiosis I produces two daughter cells. However, because each pair of homologous chromosomes was separated, neither cell has the two complete sets of chromosomes in a diploid cell. Those two sets have been shuffled and sorted almost like a deck of cards. The two cells produced by meiosis I have sets of chromosomes and alleles that differ from each other and from the diploid cell that entered meiosis I.

**Meiosis II**  The two cells now enter a second meiotic division called meiosis II, which is shown along with meiosis I in **Figure 12-17**. Unlike the first division, neither cell goes through a round of chromosome replication before entering meiosis II.

### Prophase II  🔍 *As the cells enter prophase II, their chromosomes—each consisting of two chromatids—become visible.* The chromosomes do not pair to form tetrads, because the homologous pairs were already separated during meiosis I.

### Metaphase II, Anaphase II, Telophase II, and Cytokinesis

During metaphase of meiosis II, chromosomes line up in the center of each cell. As the cell enters anaphase, the paired chromatids separate. 🔍 *The final four phases of meiosis II are similar to those in meiosis I. However, the result is four haploid daughter cells.* In the example shown here, each of the four daughter cells produced in meiosis II receives two chromosomes. These four daughter cells now contain the haploid number (N)—just two chromosomes each.

The haploid cells produced by meiosis develop into the gametes for sexual reproduction. In males, these gametes are usually called sperm. In females, they are known as egg cells.

✔️ **READING CHECK** **Interpret Graphics**  Describe the differences between meiosis I and meiosis II.

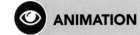

**ANIMATION**

Figure 12-17

## Meiosis I and Meiosis II

During meiosis I, a diploid cell undergoes a series of events that results in the production of two daughter cells. Neither daughter cell has the same sets of chromosomes that the original diploid cell had. The second meiotic division, called meiosis II, produces four haploid daughter cells.

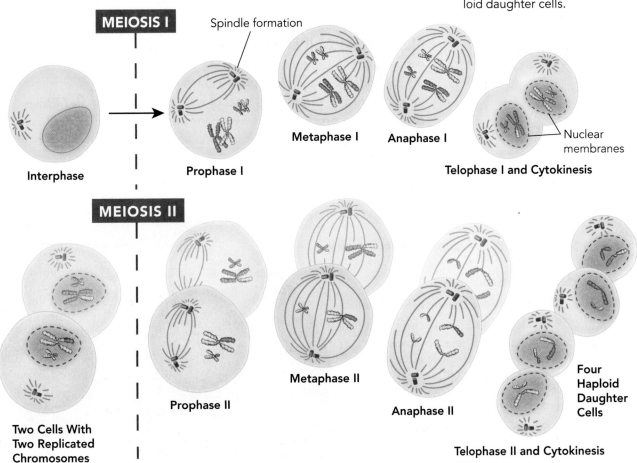

**MEIOSIS I**

Spindle formation

Interphase

Prophase I

Metaphase I

Anaphase I

Telophase I and Cytokinesis

Nuclear membranes

**MEIOSIS II**

Two Cells With Two Replicated Chromosomes

Prophase II

Metaphase II

Anaphase II

Telophase II and Cytokinesis

Four Haploid Daughter Cells

**INTERACTIVITY**

Investigate the steps of meiosis, and compare meiosis and mitosis.

**READING TOOL**

Draw and complete a two-column table to compare and contrast meiosis and mitosis.

# Comparing Meiosis and Mitosis

The words *mitosis* and *meiosis* may sound similar, but the two processes are very different, as you can see in **Figure 12-18**. Mitosis can be a form of asexual reproduction, whereas meiosis is an early step in sexual reproduction. Mitosis and meiosis also differ in the way chromosomes move and in their number of cell divisions.

**Replication and Separation of Genetic Material** A cell replicates, or copies, all of its chromosomes before entering either mitosis or meiosis. However, the next steps differ dramatically. *In mitosis, each daughter cell receives a complete diploid set of chromosomes. In meiosis, homologous chromosomes are separated, and each daughter cell receives only a haploid set of chromosomes.* As a result, in meiosis the two alleles for each gene are segregated, and end up in different gamete cells. The sorting and recombination of genes that takes place in meiosis helps to increase genetic variation from one generation to the next.

**Changes in Chromosome Number** *Mitosis does not change the chromosome number of the original cell. Meiosis reduces the chromosome number by half.* A diploid cell that enters mitosis with eight chromosomes will divide to produce two diploid daughter cells, each of which also has eight chromosomes. On the other hand, a diploid cell that enters meiosis with eight chromosomes will pass through two meiotic divisions to produce four haploid gamete cells, each with only four chromosomes.

**Number of Cell Divisions** Mitosis is a single cell division, resulting in the production of two identical daughter cells. On the other hand, meiosis requires two rounds of cell division, and, in most organisms, produces a total of four daughter cells. *Mitosis results in the production of two genetically identical diploid cells, whereas meiosis produces four genetically different haploid cells.*

HS-LS3-2

 **Modeling Lab**    Open-Ended Inquiry

### A Model of Meiosis

**Problem** How does meiosis change a diploid cell into haploid gametes?

In this lab, you will plan and develop a model of meiosis. You will choose materials to represent the cell and chromosomes, assemble and manipulate the materials to represent the stages of meiosis, and use the model to explain the process.

You can find this lab in your digital course.

**Figure 12-18**

# Comparing Mitosis and Meiosis

Mitosis and meiosis both ensure that cells inherit genetic information. Both processes begin after interphase, when chromosome replication occurs. However, the two processes differ in the separation of chromosomes, the number of cells produced, and the number of chromosomes each cell contains.

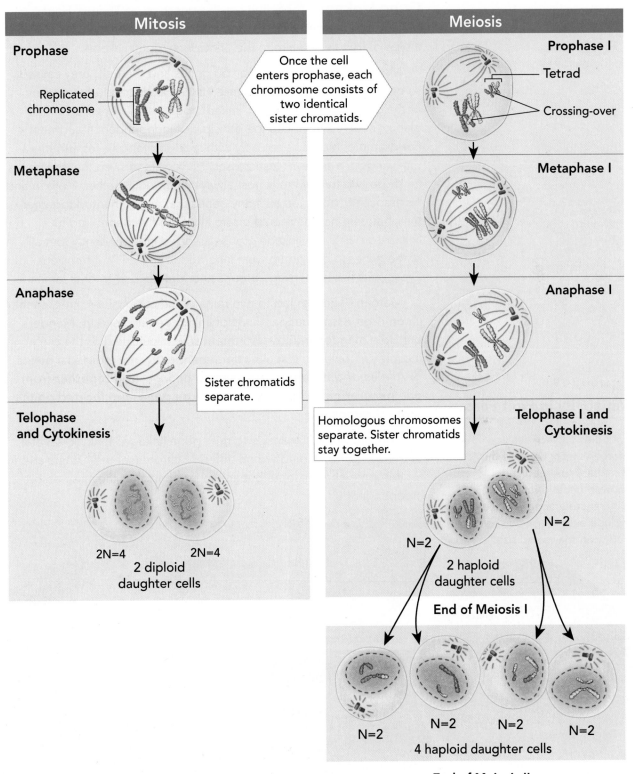

**Mitosis**

**Prophase**

Replicated chromosome

**Metaphase**

**Anaphase**

**Telophase and Cytokinesis**

2N=4    2N=4
2 diploid daughter cells

Once the cell enters prophase, each chromosome consists of two identical sister chromatids.

Sister chromatids separate.

Homologous chromosomes separate. Sister chromatids stay together.

**Meiosis**

**Prophase I**

Tetrad

Crossing-over

**Metaphase I**

**Anaphase I**

**Telophase I and Cytokinesis**

N=2    N=2
2 haploid daughter cells

**End of Meiosis I**

N=2    N=2    N=2    N=2
4 haploid daughter cells

**End of Meiosis II**

**VIDEO**

Investigate the work of
Thomas Hunt Morgan and
his colleagues.

# Gene Linkage and Gene Maps

If you think carefully about Mendel's principle of independent assortment in relation to meiosis, one question might bother you. Genes that are located on different chromosomes assort independently, but what about genes that are located on the same chromosome? Wouldn't they generally be inherited together?

**Gene Linkage**  The answer to this question, as Thomas Hunt Morgan first realized in 1910, is yes. Morgan's research on *Drosophilia*, a type of fruit fly, led him to the principle of gene linkage.

Morgan identified more than 50 genes and the traits they caused, some of which are shown in **Figure 12-19**. He discovered that many of the genes appeared to be "linked" together in ways that, at first glance, seemed to violate the principle of independent assortment. For example, Morgan used a fly with reddish-orange eyes and miniature wings in a series of test crosses. His results showed that the genes for those two traits were almost always inherited together. Morgan and his associates observed so many genes that were inherited together that, before long, they could group all of the fly's genes into four linkage groups. The linkage groups assorted independently, but all of the genes in one group were inherited together. As it turns out, *Drosophila* has four linkage groups and four pairs of chromosomes.

Morgan's findings led to two remarkable conclusions. First, each chromosome is actually a group of linked genes. Second, Mendel's principle of independent assortment still holds true. It is the chromosomes, however, that assort independently, not individual genes. ✎ *Alleles of different genes tend to be inherited together from one generation to the next when those genes are located on the same chromosome.*

How did Mendel manage to miss gene linkage? By luck, several of the genes he studied are on different chromosomes. Others are on the same chromosome but are so far apart that they also assort independently.

**Figure 12-19**
## Variability in Fruit Flies

Fruit flies proved ideal for Morgan's work because they were easy to breed and showed genetic variability. Differences among fruit flies include eye color, body color, and wing shape and size.

**Gene Mapping** In 1911, a Columbia University student was working part time in Morgan's lab. This student, Alfred Sturtevant, wondered if the frequency of crossing-over between genes during meiosis might be a clue to the genes' locations. Sturtevant reasoned that the farther apart two genes were on a chromosome, the more likely it would be that crossing-over would occur between them. If two genes are close together, then crossovers between them should be rare. If two genes are far apart, then crossovers between them should be more common, reducing the frequency with which they are linked. By this reasoning, he could use the frequency of crossing-over between genes to determine their distances from each other.

Sturtevant gathered up several notebooks of lab data and took them back to his room. The next morning, he presented Morgan with a gene map showing the relative locations of each known gene on one of the *Drosophila* chromosomes. Sturtevant's method has been used to construct gene maps, like the one in **Figure 12-20**, ever since.

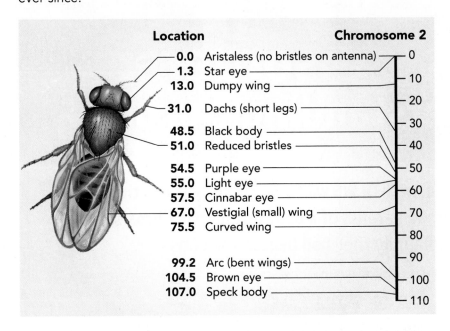

### Figure 12-20
### Gene Map

This gene map shows the location of a variety of genes on chromosome 2 of the fruit fly. The genes are named after the problems that abnormal alleles cause, not after the normal structures.

☑ **Interpret Diagrams** Where on the chromosome is the "purple eye" gene located?

HS-LS3-1, HS-LS3-2

## ☑ LESSON 12.4 Review

### ⚲ KEY QUESTIONS

1. Why are human gametes haploid instead of diploid?

2. What events occur during meiosis I and meiosis II?

3. How is meiosis similar to mitosis? How is it different?

4. Why can chromosomes be described as units of linked genes?

### CRITICAL THINKING

5. **Synthesize Information** How does meiosis help explain Mendel's principle of independent assortment?

6. **Use Models** Refer to the stages of meiosis shown in **Figure 12-17**. Events in which stages determine the assortment of genes in the gametes? Explain your answer.

7. **Construct an Explanation** In asexual reproduction, mitosis occurs but meiosis does not occur. Which type of reproduction—sexual or asexual—results in offspring with greater genetic variation? Explain your answer.

# Genetic disorders:
## understanding the odds

The birth of a foal with OLWS was a tragic surprise to the horse owner. To the proud parents of a baby girl, cystic fibrosis was a known risk, but happily they had beaten the odds.

HS-LS3-3, CCSS.ELA-LITERACY.RST.9-10.7, CCSS.ELA-LITERACY.WHST.9-10.9

## Make Your Case

Research either cystic fibrosis or overo lethal white syndrome, and learn what is known about the causes of both disorders. Find out why the overo white coat color is linked to problems in the equine digestive system. Similarly, try to find out why the sweat of children with cystic fibrosis is abnormally salty. Then, link this information to the way in which both disorders are inherited.

## Translate Scientific Information

1. **Synthesize Information** How do you explain to the horse owner why this foal was born with OLWS while two previous foals were perfectly healthy? What would you tell the new parents of the baby girl about their prospects for having more children?

2. **Support Your Explanation with Evidence** The parents of the newborn baby girl are happy that their first child was born without cystic fibrosis. But now they worry the odds have increased that their next child will suffer from the disorder. Are their concerns justified? Why or why not?

## Careers on the Case

### Work Toward a Solution

Understanding the principles of genetics is needed for a wide variety of careers. A genetic counselor is one such career.

### Genetic Counselor

Many hospitals and clinics employ counselors specially trained to help potential parents understand the chances of having children with certain inherited disabilities. Genetic counselors must have a detailed knowledge of human genetics, and must also possess exceptional personal skills to advise potential parents.

▶ **VIDEO**

Watch this video to learn more about a career in genetic counseling.

## Technology on the Case
### The Fight Against CF

Cystic fibrosis (CF) is a recessive genetic disorder caused by a defective allele for a gene on chromosome 7. This gene normally produces a cell membrane protein that allows chloride ions (Cl⁻) to enter and leave the cell. In most cases of CF, a missing or incorrect amino acid causes the protein to become misfolded so that it is not transported to the cell membrane. As a result, many tissues, such as the lungs and small intestine, cannot function properly. CF is the most common fatal genetic disorder among Americans of European ancestry.

Short of actually correcting the defective allele, researchers have tried to find ways to treat CF by going after that misfolded protein. Several teams of pharmaceutical researchers have developed drugs that help to prevent protein misfolding. In some cases, these drugs seem to "rescue" the protein by helping it to fold properly so that the cell is able to transport it to the cell membrane.

Another approach makes use of the fact that in many patients, a reduced number of the chloride ion channel proteins do find their way to the cell membrane, but don't function properly. Drugs have now been developed that help to keep these channels in an "open" position so they can function more effectively, relieving some of the symptoms of CF.

To date, while combinations of these two approaches look promising, neither provides a cure for the disorder. Therefore, knowing that more than 30,000 people in the United States suffer from cystic fibrosis, research will continue.

# Lesson Review

Go to your Biology Foundations Workbook for longer versions
of these lesson summaries.

## 12.1 The Work of Gregor Mendel

The scientific study of biological inheritance is
called genetics. Gregor Mendel's experiments
of cross-pollinating pea plants led to two basic
discoveries: first, traits or characteristics are
passed from one generation to the next by means
of genes, and second, different forms of a single
gene, called alleles, exhibit dominance and
recessiveness.

Recessive traits may disappear in one individual
or one generation because the recessive alleles
are masked by the dominant allele. During gamete formation, alleles are segregated so that each
gamete carries only one allele for each gene. If
a recessive allele is paired with another recessive
allele during fertilization, then the recessive trait
will reappear.

- genetics
- fertilization
- trait
- hybrid
- gene
- allele
- principle of dominance
- segregation
- gamete

### Cross-Pollination

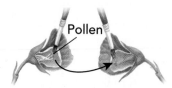

Pollen

☑ **Draw Conclusions** How can cross-pollination
be used to produce hybrid organisms?

## 12.2 Applying Mendel's Principles

Punnett squares use mathematical probability to
help predict the genotype and phenotype combinations in genetic crosses.

The principle of independent assortment states
that genes for different traits can segregate independently during the formation of gametes.

Mendel's principles of heredity, observed through
patterns of inheritance, form the basis of modern
genetics.

- probability
- homozygous
- heterozygous
- phenotype
- genotype
- Punnett square
- independent assortment

|  | TG | tG | Tg | tg |
|---|---|---|---|---|
| TG |  |  |  |  |
| tG |  |  |  |  |
| Tg |  |  |  |  |
| tg |  |  |  |  |

☑ **Interpret Diagrams** Complete the Punnett
square for the cross between two pea plants that
are heterozygous for size (*Tt*) and pod color (*Gg*).

## 12.3 Other Patterns of Inheritance

In incomplete dominance, the alleles for a particular trait are neither completely dominant nor completely recessive. Codominance is a situation in which the phenotypes produced by both alleles are clearly expressed. Many genes exist in several different forms and are therefore said to have multiple alleles. Many traits, known as polygenic traits, are produced by the interaction of several genes. Some traits follow non-Mendelian patterns of inheritance.

Environmental conditions can affect gene expression and influence genetically determined traits.

- incomplete dominance
- codominance
- multiple alleles
- polygenic trait

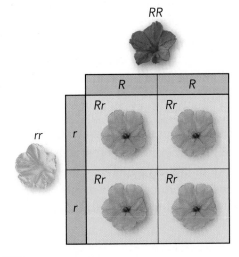

**✓ Interpret Diagrams** What pattern of inheritance is shown in the diagram above? How do you know?

## 12.4 Meiosis

In prophase I of meiosis, each replicated chromosome pairs with its corresponding homologous chromosome. During metaphase I of meiosis, paired homologous chromosomes line up across the center of the cell. During anaphase I, spindle fibers pull each homologous chromosome pair toward opposite ends of the cell. The next phase is telophase I, in which a nuclear membrane forms around each cluster of chromosomes. Cytokinesis follows, forming two new cells. As the cells enter prophase II, their chromosomes—each consisting of two chromatids—become visible. The final four phases of meiosis II are similar to those in meiosis I. However, the result is four haploid daughter cells.

In mitosis, each daughter cell receives a complete diploid set of chromosomes. In meiosis, homologous chromosomes are separated, and each daughter cell receives only a haploid set of chromosomes. Mitosis does not change the chromosome number of the original cell. Meiosis reduces the chromosome number by half. Mitosis results in the production of two genetically identical diploid cells, whereas meiosis produces four genetically different haploid cells.

Alleles of different genes tend to be inherited together from one generation to the next when those genes are located on the same chromosome. This is called gene linkage.

- homologous
- diploid
- haploid
- meiosis
- tetrad
- crossing-over

## Organize Information

Complete the table to compare mitosis and meiosis.

|  | Role in Organism | Daughter Cells | Chromosomes | Number of Cell Divisions |
|---|---|---|---|---|
| **Mitosis** | 1. | 2. | No change to chromosome number | 3. |
| **Meiosis** | 4. | Four haploid cells | 5. | 6. |

# Growing
## More and Better Corn

# Evaluating Information

HS-LS3-3, CCSS.ELA-LITERACY.WHST.9-10.2

**STEM** By observing the seeds in this photograph, can you make inferences about the traits of the adult plants that will grow from these seeds? Probably not. The key information is carried on the inside of the seeds, not the outside. The genes of the seeds code for their growth and development.

Even small changes in the genes of seeds can make a huge difference in the plants they produce. One important example comes from the corn plant (*Zea mays*). Corn is native to North America, where it was first developed by Native American farmers several thousand years ago. It is now grown worldwide.

Up until the 1930s, farmers could expect to harvest about 30 bushels of corn for every acre they planted. But then something remarkable happened. The corn yields began increasing. By the 1960s, yields of 60 bushels per acre were common. After another 40 years, average yields had doubled again. Today, farmers can expect an acre of corn plants to yield more than 140 bushels.

What caused this huge increase in corn yields? The main reason is hybrid seeds. A field of hybrid corn plants will all grow to the same size and height, making the crop easier to harvest. Hybrid plants also tend to be healthier and grow more vigorously.

Seed companies produce hybrid seeds by developing two inbred strains, meaning strains that have homozygous genotypes. Then, they cross the two strains to produce hybrid plants. The procedure is shown in the diagram and explained here.

**1** Heterozygous plants self-pollinate to produce a $F_1$ generation.

**2** In $F_1$, $\frac{1}{2}$ of the plants are homozygous (*GG* or *gg*). All of the plants self-pollinate to produce an $F_2$ generation.

**3** In $F_2$, $\frac{3}{4}$ of the plants are homozygous. With each new self-pollinated crop, more and more of the plants are homozygous.

**4** After 7 or more generations, nearly pure homozygous strains have been produced. Two such strains are then crossed to produce hybrid seeds ready for farmers to plant.

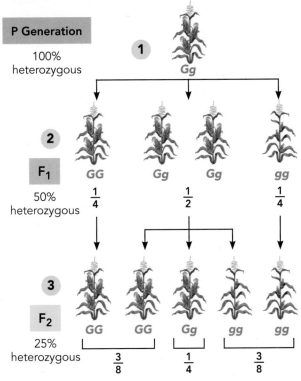

**P Generation**
100% heterozygous
*Gg*

1

2

**F₁**
50% heterozygous

*GG* ¼
*Gg* ½
*gg* ¼

3

**F₂**
25% heterozygous

*GG* *GG* ³⁄₈
*Gg* ¼
*gg* *gg* ³⁄₈

1. **Use Models** Construct four Punnett squares to represent each F₁ plant self-pollinating. Then, using colored pencils, shade *GG*, *Gg*, and *gg* (each with a different color).

2. **Patterns** Identify a pattern in the number of heterozygotes for the first three generations. What do you see? Continue the pattern for a total of 7 generations.

3. **Construct an Explanation** When Step 2 of the procedure is repeated, do the percentages of homozygous plants always increase? Explain why or why not.

4. **Identify** Why does the procedure lead to hybrid seeds after Step 4?

5. **Construct an Explanation** Which is easier to produce: a strain of plants that are homozygous dominant (*GG*) or homozygous recessive (*gg*)? Explain your reasoning.

6. **Apply Scientific Reasoning** A farmer grows a corn crop from hybrid seeds. Then, the farmer gathers and plants some of the seeds from the hybrid corn plants. How will the new corn crop compare to the first crop?

7. **Conduct Research** Choose another popular garden plant or crop plant, such as pumpkins, sunflowers, squash, or tomatoes. Research the breeding techniques for the plant. Also research the useful and variable traits of the plant, such as fruit size, shape, or color.

8. **Communicate** Present your research findings in a poster, essay, or computer slide show. Your presentation should include answers to these questions:

- How can a breeder control reproduction in the plant?

- Which traits have breeders selected to produce purebred or hybrid strains?

- What new or modified strain has proven useful for the plant, or what improvements might be developed in the future?

# ☑ASSESSMENT

## 🔑 KEY QUESTIONS AND TERMS

### 12.1 The Work of Gregor Mendel
HS-LS3-3

1. Different forms of a gene are called
   a. hybrids.
   b. dominant factors.
   c. alleles.
   d. recessive factors.

2. Organisms that have two identical alleles for a particular trait are said to be
   a. hybrid.
   b. heterozygous.
   c. homozygous.
   d. dominant.

3. Mendel had many stocks of pea plants that were true-breeding. What is meant by this term?

4. Explain how Mendel kept his pea plants from self-pollinating.

### 12.2 Applying Mendel's Principles
HS-LS3-3

5. A Punnett square is used to determine the
   a. probable outcome of a cross.
   b. actual outcome of a cross.
   c. result of incomplete dominance.
   d. result of meiosis.

6. The physical characteristics of an organism are called its
   a. genetics.
   b. heredity.
   c. phenotype.
   d. genotype.

7. What is the probability of flipping a coin twice and getting two heads?
   a. 1
   b. $\frac{1}{2}$
   c. $\frac{1}{4}$
   d. $\frac{3}{4}$

8. Summarize the four basic principles of genetics that Mendel discovered in his experiments.

9. In pea plants, the allele for yellow seeds is dominant over the allele for green seeds. Predict the genotypic ratio of offspring produced by crossing two parents that are heterozygous for this trait. Draw a Punnett square to illustrate your prediction.

### 12.3 Other Patterns of Inheritance
HS-LS3-3

10. A situation in which a gene has more than two alleles is known as
    a. complete dominance.
    b. codominance.
    c. polygenic dominance.
    d. multiple alleles.

11. A pink-flowered *Mirabilis* plant (*Rr*) is crossed with a white-flowered *Mirabilis* (*rr*). What is the chance that a seed from this cross will produce a red-flowered plant (*RR*)?
    a. 0
    b. $\frac{1}{4}$
    c. $\frac{1}{2}$
    d. 1

12. What is the difference between multiple alleles and polygenic traits?

13. Why can multiple alleles result in many different phenotypes for a trait?

14. Are an organism's characteristics determined only by its genes? Explain.

### 12.4 Meiosis
HS-LS3-1, HS-LS3-2

15. The illustration below represents which stage of meiosis?

   a. prophase I
   b. anaphase II
   c. telophase I
   d. metaphase I

16. Unlike mitosis, meiosis in male mammals results in the formation of
    a. one haploid gamete.
    b. three diploid gametes.
    c. four diploid gametes.
    d. four haploid gametes.

17. A gene map shows
    a. the number of possible alleles for a gene.
    b. the relative locations of genes on a chromosome.
    c. where chromosomes are in a cell.
    d. how crossing-over occurs.

18. Suppose that an organism has the diploid number 2N = 8. How many chromosomes do this organism's gametes contain?

19. Describe the process of meiosis.

20. Explain why chromosomes, not individual genes, assort independently.

## CRITICAL THINKING
HS-LS3-1, HS-LS3-2, HS-LS3-3

21. **Infer** Suppose Mendel crossed two pea plants and got both tall and short offspring. What could have been the genotypes of the two original plants? What genotype could not have been present?

22. **Construct an Explanation** Complete the Punnett square with the probable offspring of these two parents: RrYy × RrYy, where R is round seed shape and r is wrinkled, Y is yellow seed color and y is green. Explain how the different phenotypes are produced.

|     | RY | Ry | rY | ry |
|-----|----|----|----|----|
| **RY** |    |    |    |    |
| **Ry** |    |    |    |    |
| **rY** |    |    |    |    |
| **ry** |    |    |    |    |

F₂ Generation

23. **Compare and Contrast** Compare the phases of meiosis I and meiosis II in terms of number and arrangement of the chromosomes.

24. **Use Models** Identify the steps in meiosis that support the independent assortment of inherited genes. Make a diagram that illustrates how independent assortment ensures that the DNA in daughter cells is different from the DNA of the parent cell.

25. **Design a Solution** In sheep, the allele for white wool (A) is dominant over the allele for black wool (a). Design an experiment to determine the genotype of a white sheep.

26. **Construct an Explanation** Explain why it is possible for several offspring of the same parents to have the same phenotype but different genotypes.

27. **Draw Conclusions** In guinea pigs, the allele for a rough coat (R) is dominant over the allele for a smooth coat (r). A heterozygous guinea pig (Rr) and a homozygous recessive guinea pig (rr) have a total of nine offspring. The Punnett square for this cross shows a 50-percent chance that any particular offspring will have a smooth coat. Explain how all nine offspring can have smooth coats.

|     | R  | r  |
|-----|----|----|
| **r** | Rr | rr |
| **r** | Rr | rr |

28. **Interpret Visuals** Genes that control hair or feather color in some animals are expressed differently in the winter than in the summer. Ptarmigans are birds that live in the Arctic, where there is snow in the winter, but not in the summer. How might such a difference be beneficial to the ptarmigan shown here?

29. **Construct an Explanation** A red bull is bred with a white cow. The offspring has a coat known as roan because it is made up of both red and white hairs. Is the expression of the roan coat an example of incomplete dominance or codominance? Explain how you can identify the difference between these two patterns of inheritance.

## CROSSCUTTING CONCEPTS

**30. Cause and Effect** As Mendel concluded, what was the cause of recessive traits disappearing after a parental cross, but then reappearing in the next generation?

**31. Cause and Effect** Explain why the alleles for reddish-orange eyes and miniature wings in *Drosophila* are usually inherited together. Describe the pattern of inheritance these alleles follow, and explain the cause for this pattern as it relates to gene linkage. (**Hint:** To organize your ideas, draw a cause-effect diagram that shows what happens to the two alleles during meiosis.)

**32. Scale, Proportion, and Quantity** A scientist conducts a hybrid cross for tallness in pea plants ($Tt \times Tt$). Then, the scientist plants the seeds that the cross produces. What can the scientist predict about the new generation of plants, regardless of the number of seeds that are harvested?

## MATH CONNECTIONS

## Analyze and Interpret Data

HS-LS3-3, CCSS.MATH.CONTENT.MP2, CCSS.MATH.CONTENT.MP4

Use the paragraph and table to answer questions 33 to 35.

A researcher studying fruit flies finds a fly with brown-colored eyes. Almost all fruit flies in nature have bright red eyes. When the researcher crosses the brown-eyed fly with a red-eyed fly, all of the $F_1$ offspring have red eyes. The researcher then crosses two of the $F_1$ red-eyed flies and obtains the following results in the $F_2$ generation:

| Results of Eye Color Experiment | |
|---|---|
| **Phenotype** | **Number of Flies in $F_2$ Generation** |
| Red Eyes | 37 |
| Brown Eyes | 14 |

**33. Calculate** What is the approximate ratio of red-eyed flies to brown-eyed flies in the $F_2$ generation?
 **a.** 1 : 1          **c.** 3 : 1
 **b.** 1 : 3          **d.** 4 : 1

**34. Use Models** Based on the information in this table, how would you describe the pattern of inheritance for brown- and red-colored eyes in fruit flies? Cite data from the researcher's experiments to support your description.

**35. Reason Quantitatively** Propose genotypes for the fruit flies in the P generation and the $F_1$ generation. Then draw a Punnett square to describe the $F_2$ generation.

## LANGUAGE ARTS CONNECTIONS

## Write About Science

CCSS.ELA-LITERACY.WHST.9-10.2, CCSS.ELA-LITERACY.WHST.9-10.9

**36. Write Explanatory Texts** A litter of seven puppies is born to a female dog. No two puppies have exactly the same fur color or pattern of markings even though they all have the same parents. Write an explanation of how new genetic combinations that occur during meiosis may account for the differences in their fur.

**37. Draw Evidence** How did Mendel's observations of the traits expressed in the $F_1$ and $F_2$ generations of pea plants lead him to propose the idea of segregation of alleles?

## Read About Science

CCSS.ELA-LITERACY.RST.9-10.1, CCSS.ELA-LITERACY.RST.9-10.3

**38. Follow a Multistep Procedure** Review the steps that Mendel took starting with his crossing of tall and short pea plants to produce both $F_1$ and $F_2$ offspring. List each step in order for both crosses. Identify the question(s) Mendel was trying to answer with each cross.

**39. Cite Textual Evidence** Describe the exceptions to Mendel's principles of inheritance presented in the chapter. What evidence does the chapter offer to support the claim that these are exceptions to Mendel's principles?

1. Gregor Mendel crossed true-breeding plants that had green pea pods with true-breeding plants that had yellow pea pods. The resulting $F_1$ generation all had green pea pods. What did he observe in the $F_2$ generation?

   A. Mendel observed green and yellow pea pods in a 3:1 ratio because the $F_1$ generation was heterozygous.

   B. Mendel observed green and yellow pea pods in a 4:1 ratio because the allele for green pea pods is dominant.

   C. Mendel observed green and yellow pea pods in a 1:1 ratio because the $F_2$ generation had the same characteristics as the parent generation.

   D. Mendel observed only green pea pods because both parents had green pea pods.

   E. Mendel observed green and yellow pea pods in a 1:2 ratio because the allele for yellow pea pods is dominant.

2. Rory made the Punnett square below to show the possible genotypes of a cross between two pea plants that are heterozygous for tall stems and smooth pea pods.

   $T$ = tall stems      $S$ = smooth pod
   $t$ = short stems      $s$ = constricted pod

   |      | TS   | Ts   | tS   | ts   |
   |------|------|------|------|------|
   | TS   | TTSS | TTSs | TtSS | TtSs |
   | Ts   | TTSs | TTss | TtSs | Ttss |
   | tS   | TtSS | TtSs | ttSS | ttSs |
   | ts   | TtSs | Ttss | ttSs | ttss |

   What is the ratio of the phenotypes expressed by the offspring in this cross?

   A. 3 : 1

   B. 4 : 1

   C. 9 : 3 : 3 : 1

   D. 1 : 1

   E. 1 : 9 : 16

3. The gene map below shows some of the genes on chromosome 2 of the fruit fly *Drosophila melanogaster*.

   | Location | | Chromosome 2 |
   |------|------|------|
   | 0.0 | Aristaless (no bristles on antenna) | 0 |
   | 1.3 | Star eye | 10 |
   | 13.0 | Dumpy wing | 20 |
   | 31.0 | Dachs (short legs) | 30 |
   | 48.5 | Black body | 40 |
   | 51.0 | Reduced bristles | |
   | 54.5 | Purple eye | 50 |
   | 55.0 | Light eye | 60 |
   | 57.5 | Cinnabar eye | |
   | 67.0 | Vestigial (small) wing | 70 |
   | 75.5 | Curved wing | 80 |
   | | | 90 |
   | 99.2 | Arc (bent wings) | 100 |
   | 104.5 | Brown eye | |
   | 107.0 | Speck body | 110 |

   Which pair of traits is MOST LIKELY to be inherited together?

   A. purple eye and brown eye because they are both eye traits

   B. aristaless and speck body because they have the greatest chance of crossing over

   C. curved wing and arc (bent wings) because they have the least chance of crossing-over

   D. dachs (short legs) and black body because there are no other genes between them on the gene map

   E. black body and light eye because they are closest together on chromosome 2

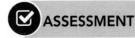 **ASSESSMENT**

For additional assessment practice, go online to access your digital course.

## If You Have Trouble With...

| Question | 1 | 2 | 3 |
|----------|---|---|---|
| See Lesson | 12.1 | 12.2 | 12.4 |
| Performance Expectation | HS-LS3-3 | HS-LS3-3 | HS-LS3-2 |

**13.1**
Identifying the
Substance of the Gene

**13.2**
The Structure of DNA

**13.3**
DNA Replication

**Go Online to access your digital course.**

▶ VIDEO

🔊 AUDIO

👆 INTERACTIVITY

📖 eTEXT

👁 ANIMATION

🧪 VIRTUAL LAB

☑ ASSESSMENT

This loggerhead turtle is one of seven species of sea turtles. Each species has unique DNA sequences that distinguish it.

# Living things don't carry ID cards... or do they?

Jamal is shopping for seafood at the supermarket. He wants to try Atlantic cod, which friends say is a common, nutritious, and great-tasting fish. The seafood counter has many fish fillets on display, each labeled with the species name. Jamal finds haddock, pollock, whiting, and then the Atlantic cod that he wanted. However, he notices that all of the fillets look very much alike. All have a pale white color with similar shapes and textures. He wonders how anyone one could tell them apart. Are the labels truly accurate?

Across town, Fiona is buying ferns at a nursery. She is looking for a certain species called a Wright's lip fern. This fern is native to North America and tolerates dry conditions, making it a popular choice for rock gardens. Fiona finds a Wright's lip fern that looks attractive and healthy. Then she starts asking herself some questions. She only knows the name of the fern from the label on the pot, and many ferns look much like another. Can the identity of the fern be confirmed?

At a Florida beach, Wendy is looking through binoculars from her perch behind some sand dunes. She finally sees what she is hoping to see, which is a sea turtle emerging from the water. Wendy is studying marine biology. As she has learned, adult female sea turtles leave the water only to lay eggs on the sand. As Wendy continues observing, she wonders if this is a loggerhead turtle, the one seen most frequently in Florida, or if it might be the less common green sea turtle. A variety of turtles live in the sea, and they can be difficult to tell apart. Can a simple test help identify a sea turtle?

Jamal, Fiona, and Wendy each have similar questions—and the answer to each question is yes. Indeed, scientists are now using the same type of procedure to identify all sorts of species. The procedure is called DNA barcoding.

At the supermarket, every package of food has a unique barcode that identifies it. Species also have unique identifiers hidden in their DNA, the molecule that makes up genes. Scientists have been identifying and recording these unique sections of DNA—or DNA barcodes—for a wide variety of species, including fishes, ferns, and turtles.

DNA barcoding has shown some surprising results. At some markets, as many as 75 percent of fish fillets were mislabeled with the wrong species. At nurseries, Australian ferns had been mislabeled as Wright's lip ferns. Marine biologists once thought that all sea turtles were the same species, but DNA barcoding shows at least seven species.

What is DNA? How was its role in living cells discovered? How does it differ from one organism to another?

**Throughout this chapter, look for connections to the** CASE STUDY **to help you answer these questions.**

# Identifying the Substance of the Gene

**HS-LS1-1:** Construct an explanation based on evidence for how the structure of DNA determines the structure of proteins which carry out the essential functions of life through systems of specialized cells.

**HS-LS3-1:** Ask questions to clarify relationships about the role of DNA and chromosomes in coding the instructions for characteristic traits passed from parents to offspring.

## VOCABULARY

**transformation**
**bacteriophage**

## READING TOOL

As you read, pay attention to the experiments that were carried out to help scientists understand genes and DNA. Take notes on the importance of each in the graphic organizer in your 📖 **Biology Foundations Workbook.**

Like other animals, this mouse began as a single fertilized cell that developed into a multicellular organism. Genes inside the mouse determined its physical traits, such as ear shape and fur color. But how do genes work? How do they determine whether that cell will become a mouse or a moose? To answer that question, the first step would be to figure out what genes are actually made of. Got any ideas? How would you try to find the molecules that carry genetic information?

## Bacterial Transformation

About 100 years ago, biologists realized that to truly understand genetics, they first had to discover the chemical nature of the gene. As with many stories in science, this discovery began with an investigator who was actually looking for something else.

In 1928, the British scientist Frederick Griffith was investigating how certain types of bacteria produce pneumonia, which is a serious lung disease. Griffith had isolated two very similar types of bacteria from mice. Both types grew very well in culture plates in Griffith's lab, but only one of them caused pneumonia. The disease-causing bacteria (the "S" type) grew into smooth-edged colonies on culture plates, whereas the harmless bacteria (the "R" type) produced colonies with rough edges. The difference in appearance made the two types easy to tell apart.

**Griffith's Experiments** When Griffith injected mice with disease-causing bacteria, the mice developed pneumonia and died. When he injected other mice with harmless bacteria, the mice remained healthy. Griffith wondered what made the first group of mice get pneumonia. Did the S-type bacteria produce a poison that made the mice sick? To find out, he ran the series of experiments shown in **Figure 13-1**.

First, Griffith killed the S-type cells by heating them, and injected these heat-killed bacteria into laboratory mice. The mice survived, suggesting that the cause of pneumonia was not a poison from the disease-causing bacteria. In Griffith's next experiment, he mixed the heat-killed, S-type bacteria with live, harmless bacteria from the R-type. He also injected this mixture into laboratory mice. By themselves, neither type of bacteria should have made the mice sick. To Griffith's surprise, however, many of the injected mice developed pneumonia and died. When he examined the lungs of these mice, he found them to be filled not with the harmless bacteria, but with the disease-causing bacteria. How could that happen if the S-type cells were dead?

## Transformation

Somehow, the heat-killed bacteria passed their disease-causing ability to the harmless bacteria. Griffith reasoned that mixing the two types of bacteria allowed a chemical factor to transfer from the heat-killed, S-type cells into the living R-type cells. This chemical compound, he concluded, must contain information that changed harmless bacteria into disease-causing ones. He called this process **transformation**, because one type of bacteria (the harmless form) had been changed permanently into another (the disease-causing form). Because the ability to cause disease was inherited by the offspring of the transformed bacteria, Griffith concluded that the transforming factor had to be a gene.

✓ **READING CHECK** **Apply Concepts** How were dead S-type cells able to transform living R-type cells?

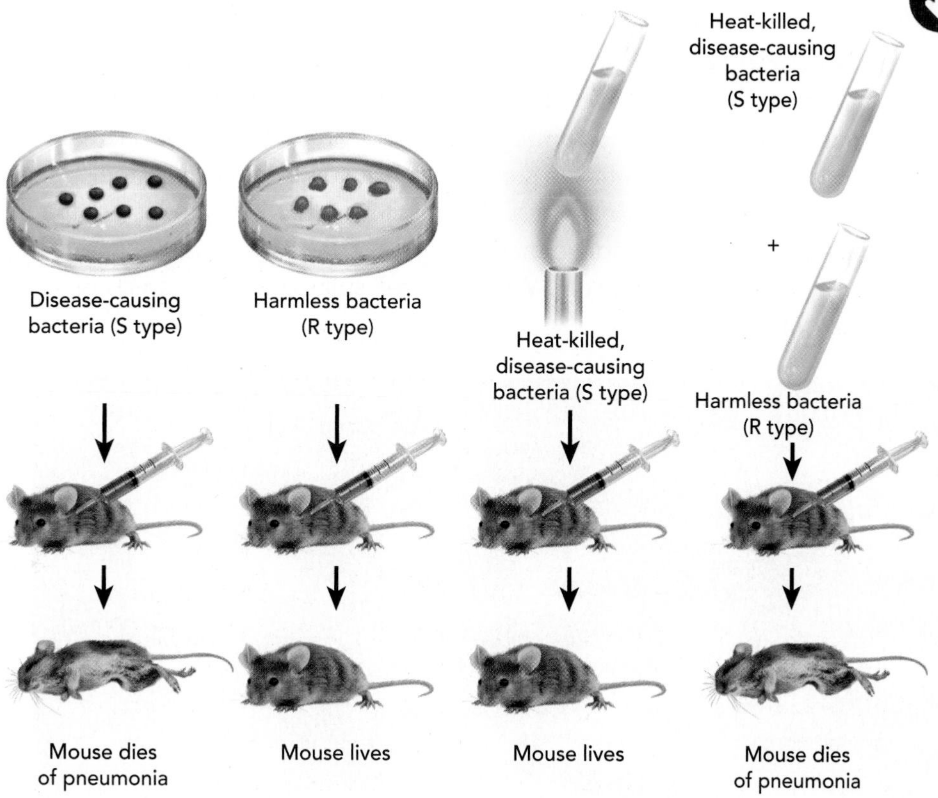

**INTERACTIVITY**

**Figure 13-1**

## Griffith's Experiments

Griffith injected mice with four different samples of bacteria. When injected separately, neither heat-killed, disease-causing bacteria nor live, harmless bacteria killed the mice. The two types injected together, however, caused fatal pneumonia. From this experiment, Griffith inferred that genetic information could be transferred from one bacterial type to another.

Disease-causing bacteria (S type)

Harmless bacteria (R type)

Heat-killed, disease-causing bacteria (S type)

Heat-killed, disease-causing bacteria (S type)

+

Harmless bacteria (R type)

Mouse dies of pneumonia

Mouse lives

Mouse lives

Mouse dies of pneumonia

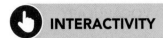

**INTERACTIVITY**

Recreate Avery's experiments and see if you come up with the same results.

**The Molecular Cause of Transformation** In 1944, a group of scientists at the Rockefeller Institute in New York decided to repeat Griffith's work. Led by Canadian biologist Oswald Avery, the scientists wanted to identify the molecule in the heat-killed bacteria that caused the transformation.

Avery and his team extracted a mixture of various molecules from the heat-killed bacteria. They carefully treated this mixture with enzymes that destroyed proteins, lipids, carbohydrates, and the nucleic acid RNA. Transformation still occurred. Clearly, none of the destroyed molecules could have been responsible for the transformation.

Avery's team repeated the experiment one more time. This time, they used enzymes that broke down a compound called deoxyribonucleic acid: DNA. When they destroyed the DNA in the mixture, transformation did not occur. Only one possible conclusion could explain these results: DNA was the transforming factor. ⚲ *By observing bacterial transformation, Avery and other scientists discovered that DNA stores and transmits genetic information from one generation of bacteria to the next.* Avery's work provided evidence that genes were made of DNA.

## Bacterial Viruses

Many biologists were skeptical of Avery's results. They pointed out that eukaryotic chromosomes actually contain more protein than DNA. However, in 1952, the genetic importance of DNA was confirmed in a dramatic experiment performed by two American scientists, Alfred Hershey and Martha Chase.

**Bacteriophages** Hershey and Chase studied viruses, which are tiny nonliving particles that can infect living cells. Their experiment was done with a **bacteriophage**, a type of virus that infects bacteria. These viruses attach to the surface of a bacterium and inject their genetic information into it, as shown in **Figure 13-2**. Once inside, the viral genes act to produce many new bacteriophages, which gradually destroy the bacterium. When the cell splits open, hundreds of new viruses burst out.

**Figure 13-2**

**Bacteriophage**

A bacteriophage is a type of virus that infects and kills bacteria. The diagram shows a bacteriophage. The micrograph shows T2 bacteriophages (green) attacking and injecting their DNA into an *E. coli* bacterium (gold).

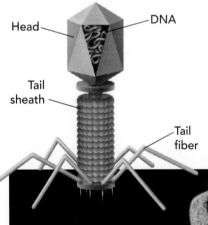

Head

DNA

Tail sheath

Tail fiber

TEM 150,000×

*E. coli* bacterium

## Figure 13-3

## The Hershey-Chase Experiment

Alfred Hershey and Martha Chase (pictured) used different radioactive markers to label the DNA and proteins of bacteriophages. The experiments showed that bacteriophages injected only DNA, not proteins, into bacterial cells.

**Martha Chase**

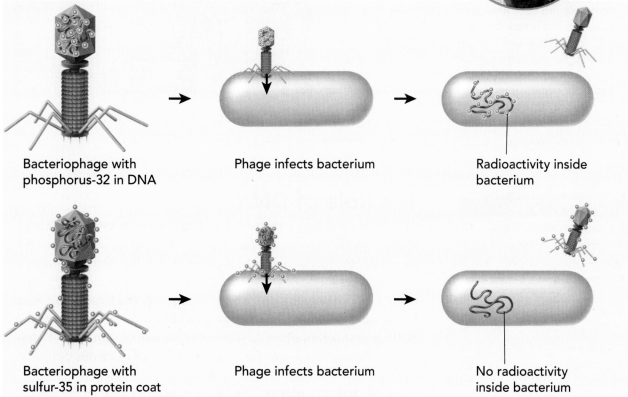

Bacteriophage with phosphorus-32 in DNA

Phage infects bacterium

Radioactivity inside bacterium

Bacteriophage with sulfur-35 in protein coat

Phage infects bacterium

No radioactivity inside bacterium

**The Hershey-Chase Experiment** Hershey and Chase designed an experiment to determine which part of a virus—its protein coat or its DNA core—entered the bacterial cell. To do this, the pair grew viruses in cultures containing radioactive isotopes of phosphorus-32 ($^{32}P$) and sulfur-35 ($^{35}S$). This was a clever strategy, because proteins contain almost no phosphorus, and DNA contains no sulfur. Therefore, these isotopes could be used as markers, telling the scientists which molecules entered the bacteria. If they found radioactivity from $^{35}S$ in the bacteria, it would mean the viral genes were made of protein. If they found $^{32}P$, then the genes were made of DNA.

They allowed the viruses to infect the bacteria and then tested them for radioactivity. **Figure 13-3** shows the steps in this experiment. The results showed that nearly all the radioactivity in the bacteria was from phosphorus ($^{32}P$), the marker found in DNA. Hershey and Chase concluded that the genetic material of the bacteriophage was indeed DNA, not protein. 🔍 *Hershey and Chase's experiment with bacteriophages confirmed Avery's conclusion that DNA was the genetic material.* Today, we know that DNA makes up the genetic material of all living cells, not just viruses and bacteria.

### INTERACTIVITY

Learn how various scientists contributed to the discovery of DNA.

✓ **READING CHECK** Identify Variables Identify the independent and dependent variables in the Hershey-Chase experiment.

## Forensics Lab — Guided Inquiry

### Using DNA to Identify Species

**Problem** How can DNA be used to identify a species?

At the Round Lake Resort, the fishing guides are surprised to find a new species of fish in the lake. In this lab, you will follow the first and last steps of DNA barcoding. For the extraction step, you will use a strawberry instead of a fish. Because each strawberry cell has eight copies of its chromosomes, you will be able to collect a large amount of DNA. Ripe strawberries also contain enzymes that help break down cell walls.

You can find this lab in your digital course.

**READING TOOL**

As you read about each role of DNA, refer to the related image shown in **Figure 13-4**.

# The Role of DNA

You might think that scientists would have been satisfied knowing that genes were made of DNA, but that was not the case at all. In fact, the discovery actually raised more questions than it answered. If genes were made of DNA, then DNA must be capable of doing some extraordinary things. ✎ *Specifically, the DNA molecule must be capable of storing and copying genetic information, as well as putting that information to work in gene expression.* The illustrations in **Figure 13-4** show the many tasks that DNA carries out.

**Storing Information** The foremost job of DNA, as the molecule of heredity, is to store genetic information. The genes that make a flower purple must have the information to produce purple pigment. Genes for blood type and eye color must have the information needed for their jobs as well. Genes control development, which means that the instructions that cause a single cell to develop into an oak tree, a sea urchin, or a dog must also be coded in DNA. But what is that code, and how does it relate to the characteristics controlled by genes?

**Copying Information** Before a cell divides, it must make a complete copy of every one of its genes. To many scientists, the most puzzling aspect of DNA was how it could be precisely copied without losing information. They could not even imagine how a molecule could copy itself, but that is exactly what DNA would have to do.

**Gene Expression** Finally, cells must be able to take the information coded in DNA and put it to work. How does that happen, and what are the cellular mechanisms by which genes are expressed? The solutions to these and many other puzzles would have to wait until the structure of the DNA molecule was figured out.

**READING CHECK** **Review** What kinds of information does DNA store?

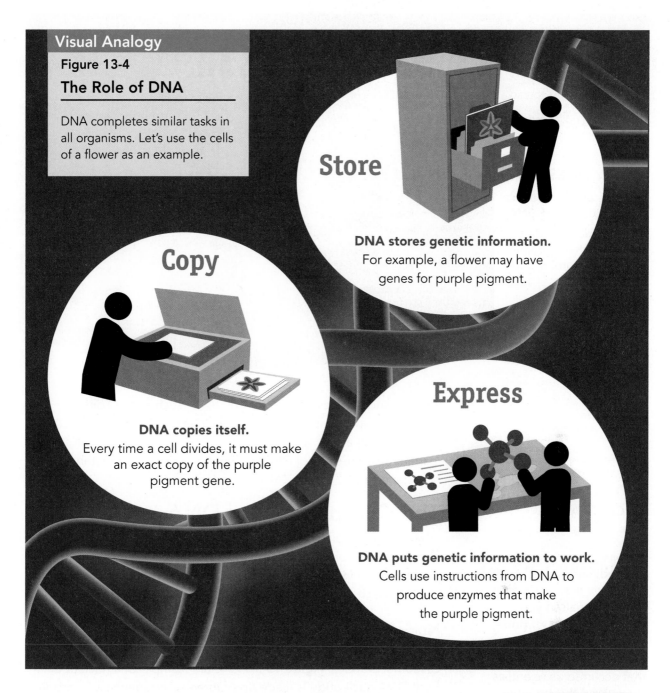

**Figure 13-4**

**The Role of DNA**

DNA completes similar tasks in all organisms. Let's use the cells of a flower as an example.

**Store**

**DNA stores genetic information.**
For example, a flower may have genes for purple pigment.

**Copy**

**DNA copies itself.**
Every time a cell divides, it must make an exact copy of the purple pigment gene.

**Express**

**DNA puts genetic information to work.**
Cells use instructions from DNA to produce enzymes that make the purple pigment.

HS-LS1-1, HS-LS3-1

## ☑ LESSON 13.1 Review

### ⚲ KEY QUESTIONS

1. What did the experiments of Griffith and Avery show about genetic information?

2. How did the results of the Hershey-Chase experiment strengthen Avery's conclusions?

3. What are the three key roles of DNA?

### CRITICAL THINKING

4. **Evaluate Reasoning** How did Hershey and Chase use radioactivity to draw a conclusion about proteins and DNA?

5. **Use Evidence to Construct an Argument** In the 1940s, many scientists were convinced that a protein was the genetic material. Refute this claim using the experiments in this lesson.

6. **Evaluate Evidence** Choose Griffith, Avery, or Hershey and Chase. Select evidence from the text to develop a flowchart that shows how that scientist or team of scientists used scientific methods. Be sure to identify each method. Use your flowchart from the Reading Tool and content from Chapter 1 as a guide.

Blue morpho butterfly

## KEY QUESTIONS

- What are the chemical components of DNA?
- What clues helped scientists determine the structure of DNA?
- What does the double-helix model show about DNA?

**HS-LS1-1:** Construct an explanation based on evidence for how the structure of DNA determines the structure of proteins which carry out the essential functions of life through systems of specialized cells.

**HS-LS3-1:** Ask questions to clarify relationships about the role of DNA and chromosomes in coding the instructions for characteristic traits passed from parents to offspring.

## VOCABULARY
**base pairing**

## READING TOOL

While you read the lesson, use the visuals in your 📖 **Biology Foundations Workbook** to help you understand the events that occurred as scientists discovered the structure of DNA.

To carry and express genetic information—such as the color of the blue morpho butterfly—DNA would have to be a very special molecule with a very special structure. And so it is. As we will see, learning the structure of DNA has been the key to understanding how genes work.

## The Components of DNA

DNA is an example of a nucleic acid, which is one of the four main categories of biological macromolecules. 🔑 *DNA is made of nucleotides joined into long strands or chains by covalent bonds.* Let's examine each of the components of DNA more closely.

**Nucleic Acids and Nucleotides**  Nucleic acids are long, slightly acidic molecules built from small monomers, or subunits called nucelotides. **Figure 13-5** shows an example of a nucleotide. Each DNA nucleotide is made up of three components: a 5-carbon sugar called deoxyribose, a phosphate group, and a nitrogenous base. Nucleotides join together to form strands of DNA, as shown in **Figure 13-6**.

## Figure 13-5

### Nucleotide

Nucleotides are the building blocks of nucleic acids. Each nucleotide consists of a sugar, a phosphate group, and a nitrogenous base. In RNA the sugar is ribose; in DNA the sugar is deoxyribose.

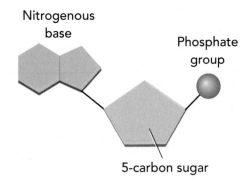

Nitrogenous base

Phosphate group

5-carbon sugar

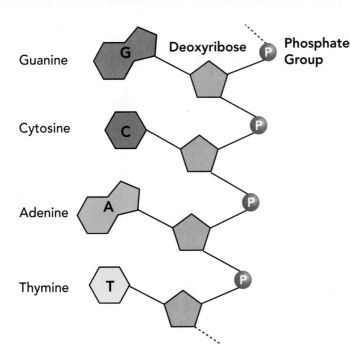

Guanine — G — Deoxyribose — P — **Phosphate Group**

Cytosine — C — P

Adenine — A — P

Thymine — T — P

**CASE STUDY**

Figure 13-6

## A Single Strand of DNA

This representation shows a portion of a single DNA strand. In this diagram, only four bases are shown. Actual DNA molecules consist of thousands or even millions of bases.

## Nitrogenous Bases

DNA uses four kinds of nitrogenous bases: adenine, guanine, cytosine, and thymine. Biologists often refer to the nucleotides in DNA by the first letters of the base names: A, G, C, and T. The nucleotides are joined by covalent bonds between the sugar of one nucleotide and the phosphate group of the next. The nucleotides can join together in any order, meaning that any sequence of bases is possible.

As you study **Figure 13-6**, do you see evidence to explain the remarkable properties of DNA? If not, don't be surprised. In the 1940s and early 1950s, the leading biologists in the world thought of DNA as little more than a string of nucleotides. They were baffled, too. The four different nucleotides, like the 26 letters of the alphabet, could be strung together in many different sequences, so it was possible they could carry coded genetic information. However, so could many other molecules, at least in principle. How could the structure of DNA allow it to carry complex information?

**READING TOOL**

As you read about each step in the discovery of the structure of DNA, relate it to the steps that came before it. Then try to predict the type of discovery that came next.

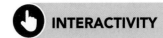 **INTERACTIVITY**

Explore the structure of a DNA molecule.

✓ **READING CHECK Interpret Diagrams** How are the nucleotides joined together to form the DNA chain? (*Hint:* Refer to **Figure 13-6.**)

## Analyzing Data

### Chargaff's Rule

Erwin Chargaff was interested in the work of Avery and did additional research on the structure of DNA. One set of results from his experiments is shown in the data table. Use the information to answer the questions.

| Percentages of Bases in Five Organisms | | | | |
|---|---|---|---|---|
| Source of DNA | A | T | G | C |
| *Streptococcus* | 29.8 | 31.6 | 20.5 | 18.0 |
| Yeast | 31.3 | 32.9 | 18.7 | 17.1 |
| Herring | 27.8 | 27.5 | 22.2 | 22.6 |
| Human | 30.9 | 29.4 | 19.9 | 19.8 |
| *E.coli* | 24.7 | 23.6 | 26.0 | 25.7 |

1. **Identify Patterns** What pattern do you identify in the data?

2. **Calculate** If a species has 35 percent adenine in its DNA, what is the percentage of the other three bases?

3. **Develop Models** All DNA is composed of the four bases shown in the table. How is the pattern in the data useful for developing a model of DNA?

**VIDEO**

Discover the contributions of various scientists in determining the structure of DNA.

# Solving the Structure of DNA

Knowing that DNA is made from long chains of nucleotides was only the beginning of understanding the structure of this molecule. The next step required an understanding of the way in which those chains are arranged in three dimensions.

**Chargaff's Rule** One of the puzzling facts about DNA was a curious relationship between its nucleotides. Years earlier, biochemist Erwin Chargaff had discovered that the percentages of the bases adenine [A] and thymine [T] are almost equal in any sample of DNA. The same relationship holds for the other two nucleotides, guanine [G] and cytosine [C]. The observation that [A] = [T] and [G] = [C] became known as "Chargaff's rule." Scientists showed that DNA samples from organisms as different as bacteria and humans obeyed this rule. However, neither Chargaff nor anyone else had the faintest idea why.

**Franklin's X-Rays** In the early 1950s, the British scientist Rosalind Franklin began to study DNA. Franklin used a technique called X-ray diffraction to study the structure of the DNA molecule. First, she stretched DNA fibers in a thin glass tube so that most of the strands were parallel. Next, she aimed a powerful X-ray beam at the concentrated DNA samples and recorded the scattering pattern of the X-rays on film. Franklin worked hard to obtain better and better patterns from DNA until the patterns became clear. In May 1952, she took an X-ray photograph known as photo 51, which is shown in **Figure 13-7**.

By itself, Franklin's X-ray pattern does not reveal every detail of the structure of DNA. However, it does provide some very important clues. The X-shaped pattern shows that the strands in DNA are twisted around each other like the coils of a spring. This shape is known as a <u>helix</u>. Also, the dark spots at the top and bottom show that the nitrogenous bases are stacked at regular intervals near the center of the molecule.

**Figure 13-7**

**Rosalind Franklin and Photo 51**

Franklin's X-ray diffraction photograph shows the pattern that indicated that the structure of DNA is helical.

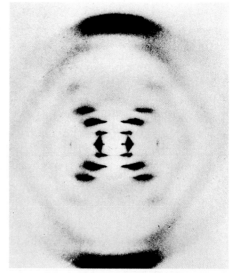

**The Work of Watson and Crick** While Franklin was continuing her research, American biologist James Watson and British physicist Francis Crick were also trying to understand the structure of DNA. They built three-dimensional models of the molecule that were made of cardboard and wire. They twisted and stretched the models in various ways, but their best efforts did nothing to explain DNA's properties.

Then, early in 1953, Watson was shown a copy of Franklin's remarkable X-ray pattern. The effect was immediate. In his book *The Double Helix*, Watson wrote: "The instant I saw the picture my mouth fell open and my pulse began to race." Photo 51 contained the clues they needed to construct a model of DNA.

🔍 *The data in Franklin's X-ray pattern enabled Watson and Crick to build a model that explained the specific structure and properties of DNA.* The pair published their results in a historic one-page paper in April 1953. Watson and Crick's breakthrough model of DNA was a double helix, shown in **Figure 13-8**, in which two strands of nucleotide sequences were wound around each other. The double helix explains many of DNA's most important properties.

✓ **READING CHECK** **Summarize** How was Rosalind Franklin's work important in the discovery of the structure of DNA?

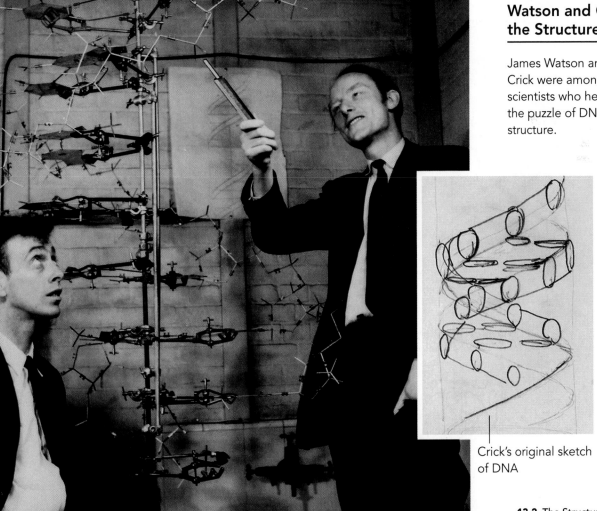

**Figure 13-8**

**Watson and Crick and the Structure of DNA**

James Watson and Francis Crick were among the many scientists who helped to solve the puzzle of DNA's molecular structure.

Crick's original sketch of DNA

## Figure 13-9

### Double Helix Structure of DNA

The structure of the DNA double helix resembles a twisted ladder. The sugar-phosphate backbones form the sides of the ladder and the nitrogenous bases form the rungs of the ladder.

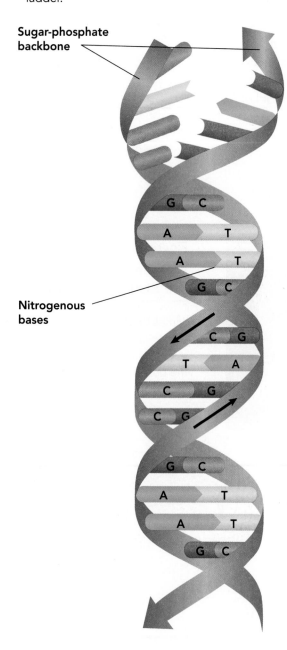

Sugar-phosphate backbone

Nitrogenous bases

# The Double-Helix Model

The DNA double helix looks a bit like a ladder with its two sides twisted around each other. Watson and Crick realized that the double helix accounted for Franklin's X-ray pattern. Further still, the shape explained many of the most important properties of DNA. ✎ *The double-helix model explains Chargaff's rule of base pairing and how the two strands of DNA are held together.* The double-helix model even hinted at how DNA can function as a carrier of genetic information. You can see the double helix structure in **Figure 13-9**.

**Antiparallel Strands** One of the most important aspects of the double-helix model is that its two strands of DNA run in opposite directions. Evidence for this had appeared in an earlier X-ray pattern of DNA, which Franklin had taken almost a year before photo 51. In the language of biochemistry, the two strands are said to be antiparallel. This arrangement enables the nitrogenous bases on both strands to come into contact near the center of the molecule. It also allows each strand of the double helix to carry a sequence of nucleotides, arranged almost like letters in a four-letter alphabet.

**Hydrogen Bonds** At first, Watson and Crick could not explain what forces held the two strands of DNA's double helix together. They then discovered that hydrogen bonds could form between certain nitrogenous bases, providing just enough force to hold the two strands together. As you may recall, hydrogen bonds are relatively weak chemical forces. However, the hydrogen bonds form only between certain base pairs: adenine with thymine and guanine with cytosine. This nearly perfect fit between A–T and G–C nucleotides is known as **base pairing**, and is illustrated in **Figure 13-10**.

Does it make sense that a molecule as important as DNA should be held together by weak bonds? Indeed, it does. If the two strands of the helix were held together by strong bonds, they might be impossible to separate. As we will see, the ability of the two strands to separate is critical to DNA's functions.

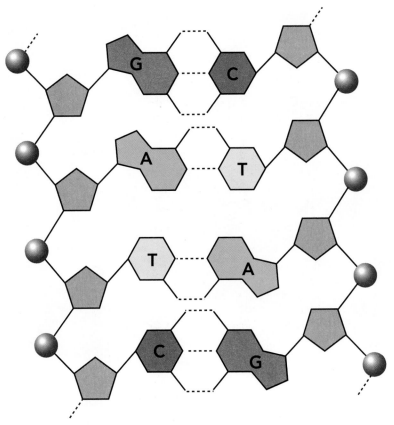

**Figure 13-10**

**Base Pairing**

The two strands of DNA are held together by hydrogen bonds between the nitrogenous bases adenine and thymine and between guanine and cytosine.

**Base Pairing** Watson and Crick realized that base pairing explained Chargaff's rule. It gave a reason why [A] = [T] and [G] = [C]. For every adenine in a double-stranded DNA molecule, there has to be exactly one thymine. For each cytosine, there is one guanine. The ability of their model to explain Chargaff's observations increased Watson and Crick's confidence that they had come to the right conclusion, with the help of Rosalind Franklin's extraordinary photo 51. In 1962 the Nobel Prize was awarded to James Watson, Francis Crick, and to Franklin's associate, Maurice Wilkins. Sadly, Franklin had died in 1958 and was not able to share the prize or fully appreciate the acclaim her work had earned.

Although the double-helix model explained many aspects of DNA structure, it still had limitations. It did not reveal how DNA carried information, nor did it explain how the cell could use this information. Answers to those questions would come later.

HS-LS1-1, HS-LS3-1

## ☑ LESSON 13.2 Review

### 🔍 KEY QUESTIONS

1. List the chemical components of DNA.

2. Describe the discoveries that led to the modeling of DNA.

3. What facts about DNA does the Watson-Crick model explain?

### CRITICAL THINKING

4. **Construct an Explanation** Why is it useful for the base pairs of DNA to be held together by hydrogen bonds and not covalent bonds?

5. **Reason Quantitatively** If a DNA sample contains 25 percent adenine (A), what percent of thymine, cytosine, and guanine must it contain? Use Chargaff's rule to construct your answer.

6. **Cite Evidence** How did Watson and Crick make a useful inference from Franklin's X-ray studies of DNA?

# DNA Replication

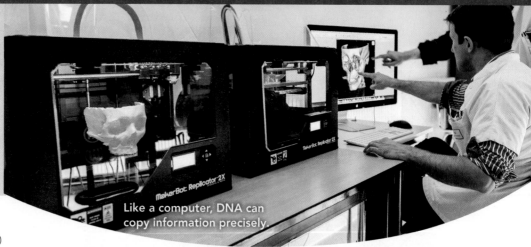
## 🔍 KEY QUESTIONS

- *What is the role of DNA polymerase in copying DNA?*
- *How does DNA replication differ in prokaryotic cells and eukaryotic cells?*

**HS-LS3-2:** Make and defend a claim based on evidence that inheritable genetic variations may result from: (1) new genetic combinations through meiosis, (2) viable errors occurring during replication, and/or (3) mutations caused by environmental factors.

## VOCABULARY

replication
DNA polymerase
telomere

## READING TOOL

As you read through this lesson, write the main ideas and supporting details in the chart in your ▄ **Biology Foundations Workbook.**

Before a cell divides, its DNA must first be copied. How might the double-helix structure of DNA make that possible? What might happen if one of the nucleotides were damaged or chemically altered just before the copying process? How might this affect the DNA inherited by each daughter cell after cell division?

## Copying the Code

When Watson and Crick discovered the structure of DNA, they immediately recognized one genuinely surprising aspect of the structure. Base pairing in the double helix explains how DNA can be copied, or replicated, because each base on one strand pairs with one—and only one—base on the opposite strand. Each strand of the double helix, therefore, has all the information needed to reconstruct the other half by the mechanism of base pairing. Because each strand can be used to make the other strand, the strands are said to be complementary.

**The Replication Process** Before a cell divides, it duplicates its DNA in a copying process called **replication** during the S phase of the cell cycle. During replication, the two strands of each DNA molecule separate. Two new complementary strands are then synthesized following the rules of base pairing. Each strand of the double helix of DNA serves as a template, or model, for the new strand. DNA replication is semiconservative, which means that each DNA molecule resulting from replication has one of the two original strands and one new strand.

Figure 13-11 shows details of DNA replication. During the S phase, the two strands of the double helix separate, allowing two replication forks to form. As each new strand is synthesized, new bases are added, following the rules of base pairing.

If the base on the original strand is adenine, then thymine is added to the newly forming strand. Likewise, guanine is always paired with cytosine. For example, a strand that has the base sequence TACGTT produces a strand with the complementary base sequence ATGCAA. The result is two DNA molecules identical to each other and to the original molecule.

**The Role of Enzymes** DNA replication is carried out during the S phase of the cell cycle by a series of enzymes. These enzymes first "unzip" a molecule of DNA by breaking the hydrogen bonds between base pairs and unwinding the two strands of the molecule. Each strand then serves as a template for the attachment of complementary bases. The principal enzyme involved in DNA replication is called **DNA polymerase** (PAHL ih mur ayz), so named because it acts to join nucleotides into the DNA polymer. 🔎 *DNA polymerase joins nucleotides to synthesize a new complementary strand of DNA.* Besides producing the sugar-phosphate bonds that join nucleotides, DNA polymerase also "proofreads" each new DNA strand, so that each molecule is a near-perfect copy of the original.

**INTERACTIVITY**

Investigate the process of DNA replication.

**BUILD VOCABULARY**

**Suffixes** The suffix *-ase* is used to name enzymes. *DNA polymerase* is the enzyme that helps add units to a DNA molecule.

**ANIMATION**

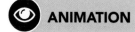

Figure 13-11

**DNA Replication**

During DNA replication, the DNA molecule produces two new complementary strands. Each strand of the double helix serves as a template for a new strand. The micrograph shows a pair of replication forks in human DNA.

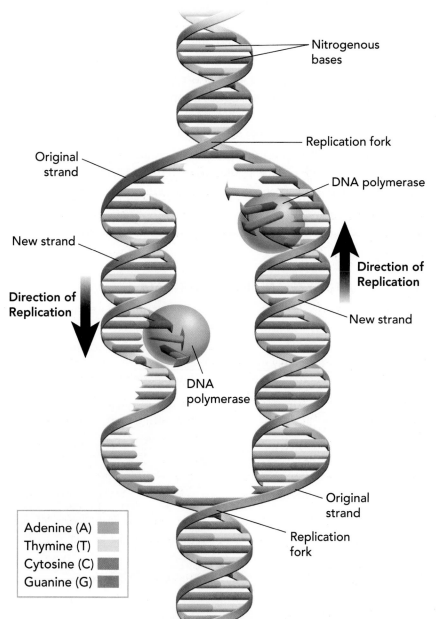

Nitrogenous bases

Replication fork

Original strand

DNA polymerase

New strand

Direction of Replication

Direction of Replication

New strand

DNA polymerase

Original strand

Replication fork

Adenine (A)
Thymine (T)
Cytosine (C)
Guanine (G)

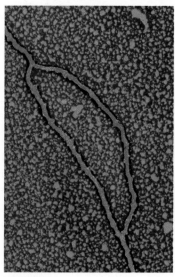

TEM 60,000×

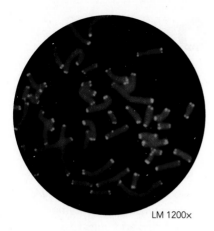

LM 1200×

**Figure 13-12**

**Telomeres**

The telomeres are the yellow (stained) parts of the red chromosomes.

 **INTERACTIVITY**

Virtually experience the technique of PCR as you replicate DNA strands.

**Telomeres** The tips of eukaryotic chromosomes are known as **telomeres**. An example of telomeres can be seen in **Figure 13-12**. Because the ends of a DNA molecule are difficult to replicate, cells use a special enzyme, called telomerase, to do the job. This enzyme adds short, repeated DNA sequences to telomeres as the chromosomes are replicated. In rapidly dividing cells, telomerase helps to prevent genes near the ends of chromosomes from being damaged or lost during replication. Telomerase is often switched off in adult cells. In cancer cells, however, the enzyme may be activated, enabling these cells to grow and proliferate rapidly.

☑ **READING CHECK** **Define** What is telomerase?

## Replication in Living Cells

DNA replication occurs during the S phase of the cell cycle. Like other events of the cell cycle, DNA replication is carefully regulated. For each daughter cell to receive a copy of DNA, replication must be completed before a cell enters mitosis or meiosis.

DNA differs somewhat between prokaryotes and eukaryotes. In most prokaryotes, the cells have a single, circular DNA molecule in the cytoplasm. It contains nearly all of the cell's genetic information. In contrast, eukaryotic cells may have up to 1000 times more DNA. Most of their DNA is found in the nucleus, where it is packaged into chromosomes. The chromosomes consist of DNA and histone proteins that are tightly packed together to form a substance called chromatin. Together, the DNA and histone molecules form beadlike structures called nucleosomes, as described in Chapter 11. Histones, you may recall, are proteins around which DNA is tightly coiled. **Figure 13-13** shows DNA replication in both prokaryotic cells and eukaryotic cells.

HS-LS3-2

---

**Quick Lab** 🧪 **Open-Ended Inquiry**

### Modeling DNA Replication

1. Cut out small squares of white and black paper to represent phosphate and deoxyribose groups. Label the white squares "phosphate" and the black squares "deoxyribose."

2. Then cut colored paper strips to represent the four nitrogenous bases. Match the colors used in **Figure 13-11**. Label each strip with its nucleotide name. Then tape together a set of five nucleotides.

3. Using your nucleotides, tape together a single strand of DNA. Exchange strands with a partner.

4. Model DNA replication by creating a strand that is complementary to your partner's original strand.

### ANALYZE AND INTERPRET DATA

1. **Use Models** The action of what enzyme was modeled by the taping together of the nucleotides?

2. **Evaluate Models** In what ways does this activity accurately model DNA replication? How could you improve the activity to better model the steps of DNA replication?

3. **Defend Your Claim** How can errors during DNA replication lead to genetic variations? Use your model to support your answer.

## Prokaryotic DNA Replication

In most prokaryotes, DNA replication begins when regulatory proteins bind to a single starting point on the chromosome. These proteins then trigger the beginning of the S phase, and DNA replication begins. ⚲ *Replication in most prokaryotic cells starts from a single point and proceeds in two directions until the entire chromosome is copied.* Often, the two chromosomes produced by replication are attached to different points inside the cell membrane and are separated when the cell splits to form two new cells.

## Eukaryotic DNA Replication

Compared to prokaryotes, eukaryotic chromosomes are generally much larger and more complex. ⚲ *In eukaryotic cells, replication may begin at dozens or hundreds of places on the DNA molecule. Then it proceeds in both directions until each chromosome is completely copied.* Several proteins check DNA for chemical damage or base pair mismatches prior to replication. However, the system is not perfect. Damaged regions of DNA are sometimes replicated, resulting in changes to DNA base sequences. The changes may alter genes, which can cause serious consequences.

The two copies of DNA remain closely associated until the cell enters prophase. At that point, the chromosomes condense, and the two chromatids in each chromosome become clearly visible. They separate from each other in anaphase of cell division, producing two cells, each with a complete set of genes coded in DNA.

## Figure 13-13
## Differences in DNA Replication

Replication in most prokaryotic cells begins at a single starting point and proceeds in two directions until the entire chromosome is copied. In eukaryotic cells, replication proceeds from multiple starting points on individual chromosomes and ends when all the chromosomes are copied.

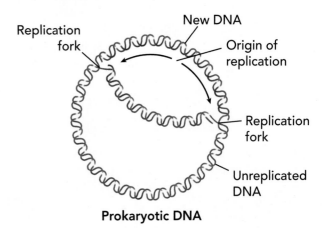

**Prokaryotic DNA**

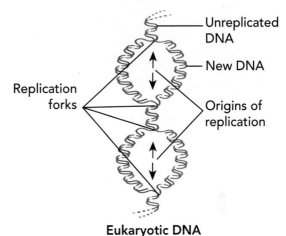

**Eukaryotic DNA**

HS-LS3-2

# ☑ LESSON 13.3 Review

### ⚲ KEY QUESTIONS

1. What is the role of DNA polymerase in the process of DNA replication?

2. How does DNA replication compare between prokaryotes and eukaryotes?

### CRITICAL THINKING

3. Form a Hypothesis  A scientist uses radioactive nitrogen to label the nitrogenous bases of the DNA of a cell. Then the DNA is allowed to replicate, and the new strands take up nonradioactive bases. Do one, both, or neither of the daughter cells have radioactive DNA? Explain.

4. Construct an Explanation  A replication fork moves about 50 times faster in prokaryotic DNA than in eukaryotic DNA. Use the structure of DNA in prokaryotes and eukaryotes to explain this difference.

5. Evaluate Models  A twisted zipper is used as a model of eukaryotic DNA. How could the model be developed to represent DNA replication in eukaryotes? Describe the limitations of merely zipping and unzipping the zipper.

# Living things don't carry ID cards... or do they?

Experts use body shape and markings to identify fish species, such as the Atlantic cod shown here. With DNA barcoding, scientists now can identify a species from only a sample of cells.

HS-ETS1-1, HS-LS3-1, CCSS.ELA-LITERACY.WHST.9-10.8

## Make Your Case

New technology allows DNA samples to be sequenced and identified very quickly and inexpensively. In closely related species, some DNA sequences are nearly identical. However, every species has short, unique DNA sequences that act like ID cards, or DNA barcodes. Specimens of fishes—or ferns, or sea turtles—can be classified into the correct species according to these DNA sequences.

## Communicating Information

1. **Conduct Research** Apart from the examples presented in this case study, what other problems do you think DNA barcoding could help solve? Conduct additional research about the technology and its potential uses.

2. **Develop Possible Solutions** Describe how DNA barcoding might be useful for addressing the problem you identified.

# Technology on the Case

## Cracking the Barcode

Supermarket barcodes are labels that identify a specific food product, like a can of peas or a box of cereal. Similarly, DNA barcodes are regions of DNA that are unique to each species, making them useful for classification.

The Barcode Initiative is an international scientific effort to identify and catalog DNA barcodes for as many species as possible. Below are the steps that the scientists are following to add a new species. Once the steps are completed, the DNA barcode can be used to identify any member of the species.

1. **Find a Known Specimen** For hundreds of years, scientists have been identifying huge numbers of plant and animal specimens. Many accurately identified specimens are kept at museums, zoos, aquariums, and botanical gardens.

2. **Sequence the DNA** Today, the entire genome of an organism can be sequenced in a matter of days. Only a small sample of cells is necessary.

3. **Store and Analyze** The sequenced genome is stored in an online database that is available to both scientists and the general public. Through rigorous analysis, a unique DNA barcode within the genome can be identified.

Like many examples of technology, DNA barcoding developed very rapidly. Canadian scientist Paul Hebert proposed the idea in 2003. Now, the technology is helping answer classification questions in both scientific research and everyday life.

# Careers on the Case

## Work Toward a Solution

DNA barcoding is being used to identify species of fishes and other organisms to prevent them from being sold or labeled incorrectly.

### Food Safety Inspector

Food safety inspectors work to make sure food is safe to eat. They work in food-processing plants, supermarkets, restaurants, and wherever else foods are produced or sold.

▶ **VIDEO**

Watch this video to learn more about careers in biology.

# Lesson Review

Go to your Biology Foundations Workbook for longer versions of these lesson summaries.

## 13.1 Identifying the Substance of the Gene

By observing bacterial transformation, Avery and other scientists discovered that the nucleic acid DNA stores and transmits genetic information from one generation of bacteria to the next.

Hershey and Chase's experiment with bacteriophages confirmed Avery's results, convincing many scientists that DNA was the genetic material found in genes—not just in viruses and bacteria, but in all living cells.

The DNA that makes up genes must be capable of storing, copying, and transmitting the genetic information in a cell.

- transformation
- bacteriophage

Bacteriophage with phosphorus-32 in DNA

Bacteriophage with sulfur-35 in protein coat

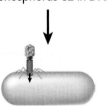

Phage infects bacterium

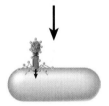

Phage infects bacterium

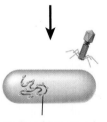

Radioactivity inside bacterium

No radioactivity inside bacterium

**☑ Interpret Diagrams** How did the experiment described here use radioactive isotopes to distinguish proteins from DNA?

## 13.2 The Structure of DNA

DNA is a nucleic acid made up of nucleotides joined into long strands or chains by covalent bonds.

The clues in Franklin's X-ray pattern enabled Watson and Crick to build a model that explained the specific structure and properties of DNA.

The double-helix model explains Chargaff's rule of base pairing and the way the two strands of DNA are held together.

- base pairing

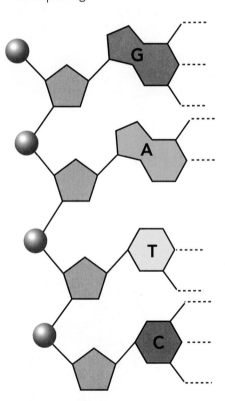

**☑ Use Models** Based on base pairing rules, which bases would you add to the right side of the drawing?

## 13.3 DNA Replication

Before a cell divides, it duplicates its DNA in a copying process called replication. During replication, the two strands of each DNA molecule separate. Two new complementary strands are then synthesized following the rules of base pairing. DNA polymerase is an enzyme that joins individual nucleotides to produce a new strand of DNA.

Telomerase is a special enzyme that replicates the telomeres, the ends of the chromosomes, in eukaryotic cells. Telomerase is often switched off in adult cells. It may be activated in cancer cells, which enables the cells to grow and proliferate rapidly.

Replication in most prokaryotic cells starts from a single point and proceeds in two directions until the entire chromosome is copied. In eukaryotic cells, replication may begin at dozens or even hundreds of places on the DNA molecule, proceeding in both directions until each chromosome is completely copied.

• replication
• DNA polymerase
• telomere

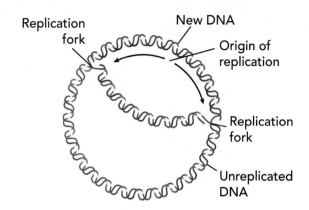

☑ **Interpret Diagrams** Is the diagram showing DNA replication in prokaryotes or eukaryotes? How do you know?

..................................................

# Organize Information

Cite evidence from the text for each statement. Then draw a model to support each statement.

| Statement | Evidence | Model |
|---|---|---|
| A bacteriophage transfers genes, not proteins, from one bacterium to another. | The Hershey-Chase experiment | 1. |
| The structure of DNA can be modeled by a double helix. | 2. | 3. |
| Nitrogenous bases pair with one another. | Chargaff's rule | 4. |
| DNA "unzips" during replication. | 5. | 6. |

# An Eight-Hour Task: How Does DNA Replicate So Quickly?

## Reason Quantitatively

HS-LS3-1, CCSS.ELA-LITERACY.WHST.9-10.8,
CCSS.MATH.CONTENT.HSN.Q.A.1

**STEM** How long does it take you to copy the letter *C* onto a piece of paper? The time is so short that you might struggle to measure it properly. However, what if you had to copy several million letter *C*'s, as well as an equal number of *A*'s, *G*'s, and *T*'s? You might spend days at this task or be forced to quit when you run out of ink or pencil lead—or patience. Nevertheless, cells complete tasks such as this one whenever they replicate DNA.

On even one chromosome of a simple eukaryotic organism, the complete DNA molecule contains many million base pairs. A single replication fork could move through the molecule and duplicate it, but not within a reasonable amount of time.

The solution is to use many replication forks. As replication begins, pairs of replication forks appear at multiple locations along the DNA molecule. The two forks in each pair move in opposite directions, forming a "replication bubble" that expands over time. Eventually, the adjacent bubbles meet, and the replication is completed.

Of course, errors in the replication process can and do occur. The cell uses enzymes and the original DNA to identify and repair incorrect base sequences. After this "proofreading" step, the number of incorrect base pairs in the DNA copy is about 1 in every 100 million—a very low error rate.

Why is it important for DNA replication to be so accurate? In a multicellular organism, the DNA in billions or even trillions of adult cells has been produced by repeated rounds of DNA replication starting with the single cell from which that organism developed. Any errors made in one round of DNA replication will be passed along to the next. Therefore, it's important to get it right every time. Accuracy matters.

In this assessment, you will compare the speed of a replication fork with your rate of completing a copying task. Then you will develop a model of DNA replication that shows replication forks and the speed at which they move.

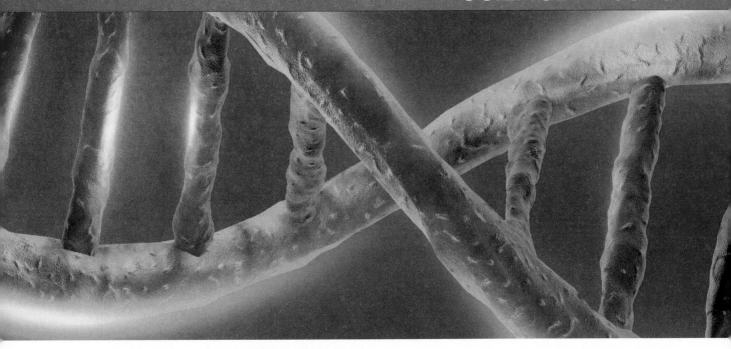

1. **Collect Data** Have a partner act as timekeeper. Measure and record the time, in seconds, that it takes you to copy the 50 letters shown in the boxes. Then divide by 60 to convert seconds into minutes.

| |
|---|
| CAGTTGACCC |
| GATCCAAAGC |
| TTACGAACTA |
| TGACAGATCG |
| ACGACGGACT |

2. **Interpret Data** Review the letters you wrote in question 1. How many errors did you make in copying them? Compare your errors with the error rate of the cell.

3. **Calculate** Divide 50 letters by the writing time to calculate your copying rate.

4. **Compare** How does your copying rate compare with the rate of a replication fork in DNA?

| Replication Speed of Human Chromosome 1 | |
|---|---|
| Chromosome length | 250,000,000 base pairs |
| Speed of a replication fork | 2000 base pairs per minute |
| Replication time | 8 hours (480 minutes) |

5. **Reason Quantitatively** You and a group of friends are asked to copy a written model of human chromosome 1 in 8 hours. How many group members are needed to complete this task? Assume that everyone copies the letters at the rate you recorded in step 3.

6. **Compare** How many replication forks does the cell need to copy chromosome 1? Compare this number with your answer to question 5.

7. **Communicate** Prepare a model of DNA replication in the form of a poster or another visual display. Include a diagram that shows pairs of replication forks in a DNA molecule. Also include the calculations you performed to determine your answers.

## 🔑 KEY QUESTIONS

### 13.1 Identifying the Substance of the Gene

HS-LS1-1, HS-LS3-1

1. The process by which one type of bacteria is changed into another type is called
   a. transcription.
   b. transformation.
   c. duplication.
   d. replication.

2. Bacteriophages are
   a. a form of bacteria.
   b. enzymes.
   c. coils of DNA.
   d. viruses.

3. Which of the following researchers used radioactive markers in experiments to show that DNA was the genetic material in cells?
   a. Frederick Griffith
   b. Oswald Avery
   c. Alfred Hershey and Martha Chase
   d. James Watson and Francis Crick

4. Before DNA could definitively be shown to be the genetic material in cells, scientists had to show that it could
   a. tolerate high temperatures.
   b. carry and make copies of information.
   c. be modified in response to environmental conditions.
   d. be broken down into small subunits.

5. Briefly describe the conclusion that could be drawn from the experiments of Frederick Griffith.

6. What evidence allowed Hershey and Chase to show that DNA alone carried the genetic information of a bacteriophage?

### 13.2 The Structure of DNA

HS-LS1-1, HS-LS3-1

7. A nucleotide does NOT contain
   a. a 5-carbon sugar.
   b. an amino acid.
   c. a nitrogen base.
   d. a phosphate group.

8. According to Chargaff's rule of base pairing, which of the following is true about DNA?
   a. [A] = [T], and [C] = [G]
   b. [A] = [C], and [T] = [G]
   c. [A] = [G], and [T] = [C]
   d. [A] = [T] = [C] = [G]

9. The bonds that hold the two strands of DNA together come from
   a. the attraction of phosphate groups for each other.
   b. strong bonds between nitrogenous bases and deoxyribose.
   c. weak hydrogen bonds between the nitrogenous bases.
   d. carbon-to-carbon bonds in the sugar portion of the nucleotides.

10. Describe the components and structure of a DNA nucleotide.

11. Explain how Chargaff's rule of base pairing helped Watson and Crick model DNA.

12. Why is it significant that the two strands of DNA are antiparallel?

13. Rosalind Franklin's X-ray diffraction photograph of DNA is shown below. What did the X-shaped pattern in the center reveal about the structure of DNA?

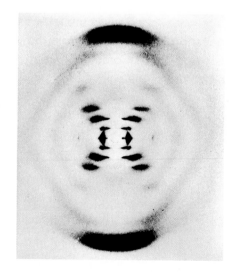

## 13.3 DNA Replication

HS-LS3-2

14. In prokaryotes, DNA molecules are located in the
    a. nucleus.
    b. ribosomes.
    c. cytoplasm.
    d. histones.

15. In eukaryotes, nearly all the DNA is found in the
    a. nucleus.
    b. ribosomes.
    c. cytoplasm.
    d. histones.

16. The main enzyme involved in linking individual nucleotides into DNA molecules is
    a. DNA protease.
    b. ribose.
    c. carbohydrase.
    d. DNA polymerase.

17. What is meant by the term *base pairing*? How is base pairing involved in DNA replication?

18. Describe the appearance of DNA in a typical prokaryotic cell.

19. Explain the process of replication. When a DNA molecule is replicated, how do the new molecules compare with the original molecule?

## CRITICAL THINKING

HS-LS1-1, HS-LS3-2

20. **Draw Conclusions** Look back at Griffith's experiment shown in **Figure 13-1**. What conclusion did Griffith draw when he saw the results of combining heat-killed S type with live R-type bacteria?

21. **Identify Variables** Avery and his team identified DNA as the molecule responsible for the transformation seen in Griffith's experiment. Identify the variables in their experiment. Cite textual evidence of how they controlled variables to make sure that only DNA caused the effect.

22. **Use Models** How did Watson and Crick's model of the DNA molecule explain base pairing?

23. **Use Models** Rosalind Franklin's X-ray pattern showed that the distance between the two strands of a DNA molecule is the same throughout the length of the molecule. How did that information help Watson and Crick determine how bases are paired?

24. **Evaluate Models** Is photocopying a document similar to DNA replication? Think of the original materials, the copying process, and the final products. Explain how the two processes are alike. Identify major differences.

25. **Evaluate Reasoning** During what phase of a cell's life cycle is DNA replicated? Why must this happen before a cell can enter mitosis?

26. **Infer** In their original paper describing the structure of DNA, Watson and Crick noted in a famous sentence that the structure they were proposing immediately suggested how DNA could make a copy of itself. Explain what Watson and Crick meant when they said this.

27. **Form a Hypothesis** There is a direct correlation between exposure to ultraviolet light and an increase in DNA replication errors. What might be some observable consequences of exposure to ultraviolet light in humans? Form a hypothesis that you can use to test the relationship between exposure to ultraviolet light and its effect on humans.

28. **Ask Questions** Clues in Rosalind Franklin's X-ray diffraction photograph of a strand of DNA led Watson and Crick to complete their model of the DNA molecule. Take a look at photo 51 on in question 13. Describe what you observe in the photograph. What questions would you ask to help analyze the image and understand how your observations relate to a DNA molecule?

The chart compares different types of gene maps. Refer to the chart to answer questions 29 and 30.

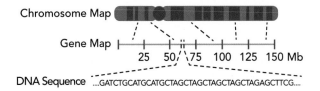

29. **Evaluate Information** In Chapter 12, you learned that gene maps show the relative locations of different genes on a chromosome. What additional information does the DNA sequence provide that is missing from the gene map?

30. **Evaluate Models** A chromosome map shows the unique banding pattern of a chromosome when stained. Like a fingerprint, the pattern and thickness of alternating light and dark bands can be used to identify specific chromosomes. How does the information provided by the DNA sequence relate to the chromosome map?

## CROSSCUTTING CONCEPTS

**31. Structure and Function** Explain how the structure of DNA causes it to be capable of storing, copying, and transmitting genetic information.

**32. Cause and Effect** As you read in Chapter 11, apoptosis is a process of programmed cell death. The shortening of telomeres has been associated with cell death and the aging process. Conduct research to find more information about the role of telomeres during DNA replication. Based on what you have read in the text and your additional research, explain the evidence that supports the idea that telomeres play a role in aging. Be sure to cite your sources.

## MATH CONNECTIONS

## Analyze and Interpret Data

CCSS.MATH.CONTENT.MP2, CCSS.MATH.CONTENT.HSN.Q.A.2

The following table shows the results of measuring the percentages of four bases in the DNA of several different organisms. Some of the values are missing from the table. Use the data table to answer questions 33–35.

| Nitrogenous Bases (%) | | | | |
|---|---|---|---|---|
| Organism | A | G | T | C |
| Human | | 19.9 | 29.4 | |
| Chicken | 28.8 | | | 12.5 |
| Bacterium (*S. lutea*) | 13.4 | | | |

**33. Interpret Tables** Based on Chargaff's rule, what is the expected percentage of adenine bases in human DNA?

**34. Reason Quantitatively** Calculate the value for the percentage of guanine bases in the bacterium.

**35. Predict** Two DNA strands of the chicken were separated. The base composition of just one of those strands was determined. Which of the following could you expect, based on the analysis of the single strand of DNA?
A. The amount of A will equal the amount of T.
B. The amount of C will equal the amount of G.
C. The strand will contain equal amounts of A, T, C, and G.
D. The four nitrogenous bases may have any value.

## LANGUAGE ARTS CONNECTION

## Write About Science

HS-LS3-1, CCSS.ELA-LITERACY.WHST.9-10.2

**36. Write Explanatory Text** Recall that Gregor Mendel concluded that factors, which we now call genes, determine the traits that pass from one generation to the next. Imagine that you could send a letter backward in time to Mendel. Write a letter to him in which you explain what a gene consists of in molecular terms.

**37. Write Procedures** Write out the steps of the Hershey-Chase experiment as a numbered list.

## Read About Science

CCSS.ELA-LITERACY.RST.9-10.1

**38. Cite Textual Evidence** Look for evidence in the text to support the descriptions of the similarities and differences between prokaryotic and eukaryotic DNA replication.

**39. Evaluate Media** Perform an online search to find a three-dimensional, animated representation of the Watson and Crick double-helix model of a DNA molecule. Look for animations that show the DNA molecule from different angles as well as undergoing separation and replication. Review the written description of the structure of DNA in the chapter. What information did you read in the text about the structure of DNA to help you understand what you saw in the animation? What did you learn about the structure of DNA from viewing the animated model?

# END-OF-COURSE TEST PRACTICE

1. In 1928 Frederick Griffith did a series of experiments that included injecting mice with different types of bacteria. The table below summarizes the results of his experiments.

| Griffith's Experiments | | | | |
|---|---|---|---|---|
| Injected Bacteria | Disease-causing bacteria | Harmless bacteria | Heat-killed, disease-causing bacteria | Heat-killed, disease-causing bacteria and harmless bacteria |
| Result | Mouse dies of pneumonia | Mouse lives | Mouse lives | Mouse dies of pneumonia |

What question was Griffith trying to answer with his experiments?

A. How do bacteria live in mice?

B. Why does heat cause bacteria to die?

C. What made the mice injected with disease-causing bacteria die?

D. What type of mice can survive when injected with bacteria?

E. How long do mice injected with bacteria live?

2. Which of the following events may result in altered genes during eukaryotic DNA replication?

A. Hydrogen bonds between base pairs are broken

B. The enzyme telomerase is switched off

C. Duplicated chromosomes crossing-over

D. Replication proceeds in two directions

E. Replication begins in multiple places on a chromosome

3. The illustration below represents a section of a DNA molecule.

What characteristic of the structure of DNA allows DNA to carry coded genetic information?

A. The sequence of nitrogenous bases

B. The sequence of 5-carbon sugars

C. The quantity of phosphate groups

D. The quantity of each type of nitrogenous base

E. The pattern of 5-carbon sugars and phosphate groups

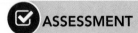 ASSESSMENT

For additional assessment practice, go online to access your digital course.

| If You Have Trouble With... | | | |
|---|---|---|---|
| **Question** | 1 | 2 | 3 |
| **See Lesson** | 13.1 | 13.3 | 13.2 |
| **Performance Expectation** | HS-LS3-1 | HS-LS3-2 | HS-LS1-1 |

CHAPTER 14

# RNA and Protein Synthesis



Go Online to access your digital course.

- VIDEO
- AUDIO
- INTERACTIVITY
- eTEXT
- ANIMATION
- VIRTUAL LAB
- ASSESSMENT

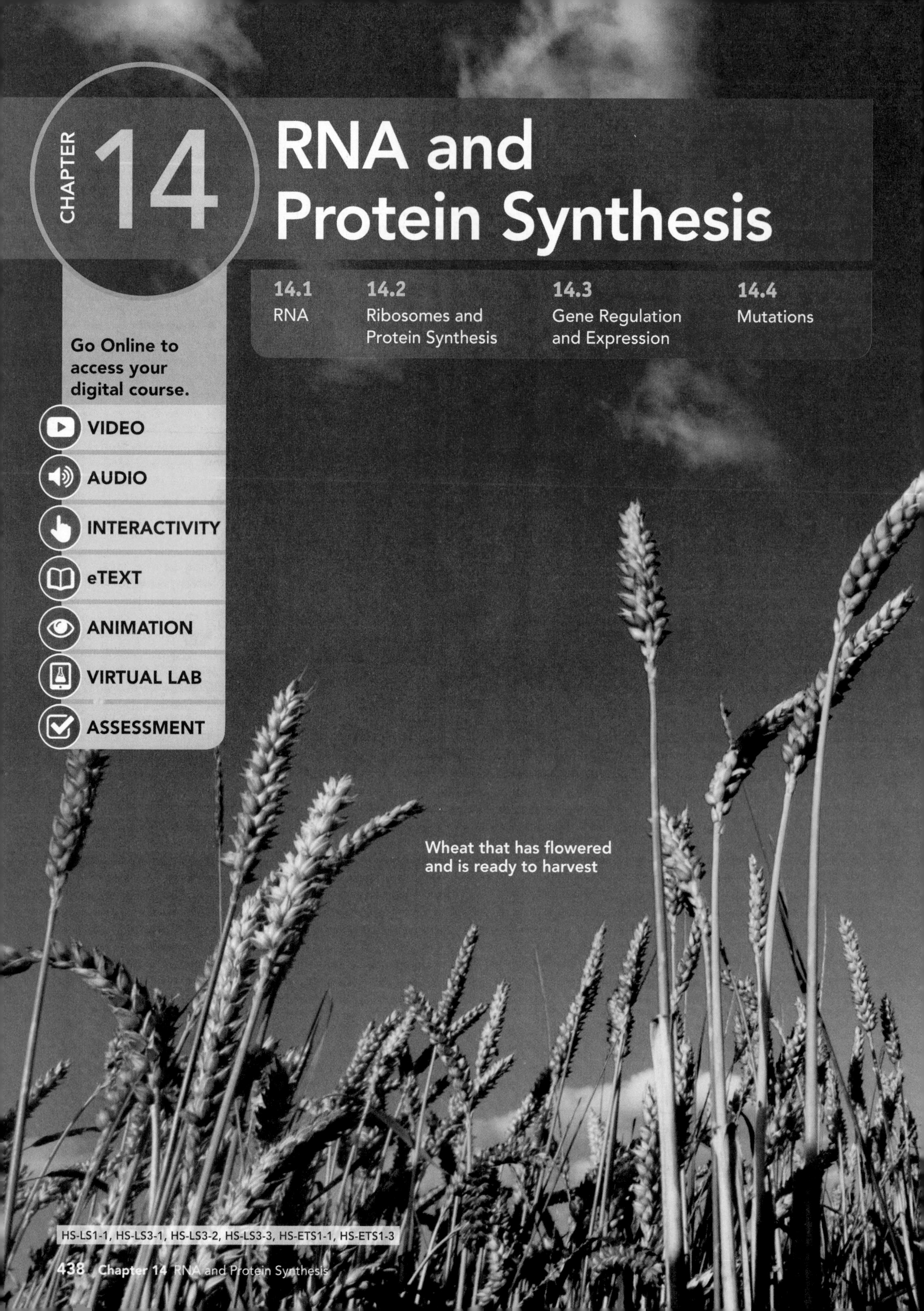

Wheat that has flowered and is ready to harvest

HS-LS1-1, HS-LS3-1, HS-LS3-2, HS-LS3-3, HS-ETS1-1, HS-ETS1-3

# How does a plant remember winter?

Winters on the prairies of the northern Great Plains can be long, cold, and brutal. When spring does come, the growing season is shorter than it is farther south, and that presents special challenges to farmers in states like North Dakota and South Dakota. They need crops that will sprout early in the spring, grow quickly, and produce a high yield.

One of the most important crops in these states is wheat. Wheat serves as a source of grain for flour to make bread, pasta, and other foods. For American farmers, wheat is a major cash crop, and is widely exported throughout the world. However, for many farmers in the northern Great Plains, the planting time for wheat is not in the spring, as you might expect.

Rather, many farmers plant a variety of wheat called "winter wheat" in September or early October. These plants sprout before the first frost and then lay dormant all winter, enduring snowstorms and extreme low temperatures. In springtime, the plants grow quickly to maturity, flower (That's right, wheat plants produce flowers!), and produce excellent yields of grain.

There are many advantages to winter wheat. One advantage is high productivity. Another advantage is the ability to evade insect pests, since the planting is done in the fall when many such pests have disappeared for the winter.

The varieties developed for winter wheat have a very interesting property. Unless they endure an extended, very cold winter, they will not produce flowers in the spring and therefore will not produce grain. In a sense, the plants are able to "remember" winter, and will not go to flower until they have passed through it. If these varieties of winter wheat are planted in year-round warm climates, they do not flower and produce grain.

How do they do this? Plants like winter wheat hold back on activating the genes needed for flowering until they have lived through a cold season. As we will see, this involves the control of gene expression by a mechanism known as epigenetics. Plants, unlike animals, don't have nervous systems, and they certainly don't "remember" seasons in the way that you or I might. So, how can a plant know that winter has passed and adjust the expression of its genes to produce flowers in the spring?

**Throughout this chapter, look for connections to the** CASE STUDY **to help you answer this question.**

# RNA

**HS-LS1-1:** Construct an explanation based on evidence for how the structure of DNA determines the structure of proteins which carry out the essential functions of life through systems of specialized cells.

**HS-LS3-1:** Ask questions to clarify relationships about the role of DNA and chromosomes in coding the instructions for characteristic traits passed from parents to offspring.

### VOCABULARY

**RNA**
**messenger RNA**
**ribosomal RNA**
**transfer RNA**
**transcription**
**RNA polymerase**
**promoter**
**intron**
**exon**

### READING TOOL

As you read, identify the similarities and differences between RNA and DNA. Complete the Venn diagram in your 📘 **Biology Foundations Workbook.**

Once it was clear that DNA was the genetic material, biologists realized that it must contain a code that living cells can read, understand, and express. But what sort of code? DNA is made of just four nucleotides joined together in double-stranded molecules that may be millions of bases in length. What exactly do those bases code for, and how does the cell "read" that code? That's where RNA comes in.

## The Role of RNA

When Watson and Crick solved the double-helix structure of DNA, they realized that the structure itself did not explain how a gene works. Eventually, scientists learned that another nucleic acid, ribonucleic acid, or RNA, helped to put the genetic code into action. **RNA**, like DNA, is a nucleic acid that consists of a long chain of nucleotides.

In a general way, genes contain coded DNA instructions that tell cells how to build proteins. The first step in decoding these genetic instructions is to copy part of the base sequence from DNA into RNA. RNA then uses these instructions to direct the production of proteins, which help to determine an organism's characteristics.

**Comparing RNA and DNA** Like DNA, RNA is made up of nucleotides. Each nucleotide consists of a 5-carbon sugar, a phosphate group, and a nitrogenous base. However, DNA and RNA differ in three important ways. 🔍 *Unlike DNA, RNA uses the sugar ribose instead of deoxyribose, RNA generally is single stranded, and RNA contains uracil in place of thymine.* These chemical differences make it easy for enzymes in the cell to tell DNA and RNA apart. The structures of DNA and RNA are shown in **Figure 14-1.**

## Figure 14-1

## Comparing RNA and DNA

Although the two molecules are similar, the differences between DNA and RNA allow them to perform separate functions in the cell. The information in DNA is always around, stored in the nucleus. In contrast, RNA is synthesized when the products of a particular gene are needed.

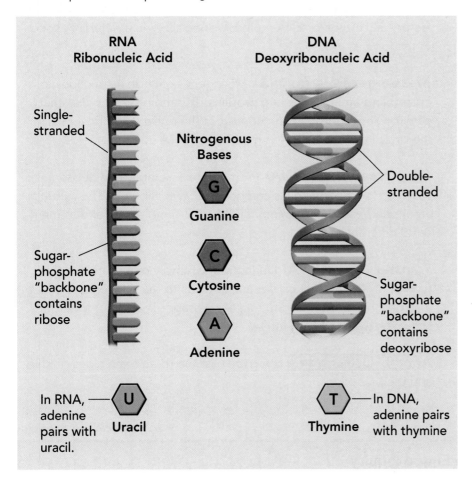

You can compare the different roles played by DNA and RNA to the two types of plans used by builders. DNA is a bit like an architect's master plan. It has all the information needed to construct a building. But builders never bring the valuable master plan to the job site, where it might be damaged or lost. Instead, they work from blueprints, which are inexpensive, disposable copies of the master plan.

In the cell, the DNA "master plan" remains safe in the cell's nucleus, where it serves as a template to make multiple RNA copies. Then those RNA "blueprints" travel to the ribosomes, which then put the coded instructions into action by assembling proteins in the cytoplasm.

 **INTERACTIVITY**

Compare the structures of RNA and DNA and learn how RNA is used to create proteins.

**READING CHECK** **Summarize** What is the role of RNA in the production of proteins?

**Three Main Types of RNA** You can think of an RNA molecule as a working copy of a gene, which is a functional segment of DNA. RNA has many roles, but for now, we will focus on just one role, which is protein synthesis. RNA controls the assembly of amino acids into proteins.

There are three main types of RNA involved in protein synthesis: messenger RNA, ribosomal RNA, and transfer RNA. Like workers in a factory, each type of RNA molecule specializes in a different aspect of the job.

**Messenger RNA (mRNA)** Most genes encode instructions for assembling amino acids into proteins. The molecules of RNA that carry copies of these instructions from the nucleus to ribosomes in the cytoplasm are known as **messenger RNA** (mRNA).

**Ribosomal RNA (rRNA)** Proteins are assembled on ribosomes, which are small organelles composed of two subunits. The subunits are made of several **ribosomal RNA** (rRNA) molecules and as many as 80 different proteins.

**Transfer RNA (tRNA)** During the assembly of a protein, a third type of RNA molecule carries amino acids to the ribosome and matches them to the coded mRNA message. These molecules are known as **transfer RNA** (tRNA).

**✓ READING CHECK** **Describe** List the three main types of RNA and their functions.

**▶ VIDEO**

Explore the phenomenon of reverse transcription using viruses and learn how AZT can be used to interfere with this process in HIV.

HS-LS1-1

---

**Quick Lab** 🧪 **Open-Ended Inquiry**

## How Can You Model DNA and RNA?

1. Work with a partner or in a group to plan models of DNA and RNA. Plan to use available materials, such as beads, toothpicks, or modeling clay. You could also choose to draw a diagram or make a computer model.

2. Have your teacher review your plan before you proceed.

3. Carry out your plan. Begin by making the model of DNA. Then use one of the DNA strands as a template to make the model of RNA.

### ANALYZE AND CONCLUDE

1. **Evaluate Models** How well do the models represent DNA and RNA? What are the limitations of the models?

2. **Use Models** How does DNA act to specify a molecule of RNA? Use your model to help demonstrate this process.

3. **Synthesize Information** Construct a graphic organizer to compare and contrast the chemical structure, properties, and functions of DNA and RNA.

# RNA Synthesis

A single DNA molecule may contain hundreds or even thousands of genes. However, only those genes being expressed are copied into RNA at any given time.

**Transcription** The process of copying a base sequence from DNA to RNA is known as **transcription**. Transcription is similar to DNA replication, but the product is an RNA molecule instead of a duplicate of DNA. 🔍 *In transcription, segments of DNA serve as templates to produce complementary RNA molecules.* As shown in **Figure 14-2**, transcription is carried out by an enzyme called **RNA polymerase**. RNA polymerase first binds to DNA and separates the DNA strands. It then uses one strand of DNA as a template to assemble nucleotides into a complementary strand of RNA. The ability to quickly copy a DNA sequence into RNA makes it possible for a single gene to produce hundreds, or even thousands, of RNA molecules.

**Promoters** How does RNA polymerase know where to start and stop making a strand of RNA? The answer is that RNA polymerase does not bind to DNA just anywhere. The enzyme binds only to **promoters**, which are regions of DNA with specific base sequences that can bind to RNA polymerase. Other regions of DNA cause transcription to stop when an RNA molecule is completed.

**READING TOOL**

After you read this section, write down the steps of RNA synthesis in the order in which they occur. Re-read the section and check your work.

**INTERACTIVITY**

**Figure 14-2**

**Transcription**

Transcription begins when RNA polymerase binds to a promoter. RNA polymerase then uses one strand of DNA as a template to assemble complementary nucleotides in a strand of RNA.

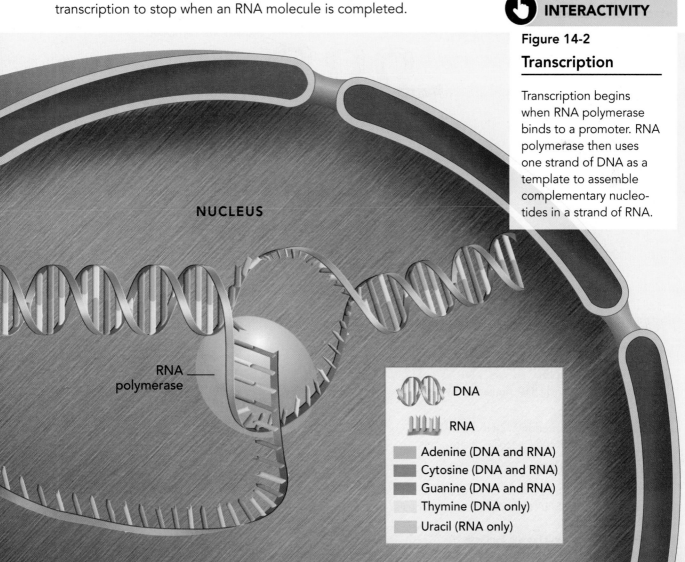

NUCLEUS

RNA polymerase

DNA

RNA

Adenine (DNA and RNA)
Cytosine (DNA and RNA)
Guanine (DNA and RNA)
Thymine (DNA only)
Uracil (RNA only)

**RNA Editing** Like a writer's first draft, new RNA molecules sometimes require a bit of editing before they are ready to be read. These pre-mRNA molecules have bits and pieces cut out of them before they can go into action. The portions that are cut out and discarded are called **introns**. In eukaryotes, introns are taken out of newly synthesized pre-mRNA molecules while they are still in the nucleus. The remaining pieces, known as **exons**, are then spliced back together to form the final mRNA, as shown in **Figure 14-3**.

What is the purpose of making a large RNA molecule and then throwing parts of that molecule away? That's a good question, and biologists still don't have a complete answer. Some pre-mRNA molecules are cut and spliced in different ways in different tissues. Because of this, a single gene can actually produce several different mRNA molecules. Introns and exons may also play a role in evolution, making it possible for very small changes in DNA sequences to have dramatic effects on how genes affect cellular function.

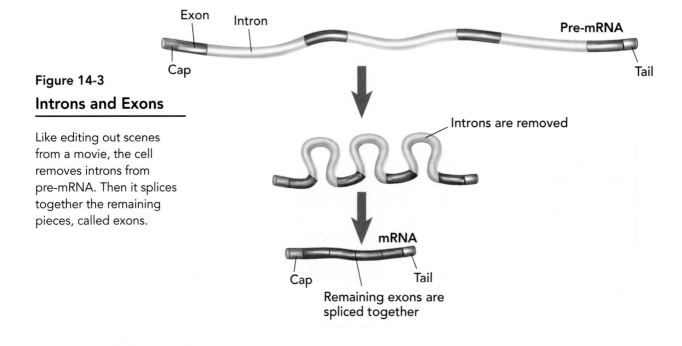

**Figure 14-3**

**Introns and Exons**

Like editing out scenes from a movie, the cell removes introns from pre-mRNA. Then it splices together the remaining pieces, called exons.

HS-LS1-1, HS-LS3-1

## ✓ LESSON 14.1 Review

### 🔍 KEY QUESTIONS

1. How are RNA and DNA similar? How do they differ?

2. How is the information in DNA passed to a molecule of mRNA? Describe this process.

### CRITICAL THINKING

3. **Construct an Explanation** How does the cell use both DNA and RNA to direct protein synthesis?

4. **Infer** Why are regions called promoters essential to RNA transcription?

5. **Infer** Why is it important for a single gene to be able to produce hundreds or thousands of the same RNA molecules?

6. **CASE STUDY** From what you have learned so far about DNA and RNA, what can you conclude about the role of RNA in the flowering of winter wheat? What questions do you still have?

# Ribosomes and Protein Synthesis

**KEY QUESTIONS**
- *How does the genetic code work?*
- *What role does the ribosome play in assembling proteins?*
- *How does molecular biology relate to genetics?*

**HS-LS1-1:** Construct an explanation based on evidence for how the structure of DNA determines the structure of proteins which carry out the essential functions of life through systems of specialized cells.

**HS-LS3-1:** Ask questions to clarify relationships about the role of DNA and chromosomes in coding the instructions for characteristic traits passed from parents to offspring.

Think of a molecule of mRNA as containing a secret code written in just four letters: A, C, G, and U. How would you go about decoding the hidden message? That's the problem every cell solves as it uses the code in mRNA to build proteins, one amino acid after another.

## The Genetic Code

As you have read, the first step in the process of decoding genetic messages is transcription, which is the copying of a nucleotide base sequence from DNA to mRNA. The next steps lead to the assembly of a protein. Proteins are made by joining amino acids together into chains called **polypeptides**. Twenty different amino acids are commonly found in polypeptides.

The specific order in which amino acids are joined together in a polypeptide chain determines the shape, chemical properties, and ultimately, function of a protein. How is the order of bases in DNA and RNA molecules translated into the order of amino acids in a polypeptide?

The four bases of RNA form a kind of language with just four letters: A, C, G, and U. We call this language the **genetic code**. How can a code with just four letters carry the instructions for 20 different amino acids? 🔍 *The genetic code is read three bases at a time. Each "word" of the code is three bases long and corresponds to a single amino acid.* This three-base "word" is known as a codon. A **codon** consists of three consecutive bases that specify a single amino acid to be added to the polypeptide chain.

**VOCABULARY**
polypeptide
genetic code
codon
translation
anticodon

**READING TOOL**

As you read, identify the steps of translation and protein synthesis. Create a flowchart in your 📓 **Biology Foundations Workbook.**

**Figure 14-4**

## Codons

A codon is a group of three nucleotide bases in messenger RNA that specifies a particular amino acid.

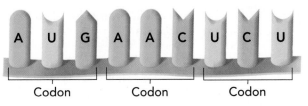

| A U G | A A C | U C U |
|-------|-------|-------|
| Codon | Codon | Codon |

# Figure 14-5

## The Genetic Code

To interpret this diagram, read each codon from the inner circle to the outer circle. For example, the codon CAC codes for the amino acid called histidine. ☑ **Use Models** Which two codons code for glutamic acid?

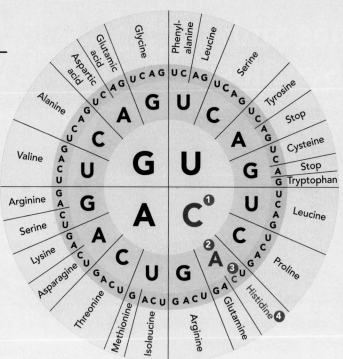

**❶** To decode the codon CAC, find the first letter in the set of bases at the center of the circle.

**❷** Find the second letter of the codon A, in the "C" quarter of the next ring.

**❸** Find the third letter, C, in the next ring, in the "C-A" grouping.

**❹** Read the name of the amino acid in that sector—in this case histidine.

**BUILD VOCABULARY**

**Academic Words** The verb specify means "to identify precisely." Each codon in the genetic code specifies the next amino acid to add to a polypeptide. Three "stop" codons specify when no amino acids should be added, and synthesis should cease.

**INTERACTIVITY**

Explore the genetic code.

**How to Read Codons** Because there are four different bases in RNA, there are 64 possible three-base codons (4 × 4 × 4 = 64) in the genetic code. Most amino acids can be specified by more than one codon. For example, six different codons—UUA, UUG, CUU, CUC, CUA, and CUG—specify leucine. But only one codon—UGG—specifies the amino acid tryptophan.

You can use **Figure 14-5** to interpret all 64 codons. Start at the middle of the circle with the first letter of the codon. Move out to the second ring to find the second letter of the codon. Then find the third and final letter among the smallest set of letters in the third ring from the center. Next to the third letter is the amino acid that the codon specifies.

**Start and Stop Codons** Whether a message is communicated in writing or the genetic code, it needs punctuation marks. In English, punctuation tells us where to pause, when to sound excited, and where to start and stop a sentence. The genetic code has punctuation marks, too. The methionine codon AUG also serves as the initiation, or "start," codon for protein synthesis. Following the start codon, mRNA is read, three bases at a time, until it reaches one of three different "stop" codons, which end translation. At that point, the polypeptide is complete.

☑ **READING CHECK Interpret Diagrams** Refer to **Figure 14-5**. What does the codon GAC code for?

Analyzing Data

## Crack the Code

The middle of an mRNA molecule contains the nucleotide sequence shown here. Much more of the mRNA is translated. Assume that the sequence is translated from left to right.

AUUUAACUGUUCUGUCUAGAG

1. **Construct an Explanation** Based only on the information provided, why could the mRNA section be translated into three different sets of amino acids, instead of just one set?

2. **Use Models** Use the genetic code to translate the sequence into each of the three possible sets of amino acids.

3. **Draw Conclusions** Which of the three sets of amino acids is the most likely to be included in the polypeptide? Explain your reasoning.

# Translation

You can think of the sequence of bases in an mRNA molecule as a set of instructions. The sequence gives the order in which amino acids should be joined to produce a polypeptide. Once the polypeptide is complete, it then folds into its final shape or joins with other polypeptides to become a functional protein.

If you've ever assembled a complex toy, you know that just reading the instructions is only the first step. You need to follow the instructions to put the parts together. A cell part that acts like a tiny factory—the ribosome—carries out the assembly tasks. **Ribosomes use the sequence of codons in mRNA to assemble amino acids into polypeptide chains.** The decoding of an mRNA message into a protein is a process known as **translation**.

**Steps in Translation** Translation begins when a ribosome attaches to an mRNA molecule in the cytoplasm. As each codon passes through the ribosome, several molecules of tRNA bring the proper amino acids into the ribosome. One at a time, the ribosome then attaches these amino acids to the growing chain. Each tRNA molecule carries just one kind of amino acid. In addition, each tRNA molecule has three unpaired bases that are together called an **anticodon**. Each anticodon is complementary to a codon on mRNA. In the case of the tRNA molecule for methionine, the anticodon is UAC, which pairs with the methionine codon, AUG.

The ribosome has a second binding site for a tRNA molecule for the next codon. If that next codon is UUC, a tRNA molecule with an AAG anticodon fits against the mRNA molecule held in the ribosome. That second tRNA molecule brings the amino acid phenylalanine into the ribosome.

 **INTERACTIVITY**

Perform a virtual activity to explore the role of mRNA in protein synthesis.

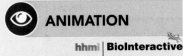
## Figure 14-6 **Translation**

All three types of RNA interact at a ribosome to form a polypeptide. A molecule of mRNA binds to the ribosome, which is made of rRNA. Then molecules of tRNA bring amino acids. The numbered diagrams show the process of translation.

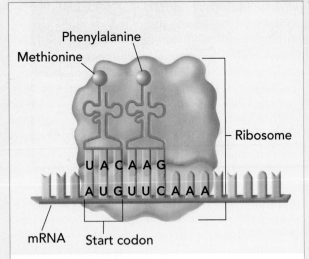

**1 Translation Begins**

Translation begins at AUG, the start codon. Each transfer RNA has an anticodon whose bases are complementary to the bases of a codon on the mRNA strand.

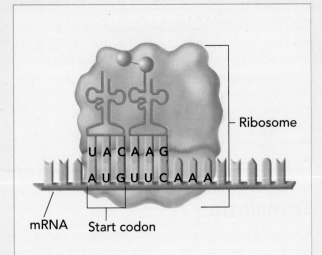

**2 Transfer RNA**

The ribosome positions the start codon to attract its anticodon, which is part of the tRNA that binds methionine. The ribosome also binds the next codon and its anticodon.

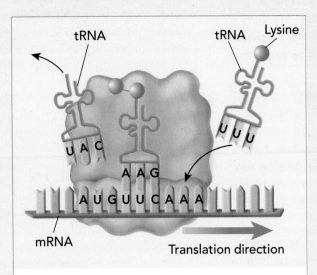

**3 The Polypeptide "Assembly Line"**

The ribosome joins the two amino acids—methionine and phenylalanine—and breaks the bond between methionine and its tRNA. The tRNA floats away from the ribosome, allowing the ribosome to bind another tRNA. The ribosome moves along the mRNA, binding new tRNA molecules and amino acids.

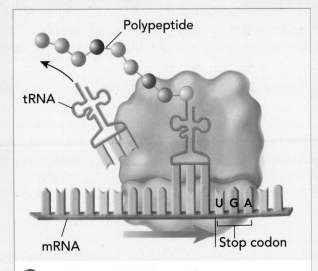

**4 Completing the Polypeptide**

The process continues until the ribosome reaches one of the three stop codons. Once the polypeptide is complete, it and the mRNA are released from the ribosome.

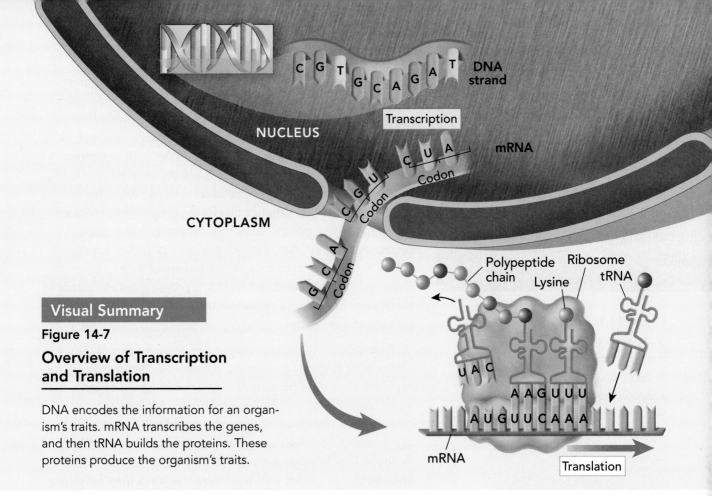

CYTOPLASM

**Visual Summary**

**Figure 14-7**

## Overview of Transcription and Translation

DNA encodes the information for an organism's traits. mRNA transcribes the genes, and then tRNA builds the proteins. These proteins produce the organism's traits.

Look at **Figure 14-6**. Like an assembly line worker who attaches one part to another, the ribosome helps form a covalent bond, called a peptide bond between the first and second amino acids. In this example, they are methionine and phenylalanine. At the same time, the bond holding the first tRNA molecule to its amino acid is broken. That tRNA then moves into a third site, from which it exits the ribosome. The ribosome then moves to the next codon, where tRNA brings in another amino acid.

The polypeptide chain continues to grow until the ribosome reaches a "stop" codon on the mRNA molecule. Then it releases both the newly synthesized polypeptide and the mRNA molecule.

### The Roles of tRNA and rRNA in Translation

The three major forms of RNA—mRNA, tRNA, and rRNA—are each involved in the process of translation. The mRNA molecule carries the coded message that directs the process. tRNA molecules deliver the amino acids, enabling the ribosome to "read" the mRNA's message and to get translation just right. Ribosomes themselves are composed of roughly 80 proteins and three or four different rRNA molecules. These rRNA molecules hold ribosomal proteins in place and carry out the chemical reactions that join amino acids together. As you can see in **Figure 14-7**, RNA molecules not only carry the genetic code, they also play a key role in translating it.

**READING CHECK** **Summarize** How do the three types of RNA work together at a ribosome to synthesize a polypeptide?

**READING TOOL**

Use **Figure 14-7** to explain the relationship among mRNA, tRNA, and ribosomes.

# Molecular Genetics

Gregor Mendel might have been surprised to learn that most genes contain nothing more than instructions for assembling proteins. He might have asked what proteins could possibly have to do with the color of a flower, the shape of a leaf, or the gender of a newborn baby. The answer is that proteins have everything to do with these traits. Remember that many proteins are enzymes, which catalyze and regulate chemical reactions. A gene that codes for an enzyme to produce pigment can control the color of a flower. Another gene produces proteins that regulate patterns of tissue growth in a leaf. Yet another may trigger the female or male pattern of development in an embryo. In short, proteins are microscopic tools, each specifically designed to build or operate a component of a living cell.

After scientists learned that genes were made of DNA, a series of other discoveries soon followed. When they explained the genetic code, a new scientific field called molecular biology had been established. Molecular biologists seek to understand living organisms by studying them at the molecular level, using molecules like DNA and RNA. 🔍 *Molecular biology provides a way to understand the links between genes and the characteristics they influence.* Scientists such as Ada Yonath, shown in **Figure 14-8**, continue to make advancements in this field.

One of the most interesting discoveries of molecular biology is the near-universal nature of the genetic code. Although some organisms show slight variations in the amino acids assigned to particular codons, the code is always read three bases at a time, always in the same direction, and is always translated on ribosomes composed of RNA and protein. Despite their enormous diversity in form and function, living organisms display remarkable unity at life's most basic level, the molecular biology of the gene.

**Figure 14-8**

## Ada Yonath

In 2009, Ada Yonath was awarded the Nobel Prize in Chemistry for mapping the structure of ribosomes.

HS-LS1-1, HS-LS3-1

##  LESSON 14.2 Review

### 🔍 KEY QUESTIONS

1. How does the cell interpret the genetic code?

2. How do ribosomes use mRNA and tRNA to assemble proteins?

3. How are proteins and genes related?

### CRITICAL THINKING

4. **Synthesize Information** Why can the same tRNA and rRNA molecules be used to synthesize a wide variety of polypeptides?

5. **Infer** How does the genetic code show a shared history among all organisms?

6. **Construct an Explanation** How do proteins determine the traits of an organism?

# Gene Regulation and Expression

## KEY QUESTIONS

- *How are prokaryotic genes regulated?*
- *How are genes regulated in eukaryotic cells?*
- *What controls the development of cells and tissues in multicellular organisms?*

**HS-LS3-1:** Ask questions to clarify relationships about the role of DNA and chromosomes in coding the instructions for characteristic traits passed from parents to offspring.

**VOCABULARY**

operon
operator
differentiation
homeotic gene
homeobox gene
Hox gene

**READING TOOL**

Identify the main ideas and details for each heading in this lesson. Record your observations in the table in your 📘 **Biology Foundations Workbook.**

Think of a library filled with how-to books. Would you ever need to consult all of these books at the same time? Of course not. If you wanted to know how to fix a leaky faucet, you'd open the book about plumbing but not the one on carpentry. Now picture a bacterium such as *E. coli* with a genetic library of more than 4000 genes. How does it pick exactly the right gene to put into action?

## Prokaryotic Gene Regulation

To conserve energy and resources, cells control which genes they express. For example, it would be wasteful for a bacterium to produce the enzymes to make a molecule it could get from its environment instead. By regulating gene expression, bacteria can respond to changes in their environment, such as the presence or absence of nutrients. How do they do this? 🔍 *DNA-binding proteins in prokaryotes regulate genes by controlling transcription.* Some of these regulatory proteins switch genes on, while others turn genes off.

How does an organism know when to turn a gene on or off? *E. coli*, shown in **Figure 14-9**, provides us with a clear example. A total of 4288 genes code for proteins in *E. coli*. Among them is a cluster of 3 genes that must be turned on together before the bacterium can break apart lactose, a type of sugar. Lactose provides food for the bacterium. Because the three genes are "operated" together, the three lactose genes in *E. coli* are called the *lac* operon. An **operon** is a group of genes that are regulated together.

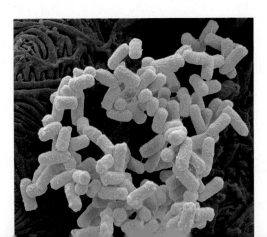

**Figure 14-9**

## *Escherichia coli*

Even "simple" organisms like *E. coli* have thousands of genes to regulate (false-colored SEM 3600x).

**451**

Figure 14-10

## Gene Regulation in Prokaryotes

The *lac* genes in *E. coli* are turned off by *lac* repressors and turned on in the presence of lactose.

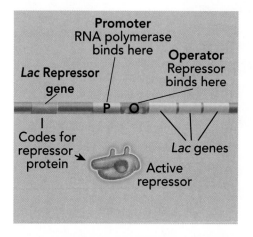

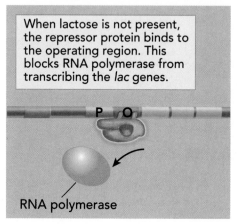

When lactose is not present, the repressor protein binds to the operating region. This blocks RNA polymerase from transcribing the *lac* genes.

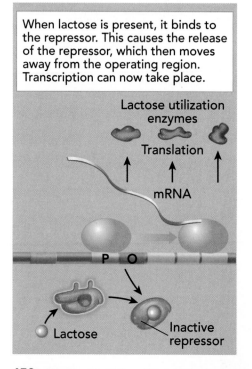

When lactose is present, it binds to the repressor. This causes the release of the repressor, which then moves away from the operating region. Transcription can now take place.

### The *Lac* Operon

Why must *E. coli* be able to switch the *lac* genes on and off? Lactose is a compound made up of two sugars: galactose and glucose. To use lactose for food, the bacterium must transport lactose across its cell membrane and then break the bond between glucose and galactose. These tasks are performed by proteins coded for by the genes of the *lac* operon.

Remarkably, the bacterium almost seems to "know" when the products of the *lac* operon genes are needed, and when they're not needed. For example, if the bacterium grows in a medium where lactose is the only food source, the genes must be transcribed to produce the proteins. However, if the environment changes to another food source, such as glucose, then the genes are not transcribed. How does the cell turn the expression of these genes on and off, and in such a useful way?

### Promoters and Operators

The secret to the control of the *lac* operon lies on one side of the operon's three genes, where there are two regulatory regions. The first is a promoter (P), which is a site where RNA polymerase can bind to begin transcription. The other region is called the **operator** (O). The O site is where a DNA-binding protein known as the *lac* repressor can bind to DNA.

### The Lac Repressor Blocks Transcription

When lactose is not present, the *lac* repressor binds to the O region and RNA polymerase cannot reach the *lac* genes to begin transcription, as shown in **Figure 14-10**. In effect, the binding of the repressor protein switches the operon "off" by preventing the transcription of its genes.

### Lactose Turns the Operon "On"

Besides its DNA binding site, the *lac* repressor protein has a binding site for lactose itself. When lactose is in the medium, some of it diffuses into the cell and attaches to the *lac* repressor. This changes the shape of the repressor protein in a way that causes it to fall off the operator. Now, with the repressor no longer bound to the O site, RNA polymerase can bind to the promoter and transcribe the genes of the operon. As a result, in the presence of lactose, the operon is automatically switched on. Messenger RNA transcribed from the *lac* genes is then translated into proteins that enable lactose to cross the cell membrane and to be broken down for use as an energy source by the cell. Many other prokaryotic genes are switched on or off by similar mechanisms.

☑ **READING CHECK** **Review** What is the function of the operator in the *lac* operon?

# Eukaryotic Gene Regulation

The general principles of gene expression in prokaryotes also apply to eukaryotes, although the regulation of many eukaryotic genes is much more complex. **Figure 14-11** shows several features of a typical eukaryotic gene. One of these is the TATA box, a short region of DNA, about 25 or 30 base pairs before the start of a gene, containing the sequence TATATA or TATAAA. The TATA box binds a protein that helps position RNA polymerase by marking a point just before the beginning of a gene.

**Transcription Factors** DNA-binding proteins known as transcription factors play an important part in regulating gene expression. Some transcription factors open up tightly packed chromatin to help attract RNA polymerase. Others block access to certain genes, much like prokaryotic repressor proteins. Sometimes multiple factors must bind to DNA sequences known as enhancers before a gene can be transcribed. ✎ *By binding DNA sequences in the regulatory regions of eukaryotic genes, transcription factors control gene expression.*

A transcription factor can activate scores of genes at once, thereby dramatically affecting patterns of gene expression. Steroid hormones, for example, are chemical messengers that enter cells and bind to receptor proteins. These hormone–receptor complexes then act as transcription factors that bind to DNA and activate multiple genes. Eukaryotic gene expression can also be regulated by many other factors, including the exit of mRNA molecules from the nucleus, the stability of mRNA, and even the breakdown of a gene's protein products.

**Cell Specialization** Why is gene regulation in eukaryotes more complex than in prokaryotes? Think about the way in which genes are expressed in a multicellular organism. The genes that code for liver enzymes, for example, are not expressed in nerve cells. Keratin, an important protein in skin cells, is not produced in blood cells. Cell differentiation requires genetic specialization, yet most of the cells in a multicellular organism carry the same DNA in their nucleus. Complex gene regulation in eukaryotes makes it possible for cells to be differentiated and specialized. Gene regulation also allows multicellular organisms to reproduce. A new organism generally begins as a single cell. Complex changes in gene expression allow the cell to develop into a functioning multicelluar organism.

## Figure 14-11
## Eukaryotic Gene Regulation

Many eukaryotic genes include a region called the TATA box that helps position RNA polymerase.

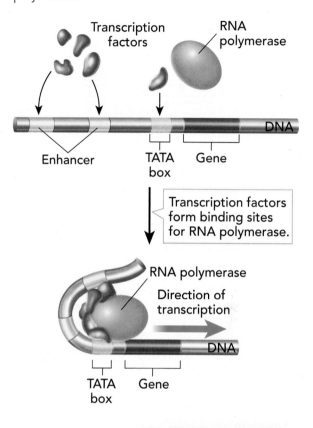

**READING TOOL**

Construct a flowchart to show how transcription factors affect gene regulation in eukaryotes.

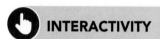 **INTERACTIVITY**

Investigate prokaryotic and eukaryotic gene regulation.

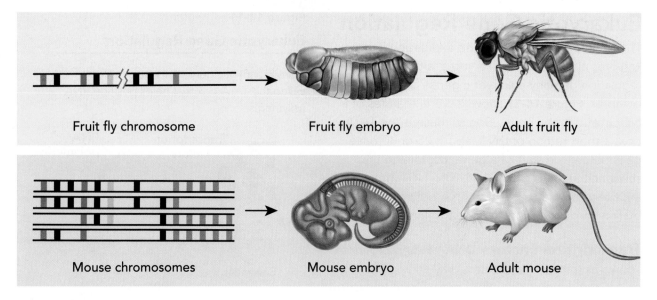

**Figure 14-12**

**Hox Genes and Body Development**

In fruit flies, a series of Hox genes along a chromosome determine the basic body structure. Mice have similar genes on four different chromosomes. The colored areas on the fly and mouse show the approximate body areas affected by genes of the corresponding colors.
☑ **Interpret Visuals** What section of the bodies of flies and mice is coded by the genes shown in blue?

**BUILD VOCABULARY**

**Word Origins** The word part *homeo* comes from the Latin and Greek part *homio*, meaning "similar to" or "the same kind." Homeobox genes are a group of similar genes that regulate specific structures.

# Genetic Control of Development

Regulating gene expression is especially important during the earliest stages of development. The activation of genes in different parts of an embryo cause cells to differentiate. The process of **differentiation** gives rise to specialized tissues and organs.

**Homeotic Genes** American biologist Edward B. Lewis was the first to show that a specific group of genes controls the identities of body parts in the embryo of the common fruit fly. Change one of these genes, and a body part like an antenna might actually be changed into a leg. From Lewis's work it became clear that a set of master control genes, known as **homeotic genes**, regulates organs that develop in specific parts of the body.

Molecular studies of homeotic genes show that they share a very similar 180-base DNA sequence, which was given the name *homeobox*. **Homeobox genes** code for transcription factors that activate other genes that are important in cell development and differentiation. In flies, a group of homeobox genes known as **Hox genes** are located side by side in a single cluster. As shown in **Figure 14-12**, Hox genes determine the identities of each segment of a fly's body. They are arranged in the exact order in which they are expressed, from anterior to posterior. A mutation in one of these genes can completely change the organs that develop in specific parts of the body.

Remarkably, clusters of Hox genes exist in the DNA of other animals, including humans. These genes are arranged in the same way—from head to tail. The function of Hox genes in humans seems to be almost the same as it is in fruit flies: They tell the cells of the body how to differentiate as the body grows. This means that nearly all animals, from flies to mammals, share the same basic tools for building the different parts of the body.

Common patterns of genetic control exist because all these genes have descended from the genes of common ancestors. 🔍 *Master control genes are like switches that trigger particular patterns of development and differentiation in cells and tissues.* The details can vary from one organism to another, but the switches are nearly identical. Recent studies have shown that the very same Hox gene that triggers the development of hands and feet is also active in the fins of certain fish.

**Epigenetics** Cells have another way to regulate gene expression. Recall that nuclear DNA is coiled around protein clusters, called nucleosomes, to form chromatin. In places where chromatin is tightly packed, transcription factors cannot access their DNA binding sites, and gene expression is blocked. By contrast, in regions where chromatin is opened up, gene expression is enhanced, as shown in **Figure 14-13**.

**INTERACTIVITY**

Investigate the science behind the genetically modified mosquito being developed to fight Zika in the United States.

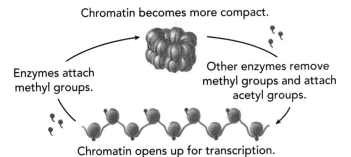

Chromatin becomes more compact.

Enzymes attach methyl groups.

Other enzymes remove methyl groups and attach acetyl groups.

Chromatin opens up for transcription.

**Figure 14-13**

## Effect of Chemical Marks

The presence or absence of chemical marks determines how compact chromatin is in a given region of DNA. For transcription to occur, the chromatin must be less compact.

Cells can regulate the state of chromatin by enzymes that attach chemical groups to DNA and to histone proteins. Specifically, the attachment of large numbers of methyl groups ($—CH_3$) will cause chromatin to condense, shutting down gene expression. Conversely, the attachment of acetyl groups ($—CO-CH_3$) will open chromatin up for transcription and gene expression.

These chemical marks on chromatin are said to be epigenetic, meaning they are above the level of the genome. Epigenetic marks do not change DNA base sequences. Instead, they influence patterns of gene expression over long periods of time. During development, for example, the marks help to determine which genes are expressed in a liver cell and which are expressed in muscle or skin cells.

☑ **READING CHECK** **Summarize** How can cells regulate gene expression?

**CASE STUDY**

**Figure 14-14**

## Epigenetics

A caterpillar, pupa, and butterfly all have exactly the same genes. Epigenetic mechanisms control which genes are on and which are off during each stage of the insect's life cycle.

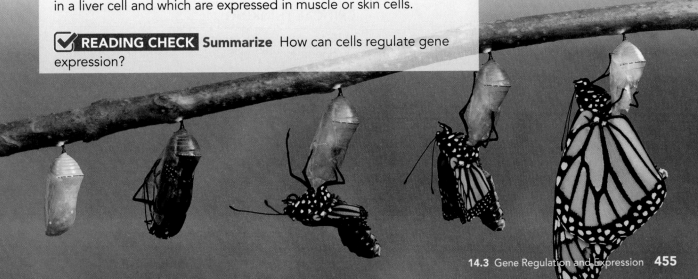

**Figure 14-15**

**Environmental Influences on Gene Expression**

The coloring of the coat of a Himalayan rabbit is one example of the effect of the environment on gene expression. ☑ **Predict** What would happen if a cold pack were strapped to a Himalayan rabbit's back while its fur was growing in?

Raised at temperatures below 25°C

Raised at temperatures above 30°C

**Environmental Influences** As you have seen, cell differentiation is controlled at least in part by the regulation of gene expression. Conditions in an organism's environment play a role too. In prokaryotes and eukaryotes, environmental factors such as temperature, salinity, and nutrient availability can regulate gene expression. For example, the *lac* operon in *E. coli* is switched on only when lactose is the sole food source in the bacteria's environment.

The environment can often influence how and when epigenetic marks are attached to chromatin. One well-known example involves Dutch children born near the end of World War II. When these children reached adulthood, they had much higher rates of obesity, diabetes, and cardiovascular disease than their parents and ancestors. Why? Because epigenetic marks had been attached to these individuals' DNA as they developed inside their malnourished mothers. Insufficient nourishment during the first three months of development changed the way genes were expressed in the growing fetus. As a result of these epigenetic changes, the body was altered so that it was better suited for an environment where food was scarce. However, life gradually returned to normal after the war, and food because plentiful again. This had a profoundly negative, lifelong impact on individuals whose gene expression was epigenetically altered to cope with food shortages.

Environmental factors can also directly affect the expression of other genes. A dramatic example involves Himalayan rabbits carrying a particular gene for fur color. In a rabbit raised at temperatures between 15°C and 25°C, the gene produces black color in the fur on the animal's nose, ears, and on the tips of its feet, as shown in **Figure 14-15**. The gene is not fully active at temperatures above 30°C, so only the coldest portions of the rabbit's body allow the gene to function. If a rabbit is raised at temperatures above 30°C, the gene is completely inactive, and the entire rabbit is white.

HS-LS3-1

☑ **LESSON 14.3 Review**

### ⚘ KEY QUESTIONS

1. What controls transcription in prokaryotes?

2. What are three mechanisms by which transcription factors regulate eukaryotic gene expression?

3. Why are master control genes almost universal and common to different organisms?

### CRITICAL THINKING

4. **Construct an Explanation** How does the *lac* operon help *E. coli* conserve energy and other resources?

5. **Engage in Argument** You are studying the genes of fruit flies. Your partner claims that each gene matches to a specific body part, such as the head, wings, and tail. How would you argue for or against this claim?

# Mutations

A mutation causes dwarfism in Bantam chickens.

## 🔍 KEY QUESTIONS

- *In what ways do mutations change genetic information?*
- *How do mutations affect genes?*

**HS-LS3-1:** Ask questions to clarify relationships about the role of DNA and chromosomes in coding the instructions for characteristic traits passed from parents to offspring.

**HS-LS3-2:** Make and defend a claim based on evidence that inheritable genetic variations may result from: (1) new genetic combinations through meiosis, (2) viable errors occurring during replication, and/or (3) mutations caused by environmental factors.

### VOCABULARY

mutation
point mutation
frameshift mutation
mutagen
polyploidy

### READING TOOL

As you read, find a brief description of each type of genetic mutation. Fill in the table in your 📖 **Biology Foundations Workbook** with the description and the possible effects.

As you've seen, the sequence of bases in DNA are like the letters of a coded message. But what would happen if a few of those letters changed accidentally, altering the message? Could the cell still understand its meaning? Think about what might happen if someone changed at random a few lines of code in a computer program. Would the program be affected, and in ways that you would notice?

## Types of Mutations

Now and then cells make mistakes in copying their own DNA. An incorrect base is inserted or a base is skipped during transcription. These variations are called **mutations**, from the Latin word *mutare*, meaning "to change." Mutations are heritable changes in genetic information. 🔍 *Mutations can involve changes in the sequence of nucleotides in DNA or changes in the number or structure of chromosomes.*

**Point Mutations** Mutations that change a single base pair are known as **point mutations** because they occur at a single point in the DNA sequence. Point mutations usually involve a substitution, in which one base is changed to a different base. Substitutions usually affect no more than a single amino acid, and sometimes have no effect at all. For example, if a mutation changed one codon of mRNA from CCC to CCA, the codon would still specify the amino acid proline. Mutations like this are known as *silent mutations*, since they don't affect amino acid sequence. But changing CCC to ACC might be more significant, since it would replace proline with the amino acid threonine. Mutations that change the amino acid specified by a codon are called *missense mutations*.

As you read about the different types of mutations in this section, create a two-column table in which you list each type of mutation and the effect it has on genetic information.

Sometimes a point mutation can have severe effects on gene expression. For example, if a mutation changed an mRNA codon from AAA to UAA, it would result in a stop codon instead of lysine. This is known as a *nonsense mutation* because it would cause translation to stop before the protein was finished. Depending on the position of the stop codon, it could result in the production of a defective protein.

**Insertions and Deletions** Mutations in which one or many bases are inserted or removed from the DNA sequence are called insertions and deletions. As shown in **Figure 14-16**, the significance of these changes can be dramatic. Remember that the genetic code is read three bases at a time. If a nucleotide is added or deleted, the bases are still read in groups of three, but now those groupings change in every codon that follows the mutation.

Insertions and deletions are also called **frameshift mutations** because they shift the "reading frame" of the genetic message. By shifting the reading frame, frameshift mutations can change every amino acid that follows the point of the mutation. They can alter a protein so much that it is unable to perform its normal functions.

**INTERACTIVITY**

Learn about the different types of point mutations and their effects.

### Figure 14-16
### Point Mutations

Point mutations involve a change in a single base pair. This change can involve the switch (substitution), loss (deletion), or gain (insertion) of a base pair. Point mutations can be classified based on how they affect the polypeptide for which the gene codes.

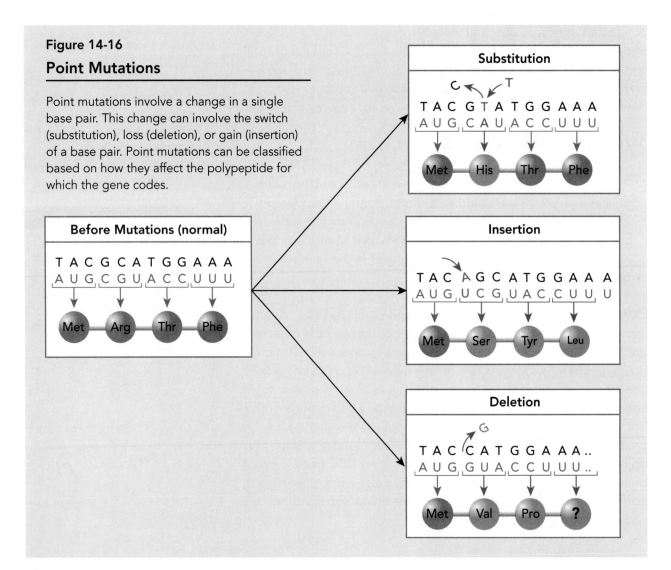

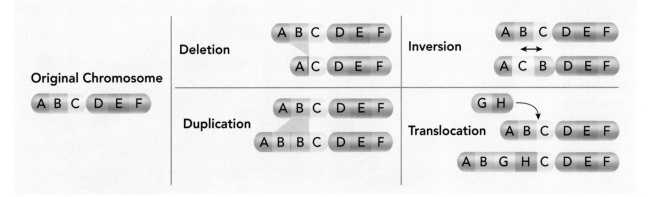

## Chromosomal Mutations

Chromosomal mutations involve changes in the number or structure of chromosomes. These mutations can change the location of genes on chromosomes and can even change the number of copies of some genes.

There are four types of chromosomal mutations: deletion, duplication, inversion, and translocation. In **Figure 14-17**, the top chromosome in each example is the original chromosome. The chromosome underneath it is the chromosome that results from the mutation. Deletion involves the loss of all or part of a chromosome; duplication produces an extra copy of all or part of a chromosome; and inversion reverses the direction of parts of a chromosome. Translocation occurs when part of one chromosome breaks off and attaches to another.

 **READING CHECK Describe** What is a frameshift mutation?

# Effects of Mutations

Genetic material can be altered by natural events or by artificial means. The resulting mutations may or may not affect an organism. And some mutations that affect individual organisms can also affect a species or even an entire ecosystem.

Many mutations are produced by errors in genetic processes. For example, some point mutations are caused by errors during DNA replication. The cellular machinery that replicates DNA inserts an incorrect base roughly once in every 10 million bases. But small changes in genes can gradually accumulate over time.

**Figure 14-17**

**Chromosomal Mutations**

Mutations that change the structure or number of chromosomes are called chromosomal mutations. ☑ **Analyze Diagrams** What is the difference between inversion and translocation?

 **INTERACTIVITY**

Investigate different types of mutations and their effects on organisms.

HS-LS3-2

## Modeling Lab

### Open-ended Inquiry

### The Effect of Mutations

**Problem** How can mutations affect a protein?

In this lab, you will be exploring different types of mutations and the possible effects they can have on a protein.

You can find this lab in your digital course.

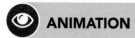

## ANIMATION

**hhmi** | **BioInteractive**

Figure 14-18

### Damage to DNA leads to mutation

The ultraviolet light in sunlight can cause mutations in skin cells, resulting in skin cancer. Sunscreen and protective clothing help shield beachgoers from harmful UV radiation.

## BUILD VOCABULARY

**Root Words** The root word *gen* means "producing." A **mutagen** is something that produces a mutation.

## VIRTUAL LAB

Identify which type of mutation can lead to a white-eyed fruit fly.

**Mutagens** Some mutations arise from **mutagens**, chemical or physical agents in the environment. Chemical mutagens include certain pesticides, a few natural plant alkaloids, tobacco smoke, and environmental pollutants. Physical mutagens include some forms of electromagnetic radiation, such as ultraviolet light, shown in **Figure 14-18**, and X-rays. If these agents interact with DNA, they can produce mutations at high rates. Cells can sometimes repair the damage; but when they cannot, the DNA base sequence changes permanently. Some compounds interfere with base-pairing, increasing the error rate of DNA replication. Other mutagens weaken the DNA strand, causing breaks and inversions that produce chromosomal mutations.

**Harmful and Helpful Mutations** As you've already seen, some mutations don't even change the amino acid specified by a codon, while others may significantly alter a complete protein or even an entire chromosome. 🔍 *The effects of mutations on genes vary widely. Some have little or no effect, some produce beneficial variations, and some negatively disrupt gene function.* Many if not most mutations are neutral; they have little or no effect on the expression of genes or the function of the proteins for which they code. Whether a mutation is negative or beneficial depends on how its DNA changes relative to the organism's situation. Mutations are often thought of as negative, since they can disrupt the normal function of genes. However, without mutations, organisms could not evolve. Mutations are the source of genetic variability in a species.

**Harmful Effects** Some of the most harmful mutations are those that dramatically change protein structure or gene activity. The defective proteins produced by these mutations can disrupt normal biological activities, and result in genetic disorders. Some cancers, for example, are the product of mutations that cause the uncontrolled growth of cells. A human genetic disorder called xeroderma pigmentosum is the result of a mutation that inactivates a protein that normally repairs DNA damaged by ultraviolet (UV) light. Individuals with this mutation have to avoid sunlight as much as possible because their skin cells can become cancerous as a result of UV damage to DNA.

**Figure 14-19**

## Effects of Mutations

Polyploidy is a condition that is generally lethal in animals. But in plants, like these limes (left), polyploidy often produces stronger plants and larger fruits. A mutation damaged the immune system of the nude mouse (bottom), making it valuable for scientific research.

**Helpful Effects** Some of the variation produced by mutations can be highly advantageous to an organism or species. ⚲ *Mutations often produce proteins with new or altered functions that can be useful to organisms in different or changing environments.* For example, over the past 20 years, mutations in the mosquito genome have made many African mosquitoes resistant to the chemical pesticides once used to control them. This may be bad news for humans, but it is highly beneficial to the insects themselves. Beneficial mutations occur in humans, too, including ones that increase bone strength and density, making fractures less likely. Some mutations increase resistance to HIV, the virus that causes AIDS.

Plant and animal breeders often make use of "good" mutations. For example, when a complete set of chromosomes fails to separate during meiosis, the gametes that result may produce triploid (3N) or tetraploid (4N) organisms. The condition in which an organism has extra sets of chromosomes is called **polyploidy**. Polyploid plants, like the one shown in **Figure 14-19**, are often larger and stronger than diploid plants. Important crop plants—including bananas, limes, and strawberries—have been produced this way. Polyploidy also occurs naturally in citrus plants, often through spontaneous mutations.

HS-LS3-1, HS-LS3-2

## ☑ LESSON 14.4 Review

### ⚲ KEY QUESTIONS

1. Describe the ways mutations can affect DNA and chromosomes.

2. What are the possible ways that a mutation may affect an organism?

### CRITICAL THINKING

3. Construct Explanations The effects of a mutation are not always visible. Choose a species and explain how you would determine whether a mutation has occurred. How might you determine what type of mutation it is?

4. Evaluate Claims A science student claims that a substitution mutation is less likely to affect gene function than an insertion or deletion mutation. Use logical reasoning to evaluate this claim.

5. Synthesize Information What are three possible ways that a mutation could change DNA, yet have no measurable effect on the organism?

6. Construct an Explanation After many years of normal function, a cell begins producing different proteins than it produced before. Propose two different explanations for this change.

# How does a plant remember winter?

The environment can exert long-term influences on gene expression by triggering epigenetic changes in DNA. Flowering in winter wheat is regulated by just such changes.

HS-ETS1-1, HS-LS3-3

## Make Your Case

As you have learned, genes are expressed through the processes of transcription and translation. But that's just one part of the story. Not all genes are expressed all the time. The study of epigenetics involves the many mechanisms that affect when and how genes are expressed. Some of these mechanisms alter the structure of DNA, while others change the histones that hold DNA in place. Even a simple change to DNA can have far-reaching consequences to the organism.

## Obtain Information

1. **Ask Questions** Starting with winter wheat as an example, research the role of epigenetic changes in other organisms. Use the "agouti mutation" in mice as a specific example.

2. **Conduct Research** Research winter wheat, vernalization, and epigenetics. Then identify a social or technological problem that epigenetics might help solve. Evaluate your sources for reliability.

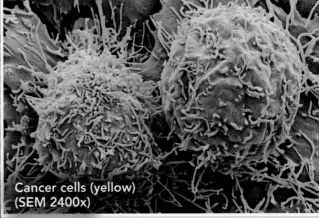

Cancer cells (yellow)
(SEM 2400x)

## Careers on the Case

### Work Toward a Solution

The study of epigenetics is being applied in some unexpected ways, such as nutrition.

### Nutritionist

To help people eat healthful diets, nutritionists study the nutrients in foods and the way they affect the body. Nutritionists may work in hospitals or doctor's offices, or work for companies that manufacture foods.

▶ **VIDEO**

Watch this video to learn about other careers in biology.

## Technology on the Case

### Epigenetics and Cancer

What causes cancer? For many years, scientists thought that the main cause was damage to DNA. Chemicals in tobacco cause this type of damage, which is why tobacco users have a high risk for cancer. However, new research shows that epigenetic mechanisms can also play a role in causing cancer. For example, some genes act to regulate the growth of the cell. If an epigenetic change "turns off" these genes, then cell growth will keep going unchecked and lead to a cancerous tumor. Another example involves the genes that help repair DNA. If these genes become deactivated, then cancer could be the result.

The good news is that epigenetic changes sometimes can be reversed. Researchers are investigating several epigenetic treatments for cancer, and the results have been encouraging. The goal of epigenetic therapy is not to kill the cancer cells, which is the goal of conventional treatments for cancer. Instead, epigenetic therapy works by reactivating the genes that help the body fight cancer naturally.

Scientists are also applying epigenetics to help explain some cancer statistics. For example, research shows that people who regularly take aspirin are less likely to get certain types of cancer. The reason might be that aspirin reduces inflammation within cells. If the inflammation affects DNA in the cell nucleus, then epigenetic changes could be the result.

# Lesson Review
Go to your Biology Foundations Workbook for longer versions of these lesson summaries.

## 14.1 RNA

Unlike DNA, RNA uses the sugar ribose instead of deoxyribose, RNA is generally single stranded, and RNA contains uracil in place of thymine. There are three main types of RNA: messenger RNA (mRNA), ribosomal RNA (rRNA), and transfer RNA (tRNA).

In transcription, segments of DNA serve as templates to produce complementary RNA molecules.

- RNA
- messenger RNA
- ribosomal RNA
- transfer RNA
- transcription
- RNA polymerase
- promoter
- intron
- exon

**RNA**
**Ribonucleic Acid**

**DNA**
**Deoxyribonucleic Acid**

✓ **Compare and Contrast** What are the differences between RNA and DNA?

## 14.2 Ribosomes and Protein Synthesis

The genetic code is a language composed of the four different bases of RNA: adenine, cytosine, guanine, and uracil. The code is read three letters at a time to carry instructions for the 20 different amino acids commonly found in polypeptides. Each three-letter combination in mRNA is a codon. Because there are four different bases, there are 64 possible three-base codons in the genetic code.

The order in which amino acids are joined together in a peptide determines the shape, the chemical properties, and ultimately the function of the protein. In the cell, ribosomes use the sequence of codons in mRNA to assemble amino acids into polypeptide chains in a process called translation. All three major forms of RNA are involved in the process of translation.

After the genetic code was discovered, the new field of molecular biology was established. Molecular biologists seek to understand the links between genes and the characteristics they influence.

- polypeptide
- genetic code
- codon
- translation
- anticodon

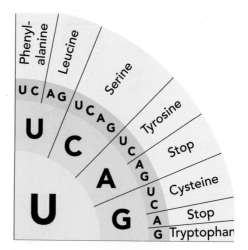

✓ **Interpret Diagrams** Which amino acid is specified by the codon UAC?

## 14.3 Gene Regulation and Expression

DNA-binding proteins in prokaryotes regulate genes by controlling transcription.

By binding DNA sequences in the regulatory regions of eukaryotic genes, transcription factors control gene expression.

Master control genes are like switches that trigger particular patterns of development and differentiation in cells and tissues.

- operon
- operator
- differentiation
- homeotic gene
- homeobox gene
- Hox gene

☑ **Apply Concepts** What is a genetic explanation for the difference in these two Himalayan rabbits?

## 14.4 Mutations

Mutations can involve changes in the sequence of nucleotides in DNA. They can also involve changes in the number or structure of chromosomes in an organism. A change in a single base pair is known as a point mutation. The insertion or deletion of one or many bases in DNA is called a frameshift mutation. These mutations shift the "reading frame" of the genetic message. Chromosomal mutations involve changes in the number or structure of chromosomes and include deletion, duplication, inversion, and translocation.

Some mutations arise from mutagens, which interact with DNA to produce cell damage. The most harmful mutations dramatically change protein structure or gene activity, producing genetic disorders, such as cancer.

- mutation
- point mutation
- frameshift mutation
- mutagen
- polyploidy

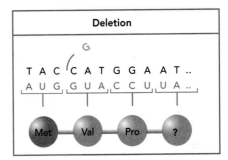

☑ **Cause and Effect** How does the deletion of a single base cause a frameshift mutation?

## Organize Information

Complete the table to describe the molecules involved in protein synthesis. One entry is completed for you.

| Molecule | Function |
|---|---|
| mRNA | 1. |
| rRNA | 2. |
| tRNA | Binds amino acids, brings them to the ribosomes, and reads the mRNA codons by base pairing |
| Introns and exons | 3. |
| Transcription factors | 4. |

# A New Kind of Drug: mRNA

## Evaluate a Solution

HS-LS1-1, HS-LS3-1, HS-ETS1-3

**STEM** What happens when you take a conventional drug, such as aspirin or penicillin? The drug travels through the blood stream, and then is absorbed by body cells or (as with penicillin) by the cells of bacteria or other invaders. The drug does its work, but eventually it goes away. Enzymes and other mechanisms break apart drugs and remove them from the body.

Today, researchers are trying to develop drugs in a very different way. The new drugs are a modified form of messenger RNA (mRNA). Instead of directly completing the tasks of the drug, the modified mRNA enters the cell and directs protein synthesis. Then the protein takes action as a drug or medicine. The protein might be a vaccine or antibody, or it might be an enzyme that the body cannot make or that it needs in an increased supply.

To develop mRNA drugs, researchers had to find a way to make the molecules last longer in the body than they generally do. They also needed to "trick" the target cell into recognizing and accepting the drug. Otherwise, the cell might attack the drug as if it were a virus.

Researchers met both challenges with the same solution. The drug is not quite the same as the natural mRNA found in cells. Instead, it uses a few nucleotides that are slightly different from the normal nucleotides found in RNA. The modifications make the mRNA both more stable and less viruslike.

The process of RNA therapy can be summarized as follows:

1. Modified mRNA is synthesized in a laboratory cell culture.

2. The mRNA is delivered into the patient. Often it is injected with a vector, or carrier, such as a deactivated virus.

3. Inside cells, the mRNA attaches to ribosomes, as if it were the natural mRNA of the cell.

4. The mRNA directs protein synthesis.

5. The protein fills a positive role in the body, just like a conventional drug or medicine.

1. **Form a Hypothesis** Would this therapy work if mRNA were replaced with other types of RNA, such as ribosomal RNA (rRNA) or transfer RNA (tRNA)? Use evidence to support your hypothesis.

2. **Evaluate a Solution** What are the advantages of using mRNA, rather than DNA, for directing the synthesis of the drug? (**HINT:** Remember the role of regulating gene expression in the cell.)

3. **Develop Models** Review the steps of administering an mRNA drug. Add illustrations to the figure to model the processes that are occuring inside the cell with the mRNA drug. Either draw the illustrations by hand or copy diagrams from the chapter.

4. **Use Models** Use your model to compare the administration of an mRNA drug to the protein synthesis that the cell normally performs.

5. **Conduct Research** Use an online search engine to research more information about mRNA drugs, their uses, and their development. Be sure to take notes and to cite your sources.

6. **Communicate Information** Share your findings about mRNA drugs in an oral report to the class, or in a written essay or computer presentation. Address these questions:

   - Why are companies investing in mRNA drugs?

   - What advances in technology have allowed mRNA drugs to be developed?

   - What kinds of proteins can mRNA drugs be used to synthesize?

## 🔑 KEY QUESTIONS AND TERMS

## 14.1 RNA

**HS-LS1-1, HS-LS3-1**

1. RNA differs from DNA in that RNA has
   a. a double strand and contains uracil.
   b. a single strand and contains adenine.
   c. a double strand and contains thymine.
   d. a single strand and contains uracil.

2. From which molecules are mRNA molecules transcribed?
   a. tRNA          c. DNA
   b. rRNA          d. protein

3. Which of the following are found in both DNA and RNA?
   a. ribose, phosphate groups, and adenine
   b. deoxyribose, phosphate groups, and guanine
   c. phosphate groups, guanine, and cytosine
   d. phosphate groups, guanine, and thymine

4. What is the function of RNA polymerase in the process of transcription?

5. Identify the three types of RNA and describe their functions.

6. What are introns and exons?

## 14.2 Ribosomes and Protein Synthesis

**HS-LS1-1, HS-LS3-1**

7. What happens during translation?
   a. Messenger RNA is made from a DNA code.
   b. The cell uses a messenger RNA code to make proteins.
   c. Transfer RNA is made from a messenger RNA code.
   d. Copies of DNA molecules are made.

8. The genetic code is always read
   a. 3 bases at a time in the same direction.
   b. 4 bases at a time in the same direction.
   c. 3 bases at a time and the direction varies.
   d. 4 bases at a time and the direction varies.

9. Ribosomes are tiny "factories" within cells that do all of the following EXCEPT
   a. decode an mRNA message into a protein.
   b. assemble amino acids into polypeptide chains.
   c. attach to mRNA molecules in the cytoplasm.
   d. translate DNA into RNA.

10. What are the four bases of the genetic code?

11. What is the difference between translation and transcription?

12. How is molecular biology related to genetics?

## 14.3 Gene Regulation and Expression

**HS-LS3-1**

13. Gene regulation in eukaryotic cells
    a. usually involves operons.
    b. is simpler than in prokaryotes.
    c. allows for cell specialization.
    d. includes the action of an operator region.

14. What is a promoter?
    a. a binding site for DNA polymerase
    b. a binding site for RNA polymerase
    c. a start signal for replication
    d. a stop signal for transcription

15. What happens to *lac* repressors in *E. coli* when lactose is present?

16. Explain the function of homeotic genes and Hox genes.

17. Describe how a TATA box helps position RNA polymerase in a eukaryotic cell.

## 14.4 Mutations

**HS-LS3-1, HS-LS3-2**

18. What is the name for a mutation that involves one nucleotide only?
    a. mutagen
    b. inversion
    c. point mutation
    d. translocation

19. When a chromosome undergoes a deletion mutation, information is
    a. repeated.          c. reversed.
    b. lost.              d. transferred.

20. A substance such as tobacco that can cause a genetic change is called a(n)
    a. polyploidy.        c. mutagen.
    b. antigen.           d. collagen.

**21.** Which kind of mutation is shown below?

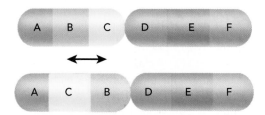

**22.** How can a mutation be beneficial to an organism?

## CRITICAL THINKING

HS-LS1-1, HS-LS3-1, HS-LS3-2

Refer to the genetic code diagram below to answer questions 23–25.

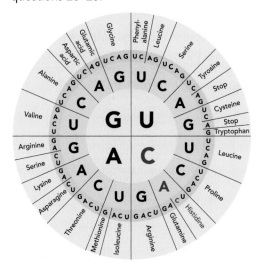

**23.** **Analyze Data** Suppose you start with the DNA strand ACCGTCACT. What three amino acids does the complementary mRNA strand code for?

**24.** **Construct a Table** Construct a two-column table that presents the possible mRNA codons for the following amino acids: alanine, valine, and leucine.

**25.** **Analyze Data** Analyze the information in the table you constructed for question 24. How would a substitution mutation in the third nucleotide position of the codons for alanine and valine affect the resulting protein?

**26.** **Defend Your Claim** During what stage of meiosis will a failure of chromosomes to separate lead to polyploidy? Use evidence from the text to defend your claim.

**27.** **Construct an Explanation** Nitrous acid is a mutagen. It can react chemically with cytosine to change it to uracil in a DNA strand. Using your knowledge of DNA replication and base pairing, explain the effect of this mutagen on a strand of DNA that undergoes replication.

**28.** **Evaluate Evidence** In eukaryotes, the number of promoter sequences and enhancer sites and the TATA box make gene regulation far more complex than regulation in prokaryotes. Why is regulation in eukaryotes so much more complex?

**29.** **Evaluate Claims** A chromosomal mutation that occurs during meiosis may or may not be expressed in an organism's offspring. A similar mutation that only occurs during mitosis of a body cell will not be expressed in the organism's offspring. Evaluate these claims. Determine whether or not they are true, and explain your reasoning.

**30.** **Form a Hypothesis** *E. coli* bacteria need the amino acid tryptophan to survive. When tryptophan is present in its growth medium, *E. coli* is able to ingest it. However, tryptophan is not always available in the *E. coli*'s environment. What are some questions you can ask regarding how *E. coli* might respond if tryptophan were not present in its growth medium? Form a hypothesis that you can test to answer one of your questions.

**31.** **Construct an Argument** A researcher identifies the nucleotide sequence AAC in a long strand of RNA inside a nucleus. In the genetic code, AAC codes for the amino acid asparagine. When that RNA becomes involved in protein synthesis, will asparagine necessarily appear in the protein? Use specific content to support your argument.

**32.** **Analyze** A mutation in the DNA of an organism changes one base sequence in a protein-coding region from CAC to CAT. What is the effect of the mutation on the final protein?

## CROSSCUTTING CONCEPTS

**33. Patterns** The word *transcribe* means "to write out." The word *translate* means "to express in another language." Review the meanings of *transcription* and *translation* in genetics. Look for patterns in the meanings of these words. How do the technical meanings of these words relate to the everyday meanings of the words?

**34. Structure and Function** Describe how the sequence of nucleotides in mRNA codes for the amino acids of a protein. How can the insertion or deletion of even one nucleotide in mRNA cause significant changes to the protein that results?

## MATH CONNECTIONS

## Analyze and Interpret Data

CCSS.MATH.CONTENT.MP2

RNA is the genetic material of many viruses. Scientists analyzed RNA from four different types of viruses. The content of the four nitrogenous bases is shown below.

| Base Percentages in Four Viruses | | | | |
|---|---|---|---|---|
| Virus | A | U | C | G |
| A | 26.3 | 29.3 | 20.6 | 23.8 |
| B | × | × | 17.6 | 17.5 |
| C | 21.9 | 12.8 | 34.3 | 31.1 |
| D | 29.8 | 26.3 | 18.5 | 25.3 |

Use the data table to answer questions 35–37.

**35. Interpret Tables** Which of the four types of viruses is most likely to use double-stranded RNA as its genetic material? Explain how you reached your conclusion.

**36. Calculate** Based on the data, calculate the values in the two boxes labeled with an ×.

**37. Reason Quantitatively** How would the percentages of the four nitrogenous bases shown in the table compare to the percentages of the nitrogenous bases found in strands of DNA?

## LANGUAGE ARTS CONNECTION

## Write About Science
HS-LS3-1, CCSS.ELA-LITERACY.WHST.9-10.1, CCSS.ELA-LITERACY.WHST.9-10.8

**38. Write Arguments** A classmate tells you that comic books are full of superheroes with powers caused by mutations. Therefore, all mutations must be beneficial. Decide whether or not you agree. Write a paragraph to argue your position regarding the benefits or harm caused by mutations.

**39. Use Information** Explain what Hox genes are and what they control. Incorporate paraphrasing from the text into your explanation.

## Read About Science
HS-LS3-1, CCSS.ELA-LITERACY.RST.9-10.1, CCSS.ELA-LITERACY.RST.9-10.9

**40. Corroborate** Research several different examples of epigenetics. Based on your understanding of epigenetics, explain how the patterns of expression are similar and how they are different.

Questions 1–2 refer to the following diagram.

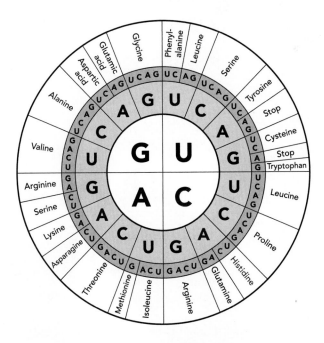

1. What is the significance of this genetic code?
   A. It describes how DNA is transcribed to RNA.
   B. It describes how RNA is translated to amino acids.
   C. It describes how RNA is translated to genes.
   D. It describes how proteins are translated to RNA.
   E. It describes how RNA is translated to DNA.

2. Two scientists are both studying RNA. One scientist is studying RNA in mice, and the other is studying RNA in *E. coli* bacteria. Which of the following **best** describes how each scientist would use a genetic code?
   A. Both scientists would use the same genetic code because all organisms have RNA.
   B. Both scientists would use the same genetic code because in all organisms the code is read three bases at a time and in the same direction.
   C. The scientists would use different genetic codes because different genes are expressed in mice and *E. coli*.
   D. The scientist studying mice would use the genetic code for mice and the scientist studying *E. coli* would use the genetic code for *E. coli* because mice are more complex multicellular organisms.
   E. The scientist studying mice would use the genetic code for eukaryotes and the scientist studying *E. coli* would use the genetic code for prokaryotes because they each have different types of chromosomes.

3. Human nerve cells and muscle cells have many structural and functional differences. What role does DNA play in these differences?
   A. Nerve cells and muscle cells contain different DNA.
   B. Nerve cells contain more DNA than muscle cells.
   C. DNA in muscle cells is condensed into chromatids.
   D. Muscle cells are more likely to have DNA mutations than nerve cells.
   E. Transcription factors and gene expression is different in nerve cells and muscle cells.

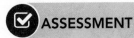 ASSESSMENT

For additional assessment practice, go online to access your digital course.

| If You Have Trouble With... | | | |
|---|---|---|---|
| Question | 1 | 2 | 3 |
| See Lesson | 14.2 | 14.2 | 14.3 |
| Performance Expectation | HS-LS1-1 | HS-LS1-1 | HS-LS3-1 |

CHAPTER 15

# The Human Genome

15.1 Human Chromosomes

15.2 Human Genetic Disorders

15.3 Studying the Human Genome

Go Online to access your digital course.

- VIDEO
- AUDIO
- INTERACTIVITY
- eTEXT
- ANIMATION
- VIRTUAL LAB
- ASSESSMENT

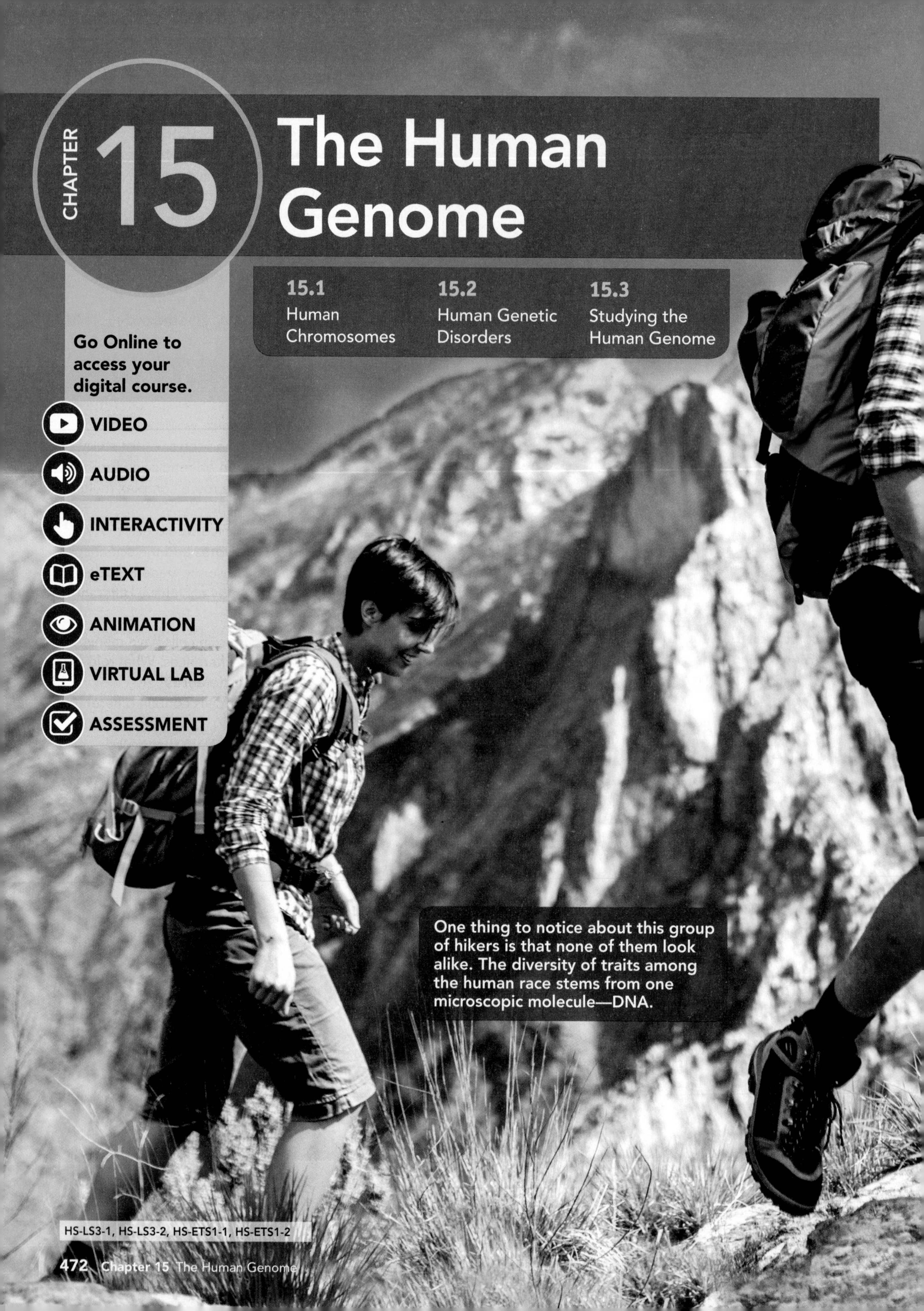

One thing to notice about this group of hikers is that none of them look alike. The diversity of traits among the human race stems from one microscopic molecule—DNA.

HS-LS3-1, HS-LS3-2, HS-ETS1-1, HS-ETS1-2

# DNA—to test or not to test?

In 1990, scientists around the world launched the Human Genome Project. The goal was to determine the complete nucleotide sequence of human DNA, and to map the location of every gene. Thirteen years later, on time and under budget, the project was completed. The scientists identified about 20,000 genes, an unexpectedly small number given the complexity of the human species.

Today, new technology allows DNA to be sequenced a lot more rapidly, and for a lot less money. Machines can now automatically sequence the human genome in a day or two for less than one thousand dollars! For much less than that, many companies will now analyze samples of your DNA to search for specific sequences that reveal ethnic ancestry and tendencies to develop certain diseases.

What has been learned from exploring the details of the human genome? One example is the way human relationships can now be traced with great precision. The genomes for all humans are similar, but individual differences show how closely two people are related, and can even solve historical mysteries. For example, the remains of Richard III, an English king who died in 1485, were identified by comparing a DNA sample with a sample from one of his living descendants. Similar studies have confirmed the fates of members of the royal family of Russia after the Russian revolution. In criminal justice, the routine use of DNA in criminal investigations has helped to identify the guilty and exonerate the innocent in many cases.

DNA sequencing also helps identify genetic diseases. An important example is Tay-Sachs disease, which destroys nerve cells in infants. About 1 in 250 people carry the allele that causes the disease, and the rate is higher among certain populations. A simple blood test is now available to couples that can determine whether either of them has the recessive disease-causing allele. As you know from basic genetics, if both parents have the allele, the probability that a child will inherit the disease is 1 out of 4. In Israel, where the disease is more prevalent than elsewhere, testing and counseling have reduced Tay-Sachs cases by nearly 90 percent.

DNA tests are now available for hundreds of genetic disorders, raising a number of important questions. Should potential parents be required to be tested for genetic disorders? If such tests show a probability that two potential parents might produce children with a genetic disorder, does a couple have the right to take a chance and have children anyway? Does government have a role in trying to eliminate these tragic and costly disorders from the population?

**Throughout this chapter, look for connections to the CASE STUDY to help you answer these questions.**

If you had to pick an ideal animal for the study of genetics, you certainly wouldn't pick one that produced very few offspring, had a long life span, and could not be grown in a lab. Yet, when we study human genetics, this is exactly the sort of organism we deal with. Given all of these difficulties, it may seem a wonder that we know as much about human genetics as we do.

## Karyotypes

What makes us human? We might try to answer that question by looking under the microscope to see what is inside a human cell. Not surprisingly, human cells look much like the cells of other animals. To find what makes us uniquely human, we have to look deep into the genetic instructions that build each new individual. This means that we have to explore the human genome. A **genome** is the full set of genetic information that an organism carries in its DNA.

The analysis of any genome starts with chromosomes, which are bundles of DNA and protein found in the nuclei of eukaryotic cells. To see human chromosomes clearly, cell biologists photograph cells in mitosis, when the chromosomes are fully condensed and easy to view. Scientists then arrange images of each chromosome to produce a **karyotype** (KAIR ee uh typ). 🔍 *A karyotype shows the complete diploid set of chromosomes grouped together in pairs, arranged in order of decreasing size.*

The karyotype shown in **Figure 15-1** is from a typical human cell, which contains 46 chromosomes, arranged in 23 pairs. Why do our chromosomes come in pairs? Remember that the first cell of a human is formed when a haploid sperm, carrying 23 chromosomes, fertilizes a haploid egg, also with 23 chromosomes. The resulting diploid cell develops into a new individual and carries the full complement of 46 chromosomes—two sets of 23.

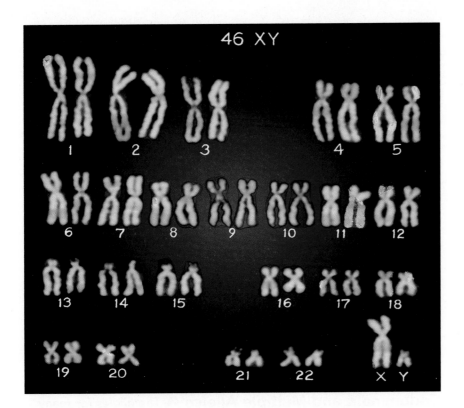

46 XY

1 2 3 4 5
6 7 8 9 10 11 12
13 14 15 16 17 18
19 20 21 22 X Y

**Figure 15-1**

**Human Karyotype**

A typical human cell has 23 pairs of chromosomes. These color-enhanced images of a complete set of chromosomes have been arranged to form a karyotype.

**Sex Chromosomes** Two of the 46 chromosomes in the human genome are known as **sex chromosomes**, because they determine an individual's sex. The two sex chromosomes in humans are shown in **Figure 15-2**. Females have two copies of the X chromosome. Males have one X chromosome and one Y chromosome.

All human egg cells carry a single X chromosome (23,X). However, half of all sperm cells carry an X chromosome (23,X) and half carry a Y chromosome (23,Y). This means that there is a 50 percent probability that an egg cell will be fertilized by an X-carrying sperm, and a 50 percent probability that it will be fertilized by a Y-carrying sperm. As a result, just about half the zygotes will be males and half will be females.

More than 1400 genes are found on the X chromosome. The Y chromosome, which is smaller, contains only about 158 genes, many of which are associated with male sex determination and sperm development.

**Autosomal Chromosomes** To distinguish them from the sex chromosomes, the remaining 44 human chromosomes are known as autosomal chromosomes, or **autosomes**. The complete human genome consists of 46 chromosomes, including 44 autosomes and 2 sex chromosomes. To quickly summarize the total number of chromosomes present in a human cell—both autosomes and sex chromosomes—biologists write 46,XX for females and 46,XY for males.

☑ **READING CHECK** Apply Concepts Why are males and females born in a roughly 50:50 ratio?

**Figure 15-2**

**X and Y Chromosomes**

The human X chromosome contains roughly ten times as many genes as the human Y chromosome. The figure shows the locations of some genes on each of the sex chromosomes.

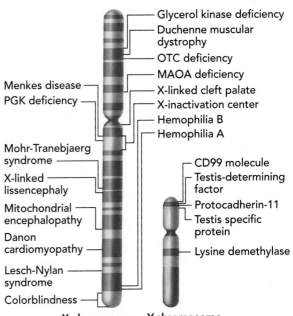

Glycerol kinase deficiency
Duchenne muscular dystrophy
OTC deficiency
MAOA deficiency
X-linked cleft palate
X-inactivation center
Hemophilia B
Hemophilia A

Menkes disease
PGK deficiency

Mohr-Tranebjaerg syndrome
X-linked lissencephaly
Mitochondrial encephalopathy
Danon cardiomyopathy
Lesch-Nylan syndrome
Colorblindness

CD99 molecule
Testis-determining factor
Protocadherin-11
Testis specific protein
Lysine demethylase

X chromosome    Y chromosome

# Transmission of Human Traits

The study of human genetics has progressed rapidly in recent years because of the use of molecular techniques for studying DNA. What have these studies shown? Human genes follow the same patterns of inheritance as the genes of other organisms.

## Dominant and Recessive Alleles ✎ *Many human traits follow a pattern of simple dominance.* For instance, a gene on chromosome 16 known as *MC1R* helps determine skin and hair color. Some of *MC1R*'s recessive alleles produce red hair, as in **Figure 15-3**. An individual with red hair usually has two of these recessive alleles, inheriting a copy from each parent. Dominant alleles for the *MC1R* gene help produce darker hair colors.

Another trait that displays simple dominance is the Rhesus, or Rh blood group. The allele for Rh factor comes in two forms: Rh+ and Rh−. Rh+ is dominant, so an individual with both alleles (Rh+/Rh−) is said to have Rh positive blood. Rh negative blood is found in individuals with two recessive alleles (Rh−/Rh−).

## Codominant and Multiple Alleles ✎ *The alleles for many human genes display codominant inheritance.* One example is the ABO blood group, determined by a gene on chromosome 9 with three alleles: $I^A$, $I^B$, and $i$. Alleles $I^A$ and $I^B$ are codominant. They produce molecules known as antigens on the surface of red blood cells. As **Figure 15-4** shows, individuals with alleles $I^A$ and $I^B$ produce both A and B antigens, making them blood type AB. The $i$ allele is recessive. Individuals with alleles $I^A I^A$ or $I^A i$ produce only the A antigen, making them blood type A. Those with $I^B I^B$ or $I^B i$ alleles are type B. Those homozygous for the $i$ allele ($ii$) produce no antigen and are said to have blood type O. If a patient has AB-negative blood, it means the individual has $I^A$ and $I^B$ alleles from the ABO gene and two Rh− alleles from the Rh gene.

**Figure 15-3**

**Recessive Alleles**

Some recessive alleles in humans produce variations, like red hair or type O blood. Other alleles result in harmful traits, like Tay-Sachs disease and cystic fibrosis.

**INTERACTIVITY**

Determine which set of parents may have children with colorblindness.

**Figure 15-4**

**Human Blood Groups**

Analyze the data in the table to see the relationship between genotype and phenotype for the ABO blood group. The table also shows which blood types can safely be transfused into people with other blood types.

| Blood Groups | | | | |
|---|---|---|---|---|
| Phenotype (Blood Type) | Genotype | Antigen on Red Blood Cell | Safe Transfusions | |
| | | | To | From |
| A | $I^A I^A$ or $I^A i$ | A | A, AB | A, O |
| B | $I^B I^B$ or $I^B i$ | B | B, AB | B, O |
| AB | $I^A I^B$ | A and B | AB | A, B, AB, O |
| O | $ii$ | None | A, B, AB, O | O |

## Sex-Linked Inheritance

🔑 Because the X and Y chromosomes determine sex, the genes located on them show a pattern of inheritance called sex-linkage. A **sex-linked gene** is a gene located on a sex chromosome. As you might expect, genes on the Y chromosome are found only in males and are passed directly from father to son. Genes located on the X chromosome are found in both sexes, but the fact that men have just one X chromosome leads to some interesting <u>consequences</u>.

For example, humans have three genes responsible for color vision, all located on the X chromosome. In males, a defective allele for any of these genes results in colorblindness, an inability to distinguish certain colors, like those shown in **Figure 15-5**. The most common form, red-green colorblindness, occurs in about 1 in 12 males. Among females, however, colorblindness affects only about 1 in 200. Why is there such a difference? In order for a recessive allele, like colorblindness, to be expressed in females, it must be present in two copies—one on each of the X chromosomes. This means that the recessive phenotype of a sex-linked genetic disorder tends to be much more common among males than among females.

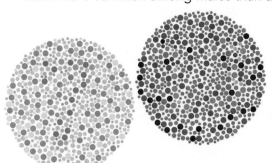

### Figure 15-5

### Eye Test

Doctors use images like these to test for colorblindness. A person who is colorblind will perceive only random dots, and not the colored numbers inside the circles.

## X-Chromosome Inactivation

If just one X chromosome is enough for cells in males, how does the cell "adjust" to the extra X chromosome in female cells? The answer was discovered by British geneticist Mary Lyon. In female cells, most of the genes in one of the X chromosomes are inactivated, forming a condensed region in the nucleus known as a Barr body. A special RNA molecule binds to the inactivated chromosome and keeps it in the condensed state.

The same process happens in other mammals. In cats, for example, a gene that controls the color of coat spots is located on the X chromosome. One X chromosome may have an allele for orange spots and the other X chromosome may have an allele for black spots. In cells in some parts of the body, one X chromosome is switched off. In other parts of the body, the other X chromosome is switched off. As a result, the cat's fur has a mixture of orange and black spots, like those in **Figure 15-6**. Male cats, which have just one X chromosome, can have spots of only one color. Therefore, if the cat's fur has three colors—white with orange and black spots, for example—you can almost be certain that the cat is female.

**✓ READING CHECK** **Apply Concepts** How does a Barr body help explain why the fur of female cats can have three colors?

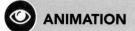

👁 **ANIMATION**

hhmi | **BioInteractive**

### Figure 15-6

### X-Chromosome Inactivation

Calico cats are tricolored. Spots are either orange or black, depending on which X chromosome is inactivated in different patches of their skin.

**INTERACTIVITY**

Investigate human inheritance with interactive pedigree charts.

# Human Pedigrees

Given the complexities of genetics, how would you determine whether a trait is caused by a dominant or recessive allele and whether the gene for that trait is autosomal or sex-linked? The answers, not surprisingly, can be found by applying Mendel's basic principles.

To analyze the pattern of inheritance followed by a particular trait, you can use a **pedigree** chart that shows the relationships within a family. A pedigree shows the presence or absence of a trait according to the relationships among parents, siblings, and offspring.

The pedigree in **Figure 15-7** shows how one human trait—a white lock of hair just above the forehead—passes through three generations of a family. The allele for the white forelock trait is dominant. At the top of the chart is a grandfather who had the white forelock trait. Two of his three children inherited the trait. Three grandchildren have the trait, but two do not.

**CASE STUDY**

**Figure 15-7**

## How to Use a Pedigree

The diagram shows what the symbols in a pedigree represent. This pedigree shows the inheritance of a white forelock. ☑ **Explain** How might a pedigree be used to study a harmful trait, like Tay-Sachs disease?

White forelock

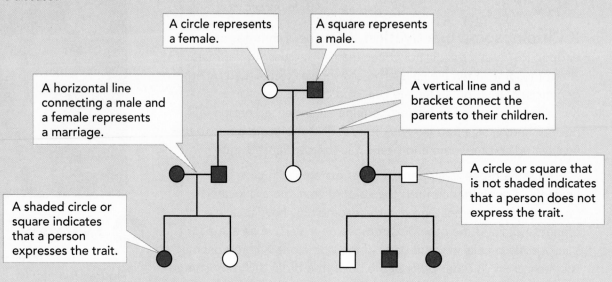

A circle represents a female.

A square represents a male.

A horizontal line connecting a male and a female represents a marriage.

A vertical line and a bracket connect the parents to their children.

A circle or square that is not shaded indicates that a person does not express the trait.

A shaded circle or square indicates that a person expresses the trait.

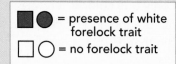

■● = presence of white forelock trait
□○ = no forelock trait

## Quick Lab — Guided Inquiry

### How Can You Analyze a Pedigree?

1. In a small group, choose one of the genetic conditions or disorders described in this chapter.

2. Construct a pedigree for the condition, such as the one for red hair shown here. Begin the pedigree with one pair of grandparents, and then add several children and grandchildren. For each family member, record a genotype for the condition or disorder.

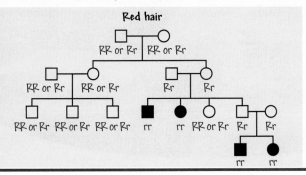

3. Draw a second pedigree, this time showing the phenotype of the condition for each family member.

4. Exchange the second pedigree with another student group.

### ANALYZE AND CONCLUDE

1. **Construct an Explanation** Study the pedigree that the other student group produced. How is the genetic condition or disorder inherited? Construct an explanation based on the information the pedigree shows.

2. **Analyze Data** Write a possible genotype for each family member shown in the pedigree.

3. **Evaluate Reasoning** Compare the genotypes you identified with those specified by the student group that produced the pedigree. Explain any differences.

By analyzing a pedigree, we can infer genotypes and predict future outcomes. Because the white forelock trait is dominant, the family members in Figure 15-7 lacking this trait must have homozygous recessive alleles. One of the grandfather's children lacks the white forelock trait, so the grandfather must be heterozygous. On this basis, we can predict that roughly half of the grandfather's children would display the trait.

With pedigree analysis, it is possible to apply the principles of Mendelian genetics to humans. **The information gained from pedigree analysis makes it possible to determine the nature of genes and alleles associated with inherited human traits.** Based on a pedigree, you can often determine if an allele for a trait is dominant or recessive, as well as autosomal or sex-linked.

## ✓ LESSON 15.1 Review

### KEY QUESTIONS

1. How is a karyotype made?

2. How are recessive traits inherited when multiple alleles or sex-linked genes are involved?

3. What does a pedigree show about human traits?

### CRITICAL THINKING

4. **Construct an Explanation** Why is colorblindness more common in men than in women?

5. **Use Models** A woman with type O blood and a man with type AB blood have children. Use **Figure 15-4** as a model to list the possible genotypes and phenotypes of their children.

6. **Identify Patterns** Is it possible that any of the individuals in the pedigree in **Figure 15-7** are homozygous dominant? Why or why not? What phenotype would you expect to see in the children of an individual who is homozygous dominant for the white forelock trait?

7. **CASE STUDY** Healthy parents may have children who suffer from Tay-Sachs disease, a genetic disorder. Based on this evidence, is Tay-Sachs caused by a dominant or recessive allele? Explain.

# Human Genetic Disorders

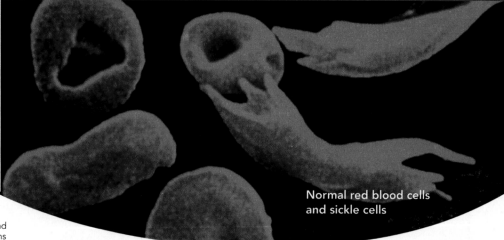

Normal red blood cells and sickle cells

**VOCABULARY**
**nondisjunction**

**READING TOOL**

As you read, identify the main ideas and details that support the main ideas. Fill in the table in your 📖 **Biology Foundations Workbook.**

 **INTERACTIVITY**

Investigate genetic disorders and how they are expressed in humans.

Have you ever heard the expression "It runs in the family"? Relatives or friends might have said that about your smile or the shape of your ears, but what could it mean when they talk of diseases and disorders? What, exactly, is a genetic disorder?

## Chromosomal Disorders

Most of the time, the process of meiosis works perfectly and each human gamete gets exactly 23 chromosomes. Every now and then, however, something goes wrong. The most common error in meiosis occurs when homologous chromosomes fail to separate. This mistake is known as **nondisjunction**, which means "not coming apart." **Figure 15-8** illustrates the process.

🔍 *If nondisjunction occurs during meiosis, gametes with an abnormal number of chromosomes may result, leading to a disorder of chromosome numbers.* For example, if two copies of an autosomal chromosome fail to separate during meiosis, an individual may be born with three copies of that chromosome. This condition is known as a trisomy, meaning "three bodies." The most common form of trisomy, involving three copies of chromosome 21, is Down syndrome, which is associated with a range of cognitive disabilities and certain birth defects.

Nondisjunction of the X chromosomes can lead to a disorder known as Turner's syndrome. A female with Turner's syndrome usually inherits only one X chromosome. Most women with Turner's syndrome are unable to reproduce because their sex organs do not develop properly at puberty. In males, nondisjunction may cause Klinefelter's syndrome, resulting from the inheritance of an extra X chromosome, which interferes with meiosis and may prevent these individuals from reproducing.

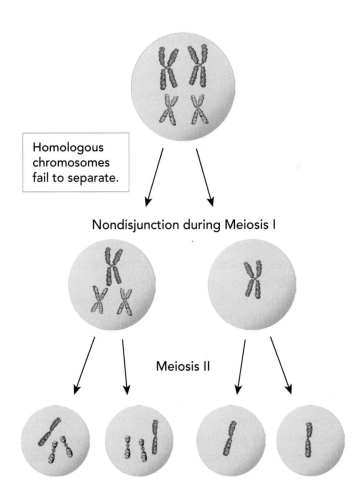

Homologous chromosomes fail to separate.

Nondisjunction during Meiosis I

Meiosis II

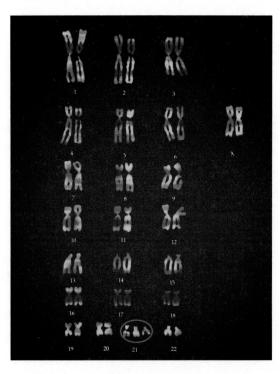

Down Syndrome

## Figure 15-8
## Nondisjunction

This failure of meiosis causes gametes to have an abnormal number of chromosomes. The karyotype shown here is that of Down syndrome. Notice that there are three copies of chromosome 21 instead of two.

# From Molecule to Phenotype

We know that genes are made of DNA and that they interact with the environment to produce an individual organism's characteristics, or phenotype. However, when a gene fails to work or works improperly, serious problems can result.

Molecular research techniques have shown us a direct link between genotype and phenotype. For example, the wax that sometimes builds up in our ear canals can be one of two forms: wet or dry. People of African and European ancestry are more likely to have wet earwax—the dominant form. Those of Asian or Native American ancestry most often have the dry form, which is recessive. The cause is a single DNA base in the gene for a membrane-transport protein. A simple base change from guanine (G) to adenine (A) causes this protein to produce dry earwax instead of wet earwax.

The connection between molecule and trait, and between genotype and phenotype, is often that simple, and just as direct. ⚲ *Changes in a gene's DNA sequence can change proteins by altering their amino acid sequences, which may directly affect an individual's phenotype.* Sometimes, however, these effects are more subtle. For example, certain alleles are associated with tendencies to develop conditions such as diabetes, heart disease, and cancer. Many other factors, such as behavior, diet, and environment, can have a profound effect on whether these conditions actually develop.

## BUILD VOCABULARY

**Prefixes** The word *nondisjunction* is formed by adding the prefixes *non-* and *dis-* to *junction*, which comes from a Latin verb that means "to join." *Non-* (not) and *dis-* (separate) also come from Latin. Put together, these word parts indicate that something joined does not come apart.

**Disorders Caused by Individual Genes** Given the size and complexity of the human genome, it shouldn't be surprising that things can sometimes go wrong. In fact, we now know of thousands of genetic disorders caused by changes in individual genes. These changes often affect specific proteins associated with important cellular functions.

*Sickle Cell Disease* Although sickle cell disease had been known for centuries in Africa, it was not described in the scientific literature until 1910. In the late 1940s, scientists made two important discoveries. The first was that sickle cell disease was hereditary and caused by a recessive allele. The second was that the hemoglobin in people with sickle cell disease was different from normal hemoglobin. Hemoglobin is the oxygen-carrying protein in red blood cells. These two discoveries revealed the links between genes and abnormal proteins, and between proteins and human disease. Sickle cell disease was one of the first recognized molecular diseases, and its discovery spurred research into the molecular origins of other diseases.

As shown in **Figure 15-9**, sickle cell disease is caused by a defective allele for beta-globin, one of two polypeptides in hemoglobin. The defective polypeptide makes hemoglobin a bit less soluble, causing hemoglobin molecules to stick together when the blood's oxygen level decreases. As a result, hemoglobin tends to clump into long fibers that push against the membranes of red blood cells and distort their shape. The physician who first observed such cells described them as "sickle-shaped," and that is how the disorder has been known ever since.

Sickle-shaped cells are more rigid than normal red blood cells, so they tend to get stuck in capillaries—the narrowest blood vessels in the body. If the blood stops moving through the capillaries, damage to cells, tissues, and even organs can result.

**ANIMATION**

hhmi | **BioInteractive**

**Figure 15-9**

**Sickle Cell Disease**

A mutation in the beta-globin gene on chromosome 11 results in the formation of aggregated fibers of hemoglobin, which produces the sickle-cell shape of red blood cells.

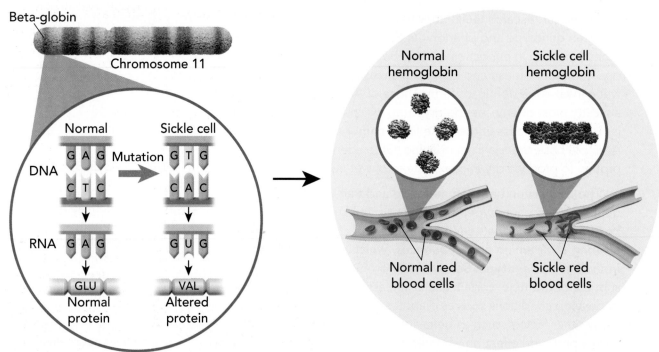

**Cystic Fibrosis** Cystic fibrosis (CF) usually results from the deletion of just three bases in the gene for a protein called cystic fibrosis transmembrane conductance regulator (CFTR). CFTR normally allows chloride ions ($Cl^-$) to pass across cell membranes. The loss of these bases removes a single amino acid—phenylalanine—from CFTR, causing the protein to fold improperly.

People with one normal copy of the CF allele are unaffected by CF because they can produce enough CFTR to allow their cells to work properly. Two copies of the defective allele are needed to produce the disorder, which means the CF allele is recessive. Children with CF have serious digestive problems and produce thick, heavy mucus that clogs their lungs and breathing passageways. A CF patient undergoing a breathing treatment is shown in **Figure 15-10**.

**Huntington's Disease** Huntington's disease is caused by a dominant allele for a protein found in brain cells. The allele for this disease contains a long string of bases in which the codon CAG—coding for the amino acid glutamine—repeats over and over again, more than 40 times. Despite intensive study, the reason why these long strings of glutamine cause disease is still not clear. The symptoms of Huntington's disease, namely mental deterioration and uncontrollable movements, usually do not appear until middle age. The greater the number of codon repeats, the earlier the disease appears, and the more severe its symptoms are.

**✓ READING CHECK Infer** Is a person who inherits a single allele for Huntington's disease likely to develop the disorder? If so, when?

**Genetic Advantages** Disorders such as CF and sickle cell disease are still common in human populations. In the United States, the CF allele is carried by roughly 1 person in 25 of European ancestry, and approximately 1 person in 12 of African ancestry carries the sickle cell allele. Why are these alleles still around if they can be fatal for those who carry them? The answers may surprise you.

**CF Allele and Typhoid** More than 1000 years ago, the cities of medieval Europe were ravaged by epidemics of typhoid fever. Typhoid is caused by a bacterium that enters the body through cells in the digestive system. The protein produced by the CF allele helps block the entry of this bacterium. Individuals who are heterozygous for CF would have had an advantage when living in cities with poor sanitation and polluted water. Because they also carried the normal allele, these individuals would not have suffered from cystic fibrosis.

**▶ VIDEO**

Explore how muscle fibers twitch at different rates and how this affects athletes.

## Analyzing Data

### The Geography of Malaria

Malaria is a potentially fatal disease transmitted by mosquitoes. Its cause is a parasite that lives inside red blood cells. The upper map shows where malaria is common. The lower map shows regions where the sickle cell allele is the most prevalent.

1. **Analyze Data** What is the relationship between the places where malaria is common and where the sickle cell allele is commonly found?

2. **Construct an Explanation** In 1805, a Scottish explorer named Mungo Park led an expedition of European geographers to find the source of the Niger River in Africa. The journey began with a party of 45 Europeans. During the expedition, most of these men perished from malaria. Their native guides and the other natives they encountered were seemingly unaffected. Use the data to construct an explanation for why the native Africans' phenotype helped them survive.

3. **Form a Hypothesis** As the map shows, the sickle cell allele is not found in African populations that are native to southern Africa. Form a hypothesis to account for this discrepancy.

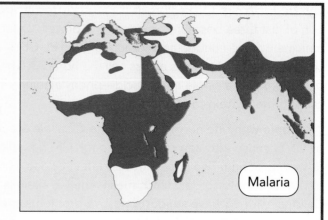

Malaria

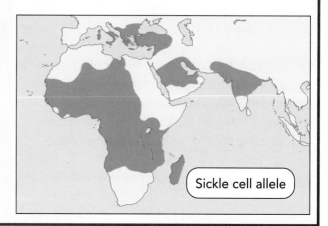

Sickle cell allele

***Sickle Cell Allele and Malaria*** Many African Americans today are descended from populations that originally lived in west central Africa, where malaria is common. Malaria is a mosquito-borne infection caused by a parasite that lives inside red blood cells. Individuals with just one copy of the sickle cell allele are generally healthy and are also highly resistant to the parasite. This resistance gives them a great advantage against malaria, which even today claims more than four hundred thousand lives every year.

## ☑ LESSON 15.2 Review

### ⚗ KEY QUESTIONS

1. How does nondisjunction affect the production of gametes?

2. How can a change in genotype affect phenotype?

### CRITICAL THINKING

3. **Use Models** What condition is modeled by the expression 47, XXY? Explain what the model shows.

4. **Synthesize Information** Is it possible for a change of a single nucleotide in DNA to have an observable effect on phenotype? Include an example to support your answer.

5. **Construct an Explanation** How can alleles that cause serious diseases, such as sickle cell disease, still provide an advantage to the human population?

# Studying the Human Genome

## 🔍 KEY QUESTIONS

- *How can scientists read DNA base sequences?*
- *What research efforts have resulted from the Human Genome Project?*

**HS-LS3-1:** Ask questions to clarify relationships about the role of DNA and chromosomes in coding the instructions for characteristic traits passed from parents to offspring.

**HS-ETS1-1:** Analyze a major global challenge to specify qualitative and quantitative criteria and constraints for solutions that account for societal needs and wants.

There are more than 6 billion base pairs of DNA in just a single human cell. If we think of each base pair as a single letter, that amounts to nearly 3000 textbooks of 1000 pages each. Just a few decades ago, that might have seemed to be an unimaginably large amount of information. Today, however, we have powerful techniques to read, store, and process that information. As a result, we know more about the human genome than ever—and are learning more every day.

## Manipulating DNA

Since the discovery of the double helix, biologists have dreamed of a time when they could read the DNA sequences in the human genome. For a long time, it seemed impossible. DNA molecules are huge—even the smallest human chromosome contains nearly 50 million base pairs. Manipulating such large molecules is difficult. In the late 1960s, however, scientists discovered natural enzymes, called **restriction enzymes**, that could cut DNA at specific sites. **Figure 15-11** shows how restriction enzymes work. 🔍 ***By using tools that cut, separate, and copy nucleic acids, scientists can now read DNA base sequences.*** Such techniques have made it possible to study the genomes of living organisms, including humans, in great detail.

**VOCABULARY**

**restriction enzyme**
**gel electrophoresis**
**genomic imprinting**

**READING TOOL**

As you read, keep track of the different steps that scientists use to read nucleotide sequences. Fill in the graphic organizer in your 📖 **Biology Foundations Workbook.**

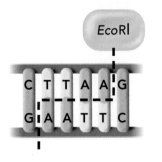
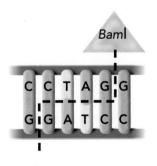
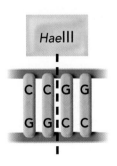

**Figure 15-11**

**Restriction Enzymes**

These enzymes recognize specific DNA sequences, and then cut both DNA strands as shown.

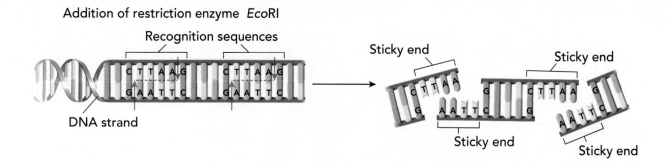

Addition of restriction enzyme *Eco*RI

Recognition sequences

Sticky end

Sticky end

C T T A A G C T T A A G

G A A T T C G A A T T C

DNA strand

Sticky end

Sticky end

Sticky end

**INTERACTIVITY**

**Figure 15-12**

## Cutting DNA

Restriction enzymes cut DNA in specific ways.

**Cutting DNA** DNA is relatively easy to extract from cells and tissues. However, DNA molecules are so large that they must first be cut into smaller pieces for analysis. Many bacteria produce restriction enzymes that do exactly that. They precisely cut DNA molecules into smaller pieces, several hundred bases in length. Bacteria use restriction enzymes to cut and inactivate the DNA of bacteriophages, viruses that infect bacteria. A restriction enzyme is like a key that fits only one lock. For example, as shown **Figure 15-12**, the *Eco*RI restriction enzyme can only recognize the base sequence GAATTC. It cuts each strand of DNA between the G and A bases, leaving single-stranded overhangs with the sequence AATT. The overhangs are called "sticky ends" because they can bond, or "stick," to a DNA fragment with the complementary base sequence.

**Figure 15-13**

## Separating DNA

An electric voltage moves DNA fragments across a gel similar to a slice of gelatin. Within an hour or two, the fragments all separate, each appearing as a band on the gel.

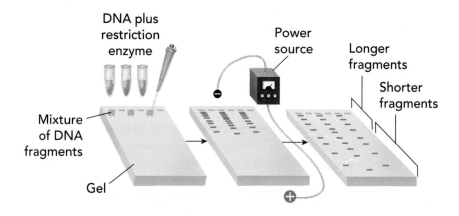

DNA plus restriction enzyme

Power source

Longer fragments

Shorter fragments

Mixture of DNA fragments

Gel

**INTERACTIVITY**

Conduct a virtual activity using restriction enzymes to isolate particular genes.

**Separating DNA** Once DNA has been cut by restriction enzymes, scientists can use a technique known as **gel electrophoresis** to separate the fragments. **Figure 15-13** illustrates this simple, yet effective, method. A mixture of DNA fragments are placed in wells on one end of a porous gel. When an electric voltage is applied to the gel, DNA molecules—which are negatively charged—move toward the positive end of the gel. The smaller the DNA fragment, the faster and farther it moves. The current is turned off after a few hours. The result is a pattern of bands based on fragment size. Specific stains that bind to DNA make these bands visible. Researchers can then remove individual restriction fragments from the gel and study them further.

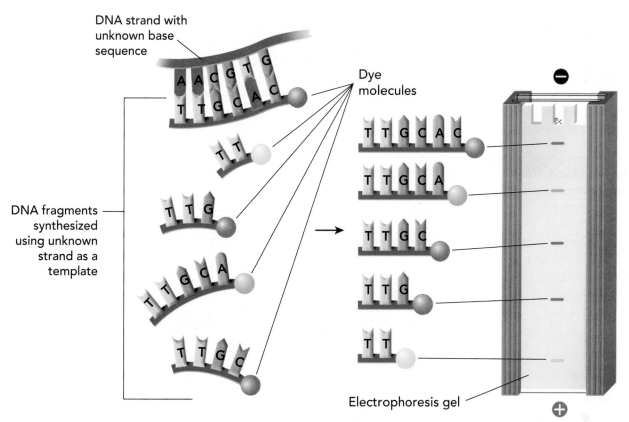

DNA strand with unknown base sequence

Dye molecules

DNA fragments synthesized using unknown strand as a template

Electrophoresis gel

**Figure 15-14**

**Reading DNA**

Fragments of DNA separated by electrophoresis and tagged with dye can be used to determine the sequence of bases in a strand of DNA.

**Reading DNA** After the DNA fragments have been separated, researchers use a clever chemical "trick" to read, or sequence, them. The single-stranded DNA fragments are placed in a test tube containing DNA polymerase—the enzyme that copies DNA—along with the four nucleotide bases, A, T, G, and C. As the enzyme goes to work, it uses the unknown strand as a template to make one new DNA strand after another. The tricky part is that researchers also add a small number of bases that have a chemical dye attached. Each time a dye-labeled base is added to a new DNA strand, the synthesis of that strand stops. When DNA synthesis is completed, the result is a series of color-coded DNA fragments of different lengths, as shown in **Figure 15-14**. Researchers can then separate these fragments, often by gel electrophoresis. The order of colored bands on the gel tells the exact sequence of bases in the DNA.

Until the late 1980s, the sequencing of DNA was done by researchers painstakingly analyzing the columns and bands on electrophoresis gels and recording their data. This was a slow process, prone to errors, and very expensive. It takes a person about a year to read a sequence of 20,000 to 50,000 bases—and the human genome contains about 3 billion base pairs. Fortunately, sequencing has been improved and automated over the decades, becoming faster, less expensive, and more accurate. Tasks that once took a person a year to do can now be done in a matter of hours. Some labs now sequence well over 100,000 billion bases per year, with hundreds of DNA fragments being sequenced simultaneously.

**READING TOOL**

After you have read this section, write down the sequence of events involved in manipulating and reading DNA. Reread the section to check your work.

**Assembling the Sequence** One common feature of most DNA sequencing techniques is that they read fragments no more than a few hundred bases in length. How are these short "reads" of DNA put together to produce a full-length map? **Figure 15-15** shows how this is done through a technique known as "shotgun" sequencing. Whole chromosomes are cut into random fragments. These are sequenced automatically, and the information is fed into a computer. A computer program analyzes the data by searching for matching sequences among the fragments, and aligns them to reassemble the fragments and complete the sequence.

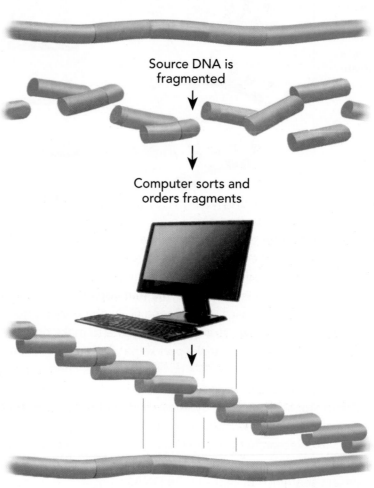

Source DNA is fragmented

Computer sorts and orders fragments

Overlapping sequences are matched and aligned to determine the complete DNA sequence.

**Figure 15-15**

**Putting the Pieces Together**

Computers can quickly find overlapping sequences, thereby determining the sequence for an entire length of DNA.

Some new sequencing technologies have even done away with the need to cut DNA into fragments. One involves drawing a strand of DNA through a tiny pore, like a thread being pulled through the eye of a needle. Each base creates a different kind of electrical signal as it passes through the pore, allowing the bases to be read one by one. As a result of all this technical progress, you might say that the "easy" part of genome analysis today is reading the DNA base sequence. The hard part is making sense of it.

**✓ READING CHECK Summarize** Describe how DNA is sequenced.

## Develop a Solution Lab — Guided Inquiry

### Gel Electrophoresis

**Problem** How can molecules be separated by electric charge?

Scientists use gel electrophoresis to separate DNA fragments. In this lab, you will practice the technique of gel electrophoresis by separating food dye into its different components.

You can find this lab in your digital course.

# The Human Genome—What's Inside?

In 2003, an international effort known as the Human Genome Project finished the first complete human DNA sequence. But scientists quickly realized there was much more to be done, and set about trying to make sense of all the data. ⚲ *Labs around the world now study which regions of DNA are transcribed into RNA, which bind to proteins, which are marked with epigenetic tags, and which vary from one individual to the next.* The Human Genome Project was only the beginning of a new era of research on human molecular genetics, but the findings so far are fascinating.

**How Many Genes?** Research on the human genome revealed many surprises. Human cells contain approximately 20,000 genes, which is not a large number compared to the cells of other species. In fact, one research team wrote that with respect to the number of genes, humans are "somewhere between a chicken and a grape." The chicken genome has about 17,000 genes, and the grape has about 30,000 genes. What do those genes code for? As **Figure 15-16** shows, the functions of more than a quarter of human genes are unknown. The other genes fall into categories such as transcription factors, metabolic enzymes, components of the cell membrane, receptors, and regulatory factors.

**Figure 15-16**

**Functions of Human Genes**

While the functions of many genes are known, we are still unsure of the functions of more than 25 percent of our genes.

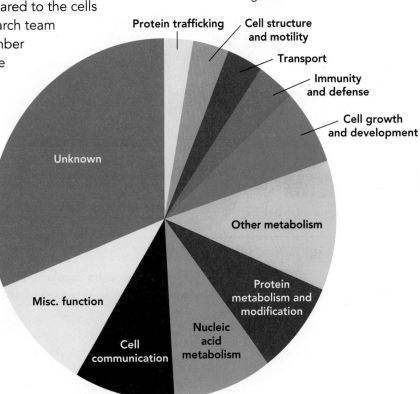

Adapted from Freeman Biological Science ©2011

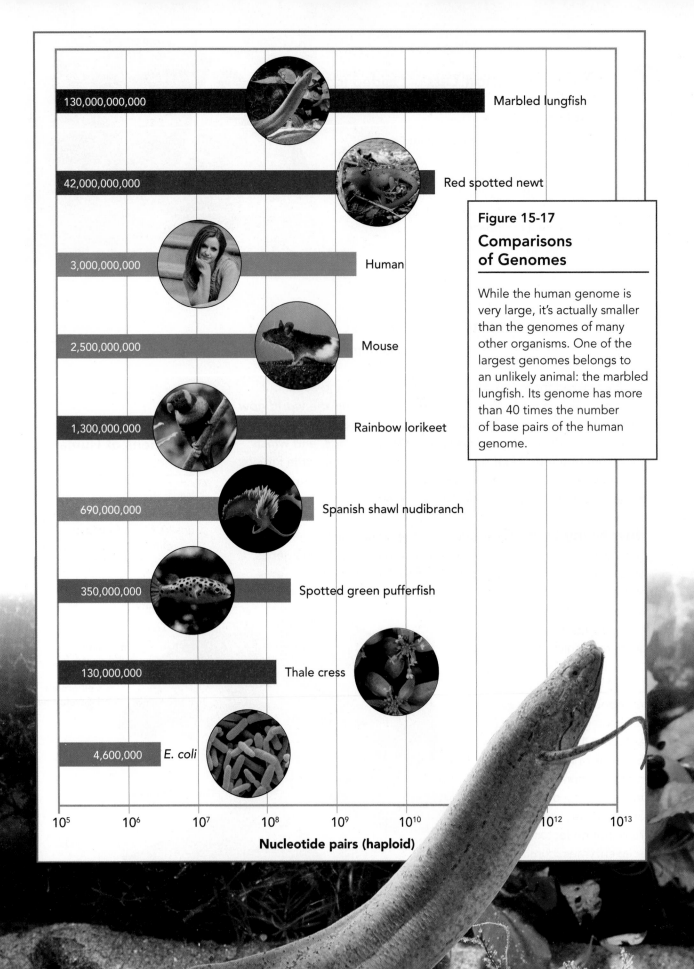

130,000,000,000 — Marbled lungfish

42,000,000,000 — Red spotted newt

3,000,000,000 — Human

2,500,000,000 — Mouse

1,300,000,000 — Rainbow lorikeet

690,000,000 — Spanish shawl nudibranch

350,000,000 — Spotted green pufferfish

130,000,000 — Thale cress

4,600,000 — *E. coli*

$10^5$  $10^6$  $10^7$  $10^8$  $10^9$  $10^{10}$  $10^{12}$  $10^{13}$

**Nucleotide pairs (haploid)**

**Figure 15-17**

## Comparisons of Genomes

While the human genome is very large, it's actually smaller than the genomes of many other organisms. One of the largest genomes belongs to an unlikely animal: the marbled lungfish. Its genome has more than 40 times the number of base pairs of the human genome.

**The Large and Small of It** At 3 billion bases, the human haploid genome is larger than the genome of many other organisms. You might be tempted to think that our unique capabilities are the result of having so much DNA. However, the cells of many organisms contain far more DNA than our cells do! The ordinary onion has nearly five times as much DNA as we have. The marbled lungfish (*Protopterus aethiopicus*) has more than 40 times as much. Curiously, another type of fish, the puffer fish (*Fugu*), has the smallest vertebrate genome discovered so far—just 350 million bases. **Figure 15-17** provides a comparison of the genome sizes of many different types of organisms.

One of the most striking aspects of the human genome is how little of it actually codes for proteins—only about 2 percent. So, what does the rest of the DNA code for? Some of it, of course, is involved in the regulation of gene expression. DNA sequences known as enhancers can bind proteins to open up genes for transcription. Other regions are involved in blocking the expression of nearby genes. Many other regions are transcribed at low frequencies, producing RNA molecules that are not translated into proteins but may play a role in gene regulation. However, all of these sequences taken together account for only about 10 percent of the genome.

Approximately 50 percent of the human genome is composed of highly repetitive DNA sequences—short stretches where the base sequence is repeated over and over again. Many, if not most, of these regions are derived from transposable elements, pieces of DNA that move from place to place in the genome and sometimes generate multiple copies of themselves. The functions, if any, of these regions, which make up more than half of the human genome, remain unknown.

**✓ READING CHECK Infer** Is there a relationship between the complexity of an organism and the number of bases in its genome?

**The Personal Genome** If you were to compare the genomes of two unrelated individuals, you would find that most—but not all—of their DNA will match base for base with each other. On average, about one base in 1200 will not match between two individuals. Biologists call these single base differences single nucleotide polymorphisms (SNPs, or "snips"). Researchers have discovered that certain sets of closely linked SNPs occur together time and time again. Some of these are associated with certain traits, including the susceptibility to particular diseases or medical conditions. Increasingly, high-speed DNA sequencing is making it possible to rapidly pinpoint SNPs and their associated alleles, enabling physicians to tailor medical treatments to a patient's genome. In addition, many private companies now offer a "personal genome" service that analyzes one's DNA for a modest price, and uses that information to determine ethnic ancestry as well as the possibility of developing certain diseases. As we further explore the human genome, the medical and social possibilities for the use of personal genomic information will only increase.

## Figure 15-18
## Collecting Genetic Information

People who are interested in learning about their ancestry or risk for certain diseases, might collect and send their DNA to private companies for analysis. Many ethical questions and decisions surround this practice.

**Use Prior Knowledge** You know that a genome refers to the genetic information carried in the DNA of an organism. An imprint is an identifying marker. Therefore, the term *genomic imprinting*, refers to marks that are carried on DNA.

**Genome Privacy** Rapid advances in gathering and analyzing genomic data have raised a number of ethical and legal questions. For example, who owns and controls the genetic information of the person in **Figure 15-18**? Who should have access to personal genetic information? In response to some of these issues, in 2008, the U.S. Congress passed the Genetic Information Nondiscrimination Act. This act makes it illegal for insurance companies and employers to discriminate based on information from genetic tests. As the science advances, other protective laws may soon follow.

**Gene Imprinting** As you read in Chapter 14, epigenetic chemical marks can be attached to DNA and histone proteins in a way that affects gene expression by altering chromatin structure. This process is known as **genomic imprinting**. In humans as well as other mammals, some of these marks can be passed from one generation to the next through either the mother or the father. This means there are some genes that are only expressed if they came from a male parent and there are some genes that are only expressed if they came from a female parent. Nearly 100 genes in humans are imprinted in this way.

One example of genomic imprinting is a condition called Angelman syndrome, which results from the deletion of a gene known as UBE3A on chromosome 15. Angelman syndrome causes seizures and an unusually happy disposition. An affected child typically inherits two copies of chromosome 15. One copy comes from the child's mother and one from the child's father.

**✓ READING CHECK Review** How does genomic imprinting lead to the expression of one allele over another?

| ■ Chromosome From Father | ■ Chromosome From Mother | ■ Silenced Region |
| --- | --- | --- |

**Angelman Syndrome**

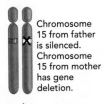

Chromosome 15 from father is silenced. Chromosome 15 from mother has gene deletion.

**Angelman Syndrome**

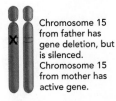

Chromosome 15 from father has gene deletion, but is silenced. Chromosome 15 from mother has active gene.

**Normal Phenotype**

**Prader-Willi Syndrome**

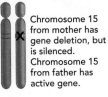

Chromosome 15 from mother has gene deletion, but is silenced. Chromosome 15 from father has active gene.

**Normal Phenotype**

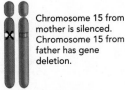

Chromosome 15 from mother is silenced. Chromosome 15 from father has gene deletion.

**Prader-Willi Syndrome**

**Figure 15-19**

## Deletions and Imprinting

Whether a child has Angelman syndrome or Prader-Willi syndrome depends on whether the defective chromosome is inherited from the mother or the father.

The region containing this gene is silenced by epigenetic imprinting in the chromosome inherited from the child's father, while the same region inherited from the mother is active. This means that if a child inherits the deletion on chromosome 15 from its mother, the child will develop Angelman syndrome, since the paternal copy of the gene is silenced, as shown in **Figure 15-19**. On the other hand, if a child inherits the deletion from its father, it will have no effect, since that region of the chromosome is silenced by imprinting, and the mother's copy of the gene is active. Interestingly, there is another genetic disorder known as Prader-Willi syndrome caused by the deletion of a nearby region of the same chromosome. This deletion mutation, however, is inherited from the paternal chromosome, because in this region it is the mother's genes that are silenced by genomic imprinting. Prader-Willi syndrome causes weak muscles and feelings of extreme hunger.

HS-LS3-1, HS-ETS1-1

## ☑ LESSON 15.3 Review

### ⚲ KEY QUESTIONS

1. How are scientists able to read DNA base sequences?

2. How does the number of genes in human cells compare with the numbers in other species?

### CRITICAL THINKING

3. **Construct an Explanation** How does gel electrophoresis work to separate DNA fragments?

4. **Apply Scientific Reasoning** A point mutation changes one nucleotide at a random location in human DNA. How likely is the mutation to cause a change in the amino acid sequence of a protein? Apply scientific reasoning to explain your prediction.

5. CASE STUDY A couple receives DNA analysis, which determines that they are both heterozygous for the gene responsible for Tay-Sachs disease. Should doctors or the government have a role in deciding if the couple can have children together? Construct an argument to explain why or why not.

**15.3** Studying the Human Genome **493**

# DNA—to test or not to test?

**Scientists now have the knowledge and tools to analyze DNA. Human relationships can be traced, crimes can be solved, and genetic diseases can be identified. However, with this knowledge comes some serious ethical and legal questions.**

HS-LS3-1, HS-ETS1-2, CCSS.ELA-LITERACY.WHST.9-10.2

## Make Your Case

DNA testing can identify carriers of the Tay-Sachs allele. In an effort to eliminate this tragic disease, couples at risk are urged to get tested for the allele before they marry or have children. Potentially, this approach could also reduce the incidence of other genetic diseases and disorders.

## Develop a Solution

1. **Ask Questions** With a partner, research two common human genetic disorders. Find out whether genetic testing is available for them, and find out whether such tests are generally offered to prospective parents.

2. **Form an Opinion** Decide whether such testing makes medical and economic sense for the disorders you have researched. Discuss whether there should be legal requirements for such testing and what the rights of prospective parents should be in cases where disease-causing alleles are found.

## Society on the Case

### Private Information?

For many years, people have been volunteering their DNA for research studies. Analyses of the DNA have been published online or in other forums, but never with the name of the volunteer included. For years, scientists assumed that they were safeguarding people's privacy. Now, new knowledge and technology are challenging this assumption.

From analyzing a DNA sample and other genetic information, scientists can now infer data about a person's weight, age, and general health. Some viral infections can be detected because they change genetic activity. Genes also show risks for Alzheimer's disease, cancer, and other diseases.

Is it possible to identify someone from only a DNA sample? In 2013, Yaniv Erlich of the Whitehead Institute in Massachusetts showed a surprising answer to this question. He selected five samples of DNA at random from a database. Using public records and a computational model he developed, he identified each of the five people by name.

Not all DNA samples are volunteered. The U.S. military catalogs the DNA of soldiers. Police officers gather DNA samples from crime scenes, and they attempt to match the samples to criminal suspects. Suspects may be forced to submit a DNA sample.

Should people have the right to keep their DNA private? Or is DNA no more private than a face or fingerprint? What do you think?

## Careers on the Case

### Work Toward a Solution

Analyzing DNA involves tracking millions, if not billions, of individual nucleotides. Computers make this kind of analysis possible, so computer specialists are essential for DNA research.

### Computational Biologist

Most scientists work with computers to organize data. For complex data analysis, however, they might consult a computational biologist. This field applies computer science and math to help solve problems in biology or biological research.

▶ **VIDEO**

Learn more about careers that combine computers and biology.

# Lesson Review

Go to your Biology Foundations Workbook for longer versions of these lesson summaries.

## 15.1 Human Chromosomes

A genome is the full set of genetic information that an organism carries in its DNA. Scientists arrange images of chromosomes in a genome to produce a karyotype, which shows the complete diploid set of chromosomes grouped together in pairs, arranged in order of decreasing size. The full complement of chromosomes in the human cell is 46—two sets of 23.

Human traits are passed on largely through dominant and recessive alleles, although some alleles display codominant inheritance. Genes located on sex chromosomes are called sex-linked genes. A pedigree chart traces the presence and absence of traits through generations of a family, and can often determine if an allele for a trait is dominant or recessive, autosomal or sex-linked.

- genome
- karyotype
- sex chromosome
- autosome
- sex-linked gene
- pedigree

| Blood Groups | | |
|---|---|---|
| **Phenotype (Blood Type)** | **Genotype** | **Antigen on Red Blood Cell** |
| A | $I^A I^A$ or $I^A i$ | 1. |
| B | 2. | B |
| 3. | 4. | A and B |
| 5. | $ii$ | 6. |

☑ **Review** Complete the table of human blood types. Which blood types are produced by two different genotypes?

## 15.2 Human Genetic Disorders

Chromosomal disorders such as nondisjunction in meiosis can produce Down syndrome, which is associated with cognitive disabilities and birth defects, or Turner's and Klinefelter's syndromes, which impair reproductive capacity.

The DNA in genes interacts with the environment to produce an individual phenotype. Changes in a gene's DNA sequence can change proteins by altering their amino acid sequences. These changes can affect an individual's phenotype or, more subtly, underlie tendencies to develop conditions such as diabetes, heart disease, and cancer. These conditions may or may not develop depending on many other factors, such as diet, behavior, and environment. Some changes in specific genes cause disorders such as sickle cell disease, cystic fibrosis, and Huntington's disease.

- nondisjunction

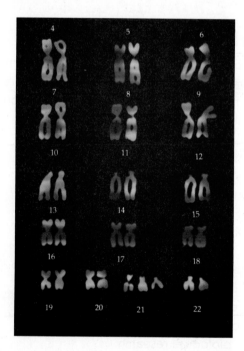

☑ **Interpret Data** Which chromosome illustrates nondisjunction? How do you know?

## 15.3 Studying the Human Genome

Scientists can use tools that cut, separate, and copy nucleic acids. These tools make it possible to study the genomes of different organisms. Restriction enzymes can be used to cut DNA molecules into smaller pieces. These DNA fragments are then separated using gel electrophoresis. The separated fragments are finally sequenced using a technique that includes copying the DNA. New sequencing technologies have allowed scientists to read DNA without cutting it into fragments.

In 2003, the Human Genome Project finished the first complete DNA sequence. Surprisingly, human cells contain approximately 20,000 genes, which is not a large number compared to other species.

Single nucleotide polymorphisms, or SNPs, are single-base base differences that are found among individuals. Some SNPs are associated with certain traits. Many private companies offer services that analyze one's DNA to determine ethnic ancestry and the possibility of developing certain diseases.

In a process known as genomic imprinting, epigenetic chemical marks on DNA can be passed from one generation to the next. These marks can affect gene expression, and some genes are only expressed if they come from a male parent while others are only expressed if they come from a female parent.

- restriction enzyme
- gel electrophoresis
- genomic imprinting

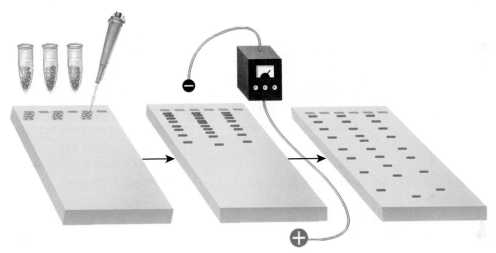

☑ **Interpret Diagrams** How does gel electrophoresis separate DNA fragments?

## Organize Information

Complete the table with definitions of the terms and explanations of how the concepts help you understand human heredity.

| Genetic term | Definition | How concept helps you understand human heredity |
|---|---|---|
| genome | 1. | 2. |
| karyotype | 3. | 4. |
| autosome | 5. | 6. |
| nondisjunction | 7. | 8. |
| genomic imprinting | 9. | 10. |

# Tracking Royal Blood

## Evaluate and Communicate Information

HS-LS3-1, CCSS.ELA-LITERACY.WHST.9-10.9

**STEM** From 1837 until her death in 1901, Queen Victoria ruled Great Britain and the lands it conquered. The queen and her family had a combination of wealth, power, and privilege that might be difficult to imagine today. Nevertheless, their lives were hardly ideal.

The queen's youngest son, Prince Leopold, was weak and sickly. So were some of the queen's grandchildren. They suffered from a disease called hemophilia, in which the blood clots poorly. With this disease, any minor injury can lead to severe bleeding or bruising. In the 1800s, few hemophiliacs lived long into adulthood. Prince Leopold died at age 30.

Today, scientists recognize hemophilia as a genetic disorder. They have identified two types of hemophilia, the specific faulty genes associated with hemophilia, and the mutations that affected them. The queen and her family, however, had no such knowledge. All they could do was recognize the pattern of inheritance and worry about the next child to be born.

Study the pedigree on the next page, which shows some of the queen's family. Notice that females could be carriers. Carriers are individuals who carry the defective gene but do not suffer from the disease. The queen and many of her descendants were carriers.

1. **Analyze Data** Identify the carriers of the gene associated with hemophilia. Explain your reasoning.

2. **Cite Evidence** Is the gene for hemophilia located on an autosome, the X chromosome, or the Y chromosome? Cite the evidence in the pedigree to support your answer.

3. **Draw Conclusions** Is the allele for hemophilia dominant or recessive? How do you know?

4. **Construct an Explanation** Using the family in the pedigree as an example, explain how the trait of hemophilia is expressed, and how it passes through generations.

5. **Construct a Simulation** Work with a partner to construct another pedigree that shows the inheritance of hemophilia, sickle cell disease, or another genetic disorder or condition presented in this chapter. Draw the pedigree and present it on a poster, or prepare a computer presentation. Share your pedigree with the class, and explain the pattern of inheritance that it shows.

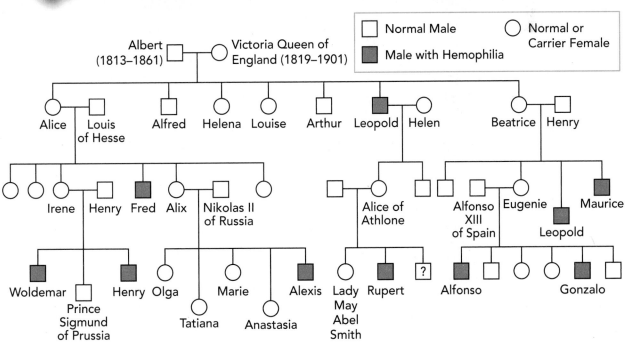

## 🔍 KEY QUESTIONS AND TERMS

### 15.1 Human Chromosomes
**HS-LS3-1, HS-LS3-2**

1. What is the number of chromosomes in a normal human karyotype?
   a. 2
   b. 23
   c. 44
   d. 46

2. Colorblindness is more common in males than in females because the allele for colorblindness is
   a. dominant and located on the X chromosome.
   b. dominant and located on the Y chromosome.
   c. recessive and located on the X chromosome.
   d. recessive and located on the Y chromosome.

3. The alleles for blood groups I^A and I^B are codominant. When paired they produce the blood type
   a. A.
   b. B.
   c. O.
   d. AB.

4. Explain why there are only 23 chromosomes in a sperm cell or an egg cell.

5. Why is blood type O considered the universal donor?

6. What phenomenon occurs in females as a result of X-chromosome inactivation?

7. How does a pedigree chart differ from a family tree?

8. How many generations are shown in this diagram?

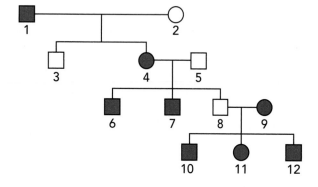

### 15.2 Human Genetic Disorders
**HS-LS3-1**

9. Which of the following diseases and conditions does not appear until later in a person's life?
   a. cystic fibrosis
   b. sickle cell disease
   c. colorblindness
   d. Huntington's disease

10. Because two copies of a defective CF allele are needed to produce cystic fibrosis,
    a. the CF allele is dominant.
    b. the CF allele is recessive.
    c. the CF allele cannot produce CFTR.
    d. the CF allele overproduces CFTR.

11. Which of the following disorders does NOT result from nondisjunction in meiosis?
    a. Down syndrome
    b. Turner's syndrome
    c. Klinefelter's syndrome
    d. sickle cell disease

12. How can being heterozygous for sickle cell disease be beneficial rather than harmful?

13. What function of the CF allele protects a carrier from contracting typhoid?

14. Nondisjunction of the X chromosomes produces what disorder in women?

15. What is Klinefelter's syndrome?

16. Why would it be useful for an adopted child to have access to his or her birth parents' health histories?

### 15.3 Studying the Human Genome
**HS-LS3-1, HS-ETS1-1**

17. The first step in sequencing the human genome is
    a. locating overlapping sequences.
    b. identifying genes by finding promoters.
    c. cutting the DNA into manageable pieces.
    d. sorting introns from exons.

18. What is the role of restriction enzymes in studying the human genome?
    a. copying pieces of DNA
    b. labeling different nucleotides with chemical dyes
    c. separating different pieces of DNA based on their size
    d. cutting large DNA molecules into smaller pieces

19. The technique known as gel electrophoresis serves to
    a. bind DNA to chemical dyes.
    b. separate DNA fragments.
    c. reproduce DNA strands.
    d. synthesize nucleotide bases.

20. Approximately how many genes make up the human genome?

21. True or false: The functions of all genes in the human genome have been identified.

22. What benefits have resulted from the identification of SNPs associated with susceptibility to certain diseases or medical conditions?

23. In 2008, Congress passed the Genetic Information Nondiscrimination Act to prevent what?

24. What is the process of genomic imprinting?

# CRITICAL THINKING

HS-LS3-1

25. **Plan an Investigation** Researchers suspect that a certain disease is caused by a recessive allele in a gene located on the X chromosome in fruit flies. Plan an investigation to test this hypothesis.

26. **Construct Tables** What are the possible genotypes of the parents of a child who is colorblind? Create a Punnett square to find out. Explain what the different possibilities are.

27. **Evaluate a Solution** Can a genetic counselor use a karyotype to identify a carrier of cystic fibrosis? Explain.

28. **Observe** The table shows the DNA sequences that are recognized by five different restriction enzymes and the locations where those enzymes cut. Which enzymes produce DNA fragments with "sticky ends"? What is the common feature of the sequences cut by these enzymes?

### DNA Sequences Cut by Enzymes

| Enzyme | Recognition Sequence |
|--------|---------------------|
| AluI | A G ↓ C T <br> T C ↑ G A |
| HaeIII | G G ↓ C C <br> C C ↑ G G |
| BamHI | G ↓ G A T C C <br> C C T A G ↑ G |
| HindIII | A ↓ A G C T T <br> T T C G A ↑ A |
| EcoRI | G ↓ A A T T C <br> C T T A A ↑ G |

29. **Plan an Investigation** Fruit fly sex is determined by X and Y chromosomes, just as it is in humans. Researchers suspect that a certain disease is caused by a recessive allele in a gene located on the X chromosome in fruit flies. Design an experiment to test this hypothesis.

30. **Ask Questions** Review the table and compare the genome sizes and estimated number of genes for each organism or virus. What are some questions that you would ask to clarify the relationship between an organism or virus and its genome size? What questions would you need answered to determine why a single-celled organism has a larger genome size than other, more complex organisms?

### Size Comparison of Various Genomes

| Organism or Virus | Genome Size (bases) | Estimated Genes |
|-------------------|--------------------|-----------------|
| Human (*Homo sapiens*) | 3.2 billion | 25,000 |
| Laboratory mouse (*M. musculus*) | 2.5 billion | 24,174 |
| Fruit fly (*D. melanogaster*) | 165.0 million | 13,600 |
| Mustard weed (*A. thaliana*) | 120.0 million | 25,498 |
| Roundworm (*C. elegans*) | 97.0 million | 19,000 |
| Yeast (*S. cerevisiae*) | 12.1 million | 6294 |
| Bacterium (*E. coli*) | 4.6 million | 4288 |
| Human immunodeficiency virus (HIV) | 9749.0 | 9 |

31. **Identify Variables** Identify what accounts for the vast differences of traits observed among different organisms, and for the complexity of these traits. Consider what you know about RNA transcription as part of your answer.

32. **Evaluate a Solution** Currently, tests are available for detecting genetic markers for different traits and syndromes. Evaluate the effectiveness of genetic testing as a solution for people facing the possibility of being a carrier for a genetic disorder. What are its limitations and advantages?

33. **Identify Patterns** Enzymes perform many different functions. Identify the different enzymes that have been mentioned in Chapters 13 through 15. What do they have in common? What are some of the different functions that they serve? What are some problems that an organism may face if its enzymes stopped working properly?

34. **Synthesize Information** How do human nondisjunction disorders explain how a male calico cat might be produced?

## CROSSCUTTING CONCEPTS

**35. Connect to Technology** Private companies often announce advances in the technologies used for genetic testing. How have the technologies changed in the past twenty years? What new technologies are being developed currently? How do these differ from technologies used in the past?

**36. Cause and Effect** Explain why a small change to a gene can affect human traits. Give an example that illustrates why the change may bestow a benefit or may be harmful.

**37. Connect to Society** Perform research to find the concerns people have about genetic testing. What potentially positive and negative effects on society do you think the increasing availability of such testing will have?

**38. Cause and Effect** Restriction enzymes are named for the bacteria in which they were first discovered. For example, *Eco*RI was discovered in *E. coli*. Why do you think bacteria have DNA-snipping enzymes? (**Hint:** Think about the Hershey-Chase experiment.)

## MATH CONNECTIONS

## Analyze and Interpret Data

HS-LS3-1, CCSS.MATH.CONTENT.MP2

**Refer to the pedigree chart to answer questions 39–41.**

Lactose intolerance results from a person's inability to produce the enzyme lactase that breaks down the sugar lactose found in milk. Many adults experience lactose intolerance as they age and rely less on milk and dairy products as sources of nutrition. There is another rare form of lactose intolerance that affects infants from birth. A mutated version of the *LCT* gene that codes for the production of lactase exists as a recessive allele.

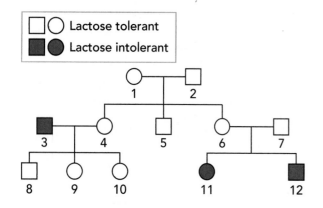

**39. Predict** Using your knowledge of Mendelian inheritance, create a Punnett square to show the possible genotypes of a child born to parents when the mother is homozygous dominant and the father is heterozygous for the *LCT* gene.

**40. Calculate** What is the ratio of the genotypes in the Punnett square you created? What is the ratio of the phenotypes?

**41. Reason Quantitatively** The pedigree shows the original parents numbered 1 and 2. They had three children. Compare the numbers in the ratios you determined to the appearance of the trait in the pedigree. Why were Persons 11 and 12 lactose intolerant while Persons 8, 9, and 10 were not?

## LANGUAGE ARTS CONNECTION

## Write About Science

HS-LS3-1, CCSS.ELA-LITERACY.WHST.9-10.5,
CCSS.ELA-LITERACY.WHST.9-10.8

**42. Write Arguments** Should people have the right to keep genetic information private? Under what circumstances, if any, should scientists have access to genetic information without the person's consent? Present an argument to support your opinions.

**43. Plan and Revise** Explain the relationship between meiosis and Down syndrome, Turner's syndrome, and Klinefelter's syndrome. Make a plan, write a first draft, and revise your answer.

## Read About Science

CCSS.ELA-LITERACY.RST.9-10.3, CCSS.ELA-LITERACY.RST.9-10.4

**44. Determine Meaning** Review the pedigree example in **Figure 15-7**. What is a pedigree? Determine the meaning of each symbol on the pedigree. What information do you need to already have that the pedigree does not provide in order to be able to understand it?

**45. Follow a Multistep Procedure** Review **Figures 15-12, 15-13,** and **15-14,** which show graphic representations of the steps of sequencing DNA. How would you describe the steps if you were to create a numbered list that someone else could follow to understand the procedure?

**For questions 1-2, refer to the following passage and diagram.**

A student traced the recurrence of a widow's peak hairline in her family. Based on her interviews and observations, she drew the pedigree shown below.

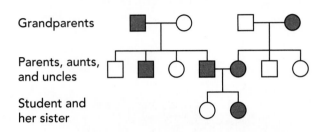

Grandparents

Parents, aunts, and uncles

Student and her sister

| | Widow's peak | No widow's peak |
|---|---|---|
| Male | ■ | □ |
| Female | ● | ○ |

1. Which pattern of inheritance is consistent with the pedigree?
   A. sex-linked
   B. multiple alleles
   C. codominant alleles
   D. recessive allele
   E. dominant allele

2. What is the function of DNA in this pattern of inheritance?
   A. Proteins containing DNA were passed from parent to offspring in each generation.
   B. DNA was not folded properly in each of the affected individuals.
   C. Mutations were induced in the widow's peak gene in each of the affected individuals.
   D. A chromosome containing the allele for a widow's peak was passed from parent to offspring in each generation.
   E. The chromosome containing the allele for a widow's peak was inactivated in each of the affected individuals.

3. The figure is a karyotype from a person with XYY Syndrome.

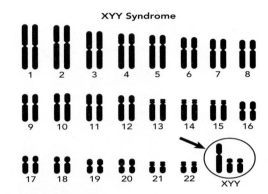

What event is MOST LIKELY to cause XYY Syndrome?
   A. A duplication of the Y chromosome
   B. Nondisjunction of chromosomes during meiosis
   C. An error in DNA replication during mitosis
   D. A change in a gene's DNA sequence
   E. Inactivation of an X chromosome

4. How do alleles that display codominance differ from alleles that display simple dominance?
   A. If two alleles are codominant then both alleles will be observed in heterozygotes.
   B. If two alleles are codominant then the heterozygous phenotype will be somewhere between the homozygous phenotypes.
   C. If two alleles display simple dominance then only the recessive allele will be observed.
   D. If two alleles display simple dominance then neither allele will be observed in heterozygotes.
   E. If two alleles display simple dominance then only the dominant allele is inheritable.

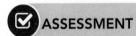 **ASSESSMENT**

For additional assessment practice, go online to access your digital course.

## If You Had Trouble With...

| Question | 1 | 2 | 3 | 4 |
|---|---|---|---|---|
| See Lesson | 15.1 | 15.1 | 15.2 | 15.1 |
| Performance Expectation | HS-LS3-1 | HS-LS3-1 | HS-LS3-1 | HS-LS3-1 |

**16.1**
Changing the
Living World

**16.2**
The Process of
Genetic
Engineering

**16.3**
Applications of
Biotechnology

**16.4**
Ethics and
Impacts of
Biotechnology

**Go Online to
access your
digital course.**

 VIDEO

 AUDIO

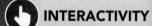 INTERACTIVITY

📖 eTEXT

👁 ANIMATION

📱 VIRTUAL LAB

☑ ASSESSMENT

These fish that glow in
the dark were produced
through genetic
engineering.

HS-ETS1-1, HS-ETS1-2, HS-LS3-1

# What will the future hold for genetically modified crops?

Throughout the twentieth century, scientists studied genes and genetic mechanisms. They investigated the genes of a huge variety of organisms, ranging from single-celled bacteria to multicellular plants and animals, including humans. All of these investigations support the same conclusion, which is that all living things use genes in very similar ways.

The similarity of genetic mechanisms led scientists to ask: Could a gene from one organism be transferred to another, and be made to function in its new home? The answer proved to be yes. In the 1970s, scientists began transferring genes between bacteria. Then in 1983, scientists announced the creation of the first transgenic plants. Genes from bacteria were successfully incorporated into plant genomes, and the plants were producing the bacterial proteins.

In the years after these experiments, scientists began developing genetically modified (GM) plants for use as farm crops. Some of the first GM plants received a gene from the bacterial species *Bacillus thuringiensis*. The gene directs the synthesis of a protein that is poisonous to certain insects, many of which are common farm pests. Potatoes, cotton, and corn were all modified with this gene. Many farmers were happy with the results. They did not need to spray their fields with pesticides because the crops made their own pesticides.

Scientists continue to develop new GM plants, and similar technology is now being applied to animals. Fast-growing GM salmon were approved for sale in 2015, and other GM animals may follow.

Many scientists and agricultural experts argue that GM plants and animals provide an effective, efficient way to feed Earth's growing human population. Many GM plants can resist insects without the need for chemical pesticides. Others are tolerant to herbicides, or weed-killing chemicals. Evidence shows that the food is likely to be safe and nutritious to eat, and is essentially the same as the food from the original crops.

However, many critics argue against GM crops. One of their arguments is that the crops may easily spread beyond farmers' fields and into the wild. If the GM plants breed with wild plants, the new genes could alter the plants—and natural ecosystems—in unforeseen ways. Their concern is that the combination of artificial and natural processes could generate a harmful plant, or even a toxic one.

How do scientists transfer genes from one organism into another? What are some of the other arguments in favor of and against the use of GM crops, as well as other genetic technologies? What ethical questions should we ask, and try to answer, about genetic technology?

**Throughout this chapter, look for connections to the CASE STUDY to help you answer these questions.**

# Changing the Living World

- *What is selective breeding used for?*
- *How do people increase genetic variation?*

**VOCABULARY**

**selective breeding**
**biotechnology**
**hybridization**
**inbreeding**

**READING TOOL**

While you read the lesson, explain the two ways that scientists carry out selective breeding practices. Fill in the graphic organizer in your 📖 **Biology Foundations Workbook.**

▶ **VIDEO**

Examine how the many breeds of dogs have originated from a common ancestor.

Visit a dog park, and what do you see? Striking contrasts are everywhere—from a tiny Chihuahua to a massive Great Dane, from the short coat of a Labrador retriever to the curly fur of a poodle, from the long muzzle of a wolfhound to the pug nose of a bulldog. The differences among breeds of dogs are so great that someone might think they are different species. They're not, of course, but where did these obvious differences come from?

## Selective Breeding

The answer is that we did it. Humans have kept and bred dogs for thousands of years, always looking to produce animals that are better hunters, better retrievers, or friendlier companions. We've done so by **selective breeding**, allowing only those animals with wanted characteristics to produce the next generation. 🔍 *Humans use selective breeding to take advantage of naturally occurring genetic variation to pass wanted traits on to the next generation of organisms.*

Selective breeding is just one example of **biotechnology**, the application of a technological process, invention, or method to living organisms. Although we tend to think of biotechnology as involving high-powered equipment in gleaming laboratories, humans have been practicing biotechnology for thousands of years as they bred domesticated plants and animals. A perfect example may be right in front of you in the form of the corn chips or popcorn we snack on.

When Europeans came to the New World, they discovered that Native Americans were cultivating corn, a productive and nutritious crop unknown to them. Where did this remarkable plant come from? The chromosomes of corn are remarkably similar to those of teosinte, a wild grass native to central Mexico. Corn can be crossed with teosinte, demonstrating that the two species are closely related.

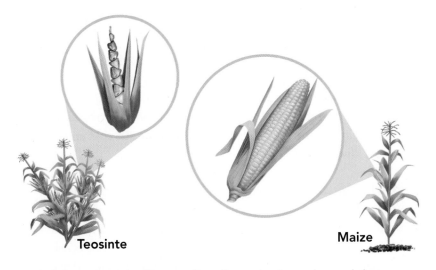

Teosinte

Maize

During its domestication, corn (maize) lost the ability to survive in the wild but gained valuable agricultural traits. For example, the hard case around the kernel disappeared over time, leaving the rows of soft corn kernels we enjoy today.

Work by geneticist George Beadle and others showed that changes in just a few genes account for the differences between corn and teosinte, as shown in **Figure 16-1**. In a sense, corn is one of humankind's first great achievements in biotechnology. Nearly 10,000 years ago, Native Americans selectively bred teosinte to select for the traits controlled by those genes, producing what is now one of the world's most important crops.

## Hybridization

American botanist Luther Burbank (1849–1926) may have been the greatest selective breeder of all time. Burbank used **hybridization**, the crossing of dissimilar individuals to bring together the best of both organisms. Many of Burbank's hybrid crosses combined the disease resistance of one plant with the food-producing capacity of another. The result was a new line of plants that led to increased food production. **Figure 16-2** shows the Russet Burbank potato, the most widely grown potato in North America.

**BUILD VOCABULARY**

**Related Words** Recall that a *hybrid* is the offspring of parents with different traits. **Hybridization** is a method to produce offspring with the desired characteristics from both parents.

## Inbreeding

To maintain desirable characteristics in a line of organisms, breeders often use a technique known as inbreeding. **Inbreeding** is the continued breeding of individuals with similar characteristics. The many breeds of dogs—from beagles to poodles—are maintained using this practice. Inbreeding helps ensure that the characteristics that make each breed unique are preserved. Although inbreeding is useful in preserving certain traits, it can be risky. Most of the members of a breed are genetically similar, which increases the chance that a cross between two individuals will bring together two recessive alleles for a genetic defect.

🖰 **INTERACTIVITY**

Figure 16-2

**Burbank's Hybrids**

Russet potatoes are just one of the 800 varieties of plants hybridized by Luther Burbank.

☑ **READING CHECK** Compare
How do hybridization and inbreeding compare?

# Increasing Variation

Selective breeding would be nearly impossible without the wide variation found in natural populations of plants and animals. But sometimes breeders want even more variation than exists in nature. 🔍 *Breeders can increase the genetic variation in a population by introducing mutations, which are the ultimate source of biological diversity.*

**Figure 16-3**

**Ploidy Numbers**

Because polyploid plants are often larger than other plants, many farmers deliberately grow polyploid varieties of crops like those listed.

| Polyploid Crops | | | |
|---|---|---|---|
| Plant | Probable Ancestral Haploid Number | Chromosome Number | Ploidy Level |
| Domestic oat | 7 | 42 | 6N |
| Peanut | 10 | 40 | 4N |
| Sugar cane | 10 | 80 | 8N |
| Banana | 11 | 22, 33 | 2N, 3N |
| Cotton | 13 | 52 | 4N |

**Bacterial Mutations** Mutations—heritable changes in DNA—occur spontaneously, but breeders can increase the mutation rate of an organism by using radiation or chemicals. While many mutations are harmful, breeders can select for those mutations that produce useful characteristics not found in the original population. This technique has been particularly useful with bacteria. Because they are small, millions of bacteria can be treated with radiation or chemicals at the same time, which increases the chances of producing a useful mutant. This technique has allowed scientists to develop hundreds of useful bacterial strains. For instance, we have known for decades that certain strains of oil-digesting bacteria are effective for cleaning up oil spills. Today scientists are working to produce bacteria that can clean up radioactive substances and metal pollution in the environment.

**Polyploid Plants** Drugs that prevent the separation of chromosomes during meiosis are very useful in plant breeding. These drugs can produce cells that have many times the normal number of chromosomes. Plants grown from these cells are called polyploid because they have many sets of chromosomes. Polyploidy is usually fatal in animals. But, for reasons that are not clear, plants are much better at tolerating extra sets of chromosomes. Polyploidy can quickly produce new species of plants that are larger and stronger than their diploid relatives. A number of important crop plants, including bananas and many varieties of citrus fruits, have been produced in this way. **Figure 16-3** lists several examples of polyploid plants.

## ✅ LESSON 16.1 Review

### 🔍 KEY QUESTIONS

1. Explain the process of selective breeding.
2. Why would breeders want to introduce mutations into a population?

### CRITICAL THINKING

3. **Evaluate Claims** What evidence supports the claim that corn plants were bred from teosinte?

4. **Construct an Explanation** How do biotechnologies such as hybridization and the introduction of mutations increase genetic variation?

5. **Interpret Tables** Look at **Figure 16-3**. Which plant has undergone the most dramatic change in chromosome number?

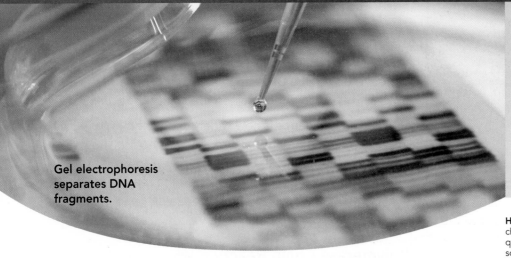

# The Process of Genetic Engineering

Gel electrophoresis separates DNA fragments.

HS-ETS1-1: Analyze a major global challenge to specify qualitative and quantitative criteria and constraints for solutions that account for societal needs and wants.

## KEY QUESTIONS

- *How do scientists copy the DNA of living organisms?*
- *How is recombinant DNA used?*
- *How are transgenic organisms produced?*

## VOCABULARY

**polymerase chain reaction**
**recombinant DNA**
**plasmid**
**genetic marker**
**transgenic**
**clone**

## READING TOOL

Before you read, skim through the lesson and note the section headings. Fill in the graphic organizer in your 📖 **Biology Foundations Workbook** with those section headings.

For nearly all of human history, plant and animal breeders were limited in what they could do. They could only work with variations that already existed in nature, or were the result of mutations, which were risky and unpredictable. Today, however, all that has changed. Genetics is not just something we study. It is something we can engineer to change the characteristics of living organisms.

## Analyzing DNA

You may recall from Chapter 15 that it is relatively easy to extract DNA from cells and tissues. The extracted DNA can be cut into fragments of manageable size using restriction enzymes. These restriction fragments can then be separated for study according to size, using gel electrophoresis or another similar technique. Finally, the base sequences of these fragments can be read, and then put back together to produce a complete genomic DNA sequence. Now the tough part: How do you find a specific gene in that DNA sequence?

The problem is huge. If we were to cut DNA from a bacterium such as *E. coli* into restriction fragments averaging 1000 base pairs in length, we would have 4000 restriction fragments. In the human genome, we would have 3 million restriction fragments. How do we find a single gene among millions of fragments? In some respects, it's the classic problem of finding a needle in a haystack—we have an enormous pile of hay and just one needle.

Actually, there is a way to find a needle in a haystack. We can toss the hay in front of a powerful magnet until something sticks. The hay won't stick, but a needle made of iron or steel will. Believe it or not, similar techniques can help scientists identify specific genes.

## Figure 16-4

## A Fluorescent Gene

The Pacific Ocean jellyfish, *Aequorea victoria*, emits a bluish glow. A protein in the jellyfish absorbs blue light from the sun and produces green fluorescence.

## Figure 16-5

## The PCR Method

Polymerase chain reaction is used to make multiple copies of a gene. This method is particularly useful when only tiny amounts of DNA are available.

| |
|---|
| ❶ DNA is heated to separate strands. |

| |
|---|
| ❷ The mixture is cooled, and primers bind to strands. |

| |
|---|
| ❸ DNA polymerase adds nucleotides to strands, producing two complementary strands. |

| |
|---|
| ❹ The procedure is repeated starting at step 1. |

**Finding a Gene** In 1987, biologist Douglas Prasher wanted to find the gene for the green fluorescent protein (GFP) found in some jellyfish, such as *Aequoria victoria*, shown in **Figure 16-4**. First Prasher predicted the mRNA base sequence that would code for some of the amino acids. Then he screened a genetic "library" with thousands of jellyfish mRNA sequences, until he found one that matched his predictions. Finally, using a gel in which DNA fragments from the jellyfish genome had been separated, he found one of the DNA fragments that matched the GFP mRNA. That fragment contained the actual gene for GFP.

The GFP sequence is now widely used to label proteins in living cells and organisms, like the glowing fish shown on the opening pages of this chapter. Today it is often quicker and less expensive for scientists to search for genes in computer databases where the complete genomes of many organisms are available.

**Polymerase Chain Reaction** When a sample contains too little DNA to be analyzed easily, scientists use a technique known as **polymerase chain reaction** (PCR) to make multiple copies of specific DNA sequences. As shown in **Figure 16-5**, short pieces of single-stranded DNA known as primers, each about 20 or 30 bases in length, are added to the sample. The base sequences of these pieces are chosen to be complementary to sequences on either end of the region of DNA to be copied. The DNA sample is heated to separate its strands. Then, as the DNA cools, the primers bind to the single strands. Next, DNA polymerase copies or replicates the region between the primers. As the cycle of heating and cooling is repeated, these copies serve as templates to make still more copies. 🔍 *Using the PCR process, just a few dozen cycles of replication can produce billions of copies of the DNA between the primers in less than a day.*

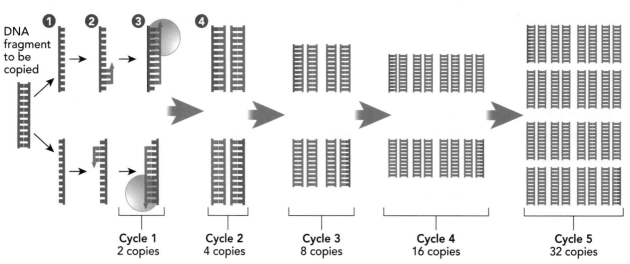

DNA fragment to be copied

| Cycle 1 | Cycle 2 | Cycle 3 | Cycle 4 | Cycle 5 |
|---|---|---|---|---|
| 2 copies | 4 copies | 8 copies | 16 copies | 32 copies |

Where did Kary Mullis, the American scientist who invented PCR, find a DNA polymerase enzyme that could stand repeated cycles of heating and cooling? Mullis found it in bacteria from the hot springs of Yellowstone National Park—a powerful example of the importance of biodiversity to biotechnology!

✅ **READING CHECK** **Identify** How does polymerase chain reaction make copies of a specific region of DNA?

# Rewriting the Genome

Just as scientists were learning how to read and analyze DNA sequences, they began to wonder if it might be possible to change the DNA of a living cell. However, this feat had already been accomplished decades earlier. Do you remember Griffith's experiments on bacterial transformation? His extract of heat-killed bacteria contained DNA fragments. When he mixed those fragments with live bacteria, a few of the bacteria took up the DNA molecules, transforming the DNA and changing the bacteria's genomes. Griffith might have been the world's first genetic engineer.

**Recombinant DNA** Today, scientists can take DNA molecules from any source—either another organism or DNA custom-built in the lab—and insert them into living cells. Usually, these sequences are first joined to other DNA molecules using enzymes like DNA ligase to splice the molecules together. As **Figure 16-6** shows, the "sticky ends" left by restriction enzymes allow DNA fragments to combine. These combined molecules are known as **recombinant DNA**, since they are produced by recombining DNA from different sources. 🔍 *Recombinant-DNA technology makes it possible to change the genetic composition of living organisms.* By manipulating DNA in this way, scientists can learn more about genome organization and function.

**Plasmids and Genetic Markers** Scientists working with recombinant DNA soon discovered that many of the DNA molecules they tried to insert into host cells simply vanished because the cells often did not copy, or replicate, the added DNA. Today scientists join recombinant DNA to another piece of DNA containing a replication "start" signal. This way, whenever the cell copies its own DNA, it copies the recombinant DNA too.

In addition to their own chromosomes, some bacteria contain small circular DNA molecules known as **plasmids**. Plasmids are widely used in recombinant DNA studies. Joining DNA to a plasmid, and then using the recombinant plasmid to transform bacteria, results in the replication of the newly added DNA along with the rest of the cell's genome.

Plasmids are also found in yeasts, which are single-celled eukaryotes that can be transformed with recombinant DNA as well. Biologists working with yeasts can construct artificial chromosomes containing centromeres, telomeres, and replication start sites. These artificial chromosomes greatly simplify the process of introducing recombinant DNA into the yeast genome.

## Figure 16-6

### Joining DNA Pieces Together

If DNA molecules from two sources are cut with the same restriction enzyme, their sticky ends will bond to a fragment of DNA that has the complementary sequence of bases.

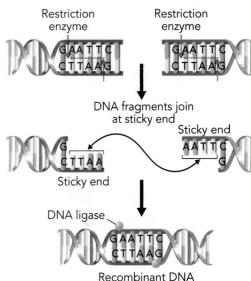

Recombinant DNA

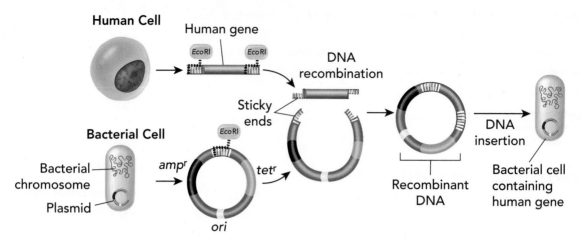

**Figure 16-7**

## Plasmid DNA Transformation

Scientists can insert a piece of DNA into a plasmid if both the plasmid and the target DNA have been cut by the same restriction enzymes to create sticky ends. With this method, bacteria can be used to produce substances such as human growth hormone.

**Figure 16-7** shows how bacteria can be transformed using recombinant plasmids. First, the DNA being used for transformation is joined to a plasmid. The plasmid DNA contains a signal for replication (*ori*) as well as genetic markers such as genes for antibiotic resistance (*ampr* and *tetr*). A **genetic marker** makes it possible to distinguish bacteria that carry the plasmid from those that don't. So, even if just a few cells in a million take up the recombinant plasmids, the markers make it possible to find those cells. After transformation, the culture is treated with the antibiotic. Only those rare cells that have been transformed survive, because only they carry the resistance gene.

✓ **READING CHECK** **Review** How are plasmids used in genetic engineering?

**CRISPR and DNA Editing** Although recombinant DNA technology has been useful, it is limited by the fact that it makes use of DNA from existing sources. Biologists have dreamed of a tool that could directly change the DNA base sequence of a gene in the way you might edit the words in an essay you are typing on your computer. Now, it seems, just such a tool is available. The technique is called CRISPR (clustered regularly interspersed short palindromic repeats), and its development began with a discovery made more than 20 years ago.

---

**Quick Lab** 🧪 **Guided Inquiry**

### Inserting Genetic Markers

1. One partner should write a random DNA sequence on a long strip of paper to model an organism's genome.

2. The other partner should write a short DNA sequence on a short strip of paper to model a genetic marker.

3. Using the chart your teacher gives you, work with your partner to figure out how to insert the marker gene into the genome.

### ANALYZE AND CONCLUDE

1. **Analyze** How did the structure of your DNA molecule change?

2. **Use Models** What kind of molecule did you and your partner model?

3. **Construct an Explanation** Suppose a cell contains the DNA sequence you modeled. Explain what will happen when the cell copies its own DNA.

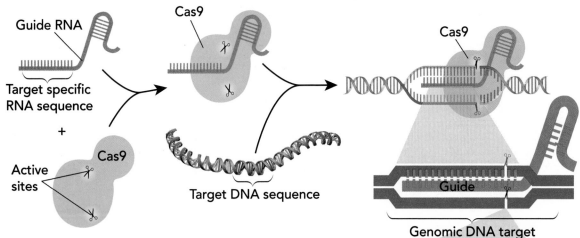

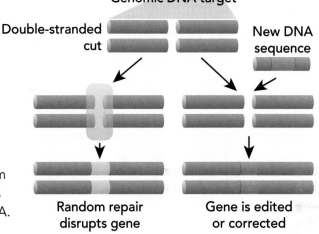

Double-stranded cut

New DNA sequence

Genomic DNA target

Random repair disrupts gene

Gene is edited or corrected

Francisco Mojica, a biology graduate student, discovered that a fragment of bacterial DNA from a salt marsh in Spain contained short, repeated base sequences similar to those found in the DNA of certain bacterial viruses. Before long, it became clear that these DNA sequences were actually part of the defense mechanism against those viruses. If DNA from such a virus enters the cell, the bacterium uses these repeated base sequences to produce its own short RNA molecules that bind to the viral DNA. Guided by that RNA, an enzyme then cuts the viral DNA, making it useless. While it might seem that this discovery was of little practical benefit (unless you happen to be a bacterium!), scientists gradually realized that this system could be used to edit DNA.

**Figure 16-8** shows how the CRISPR system is now used to edit DNA in a eukaryotic cell. A recombinant DNA molecule that contains two genes is constructed. One codes for an enzyme known as Cas9, and the other for a RNA molecule that will guide the Cas9 enzyme to a particular DNA sequence. The guide RNA enables the Cas9 enzyme to attach to DNA and cut both strands at an exact point. Enzymes in the cell then repair the broken ends by inserting random bases, which usually destroy the function of the gene. However, if a single strand of DNA with base sequences matching those at the break is also injected into the cell, the repair mechanism will use this DNA instead. In this way, scientists can rewrite the base sequence of nearly any gene in the cell.

More than a dozen laboratories around the world played a role in developing this technology, which is now widely used in research. CRISPR makes it possible to study gene function by inactivating specific genes. This technology also has the possibility of changing the DNA sequences of certain disease-causing genes, as well as re-engineering genes to perform new functions.

**ANIMATION**

**Figure 16-8**

## CRISPR Technology

CRISPR allows scientists to change the base sequence of a gene without the insertion of DNA from another source.

**INTERACTIVITY**

Practice genetic engineering by isolating particular genes and then transferring them into another organism.

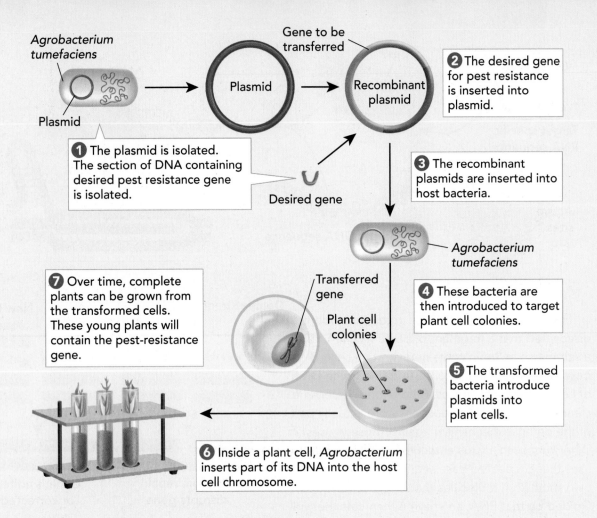

Agrobacterium tumefaciens

Plasmid

**1** The plasmid is isolated. The section of DNA containing desired pest resistance gene is isolated.

Gene to be transferred

Plasmid

Recombinant plasmid

**2** The desired gene for pest resistance is inserted into plasmid.

Desired gene

**3** The recombinant plasmids are inserted into host bacteria.

Agrobacterium tumefaciens

**7** Over time, complete plants can be grown from the transformed cells. These young plants will contain the pest-resistance gene.

Transferred gene

Plant cell colonies

**4** These bacteria are then introduced to target plant cell colonies.

**5** The transformed bacteria introduce plasmids into plant cells.

**6** Inside a plant cell, *Agrobacterium* inserts part of its DNA into the host cell chromosome.

CASE STUDY

Figure 16-9

**Transgenic Organisms**

Recombinant DNA is used to create transgenic plants.

**BUILD VOCABULARY**

**Prefixes** The prefix *trans-* means "changing thoroughly." A transgenic organism has been changed by the addition of genes from another species.

# Transgenic Organisms and Cloning

The universal nature of the genetic code makes it possible to construct organisms that are **transgenic**, containing genes from other species. 🔍 *Transgenic organisms can be produced by the insertion of recombinant DNA into the genome of a host organism.* Like bacterial plasmids, the DNA molecules used for the transformation of plant and animal cells contain genetic markers that help scientists identify which cells have been transformed. Transgenic technology was perfected using mice in the 1980s. Genetic engineers can now produce transgenic plants, animals, and microorganisms.

**Transgenic Plants** Many plant cells can be transformed using the bacterium *Agrobacterium*. In nature this bacterium inserts a small DNA plasmid that produces tumors in plant cells. Scientists can deactivate the plasmid's tumor-producing gene and replace it with a piece of recombinant DNA. The recombinant plasmid can then be used to infect and transform plant cells, as shown in **Figure 16-9**.

There are other ways to produce transgenic plants as well. When their cell walls are removed, plant cells in culture will sometimes take up DNA on their own. DNA can also be injected directly into some plant cells. If transformation is successful, the recombinant DNA is integrated into one of the plant cell's chromosomes.

**Transgenic Animals** Scientists can transform animal cells using some of the same techniques used for plant cells. The egg cells of many animals are large enough that DNA can be injected directly into the nucleus. Once the DNA is in the nucleus, enzymes that are normally responsible for DNA repair and recombination may help insert the foreign DNA into the chromosomes of the injected cell.

**Cloning** A **clone** is a population of genetically identical cells produced from a single cell. The technique of cloning uses a single cell from an adult organism to grow an entirely new individual that is genetically identical to the organism from which the cell was taken.

Cloned colonies of bacteria and other microorganisms are easy to grow, but this is not always true of multicellular organisms, especially animals. Nonetheless, in 1997 Scottish scientist Ian Wilmut announced that he had produced a sheep, called Dolly, by cloning.

**Figure 16-10** shows the basic steps by which an animal can be cloned. First, the nucleus of an unfertilized egg cell is removed. Next, the egg cell is fused with a donor cell that contains a nucleus taken from an adult. That cell develops into an embryo, which is then implanted in the uterus of a foster mother, where it develops until birth. Farmers and ranchers have used these techniques to clone champion cows, pigs, and other animals to improve the breeding stock for their herds.

**INTERACTIVITY**

Review the process of genetic engineering.

**Figure 16-10**

**Cloning Animals**

Animal cloning uses a procedure called nuclear transplantation. The process combines an egg cell with a donor nucleus to produce an embryo.

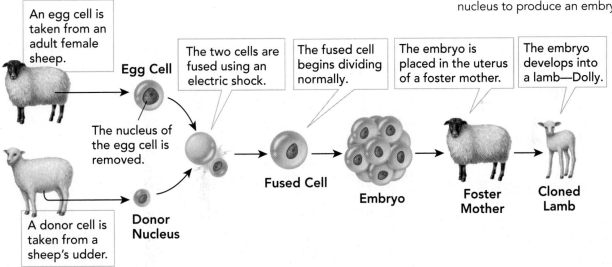

An egg cell is taken from an adult female sheep.

**Egg Cell**

The two cells are fused using an electric shock.

The nucleus of the egg cell is removed.

The fused cell begins dividing normally.

The embryo is placed in the uterus of a foster mother.

The embryo develops into a lamb—Dolly.

**Fused Cell**

**Embryo**

**Foster Mother**

**Cloned Lamb**

A donor cell is taken from a sheep's udder.

**Donor Nucleus**

HS-ETS1-1

## ☑ LESSON 16.2 Review

### 🔍 KEY QUESTIONS

1. Describe the process scientists use to make lots of copies of DNA sequences.

2. How are plasmids used to change the genetic composition of living organisms?

3. What is a transgenic organism?

### CRITICAL THINKING

4. **Construct an Explanation** Why would a scientist want to determine the sequence of a DNA molecule?

5. **Compare and Contrast** Compare the transformation of a plant cell with the transformation of an animal cell.

# Applications of Biotechnology

## KEY QUESTIONS

- How can genetic engineering benefit agriculture and industry?
- How can biotechnology improve human health?
- How is DNA used to identify individuals?

**HS-ETS1-1:** Analyze a major global challenge to specify qualitative and quantitative criteria and constraints for solutions that account for societal needs and wants.

**HS-LS3-1:** Ask questions to clarify relationships about the role of DNA and chromosomes in coding the instructions for characteristic traits passed from parents to offspring.

## VOCABULARY

**gene therapy
DNA microarray
DNA fingerprinting
forensics**

### READING TOOL

As you read, identify the main ideas and supporting details under each main heading. Fill in the table in your 📖 **Biology Foundations Workbook.**

Have you eaten any genetically modified food lately? Don't worry if you're not sure. For many years, the labeling of these foods in grocery stores or markets has not been required. But if you eat corn, potatoes, or soy products, chances are close to 100 percent that you've eaten foods modified in some way by genetic engineering.

## Agriculture and Industry

Everything we eat and much of what we wear comes from living organisms. Not surprisingly, then, researchers have used genetic engineering to try to improve the products we get from plants and animals. 🔍 *Ideally, genetic modification would lead to better, less expensive, and more nutritious food as well as less harmful manufacturing processes.*

**GM Crops** Since their introduction in 1996, genetically modified (GM) plants have become an important component of our food supply. In 2016, GM crops made up 94 percent of soybeans, 89 percent of cotton, and 89 percent of corn grown in the United States. Corn, for example, is often modified with bacterial genes that produce a protein known as Bt toxin. While it is harmless to humans and most other animals, enzymes in the digestive systems of insects convert the Bt protein to a form that kills the insects. Fields of Bt corn do not have to be sprayed with pesticides, and have been shown to produce higher crop yields.

Resistance to insects is just one useful characteristic being engineered into crops. Others include resistance to viral infections and herbicides, which are chemicals that kill weeds. Some transgenic plants may soon produce foods that are resistant to rot and spoilage. And engineers are currently developing GM plants that may produce plastics for the manufacturing industry.

**GM Animals** Transgenic animals are also becoming more important to our food supply. For example, about 30 percent of the milk in U.S. markets comes from cows that have been injected with hormones made by recombinant-DNA techniques to increase milk production. Pigs can be genetically modified to produce more lean meat or higher levels of healthy omega-3 acids. Using growth-hormone genes, scientists have developed transgenic salmon that grow much more quickly than wild salmon. These salmon are grown in captive aquaculture facilities to ensure that they do not outcompete wild populations.

When scientists in Canada combined spider genes with the cells of lactating goats, the goats began to manufacture silk along with their milk. By extracting polymer strands from the milk and weaving them into thread, we can create a light, tough, and flexible material that could be used in such applications as military uniforms, medical sutures, and tennis racket strings. Scientists are now using human genes to develop antibacterial goat milk.

✓ **READING CHECK** **Summarize** What are some ways that genetic modification have improved farm crops and animals?

# Health and Medicine

Biotechnology, in its broadest sense, has always been part of medicine. Early physicians extracted substances from plants and animals to cure their patients. Twentieth-century medicine saw the use of vaccines to save countless lives. ⚲ *Today, biotechnology is the source of some of the most important and exciting advances in the prevention and treatment of disease.*

**Genetic Testing** If two prospective parents suspect they are carrying the alleles for a genetic disorder, such as cystic fibrosis (CF), how could they find out for sure? Because the CF allele has slightly different DNA sequences from its normal counterpart, genetic tests using labeled DNA probes can distinguish the presence of CF. Like many genetic tests, the CF test uses specific DNA sequences that detect the complementary base sequences found in the disease-causing alleles. Other genetic tests search for changes in cutting sites of restriction enzymes. Some use PCR to detect differences between the lengths of normal and abnormal alleles. Genetic tests are now available for diagnosing hundreds of disorders.

**Medical Research** Transgenic animals, such as the pig shown in **Figure 16-11**, are often used as model test subjects in medical research, simulating human genetic disorders. These animal models have been used to study the onset and progression of diseases and to conduct drug testing. Although they cannot completely simulate the responses of the human body, animal models are useful, and have been used to research human disorders, such as Alzheimer's disease and arthritis.

**BUILD VOCABULARY**

**Academic Words** When you modify something, you make small changes to it, often with the purpose of improving it. Modified is the past tense of modify. A genetically modified organism has had changes made to its genome.

**Figure 16-11**

**Transgenic Pig**

This pig is greenish because it has jellyfish genes for fluorescent proteins. These jellyfish genes act as markers for genes being studied in medical research.

**Preventing and Treating Disease** Bioengineering can prevent and treat human diseases in a variety of different ways, from making our food more nutritious to creating strains of mosquitoes that are incapable of transmitting particular pathogens.

***Golden Rice*** One interesting development in transgenic technology is golden rice, shown in **Figure 16-12**. Traditional white rice does not contain provitamin A, also known as beta-carotene, which is essential for human health. Golden rice has been genetically modified to produce and accumulate beta-carotene. Provitamin A deficiencies lead to serious medical problems, including infant blindness. While there have been setbacks in bringing this new crop to the areas that could benefit from it, scientists continue to hope that provitamin A-rich golden rice will help prevent these problems.

***Human Proteins*** When recombinant-DNA techniques were developed for bacteria, biologists realized almost immediately that the technology held the promise to do something that had never been done before—to make important proteins that could prolong and even save human lives. For example, human growth hormone, which is used to treat patients suffering from pituitary dwarfism, was once scarce. Human growth hormone is now widely available because it is mass-produced by recombinant bacteria. Other products now made with genetically engineered bacteria include insulin to treat diabetes, blood-clotting factors for hemophiliacs, and potential cancer-fighting molecules, such as interleukin-2 and interferon.

In the future, transgenic animals may provide us with an ample supply of our own proteins. Several laboratories have engineered transgenic sheep and pigs that produce human proteins in their milk, making it easy to collect and refine the proteins. Many of these proteins can be used in disease prevention.

***Gene Therapy*** An even more ambitious goal of biotechnology would be to cure genetic disorders by fixing or replacing the alleles that cause them. The hope of many scientists is to make **gene therapy**, the changing of a gene to treat a disease or disorder, a routine part of medical treatment. As promising as this idea seems, there have been many problems in making it a reality. Researchers have carried out a number of experiments in which they inserted DNA containing a healthy, working gene into a modified virus. They then infected the cells of patient volunteers with the virus, hoping it would insert the healthy gene into the target cell and correct the defect. In some cases, there was modest success in reversing the effects of the disorder. But in other cases, the attempts failed and in 1999 one even took the life of a courageous young man who had volunteered for this experimental therapy. As a result, many potential plans for gene therapy were abandoned out of concern that they might actually harm, rather than help, patients.

Despite these setbacks, the development of CRISPR technology has caused many scientists to think of gene therapy once again. In 2013 a group of Chinese scientists did correct a genetic disorder in mice. The disorder was caused by a dominant allele that produced cataracts, small opaque regions that cloud the lens of the eye and interfere with vision. To knock out this dominant allele, they injected the mice with mRNA containing the Cas9 sequence and a guide RNA targeting the specific DNA sequence of the cataract allele. The guide RNA found the allele, and the Cas9 enzyme took care of the rest, inactivating the allele. When the mice developed, they were cataract free. This new approach to gene therapy is off to a promising start. It will be interesting to see what the future brings!

**GM Mosquitoes** Other techniques are targeting mosquitoes, which spread many diseases, including malaria and the Zika virus. In February 2016, Brazilian biologists released genetically modified mosquitoes. When these mosquitoes breed with wild mosquitoes, they pass on genes that prevent the mosquitoes from carrying the Zika virus. **Figure 16-13** shows a scientist releasing the genetically modified mosquitoes that were raised in the laboratory.

**Figure 16-13**

**Preventing Disease**

A scientist is releasing GM mosquitoes into a Brazilian neighborhood to help stop the spread of the Zika virus. The fluorescent mosquito larvae (inset) are part of a study to produce GM mosquitoes that cannot carry the protist that causes malaria.

## Figure 16-14

## Analyzing Gene Activity

DNA microarrays help researchers explore the underlying genetic causes of many human diseases.

### ❶ Preparing the cDNA Probe

**ⓐ** mRNA samples are isolated from two different types of cells or tissues, such as cancer cells and normal cells.

mRNA from cancer cells

mRNA from normal cells

**ⓑ** Enzymes are used to prepare complementary DNA molecules (cDNA) from both groups of mRNA. Contrasting fluorescent labels are attached to both groups of cDNA (red to one, green to the other).

cDNA from cancer cells

cDNA from normal cells

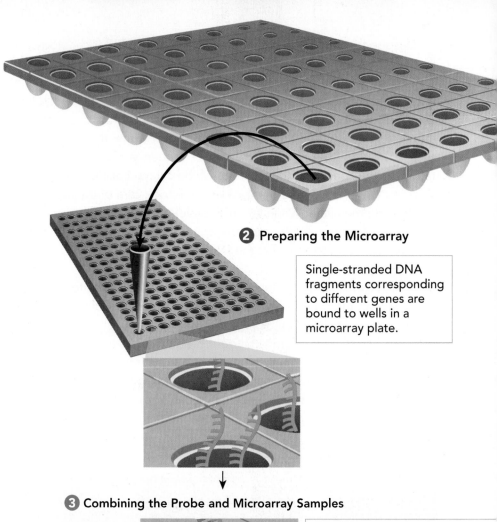

### ❷ Preparing the Microarray

Single-stranded DNA fragments corresponding to different genes are bound to wells in a microarray plate.

### ❸ Combining the Probe and Microarray Samples

**ⓐ** Color-labeled cDNA molecules from cancer and normal cells bind to complementary sequences on the plate.

**ⓑ** Red spots indicate higher levels of expression of that gene in cancer cells. Green spots indicate lower levels of gene expression. Yellow spots indicate equal gene expression in normal and cancerous cells.

**Examining Active Genes** Although each cell in a person contains the same genetic material, the same genes are not active in every cell. By studying which genes are active and which are inactive in different cells, scientists can understand how the cells function normally and what happens when genes don't work as they should. Today, scientists use **DNA microarray** technology to study hundreds or even thousands of genes at once to understand their activity levels. A DNA microarray is a glass slide or silicon chip to which spots of single-stranded DNA have been tightly attached. Typically each spot contains a different DNA fragment. **Figure 16-14** shows how a DNA microarray is constructed and used.

Suppose, for example, that you want to compare the genes expressed in cancer cells with genes in normal cells from the same tissue. After isolating mRNA from both types of cells, you would use an enzyme to copy the mRNA base sequence into single-stranded DNA labeled with fluorescent colors—red for the cancer cell and green for the normal cell. Next you would mix both samples of labeled DNA together and let them compete for binding to the complementary DNA sequences already in the microarray. If the cancer cell produces more of a particular form of mRNA, then more red-labeled molecules will bind at the spot for that gene, turning it red. Where the normal cell produces more mRNA for another gene, that spot will be green. Where there is no difference between the two cell types, the spot will be yellow because it contains both colors.

**✔ READING CHECK** **List** What are five applications of genetic engineering in the field of health and medicine?

# Personal Identification

The complexity of the human genome ensures that no individual is exactly like any other genetically—except for identical twins, who share the same genome. Molecular biology has used this fact to develop a powerful tool called **DNA fingerprinting** for use in identifying individuals. ⚷ *DNA fingerprinting analyzes sections of DNA that may have little or no function but that vary widely from one individual to another.* This method is shown in **Figure 16-15**. First, restriction enzymes cut a small sample of human DNA. Next, gel electrophoresis separates the restriction fragments by size. Then a DNA probe detects the fragments that have highly variable regions, revealing a series of variously sized DNA bands. If enough combinations of enzymes and probes are used, the resulting pattern of bands can be distinguished statistically from that of any other individual in the world. By using PCR to amplify the sequences used for DNA fingerprinting, even the tiniest trace samples of blood, sperm, or hair can provide enough DNA to work with.

**READING TOOL**

After reading the section Personal Identification, look closely at Figure 16-15. Which suspect was likely at the crime scene? Explain.

**INTERACTIVITY**

**Figure 16-15**

**DNA Fingerprinting**

DNA fingerprinting can be used to match a DNA sample to a particular person. It is especially useful in solving crimes. The diagram shows how scientists match DNA evidence from a crime scene with two possible suspects.

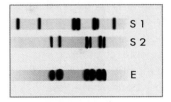

DNA fingerprint

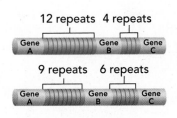

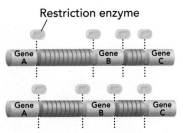

Restriction enzyme

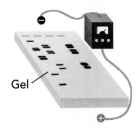

Gel

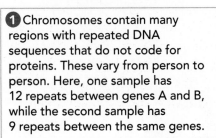

❶ Chromosomes contain many regions with repeated DNA sequences that do not code for proteins. These vary from person to person. Here, one sample has 12 repeats between genes A and B, while the second sample has 9 repeats between the same genes.

❷ Restriction enzymes are used to cut the DNA into fragments containing genes and repeats. Note that the repeat fragments from these two samples are of different lengths.

❸ The restriction fragments are separated according to size using gel electrophoresis. The DNA fragments containing repeats are then labeled using radioactive probes. This labeling produces a series of bands—the DNA fingerprint.

**INTERACTIVITY**

Practice using DNA finger-printing to determine the genome of an individual from a crime scene.

**Forensic Science** DNA fingerprinting has been used in the United States since the late 1980s. Its precision and reliability have revolutionized **forensics**—the scientific study of crime scene evidence. DNA fingerprinting has helped solve crimes, convict criminals, and even overturn wrongful convictions. DNA evidence was first used to save an innocent person from execution in 1989. Since then, DNA evidence has saved more than 180 wrongfully convicted prisoners from death sentences. DNA forensics is used in wildlife conservation as well. African elephants are a highly vulnerable species. Poachers, who slaughter the animals mainly for their tusks, have reduced their population dramatically. To stop the ivory trade, African officials now use DNA fingerprinting to identify the herds from which black-market ivory has been taken.

**Fallen Heroes** Buried at the Tomb of the Unknowns, shown in **Figure 16-16**, are the remains of unidentified American soldiers who fought our nation's wars. Biotechnology offers hope that there will never be another unknown soldier. The U.S. military now requires all personnel to give a DNA sample when they begin their service. Those DNA samples are kept on file and used, if needed, to identify the remains of individuals who perish in the line of duty. In many ways, this practice is a comfort to military families, who can be assured that the remains of a loved one can be properly identified for burial.

**Figure 16-16**

## Unknown Identities

The Tomb of the Unknowns in Arlington National Cemetery, near Washington, D.C. holds the remains of unknown American soldiers from World Wars I and II, the Korean War, and, until 1998, the Vietnam War. The tomb also serves as a focal point for the honor and remembrance of those service members lost in combat whose bodies have never been recovered.

**Establishing Relationships** In cases of disputed paternity, how does our justice system determine the rightful father of a child? DNA fingerprinting makes it easy to find alleles carried by the child that do not match those of the mother. Any such alleles must come from the child's biological father, and they will show up in his DNA fingerprint. The probability that those alleles will show up in a randomly picked male is less than 1 in 100,000. This means the likelihood that a given male is the child's father must be higher than 99.99 percent to confirm his paternity.

## Forensics Lab    Guided Inquiry

### Using DNA to Solve Crimes

**Problem** How can DNA samples be used to connect a suspect to a crime scene?

In this lab, you will make and analyze four DNA profiles using gel electrophoresis. You will then compare the DNA profile collected from a crime scene with DNA profiles from three suspects.

You can find this lab in your digital course.

When genes are passed from parent to child, genetic recombination scrambles the molecular markers used for DNA fingerprinting, so ancestry can be difficult to trace. There are two ways to solve this problem. The Y chromosome never undergoes crossing-over, and only males carry it. Therefore, Y chromosomes pass directly from father to son with few changes. The same is true of the small DNA molecules found in mitochondria. These are passed, with very few changes, from mother to child in the cytoplasm of the egg cell.

Because mitochondrial DNA (mtDNA) is passed directly from mother to child, your mtDNA is the same as your mother's mtDNA, which is the same as her mother's mtDNA. This means that if two people have an exact match in their mtDNA, then there is a very good chance that they share a common maternal ancestor. Y-chromosome analysis has been used in the same way and has helped researchers to settle a longstanding historical question—did President Thomas Jefferson father the child of a slave? DNA testing showed that one of the modern descendants of Sally Hemings, a slave on Jefferson's Virginia estate, carried his Y chromosome. This result suggests that Jefferson was indeed the father of one of Hemings's sons.

HS-ETS1-1, HS-LS3-1

## ☑ LESSON 16.3 Review

### ⚲ KEY QUESTIONS

1. Provide an example of a GM organism. What benefit does this organism provide that the non-GM organism could not provide?

2. In what ways can biotechnology prevent and treat diseases?

3. How is DNA fingerprinting useful?

### CRITICAL THINKING

4. **Construct an Explanation** Medicines in the body interact with the body's proteins. Explain how normal variations in your genes may affect your response to different medicines.

5. **Ask Questions** You are researching different companies that analyze DNA to trace ancestry. What questions would you ask each company before you decide which company to use?

# Ethics and Impacts of Biotechnology

## ⚲ KEY QUESTIONS

- *What privacy issues does biotechnology raise?*
- *What are some of the pros and cons of transgenic organisms?*
- *What are some of the ethical issues around new biotechnology?*

**HS-ETS1-1:** Analyze a major global challenge to specify qualitative and quantitative criteria and constraints for solutions that account for societal needs and wants.

## READING TOOL

As you read, identify the opposing views on each ethical issue with biotechnology. Take notes in the two-column chart in your 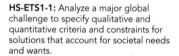 **Biology Foundations Workbook.**

We can already use biotechnology to analyze and change an organism's DNA. Should scientists be able to make any change they wish? And what should we make of a future world in which authorities might use genetics to decide a person's schooling, job prospects, and even his or her legal rights?

## Profits and Privacy

Private biotechnology companies do much of the research involving GM plants and animals, hoping to make a profit. Like most inventors, they protect their discoveries and innovations with patents. A *patent* is a legal tool that gives an individual or company the exclusive right to profit from its innovations for a number of years.

**Patenting Life** Like new machines and devices, molecules and biotechnology procedures can be patented. But sometimes patent disputes have slowed research that might be beneficial. That was the case with provitamin A-enriched golden rice, a GM plant described in the last lesson. Even after the rice was developed, patent disputes kept it out of the hands of farmers for years. However, in 2013 the United States Supreme Court unanimously ruled that genes found in nature cannot be patented. Altered, or synthetic genes, however, can be patented, allowing companies to protect novel biotechnology products.

**Genetic Privacy** A great deal can be learned about a person from a sample of his or her DNA. ⚲ *DNA can reveal private information, including ethnic heritage, the chances of developing certain diseases, and evidence for criminal cases.* As science advances, legal experts will debate ways to keep personal genetic information safe and confidential. No one wants to be denied a job or an education because of conclusions someone else might make about his or her intelligence or personality based on DNA.

# Safety of Transgenic Organisms

There is a lot of controversy concerning foods that have had their DNA altered through genetic engineering. While nearly half of all GM crops today are grown in the United States, farmers around the world are now using GM technology. Are the foods from GM crops the same as those prepared from traditionally bred crops, and how will this new area of research affect the environment?

**Arguments for GM Foods** The companies producing seeds for GM crops would say that GM plants are actually better and safer than other crops. Farmers choose them because they produce higher yields, reducing the amount of land and energy that must be devoted to agriculture and lowering the cost of food and other plant-based products for everyone.

Insect-resistant GM plants need little, if any, insecticide to grow successfully. This reduces the chance that insecticide residues will enter the food supply and reduces damage to the environment. In addition, GM foods have been widely available for more than two decades. 🔍 *Careful studies of such foods have provided no scientific support for concerns about their safety, and the scientific community regards foods made from GM plants as safe to eat.*

**Arguments Against GM Foods** Critics acknowledge some benefits of genetically modified foods, but they also point out that no long-term studies have been made of the potential hazards. Therefore, even if there is no current evidence that such products are harmful, they argue that adverse effects could appear in the future.

## INTERACTIVITY

Explore the impacts and ethics of biotechnology.

## BUILD VOCABULARY

**Related Words** *Insecticides* are chemicals that kill insects. *Pesticides* are chemicals that target a wide range of pests, including insects, weeds, fungi, rodents, and snails. An insecticide is a type of pesticide.

---

## CASE STUDY  Analyzing Data

### Genetically Modified Crops in the United States

U.S. farmers have adopted GM crops widely since their introduction in 1996. Soybeans, cotton, and corn have been modified to tolerate herbicides and resist insect damage. The graph summarizes the extent to which these crops were adopted between 1996 and 2016. The modified traits shown here include herbicide tolerance (HT) and insect resistance (Bt).

1. **Analyze Graphs** Which two crops were most widely and rapidly adopted?

2. **Draw Conclusions** Why do you think the levels of adoption of GM crops fell at certain points over the period shown in the graph?

3. **Predict** What do you think will happen to HT soybeans and HT corn over the next few years? Why? Use the graph to support your prediction.

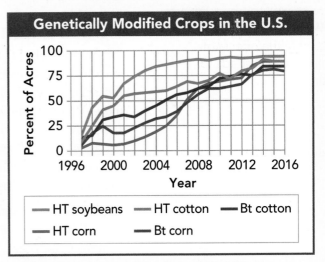

Data for each crop category include varieties with both HT and Bt (stacked) traits.
**Sources:** USDA, Economic Research Service using data from Fernandez-Cornejo and McBride (2002) for the years 1996–1999 and USDA, National Agriculture Statistics Service, *June Agriculture Survey* for years 2000–16.

**VIDEO**

Examine the ethics of bio-technology by looking at the benefits and drawbacks of the process.

**CASE STUDY**

**Figure 16-17**

**Food Labeling**

Many foods now include labeling that shows they were not produced using GM grains or other raw materials even though such labels are not yet required by law.

**READING TOOL**

Identify the effects of planting GM seeds for farmers.

New efforts to develop genetically modified animal food products, such as salmon, pork, and beef, only add to this uncertainty, and have led critics to call for a complete ban on GM meats. ⚛ *Even if GM food itself presents no hazards, there are many serious concerns about the unintended consequences that a shift to GM farming and ranching may have on agriculture.* Some worry that the insect resistance engineered into GM plants may threaten beneficial insects, killing them as well as crop pests. Others express concerns that use of plants resistant to chemical herbicides may lead to overuse of these weed-killing compounds.

Another concern is that the costly patents held on GM seeds by companies may raise the cost of seeds to the point that small farmers go out of business, especially in the developing world. It is not clear whether any of these concerns should block the wider use of these new biotechnologies, but it is certain that they will continue to prove controversial in the years ahead.

In the United States, many public interest groups have argued that GM foods should be labeled so that consumers know what they are eating. In 2016, the state of Vermont passed a law requiring such labeling, and other states considered similar laws. However, just a few months later, Congress overrode such state laws, and instructed the U.S. Department of Agriculture (USDA) to develop rules for GM food labeling that would apply across the country. At this point, the USDA has yet to finalize those rules. However, many food packages, like the one shown in **Figure 16-17**, are starting to include labeling that indicates that the food was not produced using GM materials.

✅ **READING CHECK** **Summarize** In the United States, are manufacturer required to label products that contain genetically modified foods? Explain.

## Ethics of the New Biology

"Know yourself." The ancient Greeks carved this good advice in stone, and it has been guiding human behavior ever since. Biotechnology has given us the ability to know ourselves more and more. With this knowledge, however, comes responsibility. You've seen how easy it is to move genes from one organism to another. For example, the GFP gene can be extracted from a jellyfish and spliced onto genes coding for important cellular proteins. This ability has led to significant new discoveries about how cells function.

The same GFP technology was used to create the fluorescent zebra fish shown in **Figure 16-18**. These fish—along with fluorescent mice, tadpoles, rabbits, and even cats—have all contributed to our understanding of cells and proteins. But the ability to alter life forms for any purpose, scientific or nonscientific, raises important questions. ⚛ *Just because we have the technology to modify an organism's characteristics, are we justified in doing so?*

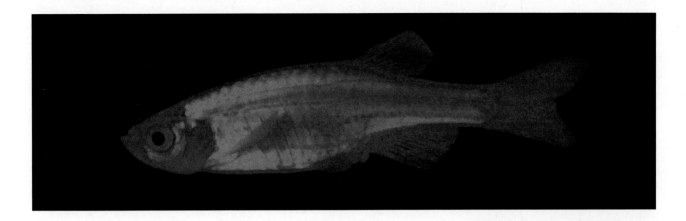

It would indeed be marvelous if new research in biotechnology enabled us to cure hemophilia, cystic fibrosis, or other genetic diseases. The technology now exists to eliminate mitochondrial diseases by transferring a zygote nucleus into the egg cytoplasm of a third person. But if human cells can be manipulated to cure disease, should biologists try to engineer taller people or change people's eye color, hair texture, sex, blood group, or appearance? What will happen to the human species when we gain the opportunity to design our bodies or those of our children? What will be the consequences if biologists develop the ability to clone human beings by making identical copies of their cells? These are questions that society must understand and deal with.

The goal of biology is to gain a better understanding of the nature of life. As our knowledge increases, however, so does our ability to manipulate the genetics of living things, including ourselves. In a democratic nation, all citizens—not just scientists—are responsible for ensuring that the tools science has given us are used wisely. This means that you should be prepared to help develop a thoughtful and ethical consensus of what should and should not be done with the human genome. To do anything less would be to lose control of two of our most precious gifts: our intellect and our humanity.

**INTERACTIVITY**

**Figure 16-18**
## Solving Problems

Fluorescent zebra fish were originally bred to help scientists detect environmental pollutants. Today, studying fluorescent fish is helping us understand cancer and other diseases. Many of these fish are also sold to the public for their home aquariums.

HS-ETS1-1

## ☑ LESSON 16.4 Review

### ⚲ KEY QUESTIONS

1. What private information can DNA reveal about a person?

2. What are some of the positive outcomes of GM agriculture?

3. What are the main concerns about genetic engineering discussed in this lesson or elsewhere in the chapter?

### CRITICAL THINKING

4. **Defend Your Claim** Do you think GM food should be labeled? Cite evidence or logical reasoning to support your claim.

5. **Construct an Argument** Plants and animals have been genetically modified for a wide variety of purposes, including scientific research, improving food crops, improving human health, and commercial profit. Discuss the ethical arguments for and against these biotechnology techniques.

6. **CASE STUDY** Biologists may one day be able to use genetic engineering to alter a child's inherited traits. Under what circumstances, if any, should this ability be used? Write a persuasive paragraph expressing your opinion.

# What will the future hold for genetically modified crops?

**The canola plants in this field look, grow, and function almost exactly the same as all other canola plants. The difference is a gene that enables them to resist chemicals used to control weeds.**

HS-ETS1-1, CCSS.ELA-LITERACY.RST.9-10.1, CCSS.ELA-LITERACY.WHST.9-10.9

## Make Your Case

Over the past 40 years, genetic technology has been changing the way we raise farm crops. These changes have brought many benefits to farmers and consumers alike. Yet critics of genetically modified (GM) foods have raised a variety of concerns. Research the arguments both in favor of and against this technology. Be sure to evaluate the sources you reference, and look for evidence that supports the arguments.

## Construct an Argument

1. **Form an Opinion** What is your opinion about the use of GM crops in agriculture, as well as the development of new GM crops? Cite evidence from your research and use logical reasoning to construct an argument in support of your opinion.

2. **Conduct Peer Review** Work with a partner to discuss your arguments. Then evaluate your partner's argument. Verify the evidence that supports the argument, and evaluate the reasoning. If possible, suggest ways to strengthen either your partner's argument or your own.

A field of canola. Canola seeds (inset) change from green to brown as they mature.

## Careers on the Case

### Work Toward a Solution

Scientists in several fields work together to invent, distribute, and manage GM farm crops. Yet ultimately the crops are in the hands of farmers. The economic and social demands of farming make science knowledge essential for farmers to succeed.

### Farmer

The job of a farmer involves much more than merely planting seeds and then harvesting the crop. Farmers must now decide which crops to farm and if they want to raise GM crops. Many farmers and future farmers are now studying science at the college level. Their knowledge will help them run farms as effectively as possible.

▶ **VIDEO**

Watch this video to learn about scientists who are working with genetically modified mosquitoes.

## Technology on the Case

### Old Problem, New Solution

One hundred years ago, botanist George Washington Carver worked tirelessly to improve farming in the southeastern United States. Most farmers were growing cotton, which depleted the soil of nutrients. Carver encouraged farmers to alternate cotton with crops that restored nutrients to the soil, such as soybeans and peanuts. Carver also developed many new uses for peanuts to make them more valuable.

Today, huge volumes of fertilizer are spread on cotton and many other crops. The fertilizer supplies the nutrients and minerals that plants need. One of these nutrients is "fixed" nitrogen, which is the name for the nitrogen compounds that plants can use. Peanuts, and other legume plants, are able to supply their own fixed nitrogen because of certain bacteria that live on their roots.

Fertilizer is expensive to make and use, and it can pollute the environment. Genetic technology may offer an alternative. Scientists have identified three bacterial genes that produce the proteins involved in nitrogen fixation. Now their goal is to transfer those proteins into crop plants. If they succeed, then the modified crops would fix nitrogen from the atmosphere, just like bacteria do for legume plants. What would George Washington Carver think about that?

# Lesson Review

Go to your Biology Foundations Workbook for longer versions of these lesson summaries.

## 16.1 Changing the Living World

Biotechnology is the application of a technological process, invention, or method to living organisms. One example of biotechnology is selective breeding. Both hybridization and inbreeding are methods of selective breeding.

Sometimes breeders want even more variation than exists in nature and therefore introduce mutations into a population. Bacteria can be treated with radiation or chemicals to produce a useful mutant.

- selective breeding
- biotechnology
- hybridization
- inbreeding

## 16.2 The Process of Genetic Engineering

Scientists use computer databases to search for specific genes they wish to study. When a sample of DNA is too small to analyze, scientists use polymerase chain reaction (PCR) to produce billions of copies of DNA. Scientists can isolate genes and insert genes from one organism into another. Combined DNA from two or more organisms is called recombinant DNA.

Recombinant DNA can change the genetic composition of a living organism. Plasmids are small circular DNA molecules found in some bacteria and yeasts. Plasmids are used in recombinant DNA studies.

CRISPR technology allows scientists to edit DNA in a eukaryotic cell and makes it possible to study gene function by inactivating specific genes.

Transgenic organisms contain genes from other species. A clone is a population of genetically identical cells produced from a single cell. Cloning allows a single cell from an adult organism to grow an entirely new individual that is genetically identical to the organism from which the cell was taken.

- polymerase chain reaction
- recombinant DNA
- plasmid
- genetic marker
- transgenic
- clone

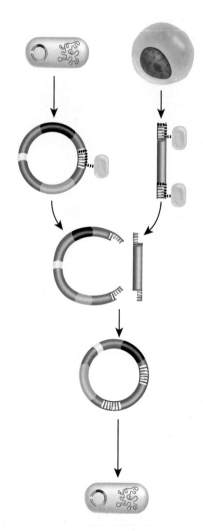

☑ **Interpret Diagrams** Describe the process of inserting a gene for human growth hormone into a bacterial cell, as shown here.

## 16.3 Applications of Biotechnology

Genetic modification of plants and animals could lead to more nutritious food that is less expensive to grow or raise. Some GM plants make it possible for farmers to use less pesticides that can be harmful to the environment. Other GM plants can resist diseases that the natural varieties cannot. GM animals can produce human proteins in milk that can fight disease. Or they may be able to produce materials that are useful to industry.

Biotechnology has led to important advances in the prevention and treatment of diseases. Gene therapy, the changing of a gene to treat a disease or disorder, is a goal of biotechnology. DNA microarray technology allows scientists to study thousands of genes at once to understand their activity levels.

DNA fingerprinting analyzes sections of DNA that may have little or no function but that vary widely from one individual to another. DNA fingerprinting has applications in forensics, in identifying individuals, and in tracing ancestry.

- gene therapy
- DNA microarray
- DNA fingerprinting
- forensics

☑ **Construct an Explanation** Explain how DNA microarray can help researchers determine differences between how cancer cells and normal cells function.

## 16.4 Ethics and Impacts of Biotechnology

Private biotechnology and pharmaceutical companies do much of the research involving GM plants and animals. They have often sought to protect their research by patenting discoveries. However, in 2013, the U.S. Supreme Court ruled that human genes cannot be patented.

There is much controversy surrounding foods that contain GM ingredients. Studies have provided no scientific support for concerns about their safety. However, there are serious concerns about the unintended consequences that farming and ranching with genetically modified organisms may have on agriculture.

The ability to alter life forms for any purpose raises important ethical questions. Just because something can be done doesn't mean it should be done. Should we manipulate human cells to engineer body design or appearance? How do we ensure that the tools of biotechnology are used wisely? A thoughtful and ethical consensus needs to be developed to preserve our intellect and our humanity.

☑ **Make Generalizations** How do you evaluate the ethics of genetic technologies?

# Organize Information

List the correct order of the lettered phrases to match the type of biotechnology with its application.

| Type of Biotechnology | Used to ... |
|---|---|
| Selective breeding | a. transfer genes from one organism to another organism |
| Recombinant DNA | b. match a DNA sample to an individual |
| CRISPR | c. select for wanted characteristics from one generation to the next |
| DNA microarray | d. edit an organism's DNA |
| DNA fingerprinting | e. examine the activity level of a gene |

# Gene Therapy

1990
Dr. Kenneth Culver and Dr. Michael Blaese treated the first gene therapy patients.

Adenoviruses are often used to deliver genes to the cells of gene-therapy patients.

# Evaluate a Solution

HS-ETS1-2, CCSS.ELA-LITERACY.RST.9-10.2, CCSS.ELA-LITERACY.WHST.9-10.2

**STEM** It all seemed so simple. To cure a disease caused by a defective gene, why not replace it with a healthy version of the same gene? In 1990, Dr. Kenneth Culver and Dr. Michael Blaese had done just that for a four-year-old girl with a genetic disorder called adenosine deaminase deficiency. Given such success, in 1999, researchers at the University of Pennsylvania thought they might be able to do something similar for eighteen-year-old Jessie Gelsinger.

Jessie suffered from ornithine transcarbamylase deficiency (OTCD), which prevents the liver from processing ammonia as it should. Although drugs had enabled Jessie to lead a fairly normal life, he volunteered to be a test subject for experimental gene therapy. His parents went along with his wishes, in the hope of helping children with potentially fatal versions of the same disease.

The treatment involved medical researchers inserting copies of the healthy gene into a virus. They expected that the virus would carry the replacement gene into Jessie's liver cells, curing him of OTCD. The virus had been carefully engineered for this purpose, and the researchers were confident that it would be harmless. But shortly after they injected this virus into the artery leading to Jessie's liver, something went terribly wrong.

Within days of the treatment, his immune system reacted against the virus so strongly that his liver and other organs underwent a complete shutdown. Five days later, this courageous volunteer was removed from life support, and died.

# NEW Technology, NEW Challenges

**1999**
Jessie Gelsinger dies as a result of a gene therapy trial.

**2017**
Dr. Marina Cavazzana led a team that has developed a promising gene therapy treatment for sickle cell disease. The treatment uses the patient's stem cells.

You are a member of a journalism organization that has been assigned to write and produce a 10-minute feature broadcast about the history and future of gene therapy. Follow the steps to help you gather the information you will need to develop a script for your broadcast.

1. **Define the Problem** Jessie was the first reported patient to die during a gene therapy trial, and his death had an impact on the direction of the technology.

   • Research the gene therapy treatment that was given to Jessie Gelsinger. Prepare a description of the treatment and an explanation of what may have gone wrong.

   • Why did it seem as though gene therapy would be a promising treatment for people with disorders caused by a single gene?

   • Did the field of gene therapy head in a different direction after Jessie's death in 1999? Have there been any other tragedies or examples of success stories?

2. **Evaluate a Solution** How might CRISPR technology offer hope for the future of gene therapy? What problems might be solved by delivering replacement genes via CRISPR rather than using other types of vectors?

3. **Communicate Information** As a group, prepare a script for a 10-minute video to explain the information you gathered to a general audience. Decide how you will deliver the information. For example, one member of your group could be an interviewer and another member could be a scientist being interviewed. Consider any props you will need to explain gene therapy techniques and CRISPR to a general audience, such as images or models. Once your plan and script are complete, make your video to present to your teacher and class.

## 🔑 KEY QUESTIONS AND TERMS

### 16.1 Changing the Living World

1. Crossing dissimilar individuals to bring together their best characteristics is called
   a. domestication.
   b. inbreeding.
   c. hybridization.
   d. polyploidy.

2. Crossing individuals with similar characteristics so that those characteristics will appear in their offspring is called
   a. inbreeding.
   b. hybridization.
   c. recombination.
   d. polyploidy.

3. Taking advantage of naturally occurring variations in organisms to pass wanted traits on to future generations is called
   a. selective breeding.
   b. inbreeding.
   c. hybridization.
   d. mutation.

4. How do breeders produce genetic variations that are not found in nature?

5. What is polyploidy? When is this condition useful to researchers?

### 16.2 The Process of Genetic Engineering

HS-ETS1-1

6. Organisms that contain genes from other organisms are called
   a. transgenic.
   b. mutagenic.
   c. donors.
   d. clones.

7. When cell transformation is successful, the recombinant DNA
   a. undergoes mutation.
   b. is treated with antibiotics.
   c. becomes part of the transformed cell's genome.
   d. becomes a nucleus.

8. Bacteria often contain small circular molecules of DNA known as
   a. clones.
   b. chromosomes.
   c. plasmids.
   d. hybrids.

9. A member of a population of genetically identical cells produced from a single cell is a
   a. clone.
   b. plasmid.
   c. mutant.
   d. sequence.

10. Describe what happens during polymerase chain reaction.

11. Explain what genetic markers are and describe how scientists use them.

12. How does a transgenic plant differ from a hybrid plant?

### 16.3 Applications of Biotechnology

HS-ETS1-1, HS-LS3-1

13. Which of the following characteristics is often genetically engineered into crop plants?
    a. improved flavor
    b. resistance to herbicides
    c. shorter ripening times
    d. thicker stems

14. A substance that has been genetically engineered into transgenic rice has the potential to treat
    a. cancer.
    b. high blood pressure.
    c. vitamin A deficiency.
    d. malaria.

15. Which of the following techniques would scientists most likely use to understand the activity levels of hundreds of genes at once?
    a. a DNA microarray
    b. PCR
    c. restriction enzyme analysis
    d. DNA sequencing

16. Describe how a DNA microarray might be used to distinguish normal cells from cancer cells.

17. Describe two important uses for DNA fingerprinting.

## 16.4 Ethics and Impacts of Biotechnology

**HS-ETS1-1**

18. The right to profit from a new genetic technology is protected by
    a. getting a copyright for the method.
    b. discovering a new gene.
    c. obtaining a patent.
    d. publishing its description in a journal.

19. Give an example of a disadvantage associated with patenting genes.

20. What is one argument used by critics of genetically modified foods?

## CRITICAL THINKING

**HS-ETS1-1, HS-LS3-1**

21. **Communicate Information** Suppose a plant breeder has a thornless rose bush with scentless pink flowers, a thorny rose bush with sweet-smelling yellow flowers, and a thorny rose bush with scentless purple flowers. How might this breeder develop a pure variety of thornless, sweet-smelling, purple flowers?

22. **Compare and Contrast** Hybridization and inbreeding are important methods used in selective breeding. Evaluate these methods to determine how they are similar and different.

23. **Design a Solution** *Salmonella* is a type of bacteria that may cause illness in humans. Some strains of *Salmonella* have been shown to cause tumors to shrink. Researchers think that when *Salmonella* enter tumor cells, they cause the tumor cells to create proteins that enable immune cells to connect to the tumor and kill them. How would you design a solution to use *Salmonella* as an agent for fighting tumor cells?

24. **Define the Problem** About 120,000 people in the United States are on a waiting list to receive an organ donation. Every day, about 22 people die due to a lack of available organs. One solution that may help alleviate this problem is xenotransplantation, or the removal of an organ or tissues from an organism of one species and the placing of it into the body of an organism of a different species. Pigs have been seen as suitable donor animals for humans for several reasons. However, organ rejection is a major obstacle to successful transplantation. Pig cells contain a sugar molecule called α-1,3-galactose that triggers the human immune response. Define the problem and identify a solution to solve this problem.

25. **Summarize** If a human patient's bone marrow were removed, altered genetically, and reimplanted, would the change be passed on to the patient's children? Defend your claim.

26. **Apply Concepts** Bacteria and humans are very different organisms. Why is it sometimes possible to combine their DNA and use a bacterium to make a human protein?

27. **Infer** Briefly describe the biotechnological methods that are used to match a DNA sample to a particular person.

28. **Compare and Contrast** For hundreds of years, farmers have used selective breeding to increase the usefulness of crop plants and livestock. How do these efforts compare with the use of genetic technology to produce GM crops and livestock?

29. **Construct an Explanation** How is mitochondrial DNA useful for identifying family relationships?

Questions 30–32 refer to the diagram, which shows the results of a criminal laboratory test.

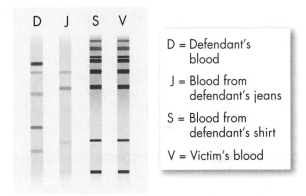

D = Defendant's blood

J = Blood from defendant's jeans

S = Blood from defendant's shirt

V = Victim's blood

30. **Infer** Briefly describe the biotechnological methods that would have been used to produce these results.

31. **Compare and Contrast** How are the bands from the jeans and the shirt similar? How are they different?

32. **Draw Conclusions** Based on these results, what conclusions might a prosecutor present to a jury during a criminal trial?

## CROSSCUTTING CONCEPTS

**33. Connect to Society** You have a friend who claims that no one should eat GM crops. Construct an argument that connects the growing of golden rice to benefits for society. In fairness to your friend, consider alternatives to GM crops that might yield the same benefits. What might be some of the challenges in the implementation of these alternative solutions?

**34. Connect to Technology** Evaluate the production of insulin and other proteins through genetic engineering. Be sure to include advantages and disadvantages. Perform additional research as needed to answer this question.

**35. Structure and Function** How do the DNA sequences included in a plasmid help ensure that recombinant DNA molecules are reproduced when they are inserted into a host cell?

## MATH CONNECTIONS

## Analyze and Interpret Data

CCSS.MATH.CONTENT.HSS.IC.B.6

The table shows the impact of GM crop adoption on different aspects of farming. The data show the percentages of change in different factors when farmers switched from planting non-GM crops to GM crops. Use the table to answer questions 36 and 37.

| Impact of GM Crops | |
|---|---|
| **Measurement** | **Percent Change** |
| Crop yield | +21.6 |
| Pesticide quantity | −36.9 |
| Pesticide cost | −39.2 |
| Total production cost | +3.3 |
| Profit for the farm | +68.2 |

**Data from:** Wilhelm Klümper, Matin Qaim, November 3, 2014, doi.org/10.1371/journal.pone.0111629

**36. Interpret Tables** What were the effects of using GM crops in terms of yield?

**37. Interpret Tables** What were the effects of using GM crops in terms of farmer profit?

## LANGUAGE ARTS CONNECTION
## Write About Science

CCSS.ELA-LITERACY.WHST.9-10.1, CCSS.ELA-LITERACY.WHST.9-10.2

**38. Write Arguments** A friend blogs about genetically modified organisms. She asserts that GM is still too new, and traditional selective breeding can accomplish the same results as GM. Write a response to your friend's blog either supporting or opposing this position.

**39. Write Technical Processes** Describe the major steps involved in inserting a human gene into a bacterium.

## Read About Science

CCSS.ELA-LITERACY.RST.9-10.1, CCSS.ELA-LITERACY.RST.9-10.4

**40. Determine Meaning** Many words and terms used in this chapter are based on the word *gene*. Examples include *genetic*, *transgenic*, and *genetically modified*. Look up the origins of the words *gene* and *genetics*. What is the original source of these words? Find as many variations as you can in the chapter. Determine their meanings and identify each word's part of speech.

**41. Cite Textual Evidence** Should a vegetarian be concerned about eating a GM plant that contains DNA from an animal gene? Support your answer with details from the text.

## Questions 1-2

DNA fingerprinting is a technology that is used for many different purposes. The diagram below is an illustration of what DNA fingerprinting data may look like.

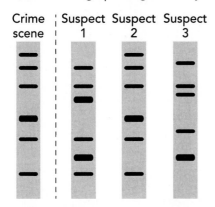

Crime scene | Suspect 1 | Suspect 2 | Suspect 3

1. Police departments and other agencies are often tasked with investigating crimes. Which of the following describes a solution to a problem investigators face that DNA fingerprinting can help solve?
   A. DNA fingerprinting can be used to treat criminals who have a genetic disease or disorder.
   B. DNA fingerprinting can be used to identify persons who were wrongly convicted of a crime.
   C. DNA fingerprinting can be used to identify which genes are active in persons who commit crimes.
   D. DNA fingerprinting can allow persons who commit crimes to be used as animal models in medical research studies.
   E. DNA fingerprinting allows investigators to identify suspects without evidence.

2. What do the dark bands in each sample represent?
   A. chromosomes
   B. active DNA fragments
   C. clones
   D. DNA fragments of different lengths
   E. Cas9 enzymes

3. One of the challenges facing the world today is supplying enough food for the human population. Farming with genetically modified plants is a possible solution to this challenge. What is a concern with using GM plants?
   A. GM plants produce higher yields, which may lead to an increase in the amount of wasted food.
   B. Farming with GM plants that are resistant to chemical herbicides may lead to overuse of weed-killing compounds.
   C. Farming with GM plants requires less land and energy, which may lead to lower food costs and an economic crisis for farmers.
   D. GM plants require more insecticide use, which may increase the chance of chemical residues in the food supply.
   E. Scientific studies on GM plants are not available, so the effects of GM plants are unknown.

4. A medical researcher hopes to cure a disease in mice by changing a gene. How can the researcher change the sequence of a gene?
   A. CRISPR
   B. cloning
   C. gel electrophoresis
   D. DNA fingerprinting
   E. DNA sequencing

5. Farmer Jones noticed that some of his chickens grow much faster than the others. What can he use to increase the frequency of this trait in his chickens?
   A. mutations
   B. genetic engineering
   C. DNA fingerprinting
   D. selective breeding
   E. gene therapy

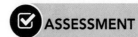 **ASSESSMENT**

For additional assessment practice, go online to access your digital course.

## If You Have Trouble With...

| Question | 1 | 2 | 3 | 4 | 5 |
|---|---|---|---|---|---|
| See Lesson | 16.3 | 16.3 | 16.4 | 16.2 | 16.1 |
| Performance Expectation | HS-ETS1-1 | HS-ETS1-1 | HS-ETS1-1 | HS-ETS1-1 | HS-ETS1-1 |

# UNIT 5 Evolution

Bridalveil Fall, Yosemite
Valley, California

**Crosscutting Concepts** Darwin's theory of evolution by natural selection, whose development beautifully demonstrates the nature of science, is the best scientific explanation for many kinds of patterns among organisms. Evolutionary theory demonstrates and explains relationships between structures of living things and their functions, mechanisms of change and their effects, and patterns of change over time.

**BOUNCE TO ACTIVATE**

**VIDEO**

Author Joe Levine describes the observations that naturalist Charles Darwin made in the Galápagos.

# Fossilized

## EVIDENCE OF LIFE LONG AGO

**Imagine you wanted to know** about life in your town one hundred years ago. You could read newspapers or look at photographs from that time. Or you could talk to people who know stories from that time. But what if you want to know what the place you live in was like millions of years ago? Earth's first living things arose over 3 billion years ago. Ever since, new species have evolved, and most of them have also gone extinct. We know they existed because a few organisms left behind fossils, which are preserved traces or remains. Fossils provide evidence for the history of life on Earth, as well as explanations for how life has changed over time.

**PROBLEM LAUNCH**
Conduct research on a fossil found in your region. Gather information to create a natural history display of your fossil.

▶ **VIDEO**

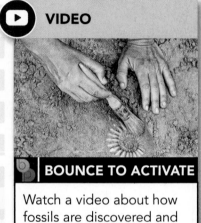

**BOUNCE TO ACTIVATE**

Watch a video about how fossils are discovered and the information that can be gathered from fossils.

# PROBLEM: What can a **fossil tell** you **about life long ago?**

➤ **TO SOLVE THIS PROBLEM, perform these activities as they come up in the unit, and record your findings in your ▱ Explorer's Journal.**

## INTERACTIVITY

Learn how fossils provide evidence of evolution.

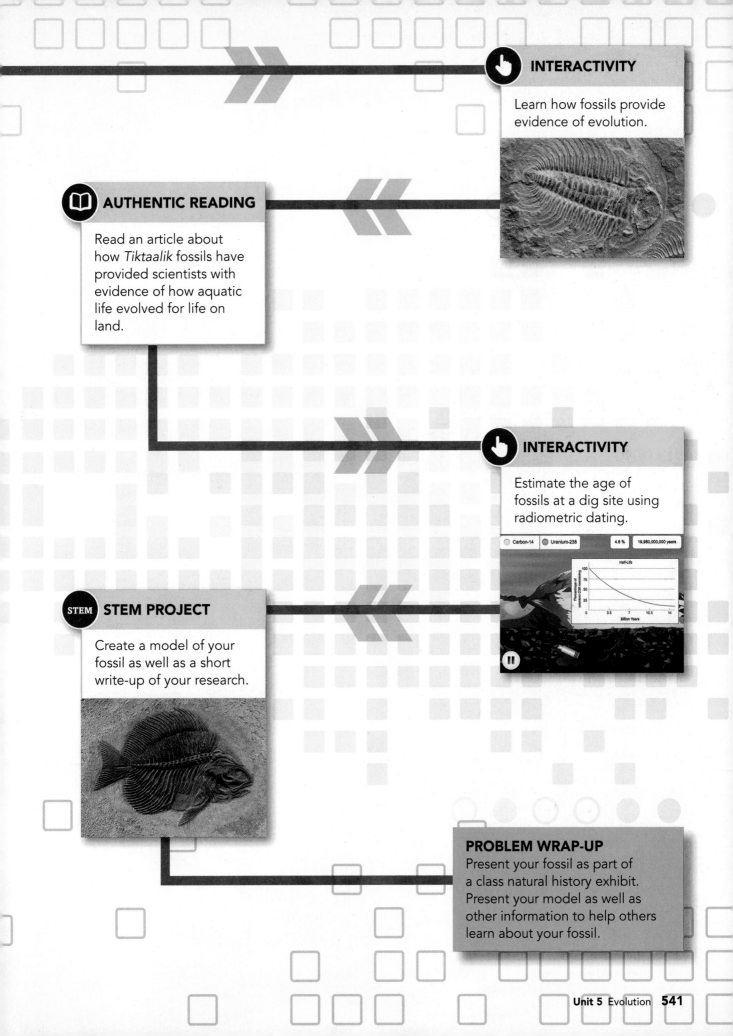

## AUTHENTIC READING

Read an article about how *Tiktaalik* fossils have provided scientists with evidence of how aquatic life evolved for life on land.

## INTERACTIVITY

Estimate the age of fossils at a dig site using radiometric dating.

## STEM PROJECT

Create a model of your fossil as well as a short write-up of your research.

## PROBLEM WRAP-UP

Present your fossil as part of a class natural history exhibit. Present your model as well as other information to help others learn about your fossil.

# 17

# Darwin's Theory of Evolution

**17.1**
A Voyage of Discovery

**17.2**
Ideas That Influenced Darwin

**17.3**
Darwin's Theory: Natural Selection

**17.4**
Evidence of Evolution

**Go Online to access your digital course.**

 **VIDEO**

 **AUDIO**

 **INTERACTIVITY**

 **eTEXT**

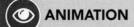 **ANIMATION**

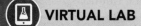 **VIRTUAL LAB**

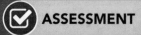 **ASSESSMENT**

The green anole (*Anolis carolinensis*) is one of almost 400 species of anoles.

HS-LS4-1, HS-LS4-2, HS-LS4-3, HS-LS4-4

# Lizards, Legs, and the Diversity of Life

Biologists looking at the living world are amazed at the variety of different living things that share our planet. Recognizing and naming all those organisms is tough enough. Figuring out how biological diversity arose has challenged scientists since science began. Some clues to the puzzle can be found in ancient fossils, while others, depending on where you live, may be staring at you, camouflaged in a nearby tree.

Some biologists try to study life's "big picture" by examining patterns that encircle the globe and changes in those patterns that span millions of years. Others focus on smaller subjects and changes that occur in just a few years.

Professor Jonathan Losos of Harvard University focuses his research on anoles, a group of small lizards found across the southeastern United States, the Caribbean, Central America, and northern South America. There are almost 400 anole species, 150 of which live in Florida and the Caribbean. Why do these lizards come in such a bewildering variety? That's the question Losos and like-minded biologists hope to answer through observation and experimentation. Two patterns seen in anole species fascinate biologists.

First pattern: Anole species living on the same island differ in body shape, behavior, and choice of niche. Species that prefer tree trunks near the ground, for example, have long back legs that enable them to jump long distances and run quickly. Species that live high in trees have very short legs and stickier toe pads. These species hang on to small twigs and creep slowly to avoid being spotted by predators.

Second pattern: Anoles living in the same niches on different islands have the same characteristics. BUT … the low-living species on different islands are different species, even though their body shapes and behaviors are similar. What's more, they are usually not closely related to the low-living species on other islands.

How do these patterns emerge? As part of his efforts to explain those patterns, Losos conducted ingenious experiments on small islands along Florida's Intracoastal Waterway. First, he studied the height of perches chosen by resident anoles of a native species, *Anolis carolinensis*. He also measured their legs and toe pads. He then introduced a small population of another species, *A. sagrei*, which had recently crossed to southern Florida from Cuba. What would happen? Would competition cause evolutionary change to occur? If so, how long would that take?

In only a few years, Losos saw evolution taking place before his eyes! The native anoles were moving higher in the trees than they had been before. Their legs and toe pads were also steadily changing to the forms found in higher tree-dwelling species! How do these kinds of changes help to explain the diversity of life on Earth?

**Throughout this chapter, look for connections to the CASE STUDY to help you answer these questions.**

# A Voyage of Discovery

Charles Darwin sailed on the HMS *Beagle*.

### 🔍 KEY QUESTIONS

- *What did Charles Darwin contribute to science?*
- *What three patterns of biodiversity did Darwin observe?*

**VOCABULARY**
evolution
fossil

**READING TOOL**

As you read the lesson, complete the main idea and details table in your 📘 **Biology Foundations Workbook**.

If you'd met young Charles Darwin, you wouldn't have guessed that his ideas would shake the world. He wasn't a star student. He preferred nature watching and hunting over studying. His father complained, "You care for nothing but shooting, dogs, and rat-catching, and you will be a disgrace to yourself and all your family." Yet Darwin would come up with what has been called "the single best idea that anyone has ever had." That didn't happen because Darwin sailed to exotic places and saw strange things. Europeans had been exploring and cataloging exotic creatures for years. Darwin did something that scientific thinkers described as the true essence of discovery. He saw things that many before him had seen, and came up with entirely new ways of thinking about them. And he asked questions. That's what Darwin did.

## Darwin's Epic Journey

Charles Darwin was born in England on February 12, 1809. Eager to see the world, he got his chance in 1831 when he was invited to join the HMS *Beagle* on the five-year voyage shown in **Figure 17-1**. The captain's job was to map coastlines and harbors. Darwin was added to keep the captain company during the long trip. No one knew it, but Darwin's presence on the *Beagle* would make this perhaps the single most important scientific voyage of all time.

The *Beagle* set sail at a time when scientists in several fields were revolutionizing scientific understanding of the natural world. Geologists were suggesting that Earth was ancient and had changed over time. Biologists were suggesting that life had also changed, through a process they called **evolution**. But although those other scientists had argued long before Darwin's voyage that organisms *could* change over time, none of them had offered a scientific description of *how* that change could happen.

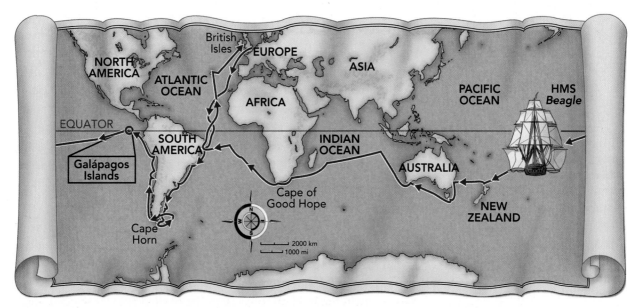

Darwin developed a theory of biological evolution that offered a scientific explanation for the unity and diversity of life, by proposing how modern organisms evolved through descent from common ancestors. Recall that a scientific theory is not a guess, a hunch, or a proposal. A scientific theory is a well-established, scientific explanation of events in the natural world. Scientific theories can be used to make predictions about events in the natural world that can be tested by experiments and observations. Darwin's work confirmed that the living world is constantly changing. Evolutionary theory helps us understand events such as the emergence and spread of drug-resistant bacteria and new strains of influenza. It helps us predict the dangers we will face if human actions drive too many species to extinction. For these reasons, all the biological and biomedical sciences are organized around the key ideas that Darwin developed more than 150 years ago.

**READING CHECK Summarize** How have scientists applied Darwin's theory of evolution?

## Figure 17-1
## Darwin's Journey

Darwin's life's work involved analyzing the many discoveries and observations he made on this journey. He was fortunate to visit a wide variety of habitats, especially the remote and isolated Galápagos Islands.

▶ **VIDEO**

Tour the Galápagos and discover the intriguing organisms that Darwin observed.

HS-LS4-1

### Analyzing Data

## Darwin's Voyage

1. Using the biome map in Chapter 3 as a model, identify three different biomes that Darwin visited on his voyage.

2. Find an example of when Darwin visited the same biome on two different continents.

### ANALYZE AND INTERPRET DATA

1. **Identify Patterns** Which biome did you identify as the same on two continents? Are similar types of animals found on both continents?

2. **Infer** How was a round-the-world voyage useful to Darwin for developing his theory of evolution?

3. **Evaluate Evidence** How does evidence from many places around the world, instead of only a single habitat or biome, help strengthen Darwin's theory of evolution?

# Observations from the Voyage

Darwin was fascinated by the diversity of life he saw during his trip. During a single day in a Brazilian forest he collected 68 species of beetles … and he wasn't even particularly looking for beetles! He was intrigued by how well suited to their local environments plants and animals seemed to be. He was impressed by the many ways that different organisms obtained food, protected themselves, and produced offspring. He was also puzzled by where different species lived—and did not live. He filled his notebooks with observations.

But Darwin wasn't content just to *describe* the diversity he saw. He wanted to *explain* it in a scientific way. He kept observing, asking questions, and formulating hypotheses. Those hypotheses guided him in making more observations to test those hypotheses. He kept looking for larger patterns into which his observations might fit. Over time, Darwin focused on three patterns of diversity: (1) species vary globally, (2) species vary locally, and (3) species vary over time.

**Species Vary Globally** Wherever Darwin went, he observed and asked questions. In the grasslands of South America, he found flightless, ground-dwelling birds called rheas, as shown in **Figure 17-2**. Rheas look and act a lot like ostriches. Yet rheas live only in South America, and ostriches live only in Africa. Why? Then, when Darwin visited Australia's grasslands, he found another large flightless bird, the emu. Darwin also noticed that rabbits and other species that lived in the grasslands of Europe did not live in the grasslands of South America and Australia. And when Darwin visited Australian grasslands, he saw kangaroos and other animals that are found nowhere else.

🔍 *Darwin noticed that different, yet ecologically similar, species inhabited separated, but ecologically similar, habitats around the globe.* What did these patterns of geographic distribution mean? Why did different flightless birds live in South America, Australia, and Africa, but not in the Northern Hemisphere? Why weren't there any rabbits in Australian habitats that seemed ideal for them? For that matter, why didn't kangaroos live in England?

**READING TOOL**

Make a table summarizing the observations made by Darwin during his travels. What types of variations did he notice globally, locally, and over time?

**INTERACTIVITY**

**Figure 17-2**

**Species Vary Globally**

Ostriches and rheas live in similar habitats on separate continents. Darwin wondered why the two species were similar, yet not identical.

Ostrich

Rhea

**Species Vary Locally** There were other puzzles, too. ⚲ *Darwin noticed that different, yet related, species often occupied different habitats within a local area.* For example, Darwin found *two* species of rheas in South America. One thrived in Argentina's grasslands, while a smaller species was adapted to the colder, harsher grass and scrubland to the south.

Darwin observed other examples of local variation in the Galápagos Islands, about 1000 kilometers off the Pacific coast of South America. These islands are relatively close to one another, but are ecologically different. Darwin was impressed and fascinated by the Galápagos, a region that he described as "a little world within itself" and "very remarkable" because it was home to a number of peculiar animals, including giant land tortoises such as those shown in **Figure 17-3**. At first, Darwin didn't think much about these beasts. In fact, like other travelers, Darwin ate several of them and tossed their remains overboard without studying them closely! Then the islands' vice-governor told Darwin that tortoises living on different islands were so different from one another that he could tell which island a tortoise came from just by looking at the shape of its shell. Darwin later admitted, "I did not for some time pay sufficient attention to this statement."

Darwin also observed that different islands had different varieties of mockingbirds, all of which resembled mockingbirds he had seen in South America. He also noticed several types of small brown birds with beaks of different shapes. He thought some of these birds were wrens, some were warblers, and some were blackbirds. He didn't consider them to be especially unusual or important—at first.

**Species Vary Over Time** In addition to collecting specimens of living species, Darwin also collected **fossils**, preserved remains or traces of ancient organisms. Scientists already knew that these remains formed a fossil record of organisms no longer living, although researchers in Darwin's day didn't yet know how to read and interpret that record.

⚲ *Darwin noted that the fossil record included many extinct animals that were similar to, yet different from, living species.* Among the most striking examples were fossils of extinct giant armored animals called glyptodonts. You can see in **Figure 17-4** that glyptodonts look like giant versions of modern armadillos, which live in the same area today. But why had glyptodonts disappeared? And why did modern armadillos resemble them? Could these animals have had a common ancestor? Darwin wrote: "This wonderful relationship in the same continent between the dead and the living, will, I do not doubt, hereafter throw more light on the appearance of organic beings on our Earth, and their disappearance from it, than any other class of facts."

☑ **READING CHECK** **Identify** What evidence did Darwin have to suggest that extinct species were similar to living species?

Figure 17-3

## Galápagos Tortoises

These two tortoise species live on different Galápagos Islands. Like anole lizards, the tortoises have traits that vary. ☑ **Compare and Contrast** Describe differences and similarities between these two tortoises.

Isabela Island Tortoise

Hood Island Tortoise

**BUILD VOCABULARY**

**Word Origins** The word *fossil* comes from the Latin word *fossilis*, meaning "dug up." Fossils are often dug out of the ground.

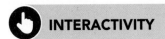

**INTERACTIVITY**

Explore Darwin's observations during his voyage aboard the *Beagle*.

**Putting the Puzzle Together** On the voyage home, Darwin thought about the patterns he had seen. When he returned to London, he visited experts to whom he he sent his specimens for identification. Those experts' evaluation of Darwin's specimens set the scientific community abuzz. It turned out that Galápagos mockingbirds belonged to three separate species found nowhere else on Earth! The little brown birds Darwin thought were wrens, warblers, and blackbirds were actually all species of finches! They, too, lived nowhere else, although they all resembled a single common finch species from South America. Yet in addition to being different from each other, those island species were different from that mainland species too. The same was true of Galápagos tortoises, marine iguanas, and many island plants.

Darwin was stunned by these discoveries. The evidence caused him to wonder whether species were really fixed and unchanging, as people thought back then. Could organisms change over time, through some natural process? Could Galápagos species have evolved from common South American ancestors? Darwin spent years researching and filling notebooks with ideas about species and evolution.

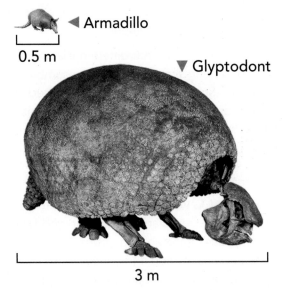

◀ Armadillo

0.5 m

▼ Glyptodont

3 m

**Figure 17-4**

**Glyptodont vs. Armadillo**

Fossils show that ancient organisms differed in important ways from those alive today, yet shared many similarities. ☑ **Ask Questions** What questions would you ask about the relationship between the ancient glyptodont and the modern armadillo?

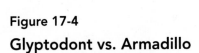

## ☑ LESSON 17.1 Review

### 🔍 KEY QUESTIONS

1. What does Darwin's theory of evolution explain about the natural world?

2. What three kinds of variations among organisms did Darwin observe during his voyage?

### CRITICAL THINKING

3. **Identify Patterns** Buffalo graze on the grasses of the North American plains, while yaks graze on grass in northern Asia. How do Darwin's categories of species variation apply to this comparison?

4. **Ask Questions** Suppose you visited the Galápagos Islands and observed several finch species, each different from one another and from mainland species. What questions would you ask about the history of the finches?

5. **CASE STUDY** How are the tortoises that Darwin observed on the Galápagos Islands similar to the anoles that Losos studied?

# Ideas That Influenced Darwin

The Grand Canyon provides evidence of Earth's long history.

## 🔍 KEY QUESTIONS

- *What did Hutton and Lyell conclude about Earth's history?*
- *How did Lamarck propose that species evolve?*
- *How did Malthus explain population growth?*
- *How is inherited variation used in artificial selection?*

**VOCABULARY**
artificial selection

**READING TOOL**

As you read, identify the science concepts and ideas that influenced Darwin. Complete the graphic organizer in your 📖 Biology Foundations Workbook.

Like all great scientific thinkers, Darwin was profoundly influenced by the work of other scientists. The *Beagle's* voyage came during one of the most exciting periods in the history of science. Geologists studying Earth's structure and history were making new observations and inferences about forces that have shaped our planet. Naturalists were describing and analyzing connections between organisms and their environments. These and other new ways of thinking about the natural world helped shape and guide Darwin's thoughts as he proposed hypotheses and gathered data to test them.

## An Ancient, Changing Earth

Many Europeans in Darwin's day thought that Earth was only a few thousand years old, and that it hadn't changed much during that time. By Darwin's time, however, a new generation of geologists were thinking in very different ways about Earth's history. Geologists James Hutton and Charles Lyell proposed important hypotheses based on the work of other researchers, and on data they uncovered themselves. 🔍 *Hutton and Lyell concluded that Earth is extremely old and that the processes that changed Earth in the past are the same processes that operate in the present.* In 1785, Hutton pre-sented his hypotheses about how geological processes have shaped Earth. Lyell, who built on the work of Hutton and others, published the first volume of his great work, *Principles of Geology*, in 1830.

View of the Valle del Bove Etna.

Illustration of Valle del Bove near Mt. Etna, *Principles of Geology*

## Hutton and Geological Change

Hutton recognized the connections between geological processes and features, like mountains, valleys, and layers of rock that seemed to be bent or folded. Hutton realized, for example, that certain kinds of rocks are formed from molten lava. He also realized that some other kinds of rocks, like those shown in **Figure 17-5**, form very slowly, as sediments build up and are squeezed into layers.

Hutton also proposed that forces beneath Earth's surface can push rock layers upward, tilting or twisting them in the <u>process</u>. Over long periods, those forces can build mountain ranges. Mountains, in turn, can be worn down by rain, wind, heat, and cold. Most of these processes, shown in Figure 17-5, operate very slowly. For these processes to have shaped Earth as we know it, Hutton concluded that our planet must be much older than a few thousand years. These data and inferences moved him to introduce a concept called *deep time*—the idea that our planet's history stretches back over a period of time so long that it is difficult for the human mind to imagine.

## Lyell's *Principles of Geology*

Lyell's great contribution was to argue that laws of nature are constant over time, so scientists must explain past events in terms of processes they can observe in the present. This way of thinking, called *uniformitarianism*, holds that the geological processes we see in action today are the same processes that shaped Earth millions of years ago. Ancient volcanoes released lava and gases, just as volcanoes do now. Ancient rivers slowly dug channels and carved canyons, just as they do today. Lyell's theories required enough time for these changes to occur. Like Hutton, Lyell argued that Earth is much older than a few thousand years. Otherwise, how would a river have enough time to carve out a valley?

Darwin read Lyell's books during his *Beagle* voyage. With Lyell's ideas fresh in his mind, Darwin had some spectacular good fortune. He saw a volcano erupt in Chile, and later learned that another volcano 480 miles away had blown its top the same night. Just over a month later, he experienced an earthquake that threw him to the ground and lifted a stretch of rocky shoreline more than 3 meters out of the sea with mussels and other sea animals clinging to it. Still later, when Darwin travelled inland, he observed beds of fossil marine animals in mountains thousands of feet above sea level.

Those experiences amazed Darwin and his companions. But only Darwin turned his observations into a brilliant scientific insight. Geological events like the earthquake he'd seen, repeated many times over many years, could push rocks upward a few feet at a time, forming mountains from rocks that had once been beneath the sea. He could see Lyell's principle of geological uniformitarianism in action, with his own eyes! Darwin asked himself, "If Earth can change over time, could life change too?"

✅ **READING CHECK** **Infer** What evidence or logical reasoning suggested that Earth was much more than a few thousand years old?

### BUILD VOCABULARY

**Academic Words** The noun <u>process</u> means "a series of actions or changes that take place in a definite manner." The processes that shape Earth are actions and changes that build mountains, carve valleys, and otherwise change the landscape.

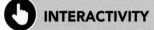

### INTERACTIVITY

Compare the different ideas of how Earth, and the life on it, came to be over time.

**Figure 17-5**

## Processes That Shape Earth

James Hutton described how geological processes could form and transform rocks, twist them, and lift them to the surface from deep within Earth. ☑**Infer** How were geologic principles important to Darwin's work?

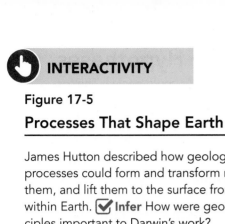

Rocks in this formation were folded and twisted by intense pressure and movement along the San Andreas fault—a place where two continental plates are sliding past one another.

Water and wind wear down rock over time. The pieces that break away become sediment that is moved to a different area, also by water and wind.

Molten lava, emerging at the surface, creates new rocks and can build large land masses.

# Lamarck's Evolutionary Hypotheses

Darwin wasn't the first to suggest that species could evolve. The fossil record already provided strong evidence that life had changed over time. Ideas about how species could evolve, however, differed. French naturalist Jean-Baptiste Lamarck proposed two of the first hypotheses about how species could change over time. 🔍 *Lamarck suggested that individual organisms could change during their lifetimes by selectively using or not using various parts of their bodies. He also suggested that individuals could pass these acquired traits on to their offspring, enabling species to change over time.* Lamarck published these hypotheses in 1809, the year Darwin was born.

**Lamarck's Ideas** Lamarck proposed that all organisms have an inborn urge to become more complex and perfect. As a result, organisms change and acquire features that help them live more successfully in their environments. He thought that organisms could change the size or shape of their organs by using their bodies in new ways. According to Lamarck, for example, water birds could have acquired long legs because they began to wade in deeper water looking for food. As a bird stretched its legs to stay above the water's surface, its legs would grow a little longer. Structures of individual organisms could also shrink if they were not used. If a bird stopped using its wings to fly, for example, its wings would become smaller. Lamarck called traits altered by an individual organism during its life *acquired characteristics*.

Lamarck also suggested that if a bird acquired a trait, like longer legs, during its lifetime, it could pass that trait on to its offspring. This principle is called *inheritance of acquired characteristics*. Over a few generations, species like the flamingo shown in **Figure 17-6** would evolve longer legs than their ancestors.

**Evaluating Lamarck's Hypotheses** Today, we know that Lamarck's hypotheses are completely unsupported. Organisms do not have an inborn drive to become perfect. Evolution does not mean that a species becomes "better" over time. Also, evolution does not progress in a predetermined direction. We also know that traits acquired by individuals during their lifetime (such as loss of a limb), are not inherited by their offspring.

Still, Lamarck was one of the first naturalists to argue strongly that species are not fixed. He was among the first to propose a scientific description of natural processes he thought could enable species to change over time. Lamarck also recognized that organisms' adaptations are related to their environments and the way they "make a living." So, although Lamarck's hypotheses about evolutionary change were wrong, his ideas paved the way for later biologists, including Darwin.

✓ **READING CHECK** Draw Conclusions What evidence refutes Lamarck's ideas about passing on acquired traits?

**Figure 17-6**

## Always Improving?

Lamarck thought that organisms such as these flamingos could improve their traits during their lifetimes, and then pass the improvements to their offspring.

**READING TOOL**

Create a flowchart to show the sequence of events that would have had to occur for flamingos to gain longer legs, according to Lamarck's ideas.

# Population Growth

In 1798, English economist Thomas Malthus noted that people were being born faster than people were dying, causing overcrowding, as shown in **Figure 17-7**. ⚘ *Malthus reasoned that if the human population grew unchecked, there wouldn't be enough living space and food for everyone.* The forces that work against population growth, Malthus suggested, include war, famine, and disease.

Darwin was thunderstruck when he read Malthus's work. He realized that if Malthus's reasoning applied to people, it applied even more to other organisms. Why? Because many organisms can produce lots more offspring than humans, and therefore have the potential to produce many more offspring than can survive. A maple tree produces thousands of seeds. An oyster can produce millions of eggs. Evaluating these facts, Darwin realized that if all descendants of even one pair of oysters survived, they would eventually overrun Earth. Obviously, this wasn't happening. In the struggle for existence, many die and only a few survive and reproduce. This is known in the language of evolutionary biology as differential reproductive success.

Why was this realization important? Darwin was convinced that species evolved. But he needed a *mechanism*—a scientific explanation based on a natural process—that could produce evolutionary change. So Darwin did what good scientists do: he asked important questions. Which individuals survive? And why?

## Figure 17-7

## So Many People

This engraving shows the crowded conditions in London during Darwin's lifetime. ☑ **Cause and Effect** According to Malthus, what would happen if the population of London continued to grow?

HS-LS4-2

---

## Quick Lab    Open Ended Inquiry

### Variation in Peppers

1. Obtain a green, yellow, red, or purple bell pepper.

2. Slice open the pepper and count the number of seeds it contains. *CAUTION: Always direct a sharp edge or point away from yourself and others.*

#### ANALYZE AND CONCLUDE

1. **Construct Tables** Collect data from your class and construct a data table. Compare your data with the data of other students who have peppers of a different color.

2. **Analyze Data** Calculate the average (mean) number of seeds in your class's peppers. By how much does the number of seeds in each pepper differ from the average number of seeds?

3. **Ask Questions** Think about the kinds of variations among organisms that Darwin observed. Suppose Darwin analyzed your class data. What questions might he have asked?

**VIDEO**

Explore the evidence that was used by Charles Darwin to formulate his ideas about evolution.

# Artificial Selection

Darwin combined ideas about population growth with observations that individual organisms in nature differed from one another. Plant and animal breeders confirmed his observations. Some plants bear larger or smaller fruit than average for their species. Some cows give more or less milk than others in their herd. Farmers also told Darwin that some of these differences were inherited variation—meaning that they could be passed from parents to offspring.

Farmers used this variation to their advantage. They would select for breeding only trees that produced the largest fruit, or cows that produced the most milk. Over time, this selective breeding, which Darwin called **artificial selection**, would produce trees with even bigger fruit and cows that gave even more milk. ⚲ *In artificial selection, nature provides the inherited variations, and humans select those variants they find useful.* Darwin tested artificial selection himself by breeding plants and fancy pigeon varieties, like those in **Figure 17-8**.

**Figure 17-8**

**Fancy Pigeons**

By choosing which parents to mate, Darwin was able to produce unusual pigeons like these.

Darwin had no idea how heredity worked, or what caused inherited variation. But he did know that inherited variation occurs in wild species as well as in domesticated plants and animals. Before Darwin, scientists viewed variations among individuals as unimportant, minor defects. Darwin made a breakthrough by recognizing that inherited variation was actually very important, because it could provide raw material for a natural mechanism that could drive evolution.

Finally, Darwin had all the information he needed. His scientific explanation for evolution was formed. When it was published, it would change the way people understood the living world.

## ☑ LESSON 17.2 Review

### ⚲ KEY QUESTIONS

1. What did Hutton and Lyell conclude about Earth's history?

2. What role did Lamarck think acquired characteristics played in evolution?

3. According to Malthus, what factors limit human population growth?

4. What is involved in the process of artificial selection?

### CRITICAL THINKING

5. **Construct an Explanation** What events must have occurred for fossils of marine organisms to be in a mountain far above sea level?

6. **Evaluate** Explain why Lamarck made a significant contribution to science even though his explanation of evolution was wrong.

7. **Infer** Could artificial selection occur without inherited variation? Explain your answer.

# Darwin's Theory: Natural Selection

Variation within a population is necessary for natural selection to occur.

### 🔍 KEY QUESTIONS

- *Under what conditions does natural selection occur?*
- *What does evolutionary theory suggest about the unity and diversity of life?*

**HS-LS4-2:** Construct an explanation based on evidence that the process of evolution primarily results from four factors: (1) the potential for a species to increase in number, (2) the heritable genetic variation of individuals in a species due to mutation and sexual reproduction, (3) competition for limited resources, and (4) the proliferation of those organisms that are better able to survive and reproduce in the environment.

**HS-LS4-3:** Apply concepts of statistics and probability to support explanations that organisms with an advantageous heritable trait tend to increase in proportion to organisms lacking this trait.

**HS-LS4-4:** Construct an explanation based on evidence for how natural selection leads to adaptation of populations.

### VOCABULARY

adaptation
fitness
natural selection

### READING TOOL

As you read, complete the natural selection concept map in your 📙 **Biology Foundations Workbook.**

Darwin worked out the main elements of evolution by natural selection soon after reading Malthus and thinking about artificial selection. His scientific friends urged him to publish his brilliant arguments. Darwin did write up a complete draft of his ideas, but he put the work aside and didn't publish it for another 20 years. Why? Darwin knew that many scientists, including some of his own teachers, ridiculed Lamarck's ideas. Darwin's theory was even more radical, so he wanted to gather as much evidence as he could to support his ideas before he made them public.

Then, in 1858, Darwin reviewed an essay by Alfred Russel Wallace, a British naturalist working in Malaysia. Wallace's thoughts about evolution were almost identical to Darwin's! Not wanting to get "scooped," Darwin moved forward with his own work. Wallace's essay was presented together with some of Darwin's observations at a scientific meeting in 1858. The next year, Darwin published *On the Origin of Species*, which described his ideas in detail. Wallace had the right idea, but Darwin had data and observations to support his hypotheses.

## Evolution by Natural Selection

Darwin's contribution was to describe a natural process, a scientific mechanism, that could operate like artificial selection. In *On the Origin of Species*, he supported his ideas with arguments from Malthus and Lamarck.

**The Struggle for Existence** Malthus's work had convinced Darwin that if all populations have the potential to produce more offspring than can survive, members of a population will compete for a finite supply of environmental resources. Darwin described this competition as *the struggle for existence*. But which individuals would succeed in surviving and reproducing?

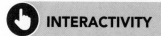
**INTERACTIVITY**

Simulate the various adaptations of bird beaks and how they impact a bird's diet.

**Variation and Adaptation** Here's where natural inheritable variation took center stage. Darwin hypothesized that individuals with certain types of inherited variation are better suited, or adapted, to life in their environment than other individuals. Members of a predatory species that are faster or have longer claws or sharper teeth can catch more prey. And members of a prey species that are faster or better camouflaged can avoid being caught.

Any heritable characteristic that increases an organism's ability to survive and reproduce in its environment is called an **adaptation**. Adaptations can involve body parts or structures, like a tiger's claws. Adaptations can involve colors, like those that make camouflage possible. Some adaptations are physiological, like the way a plant carries out photosynthesis, or the way an animal hibernates to survive harsh winters. Many adaptations also involve behaviors, such as social behavior and avoidance of predators. All of the animals shown in **Figure 17-9** have adaptations that help them feed on insects that live in wood.

**Survival of the Fittest** Darwin, like Lamarck, recognized that there must be a connection between the way an organism "makes a living" and the environment in which it lives. According to Darwin, differences in adaptations affect an individual's fitness. **Fitness** describes how well an organism can survive and reproduce in its environment.

Individuals with adaptations that are well suited to their environment can survive and reproduce and are said to have high fitness. Individuals with characteristics that are not well suited to their environment either die without reproducing or leave relatively few offspring and are said to have low fitness. This results in differential reproductive success, or, as some call it, *survival of the fittest*. Note that *survival* here means more than just staying alive. In evolutionary terms, *survival* means surviving, reproducing, and passing adaptations on to the next generation.

**Figure 17-9**

## Many Adaptations

All of these animals are adapted to feed on insects that tunnel in trees. Long beaks and fingers can probe for food, as can thorns, when used as tools.

**Aye-Aye, Madagascar**
Uses its long middle finger to tap trees and listen for a hollow area that indicates an insect nest; then uses the long finger to probe for food

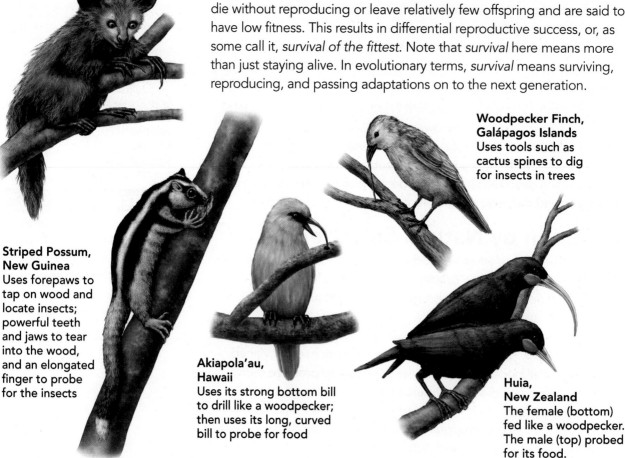

**Striped Possum, New Guinea**
Uses forepaws to tap on wood and locate insects; powerful teeth and jaws to tear into the wood, and an elongated finger to probe for the insects

**Akiapola'au, Hawaii**
Uses its strong bottom bill to drill like a woodpecker; then uses its long, curved bill to probe for food

**Woodpecker Finch, Galápagos Islands**
Uses tools such as cactus spines to dig for insects in trees

**Huia, New Zealand**
The female (bottom) fed like a woodpecker. The male (top) probed for its food.

This grasshopper population has green and yellow individuals.

Hungry birds can easily spot yellow grasshoppers. Green grasshoppers blend into their surroundings, so more of them survive and reproduce.

Over time, green grasshoppers become more common. Yellow grasshoppers, which are more likely to be eaten by birds, are less likely to pass their genes onto the next generation.

**Natural Selection** Darwin named his mechanism for evolution *natural selection*. **Natural selection** is the process by which organisms in nature with variations most suited to their local environment survive and leave more offspring. In both artificial and natural selection, only certain individuals produce offspring. But in natural selection, the environment—not a farmer or animal breeder—influences fitness.

When does natural selection occur? *Natural selection occurs in any situation in which more individuals are born than can survive (the struggle for existence), natural heritable variation affects the ability to survive and reproduce (variation and adaptation), and fitness varies among individuals (differential reproductive success).* Well-adapted individuals survive and reproduce. From generation to generation, populations continue to change as they become better adapted, or as their environment changes. **Figure 17-10** shows a hypothetical example of natural selection. Note that natural selection acts only on inherited traits because those are the only characteristics that parents can pass on to their offspring.

Natural selection does not make organisms "better." Adaptations don't have to be perfect—just good enough to enable an organism to pass its genes on to the next generation. Natural selection also doesn't move in a fixed direction. If local environmental conditions change, some traits that were once adaptive may no longer be useful, and different traits may become adaptive. This can lead to a great diversity of adaptations in species living in different environments. Importantly, if environmental conditions change faster than a species can adapt to those changes, the species may become extinct. Since Darwin's time, we have learned that natural selection is not the only mechanism that leads to evolutionary change. You will learn about other mechanisms in the next chapter.

**✓ READING CHECK Compare** How is natural selection different from artificial selection?

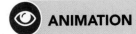

**ANIMATION**

**Figure 17-10**

**Natural Selection**

Forces in the environment, including those caused by humans, cause individuals with less favorable traits to pass on fewer or none of their genes. ☑ **Use Models** What selective forces are acting upon the grasshopper population shown here? What is the end result?

**READING TOOL**

Before you read the section Natural Selection, look at **Figure 17-10**. Read the information in the figure, and then write three questions you have about it. As you read, answer the questions.

Similar to the Galápagos finches, the Hawaiian honey-creepers are a group of diverse birds that are descended from a common ancestor. Over time, different adaptations evolved for feeding and mating in their respective habitats.

☑ **Compare** How does common ancestry explain Losos's observations of anoles?

**Multiple Meanings** To descend can mean to move downward, such as an airplane descending before it lands. In evolutionary theory, a *descent* refers to a line of ancestors.

**⤴ INTERACTIVITY**

Investigate how natural selection can lead to change over time.

# Common Ancestry

Natural selection depends on individuals' ability to reproduce and leave descendants. Every organism alive is descended from parents who survived and reproduced. Those parents 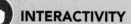descended from their parents, and so forth back through time. Just as well-adapted individuals in a species survive and reproduce, well-adapted species survive over time. Darwin proposed that living species are descended, with changes over time, from common ancestors—an idea called *descent with modification*. Over many generations, different sets of changing environmental conditions could lead to adaptations that could cause a single species to split into two or more new species, as with the honeycreepers in **Figure 17-11**. For evidence of descent with modification over long periods of time, Darwin pointed to the fossil record. Note that this process requires enough time for descent with modification to occur! This reminds us how Hutton and Lyell's work supported Darwin's theory: Deep time gave enough time for natural selection to act.

Darwin's idea that natural selection and adaptation can produce new species offered an explanation for both the unity and diversity of life. Darwin's sketched his thoughts about descent from common ancestors in the form of a branching tree. His evolutionary tree sketch is shown in **Figure 17-12**. This "tree-thinking" implies that all organisms are related. Look back in time, and you will find common ancestors shared by tigers, panthers, and cheetahs. Look farther back, and you will find ancestors that these felines share with dogs, then horses, and then bats. Farther back still is the common ancestor that all mammals share with birds, alligators, and fish. Far enough back are the common ancestors of all living things. **⚲ *According to the principle of common descent, all species—living and extinct—are united by descent from ancient common ancestors, and exhibit diversity due to natural selection and adaptation*.** A single "tree of life" links all living things.

## Figure 17-12

## The Tree Model

As shown by the illustration (below), all the finches of the Galápagos Islands descended from a common ancestor. Darwin was the first to use a tree-like model to represent common descent (right). The very first organisms form the base of the tree, and their descendants form the trunk and branches.

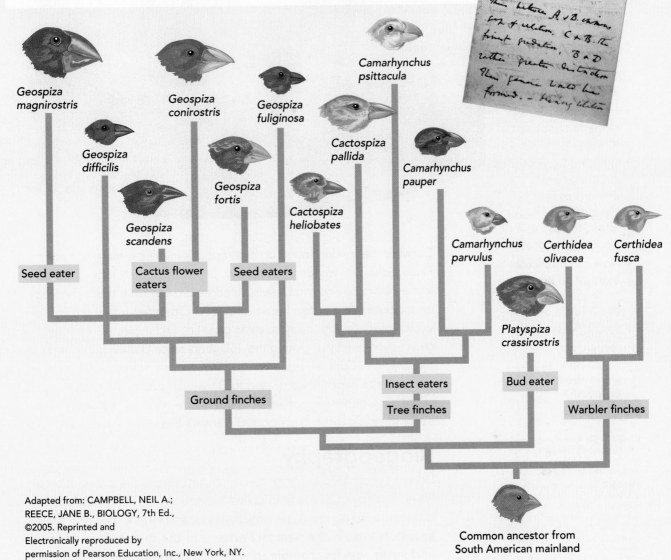

Adapted from: CAMPBELL, NEIL A.; REECE, JANE B., BIOLOGY, 7th Ed., ©2005. Reprinted and Electronically reproduced by permission of Pearson Education, Inc., New York, NY.

Common ancestor from South American mainland

HS-LS4-2, HS-LS4-3, HS-LS4-4

## ☑ LESSON 17.3 Review

### ⚲ KEY QUESTIONS

1. What three conditions are necessary for natural selection to occur?

2. How does evolution explain both the unity and the diversity of all living things?

### CRITICAL THINKING

3. **Construct an Explanation** Why is high fitness a function of an organism's environment? Include animals from a specific environment, such as polar bears in the arctic tundra or frogs in the tropical rain forest, as evidence to support your explanation.

4. **CASE STUDY** What adaptations might help different anole species survive in their environments?

# Evidence of Evolution

*Coelacanth* resembles fishes that lived millions of years ago.

Darwin's theory depended on assumptions involving many scientific fields. Scientists working in geology, physics, paleontology, chemistry, and embryology during Darwin's lifetime did not have the technology or understanding to test his assumptions. Other fields that are part of evolutionary theory today, such as genetics and molecular biology, didn't even exist yet! During the 160 years since Darwin published *On the Origin of Species*, research in all these fields has provided independent tests of hypotheses related to Darwinian theory. All of these tests could have either supported or refuted Darwin's work. Astonishingly, every scientific test has supported Darwin's basic ideas about evolution.

## Biogeography

Darwin recognized the importance of patterns in the distribution of life—the subject of the field called biogeography. **Biogeography** is the study of where organisms live now and where they and their ancestors lived in the past. 🔍 *Patterns in the distribution of fossils and living species, combined with information from geology, tell us how modern organisms evolved from their ancestors.* Recall that two observations involving biogeography were important to Darwin's thinking. First, closely related species can evolve diverse adaptations in different environments. Second, very distantly related species can evolve similar adaptations if they live in similar environments or face similar challenges in the struggle for existence.

**Closely Related but Different** To Darwin, the biogeography of Galápagos bird species suggested that populations of several island species had all evolved from a single mainland species. Over time, natural selection on different islands selected among individuals with different inherited variations. That caused populations on different islands to evolve into different, but closely related, species.

**Distantly Related but Similar** In contrast, Darwin noted that ground-dwelling birds in ecologically similar grasslands in Europe, Australia, and Africa resembled one another, although they were not closely related. Differences in those birds' body structures provide evidence that they evolved from different ancestors. But natural selection in similar habitats led to similar adaptations, such as long legs and feet with toes adapted to running.

# The Age of Earth and Fossils

Two potential difficulties for Darwin's theory involved the age of Earth and gaps in the fossil record. Data collected since Darwin's time addressed those difficulties and provided dramatic support for an evolutionary view of life.

**The Age of Earth** Darwin knew that for life to have evolved the way he thought it had, Earth must be very old. Hutton and Lyell had argued that Earth was a lot older than people used to think, but couldn't determine just *how* old. The discovery of radioactivity and the technique of radioactive dating enabled geologists to establish the age of certain rocks and fossils starting in the early twentieth century. If this technique had shown that Earth was young, Darwin's ideas would have been refuted. Instead, radioactive dating indicates that Earth is about 4.5 billion years old—plenty of time for evolution by natural selection to take place.

**Recent Fossil Finds** Darwin also struggled with what he called the "imperfection of the geological record." Paleontologists in Darwin's time hadn't found enough fossils to document the evolution of modern species from their ancestors. But that's changed with the discovery of hundreds of fossils, like the ancient whale skeleton shown in **Figure 17-13**. 🔍 *Many recently discovered fossils now show clearly how modern species evolved from extinct ancestors.* A fossil series shown on the next page in **Figure 17-14** documents the evolution of whales from ancient land mammals. Other recent fossil finds connect the dots between dinosaurs and birds, and between fishes and four-legged land animals. So many intermediate forms have been found that it is often hard to tell where one group begins and another ends. All historical records are incomplete, and the history of life is no exception. The evidence we do have, however, tells an unmistakable story of evolutionary change.

✅ **READING CHECK** **Identify** What technology helped to support Hutton and Lyell's hypothesis that Earth is much older than many people thought?

**Figure 17-13**
**Fossil Discoveries**

This fossil of *Basilosaurus*, discovered in Egypt, provides evidence of the evolution of whales from land mammals. It also provides evidence for how Earth has changed over time. This site was once an ancient sea.

## Figure 17-14

## Whale Evolution

Researchers have found more than 20 related fossils that document the evolution of whales from ancestors that walked on land. Several reconstructions, based on fossil evidence, are shown here. ☑ **Infer** Which of the animals shown was probably the most recent to live primarily on land?

*Basilosaurus* had a streamlined body and reduced hind limbs. These skeletal features suggest that *Basilosaurus* spent its entire life swimming in the ocean.

The limb structure of *Ambulocetus* ("walking whale") suggests that these animals could both swim in shallow water and walk on land.

The hind limbs of *Rodhocetus* were short and probably not able to bear much weight. Paleontologists think that these animals spent most of their time in the water.

*Ambulocetus*

*Pakicetus*

Ancient artiodactyl

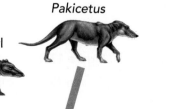

*Rodhocetus*

# Comparing Anatomy and Development

By Darwin's time, scientists had noted that the bones in all vertebrate limbs resembled each other to a surprising degree, as shown in **Figure 17-15**. That resemblance was clear, even though some of those limbs were used for crawling, some for climbing, some for running, and others for flying. Why do the same basic structures appear over and over again with such different purposes?

**Homologous Structures** Similar structures, like the bones of vertebrate limbs, that are shared by related species and have been inherited from a common ancestor are called **homologous structures**. ⚲ *Evolutionary theory explains the existence of homologous structures adapted to different purposes as the result of descent with modification from a common ancestor.* Biologists test whether structures are homologous by studying anatomical details, the way structures develop in embryos, and the pattern in which they appeared over evolutionary history.

Similarities and differences among homologous structures help determine how recently species shared a common ancestor. For example, many bones of reptiles and birds are more similar to one another in structure and development than they are to homologous

**READING TOOL**

As you read about homologous structures, look for examples in the illustrations shown in Figure 17-14.

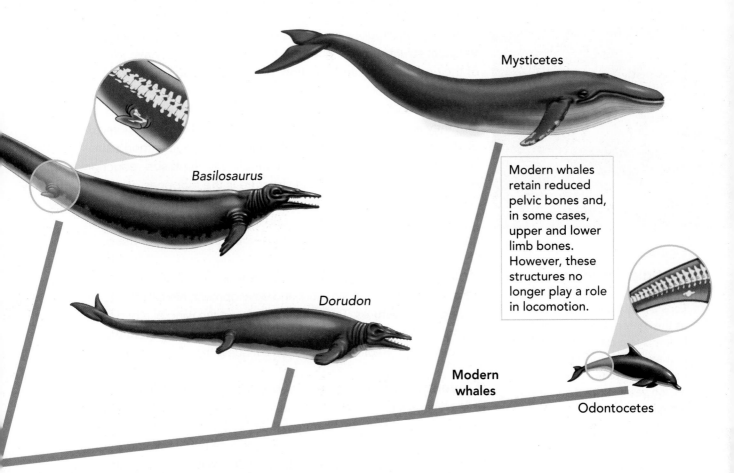

Mysticetes

*Basilosaurus*

Modern whales retain reduced pelvic bones and, in some cases, upper and lower limb bones. However, these structures no longer play a role in locomotion.

*Dorudon*

Modern whales

Odontocetes

bones of mammals. This shows that the common ancestor of reptiles and birds lived more recently than the common ancestor of reptiles, birds, and mammals. So birds are much more closely related to crocodiles than they are to bats, even though both birds and bats have wings! Note that the key to identifying homology is common structure and origin during development, not common function. A bird's wing and a horse's front limb (which are homologous structures) have similar structures and development, but different functions. Homology occurs among plants, too. Certain groups of plants share homologous stems, roots, leaves, and flowers.

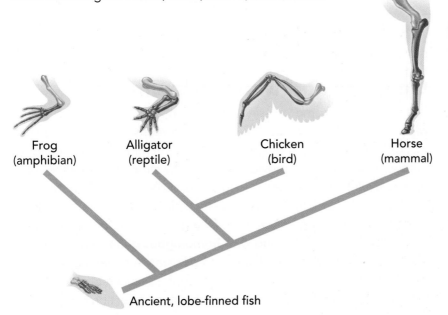

Frog (amphibian)

Alligator (reptile)

Chicken (bird)

Horse (mammal)

Ancient, lobe-finned fish

**INTERACTIVITY**

Figure 17-15

**Homologous Structures**

Color-coding is used to show the homologous bones in the forelimbs of select modern vertebrates. These limbs evolved from the front limbs of a common ancestor whose bones resembled those of an ancient fish. If these animals had no recent common ancestor, they would be unlikely to share so many common structures.

**Figure 17-16**

**Vestigial Structures**

*Lerista lineopunctulata*, known as the dotted-line robust slider, belongs to a clade of skinks that are known for their limb reduction over the past several million years. Note the small remnant of a limb resting on the leaf.

Some homologous structures don't serve important functions. **Vestigial structures** are inherited from ancestors, but have lost much of their original size and function. Recently, researchers in Australia studied a clade of skinks, a type of lizard. This group of skinks has elongated bodies like snakes. Many of them have remnants of limbs that they no longer use, as shown in **Figure 17-16**. Using molecular evidence, the researchers hypothesized relationships among species of this clade and developed a timeline for limb size reduction. Another example of a vestigial structure is the hipbones of dolphins. You can see a dolphin hipbone in Figure 17-14. Why do these vestigial structures persist? One possibility is that they don't affect an organism's fitness, so selection does not act to eliminate them.

**Analogous Structures** Body parts that serve similar functions, but do not share structure and development, are called **analogous structures**. The wing of a bee and the wing of a bird are examples of <u>analogous</u> structures. Both are used for flight, but they grow and develop from different embryonic tissues.

**Development** Researchers noticed long ago that early developmental stages of many vertebrates look similar. Recent observations make clear that the same groups of embryonic cells develop in the same order and in similar patterns to produce many homologous tissues and organs. For example, the very differently shaped limb bones in Figure 17-15 all develop from the same clump of embryonic cells. Darwin recognized that evolutionary theory offers the most logical explanation for these similarities. *Similar patterns of embryological development provide further evidence that organisms have descended from a common ancestor.*

Darwin could not have anticipated, however, the support for his theory that would come from evidence he couldn't see. An incredible amount of evidence regarding homology has been found from studies in genetics and molecular biology that investigate genes that control the development of both visible and microscopic homologous structures.

**BUILD VOCABULARY**

**Academic Words** The word <u>analogous</u>, meaning "comparable," relates to the word *analogy*, meaning "a comparison between two things that are alike in *some* respects." In biology, analogous structures have a similar function but a different evolutionary origin.

☑ **READING CHECK** **Summarize** How do homologous structures provide evidence for evolutionary relationships?

# Genetics and Molecular Biology

The most troublesome "missing information" for Darwin had to do with inheritance. Darwin had no idea how heredity worked, and he was deeply worried that this lack of knowledge might prove fatal to his theory. Today, genetics provides some of the strongest evidence supporting evolutionary theory. A long series of discoveries, from Mendel to Watson and Crick to genomics, help explain how evolution works. *At the molecular level, overwhelming similarities in the genetic code of all organisms, along with homologous genes and molecules, provide evidence of common descent.* Also, we now understand how mutation and gene shuffling during sexual reproduction produce the heritable variation on which natural selection operates.

##  Exploration Lab    Open Ended Inquiry

### Evidence of Evolution

**Problem** What kinds of evidence support common ancestry and biological evolution?

In this lab, you will be investigating several types of evidence for evolution. Your goal is to determine the most likely evolutionary relationship between four living species.

You can find this lab in your digital course.

**Life's Common Genetic Code** One example of molecular evidence for evolution is so basic that by this point in your study of biology you might take it for granted. All living cells use information coded in DNA and RNA to carry information from one generation to the next and to direct protein synthesis. This genetic code is nearly identical in almost all organisms, including bacteria, plants, fungi, and animals. This is powerful evidence that all organisms evolved from common ancestors that shared this code.

**Molecular Homology** In Darwin's day, biologists could only study similarities and differences in structures they could see. But physical body structures can't be used to compare mice with yeasts or bacteria. Today, we know that homology resulting from common ancestors shows up at the molecular level, too.

One spectacular example of homologous genes is a set of genes called Hox genes that determine the destinies of body parts. Hox genes help determine which part of an embryo becomes the head, and which part becomes the tail. In all vertebrates, sets of homologous Hox genes direct the growth of front and hind limbs. Small changes in these "master control genes," as they are sometimes called, can produce dramatic changes in the size and shape of the structures they control. So relatively minor mutations in an organism's genome can produce major changes in an organism's structure and the structure of its descendants. At least some homologous Hox genes are found in almost all multicellular animals, from fruit flies to humans. This widespread distribution of homologous Hox genes indicates that these genes have been inherited from ancient common ancestors.

 **INTERACTIVITY**

Explore the evidence for evolution.

## Testing Natural Selection

One way to gather evidence for evolutionary change is to observe natural selection in action. But is it possible to observe natural selection happening in nature? Darwin didn't think so, because he thought evolutionary change always happens very slowly. "We see nothing of these slow changes in progress," he wrote, "until the hand of time has marked the lapse of ages." In recent years, however, several biologists have designed experiments to study natural selection in the wild.

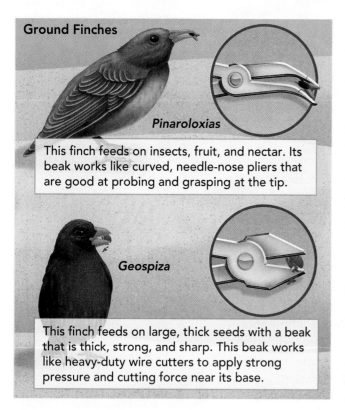

**Ground Finches**

*Pinaroloxias*

This finch feeds on insects, fruit, and nectar. Its beak works like curved, needle-nose pliers that are good at probing and grasping at the tip.

*Geospiza*

This finch feeds on large, thick seeds with a beak that is thick, strong, and sharp. This beak works like heavy-duty wire cutters to apply strong pressure and cutting force near its base.

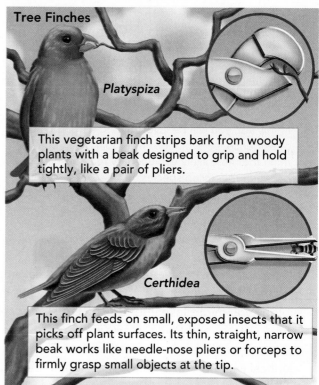

**Tree Finches**

*Platyspiza*

This vegetarian finch strips bark from woody plants with a beak designed to grip and hold tightly, like a pair of pliers.

*Certhidea*

This finch feeds on small, exposed insects that it picks off plant surfaces. Its thin, straight, narrow beak works like needle-nose pliers or forceps to firmly grasp small objects at the tip.

**Visual Analogy**

**Figure 17-17**

**Finch Adaptations**

Darwin had noted that different Galápagos finch species have beaks of very different sizes and shapes. Each species uses its beak just like a specialized tool to pick up and handle its preferred food.

**INTERACTIVITY**

Demonstrate your understanding of natural selection by investigating Darwin's finches.

**READING TOOL**

Write a three-part summary of the studies performed by the Grants. Summarize the tests performed, the results, and the conclusions.

**Back to the Galápagos** The longest-running and most detailed study of evolution in a natural environment is the ongoing work on Darwin's finches by Peter and Rosemary Grant of Princeton University. The Grants have been studying the finches that live on an island called Daphne Major. That tiny slab of volcanic rock is home to a total finch population of a few hundred individuals. That's enough birds to provide plenty of data, but not so many as to be unmanageable. *Manageable*, of course, is a relative term. What the Grants have been doing for more than 40 years is pretty amazing. They have regularly captured, identified, and measured every single individual bird on the island! When new birds hatch, the Grants note their parents, and tag the infant birds to add them to their list of known individuals. Meanwhile, the Grants and their assistants have also counted and measured all the different kinds of seeds the birds depend on for food. They even created their own device to measure the hardness of those seeds. The results of their many studies have been fascinating. We'll just look at a very small part of one study here.

**A Testable Hypothesis** Darwin had noted that different Galápagos finch species have beaks of very different sizes and shapes, as shown in **Figure 17-17**. Darwin hypothesized that natural selection had shaped the beaks of different bird populations as they became adapted to eat different foods. The Grants realized that this hypothesis rested on two testable assumptions. First, in order for beak size and shape to evolve, there must be enough heritable variation in those traits to provide raw material for natural selection. Second, if those differences were involved in natural selection, birds with different beak size and shape should show differential survival and reproduction.

**Natural Selection** The Grants' data showed that there is lots of heritable variation in beak size and shape in finch populations. But is that variation related to differential survival and reproduction? Luck was on the Grants' side, because during their study, a severe drought hit the islands. Plants produced fewer seeds, so the number of seeds dropped steadily. Here's where things got interesting. As the drought continued, the birds ate the smaller and softer seeds first. So, over time, only the largest, hardest seeds remained. Many birds starved, and the total number of birds on the island fell. But the Grants' data showed that certain birds were more likely to survive than others. Individuals with the largest beaks had higher evolutionary fitness. Drought caused the average beak size in this finch population to change dramatically over just a few years. **Figure 17-18** shows the trends that the Grants observed during the drought.

This amazing study supported two important hypotheses. ⚲ *The Grants documented that natural selection takes place in wild finch populations frequently, and sometimes rapidly.* One of the Grants' colleagues calculated that it might take no more than 12 to 20 such droughts to change the birds' beak size enough to transform one species into another. Also, this work showed the importance of variation in providing raw material on which natural selection can operate. Variation within a species increases a population's ability to adapt to, and survive, environmental change. If the finch population hadn't had enough variation in beak size when the drought started, they would not have been able to adapt and change.

**Evolutionary Theory Evolves** Many scientific advances have confirmed and expanded Darwin's hypotheses. Today, evolutionary theory is vital to all biological and biomedical sciences, and is often called the grand unifying theory of the life sciences. Like any scientific theory, evolutionary theory is constantly reviewed as new data are gathered. However, any questions that remain are about *how* evolution works—not *whether* evolution occurs.

**Figure 17-18**

## Data From the Galápagos

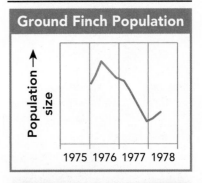

Ground Finch Population

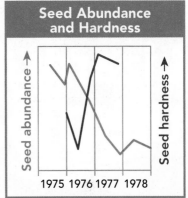

Seed Abundance and Hardness

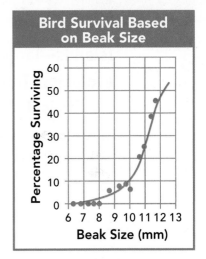

Bird Survival Based on Beak Size

HS-LS4-1, HS-LS4-2, HS-LS4-3, HS-LS4-4

---

## ✓ LESSON 17.4 Review

### ⚲ KEY QUESTIONS

1. How is biogeography useful for identifying evolutionary relationships?

2. What have scientists learned from fossils that have been discovered since Darwin's time?

3. How do vestigial structures provide evidence for evolution?

4. What is the relationship between Hox genes and embryological development?

5. What hypothesis have the Grants been testing?

### CRITICAL THINKING

6. **Construct an Explanation** Use evidence from the text to explain how evidence since Darwin's time has strengthened his theories.

7. **CASE STUDY** Jonathan Losos introduced a species of anole onto a Florida island that already had another species, and then studied their descendants. How are his investigation and observations similar to the work of the Grants on the Galápagos Islands?

# Lizards, Legs, and the Diversity of Life

**Islands—large, small, and tiny—are superb places to study evolution. In the Galápagos, Darwin worked with finches and tortoises. In the Caribbean, Losos and his colleagues study anoles.**

HS-LS4-2, HS-LS4-3, CCSS.ELA-LITERACY.RST.9-10.1, CCSS.ELA-LITERACY.RST.9-10.6, CCSS.ELA-LITERACY.WHST.9-10.1

## Make Your Case

To answer important questions related to evolution and biodiversity of all life on Earth, Jonathan Losos focused on anoles. Why? Losos and his colleagues realized that the existence of roughly 400 known anole species suggested that these animals might evolve quickly. In addition, anoles' ability to live on small islands, and their choice of niches, offered excellent opportunities to study evolution in action in natural environments.

Go online to learn more about Losos's work on anoles and how it relates to Darwinian theory.

## Construct an Argument

1. **Cite Evidence** Do interactions among anole species lead to selection pressure that drives evolution? Do anoles evolve rapidly? Cite evidence that Losos gathered to answer those questions.

2. **Defend Your Claim** How do Losos's studies relate to classical evolutionary theory? Defend your claim by citing his team's results and by applying the concepts of adaptation, fitness, and natural selection.

## Technology on the Case

### Tools of the Trade

When you think about the things Jonathan Losos does during his studies, it could be easy to overlook the technology essential to his team's work. His animal subjects are small, and can be caught with very simple "technology"—a small noose at the end of a kind of "lizard-fishing-pole." Once he collects his animals, it's fairly simple for him to store them in ventilated containers until he has time to take measurements.

But if you think technology isn't used in this case, guess again. It's just that some of that technology is similar to tools you use all the time too! Digital imaging is used in several ways. Photographs document individual anole's colors, and record shapes of body parts, ranging from skin on their backs to brightly colored neck flaps, or dewlaps, they use in mating displays. High-resolution images can be blown up to reveal intricate details such as the hairs and other features on toe pads that enable anoles to hang on to leaves and twigs.

Another way that technology helps in this work is in data analysis. Capturing, measuring, releasing, recapturing, and gathering lots of data points repeatedly over several years generates enormous amounts of data. Those data need to be logged, stored, and finally analyzed and graphed. Although all of that could be done with pencil, paper, and calculator, software now enables portable digital devices to do that work much more quickly and efficiently.

## Careers on the Case

### Work Toward a Solution

Taking outstanding animal images requires a wide knowledge of biology, especially behavior and ecology. Behavior is often best documented using photos and videos.

### Wildlife Photographer

The best wildlife photographers do much more than just stalk their subjects. They need to know when and where to look for those magic moments of behavior, and how to capture the right images.

▶ **VIDEO**

Learn about the techniques used to find fossils of dinosaurs.

hhmi | **BioInteractive**

# Lesson Review

Go to your Biology Foundations Workbook for longer versions of these lesson summaries.

## 17.1 A Voyage of Discovery

Charles Darwin's voyage on the HMS *Beagle* opened his eyes to the natural world. From the observations he made, Darwin developed a scientific theory of biological evolution that explains how modern organisms evolved over long periods of time through descent from common ancestors.

Darwin noticed that different, yet ecologically similar, animal species inhabited separated, but ecologically similar, habitats around the globe. He also observed that different, yet related, animal species often occupied different habitats within a local area. He also noted that some fossils of extinct animals were similar to living species.

- evolution
- fossil

☑ **Summarize** What observations did Darwin make about large flightless birds during his voyage?

## 17.2 Ideas That Influenced Darwin

As Darwin worked out his theory of evolution, he was influenced by other scientists of his time. Hutton and Lyell concluded that Earth is extremely old and that the processes that changed Earth in the past are the same processes that operate in the present. Darwin wondered, if Earth's surface could change over time, could life also change over time?

Lamarck suggested that organisms could change during their lifetimes by selectively using or not using various parts of their bodies. He also suggested that individuals could pass these acquired traits on to their offspring, enabling species to change over time. Lamarck's hypotheses were not correct, but he did recognize that there is a connection between an organism's environment and body structures.

Malthus reasoned that if the human population grew unchecked, there wouldn't be enough living space and food for everyone. Darwin realized this was true for other organisms. If more offspring are born than can survive, what causes some to survive and others to die?

In artificial selection, nature provides the variations, and humans select those they find useful. Darwin realized that these natural variations also provide the raw material for evolution.

- artificial selection

☑ **Summarize** Explain how artificial selection was used to produce a pigeon with such unusual features.

## 17.3 Darwin's Theory: Natural Selection

Darwin named his mechanism of evolution *natural selection*. Natural selection occurs in any situation in which more individuals are born than can survive, there is natural heritable variation, and there is variable fitness among individuals. Natural selection depends on the ability of organisms to leave descendants.

Darwin proposed that adaptation could cause successful species to evolve into new species. According to the principle of common descent, all species—living and extinct—are descended from ancient common ancestors.

- adaptation
- fitness
- natural selection

✅ **Apply Concepts** How is fitness related to natural selection? Use the picture to give an example.

## 17.4 Evidence of Evolution

Since Darwin's time, scientific discoveries have continued to support his theory of evolution. For example, patterns in the distribution of living and fossil species tell us how modern organisms evolved from their ancestors.

Evolutionary theory explains the existence of homologous structures adapted to different purposes as the result of descent with modification

from a common ancestor. Homologous structures have similar structures, even if their functions are different (arm bones in humans and dolphins). Analogous structures have similar functions, but very different structures (wings of bees and birds). The universal genetic code and homologous molecules also provide evidence of common descent.

The Grants have documented that natural selection takes place in wild Galápagos finch populations frequently, and sometimes rapidly. They also noted that variation within a species increases the likelihood of the species' adapting to and surviving environmental change.

- biogeography
- homologous structure
- vestigial structure
- analogous structure

✅ **Compare and Contrast** Which beak would be useful in getting food from a crevice in tree bark? Which beak would be good for crushing a large seed? Explain your choices.

## Organize Information

The factors that are required for natural selection to occur are listed in the table. In the right column, describe these factors and how they contribute to Darwin's theory of evolution by natural selection.

| Factor | Contribution to Natural Selection |
|---|---|
| Struggle for existence | 1. |
| Variation and adaptation | 2. |
| Differential reproductive success | 3. |

# Evolution in Action
## Beak Size Among Darwin's Finches

## Analyze Data

HS-LS4-2, HS-LS4-3, HS-LS4-4,
CCSS.MATH.CONTENT.MP4

**STEM** ▸ Darwin was just the first scientist to be puzzled and inspired by Galápagos finches. Peter and Rosemary Grant have been studying free-living birds there for decades. Their careful tagging and releasing of individual birds, combined with detailed measurements of beak size, have produced an amazing wealth of data. Those measurements have provided what researchers call "baseline data" on beak sizes. As you can see from the graphs shown here, beak size varies a lot. That's important, because beak size determines how efficiently birds can eat seeds of different sizes and levels of hardness.

When a severe drought hit, plants on the island produced fewer seeds. Hungry birds soon devoured the smaller, softer seeds they prefer. What was left? Larger seeds

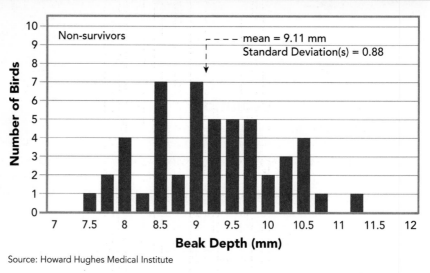

**Beak Depths of 50 Medium Ground Finches that Did Not Survive the Drought**

Non-survivors

mean = 9.11 mm
Standard Deviation(s) = 0.88

Number of Birds

Beak Depth (mm)

Source: Howard Hughes Medical Institute

that were harder to eat. What happened? Only half the tagged birds survived. But which half? Study the graphs. Then use the data and your knowledge of evolution to answer these questions.

1. **Interpret Graphs** How did the average and range of beak size differ between birds that survived the drought and birds that died?

2. **Form a Hypothesis** How could the change in food supply have led to a change in beak size? Form a hypothesis that explains the relationship.

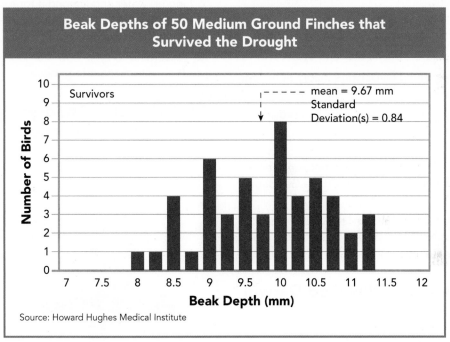

**Beak Depths of 50 Medium Ground Finches that Survived the Drought**

Survivors

mean = 9.67 mm
Standard Deviation(s) = 0.84

Number of Birds (y-axis: 0, 1, 2, 3, 4, 5, 6, 7, 8, 9, 10)

Beak Depth (mm) (x-axis: 7, 7.5, 8, 8.5, 9, 9.5, 10, 10.5, 11, 11.5, 12)

Source: Howard Hughes Medical Institute

3. **Construct an Explanation** Explain how the following factors caused the finch population to evolve: the potential for the finches to reproduce, the existence of genetic variation related to beak size in the population, the competition for limited resources, and the differential reproductive success of the individuals that survive.

4. **Develop a Model** The data in the table show only a small evolutionary change. Use these data to develop a model of evolutionary change in finches that might occur over several decades, and that includes the evolution of a new finch species. For example, you may choose to model the effects of many droughts, each repeating the the selective pressure caused by a single drought.

Begin by choosing a method to represent the variety of bird beaks and seeds. You may use illustrations, a mathematical model, or physical models. For example, pencils of various sizes could represent the beaks, and counters or game pieces could represent the seeds.

5. **Communicate** Demonstrate your working model to classmates. Ask them to evaluate how well it models evolution by natural selection, as well as its limitations.

# ☑ASSESSMENT

## ⚷ KEY QUESTIONS AND TERMS

## 17.1 A Voyage of Discovery

1. The glyptodont fossils and living armadillos that Darwin observed during his voyage are related to which pattern of biodiversity?
   a. species vary globally
   b. species vary locally
   c. species vary over time
   d. all of the above

2. In addition to observing living organisms, Darwin studied the preserved remains of ancient organisms called
   a. fossils.
   b. adaptations.
   c. homologies.
   d. vestigial structures.

3. In your own words, define the term *evolution*.

4. What was explained by Darwin's theory of biological evolution?

5. Describe two large flightless birds that provide evidence that species vary globally.

6. From what you have read, interpret the connection between structural differences in tortoise species and the differing environments on the Galápagos Islands.

7. Why was Darwin's trip aboard the *Beagle* so important to his development of the theory of natural selection?

## 17.2 Ideas That Influenced Darwin

8. According to Malthus, what would occur if the human population grew unchecked?
   a. evolution of a new species
   b. extinction of humans
   c. disease, war, or famine
   d. development of new traits in humans

9. Which of the following would an animal breeder use to increase the number of cows that give the most milk?
   a. overproduction
   b. genetic isolation
   c. acquired characteristics
   d. artificial selection

10. Describe an example of selective breeding.

11. The curved beak of a flamingo is useful for scooping up water and filtering it for food. According to Lamarck's ideas, how could the flamingo have acquired its curved beak?

12. According to Lyell, how did geologic processes of the past compare to geologic processes today?

## 17.3 Darwin's Theory: Natural Selection

HS-LS4-2, HS-LS4-3, HS-LS4-4

Akiapola'au, Hawaii

13. The akiapola'au uses its long top bill to probe for insects in trees. This beak is an example of
   a. an adaptation.     c. an acquired characteristic.
   b. fitness.            d. a variation.

14. During the process of natural selection, what determines which organisms survive and reproduce?
   a. number of adaptations
   b. variety of adaptations
   c. evolutionary fitness
   d. population size

**15.** How does natural variation affect evolution?

**16.** According to the principle of common descent, what explains the diversity among organisms today?

**17.** Do all adaptations involve body structures? Give an example to support your answer.

## 17.4 Evidence of Evolution

**HS-LS4-1, HS-LS4-2, HS-LS4-3, HS-LS4-4**

**18.** Intermediate fossil forms are important evidence of evolution because they show
a. how organisms changed over time.
b. how animals behaved in their environments.
c. how the embryos of organisms develop.
d. molecular homologies.

**19.** The wing of a bat and the wing of a bee or another insect are examples of what type of structures?
a. analogous structures
b. homologous structures
c. vestigial structures
d. unrelated structures

**20.** What evidence for evolution is provided by the hip bones of a dolphin?

**21.** How do homologous structures develop?

**22.** What evidence at the molecular level supports the theory of evolution?

**23.** What evidence for evolution did Peter and Rosemary Grant provide?

## CRITICAL THINKING

**HS-LS4-1, HS-LS4-2, HS-LS4-3, HS-LS4-4.**

**24. Integrate Information** Many scientists of Darwin's time were experts at identifying plant and animal species. How did Darwin's work differ from the work of these other experts?

**25. Infer** In all animals with backbones, oxygen is carried in blood by a molecule called hemoglobin. What could this physiological similarity indicate about the evolutionary history of vertebrates (animals with backbones)?

**26. Construct an Explanation** How does Darwin's theory of evolution help to explain the spread of drug-resistant bacteria?

Use the illustration of mice shown below to answer questions 27 to 29.

**27. Interpret Visuals** Which of the mice might be better adapted to their environment? Explain your answer.

**28. Construct an Explanation** What event might change the relative fitness of the different mice? Explain how the change in fitness could occur.

**29. Synthesize Information** Consider possible changes that could affect the mice. How is the variation among the mice useful to the mouse population?

**30. Evaluate Models** According to Lamarck's ideas, an animal's actions could affect inheritance. An example is a wading bird that stretches its legs, who then passes the trait of longer legs on to its offspring. Cite evidence to evaluate this model of inheritance.

**31. Develop Models** Darwin used the concept of artificial selection to model animal breeding, in which humans selected the traits that animals pass to offspring. How did Darwin develop this model to explain evolution in natural systems?

**32. Use Scientific Reasoning** A scientist discovers a new species of vertebrate, or animal with a backbone, in a desert ecosystem. According to Darwin and to modern ideas about evolution, what kinds of traits can the species be expected to display? Include traits at the molecular level.

# ☑ASSESSMENT

## CROSSCUTTING CONCEPTS

**33. Patterns** Describe one of the patterns among species that Darwin identified. How did this pattern help him develop his ideas about evolution?

**34. Cause and Effect** According to Darwin's ideas, what is the cause of a change in the adaptations of a species over time? Describe a specific example.

## MATH CONNECTIONS

## Analyze and Interpret Data

CCSS.MATH.CONTENT.HSS.IC.A.1, CCSS.MATH.CONTENT.MP4

Use the following paragraph and the line graph to answer questions 35 to 37.

In the 1990s, scientists were studying a colony of brown anoles (*Anolis sagrei*) on a Caribbean island. These brown anoles live in trees and perch on branches. In 1996, a large, predatory lizard species arrived on the island, and they began hunting the brown anoles. The graph shows the change in the average diameter of the tree branches where the scientists found brown anoles.

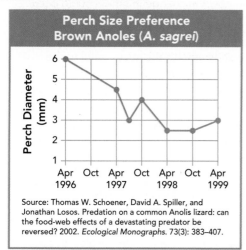

**Perch Size Preference Brown Anoles (*A. sagrei*)**

Source: Thomas W. Schoener, David A. Spiller, and Jonathan Losos. Predation on a common Anolis lizard: can the food-web effects of a devastating predator be reversed? 2002. *Ecological Monographs.* 73(3): 383–407.

**35. Interpret Graphs** How did the average branch diameter of the brown anoles' perches change during the time of this study?

**36. Construct an Explanation** How might the introduction of the predatory lizard species have caused the change in perch diameter shown in the graph?

**37. Predict** As a result of the introduction of the new predator, what other changes may occur to the brown anole population over time? Use the concepts of fitness, adaptation, and natural selection to justify your prediction.

Use the following paragraph and the chart to answer questions 38 and 39.

Cytochrome c is a small protein that takes part in cellular respiration. The table compares the cytochrome c of various organisms to that of chimpanzees.

| Organism | Number of Amino Acids That Are Different From Chimpanzee Cytochrome c |
|---|---|
| Dog | 10 |
| Moth | 24 |
| Penguin | 11 |
| Yeast | 38 |

**38. Interpret Data** How can you interpret the data in the chart to draw a conclusion about the evolutionary relationships among the species?

**39. Draw Conclusions** A chimpanzee is a larger and more complex organism than yeast. Can you draw a conclusion about the usefulness or adaptive value of cytochrome c in the two species? Explain.

## LANGUAGE ARTS CONNECTION

## Write About Science

CCSS.ELA-LITERACY.WHST.9-10.2, CCSS.ELA-LITERACY.WHST.9-10.1

**40. Write Informative Texts** Write a paragraph to explain how studies in genetics and molecular biology provide evidence for the theory of evolution. Include specific examples in your explanation.

**41. Write Explanatory Texts** Summarize the conditions under which natural selection occurs. Then, describe three lines of evidence that support the theory of evolution by natural selection.

## Read About Science

CCSS.ELA-LITERACY.RST.9-10.2

**42. Determine Conclusions** What conclusion did Darwin reach about the patterns he observed among Earth's living things?

# END-OF-COURSE TEST PRACTICE

1. A pond has several varieties of a species of frog that all eat the same kind of bug. Most of the frogs are fast-growing varieties that need to eat more bugs each day than the slow-growing variety. A drought drastically reduces the number of bugs, and the population of the fast-growing frogs declines drastically while the population of slow-growing frogs declines only slightly, so that most of the frogs in the pond are now the slow-growing variety. This is an example of which of the following?
   A. mutation
   B. natural selection
   C. biogeography
   D. artificial selection
   E. acquired characteristics

2. Thomas Malthus argued that if the human population grew unchecked, then supplies of food and other resources would be exhausted. Which of these ideas about evolution did Darwin adapt from Malthus's work?
   A. An organism passes many of its traits to its offspring.
   B. All organisms fill a niche, or a role in their environment.
   C. Variations within a species are necessary for evolutionary change.
   D. Organisms are able to produce many more offspring than will survive.
   E. The environment selects the traits that an organism passes to offspring.

3. Two species of fish are introduced to the same lake. Over time, only one species survives. According to Darwin's theory of evolution, what should characterize the surviving species?
   A. greater genetic variation
   B. more abundant food supply
   C. a better ability to survive and reproduce in the lake
   D. a better ability to withstand seasonal changes in the lake
   E. common ancestors with other fish in the lake

4. Darwin's theory of evolution offers a scientific explanation for which of the following?
   A. how genetic information is inherited
   B. changes in species over time
   C. human effects on biodiversity
   D. the age of Earth
   E. the origin of life

5. Bernice is preparing a report on evidence for the common ancestry of species. She includes the figure of forelimbs shown.

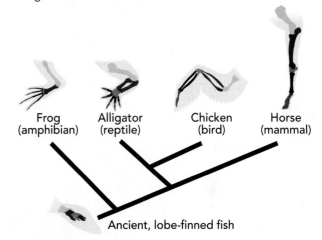

Frog (amphibian)   Alligator (reptile)   Chicken (bird)   Horse (mammal)

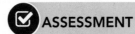

Ancient, lobe-finned fish

The forelimbs are an example of which of the following?
   A. analogous structures
   B. vestigial structures
   C. homologous structures
   D. convergent structures
   E. mutated structures

☑ **ASSESSMENT**

For additional assessment practice, go online to access your digital course.

## If You Have Trouble With...

| Question | 1 | 2 | 3 | 4 | 5 |
|---|---|---|---|---|---|
| See Lesson | 17.3 | 17.2 | 17.1 | 17.4 | 17.4 |
| Performance Expectation | HS-LS4-2 | HS-LS4-2 | HS-LS4-4 | HS-LS4-3 | HS-LS4-1 |

# 18

# Evolution of Populations

**18.1**
Genes and
Variation

**18.2**
Evolution as
Genetic Change

**18.3**
The Process
of Speciation

**18.4**
Molecular
Evolution

**Go Online to
access your
digital course.**

▶ **VIDEO**

◀ **AUDIO**

👆 **INTERACTIVITY**

📖 **eTEXT**

👁 **ANIMATION**

⚗ **VIRTUAL LAB**

☑ **ASSESSMENT**

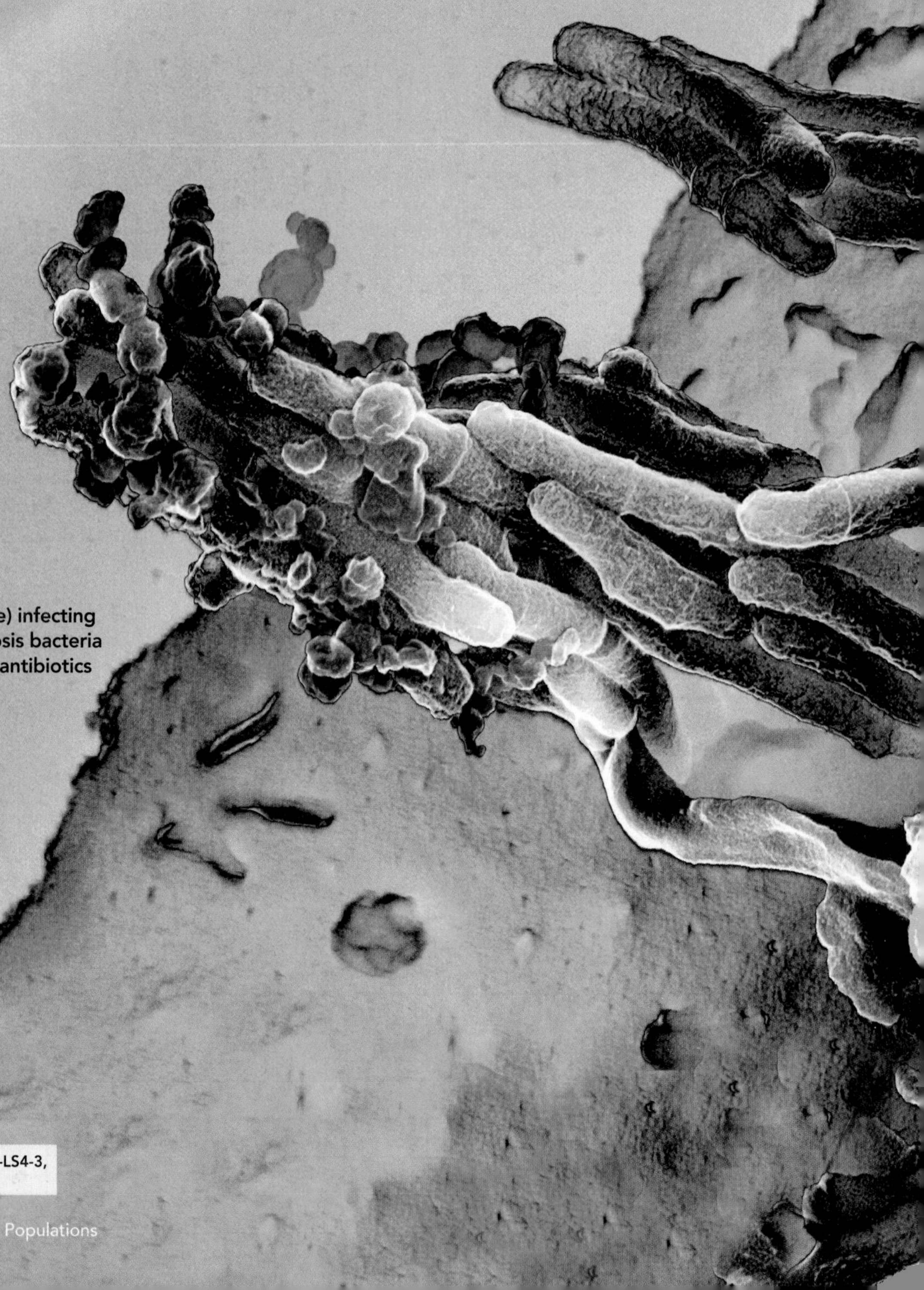

Tuberculosis bacteria (orange) infecting
a white blood cell. Tuberculosis bacteria
can become resistant to the antibiotics
that are used to treat it.

HS-LS3-2, HS-LS3-3, HS-LS4-2, HS-LS4-3,
HS-LS4-4, HS-LS4-5, HS-ETS1-1

# How can antibiotics keep up with drug-resistant bacteria?

"When I woke up just after dawn ..." biologist Alexander Fleming once said, " I certainly didn't plan to revolutionize all medicine by discovering the world's first antibiotic ..." Yet that's precisely what Fleming did that day. Returning to his laboratory after a vacation, he noticed that one of his bacterial cultures had been contaminated by a mold. Another scientist might have thought the culture was ruined. But Fleming observed something happening in that dish that got him thinking.

Fleming noticed that bacteria near the mold were dying. "That's funny," he remarked. But instead of just tossing the dish away, he did what scientists do. He proposed a hypothesis to explain his observation, and gathered data to test that hypothesis.

Fleming hypothesized that the mold produced something that killed bacteria. He identified the mold as *Penicillium*, grew it in culture, and isolated that "something," which he called penicillin.

Years later, researchers learned to mass-produce a form of penicillin that could be used to treat bacterial infections. Antibiotics saved thousands of lives during World War II by controlling bacterial infections among wounded soldiers. Soon, many bacterial diseases, such as pneumonia, posed much less of a threat. That's why antibiotics were called "magic bullets" and "wonder drugs."

Doctors began prescribing antibiotics widely. Farmers started giving antibiotics to farm animals such as cattle to prevent infections so they could fatten them up quickly. As a result, antibiotics are now a regular part of the environment for bacteria.

But the magic is fading as bacteria evolve. Today, the original form of penicillin is no longer effective. Newer antibiotics are failing too. The Centers for Disease Control (CDC) estimates that 2 million Americans each year become infected with antibiotic-resistant bacteria, and as many as 23,000 die from those infections.

Bacterial populations have always contained a few individuals with mutations that enabled them to destroy, inactivate, or eliminate antibiotics. But those individuals didn't have higher fitness, so those mutant alleles didn't become common.

What's happening? Evolution! In this new environment, individuals with resistance alleles have higher fitness, so the resistance alleles increase in frequency. Also, resistance alleles can be transferred from one bacterial species to another species on their plasmids. Thus, disease-causing bacteria can pick up resistance from harmless strains.

Many bacteria, including those that cause tuberculosis and certain forms of staph infections, are evolving resistance to not just one type of antibiotic, but to almost all medicines known. This prospect terrifies doctors. They fear the loss of one of the vital weapons against bacterial disease and the impact that could have.

Just how do populations evolve over time? How do new traits, such as antibiotic resistance, appear and become more common in a population, while other traits become less common, or disappear? Is it possible for new genes to appear, and if so, how?

**Throughout this chapter, look for connections to the** CASE STUDY **to help you answer these questions.**

# Genes and Variation

These ladybugs show some of the genetic variation typically present in their populations.

## KEY QUESTIONS

- *How is evolution defined in genetic terms?*
- *What are the sources of genetic variation?*
- *What determines the number of phenotypes for a given trait?*

HS-LS3-2: Make and defend a claim based on evidence that inheritable genetic variations may result from: (1) new genetic combinations through meiosis, (2) viable errors occurring during replication, and/or (3) mutations caused by environmental factors.
HS-LS3-3: Apply concepts of statistics and probability to explain the variation and distribution of expressed traits in a population.
HS-LS4-2: Construct an explanation based on evidence that the process of evolution primarily results from four factors: (1) the potential for a species to increase in number, (2) the heritable genetic variation of individuals in a species due to mutation and sexual reproduction, (3) competition for limited resources, and (4) the proliferation of those organisms that are better able to survive and reproduce in the environment.

**VOCABULARY**

**gene pool**
**allele frequency**
**single-gene trait**
**polygenic trait**

**READING TOOL**

Use the section headings to help you understand the information. Fill in the outline in your 📖 Biology Foundations Workbook.

Darwin knew that in order for traits to evolve, they had to be heritable. He also knew that to change over time, those traits had to vary among individuals. But he had no idea how heritable traits pass from one generation to the next, or where that all-important variation came from. Mendel's studies of inheritance were published during Darwin's lifetime, but no one, including Darwin, realized how important that work was. After Mendel's work was rediscovered around 1900, genetics took off like a rocket. One discovery after another tested evolutionary theory. Would new data support or refute Darwin's work?

## Genetics Joins Evolutionary Theory

Twentieth-century geneticists discovered that heritable traits are controlled by genes carried on chromosomes. They also learned that changes in genes and chromosomes generate variation. Molecular genetic techniques can now test hypotheses about variation and selection, and help us understand evolutionary change better than Darwin ever could. Studies in population genetics reinforce Darwin's understanding that populations—not individual organisms—evolve over time. All these discoveries give biologists a deeper understanding of how evolution works. To discuss that understanding properly, we need genetically based definitions of some important concepts.

**Genes, Populations, and Species** With insights from modern genetics, we can refine our definitions of important evolutionary terms. The genetic definition of a *species* is a population (or group of populations) of physically similar, interbreeding organisms that do not interbreed with other such groups. And in genetic terms, a *population* is a group of individuals of the same species that mate and produce offspring.

## Populations and Gene Pools

Here's where population genetics comes in. Because members of a population interbreed with one another, they share a common group of genes called a gene pool. A **gene pool** consists of all genes present in a population, including all alleles for each gene. Researchers describe gene pools by the numbers of different alleles they contain. The number of times an allele occurs in a gene pool, as a percentage of the total occurrence of all alleles for that gene in that gene pool, is called **allele frequency**. For example, in the mouse population in **Figure 18-1**, the allele frequency of the dominant *B* allele (black fur) is 40 percent (8 out of 20), and the allele frequency of the recessive *b* allele (brown fur) is 60 percent (12 out of 20). Note that allele frequency has nothing to do with whether the allele is dominant or recessive. In this mouse population, the recessive allele occurs more frequently than the dominant allele.

With this understanding as background, we can now define evolution in genetic terms. ⚲ *Evolution involves any change in the frequency of alleles in a population over time.* If the frequency of the *B* allele in Figure 18-1, for example, drops to 30 percent, the population is evolving. Again, it's important to note that populations, not individuals, evolve. Natural selection can act by increasing or decreasing the relative fitness of individual organisms. But those individuals don't evolve during their lifetimes. The results of natural selection show up as changes in allele frequencies in populations over time.

## Genotype, Phenotype, and Evolution

It is important to remember that natural selection "selects" an entire organism, either to survive and reproduce or to die without reproducing. Recall that the combination of alleles an individual carries is called its genotype. An individual's genotype, together with environmental conditions during its lifetime, produces its phenotype. A phenotype includes all physical, physiological, and behavioral characteristics of an organism, such as eye color or height. Natural selection acts directly on an organism's phenotype, not its genotype.

In any population, some individuals have phenotypes that are better suited to their environment than the phenotypes of other individuals. Better-suited individuals have higher fitness, produce more offspring, and pass more copies of their genes to the next generation. Thus, inherited variation can lead to natural selection because it can result in differential reproductive success. In genetics terms, evolutionary fitness is an individual's success in passing genes to the next generation. And an evolutionary adaptation is any genetically controlled trait that increases an individual's fitness.

✓ **READING CHECK** Cause and Effect Describe how natural selection affects genotypes by acting on phenotypes.

## Figure 18-1
## Alleles in a Population

When scientists try to determine whether a population is evolving, they study its allele frequencies. This diagram shows allele frequencies for fur color in a mouse population. ✓ **Calculate** Using the circle graph, what are the percentages of brown and black alleles in this population? (**Hint:** The homozygous black mice represent 16% of all black alleles in the population. What percentages of all black alleles are found in the heterozygous black mice?)

**Sample Population**

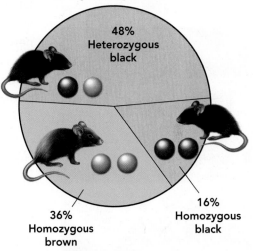

48% Heterozygous black

36% Homozygous brown

16% Homozygous black

**Frequency of Alleles**

⬤ Allele for brown fur  ⬤ Allele for black fur

👆 **INTERACTIVITY**

Explore how the same species of organisms can express similar, yet different, traits through genetic variation.

Figure 18-2

## Genetic Variation

A mutation that stopped the production of pigment resulted in the white deer. Mutations in bacteria can make them resistant to antibiotics. The puggle is a result of breeding of a pug and a beagle.

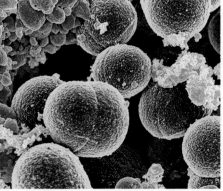

SEM 20,000×

# Sources of Genetic Variation

Understanding how genes and chromosomes work enables us to understand how the heritable variation so important in evolutionary change is produced. ✎ *Genetic variation is produced in three main ways: mutation, genetic recombination during sexual reproduction, and lateral gene transfer.* These mechanisms can all generate diversity within species. Let's see how that works.

**Mutations** Much of the time, genes are duplicated and passed from one generation to the next without change. But every so often an error occurs. A mutation is a heritable change in genetic information.

Many early geneticists assumed that mutations were usually "bad," because the kinds of mutations that first came to their attention didn't function as well as "wild-type" alleles. But "mistakes" in DNA replication are actually essential to a species' long-term survival. A population in which DNA replicates flawlessly, producing new generations without any genetic change, would lack much of the variation on which natural selection operates. That kind of population wouldn't evolve. And in a world where environments change, populations that can't evolve don't survive for long.

Some mutations—called neutral mutations—do not affect phenotype, and therefore don't affect fitness. Mutations that do produce changes in phenotype may or may not affect fitness. Some mutations may lower fitness by decreasing an individual's ability to survive and reproduce. Other mutations, such as those that cause genetic diseases, may be lethal. Still other mutations may result in adaptations that improve an individual's ability to survive and reproduce.

Note that mutations, such as those shown in **Figure 18-2**, matter in evolution only if they can be passed from generation to generation. For that to happen in plants and animals, mutations must occur in gametes (eggs or sperm). A mutation in a skin cell that produces skin cancer, for example, will not be passed to the next generation. Research suggests that each of us carries roughly 300 mutations that make our DNA different from that of our parents.

## Genetic Recombination During Sexual Reproduction

Mutations aren't the only source of heritable variation. You don't look exactly like your biological parents, even though they gave you all your genes. You probably look even less like any brothers or sisters you may have. Yet no matter how you feel about your relatives, they don't look different from you because either they (or you) are mutants! Most heritable differences within families are caused by genetic recombination. The puggle shown in **Figure 18-2** is a result of the combination of genes from its pug and beagle parents. Remember that during meiosis one member of each chromosome pair is shuffled randomly into each egg or sperm with one member of every other chromosome pair. In humans, who have 23 pairs of chromosomes, this can produce 8.4 million gene combinations!

Crossing-over is another mechanism that can produce genetic recombination. Recall that during meiosis, paired chromosomes often swap lengths of DNA at random. This crossing-over further increases the number of new genotypes created in each generation. You can now understand why, in species that reproduce sexually, no two siblings (except identical twins) look exactly alike. With all that recombination, you can end up with your mother's eyes, your father's nose, and hair that combines qualities from both parents.

**Lateral Gene Transfer** Most of the time, genes are passed only from parents to offspring during reproduction. Sometimes, however, genes pass from one individual to another individual that is not its offspring. This passing of genes produces a kind of gene flow called *lateral gene transfer*. Lateral gene transfer can occur between individuals of the same species or individuals of different species.

Gene flow can increase genetic variation, and therefore increase diversity, in any species that picks up "new" genes. Many bacteria, for example, swap genes on plasmids. This kind of lateral gene transfer is important in the evolution of antibiotic resistance. Lateral gene transfer among single-celled organisms has been common, and important, in generating diversity among species during the history of life.

**READING CHECK Describe** Explain how different sources of genetic variation contribute to the total diversity of individuals in a population.

# Single-Gene and Polygenic Traits

Genes relate to phenotypes in different ways. In some cases, a single gene produces a simple trait. Mendel was very lucky that several of the traits he studied in pea plants were controlled by a single gene. Other times, several genes interact to control a more complex trait. ✎ *The number of phenotypes produced for a trait depends on how many genes control the trait.*

**Single-Gene Traits** Traits controlled by a single gene may have only two or three distinct phenotypes, depending on the number of alleles involved. In the snail species shown in **Figure 18-3**, some snails have dark bands on their shells, and other snails don't. Shell banding is controlled by a single gene that has two alleles, and is therefore a **single-gene trait**—a trait controlled by only one gene. The allele for no bands is dominant over the allele for dark bands. All genotypes for this trait have one of two phenotypes: bands or no bands.

**READING TOOL**

As you read this section, write down questions you have about how the three main sources of genetic variation play a role in evolution. Answer your questions as you continue reading the chapter.

**INTERACTIVITY**

**Figure 18-3**

**Two Phenotypes**

In this species of snail, a single gene with two alleles controls whether or not a snail's shell has bands. The graph shows the percentage, in one population, of snails with bands, and snails without bands.

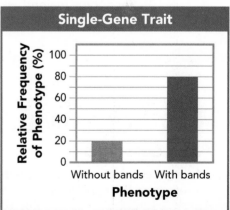

**Single-Gene Trait**

Relative Frequency of Phenotype (%)

Phenotype: Without bands, With bands

## INTERACTIVITY

Simulate how the frequency of alleles results in the expression of traits and the selective pressures that can cause these frequencies to change.

## BUILD VOCABULARY

**Prefixes** The prefix *poly-* means "many." **Polygenic traits** are traits controlled by many genes.

**Figure 18-4**

## A Range of Phenotypes

The graph shows the distribution of phenotypes that would be expected for a trait if many genes contributed to the trait. The photograph shows the actual distribution of heights in a group of young men.

The bar graph in Figure 18-3 shows the relative frequency of phenotypes for this trait in one snail population. This graph shows that the presence of dark bands may be more common in a population than the absence of bands. This is true even though the allele for shells without bands is the dominant form. In populations, phenotypic ratios are determined by the frequency of alleles in the population as well as by whether the alleles are dominant or recessive.

**Polygenic Traits** Many traits are controlled by two or more genes and are called **polygenic traits**. Each gene of a polygenic trait often has two or more alleles. As a result, a single polygenic trait often has many possible genotypes and an even greater variety of phenotypes. Often those phenotypes are not clearly distinct from one another.

Height in humans is one example of a polygenic trait. Height varies from very short to very tall and everywhere in between. You can sample phenotypic variation in this trait by measuring the height of all the students in your class. You can then calculate average height for this group. Many students will be just a little taller or shorter than average. Some, however, will be very tall or very short. If you graph the number of individuals of each height, you may get a graph similar to the one in **Figure 18-4**. The symmetrical bell-like shape of this curve is typical of polygenic traits. A bell-shaped curve is also called a normal distribution.

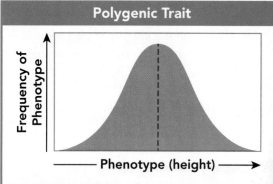

**Polygenic Trait**

Frequency of Phenotype

← Phenotype (height) →

HS-LS3-2, HS-LS3-3, HS-LS4-2

## ☑ LESSON 18.1 Review

### 🔍 KEY QUESTIONS

1. In genetic terms, what indicates that evolution is occurring in a population?

2. How do mutation, genetic recombination during sexual reproduction, and lateral gene transfer produce genetic variation?

3. What is the difference between a single-gene trait and a polygenic trait?

### CRITICAL THINKING

4. **Construct an Explanation** A bright orange color begins to appear in a population of butterflies. How could evolutionary fitness help explain this change?

5. **Develop Models** In a model of genetic inheritance, how do mutations help explain genetic variability?

6. **CASE STUDY** How does lateral gene transfer help explain the evolution of antibiotic resistance in bacteria?

# Evolution as Genetic Change

Spraying pesticide on a field of corn

## 🔍 KEY QUESTIONS

- *How does natural selection affect single-gene and polygenic traits?*
- *What is genetic drift?*
- *What conditions are required to maintain genetic equilibrium?*

**HS-LS3-3:** Apply concepts of statistics and probability to explain the variation and distribution of expressed traits in a population.

**HS-LS4-2:** Construct an explanation based on evidence that the process of evolution primarily results from four factors: (1) the potential for a species to increase in number, (2) the heritable genetic variation of individuals in a species due to mutation and sexual reproduction, (3) competition for limited resources, and (4) the proliferation of those organisms that are better able to survive and reproduce in the environment.

**HS-LS4-3:** Apply concepts of statistics and probability to support explanations that organisms with an advantageous heritable trait tend to increase in proportion to organisms lacking this trait.

## VOCABULARY

**directional selection**
**stabilizing selection**
**disruptive selection**
**genetic drift**
**bottleneck effect**
**founder effect**
**genetic equilibrium**
**Hardy-Weinberg principle**
**sexual selection**
**gene flow**

## READING TOOL

Focusing on the similarities and differences of each subject in the lesson, fill in the chart in your 📘 **Biology Foundations Workbook** to differentiate the concepts for each section.

Farmers have battled crop-eating insects since the dawn of agriculture. Many now use chemicals called insecticides to kill pests. At first, the early insecticides, like DDT, killed most insects. But after a few years, the poisons stopped working. These days, scientists develop new insecticides, but insects become resistant to those new weapons too. Doctors face a similar challenge. Bacteria once controlled by antibiotics are becoming resistant to almost every antibiotic known. This is often called an "arms race," because as soon as farmers and doctors develop new "weapons," the organisms they are fighting develop ways to resist their effects. This arms race is a result of evolution in response to natural selection.

## How Natural Selection Works

In evolutionary terms, when insecticides or antibiotics are introduced, those compounds become part of the environment. They dramatically reduce the fitness of any individuals susceptible to their effects. But almost always, just by chance, some individuals in the pest population carry one or more genetic variations that enable them to resist the pesticide. Similarly, a few bacteria, also by chance, carry genetic variation that lets them resist antibiotics. Both of these kinds of resistance are adaptations that enable individuals to survive and reproduce.

So, how does this happen? The presence of the pesticide or antibiotic increases the relative fitness of the few individuals that carry the resistance adaptation. The resistant individuals survive and thrive, because in dramatically reduced populations, there is less competition for resources. Resistant insects and bacteria reproduce, passing resistance alleles to their offspring. Nonresistant individuals die without reproducing. Over time, the frequency of resistance alleles increases in the population. This differential survival and reproduction of individuals with beneficial characteristics is called natural selection.

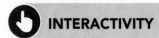
**Figure 18-5**

## Selection on a Single-Gene Trait

Natural selection on a single-gene trait can lead to changes in allele frequencies and, thus, to evolution. This type of evolution can occur in bacteria as well. ☑**Apply Concepts** What kind of mutation in disease-causing bacteria would lead to a change in allele and phenotype frequencies?

## Natural Selection on Single-Gene Traits

When natural selection produces differential reproductive success, the effects on phenotype can look different for single-gene and polygenic traits. ⚲ *Natural selection on single-gene traits can produce changes in allele frequencies that may be reflected by simple changes in phenotype frequencies.* Imagine, for example, that a population of brown lizards undergoes mutations in a gene that determines body color. The mutations produce red and black forms, as shown in **Figure 18-5**. What happens to allele and phenotype frequencies?

If red lizards are more visible to predators, they might be less likely to survive and reproduce, and the allele for red coloring might not become common. Black coloration might enable individuals to absorb more sunlight and warm up faster. If high body temperature allows individuals to move faster when feeding and avoid predators, black coloration might act as an adaptation that increases fitness. Then the allele for black coloration and the black phenotype will both increase in frequency. If black coloration has no effect on fitness, the phenotype produced by the mutant allele will not act as an adaptation. The allele will not be under pressure from natural selection.

| Effect of Color Mutations on Lizard Survival | | | |
|---|---|---|---|
| **Initial Population** | **Generation 10** | **Generation 20** | **Generation 30** |
| 80% | 80% | 70% | 40% |
| 10% | 0% | 0% | 0% |
| 10% | 20% | 30% | 60% |

## Natural Selection on Polygenic Traits

When a trait is controlled by more than one gene, both the trait and the effects of natural selection on the trait are more complex. Polygenic traits often display a range of phenotypes that form a bell curve. The fitness of individuals may vary from one end of such a curve to the other, and natural selection can act in one of three ways. ⚲ *Natural selection on polygenic traits can affect the relative fitness of phenotypes in three types of selection: directional selection, stabilizing selection, or disruptive selection.* These three types of selection are shown in **Figure 18-6**.

**Directional Selection** When individuals at one end of the curve have higher fitness than individuals elsewhere in the curve, **directional selection** occurs. The range of phenotypes shifts because individuals with adaptations that result in higher fitness experience higher reproductive success.

Think back to the experiments on the seed-eating Galápagos finches. Birds with big, thick beaks can feed more easily on large, hard, thick-shelled seeds than birds with smaller beaks. When the supply of small- and medium-sized seeds runs low, only larger seeds are left. Under these conditions, big-beaked birds can feed more easily than small-beaked birds. The big-beaked adaptation produces higher fitness, and greater reproductive success. Over time, the average beak size of this population will increase.

**Stabilizing Selection** If individuals near the center of the curve have higher fitness than individuals at either end, **stabilizing selection** takes place. The center of the curve remains at its current position, but the curve overall becomes more narrow.

Suppose that, on some islands, supplies of both big and small seeds varied between wet and dry seasons, but sizes of available seeds stayed fairly constant. Individuals with either very large or very small beaks might be outcompeted by birds that can eat both kinds of seeds. Over time, a greater proportion of the population would have a beak size in between the two extremes.

**Disruptive Selection** When phenotypes at both the upper and lower ends of the curve have higher fitness than individuals near the middle, **disruptive selection** can occur. Disruptive selection lowers the fitness of intermediate phenotypes. If the pressure of natural selection is strong and lasts long enough, the single curve can split. Two distinct phenotypes are created, increasing diversity within species.

Suppose a bird population lived in an area where medium-sized seeds became less common than large and small seeds. Birds with unusually small or unusually large beaks would both have higher fitness. As shown in the graph, the population might split into two groups: one with smaller beaks and one with larger beaks.

☑ **READING CHECK** **Compare and Contrast** How is the action of natural selection similar for single-gene and polygenic traits? How is it different?

### Figure 18-6

## Selection on Polygenic Traits

Natural selection on polygenic traits has one of three patterns: directional selection, stabilizing selection, or disruptive selection. These graphs describe the evolution of beak size in birds.

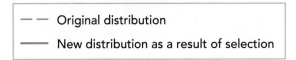
- - -   Original distribution
———   New distribution as a result of selection

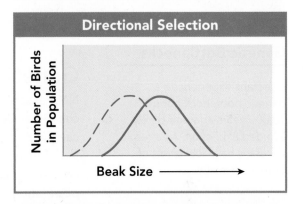

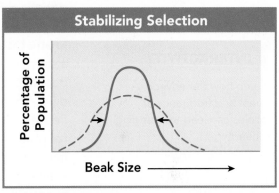

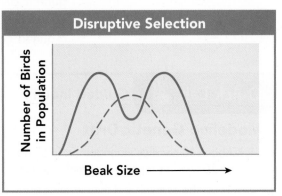

**Figure 18-7**

**Genetic Bottlenecks**

Cheetahs experienced a genetic bottleneck about 10,000 years ago and barely avoided extinction. As a result, cheetahs have low levels of genetic diversity.

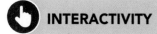

**INTERACTIVITY**

Learn how the environment and frequency of alleles can lead to changing phenotypes.

# Genetic Drift

Natural selection is not the only evolutionary mechanism that can change allele frequencies. *In small populations, individuals that carry a particular allele may leave more descendants than other individuals, just by chance. Over time, a series of chance occurrences can cause an allele to become more or less common in a population.* This kind of random change in allele frequency is called **genetic drift**.

**Genetic Bottlenecks** Sometimes a natural disaster, such as a storm or flood, kills many individuals in a population. The gene pool of the surviving population may have allele frequencies that differ from those of the original gene pool just by chance. The allele frequencies of the population may thus be different from the original population. This kind of **bottleneck effect** is a change in allele frequency following a dramatic reduction in the size of a population. A severe population bottleneck can sharply reduce a population's genetic diversity, and thus decrease diversity within the species. The cheetah shown in **Figure 18-7** is often used as an example of reduced genetic diversity.

HS-LS3-3

---

**Quick Lab** **Guided Inquiry**

## Modeling Genetic Drift

1. Choose 10 candies at random from a bag of colored candies. The 10 candies represent a small population of a species.

2. Mix up the candies and then arrange them in a single row. Record the number of candies of each color.

3. Model the growth of the population. For each of the 5 candies on the left side of the row, add another candy of the same color.

4. Repeat steps 2 and 3 two more times.

5. Now remove 20 candies at random, leaving only 5 candies. Then again repeat steps 2 and 3 two more times.

### ANALYZE AND INTERPRET DATA

1. **Reason Quantitatively** How did the distribution of colors change during the procedure?

2. **Use Models** How does the model represent the evolution and change in allele frequency of the population?

3. **Evaluate Models** What evolutionary mechanism is shown by step 5 of the model? Describe this mechanism.

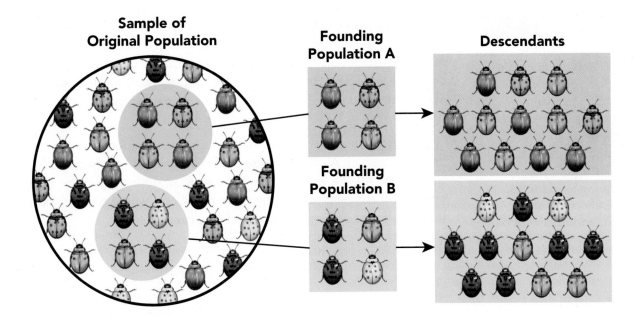

**Sample of Original Population**

**Founding Population A**

**Founding Population B**

**Descendants**

## The Founder Effect

Genetic drift may also occur when a few individuals colonize a new habitat. These founding individuals may carry alleles that differ in relative frequencies from those of the main population, just by chance. The new gene pool therefore starts out with allele frequencies that differ from those of the parent gene pool, as shown in **Figure 18-8**. This situation, in which allele frequencies change as a result of the migration of a small subgroup of a population, is known as the **founder effect**.

One example of the founder effect is found in the evolution of several hundred species of fruit flies on different Hawaiian islands. Genetic and molecular evaluation of these flies suggests that they are descended from the same mainland fruit fly population. However, species on different islands have allele frequencies that are different from those of the original species.

☑ **READING CHECK** **Describe** What are two circumstances under which genetic drift may occur?

## Evolution Versus Genetic Equilibrium

How and why do populations evolve? And when might a population *not* evolve? One way to answer this question is to imagine a model of a hypothetical population that does not evolve. What would that population look like in terms of population genetics? If the population is not evolving, allele frequencies in its gene pool are not changing, and that population is in **genetic equilibrium**.

### Sexual Reproduction and Allele Frequency

Gene shuffling during sexual reproduction can produce many different gene combinations. But a century ago, researchers realized that meiosis and fertilization, by themselves, do not change allele frequencies. So, hypothetically, a population of sexually reproducing organisms could remain in genetic equilibrium.

**INTERACTIVITY**

**Figure 18-8**

**Founder Effect**

This illustration shows how two small groups from a large, diverse population could produce new populations that differ from the original group.
☑ **Compare and Contrast** Explain why the two populations of descendants are so different from one another.

**BUILD VOCABULARY**

**Word Origins** The word *equilibrium* originates from the Latin word *aequilibrium*, which means "balance."

As you read about the Hardy-Weinberg principle, draw upon your prior knowledge in solving mathematical expressions. Remember when solving expressions to use the correct order of operations: parentheses, exponents, multiplication, division, addition, and subtraction.

## The Hardy-Weinberg Principle

According to the **Hardy-Weinberg principle**, allele frequencies in a population should remain constant unless one or more factors causes those frequencies to change. The Hardy-Weinberg principle makes predictions like Punnett squares—but for populations, not individuals. Here's how it works.

Suppose that there are two alleles for a gene: A (dominant) and a (recessive). A cross of these alleles can produce three possible genotypes: AA, Aa, and aa. The frequencies of genotypes in the population can be predicted by these equations, where p and q are the frequencies of the dominant and recessive alleles:

In symbols:

$$p^2 + 2pq + q^2 = 1 \text{ and } p + q = 1$$

In words:

(frequency of AA) + (frequency of Aa) + (frequency of aa) = 100%
and (frequency of A) + (frequency of a) = 100%

Here's how the Hardy-Weinberg equation can be used to evaluate the likelihood that evolution is taking place in a population. Suppose that, in one generation, the frequency of the A allele were 40 percent ($p = 0.40$) and the frequency of the a allele were 60 percent ($q = 0.60$). If this population were in genetic equilibrium, the chances of an individual in the next generation having genotype AA would be 16% ($p^2 = 0.40^2 = 0.16$ or 16%). The probability of genotype aa would be 36% ($q^2 = 0.60^2 = 0.36$). The probability of genotype Aa would be 48% ($2pq = 2 (0.40) (0.60) = 0.48$). If a population doesn't show these predicted phenotype frequencies, evolution is taking place. 🔍 *The Hardy-Weinberg principle predicts that five conditions can disturb genetic equilibrium and cause evolution to occur: (1) nonrandom mating, (2) small population size, (3) gene flow from immigration or emigration, (4) mutations, or (5) natural selection.*

**Nonrandom Mating** In genetic equilibrium, individuals must mate at random. But females of many animal species select mates based on size, strength, or coloration, as shown in **Figure 18-9**, a practice known as **sexual selection**. When sexual selection occurs, genes for traits selected for or against are not in equilibrium.

**Figure 18-9**

## Sexual Selection

When the gene pools shifts, populations evolve. Bright, colorful feathers and large antlers help males attract females. Males with plain feathers, or males with smaller antlers, are less likely to mate. ☑ **Apply Concepts** How does nonrandom mating explain why male ducks, but not females, evolved bright, colorful feathers?

**Figure 18-10**

**Small Population Size**

The population of black-footed ferrets was once as low as 18 individuals, all in captivity. By 2013, the population had increased to 500, but much genetic diversity had been lost.

**Small Population Size** Genetic drift does not usually have major effects in large populations, but can affect small populations. Evolution due to genetic drift thus happens more easily in small populations. An example is described in **Figure 18-10**.

**Gene Flow from Immigration or Emigration** Changes in allele frequency can be produced by **gene flow**, the movement of genes into or out of a population. Individuals who join a population (through immigration) may introduce new alleles, and individuals who leave (through emigration) may remove alleles. If allele frequency in the population changes, gene flow has caused evolution to occur.

**Mutations** Mutations can introduce new alleles into a gene pool, changing allele frequencies and causing evolution to occur.

**Natural Selection** If different genotypes have different fitness, natural selection will disrupt genetic equilibrium, and evolution will occur.

If you think about it, almost any population in nature is likely to experience one or more of these conditions. So, most of the time, in most populations, in typical habitats, evolution happens.

HS-LS3-3, HS-LS4-2, HS-LS4-3

## ☑ LESSON 18.2 Review

### ⚲ KEY QUESTIONS

1. How does natural selection affect a single-gene trait?

2. Define genetic drift.

3. What five conditions are necessary to maintain genetic equilibrium?

### CRITICAL THINKING

4. **Compare and Contrast** Compare directional selection and disruptive selection.

5. **Infer** Do you think populations stay in genetic equilibrium after the environment has changed significantly? Explain your answer.

6. **CASE STUDY** Use the concepts of natural selection, genetic variation, and relative fitness to explain how antibiotic resistance evolves in bacteria.

# The Process of Speciation

Marine iguanas, like this one, are found only in the Galápagos.

## KEY QUESTIONS

- *What types of isolation lead to the formation of new species?*
- *What is a current hypothesis about Galápagos finch speciation?*

**HS-LS4-2:** Construct an explanation based on evidence that the process of evolution primarily results from four factors: (1) the potential for a species to increase in number, (2) the heritable genetic variation of individuals in a species due to mutation and sexual reproduction, (3) competition for limited resources, and (4) the proliferation of those organisms that are better able to survive and reproduce in the environment. **HS-LS4-5:** Evaluate the evidence supporting claims that changes in environmental conditions may result in: (1) increases in the number of individuals of some species, (2) the emergence of new species over time, and (3) the extinction of other species.

## VOCABULARY

speciation
reproductive isolation
behavioral isolation
geographical isolation
temporal isolation

## READING TOOL

As you read, think about the three types of reproductive isolation and what causes them. Fill in the flowchart in your 📘 **Biology Foundations Workbook.**

In his book, *On the Origin of Species*, Darwin describes how species adapt to changing environments. But despite the book's title, it says little about the origin of new species—the process called **speciation**.

Darwin made observations whenever he found unusual species. And he described the Galápagos Islands as "a little world within itself" and "very remarkable" in its species. Years later, he suggested that those islands might hold the clues to "…that mystery of mysteries—the first appearance of new beings on this Earth." Darwin's intuition was on target. He had a sense that something about the islands was connected, somehow, with speciation. We now know that a lot of isolated island groups are home to species found nowhere else. So what gives with islands and speciation? Again, gene pools and evolution as genetic change help to answer that question.

## Isolating Mechanisms

To understand how a species can give rise to a new species, recall that evolution is any change in relative frequencies of alleles in a population's gene pool. Interbreeding enables any genetic change that occurs in a population to spread throughout that population.

But what would happen if some members of a population were to stop breeding with other members? If that occurred, the species gene pool could split into two populations, as shown in **Figure 18-11**. And if, over time, members of those two populations stopped interbreeding altogether, changes in one gene pool could not spread to the other. When this happens, we say that those populations have become reproductively isolated from one another. If this **reproductive isolation** lasts long enough, those populations may split into two separate species. *Reproductive isolation can develop in several ways, including behavioral isolation, geographic isolation, and temporal isolation.*

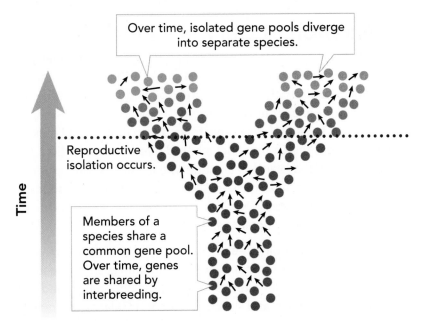

Over time, isolated gene pools diverge into separate species.

Time

Reproductive isolation occurs.

Members of a species share a common gene pool. Over time, genes are shared by interbreeding.

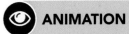
### An Example of Speciation

If two populations of a species become reproductively isolated, their gene pools can diverge, producing new species.

**Behavioral Isolation** If two populations that were once able to interbreed evolve differences in courtship rituals or other behaviors, **behavioral isolation** can occur. For example, eastern and western meadowlarks are similar birds whose habitats overlap. But members of the two species will not mate with each other, partly because they use different songs to attract mates.

**Geographic Isolation** When two populations are separated by geographic barriers such as rivers, mountains, or bodies of water, **geographic isolation** occurs. The Galápagos Islands, for example, are far enough from the mainland of South America that small birds like finches very rarely make the crossing. The islands are also isolated from one another.

Biological islands come in many more "flavors" than just chunks of land surrounded by water. A biological island is any habitat that is isolated in some way from other, similar habitats. Punctuating the tropical forests of Venezuela and Guyana, for example, are craggy, tabletop mountains called tepuis, as shown in **Figure 18-12**. The cool, misty environment on the summits of these steep-walled mountains differs dramatically from the steamy, lowland jungle surrounding their bases. Organisms on each plateau are isolated by jungle.

Geographic barriers do not always guarantee isolation. Floods, for example, may link separate lakes, enabling their fish populations to mix and interbreed. Also, a geographic barrier may separate certain organisms but not others. A large river may keep squirrels and other rodents apart, but probably won't isolate bird populations.

**Temporal Isolation** A third isolating mechanism, known as **temporal isolation**, happens when two or more species reproduce at different times. For example, suppose three similar species of orchids live in the same rain forest. Each species has flowers that last only one day. If the species bloom at different times of the year, they cannot pollinate one another.

**INTERACTIVITY**

Investigate the three types of isolation that lead to speciation.

**Figure 18-12**

### Geographic Isolation

Tepuis are like isolated islands in a sea of jungle. Organisms that live on top of these tepuis are not found anywhere else in the world.

# Speciation in Darwin's Finches

Recall that Peter and Rosemary Grant spent years in the Galápagos studying finch populations. They measured and recorded anatomical characteristics such as beak length, beak depth, and other traits. When data for each trait were graphed, they formed bell-shaped distributions typical of polygenic traits. As environmental conditions changed, the Grants documented directional selection. When drought struck the island of Daphne Major, finches with larger beaks capable of cracking the thickest seeds survived and reproduced more often than others. Over many generations, the proportion of large-beaked finches increased.

We can now combine these studies by the Grants with evolutionary concepts to form a hypothesis that answers a question: How might the founder effect and natural selection have led to reproductive isolation and speciation among Galápagos finches? *Speciation in Galápagos finches occurred by the founding of a new population, geographic isolation, changes in the new population's gene pool, behavioral isolation, and ecological competition.*

**Founders Arrive**

**Founders Arrive** Many years ago, a few finches from South America—species M—arrived on one of the Galápagos Islands. These birds may have gotten lost or been blown off course by a storm. Once on the island, they survived and reproduced. Because of the founder effect, allele frequencies of this founding finch population could have differed from allele frequencies in the original South American population.

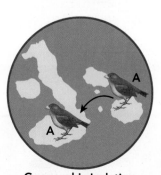

**Geographic Isolation**

**Geographic Isolation** The environment the birds encountered in the Galápagos was different from the environment they came from on the mainland of South America. Some combination of the founder effect, geographic isolation, and natural selection resulted in differential reproductive success, adaptation, and evolution of this island population into a new species—species A. Later, a few birds of species A crossed to another island. Because these birds do not usually fly over open water, they move from island to island very rarely. Thus, finch populations on the two islands were geographically isolated, and no longer shared a common gene pool.

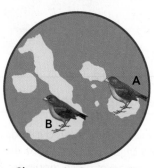

**Changes in Gene Pools**

**Changes in Gene Pools** Over time, populations on each island further adapted to local environments. Plants on the first island may have produced small, thin-shelled seeds, whereas plants on the second island may have produced larger, thick-shelled seeds. On the second island, directional selection would have favored individuals with larger, heavier beaks. These birds could crack open and eat the large seeds more easily. Thus, birds with large beaks would be better able to survive on the second island. Over time, natural selection would have caused that population to evolve larger beaks, forming a new population, B, with a new phenotype.

## Modeling Lab    Guided Inquiry

### Competing for Resources

**Problem** How can competition lead to speciation?

In this lab, you will model variation in the size and shape of finch beaks using different tools. You will determine which "beaks" are better adapted to small seeds and large seeds. You will also observe how competition and the abundance or scarcity of food affects survival.

You can find this lab in your digital course.

**Behavioral Isolation** Now, imagine that a few birds from the second island cross back to the first island. Will population A birds breed with population B birds? Probably not. During courtship, these finches closely inspect a potential partner's beak. Finches prefer to mate with birds that have the same size beak as they do. Big-beaked birds prefer to mate with other big-beaked birds, and smaller-beaked birds prefer to mate with other smaller-beaked birds. Because the populations on the two islands have evolved different-sized beaks, they would probably not mate with each other.

Thus, differences in beak size, combined with mating behavior, could lead to reproductive isolation. The gene pools of the two bird populations remain isolated—even when individuals live in the same place. The populations have now become two distinct species.

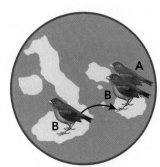

**Behavioral Isolation**

**Competition and Continued Evolution** As these two new species live together on the first island, they compete for seeds. During the dry season, birds that are most different from each other have the highest fitness. That is because the more specialized birds experience less competition for certain kinds of seeds and other foods. Over time, the species evolve in a way that increases the differences between them. Birds on the first island that once belonged to species B may evolve into a new species, C.

These processes of geographic isolation, genetic change, and behavioral isolation could have repeated again and again across the Galápagos chain. Over many generations, therefore, natural selection could have produced the diversity among the 13 different finch species found there today.

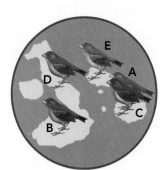

**Competition and Continued Evolution**

**INTERACTIVITY**

Study speciation by investigating ring species.

HS-LS4-2, HS-LS4-5

## LESSON 18.3 Review

### ⚲ KEY IDEAS

1. What is geographic isolation?

2. What types of reproductive isolation may have been important in Galápagos finch speciation? Explain.

### CRITICAL THINKING

3. Apply Scientific Reasoning On the Galápagos Islands, different types of seeds are common on different islands. How did the seed types affect the evolution of Darwin's finches?

# Molecular Evolution

🔑 KEY QUESTIONS

- *Where do new genes come from?*
- *How may Hox genes be involved in evolutionary change?*
- *How do molecular clocks work?*

HS-LS3-2: Make and defend a claim based on evidence that inheritable genetic variations may result from: (1) new genetic combinations through meiosis, (2) viable errors occurring during replication, and/or (3) mutations caused by environmental factors.

**VOCABULARY**
**Hox gene**

**READING TOOL**

As you read, identify the details that describe the headings listed in your 📖 **Biology Foundations Workbook.**

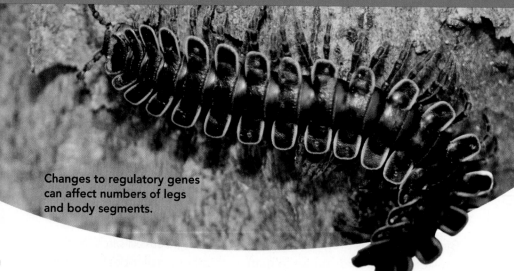

Changes to regulatory genes can affect numbers of legs and body segments.

Charles Darwin worked almost a century before the DNA double helix was discovered. Yet Darwinian theory applies just as much to molecules as it does to the animals and plants that Darwin studied. Today, as we study and compare genomes, we can evaluate evolutionary theory by making testable predictions about evolutionary change in genes and genomes.

## New Genes, New Functions

Consider one of the most basic questions in biology: Where did the roughly 25,000 genes in the human genome come from? Modern genes descended from a much smaller number of genes in early life forms. But how could that have happened? 🔑 *One way new genes can evolve is through duplication, followed by modification, of existing genes.*

**Gene Duplication** Recall that during meiosis, paired chromosomes swap DNA in a process called crossing-over. Sometimes, an unequal swap gives one chromosome in the pair an "extra" copy of one or more genes. If mutations occur in those duplicate copies, they don't affect the function of the original gene. **Figure 18-13** shows how this happens. The evolving duplicate genes, however, can gain new functions over time.

**Figure 18-13**

**Gene Duplication**

In this diagram, a gene is first duplicated, and then one of the two resulting genes undergoes mutation.

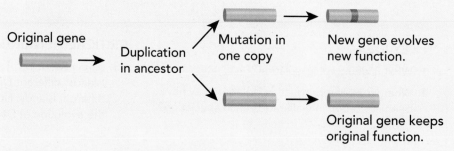

Original gene → Duplication in ancestor → Mutation in one copy → New gene evolves new function.

Original gene keeps original function.

One way to evaluate this idea is to check to see if genomes of living organisms contain duplicate genes. It turns out that they do! For example, the human genome contains six copies of the gene for beta-globin, one of the polypeptides in the blood protein hemoglobin. Although these six beta-globin genes are similar, mutations have slightly changed their characteristics since they were produced by duplication of a single ancestral globin gene. In other cases, gene duplication has allowed copies of genes to acquire completely new functions.

**Genetic Rearrangement** Chromosomes are not static DNA sequences. They can break and reconnect, lose bits and pieces of DNA, and acquire DNA sequences from viruses, microorganisms, and even other chromosomes. In fact, exons from one gene can mix and combine with exons from other genes. These changes can produce new genes that code for completely different proteins.

Over time, gene duplications and rearrangements have greatly increased the size and complexity of eukaryotic genomes. They have also left evidence for evolution in the form of gene "families." These gene families can be analyzed to trace the course of evolution, and to help establish evolutionary relationships between different species.

✓ **READING CHECK** **Review** Describe how new genes are created through duplication and rearrangement.

# Developmental Genes and Body Plans

One exciting new research area is nicknamed "evo-devo" because it studies the relationship between evolution and development. Researchers have now shown how small changes in master control genes can produce the kinds of evolutionary changes seen in the fossil record.

**Hox Genes and Evolution** A group of regulatory genes known as **Hox genes** determines which parts of an embryo develop into arms, legs, or wings. Groups of Hox genes also control the sizes and shapes of those structures. In fact, homologous Hox genes shape the bodies of animals as different as insects and humans—even though those animals last shared a common ancestor no fewer than 500 million years ago!

🔍 *Small changes in Hox gene activity during embryological development can produce large changes in adult animals.* For example, insects and crustaceans are related to ancient common ancestors that possessed dozens of legs. Today's crustaceans, including shrimp and lobsters, have 5 pairs of legs, and insects have just 3 pairs. What happened to all those extra legs? Recent studies have shown that mutations in a single Hox gene, known as *Ubx*, turns off the growth of legs in the abdominal regions of insects. Thus, a small change in one Hox gene accounts for a major evolutionary difference between two important animal groups, as shown in **Figure 18-14**.

👆 **INTERACTIVITY**

Investigate how evolution changes the appearance of organisms over time as the result of new genes being formed.

**BUILD VOCABULARY**
**Academic Words**
Sequence refers to a set of related events, movements, or things that follow each other in a particular order.

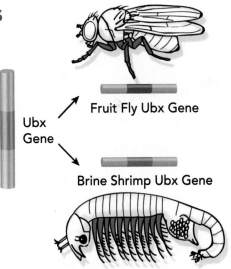

Ubx Gene

Fruit Fly Ubx Gene

Brine Shrimp Ubx Gene

**Figure 18-14**

**Change in a Hox Gene**

In the illustration, the legs of the fruit fly and the legs of the brine shrimp are the same color (red) because a variant of the same Hox gene, *Ubx*, directs the development of the legs of both animals.

**Timing Is Everything** Each part of an embryo starts to grow at a specific time, grows for a specific length of time, and stops growing at a specific time. Small changes in start and stop times can make a big difference in adult body shape. For example, small timing changes can make the difference between long, slender fingers and short, stubby toes. No wonder "evo-devo" is one of the hottest areas in evolutionary biology!

✓ **READING CHECK** **Summarize** How do Hox genes affect the development of embryos?

# Molecular Clocks

Because changes in DNA drive evolution and record organisms' common ancestors, we can compare the DNA sequences of different organisms to determine their evolutionary relationships. If two species share a common ancestor, changes in their DNA should have accumulated since they became separate species. Biologists can use these differences as a kind of "molecular clock" to mark the passage of evolutionary time. ✎ *A molecular clock uses mutation rates in DNA to estimate the time that two species have been evolving independently.*

**Neutral Mutations as "Ticks"** To understand molecular clocks, think about mechanical clocks. They mark time with a mechanism that clicks every second, creating the ticking sound. A molecular clock also relies on a repeating process—mutation—to mark time. Simple mutations occur all the time, causing slight changes in DNA sequences.

Some mutations have a major positive or negative effect on an organism's phenotype. These mutations are under powerful pressure from natural selection. Many small mutations, however, have no effect on phenotype. These neutral mutations tend to accumulate in the DNA of different species at about the same rate. Researchers can compare such DNA sequences in two species. The comparison can reveal how many mutations have occurred independently in each group, as shown in **Figure 18-15**. The more differences there are between the DNA sequences of the two species, the more time has elapsed since the two species shared a common ancestor.

👆 **INTERACTIVITY**

**Figure 18-15**
**Molecular Clock**

By comparing the DNA sequence of two or more species, biologists estimate how long the species have been separated. ✓ **Analyze** What evidence indicates that species C is more closely related to species B than to species A?

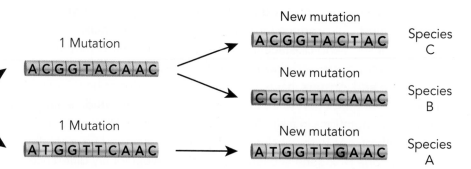

Section of DNA in a common ancestor

## Analyzing Data

### Variation of Expressed Traits

Suppose that in a population of a mammal species, almost all of the animals have brown fur, but occasionally an animal with white fur appears. One explanation is that fur color is controlled by a single gene with two alleles: a dominant allele for brown fur and a recessive allele for white fur. Use this model to generate and analyze statistics on the variation of fur color.

1. Read the procedure. Prepare a data table to record the results.

2. Prepare two paper bags, each with 7 brown counters and 3 white counters. Each bag represents the alleles for fur color in the population.

3. Randomly pick a counter from each bag to model the genes of an offspring. Record the two alleles, and the fur color they produce.

4. Repeat step 3 to generate 20 samples.

### ANALYZE AND INTERPRET DATA

1. Calculate  Find the percentages of brown and white animals among the first 5 offspring, the first 10 offspring, and all 20 offspring in your model.

2. Evaluate Models  Why is it more useful to generate and analyze data from 20 offspring compared to a smaller number?

3. Construct an Explanation  As shown by your model, how do allele frequencies help explain the variation and distribution of the trait of fur color?

4. Predict  What events in nature might change the percentages of fur color in this species? Explain your prediction.

**Calibrating the Clock**  The use of molecular clocks is not simple, because there is not just one molecular clock in a genome. There are many different clocks, each of which "ticks" at a different rate. This is because some DNA sequences accumulate mutations faster than others. Think of a conventional clock. If you want to time a brief event, you use the second hand. To time an event that lasts longer, you use the minute hand or the hour hand. In the same way, researchers choose a different molecular clock for comparing great apes than for estimating when mammals and fishes shared a common ancestor. Researchers check the accuracy of molecular clocks by trying to estimate how often mutations occur. In other words, they estimate how often the clock they have chosen "ticks." To do this, they compare the number of mutations in a particular gene in species whose ages have been determined by other methods.

## ✓ LESSON 18.4 Review

### ⚗ KEY QUESTIONS

1. How can crossing-over result in gene duplication?

2. In evolution, why have small changes in Hox genes had a significant impact?

3. How does a molecular clock allow scientists to study evolutionary history?

### CRITICAL THINKING

4. Construct an Explanation  How can duplicated genes lead to the development of new adaptations in a species?

5. Evaluate Models  A computer simulation is used to predict the effect of a mutation in a Hox gene in fruit flies. Why is it important for the model to specify the timing of the mutation?

6. Ask Questions  You are studying corresponding DNA sequences from three species of trout, which is a type of fish. What questions can you ask, and then investigate, to help determine the evolutionary relationship among the trout species?

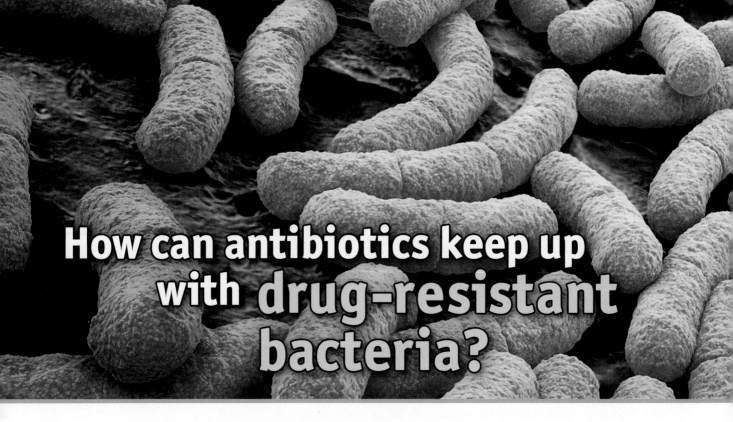

# How can antibiotics keep up with drug-resistant bacteria?

**A new antibiotic may be very effective at first. Then, over time, bacterial populations evolve resistance to it.**

HS-LS4-4, HS-LS4-5

## Make Your Case

Natural selection can drive changes in gene frequency in populations—especially if organisms' environment changes in a dramatic way. The widespread use and overuse of antibiotics created just such a change by making antibiotics part of the environment. Unfortunately, antibiotic resistance poses a very serious threat to human health. As old antibiotics become less effective, new ones are needed to replace them. Some good news came in 2015 with the discovery of a new antibiotic called teixobactin. It is the first new antibiotic in decades.

## Construct an Argument

1. **Conduct Research** Look for reliable data that show how and why the effectiveness of an antibiotic changes if that antibiotic is widely used.

2. **Construct an Explanation** When an antibiotic is used for many years, how does natural selection lead to bacteria that are resistant to it? Use the data you researched as evidence to support your explanation.

3. **Engage in Argument** When new antibiotics such as teixobactin are developed, when and how widely should they be used? Cite evidence and use logical reasoning in your argument.

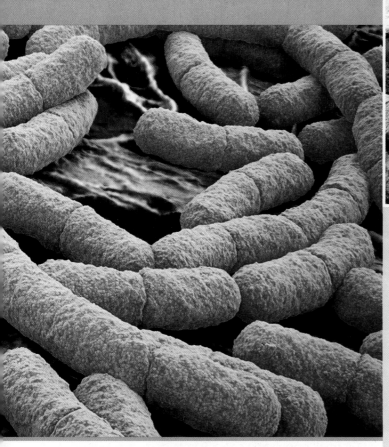

## Society on the Case

### Drugs for Livestock

Bacteria can and do infect livestock. In fact, modern practices for raising livestock make them especially prone to bacterial infections. The animals are often kept in very crowded, stressful conditions. Bacteria can spread quickly within a crowded cattle pen or chicken coop.

For these reasons, closely packed livestock are generally given heavy doses of antibiotics. The U.S. government regulates this practice. The stated goals of the regulations are to keep the food supply safe and keep antibiotic resistance at a minimum. Critics, however, argue that the laws and regulations are not strict enough. Several organizations are working to reduce or eliminate the need for heavy antibiotic use on livestock, such as by decreasing the density of animals kept in close quarters.

In 2015, California became the first state to ban the use of antibiotics in feedlots to speed up an animal's growth. The law allows animals to receive certain antibiotics only when it is necessary for their health.

Consumers are becoming more aware of the use of antibiotics in livestock that is raised for food. As a result, some American poultry producers have begun to voluntarily reduce or limit the routine use of antibiotics.

## Careers on the Case

### Work Toward a Solution

The problem of antibiotic resistance means that new antibiotics are always needed. People in many careers work together to find or invent a new drug, test it carefully, and develop ways to manufacture it for wide distribution.

### Pharmaceutical Scientist

Some potential drugs are found in nature, while others involve chemical changes to existing drugs. Pharmaceutical scientists work in teams to develop new drugs. Most people with this career work for drug companies. Pharmaceutical scientists may also work at universities or for government agencies.

### ▶ VIDEO

Watch this video to learn about other careers in biology.

hhmi | BioInteractive

# STUDY GUIDE

## Lesson Review

Go to your Biology Foundations Workbook for longer versions of these lesson summaries.

### 18.1 Genes and Variation

Evolution is a change in the frequency of alleles in a population over time. In genetics terms, evolutionary fitness is an individual's success in passing genes to the next generation.

Genetic variation is produced in three main ways. Mutation is a change in a genetic sequence. Sexual reproduction creates new combinations of genes. Lateral gene transfer occurs when one individual passes genes to another that is not its offspring, as when a bacterium transfers a plasmid.

The number of phenotypes produced for a trait depends on how many genes control the trait. Traits can be determined by a single gene or by many genes.

- gene pool
- allele frequency
- single-gene trait
- polygenic trait

**Sample Population**

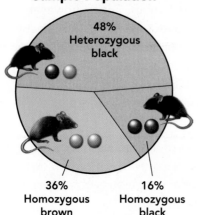

48%
Heterozygous
black

36%
Homozygous
brown

16%
Homozygous
black

☑ **Calculate** In a population of 200 mice, how many are heterozygous black? how many are homozygous brown? how many are homozygous black?

### 18.2 Evolution as Genetic Change

Natural selection on single-gene traits can lead to changes in allele frequencies and, thus, to changes in phenotype frequencies.

Natural selection on polygenic traits can affect the relative fitness of phenotypes and thereby produce one of three types of selection: directional selection, stabilizing selection, or disruptive selection.

In small populations, individuals that carry a particular allele may leave more descendants than other individuals leave, just by chance. Over time, a series of chance occurrences can cause an allele to become more or less common in a population.

The Hardy-Weinberg principle predicts that five conditions can disturb genetic equilibrium and cause evolution to occur: (1) nonrandom mating, (2) small population size, (3) immigration or emigration, (4) mutations, or (5) natural selection.

- directional selection
- stabilizing selection
- disruptive selection
- genetic drift
- bottleneck effect
- founder effect
- genetic equilibrium
- Hardy-Weinberg principle
- sexual selection
- gene flow

☑ **Summarize** Which process of evolution does the figure show? Explain the events that occur.

**Original Population**

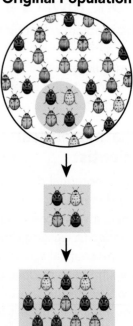

**Descendants**

## 18.3 The Process of Speciation

When populations become reproductively isolated, they can evolve into two separate species. Reproductive isolation can develop in several ways, including behavioral isolation, geographic isolation, and temporal isolation.

The classic example of speciation is seen in the 13 species of Galápagos finches. Speciation resulted from the founding of a new population, geographic isolation, changes in the new population's gene pool, behavioral isolation, and ecological competition.

- speciation
- reproductive isolation
- behavioral isolation
- geographic isolation
- temporal isolation

## 18.4 Molecular Evolution

One way new genes can evolve is through the duplication, followed by modification, of existing genes.

Small changes in Hox gene activity during embryological development can produce large changes in adult animals.

A molecular clock uses mutation rates in DNA to estimate the time that two species have been evolving independently.

- Hox gene

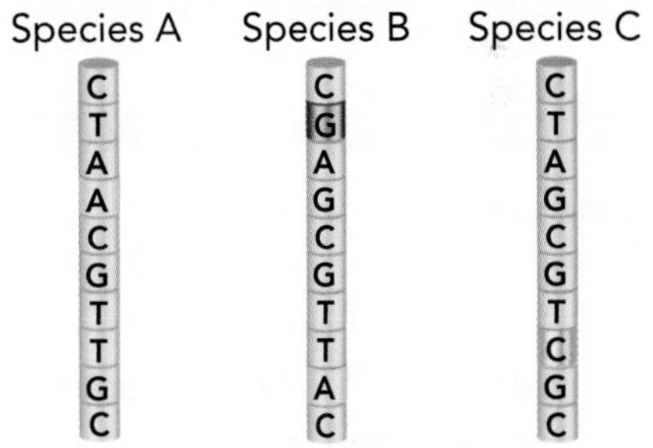

Species A    Species B    Species C

☑ **Interpret Diagrams** The colored bands in the diagrams represent mutations in a segment of DNA in species A, B, and C. Which two of the three species probably share the most recent common ancestor?

# Organize Information

Complete the graphic organizer about sources of genetic variation.

| Sources of Genetic Variation | Description | Example |
| --- | --- | --- |
| Mutations | 1. | 2. |
| 3. | In independent assortment, each chromosome in a pair moves independently during meiosis. During crossing-over, paired chromosomes often swap lengths of DNA. | 4. |
| 5. | 6. | Many bacteria swap genes on plasmids, leading to antibiotic-resistant bacteria. |

# When Weeds Fight Back!

# Construct an Explanation

HS-LS3-3, HS-LS4-3, HS-ETS1-1

**STEM** ▶ For cotton farmers, a green tassel-like weed called Palmer amaranth is bad news. This invasive weed, native to the southwest, spread across the Midwest and into the southeast. Each female plant can produce up to 600,000 seeds, which germinate throughout the season. It competes with cotton for space, light, soil, water, and nutrients.

During the 1970s, cotton farmers began using a weed-killing chemical called glyphosate, which is sold to both the commercial and consumer market. It worked temporarily to keep weed growth down and to slow the invasive's spread. It wasn't a perfect solution, as weed-killing chemicals can have negative effects on the environment, and on human health. But even that imperfect solution didn't last.

In 2004, a farmer in Georgia reported glyphosate-resistant weeds. That resistance spread rapidly. By 2011, weeds were decreasing cotton yields by 50 percent. Today, farmers must use a variety of herbicides. Still, Palmer amaranth remains a nuisance.

The series of circle graphs describe a model of a weed population that evolves resistance to an herbicide. The width of each circle shows the relative size of the weed population, and the colors show the percentages of normal and herbicide-resistant weeds. Study the graphs, and then apply your knowledge of evolution by natural selection to answer these questions.

1. **Interpret Graphs** What do the circle graphs show about the effect of herbicide on the weed population in the model?

2. **Support an Explanation** Consider this explanation of natural selection:

   When a heritable trait provides some individuals in a population with higher fitness under specific conditions, organisms with that trait tend to become more common.

   Support this explanation using the data shown in the circle graphs, and by applying concepts of statistics and probability.

Cotton farmers face many challenges, including weeds.

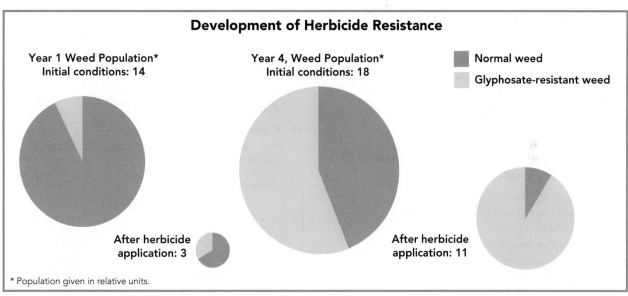

**Development of Herbicide Resistance**

Year 1 Weed Population*
Initial conditions: 14

Year 4, Weed Population*
Initial conditions: 18

■ Normal weed
□ Glyphosate-resistant weed

After herbicide
application: 3

After herbicide
application: 11

* Population given in relative units.

Based on information from Grains Research & Development Corporation

3. **Conduct Research** One company has recently been given approval to produce genetically modified varieties of cotton and soybeans that are resistant to the weeds. Research these new weed-resistant varieties. What are the pros and cons of the commercial use of these genetically modified crops?

4. **Communicate** Prepare a poster, an oral or a written report, or a computer presentation to communicate your findings. Share your knowledge and conclusions with classmates.

## 🔍 KEY QUESTIONS AND TERMS

### 18.1 Genes and Variation

**HS-LS3-2, HS-LS3-3, HS-LS4-2**

1. The combined genetic information of all members of a particular population forms a
   a. gene pool.
   b. niche.
   c. phenotype.
   d. population.

2. Mutations that improve an individual's ability to survive and reproduce are
   a. harmful.
   b. neutral.
   c. beneficial.
   d. chromosomal.

3. Traits, such as human height, that are controlled by more than one gene are known as
   a. single-gene traits.
   b. polygenic traits.
   c. recessive traits.
   d. dominant traits.

4. Explain what the term *allele frequency* means. Include an example illustrating your answer.

5. Explain what determines the number of phenotypes for a given trait.

6. What is *lateral gene transfer*?

7. Define evolution in genetic terms.

### 18.2 Evolution as Genetic Change

**HS-LS3-3, HS-LS4-2, HS-LS4-3**

8. The type of selection in which individuals of average size have greater fitness than small or large individuals is called
   a. disruptive selection.
   b. stabilizing selection.
   c. directional selection.
   d. neutral selection.

9. A random change in a small population's allele frequency is known as
   a. a gene pool.
   b. genetic drift.
   c. variation.
   d. fitness.

10. The situation in which allele frequencies change as a result of the migration of a small subgroup of a population is known as
    a. the bottleneck effect.
    b. the founder effect.
    c. genetic equilibrium.
    d. sexual selection.

11. What effect does natural selection have on single-gene traits?

12. How do stabilizing selection and disruptive selection differ?

13. What is genetic equilibrium? In what kinds of situations is it likely to occur?

### 18.3 The Process of Speciation

**HS-LS4-2, HS-LS4-5**

14. Temporal isolation occurs when two different populations
    a. develop different mating behaviors.
    b. become geographically separated.
    c. reproduce at different times.
    d. interbreed.

15. When two populations no longer interbreed, what is the result?
    a. genetic equilibrium
    b. reproductive isolation
    c. stabilizing selection
    d. artificial selection

16. If coat color in a rabbit population is a polygenic trait, which process might have produced the graph below?

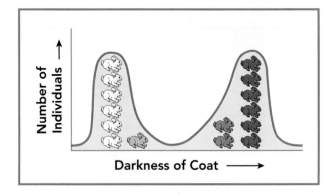

17. Describe three ways populations can become reproductively isolated.

18. List three types of geographic barriers that may lead to the geographic isolation of a species.

## 18.4 Molecular Evolution

HS-LS3-2

**19.** A group of regulatory genes that determine which parts of an embryo develop into arms, legs, or wings are known as
**a.** polygenic genes.
**b.** molecular clocks.
**c.** neutral genes.
**d.** Hox genes.

**20.** Each "tick" of a molecular clock is an occurrence of
**a.** genetic drift.  **c.** DNA mutation.
**b.** crossing-over.  **d.** mitosis.

**21.** How do chromosomes gain an extra copy of a gene during meiosis?

**22.** What is the study of "evo-devo," and how is it related to evolution?

**23.** What are neutral mutations?

## CRITICAL THINKING

HS-LS3-3, HS-LS4-3, HS-LS4-4, HS-LS4-5

**24.** **Cite Evidence** In the DNA of any individual human, about 300 mutations may differentiate the genome from either parent. As a result of the mutations, should an individual expect 300 distinct effects in phenotype? Or is the number of effects much fewer? Cite evidence about DNA and its role in controlling traits to support your answer.

**25.** **Infer** A black guinea pig and a white guinea pig mate and have offspring. All the offspring are black. Is the trait of coat color probably a single-gene trait or a polygenic trait? Explain.

**26.** **Predict** A newly formed lake divides a population of a beetle species into two groups. What other factors besides isolation might lead to the two groups becoming separate species?

**27.** **Use Models** The Hardy-Weinberg principle provides a model for genetic equilibrium in a species. Why is random mating a necessary assumption for this model?

**28.** **Synthesize Information** Why are many islands, such as the Galápagos Islands, home to species that differ from those on the nearby mainland?

**29.** **Predict** Pine trees grow throughout a large tract of forest. Suppose a highway is built through the forest, effectively dividing it in half. Is it likely that the two groups of pine trees will evolve separately? Explain your prediction.

**30.** **Construct an Explanation** How are changes in Hox genes significant in the evolution of species?

**31.** **Apply Scientific Reasoning** Scientists compare the DNA of two species to draw conclusions about their evolutionary relationship, and determine when the species diverged from a common ancestor. What assumption about mutations is necessary to support these types of conclusions?

In turkeys, feather color is controlled by several genes, each with at least two alleles. In a population of turkeys, the trait of black feathers is gradually becoming more common than the trait of bronze feathers. Use this information to answer questions 32–34.

**32.** **Draw Conclusions** Can you conclude that the gene pool for feather color is changing in the turkey population? Explain your reasoning and identify a possible change in the gene pool that could be occurring.

**33.** **Construct an Explanation** Apply Darwin's theory of natural selection to explain why the trait of black feathers might be becoming more common.

**34.** **Integrate Information** Some turkeys live in the wild, while others are domesticated. How does the type of turkey population (wild or domesticated) affect the explanation you constructed about the changes to the population?

## CROSSCUTTING CONCEPTS

**35. Cause and Effect** Why does sexual reproduction provide more opportunities for genetic variation than asexual reproduction?

**36. Connect to Society** Why is it important for physicians to keep some antibiotics in reserve, using them only for the most serious infections?

## MATH CONNECTIONS

### Analyze and Interpret Data

HS-LS3-3, HS-LS4-3, CCSS.MATH.CONTENT.MP4,
CCSS.MATH.CONTENT.HSS.IC.B.6

A research team studied two lakes in an area that sometimes experiences flooding. Each lake contained two types of similar fishes: a dull brown form and an iridescent gold form. The team wondered how all the fishes were related, and they considered the two hypotheses in the diagram. Use this information and the diagram to answer questions 37–39.

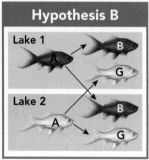

A = Possible ancestor
B = Contemporary brown form
G = Contemporary gold form

→ Shows possible line of descent

**37. Use Models** Study the two diagrams. What does hypothesis A indicate about the ancestry of the fishes in Lake 1 and Lake 2? What does hypothesis B indicate?

**38. Compare and Contrast** According to the two hypotheses, what is the key difference in the way the brown and gold fish populations might have formed?

**39. Construct Explanations** A DNA analysis showed that the brown and gold fishes from Lake 1 are the most closely related. Which hypothesis does this evidence support?

Use the data table to answer questions 40 and 41.

| Frequency of Alleles | | |
|---|---|---|
| Year | Frequency of Allele B | Frequency of Allele b |
| 1910 | 0.81 | 0.19 |
| 1930 | 0.49 | 0.51 |
| 1950 | 0.25 | 0.75 |
| 1970 | 0.10 | 0.90 |

**40. Interpret Data** Describe the trend shown by the data in the table.

**41. Analyze Data** What might account for the trend shown by the data?

## LANGUAGE ARTS CONNECTION

### Write About Science

HS-LS4-4, CCSS.ELA-LITERACY.WHST.9-10.2,
CCSS.ELA-LITERACY.WHST.9-10.9

**42. Write Explanatory Texts** Write a paragraph to explain how reproductive isolation may lead to speciation. Include references to **Figure 18-8** to help support your explanation.

**43. Draw Evidence** At least 13 species of finches live on the Galápagos Islands. Did a small population of finches colonize the islands, and then evolve into the 13 species? Write an argument for or against this conclusion. Draw evidence and use logical reasoning to support your answer.

### Read About Science

CCSS.ELA-LITERACY.RST.9-10.2

**44. Summarize Text** How can random events affect evolution?

# END-OF-COURSE TEST PRACTICE

1. The table provides information about a population in which natural selection acts on a single-gene trait.

| Frequency of Alleles | | |
|---|---|---|
| Year | Frequency of Allele *B* | Frequency of Allele *b* |
| 1910 | 0.81 | 0.19 |
| 1930 | 0.49 | 0.51 |
| 1950 | 0.25 | 0.75 |
| 1970 | 0.10 | 0.90 |

What can be inferred from the information in the table?

A. Diversity in the gene pool increased over time.

B. Allele *B* was dominant in 1910 but became recessive over time.

C. The population was in genetic equilibrium during this time period.

D. The probability of genotype *Bb* increased over time.

E. The likelihood of surviving and reproducing became higher for individuals with Allele *b* than for individuals with Allele *B*.

2. Scientists want to estimate the time when two species began evolving separately from a common ancestor. What would be the most useful strategy for calculating this estimate?

A. comparing DNA sequences from each species for the same gene

B. comparing DNA sequences from each species for different genes

C. comparing the length, size, or weight of an average member of each species

D. identifying the traits of the common ancestor

E. identifying the genetic diversity of each species

3. The graphs below show the changes in crab color at one beach.

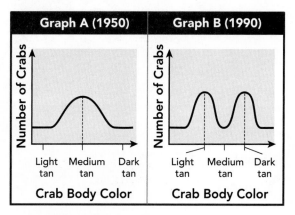

Which of the following is most likely to have caused the change in the distribution?

A. A new predator arrived that preferred dark-tan crabs.

B. A new predator arrived that preferred light-tan crabs.

C. A change in beach color made medium-tan crabs the least visible to predators.

D. A change in beach color made medium-tan crabs the most visible to predators.

E. A change in beach color made light-tan crabs the most visible to predators.

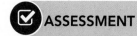 **ASSESSMENT**

For additional assessment practice, go online to access your digital course.

| If You Have Trouble With... | | | |
|---|---|---|---|
| Question | 1 | 2 | 3 |
| See Lesson | 18.2 | 18.4 | 18.2 |
| Performance Expectation | HS-LS3-3 | HS-LS4-5 | HS-LS4-3 |

CHAPTER

19

# Biodiversity and Classification

19.1
Finding Order in Biodiversity

19.2
Modern Evolutionary Classification

**Go Online to access your digital course.**

▶ VIDEO

🔊 AUDIO

👆 INTERACTIVITY

📖 eTEXT

👁 ANIMATION

⚗ VIRTUAL LAB

☑ ASSESSMENT

# It's a duck! No, it's a beaver! No, it's a platypus!

> The first European scientist to see a specimen labeled it a hoax—although he did give it a scientific name. An anatomist called it an "amphibious creature of the mole kind." It had webbed feet with claws, an otter's body, a beaver's tail, and a duck's beak. Males carried spurs that delivered snake-like venom. Was it fake? Or was it real?

Australia's native people have known about the curious creature we call a platypus for a very long time. One of their myths suggests that a particularly determined water rat somehow managed to mate with a female duck. The off-spring combine their father's four legs and fur, with their mother's beak and webbed feet. (Not likely in the real world.)

When a scientist at the British Museum first saw a dried specimen, he doubted "the genuine nature of the animal." In fact, he cut around the beak, trying to show that someone had sewn a bird's beak onto a mammal skin. (He failed.)

Only after many specimens showed up in museums, and lots more reports of live platypus came in from Australia, did Europeans finally admit that the creatures were real. They then tried to figure out where this oddball animal belonged in the scheme of life they were constructing. (They got very confused.)

A platypus is about the size of a beaver, with a furry body and a broad tail. It lives in rivers, lakes, and streams. Females produce and feed their young milk. And males' reproductive organs resemble those of mammals.

So … are they mammals? Maybe. But females' reproductive organs share a mix of reptilian and mammalian traits. They lay eggs with leathery shells. Males' venom resembles that of snakes and other reptiles. And their four limbs point outward from the sides of their bodies like those of alligators and crocodiles.

So … are they reptiles? Perhaps. But the platypus also has features more often seen in birds, such as a beak that looks remarkably like the ones ducks use to dig through the muck of rivers and streams. Females incubate eggs for about 10 days.

Eventually, biologists decided—correctly—that these strange creatures were very odd mammals. They are further placed into an ancient group of egg-laying mammals called monotremes, whose ancestors split off from ancestors of other mammals back during the days of the dinosaurs. Why mammals? Hair or fur and the production of milk for young are characteristics that distinguish all mammals from all other animal groups. Recent studies of the platypus genome confirm that they carry some genes similar to those of birds, some similar to genes of reptiles, and some like those of other mammals.

What can the platypus teach us about the evolution of mammals? Why are monotremes classified as mammals?

**Throughout this chapter, look for connections to the** CASE STUDY **to help you answer these questions.**

# Finding Order in Biodiversity

*Puma concolor*

## KEY QUESTIONS

- *What are the goals of binomial nomenclature and taxonomy?*
- *How did Linnaeus group species into larger taxa?*
- *What are the six kingdoms of life as they are now identified?*

## VOCABULARY

**taxonomy**
**binomial nomenclature**
**genus**
**systematics**
**taxon**
**family**
**order**
**class**
**phylum**
**kingdom**
**domain**

### READING TOOL

In your 📖 **Biology Foundations Workbook**, order the events listed to describe the history of how scientists have organized and labeled living organisms.

As European scientists traveled the world, they discovered plants and animals they had never seen before. They were eager to communicate with each other about their discoveries. But the common names for organisms back then varied a lot from place to place. In fact, common names can still be confusing today. For example, in the United States, this big cat may be known as a cougar, a mountain lion, or a puma. Some of its Spanish common names are león Americano, león bayo, león Colorado, and onza bermeja! So, it isn't surprising that biologists need a scientific system to universally identify species.

## Assigning Scientific Names

Biologists now identify and organize biodiversity through a standardized system. **Taxonomy** is a system of naming and classifying organisms based on shared characteristics and universal rules. Each scientific name must refer to one and only one species. Scientists must all agree to use the same name for that species.

At first, European scientists tried to assign Latin or Greek names to each species. Unhappily, that idea didn't work well. Early scientific names often described species in great detail, so names could be ridiculously long. For example, the English translation of the scientific name of a tree might be "Oak with deeply divided leaves that have no hairs on their undersides and no teeth around their edges." It was also difficult to standardize these names.

**Binomial Nomenclature** In the 1730s, Swedish botanist Carolus Linnaeus developed a naming system called **binomial nomenclature**. The system proved very successful and popular, and is still in use today. 🔍 *In binomial nomenclature, each species is assigned a two-part scientific name.* Scientific names are written in italics. The first word begins with a capital letter, and the second word is in lowercase.

For example, the scientific name of the polar bear shown in **Figure 19-1** is *Ursus maritimus*. The first part of that name—*Ursus*—is the genus to which the species belongs. A **genus** (plural: genera, JEN ur uh) is a group of similar species. The genus *Ursus* contains five other species of bears, such as *Ursus arctos*, the brown bear or grizzly bear, and *Ursus americanus*, the American black bear. The second part of a scientific name is often a description of an important trait or the organism's habitat. The Latin word *maritimus* refers to the sea, because polar bears often live on pack ice that floats in the sea.

**VIDEO**

Discover what it is like to find a new species.

**Classifying Species into Larger Groups** In addition to naming organisms, biologists classify living and fossil species into larger groups. Whether you realize it or not, you classify things all the time. You may, for example, talk about "teachers" or "mechanics." Sometimes you refer to a more specific group, such as "biology teachers" or "auto mechanics." When you do this, you refer to these groups using widely accepted names and characteristics that many people understand.

The science of naming and grouping organisms is called **systematics** (sis tuh MAT iks). ✎ *The goal of systematics is to organize living things into groups that have biological meaning.* Biologists often refer to these groups as **taxa** (singular: taxon).

✓ **READING CHECK** **Synthesize** What are the parts of a scientific name for an organism?

**Figure 19-1**

**Binomial Nomenclature**

Different species within the same genus, such as these bears, lemurs, and oak trees, share many characteristics in common, but differ from each other in distinctive ways.

*Ursus arctos*

*Ursus maritimus*

*Eulemur coronatus*

*Eulemur macaco*

*Quercus robur*

*Quercus virginiana*

# The Linnaean Classification System

Linnaeus developed a classification system that organized species into taxa based on similarities and differences he could see. ✎ *Over time, Linnaeus's original classification system expanded to include seven hierarchical taxa: species, genus, family, order, class, phylum, and kingdom.*

**Species and Genus** Let's explore this classification system using camels as our subject. The scientific name of a camel with two humps is *Camelus bactrianus*. The second part of the name refers to Bactria, an ancient country in Asia. As you can see in **Figure 19-2**, the genus *Camelus* also includes another species, *Camelus dromedarius*, the dromedary, which has only one hump.

**Family** Bactrian camels and dromedaries resemble llamas, which live in South America. But llamas are more similar to other South American species than they are to Asian and African camels. Therefore, llamas are placed in a different genus, *Lama*, and their species name is *Lama glama*. The genera *Camelus* and *Lama* are grouped with other genera that share many similarities into a larger taxon, the **family** Camelidae.

**Order** Closely related families are grouped into the next larger taxon, called an **order**. Camels and llamas (family Camelidae) are grouped with several other animal families, including deer (family Cervidae) and cattle (family Bovidae). They form the order Artiodactyla, which includes hoofed animals with an even number of toes.

**INTERACTIVITY**

Explore classification using the Linnaean system.

**CASE STUDY**

Figure 19-2

**From Species to Kingdom**

From species to kingdom, *Camelus bactrianus* is organized in larger and larger groups. ☑ **Interpret Visuals** What is the most specific group to which both camels and platypuses belong?

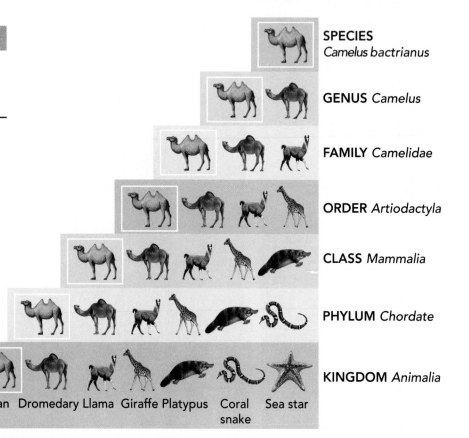

**SPECIES** *Camelus bactrianus*

**GENUS** *Camelus*

**FAMILY** *Camelidae*

**ORDER** *Artiodactyla*

**CLASS** *Mammalia*

**PHYLUM** *Chordate*

**KINGDOM** *Animalia*

Bactrian camel   Dromedary   Llama   Giraffe   Platypus   Coral snake   Sea star

**Class** Similar orders, in turn, are grouped into the next larger rank, a **class**. The order Artiodactyla is placed in the class Mammalia. The mammals include all animals that are warmblooded, have body hair, and produce milk for their young.

**Phylum** Classes are grouped into a **phylum**. A phylum includes organisms that can look different, but share important characteristics. The class Mammalia is placed in the phylum Chordata. The chordates are animals that share a body feature called a nerve cord along the back and other important body features. Phylum Chordata includes mammals, birds (class Aves), reptiles (class Reptilia), amphibians (class Amphibia), and all classes of fishes.

**Kingdom** The largest and most inclusive of traditional taxonomic categories is the **kingdom**. All multicellular animals are placed in the kingdom Animalia.

**Classification Changes with New Discoveries** In a sense, organisms determine on their own who belongs to their species. How? By deciding with whom they mate! If individuals living under natural conditions mate and produce fertile offspring, those parents and offspring are members of the same species. That's a simple "natural" way to define species, the smallest important taxon.

Higher taxa, on the other hand, are defined by rules created by researchers like Linnaeus. He classified organisms according to rules based on similarities and differences he could see. But that can get tricky. Look at the animals in **Figure 19-3**. Adult barnacles and limpets both live attached to rocks, and have similar-looking shells. Adult crabs, on the other hand, scramble around on jointed legs. Based on these easily visible characteristics, would you classify limpets and barnacles together, and put crabs in a different group?

As biologists attempted to classify more and more organisms, these kinds of questions arose frequently. Which characteristics are most important? In addition, ongoing discoveries in genetics, cell biology, and development revealed scores of new and different characteristics. Rules for ranking the importance of those characteristics in forming higher taxa groups have changed over time. In addition, biologists today want classification to reflect Darwinian theory by grouping organisms into taxa that reflect how closely related they are to each other.

**READING CHECK** Synthesize What are the seven taxa in hierarchical order, from most general to most specific?

**BUILD VOCABULARY**

**Multiple Meanings** The words *family*, *order*, *class*, and *kingdom* all mean something different in everyday usage than they do in biological classification. For example, in everyday usage, a *family* is a group of people who are related to one another. In systematics, a *family* is a group of genera. Use a dictionary to find the common meanings of *order*, *class*, and *kingdom*.

**INTERACTIVITY**

Figure 19-3

## Classifying Organisms by Appearance

Barnacles may appear similar to limpets, but their interiors show more structural similiarity to crabs. These animals show the difficulty of classifying organisms by appearances alone.

Crab

Limpets

Barnacles

## Quick Lab — Guided Inquiry

### Using a Dichotomous Key

A.     B.     C.

A dichotomous key is a series of steps that lead to a classification of an organism. It consists of a series of paired statements that describe alternative characteristics of organisms. Use the key to identify the type of tree that produced each leaf. Begin with Step 1. Your answer to each step will either bring you to the next step or identify the tree. The results will show either the next step or the name of the tree.

### ANALYZE AND CONCLUDE

1. **Classify** Identify the type of tree that produced leaves A, B, and C.
2. **Identify Patterns** Use the objects provided by your teacher to make your own dichotomous key.

| Dichotomous Key for Classifying Leaves | | |
|---|---|---|
| **Step** | **Leaf Characteristics** | **Result** |
| 1a | Compound leaf, divided into leaflets | Go to step 2 |
| 1b | Simple leaf, not divided into leaflets | Go to step 4 |
| 2a | Leaflets all attached at a central point | Buckeye |
| 2b | Leaflets attached at several points | Go to step 3 |
| 3a | Leaflets tapered with pointed tips | Pecan |
| 3b | Leaflets oval with rounded tips | Locust |
| 4a | Veins branched out from one central point | Go to step 5 |
| 4b | Veins branched off main vein in middle of the leaf | Go to step 6 |
| 5a | Heart-shaped leaf | Redbud |
| 5b | Star-shaped leaf | Sweet gum |
| 6a | Leaf with jagged edges | Birch |
| 6b | Oval leaf | Magnolia |

# Changing Ideas About Kingdoms

During Linnaeus's time, the only known fundamental differences among living things were the characteristics that separated animals from plants. For this reason, the two kingdoms of this time were Animalia and Plantae. Over time, biologists learned more about the natural world. The classification systems have changed dramatically, as shown in **Figure 19-4**.

**From Two to Six Kingdoms** Researchers found faults with the two-kingdom system when they began to study microorganisms. They discovered that single-celled organisms were significantly different from plants and animals. At first, they placed all microorganisms in a single kingdom, called Protista. Then yeasts, molds, and multicellular mushrooms were placed in the new kingdom Fungi.

Later still, scientists realized that bacteria lack the nuclei, mitochondria, and chloroplasts found in other forms of life. All prokaryotes were placed in another new kingdom, called Monera. Single-celled eukaryotic organisms remained in the kingdom Protista. This process produced five kingdoms: Monera, Protista, Fungi, Plantae, and Animalia.

By the 1990s, researchers had learned enough about bacteria to realize that some organisms lumped together as Monera were very different from one another genetically and biochemically. As a result, monerans were separated into two kingdoms, Eubacteria and Archaebacteria. The total number of kingdoms is now six. ☌ **The six-kingdom system of classification includes the kingdoms Eubacteria, Archaebacteria, Protista, Fungi, Plantae, and Animalia.** This system of classification is shown in the bottom row of the chart in **Figure 19-4**.

## Visual Summary
### Figure 19-4
## Kingdoms Over Time

This diagram shows some of the ways in which organisms have been classified into kingdoms since the 1700s.

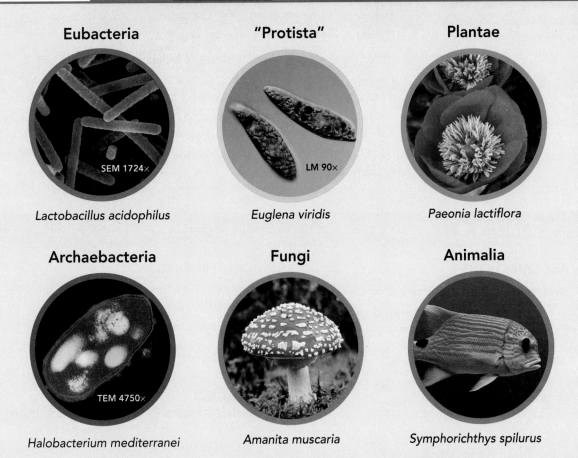

| Kingdoms of Life, 1700s–1990s | | | | | | |
|---|---|---|---|---|---|---|
| **First Introduced** | **Names of Kingdoms** | | | | | |
| 1700s | Plantae | | | | | Animalia |
| Late 1800s | Protista | | | Plantae | | Animalia |
| 1950s | Monera | | "Protista" | Fungi | Plantae | Animalia |
| 1990s | Eubacteria | Archaebacteria | "Protista" | Fungi | Plantae | Animalia |

**Eubacteria**

SEM 1724×

*Lactobacillus acidophilus*

**"Protista"**

LM 90×

*Euglena viridis*

**Plantae**

*Paeonia lactiflora*

**Archaebacteria**

TEM 4750×

*Halobacterium mediterranei*

**Fungi**

*Amanita muscaria*

**Animalia**

*Symphorichthys spilurus*

| Classification of Living Things | | | | | | |
|---|---|---|---|---|---|---|
| **DOMAIN** | **Bacteria** | **Archaea** | **Eukarya** | | | |
| **KINGDOM** | **Eubacteria** | **Archaebacteria** | **"Protista"** | **Fungi** | **Plantae** | **Animalia** |
| **CELL TYPE** | Prokaryote | Prokaryote | Eukaryote | Eukaryote | Eukaryote | Eukaryote |
| **CELL STRUCTURES** | Cell walls with peptidoglycan | Cell walls without peptidoglycan | Cell walls of cellulose in some; some have chloroplasts | Cell walls of chitin | Cell walls of cellulose; chloroplasts | No cell walls or chloroplasts |
| **NUMBER OF CELLS** | Unicellular | Unicellular | Most unicellular; some colonial; some multicellular | Most multicellular; some unicellular | Most multicellular; some green algae unicellular | Multicellular |
| **MODE OF NUTRITION** | Autotroph or heterotroph | Autotroph or heterotroph | Autotroph or heterotroph | Heterotroph | Autotroph | Heterotroph |
| **EXAMPLES** | *Streptococcus, Escherichia coli* | Methanogens, halophiles | *Amoeba, Paramecium,* slime molds, giant kelp | Mushrooms, yeasts | Mosses, ferns, flowering plants | Sponges, worms, insects, fishes, mammals |

**Figure 19-5**

**Three Domains**

Today, organisms are commonly grouped into three domains and six kingdoms. This table summarizes the key characteristics used to classify organisms into these higher taxa.

**Three Domains** Still more recent genomic analysis has revealed that the two main prokaryotic groups are even more different from each other, and from eukaryotes, than previously thought. So biologists established a new taxonomic category—the domain. A **domain** is even larger than a kingdom. The three are Bacteria (the old kingdom Eubacteria), Archaea (the old kingdom Archaebacteria), and Eukarya (kingdoms Fungi, Plantae, Animalia, and "Protista"), as shown in **Figure 19-5**.

Why do we put quotation marks around the old kingdom Protista? Recent research shows that there is no way to put all unicellular eukaryotes into a taxon that contains a single common ancestor, all of its descendants, and only those descendants. Since only that kind of taxon is valid under evolutionary classification, quotation marks are used to show that this is not a taxon of the sort modern biologists prefer.

## ☑ LESSON 19.1 Review

### 🔍 KEY QUESTIONS

1. Identify two goals of systematics.

2. In which group of organisms are the members more closely related—all of the organisms in the same kingdom or all of the organisms in the same order? Explain your answer.

3. How do the six kingdoms fit into the three domains?

### CRITICAL THINKING

4. **Define the Problem** What problem is solved by the Linnaean system of classification?

5. **Identify Patterns** A starfish and a sea cucumber are both members of the same phylum, called Echinodermata. From this information, what other taxa can you conclude that they share?

6. **CASE STUDY** The platypus is the only living member of the family Ornithorhynchidae. Based on this information, what conclusion can you make about its genus?

# Modern Evolutionary Classification

## KEY QUESTIONS

- *What is the goal of evolutionary classification?*
- *What is a cladogram?*
- *How are DNA sequences used in classification?*
- *What does the tree of life show?*

HS-LS4-1: Communicate scientific information that common ancestry and biological evolution are supported by multiple lines of empirical evidence.

**VOCABULARY**

phylogeny
clade
cladogram
**derived character**

**READING TOOL**

As you read, define and give examples of derived characters and lost traits. Fill in the table in your 📖 **Biology Foundations Workbook.**

Darwin's "tree of life" suggests a way to classify organisms based on how closely related they are. When taxa are rearranged this way, some old Linnaean ranks fall apart. For example, the Linnaean class Reptilia isn't valid unless birds are included—which means birds are reptiles! And not only are birds reptiles, they are also descended from dinosaurs! Wondering why? To understand, we need to look at the way evolutionary classification works.

## Evolutionary Classification

The core Darwinian concept of descent with modification revolutionized classification. First, Darwinian theory gave birth to the field of phylogeny. **Phylogeny** (fy LAHJ uh nee) is the study of the evolutionary history of lineages of organisms. Advances in phylogeny, in turn, led to evolutionary classification. 🔑 *The goal of evolutionary classification is to group species into larger categories that reflect lines of evolutionary descent, rather than overall similarities and differences.*

Evolutionary classification places organisms into higher taxa whose members are more closely related to one another than they are to members of any other group. The larger a taxon is, the farther back in time all of its members shared a common ancestor. This is true all the way up to the largest taxa—the domains described in the last lesson.

Classifying organisms according to these rules places them into groups called clades. A **clade** is a group of species that includes a single common ancestor and all descendants of that ancestor—living and extinct. Some of the old higher taxa fit those requirements well. Other old taxa are not proper clades. Certain taxa fail the "clade test" because they include species descended from more than one different ancestor. Others (like the Linnaean class Reptilia) are not valid because they exclude some descendants of a single common ancestor (like birds).

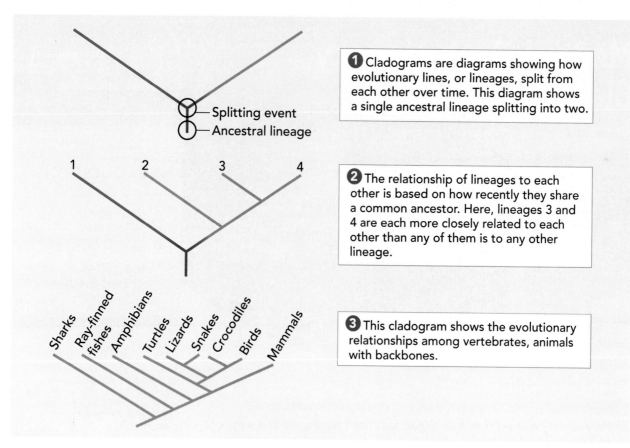

**1** Cladograms are diagrams showing how evolutionary lines, or lineages, split from each other over time. This diagram shows a single ancestral lineage splitting into two.

**2** The relationship of lineages to each other is based on how recently they share a common ancestor. Here, lineages 3 and 4 are each more closely related to each other than any of them is to any other lineage.

**3** This cladogram shows the evolutionary relationships among vertebrates, animals with backbones.

**Figure 19-6**

**Building a Cladogram**

A cladogram shows relative degrees of relatedness among lineages.

**INTERACTIVITY**

Complete a cladogram that shows the evolutionary history of plants.

# Cladograms

Modern evolutionary classification uses a method called cladistic analysis. Cladistic analysis compares carefully selected traits to determine the order in which groups of organisms branched off from their common ancestors. This information is then used to link clades together into a diagram called a **cladogram**. 🔍 *A cladogram links groups of organisms by showing current hypotheses about how evolutionary lines, or lineages, branched off from common ancestors.*

**Building Cladograms** To understand how cladograms are constructed, think back to the process of speciation and look at part 1 of **Figure 19-6**. Part 1 represents how one ancestral species branches into two species, each of which could found a new lineage. Now look at part 2. The bottom, or "root" of this cladogram, represents the common ancestor shared by all organisms in the cladogram. The branching pattern shows how closely related various lineages are. Each branch point represents the last point at which species in lineages above that point shared a common ancestor. Lineages 3 and 4 share a common ancestor more recently with each other than they do with lineage 2. So you know that lineages 3 and 4 are more closely related to each other than either is to lineage 2. The same is true for lineages 2, 3, and 4. All three of these groups are more closely related to each other than any of them is to lineage 1. Now look at part 3 of the figure. Does it surprise you that amphibians are more closely related to mammals than they are to ray-finned fish?

**Derived Characters** Cladistic analysis focuses on certain kinds of characters, called derived characters. A **derived character** is a trait that arose in the most recent common ancestor of a lineage and was passed to its descendants.

Whether or not a character is derived depends on the level at which you're grouping organisms. Here's what we mean. **Figure 19-7** shows several traits shared by coyotes and lions, members of the clades Tetrapoda, Mammalia, and Carnivora. Four limbs is a derived character for the entire clade Tetrapoda, because the common ancestor of all tetrapods had four limbs. But if we look just at mammals, four limbs is *not* a derived character. If it were, *only* mammals would have four limbs. Hair, on the other hand, is a derived character for the clade Mammalia. But neither four limbs nor hair is a derived character for clade Carnivora. Why? Other species not in this clade also have four limbs (i.e. frogs) or hair (i.e. rodents). Specialized shearing teeth, however, is a derived character for Carnivora. What about retractable claws? This trait is found in lions, but not in coyotes. Thus, retractable claws is a derived character for the clade Felidae, a subgroup of Carnivora that consists of cats.

**Losing Traits** As stated, four limbs is a derived character for clade Tetrapoda. But what about snakes? Snakes are reptiles, which are tetrapods. But snakes don't have four limbs! The *ancestors* of snakes, however, did have four limbs. Somewhere in the lineage leading to modern snakes, that trait was lost. Because distantly related groups can sometimes lose a character, systematists are cautious about using the *absence* of a trait as a character in their analyses. After all, whales don't have four limbs either, but snakes are certainly more closely related to other reptiles than they are to whales.

✅ **READING CHECK** **Classify** Are both coyotes and lions a member of the clade Carnivora? Explain.

**BUILD VOCABULARY**

**Academic Words** The term underlined derived refers to a beginning or origin. Some English words, for example, are derived from other languages. A **derived character** is a trait that has a common origin in a clade.

**Figure 19-7**
**Derived Characters**

Shared characters put both lions and coyotes in several clades, including Tetrapoda (four legs), Mammalia (hair), and Carnivora (shearing teeth). Only the lion, however, has retractable claws, a derived character for the clade Felidae.

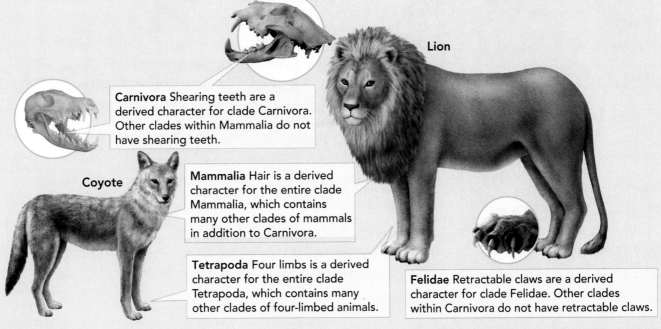

**Carnivora** Shearing teeth are a derived character for clade Carnivora. Other clades within Mammalia do not have shearing teeth.

Lion

Coyote

**Mammalia** Hair is a derived character for the entire clade Mammalia, which contains many other clades of mammals in addition to Carnivora.

**Tetrapoda** Four limbs is a derived character for the entire clade Tetrapoda, which contains many other clades of four-limbed animals.

**Felidae** Retractable claws are a derived character for clade Felidae. Other clades within Carnivora do not have retractable claws.

**Interpreting Cladograms** Look at **Figure 19-8**, which shows a simplified phylogeny of the cat family. The lowest branching point represents the last common ancestor of all four-limbed animals, which are members of the clade Tetrapoda. The forks in this cladogram show the order in which various groups branched off from the tetrapod lineage. The positions of various characters in the cladogram reflect the order in which those characteristics arose. Hair, for example, is a defining character for the clade Mammalia. In the lineage leading to cats, specialized shearing teeth evolved before retractable claws.

Furthermore, each derived character listed along the main trunk of the cladogram defines a clade. Retractable claws is a derived character shared only by the clade Felidae. Derived characters that occur "lower" on the cladogram than the branch point for a clade are not derived for that particular clade. Note that hair is a derived character for the entire clade Mammalia, but it is not a derived character for the branch of mammals in the clade Carnivora.

## Clades and Traditional Groups

Which Linnaean groupings form clades, and which do not? Remember that a true clade must contain an ancestral species and *all* of its descendants, with no exceptions. It also must exclude all species that are not descendants of the original ancestor. Cladistic analysis shows that many traditional taxonomic groups form valid clades. For example, Linnaean class Mammalia corresponds to clade Mammalia.

**CASE STUDY**

Figure 19-8

## Interpreting a Cladogram

In a cladogram, all organisms in a clade share a set of derived characters. Notice that smaller clades are nested within larger clades. ☑**Interpret Visuals** For which clade is an amniotic egg a derived character? Is the duck-billed platypus a member of the clade Amniota? Explain.

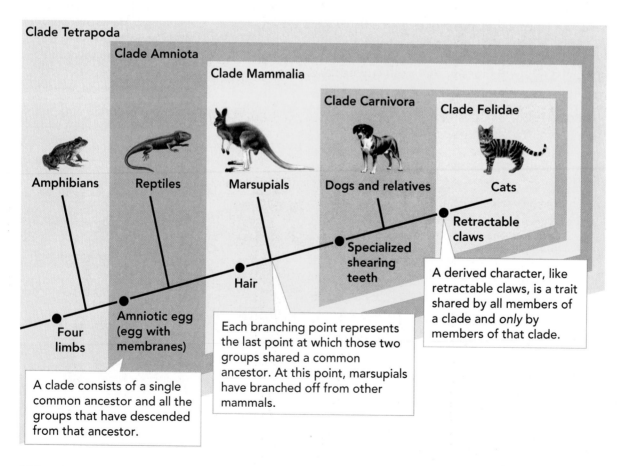

Clade Tetrapoda

Clade Amniota

Clade Mammalia

Clade Carnivora

Clade Felidae

Amphibians    Reptiles    Marsupials    Dogs and relatives    Cats

Retractable claws

Specialized shearing teeth

Hair

Four limbs

Amniotic egg (egg with membranes)

A derived character, like retractable claws, is a trait shared by all members of a clade and *only* by members of that clade.

Each branching point represents the last point at which those two groups shared a common ancestor. At this point, marsupials have branched off from other mammals.

A clade consists of a single common ancestor and all the groups that have descended from that ancestor.

**Figure 19-9**

# Clade or Not?

A clade includes an ancestral species and all its descendants. Linnaean class Reptilia is not a clade because it does not include modern birds. Clades Reptilia and Aves are valid clades. Note that these cladograms include living groups only.

**Class Reptilia: Not a Clade**

**Clade Reptilia**

**Clade Aves**

In other cases, however, traditional groups are not valid clades, as **Figure 19-9** shows. Today's reptiles are all descended from a common ancestor. Birds were traditionally treated as a separate class, Aves. But birds are descended from that same common ancestor as reptiles. So class Reptilia, without birds, is not a clade. There are several valid clades that *do* include birds: Aves, Dinosauria, and the clade Reptilia. Can you now see why biologists say that birds are dinosaurs?

You may wonder: class Reptilia, clade Reptilia—who cares? But these names represent important concepts in classification. Remember that modern biologists want classification systems to represent the evolutionary relationships among organisms. Accurate understanding of those relationships can be very helpful in comparing and contrasting characteristics among and between clades.

✔ **READING CHECK** Compare What do all clades have in common, regardless of their size?

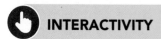

**INTERACTIVITY**

Classify five shark species based on morphology and DNA analysis.

# DNA in Classification

The examples of cladistic analysis we've discussed so far are based largely on physical characteristics like skeletons and teeth. However, the goal of modern systematics is to understand the evolutionary relationships of *all* life on Earth, including bacteria, plants, worms, and octopuses. How can we devise hypotheses about the common ancestors of organisms that have no physical similarities?

**Genes as Derived Characters**  Remember that all organisms carry genetic information in DNA. They inherit genes from earlier generations. As scientists have discovered, a wide range of organisms share genes that can be used to determine evolutionary relationships.

For example, all eukaryotic cells have mitochondria, and all mitochondria have their own genes. Because all genes mutate over time, shared genes contain differences that can be treated as derived characters in cladistic analysis. For that reason, similarities and differences in DNA can be used to develop hypotheses about evolutionary relationships. ⚲ *In general, the more derived genetic characters two species share, the more recently they shared a common ancestor and the more closely they are related in evolutionary terms.*

### Figure 19-10

### DNA and Classification

The two vultures appear very different from the stork. However, DNA analysis suggests that American vultures, such as the turkey vulture, are more closely related to storks than they are to other vultures.

American turkey vulture (*Cathartes aura*)

African hooded vulture
(*Necrosyrtes monachus*)

Saddle-billed stork (*Ephippiorhynchus senegalensis*)

Racoons
(*Procyon lotor*)

Red pandas
(*Ailurus fulgens*)

Giant pandas
(*Ailuropoda melanoleuca*)

Polar bears
(*Ursus maritimus*)

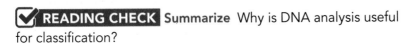

Common Ancestor

### Figure 19-11
### Classification of Pandas

Biologists used to classify the red panda and the giant panda together. However, cladistics analysis using DNA suggests that the giant panda shares a more recent common ancestor with bears than with either red pandas or raccoons.

**New Techniques Suggest New Trees** DNA analysis has helped to make evolutionary trees more accurate. Consider, for example, the birds shown in **Figure 19-10**. The hooded vulture from Africa looks a lot like the American turkey vulture. Both were traditionally classified in the Falcon clade. However, American vultures have a peculiar behavior: When they get overheated, they urinate on their legs, allowing evaporation to cool them down. Storks share this behavior, while hooded vultures and other vultures from Africa do not. Could the behavior be a clue to the real relationships between these birds?

Biologists solved the puzzle by analyzing DNA from all three species. Molecular analysis showed that the DNA from American vultures is more similar to the DNA of storks than to the DNA of African vultures. DNA evidence therefore suggests that American vultures and storks share a more recent common ancestor than the American and African vultures do.

Often, scientists use DNA evidence when anatomical traits alone cannot provide clear answers. Giant pandas and red pandas, for example, puzzled taxonomists for many years. These species share anatomical similarities with both bears and raccoons, and both have peculiar wrist bones that work like a human thumb. DNA analysis revealed that the giant panda shares a more recent common ancestor with bears than with raccoons. DNA places red pandas, however, outside the bear clade. So giant pandas have been reclassified, and are now placed with other bears in the clade Ursidae, as shown in **Figure 19-11**. The red panda is now placed in a different clade that also includes raccoons, seals, and weasels.

**READING CHECK** **Summarize** Why is DNA analysis useful for classification?

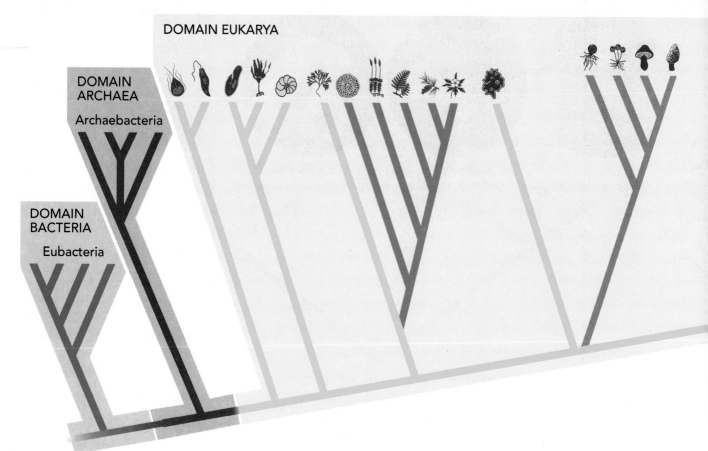

DOMAIN EUKARYA

DOMAIN ARCHAEA

Archaebacteria

DOMAIN BACTERIA

Eubacteria

**Figure 19-12**

**Tree of Life**

The tree of life shows the latest hypothesis about how major groups of organisms are related to one another. Note that both domain and kingdom designations are shown. ✅ **Classify** Which of the six kingdoms contains organisms that are not all in the same clade?

# The Tree of All Life

Modern evolutionary classification is a rapidly changing science with a difficult goal—to present all life on a single evolutionary tree. As new discoveries are made, biologists change the way organisms are grouped. Sometimes they change the names of groups. Remember that cladograms are visual presentations of hypotheses about relationships, and not final. 🔍 *The tree of all life illustrates current hypotheses regarding evolutionary relationships among the taxa within the three domains of life.* **Figure 19-12** shows a simplified version of the tree.

**Domain Bacteria** Members of the domain Bacteria are unicellular and prokaryotic. Their cells have thick, rigid walls that surround a cell membrane. The cell walls contain a substance known as peptidoglycan (pep tih doh GLY kun). These bacteria range from free-living soil organisms to deadly parasites. Some photosynthesize, while others do not. Some need oxygen to survive, while others are killed by oxygen. This domain corresponds to the old kingdom Eubacteria.

**Domain Archaea** Like Bacteria, members of the domain Archaea (ahr KEE uh) are also unicellular and prokaryotic. However, Archaea live in some of Earth's most extreme environments, such as volcanic hot springs, brine pools, and black organic mud totally devoid of oxygen. Indeed, many archaea can survive only in the absence of oxygen. Their cell walls lack peptidoglycan, and their cell membranes contain unusual lipids that are not found in any other organisms. The domain Archaea corresponds to the old kingdom Archaebacteria.

| | |
|---|---|
| ■ Eubacteria | ■ Plantae |
| ■ Archaebacteria | ■ Fungi |
| ■ "Protists" | ■ Animalia |

**Domain Eukarya** The domain Eukarya consists of all organisms that have a nucleus. It comprises the four remaining major groups of the old six-kingdom system: Protista, Fungi, Plantae, and Animalia.

*"Protists": Unicellular Eukaryotes* Remember that this old kingdom is *not* a valid clade. People still use the name "protists" casually to refer to these organisms. However, scientists have known for years that many of these organisms are fundamentally different from one another, so the casual name has little meaning. Figure 19-12 shows that current cladistic analysis divides these organisms into at least five clades. The positions of these groups on the cladogram reflect current hypotheses about their evolutionary histories.

The protists are divided into several separate clades that also include other types of species. Most clades are unicellular, but one clade, the brown algae, is multicellular. Some are photosynthetic, while others are heterotrophic.

*Fungi* Members of the kingdom Fungi are heterotrophs with cell walls containing chitin. Mushrooms are multicellular. Some fungi, including yeasts, are unicellular. Fungal ecology is complicated, although most obtain nutrients from organic matter. Many fungi once thought to be just decomposers also act as symbionts with the roots of plants.

*Plantae* Members of the kingdom Plantae are autotrophs with cell walls that contain cellulose. Autotrophic plants photosynthesize using chlorophyll. The plant kingdom includes green algae, mosses, ferns, cone-bearing plants, and flowering plants. Some species of green algae are unicellular, and others are multicellular. All other types of plants are multicellular.

*Animalia* Members of the kingdom Animalia are multicellular and heterotrophic. Animal cells do not have cell walls. Most animals can move about, at least for some part of their life cycle. There is incredible diversity within the animal kingdom.

**READING TOOL**

Use the visual to explain why "Protists" do not form a valid clade.

## Argument-Based Inquiry  Guided Inquiry

### Construct a Cladogram

**Problem** How can you use a cladogram to model the evolutionary relationship among species?

In this lab, you will make models of organisms to show evolutionary relationships. Then you will study a model made by another group. You will use your skills of observation and logical reasoning to identify the derived characters and construct a cladogram.

You can find this lab in your digital course.

### A Revised Tree of Life

The tree shown in Figure 19-12 is drawn to clearly illustrate current hypotheses about relationships among the groups of organisms that you are likely to know. That kind of tree, however, gives a couple of incorrect impressions. For one thing, its style of presentation suggests that mammals are the latest and greatest living things. It also misrepresents the relative numbers of organisms belonging to different clades. There are almost unimaginably large numbers of species in domains Eubacteria and Archaea, and equally overwhelming numbers of single-celled eukaryotes. Those clades literally dwarf the clades of multicellular fungi, plants, and animals that most people know best.

So what's the solution? What kind of cladogram could show a more accurate picture of the full diversity of life? To more accurately portray the living world, that kind of tree would spread organisms out to reflect the genetic diversity that underlies major differences in biochemistry and cell structure. The difficulty is that if we draw such a tree in the "normal" style for cladograms, it would spread out over several pages. One solution, proposed by biologist David Hillis, of the University of Texas at Austin, is shown in **Figure 19-13**. It provides a truer representation of the full diversity we know exists among living organisms.

## ✓ LESSON 19.2 Review

### ⚲ KEY IDEAS

1. How is the goal of evolutionary classification different from Linnaean classification?

2. What is the relationship between a clade and a cladogram?

3. How do taxonomists use the DNA sequences of species to determine how closely two species are related?

4. How is the tree of life related to the work of Charles Darwin?

### CRITICAL THINKING

5. Apply Scientific Reasoning  The family Camelidae includes camels and llamas. Do all the living members of the family form a clade? Explain.

6. CASE STUDY  A scientist studies the DNA in corresponding genes of a platypus, a beaver, and a duck. The DNA from which two species are most likely to be most similar? Explain your answer.

Figure 19-13

**Circular Model of the Diversity of Life**

This circular model shows how the diversity of life has increased over time.

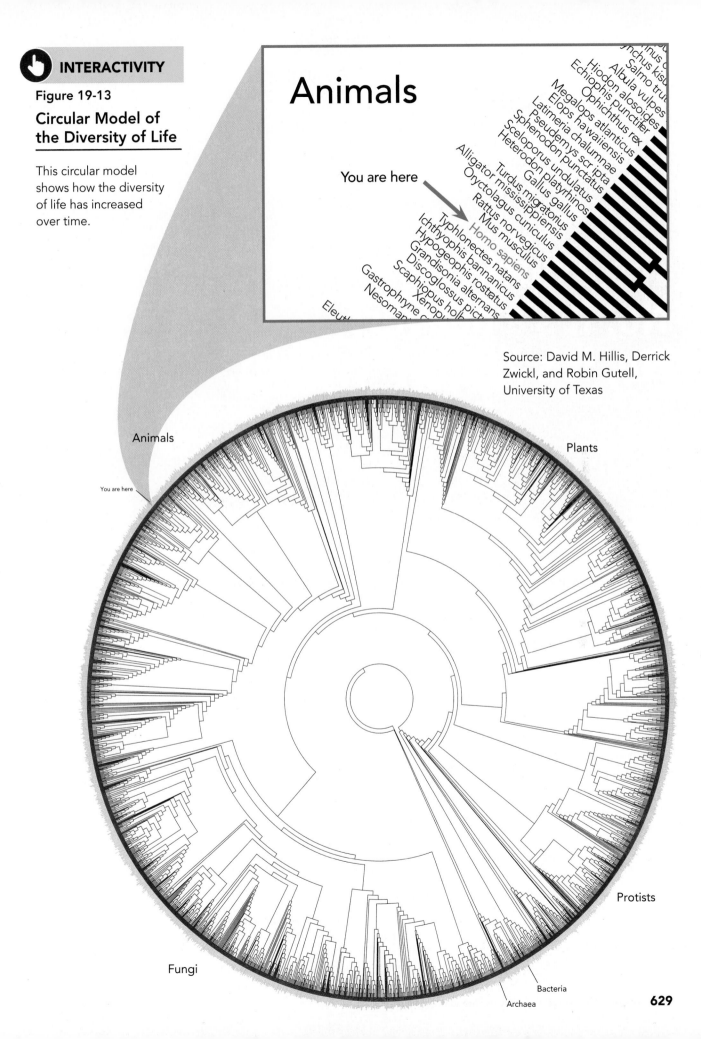

Animals

You are here

Source: David M. Hillis, Derrick Zwickl, and Robin Gutell, University of Texas

Animals

You are here

Plants

Protists

Fungi

Bacteria

Archaea

# It's a duck!
# No, it's a beaver!
# No, it's a platypus!

**Platypus lay eggs, yet suckle their young. These characteristics show how mammalian reproductive systems have evolved over time.**

HS-LS4-1

## Make Your Case

Carolus Linnaeus lived long before evolutionary theory and genetics provided a framework for biology. So, Linnaeus classified organisms based on shared visible characteristics, and had no scientific way to determine the relative importance of those characteristics in grouping organisms. No wonder it was difficult to use his system to classify oddballs like the platypus! Modern taxonomy includes anatomical, physiological, and genetic characteristics, and uses evolutionary theory to evaluate the relative importance of those traits in classification.

## Develop a Solution

1. **Construct an Explanation** Why did scientists in the 1800s struggle to classify the platypus, and how does evolutionary classification inform that task?

2. **Develop a Model** All mammals except monotremes give birth to live young. Research other shared and derived mammalian traits and construct a simple cladogram that shows the relationships among the three main groups of mammals: marsupials, monotremes, and placentals.

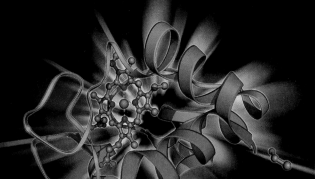

# Technology on the Case

## Genes, Computers, and Taxonomy

Early taxonomists relied on visible differences among organisms that could be seen with the naked eye. The invention and refinement of microscopes, the development of evolutionary theory, the ability to study amino acid sequences of ancient proteins, and techniques that enabled us to "read" information coded in DNA all triggered dramatic changes in the ways scientists name and classify organisms.

In recent years, advances in molecular biology and computer science have fueled incredible growth and change in taxonomy. A few decades ago, scientists struggled to study the amino acid sequences in ancient proteins like cytochrome c. Today, automated technology is able to sequence entire genomes in a few hours! This technology puts an astonishing amount of data at the disposal of taxonomists. A great gift to taxonomy? Absolutely! But the volume of those data creates a question: How do we understand and interpret all that information?

Recall that modern taxonomy attempts to classify organisms into groups that represent evolutionary lines of descent. For traits such as bones and teeth, fossils can help determine which traits are old and shared by many organisms, and which are newer and shared only by smaller taxa.

But how can researchers make those kinds of determinations with DNA sequences? Computers can sort through vast amounts of data … but HOW should they do the sorting? Which DNA sequences are old, shared traits? Which are newer, derived traits? The emerging rules are complicated … and the evolving science of taxonomy is rising to the challenge!

# Careers on the Case

## Work Toward a Solution

Many scientists might study the platypus or another species that poses puzzling questions. However, the task of classifying the species belongs to the taxonomist.

### Taxonomist

Studying biology in high school and college is the first step to becoming a taxonomist. Taxonomists study further to specialize in the taxonomy of plants, insects, or other animals. Taxonomists may work for universities, the government, museums and, zoos or research firms. Strong research skills and a love of nature are keys to success in this career.

 **VIDEO**

Learn more about taxonomists and related careers.

# Lesson Review
Go to your Biology Foundations Workbook for longer versions of these lesson summaries.

## 19.1 Finding Order in Biodiversity

Scientists found that they needed a universal naming system to clearly communicate with each other about the organisms they discovered and studied. In the Linnaean system of organization, each living thing is given a two-part name consisting of its genus and species. This system is called binomial nomenclature.

In addition to naming organisms, biologists try to classify them into larger groups that have biological meaning. The science of naming and grouping organisms is systematics.

Linnaeus's original classification system eventually expanded to include seven hierarchical taxa: species, genus, family, order, class, phylum, and kingdom. The first classification system consisted of only two kingdoms, Plantae and Animalia.

Over time, the classification system expanded from a two-kingdom system to a six-kingdom system. Then biologists added a new level that is larger and more inclusive than a kingdom—the domain. Under this system there are three domains: Bacteria, Archaea, and Eukarya.

- taxonomy
- binomial nomenclature
- genus
- systematics
- taxon
- family
- order
- class
- phylum
- kingdom
- domain

Dromedary    Llama    Platypus

☑**Review** What is the name of the most specific taxon that contains all these animals?

## 19.2 Modern Evolutionary Classification

In modern evolutionary classification, organisms are grouped into categories that reflect their evolutionary descent. This system places organisms into higher taxa whose members are more closely related to one another than they are to members of any other group. The larger the taxon, the more ancient the common ancestor of the group.

A cladogram shows evolutionary lineages that branched off from common ancestors. Each branch in a cladogram is associated with a derived character, a trait that arose in the most recent common ancestor and was passed to its descendants. In general, the more derived characteristics two species share, the more closely they are related.

Cladograms can be assembled into a tree of all life. Whether displayed as a form that branches outward and upward or as a circle branching from the center, the tree of all life shows the current hypotheses regarding evolutionary relationships within the three domains of life: Archaea, Bacteria, and Eukarya.

- phylogeny
- clade
- cladogram
- derived character

☑**Apply Concepts** Coyotes and lions are both members of the clade Carnivora. What other clades include both animals? Name some other animals that are members of these clades.

# Organize Information

Complete the Cornell notes for this chapter. First, finish the notes on main ideas and details. Next, select the key points from your notes. Finally, write a summary of the chapter based on your key points.

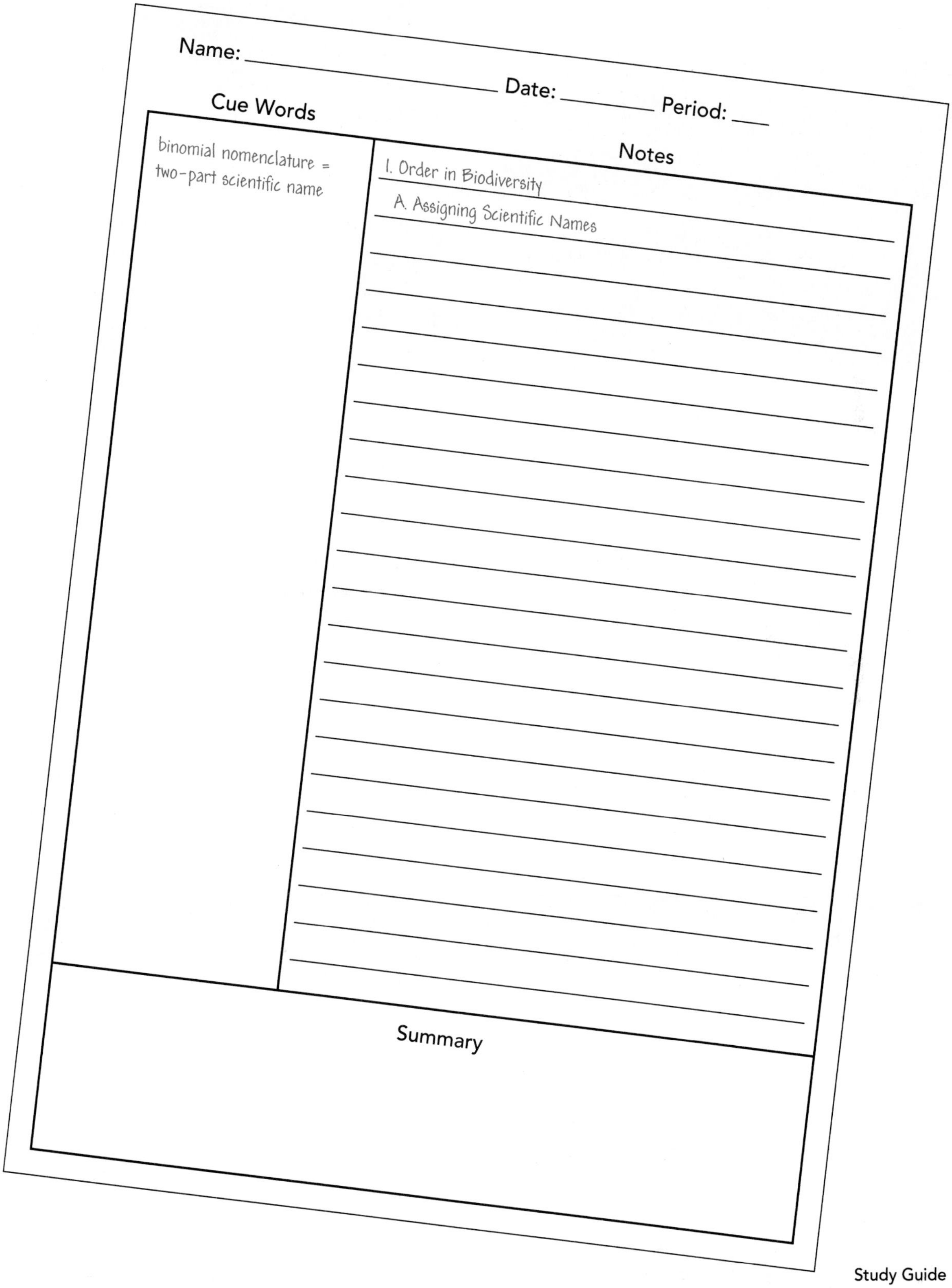

Name: _____

Date: _____ Period: ____

## Cue Words

binomial nomenclature = two-part scientific name

## Notes

I. Order in Biodiversity

  A. Assigning Scientific Names

## Summary

# Build a Cladogram

## Construct a Model

HS-LS4-1, CCSS.ELA-LITERACY.SL.9-10.4, CCSS.ELA.LITERACY.SL9-10.5, CCSS.ELA-LITERACY.RST.9-10.7, CCSS.ELA-LITERACY.WHST.9-10.2

**STEM** A cladogram is a model that presents a hypothesis about how groups of organisms are related. Members of each clade should be more closely related to each other than they are to members of any other clade.

To construct a cladogram, scientists focus on derived characters that define evolutionary lineages. For example, a backbone, or vertebral column, formed by vertebrae is a derived character for the clade Vertebrata.

All members of that clade, and only members of that clade, have a vertebral column. This means that a vertebral column evolved once in the common ancestor shared by all vertebrates. That character was then passed on to all descendants of that common ancestor.

How is the clade Vertebrata divided into smaller clades? By using other traits that later evolved in some, but not all, vertebrates. Use the table of characters to build a cladogram model that shows the evolution of vertebrates.

|  | Vertebrate? | Bony skeleton? | Four limbs? | Amniotic egg? | Hair? | Eggs with shells? |
|---|---|---|---|---|---|---|
| Sharks and relatives | Yes | No | No | No | No | No |
| Ray-finned fishes | Yes | Yes | No | No | No | No |
| Amphibians | Yes | Yes | Yes | No | No | No |
| Crocodiles | Yes | Yes | Yes | Yes | No | Yes |
| Dinosaurs and birds | Yes | Yes | Yes | Yes | No | Yes |
| Primates | Yes | Yes | Yes | Yes | Yes | No |
| Rodents | Yes | Yes | Yes | Yes | Yes | No |

1. **Draw Conclusions** Of the six characters listed in the table, which was found in the common ancestor of all seven groups? Explain your inference.

2. **Infer** Traits found in some or all vertebrate groups include a bony skeleton, four limbs, and an amniotic egg. Which evolved first? Which evolved next? Explain your inference.

3. **Use a Model** The diagram shows a small section of the cladogram that explains the evolution of the seven animal groups. What does this section show about the evolution of primates, rodents, and rabbits?

4. **Develop a Model** Expand your cladogram to show the evolutionary lineages of all seven groups listed in the table. Use labels at branch points in the lineages to show the derived characters that evolved over time.

5. **Communicate Information** Research the evolution of vertebrates, focusing on the evolution of the traits used in your model in the fossil record. In an oral report or written paragraph, use the cladogram to organize and present the results of your study.

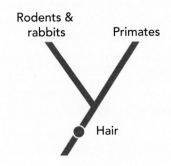

## 🔍 KEY QUESTIONS AND TERMS

### 19.1 Finding Order in Biodiversity

1. The scientific name for a species has how many parts?
   a. one       c. three
   b. two       d. four

2. Arrange the taxa from most specific to most general.

   class       family       genus       kingdom

   order       phylum       species

3. Study the picture.

Bactrian camel   Dromedary   Llama   Giraffe   Platypus   Coral snake   Sea star

   The animals shown here are grouped together in the same
   a. family.       c. genus.
   b. phylum.       d. kingdom.

4. How does the modern system of classification compare to Linnaeus's original system?

5. How have the organisms in the old Kingdom Monera been reclassified today?

6. What are the three domains?

7. Which four of the six kingdoms are grouped together in the same domain?

8. Identify the kingdom for each of these organisms.

a.

c.

b.

d.

### 19.2 Modern Evolutionary Classification

HS-LS4-1

9. A common ancestor and all its descendants make up a
   a. clade.       c. kingdom.
   b. domain.      d. order.

10. The members of which domain are most apt to live in harsh habitats, such as brine pools or volcanic hot springs?
    a. Archaea      c. Eukarya
    b. Bacteria     d. Monera

11. Which cell structure distinguishes members of domain Eukarya from other organisms?
    a. cell wall
    b. cell membrane
    c. cytoplasm
    d. nucleus

Use the diagram to answer questions 12 and 13.

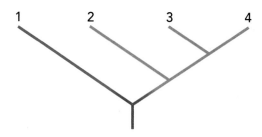

12. What do the lines in the diagram represent?

13. What is represented by the intersection of two lines in the diagram?

14. How do derived genetic characters help reveal evolutionary relationships?

15. Why can differences in mitochondrial DNA be used as derived characters?

16. What does a model called the tree of life show about all living things?

17. Give an example of a kingdom from an older classification scheme that is not a valid clade. Why is it not valid?

18. What does the term *phylogeny* describe about organisms?

19. How is a derived character different from other shared traits of a clade?

# CRITICAL THINKING

HS-LS4-1

20. **Compare and Contrast** How are members of the domains Bacteria and Archaea alike? How are they different?

21. **Apply Concepts** Both snakes and worms are tube shaped and lack legs. How could you determine whether their similarity in shape means that they share a recent common ancestor?

22. **Ask Questions** What questions would Linnaeus ask to determine a classification? What questions would a modern taxonomist ask?

23. **Construct an Explanation** What are the advantages of classifying species according to their evolutionary relationships, rather than their physical or behavioral similarities?

24. **Use Models** Taxa act as a model of evolutionary relationships. Scientists now use the taxonomic category of the domain to organize the kingdoms of life. How is the domain an improvement to the model?

25. **Apply Scientific Reasoning** A cladogram for bats includes the development of wings for flight. Birds also fly, so should they also be included in the cladogram? Explain your reasoning.

26. **Synthesize Information** Why is kingdom "Protista" not an example of a clade?

27. **Ask Questions** Corals are multicellular organisms that live underwater. As adults they do not move from place to place. What questions would you ask to help you classify them into the proper kingdom?

28. **Evaluate Claims** A student claims that beaks, hollow bones, and feathers are derived characters of birds, which are members of the clade *Theropoda*. What evidence would support this claim?

29. **Compare and Contrast** People often use a diagram called a family tree as a model of their extended family. The diagram shows parents, children, siblings, and other family relationships. How does a family tree compare to the tree of life?

30. **Infer** Birds, reptiles, and mammals are each members of one class only. Fishes, however, are organized into three classes. What can you infer about fishes from their diverse classifications?

Use the cladogram shown below to answer questions 31–33.

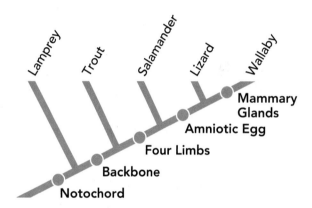

31. **Interpret Diagrams** Of the characteristics listed in the cladogram, which do lizards and salamanders have in common?

32. **Draw Conclusions** The diagram identifies five derived characters. What conclusion does the diagram support about the order in which the five derived characters evolved?

33. **Integrate Information** A tuatara has a backbone and four limbs, but does not develop from an amniotic egg. Where does it fit in the cladogram? Explain.

## CROSSCUTTING CONCEPTS

**34. Systems and System Models** How is the classification of an organism in the Linnaean system similar to the street address of a house? (**Hint:** Think of an address used for international mail.)

**35. Patterns** What evolutionary pattern does every cladogram show?

Use the diagram to answer questions 36–38.

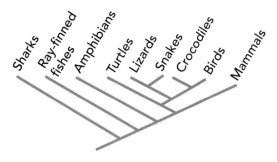

**36. Systems and System Models** Turtles, lizards, snakes, and crocodiles are all classified as reptiles. Why is this group of animals not a clade?

**37. Stability and Change** Did ray-finned fishes evolve from sharks? Use the diagram to support your answer.

**38. Systems and System Models** Mammals have four limbs, give birth to live young, and make milk for their young. How could you determine which of these traits, if any, is a derived character of the clade of mammals?

## MATH CONNECTIONS

## Analyze and Interpret Data

CCSS.MATH.CONTENT.MP4

The table describes the characteristics of five different organisms. Use the table to answer questions 39–41.

|  | Turtle | Lamprey | Frog | Fish | Cat |
|---|---|---|---|---|---|
| Hair | No | No | No | No | Yes |
| Amniotic egg | Yes | No | No | No | Yes |
| Four legs | Yes | No | Yes | No | Yes |
| Jaw | Yes | No | Yes | Yes | Yes |
| Vertebrae | Yes | Yes | Yes | Yes | Yes |

**39. Interpret Data** The first column lists derived characters that can be used to make a cladogram of vertebrates. Which characteristic is shared by the most organisms? Which is shared by the fewest?

**40. Develop a Model** Use the data to sequence the organisms from the most recently evolved to the most ancient.

**41. Draw Conclusions** Which of the characteristics shown in the table was the most likely to have evolved first? Which evolved most recently? Explain.

A scientist analyzes the DNA of complementary mitochondrial genes from five organisms, labeled A to E. Each organism represents a different species. The data table shows the number of base-pair differences in the DNA of any two of the organisms. Use the data table to answer questions 42–44.

|  | A | B | C | D | E |
|---|---|---|---|---|---|
| A | × | 18 | 3 | 29 | 10 |
| B | 18 | × | 26 | 4 | 12 |
| C | 3 | 26 | × | 20 | 13 |
| D | 29 | 4 | 20 | × | 11 |
| E | 10 | 12 | 13 | 11 | × |

**42. Interpret Data** Identify the two most recent evolutionary events that the data suggest.

**43. Develop Models** Draw a cladogram that is supported by the data.

**44. Evaluate Models** What aspects of the cladogram are strongly supported by the data? Which are more weakly supported? Explain your evaluation.

## LANGUAGE ARTS CONNECTION

## Write About Science
CCSS.ELA-LITERACY.WHST.9-10.1, CCSS.ELA-LITERACY.WHST.9-10.2

**45. Write Explanatory Texts** Write a paragraph to explain how species are classified into clades.

**46. Write Arguments** How is the clade system of classification more useful than the Linnaean taxonomic system?

## Read About Science
CCSS.ELA-LITERACY.RST.9-10.1

**47. Key Ideas and Details** You are a reviewer of a paper on the discovery of new species in the Amazon jungle. Two new species of beetles have been found, beetle A and beetle B, that closely resemble each other but have somewhat different markings on their wings. In addition, both beetles resemble beetle C, a species that has already been identified. How could DNA similarities be used to help determine whether beetle A and beetle B are more closely related to each other or to beetle C? Cite evidence from the text to support your analysis.

**Questions 1–3** refer to the following diagram.

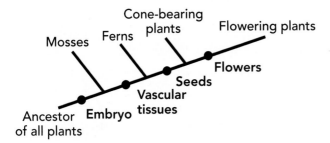

1. According to the cladogram, which of these organisms appeared before all the others?
   A. mosses
   B. a plant with vascular tissue
   C. an organism that developed from an embryo
   D. a plant that made seeds
   E. ferns

2. What conclusion about flowers is supported by the evidence in the cladogram?
   A. Flowers evolved more recently than seeds and vascular tissue.
   B. Flowering plants have a reproductive advantage over cone-bearing plants
   C. Most plants alive today produce flowers.
   D. Flowers are a trait of living plant species, but not extinct species.
   E. Flowers evolved from cone-bearing plants.

3. Two students are studying plants to determine the closest relatives to cone-bearing plants. Which conclusion could they make based on the cladogram?
   A. Cone-bearing plants are most closely related to ferns because they both have vascular tissues.
   B. Cone-bearing plants are most closely related to ferns because they share the most recent common ancestor.
   C. Cone-bearing plants are equally related to mosses, ferns, and flowering plants because they are all in the same clade.
   D. Cone-bearing plants are most closely related to flowering plants because they both have flowers.
   E. Cone-bearing plants are most closely related to flowering plants because they share the most recent common ancestor.

4. Compared to the Linnaean system of classification, what is the advantage of classifying species into clades?
   A. Clades show evolutionary relationships.
   B. Clades identify domains and kingdoms.
   C. Clades group single-celled organisms separately from multicellular organisms.
   D. Clades include more species.
   E. Clades exclude species that are now extinct

5. Scientists struggled with classifying red pandas and giant pandas because they have physical similarities to both raccoons and bears. How has the availability of DNA evidence affected the evolutionary classification of organisms such as the pandas?
   A. Organisms with the most shared derived genetic characters are considered the most closely related.
   B. Organisms with the most shared derived genetic characters are classified in the most clades.
   C. DNA evidence has had little impact because derived physical characters are still more important than derived genetic characters.
   D. Derived genetic characters can be used to identify evolutionary relationships, but only if organisms have some shared physical characteristics.
   E. DNA analysis has confirmed species classifications based on derived physical characters, but no new classifications have been suggested.

✓ **ASSESSMENT**

For additional assessment practice, Go Online to access your digital course.

## If You Have Trouble With...

| Question | 1 | 2 | 3 | 4 | 5 |
|---|---|---|---|---|---|
| See Lesson | 19.2 | 19.2 | 19.2 | 19.2 | 19.2 |
| Performance Expectation | HS-LS4-1 | HS-LS4-1 | HS-LS4-1 | HS-LS4-1 | HS-LS4-1 |

CHAPTER 20

# History of Life

20.1 The Fossil Record

20.2 Evolutionary Patterns and Processes

20.3 Earth's Early History

**Go Online to access your digital course.**

- VIDEO
- AUDIO
- INTERACTIVITY
- eTEXT
- ANIMATION
- VIRTUAL LAB
- ASSESSMENT

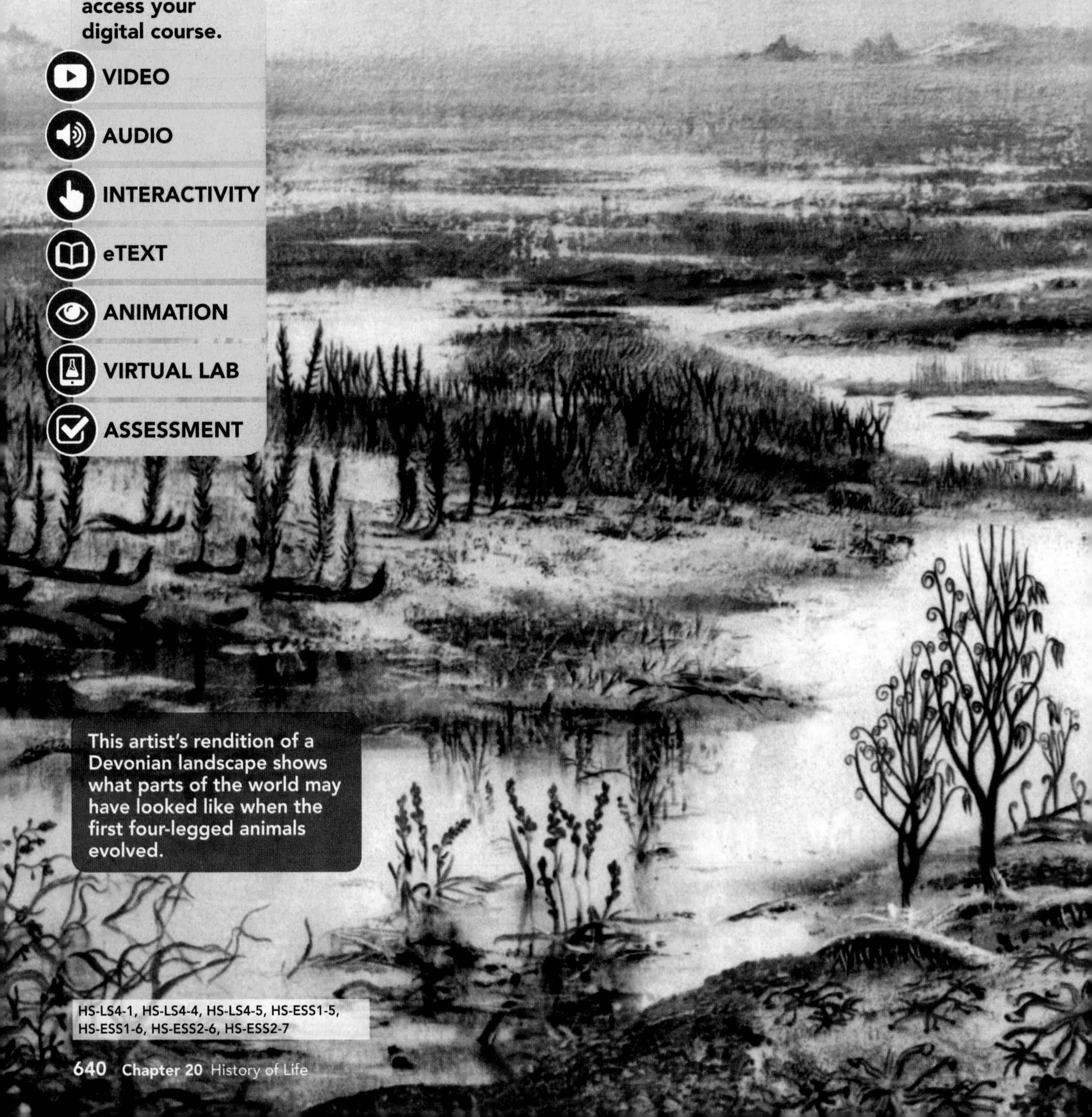

This artist's rendition of a Devonian landscape shows what parts of the world may have looked like when the first four-legged animals evolved.

HS-LS4-1, HS-LS4-4, HS-LS4-5, HS-ESS1-5, HS-ESS1-6, HS-ESS2-6, HS-ESS2-7

# How did fossil hunters find *Tiktaalik*?

If social media had existed 375 million years ago, one popular meme could well have been "A small step for fishes … a great leap for animals with backbones!" Why? Because around that time, adaptations that made life on land possible (including legs that could take steps) developed in the ancestors of modern four-limbed animals. But who took that crucial first step?

Life began in the sea, and remained underwater for a long time. By around 430 million years ago, ancestors of land plants and insects had colonized the land. By 100 million years later, land animals with four limbs—called tetrapods—were common. Fossil evidence suggested that the first tetrapods evolved from a group of ancient fishes. The fins of those fishes had some bones that were homologous to the bones of modern animals' arms and legs. But some steps in the evolutionary transformation from fins to limbs were missing.

Could anyone find an ancient four-legged fish that would document this transition? One team, headed by researchers Neil Shubin, Edward Daeschler, and Farish Jenkins, was determined to try. First came intensive studies of geology, geography, and fossils. Then came years of difficult fieldwork in northern Canada, just 600 miles from the North Pole. Finally, in 2004, they announced the discovery of an amazing fossil. They named it *Tiktaalik* (TIK-ta-lik), which means "large, freshwater fish" in the local First Nations language.

*Tiktaalik* shared some traits with fishes. It had scales and fins, and it used gills to breathe. But its skeleton differed from those of other fishes in important ways. *Tiktaalik's* fins were connected to its backbone by bony structures that look like a shoulder and pelvis. These structures would have helped those fins to support the animal's weight. *Tiktaalik* also had rib bones that attached to one another, like those of land animals. Taken together, these skeletal features show that *Tiktaalik* could hold its body against the pull of gravity. *Tiktaalik* also had neck bones that allowed it to move its head from side to side. Many land animals today have moveable necks, but fishes don't.

*Tiktaalik* wasn't the common ancestor of land-dwelling vertebrates, but it gives us a good idea of what that common ancestor might have looked like. Its discoverers dubbed it "fish-a-pod" to emphasize that it represented a stage between fishes and modern tetrapods. They suggest that *Tiktaalik* lived in shallow water, where it propped itself up to snatch prey.

The discovery of *Tiktaalik* was no accident. The research Shubin and his team performed before heading out into the field convinced them that they knew just where to look. Their determination was important, because they searched for four years before finding what they were after! How did they know where to look? What evidence can fossils provide about ancient life and the history of life on Earth? What kinds of patterns do fossils form?

**Throughout this chapter, look for connections to the** CASE STUDY **to help you answer these questions.**

### KEY QUESTIONS

- *What do fossils reveal about ancient life?*
- *How do we date events in Earth's history?*
- *How was the geologic time scale established, and what are its major divisions?*
- *How have Earth's physical and biological environments shaped the history of life?*

**HS-LS4-1:** Communicate scientific information that common ancestry and biological evolution are supported by multiple lines of empirical evidence.

**HS-ESS1-5:** Evaluate evidence of the past and current movements of continental and oceanic crust and the theory of plate tectonics to explain the ages of crustal rocks.

**HS-ESS2-7:** Construct an argument based on evidence about the simultaneous coevolution of Earth's systems and life on Earth.

### VOCABULARY

extinct
relative dating
index fossil
radiometric dating
half-life
geologic time scale
era
period
plate tectonics

### READING TOOL

As you read through this lesson, pay special attention to how fossils form and fill in the graphic organizer in your 📓 **Biology Foundations Workbook.**

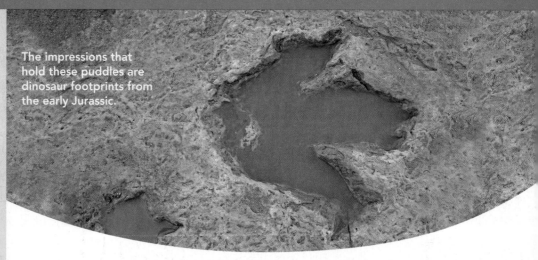

The impressions that hold these puddles are dinosaur footprints from the early Jurassic.

If you know how to interpret fossils, looking at them can be like watching a documentary about the history of life on Earth. Holding one in your hand can be an emotional experience. As scientist and philosopher Loren Eiseley once wrote, "…every bone that one holds in one's hands is a fallen kingdom, a veritable ruined world, a totally unique object that will never return through time."

## Fossils and Ancient Life

Fossils provide vital information about **extinct** species—species that have died out. Fossils form rarely and only under certain conditions. The fossil record is incomplete because for every organism preserved as a fossil, many more die without leaving a trace. Still, the fossil record contains an enormous amount of information for paleontologists (pay lee un TAHL uh jists), researchers who study fossils, to learn about ancient life.

**Types of Fossils** Fossils can be as large and perfectly preserved as an entire animal, complete with skin, hair, scales, or feathers, and sometimes even internal organs. They can also be as tiny as bacteria, embryos, or pollen grains. Many fossils are mere fragments of an organism—teeth, pieces of a jawbone, or bits of leaf. Sometimes, an organism leaves only trace fossils—casts of footprints, burrows, tracks, or even droppings.

**Fossils in Sedimentary Rock** Most fossils are preserved in sedimentary rock, as shown **Figure 20-1**. Sedimentary rock usually forms when small particles of sand, silt, clay, or lime settle to the bottom of a body of water. Sedimentary rock can also form from compact desert sand. If sediments build up quickly, they can bury dead organisms before the remains are eaten or scattered by scavengers.

Soft body structures usually decay after death, so most of the time only wood, shells, bones, or teeth remain. These hard structures can be preserved if they are saturated or replaced with mineral compounds. Sometimes, however, organisms are buried so quickly that soft tissues are protected from aerobic decay. When this happens, fossils may preserve detailed imprints of soft-bodied animals and structures like skin or feathers. As layers of sediment build up over time, the remains are buried deeper. Over many years, pressure gradually compresses the lower layers. This pressure, along with chemical activity, can turn the soft sediment into rock.

## Evaluating Evidence in the Fossil Record

By comparing fossils to each other and to living organisms, paleontologists can propose and test evolutionary hypotheses. ⚲ *Fossils reveal information about the structures of ancient organisms, the sequential nature of groups in the fossil record, evolution from common ancestors, and the ecology of ancient environments.*

Comparisons of body structures test hypotheses about the appearance, evolution, and history of groups in the fossil record. Studies of evolutionary change in body structures can also test hypotheses about the evolution of living species from extinct common ancestors and the evolution of diversity. Bone structures and footprints can indicate how animals moved. Fossilized plant leaves and pollen suggest whether an area was a swamp, a lake, a forest, or a desert. Also, when different kinds of fossils are found together, researchers can sometimes reconstruct entire ancient ecosystems.

☑ **READING CHECK Explain** Why does a fossil most often form in sediment?

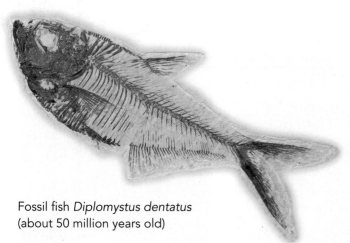

Fossil fish *Diplomystus dentatus* (about 50 million years old)

**VIDEO**

Learn how scientists construct skeletons from fossilized remains.

**INTERACTIVITY**

Explore the fossil record and learn how it provides evidence for evolution.

**Figure 20-1**

## Fossil Formation

Most fossils form in sedimentary rock.

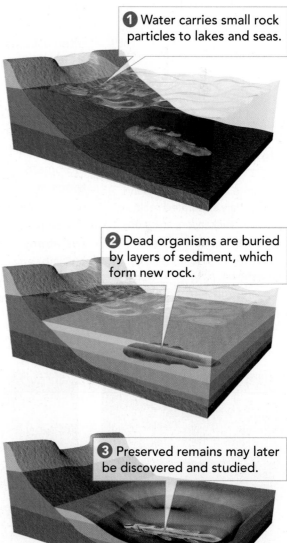

❶ Water carries small rock particles to lakes and seas.

❷ Dead organisms are buried by layers of sediment, which form new rock.

❸ Preserved remains may later be discovered and studied.

# Dating Earth's History

The fossil record would not be as useful if we had no way to figure out what happened when. Researchers use several techniques to put fossils in order from oldest to newest and to figure out how old those fossils are.

**Relative Dating** Because sedimentary rock is formed as layers, lower layers and fossils they contain are generally older than upper layers. **Relative dating** places rock layers and their fossils in a time sequence, as shown in **Figure 20-2**. ✎ *Relative dating helps paleontologists to determine whether a fossil is older or younger than other fossils.*

To help establish the relative age of rock layers and their fossils, scientists use **index fossils**. Index fossils are distinctive fossils used to establish and compare the relative age of rock layers and the fossils they contain. A useful index fossil must be easy to recognize and occur only in a few rock layers (meaning the species existed only for a brief span of geologic time), but layers from that time period must be found in many places (meaning the organism was widely distributed). Trilobites, a large group of distinctive marine organisms, are often used as index fossils. There are more than 15,000 recognized species of trilobite. Together, they can be used to establish the relative dates of rock layers over a time span of nearly 300 million years.

**Radiometric Dating** Relative dating tells us the order in which fossil organisms first appeared, but provides no information about a fossil's absolute age in years. One way to date rocks and fossils is radiometric dating. **Radiometric dating** relies on radioactive isotopes, which decay or break down into stable isotopes at a steady rate. A **half-life** is the time required for half of the radioactive atoms in a sample to decay. After one half-life, half of the original radioactive atoms have decayed, as shown in **Figure 20-3**. After another half-life, another half of the remaining radioactive atoms will have decayed. ✎ *Radiometric dating uses the proportion of radioactive isotopes to stable isotopes to calculate the age of a sample.*

**Figure 20-2**

**Index Fossils**

If the same index fossil is found in two widely separated rock layers, the rock layers are probably similar in age. ☑**Draw Conclusions** Using the index fossils shown, determine which layers are "missing" from each location. Layers may be missing because they never formed, or because they eroded.

A 🐚 B 🦪 C 🐚 D 🐚 E 🐚 F 🦐

Location 1

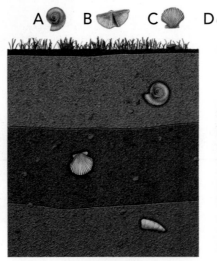

Location 2

Location 3

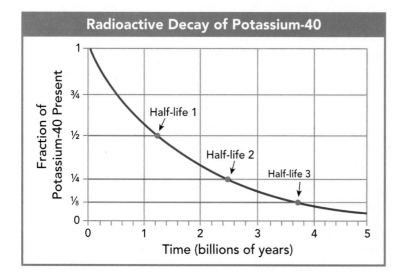

**Radioactive Decay of Potassium-40**

Fraction of Potassium-40 Present (y-axis): 0, ⅛, ¼, ½, ¾, 1

Half-life 1
Half-life 2
Half-life 3

Time (billions of years) (x-axis): 0, 1, 2, 3, 4, 5

**Figure 20-3**

## Radioactive Decay

The time it takes for half the radioactive atoms in a sample to decay is a half-life. The half-life of potassium-40 is 1.26 billion years.

Different radioactive isotopes decay at different rates. Elements with short half-lives are used to date very recent fossils. Elements with long half-lives are used to date older fossils. Consider how we time sporting events. For a 100-meter dash, a coach depends on the fast-moving second hand of a stopwatch. To time a marathon, the slower-moving hour and minute hands are more useful.

An isotope known as carbon-14, which has a half-life of roughly 5730 years, is useful for directly dating recent fossils. Carbon-14 is produced at a steady rate in the upper atmosphere. Air contains a tiny amount of carbon-14 in addition to the more common, stable, nonradioactive form, carbon-12. Plants take in carbon-14 when they absorb carbon dioxide during photosynthesis, and animals acquire it when they eat plants or other animals. Once an organism dies, it no longer takes in this isotope, so its age can be determined by the amount of carbon-14 remaining in tissues, such as bone or wood. The relatively short half-life of carbon-14 limits its use to organisms that lived during the last 60,000 years. After 10 half-lives have passed, less than one thousandth (1/1000) of the original carbon-14 remains in a sample.

**INTERACTIVITY**

Use radiometric dating techniques to determine the ages of different objects.

---

## Quick Lab — Guided Inquiry

### How Can You Model Half-Life?

1. Construct a data table with two columns and five rows. Label the columns "Spill Number" and "Number of Squares Returned." Enter the numbers 1 to 5 for the spill numbers.

2. Cut out 100 squares with side lengths of about 1 cm. Write an X on one face of each square. Mix the squares thoroughly in a cup.

3. Spill out the squares, and then remove all the squares on which the X faces up. Count and record the number of squares that do not have the X facing up, and return these squares to the cup.

4. Repeat Step 3 four times, or until no squares remain.

### ANALYZE AND CONCLUDE

1. **Construct Graphs** Make a line graph to organize the data you recorded. Plot the number of squares returned on the *y*-axis, and the spill numbers 1 to 5 on the *x*-axis.

2. **Interpret Graphs** How does the line graph show a model of half-life for this activity?

3. **Evaluate Models** How well does this model represent the half-life of a radioactive element? What are the limitations of the model?

Older fossils can be dated indirectly, using isotopes with longer half-lives to date the rock layers in which the fossils are found. Isotopes useful for dating include potassium-40 (1.26 billion years), uranium-238 (4.5 billion years), and rubidium-87 (48.8 billion years). These studies provide direct physical evidence for the ages of index fossils that identify periods in Earth's history. They also provide information used to document the rates at which groups appear, evolve, and become extinct.

✅ **READING CHECK** **Explain** Why can't carbon-14 be used to estimate the age of very old fossils?

# Geologic Time Scale

Geologists and paleontologists have built a timeline of Earth's history called the **geologic time scale**. The most recent version is shown in **Figure 20-4**. 🔍 *The geologic time scale is based on both relative and absolute dating. The major divisions of the geologic time scale are eons, eras, and periods.*

**Establishing the Time Scale** By studying rock layers and index fossils, early paleontologists placed Earth's rocks and fossils in order by relative age. As they worked, they noticed major changes in the fossil record at boundaries between certain rock layers. Geologists used rock-layer boundaries to determine where one division of geologic time ended and the next began. Because these divisions of geologic time were described in this way, the lengths of ages are not consistent. The Cambrian Period, for example, began 542 million years ago and continued until 488 million years ago, which makes it 54 million years long. The Cretaceous Period was 80 million years long.

Years after the time scale was established, radiometric dating was used to assign specific ages to the various rock layers. The time scale is constantly being tested, verified, and adjusted.

**Divisions of the Geologic Time Scale** Geologists recognize four eons. The Hadean Eon, during which the first rocks formed, spanned the time from Earth's formation to about 4 billion years ago. The Archean Eon, during which life first appeared, followed the Hadean. During the Proterozoic Eon, stable continents began to form and eukaryotic cells evolved. The Phanerozoic (fan ur uh ZOH ic) Eon began at the end of the Proterozoic and continues to the present.

Eons are divided into **eras**. The Phanerozoic Eon, for example, is divided into the Paleozoic, Mesozoic, and Cenozoic Eras. Eras are subdivided into **periods**, which range in length from nearly 100 million years to just under 2 million years.

During the Cambrian Period, multicellular life experienced its greatest adaptive radiation in what is called the Cambrian explosion. The Cambrian ended with a large mass extinction in which nearly 30 percent of all animal groups died.

## Geologic Time Scale

| Eon | Era | Period | Time (millions of years ago) |
|---|---|---|---|
| Phanerozoic | Cenozoic | Quaternary | 1.8–present |
| Phanerozoic | Cenozoic | Neogene | 23–1.8 |
| Phanerozoic | Cenozoic | Paleogene | 65.5–23 |
| Phanerozoic | Mesozoic | Cretaceous | 146–65.5 |
| Phanerozoic | Mesozoic | Jurassic | 200–146 |
| Phanerozoic | Mesozoic | Triassic | 251–200 |
| Phanerozoic | Paleozoic | Permian | 299–251 |
| Phanerozoic | Paleozoic | Carboniferous | 359–299 |
| Phanerozoic | Paleozoic | Devonian | 416–359 |
| Phanerozoic | Paleozoic | Silurian | 444–416 |
| Phanerozoic | Paleozoic | Ordovician | 488–444 |
| Phanerozoic | Paleozoic | Cambrian | 542–488 |
| Precambrian Time | Proterozoic | | 2500–542 |
| Precambrian Time | Archean | | 4000–2500 |
| Precambrian Time | Hadean | | About 4600–4000 |

◀ Tiktaalik *(indicated at Devonian, 416–359)*

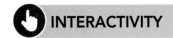

**INTERACTIVITY**

**Figure 20-4**

## Geologic Time Scale

The basic divisions of the geologic time scale are eons, eras, and periods. Precambrian time was the name originally given to all of Earth's history before the Phanerozoic Eon. Note that the Paleogene and Neogene are sometimes called the Tertiary Period, but this term is considered outdated.

**Naming the Divisions** The divisions of the geologic time scale were named in different ways. The Cambrian Period was named after Cambria—an old name for Wales, which is where rocks from that time were first identified. The Carboniferous ("carbon-bearing") Period is named for large coal deposits that formed during that time. Geologists started to name divisions of the time scale before any rocks older than the Cambrian Period had been identified. For this reason, all of geologic time before the Cambrian was simply called Precambrian Time. Precambrian Time covers about 90 percent of Earth's history. See Appendix C: Illustrated History of Life for more detailed information about each division.

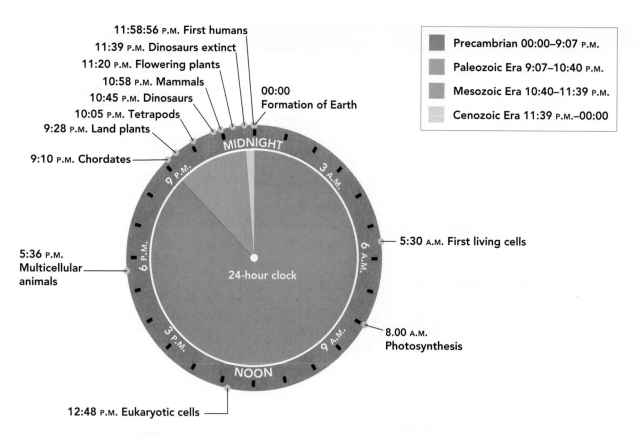

11:58:56 P.M. First humans
11:39 P.M. Dinosaurs extinct
11:20 P.M. Flowering plants
10:58 P.M. Mammals
10:45 P.M. Dinosaurs
10:05 P.M. Tetrapods
9:28 P.M. Land plants
9:10 P.M. Chordates

00:00 Formation of Earth

MIDNIGHT

5:36 P.M. Multicellular animals

5:30 A.M. First living cells

24-hour clock

8.00 A.M. Photosynthesis

NOON

12:48 P.M. Eukaryotic cells

Precambrian 00:00–9:07 P.M.
Paleozoic Era 9:07–10:40 P.M.
Mesozoic Era 10:40–11:39 P.M.
Cenozoic Era 11:39 P.M.–00:00

**Visual Analogy**

**Figure 20-5**

**Geologic Time as a Clock**

To help visualize the enormous span of time since Earth formed, this model compresses the history of Earth into a 24-hour period. Notice the relative length of Precambrian Time—almost 22 hours. ☑ **Use Analogies** Using this model, about what time did life appear? The first plants? The first humans?

**Comparing Time** What do you think is a long period of time? Would you describe a year as a long time, or a decade, or a century? On the geologic time scale, even a thousand years is like a passing moment. The model shown in **Figure 20-5** represents all of Earth's history on the face of a clock. Notice that Precambrian Time, when life was just beginning, covers about 90 percent of the clock face. In contrast, the history of modern humans fits into about a minute.

☑ **READING CHECK** **Use an Analogy** How does the time span of human history compare to the history of Earth? Use an analogy to compare them.

# Life on a Changing Planet

During a human lifetime, environments seem constant. Areas around the Gulf of Mexico are usually hot and humid. Antarctica is usually cold. But Earth's environments and climate changed dramatically over millions of years, and those changes profoundly affected the history of life. Life, in turn, has also had profound effects on Earth.

**Changes in Climate** Earth's regional climates have changed repeatedly over time because of nonhuman causes of global change. Many dramatic changes in regional environments were triggered by fairly small shifts in global temperature. For example, during a global "heat wave" of the Mesozoic era, average global temperatures were only 6 to 12 degrees Celsius higher than they were in the twentieth century. During the great ice ages, which chilled the globe as recently as 10,000 years ago, temperatures were only about 5 degrees Celsius cooler than they are now.

**Geologic Forces** Regional and global environments are influenced by interactions between wind and ocean currents, as well as by geological features like mountains and plains. Over long periods of time, geological forces built mountains, moved continents, and created volcanic island chains like the Galápagos. The movement of continents produced even more dramatic changes in Earth's landscape, as shown in **Figure 20-6**. The theory of **plate tectonics** explains the movements of continents and oceans. They are the result of solid "plates" moving slowly, about 3 centimeters per year, over Earth's mantle.

In addition, comets and large meteors have crashed into Earth many times in the past. Some of these impacts were so violent that they kicked enough dust and debris into the atmosphere to cause or contribute to climate change that drove major extinctions.

### Ordovician Period 488–444 mya

During the Ordovician, continents were separated and ringed by shallow seas rich in marine life.

**Figure 20-6**

## The Changing Face of Earth

Over the last several hundred million years, the face of Earth has changed dramatically due to the movement of tectonic plates. Continents once collided to form "super continents" and then drifted apart again. These actions changed the flow of ocean currents and altered global climate, albeit very gradually. These plates continue to move today.

### Carboniferous Period 359–299 mya

In the Carboniferous, continents began to come together. Eventually, they would fuse into the super continent, Pangaea.

### Triassic Period 251–200 mya

During the Triassic, Pangaea started to break apart.

### Cretaceous Period 146–65.5 mya

By the end of the Cretaceous, the continents as we know them, began to drift apart from each other.

**Present Day**

## Figure 20-7

### Changing Habitats

Mountains in South Africa hold fossils of sea stars and marine mollusks that are about 400 million years old. The fossils are evidence that these rocks were once part of a shallow sea floor teeming with life, such as the modern day ocean floor shown.

Off the coast of the Galápagos Islands, Pacific Ocean

**Effects on Life** As Earth's land changed, the habitats it provided changed as well. 🔍 *Global climate change, mountain building, the emergence of islands, continental drift, changes in levels of continents and oceans, and meteor impacts have altered Earth's habitats, with major effects on the history of life.* These environmental changes altered ecological interactions among organisms and between organisms and their environments. Those altered interactions, in turn, changed the pressures of natural selection, favoring adaptation to new conditions. In addition, both the emergence of new habitats and changes in the environment of existing habitats created new ecological niches. Those new niches offered opportunities for natural selection to increase diversity among species.

The movement of tectonic plates also shaped biogeography, or the distribution of fossils and living organisms. For example, the continents of Africa and South America are now separated by the Atlantic Ocean, but fossils of *Mesosaurus*, an aquatic reptile, have been found in Africa and South America. The presence of the same fossils on both continents indicates that they were joined at the time those organisms lived. **Figure 20-7** shows an example of a current land mass that was once the site of a shallow sea.

**Figure 20-8**

**Blue-Green Algae**

**Figure 20-8**

**Blue-Green Algae**

Earth's first atmosphere had very little oxygen. The first photosynthetic organisms, which were like the algae shown here, caused carbon dioxide levels to fall and oxygen levels to rise—and forever changed life on Earth (LM 160x).

**Biological Forces** Life is definitely affected by changes in Earth's physical environment. But life also plays a major role in shaping that environment. Today, plants, animals, and microorganisms are active players in global cycles of key elements, including carbon, nitrogen, and oxygen. That has been true ever since life evolved. For example, Earth's early atmosphere contained much more carbon dioxide than it does today—and little or no oxygen. Then early photosynthetic organisms began absorbing carbon dioxide and releasing oxygen. Our planet has never been the same since. Earth cooled as carbon dioxide levels dropped. The iron content of the oceans fell, as soluble iron ions reacted with oxygen to form insoluble compounds (rust) that settled to the ocean floor. These changes affected climate and ocean chemistry in many ways.

🔍 *The actions of living organisms over time have changed conditions in the atmosphere, the oceans, and the land.* Those changes altered the pressures of natural selection in ways that favored the evolution of different adaptations in existing species. The changes caused pressures that led to the emergence of new species and new groups of species. The presence of oxygen, for example, led to the evolution of aerobic metabolism, transforming life on Earth.

HS-LS4-1, HS-ESS1-5, HS-ESS2-7

## ☑ LESSON 20.1 Review

### 🔍 KEY QUESTIONS

1. What can fossils reveal about the ecosystems in which the organisms once existed? Include an example.

2. How is relative dating of fossils different from absolute dating?

3. How does geologic time compare to the time scales we use in everyday life?

4. Explain how life both has been affected by geologic change and has affected geologic change.

### CRITICAL THINKING

5. **Evaluate Reasoning** Using radiometric dating, the age of a sedimentary rock in a rock layer is dated to 530 million years ago. A science student concludes that the fossils in the rock layer are also 530 million years old. Explain whether or not this conclusion is reasonable.

6. **Construct an Explanation** Earth's climate has changed many times throughout its long history. How does continental climates change as a result of continental drift?

7. **CASE STUDY** What techniques do you think Shubin and his fellow researchers used to determine how deep they should dig to look for *Tiktaalik*?

Some animals and plants evolve in response to each other.

# Evolutionary Patterns and Processes

**LESSON 20.2**

## 🔍 KEY QUESTIONS

- *What patterns describe the sequential nature of groups in the fossil record?*
- *What does the fossil record show about periods of stasis and rapid change?*
- *What are two patterns of macroevolution?*
- *What evolutionary characteristics are typical of coevolving species?*

**HS-LS4-1:** Communicate scientific information that common ancestry and biological evolution are supported by multiple lines of empirical evidence.

**HS-LS4-4:** Construct an explanation based on evidence for how natural selection leads to adaptation of populations.

**HS-LS4-5:** Evaluate the evidence supporting claims that changes in environmental conditions may result in: (1) increases in the number of individuals of some species, (2) the emergence of new species over time, and (3) the extinction of other species.

### VOCABULARY

**macroevolutionary pattern**
**background extinction**
**mass extinction**
**gradualism**
**punctuated equilibrium**
**adaptive radiation**
**convergent evolution**
**coevolution**

### READING TOOL

Use the section headings to guide you through this lesson. Take notes on the important vocabulary terms in your 📖 **Biology Foundations Workbook.**

The fossil record documents that life has changed in a chronological sequence. Species and larger clades evolved, survived for a time, and either continued to evolve or became extinct. The fossil record also documents that more than 99 percent of all species that have ever lived are extinct. How have so many species and larger clades evolved? Why are so many extinct?

## Speciation and Extinction

The fossil record provides evidence about the nature and rate of evolutionary change in species and larger clades. Major transformations in anatomy, phylogeny, ecology, and behavior, which usually take place in larger clades, are known as **macroevolutionary patterns**. 🔍 *The emergence, growth, and extinction of larger clades, such as dinosaurs, mammals, or flowering plants, are examples of macroevolutionary patterns.*

**Macroevolution and Cladistics** Fossils are classified using the same cladistic techniques used to classify living species. In some cases, fossils are placed in clades that contain only extinct organisms. In other cases, fossils are placed in clades that include living organisms. Cladograms illustrate hypotheses about how closely related organisms are, by proposing relationships among living species, extinct species, and common ancestors that they share. Note that hypothesizing that an extinct species is *related* to a living species is *not* the same thing as claiming that the extinct organism is a direct *ancestor* of that living species. For example, **Figure 20-9** does not suggest that any extinct species shown are direct ancestors of modern birds. Instead, the extinct species shown descended over time from a line of common ancestors that they share with modern birds.

**Adaptation and Extinction** When environmental conditions change, natural selection and other evolutionary mechanisms enable some species to evolve adaptations to the new conditions. Species that evolve such adaptations thrive. Species that fail to adapt to changing environments become extinct. Interestingly, the rates at which species appear, adapt, and become extinct vary from one clade to another and from one period of geologic time to another.

Why have some clades produced many species and survived for long periods, while other clades have given rise to only a few species that vanished? Paleontologists look for part of the answer by studying patterns of speciation and extinction in different clades. One way to think about this process is in terms of species diversity. High species diversity within a clade can serve as "raw material" for macroevolutionary change in that clade. In some cases, the more varied the adaptations of species in a clade are, the more likely the clade is to survive environmental change. This is similar to the way in which genetic diversity serves as raw material for evolutionary change for populations within a species. If the rate of speciation in a clade is equal to or greater than the rate of extinction, the clade will continue to exist. If the rate of extinction in a clade is greater than the rate of speciation, the clade will eventually become extinct.

The clade Reptilia is one example of a highly successful clade. The reptile cladogram in Figure 20-9 includes living snakes, lizards, turtles, and crocodiles, and also dinosaurs that thrived for tens of millions of years. It also includes the common ancestors shared by all members of this clade. Most species in the clade Dinosauria are now extinct, but the clade survived because it produced groups of new species that adapted to changing conditions. One small dinosaur clade survives today—we call them birds.

**Figure 20-9**

## The Lineage of Modern Birds

This cladogram shows some of the clades within the large clade Reptilia. The photograph shows fossilized feathers in amber. Notice that clade Dinosauria is represented today by modern birds.
☑ **Classify** What are the two major clades of dinosaurs shown in this figure?

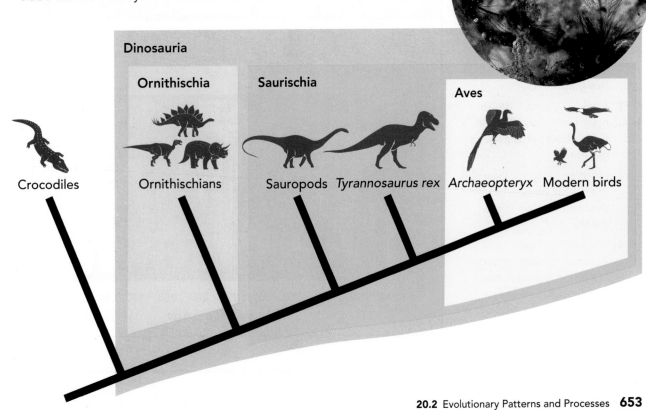

Dinosauria

Ornithischia

Saurischia

Aves

Crocodiles  Ornithischians  Sauropods  *Tyrannosaurus rex*  *Archaeopteryx*  Modern birds

**READING TOOL**

Compare the causes and effects of background extinction and mass extinction.

**Patterns of Extinction** Species become extinct when they fail to adapt to competition and changing environments. Paleontologists describe this kind of "business as usual" extinction as **background extinction**. Rates of background extinction vary over time, but tend to leave functioning ecosystems and many species intact.

However, every few hundred million years or so, something dramatic happens that affects species and ecosystems on a global scale. This type of event is called a **mass extinction**. In a mass extinction, a large number of species become extinct over a relatively short time. A mass extinction isn't just a small increase in background extinction. Entire ecosystems vanish, and whole food webs collapse. Species become extinct because their environment breaks down and the ordinary process of natural selection cannot compensate quickly enough.

Mass extinctions reduce biodiversity rapidly and dramatically. Some groups of organisms survive while other groups do not. What happens then? Survivors face a changed world. There is less competition. Climate may have changed. Many new ecological niches open up. As adaptation and speciation produce new species that fill those niches, biodiversity slowly recovers—typically over 5 to 10 million years.

☑ **READING CHECK Describe** What is the difference between background extinction and mass extinction?

HS-LS4-5

**Analyzing Data**

## Extinctions Through Time

The graph shows how the rate of extinction has changed over time.

1. **Analyze Data** What is the likely source for the data in this graph?

2. **Analyze Graphs** Which mass extinction killed off the highest percentage of genera?

3. **Identify Patterns** Describe the overall pattern of extinction shown in the graph.

4. **Apply Scientific Reasoning** What changes in environmental conditions could have led to these mass extinctions?

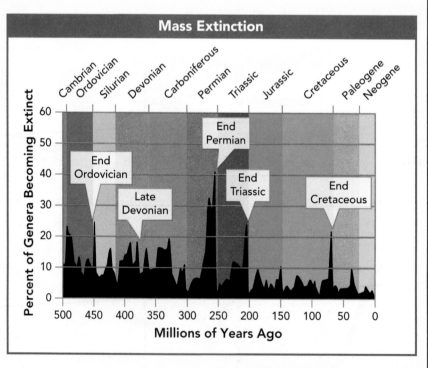

# Rate of Evolution

Evolution does not occur at exactly the same rate for all species all of the time. ✎ *Fossil evidence supports the hypothesis that evolution can occur at different rates in different clades, and at different times.* Species may evolve gradually or rapidly, or appear or disappear suddenly. Those data support the hypothesis that, at certain times, some organisms have experienced periods of little or no visible evolutionary change. Other times, the fossil record documents the relatively sudden appearance or disappearance of certain species and supports a dynamic model of evolutionary change. Two models of evolutionary change are shown in **Figure 20-10**.

**Gradualism** Darwin suggested that evolution proceeded slowly and steadily, an idea called **gradualism**. The fossil record shows that many organisms have indeed changed gradually. Sometimes, however, the physical structures preserved in the fossil record don't appear to have changed much over long periods of time. Major body structures of horseshoe crabs, for example, have changed little from the time these species first appeared in the fossil record. For much of their history, these species are said to have been in a state of equilibrium, or *stasis*. This means that their structures do not change much even though they continue to evolve genetically.

**Punctuated Equilibrium** ✎ *Now and then, the fossil record shows that equilibrium can be interrupted by brief periods of geologically rapid change.* This pattern is called **punctuated equilibrium**. During such "punctuations," existing species may change and new species may appear rapidly. In fact, some biologists suggest that many new species evolve during periods of relatively rapid change. It is important to remember that words like "rapid" and "relatively rapid" here are in relation to time measured by the 4.5-billion-year geologic time scale. The meaning of "rapid change" in paleontology is different from what you think of when you hear about a rapid change in your daily life. Geologically "rapid" change can take place over many thousands or millions of years.

**INTERACTIVITY**

**Figure 20-10**

## Gradualism and Punctuated Equilibrium

Biologists have considered two different patterns for the rate of evolution: gradualism and punctuated equilibrium. These illustrations are simplified to show the general trend of each model.

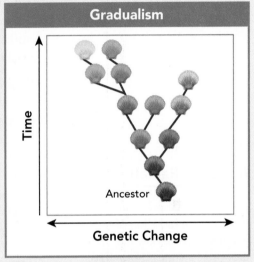

Gradualism involves a slow, steady change in a particular line of descent.

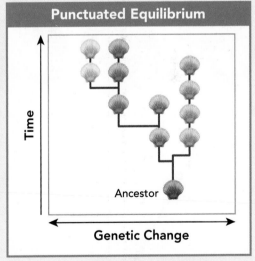

Punctuated equilibrium involves stable periods interrupted by rapid changes.

## Rapid Evolution After Equilibrium

Evolution of species may proceed at different rates at different times. You learned earlier in this unit about some mechanisms that can explain this variation in rates of change. Two types of events that can lead to rapid evolution are genetic drift and mass extinctions.

**Genetic Drift** Recall that in small populations, a trait can become more or less common simply by chance. Rapid evolution may occur after a small population becomes isolated from the main population. This founder effect could happen when a small population colonizes a new environment, such as the finches that left South America and colonized the Galápagos Islands.

A genetic bottleneck may occur when a disease or natural disaster greatly reduces the size of a population. By chance, the smaller population may have a different allele frequency than the larger population had.

**Mass Extinction** Mass extinctions open ecological niches, creating new opportunities for many populations of surviving organisms. Groups of organisms that survive mass extinctions can evolve "rapidly" during the first several million years after the extinction. At the end of the Permian Period, for example, a mass extinction occurred, known as "The Great Dying." A large majority of species on Earth became extinct. Evidence suggests that life rebounded relatively quickly after the Permian extinction as the survivors thrived in environments with limited competition.

☑ **READING CHECK** **Compare and Contrast** How do patterns of change differ in gradualism and punctuated equilibrium?

## Figure 20-11
## Adaptive Radiation

This diagram shows part of the adaptive radiation of mammals. Note how the groups of animals shown have adapted to different ways of life—including two groups that became aquatic.

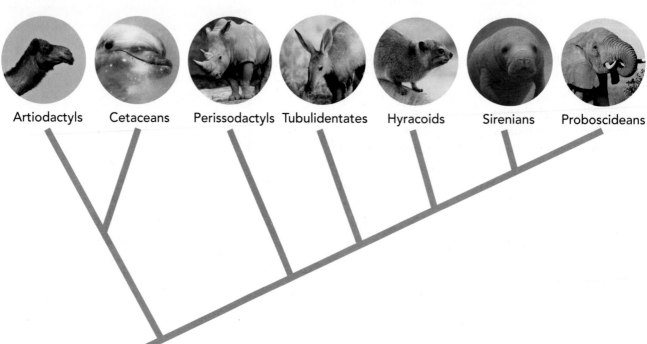

Artiodactyls   Cetaceans   Perissodactyls   Tubulidentates   Hyracoids   Sirenians   Proboscideans

Mammal ancestor

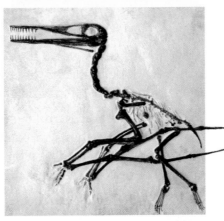

**Figure 20-12**
**Convergent Evolution**

Animals from different lineages may independently evolve structures or systems that perform similar functions. Flight, for example, has evolved in many different animal lineages. Animals in these pictures are all said to have "wings." But the structures used in flight are made of different parts, and operate in different ways. The pterodactyl, whose fossil is shown here, is an extinct flying reptile.

# Macroevolutionary Patterns

As evolutionary biologists study the fossil record, they look for patterns. ✎ *Two important patterns of macroevolution are adaptive radiation and convergent evolution.*

**Adaptive Radiation** Descendants of an ancestral species may diversify over time into related species adapted to different niches. This process, where a single species evolves into several distinct species, is called **adaptive radiation**. Adaptive radiation may occur when species migrate to new environments or when extinction eliminates competing species.

Dinosaurs underwent adaptive radiations during the Mesozoic Era. After most dinosaurs became extinct, mammals began a new adaptive radiation, as shown in **Figure 20-11**. Galápagos finches also experienced an adaptive radiation, as they adapted to islands with different kinds of available food.

**Convergent Evolution** Unrelated organisms in similar environments may evolve adaptations to similar niches. The appearance of similar characteristics in unrelated organisms is known as **convergent evolution**. For example, mammals that feed on ants and termites evolved five times in different regions across the world. Large grassland birds, such as the emus, rheas, and ostriches Darwin observed, are also examples of convergent evolution. Flight has also evolved in unrelated species, as shown in **Figure 20-12**.

**BUILD VOCABULARY**

**Prefixes** The prefix *macro-* comes from the Greek *makro-*, meaning "large." Macroevolutionary patterns are large patterns of evolution.

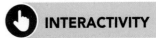 **INTERACTIVITY**

Build and analyze clado-grams to determine evolutionary relationships between bats and birds.

**Figure 20-13**

**Plants and Herbivorous Insects**

Milkweed plants produce toxic chemicals. However, they are the only food source for monarch caterpillars. The caterpillars can tolerate the toxin and store it in their own body tissues as a defense against predators.

# Coevolution

Sometimes two or more species are so closely connected ecologically that they evolve together. The process by which two species evolve in response to changes in each other over time is called **coevolution**. Many flowering plants, for example, can reproduce only if their flowers attract a specific pollinator species. Pollinators, in turn, may depend on the flowers of certain plants for pollen or nectar. ⚲ *The relationship between coevolving organisms often becomes so specific that neither organism can survive without the other. Evolutionary change in one organism is usually followed by a change in the other organism.*

**Flowers and Pollinators** Coevolution of flowers and pollinators can lead to unusual results. For example, Darwin described an orchid whose nectar was at the bottom of a tube nearly 40 centimeters long. He predicted the existence of an insect with a feeding structure long enough to reach that nectar.

Darwin never discovered the insect. However, about 40 years after Darwin's hypothesis, researchers discovered a moth with a 40-centimeter-long feeding tube that was eating the nectar of the orchid. The discovery was exactly what Darwin predicted!

**Plants and Herbivorous Insects** Plants and herbivorous insects also coevolve. Insects have been feeding on flowering plants since both groups emerged. Over time, many plants have evolved bad-tasting or poisonous compounds that discourage insects from eating them. But once plants produce poisons, natural selection on herbivorous insects favors any variants that can alter, inactivate, or eliminate those poisons. Time and again, a group of insects, like the caterpillar shown in **Figure 20-13**, have evolved a way to deal with the particular poisons produced by a certain group of plants.

HS-LS4-1, HS-LS4-4, HS-LS4-5

# ✓ LESSON 20.2 Review

## ⚲ KEY QUESTIONS

1. How does variation within a clade affect the clade's chance of surviving environmental change?

2. What patterns, if any, are formed by the rates of evolution in different lineages?

3. How does adaptive radiation compare to convergent evolution?

4. How can evolutionary change in one species lead to evolutionary change in another species that it is associated with? Include an example to support your answer.

## CRITICAL THINKING

5. **Stability and Change** Major geologic changes often go hand in hand with mass extinctions. Why do you think this is true?

6. **Draw Conclusions** Mammals that have horns or antlers include deer, antelope, goats, and sheep. Is it reasonable to conclude that the trait of horns evolved in a common ancestor of all these mammals? Explain.

7. CASE STUDY During the Devonian Period, when *Tiktaalik* lived, the only land animals were invertebrates, such as worms and insects. Which macroevolutionary pattern do you think occurred once animals were able to survive outside of the water? Explain your answer.

# Earth's Early History

## KEY QUESTIONS

- *What do scientists hypothesize about early Earth and the origin of life?*
- *What theory explains the origin of eukaryotic cells?*

**HS-ESS1-6:** Apply scientific reasoning and evidence from ancient Earth materials, meteorites, and other planetary surfaces to construct an account of Earth's formation and early history.

**HS-ESS2-6:** Develop a quantitative model to describe the cycling of carbon among the hydrosphere, atmosphere, geosphere, and biosphere.

**HS-ESS2-7:** Construct an argument based on evidence about the simultaneous coevolution of Earth's systems and life on Earth.

**VOCABULARY**

endosymbiotic theory

**READING TOOL**

List the events described in the text in the order in which they occur. Take notes in your 📕 Biology Foundations Workbook.

▶ **VIDEO**

Learn how scientists classify a new organism from fossil records.

---

How did life on Earth begin? What were the earliest forms of life? Origin-of-life research is a dynamic field. Current hypotheses will probably change as our understanding of the story continues to grow.

## Mysteries of Life's Origins

Geological and astronomical evidence suggest that Earth formed as pieces of cosmic debris collided. The rest of the solar system formed in much the same way, and at the same time. For millions of years, volcanic activity rocked Earth, as comets and asteroids bombarded its surface. About 4.2 billion years ago, Earth cooled enough to allow solid rocks to form. The cooling allowed water to condense as rain, which formed the oceans. Liquid water on the surface was essential for the first living things, just as it is essential today.

This infant planet was very different from Earth today. 🔑 *Earth's early atmosphere contained little or no oxygen. It was mainly composed of carbon dioxide, water vapor, and nitrogen, with smaller amounts of carbon monoxide, hydrogen sulfide, and hydrogen cyanide.* Because of these gases, the sky was probably pinkish-orange. If you had been there, a deep breath might have killed you! Even though the young planet seems like it would have been inhospitable to life, this was the Earth on which life began.

**Organic Molecules in Space** We now know that many basic building blocks of life form naturally in our solar system. Meteorites and comets contain several amino acids, including those used by living organisms to make proteins. These data suggest that similar molecules were present on early Earth.

## Figure 20-14

## The Miller-Urey Experiment

Miller and Urey produced amino acids, which are needed to make proteins, by passing sparks of electricity through a mixture of hydrogen, methane, ammonia, and water vapor. Evidence now suggests that the composition of Earth's atmosphere was different from their 1953 experiments. More recent experiments with different mixtures of gases have produced similar amino acids.

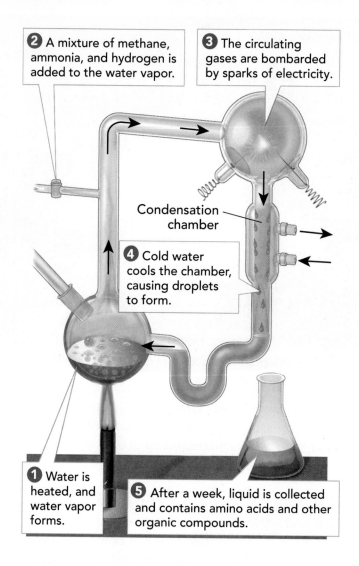

**2** A mixture of methane, ammonia, and hydrogen is added to the water vapor.

**3** The circulating gases are bombarded by sparks of electricity.

Condensation chamber

**4** Cold water cools the chamber, causing droplets to form.

**1** Water is heated, and water vapor forms.

**5** After a week, liquid is collected and contains amino acids and other organic compounds.

**INTERACTIVITY**

Investigate the origin of life on Earth.

**The Miller-Urey Experiment** In 1953, chemists Stanley Miller and Harold Urey tried to test the hypothesis that organic compounds could have been produced on early Earth. They warmed water in a sterile flask and added methane, ammonia, and hydrogen to simulate Earth's early atmosphere. Then, as shown in **Figure 20-14**, they passed sparks of electricity through the gases to simulate lightning. The liquid circulated through the experimental apparatus for a week.

The results were spectacular. Miller and Urey's analysis revealed that 21 amino acids had been produced in their apparatus. A more recent analysis of one of Miller's experiments not only confirmed that result, but also found that the experiment had produced two additional amino acids for a total of 23! *Miller and Urey's experiment suggests that organic compounds necessary for life could have arisen from simpler compounds on a primitive Earth.*

While Miller and Urey's hypotheses about the composition of the early atmosphere were incorrect, more recent experiments using current ideas about the early atmosphere have validated their conclusion: Organic compounds could have been produced on early Earth. The discovery of organic compounds on meteorites and comets has confirmed these lab experiments.

**Formation of Protocells** Amino acids may be easy to make, but what about membranes? Studies show that molecules similar to fatty acids—the building blocks of membrane lipids—can form spontaneously under certain conditions. These molecules can then assemble to form membrane-like vesicles. Similar compounds from a meteorite that fell in Australia in 1969 also formed vesicles in laboratory experiments. Nobel Prize–winner Jack Szostak, an origin-of-life researcher at Harvard University, calls these structures protocells. He suggests that protocells may have formed around molecules similar to RNA, which may have been able to copy themselves.

**RNA First?** Several lines of evidence suggest that RNA, rather than DNA, was the first information-carrying molecule. ⚲ *The "RNA world" hypothesis proposes that RNA existed before DNA. From this simple RNA-based system, several steps could have led to today's DNA-directed protein synthesis.* This hypothesis, shown in **Figure 20-15**, is still being tested, but a number of facts make it credible. Recent experiments show that at least two RNA nucleotides can form in the absence of life. Other experiments show how simple clay minerals can bind nucleotides, which can polymerize to form RNA polynucleotides. In addition, certain RNA sequences are capable of catalyzing chemical reactions that include RNA self-replication.

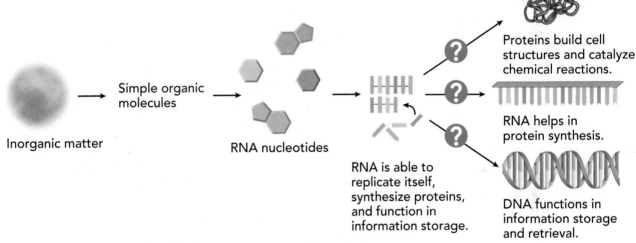

Inorganic matter → Simple organic molecules → RNA nucleotides → RNA is able to replicate itself, synthesize proteins, and function in information storage.

Proteins build cell structures and catalyze chemical reactions.

RNA helps in protein synthesis.

DNA functions in information storage and retrieval.

Furthermore, several molecules important to cell metabolism, such as ATP, NADH, and coenzyme A, are built around RNA-like nucleotides. All cells make proteins by first copying genetic information into RNA. DNA nucleotides themselves are first synthesized as RNA nucleotides. Finally, the ribosomes that build proteins in all cells are "RNA machines" in which RNA, not DNA, performs the key function of linking amino acids together. All these data support the hypothesis that an "RNA world" was a stage in the origin of life on Earth.

Researchers have made major progress in understanding the origin of life. Still, Szostak himself has written that "the exact circumstances of the origin of life may be forever lost to science." That may be true, but experiments have shown that complex molecules like RNA can form in the absence of life, replicate, and carry information. These data give many scientists confidence that, as Szostak has also said, "Research can at least help us understand what is possible."

**Figure 20-15**

## Origin of RNA and DNA

The "RNA world" hypothesis about the origin of life suggests that RNA evolved before DNA. Scientists have not yet demonstrated the later stages of this process in a laboratory setting. ☑ **Interpret Visuals** How would RNA have stored genetic information?

**Figure 20-16**

**Banded Iron Formation**

When photosynthesis evolved, early life began to release oxygen. Oxygen reacted with dissolved iron in the oceans, which led to the formation of iron oxide minerals. This rock, with its layers of red jasper and iron magnetite, was formed billions of years ago as part of that process.

**VIDEO**

Learn how microorganisms changed Earth's atmosphere and made the planet more hospitable for higher life forms.

**READING TOOL**

Recall the symbiotic relationships you learned about in Chapter 6 and describe how the concept relates to the evolution of eukaryotic cells.

**Life Changes the Atmosphere** Microscopic fossils of prokaryotes have been found in rocks more than 3.5 billion years old. When these first life forms evolved, and for more than a billion years afterward, Earth's atmosphere contained very little oxygen. Then, during the early Proterozoic Eon, roughly 2.2 billion years ago, photosynthesis evolved, and photosynthetic bacteria began to churn out oxygen. This highly reactive gas had dramatic effects. Oxygen combined with iron in the oceans, producing iron oxide. The iron oxide sank to the ocean floor and is now the source of most iron ore mined today. You can see bands of iron oxide that formed billions of years ago in **Figure 20-16**.

Next, oxygen accumulated in the atmosphere, forming the ozone layer, which turned the sky a shade of blue. Over several hundred million years, the concentration of oxygen in the atmosphere increased to the point where it drove some early anaerobic life forms to extinction. Other organisms, however, evolved new metabolic pathways that used oxygen for respiration. These organisms also evolved ways to protect themselves from oxygen's powerful reactive properties.

**☑ READING CHECK Summarize** How did photosynthesis change the composition of the atmosphere?

# Origin of the Eukaryotic Cell

Eukaryotic cells, as you've learned, contain several kinds of complex cytoplasmic organelles, including lysosomes, endoplasmic reticula, cilia, and flagella. Two other organelles—chloroplasts and mitochondria—are even more complicated. The evolution of these complex eukaryotic cells from much simpler prokaryotic cells was one of the most important events in the history of life. How did this cellular complexity evolve?

**The Earliest Eukaryotes** The fossil record provides few clues to the evolution of cells. The oldest eukaryotic cell fossils have been found in rocks 2.1 billion years old. Unfortunately, these microscopic fossils don't usually show details of internal cell structure, so they provide few clues about early eukaryote evolution.

Studies of living cells, however, have led to several ideas. The **endosymbiotic theory**, developed in the 1960s by Lynn Margulis of the University of Massachusetts, proposes that organelles in eukaryotic cells were formed when different types of cells joined in a kind of merger, as shown in **Figure 20-17**. Margulis called her idea endosymbiosis, which literally means "living together within." In recent years, molecular biology has been able to evaluate this theory with new techniques and greater precision. ✱ *A great deal of evidence now supports the theory that many of the complex features of eukaryotic cells evolved through endosymbiosis.* The fact that some cells today contain bacteria and algae living as endosymbionts further supports this theory.

Mitochondria, for example, are similar in size to bacteria, have their own DNA genomes, synthesize some of their own proteins, and are formed when preexisting mitochondria divide. Most biologists now agree with Margulis's evaluation that mitochondria are the descendants of free-living bacteria that took up residence in the earliest eukaryotes.

Similar evidence supports an endosymbiotic origin for chloroplasts. Chloroplast membranes resemble those of photosynthetic prokaryotes. Chloroplast DNA has many similarities to prokaryotes as well. This suggests that chloroplasts evolved from free living photosynthetic cells that paired with the earliest eukaryotes.

Living cells are filled with complex biochemical systems. Some of these are biochemical pathways like the Krebs cycle. Others are complex processes like mitotic cell division. Still others are complicated structures, such as ribosomes, cilia, and flagella. Many of these systems date back billions of years, so it is difficult to determine their exact origins. Nonetheless, analysis of these systems in living cells today provides some interesting clues.

**Figure 20-17**

## The Endosymbiotic Theory

Ancient prokaryotes may have entered primitive eukaryotic cells, remained there, and evolved into organelles. ☑**Infer** Is it likely that nonphotosynthetic prokaryotes could have evolved into chloroplasts? Explain your answer.

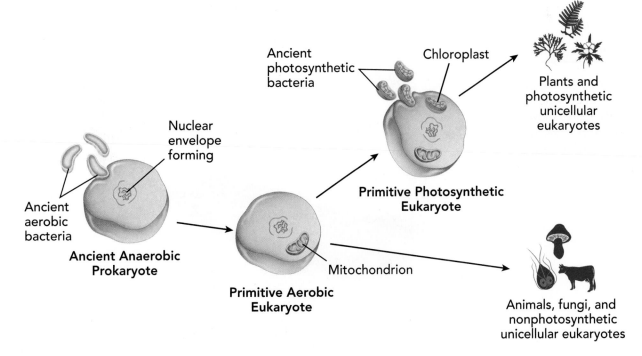

Ancient photosynthetic bacteria

Chloroplast

Plants and photosynthetic unicellular eukaryotes

Nuclear envelope forming

Ancient aerobic bacteria

**Ancient Anaerobic Prokaryote**

Mitochondrion

**Primitive Aerobic Eukaryote**

**Primitive Photosynthetic Eukaryote**

Animals, fungi, and nonphotosynthetic unicellular eukaryotes

### The Ribosome

Ribosomes are complex organelles used by all living cells to translate the coded instructions of mRNA molecules into the sequences of amino acids that make up proteins. Ribosomes in eukaryotic cells consist of four ribosomal RNA molecules and more than 80 different proteins. The origin of this complex structure has long been a mystery. New research, however, has led to some surprising findings. One of these is that the part of the ribosome where chemical bonds are formed between amino acids completely lacks proteins. This is true of other key places in the ribosome as well, so it is now clear that ribosomal RNA itself carries out the most important tasks in protein synthesis. As a result, the evidence suggests that the earliest cells may have produced proteins using RNA alone. Over time, proteins were added to that RNA in ways that improved the efficiency of the process, leading to today's complex ribosomes.

### Cilia and Flagella

Cilia and flagella are complex structures that enable cells to move. **Figure 20-18** shows an example of a bacterium with flagella. The two main groups of prokaryotes have two types of flagella that differ biochemically. The flagella of Eubacteria contain 30 to 40 proteins, while the flagella of Archaea contain 10 to 20 proteins. Yet these flagella share a common feature that helps explain their origin. Each type of flagellum is assembled from protein subunits that serve other purposes elsewhere in the cell. For example, the flagella of Archaea contain proteins resembling those found in structures on the cell surface known as pili. Nearly every protein in the flagella of Eubacteria resembles proteins that are used for other purposes in bacteria that lack flagella. This suggests that these cells "borrowed" copies of these proteins as the flagellum evolved. In fact, a group of ten such proteins so closely resembles a channel structure in the cell membrane that the channel structure and the flagellum may share a common ancestor.

### Figure 20-18
### Bacterium with Flagella

Cilia and flagella remain features of bacteria today. Their structures show how cells can reuse proteins for new purposes (TEM 14,000x).

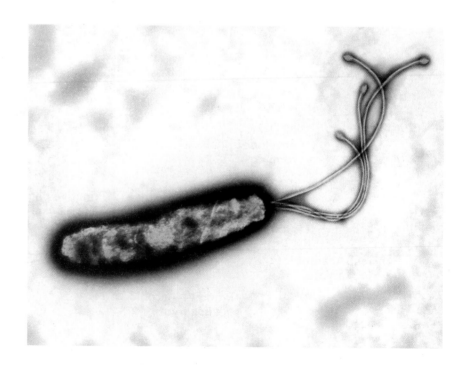

**Argument-Based Inquiry**     **Guided Inquiry**

### Modeling Coacervates

**Problem** How can you model the early stages of life?

Coacervates are beadlike collections of amino acids, carbohydrates, and other compounds. In this lab, you will make a model of coacervates. Then you will analyze your model to make inferences about the role of coacervates in developing the first cells.

You can find this lab in your digital course.

In eukaryotes, these structures contain several hundred different proteins. The key proteins in eukaryotic cilia and flagella are tubulin and dynein. Both of these proteins are involved in many other systems in the cell that produce movement, including the movements of chromosomes during mitosis. This suggests that the major protein components of cilia and flagella were present before these structures evolved. With time, complex systems evolved by reusing old existing parts in new ways.

### Do We Understand the Cell Completely? Of course not.

Many uncertainties remain in our current understanding of cellular complexity. Biologists are still learning how cells function in response to their environments and how they interact with each other. Such uncertainties are as much a part of biology as they are for any other experimental science. In many ways, this is good news, because it means that there are plenty of mysteries to be solved by the next generation of biologists. Meanwhile, what we do understand suggests that complex cell structures and pathways were produced by known mechanisms of evolutionary change.

HS-ESS1-6, HS-ESS2-6, HS-ESS2-7

## ☑ LESSON 20.3 Review

### ⚲ KEY QUESTIONS

1. What was Earth's early atmosphere like?

2. How could the basic compounds necessary for life have been formed on early Earth?

3. What does the endosymbiotic theory propose?

### CRITICAL THINKING

4. **Construct an Explanation** Did the first living cell evolve suddenly in a single step or gradually as the result of many intermediate steps? Explain.

5. **Cite Evidence** What evidence and logical reasoning support the conclusion that anaerobic organisms evolved first, followed much later by aerobic organisms?

6. **Develop Models** What evidence supports the model of endosymbiotic origin for mitochondria and chloroplasts?

Neil Shubin

# How did fossil hunters find *Tiktaalik?*

Finding *Tiktaalik* was as amazing as it is scientifically important. That discovery followed years of careful research and preparation, that helped Shubin and his colleagues to figure out where to look!

## Make Your Case

Based on other fossils and radiometric dating, Neil Shubin and his colleagues knew that vertebrates first made the move from water to land during the Devonian period, between 380 and 363 million years ago. The island of Ellesmere, in the Canadian Arctic, had freshwater sedimentary rocks of exactly that age, so that's where they began their explorations. After four summers of hard work, one member of the group noticed something unusual in a rocky hillside. As they carefully chipped away at the rock, they discovered the first of many *Tiktaalik* fossils.

## Construct an Explanation

1. **Cite Evidence** Shubin concluded that the fossil he sought was buried in rocks from the Devonian Period. What evidence supported this conclusion?

2. **Apply Scientific Reasoning** How does *Tiktaalik* provide evidence for the evolution of tetrapods and land-dwelling vertebrates?

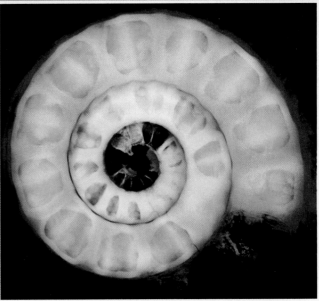

## Technology on the Case

### X-Rays for Fossils

After technology is developed for one purpose, it often becomes useful in new ways. One example is X-ray technology. X-rays are a form of high-energy electromagnetic radiation. They pass through soft materials, but are stopped by hard, dense matter, such as bone. After their initial discovery, technology that uses X-rays was developed for doctors to identify broken bones and for dentists to find tooth decay. Now, paleontologists are using X-rays to study fossils.

In 2009, scientists at Stanford University used extremely powerful X-rays to study a fossil of *Archaeopetryx*. This animal was an intermediate species between dinosaur and bird. The X-rays showed the presence of trace elements that might have been a part of muscles or feathers.

In 2015, researchers studied a fossil of a sea urchin using computed tomography (CT). This technology uses X-rays to generate three-dimensional images of an object's interior. The results showed that a colony of tiny mollusks had lived inside the sea urchin.

In 2016, scientists at the University of Florida began using a micro-CT scanner. This scanner can resolve images to a micrometer, which is one millionth of a meter. In one project, the scanner is helping to depict the brain of an animal that lived 45 million years ago.

## Careers on the Case

### Work Toward a Solution

Neil Shubin is a paleontologist, a scientist who studies ancient life. People in other careers work with paleontologists to help find, study, prepare, and communicate about fossils.

### Fossil Preparator

If you have enjoyed seeing fossils at a museum, then you have benefited from the work of a fossil preparator. Fossil preparators specialize in preparing fossils to study or for display. Sometimes, they remove a fossil from its surrounding rock. They may also repair damaged fossils.

▶ **VIDEO**

Learn more about careers related to studying the history of life.

**hhmi | BioInteractive**

# Lesson Review

Go to your Biology Foundations Workbook for longer versions of these lesson summaries.

## 20.1 The Fossil Record

From the fossil record, paleontologists learn about the structure of ancient organisms, their environment, and the ways in which they lived. The fossil record is incomplete because the remains of many organisms decay before they can be fossilized, or the organisms die in an environment where fossils are unlikely to form.

Relative dating allows paleontologists to determine whether a fossil is older or younger than other fossils. Radiometric dating uses the proportion of radioactive to stable isotopes to calculate the age of a sample.

The geologic time scale is based on both relative and absolute dating. The major divisions of the geologic time scale are eons, eras, and periods.

Rising mountains, changing coastlines, changing climates, and geological forces have altered habitats of living organisms repeatedly throughout Earth's history. In turn, the actions of living organisms over time have changed conditions in the land, water, and atmosphere.

- extinct
- relative dating
- index fossil
- radiometric dating
- half-life
- geologic time scale
- era
- period
- plate tectonics

☑ **Summarize** What environmental conditions are important in order for intricate structures to be preserved in a fossil?

## 20.2 Evolutionary Patterns and Processes

If the rate of speciation in a clade is equal to or greater than the rate of extinction, the clade will continue to exist. If the rate of extinction in a clade is greater than the rate of speciation, the clade will eventually become extinct.

Evidence shows that evolution has often proceeded at different rates for different organisms at different times over the long history of life on Earth. Sometimes species change gradually over time. Sometimes an event occurs that disrupts the species equilibrium and change becomes relatively rapid.

Two important patterns of macroevolution are adaptive radiation and convergent evolution. Adaptive radiation occurs when a single species or a small group of species evolves over a relatively short time into several different forms that live in different ways. Convergent evolution occurs when unrelated organisms evolve into similar forms, such as the large grassland birds that Darwin observed.

The relationship between two coevolving organisms often becomes so specific that neither organism can survive without the other. Thus, an evolutionary change in one organism is usually followed by a change in the other organism.

- macroevolutionary pattern
- background extinction
- mass extinction
- gradualism
- punctuated equilibrium
- adaptive radiation
- convergent evolution
- coevolution

☑ **Explain** How do the concepts of gradualism and punctuated equilibrium help to explain the fossil record?

## 20.3 Earth's Early History

The early Earth was very hot and experienced intense volcanic activity. Eventually Earth cooled which allowed solid rock and oceans to form. Earth's early atmosphere contained little or no oxygen. It was principally composed of carbon dioxide, water vapor, and nitrogen, with lesser amounts of carbon monoxide, hydrogen sulfide, and hydrogen cyanide.

Scientists have long wondered how life began on Earth. Miller and Urey's experiment suggested how mixtures of the organic compounds necessary for life could have arisen from simpler compounds on a primitive Earth. The "RNA world" hypothesis proposes that RNA existed by itself before DNA. From this simple RNA-based system, several steps could have led to DNA-directed protein synthesis.

The evolution of photosynthetic microorganisms changed Earth's oceans and atmosphere. The microorganisms removed carbon dioxide from the atmosphere and added oxygen to it. Over several hundred millions of years, this allowed for the evolution of microorganisms that use oxygen for respiration.

The endosymbiotic theory explains the evolution of eukaryotic cells by proposing that a symbiotic relationship evolved over time between primitive eukaryotic cells and the prokaryotic cells within them.

Research has shown that the structure of ribosomes would have allowed early cells to use RNA alone to produce proteins. Cellular research has also shown that cilia and flagella may have evolved from protein subunits that served other purposes in the cell.

- endosymbiotic theory

☑**Summarize** How does this photo help explain the history of life on Earth?

## Organize Information

Cite evidence for each statement from the text. Then draw a model to support each statement.

| Statement | Evidence | Model |
|---|---|---|
| Fossils are a roadmap of evolution. | 1. | 2. |
| Evolution does not proceed at a constant rate. | 3. | 4. |
| Symbiosis was crucial to cell development. | 5. | 6. |

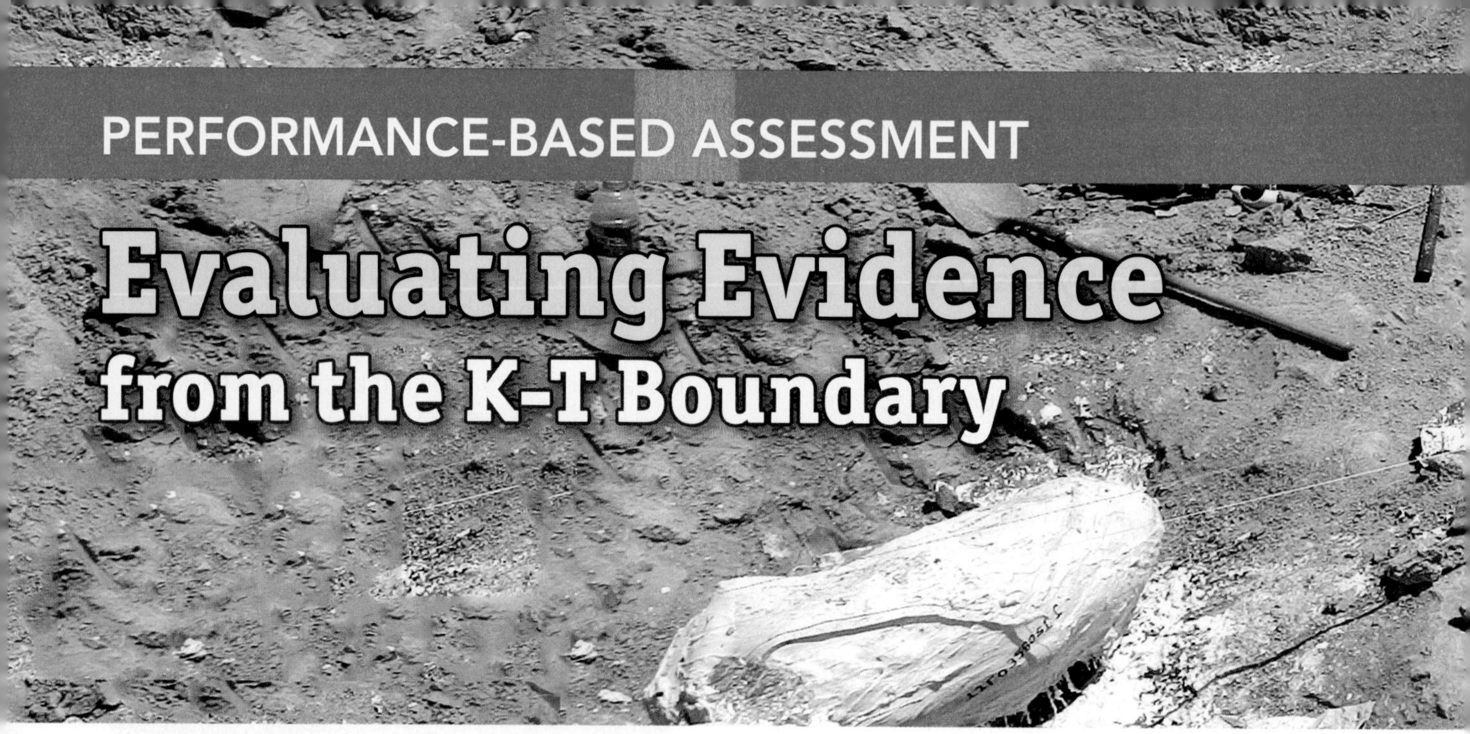

# Evaluating Evidence from the K-T Boundary

## Apply Scientific Reasoning

HS-LS4-5

The fossil record shows that dinosaurs once lived in nearly every habitable part of Earth. Fossils of widely known dinosaurs are particularly common in rocks dating from the Mesozoic Era, which ended around 66 million years ago. But after the Mesozoic, dinosaur fossils are nowhere to be found. What's more, many other Mesozoic species—plant and animal, terrestrial and marine—also disappeared.

What could have caused that mass extinction? Scientists been debating this question for many years, and new data are still being gathered to test two competing hypotheses.

The hypothesis that most people are familiar with was proposed by a father-son team: physicist Luis Alvarez and geologist Walter Alvarez. They were studying a layer of rocks called the K-T boundary, which marks the end of the Cretaceous Period ("K"), and the beginning of the Tertiary Period ("T"). (Recall that the Tertiary Period is now split into the Paleogene and Neogene Periods). They found that the K-T layer was rich in iridium, an element that is rare on Earth's surface, but common in objects from space such as meteorites. What could this mean?

Other studies showed that K-T boundary rocks from elsewhere, especially in North America, contain a type of deformed quartz called shocked quartz, along with glassy beads called spherules. Shocked quartz can form when powerful pressure waves move through rocks, and spherules form when rock vaporizes, then solidifies. They put these clues together with other evidence. In 1991, scientists discovered a huge crater just off the Yucatan peninsula, where an asteroid had punched through the floor of the Gulf of Mexico.

Some of the evidence from the K-T boundary is summarized in the table. Based in part on this evidence, the Alvarez team and other scientists propose the following hypothesis for the K-T mass extinction.

- For millions of years near the end of the Cenozoic Era, Earth's climate was relatively constant. Dinosaurs lived in many places around the world, and were diverse and numerous.

- About 65 million years ago, an asteroid struck Earth, in the region that is now Mexico's Yucatán peninsula. The asteroid strike raised a huge cloud of dust and ash that spread around the world. Sudden changes to the climate and other environmental factors caused most species to go extinct.

- Within 10 million years of the asteroid strike, mammalian diversity exploded, as surviving mammals evolved and filled the ecological niches left empty by the extinct dinosaurs.

| Evidence from the K-T Boundary | |
|---|---|
| **Rock Layers** | **Observations** |
| Beneath the K-T Boundary | • Contains fossils from a wide variety of dinosaurs, as well as other animals and plants<br>• Thick rock layers are relatively uniform, indicating consistent conditions over millions of years |
| At the K-T Boundary | • Rocks are high in iridium<br>• Rocks in North America contain shocked quartz and spherules |
| Above the K-T Boundary | • No fossils from 80% of Cretaceous animal species, including all dinosaur species<br>• Fossil pollen shows 60% fewer plant species than during the Cretaceous Period<br>• Fossils of small animals are common |

1. **Apply Scientific Reasoning** How do observations of the K-T boundary support the conclusion that an asteroid hit Earth about 65 million years ago?

2. **Infer** Why might spherules and shocked quartz be common in K-T boundary rocks in North America, but not in other continents?

3. **Evaluate Evidence** Evaluate the evidence presented as support for the Alvarez hypothesis about the K-T extinction. Does this evidence support this hypothesis? Search for other scientific evidence about the K-T extinction that appears to support an alternative hypothesis. What does your research tell you about the current scientific consensus about this extinction?

4. **Construct an Explanation** After the extinction, mammals underwent a dramatic adaptive radiation from a few, mostly small species to the large-bodied, diverse forms we know today. Explain how a change in the environment made this possible.

5. **Communicate** Prepare a written or oral report, or a computer presentation, to share your evaluation of the evidence of the evolutionary changes that occurred 65 million years ago. In your evaluation, discuss these concepts from the chapter.
   - extinction
   - mass extinction
   - macroevolutionary patterns
   - adaptive radiation

## 🔑 KEY QUESTIONS AND TERMS

### 20.1 The Fossil Record
HS-LS4-1, HS-ESS1-5, HS-ESS2-7

1. Fossils are most often found in
   a. soil.　　　　　c. igneous rock.
   b. sedimentary rock. d. clay.

2. Trilobite fossils are found in only a few rock layers, so they are useful
   a. index fossils.
   b. means of absolute dating.
   c. indicators of stratification.
   d. means of radiometric dating.

3. What type of information do fossils provide?

4. What is measured by the half-life of an element?

5. What changes to Earth's surface are explained by the theory of plate tectonics?

6. How did scientists determine the eras of the geologic time scale?

7. Compare the information learned from relative dating and absolute dating.

### 20.2 Evolutionary Patterns and Processes
HS-LS4-1, HS-LS4-4, HS-LS4-5

8. In convergent evolution, similar traits develop in two species that are
   a. closely related.
   b. not closely related.
   c. extinct.
   d. living.

9. A variety of bear species, including the polar bear, evolved from a common bear ancestor. This pattern of evolution is an example of
   a. adaptive radiation.
   b. convergent evolution.
   c. punctuated equilibrium.
   d. gradualism.

10. Cladograms that are based on the fossil record always show
    a. which organisms are direct ancestors of the others.
    b. relationships based on shared derived characteristics.
    c. that clades are made up of only extinct species.
    d. relative ages of organisms in the clade.

11. The evolution of species at a slow, relatively constant rate is called
    a. background extinction.
    b. mass extinction.
    c. gradualism.
    d. punctuated equilibrium.

12. Evolution by punctuated equilibrium is characterized by
    a. minor genetic change.
    b. slow, gradual change.
    c. varying rates of change.
    d. a constant rate of change.

13. Describe a biological example of a macroevolutionary pattern.

14. How does coevolution link a pair of species?

### 20.3 Earth's Early History
HS-ESS1-6, HS-ESS2-6, HS-ESS2-7

15. Earth's early atmosphere contained
    a. carbon dioxide, water vapor, nitrogen, and oxygen.
    b. carbon dioxide, water vapor, carbon monoxide, and oxygen.
    c. hydrogen sulfide, carbon monoxide, hydrogen cyanide, and water vapor.
    d. oxygen, carbon monoxide, water vapor, and nitrogen.

16. The Miller-Urey experiment demonstrated that the atmosphere of early Earth could support the development of
    a. amino acids.　　c. fatty acids.
    b. proteins.　　　　d. protocells.

17. The origin of the eukaryotic cell is explained by
    a. the RNA world hypothesis.
    b. protocells.
    c. the Miller-Urey experiment.
    d. the endosymbiotic theory.

18. How are protocells similar to living cells?

19. The sky of early Earth was probably pinkish-orange. As life became established, the sky turned blue. What was responsible for the color change?

**20.** What conclusion about life on Earth is supported by the Miller-Urey experiment?

## CRITICAL THINKING

HS-LS4-1, HS-LS4-4, HS-LS4-5, HS-ESS1-5, HS-ESS1-6, HS-ESS2-7

**21. Construct an Explanation** Why do gaps exist in the fossil record?

**22. Evaluate Evidence** The fossil record shows that dinosaurs became extinct about 65 million years ago, after which mammals became more diverse. How does the fossil record support conclusions about environmental changes that began 65 million years ago?

**23. Construct an Argument** After a mass extinction, does evolution generally occur rapidly or slowly? Cite evidence and logical reasoning to support your argument.

**24. Evaluate Models** The diagram shows part of the apparatus used in the Miller-Urey investigations on the origin of life on Earth. How does the apparatus represent early Earth? What are the limitations of the model?

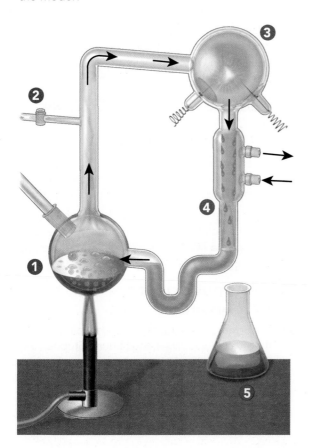

**25. Draw Conclusions** How did the evolution of photosynthesis change Earth's atmosphere and living things?

Use the diagram of rock layers to answer questions 26 and 27. The diagram shows rock layers in two different places.

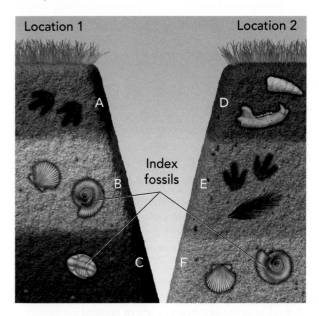

**26. Apply Scientific Reasoning** How do the ages of the fossils from layer A and layer C compare? Explain your reasoning.

**27. Synthesize Information** Which fossils in Location 2 are most likely the same age as the fossils in layer B? Explain.

**28. Apply Scientific Reasoning** Use the example of body shape in sharks, dolphins, and penguins to explain convergent evolution.

**29. Engage in Argument** A student claims that monarch butterflies and milkweed plants evolved together as an example of coevolution. What type of evidence could support this claim?

**30. Predict** Where are fossils most likely to be found: in rocks along the walls of a river canyon, along the mouth of an active volcano, or in the soil of a tropical rain forest? Explain your prediction.

**31. Evaluate Evidence** A scientist digs for fossils in the dry, dusty land in the state of Wyoming. She finds a fossil of fern leaves. What does the fossil evidence show about the natural history of Wyoming?

# ☑ASSESSMENT

## CROSSCUTTING CONCEPTS

**32.** **Cause and Effect** Describe the cause-and-effect relationship between changes in the environment and adaptations in living things.

**33.** **Stability and Change** How is the concept of background extinction an example of both stability and change?

## MATH CONNECTIONS

### Analyze and Interpret Data
CCSS.MATH.CONTENT.MP2

**34.** **Reason Quantitatively** In the analogy of a 24-hour clock for geologic time, the Cenozoic Era would last from 11:39 PM to midnight. What percentage of geologic time is taken up by this era?

**35.** **Interpret Data** A recent newspaper article lists 12 species that were once common in your region, but have gone extinct during the past few years. Classify the type of extinction that the newspaper is reporting. What additional facts would help you evaluate the information?

The table identifies the half-life of several isotopes. Use the table to answer questions 36 and 37.

| Isotope and Decay Product | Half-Life (yrs) |
|---|---|
| Potassium-40 ➝ Argon-40 | 1.25 billion |
| Rubidium-87 ➝ Strontium-87 | 48.8 billion |
| Thorium-232 ➝ Lead-208 | 14.0 billion |
| Uranium-235 ➝ Lead-207 | 704.0 million |
| Uranium-238 ➝ Lead-206 | 4.5 billion |

**36.** **Interpret Data** A sample of thorium-232 has a mass of 12.0 micrograms. What can be concluded about the sample after 14.0 billion years has passed?

**37.** **Calculate** Earth is now about 4.5 billion years old. When will Earth have 1/4 of the uranium-238 that it had when the planet formed?

The diagram shows an example of evolution by punctuated equilibrium. Use the diagram to answer questions 38 and 39.

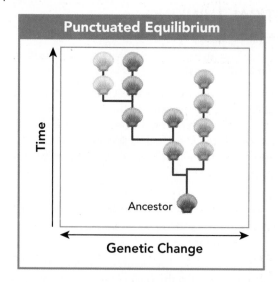

**Punctuated Equilibrium**

Time

Ancestor

Genetic Change

**38.** **Interpret Graphs** What does the graph show about the relationship between time and genetic change when species evolve in a pattern of punctuated equilibrium?

**39.** **Evaluate Conclusions** In this example, does the evidence support the conclusion that punctuated equilibrium will continue in this species as time goes on? Explain your evaluation.

## LANGUAGE ARTS CONNECTION

### Write About Science
HS-ESS2-7, CCSS.ELA-LITERACY.WHST.9-10.1, CCSS.ELA-LITERACY.WHST.9-10.2

**40.** **Write Explanatory Texts** Write a paragraph to explain how fossils may form in sedimentary rock.

**41.** **Write Arguments** Could life have evolved from nonliving compounds? Include evidence, such as from the Miller-Urey experiment, to support your argument.

### Read About Science
CCSS.ELA-LITERACY.RST.9-10.2

**42.** **Determine Meaning** When describing their theory of punctuated equilibrium, Stephen Jay Gould and Niles Eldredge often used the motto "Stasis is data." *Stasis* is another word for *equilibrium*. Explain what Gould and Eldredge meant.

1. The diagram shows fossil layers in different locations. The different shading in the diagram indicates different types of rock.

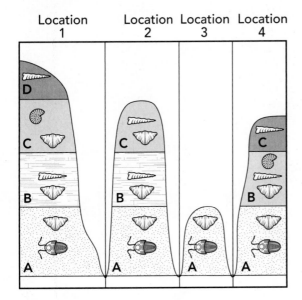

Location 1   Location 2   Location 3   Location 4

How could fossils like the ones shown support the theory of evolution?

A. Fossil evidence supports the hypothesis that evolution can occur at different rates in different clades.

B. Fossil evidence supports the hypothesis that individual organisms and populations evolve to adapt to a changing environment.

C. Fossil evidence provides a complete record of the organisms that once lived and are ancestors to other organisms.

D. Fossil evidence provides information on the allele frequency in ancestral populations.

E. Fossil evidence supports the hypothesis that behavioral isolation contributes to evolutionary change.

2. At the end of the Permian Period, a mass extinction occurred known as "The Great Dying." How do mass extinctions affect the rate of evolutionary change?

A. Species that survive mass extinctions adapt rapidly because they face limited competition.

B. Species that survive mass extinctions adapt rapidly because they have been exposed to mutagens.

C. Species adapt quickly after mass extinctions because the environment has often changed significantly.

D. Species evolve slowly after mass extinctions because the environment has often changed significantly.

E. Evolutionary change occurs slowly after mass extinctions because a large number of species have become extinct over a relatively short time.

3. Over the course of Earth's history, Earth and the organisms that live on it have changed. How did early life on Earth affect Earth's systems?

A. As prokaryotes evolved, methane and ammonia in Earth's atmosphere were replaced with amino acids.

B. As the number of organisms increased, the size of the ozone layer in Earth's atmosphere decreased.

C. As the remains of early organisms accumulated, iron oxide formed in rock layers.

D. As prokaryotes evolved, Earth's atmosphere changed from having little oxygen to having enough oxygen to support cellular respiration.

E. As organisms produced organic compounds, the compounds were released into the atmosphere and formed meteorites and comets.

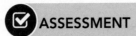 **ASSESSMENT**

For additional assessment practice, go online to access your digital course.

## If You Have Trouble With...

| Question | 1 | 2 | 3 |
|---|---|---|---|
| See Lesson | 20.1 | 20.2 | 20.3 |
| Performance Expectation | HS-LS4-1 | HS-LS4-5 | HS-ESS2-7 |

# UNIT 6 Diversity of Life

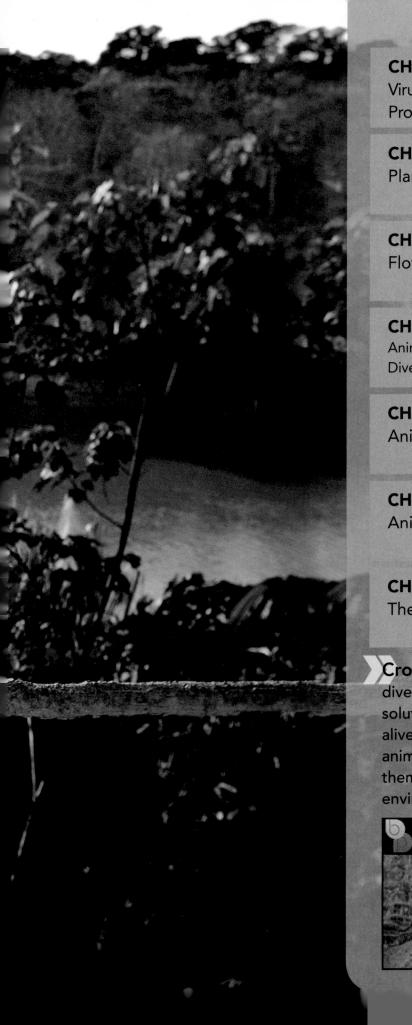

> **Crosscutting Concepts** The great diversity of animal life presents many solutions to the challenges of staying alive. The tissues, organs, and systems of animals are structured in ways that enable them to function in an ever-changing environment.

**BOUNCE TO ACTIVATE**      ▶ **VIDEO**

Author Ken Miller discusses Scale and Proportion as he explains why an elephant can't jump like a grasshopper.

# Recovery

## PLANS FOR ENDANGERED SPECIES

**The bald eagle, the timber** wolf, and the American alligator are all species that teetered on the brink of extinction due to human activities such as pollution, overhunting, and habitat destruction. For the bald eagle, loss of habitat, illegal hunting, and contamination of the animals' food source with the pesticide DDT nearly wiped out the population. In the 1960s fewer than 500 nesting pairs remained. Intentional actions designed to protect bald eagle habitats and eliminate DDT from the environment have resulted in an impressive recovery. The bald eagle is an example of a species saved by a successful recovery plan.

**PROBLEM LAUNCH**
Conduct research and develop a recovery plan on an endangered species in your region.

▶ **VIDEO SAFARI**

**BOUNCE TO ACTIVATE**

Watch a video about the contributing factors that might lead to a species becoming endangered.

# PROBLEM: How can you develop a species recovery plan?

≫ **TO SOLVE THIS PROBLEM,** perform these activities as they come up in the unit and record your findings in your ⬧ Explorer's Journal.

## INTERACTIVITY

Explore captive breeding and reintroduction of endangered species.

## LAB INVESTGATION

Investigate the effect of environmental conditions on plants.

## AUTHENTIC READING

Read an article about how climate change impacts the growth of walnut trees.

### STEM STEM PROJECT

Research your endangered species and design a plan for its recovery.

## INTERACTIVITY

Investigate how pollution can affect an animal's body systems.

## PROBLEM WRAP-UP

Evaluate and revise your recovery plan, and then present your findings as a report.

| **21.1** Viruses | **21.2** Prokaryotes | **21.3** Protists | **21.4** Fungi |
|---|---|---|---|

**Go Online to access your digital course.**

▶ **VIDEO**

🔊 **AUDIO**

👆 **INTERACTIVITY**

📖 **eTEXT**

👁 **ANIMATION**

⚗ **VIRTUAL LAB**

☑ **ASSESSMENT**

Controlling the mosquito population helps slow the spread of the disease-causing organisms they carry.

# Preventing the next epidemic

The plot could come from a horror movie. *They* are silent, invisible, always in the background. At first, they do no harm. Then something small happens. Perhaps a new animal arrives in the neighborhood, one that becomes their ideal host, and they stop being harmless.

*They* are the microscopic organisms, or microbes, with whom we share this planet. In fact, these organisms actually *dominate* the planet. They are found everywhere, from the cleanest home to the most extreme environments on earth.

Most of the time, their actions are harmless or even helpful. In nature, they help to recycle dead organic material, such as when they break down a dead tree to help enrich the soil. Microbes known as bacteria also live closely with plants and animals. In fact, the human body may be home to more bacterial cells than human cells!

Centuries ago, Europeans first made their way into North and South America. They brought horses and guns, both of which were unknown to the native peoples. Unwittingly, they also brought along microscopic cargo that was to prove far deadlier than any weapon. For the first time, Native Americans were exposed to the infectious diseases smallpox, cholera, and influenza. The Europeans had lived with these diseases for centuries, but the native peoples had not, and had no immunity to them. The toll was devastating. These microscopic pathogens laid waste to indigenous civilizations in just decades.

Some diseases, such as Zika and Ebola, are caused by viruses. Others, such as cholera, are caused by bacteria that infect food and drinking water. Malaria—among the deadliest killers of children—is the result of a unicellular eukaryote carried by mosquitoes in tropical regions.

In many cases, modern medicine has developed effective ways to cure or prevent these diseases. Yet that has not always prevented these diseases from breaking out of the background to produce mass epidemics. Sometimes a disease spreads so quickly that it is out of control before public health authorities realize it has become a problem. For others, preventive measures like vaccines have become so effective that people lose sight of just how dangerous these diseases can be. And tragically, many poor and underdeveloped regions of the world lack the resources to prevent the spread of disease and to react effectively when an epidemic threatens.

What are the types of microscopic organisms responsible for such diseases and how do they differ from one another? Just as importantly, how can understanding these microbes help us to control them and to prevent new outbreaks of disease?

**Throughout this chapter, look for connections to the CASE STUDY to help you answer these questions.**

# Viruses

Leaf infected with tobacco mosaic virus

Imagine that you have been presented with a great puzzle. Farmers have begun to lose their valuable tobacco crop to a disease that causes infected leaves to wither and die, killing the plants. You take leaves from a diseased plant and crush them to produce a liquid extract. You place a few drops of that liquid on the leaves of healthy plants. A few days later, these leaves also turn yellow and die.

You use a light microscope to look for a germ that might cause the disease, but none can be seen. In fact, when even the tiniest of cells are filtered out of the liquid, a drop of it still causes the disease. You figure the liquid must contain disease-causing agents so small that they are not visible under the microscope and can pass right through the filter. What do you do next? How do you deal with something invisible but deadly?

## What Is a Virus?

If you think you know the answer to this puzzle, congratulations! You're walking in the footsteps of a 28-year-old Russian biologist, Dmitri Ivanovski. In 1892, Ivanovski showed that the cause of this plant disease—called tobacco mosaic disease—was found in the liquid extracted from infected plants. But what was in the liquid?

**Discovery of Viruses** In 1897, Dutch scientist Martinus Beijerinck suggested that tiny particles in the juice caused the disease, and he named these particles *viruses*, after a Latin word for "poison." Then, in 1935, the American biochemist Wendell Stanley isolated crystals of tobacco mosaic virus. Living organisms do not crystallize, so Stanley inferred that viruses were not truly alive. This is a conclusion that biologists still recognize as being valid today. A **virus** is a nonliving particle made of proteins, nucleic acids, and sometimes lipids. ⚲ *Viruses can reproduce only by infecting living cells.*

**Structure and Composition** Viruses are very different from living cells, and are so small they can be seen only with the aid of a powerful electron microscope. Viruses differ widely in terms of size and structure, as you can see in **Figure 21-1**. Viruses contain genetic information in the form of RNA or DNA, surrounded by a protein coat known as a **capsid**. Some viruses, such as the influenza virus, also have a membrane surrounding the capsid. The simplest viruses contain only a few genes, whereas the most complex may have hundreds.

☑ **READING CHECK** **Explain** How did scientists conclude that viruses are not alive?

**Figure 21-1**

## Diversity of Viral Forms

Viruses come in a wide variety of sizes and shapes. Three types of viruses are shown here.
☑ **Interpret Diagrams** What kind of nucleic acid does each virus type have?

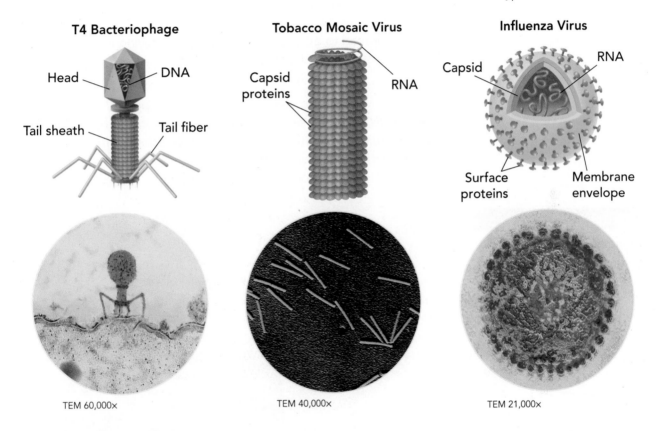

**T4 Bacteriophage**

Head — DNA

Tail sheath — Tail fiber

TEM 60,000×

**Tobacco Mosaic Virus**

Capsid proteins — RNA

TEM 40,000×

**Influenza Virus**

Capsid — RNA

Surface proteins — Membrane envelope

TEM 21,000×

---

## Quick Lab — Guided Inquiry

### How Do Viruses Differ in Structure?

1. Make models of two of the viruses shown in **Figure 21-1**.

2. Label the parts of each of your virus models.

3. Measure and record the length of each of your virus models in centimeters. Convert the length of each model into nanometers by using the following formula:
   1 cm = 10 million nm.

4. Measure the actual length of each virus you modeled. Divide the length of each model by the length of the actual virus to determine how much larger each model is than the virus it represents.

### ANALYZE AND CONCLUDE

1. **Use Models** Which structures of your models are found in all viruses?

2. **Identify Patterns** Which characteristics of one or both of your models are found in only some viruses?

3. **Reason Quantitatively** How many times larger are your models than the viruses they represent?

# Viral Infections

If you have access to a personal computer, you may know that they can easily be infected by pieces of code known as computer viruses. These usually enter a computer system by trickery, masquerading as an email attachment or an application program. Once they gain entry to a system, they can "reproduce" by making copies of their own code, and can even spread to other computers by instructing the operating system to send these copies to other computers on a network. The viruses that infect living cells work in ways that are remarkably similar to this, as described in **Figure 21-2**.

To enter a host cell, most viruses have proteins on their surfaces that bind to receptors on a cell. These proteins "trick" the cell to take in the virus. Once inside the cell, the virus makes copies of itself that can spread to other cells, sometimes destroying the host cell in the process. Nearly every type of organism, whether plant, animal, or bacterium, can be infected by viruses.

After a virus has entered a host cell, what happens? ⚲ *Inside living cells, viruses use their genetic information to reproduce. Some viruses replicate immediately, while others initially persist in an inactive state within the host.* These two patterns of infection are called lytic infection and lysogenic infection.

## Visual Analogy

**Figure 21-2**

## How Viruses Enter Living Cells

Viruses gain entry to cells by "tricking" their hosts. First the host cell takes in the virus, and then it follows the harmful instructions the virus contains.

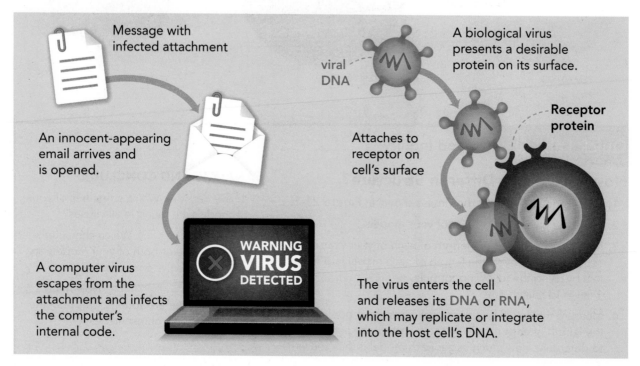

Message with infected attachment

viral DNA

A biological virus presents a desirable protein on its surface.

Receptor protein

An innocent-appearing email arrives and is opened.

Attaches to receptor on cell's surface

WARNING VIRUS DETECTED

A computer virus escapes from the attachment and infects the computer's internal code.

The virus enters the cell and releases its DNA or RNA, which may replicate or integrate into the host cell's DNA.

## Lytic Infection

In a **lytic infection**, a virus enters a bacterial cell, makes copies of itself, and causes the cell to burst, or lyse. *T4*, a bacterial virus, or **bacteriophage**, causes just such an infection. The virus binds to the surface of a bacterium, injects its DNA into the cell, and then begins to make messenger RNA (mRNA) from its own genes. These mRNAs are translated into proteins that act like a molecular wrecking crew, chopping up the cell's DNA.

Under the control of viral genes, the host cell now makes thousands of copies of viral nucleic acid and capsid proteins, enabling the virus to reproduce. Before long, the infected cell lyses, releasing hundreds of virus particles that may go on to infect other cells.

## Lysogenic Infection

Some bacterial viruses, including the bacteriophage *lambda*, cause a **lysogenic infection**, in which a host cell is not immediately taken over. Instead, the viral nucleic acid is inserted into the host cell's DNA, where it is replicated along with the host DNA without damaging the host.

Bacteriophage DNA that becomes embedded in the bacterial host's DNA is called a **prophage**. That DNA may remain in the host genome for many generations. Influences from the environment—including radiation, heat, and certain chemicals—trigger the prophage to become active. It then removes itself from the host cell DNA and reproduces by forming new virus particles. The lysogenic infection now becomes an active lytic infection, as shown in **Figure 21-3**. The details of viral infection in eukaryotic cells differ in many ways from infections of bacteria. However, the basic patterns are similar.

### INTERACTIVITY

Figure 21-3

## Comparing Two Types of Bacteriophage Infection

Viruses that infect bacteria, called bacteriophages, may infect cells in one of two ways: lytic infection or lysogenic infection. ☑ **Compare** How are the two main patterns of viral infection alike and different?

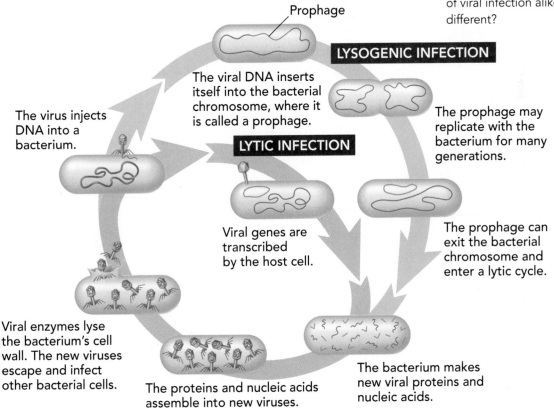

Prophage

**LYSOGENIC INFECTION**

The viral DNA inserts itself into the bacterial chromosome, where it is called a prophage.

The prophage may replicate with the bacterium for many generations.

**LYTIC INFECTION**

The virus injects DNA into a bacterium.

Viral genes are transcribed by the host cell.

The prophage can exit the bacterial chromosome and enter a lytic cycle.

Viral enzymes lyse the bacterium's cell wall. The new viruses escape and infect other bacterial cells.

The proteins and nucleic acids assemble into new viruses.

The bacterium makes new viral proteins and nucleic acids.

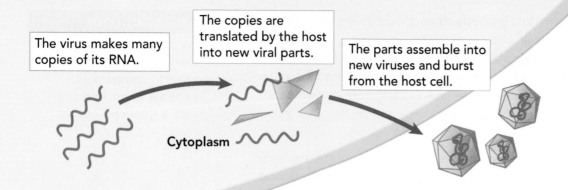

The virus makes many copies of its RNA.

The copies are translated by the host into new viral parts.

The parts assemble into new viruses and burst from the host cell.

Cytoplasm

**Figure 21-4**

## Common Cold Infection Mechanism

Once the cold virus has penetrated the host's cells, it uses the host's cellular machinery to replicate itself.

**Figure 21-5**

## HIV Infection Mechanism

In contrast to the cold virus, a retrovirus such as HIV makes a DNA copy of itself that inserts into the host's DNA. There, it may remain inactive for many cell cycles.

**A Closer Look at Two RNA Viruses** About 70 percent of viruses contain RNA rather than DNA. In humans, RNA viruses cause a wide range of infections, from relatively mild colds to influenza and AIDS. Certain kinds of cancer also begin with an infection by viral RNA.

*The Common Cold* What happens when you get a cold? Cold viruses attack with a very simple, fast-acting infection, as shown in **Figure 21-4**. A virus settles on a cell, often in the lining of the nose, and is brought inside the cell. The host cell's ribosomes translate the viral RNA into capsids and other viral proteins. These proteins assemble around copies of viral RNA, and within eight hours, the host cell releases hundreds of new virus particles to infect other cells.

*HIV* The deadly disease called acquired immune deficiency syndrome (AIDS) is caused by an RNA virus called human immunodeficiency virus (HIV), shown in **Figure 21-5**. HIV belongs to a group of RNA viruses that are called **retroviruses**. The genetic information of a retrovirus is copied from RNA to DNA, and may become inserted into the DNA of the host cell. Retroviral infections are similar to lysogenic infections of bacteria. The viral genes may remain inactive for many cell cycles before making new virus particles and damaging the cells of the host's immune system. Once activated, HIV begins to destroy the very cells that would normally fight infections.

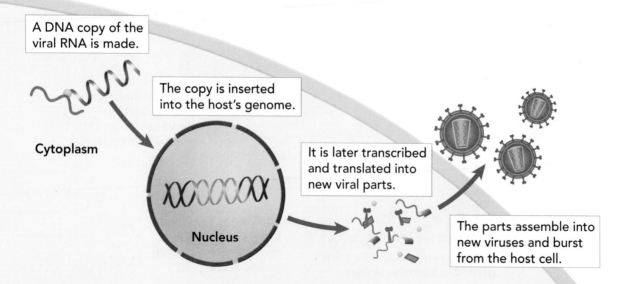

A DNA copy of the viral RNA is made.

The copy is inserted into the host's genome.

Cytoplasm

It is later transcribed and translated into new viral parts.

The parts assemble into new viruses and burst from the host cell.

Nucleus

# Viral Diseases

Viruses produce disease by disrupting the body's normal homeostasis. **Figure 21-6** lists some common human diseases caused by viruses. Viruses produce serious animal and plant diseases as well.

**Disease Mechanism** In many viral infections, viruses attack and destroy certain cells in the body, causing the symptoms of the associated disease. Poliovirus, for example, destroys cells in the nervous system, producing paralysis. Other viruses cause infected cells to change their patterns of growth and development, sometimes leading to cancer. 🔍 *Viruses cause disease by directly destroying living cells or by affecting cellular processes in ways that upset homeostasis.*

**Prevention and Treatment** Many viral diseases can be prevented by vaccines prepared from weakened or inactivated virus particles. Vaccines stimulate the body's immune system to recognize and destroy such viruses before they can cause disease. Personal hygiene matters, too. Studies show that cold and flu viruses are often transmitted by hand-to-mouth contact, so washing your hands as well as controlling coughs and sneezes can help prevent the spread of viruses.

While viral diseases are very difficult to treat, in recent years limited progress has been made in developing a handful of antiviral drugs that attack specific viral enzymes that host cells do not have. These treatments include an antiviral medication that can help speed recovery from the flu virus, and others that have helped prolong the lives of people infected with HIV.

✔️ **READING CHECK** Explain How do viruses cause disease?

### Figure 21-6

### Common Human Viral Diseases

Some common viral diseases are shown in the table below.

| Common Human Viral Diseases | | |
|---|---|---|
| **Disease** | **Effect on Body** | **Transmission** |
| Common cold | Sneezing, sore throat, fever, headache, muscle aches | Contact with contaminated objects; droplet inhalation |
| Influenza | Body aches, fever, sore throat, headache, dry cough, fatigue, nasal congestion | Flu viruses spread in respiratory droplets caused by coughing and sneezing. |
| AIDS (HIV) | Helper T cells, which are needed for normal immune-system function, are destroyed. | Sexual contact; contact with contaminated blood or body fluids; can be passed to babies during delivery or during breastfeeding |
| Hepatitis B | Jaundice, fatigue, abdominal pain, nausea, vomiting, joint pain | Contact with contaminated blood or bodily fluids |
| West Nile Virus | Fever, headache, body ache | Bite from an infected mosquito |
| Ebola | Fever and body aches, followed by rash and digestive symptoms impacting kidney and liver function | Contact with contaminated blood or bodily fluids |
| Zika | Fever, rash, joint pain, reddened eyes; can interfere with fetal development in pregnant women | Bite from an infected mosquito |

**INTERACTIVITY**

Investigate the structure of a virus and compare its traits to a living organism.

# Viruses and Cells

Viruses must infect living cells in order to grow and reproduce, taking advantage of the nutrients and cellular machinery of their hosts. This means that all viruses are parasites. Parasites depend entirely upon other living organisms for their existence, harming these organisms in the process.

🔍 **Despite the fact that they are not alive, viruses have many of the characteristics of living things.** After infecting living cells, viruses can reproduce, regulate gene expression, and even evolve. In fact, viral evolution is one of the reasons we need a new flu shot every year. A comparison of the principal differences between cells and viruses is shown in **Figure 21-7**.

Although viruses are smaller and simpler than the smallest cells, it is unlikely that they were the first organisms. Because viruses are dependent upon living organisms, it seems more likely that viruses developed after living cells. In fact, the first viruses may have evolved from the genetic material of living cells. Viruses have continued to evolve, along with the cells they infect, for billions of years.

Figure 21-7

## Comparing Viruses and Cells

The differences between viruses and cells are listed in this chart. ✔ **Form an Opinion** Based on this information, would you classify viruses as living or nonliving? Explain

| Viruses and Cells | | |
| --- | --- | --- |
| Characteristic | Virus | Cell |
| Structure | DNA or RNA in capsid, some with envelope | Cell membrane, cytoplasm; eukaryotes also contain nucleus and many organelles |
| Reproduction | Only within a host cell | Independent cell division, either asexually or sexually |
| Genetic Code | DNA or RNA | DNA |
| Growth and Development | No | Yes; in multicellular organisms, cells increase in number and differentiate |
| Obtain and Use Energy | No | Yes |
| Response to Environment | No | Yes |
| Change Over Time | Yes | Yes |

HS-ETS1-1

# ☑ LESSON 21.1 Review

## 🔍 KEY QUESTIONS

1. What do viruses depend on for their reproduction?

2. Describe each of the two paths viruses may follow once they have entered a cell.

3. Name three human diseases caused by viruses.

4. What characteristics of living things do viruses have?

## CRITICAL THINKING

5. **Compare and Contrast** How is viral reproduction different from that of cell-based organisms?

6. **Compare and Contrast** Compare the structure of a virus to the structure of both a prokaryotic cell and a eukaryotic cell. Use a graphic organizer of your choice to organize the information. You may wish to use primary scientific references or to refer to Chapter 8, which discusses the structures of cells in detail.

# Prokaryotes

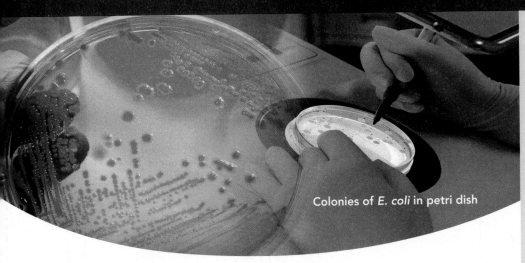

Colonies of *E. coli* in petri dish

Imagine living all your life as a member of what you believe is the only family on your street. Then, one morning, you open the front door and see neighbors tending their gardens and children walking to school. Where did all the people come from? What if the answer turned out to be that they had always been there—you just hadn't seen them? When the microscope was first invented, we humans had just such a shock. Suddenly, the street was very crowded! Microorganisms like bacteria are all around us—in fact, they even live inside our bodies.

## What Are Prokaryotes?

Microscopic life covers nearly every square centimeter of Earth. The smallest and most abundant of these microorganisms are **prokaryotes** (pro KAR ee ohts)—unicellular organisms that lack a nucleus. Unlike eukaryotes, the DNA of prokaryotes is located directly in the cytoplasm.

For many years, most prokaryotes were simply called "bacteria." Today, however, biologists divide prokaryotes into two very distinct groups: Bacteria and Archaea. These groups are as different from each other as both are from eukaryotes. **🔍 *Prokaryotes are classified as Bacteria or Archaea—two of the three domains of life.*** Eukarya is the third domain. The domain Bacteria corresponds to the kingdom Eubacteria. The domain Archaea corresponds to the kingdom Archaebacteria.

**Bacteria** The larger of the two domains of prokaryotes is Bacteria. Bacteria include a range of organisms with lifestyles so different that biologists do not agree on exactly how to classify them within the group. Bacteria live almost everywhere, in fresh water, in salt water, on land, and on and within the bodies of humans and other eukaryotes.

Bacteria are usually surrounded by a cell wall that protects the cell from injury and determines its shape. The cell walls of bacteria contain peptidoglycan—a polymer of sugars and amino acids that surrounds the cell membrane. Some bacteria, such as *E. coli*, shown in **Figure 21-8**, have a second membrane outside the peptidoglycan wall that makes the cell especially resistant to damage. In addition, some prokaryotes have flagella that they use for movement, or pili (singular: pilus), which in *E. coli* serve mainly to anchor the bacterium to a surface or to other bacteria.

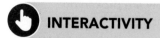 INTERACTIVITY

Figure 21-8

**Typical Bacterial Structure**

A bacterium such as *E. coli* has the basic structure typical of most prokaryotes. *E. coli* also has an outer membrane composed of lipids. This outer membrane is not present in all bacteria.

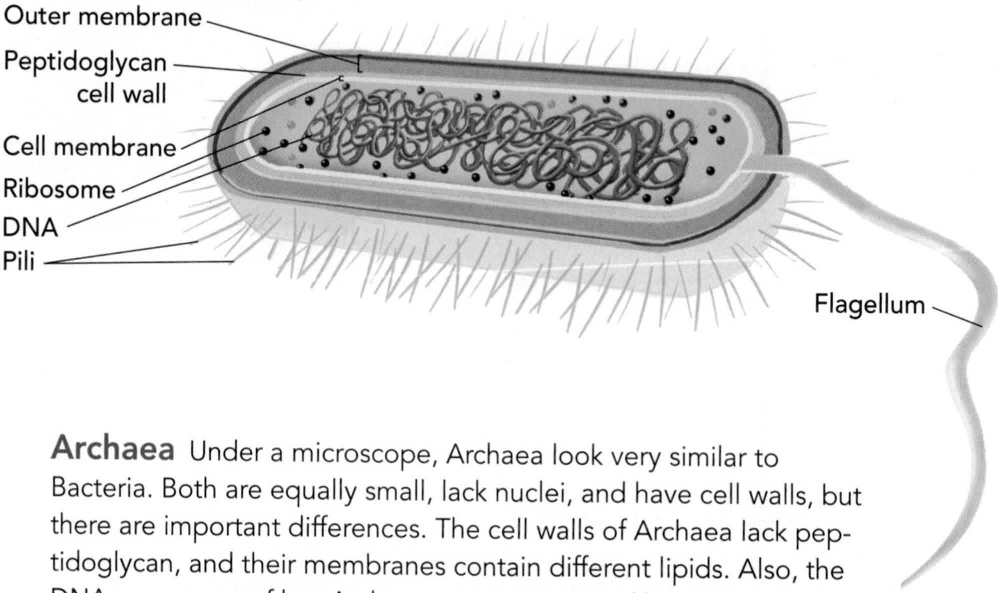

Outer membrane

Peptidoglycan cell wall

Cell membrane

Ribosome

DNA

Pili

Flagellum

**Archaea** Under a microscope, Archaea look very similar to Bacteria. Both are equally small, lack nuclei, and have cell walls, but there are important differences. The cell walls of Archaea lack peptidoglycan, and their membranes contain different lipids. Also, the DNA sequences of key Archaea genes are more like those of eukaryotes than those of bacteria.

Many Archaea live in extremely harsh environments. One group of Archaea produce methane gas and live in environments with little or no oxygen, such as thick mud or the digestive tracts of animals. Other Archaea live in extremely salty environments, such as Utah's Great Salt Lake, or in hot pools where temperatures approach the boiling point of water, such as the one shown in **Figure 21-9**.

Figure 21-9

**Archaea**

A thermal hot pool in Yellowstone National Park can reach scalding temperatures yet still be home to Archaea.

✓ **READING CHECK** **Classify** How are prokaryotes classified into groups?

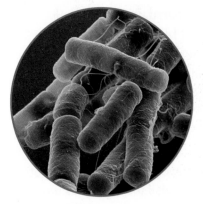
Bacilli (SEM 8500×)

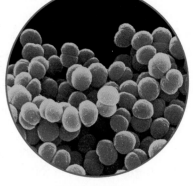
Cocci (SEM 9200×)

Spirilla (SEM 3000×)

# Structure and Function of Prokaryotes

Because prokaryotes are so small, it may seem hard to tell them apart. ⚲ *Prokaryotes vary in their size and shape, in the way they move, and in the way they obtain and release energy.*

Prokaryotes range in size from 1 to 5 micrometers, making them much smaller than most eukaryotic cells. Prokaryotes come in a variety of shapes, as shown in **Figure 21-10**. Rod-shaped prokaryotes are called bacilli (buh SIL eye). Spherical prokaryotes are called cocci (KAHK sy). Spiral and corkscrew-shaped prokaryotes are called spirilla (spy RIL uh). You can also distinguish prokaryotes by whether they move and how they move. Some prokaryotes do not move at all. Others are propelled by flagella. Some glide slowly along a layer of slimelike material they secrete.

**Nutrition and Metabolism** Like all organisms, prokaryotes need a supply of chemical energy, or food. They release energy from food molecules by cellular respiration, fermentation, or both. The diverse ways prokaryotes obtain and release energy are compared in **Figure 21-11**.

**Figure 21-10**
## Prokaryotic Shapes

Prokaryotes usually have one of these three basic shapes: bacilli, cocci, or spirilla.

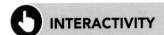 **INTERACTIVITY**

Investigate the structure and function of prokaryotes.

**Figure 21-11**
## Energy Capture and Release by Prokaryotes

Prokaryotes vary in the way they capture energy and in the way they release it.

| Energy Capture by Prokaryotes | |
| --- | --- |
| **Mode of Nutrition** | **How Energy Is Captured** |
| **Heterotroph** "other feeder" | Take in organic molecules from environment or other organisms to use as both energy and carbon supply |
| **Photoheterotroph** "light and other feeder" | Like basic heterotrophs, but also use light energy |
| **Photoautotroph** "light self-feeder" | Use light energy to convert $CO_2$ into carbon compounds |
| **Chemoautotroph** "chemical self-feeder" | Use energy released by chemical reactions involving ammonia, hydrogen sulfide, etc. |

| Energy Release by Prokaryotes | |
| --- | --- |
| **Mode of Metabolism** | **How Energy Is Released** |
| **Obligate aerobe** "requiring oxygen" | Cellular respiration; must have ready supply of oxygen to release fuel energy |
| **Obligate anaerobe** "requiring a lack of oxygen" | Fermentation; die in presence of oxygen |
| **Facultative anaerobe** "surviving without oxygen when necessary" | Can use either cellular respiration or fermentation as necessary |

**READING TOOL**

As you read about prokaryotes, recall your prior knowledge about life at the cellular level. Relate bacterial growth and reproduction to similar processes in plant and animal cells.

## Growth, Reproduction, and Recombination

Most prokaryotes reproduce by the process of **binary fission**, shown in **Figure 21-12**. In this process, the cell replicates its DNA and then divides in half to produce two identical cells. Because binary fission does not involve the exchange or recombination of genetic information, it is a form of asexual reproduction. When conditions are favorable, some prokaryotes can grow and divide as often as once every 20 minutes!

When growth conditions become unfavorable, many prokaryotic cells form an **endospore**—a thick internal wall that encloses the DNA and a portion of the cytoplasm. Endospores can remain dormant for months or even years. The ability to form endospores makes it possible for some prokaryotes to survive very harsh conditions. The bacterium *Bacillus anthracis*, which causes the disease anthrax, is one such bacterium.

As in any organism, adaptations that increase the survival and reproduction of a particular prokaryote are favored. Recall that in organisms that reproduce sexually, genes are shuffled and recombined during meiosis. But many prokaryotes reproduce asexually. So, how do their populations evolve?

*Mutations* Mutations are one of the main ways prokaryotes evolve. Recall that mutations are heritable changes in DNA. In prokaryotes, mutations are inherited by daughter cells produced by binary fission.

*Conjugation* Many prokaryotes exchange genetic information by a process called conjugation. During **conjugation**, a hollow bridge forms between two bacterial cells, and genetic material, usually in the form of a plasmid, moves from one cell to the other. Many plasmids carry genes that enable bacteria to survive in new environments or to resist antibiotics that might otherwise prove fatal. This transfer of genes increases genetic diversity in populations of prokaryotes.

☑ **READING CHECK** **Explain** How is forming an endospore useful for many bacteria?

**Figure 21-12**

**Binary Fission, Endospores, and Conjugation**

An *E. coli* bacterium has almost completed the process of binary fission (left.) Another bacterium has developed an endospore, the green region (middle.) In conjugation, tiny bridges allow bacteria to transfer genetic information (right.) All three micrographs have been false-colored.

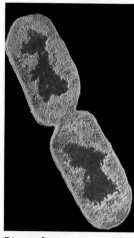 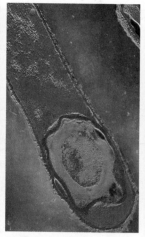 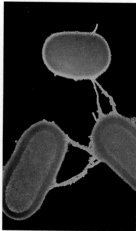

Binary fission (TEM 38,000×)   Endospore (TEM 20,000×)   Conjugation (TEM 11,000×)

# Prokaryotes in the Environment

You may remember the star actors in the last movie you saw, but have you ever thought about a film's behind-the-scene production crew? Prokaryotes are just like those unseen workers. 🔑 *Prokaryotes are essential in maintaining every aspect of the ecological balance of the living world. In addition, some species have specific uses in human industry.*

**Decomposers** Every living thing depends on a supply of raw materials for its survival. By breaking down, or decomposing, dead organisms, prokaryotes supply raw materials to the environment. Bacterial decomposers are also essential to industrial sewage treatment, helping to produce purified water and chemicals that can be used as fertilizers.

**Producers** Photosynthetic prokaryotes are among the most important producers on the planet. The tiny cyanobacterium *Prochlorococcus* (**Figure 21-13**) alone may account for more than half of the primary production in the open ocean. Food chains everywhere are dependent upon prokaryotes as producers of food and biomass.

**Nitrogen Fixers** All organisms need nitrogen to grow. But while nitrogen gas ($N_2$) makes up 80 percent of Earth's atmosphere, only a few organisms—all of them prokaryotes—can convert $N_2$ into useful forms. This process, known as nitrogen fixation, provides up to 90 percent of the nitrogen used by other organisms. Some plants have vital symbiotic relationships with nitrogen-fixing prokaryotes. As shown in **Figure 21-13**, the bacterium *Rhizobium* grows in nodules, or knobs, on the roots of legume plants such as clover and soybean. The *Rhizobium* bacteria within these nodules convert nitrogen in the air into the nitrogen compounds essential for plant growth. In effect, these plants have fertilizer factories in their roots!

**Human Uses of Prokaryotes** Prokaryotes, especially bacteria, are used in the production of a wide variety of foods and other commercial products. For example, yogurt is produced by the bacterium *Lactobacillus*. Some bacteria can even digest petroleum and remove human-made waste products and poisons from water. Others are used to synthesize drugs and chemicals through the techniques of genetic engineering.

**The Microbiome** Bacteria live just about everywhere, but one of their favorite places turns out to be the human body. Bacteria live on the skin, on the hair, inside the mouth and nose, and especially inside our digestive systems. In a typical human intestine there may be as many as 30 trillion bacteria belonging to 150 different species. Throughout the body these organisms form what scientists now call the "microbiome," a huge collection of prokaryotic genomes that rivals the human genome in size and complexity.

## Figure 21-13
### Ecological Roles Played by Prokaryotes

Prokaryotes play many important roles in the environment. Cyanobacteria in the ocean (top) provide oxygen to the atmosphere and food for ocean food chains. *Rhizobium* nodules on soybean roots (bottom) convert atmospheric nitrogen into useful compounds.

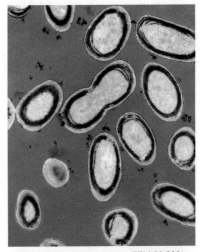

TEM 23,000×

This great diversity of microorganisms helps us to digest food, synthesizes certain vitamins, and maintains a balance that is important to good health. There is growing evidence that disorders such as diabetes, obesity, and even cancer can be linked to abnormal microbiomes. An emerging area of medical science is now dedicated to understanding and correcting imbalances in the microbiome.

**INTERACTIVITY**

Conduct a simulation of an outbreak of cholera, a deadly bacterial disease.

# Bacterial Diseases

We share this planet with prokaryotes and viruses, and most of the time we are never aware of our relationships with them. Often, these relationships are highly beneficial, but in a few cases, sharing simply doesn't work—and disease is the result.

Disease-causing agents are called **pathogens**. Although pathogens can come from any taxonomic group, nearly all known prokaryotic pathogens are bacteria. The French chemist Louis Pasteur was the first person to show convincingly that bacteria cause disease. Pasteur helped to establish what has become known as the *germ theory of disease* when he showed that bacteria were responsible for a number of human and animal diseases.

**Figure 21-14**

## Common Human Bacterial Diseases

Some common bacterial diseases are shown in the table below. ☑ **Infer** Why do bacterial meningitis outbreaks sometimes occur in college dormitories?

**Disease Mechanisms** Bacteria produce disease in one of two general ways. ✎ *Bacteria disrupt health and cause disease by destroying living cells or by releasing chemicals that upset homeostasis.* Some bacteria destroy living cells and tissues of the infected organism directly, while some cause the immune system to overreact, causing it to attack the body's own tissues. Other bacteria release toxins (poisons) that interfere with the normal activity of the host. **Figure 21-14** lists some common human diseases caused by bacteria.

| Some Human Bacterial Diseases | | |
|---|---|---|
| **Disease** | **Effect on Body** | **Transmission** |
| Lyme disease | "Bull's-eye" rash at site of tick bite, fever, fatigue, headache | Ticks transmit the bacterium *Borrelia burdorferi*. |
| Tetanus | Lockjaw, stiffness in neck and abdomen, difficulty swallowing, fever, elevated blood pressure, severe muscle spasms | Bacteria enter the body through a break in the skin. |
| Tuberculosis | Fatigue, weight loss, fever, night sweats, chills, appetite loss, bloody sputum from lungs | Bacteria particles are inhaled. |
| Bacterial meningitis | High fever, headache, stiff neck, nausea, fatigue | Bacteria are spread in respiratory droplets caused by coughing and sneezing; close or prolonged contact with someone infected with meningitis |
| Strep throat | Fever, sore throat, headache, fatigue, nausea | Direct contact with mucus from an infected person or direct contact with infected wounds or breaks in the skin |

| Controlling Bacteria | |
|---|---|
| **Method** | **Description** |
| Physical Removal | Washing hands or other surfaces with soap under running water doesn't kill pathogens, but it helps dislodge both bacteria and viruses. |
| Disinfectants | Chemical solutions that kill bacteria can be used to clean bathrooms, kitchens, hospital rooms, and other places where bacteria may flourish. |
| Food Storage | Low temperatures slow the growth of bacteria and keep most foods fresher for a longer period of time than room temperature. |
| Sanitation | Well-designed sanitary sewage and septic systems can protect drinking water and prevent the spread of disease. |
| Food Processing | Boiling, frying, or steaming can sterilize many kinds of food by raising the temperature of the food to a point where bacteria are killed. |
| Sterilization by Heat | Sterilization of objects such as medical instruments at temperatures well above 100° Celsius can prevent the growth of potentially dangerous bacteria. Most bacteria cannot survive such temperatures. |

**Controlling Bacteria** Although most bacteria are harmless, and many are beneficial, the everyday risks of any person acquiring a bacterial infection are great enough to warrant efforts to control bacterial growth. Some methods of controlling bacteria are shown in **Figure 21-15**.

**Preventing Bacterial Diseases** Many bacterial diseases can be prevented by stimulating the body's immune system with vaccines. A **vaccine** is a preparation of weakened or killed pathogens or inactivated toxins. When injected into the body, a vaccine prompts the body to produce immunity to a specific disease. Immunity is the body's ability to recognize and destroy pathogens before they cause disease.

**Treating Bacterial Diseases** A number of drugs can be used to attack a bacterial infection. These drugs include **antibiotics**, such as penicillin and tetracycline, that block the growth and reproduction of bacteria. Antibiotics disrupt proteins or cell processes that are specific to bacterial cells. In this way, they do not harm the host's cells.

**"Superbugs"** When first introduced in the 1940s, penicillin, an antibiotic derived from fungi, was a miracle drug. Conquest of bacterial diseases seemed to be in sight. Within a few decades, however, penicillin lost much of its effectiveness, as have other antibiotics. The culprit is evolution. Natural selection and the widespread use of antibiotics have led to the emergence of antibiotic resistance. Physicians now must fight "superbugs" that are resistant to multiple antibiotics.

One example is methicillin-resistant *Staphylococcus aureus*, known as MRSA (pronounced MURS uh), which can cause infections that are especially difficult to control. MRSA skin infections can be spread by close contact, including the sharing of personal items such as towels and athletic gear. In hospitals, MRSA bacteria can infect surgical wounds and spread from patient to patient.

**Figure 21-15**

**Controlling Bacteria**

Bacteria cannot—and should not—be eliminated from the environment, but many methods will control their growth.

**BUILD VOCABULARY**

**Root Words** The prefix *anti-* means "opposed," and *biotic* refers to "life." However, antibiotics fight bacterial life only, and not other types of living things.

☑ **READING CHECK** Infer Why has penicillin become less useful?

## MRSA—Fighting Back

Infection by methicillin-resistant *Staphylococcus aureus* (MRSA) rose quickly in the years leading up to 2005. The table shows the incidence of MRSA infections in U.S. hospitals between 2005 and 2011.

1. **Construct Graphs** Prepare a line graph showing the number of MRSA infections in U.S. hospitals over time. Describe the trend shown by your graph.

2. **Reason Quantitatively** By what percentage did MRSA infections in U.S. hospitals increase or decrease between 2005 and 2011?

3. **Form a Hypothesis** What do you think led to the trend in the data observed between 2005 and 2011? If the average hospital stay in the United States lasted 4.6 days, while that of the average MRSA-infected patient was 10.0 days, what effect did this trend have on hospital costs?

| Incidence of MRSA ||
|---|---|
| **Year** | **MRSA Infections** |
| 2005 | 111,261 |
| 2006 | 106,811 |
| 2007 | 100,876 |
| 2008 | 93,460 |
| 2009 | 86,041 |
| 2010 | 83,287 |
| 2011 | 80,461 |

## BUILD VOCABULARY

**Academic Words** An epidemic is a rapid outbreak of a disease, meaning that the disease spreads quickly among many people. If the disease is fatal, many people may die in a short span of time.

# Emerging Disease

🔍 *A previously unknown disease that appears in a population for the first time or a well-known disease that suddenly becomes harder to control is called an emerging disease.* To Native Americans, the smallpox virus that Europeans brought to the new world was just such a disease. In 1521, an epidemic of this viral disease so weakened the mighty Aztec empire that Spaniard Hernán Cortés was able to conquer what is now Mexico with just a few hundred soldiers. Similar epidemics ravaged the Native American populations of New England as well in the early 1600s.

**The Threat Today** Emerging diseases remain a threat today. **Figure 21-16** shows locations worldwide where specific emerging diseases have broken out in recent years. Changes in lifestyle and commerce have made the health disruptions caused by emerging diseases even more of a threat. One recent example is the Zika virus, named for the forest in Uganda, Africa, where it was first discovered in monkeys. Over several decades, this mosquito-borne virus made the jump to humans, spreading across central Africa to Southeast Asia, and them to islands in the Pacific Ocean. Finally, in 2015, it emerged for the first time in South America. Because the population had no immunity to the virus, it spread quickly. In Brazil, there was a sudden increase in serious birth defects among children born to mothers who had been infected with the virus. Once the serious nature of the threat from Zika became known, public health officials moved quickly to try to stop the spread of the virus and the mosquitoes that carry it.

Because viruses replicate so quickly, their genetic makeup can change rapidly, sometimes allowing a virus to evolve in ways that enables it to jump from one species to another. Researchers have evidence that this is how the virus that causes AIDS originated, moving from nonhuman primates into humans.

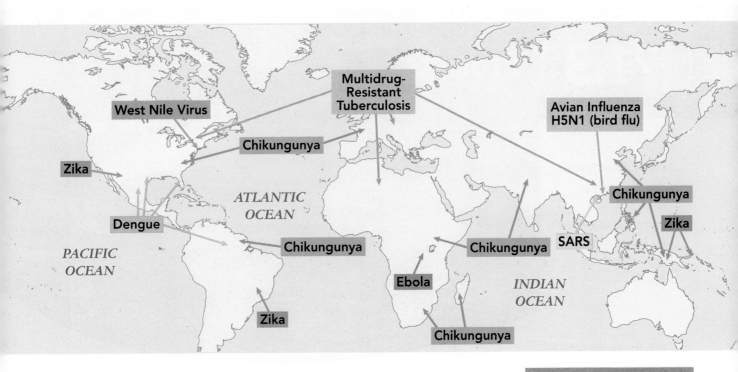

West Nile Virus

Multidrug-Resistant Tuberculosis

Chikungunya

Zika

Dengue

ATLANTIC OCEAN

Avian Influenza H5N1 (bird flu)

Chikungunya

Zika

PACIFIC OCEAN

Chikungunya

Chikungunya

SARS

Ebola

INDIAN OCEAN

Zika

Chikungunya

Public health officials are especially worried about the flu virus. This RNA virus infects cells in the respiratory system, and can lead to severe illness and even death, especially among the elderly. Gene shuffling among different flu viruses infecting wild and domesticated bird populations has led to the emergence of a dangerous "bird flu." This bird flu is similar to the flu that spread worldwide and killed millions of people in 1918. In a few cases, bird flu has indeed infected humans, and health officials warn that a major "jump" into the human population remains possible in the future.

**Prions** In 1972, American scientist Stanley Prusiner became interested in scrapie, an infectious disease in sheep, the exact cause of which was unknown. At first, he suspected a viral cause, but experiments revealed clumps of tiny protein particles in the brains of infected sheep. Prusiner called these particles prions, short for "protein infectious particles." Although prions were first discovered in sheep, many animals, including humans, can become infected with prions. Prions are formed when a protein known as PrP is improperly folded. Prions themselves can cause PrP proteins to misfold, producing even more prions. An accumulation of prions can damage nerve cells.

HS-LS1-1, HS-LS4-1

# ☑ LESSON 21.2 Review

## ⚗ KEY QUESTIONS

1. Describe the characteristics of the two kingdoms of prokaryotes.

2. In what ways do prokaryotes differ from one another?

3. List three ecological roles of prokaryotes.

4. What are two ways that bacteria cause disease?

5. Why are emerging diseases of particular concern?

## CRITICAL THINKING

6. **Apply Scientific Reasoning** You think you might have a bacterial infection. Would you ask for a vaccination against the bacteria? Why or why not?

# Protists

Dinoflagellates illuminating the seawater in China

## Key Questions

- How are protists classified?
- How do protists move and reproduce?
- What role do protists play in the environment?

HS-LS1-1: Construct an explanation based on evidence for how the structure of DNA determines the structure of proteins which carry out the essential functions of life through systems of specialized cells.

HS-LS1-2: Develop and use a model to illustrate the hierarchical organization of interacting systems that provide specific functions within multicellular organisms.

HS-LS4-1: Communicate scientific information that common ancestry and biological evolution are supported by multiple lines of empirical evidence.

## VOCABULARY

cilium
flagellum
alternation of generations

## READING TOOL

Preview the headings in this lesson to construct an outline. As you read, fill in supporting details for each heading in the outline in your 📗 Biology Foundations Workbook.

Some of the organisms we call "protists" live quietly on the bottom of shallow ponds, soaking up the energy of sunlight. Others sparkle like diamonds in coastal waters, but still others drift in the human bloodstream, destroying blood cells and killing nearly a million people a year. What kind of life is this, capable of such beauty and such destruction?

## What Are Protists?

More than a billion years ago, a new form of organism appeared on Earth. Subtle clues in the microscopic fossils of these single cells mark them as the very first eukaryotes. Single-celled eukaryotes are still with us today and are often called "protists"—a name that means "first." 🔍 **Protists are eukaryotes that are not members of the plant, animal, or fungi kingdoms.** Although most protists are unicellular, quite a few are not. The largest protists—brown algae called kelp—are multicellular organisms that contain millions of cells.

**Protists: The First Eukaryotes** Microscopic fossils of eukaryotic cells have been found in rocks as old as 1.5 billion years. Genetic and fossil evidence indicates that eukaryotes evolved from prokaryotes and are more closely related to present-day organisms in the domain Archaea than to those in the domain Bacteria. The actual split between Archaea and Eukarya may have come as early as 2.5 billion years ago. Since that time, protists have diversified into as many as 300,000 species found on every corner of the planet. Most of the major protist groups have remained unicellular, but two have produced organisms that developed true multicellularity. It is from the ancestors of these groups that plants, animals, and fungi arose. Today's protists include groups whose ancestors were among the very last to split from the organisms that gave rise to plants, animals, and fungi.

## The "Protist" Dilemma

In the past, scientists sorted protists into three groups: plantlike protists, animal-like protists, and fungus-like protists. But this simple solution began to fail as biologists learned that many protists do not fit into any of these groups. In fact, the so-called protists display a far greater degree of diversity than any other eukaryotic kingdom. These findings made it necessary to reclassify these remarkable organisms.

The most recent studies of protists divide them into six major clades, shown in **Figure 21-17**, each of which could be considered a living kingdom in its own right. Where would that leave the plant, animal, and fungi kingdoms? Surprisingly, they would fit right into these six clades, and two of them, animals and fungi, actually emerge from the same protist ancestors.

## What "Protist" Means Today

Today biologists assembling what is often called the *Tree of Life* favor the classification described. But the word *protist* remains in such common usage, even among scientists, that we continue to use it here. Bear in mind, however, that the *protist* are not a single kingdom but a collection of organisms that includes several distinct clades. This is why the term is sometimes surrounded by quotation marks.

✓ **READING CHECK** **Interpret Diagrams** Which group of "protists" in **Figure 21-17** is most closely related to plants? Which group is most closely related to animals? To fungi?

⬆ **INTERACTIVITY**

**Figure 21-17**
## Protists Classification—Work in Progress

This cladogram represents an understanding of protist relationships supported by current research.

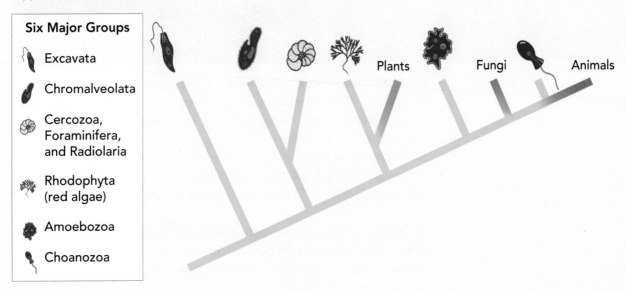

| Six Major Groups |
| --- |
| Excavata |
| Chromalveolata |
| Cercozoa, Foraminifera, and Radiolaria |
| Rhodophyta (red algae) |
| Amoebozoa |
| Choanozoa |

**READING TOOL**

Use the visuals in this section to help you understand protist movement, alternation of generations, and other topics.

# Structure and Function of Protists

Before they gave rise to multicellular eukaryotes, protists evolved just about every form of cellular movement known to exist. *Some protists move by changing their cell shape, and some move by means of specialized organelles. Other protists do not move actively but are carried by wind, water, or other organisms.*

**Movement** Many unicellular protists move like amoebas, changing their shape in a process that makes use of cytoplasmic projections known as pseudopods (SOO doh pahdz). This type of locomotion is called amoeboid movement and is found in many protists.

*Cilia and Flagella* Many protists move around by means of cilia and flagella—structures supported by microtubules. Cilia and flagella have nearly identical internal structures, but they produce cellular motion differently, as described in **Figure 21-18**. **Cilia** (singular: cilium) are short and numerous, and they move somewhat like oars on a boat. **Flagella** (singular: flagellum) are relatively long and usually number only one or two per cell. Some flagella spin like tiny propellers, but most produce a wavelike motion from base to tip.

**Visual Analogy**

**Figure 21-18**

**How Cells Move Like Boats**

The forward motion generated by cilia or flagella is similar to the way oars propel a boat.

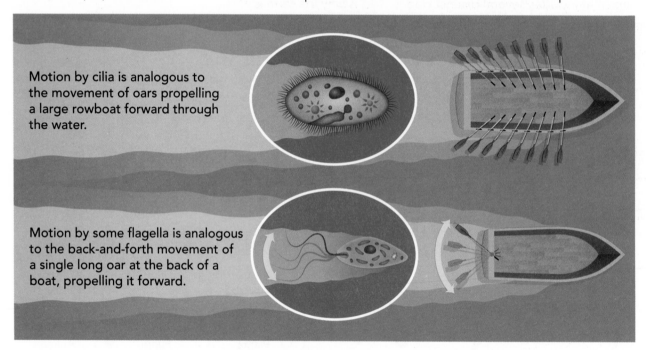

Motion by cilia is analogous to the movement of oars propelling a large rowboat forward through the water.

Motion by some flagella is analogous to the back-and-forth movement of a single long oar at the back of a boat, propelling it forward.

*Passive Movement* Some of the most important protists are nonmotile—they depend on air or water currents and other organisms to carry them around. These protists form reproductive cells called spores that can enter the cells of other organisms as parasites. Spore-forming protists include *Plasmodium*, which is carried by mosquitoes and causes malaria, and *Cryptosporidium*, which spreads through contaminated drinking water and causes severe intestinal disease.

**Reproduction** The incredible variety of protists is reflected in their varied life cycles. *Some protists reproduce asexually by mitosis. Others have life cycles that combine asexual and sexual forms of reproduction.*

**Asexual Reproduction** Most protists reproduce by mitosis: They duplicate their genetic material and then simply divide into two genetically identical cells. Other protists have phases in their life cycle in which they also produce new individuals by mitosis. Mitosis enables protists to reproduce rapidly, especially under ideal conditions, but it produces cells that are genetically identical to the parent cell, and thus limits the development of genetic diversity.

Paramecia and most ciliates also reproduce asexually by mitotic cell division. However, under stress, paramecia can remake themselves through conjugation—a process in which two organisms exchange genetic material. After conjugating, the cells then reproduce by mitosis. Paramecia have two types of nuclei: a macronucleus and one or more smaller micronuclei. The micronucleus is a bit like a reference library holding a "reserve copy" of every gene in the cell. The macronucleus is more like a lending library—it has multiple copies of the genes the cell uses in its day-to-day activities. Conjugation helps to produce and maintain genetic diversity, the raw material for evolution.

**Sexual Reproduction** Many protists have sexual life cycles in which they switch between a diploid and a haploid phase, a process known as **alternation of generations**. An example is the life cycle of a type of protist known as a water mold. Water molds thrive on dead and decaying organic matter in water or as parasites of plants on land. The life cycle of a water mold is shown in **Figure 21-19**. Water molds—and many other protists—reproduce asexually by producing spores in a structure called a sporangium. Water molds also reproduce sexually by undergoing meiosis and producing male and female gametes. These gametes fuse during fertilization, forming a zygote that begins a new life cycle.

**INTERACTIVITY**

Investigate the kingdom Protista and the characteristics of each of its major groups.

**Figure 21-19**

**Water Mold Life Cycle**

Water molds reproduce both asexually and sexually.

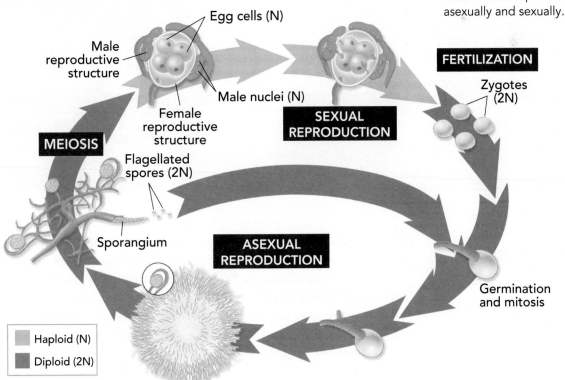

# Protists in the Environment

If you've seen greenish scum growing along the banks of a pond or maybe even at the edges of a poorly maintained swimming pool, you might have called it "algae" without thinking. The organisms we call "algae" actually belong to many different groups. Some (the cyanobacteria) are prokaryotes, and some (the green algae) belong to the plant kingdom, but many are protists.

**Autotrophic Protists** Photosynthetic protists include many phytoplankton species and the red and brown algae, as well as euglenas and dinoflagellates. These organisms share an autotrophic lifestyle, marked by the ability to use the energy from light to make a carbohydrate food source.

Photosynthetic protists play major roles in maintaining the health and wellbeing of many organisms and ecosystems. Some examples of these ecological roles played by photosynthetic protists are shown in **Figure 21-20**. ✎ *The position of photosynthetic protists at the base of the food chain makes much of the diversity of aquatic life possible.*

| Ecological Roles of Protists | | |
|---|---|---|
| Providing Food | Photosynthetic protists make up a large portion of phytoplankton found near the surface of oceans and lakes. About half of the photosynthesis that takes place on Earth is carried out by phytoplankton, providing nourishment for organisms as diverse as shrimp and baleen whales. |  |
| Supporting Coral Reefs | Coral reefs provide food and shelter to large numbers of fish and other organisms. Protists known as zooxanthellae provide most of the coral's energy needs by photosynthesis. By nourishing coral animals, these algae help maintain the health and equilibrium of the coral ecosystem. Coralline red algae also help to provide calcium carbonate to stabilize growing coral reefs. |  |
| Providing Shelter | The largest known protist is giant kelp, a brown alga. Kelp forests provide shelter for many marine species, and the kelp itself is a source of food for sea urchins. |  |

**Figure 21-20**

**Ecological Roles of Photosynthetic Protists**

Photosynthetic protists play many roles in the environment.

**Mutualists** Given the great diversity of protists, it should come as no surprise that many of them are involved in symbiotic relationships with other organisms. ✎ *Many protists are involved in mutualistic symbioses, in which they and their hosts both benefit.* One example is a mutualistic relationship involving *Trichonympha*. This protist lives within the digestive systems of termites and helps to produce enzymes that enable the termites to digest wood.

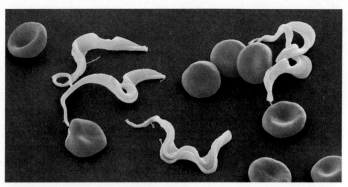

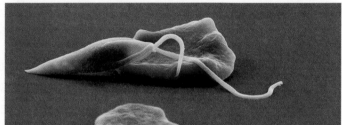

Trypanosoma brucei (yellow) and red blood cells (SEM 3600×)

Leishmaniasis (purple) and red blood cell (SEM 6600×)

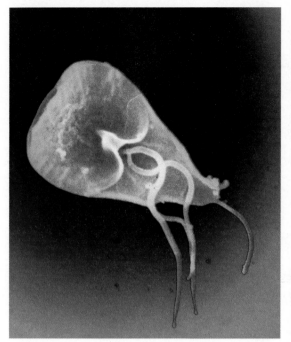

Giardia (SEM 4500×)

**Parasites** Some protists are parasites that cause serious problems. In the United States, some streams and lakes are home to *Giardia*, a protist that causes a range of intestinal problems. ⚲ *Parasitic protists are responsible for some of the world's most deadly diseases, including several kinds of debilitating intestinal diseases, African sleeping sickness, and malaria.*

In much of the world, one of the greatest threats to human health is a disease known as malaria, caused by a protist known as *Plasmodium*. This parasite lives in the human bloodstream, and is passed from person to person by the bite of the *Anopheles* mosquito, which is common in tropical regions. In years past, malaria killed as many as a million people a year, many of them children. Developing drugs and vaccines to fight this killer has been a major effort of the World Health Organization. This effort has cut the death rate from malaria by as much as 50 percent in some regions.

**Figure 21-21**

## Disease-Causing Protists

Protist parasites, such as *Giardia*, cause serious and sometimes deadly outbreaks of intestinal disease. Protists of the genus *Trypanosoma* cause African sleeping sickness. Leishmaniasis is caused by *Leishmania* protists and is common in tropical regions of the world.

 **VIDEO**

Learn about malaria and how it is transmitted.

HS-LS1-1, HS-LS1-2, HS-LS4-1

 **LESSON 21.3** Review

### ⚲ KEY QUESTIONS

1. How does the updated classification of protists differ from the older classification?

2. How is movement by means of flagella different from movement by means of cilia?

3. How would ocean food chains change in the absence of photosynthetic protists?

### CRITICAL THINKING

4. **Evaluate Models** Compare **Figure 21-17** with the model of the Tree of Life presented in Chapter 19. What simplification does **Figure 21-17** make? How could this simplification be misinterpreted? Explain your answer.

5. **Compare and Contrast** Compare asexual and sexual processes in paramecia. Include the terms *mitosis* and *meiosis* in your answer. You may want to refer back to Chapters 11 and 12 to review mitosis and meiosis.

## KEY QUESTIONS
- *What are the basic characteristics of fungi?*
- *How do fungi affect homeostasis in other organisms and the environment?*

**HS-LS1-1:** Construct an explanation based on evidence for how the structure of DNA determines the structure of proteins which carry out the essential functions of life through systems of specialized cells.

**HS-LS1-2:** Develop and use a model to illustrate the hierarchical organization of interacting systems that provide specific functions within multicellular organisms.

**HS-LS4-1:** Communicate scientific information that common ancestry and biological evolution are supported by multiple lines of empirical evidence.

### VOCABULARY

**chitin**
**hyphae**
**fruiting body**
**mycelium**
**lichen**
**mycorrhiza**

### READING TOOL

As you read, complete the chart in your 📖 **Biology Foundations Workbook** that describes the form and structure of fungi.

Bracket fungi

How many organisms are shown in the photo? You might guess 50 or 60, one for each mushroom. However, the whole ring of mushrooms is actually part of a large single organism. Most of the mass of the fungus is underground, spanning at least the width of the ring of mushrooms, and extending more than 2 meters into the ground.

## What Are Fungi?

Like the ring of mushrooms, many fungi grow from the ground. This once led scientists to classify them as nonphotosynthetic plants. But they aren't plants at all. Instead of carrying out photosynthesis, fungi produce powerful enzymes that digest food outside their bodies. Then they absorb the small molecules released by the enzymes. Many fungi feed by absorbing nutrients from decaying matter in the soil. Others live as parasites, absorbing nutrients from the bodies of their hosts.

Another defining characteristic of fungi is the composition of their cell walls, which contain chitin. **Chitin** is a polymer made of modified sugars that is also found in the external skeletons of insects. The presence of chitin is one of several features that show fungi are more closely related to animals than to plants. 🔑 *Fungi are heterotrophic eukaryotes with cell walls that contain chitin.*

**Structure and Function** Some fungi, known as yeasts, live most of their lives as single cells. But mushrooms and other fungi grow much larger, their bodies made up of cells that form long, slender branching filaments called **hyphae** (singular: hypha), as shown in **Figure 21-22**. In most fungi, cross walls divide the hyphae into compartments resembling cells, each containing one or two nuclei. In the cross walls, there are openings through which cytoplasm and organelles such as mitochondria can move.

What you recognize as a mushroom is actually the **fruiting body**, the reproductive structure of the fungus. The fruiting body grows from the **mycelium** (plural: mycelia), the mass of branching hyphae below the soil. Clusters of mushrooms are often part of the same mycelium, which means that they are actually part of the same organism.

**Figure 21-22**

**Structure of a Mushroom**

The body of a mushroom is its reproductive structure, also called a fruiting body. The major portion of the organism is the mycelium, which grows underground.

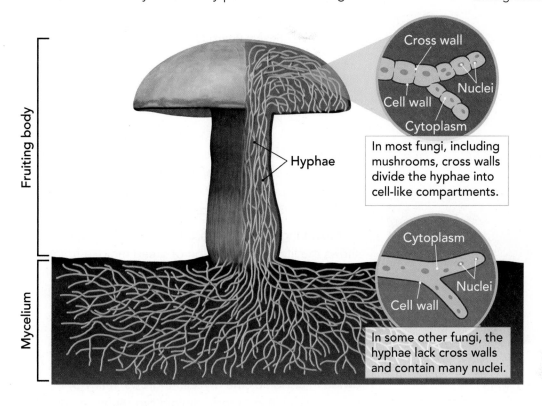

Fruiting body

Mycelium

Hyphae

Cross wall

Nuclei

Cell wall

Cytoplasm

In most fungi, including mushrooms, cross walls divide the hyphae into cell-like compartments.

Cytoplasm

Nuclei

Cell wall

In some other fungi, the hyphae lack cross walls and contain many nuclei.

 **Exploration Lab**   Open-Ended Inquiry

### Mushroom Farming

**Problem** How does the amount of available light affect mushroom growth?

In this lab, you will design an experiment to determine the effect of light on the growth of a fruiting body. Your group will monitor one of three experimental setups and share your results. You will then analyze the pooled data from the entire class to determine the optimal conditions for mushroom growth.

You can find this lab in your digital course.

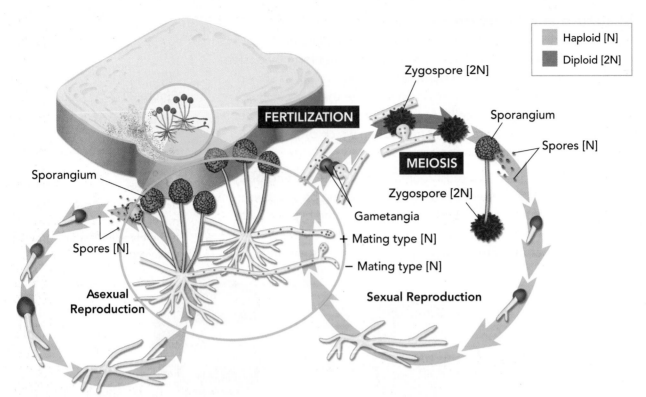

Zygospore [2N]

Sporangium

FERTILIZATION

MEIOSIS

Spores [N]

Zygospore [2N]

Sporangium

Gametangia

Spores [N]

+ Mating type [N]

− Mating type [N]

Asexual Reproduction

Sexual Reproduction

Haploid [N]

Diploid [2N]

**Figure 21-23**

## Bread Mold Life Cycle

During sexual reproduction in the black bread mold *Rhizopus stolonifer*, hyphae from two different mating types form gametangia. The gametangia fuse, and zygotes form within a zygospore. The zygospore eventually germinates, and a sporangium emerges.

**INTERACTIVITY**

Learn about the characteristics of the different groups of fungi.

**Reproduction** Fungi can reproduce asexually, primarily by releasing spores that travel through air and water. Simply breaking off a hypha or budding off a cell can also serve as asexual reproduction.

Most fungi also can reproduce sexually. **Figure 21-23** shows the life cycle of a type of bread mold, a fungus called *Rhizopus stolonifer*. Sexual reproduction in fungi often involves two different mating types. In *Rhizopus*, as in most fungi, gametes of both mating types are about the same size and are not usually called male and female. Instead, one mating type is called "+" (plus) and the other "−" (minus). The + and − nuclei form pairs that divide in unison as the mycelium grows. Many of the paired nuclei fuse to form diploid zygote nuclei, which go through meiosis to make haploid spores. Each spore has a different combination of parental genes, and each can make a new mycelium.

**Diversity of Fungi** More than 100,000 species of fungi are known. Of course, they all share the characteristics that define them as fungi but they differ from one another in important ways. Biologists have used these similarities and differences, along with DNA comparisons, to place the fungi into several distinct groups. The major groups of fungi differ from one another in their reproductive structures, as summarized in **Figure 21-24**.

**READING CHECK Describe** What is the structure of a typical fungus?

| The Major Phyla of Fungi | | |
|---|---|---|
| Phylum | Distinguishing Features | Examples |
| Basidomycota (club fungi) | Sexual spores found in club-shaped cell called a basidium | Mushrooms, puffballs, earthstars, shelf fungi, jelly fungi, rusts |
| Ascomycota (sac fungi) | Sexual spores found in saclike structure called an ascus | Morels, truffles, *Penicillium* species, baker's yeast |
| Zygomycota (common molds) | Tough zygospore produced during sexual reproducing that can stay dormant for long periods | *Rhizopus stalonifer* (black bread mold), molds found on rotting strawberries and other soft fruits, mycorrhizae associated with plant roots |
| Chytridomycota (chytrids) | Only fungi with flagellated spores | Many species are decomposers found in lakes and moist soil. |

# Fungi in the Environment

Fungi play an essential role in maintaining ecosystem health and equilibrium. But there are also some species that disrupt health by causing disease in plants and animals.

**Decomposition** Many fungi feed by releasing digestive enzymes that break down leaves, fruit, and other organic material into simple molecules they can absorb as food. This has the effect of recycling important minerals and nutrients into the soil. ✺ *Fungi help ecosystems maintain homeostasis by breaking down dead organisms and recycling essential elements and nutrients.*

**Parasitism** As useful as many fungi are, others can infect plants and animals. ✺ *Parasitic fungi can cause serious diseases in plants and animals by disrupting homeostasis.*

***Plant Diseases*** A number of parasitic fungi cause diseases that threaten food crops. Corn smut, for example, destroys corn kernels, and wheat rust affects one of the most important crops grown in North America. Fungal diseases are responsible for the loss of approximately 15 percent of the crops in temperate regions of the world and even more of the crops grown in tropical areas.

***Animal Diseases*** Fungal diseases also affect insects, frogs, and mammals. Amphibians worldwide have been impacted by one deadly fungus—*Batrachochytrium dendrobatidis* (*Bd*). This fungus typically lives in water or soil. It reproduces asexually and the resulting spores are present in the water. When an amphibian comes into contact with the water that contains the spores, the fungus invades the outer layer of the skin, disrupting the immune system and ultimately causing death. *Bd* has been blamed for the extinction of hundreds of amphibian species and poses a threat to up to one third of the world's amphibian populations.

**Figure 21-24**

**The Major Phyla of Fungi**

The table summarizes the main differences among the four major phyla of fungi.
☑ **Infer** Would you expect to find chytrids in aquatic or terrestrial habitats? Explain your answer.

**INTERACTIVITY**

Investigate how invasive pathogens impact species recovery programs.

**READING TOOL**

As you read this section, compare the roles of fungi with those of prokaryotes and protists. Think about the benefits and diseases caused by all three groups.

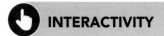

### Figure 21-25

## Parasitic Fungi

Corn smut infests the kernels of a corn plant, reducing the farmer's crop yield (left). Athlete's foot is caused by the fungus *Tinea pedis* (right.)

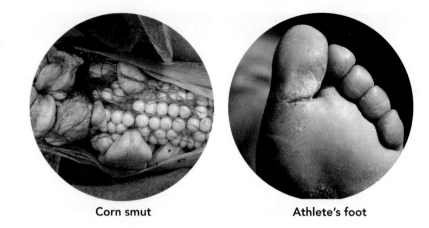

**Corn smut**          **Athlete's foot**

Parasitic fungi can also infect humans, as shown in **Figure 21-25**. The fungus that causes athlete's foot forms a mycelium in the outer layers of the skin, which produces a red, inflamed sore from which the spores can easily spread from person to person. Fungi are also responsible for vaginal yeast infections and for infections of the mouth called thrush. Fungi in these regions of the body are usually kept in check by competition from bacteria and by the body's immune system. This balance can be upset by the use of antibiotics, which kill bacteria, or by damage to the immune system.

## Lichens

The close relationships fungi form with members of other species are not always parasitic in nature. Some fungi form mutualistic associations with photosynthetic organisms in which both partners benefit. For example, a **lichen** is a symbiotic association between a multicellular fungus, a yeast, and a photosynthetic organism. The photosynthetic organism is either a green alga or a cyanobacterium, or both. **Figure 21-26** shows the structure of a lichen.

Lichens are often the first organisms to enter barren environments, gradually breaking down the rocks on which they grow. In this way, lichens help in the early stages of soil formation. Lichens are also remarkably sensitive to air pollution: They are among the first organisms to be affected when air quality deteriorates.

### Figure 21-26

## Inside a Lichen

The protective upper surface of a lichen is made up of densely packed fungal hyphae. Below this are layers of green algae or cyanobacteria and loosely woven hyphae. The bottom layer contains small projections that attach the lichen to a rock or tree. ☑ **Infer** How do lichens assist in soil formation?

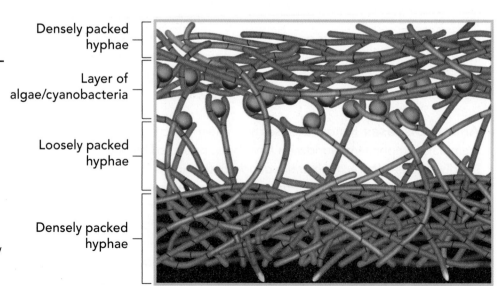

Densely packed hyphae

Layer of algae/cyanobacteria

Loosely packed hyphae

Densely packed hyphae

**Mycorrhizae** Fungi also form mutualistic relationships with plant roots. Almost half of the tissues of trees are hidden beneath the ground in masses of tangled roots. These roots are woven into a partnership with an even larger web of fungal mycelia. These symbiotic associations of plant roots and fungi are called **mycorrhizae** (my koh RY zee; singular: mycorrhiza).

Researchers now estimate that 80 to 90 percent of all plant species form mycorrhizae with fungi. Mycorrhizae gather water and nutrients from the soil, and are essential for the growth of many plants. The seeds of orchids, for example, cannot germinate in the absence of mycorrhizal fungi. Many trees are unable to survive without fungal symbionts. Interestingly, the partnership between plant and fungus does not end with a single plant. The roots of each plant are plugged into mycorrhizal networks that connect many plants. What's more astounding is that these networks appear to connect plants of different species.

A recent experiment showed that carbon atoms from one tree often end up in another tree nearby. In an experiment using isotopes to trace the movement of carbon, ecologist Suzanne Simard found that mycorrhizal fungi transferred carbon from paper birch trees growing in the sun to Douglas fir trees growing in the shade. As a result, the sun-starved fir trees thrived, basically by being "fed" carbon from the birches. Simard's findings suggest that plants—and their associated fungi—may be evolving as a partnership essential to ecosystem health.

**Human Uses of Fungi** Humans have used mushrooms and other fungi as food for thousands of years. While some wild mushrooms are poisonous, many other species are not only highly nutritious, but delicious to eat. Fungi also help to make two of the most ancient forms of human food and drink. Bread and wine are both formed by the action of those single-celled fungi known as yeasts.

**Figure 21-27**

**Birch Trees**

Studies have shown that mycorrhizal relationships between birch trees and Douglas fir trees might help maintain ecosystem health.

HS-LS1-1, HS-LS1-2, HS-LS4-1

 **LESSON 21.4** Review

**KEY QUESTIONS**

1. Identify the characteristics that all fungi have in common.

2. Summarize the role of fungi in maintaining homeostasis in a forest ecosystem.

**CRITICAL THINKING**

3. Identify Both bacteria and fungi are decomposers. What characteristics do these two groups share that allow them to function in this ecological role?

4. Construct an Explanation You notice several mushrooms growing in a ring in a grassy yard. Are you likely observing many organisms or a single organism? Explain.

# Preventing the next epidemic

**Throughout history, humans have suffered from a wide variety of infectious diseases. New and emerging diseases continue to be a threat. What can be done to help combat disease outbreaks?**

HS-ETS1-1, HS-ETS1-3, CCSS.ELA-LITERACY.RST.9-10.1, CCSS.ELA-LITERACY.RST.9-10.2, CCSS.ELA-LITERACY.WHST.9-10.1, CCSS.ELA-LITERACY.WHST.9-10.2, CCSS.ELA-LITERACY.WHST.9-10.7, CCSS.ELA-LITERACY.WHST.9-10.8, CCSS.ELA-LITERACY.WHST.9-10.9

## Make Your Case

The human population is more connected than ever before. Vehicles carry people and cargo from place to place, and all over the world. All of these vehicles carry unintended microscopic passengers, some of which may cause disease.

Choose one of the infectious diseases that has recently been in the news, such as Ebola or Zika. Do some library or Internet research to find out what pathogen causes the disease, where it first was discovered, and what is being done to control the outbreak.

## Communicate Information

1. **Construct an Explanation** What was the response to the disease you researched? Was the disease controlled or contained?

2. **Evaluate a Solution** Based on your research, how effective was the solution that was implemented? Is there another solution or recommendation you would suggest based on your research? Cite evidence to support your ideas.

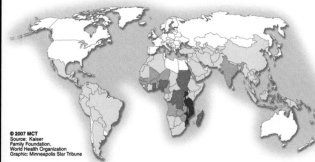

# Technology on the Case

## The Internet to the Rescue

Many people use the Internet to self-diagnose an injury or illness. Depending on the site you use, you might get good advice or maybe not-so-good advice. However, in this age of technology, the Internet is often your first choice in obtaining a lot of information quickly.

Millions of people turn to the Internet when they are feeling sick—and so do healthcare professionals. John Brownstein works at Boston Children's Hospital and is a professor at Harvard Medical School. He and his colleagues developed a system for tracking infectious diseases online. The system automatically scans a wide variety of Web sites and social media for reports of diseases and overall health. Then it plots the reports on a global map. Outbreaks are shown almost exactly at the same time as they occur. In comparison, traditional methods of tracking diseases involve analyzing reports from doctors and hospitals. Traditional reports identify outbreaks about two weeks after they start.

Epidemiologists are also looking at another unlikely source of health data: mobile phones. People often leave an area when a health crisis strikes—and they take their mobile phones with them. By tracking changes in the location of mobile phones, officials can determine where a health crisis is striking and where to invest resources.

# Careers on the Case

## Work Toward a Solution

Physicians and nurses are trained to diagnose and treat diseases in individuals. Some medical specialists, however, work to protect the entire human population from diseases.

### Epidemiologist

You can think of an epidemiologist as a disease detective. Epidemiologists analyze the cause of disease outbreaks and take action to prevent them. They are employed by hospitals, universities, and government agencies, and work closely with hospitals and other community groups who interact directly with the public.

▶ **VIDEO**

Watch this video to learn about other careers in biology.

hhmi | BioInteractive

# STUDY GUIDE

## Lesson Review
Go to your Biology Foundations Workbook for longer versions of these lesson summaries.

### 21.1 Viruses
A typical virus is composed of a core of DNA or RNA surrounded by a protein coat.

Viruses can reproduce only by infecting living cells. In a lytic infection, a virus enters a cell, makes copies of itself, and causes the cell to burst. In a lysogenic infection, a virus integrates its DNA into the DNA of the host cell, and the viral genetic information replicates along with the host cell's DNA.

Viruses cause disease by directly destroying living cells or by affecting cellular processes in ways that upset homeostasis. Despite the fact that they are not alive, viruses have many of the characteristics of living things.

- virus
- capsid
- lytic infection
- bacteriophage
- lysogenic infection
- prophage
- retrovirus

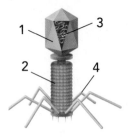

☑ **Use Visuals** Label the parts of this typical bacteriophage.

### 21.2 Prokaryotes
Prokaryotes are classified as Bacteria or Archaea—two of the three domains of life. Bacteria have cell walls made of peptidoglycan. Archaea do not contain peptidoglycan.

Prokaryotes vary in their size and shape, in the way they move, and in the way they obtain and release energy.

Prokaryotes are essential in maintaining every aspect of the ecological balance of the living world. Some prokaryotes are producers that capture energy by photosynthesis. Others break down the nutrients in dead matter and the atmosphere. Some species of prokaryotes have specific uses in human industry. Other bacteria disrupt health and cause disease by destroying living cells or by releasing chemicals that upset homeostasis.

An emerging disease is either a previously unknown disease that appears in a population for the first time or a well-known disease that suddenly becomes harder to control.

- prokaryote
- binary fission
- endospore
- conjugation
- pathogen
- vaccine
- antibiotic

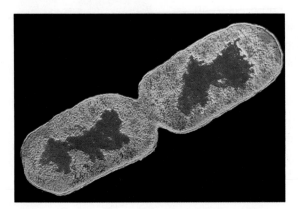

☑ **Interpret Photos** What process is being shown in this photograph?

## 21.3 Protists

Protists are eukaryotes that are not members of the plant, animal, or fungi kingdoms.

Protists vary in their structure and function. Some protists move by changing their cell shape, and some move by means of specialized organelles. Other protists do not move actively but are carried by wind, water, or other organisms. Some protists reproduce asexually by mitosis. Others have life cycles that combine asexual and sexual forms of reproduction.

Protists can help maintain homeostasis in an environment, but they also can disrupt homeostasis. Photosynthetic protists make much of the diversity of aquatic life possible. In addition, many protists are involved in mutualistic symbioses, in which they and their hosts both benefit. However, parasitic protists are responsible for some of the world's most deadly diseases, including several kinds of debilitating intestinal diseases, African sleeping sickness, and malaria.

- cilium
- flagellum
- alternation of generations

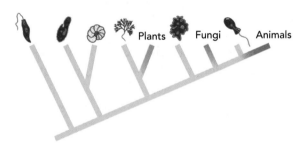

☑ **Interpret Diagrams** What does this cladogram tell you about the classification of protists?

## 21.4 Fungi

Fungi are heterotrophic eukaryotes with cell walls that contain chitin.

Fungi help ecosystems maintain homeostasis by breaking down dead organisms and recycling essential elements and nutrients. Parasitic fungi can cause serious diseases in plants and animals by disrupting homeostasis.

- chitin
- hyphae
- fruiting body
- mycelium
- lichen
- mycorrhiza

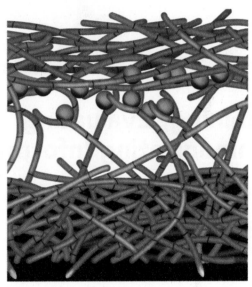

☑ **Interpret Visuals** Describe the relationship that forms the lichen.

# Organize Information

Complete the table that lists the characteristics of both protists and fungi.

|  | Movement | Reproduction | Method of Obtaining Food | Beneficial Roles | Harmful Roles |
| --- | --- | --- | --- | --- | --- |
| **Protists** | 1. | Some reproduce asexually by mitosis. Some reproduce sexually and alternate between diploid and haploid phases. | 2. | 3. | 4. |
| **Fungi** | 5. | 6. | Heterotrophic; absorb nutrients through cell wall or hyphae | 7. | 8. |

# Cholera in Haiti
## Managing a Crisis

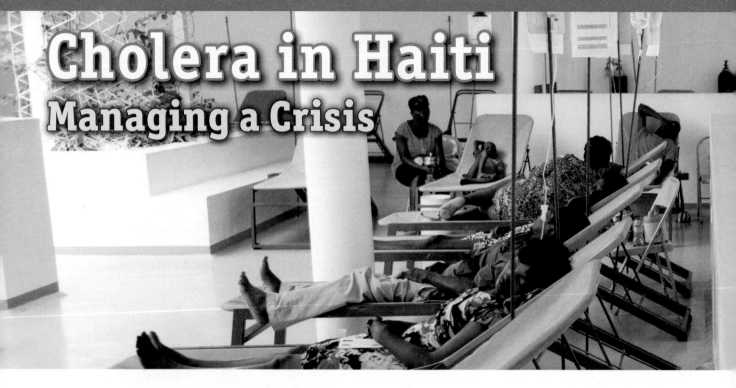

# Obtaining, Evaluating, and Communicating Information

HS-ETS1-1, HS-ETS1-3, CCSS.ELA-LITERACY.RST.9-10.1, CCSS.ELA-LITERACY.RST.9-10.2, CCSS.ELA-LITERACY.WHST.9-10.1,
CCSS.ELA-LITERACY.WHST.9-10.2, CCSS.ELA-LITERACY.WHST.9-10.6, CCSS.ELA-LITERACY.WHST.9-10.7, CCSS.ELA-LITERACY.WHST.9-10.8

**STEM** The country of Haiti has suffered many problems over the years, but cholera had not been one of them. Then, in 2010, a strong earthquake struck the island. Rescue workers arrived to help victims recover. Unfortunately, the workers likely brought with them the bacteria that cause cholera. Haiti soon was suffering its first cholera epidemic—and others would follow. By 2016, cholera had killed about 10,000 Haitians. Whole communities were wiped out.

Cholera is a bacterial infection of the digestive tract that causes watery diarrhea. Without treatment, victims can die quickly from dehydration. The bacteria, named *Vibrio cholerae*, spread through contaminated drinking water. For this reason, cholera outbreaks can be common in places, such as Haiti, where sanitation is poor and people live close together. How should cholera be managed in Haiti today? Public health officials are struggling to find the best combination of separate strategies. Some possible strategies include vaccination, education, and improved sanitation.

- **Vaccine** In 2016, health officials in Haiti launched a campaign to administer the vaccine against cholera in high-risk areas. Their goal was to vaccinate 800,000 people, which is about 8 percent of the population.

- **Education** Haitians are learning how to prevent cholera by treating drinking water with chlorine and washing hands before they eat.

- **Improved Sanitation** Installing and maintaining modern sewage systems is perhaps the most effective way to prevent cholera and similar diseases. However, these systems are expensive.

1. **Define the Problem** Why does cholera remain a problem in Haiti?

2. **Conduct Research** Find out how public health officials are preventing and treating cholera in Haiti today. Work in a small group to research the variety of strategies used in Haiti, including vaccination programs, quarantines to contain cholera outbreaks, treatment methods for cholera victims, and efforts to provide clean drinking water and improved sanitation throughout the country. Record your findings. Be sure to evaluate your sources for accuracy.

3. **Connect to Society** A great cholera epidemic ravaged the city of London in 1854. The epidemic was ended by the work of a physician named Dr. John Snow. Consult historical resources to learn how Dr. Snow discovered the source of the epidemic and also how he helped public health authorities to end it. Does the history of the London epidemic suggest any lessons for the best way to combat cholera in Haiti?

4. **Evaluate** Review the results of your research. How do you evaluate the different strategies and methods for fighting cholera in Haiti? In your evaluation, consider the importance of containing a cholera epidemic if it occurs, as well as preventing future epidemics.

5. **Construct an Argument** Based on your research, what actions or policies for fighting cholera would you recommend to the government, public health officials, and people of Haiti? Describe both the costs and benefits of your recommendations, as well as the potential consequences if no new actions were taken. Try to include scientific evidence, logical reasoning, and an economic analysis to support your argument.

6. **Communicate** Organize your research findings and your argument for a solution in an essay or computer presentation. Share your report with classmates.

## 🔑 KEY QUESTIONS AND TERMS

### 21.1 Viruses

HS-LS4-2

1. Particles made up of proteins, nucleic acids, and sometimes lipids that can reproduce only by infecting living cells are called
   a. bacteria.
   b. capsids.
   c. prophages.
   d. viruses.

2. One group of viruses that contain RNA as their genetic information is the
   a. bacteriophages.
   b. retroviruses.
   c. capsids.
   d. prophages.

3. What characteristics do all viruses have in common?

4. How are capsid proteins important to the way a virus functions?

5. Describe the sequence of events that occurs during a lytic infection.

6. What is a prophage?

7. What is the best way for people to protect themselves against most viral diseases?

### 21.2 Prokaryotes

HS-LS4-2

8. Prokaryotes are unlike all other organisms in that their cells
   a. lack nuclei.
   b. have organelles.
   c. have cell walls.
   d. lack nucleic acids.

9. Prokaryotes reproduce asexually by
   a. binary fission.
   b. endospores.
   c. conjugation.
   d. mutation.

10. What are the two distinguishing characteristics of prokaryotes?

11. Describe the three main cell shapes of prokaryotes.

12. Describe two methods by which prokaryotes move.

13. What is meant by the term *emerging disease*? Give three examples of emerging diseases.

### 21.3 Protists

HS-LS4-2

14. The fossil record shows that the first eukaryotes may have appeared on Earth
   a. more than 4 billion years ago.
   b. more than 1 billion years ago.
   c. about 500 million years ago.
   d. about 100 million years ago.

15. Which of the following statements is most accurate?
   a. Protists are more closely related to one another than to other organisms in other kingdoms.
   b. Protists are the direct descendants of bacteria.
   c. The classification of protists is a work in progress.
   d. Scientists are debating between two classification schemes for protists.

16. Alternation of generations is the process of alternating between
   a. mitosis and meiosis.
   b. asexual and sexual reproduction.
   c. male and female reproductive structures.
   d. diploid and haploid phases.

17. What is the problem with the traditional classification of protists into plantlike, animal-like, and funguslike groups?

18. Why do scientists think that all modern plants, animals, and fungi can be traced to protist ancestors?

19. What function do the cilia and flagella in protists carry out? How do they differ in structure?

20. Summarize the process of conjugation. Is conjugation a form of reproduction? Explain.

## 21.4 Fungi

HS-LS4-2

21. Which of the following statements about fungi is false?
    a. All fungi are unicellular.
    b. All fungi have cell walls.
    c. All fungi are eukaryotic.
    d. All fungi are heterotrophs.

22. A symbiotic relationship between a fungus and a green alga or a cyanobacterium is a
    a. mycorrhiza.
    b. fruiting body.
    c. lichen.
    d. mushroom.

23. Distinguish between the terms *hypha* and *mycelium*.

24. What is the evolutionary significance of mycorrhizae?

## CRITICAL THINKING

HS-LS4-2

25. **Compare and Contrast** In terms of their mechanism of infection, how does a cold virus differ from the HIV virus?

26. **Construct Explanations** Explain how a virus can spread in a bacterial population during the lysogenic phase of infection.

27. **Construct Explanations** Bacteria that live on teeth produce an acid that causes decay. Why do people who do not brush their teeth regularly have more cavities than those who do?

28. **Compare and Contrast** Explain how the outcome of binary fission differs from that of both endospore formation and conjugation.

29. **Apply Concepts** What advantages does the physical removal of infectious microbes by hand washing have over the use of disinfectants? Explain.

30. **Use Analogies** You might have a drawer in your kitchen that is a "junk drawer": a drawer filled with keys, rubber bands, pens, string, rulers, and other items that aren't easy to categorize. How is the protist kingdom like a "junk drawer," and why do you think scientists would like to change that situation?

31. **Predict** Holes in Earth's ozone layer may increase the amount of radiation that reaches the surface of the ocean. If this radiation affects the growth of phytoplankton, what do you think the long-term consequences would be for Earth's atmosphere? Explain your answer.

32. **Construct Explanations** The antibiotic penicillin is a natural secretion of a certain kind of fungus—a green mold called *Penicillium*. Penicillin kills bacteria. Why do you think a mold species has evolved a way to kill bacteria?

A scientist is investigating the effect of three hygiene treatments on bacterial growth. In an experiment, a person's treated hand is swabbed with a sterile cotton ball. Then the cotton is rubbed across a petri dish containing a growth medium. The table shows the results of two trials of the experiment.

Use the data table to answer questions 33 and 34.

| Hand Treatment | Trial 1: Number of Colonies | Trial 2: Number of Colonies |
|---|---|---|
| Unwashed | 247 | 210 |
| Rinsed in warm water | 190 | 220 |
| Washed with soap and warm water | 21 | 15 |
| Rinsed in alcohol and air-dried | 3 | 0 |

33. **Calculate** Determine the average number of bacteria colonies for each treatment.

34. **Analyze Data** Compare the effectiveness of the three treatments.

# ☑ASSESSMENT

## CROSSCUTTING CONCEPTS

**35. Cause and Effect** Explain how a mutation in a bacterial cell could help it become resistant to infection by a bacteriophage.

**36. Cause and Effect** Suppose certain bacteria lost the ability to fix nitrogen. How would this affect other organisms in their ecosystem?

**37. Patterns** A newly discovered organism is unicellular, has a cell wall containing peptidoglycan, has a circular DNA molecule, and lacks a nucleus. Based on those characteristics, to which domain does it belong?

## MATH CONNECTIONS

## Analyze and Interpret Data

CCSS.MATH.CONTENT.MP2, CCSS.MATH.CONTENT.MP4

South Africa is a country located at the southern tip of Africa. Beginning in 2000, the South African government enacted several policies for controlling malaria. The policies included improved mosquito control.

The graphs show the cases of malaria and deaths from malaria in South Africa from 2000 to 2012. Use the graphs to answer questions 38–40.

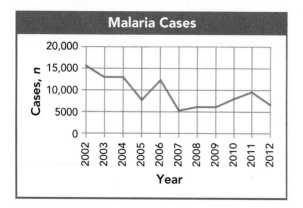

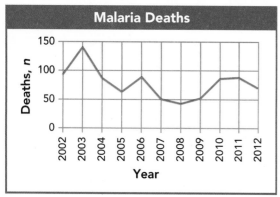

Source: Malaria Research Unit, Medical Research Council

**38. Identify Patterns** Describe the pattern in malaria cases and deaths shown in the graph.

**39. Reason Quantitatively** For the year 2006 in South Africa, what percentage of malaria cases were fatal?

**40. Evaluate a Claim** A scientist claims that improved mosquito control caused the decrease in malaria in South Africa. Use the data shown in the graph and your knowledge of malaria to evaluate this claim.

## LANGUAGE ARTS CONNECTIONS

## Write About Science

CCSS.ELA-LITERACY.WHST.9-10.2

**41. Write Procedures** A middle-school student is using a microscope to observe several single-celled organisms. The student wants to classify each organism as either a prokaryote or a protist. Write a procedure for the student to follow to complete this task.

**42. Write Informative Texts** Write a paragraph that describes a symbiotic relationship formed by bacteria, protists, or fungi.

## Read About Science

CCSS.ELA-LITERACY.RST.9-10.2, CCSS.ELA-LITERACY.RST.9-10.4,
CCSS.ELA-LITERACY.RST.9-10.6

**43. Summarize Text** Describe the main properties of viruses, prokaryotes, protists, and fungi.

**44. Determine Meaning** Explain the meanings of the terms *pathogen*, *emerging disease*, *epidemic*, and *vaccine*. Why are diseases an important topic for this chapter?

**45. Author's Purpose** Near the end of the lesson on fungi, the text discusses an experiment that showed how trees can share carbon atoms. What do you think was the author's purpose in discussing this experiment?

# END-OF-COURSE TEST PRACTICE

1. What is one of the main ways that evolution occurs in prokaryotes?
   A. Crossing over during DNA replication
   B. Exposure to pathogens that change DNA
   C. Mutations that occur during binary fission
   D. Exchanging DNA during alternation of generations
   E. Decomposing dead organisms

2. Every year in the U.S. millions of people are sickened by the flu. What is one way a person can try to prevent the flu?
   A. Get a flu vaccine every year.
   B. Take antibiotics every year.
   C. Apply sunscreen when exposed to the sun.
   D. Apply mosquito repellent when outdoors.
   E. Store foods at temperatures lower than room temperature.

3. Organisms can be classified into one of three domains: Bacteria, Archaea, or Eukarya. What characteristics distinguish Bacteria from Archaea?
   A. Organisms in the domain Archaea have cell walls, and those in the domain Bacteria do not.
   B. Organisms in the domain Bacteria have nuclei, and those in the domain Archaea do not.
   C. Organisms in the domain Bacteria are prokaryotes, and those in the domain Archaea are eukaryotes.
   D. The DNA sequences of Archaea genes are more similar to eukaryotes than to bacteria.
   E. Organisms in the domain Archaea are more likely than those in the domain Bacteria to be disease-causing pathogens.

4. Scientists once classified fungi as types of plants. Today, fungi are classified in their own kingdom. Which of these traits distinguishes fungi from plants?
   A. Fungi are prokaryotes.
   B. Fungi are autotrophs.
   C. Fungi grow in the ground and are photosynthetic.
   D. Fungi reproduce by asexual reproduction.
   E. Fungi have cell walls made of chitin, a polymer that's also found in insects.

5. Protists have been evolving for over a billion years. The major groups of protists are shown in the cladogram below.

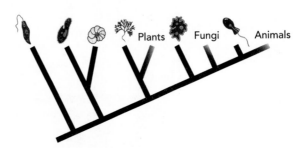

How does this cladogram represent the present-day classification of protists?
   A. Protists used to be in the animal kingdom, and now they are in the plant kingdom.
   B. Protists used to be classified with eukaryotes and are now classified with prokaryotes.
   C. Protists used to be classified with Eukarya and are now classified with Archaea.
   D. Protists used to be classified separately from plants, fungi, and animals and are now classified as plants, fungi, or animals.
   E. Protists used to be classified as similar to plants, fungi, or animals, and now some are classified into other groups.

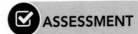 ASSESSMENT

For additional assessment practice, go online to access your digital course.

| If You Have Trouble With... | | | | | |
|---|---|---|---|---|---|
| Question | 1 | 2 | 3 | 4 | 5 |
| See Lesson | 21.2 | 21.1 | 21.2 | 21.4 | 21.3 |
| Performance Expectation | HS-LS4-2 | | | | |

**22.1**
What Is a Plant?

**22.2**
Plant Diversity

**22.3**
Flowers, Fruits, and Seeds

Go Online to access your digital course.

▶ **VIDEO**

🔊 **AUDIO**

👆 **INTERACTIVITY**

📖 **eTEXT**

👁 **ANIMATION**

⚗️ **VIRTUAL LAB**

☑️ **ASSESSMENT**

HS-LS1-1, HS-LS1-2, HS-LS1-4, HS-LS4-1, HS-LS4-6, HS-ETS1-2

# How did plants conquer the land?

In 1988, a tremendous fire burned vast tracts of forest in Yellowstone National Park. Many people were upset, thinking that a large area of the park had been permanently destroyed. Forest rangers reminded the public that fire is a natural event and the forest is adapted to survive fire. In fact, one type of tree in Yellowstone depends on fire to reproduce. This tree is the lodgepole pine. A resin seals the tree's seeds within cones. The resin only melts at the high temperature of a forest fire.

A few years after the Yellowstone fire, the forest floor was covered with tiny saplings of lodgepole pines. Today, the Yellowstone forests are filled with tall pines, and the ecosystem is as diverse and healthy as ever.

The forests of Yellowstone provide merely one example of the hardiness of plants on Earth's land. When fire burns down a forest, the trees eventually grow back. When a parking lot is abandoned, grasses and weeds eventually emerge from cracks in the asphalt. Cacti and sagebrush thrive in deserts where water and nutrients are scarce. In the far north and on mountaintops, pines and spruces withstand extreme cold. Other plants thrive in rain forests where the temperatures are warm and the climate is wet. The trees and vines of the rain forest compete with one another for sunlight and room to grow.

Much like other branches of life, the evolutionary history of plants begins in the water. Plants arose from green algae, which lived as single cells or clusters of cells that perform photosynthesis. Over time, the traits of plants as we know them today evolved in the descendants of green algae. Curiously, once they had invaded the land, plants came to dominate these habitats to an extent they never achieved in marine environments, producing great forests, jungles, and grasslands that shaped entirely new ecosystems.

How did plants evolve from single-celled algae to towering trees? How were plants able to colonize nearly all environments on land, including places very hot and very cold, and very wet and very dry? What structures allow plants to take in water, perform photosynthesis, and reproduce?

**Throughout this chapter, look for connections to the CASE STUDY to help you answer these questions.**

**Plant life regrows after a fire in Yellowstone National Park.**

# What Is a Plant?

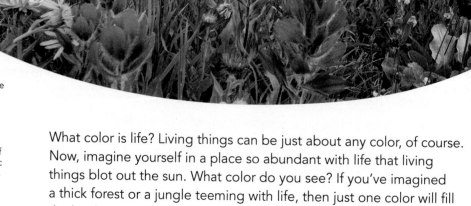

## KEY QUESTIONS

- *What are the basic needs of plants?*
- *How did plants adapt to life on land?*
- *What feature defines most plant life cycles?*

**HS-LS1-1:** Construct an explanation based on evidence for how the structure of DNA determines the structure of proteins which carry out the essential functions of life through systems of specialized cells.

**HS-LS1-2:** Develop and use a model to illustrate the hierarchical organization of interacting systems that provide specific functions within multicellular organisms.

**HS-LS4-1:** Communicate scientific information that common ancestry and biological evolution are supported by multiple lines of empirical evidence.

**VOCABULARY**

alternation of generations
sporophyte
gametophyte

**READING TOOL**

As you read this lesson, identify the things that plants need to survive. Fill in the graphic organizer in your ▣ Biology Foundations Workbook.

**INTERACTIVITY**

Explore what makes a plant a plant.

What color is life? Living things can be just about any color, of course. Now, imagine yourself in a place so abundant with life that living things blot out the sun. What color do you see? If you've imagined a thick forest or a jungle teeming with life, then just one color will fill the landscape of your mind: green—the color of plants. You know that plants dominate this planet. Have you ever wondered why?

## What Do Plants Need to Survive?

Life is tough, especially for a plant that is literally rooted in just one place. As a result, plants have developed adaptations to their stationary lifestyle that enable them to fulfill each of their basic needs, as shown in **Figure 22-1**. ⚲ *The lives of plants depend upon sunlight, gas exchange, water, and minerals.*

**Sunlight** Plants use the energy from sunlight to carry out photosynthesis. As a result, every plant displays adaptations shaped by the need to gather sunlight.

**Gas Exchange** Plants require oxygen to support cellular respiration as well as carbon dioxide to carry out photosynthesis. Therefore, they need to be able to exchange these gases with the atmosphere.

**Water and Minerals** Water is one of the raw materials of photosynthesis. So, land plants have evolved structures to draw water from the ground that also enable them to take in essential minerals from the soil. Many plants have specialized tissues that carry water and minerals upward from the soil and distribute them throughout the plant.

✓ **READING CHECK** **Infer** Why are plants not found in deep underground caves?

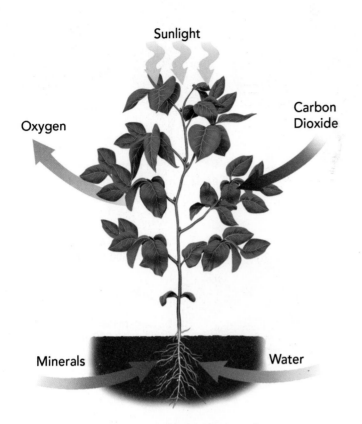

Sunlight

Oxygen

Carbon Dioxide

Minerals

Water

**Figure 22-1**

**Basic Needs of a Plant**

All plants have the same basic needs: sunlight, water, minerals, and a way to exchange gases with the surrounding air.  **Observe** Where do water and minerals enter the plant?

# The History and Evolution of Plants

For most of Earth's history, land plants did not exist. Life was concentrated in oceans, lakes, and streams. Photosynthetic prokaryotes added oxygen to our planet's atmosphere and provided food for consumers.

**Origins in the Water** The fossil record indicates that the ancestors of land plants were water-dwelling organisms similar to today's green algae. Most of these microorganisms were unicellular, but some were composed of multiple cells. At one time biologists classified green algae as protists. But since green algae have cell walls and photosynthetic pigments identical to those of land plants, they are now considered to be part of the plant kingdom.

**The First Land Plants** The oldest traces of land plants date to 472 million years ago. These plants, such as *Cooksonia*, shown in **Figure 22-2**, lacked leaves and roots and were only a few centimeters tall. The greatest challenge they faced was obtaining water. They solved this challenge by growing close to the ground in damp locations. ⚲ *The demands of life on land favored the evolution of plants that were able to draw water from the soil, resist drying out, and reproduce without water.*

The appearance of plants on land changed the rest of life on Earth. New ecosystems emerged, and organic matter began to form soil. From the first pioneering land plants, one group developed into mosses. Another lineage gave rise to ferns, cone-bearing plants, and the most successful group of all—the flowering plants.

▶ **VIDEO**

Investigate the interrelationship between a changing Earth and major stages of plant evolution.

**Figure 22-2**

**A Fossilized Plant**

One of the earliest fossilized vascular plants was *Cooksonia*, which dates back 425 million years. This fossil shows the branched stalks that bore reproductive structures at their tips.

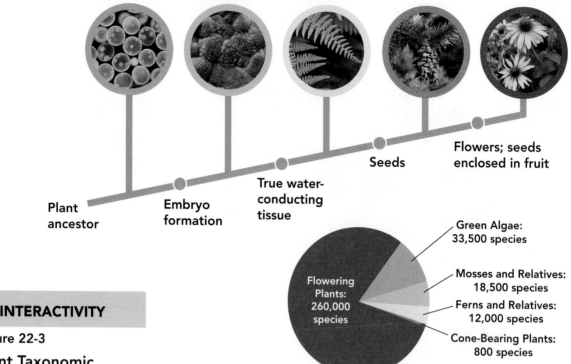

Plant ancestor

Embryo formation

True water-conducting tissue

Seeds

Flowers; seeds enclosed in fruit

Green Algae: 33,500 species

Mosses and Relatives: 18,500 species

Ferns and Relatives: 12,000 species

Cone-Bearing Plants: 800 species

Flowering Plants: 260,000 species

**INTERACTIVITY**

**Figure 22-3**

**Plant Taxonomic Diagram**

There are five main groups of plants in existence today. Note that the colors of the plant groups in the circle graph correspond to the colors of the same groups in the cladogram. ☑ **Ask Questions** What questions about plant evolution would you ask based on the data in the graph?

**An Overview of the Plant Kingdom** All plants are eukaryotes, have cell walls containing cellulose, and carry out photosynthesis using chlorophyll *a* and *b*. Botanists divide the plant kingdom into five major groups based on four important features: embryo formation, specialized water-conducting tissues, seeds, and flowers. The relationship of these taxonomic groups to one another is shown in **Figure 22-3**. Plants that form embryos are often referred to as "land plants," even though some of them now live in watery environments. Why was the development of these four features so important to plant evolution?

- Embryos that develop within a plant have protection from harsh elements on land.
- Plants with water-conducting tissue can draw water to greater heights than allowed by simple diffusion, allowing them to grow much larger.
- Seeds provide food and protection from drying out for the developing embryo. Seeds can be widely dispersed from the parent plant to grow in new locations.
- The successes of flowering plants, as shown in the circle graph in Figure 22-3, are due to the reproductive advantage they receive from their flowers and from the fruits they form around their seeds.

Plant scientists classify plants into finer groups within these major branches by comparing DNA sequences of various species.

☑ **READING CHECK Review** What are the five major groups in the plant kingdom?

# The Plant Life Cycle

Plants have a distinctive sexual life cycle that sets them apart from most other living organisms. 🔑 *The life cycle of plants has two alternating phases—a diploid (2N) phase and a haploid (N) phase.* This shift between the haploid phase and the diploid phase is known as the **alternation of generations**.

The multicellular diploid (2N) phase is known as the **sporophyte** (SPOH ruh fyt), or spore-producing plant. The multicellular haploid (N) phase is known as the **gametophyte** (guh MEE tuh fyt), or gamete-producing plant. Recall from Chapter 12 that haploid (N) organisms carry a single set of chromosomes in their cell nuclei, while diploid (2N) organisms have two sets of chromosomes.

As shown in **Figure 22-4**, a sporophyte produces haploid spores through meiosis. These spores grow into multicellular structures called gametophytes. Each gametophyte produces reproductive cells called gametes—sperm and egg cells. During fertilization, a sperm and egg fuse with each other, producing a diploid zygote. The zygote develops into a new sporophyte, and the cycle begins again.

**BUILD VOCABULARY**

**Suffixes** The suffixes *-phyta* and *-phyte* come from the Greek word *phyton*, which means "plant."

**READING TOOL**

After reading this page, use Figure 22-4 to write a paragraph in your own words that describes alternation of generations. Start your paragraph with a sporophyte plant.

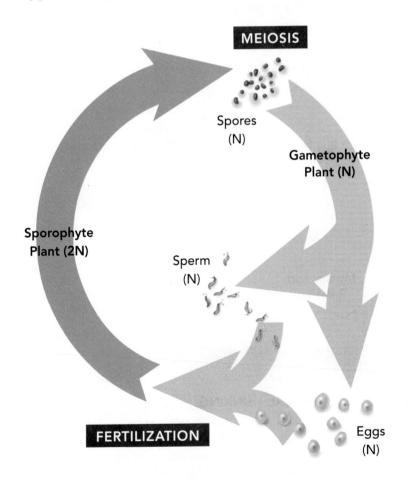

**MEIOSIS**

Spores (N)

Gametophyte Plant (N)

Sporophyte Plant (2N)

Sperm (N)

**FERTILIZATION**

Eggs (N)

**Figure 22-4**

## Alternation of Generations

Most plants have a life cycle with alternation of generations in which the haploid gametophyte phase alternates with the diploid sporophyte phase.

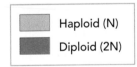

Haploid (N)

Diploid (2N)

## Comparing Adaptations of Ferns and Mosses

**Problem** How are mosses and ferns able to survive on land?

In this lab, you will compare a moss and a fern to determine which plant is better adapted to grow when conditions become dry.

You can find this lab in your digital course.

**Figure 22-5** shows an important trend in plant evolution—the reduction in size of the gametophyte and the increasing size of the sporophyte. Although many green algae have a diploid sporophyte phase, some do not; their only multicellular bodies are gametophytes. Mosses and their relatives consist of a relatively large gametophyte and smaller sporophytes. Ferns and their relatives have a small gametophyte and a larger sporophyte. Seed plants have an even smaller gametophyte.

**Figure 22-5**

## Trends in Plant Evolution

An important trend in plant evolution is the reduction in size of the gametophyte and the increase in size of the sporophyte. ☑ **Interpret Visuals** How does the relative size of the haploid and diploid stages differ between mosses and seed plants?

| | Haploid gametophyte (N) |
| | Diploid sporophyte (2N) |

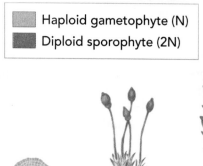

Green Algae | **Mosses and Relatives** | **Ferns and Relatives** | **Seed Plants**

HS-LS1-1, HS-LS1-2, HS-LS4-1

## ☑ LESSON 22.1 Review

### ⚲ KEY QUESTIONS

1. Why do plant cells need sunlight, carbon dioxide, and water?

2. How did the relative lack of water on land affect how plants evolved?

3. Use the terms *sporophyte* and *gametophyte* to describe the alternation of generations in plants.

### CRITICAL THINKING

4. **Construct an Explanation** Most plants have their leaves aboveground and their roots buried in the soil. How does this organization of structures help the plant survive?

5. **Identify Patterns** What pattern is formed by sporophytes and gametophytes in plant evolution?

6. **CASE STUDY** List and describe the four main adaptations that helped plants to thrive on land.

# Plant Diversity

## KEY QUESTIONS

- *What are the characteristics of green algae?*
- *What factor limits the size of bryophytes?*
- *How is vascular tissue important?*
- *What adaptations allow seed plants to reproduce without standing water?*

Like the mosses clinging to the moist rocks in the photograph, the earliest land plants were seedless, were restricted to damp environments, and grew only a few centimeters tall. Even today, many groups of seedless plants are still around. How do these plants continue to thrive, and how do their reproductive patterns differ from plants that produce seeds?

## Green Algae

What do you think of when you hear the word *algae*? As we use the word today, the algae are not a single group of organisms. Some algae are prokaryotes, like cyanobacteria, and some are protists, like the dinoflagellates. The *green algae*, however, are the ones that belong to the plant kingdom.

**The First Plants** Fossil evidence suggests that the green algae appeared well before plants first emerged on land. Fossil formations from more than 550 million years ago during the Cambrian Period show evidence of large mats of green algae. See **Figure 22-6**.

HS-LS1-4: Use a model to illustrate the role of cellular division (mitosis) and differentiation in producing and maintaining complex organisms.

**VOCABULARY**
bryophyte
vascular tissue
archegonium
antheridium
sporangium
tracheophyte
tracheid
xylem
phloem
seed
gymnosperm
angiosperm
pollination
ovule

**READING TOOL**

Compare and contrast the different types of plants. List each plant's characteristics and describe their similarities on the table in your 🔲 **Biology Foundations Workbook.**

## Figure 22-6
### Early Plants and Animals

Primitive green algae shared the ocean floor with corals and sponges in the Middle Cambrian Period, about 500 million years ago.

The green algae share many characteristics—including their photosynthetic pigments and cell wall composition—with larger, more complex plants. ⚘ *Green algae are mostly aquatic. They are found in fresh and salt water, and in some moist areas on land.* Because most green algae are single cells or branching filaments, they are able to absorb moisture and nutrients directly from their surroundings. Therefore, most green algae do not contain the specialized tissues found in other plants.

**Life Cycle** Like land plants, many green algae have life cycles that switch back and forth between haploid and diploid phases. For example, so long as living conditions are suitable, the haploid green alga *Chlamydomonas* reproduces asexually by mitosis, as shown in the left half of **Figure 22-7**. If environmental conditions become unfavorable, *Chlamydomonas* can switch to a stage that reproduces sexually, as shown in the right half of the figure.

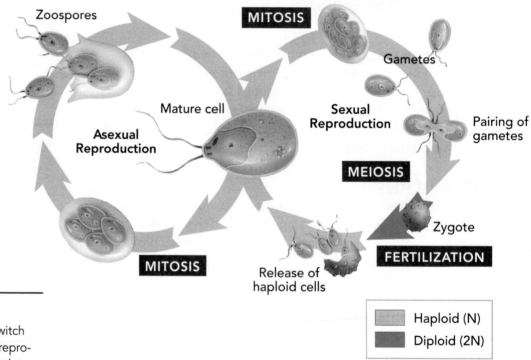

**Figure 22-7**

**Life Cycle of *Chlamydomonas***

The green alga *Chlamydomonas* can switch from asexual to sexual reproduction as environmental conditions change. ☑ **Interpret Visuals** Which form of reproduction includes a diploid organism that can survive harsh conditions?

**Multicellularity** Many green algae form colonies, and they provide a hint about how the first multicellular plants may have evolved. Two examples of colonial algae are shown in **Figure 22-8**. The freshwater alga *Spirogyra* forms long, threadlike colonies constructed of filaments. The cells of a colony are stacked almost like soda cans placed end to end. *Volvox* colonies, shown on the right, are more complex than those of *Spirogyra*, consisting of as few as 500 to as many as 50,000 cells arranged to form hollow spheres.

☑ **READING CHECK** **Review** How do green algae get moisture and nutrients?

Spirogyra (LM 80×)

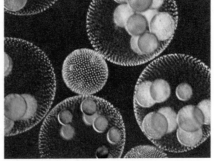
Volvox (LM 50×)

**Figure 22-8**
## Multicellular Green Algae

Colonial algae such as *Spirogyra* and *Volvox* provide evidence that multicellular organisms could evolve from single-celled versions.

# Mosses and Other Bryophytes

In the cool forests of the northern United States, the moist ground feels almost like a spongy green carpet. Look closely, however, and you will see clusters of short plants known as mosses. Mosses have a waxy coating that resists drying and thin filaments known as rhizoids (RY zoydz) that anchor them to the soil and absorb water and nutrients. **Figure 22-9** shows the common structure of a moss.

Mosses belong to a group of plants known as **bryophytes** (BRY oh fyts). Unlike algae, the bryophytes have specialized reproductive organs and grow from embryos. The bryophytes were among the first plants to become established on land. In addition to mosses, the bryophytes include two other groups, known as hornworts and liverworts. Bryophytes are generally small and found only in damp soil. This is because they lack water-conducting **vascular tissue**. Vascular tissue makes it possible for other plants to draw water up against the pull of gravity. ✎ *The lack of vascular tissue limits the height of most bryophytes to just a few centimeters.*

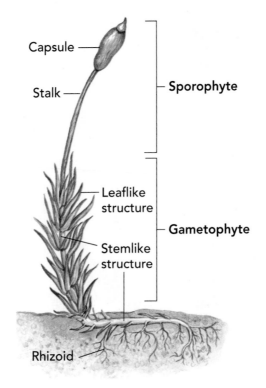

Capsule — 
Stalk — 
— **Sporophyte**
— Leaflike structure
— **Gametophyte**
— Stemlike structure
Rhizoid —

**Figure 22-9**
## Structure of Moss

In bryophytes, the gametophyte is the dominant, more familiar stage of the life cycle.

**Life Cycle** Like all land plants, bryophytes display alternation of generations. In bryophytes, the gametophyte is the dominant stage of the life cycle. It also carries out most of the plant's photosynthesis. As shown in **Figure 22-10**, the sporophyte grows out of the body of the gametophyte and is dependent on it for water and nutrients. When a moss spore lands in a moist place, it sprouts and grows into a tangled mass of green filaments that develop into the familiar green moss plants. Gametes are formed in reproductive structures at the tips of the gametophytes. Eggs are produced in a type of organ called **archegonia** (ahr kuh GOH nee uh; singular: archegonium). Sperm are produced in **antheridia** (an thur ID ee uh; singular: anther-idium) and need standing water to swim to the egg cells. When they meet, sperm and egg cells fuse to produce a diploid zygote.

That zygote then grows into a sporophyte, capped by a spore capsule called a **sporangium** (spoh RAN jee um; plural: sporangia). Inside the capsule, haploid spores are produced by meiosis. When the capsule ripens, it opens, and haploid spores are scattered to the wind to start the cycle again.

**READING CHECK** **Cite Evidence** Identify evidence that supports the claim that the gametophyte carries out most of a bryophyte's photosynthesis.

**Figure 22-10**

**Moss Life Cycle**

This life cycle shows the dominance of the gameto-phyte stage that is typical of mosses and other bryophytes. **Interpret Visuals** In which structure are eggs found?

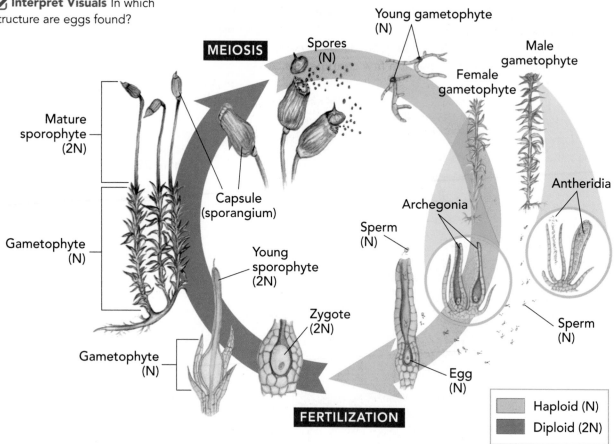

# Ferns and Their Relatives

For millions of years, plants grew no taller than a meter because they lacked vascular tissue. Then, about 420 million years ago, something remarkable happened. The small, mosslike plants on land were joined by new plants, some as large as trees. What happened? Fossil evidence shows that these new plants were the first to have a transport system with true vascular tissue. For the first time, plants were able to grow high above the ground.

**CASE STUDY**

Figure 22-11

**Vascular Tissue**

Horsetails are among the most primitive plant species to have developed specialized vascular tissue. These tissues are able to carry water and nutrients against the pull of gravity.
☑ **Infer** How can height be an advantage to plants?

**Evolution of a Transport System** Vascular plants, such as the horsetails shown in **Figure 22-11**, are also known as **tracheophytes** (TRAEY kee uh fyts). They are named after a specialized type of water-conducting cell, called a **tracheid** (TRAY kee id). Tracheids are hollow tubelike cells with thick cell walls strengthened by lignin. They are one of the great evolutionary innovations of the plant kingdom.

Tracheids are found in **xylem** (ZY lum), a tissue that carries water upward from the roots to every part of a plant. Tracheids are long, slender cells with regions on the ends and sides known as pits. The cell walls in pit regions are extremely thin, which allows water to pass through from one tracheid to the next.

Vascular plants also have a second transport tissue called phloem. **Phloem** (FLOH um) transports nutrients and carbohydrates produced by photosynthesis. Like xylem, the main cells of phloem are long and specialized to move fluids throughout the plant body. 🔍 *Vascular tissues—xylem and phloem—make it possible for vascular plants to move fluids through their bodies against the force of gravity.* Vascular plants can grow tall, but not indefinitely tall. One reason is the limits of vascular transport. Scientists estimate that the tissues can lift water to a maximum height of about 130 meters. That is about the height of the tallest trees.

**READING TOOL**

Create a two-column chart that compares and contrasts xylem and phloem. You can add information to this chart throughout the chapter.

## Figure 22-12

### Fern Fronds and Sporangia

Fronds are the leaves of ferns. Sori, which are clusters of sporangia, often form on the underside of a frond.

## Seedless Vascular Plants

**Seedless Vascular Plants** Although the tracheophytes include all seed-bearing plants, three groups of seedless vascular plants are alive today: club mosses, horsetails, and ferns.

The most numerous seedless plants, with 11,000 species, are the ferns. Ferns have true vascular tissues, strong roots, creeping or underground stems called rhizomes (RY zohmz), and large leaves called fronds, shown in **Figure 22-12**. Ferns can thrive in areas with little light. They are most abundant in wet, or at least seasonally wet, habitats.

**Life Cycle** The large plants easily recognized as ferns are actually the diploid sporophyte phase of the fern life cycle. The fern life cycle is shown in **Figure 22-13**. Spores produced by these plants grow into thin, heart-shaped haploid gametophytes, which live independently of the sporophyte. As in bryophytes, sperm and eggs are produced on these gametophytes in antheridia and archegonia, respectively. Fertilization requires a thin film of water, so that the sperm can swim to the eggs. The diploid zygote produced by fertilization develops into a new sporophyte plant, and the cycle begins again.

✓ **READING CHECK** **Cause and Effect** Why are ferns able to grow so much taller than bryophytes?

## Figure 22-13

### Fern Life Cycle

In the life cycle of a fern, the dominant and recognizable stage is the diploid sporophyte. ✓**Interpret Visuals** Are the spores haploid or diploid?

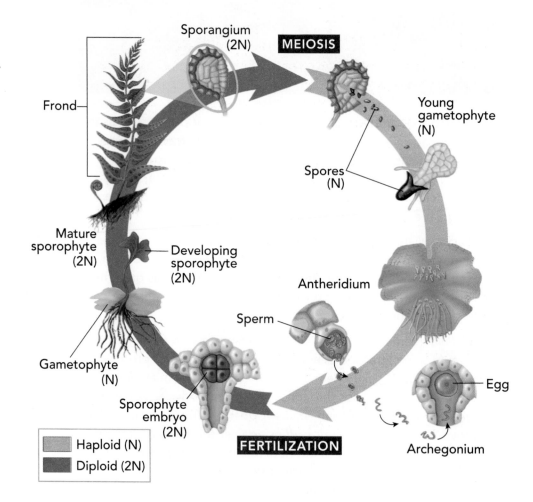

## Keeping Ferns in Check

*Dennstaedtia punctilobula* is a fern that grows on the forest floor and often crowds out tree seedlings, blocking efforts to regrow trees after logging or other work in a forest. To understand the fern better, scientists measured the number of viable fern spores per square centimeter of soil at various distances from a plot of existing fern plants. They counted spores in the soil in July, as the ferns were just beginning to grow, and in November, after they had released their spores.

| | Number of Spores in Soil | |
|---|---|---|
| Distance From Plot of Ferns (meters) | Before Dispersal (July) | After Dispersal (November) |
| 0 | 14 | 54 |
| 2 | 16 | 18 |
| 4 | 5 | 9 |
| 10 | 10 | 17 |
| 50 | 2 | 7 |

1. **Construct Graphs** Place the data from the table on a scatterplot showing the number of spores per square centimeter versus their distance from the plot. Use different colors for the before and after dispersal data points.

2. **Calculate** What percentage of the spores after dispersal are found within 4 meters of the parent plants?

3. **Interpret Graphs** Are spore numbers higher before dispersal or after dispersal? Explain.

4. **Use Evidence to Construct an Argument** Would cutting down nearby clusters of ferns prevent ferns from invading patches of the forest that have just been cut for timber? Explain your reasoning on the basis of the data.

# Seed Plants

Whether they are acorns, pine nuts, dandelion seeds, or the peas shown in **Figure 22-14**, seeds can be found everywhere. What are seeds? Are they gametes? Reproductive structures? Do they contain sperm or eggs? The truth is that they are none of the above.

A **seed** is a plant embryo and its food supply encased in a protective covering. Each and every seed contains a living plant ready to sprout as soon as it encounters the proper conditions for growth. The production of seeds has been one key to the ability of plants to colonize even the driest environments on land. The living plant within a seed is diploid and represents an early stage of the sporophyte phase of the plant life cycle.

**The First Seed Plants** There exist fossils of seed-bearing plants that lived almost 360 million years ago. These fossils document several evolutionary stages in the development of the seed. The fossil record indicates that ancestors of seed plants evolved new adaptations that enabled them to survive in many environments on dry land. Similarities in DNA sequences from modern plants provide evidence that today's seed plants are all descended from common ancestors. Unlike mosses and ferns, the gametes of seed plants do not need standing water for fertilization. ⚲ *Adaptations that allow seed plants to reproduce without standing water include a reproductive process that takes place in cones or flowers, the transfer of sperm by pollination, and the protection of embryos in seeds.*

**Figure 22-14**

## Seeds

The seeds of pea plants develop in pea pods. If conditions are right, each pea could grow into a new plant.

## Cones and Flowers

In seed plants, the male gametophytes and the female gametophytes grow and mature directly within the sporophyte. The gametophytes develop inside reproductive structures known as cones or flowers. In fact, seed plants are divided into two groups on the basis of which of these structures they have.

**Gymnosperms** (JIM noh spurmz) bear their seeds directly on the scales of cones. These were the first seed-bearing plants to appear in the fossil record. Today, highly successful gymnosperms include trees such as pine, spruce, and fir that grow in the great forests of North America.

**Angiosperms** (AN jee oh spurmz), or flowering plants, bear their seeds in flowers inside a special layer of tissue that surrounds and protects the seed. **Figure 22-15** compares the reproductive structures of gymnosperms and angiosperms. Flowering plants include nearly all of the crops grown for food around the world, such as wheat, corn, and rice, as well as fruits like apples and oranges. While many flowers are large and colorful, others, like the flowers produced by grasses and many trees, have more subtle shapes and colors, and are easy to overlook.

**Gymnosperms**

**Angiosperms**

Most flowers produce both male gametophytes (pollen grains) and female gametophytes in each flower. Some species have separate male and female flowers.

Male cones produce male gametophytes (pollen grains).

Female cones produce female gametophytes.

SEM 263×

Ovary

SEM 175×

Wind distributes the pollen of some species. But, in many species, animals carry pollen directly to other flowers.

Wind carries pollen to seed cones.

After fertilization, female cones bear seeds directly on the inside surfaces of scales.

An ovary develops into a fruit that protects the seeds.

**Pollen** The entire male gametophyte of a seed plant is contained in a tiny structure called a pollen grain. Sperm produced by this gametophyte do not swim through water to fertilize the eggs. Instead, pollen grains are carried to the female reproductive structure by wind or animals such as insects. The transfer of pollen from the male reproductive structure to the female reproductive structure is called **pollination**.

**Seeds** After fertilization, the zygote contained within a seed grows into a tiny plant—the sporophyte embryo. A tough seed coat surrounds and protects the embryo and keeps the contents of the seed from drying out. Seeds can survive long periods of bitter cold, extreme heat, or drought until it is time to sprout.

**Figure 22-16**

**Pollen Cone**

This pollen cone on a pine tree is shedding pollen, which will be carried by wind to seed cones.

**The Life Cycle of a Gymnosperm** The word *gymnosperm* actually means "naked seed." The name reflects the fact that gymnosperms produce seeds that are exposed on the scales within cones. Gymnosperms alive today include relatively rare plants such as cycads and the much more abundant plants known as conifers, which include pines and firs.

*Pollen Cones and Seed Cones* Conifers produce two types of cones: pollen cones and seed cones. Meiosis takes place in pollen cones—also called male cones—to produce pollen grains, as shown in **Figure 22-16**. As tiny as it is, a pollen grain contains the entire male gametophyte stage of the life cycle.

Seed cones are larger than pollen cones and produce the female gametophytes. Near the base of each scale of the seed cones are two **ovules** (AHV yoolz). Within the ovules, meiosis produces haploid cells that grow and divide to produce female gametophytes. These gametophytes may contain hundreds or thousands of cells. When mature, each gametophyte contains a few large egg cells, each ready for fertilization by sperm.

*Pollination and Fertilization* The conifer life cycle, shown in **Figure 22-17**, typically takes two years to complete. The cycle begins in the spring as male cones release enormous numbers of pollen grains carried away by the wind. Some of these pollen grains reach female cones. There, the pollen grains are caught in a sticky secretion produced by the ovules within the female cones and pulled inside the ovules.

If a pollen grain lands near an ovule, the grain splits open and begins to grow a pollen tube. Once the pollen tube reaches the female gametophyte, one sperm nucleus disintegrates; the other fertilizes the egg contained within the female gametophyte. Fertilization produces a diploid zygote, which grows into an embryo. The embryo is then encased in a protective covering to form a seed that is ready to be scattered.

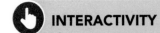

**INTERACTIVITY**

Explore the variations in the reproductive cycles of the major plant groups.

**Figure 22-17**

## Pine Life Cycle

In the life cycle of pine trees and other gymnosperms, the mature sporophyte trees produce male and female cones containing the gametophytes.

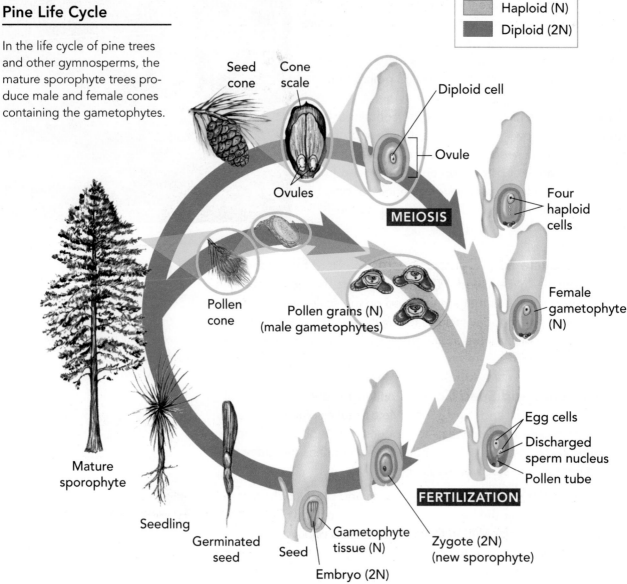

Haploid (N)
Diploid (2N)

Seed cone
Cone scale
Ovules

Diploid cell
Ovule

MEIOSIS

Four haploid cells

Pollen cone
Pollen grains (N) (male gametophytes)

Female gametophyte (N)

Egg cells
Discharged sperm nucleus
Pollen tube

FERTILIZATION

Mature sporophyte

Seedling
Germinated seed
Seed
Gametophyte tissue (N)
Embryo (2N)
Zygote (2N) (new sporophyte)

HS-LS1-4

## ✓ LESSON 22.2 Review

### ⚲ KEY QUESTIONS

1. Describe the characteristics of green algae.
2. Why are bryophytes small?
3. How did the evolution of vascular tissue function in the success of land plants?
4. What is a seed?

### CRITICAL THINKING

5. **Construct an Explanation** Why are ferns common in damp forests, but not in grasslands, deserts, and other dry environments?

6. **Classify** Make a table with two columns—labeled haploid and diploid—and assign each of the following structures from the pine life cycle to the appropriate column: pollen tube, seed cone, embryo, ovule, and seedling.

7. **CASE STUDY** How do seeds make angiosperms and gymnosperms more fit to reproduce on land than ferns and mosses?

# Flowers, Fruits, and Seeds

## 🔍 KEY QUESTIONS

- *How are different angiosperms classified?*
- *What are flowers?*
- *How does fertilization in angiosperms differ from fertilization in other plants?*
- *What is vegetative reproduction?*
- *How do fruits form?*

"Flower Power" may have been a slogan from the San Francisco "hippie" movement of the 1960s, but to biologists, flower power is a real thing. As a result of it, flowering plants dominate the land and are the most abundant organisms in the plant kingdom. What are the secrets of their success? As you will see, it all has to do with the unique way in which they reproduce.

## Angiosperms

Angiosperms first appeared during the Cretaceous Period about 135 million years ago, making their origin the most recent of any phylum, plant or animal. Flowering plants originated on land and soon came to dominate Earth's plant life. Angiosperms make up the vast majority of plant species.

Angiosperms produce sexual reproductive organs known as flowers. Flowers contain **ovaries**, which surround and protect the seeds. The presence of an ovary gives angiosperms their name: *Angiosperm* means "enclosed seed." After fertilization, ovaries within flowers develop into fruits that surround, protect, and help disperse the seeds. The angiosperm **fruit** is a structure containing one or more matured ovaries. The wall of the fruit helps disperse the seeds inside it, carrying them away from the parent plant.

**Angiosperm Classification** For many years, flowering plants were classified according to the number of seed leaves, or **cotyledons** (kaht uh LEED uns), in their embryos. Those with one seed leaf were called **monocots**. Those with two seed leaves were called **dicots**. At one time, these two groups were considered classes within the angiosperm phylum, and all angiosperms were placed in one class or the other.

**HS-LS1-1:** Construct an explanation based on evidence for how the structure of DNA determines the structure of proteins which carry out the essential functions of life through systems of specialized cells. **HS-LS1-2:** Develop and use a model to illustrate the hierarchical organization of interacting systems that provide specific functions within multicellular organisms. **HS-LS1-4:** Use a model to illustrate the role of cellular division (mitosis) and differentiation in producing and maintaining complex organisms.

### VOCABULARY

**ovary • fruit • cotyledon • monocot • dicot • embryo sac • pollination • double fertilization • endosperm • vegetative reproduction • dormancy germination**

### READING TOOL

Complete the chart in your 📖 **Biology Foundations Workbook** to compare and contrast monocots and dicots.

### ▶ VIDEO

Learn about the two main categories of flowering plants.

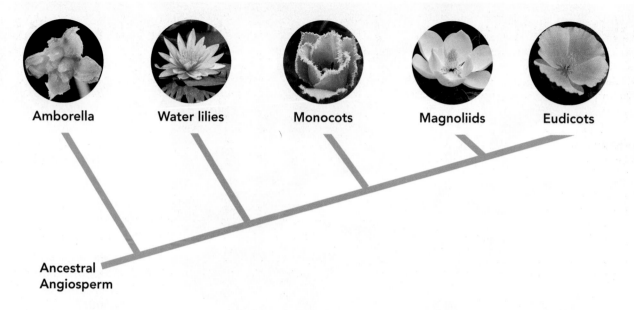

Amborella   Water lilies   Monocots   Magnoliids   Eudicots

Ancestral
Angiosperm

## Figure 22-18

### Angiosperm Clades

Five of the major clades of angiosperms are represented here. Scientists are still working out the relationships among these groups.

### INTERACTIVITY

Investigate the great diversity of angiosperms.

More recent studies of plant genomes and new fossil discoveries have shown that things are actually a little more complicated. Around 135 million years ago, the oldest known angiosperm, *Archaefructus*, whose name means "ancient fruit," first appeared. While it is a true angiosperm, it is neither a monocot nor a dicot. Other evidence suggests that *Amborella*, a plant found on the Pacific island of New Caledonia, belongs to yet another lineage of flowering plants. Information gained from the *Amborella* discovery led scientists to place other plants, such as the water lilies, near the base of angiosperm evolution.

**Figure 22-18** summarizes the modern view of angiosperm classification. While the monocots form a single group, the dicots fall into a number of different categories. This means, of course, that the term *dicot* is no longer used for classification. However, it can still be used to describe many of the characteristics of plant structure, and that is how it is used in this book.

**Angiosperm Diversity** The people who work with plants, including farmers, botanists, and foresters, categorize angiosperms according to a variety of characteristics. 🔎 *Angiosperms differ in the number of their seed leaves, the strength and composition of their stems, and the number of growing seasons they live.* An iris, for example, has a single seed leaf, is a nonwoody plant, and may live for many years.

**Monocots and Dicots** Angiosperms are called either monocots or dicots based on the number of seed leaves they produce. They also differ in characteristics such as stem structure and the number of petals per flower. **Figure 22-19** illustrates the differences between monocots and dicots. Monocots include plants such as corn, wheat, lilies, orchids, and palms. Monocot grasses—especially wheat, corn, and rice—are cultivated in mass quantities for food. Dicots include roses, clover, tomatoes, oaks, and daisies.

| Characteristics of Monocots and Dicots | | | | |
|---|---|---|---|---|
| | **Seeds** | **Leaves** | **Flowers** | **Stems** | **Roots** |
| **Monocots** | Single cotyledon | Parallel veins | Floral parts often in multiples of 3 | Vascular bundles scattered throughout stem | Fibrous roots |
| **Dicots** | Two cotyledons | Branched veins | Floral parts often in multiples of 4 or 5 | Vascular bundles arranged in a ring | Taproot |

**Woody and Herbaceous Plants** Flowering plants also differ in terms of the woodiness of their stems. Woody plants are made primarily of cells with thick cell walls that support the plant body. These include trees, shrubs, and vines. Shrubs are typically smaller than trees, and vines have stems that are long and flexible. Herbaceous (hur BAY shus) plants do not produce true wood, and therefore have nonwoody stems. Examples of herbaceous plants include dandelions, zinnias, petunias, and sunflowers.

**Annuals, Biennials, and Perennials** If you've ever planted a garden, you know that many flowering plants live for just a single season while others grow year after year. The life span of plants is determined by a combination of genetic and environmental factors. The types of plant life spans—annual, biennial, and perennial—are described in **Figure 22-20**.

✓ **READING CHECK** Review How do woody plants differ from herbaceous plants?

**Figure 22-19**

**Comparing Monocots and Dicots**

This table compares the characteristics of monocots and dicots. ✓ **Interpret Tables** How do the flowers of monocots and dicots typically differ?

**Figure 22-20**

**Comparing Plants by Life Span**

Categories of plant life spans include annuals, biennials, and perennials.

Annuals pass through their entire life cycle in one growing season.

Biennials live for two growing seasons. Seeds and flowers form in the second season.

Perennials regrow year after year.

# Flower Structure

What makes a flower beautiful? Is it the symmetry of its petals, its rich colors, or its fragrance? These things may matter to us, but to a plant, the whole point of a flower is to bring gametes together for reproduction and to protect the resulting embryo.

Flowers are an evolutionary advantage to plants because they attract animals such as bees, moths, or hummingbirds. These animals—drawn by the color, scent, or even the shape of the flower—carry pollen with them as they leave. Because these animals go directly from flower to flower, they can carry pollen to the next flower they visit. This type of pollination is much more efficient than the wind pollination of most gymnosperms.

Flowers are reproductive organs, and their beauty reflects the stunning evolutionary success of the angiosperms. The basic structure of a angiosperm flower is shown in **Figure 22-21**. ⚲ *Flowers are reproductive organs that are composed of four different kinds of specialized leaves: sepals, petals, stamens, and carpels.*

## Sepals

The outermost portion of a flower consists of modified leaves called sepals (SEE pulz). They enclose the bud before it opens and protect the flower as it develops. Petals, which are often brightly colored, are found just inside the sepals. The colors and shapes of petals help to attract insects and other pollinators to the flower.

Petals generally fall off a flower after several days. Losing petals also helps the plant reproduce. After pollination occurs, animal visitors are not useful until much later in the process.

---

**Quick Lab**    Guided Inquiry

### What Is the Structure of a Flower?

1. Examine a flower carefully. Make a detailed drawing of the flower and label as many parts as you can. Note whether the anthers are above or below the stigma.

2. Remove an anther and place it on a slide. While holding the anther with forceps, use a scalpel to cut one or more thin slices across the anther. **CAUTION:** *Be careful with sharp tools. Place the slide on a flat surface before you start cutting.*

3. Lay the slices flat on the microscope slide and add a drop of water and a coverslip. Observe the slices with the microscope at low power. Make a labeled drawing of your observations.

4. Repeat steps 2 and 3 with the ovary.

### ANALYZE AND CONCLUDE

1. **Observe** Are the anthers in this flower located above or below the stigma? How could this location affect what happens to the pollen produced by the anthers? Explain your answer.

2. **Apply Concepts** What structures did you identify in the anther? What is the function of these structures?

3. **Apply Concepts** What structures did you identify in the ovary? What is the function of these structures?

4. **Draw Conclusions** Which parts of the flower will become the seeds? Which parts will become the fruit?

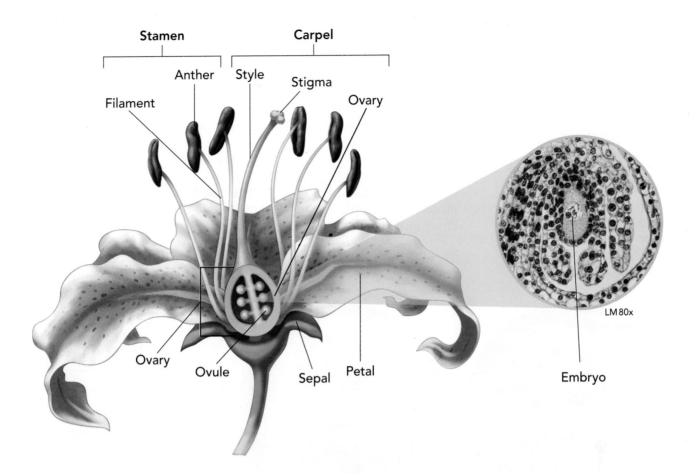

**Figure 22-21**

**The Parts of a Flower**

This diagram shows the parts of a typical flower. The flowers of some angiosperm species do not have all the parts shown here.

**Stamens and Carpels** Inside the ring of petals are organs that produce male and female gametophytes. The stamens are the male parts of the flower. Each stamen consists of a stalk called a filament with an anther at its tip. Anthers are the structures in which pollen grains—the male gametophytes—are produced. In most angiosperm species, the flowers have several stamens. If you rub your hand on the anthers of a flower, a yellow-orange dust may stick to your skin. This dust is made up of thousands of individual pollen grains.

The innermost floral parts are the carpels, which produce female gametophytes and, later, seeds. The carpels are fused into a broad base, forming an ovary where the female gametophytes are produced. The diameter of the carpel narrows into a stalk called the style. At the top of the style is a sticky or feathery portion known as the stigma, which is specialized to capture pollen. Botanists sometimes call a single carpel or several fused carpels a pistil.

**READING CHECK Classify** Make a two-column table with the columns labeled Male and Female. Then list and define the structures that make up a flower in the appropriate column.

## Figure 22-22

## Variety Among Flowers

Flowers vary greatly in structure. Some flowers have adaptations that are so specific that they can only be pollinated by one particular animal.

**Variety in Flowers** Flowers vary greatly in shape, color, and size, as shown in **Figure 22-22**. While most flowering plants produce both male and female gametophytes, in some species the male and female gametophytes are produced on different plants. In some plants, many flowers grow close together to form a composite structure that looks like a single flower. Other flowers might attract a wide variety of pollinators.

**✓ READING CHECK** **Form a Hypothesis** How might it be an advantage for a plant to have many flowers clustered in a single structure? (Hint: Refer to the allium in **Figure 22-22**.)

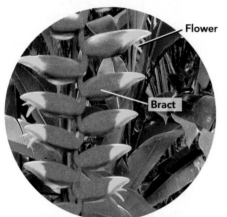

Flower

Bract

**Lobster Claw Heliconia**
*Heliconia* **flowers are protected within colorful leaf structures called bracts.**

**Allium**

**Wild Rose**

**Passion flower**

**Kuri Squash**

# The Angiosperm Life Cycle

Like other plants, angiosperms have a life cycle that shows an alternation of generations. The diploid sporophyte produces haploid gametophytes inside the tissues of the flower.

**Male Gametophytes** Male gametophytes—the pollen grains—develop inside anthers, as shown in **Figure 22-23**. First, meiosis produces four haploid spore cells. Each spore then divides again to produce two cells, a generative cell and a tube cell. The male gametophyte with its two cells is then surrounded by a thick wall that protects it from damage.

**Female Gametophytes** Female gametophytes develop inside the carpels. The ovules—the future seeds—are enveloped in a protective ovary—the future fruit. A single diploid cell goes through meiosis to produce four haploid cells, three of which disintegrate. The remaining cell undergoes mitosis, producing eight nuclei. Next, cells walls form, which produce a total of seven cells, six with one nucleus and a seventh with two nuclei. These seven cells are the female gametophyte, also known as the **embryo sac**. One of the eight nuclei, near the base of the gametophyte, is the actual egg cell—the female gamete. If fertilization takes place, this egg cell will fuse with the male gamete to become the zygote that grows into a new sporophyte plant.

**READING TOOL**

List the sequence of events that occur during the life cycle of an angiosperm.

 **ANIMATION**

Figure 22-23

## The Development of Gametophytes

The diagrams show the development of the male gametophyte inside an anther and the development of the female gametophyte inside a single ovule.

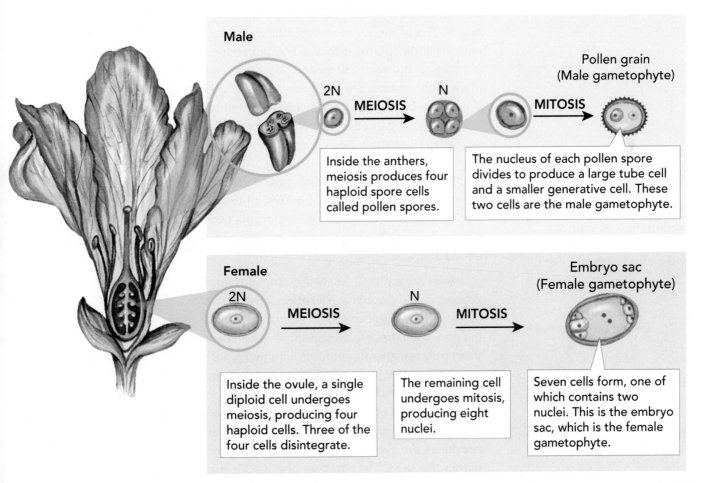

**Male**

2N → **MEIOSIS** → N → **MITOSIS** → Pollen grain (Male gametophyte)

Inside the anthers, meiosis produces four haploid spore cells called pollen spores.

The nucleus of each pollen spore divides to produce a large tube cell and a smaller generative cell. These two cells are the male gametophyte.

**Female**

2N → **MEIOSIS** → N → **MITOSIS** → Embryo sac (Female gametophyte)

Inside the ovule, a single diploid cell undergoes meiosis, producing four haploid cells. Three of the four cells disintegrate.

The remaining cell undergoes mitosis, producing eight nuclei.

Seven cells form, one of which contains two nuclei. This is the embryo sac, which is the female gametophyte.

## Figure 22-24
## Pollination

The appearance of a flower often indicates how it is pollinated. The flowers of an animal-pollinated flower are often large and brightly colored. In contrast, the flowers of a slender meadow foxtail are typical of wind-pollinated flowers in that they are small and not very showy but produce vast amounts of pollen.

**BUILD VOCABULARY**

**Related Word Forms** Several word forms are derived from the word *pollen*. **Pollination** is the transfer of pollen from one flower to another. A *pollinator* is an animal that moves pollen.

## Figure 22-25
## Inside a Corn Kernel

Distinct fertilization events produce the two main parts of the seed: the plant embryo and the endosperm.

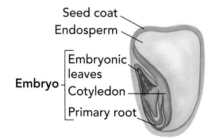

Seed coat
Endosperm
Embryo—
Embryonic leaves
Cotyledon
Primary root

**Pollination** The transfer of pollen to the female portions of the flower is called **pollination**. Some angiosperms are wind pollinated. Most angiosperms, however, are pollinated by animals, such as the bee in **Figure 22-24**, that carry pollen from one flower to another. Animal-pollinated plants have adaptations such as bright colors and sweet nectar to attract and reward animals. In turn, many animals have evolved bodies that enable them to reach nectar deep within certain flowers. For example, hummingbirds have long, thin beaks that can probe deeply into flowers to reach their nectar.

Insect pollination is beneficial to insects such as bees because it provides a dependable source of food—pollen and nectar. Plants benefit because these insects take the pollen directly from flower to flower. The efficiency of insect pollination may be one of the main reasons angiosperms displaced gymnosperms as the dominant land plants over the past 130 million years. However, it also means that many plant species are highly dependent upon insect pollinators. When bee populations, for example, are threatened by diseases or insecticides, it can adversely affect plant populations and lower the productivity of agricultural crops.

**Fertilization** When a pollen grain lands on the stigma of a flower, it begins to grow a pollen tube. One of the pollen grain's two cells—the "generative" cell—divides and forms two sperm cells. The pollen tube grows into the style, where it eventually reaches the ovary and enters an ovule.

Inside the embryo sac, two distinct fertilizations take place in a process called **double fertilization**. First, one of the sperm nuclei fuses with the egg nucleus to produce a diploid zygote that becomes the new plant embryo. Second, the other sperm nucleus does something truly remarkable—it fuses with two polar nuclei in the embryo sac to form a triploid (3N) cell. This cell will grow into a food-rich tissue known as **endosperm**, which nourishes the seedling as it grows. 🔍 *The process of fertilization in angiosperms is distinct from that found in other plants. Two fertilization events take place—one that produces the zygote and the other that produces the endosperm within the seed.* The structure of a seed is shown in **Figure 22-25**.

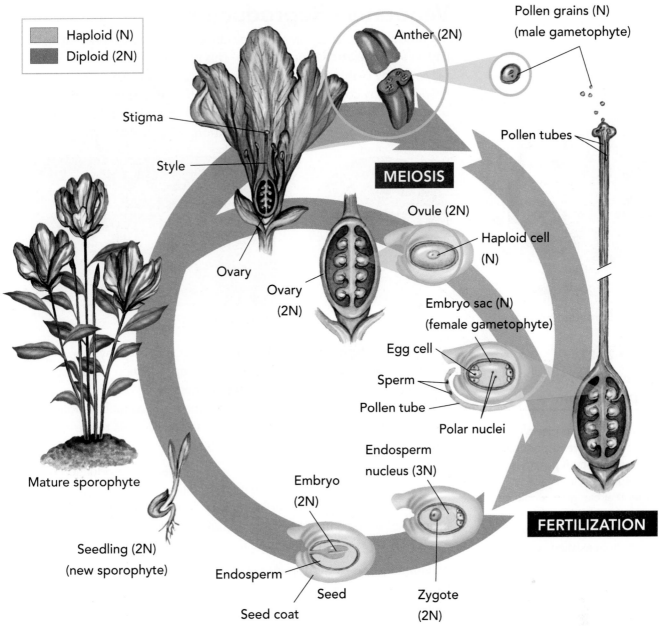

**Figure 22-26**
**Angiosperm Life Cycle**

In the life cycle of a typical angiosperm, the developing seeds of a flower are protected and nourished inside the ovary.

Double fertilization may be another reason why the angiosperms have been so successful. By using endosperm to store food, the flowering plant spends very little energy producing seeds from ovules until double fertilization has actually taken place. The energy saved can be used to make many more seeds. **Figure 22-26** summarizes the life cycle of a typical angiosperm.

☑ **READING CHECK** **Cause and Effect** What are the products of double fertilization?

# Vegetative Reproduction

Many flowering plants can also reproduce asexually by a process known as **vegetative reproduction**. This process takes place naturally in many plants, and horticulturists also use it as a technique to produce many copies of an individual plant. 🔍 *Vegetative reproduction is the formation of new individuals by mitosis. It does not require gametes, flowers, or fertilization.*

Sprouting potato

Cholla cactus

Strawberry plant

## Figure 22-27

### Examples of Vegetative Reproduction

Stem adaptations play a role in the vegetative reproduction of these plants. A potato is an underground stem called a tuber that can grow whole new plants from buds, called eyes. Some cacti can grow new plants from existing stems that fall from the plant. Strawberry plants send out long, trailing stems called stolons, or runners. Nodes that rest on the ground produce roots and upright stems and leaves.

Vegetative reproduction takes place in a number of ways, as shown in **Figure 22-27**. Because vegetative reproduction does not involve seed formation, a single plant can reproduce quickly. In addition, asexual reproduction allows a single plant to produce genetically identical offspring. This enables well-adapted individuals to rapidly fill a favorable environment.

Horticulturists often take advantage of vegetative reproduction by using cuttings or grafting to make many identical copies of a plant or to produce offspring from seedless plants. A grower may simply cut a length of stem containing meristem tissue and bury it in a sterile medium such as perlite or sand to encourage root formation.

Grafting is used to reproduce seedless plants and varieties of woody plants that will not grow from cuttings. A grower cuts a piece of stem or a lateral bud from a parent plant and attaches it to another plant, as shown in **Figure 22-28**. Grafting works best when the two plants are closely related, such as when a bud from a lemon tree is grafted onto an orange tree.

✅ **READING CHECK** **Apply Concepts** Describe how asexual reproduction might allow a plant to become rapidly established in a new area.

## Figure 22-28

### Grafting

When just starting to bud, a branch from a lemon tree is grafted onto the branch of an established orange tree. Months later, the mature branch bears lemon fruit. Grafting can lead to a single plant bearing more than one type of fruit.

# Fruits and Seeds

Would it surprise you to learn that if you ate a meal of corn on the cob and baked beans, from the point of view of a biologist, you were actually eating fruits? The development of the seed, which protects and nourishes the plant embryo, contributed greatly to the success of plants on land. But the *angiosperm* seed, protected by a fruit, was an even better adaptation, as we will see.

**Fruit and Seed Development** Once fertilization of an angiosperm is complete, nutrients flow from the vascular system into the flower to support the growing embryo within the seed. **As angiosperm seeds mature, ovary walls thicken to form a fruit that encloses the developing seeds.** A fruit is simply a matured angiosperm ovary, usually containing seeds. An exception is found in commercially grown fruits that are selectively bred to be seedless, such as some varieties of grapes. Examples of fruits are shown in **Figure 22-29**.

In everyday language, the term *fruit* applies to sweet plant products such as apples, grapes, and strawberries. However, think about foods such as string beans, corn, beans, cucumbers, and tomatoes, which we commonly call vegetables. Since these vegetables contain the seeds of plants, they are also fruits. The ovary wall surrounding a fruit may be fleshy, as it is in grapes and tomatoes, or tough and dry, like the shell that surrounds peanuts. The peanuts themselves are seeds.

While fruits and seeds are developing, it generally benefits the plant to keep animals away. Bright flower petals have fallen away, and the appearance of the remains of the flower generally blends in with the rest of the plant. The developing fruits and seeds are also not especially tasty. In many cases, they are tough and bitter. Many fruits, including tomatoes, oranges, and bananas, begin with green rinds that match the colors of the plant leaves. When they ripen, they take on brighter colors.

**Figure 22-29**
## Variety Among Fruits

Like the flowers from which they develop, fruits vary in structure.

**Pomegranate**

**Plum**

**Maple**

**Peanut**

**Lychee**

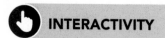
Investigate the conditions that could make flowers suddenly bloom in a hot, dry landscape.

**CASE STUDY**

**Figure 22-30**

**Mechanisms of Seed Dispersal**

Angiosperm seeds are dispersed in a variety of ways.

☑ **Construct an Explanation**
How did the adaptations that lead to a variety of seed dispersal methods contribute to the success of angiosperms on land?

**Seed Dispersal** Fruits are not there to nourish the seedling—the endosperm does that. So why should plants have seeds that are wrapped in an additional layer of nutrient-packed tissue? Think of the blackberries that grow wild in the forests of North America. Each seed is enclosed in a sweet, juicy fruit, making it a tasty treat for all kinds of animals. What good is such sweetness if all it does is get the seed eaten? Well, believe it or not, that's exactly the point.

The seeds of many plants, especially those encased in sweet, fleshy fruits, are often eaten by animals. The seeds are covered with tough coatings, allowing them to pass through an animal's digestive system unharmed. The seeds then sprout in the feces eliminated from the animal. These fruits provide nutrition for the animal and also help the plant disperse its seeds—often to areas where there is less competition with the parent plant. Several mechanisms of seed dispersal are shown in **Figure 22-30**.

Animals are not the only means by which plants can scatter their seeds. Seeds are also adapted for dispersal by wind and water. A dandelion seed, for example, is attached to a dry fruit that has a parachute-like structure. This adaptation allows the seed to glide a considerable distance away from the parent plant. Some seeds, like the coconut, are dispersed by water. Coconut fruits are buoyant enough to float in seawater for many weeks, enabling them to reach remote islands.

Birds and other animals may drop seeds as they eat the fruit.

The wind carries the tiny seeds of dandelions.

Palm trees colonize tropical islands because of their floating fruit—the coconut.

The burrs on this goat are the fruits of the burdock plant. The sticky fruits hitch a ride to new places.

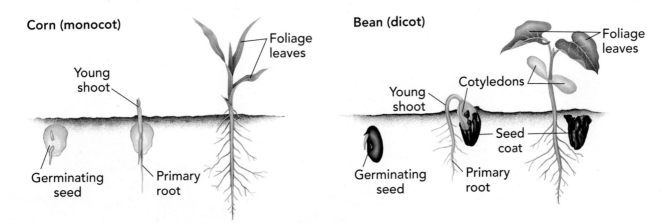

**Corn (monocot)**

Foliage leaves

Young shoot

Germinating seed

Primary root

**Bean (dicot)**

Foliage leaves

Young shoot

Cotyledons

Seed coat

Germinating seed

Primary root

**Figure 22-31**

**Germination: A Comparison**

The monocot corn seedling (left) grows directly upward, protected by a sheath of tissue that surrounds the developing leaves. In contrast, the garden bean (right) forms a hook in its stem that gently pulls the new plant tissues out of the soil.

**Seed Germination** All seeds contain plant embryos in a state of **dormancy**, during which the embryo is alive but not growing. **Germination** takes place when growth of the embryo resumes and the seed sprouts into a plant. The seeds of some plants may remain dormant for many weeks or even months. The timing of germination can be critical for a plant, especially in climates where growing conditions change with the seasons. The seeds of many temperate plants, for example, germinate only in the spring, when conditions are best for growth. In some species, the seeds depend on a period of cold temperatures. The seeds are dormant while cold, and then begin growing when temperatures warm. Dormancy also can allow for long-distance seed dispersal, making it possible for seeds to germinate under ideal conditions.

When germination does begin, the growing plant unfolds its first leaves, the cotyledons. Some cotyledons, like those of garden beans, store nutrients during dormancy. Then they transfer the nutrients to the rest of the plant as the seed germinates. **Figure 22-31** compares germination in a monocot and a dicot.

HS-LS1-1, HS-LS1-2, HS-LS1-4

## ✓ LESSON 22.3 Review

### ⚲ KEY QUESTIONS

1. Describe three general ways that angiosperms may differ from one another.

2. What are the functions of stamens and carpels?

3. Describe the features of fertilization that are characteristic of angiosperms.

4. What is the result of vegetative reproduction?

5. Describe how fruits form.

### CRITICAL THINKING

6. **Construct an Explanation** How does the life cycle of some angiosperms depend on animals? Include two specific examples to support your answer.

7. **Compare and Contrast** How is vegetative (asexual) reproduction similar to sexual reproduction in angiosperms? How is it different?

# How did plants conquer the land?

A forest fire may kill thousands of trees all at once, but the destruction is not permanent. Trees, like other plants, have a variety of adaptations that allow them to survive on land—and to repopulate the land when the opportunity arises.

HS-LS1-1, HS-LS1-2, CCSS.ELA-LITERACY.RST.9-10.2, CCSS.ELA-LITERACY.WHST.9-10.1

## Make Your Case

Green algae are small organisms that live only in the water or very moist environments. However, step by step, the descendants of algae became towering trees, vines with delicious fruit, and all the other diverse plants that live across the land today. The adaptations that evolved in plants are an amazing story. The story also involves the evolution of animals. Many plant parts, such as showy flowers and sweet fruits, are adaptations for attracting help in reproduction.

## Construct an Explanation

1. **Compare and Contrast** How do the structures and functions of a typical land plant, such as a lodgepole pine, compare and contrast with green algae?

2. **Synthesize Information** Based on your knowledge of plants, and additional research if necessary, describe in order the important events in the evolution of plants. Include at least five events in your history.

Recovery can be slow after a devastating natural disaster such as a volcanic eruption. Some areas of Mt. St. Helens are still recovering decades after the 1980 eruption.

## Careers on the Case

### Work Toward a Solution

In natural ecosystems, plants are distributed and grow in patterns that nature determines. In some careers, however, people work with plants directly.

### Landscaper

Landscapers apply their own ideas to choose and arrange plants. They work to place plants in yards and parks, along sidewalks, and in other public spaces. To be successful, landscapers need to combine a sense of design, and a knowledge of a variety of plants and how they grow.

### ▶ VIDEO

Learn more about landscaping and related careers.

## Society on the Case

### Of Lawns and Elms

When Europeans began settling North America, they brought their ideas about lawns with them. Today, grassy lawns surround houses and other buildings across the United States. Lawns can be attractive, but they displace the natural ecosystem, which may have been a forest, prairie, wetland, or desert. Lawns also require maintenance that has consequences for the environment. In hot, dry climates, a healthy lawn might require watering as often as once a day. The fertilizer that is spread on lawns may wash into lakes and streams where it can spur the growth of algae. Fertilizer can also pollute groundwater.

Some popular plants in landscaping have led to unintended results. For example, elm trees were once very popular for lining city sidewalks. The tall, arching branches of the elms formed green canopies over the streets. By 1930, North America was home to more than 70 million elm trees. Then they were ravaged by Dutch elm disease. Beetles spread this fungal-borne disease from tree to tree. By 1989, more than three quarters of the elms in North America were dead.

The best way to make a landscape sustainable is to use plants that are native to the region. In California and Arizona this could mean planting native succulents, which are plants that have fleshy parts that hold water. Southern Florida is home to many native grasses that grow in the sandy soil without excess fertilizer. Many people who live by forests choose to forgo any type of a lawn at all. They let the forest grow around their houses and clear trees only when they pose safety hazards.

# Lesson Review

Go to your Biology Foundations Workbook for longer versions of these lesson summaries.

## 22.1 What Is a Plant?

Plants depend upon sunlight, gas exchange, water, and minerals. Plants use the energy from sunlight to carry out photosynthesis. They require oxygen to support cellular respiration as well as carbon dioxide to carry out photosynthesis. Plants also need a way to access water and minerals.

Over time, the demands of life on land favored the evolution of plants more resistant to the drying rays of the sun, more capable of conserving water, and more capable of reproducing without water.

Most plant life cycles have two alternating phases, a diploid and a haploid phase. The multicellular diploid phase is the sporophyte, or spore-producing plant. The multicellular haploid phase is the gametophyte, or gamete-producing plant. The cycle is known as the alternation of generations.

- alternation of generations
- sporophyte
- gametophyte

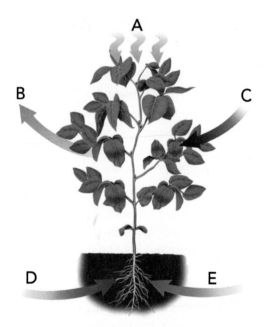

☑ **Interpret Visuals** Identify each of the labeled needs of a plant and explain the function of each.

## 22.2 Plant Diversity

Fossil evidence suggests that the first plants were similar to modern-day green algae. The first land plants were bryophytes, which include mosses, hornworts, and liverworts. Because they lack water-conducting vascular tissue, they grow in damp soil and low to the ground.

About 420 million years ago, plants with true vascular tissue evolved. Vascular plants are known as tracheophytes, because they contain tracheids. Tracheophytes include all seed-bearing plants as well as seedless vascular plants: club mosses, horsetails, and ferns. Seedless vascular plants produce spores. They require a thin film of water to carry out fertilization.

Gymnosperms and angiosperms are seed plants. A seed is a plant embryo and food supply encased in a protective covering. In seed plants, the male and female gametophytes grow and mature directly in the sporophyte, within structures known as cones or flowers. Gymnosperms bear their seeds in cones. Angiosperms bear their seeds in flowers.

- bryophyte
- vascular tissue
- archegonium
- antheridium
- sporangium
- tracheophyte
- tracheid
- xylem
- phloem
- seed
- gymnosperm
- angiosperm
- pollination
- ovule

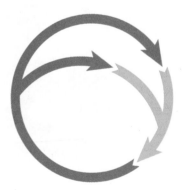

☑ **Identify Patterns** Does this life cycle follow the pattern of green algae, seedless plants, or seed plants? Explain.

## 22.3 Flowers, Fruits, and Seeds

Scientific classification best reflects evolutionary relationships among flowering plants. However, people that work with flowering plants, or angiosperms, categorize them in different ways. Angiosperms are often grouped by the number of their seed leaves—plants with one seed leaf are called monocots; those with two seed leaves are called dicots. Flowering plants can have woody or herbaceous stems (which are smooth and non-woody). Angiosperms are also classified by their life span. Annuals grow, flower, and die in one season; biennials grow over two seasons before they die; perennials continue to flower from year to year.

Flowers are reproductive organs that are composed of four different kinds of specialized leaves: sepals, petals, stamens, and carpels. Sepals protect the bud before it opens and protect the flower while it is developing. Petals are the bright-colored leaves that attract pollinators. The stamens are the male part of the flower and contain the anthers. Carpels are the innermost part of the flower that houses the ovules.

The process of fertilization in angiosperms is distinct from that found in other plants. Two fertilization events take place—one produces the zygote and the other a tissue, called the endosperm, within the seed.

Vegetative reproduction is the formation of new individuals by mitosis. It does not require gametes, flowers, or fertilization.

As angiosperm seeds mature, the ovary walls thicken to form a fruit that encloses the developing seeds. The seeds contained within the fruit are often dispersed by animals. Other methods of seed dispersal include wind and water.

- ovary
- fruit
- cotyledon
- monocot
- dicot
- embryo sac
- pollination
- double fertilization
- endosperm
- vegetative production
- dormancy
- germination

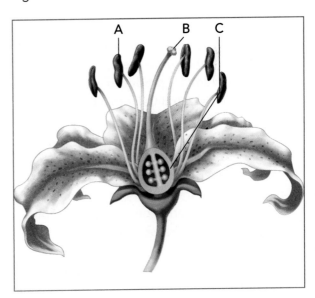

☑ **Infer** Explain how the three lettered structures are involved in fertilization.

# Organize Information

Complete the table by indicating if each group of plants exhibits the listed characteristics.

| Group of plant | Green algae | Mosses and relatives | Ferns and relatives | Cone-bearing plants | Flowering plants |
|---|---|---|---|---|---|
| Seeds? | 1. | 2. | 3. | 4. | 5. |
| Vascular tissue? | 6. | 7. | 8. | 9. | 10. |
| Fruit? | 11. | 12. | 13. | 14. | 15. |

# Keeping the Buzz On

## Communicate a Solution

HS-LS4-6, HS-ETS1-2, CCSS.ELA.LITERACY.WHST.9-10.1, CCSS.ELA.LITERACY.WHST.9-10.7

**STEM** Do you like almonds? They're healthy and they taste great, but did you know they couldn't be produced without the help of insects? Central California produces 80 percent of the world's supply of almonds. Each year, millions of bees are transported to that region to pollinate the almond groves. Honeybees also pollinate scores of other food crops throughout the country, from tomatoes and peppers to watermelons and cantaloupes. But all is not well in the world of bees.

Increasingly, honeybees in North America are threatened by colony collapse disorder, a condition in which worker bees abandon their hives and eventually die. According to the Department of Agriculture, nearly 42 percent of U.S. bee colonies died off in 2015, many due to colony collapse disorder. Concern is now so great that a Presidential Task Force was established to recommend a plan to prevent the loss of these essential insects and the crops that depend upon them.

Researchers think that a number of factors may be contributing to colony collapse disorder. These include climate-induced changes in the growing season, loss of natural habitat, parasitic mites that attack the bees' nervous systems, and the use of a class of pesticides known as neonicotinoids. Worries about the survival of these critical insects have prompted governments around the world to propose programs of habitat conservation and to consider banning pesticides that may be dangerous to bee populations.

A honeybee heads for an almond flower.

This mobile apiary is transporting bees to a grove or farm that needs pollinators.

| Possible Causes of Colony Collapse Disorder | |
| --- | --- |
| **Possible Cause** | **Leads to ...** |
| Pesticides (specifically, neonicotinoids) | Death of some bees that consume pollen or nectar tainted with the pesticide |
| Climate change | Alteration of seasonal timing for flowering |
| Habitat loss | Reduction in the abundance of wildflowers and other sources of nectar for bees |
| Parasitic mites (such as Varroa) | Death of bees by infestation |
| Stress from beekeeping practices such as transportation across the country | Weakened bees that are more susceptible to other stressors |

1. **Define the Problem** What food crops depend on bees and other pollinating insects? What would be the result if these pollinators disappeared?

2. **Ask Questions** What actions have U.S. government agencies, such as the Department of Agriculture, taken to study colony collapse disorder?

3. **Conduct Research** Use print and online reference sources to research the possible causes of colony collapse disorder, as well as possible solutions. Be sure to evaluate the credibility and accuracy of the reference sources.

4. **Develop an Argument** Choose the possible cause that you think is a likely explanation for colony collapse disorder. Then, based on the evidence you researched, develop an argument to support the explanation, as well as an action plan to address the problem.

5. **Communicate** Present your argument in a speech to classmates. Try to convince them that your action plan is worthwhile. Be sure to describe the following:

   - The specific nature of the threat to the bee population

   - Areas of the United States where this threat may be most severe

   - How your plan of action would counteract this threat, and help to improve the health of bees and other pollinating insects

As you listen to the arguments of classmates, evaluate their points of view, reasoning, and use of evidence and rhetoric. Try to identify any faulty reasoning or distorted evidence.

## 🔍 KEY IDEAS AND TERMS

## 22.1 What Is a Plant?

HS-LS1-1, HS-LS1-2, HS-LS4-1

1. The ancestors of land plants likely evolved from
   a. mosses that lived in the water.
   b. an organism similar to green algae.
   c. a protist that lived on land.
   d. prokaryotes that carried on photosynthesis.

2. Recent changes in the classification of the plant kingdom are based on
   a. studies comparing DNA sequences.
   b. comparison of physical structures.
   c. differences and similarities in life cycles.
   d. whether or not a plant uses seeds to reproduce.

3. What is the basic difference between a sporophyte and a gametophyte?
   a. A sporophyte is a reproductive structure, while a gametophyte is not.
   b. A sporophyte undergoes sexual reproduction, while a gametophyte undergoes asexual reproduction.
   c. A sporophyte is the diploid phase, while a gametophyte is the haploid phase of the plant life cycle.
   d. A sporophyte is much smaller than a gametophyte.

4. What do plants need to survive?

Use the following diagram to answer questions 5 and 6.

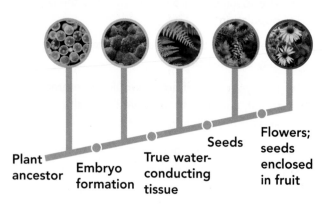

Plant ancestor — Embryo formation — True water-conducting tissue — Seeds — Flowers; seeds enclosed in fruit

5. Which group of plants is most closely related to the ancestor of all plants?

6. What distinguishes the mosses group from the fern group of plants?

## 22.2 Plant Diversity

HS-LS1-4

7. Which answer describes a reason that bryophytes need to live in moist areas?
   a. Bryophytes need the extra water for photosynthesis.
   b. The sperm of bryophytes need water to swim to an egg.
   c. Gas exchange is more efficient in wet areas.
   d. Without moisture, rhizoids cannot anchor the plants.

8. Water is carried upward from the roots to every part of a vascular plant by
   a. rhizoids.
   b. phloem.
   c. cuticle.
   d. xylem.

9. Seed-bearing plants differ from all other plants in that
   a. they have only xylem and no phloem.
   b. they have a gametophyte generation.
   c. their gametes do not require water for fertilization to occur.
   d. they have true roots, stems, and leaves.

10. In the life cycle of a moss, what environmental conditions are necessary for fertilization?

11. How was the ability to produce lignin significant to the evolution of plants?

12. Why does the conifer life cycle take two years to complete?

13. Describe a fern gametophyte.

## 22.3 Flowers, Fruits, and Seeds

HS-LS1-1, HS-LS1-2, HS-LS1-4

14. In angiosperms, the structures that produce the male gametophyte are called the
    a. anthers.          c. pollen tubes.
    b. sepals.           d. stigmas.

15. The process in which a single plant produces many offspring genetically identical to itself is
    a. sexual reproduction.
    b. agriculture.
    c. dormancy.
    d. vegetative reproduction.

16. The thickened ovary wall of a plant may join with other parts of the flower to become the
    a. fruit.            c. endosperm.
    b. seed.             d. cotyledon.

**17.** What is a carpel? Where is it located in a typical flower?

**18.** What are the products of double fertilization? Describe them.

**19.** Give examples of seed dispersal by animal, wind, and water.

**20.** What is the function of dormancy?

**21.** The diagram shows the parts of a typical flower.
   **a.** Inside which structure is pollen produced?
   **b.** What structure does label A represent? What is its function?
   **c.** In which structure do seeds develop?
   **d.** What is the name of structure G?

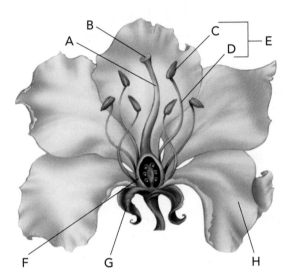

## CRITICAL THINKING

**22. Classify** How do botanists classify the five major groups of plants?

**23. Draw Conclusions** If all you know about a plant is that it lives almost all of its life as a multicellular haploid organism, what can you conclude about the kind of plant it is?

**24. Construct an Explanation** How does alternation of generations differ among the various types of plants, such as mosses and flowering plants?

**25. Compare and Contrast** How are green algae similar to other plants? How are they different?

**26. Compare and Contrast** Moss plants are small, but ferns can grow as tall as small trees. Explain why this is so.

**27. Apply Scientific Reasoning** How is it helpful for vascular plants to have two transport systems—xylem and phloem—instead of just one system?

**28. Construct an Explanation** Why are seeds not classified as the reproductive structures of a plant?

**29. Cite Evidence** During the age of the dinosaurs, the vast majority of land plants were ferns and mosses. Today, the vast majority of land plants are seed plants. Cite evidence from the text and provide an explanation for this change based on the basic requirements of plants.

**30. Apply Concepts** A friend of yours lives in one of the desert areas of New Mexico and wants to grow a garden of bryophytes. What environmental conditions would your friend need to provide the garden for it to be successful?

**31. Construct an Explanation** The seeds of lupines, a tundra plant, can remain dormant for thousands of years, and still germinate when conditions are favorable. How might this trait provide an advantage to lupines in their environment?

**32. Revise Models** A student is developing a model of the life cycle of gymnosperms. The model includes a pine cone, such as the one shown here. How could adding a second pine cone improve the model?

**33. Predict** Some plants form flowers that produce stamens but no carpels. Could fruit form on one of these flowers? Cite textual evidence to support your answer.

**34. Integrate Information** Pollen and seeds are the most reliable plant-related evidence at archaeological sites and at modern-day crime scenes because they are long-lasting. Relate this quality to their structure and function in living plants.

## CROSSCUTTING CONCEPTS

**35. Structure and Function** At first glance, an oak tree and a zebra hardly seem similar in any way. Describe the characteristics that they do share. What are the characteristics of the oak tree that distinguish it from organisms in the other kingdoms of living things?

**36. Stability and Change** Compare the benefits and drawbacks of sexual reproduction and vegetative reproduction for a plant.

## MATH CONNECTIONS

## Analyze and Interpret Data

CCSS.MATH.CONTENT.MP2, CCSS.MATH.CONTENT.HSS.IC.B.6

Refer to the text and data table to answer questions 37 and 38. In a laboratory experiment, fruits from 5 different types of trees were dropped from a height of 4 meters. The falling time was measured and recorded in the data table shown here. Assume that for every second that a fruit falls, the wind carries it 1.5 meters away from the parent tree.

| Fruit Type Versus Dispersal Time | |
|---|---|
| **Type of Tree** | **Average Time (s) for Seed to Fall 4 m** |
| Norway maple | 5.2 |
| Silver maple | 4.9 |
| White ash | 3.1 |
| Shagbark hickory | 0.9 |
| Red oak | 0.9 |

**37. Analyze Data** Given the same wind, which of the fruits shown in the table is most likely to be carried farthest from the parent tree? Explain.

**38. Draw Conclusions** Based on the data and illustrations of the fruit structures, which of the following conclusions is most reasonable?
   **a.** Winged seeds carry more nutrition for the growing embryo than seeds without wings.
   **b.** Wind is not very effective in carrying seeds away from the parent plant.
   **c.** Acorns are more likely to germinate if they fall close to the parent plant.
   **d.** Red oak and hickory depend on factors other than wind to achieve dispersal.

For several years, a homeowner notices moss growing in the backyard in areas where grass otherwise would grow. Half of the yard receives direct sunlight, while the other half is shady. The table shows the data that the homeowner collects. Use the table to answer questions 39 and 40.

| Growth of Moss in Sun and Shade | | | | | | |
|---|---|---|---|---|---|---|
| | **Year** | | | | | |
| | 1 | 2 | 3 | 4 | 5 | 6 |
| Area of Moss in Sun (m²) | 0 | 0 | 1 | 2 | 1 | 1 |
| Area of Moss in Shade (m²) | 0 | 2 | 5 | 7 | 6 | 9 |

**39. Draw Conclusions** What conclusion about the growth of moss does the data support?

**40. Apply Scientific Reasoning** The area of moss in the shade ranges from none to 9 square inches. What are some possible explanations for this range of values?

## LANGUAGE ARTS CONNECTIONS

## Write About Science

CCSS.ELA-LITERACY.WHST.9-10.2

**41. Write Explanatory Texts** Describe how seeds form from a process of double fertilization.

**42. Write Procedural Texts** Write a step-by-step procedure for distinguishing the major types of plants: green algae, mosses and their relatives, ferns, gymnosperms, and angiosperms.

## Read About Science

CCSS.ELA-LITERACY.RST.9-10.2

**43. Summarize Text** Trace the text's explanation of why flowers are the key to the evolutionary success of the angiosperms.

# END-OF-COURSE TEST PRACTICE

**Questions 1–2**

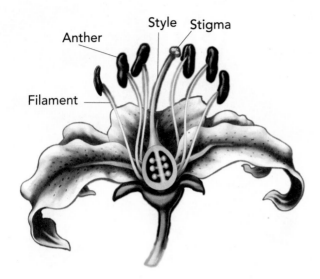

Style   Stigma

Anther

Filament

1. A student wants to determine whether or not the flower is pollinated by an animal, such as an insect or bird. Which property of the flower would be most useful for making this inference?
   A. Number of stamens
   B. Location of the style
   C. Color and shape of the petals
   D. Location and size of the ovary
   E. Amount of pollen that it produces

2. In an experiment, Marlene removes the six anthers from the flower shown here. What best describes the ability of the altered flower to form seeds?
   A. The flower cannot form seeds because it cannot be pollinated.
   B. The flower cannot form seeds because it cannot produce male gametophytes.
   C. The flower may form seeds because the stigma produces pollen.
   D. The flower may form seeds if it receives pollen made by another flower.
   E. The flower may form seeds if it receives enough nutrients from the soil.

3. Mosses and other bryophytes never grow taller than a few centimeters. The height of bryophytes is limited because they lack which of these structures?
   A. Haploid gametophytes
   B. Diploid sporophytes
   C. Flowers and cones
   D. Cells that perform photosynthesis
   E. Vascular tissue

4. The life cycle of a plant includes two alternating phases: a diploid (2N) phase and a haploid (N) phase. As plants evolved in many stages from green algae to seed plants, what trend occurred in the alternating phases?
   A. The haploid phase became larger.
   B. The diploid phase became larger.
   C. The two phases became more alike.
   D. The two phases each became smaller.
   E. The two phases became less dependent on one another.

5. When the first seed plants evolved, they became the first plants to complete which of these tasks?
   A. Transporting water against gravity
   B. Growing directly out of the soil
   C. Reproducing without flowers
   D. Reproducing without cones
   E. Reproducing without standing water

6. A cucumber is often called a vegetable because of the way it is used as a food. What property of the cucumber shows that it is properly classified as a fruit?
   A. It has a rounded shape.
   B. It develops aboveground.
   C. It has a fleshy, edible center.
   D. It contains the seeds of the plant.
   E. It develops from the sepals of a flower.

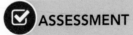 **ASSESSMENT**

For additional assessment practice, go online to access your digital course.

| If You Have Trouble With... | | | | | | |
|---|---|---|---|---|---|---|
| **Question** | 1 | 2 | 3 | 4 | 5 | 6 |
| **See Lesson** | 22.3 | 22.3 | 22.2 | 22.1 | 22.2 | 22.3 |

CHAPTER 23

# Plant Structure and Function

23.1 Roots, Stems, and Leaves

23.2 Plant Hormones and Tropisms

23.3 Plants and People

**Go Online to access your digital course.**

- VIDEO
- AUDIO
- INTERACTIVITY
- eTEXT
- ANIMATION
- VIRTUAL LAB
- ASSESSMENT

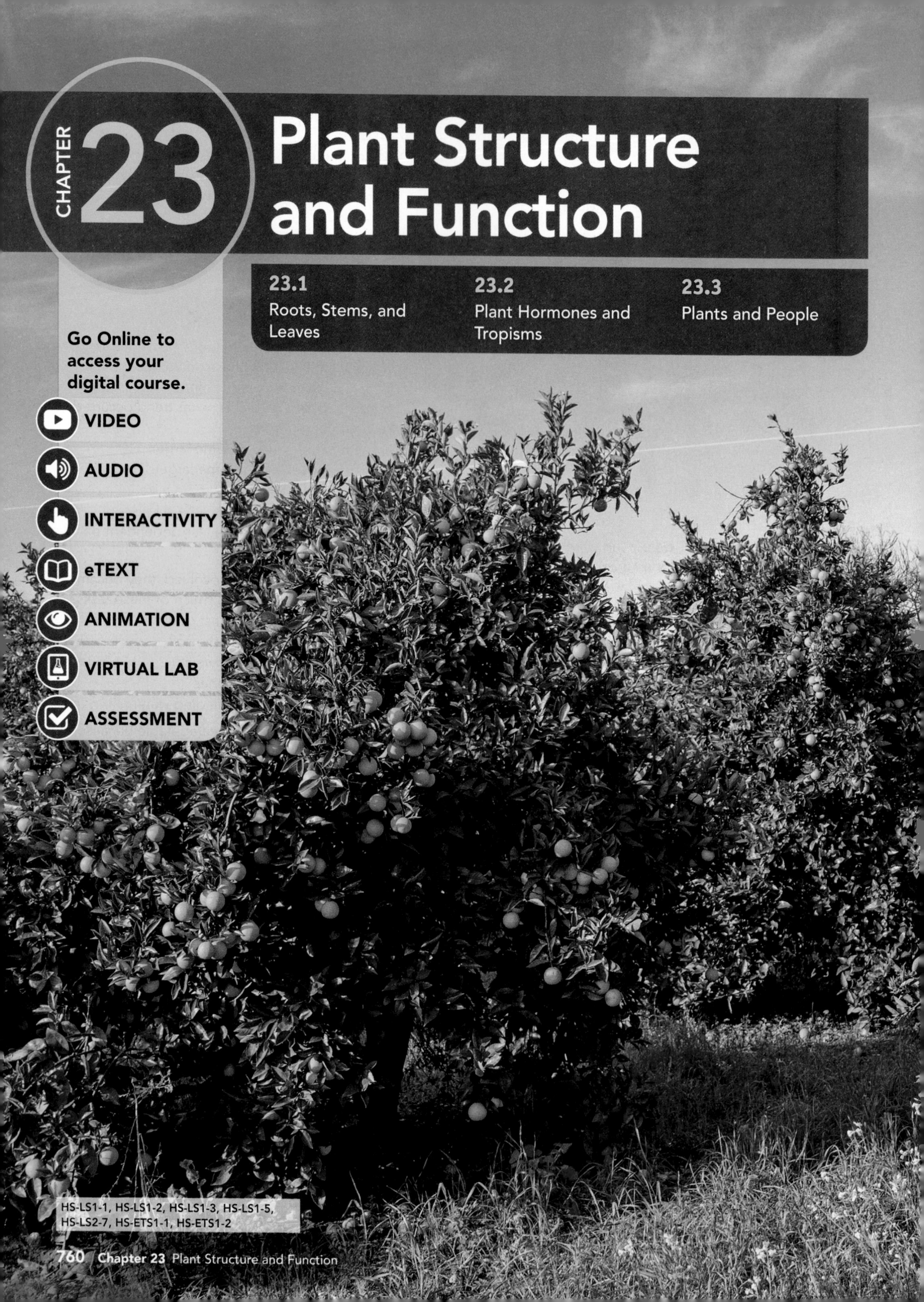

HS-LS1-1, HS-LS1-2, HS-LS1-3, HS-LS1-5, HS-LS2-7, HS-ETS1-1, HS-ETS1-2

# How can we save the crops we depend upon?

You might not realize it after a trip to your local supermarket, but nearly 50,000 species of plants are edible, at least in part. Despite this, only a small number of species appear regularly on most dinner tables. In fact, experts estimate that 60 percent of the food energy in the human diet comes from just three crops: wheat, corn, and rice.

Our dependency on such a small number of crops could pose huge problems if any of the crops fail. Raising a single crop in a large field is called monoculture. A monoculture can cause the soil to lose nutrients from year to year. It also encourages the spread of diseases and insect pests.

For example, consider the history of one of the world's favorite foods: the banana. Like other food plants, bananas have many different strains and varieties. By the 1950s, however, commercial plantations were raising only one variety of banana, the *Gros Michel*. Everyone agreed that the *Gros Michel* produced the largest and tastiest fruit, and it proved very profitable. Unfortunately, the *Gros Michel* was doomed by a tiny enemy, a soil fungus of the genus *Fusarium*. The fungus infected the roots of the *Gros Michel*, and then spread up the vascular system. The fungal infection was called Panama disease, and it ruined one banana plantation after another. By 1965, the *Gros Michel* was all but extinct.

The banana industry found another variety, the *Cavendish* banana, that was resistant to Panama disease. The *Cavendish* is the variety that most of us eat today. The bad news, however, is that new strains of the *Fusarium* fungus have evolved to infect the *Cavendish*. In southeast Asia, the fungus already has destroyed tens of thousands of acres of banana plantations. Experts are worried that the fungus could spread to the plantations in Africa and South America. Currently, there is no reasonable treatment for Panama disease. Once the fungus arrives, it cannot be stopped.

Similar problems are troubling citrus trees. Citrus fruits include oranges, lemons, and grapefruit. A disease called citrus greening has ruined millions of acres of citrus crops in the United States and elsewhere. The disease is caused by bacteria that are spread by very tiny insects, each no larger than the head of a pin. The disease is named for the green, ruined fruit that it causes. The fruits are bitter and not edible. Other diseases that threaten citrus crops include citrus canker, citrus black spot, and sweet orange scab. All are infections of bacteria and fungi, and all can spread quickly through an orchard. None can be treated after a tree is infected.

Managing diseases is just one of the challenges of agriculture, the systematic raising of plants. How did agriculture begin, and how has it changed over time? What challenges face agriculture today, and how will we meet these challenges? Should we change the way we grow food crops?

**Throughout this chapter, look for connections to the** CASE STUDY **to help you answer these questions.**

Oranges, as well as other citrus fruits, are being threatened by citrus greening disease.

### 🔑 KEY QUESTIONS

- What are the main tissue systems of plants?
- What are the different structures and functions of roots?
- What are the functions of stems and how does growth in stems occur?
- What are the different structures and functions of leaves?
- What are the major forces that transport water and nutrients in a plant?

**HS-LS1-1:** Construct an explanation based on evidence for how the structure of DNA determines the structure of proteins which carry out the essential functions of life through systems of specialized cells. **HS-LS1-2:** Develop and use a model to illustrate the hierarchical organization of interacting systems that provide specific functions within multicellular organisms. **HS-LS1-3:** Plan and conduct an investigation to provide evidence that feedback mechanisms maintain homeostasis. **HS-LS1-5:** Use a model to illustrate how photosynthesis transforms light energy into stored chemical energy.

### VOCABULARY

epidermis • meristem
taproot • fibrous root
Casparian strip • node
vascular bundle
primary growth
secondary growth
mesophyll • stoma
transpiration • guard cells
capillary action

### READING TOOL

In your 📖 **Biology Foundations Workbook,** explain how each of the listed systems work to make plants grow and thrive.

Compared to animals, plants don't seem to do much. But look deeper. Plants transport material, grow, repair themselves, and respond to the environment. They may act at a pace that seems slow to us, but their cells and tissues interact in remarkably effective ways.

## Plant Tissue Systems

Within the roots, stems, and leaves of plants are specialized tissue systems, shown in **Figure 23-1**. Dermal tissue covers a plant almost like a skin. Vascular tissue helps to support the plant and serves as its "bloodstream," transporting water and nutrients. Ground tissue produces and stores food.

### Figure 23-1

### Principal Organs of Plants

These cross sections of the principal organs of seed plants show that all three organs contain dermal tissue, vascular tissue, and ground tissue.

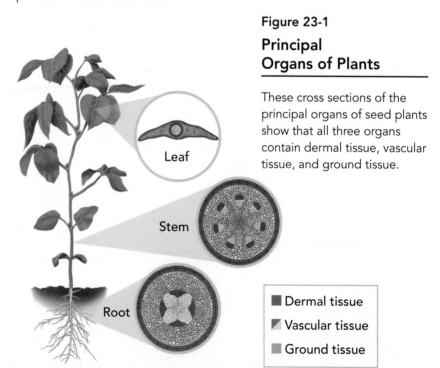

Leaf

Stem

Root

■ Dermal tissue
◣ Vascular tissue
■ Ground tissue

**Dermal Tissue** Dermal tissue in young plants consists of a single layer of cells called the **epidermis**. The outer surfaces of epidermal cells are covered with a waxy layer called the cuticle, which protects against water loss. 🔑 *Dermal tissue is the protective outer covering of a plant.* In some plants, dermal tissue may be many cell layers deep and may be covered with bark. In roots, dermal tissue includes root hair cells that absorb water, passing it along to ground and vascular tissue, where it is carried to the rest of the plant.

**Vascular Tissue** Vascular tissue includes xylem, a water-conducting tissue, and phloem, a tissue that carries nutrients. As you can see in **Figure 23-2**, xylem and phloem consist of long, slender cells that connect almost like sections of pipe. 🔑 *Interactions between vascular tissues support the plant body and transport water and nutrients throughout the plant.*

 **VIDEO**

Learn why leaves change color.

**Vessel Elements** Angiosperms have a second type of xylem cell known as a vessel element. After vessel elements mature and die, cell walls at both ends are left with slitlike openings through which water can move freely.

**Cross Section of a Stem**

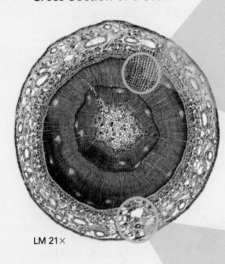

LM 21×

**Up Close**

**Figure 23-2**

**Vascular Tissue**

Xylem and phloem form the vascular transport system that moves water and nutrients throughout a plant.

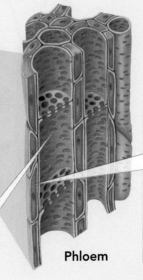

Xylem

Phloem

**Tracheids** All seed plants have xylem cells called tracheids. As they mature, tracheids die, leaving only their cell walls. These cell walls contain lignin, a complex molecule that resists water and gives wood much of its strength. The inner regions of the wall, known as pits, allow water to diffuse from tracheids into surrounding ground tissue.

**Companion Cells** The cells that surround sieve tube elements are called companion cells. Companion cells keep their nuclei and other organelles through their lifetime. Companion cells support the phloem cells and aid in the movement of substances in and out of the phloem.

**Sieve Tube Elements** Phloem cells include sieve tube elements, which are arranged end to end, forming sieve tubes. The end walls of sieve tube elements have many small holes through which nutrients move from cell to cell in a watery stream. As sieve tube elements mature, they lose their nuclei and most other organelles. The remaining organelles hug the inside of the cell wall and are kept alive by companion cells.

**Ground Tissue** The edible portions of plants—like potatoes, squash, and asparagus—are mostly ground tissue. ✎ *Ground tissue produces and stores sugars, and contributes to physical support of the plant.* Ground tissue is divided into three types based on the characteristics of the cell wall. Most ground tissue consists of parenchyma (puh RENG kih muh) cells with thin cell walls and a central vacuole surrounded by cytoplasm.

Ground tissue may also contain two other cell types. Collenchyma (kuh LENG kih muh) cells have strong, flexible cell walls that help support plant organs. Chains of such cells make up the familiar "strings" of a stalk of celery. Sclerenchyma (sklih RENG kih muh) cells have extremely thick, rigid cell walls that make tissue like the shells around a walnut seed tough and strong.

**Plant Tissues and Growth** Unlike animals, even the oldest trees produce new tissue and new reproductive organs every year, almost as if they remained "forever young." How do they do it? The secrets of plant growth are found in meristems, tissues that, in a sense, really do stay young. **Meristems** are regions of unspecialized cells in which mitosis produces new cells that are ready for differentiation. Meristems are found in places where plants grow rapidly, such as the tips of stems and roots. Because the tip of a stem or root is known as its apex, meristems in these rapidly growing regions are called apical meristems. **Figure 23-3** shows examples of stem and root apical meristems.

**BUILD VOCABULARY**

**Related Word Forms** *Apex* and *apical* are related word forms. *Apex* is a noun meaning the "narrowed or pointed end," or tip, and *apical* is an adjective describing "something related to or located at the apex."

**Figure 23-3**

**Apical Meristems**

Apical meristems are found in the growing tips of stems and roots. Within these meristems, unspecialized cells are produced by mitosis.

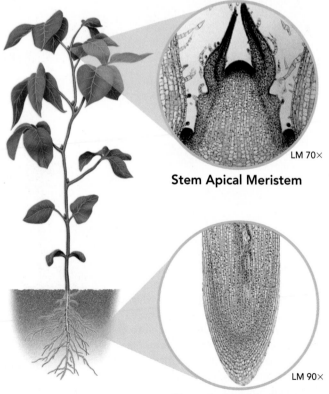

LM 70×

**Stem Apical Meristem**

LM 90×

**Root Apical Meristem**

**Meristems and Flower Development** Flower development begins when the pattern of gene expression changes to transform the apical meristem of a plant into a floral meristem. Floral meristems produce the plant's reproductive organs as well as the colorful petals that surround them.

> ✓ **READING CHECK** **Infer** How do meristems differ from other regions of a plant?

# Roots

Can you guess how large a typical plant's root system is? In a 1937 study of a single rye plant, botanist Howard Dittmer showed that the length of all the branches in the rye plant's root system was an astonishing 623 kilometers (387 miles). The surface area of these roots was more than 600 square meters—130 times greater than the combined areas of its stems and leaves!

As soon as a seed begins to sprout, it puts out its first roots to draw water and nutrients from the soil. Rapid cell growth pushes the tips of the growing roots into the soil, providing raw materials for the developing stems and leaves.

**Types of Root Systems** The two main types of root systems are taproot systems and fibrous root systems, shown in **Figure 23-4**. In some plants, the primary root grows long and thick and gives rise to smaller branch roots. The large primary root is called a **taproot**. Taproots of oak and hickory trees grow so long that they can reach water several meters down.

In plants like grasses, the primary root is replaced by branched roots that grow from the base of the stem. These **fibrous roots** branch to such an extent that no single root grows larger than the rest. The extensive fibrous root systems produced by many plants help anchor topsoil in place.

**READING TOOL**

Make a three-column chart to summarize information about roots, stems, and leaves.

**Figure 23-4**

## A Comparison of Two Root Systems

Dandelions have a taproot system, while grasses have a fibrous root system.

**Structure and Function of Roots** Dermal, vascular, and ground tissue are all found in roots, as shown in **Figure 23-5**. 🔍 *A mature root has an outside layer, called the epidermis, and also contains vascular tissue and a large area of ground tissue.*

How does a root go about the job of absorbing water and minerals from the soil? Although it might seem to, water does not just "soak" into the root from soil. It takes energy on the part of the plant to absorb water. 🔍 *Roots support a plant, anchor it in the ground, store food, and absorb water and dissolved nutrients from the soil.*

**CASE STUDY**

**Figure 23-5**

## Anatomy of a Root

A root consists of a central vascular cylinder surrounded by ground tissue and the epidermis. When bananas are infected with Panama disease, the *Fusarium* fungus colonizes the xylem and blocks the flow of water.

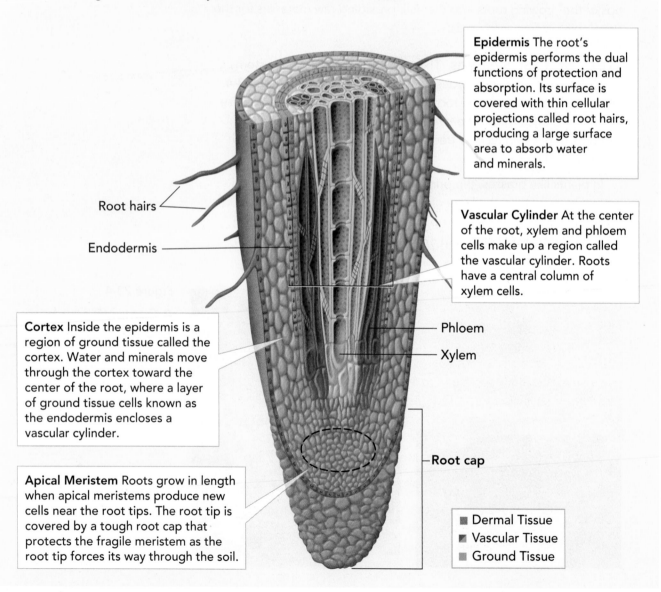

**Epidermis** The root's epidermis performs the dual functions of protection and absorption. Its surface is covered with thin cellular projections called root hairs, producing a large surface area to absorb water and minerals.

Root hairs

Endodermis

**Vascular Cylinder** At the center of the root, xylem and phloem cells make up a region called the vascular cylinder. Roots have a central column of xylem cells.

**Cortex** Inside the epidermis is a region of ground tissue called the cortex. Water and minerals move through the cortex toward the center of the root, where a layer of ground tissue cells known as the endodermis encloses a vascular cylinder.

Phloem

Xylem

Root cap

**Apical Meristem** Roots grow in length when apical meristems produce new cells near the root tips. The root tip is covered by a tough root cap that protects the fragile meristem as the root tip forces its way through the soil.

■ Dermal Tissue
■ Vascular Tissue
■ Ground Tissue

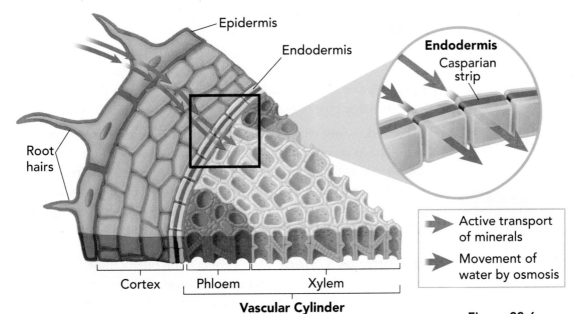

Epidermis

Endodermis

Root hairs

Cortex

Phloem

Xylem

**Vascular Cylinder**

**Endodermis**

Casparian strip

→ Active transport of minerals

→ Movement of water by osmosis

Figure 23-6

**Water Passage Into a Root**

A root absorbs water and dissolved nutrients from the soil. ☑ **Interpret Visuals** What is the function of the Casparian strip?

***Uptake of Plant Nutrients*** Soil is a complex mixture of sand, silt, clay, air, and organic matter. Plants must absorb from the soil a variety of inorganic nutrients, such as nitrogen, phosphorus, potassium, magnesium, sulfur, and calcium. In addition, smaller amounts of other nutrients, called trace elements, are just as important. The cell membranes of root hairs and other cells in the root epidermis contain active transport proteins that use energy from ATP to pump dissolved nutrient ions from the soil into the plant.

***Water Movement and the Vascular Cylinder*** You may recall that osmosis is the movement of water across a membrane toward an area where the concentration of dissolved material is higher. As the plant pumps mineral ions into its cells, water moves by means of osmosis into the root and toward the vascular cylinder, as shown in **Figure 23-6**. In this way, cells in all three tissue systems of the plant interact to transport water into the root.

The vascular cylinder is enclosed by a layer of cells known as the endodermis. Where these cells meet, their cell walls form a special waterproof zone called the **Casparian strip**. Most of the time, water can diffuse through cell walls, but not here. The strip is almost like a layer of waterproof cement between the bricks in a wall. The waxy Casparian strip forces water and minerals to move through the cell membranes of endodermis cells rather than in between the cells. As a result, there is a one-way passage of water and nutrients into the vascular cylinder.

***Root Pressure*** Contained within the Casparian strip, the water has just one place to go—up. Root pressure forces water through the vascular cylinder and into the xylem. As more water moves from the cortex into the vascular cylinder, water in the xylem is forced upward through the root into the stem.

☑ **READING CHECK Explain** How does water move into roots?

## Figure 23-7

### Anatomy of a Stem

Stems produce leaves from their nodes and new branches from buds. Stems hold leaves up to the sunlight, which is needed for the plant to carry out photosynthesis.

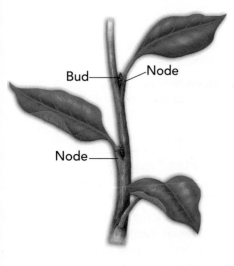

# Stems

While visiting the salad bar for lunch, you decide to add some sliced water chestnuts and bamboo shoots on top. Then you place some asparagus and potato salad on the side. These good things all come from the same part of the plant. Can you guess which one?

What do water chestnuts, bamboo shoots, asparagus, and potatoes all have in common? They are all types of stems. Stems vary in size, shape, and method of development. Some grow entirely underground; others reach high into the air. 🔍 *Stems produce leaves, branches, and flowers, hold leaves up to the sun, and transport substances throughout the plant.*

**Anatomy of a Stem** Stems contain the plant's three tissue systems: dermal, vascular, and ground tissue. Growing stems contain distinct **nodes**, where leaves are attached, as shown in **Figure 23-7**. Small buds where leaves attach to the nodes contain apical meristems that produce new stems and leaves. In larger plants, stems develop woody tissue that helps support leaves and flowers.

The arrangement of tissues in a stem follows two basic patterns. In monocots, clusters of xylem and phloem tissue, called **vascular bundles**, are scattered throughout ground tissue within the stem. Among gymnosperms and dicots, vascular bundles are arranged in a ring. Parenchyma cells inside the ring of vascular tissue are known as pith, while those outside form the cortex of the stem. You can see a comparison of monocot and dicot stems in **Figure 23-8**.

## Figure 23-8

### Comparing Monocot and Dicot Stems

These cross sections of monocot and dicot stems show their similarities and differences. ✅**Observe** How does the arrangement of the vascular bundles differ?

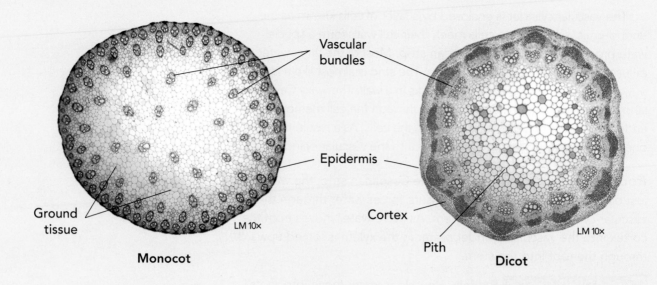

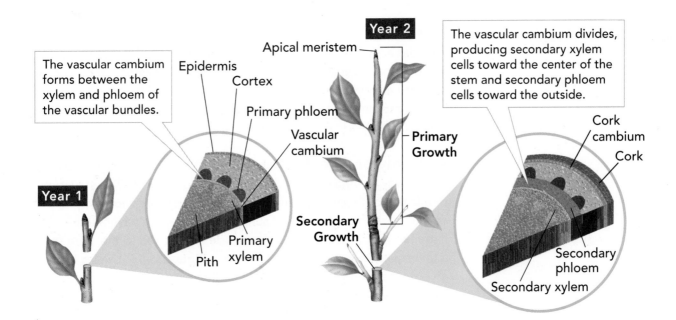

The vascular cambium forms between the xylem and phloem of the vascular bundles.

Epidermis
Cortex
Primary phloem
Vascular cambium

Year 1

Pith
Primary xylem

Year 2

Apical meristem

Primary Growth

Secondary Growth

The vascular cambium divides, producing secondary xylem cells toward the center of the stem and secondary phloem cells toward the outside.

Cork cambium
Cork

Secondary phloem
Secondary xylem

## Primary and Secondary Growth

Cows have four legs, ants have six, and spiders have eight, but roses and tomatoes don't have a set number of leaves or branches. However, plant growth is still carefully controlled and regulated, following patterns that produce the characteristic size and shape of the adult plant.

**Primary Growth** The growth of new cells produced by the apical meristems at the ends of a plant is called **primary growth**. The increase in length in a plant due to primary growth is shown in **Figure 23-9**. ⚷ *Primary growth of stems is the result of elongation of cells produced in the apical meristem.*

**Secondary Growth** As a plant grows larger, the older stems and roots must increase in thickness as well as in length. This increase in the thickness of stems and roots is known as **secondary growth**. Meristems within stems and roots are responsible for this secondary growth.

A tissue known as vascular cambium produces vascular tissues and increases the thickness of stems over time. Cork cambium produces the outer covering of stems. ⚷ *Secondary growth takes place in meristems called the vascular cambium and cork cambium.*

When secondary growth first begins, the vascular cambium is just a thin layer of cells. Divisions in the vascular cambium then give rise to new layers of xylem and phloem, thickening the stem and producing secondary xylem, which becomes the tissue we call "wood." In woody trees and shrubs, tissues outside the vascular cambium produce a thick bark that protects the growing stem.

✓ **READING CHECK** **Compare and Contrast** How is secondary growth different from primary growth?

### Figure 23-9

### Primary and Secondary Growth

New cells produced by the apical meristem cause stems to grow in length (primary growth). Meanwhile, the vascular cambium increases the stem's width (secondary growth).

**INTERACTIVITY**

Explore the internal structures of roots and stems.

# Leaves

We hear a lot these days about "green industry," such as biofuels and material recycling, but the most important manufacturing sites on Earth are already green. They are the leaves of plants. Using energy captured in their leaves, plants make the sugars, starches, and oils that feed virtually all animals, including us.

**Anatomy of a Leaf** To carry out photosynthesis, leaves must have a way of obtaining carbon dioxide and water. 🔍 *The structure of a leaf is optimized to absorb light and carry out photosynthesis.* To maximize the collection of sunlight, most leaves have a thin, flattened part called a blade. The blade is attached to the stem by a thin stalk called a petiole, as shown in **Figure 23-10**. Leaves have an outer covering of dermal tissue and inner regions of ground and vascular tissues.

**Dermal Tissue** Leaf epidermis is a specialized layer of tough, irregularly shaped cells with thick outer walls that resist tearing. The epidermis of most leaves is protected by a waxy cuticle that limits the loss of water through evaporation.

**Vascular Tissue** Cells in the vascular tissues of leaves are connected directly to the vascular tissues of stems, making them part of the plant's fluid transport system. Xylem and phloem cells are bundled in leaf veins that run from the stem throughout the leaf.

**Ground Tissue** The area between leaf veins is filled with specialized ground tissue cells known as **mesophyll**, where photosynthesis occurs. The sugars produced in mesophyll move to leaf veins, where they enter phloem tubes for transport to the rest of the plant.

### Figure 23-10

### Anatomy of a Leaf

Leaves absorb light and carry out most of the photosynthesis in a plant. ☑ **Compare and Contrast** Compare the structure of the two types of mesophyll cells in a leaf.

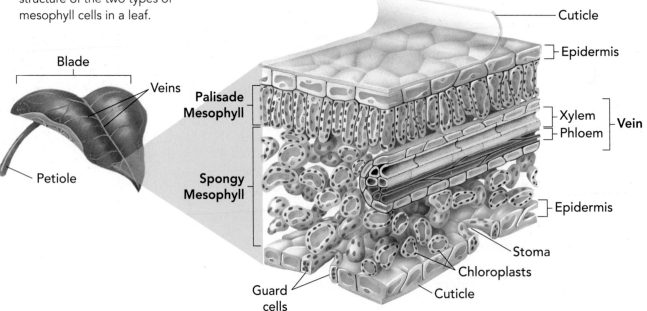

Figure 23-11
**Photosynthesis**

To perform photosynthesis, leaves need water, carbon dioxide, and the energy of sunlight. Only a small fraction of the water that plants bring to leaves is used for photosynthesis. The rest is lost through transpiration.

**Photosynthesis** The mesophyll tissue in leaves like those shown in **Figure 23-11** is highly specialized for photosynthesis. Beneath the upper epidermis is a layer of cells called the palisade mesophyll, containing closely packed cells that absorb light that enters the leaf. Beneath the palisade layer is a loose tissue called the spongy mesophyll, which has many air spaces between its cells. These air spaces connect with the exterior through **stomata** (singular: stoma). Stomata are small openings in the epidermis that allow carbon dioxide, water, and oxygen to diffuse into and out of the leaf.

**Transpiration** The walls of mesophyll cells are kept moist so that gases can enter and leave the cells easily. The trade-off to this feature is that water evaporates from these surfaces and is lost to the atmosphere. **Transpiration** is the loss of water through leaves. This lost water may be replaced by water drawn into the leaf through xylem vessels in the vascular tissue. Transpiration helps to cool leaves on hot days, but it may also threaten the leaf's survival if water is scarce.

**Gas Exchange and Homeostasis** You might not think of plants as "breathing" the same way that animals do, but plants need to exchange gases with the atmosphere, too. Plants, in fact, can even be suffocated by lack of oxygen, something that often happens during flooding or over-watering. A plant's control of gas exchange is actually one of the most important elements of homeostasis for these remarkable organisms.

***Gas Exchange*** Leaves take in carbon dioxide and give off oxygen during photosynthesis. When plant cells use the food they make, the cells respire, taking in oxygen and giving off carbon dioxide (just as animals do). Plant leaves allow gas exchange between air spaces in the spongy mesophyll and the exterior by opening their stomata.

***Homeostasis*** It might seem that stomata should be open all the time, allowing gas exchange to take place and photosynthesis to occur at top speed. However, this is not what happens! If stomata were kept open all the time, water loss due to transpiration would be so great that few plants would be able to take in enough water to survive. So plants maintain a kind of balance. 🔑 *Plants maintain homeostasis by keeping their stomata open just enough to allow photosynthesis to take place but not so much that they lose an excessive amount of water.*

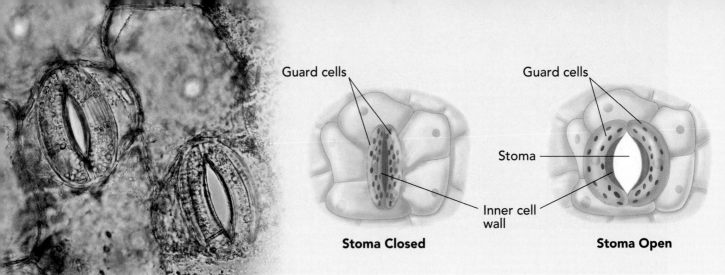

Guard cells

Guard cells

Stoma

Inner cell wall

**Stoma Closed**

**Stoma Open**

100x at 35mm

## INTERACTIVITY

**Figure 23-12**

## How Guard Cells Function

Plants regulate the opening and closing of their stomata to balance water loss with rates of photosynthesis.

Guard cells in the epidermis of each leaf are the key to this balancing act. **Guard cells** are highly specialized cells that surround the stomata and control their opening and closing. Guard cells regulate the movement of gases, especially water vapor and carbon dioxide, into and out of leaf tissues.

The stomata open and close in response to changes in water pressure within the guard cells, as shown in **Figure 23-12**. When water is abundant, it flows into the leaf, raising water pressure in the guard cells, which then open the stomata. The thin outer walls of the cells are forced into a curved shape, which pulls the thick inner walls of the guard cells away from one another, opening the stoma. Carbon dioxide can then enter through the stoma, and water is lost by transpiration.

When water is scarce, the opposite occurs. Water pressure within the guard cells decreases, the inner walls pull together, and the stoma closes. This reduces further water loss by limiting transpiration.

In general, stomata are open during the daytime, when photosynthesis is active, and closed at night, when open stomata would only lead to water loss. However, stomata may be closed even in bright sunlight under hot, dry conditions in which water conservation is a matter of life and death. Guard cells respond to conditions in the environment, such as wind and temperature, helping to maintain homeostasis within a leaf.

***Transpiration and Wilting*** Osmotic pressure keeps a plant's leaves and stems rigid, or stiff. High transpiration rates can lead to wilting. Wilting results from the loss of water—and therefore pressure—in a plant's cells. Without this internal pressure to support them, the plant's cell walls bend inward, and the plant's leaves and stems wilt. When a leaf wilts, its stomata close. As a result, transpiration slows down significantly. Thus, wilting helps a plant to conserve water.

✓ **READING CHECK** **Describe** What determines when the stoma are open and when they are closed?

# Transport in Plants

Look at a tall tree. Think about how much work it would be if you had to haul water up 15 or 20 meters to the top of that tree. Now think of a giant redwood, a hundred meters high. How does water get to the top?

Recall that active transport and root pressure cause water to move from soil into plant roots. The pressure created by water entering the tissues of a root can push water upward in a plant stem. However, this pressure does not exert nearly enough force to lift water up into trees. Other forces are much more important.

**Transpirational Pull** The major force in water transport is provided by the evaporation of water from leaves during transpiration. As water evaporates through open stomata, the cell walls within the leaf begin to dry out. Cell walls contain cellulose, the same material used in paper. As you know, dry paper towels strongly attract water. Similarly, the dry cell walls draw water from cells deeper inside the leaf. The pull extends into vascular tissue so that water is pulled up through xylem.

How important is transpirational pull? On a hot day, even a small tree may lose as much as 100 liters of water to transpiration. The hotter and drier the air, and the windier the day, the greater the amount of water lost. As a result of this water loss, the plant draws up even more water from the roots. **Figure 23-13** shows an analogy for transpirational pull.

**Visual Analogy**

**Figure 23-13**

**Transpiration Pull**

Imagine a chain of circus clowns who are tied together as they climb a ladder. When the clowns at the top fall off the ladder, they pull up the clowns behind them. Similarly, a chain of water molecules extends from the leaves of a plant down to the roots. As water exits the leaves through transpiration, they pull up the molecules behind them.

**Figure 23-14**

## Capillary Action

Capillary action causes water to move much higher in a narrow tube than in a wide tube.

### How Cell Walls Pull Water Upward

*How Cell Walls Pull Water Upward* To pull water upward, plants take advantage of some of water's most interesting physical properties. Water molecules are attracted to one another by a force called cohesion. Recall that cohesion is the attraction of molecules of the same substance to each other. Water cohesion is especially strong because of the tendency of water molecules to form hydrogen bonds with each other. Water molecules can also form hydrogen bonds with other substances. This results from a force called adhesion, which is attraction between unlike molecules.

If you were to place empty glass tubes of various diameters into a dish of water, you would see both cohesion and adhesion at work. The tendency of water to rise in a thin tube is called **capillary action**. Water is attracted to the walls of the tube, and water molecules are attracted to one another. The thinner the tube, the higher the water will rise inside it, as shown in **Figure 23-14**.

*Putting It All Together* What does capillary action have to do with water movement through xylem? Recall that xylem tissue is composed of tracheids and vessel elements that form many hollow connected tubes. These tubes are lined with cellulose cell walls, to which water adheres very strongly. So, when transpiration removes some water from the exposed walls, strong adhesion forces pull in water from the wet interior of the leaf. That pull is so powerful that it extends even down to the tips of roots and, through them, to the water in the soil. ⚬ *The combination of transpiration and capillary action lifts water upward through the xylem tissues of a plant.*

---

**Quick Lab**  Guided Inquiry

## What Is the Role of Leaves in Transpiration?

1. Put on your apron and safety goggles. Use a scalpel to cut 1 cm off the bottoms of three celery stalks. *CAUTION:* Use the scalpel with care. Always direct a sharp edge or point away from yourself and others.

2. Remove the leaves from one stalk. Use a cotton swab to apply petroleum jelly to both sides of all the leaves on another stalk. Place all three stalks into a plastic container holding about 200 mL of water and several drops of food coloring.

3. Place the plastic container in a sunny location. Observe the celery at the end of the class and the next day. Record your observations each day.

### ANALYZE AND CONCLUDE

1. **Observe** In which stalk did the colored water rise the most? The least?

2. **Infer** What effect did the petroleum jelly have on transpiration? What part of the leaf did the petroleum jelly affect?

3. **Construct Explanations** Based on your findings in this investigation, how are leaves involved in transpiration?

**Nutrient Transport** How do sugars move in the phloem? The leading explanation of phloem transport is known as the pressure-flow hypothesis, shown in **Figure 23-15**. As you know, unlike the cells that form xylem, the sieve tube cells in phloem remain alive. Transport in the phloem involves three steps. ❶ Active transport moves sugars into the sieve tube from surrounding tissues. ❷ Water then follows by osmosis, creating pressure in the tube at the source of the sugars. ❸ If another region of the plant has a need for sugars, they are actively pumped out of the tube and into the surrounding tissues. Osmosis then causes water to leave the tube, reducing pressure in the tube at such places. The result is a pressure-driven flow of nutrient-rich fluid from the sources of sugars (source cells) to the places in the plants where sugars are used or stored (sink cells). Changes in nutrient concentration drive the movement of fluid through phloem tissue in directions that meet the nutritional needs of the plant.

The pressure-flow system gives plants enormous flexibility in responding to changing seasons. During the growing season, sugars from the leaves are directed into ripening fruits or into roots for storage. As the growing season ends, the plant drops its fruits and stores nutrients in the roots. As spring approaches, chemical signals stimulate phloem cells in the roots to pump sugars back into phloem sap. Then the pressure-flow system raises these sugars into stems and leaves to support rapid growth.

## Figure 23-15

### Pressure-Flow Hypothesis

The diagram shows the movement of sugars as explained by the pressure-flow hypothesis.

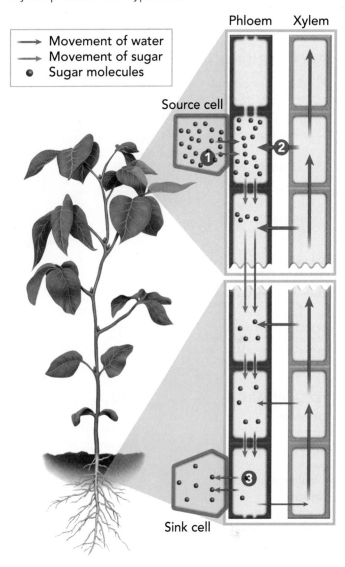

→ Movement of water
→ Movement of sugar
● Sugar molecules

Phloem    Xylem

Source cell

Sink cell

HS-LS1-1, HS-LS1-2, HS-LS1-3, HS-LS1-5

---

# ✓) LESSON 23.1 Review

## 🔍 KEY QUESTIONS

1. Describe the functions and organization of tissue systems in a seed plant.

2. Describe the main function of roots.

3. What are three important functions of stems?

4. Relate the structure and purpose of a leaf.

5. Describe the mechanisms that move water and sugars through a plant.

## CRITICAL THINKING

6. Predict  Describe what would happen over time to a tree sapling that could grow only taller, not wider.

7. Construct an Explanation  Only a small fraction of the water that plants take in is used as a reactant for photosynthesis. What happens to the rest of the water? How does a plant benefit from this use of water?

8. Develop Models  Draw a model of a plant that shows the movement of materials in and out of the plant, as well as between roots, stems, and leaves.

# Plant Hormones and Tropisms

🔍 **KEY QUESTIONS**

- *What roles do plant hormones play?*
- *What are examples of environmental stimuli to which plants respond?*
- *How do plants respond to seasonal changes?*

**HS-LS1-1:** Construct an explanation based on evidence for how the structure of DNA determines the structure of proteins which carry out the essential functions of life through systems of specialized cells.

**HS-LS1-3:** Plan and conduct an investigation to provide evidence that feedback mechanisms maintain homeostasis.

## VOCABULARY

hormone
target cell
receptor
auxin
apical dominance
tropism
phototropism
thigmotropism
gravitropism
photoperiodism

## READING TOOL

Compare the different vocabulary terms from this lesson in your 📖 **Biology Foundations Workbook.** Explain how they are similar or different in the way they support plants.

Plants grow in response to environmental factors such as light, moisture, temperature, and gravity. But how do roots "know" to grow down, and how do stems "know" to grow up? How do the tissues of a plant determine the right time of year to produce flowers? Somehow, plant cells manage to act together as a single organism.

## Hormones

**Hormones** are chemical signals that affect the growth, activity, and development of cells and tissues. In plants, hormones may act on the same cells in which they are made, or they may travel to different cells and tissues. 🔍 *Plant hormones serve as signals that control the development of cells, tissues, and organs. They also coordinate responses to the environment.* These two functions fit together well, because plants respond to the environment mainly by changing their development.

Cells affected by a particular hormone are called **target cells**. To respond to a hormone, a target cell must contain hormone **receptors**—usually proteins—to which hormone molecules bind. The response will depend on what kinds of receptors are present in the target cell. One kind of receptor might alter metabolism; a second might speed growth; a third might inhibit cell division. Thus, depending on the receptors present, a given hormone may cause a different response in roots than it does in stems or flowers, and the effects may change as cells add or remove receptors. Cells that do not contain receptors are generally unaffected by hormones.

**Auxins** The first step in the discovery of plant hormones came more than a century ago, and was made by a scientist already familiar to you. In 1880, Charles Darwin and his son Francis published the results of a series of experiments exploring the mechanism behind a grass seedling's tendency to bend toward light as it grows.

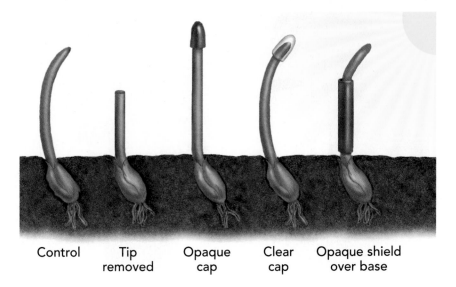

Control | Tip removed | Opaque cap | Clear cap | Opaque shield over base

**Figure 23-16**

## How Plants Detect Light

The Darwins conducted controlled experiments to determine which region of a plant senses light. When they removed the seedling tip or placed an opaque cap over the tip, they observed no bending toward light. But when they placed a clear cap on the tip or an opaque shield around the base, they observed bending similar to that seen in the control. ☑ **Control Variables** What variable did the Darwins control for by comparing the results of seedlings treated with a clear cap versus no cap?

The results of their experiments, shown in **Figure 23-16**, suggested that the tip of the seedling somehow senses light. The Darwins hypothesized that the tip produces a substance that regulates cell growth. More than forty years later, the regulatory substances produced by the tips of growing plants were identified and named *auxins*. **Auxins** stimulate cell elongation and the growth of new roots, among other roles that they play. They are produced in the shoot apical meristem and transported to the rest of the plant.

*Auxins and Cell Elongation* One of the effects of auxins is to stimulate cell elongation. As the Darwins saw in their experiment, when light hits one side of the shoot, auxins collect in the shaded part of the shoot. This change in concentration stimulates cells on the dark side to lengthen. As a result, the shoot bends away from the shaded side and toward the light, as shown in **Figure 23-17**.

 **READING CHECK Identify** What are auxins?

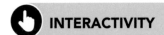 **INTERACTIVITY**

Investigate how hormones affect plant growth.

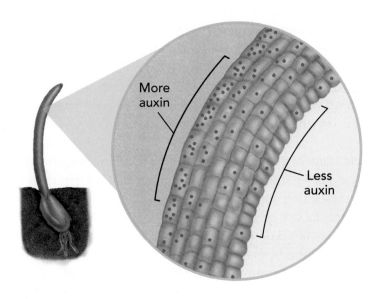

More auxin

Less auxin

**Figure 23-17**

## Auxins and Cell Elongation

Cells elongate more on the shaded side of the shoot, where there is a higher concentration of auxins.

**Figure 23-18**

## Apical Dominance

The basil plant on the right has had its apical meristem pinched off, in contrast to the plant on the left, which hasn't.
☑ **Observe** How are the two plants different?

**READING TOOL**

Compare and contrast the effects of auxins and cytokinins on plant growth.

*Auxins and Branching* Auxins also regulate cell division in meristems. As a stem grows in length, it produces lateral buds. As you may have noticed, the buds near the top of the plant grow more slowly than those near the base of a plant. The reason for this delay is that growth at the lateral buds is inhibited by auxins. Because auxins move out from the apical meristem, the closer a bud is to the stem's tip, the more it is inhibited. This phenomenon is called **apical dominance**. If you snip off the tip of a plant, these lateral buds begin to grow more quickly and the plant becomes bushier, as you can see in **Figure 23-18**. This is because the apical meristem—the source of the growth-inhibiting auxins—has been eliminated.

**Cytokinins** Cytokinins are plant hormones that are produced in growing roots and in developing fruits and seeds. Cytokinins stimulate cell division, interact with auxins to help to balance root and shoot growth, and stimulate regeneration of tissues damaged by injury. Cytokinins also delay the aging of leaves and play important roles in the early stages of plant growth.

Cytokinins often produce effects opposite to those of auxins. For example, root tips make cytokinins and send them to shoots; shoot tips make auxins and send them to roots. This exchange of signals keeps root and shoot growth in balance. Auxins stimulate the initiation of new roots, and they inhibit the initiation and growth of new shoot tips. Cytokinins do just the opposite. So if a tree is cut down, the stump will often make new shoots because auxins have been removed and cytokinins accumulate near the cut.

**Ethylene** One of the most interesting plant hormones, ethylene, is actually a gas. Fruit tissues release small amounts of the hormone ethylene, stimulating fruits to ripen. Ethylene also plays a role in causing plants to seal off and drop organs that are no longer needed. For example, petals drop after flowers have been pollinated, leaves drop in autumn, and fruits drop after they ripen. Ethylene signals cells at the base of the structure to seal off from the rest of the plant by depositing waterproof materials in their walls.

**Gibberellins** For years, farmers in Japan knew of a disease that weakened rice plants by causing them to grow unusually tall. The plants would flop over and fail to produce a high yield of rice grain. Farmers called the disease the "foolish seedling" disease. In 1926, Japanese biologist Eiichi Kurosawa discovered that a fungus, *Gibberella fujikuroi,* caused this extraordinary growth. His experiments showed that the fungus produced a growth-promoting substance.

In fact, the chemical produced by the fungus mimicked hormones produced naturally by plants. These hormones, called gibberellins, stimulate growth and may cause dramatic increases in size, particularly in stems and fruits. An example of the effect of gibberellins is shown in **Figure 23-19**.

**Abscisic Acid** Gibberellins also interact with another hormone, abscisic acid, to control seed dormancy. Abscisic acid inhibits cell division and halts growth. Recall that seed dormancy allows the embryo to rest until conditions are right for growth. When seed development is complete, abscisic acid stops the seed's growth and shifts the embryo into a dormant state. The embryo rests until environmental events shift the balance of hormones. Such events may include a strong spring rain that washes abscisic acid away. (Gibberellins do not wash away as easily.) Without the opposing effect of abscisic acid, the gibberellins can signal germination.

✅ **READING CHECK** **Summarize** Describe the roles of cytokinins, ethylene, gibberellins, and abscisic acid in plants.

**Figure 23-19**

# Gibberellins

Gibberellin hormones can cause incredible growth spurts, like those seen in the cabbage plants on the right.

---

### Analyzing Data

## Auxins and Plant Growth

This graph shows the results of experiments in which carrot cells were grown in the presence of varying concentrations of auxins. The blue line shows the effects on root growth. The red line shows the effects on stem growth.

1. **Analyze Graphs** At what auxin concentration are the stems stimulated to grow the most?

2. **Analyze Graphs** How is the growth of the roots affected by the auxin concentration at which stems grow the most?

3. **Apply Scientific Reasoning** If you were a carrot farmer, what concentration of auxin should you apply to your fields to produce the largest carrot roots?

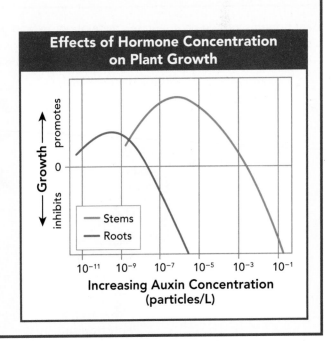

**Effects of Hormone Concentration on Plant Growth**

Growth — promotes / inhibits
— Stems
— Roots

$10^{-11}$  $10^{-9}$  $10^{-7}$  $10^{-5}$  $10^{-3}$  $10^{-1}$

**Increasing Auxin Concentration (particles/L)**

# Tropisms and Rapid Movements

Like other living things, plants move to respond to the environment. Many plant movements are slow, but some are so fast that even animals cannot keep up with them.

**BUILD VOCABULARY**

**Word Origins** The word **tropism** comes from a Greek word that means "turning."

**Tropisms** Plant sensors that detect environmental stimuli signal elongating organs to reorient their growth. These growth responses are called **tropisms**. 🔍 *Plants respond to environmental stimuli such as light, touch, and gravity.* These three tropisms are shown in **Figure 23-20**.

**Light** The tendency of a plant to grow toward a light source is called **phototropism**. This response can be so quick that young seedlings reorient themselves in a matter of hours. Recall that changes in auxin concentration are responsible for phototropism. Experiments have shown that auxins migrate toward shaded tissue, possibly due to changes in membrane permeability in response to light.

**Touch** Some plants even respond to touch, a process called **thigmotropism**. Vines and climbing plants exhibit thigmotropism when they encounter an object, such as a tree or trellis, and wrap around it. Other plants, such as grape vines, have extra growths called tendrils that emerge near the base of the leaf and wrap tightly around any object they encounter.

**Gravity** Auxins also affect **gravitropism**, the response of a plant to gravity. For reasons still not understood, auxins migrate to the lower sides of horizontal roots and stems. In horizontal stems, the migration causes the stem to bend upright. In horizontal roots, however, the migration causes roots to bend downward.

👆 **INTERACTIVITY**

**Figure 23-20**

**Three Tropisms**

---

Plant tropisms include phototropism, thigmotropism, and gravitropism. Phototropism causes a plant to grow toward a light source. One effect of a thigmotropism is that plants curl and twist around objects, such as the trellis. Gravitropism is the response of a plant to gravity.

Phototropism          Thigmotropism          Gravitropism

## Figure 23-21

## Rapid Movements

The leaves of the Venus flytrap can close quickly onto an unsuspecting insect, which the plant then breaks apart for its nitrogen and other nutrients. The mimosa plant responds to touch by folding in its leaves quickly. This response is produced by decreased osmotic pressure in cells near the base of each leaflet. ☑ **Infer** What adaptive value might this response have?

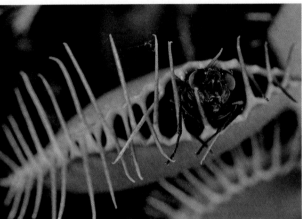

**Rapid Movements** Some plant responses are so rapid that it would be a mistake to call them tropisms. One example of a rapid response is what happens if you touch a leaf of the *Mimosa pudica*, appropriately called the "sensitive plant." Within only two or three seconds of being touched, its two leaflets fold together completely.

The carnivorous Venus flytrap, shown in **Figure 23-21**, also demonstrates a rapid response. When an insect lands on a flytrap's leaf, it triggers sensory cells on the inside of the leaf, sending electrical signals from cell to cell. A combination of changes in osmotic pressure and cell wall expansion interact, snapping the leaf shut so quickly that the insect is trapped inside—and digested.

☑ **READING CHECK** **Integrate Information** How do tropisms help plants survive in their environments?

**INTERACTIVITY**

Explore how photoperiod-ism affects plants.

# Response to Seasons

"To every thing there is a season." Nowhere is this more evident than in the regular cycles of plant growth. Year after year, some plants flower in the spring, others in the summer, and still others in the fall. Plants such as chrysanthemums and poinsettias flower when days are short and are therefore called short-day plants. Plants such as spinach and irises flower when days are long and are therefore known as long-day plants.

**Photoperiod and Flowering** How do all these plants manage to time their flowering so precisely in response to the environment? In the early 1920s, scientists discovered that tobacco plants flower according to their photoperiod, the number of hours of light and darkness they receive. Additional research showed that many other plants also respond to changing photoperiods, a response called **photoperiodism**. This type of response is summarized in **Figure 23-22**. ✿ *Photoperiodism is a major factor in the timing of seasonal activities such as flowering and growth.*

It was later discovered that a plant pigment called phytochrome (FYT oh krohm) is responsible for plant responses to photoperiod. Phytochrome absorbs red light and activates a number of signaling pathways within plant cells. By mechanisms that are still not understood completely, plants respond to regular changes in these pathways. These changes determine the patterns of a variety of plant responses.

**Figure 23-22**

**Effects of Photoperiod**

Changes in the photoperiod can affect the seasonal timing of flowering. ☑ **Form an Opinion** Are "short-day plant" and "long-day plant" the best names for categorizing these plants, or would it be better to name plants after their responses to night length? Explain your reasoning.

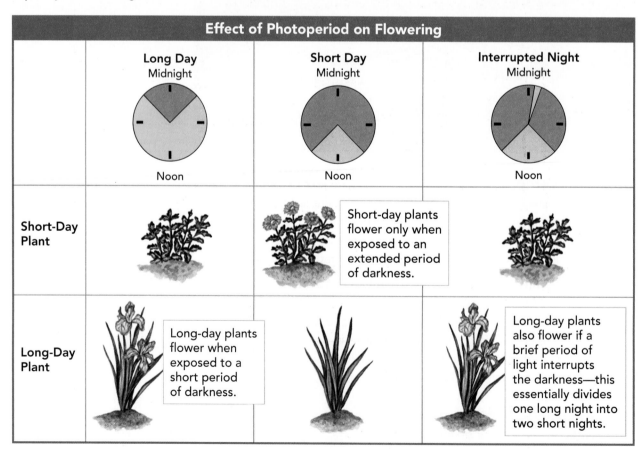

**Effect of Photoperiod on Flowering**

|  | Long Day Midnight / Noon | Short Day Midnight / Noon | Interrupted Night Midnight / Noon |
|---|---|---|---|
| **Short-Day Plant** |  | Short-day plants flower only when exposed to an extended period of darkness. |  |
| **Long-Day Plant** | Long-day plants flower when exposed to a short period of darkness. |  | Long-day plants also flower if a brief period of light interrupts the darkness—this essentially divides one long night into two short nights. |

**Winter Dormancy** Phytochrome also regulates the changes in activity that prepare many plants for dormancy as winter approaches. Recall that dormancy is the period during which an organism's growth and activity decrease or stop. 🔍 *As cold weather approaches, many plants prepare by turning off photosynthetic pathways, transporting materials from leaves to roots, and sealing off leaves from the rest of the plant.*

**Leaf Loss** In temperate regions, many flowering plants lose their leaves during the colder months. At summer's end, the phytochrome in leaves absorbs less light as days shorten and nights become longer. Auxin production drops, but the production of ethylene increases. This triggers a series of events that gradually shut down the leaf. As chlorophyll breaks down, other pigments—including yellow carotenoids and red anthocyanins—become visible, producing the beautiful colors of autumn.

**Figure 23-23**
**Adaptations for Winter**

In autumn, leaves shut down photosynthesis and fall from deciduous trees. Meanwhile, meristems at the tips of the branches produce thick, waxy scales that cover and protect new stem and leaf buds through the harsh winter.

*Changes to Meristems* Hormones also produce changes in apical meristems. Instead of continuing to produce leaves, meristems produce thick, waxy scales that form a protective layer around new leaf buds. Enclosed in its coat of scales, a terminal bud can survive the coldest winter days, as shown in **Figure 23-23**. At the onset of winter, xylem and phloem tissues pump themselves full of ions and organic compounds. The resulting solution acts like antifreeze in a car, preventing the tree's sap from freezing. This is one of several mechanisms plants use to survive the bitter cold.

HS-LS1-1, HS-LS1-3

# ✅ LESSON 23.2 Review

## 🔍 KEY QUESTIONS

1. Describe how hormones contribute to homeostasis.
2. Describe three examples of tropisms in plants.
3. Summarize plant responses to seasonal changes.

## CRITICAL THINKING

4. **Plan an Investigation** How could a garden-store owner determine what light conditions are needed for a particular flowering plant to bloom?

5. **Apply Scientific Reasoning** Review what you learned about evolution by natural selection in Chapter 17. Then, using what you know about natural selection, describe how plant adaptations for dormancy may have developed over time.

🔍**KEY QUESTIONS**
- *Which crops are the major food supply for humans?*
- *What are some examples of benefits besides food that humans derive from plants?*

**HS-ETS1-1:** Analyze a major global challenge to specify qualitative and quantitative criteria and constraints for solutions that account for societal needs and wants.

**READING TOOL**

For each section within the lesson, identify the main idea and one to three supporting details. Fill in the table in your 📖 **Biology Foundations Workbook.**

 **VIDEO**

Discover what an ethnobotanist found out about regarding plants and zombies.

A stroll through the produce section of a grocery store will convince you that plants are important. Even a medium-sized store will contain products made from scores of different plants. But which ones are the most important? Are there certain plants that we simply couldn't live without?

## Agriculture

Agriculture—the systematic cultivation of plants—did not begin with humans. In fact, the very first animals to practice agriculture may have been ants. On the island of Fiji, ants not only live inside a plant called *Squamellaria*, but they harvest its seeds, spread them around, and fertilize them. Evidence indicates that ants began "farming" this way several million years before humans first tried to grow plants for food.

**Worldwide Patterns** Many scholars now trace the beginnings of human civilization to the cultivation of crop plants. Evidence suggests that agriculture developed separately in many parts of the world about 10,000 to 12,000 years ago. Once people discovered how to grow plants for food, the planting and harvesting of crops tended to keep them in one place for much of the year, leading directly to the establishment of social institutions. Even today, agriculture is the principal occupation of more human beings than any other occupation.

Today, farming is the foundation on which human society is built. North America has some of the richest, most productive cropland in the world. As a result, farmers in the United States and Canada produce so much food that they are able to feed millions of people around the world as well as their own citizens.

Hundreds of different plants—nearly all of which are angiosperms—are raised for food in various parts of the world. Yet, despite this diversity, much of human society depends upon just a few of these plants. ♦ *Worldwide, most people depend on a few crop plants, such as rice, wheat, soybeans, and corn, for the bulk of their food supply.* The same crops are also used to feed livestock.

You may not have thought of it this way, but the food we eat from most crop plants comes from their seeds. For nutrition, most of humanity worldwide depends on the endosperm of only a few carefully cultivated species of grass. The pattern in the United States follows this trend. Roughly 80 percent of all U.S. cropland is used to grow just four crops: wheat, corn, soybeans, and hay. Of these crops, three—wheat, corn, and hay—are derived from grasses.

Devoting so much land to just a few crops can boost efficiency, but it presents certain dangers as well. Growing the same crop year after year depletes the soil of the same set of nutrients each season and increases dependency on chemical fertilizers. It also makes it more likely that insect pests and diseases associated with those crops will become more common, threatening the food supply.

**New Plants** The discovery and introduction of new crop plants has frequently changed human history. Potatoes are native to South America. Before they were discovered in the Americas, many important crops—including corn, peanuts, and potatoes—were unknown in Europe. The introduction of these plants changed European agriculture rapidly. We think of boiled potatoes, for example, as a traditional staple of German and Irish cooking, but 400 years ago, potatoes were new to the diets of Europeans.

By continuing to introduce such new plants into cultivation, the genetic diversity of the food supply can be strengthened and the likelihood that a single pest or disease will devastate farming can be reduced. Current trends along these lines have included the reintroduction of "heirloom" plants that were once cultivated but are not currently used in large-scale agriculture, such as the "heirloom" potatoes shown in **Figure 23-24**.

**READING TOOL**

As you read, write down the important events that have occurred in the history of agriculture.

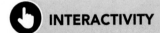

**INTERACTIVITY**

Explore how developments in agriculture have affected human life.

## Figure 23-24

## Heirloom Potatoes

Potatoes that were once common have been reintroduced into the marketplace.

**Figure 23-25**

**Seed Banks**

Seed banks help safeguard biodiversity. If stored properly, seeds could remain viable for hundreds, even thousands of years.

**Changes in Agriculture** Between 1950 and 1970, a worldwide effort to combat hunger and malnutrition led to dramatic improvements in farming techniques and crop yields. This effort came to be called the green revolution because it greatly increased the world's food supply. Green revolution technologies enabled many countries to end chronic food shortages and, in some cases, become exporters of surplus food.

At the heart of the green revolution was the use of high-yield varieties of seed and fertilizer. While some farmers today still use traditional fertilizers such as manure, artificial fertilizers helped to make the green revolution possible.

Fertilizers and pesticides must be used with great care. When large amounts of nitrogen- and phosphate-containing fertilizer are used near wetlands and streams, runoff from the fields may contaminate the water. Pesticides can also pose a health risk. Chemical pesticides are poisons, and have the potential to harm wildlife and leave dangerous chemical residues in food.

**Industrial Agriculture** Improved farming methods have made it possible to increase crop yields and produce food more cheaply, helping to alleviate hunger throughout the world. However, the large-scale cultivation of a small number of crop species has also reduced genetic diversity and left much of our food supply vulnerable to insects and disease. In certain parts of the world, whole forests have been slashed and burned to make room for immense plantations devoted to products like palm oil to be exported to developed countries. As the world population continues to increase, it will be necessary to safeguard the genetic diversity of crop plants and to deal with the challenges posed by industrial farming methods. Seed banks, as shown in **Figure 23-25**, are one of these safeguards.

 **Exploration Lab** Open-ended Inquiry

**How Do Plant Adaptations Compare?**

**Problem** How have the plants in your area adapted to their environment?

Plants have adaptations that enable them to survive in their specific environments. In this investigation, you will take a field trip to explore and observe plants in your neighborhood. You will identify how these plants reproduce, grow, and develop. You will also investigate adaptations of the plants to their environment.

You can find this lab in your digital course.

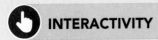
Figure 23-26

**Products from Plants**

Plant products include wood for musical instruments and cotton for clothing. The rosy periwinkle provides drugs for treating cancer.

# Fiber, Wood, and Medicine

Some of the most important uses of plants have nothing to do with food. 🔍 *Plants produce the raw materials for our homes and clothes, and some of our most powerful and effective medicines.* Some examples of plant products are shown in **Figure 23-26**. If you're reading this page out of the printed book, you are turning paper pages made from the conifer forests of North America, possibly sitting on a chair made from oak tree xylem, and probably wearing at least one piece of clothing made from the fibers of the cotton plant. Plants are also the source of many medicines and powerful drugs, including some that can be used to fight cancer.

## ▶ VIDEO

Examine the interactions plants and people have had over time.

HS-ETS1-1

## ☑ LESSON 23.3 Review

### 🔍 KEY QUESTIONS

1. Name four crops that make up the base of the world's food supply.

2. Describe the importance of plants in modern life.

### CRITICAL THINKING

3. **Evaluate Claims** The textbook claims that farming is the foundation on which human society is built. Use evidence and logical reasoning to support this claim.

4. **Synthesize Information** How are food crops different from wild plants? Include specific examples to support your answer.

5. **CASE STUDY** What are some of the drawbacks of the modern, large-scale cultivation of food crops? Cite a specific example to support your answer.

# How can we save the crops we depend upon?

**Modern agriculture has brought many benefits as well as drawbacks.**

HS-LS2-7, HS-ETS1-1, CCSS.ELA-LITERACY.RST.9-10.1, CCSS.ELA-LITERACY.WHST.9-10.7

## Make Your Case

As we've seen, fully 60 percent of the food energy found in the human diet comes from just three crops: wheat, corn, and rice. What would happen if the soil could no longer support these crops? Or if a disease decimated the harvests upon which millions depend? Should we grow more varieties of edible plants instead of concentrating on just a few?

## Engaging in Argument from Evidence

1. **Research a Problem** Go to your local supermarket or produce stand and make a list of the plant products (produce) that are sold. Then, determine which of these plants can grown locally and which plants cannot.

2. **Support Your Explanation with Evidence** Would you recommend growing some alternative varieties of plants in your local area? Based on your research, make a recommendation and support your recommendation with evidence.

## Society on the Case

### Eat Local!

The next time you buy tomatoes at the supermarket, take a look at their skins. Commercially raised tomatoes tend to be varieties with relatively thick skins, which protect them from jostling. After the tomatoes are picked from the vine, they are processed, packaged, and shipped. Then they travel hundreds, even thousands of miles to market. The tomatoes lose freshness on their journey, and the cost of transport is included in their price.

How can you find a fresh, tasty tomato, with thin skin and a rich, juicy texture? One way is to buy it from a local farm. Today, many small farms grow fruits and vegetables specifically to sell in their communities or at farmers' markets in nearby cities. Their customers get fresh produce of high quality, at a competitive price.

Beginning in the 1980s, small-scale farmers in the United States began using an economic model called community supported agriculture (CSA). In this model, community members pay a seasonal fee, or subscription, to the farmer or to a group of farmers. The subscription entitles them to a share of the harvest. This allows the farmer and the community to share the risks and benefits of farming. The subscribers may also pledge to contribute time and effort to raising the crop.

Of course, you could also raise your own tomatoes or other favorite fruits and vegetables. Many communities are establishing gardens in parks, vacant lots, and the rooftops of city buildings. You can even grow many vegetables in a pot on a patio or any other open space.

## Careers on the Case

### Work Toward a Solution

Agriculture involves the efforts of more than one specialist. For example, orchard growers know the best ways to raise fruit trees, prevent infestations, and harvest the fruit. To pollinate the flowers, however, they rely on people who know all about bees.

### Beekeeper

Beekeepers manage colonies of bees who live in hives in order to provide honey and other related products. They must maintain the health of the hives so that the bees survive. Beekeepers can work for themselves or as part of a larger commercial organization.

 **VIDEO**

Watch this video to learn about other careers in biology.

# Lesson Review

Go to your Biology Foundations Workbook for longer versions of these lesson summaries.

## 23.1 Roots, Stems, and Leaves

Plants have three main tissue systems: dermal, vascular, and ground. Dermal tissue is the protective outer covering of a plant. Vascular tissues support the plant body and transport water and nutrients throughout the plant. Ground tissue produces and stores sugars, and contributes to the physical support of the plant.

The root system of a plant plays a key role in water and mineral transport. Roots support a plant, anchor it in the ground, store food, and absorb water and dissolved nutrients from the soil. The cells and tissues of a root are specialized to carry out these functions. A mature root has an outside layer, called the epidermis, and also contains vascular tissue and a large area of ground tissue.

Stems produce leaves, branches, and flowers, hold leaves up to the sun, and transport substances throughout the plant. Primary growth of stems is the result of elongation of cells produced in the apical meristem. Secondary growth takes place in meristems called the vascular cambium and cork cambium.

The structure of a leaf is optimized to absorb light and carry out photosynthesis. Plants maintain homeostasis by keeping their stomata open just enough to allow photosynthesis to take place but not so much that they lose an excessive amount of water.

The combination of transpiration and capillary action lifts water upward through the xylem tissues of a plant. Changes in nutrient concentration drive the transport of fluid through phloem tissue in directions that meet the nutritional needs of the plant.

- epidermis
- meristem
- taproot
- fibrous root
- Casparian strip
- node
- vascular bundle
- primary growth
- secondary growth
- mesophyll
- stoma
- transpiration
- guard cells
- capillary action

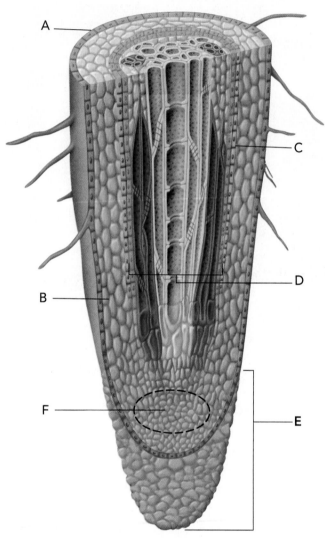

☑ **Interpret Visuals** Identify the structures labeled A through F to complete the diagram of root structure.

## 23.2 Plant Hormones and Tropisms

Plant hormones serve as signals that control development of cells, tissues, and organs. They also coordinate responses to the environment. Plant hormones include auxins, cytokinins, gibberellins, abscisic acid, and ethylene.

Plants respond to environmental stimuli through tropisms. Phototropism is the tendency of a plant to grow toward the light; gravitropism is the response of a plant to gravity; and thigmotropism is the response to touch.

Plants also respond to seasonal changes by reacting to differences in to the number of hours of lightness and darkness. Photoperiodism is a major factor in the timing of seasonal activities such as flowering and growth.

As cold weather approaches, many plants prepare by turning off photosynthetic pathways, transporting materials from leaves to roots, and sealing off leaves from the rest of the plant.

- hormone
- target cell
- receptor
- auxin
- apical dominance

- tropism
- phototropism
- thigmotropism
- gravitropism
- photoperiodism

☑️ **Identify** Label and describe each of the tropisms illustrated.

## 23.3 Plants and People

Worldwide, most people depend on a few crop plants, such as rice, wheat, soybeans, and corn, for the bulk of their food supply.

Plants produce the raw materials for our homes and clothes, and some of our most powerful and effective medicines

☑️ **Construct an Explanation** How are seed banks useful for modern agriculture?

## Organize Information

Complete the table by filling in the missing information.

| Plant Organ | Structures | Function |
|---|---|---|
| Roots | 1. | 2. |
| Stems | 3. | 4. |
| Leaves | 5. | 6. |

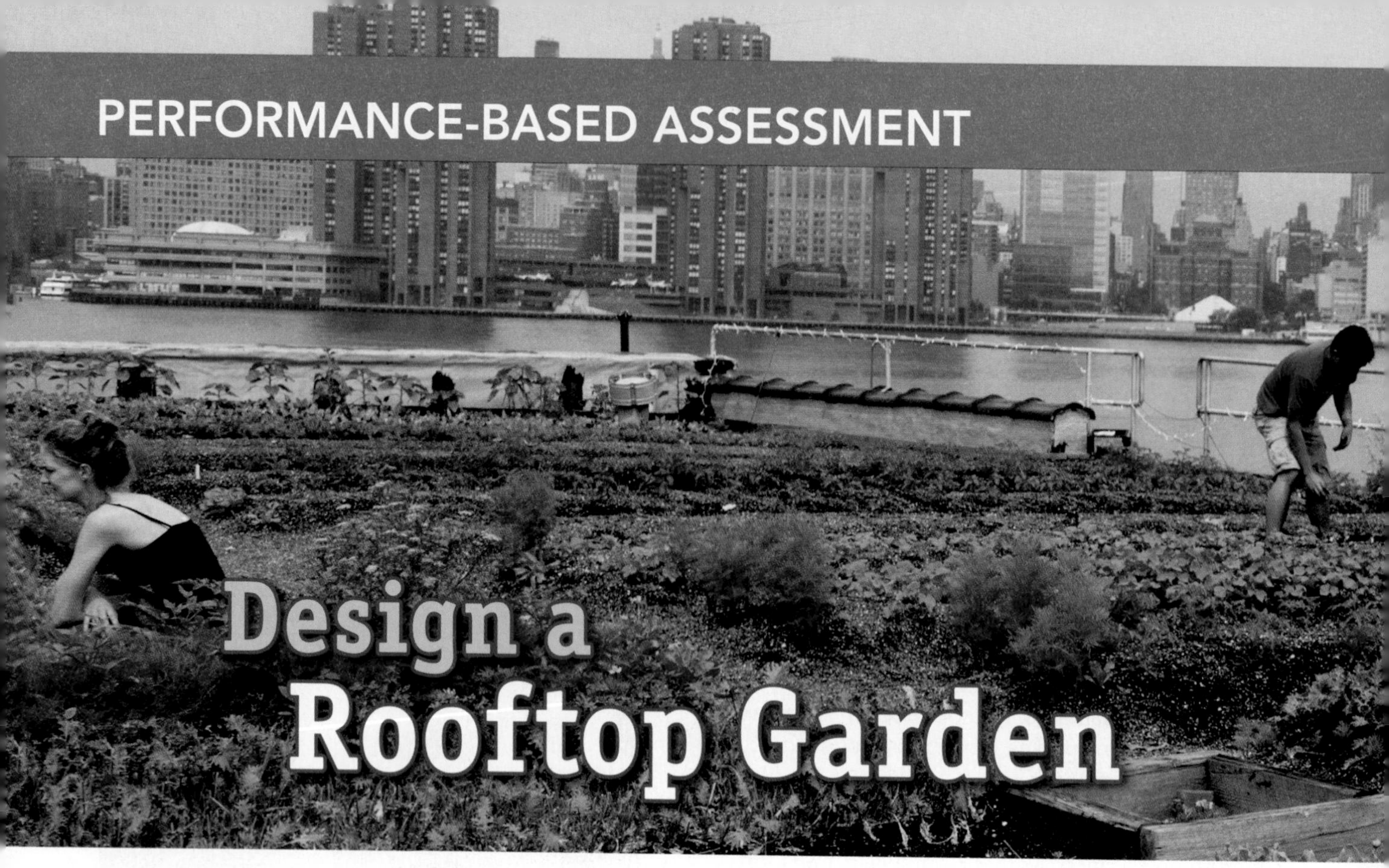

# Design a Rooftop Garden

## Design a Solution

HS-LS2-7, HS-ETS1-2, CCSS.ELA-LITERACY.RST.9-10.10, CCSS.ELA-LITERACY.WHST.9-10.2, CCSS.ELA-LITERACY.WHST.9-10.8

**STEM** Imagine covering the rooftop of a building with live plants. This idea has been developed into the technology known as a green roof. When designing a green roof, an architect must consider not only the structural properties of the building, but also the ecology of the site and its surroundings.

The area and depth of a green roof depend on many factors, including the roof's accessibility, the plants selected, the load capacity of the building, and the budget for installation and upkeep. The types of plants selected for a green roof depend on the climate of the area. The climate also determines what type of irrigation system is needed to keep the plants healthy.

Rainstorms can overwhelm wastewater systems in urban areas because water runs off buildings. A green roof retains more water than a conventional roof. This results in less runoff volume, which puts less stress on wastewater systems.

Asphalt and concrete surfaces of buildings and infrastructure absorb solar energy and re-radiate it to the environment. This process contributes to hotter summer temperatures in cities compared to surrounding areas. Solar energy can also raise the temperature inside a building. Green roofs can help reduce these warming effects.

Your task is to design a green roof system for a building of your choosing. The building may be one that you are already familiar with, such as your home or your school, or it may be a place that you have never visited before. Your design plan should explain the problem you aim to solve, the factors that guide your decision making, and details about the installation, materials, and cost of your green roof.

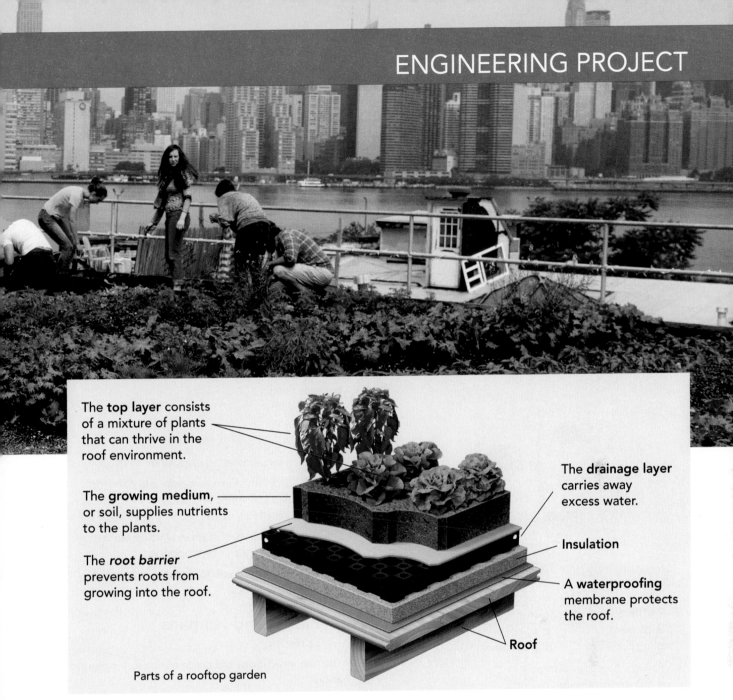

The **top layer** consists of a mixture of plants that can thrive in the roof environment.

The **growing medium**, or soil, supplies nutrients to the plants.

The *root barrier* prevents roots from growing into the roof.

The **drainage layer** carries away excess water.

**Insulation**

A **waterproofing** membrane protects the roof.

**Roof**

Parts of a rooftop garden

1. **Define the Problem** Research the site of your proposed green roof installation. What problem are you trying to solve? In what ways is the problem ecological? In what ways is the problem economic? Explain.

2. **Develop Models** Research the different types of green roof systems available and the materials used in their construction. Compare the advantages and disadvantages of each system. With the help of your class, brainstorm ways to "green" your roof.

3. **Design a Solution** Your green roof must meet certain performance requirements in order to successfully solve the problem.

These requirements are your design criteria. You also must specify the constraints that limit the scope of your design solution. Modify your model to meet your design criteria and constraints. Use your classmates' feedback to help you further modify and refine your roof design. Explain how your revised design optimizes the achievement of your design criteria.

4. **Communicate Information** Write a proposal to the owner of the site of your green roof design. Your proposal should outline the costs and benefits of installing the green roof and make a convincing case for adopting your design.

## 🔍 KEY IDEAS AND TERMS

### 23.1 Roots, Stems, and Leaves

**HS-LS1-1, HS-LS1-2, HS-LS1-3, HS-LS1-5**

1. The plant organ that supports the plant body and carries nutrients between different parts of the plant is the
   **a.** root.      **c.** leaf.
   **b.** stem.      **d.** flower.

2. Which type of plant tissue would be found ONLY in the circled areas of the plant shown?
   **a.** meristem tissue
   **b.** vascular tissue
   **c.** dermal tissue
   **d.** ground tissue

3. Tracheids and vessel elements make up
   **a.** phloem.      **c.** xylem.
   **b.** trichomes.      **d.** meristem.

4. Phloem functions primarily in
   **a.** transport of water.
   **b.** growth of the root.
   **c.** transport of products of photosynthesis.
   **d.** increasing stem width.

5. What is the principal difference between mature xylem and mature phloem cells?

6. What are the three main functions of leaves?

7. Explain how movement of sugars in the phloem contributes to the homeostasis in a plant.

8. How does the arrangement of vascular bundles in monocot stems differ from that of dicot stems?

### 23.2 Plant Hormones and Tropisms

**HS-LS1-1, HS-LS1-3**

9. Chemical signals in plants affecting the growth, activity, and development of cells and tissues are called
   **a.** hormones.
   **b.** enzymes.
   **c.** auxins.
   **d.** phytochromes.

10. Substances that stimulate cell division and cause dormant seeds to sprout are
    **a.** gibberellins.
    **b.** auxins.
    **c.** cytokinins.
    **d.** phytochromes.

11. Photoperiod is a measurement of
    **a.** water level.
    **b.** day length.
    **c.** gravity.
    **d.** nutrients.

12. Explain how auxins act in opposition to cytokinins.

13. What is a tropism? Give one example of a tropism that affects plant stems and another example of a tropism that affects roots.

14. Describe two different ways in which a plant may respond to changes in photoperiod.

15. Describe what happens to deciduous plants during winter dormancy.

### 23.3 Plants and Humans

**HS-ETS1-1**

16. The first indications of human agriculture occurred about
    **a.** 1000 years ago.
    **b.** 10,000 years ago.
    **c.** 100,000 years ago.
    **d.** 1,000,000 years ago.

17. What effect could plant species extinction have on therapeutic drug development?

18. What is an advantage of "heirloom" plants?

## CRITICAL THINKING

19. **Construct an Explanation** The seeds of lupines, an Arctic plant, can remain dormant for thousands of years, and still germinate when conditions are favorable. How might this trait provide an advantage to lupines in their environment?

20. **Predict** How would the function of a plant root be affected if it lacked a Casparian strip?

21. **Form a Hypothesis** While transplanting a houseplant to a larger pot, you notice that the roots had been very crowded in the old pot. Over the next few weeks, the plant's growth and overall appearance improve greatly. Develop a testable hypothesis that explains this observation.

22. **Apply Concepts** In the art of bonsai, gardeners keep trees small by cutting the roots and tips of the branches. The trunk of the tree, however, continues to increase in width. How do you explain the ever-increasing width of the trunk?

23. **Communicate Information** Describe a particular plant thigmotropism and hypothesize how it benefits the plant.

24. **Infer** The bulk of human plant foods comes from seeds, which constitute only a small part of the plant body. Explain how this is possible.

25. **Compare and Contrast** Compare and contrast the benefits and the dangers of using pesticides and fertilizers to grow food crops.

26. **Form a Hypothesis** Form a hypothesis to explain why plants are a good source of medicines.

27. **Apply Scientific Reasoning** How is it helpful for seed dormancy to be controlled by two types of hormones—gibberellins and abscisic acid—instead of just one type of hormone?

28. **Construct an Explanation** Spinach is a long-day plant that grows best with a night length of 10 hours or less. How does this fact explain the range of locations and seasons in which spinach plants can thrive?

29. **Compare and Contrast** Describe the benefits and drawbacks of using fertilizers and pesticides on gardens and farms.

Use the diagram to answer questions 30–33.

Recall that growth responses of plants to external stimuli are called *tropisms*. A tropism is positive if the affected plant part grows toward the stimulus. The response is negative if the plant part grows away from the stimulus. The experiment shown below was intended to test the effect of gravitropism on plant growth. The conclusion drawn from the experiment was that the plant stems grow upward due to negative gravitropism.

30. **Interpret Data** Describe the three experimental setups and the result of each.

31. **Form a Hypothesis** What was the probable hypothesis for this experiment?

32. **Interpret data** From the experimental setups shown, was the hypothesis successfully tested? Explain.

33. **Evaluate Information** Indicate what kinds of changes you would make to improve this experimental design.

# ☑ ASSESSMENT

## CROSSCUTTING CONCEPTS

**34. Systems and System Models** How does transpiration pull water up a plant?

**35. Cause and Effect** Describe the mechanism that opens and closes guard cells on leaves. Explain how the plant benefits from this mechanism.

## MATH CONNECTIONS

### Analyze and Interpret Data

CCSS.MATH.CONTENT.MP2, CCSS.MATH.CONTENT.HSS.IC.B.6

Refer to the text and circle graph below to answer questions 36 and 37.

Methyl bromide is a chemical used to kill both weeds and insects. In the United States, a total of 27,000 tons of methyl bromide are used annually on farms and orchards, mostly in Florida and California. The circle graph shows the use of methyl bromide by state.

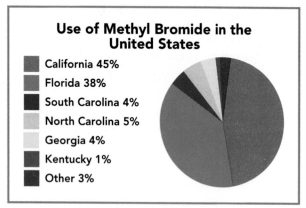

**Use of Methyl Bromide in the United States**

- California 45%
- Florida 38%
- South Carolina 4%
- North Carolina 5%
- Georgia 4%
- Kentucky 1%
- Other 3%

Source: U.S. Geological Survey

**36. Calculate** About how many tons of methyl bromide are used on Florida farms every year?

**37. Draw Conclusions** A scientist wants to compare the use of methyl bromide in Florida with its use in other states. Which information would be most useful for the scientist to research?
   **a.** the acres of farms and orchards in each state
   **b.** the most common crops grown in each state
   **c.** the percentages of methyl bromide used in states not named in the graph.
   **d.** the specific Florida farms or orchards that use the most methyl bromide

## LANGUAGE ARTS CONNECTIONS

### Write About Science

CCSS.ELA-LITERACY.WHST.9-10.2, CCSS.ELA-LITERACY.WHST.9-10.8

**38. Write Explanatory Texts** Describe how several different types of tissues in a leaf work together to help the leaf function.

**39. Gather Information** Choose a plant that is important in your region. Examples could include a crop plant, a plant used in landscaping, or a weed or other pest. Research the classification, origins, and life cycle of this plant, as well as any strategies for raising or controlling the plant. Write an essay to communicate your research. Use digital media to enhance your essay and add interest.

### Read About Science

CCSS.ELA-LITERACY.RST.9-10.2

**40. Summarize Text** Review Lesson 23.1 and the notes you took. How do roots, stems, and leaves work together to support a plant?

1. Primary growth and secondary growth both contribute to the growth of plants. Some of the tissues involved in plant growth are shown in the illustration below.

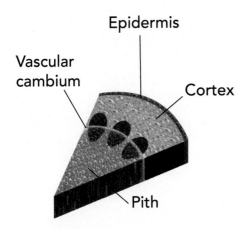

How does cell division in the vascular cambium contribute to plant growth?

I. Cell division in the vascular cambium results in an increase in stem thickness.

II. Cell division in the vascular cambium results in secondary xylem.

III. Cell division in the vascular cambium results in secondary phloem.

A. I. only
B. II. only
C. I. and III. only
D. II. and III. only
E. I., II., and III.

2. A plant pumps mineral ions into its root cells. Which of the following describes one of the functions of these ions?

A. The ions allow water to enter the roots by osmosis.

B. The ions absorb light so the plant can carry out photosynthesis.

C. The ions form the apical meristem, where water is absorbed.

D. The ions are stored in the ground tissue to provide support for the plant.

E. The ions form the pith, where water is absorbed.

3. Kate places her new houseplant near a window in her room. After a few weeks she notices the plant stems are bent toward the window. Which of the following explains how the stems are able to bend?

A. Cytokinin stimulates cell division on the sunny side of the plant's roots.

B. Abscisic acid inhibits cell division on the sunny side of stems.

C. *Gibberella fujikuroi* stimulates the plant to grow unusually tall.

D. Auxin stimulates cell elongation on the shady side of the stems.

E. Auxin concentrates at the tip of a shoot and direct growth towards light.

4. An environmental scientist is concerned about the reduced biodiversity of farm crops due to modern agricultural practices. Which would be the most effective solution to safeguard against a loss of biodiversity?

A. concentrating on a few crops to plant every year

B. developing hybrid crops that improve yields

C. establishing a seed bank to preserve wild relatives of farm crops

D. draining wetlands for use as farm land

E. promoting the use of powerful chemicals to kill farm pests

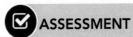 ASSESSMENT

For additional assessment practice, go online to access your digital course.

## If You Have Trouble With...

| Question | 1 | 2 | 3 | 4 |
| --- | --- | --- | --- | --- |
| See Lesson | 23.1 | 23.1 | 23.2 | 23.3 |
| Performance Expectation | HS-LS1-2 | HS-LS1-2 | HS-LS1-3 | HS-LS2-7 |

CHAPTER

# 24

# Animal Evolution, Diversity, and Behavior

**24.1**
Introduction to Animals

**24.2**
Animal Evolution and Diversity

**24.3**
Primate Evolution

**24.4**
Social Interactions and Group Behavior

**Go Online to access your digital course.**

▶ VIDEO

🔊 AUDIO

👆 INTERACTIVITY

📖 eTEXT

👁 ANIMATION

🧪 VIRTUAL LAB

☑ ASSESSMENT

Global climate change is threatening coral reefs all over the world. This reef is in the Indian Ocean.

HS-LS1-1, HS-LS1-2, HS-LS1-3, HS-LS2-7, HS-LS2-8, HS-LS4-1, HS-LS4-2, HS-LS4-3, HS-LS4-4, HS-LS4-6, HS-ESS2-4, HS-ESS3-5, HS-ETS1-2, HS-ETS1-3

# How are reefs affected by global change?

Articles about Australia's Great Barrier Reef have always described this diverse community as "magnificent," "enormous," or "spectacular." Like other modern reefs, Australia's is built by remarkable organisms called corals. Over the long history of life, different kinds of reef ecosystems, not based on corals, have evolved, thrived, and disappeared. The history of those ancient reef ecosystems can offer important insights into the state of modern coral reefs. Why? Because these days, journalists describe the Great Barrier Reef in ways that bring tears to biologists' eyes: "Dead." "Dying." "Bleached." What might we learn about the future of reefs today by studying ancient reefs and their inhabitants?

Modern coral reefs are diverse and productive ecosystems. They inhabit less than 2 percent of the ocean, yet they provide food or shelter for 25 percent of marine species. In fact, a list of all species that live on reefs would include at least one member of nearly every animal group you'll learn about in this chapter! Reefs also provide ecosystem services, such as food and jobs based on tourism, for millions of people.

Where does reef productivity come from? Corals are a group of "hybrid" organisms that are a partnership between animals and single-celled algae. Together, the organisms extract limiting nutrients from seawater and build solid skeletons of calcium carbonate from carbonate ions. Those skeletons form the structure of the reef, which provides shelter for scores of animals and algae. The coral partnership also provides food for other reef organisms. So, the reef consists of partnerships, built by partnerships, built on partnerships!

But reefs everywhere are in trouble. In 2017, *The New York Times* ran an "ecosystem obituary" in the form of an article entitled "Large Sections of Australia's Great Reef Are Now Dead."

Back in the days of the dinosaurs, a completely different reef community thrived in shallow seas. Those reefs were based not on corals, but on peculiar sorts of clamlike animals called rudists. Although they thrived for millions of years worldwide, they disappeared—both before and during the mass extinction that also wiped out the dinosaurs.

To understand what happened to rudists, and what is happening to corals, you need to understand animal body plans, their evolutionary adaptations, and their relationships to the environments.

Why should we care about what is happening to coral reefs today? And what might we learn about the state of our planet today by studying ancient communities that thrived in similar shallow-water marine ecosystems?

**Throughout this chapter, look for connections to the CASE STUDY to help you answer these questions.**

# Introduction to Animals

## KEY QUESTIONS

- *What characteristics do all animals share?*
- *What essential functions must animals perform to survive?*
- *What are some features of animal body plans?*

**HS-LS1-1:** Construct an explanation based on evidence for how the structure of DNA determines the structure of proteins which carry out the essential functions of life through systems of specialized cells.

**HS-LS1-2:** Develop and use a model to illustrate the hierarchical organization of interacting systems that provide specific functions within multicellular organisms.

**HS-LS1-3:** Plan and conduct an investigation to provide evidence that feedback mechanisms maintain homeostasis.

**HS-LS4-1:** Communicate scientific information that common ancestry and biological evolution are supported by multiple lines of empirical evidence.

## VOCABULARY

invertebrate
chordate
vertebrate
feedback inhibition
radial symmetry
bilateral symmetry
zygote
coelom
cephalization

### READING TOOL

As you read, keep track of the five things that animals do to survive. Describe each process in the graphic organizer in your Biology Foundations Workbook.

Is that a white flower? No, it is an insect called the orchid mantis.

We all know an animal when we see one—or do we? Four legs and fur may be what first comes to mind. However, other animals have scales and fins or feathers and talons. A few animals are easily mistaken for plants. Still other animals are too small to be seen with the unaided eye. It's a whole different world under the microscope!

## What Is an Animal?

Although animals may look very different from one another, they all share certain characteristics. **Animals are multicellular, heterotrophic, eukaryotic organisms with cells that lack cell walls.** Animals are often classified into two broad categories: invertebrates and chordates.

**Invertebrates** More than 95 percent of animal species are informally called invertebrates. **Invertebrates** include all animals that lack a vertebral column, such as worms, jellyfishes, and spiders. Because this category lumps organisms that lack a characteristic, rather than those that share a characteristic, "invertebrates" are not a clade.

**Chordates** Fewer than 5 percent of animal species are **chordates**, members of the clade known as phylum Chordata. All members of the phylum Chordata exhibit certain characteristics during at least one stage of life: a dorsal, hollow nerve cord; a tail that extends beyond the anus; and pharyngeal pouches. Most chordates—including fishes, amphibians, reptiles, birds, and mammals—are **vertebrates** that develop a backbone, or vertebral column, made of bones called vertebrae (singular: vertebra). Nonvertebrate chordates do not have backbones. As you see in **Figure 24-1**, the hollow nerve cord runs along the dorsal (back) part of the body. Nerves branch from this cord at intervals. At some point in their lives, all chordates have a tail that extends beyond the anus. Pharyngeal pouches are paired structures in the throat region or pharynx that may develop into gills.

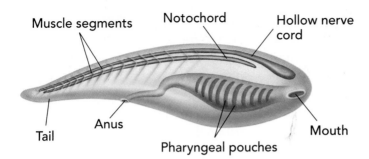

Muscle segments  Notochord  Hollow nerve cord

Tail  Anus  Pharyngeal pouches  Mouth

**Figure 24-1**

## Characteristics of Chordates

All chordates have a dorsal, hollow nerve cord; a notochord; pharyngeal pouches; and a tail that extends beyond the anus. Some chordates possess all these traits as adults; others possess them only as embryos.

# What Animals Do to Survive

All organisms keep their internal environment stable, a process known as maintaining homeostasis. ✎ *Animals maintain homeostasis by gathering and responding to information, obtaining and distributing oxygen and nutrients, and collecting and eliminating carbon dioxide and other wastes. They must also reproduce.*

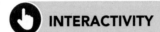

**INTERACTIVITY**

Investigate what it means to be an animal.

**Maintaining Homeostasis** If your house gets too cold, the thermostat turns the heat on. As heat warms the house, the thermostat turns the heater off. This is an example of **feedback inhibition**, or negative feedback, which occurs when the product or result of a process limits the process. Homeostasis in your body often works the same way. If you get cold, your body's thermostat makes you shiver, which uses muscle activity to generate heat. When you are no longer cold, the shivering stops. If you get too hot, you sweat, which helps you lose heat.

## Gathering and Responding to Information

The nervous system gathers information using cells called receptors that respond to sound, light, chemicals, and other stimuli. Other nerve cells collect and process that information and determine how to respond. Responding quickly and appropriately to the environment can be a matter of life—or death. Thanks to its nervous system, the pheasant in **Figure 24-2** has narrowly escaped becoming lunch for a hungry hawk. In some invertebrates, such as sponges, individual cells sense and respond to the environment. Some invertebrates have only a loose network of nerve cells. Other invertebrates and most chordates have large numbers of nerve cells concentrated into a brain.

The nervous system interacts with other systems to help animals respond to their environment. Muscle tissue generates force by becoming shorter when stimulated by the nervous system. Muscles work together with a supporting skeleton to make up the musculoskeletal system. Some invertebrates, such as earthworms, have flexible skeletons that function through the use of fluid pressure. Insects and some other invertebrates have external skeletons. The bones of vertebrates form an internal skeleton.

**Figure 24-2**

## Responding to the Environment

The hawk's nervous system helps it to spot prey and swoop down to capture it. The pheasant's nervous system helps it to elude the hawk's strike and to flee. ☑ **Infer** In what other ways do animals respond to their environment?

**Figure 24-3**

**Gas Exchange**

All animals must take in oxygen and eliminate carbon dioxide. Fishes exchange gases directly with water across their gills.

## Obtaining and Distributing Oxygen and Nutrients

All animals must obtain oxygen to perform cellular respiration, including the fish shown in **Figure 24-3**. Oxygen can diffuse across the skin of small animals in water or wet places. Larger animals use a respiratory system based on gills, lungs, or air passages. In addition, almost all animals eat to obtain nutrients, and they have a digestive system that breaks down food into usable forms. After acquiring oxygen and nutrients, animals must transport them throughout their bodies. This task often requires interactions between some kind of circulatory system and a respiratory system or digestive system. Several internal feedback mechanisms control these interactions to maintain homeostasis.

## Collecting and Eliminating Carbon Dioxide and Other Wastes

Animals' metabolic processes generate carbon dioxide and other wastes that must be eliminated. Many animals get rid of carbon dioxide through respiratory systems. Most complex animals have a specialized excretory system that concentrates or processes other wastes and expels them or stores them before eliminating them.

**Reproducing** Most animals reproduce sexually, a process that helps create and maintain genetic diversity. Many invertebrates and a few vertebrates can also reproduce asexually, usually producing offspring genetically identical to the parent.

**☑ READING CHECK Identify** How do the various body systems work together to maintain homeostasis?

# Animal Body Plans

Each animal clade has a unique organization of particular body structures, often called a body plan. Body plans are an important part of biological classification. Follow the cladogram in **Figure 24-4** as you read through the different types of body plans. ⚲ *Features of animal body plans include levels of organization, body symmetry, formation of body cavities, patterns of embryological development, segmentation, cephalization, and limb formation.*

**Levels of Organization** As the cells of most animals develop, they differentiate into specialized cells organized into tissues. Animals typically have several types of tissues. Epithelial tissues cover both the inside and outside of body surfaces. Muscle tissue is organized to move the body. Nervous tissue sends messages. Connective tissue, which includes bone and cartilage, has a variety of functions.

During growth and development, tissues combine to form organs. Organs together make up organ systems that carry out complex functions. Organ systems work together to maintain homeostasis in the organism.

**READING TOOL**

Use the key idea and the headings to help you organize the features of animal body plans.

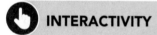 **INTERACTIVITY**

Practice your classification skills as you identify an unknown animal.

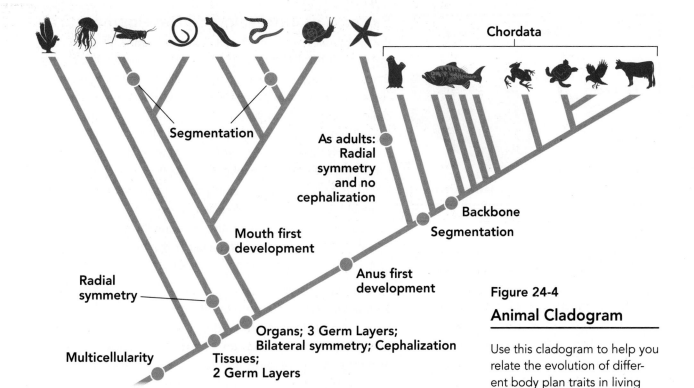

Chordata

Segmentation

As adults:
Radial
symmetry
and no
cephalization

Backbone

Segmentation

Mouth first
development

Anus first
development

Radial
symmetry

Organs; 3 Germ Layers;
Bilateral symmetry; Cephalization

Multicellularity

Tissues;
2 Germ Layers

Single-celled animal ancestor

## Figure 24-4
## Animal Cladogram

Use this cladogram to help you relate the evolution of different body plan traits in living groups of animals.

**Body Symmetry** Most animals exhibit some type of symmetry. The sea anemone in **Figure 24-5** has **radial symmetry**, with body parts that extend outward from the center like spokes of a bicycle wheel. Any number of imaginary planes drawn through the center of the body could divide it into equal halves. Many animal groups exhibit **bilateral symmetry**, in which a single imaginary plane divides the body into left and right sides that are mirror images of each other. Animals with bilateral symmetry have a front, or anterior, end and a back, or posterior, end. Bilaterally symmetrical animals also have an upper, or dorsal, side and a lower, or ventral, side. When you ride a horse, you are riding on its dorsal side.

## BUILD VOCABULARY

**Use Prior Knowledge** A radius is a line from the center of a circle to its edge. In radial symmetry, body parts follow lines that extend from a center.

## Radial Symmetry

## Bilateral Symmetry

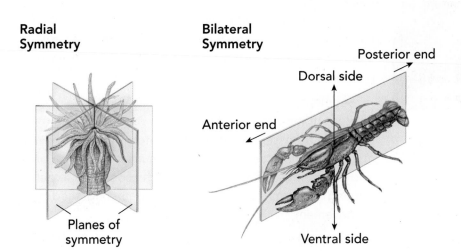

Posterior end

Dorsal side

Anterior end

Ventral side

Planes of symmetry

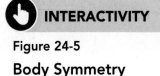 **INTERACTIVITY**

## Figure 24-5
## Body Symmetry

Animals with radial symmetry have body parts that extend from a central point. Animals with bilateral symmetry have distinct anterior and posterior ends and right and left sides.

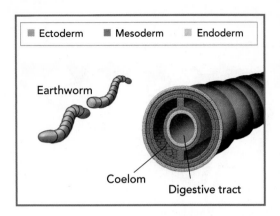

**Figure 24-6**

## Body Cavity

Earthworms are some of the simplest animals with a coelom.

# Patterns of Embryological Development

Every animal that reproduces sexually begins life as a **zygote**, or fertilized egg. As the zygote develops, it forms a hollow ball of cells like an inflated balloon. As that ball develops, it folds in on itself, as if you were holding the balloon and pushing your thumbs toward the center. This folding changes a ball of cells into an elongated structure with a tube that runs from one end to the other. This tube becomes the digestive tract. At first, this digestive tract has only a single opening to the outside. An efficient digestive tract, however, needs two openings: a mouth through which food enters and an anus through which wastes leave. In some animal clades the mouth develops first. In other animal clades, the anus develops first.

During embryological development, the cells of most animal embryos differentiate into three layers, called germ layers: the endoderm, mesoderm, and ectoderm. The endoderm develops into the lining of the digestive tract and most of the respiratory system. The mesoderm develops into the muscles and much of the circulatory, reproductive, and excretory systems. The ectoderm develops into the nervous system and the outer layer of the skin. Animals with radial symmetry have two germ layers—the endoderm and the ectoderm.

Most animals have some kind of body cavity—a fluid-filled space between the digestive tract and body wall, which contains internal organs. Your stomach and other digestive organs are suspended in your body cavity. Most complex animals have a type of body cavity called a **coelom** (see lum) as shown in **Figure 24-6**. Some invertebrates lack a body cavity, while others have only a primitive jellylike layer.

**Segmentation** As many bilaterally symmetrical animals develop, their bodies divide into repeated parts, or segments. Segmented animals typically have at least some internal and external body parts that repeat on each side of the body. Bilateral symmetry and segmentation are found together in many animal groups. The millipede in **Figure 24-7** provides one example.

Segmentation has been important in animal evolution because of the way genes control the production and growth of body segments. In segmented animals, simple mutations can cause changes in the number and form of body segments. Different segments can specialize in performing functions such as information gathering, feeding, or movement.

**Figure 24-7**

## Segmentation

In this colorful millipede, most of the segments are functionally alike. In other animals, the segments are more specialized.

## How Can Body Symmetry Affect Movement?

1. Use modeling clay to make models of two animals. Make one model radially symmetrical and the other long, narrow, and bilaterally symmetrical.

2. Make grooves to divide each model into similar segments.

3. Add legs to some segments of your models.

### ANALYZE AND CONCLUDE

1. **Infer** Which type of body symmetry is more suited to walking forward?

2. **Use Models** How is bilateral symmetry an advantage to animals that walk or run?

## Cephalization

Animals with bilateral symmetry typically exhibit **cephalization**, the concentration of sense organs and nerve cells at their anterior end. This anterior end is often different enough from the rest of the body that it is called a head. You could say that arthropods and vertebrates have gotten ahead by "getting a head"! Both insect and vertebrate heads are formed by fusion and specialization of body segments during development.

As segments fuse, internal and external parts combine in ways that concentrate sense organs, such as eyes, in the head. Nerve cells that process information and "decide" what the animal should do also become concentrated in the head. Animals with heads usually move in a "head-first" direction, which allows for sense organs and nerve cells to come in contact with new parts of the environment first.

## Limb Formation

Segmented, bilaterally symmetrical animals typically have external appendages on both sides of the body. These appendages vary from simple bristles in some worms to spiders' jointed legs, dragonfly wings, bird wings, dolphin flippers, and monkey arms. These very different appendages have evolved several times, and have been lost several times, in various animal groups.

HS-LS1-1, HS-LS1-2, HS-LS1-3, HS-LS4-1

## ☑ LESSON 24.1 Review

### ⚲ KEY QUESTIONS

1. A classmate is looking at a unicellular organism under a microscope. She asks you if it is an animal. What would you say, and why?

2. Why must waste products produced by metabolic processes be eliminated from an animal's body?

3. List five features of animal body plans.

### CRITICAL THINKING

4. **Compare and Contrast** How do vertebrates differ from other chordates?

5. **Synthesize Information** What happens to a clade over time if its body plan doesn't enable its members to survive and reproduce?

6. **CASE STUDY** Adult corals do not travel from place to place. How can this impact their ability to maintain homeostasis in changing environmental conditions?

LESSON 24.2

# Animal Evolution and Diversity

**KEY QUESTIONS**

- *How are animal clades defined?*
- *What does the cladogram of invertebrates illustrate?*
- *What can we learn by studying the chordate cladogram?*

**HS-LS4-1:** Communicate scientific information that common ancestry and biological evolution are supported by multiple lines of empirical evidence.

**VOCABULARY**
**cartilage**
**tetrapod**

**READING TOOL**

Identify the major events in animal evolution. As you read, take notes in the chart in your **Biology Foundations Workbook.**

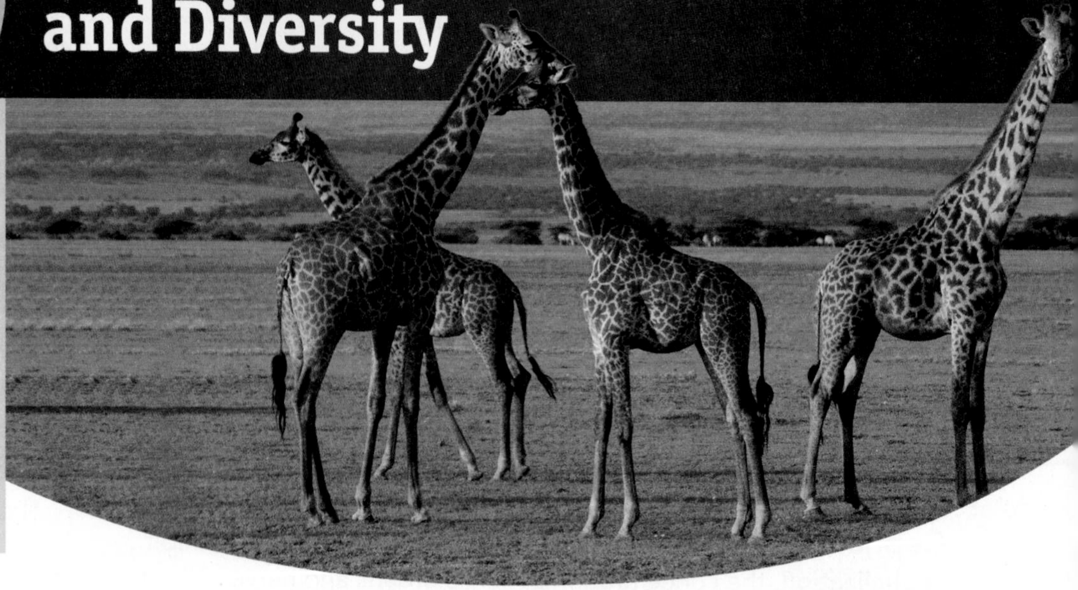

New genetics data suggests that "giraffes" are actually four separate species, roughly as genetically different from one another as polar bears are from brown bears. That's interesting, but is this information useful? Yes! Two of those giraffe species have very small populations, so they are at high risk for extinction and require extra effort at conservation. These kind of genetic studies also help us understand evolutionary relationships among larger clades.

## The Cladogram of Animals

The features of animal body plans provide information for building the cladogram shown in **Figure 24-8**, showing current hypotheses of relationships among animal clades. ***Animal clades are typically defined according to adult body plans and patterns of embryological development.***

**Differences Between Clades** Every clade has a unique combination of ancient traits inherited from its ancestors and new traits found only in that clade. It is tempting to think of this cladogram as a story about "improvements" over time. But complex body systems of vertebrates aren't necessarily better than "simpler" invertebrate systems. Any body system in living animals functions well enough to enable those animals to survive and reproduce.

**Evolutionary Experiments** You can think of each clade's body plan as an evolutionary "experiment," in which a set of body structures perform essential functions. The first appearance of a clade represents the beginning of this "experiment." The original versions of most major animal body plans were established hundreds of millions of years ago. They have been modified over time as species have adapted to changing conditions.

Land vertebrates, for example, typically have four limbs. Many, such as frogs, walk (or hop) on four limbs we call "legs." Among birds, front limbs have evolved into wings. In many primates, front limbs have evolved into "arms." Both wings and arms evolved through changes in the standard vertebrate forelimb.

# Origins of the Invertebrates

In Darwin's time, paleontologists defined the Cambrian Explosion, which started about 542 million years ago, as a time when many modern phyla seemed to appear suddenly in the fossil record. We use the word "suddenly" in the geological sense, because the Cambrian Explosion lasted over 15 million years! It looked like an "explosion" to early paleontologists because few older fossils had then been found. Why? Earlier animals were tiny, and were composed of soft tissues rarely preserved as fossils.

**The Earliest Animals** For roughly 3 billion years after the first prokaryotic cells evolved, all life remained single-celled. Current data support the hypothesis that the first animals evolved from ancestors they shared with living choanoflagellates, which share several characteristics with sponges, the simplest animals.

Our oldest evidence of multicellular life comes from recently discovered microscopic fossils roughly 600 million years old. The fossil record indicates that the first animals began evolving long before the Cambrian Explosion. These fossils include eggs, embryos, and small body parts, as well as "trace fossils" such as tracks and burrows.

**Figure 24-8**

## Cambrian Animals

This illustration shows what some of the Cambrian animals may have looked like.

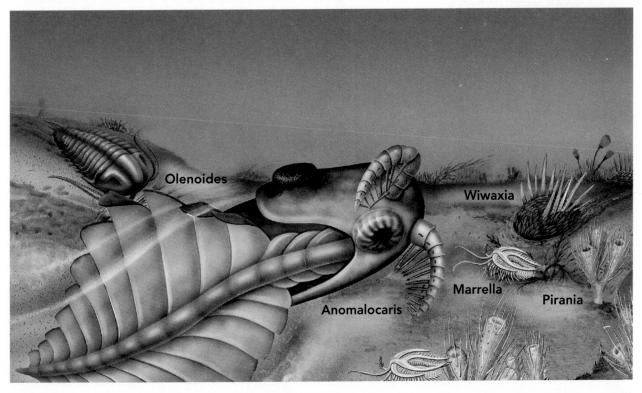

**The Ediacaran Fauna** Exciting and important fossil evidence of animal life before the Cambrian comes from Australia's Ediacara Hills. These fossils date from roughly 565 to about 544 million years ago, and formed during the Ediacaran Period at the end of the Proterozoic Eon. Most Ediacaran animals had body plans different from anything alive today, although some seem to be related to jellyfishes and worms.

**The Cambrian Explosion** Some of the best fossils from the Cambrian Period, which began about 542 million years ago, are found in Chengjiang, China, and in the Burgess Shale of Canada. These animals evolved complex body plans, including specialized cells, tissues, and organs. Many had body symmetry, segmentation, a front and back end, and appendages such as legs or antennae. Some Cambrian animals also evolved shells, skeletons, and other hard body parts that fossilize well. That's one reason Cambrian fossils are more numerous than, and were discovered before, Ediacaran fossils.

Some early Cambrian fossils are so peculiar that no one knows what to make of them! Others are classified as ancient members of modern invertebrate clades such as arthropods. Others appear to be early chordates. By the end of the Cambrian, the basic body plans of many modern clades had been established. But this does not mean that we would recognize Cambrian organisms as modern members of these phyla. Many millions of years passed before evolutionary change produced the familiar body structures of modern animals.

**Cladogram of Invertebrates** The major clades of living invertebrates are shown in **Figure 24-9**. ✎ *This cladogram shows current hypotheses about evolutionary relationships among major living invertebrate groups, and indicates the order in which important features evolved.* The invertebrates alive today are summarized in **Figure 24-10**.

**Figure 24-9**

**Cladogram of Invertebrates**

This diagram shows current hypotheses of evolutionary relationships among major groups of animals. During the course of evolution that produced these different groups, important traits evolved. These are shown by the red circle (nodes). Note that invertebrates do not form a clade.

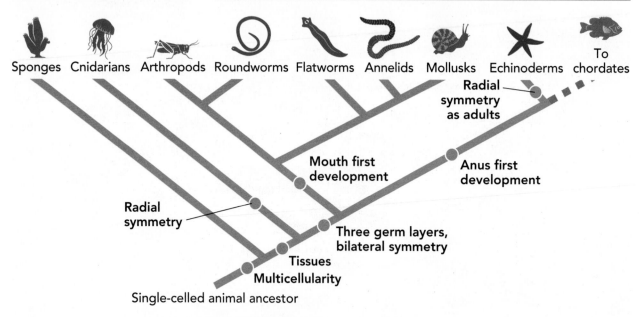

## Figure 24-10 **Modern Invertebrate Diversity**

Invertebrates live nearly everywhere, participate in nearly every food web, and vastly outnumber vertebrates.

**Sponges** Sponges are members of the clade Porifera, Latin for "pore bearers," named for the tiny openings, or pores, they have all over their bodies. Sponges are among the simplest organisms in the clade Metazoa, with all other multicellular animals.

**Cnidarians** Jellyfishes, sea fans, sea anemones, hydras, and corals are members of the clade Cnidaria. Cnidarians are aquatic, mostly soft-bodied, carnivorous, radially symmetrical animals with stinging tentacles arranged in circles around their mouths. Some, such as corals, have skeletons. Some live as independent individuals, while others live in colonies.

**Arthropods** Members of the clade Arthropoda include spiders, centipedes, insects, and crustaceans. Arthropods have segmented bodies, a tough external skeleton, cephalization, and jointed appendages. At least a million species have been identified—more than three times the number of all other animal species combined!

**Roundworms** The roundworms, or nematodes, are unsegmented worms with specialized tissues and organ systems, and digestive tracts with two openings—a mouth and an anus. Some are free-living and live in soil or water. Others are parasites that infect plants and animals.

**Flatworms** Members of clade Platyhelminthes, or flatworms, include planarians, tapeworms, and flukes. Flatworms are soft, flattened, unsegmented worms that lack a coelom and an anus.

**Annelids** The clade Annelida contains segmented worms such as earthworms and bloodsucking leeches. The name Annelida is derived from the Latin *annellus*, which means "little ring," referring to the ringlike appearance of their body segments.

**Mollusks** Members of clade Mollusca, or mollusks, include snails, slugs, clams, squids, and octopi. Mollusks are soft-bodied animals that typically have an internal or external shell and complex organ systems.

**Echinoderms** The marine clade Echinodermata includes sea stars, sea urchins, and sand dollars. Adult echinoderms have spiny skin, five-part radial symmetry, an internal skeleton of calcium carbonate plates, and a network of water-filled tubes called a water vascular system. This water vascular system is used for walking and for gripping prey.

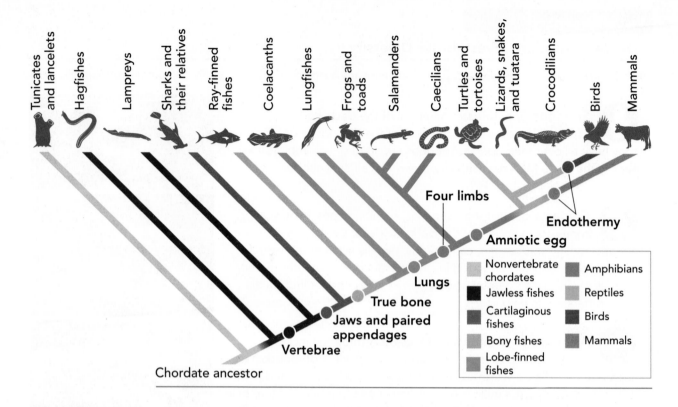

**Figure 24-11**

**Cladogram of Chordates**

The cladogram labels include: Tunicates and lancelets, Hagfishes, Lampreys, Sharks and their relatives, Ray-finned fishes, Coelacanths, Lungfishes, Frogs and toads, Salamanders, Caecilians, Turtles and tortoises, Lizards, snakes, and tuatara, Crocodilians, Birds, Mammals.

**Four limbs**

**Endothermy**

**Amniotic egg**

**Lungs**

**True bone**

**Jaws and paired appendages**

**Vertebrae**

Chordate ancestor

Key:
- Nonvertebrate chordates
- Jawless fishes
- Cartilaginous fishes
- Bony fishes
- Lobe-finned fishes
- Amphibians
- Reptiles
- Birds
- Mammals

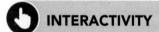

**INTERACTIVITY**

**Figure 24-11**

**Cladogram of Chordates**

The different-colored lines represent the traditional groupings of these animals, as listed in the key. The circles (nodes) indicate the evolution of some important chordate adaptations.

**READING TOOL**

As you read about the chordates, find them on the cladogram and identify their derived characters.

# Origins of the Chordates

The most ancient chordates were related to the ancestors of echinoderms. The rich Cambrian fossil record includes some early chordate fossils, such as *Pikaia* (pih KAY uh). When *Pikaia* was first discovered, it was thought to be a worm. Then scientists determined that it had paired muscles arranged in a series, similar to those of simple modern chordates. In 1999, fossil beds from later in the Cambrian yielded fossils of the earliest known vertebrate. These fossils show muscles arranged in a series, traces of fins, sets of feathery gills, a head with paired sense organs, and a skull and skeletal structures likely made of cartilage. **Cartilage**, a strong connective tissue, is softer and more flexible than bone. These characteristics are shared—during some part of the life cycle—by all chordates.

**Cladogram of Chordates** Modern chordates consist of six groups: nonvertebrate chordates and five groups of vertebrates—fishes, amphibians, reptiles, birds, and mammals. Almost all living chordates are vertebrates, and most of those are fishes. Because hard body structures fossilize well, this clade has an excellent fossil record. ⚲ *The chordate cladogram in Figure 24-11 presents current hypotheses about evolutionary relationships among chordate groups.* The circles (nodes) in the cladogram represent the appearance of important characteristics during evolution. Each new adaptation—jaws, true bone, and paired appendages—jump-started a major adaptive radiation.

**Nonvertebrate Chordates** Tunicates and lancelets are chordates that lack backbones. Cambrian fossil evidence suggests that their ancestors diverged from vertebrate ancestors more than 550 million years ago. Adult tunicates, such as the salps shown in **Figure 24-12**, look like sponges, but their larvae all have key chordate characteristics. The small, fishlike lancelets live on the sandy ocean bottom.

**Jawless Fishes** The earliest fishes appeared about 510 million years ago. They had no true jaws or teeth, and their skeletons were made of cartilage. However, fossils reveal that many had bony shields on their heads and other armor. Two other clades gave rise to modern lampreys and hagfishes. Lampreys, shown in **Figure 24-13**, are filter feeders as larvae and parasites as adults. Hagfishes have pinkish-grey, wormlike bodies, secrete lots of slime, and tie themselves into knots!

**Figure 24-12**
**Nonvertebrate Chordates**

Salps are colonial nonvertebrate chordates.

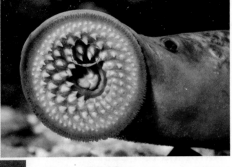

**Figure 24-13**
**Jawless Fishes**

An adult lamprey uses its teeth-filled mouth to attach to a host.

**Sharks and Their Relatives** Other ancient fishes evolved jaws, which make it possible to bite and chew. Early fishes also evolved paired pectoral (anterior) and pelvic (posterior) fins attached to supporting structures called limb girdles. Paired fins offer more control of body movement, while tail fins and muscles gave greater thrust. These adaptations launched the adaptive radiation of the Chondrichthyes (kahn DRIK theez): sharks, rays, and skates. The hundreds of cartilaginous fishes include the shark shown in **Figure 24-14**.

**Figure 24-14**
**Sharks**

The great white shark is one of the fiercest predators of the ocean.

**✓ READING CHECK** **Review** Why were jaws a significant evolutionary development?

## Figure 24-15
## Bony Fishes

Bony fishes, such as these examples, have skeletons made of true bone. Most fishes alive today are bony fishes.

Coelacanth

Cobia

**INTERACTIVITY**

Investigate biodiversity on a coral reef.

## Figure 24-16
## From Fins to Feet

The cladogram shows a few of the animal groups in the evolution of the feet of tetrapods from the fins of ancient bony fishes. All of the illustrated animal groups are extinct.

**Bony Fishes** Another group of ancient fishes evolved skeletons of true bone, launching the radiation of bony fishes, the Osteichthyes (ahs tee ɪk theez), as shown in **Figure 24-15**.

**Ray-finned Fishes** Most modern bony fishes belong to a huge group called ray-finned fishes, referring to fins formed from bony rays connected by a layer of skin.

**Lobe-finned Fishes** Lobe-finned fishes evolved fleshy fins supported by larger bones. Modern lobe-finned fishes include lungfishes and coelacanths (SEE luh kanths). One group of ancient lobe-finned fishes evolved into the ancestors of four-limbed vertebrates, or **tetrapods**.

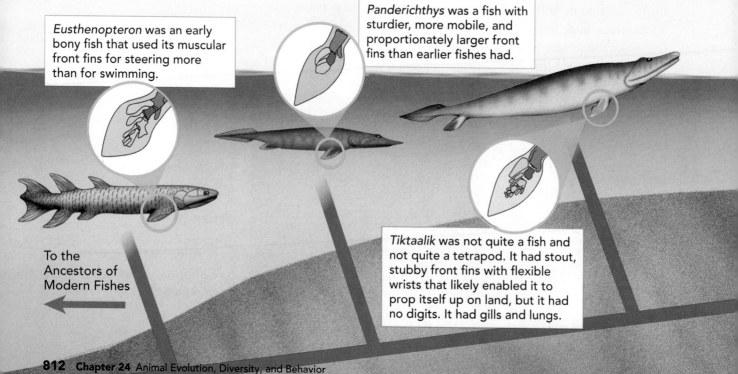

*Eusthenopteron* was an early bony fish that used its muscular front fins for steering more than for swimming.

*Panderichthys* was a fish with sturdier, more mobile, and proportionately larger front fins than earlier fishes had.

*Tiktaalik* was not quite a fish and not quite a tetrapod. It had stout, stubby front fins with flexible wrists that likely enabled it to prop itself up on land, but it had no digits. It had gills and lungs.

To the Ancestors of Modern Fishes

Salamander (juvenile)

Golden toad

Caecilian

The three living orders of amphibians are salamanders, frogs and toads, and caecilians (see SIL ee uhnz). Because amphibians are particularly sensitive to changes in their environment, species have been disappearing at an alarming rate. The Costa Rican golden toad is one of the earliest well-known amphibian species to become extinct due global change.

**The "Fishapod"** A series of spectacular transitional fossils shows how lines of lobe-finned fishes evolved sturdier appendages, as shown in **Figure 24-16**. One of these, *Tiktaalik*, has such a mix of fish and tetrapod features that it could be called a "fishapod"—part fish, part tetrapod.

**Amphibians** The word *amphibian* means "double life," because most amphibians live in water as larvae but on land as adults. Most require water for reproduction, breathe with lungs as adults, have moist skin with mucous glands, and lack scales and claws.

Early amphibians were the ancestors of reptiles, birds, and mammals. Their adaptations to breathe air and protect themselves from drying out fueled another adaptive radiation. Although they were once the dominant land vertebrates, only three orders of amphibians survive today. **Figure 24-17** shows examples of amphibians.

**BUILD VOCABULARY**

**Root Words** The prefix *tetra-* means "four," and the suffix *-pod* means "foot." Tetrapods have four feet or other types of limbs.

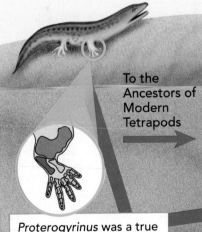

To the Ancestors of Modern Tetrapods

*Acanthostega* had digits on its front feet but spent most of its time in the water. Though it had gills, it may have used its limbs to prop itself out of oxygen-poor water so it could breathe air with its lungs.

*Ichthyostega* had sturdy hind feet with several digits, but it probably used them more often to paddle through the water than to walk on land. It may have moved like a seal on land.

*Proterogyrinus* was a true tetrapod and agile both in water and on land, much as today's alligators are.

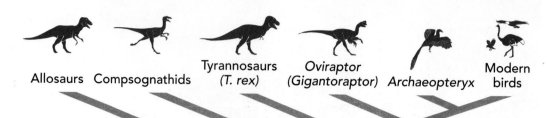

Allosaurs  Compsognathids  Tyrannosaurs *(T. rex)*  *Oviraptor* *(Gigantoraptor)*  *Archaeopteryx*  Modern birds

**Figure 24-18**

## Dinosaurs and Birds

The cladogram shows current hypotheses about the relationship between dinosaurs and modern birds.

**Reptiles** Reptiles evolved from ancient amphibians with dry scaly skin, well-developed lungs, strong limbs, and shelled eggs that do not develop in water. There are five groups of living reptiles: lizards and snakes, crocodilians, turtles and tortoises, the tuatara, and birds.

**Enter the Dinosaurs** A great adaptive radiation of reptiles continued through the Triassic and Jurassic Periods. Some ate plants; others were carnivorous. Fossils show that some lived in family groups and cared for eggs and young. Some dinosaurs even had feathers, which may have first served as a means of regulating body temperature. The evolutionary lineage that led to modern birds came from one group of feathered dinosaurs.

**Exit the Dinosaurs** The Cretaceous Period ended with a mass extinction during which most dinosaurs disappeared, along with many other animal and plant groups. This extinction was probably caused by a combination of natural disasters, including massive and widespread volcanic eruptions, a fall in sea level, and a huge asteroid smashing into what is now the Yucatán Peninsula in Mexico.

**Birds** A series of well-preserved ancient birds and feathered dinosaurs has "connected the dots" between modern birds and their dinosaur ancestors. Look at **Figure 24-18**, and you will see that modern birds form a clade within the clade containing dinosaurs. Because dinosaurs are part of a larger clade of reptiles, modern birds are also reptiles. The first birdlike fossil discovered was *Archaeopteryx* (ahr kee AHP tur iks), from about 150 million years ago during the late Jurassic. *Archaeopteryx* looked so much like a small, running dinosaur that it would be classified as a dinosaur except for its highly evolved feathers. Characteristics of birds include feathers; strong, lightweight bones; two scale-covered legs used for walking or perching; and front limbs modified into wings. Birds also are endotherms. Other living reptiles are almost all ectotherms.

### Analyzing Data

## Feather Evolution

The information in the table shows the evolution of feathers in some groups of dinosaurs that preceded modern birds.

| Group (listed alphabetically) | Feather Status |
|---|---|
| Allosaurs | None |
| *Archaeopteryx* | Flight feathers |
| Compsognathids | Hairlike feathers |
| Oviraptors | True feathers |
| Tyrannosaurs | Branched feathers |

1. **Develop Models** Use the information in the table to place these traits correctly on a cladogram. (**Hint:** Use Figure 24-18 as a guide.)

2. **Draw Conclusions** Which type of feathers would you expect modern birds to possess?

Short-beaked echidna

Female opossum carrying young

Sika deer doe with newborn fawn

**Mammals** Members of the clade Mammalia include about 5000 species that range in size from mice to whales and that share characteristics, including mammary glands, which produce milk to nourish young, and hair. Mammals breathe air, have four-chambered hearts, and are endotherms.

*The First Mammals* True mammals first appeared during the late Triassic, about 220 million years ago. They were very small and resembled modern tree shrews. While dinosaurs ruled, mammals remained small and were probably active mostly at night. New fossils and DNA analyses suggest, however, that the first members of modern mammalian groups, including primates, rodents, and hoofed mammals, evolved during this period. After the great dinosaur extinction at the end of the Cretaceous, mammals underwent a long adaptive radiation. The Cenozoic Era, which began at the end of the Cretaceous, is often called the Age of Mammals.

*Modern Mammals* By the beginning of the Cenozoic, three major mammal groups had evolved—monotremes, marsupials, and placentals. These three groups differ in their means of reproduction and development.

The egg-laying monotremes, which exist today only in Australia and New Guinea, include the duckbill platypus and four species of echidnas. A short-beaked echidna is shown in **Figure 24-19**. Marsupials, which include kangaroos and koalas, bear live young that usually complete their development in an external pouch. Most familiar mammals are placental mammals, which have embryos that develop completely inside the mother.

**Figure 24-19**

**Mammals**

Modern mammals include monotremes, such as echidnas; marsupials, such as opossums; and placentals, such as deer.

HS-LS4-1

# ✓ LESSON 24.2 Review

## 🔍 KEY QUESTIONS

1. What two features define animal phyla?

2. According to fossil evidence, when did the first animals evolve?

3. Did true bones or lungs evolve first? Explain how Figure 24-11 shows the answer.

## CRITICAL THINKING

4. **Develop Models** Design a "new" invertebrate. Create an illustration on which you point out its body plan features. Then show its place on the cladogram of invertebrates, and write a caption explaining how its features helped you decide where it belongs.

5. **CASE STUDY** Corals live in a symbiotic relationship with photosynthetic algae. Based on what you know about photosynthesis and the needs of animals, how do you think this relationship benefits these cnidarians?

# Primate Evolution

Tarsiers, Chocolate Hills, Philippines

**KEY QUESTIONS**
- *What characteristics do all primates share?*
- *What are the major groups of primates?*
- *What adaptations enable later hominin species to walk upright?*
- *What is the current scientific thinking about the genus Homo?*

**HS-LS4-1:** Communicate scientific information that common ancestry and biological evolution are supported by multiple lines of empirical evidence.

**VOCABULARY**
hominoid
opposable thumb
bipedal

**READING TOOL**

Use the timeline in your
📖 Biology Foundations
Workbook to identify in
which order each species of
primate developed.

 **VIDEO**

Travel to Kenya to learn
about baboons.

Human beings are part of the family of primates. Primates are intelligent and social creatures who exhibit complex behaviors. Many primates live in tropical and subtropical regions and are well adapted to living in trees, but humans are an exception to this.

## What Is a Primate?

Primates, including lemurs, monkeys, and apes, share several adaptations for a life spent in trees. 🔑 *In general, a primate is a mammal with relatively long fingers, toes with nails instead of claws, arms that can rotate around shoulder joints, a strong clavicle, binocular vision, and a well-developed cerebrum.*

**Fingers, Toes, and Shoulders** Primates typically have five flexible fingers and toes on each hand or foot that can curl to grip objects firmly and precisely. Most primates also have thumbs and big toes that can move against the other digits. Primates' arms are well suited for climbing because they can rotate in broad circles around a strong shoulder joint attached to a strong collarbone, or clavicle.

**Binocular Vision** Both eyes of many primates face forward, with overlapping fields of view that provide excellent binocular vision. This offers depth perception and a three-dimensional view of the world—a handy thing to have for judging the locations of tree branches, from which many primates swing.

**Well-Developed Cerebrum** In primates, the "thinking" part of the brain—the cerebrum—is large and intricate, enabling complex behaviors. Many primate species create elaborate social systems that include extended families, adoption of orphans, and even warfare between rival troops.

# Evolution of Primates

Humans and other primates evolved from a common ancestor that lived more than 65 million years ago. Early on, primates split into two groups, as shown in **Figure 24-20**. 🔍 *Primates in one group, which contains the lemurs and lorises, don't look much like typical monkeys. The other group includes tarsiers and the anthropoids, or humanlike primates.*

**Lemurs and Lorises** With few exceptions, lemurs and lorises are small and nocturnal. They have large eyes adapted to seeing in the dark and long snouts. Living members include the bush babies of Africa, the lemurs of Madagascar, and the lorises of Asia.

**Tarsiers and Anthropoids** Primates more closely related to humans than to lemurs belong to a different group, members of which have broader faces and widely separated nostrils. This group includes the tarsiers of Asia and the anthropoids. Anthropoids split into two groups around 45 million years ago, as the continents on which they lived moved apart.

*New World Monkeys* Members of one anthropoid branch, the New World monkeys, are found in Central and South America. (Europeans called the Americas the "New World.") Members of this group, which include spider monkeys and squirrel monkeys, live mainly in trees. They have long flexible arms that help them swing from branch to branch. They also have a long prehensile tail that can coil tightly around a branch to serve as a "fifth hand."

*Old World Monkeys and Great Apes* The other anthropoid branch, which evolved in Africa and Asia, includes Old World monkeys and great apes. Old World monkeys, such as langurs and macaques, spend time in trees but lack prehensile tails. Great apes, also called **hominoids**, include gibbons, orangutans, gorillas, chimpanzees, and humans. Recent DNA analyses confirm that among the great apes, chimpanzees are humans' closest living relatives.

**READING TOOL**

As you read about primate evolution, use the cladogram in Figure 24-20 to identify and compare the groups.

**INTERACTIVITY**

Investigate the evolution of primates.

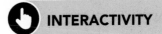
**INTERACTIVITY**

Figure 24-20
**Cladogram of Primates**

The diagram illustrates current hypotheses about evolutionary relationships among modern primates.

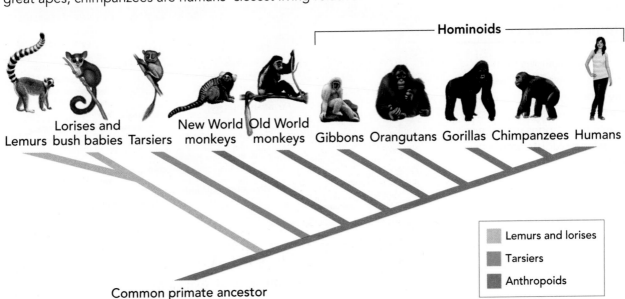

Lorises and Lemurs bush babies · Tarsiers · New World monkeys · Old World monkeys · Gibbons · Orangutans · Gorillas · Chimpanzees · Humans

Hominoids

Common primate ancestor

- Lemurs and lorises
- Tarsiers
- Anthropoids

# Hominin Evolution

Between 6 and 7 million years ago, hominins, the lineage that includes modern humans and closely related species, split from the lineage that led to chimpanzees. Hominins evolved grasping thumbs and large brains. 🔍 *The skull, neck, spinal column, hip bones, and leg bones of early hominin species changed shape in ways that enabled later species to walk upright.* Hominins also evolved an **opposable thumb** that could touch other fingertips, enabling them to grasp objects and use tools.

In addition, hominins evolved much larger brains. The brains of chimpanzees range in volume from 280 to 450 cubic centimeters. Our brains, on the other hand, range from 1200 to 1600 cubic centimeters! Most differences in brain size between species result from a greatly expanded cerebrum.

**Hominin Relationships** Most paleontologists agree that the hominin fossil record includes seven genera—*Sahelanthropus, Orrorin, Ardipithecus, Australopithecus, Paranthropus, Kenyanthropus,* and *Homo*—at least 20 species, and a few subspecies. All these hominin species are *relatives* of modern humans, but not all are human *ancestors*. To understand that distinction, think of your family. Your aunts, uncles, cousins, parents, grandparents, and great-grandparents are all your relatives. But only parents, grandparents, and great-grandparents are your ancestors.

Distinguishing hominin relatives from ancestors is an ongoing challenge. Researchers once thought that human evolution took place in simple steps in which hominin species evolved more human-like traits over time. But it is now clear that hominin adaptive radiations produced a number of species whose relationships are not at all clear. At present, there is no single, universally accepted hypothesis about the hominin family tree, so **Figure 24-21** presents current data in the form of a timeline, rather than as a cladogram.

## INTERACTIVITY

Explore the traits that distinguish primates from one another.

**Figure 24-21**

## Hominin Time Line

The diagram shows hominin species known from fossils and the time ranges during which each species probably existed. These time ranges may change as paleontologists gather new data.

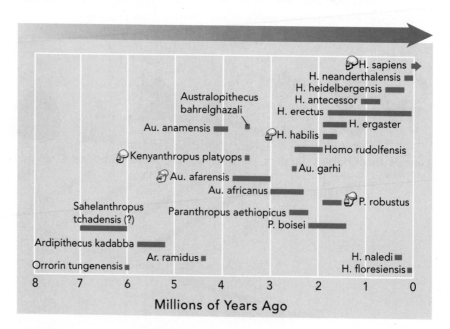

**New Findings and New Questions** The study of human ancestors, which now includes both traditional studies of fossils and DNA analysis, is constantly changing. Since the 1990s, fossil discoveries more than doubled the number of known hominin species. The oldest hominin may be *Sahelanthropus*, known from a skull roughly 7 million years old that was discovered in 2002. Scientists still debate whether *Sahelanthropus* was a hominin, and how it and other fossil hominins are related to one another, and to humans. Exciting breakthroughs in recovery and analysis of ancient DNA have recently made it possible to piece together significant amounts of genetic material from some hominin fossils. Researchers are now comparing those partial genomes with each other, and with modern human DNA. Early results suggest strongly that at least one, and possibly three other species in the genus *Homo* interbred with each other and with the ancestors of modern humans! Stay tuned for further developments!

*Australopithecus* The genus *Australopithecus* lived from about 4 million to about 1.5 million years ago. They were **bipedal** apes, which means they walked on two feet. Their skeletons suggest that they probably spent time in trees. Their tooth structure suggests a diet rich in fruit. The best-known species is *Australopithecus afarensis*, which lived from roughly 4 million to 2.5 million years ago. Other fossils of this genus indicate that males were much larger than females. The best-known *A. afarensis* specimen is a female nicknamed "Lucy," discovered in 1974, and shown in **Figure 24-22**. Lucy stood about 1 meter tall and lived about 3.2 million years ago.

In 2006, an Ethiopian researcher announced the discovery of well-preserved 3.3-million-year-old fossils of a young female hominin. This fossil was assigned to *A. afarensis*, the same species as Lucy, and nicknamed "the Dikika Baby," after the region in Africa where it was discovered. Leg bones confirmed that the Dikika Baby walked bipedally, while her arm and shoulder bones suggest that she would have been a better climber than modern humans.

# The Road to Modern Humans

Hominins that we have discussed so far lived millions of years before modern humans. ⚷ *Many species in our genus existed before Homo sapiens, and at least three other Homo species existed alongside early humans at the same time.* Paleontologists still don't fully understand the evolutionary and genetic relationships among species in our genus.

**Figure 24-22**
## Lucy and the Dikika Baby

"Lucy" and "the Dikika Baby" are nicknames of two very important fossils of the hominin *A. afarensis*. These two fossils were discovered just 6 miles apart in Ethiopia.

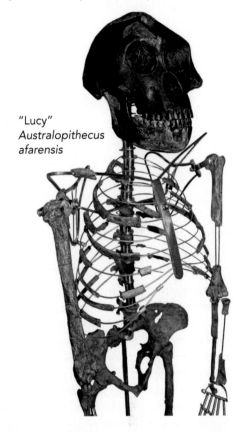

"Lucy"
*Australopithecus afarensis*

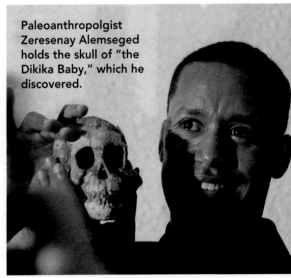

Paleoanthropolgist Zeresenay Alemseged holds the skull of "the Dikika Baby," which he discovered.

## BUILD VOCABULARY

**Multiple Meanings** The prefix *homo-* can mean "alike," as in *homologous* or *homogenous*. This prefix has Greek origins. In this lesson, *Homo*, which has a Latin origin, refers to the genus for humans.

**The Genus *Homo*** About 2 million years ago, a new group of hominin species appeared in the fossil record. Several resemble modern humans closely enough to be classified in the genus *Homo*. One set of fossils was found with tools made of stone and bone, so it was named *Homo habilis*, which means "handy man" in Latin. The earliest fossils most researchers definitely assign to the genus *Homo* have been called *Homo ergaster*. *H. ergaster* was larger than *H. habilis* and had a bigger brain and downward-facing nostrils that resemble those of modern humans. *Homo rudolfensis* appeared before *H. ergaster*, but some researchers choose to classify it in the genus *Australopithecus* instead of *Homo*.

**Homo naledi** In 2015, researchers announced the discovery of an astonishing collection of hominin remains in a cave near Johannesburg, South Africa. This fossil treasure-trove included several remarkably complete skeletons from several small-brained hominins with a confusing mix of ape-like and human-like characteristics. These specimens have been named *Homo naledi*.

**Homo neanderthalensis (or *H. sapiens neanderthalensis*)** Neanderthals—which some scientists consider a separate species, and others consider a sub-species of *H. sapiens*—flourished in Europe and western Asia beginning about 200,000 years ago. Evidence suggests that they made stone tools, lived in complex social groups, had controlled use of fire, and were excellent hunters. They buried their dead with simple rituals. Individuals whose fossils have been identified as Neanderthals survived in parts of Europe until about 28,000 to 24,000 years ago.

**Out of Africa—But When and Who?** Researchers agree that our genus originated in Africa and migrated from there to populate the world. But several questions remain about the evolution and migrations of species within our genus. Some of those questions have been complicated by recent genetic evidence for interbreeding among early humans and their relatives. You can explore some current hypotheses with **Figure 24-23**.

### Figure 24-23
### Out of Africa

Data show that relatives and ancestors of modern humans left Africa in waves. But when—and how far did they travel? By comparing the mitochondrial DNA of living humans and continuing to study the fossil record, scientists hope to improve our understanding of the complex history of *Homo sapiens*. (Note: The skull symbol represents any hominin fossils found—they might not have included skulls.)

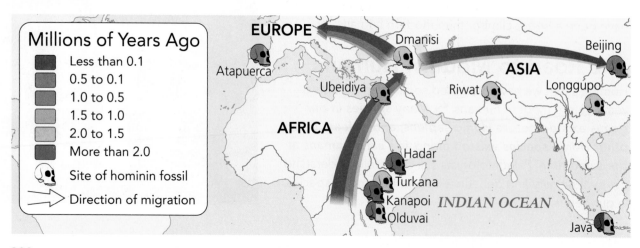

**Millions of Years Ago**

- Less than 0.1
- 0.5 to 0.1
- 1.0 to 0.5
- 1.5 to 1.0
- 2.0 to 1.5
- More than 2.0
- Site of hominin fossil
- Direction of migration

Fossil and molecular evidence both suggest that some hominins left Africa long before *Homo sapiens* evolved. It also appears that several *Homo species* made the trip later, in waves. Experts differ about the identity of some fossils, but agree that hominins began leaving Africa at least 1.8 million years ago.

**Homo erectus in Asia** According to some researchers, groups of *Homo erectus* left Africa and traveled across India and China to Southeast Asia. In fact, some of the oldest specimens of *H. erectus* were uncovered on the Indonesian island of Java. This suggests that these ancient wanderers spread rapidly once they left Africa.

**The First Homo sapiens** Paleontologists debate where and when *Homo sapiens* arose. The multiregional hypothesis suggests that modern humans evolved independently, in several places, from separated *H. erectus* populations. Still-emerging genetic evidence suggests that some differences among populations of modern humans can be traced back to interbreeding among hominin species and different groups of ancient humans. The "out-of-Africa" hypothesis proposes that modern humans evolved in Africa about 200,000 years ago, migrated through the Middle East, and replaced descendants of earlier hominin species.

Molecular biologists have analyzed mitochondrial DNA from living humans around the world to determine when we last shared a common ancestor. The estimated date for that African common ancestor is between 200,000 and 150,000 years ago. More recent DNA data suggest that a subset of those African ancestors left northeastern Africa between 65,000 and 50,000 years ago.

**Modern Humans** Homo sapiens with modern skeletons arrived in the Middle East about 100,000 years ago. By about 50,000 years ago, they were using sophisticated tools of stone, bones, and antlers. They produced cave paintings, and buried their dead with rituals. In other words, these people, began to behave like modern humans. Neanderthals and *H. sapiens* lived side by side for thousands of years. Researchers once thought that Neanderthals disappeared. More recent genetic evidence suggests Neanderthals interbred with *H. sapiens* ... and survive today as parts of our modern human genomes! For whatever reason, our species, *Homo sapiens*, is the only surviving member of the once large and diverse hominin clade.

HS-LS4-1

## ☑ LESSON 24.3 Review

### ⚲ KEY QUESTIONS

1. How do the characteristics of primates help them to survive in their environment?

2. At what point did the two groups of anthropoids split, and why?

3. How was bipedal locomotion important to hominin evolution?

4. List other *Homo* species that existed at the same time as *Homo sapiens*.

### CRITICAL THINKING

5. Compare and Contrast How are modern humans similar to other primates? What traits set humans apart?

# Social Interactions and Group Behavior

## ⚲ KEY QUESTIONS

- *How can behavior serve as an adaptation that affects reproductive success?*
- *What are the major types of learning?*
- *How do periodic environmental changes affect behavior?*
- *How can social behaviors increase evolutionary fitness?*
- *How do animals communicate?*

**HS-LS2-8:** Evaluate the evidence for the role of group behavior on individual and species' chances to survive and reproduce.

**HS-LS4-4:** Construct an explanation based on evidence for how natural selection leads to adaptation of populations.

### VOCABULARY
behavior
society
kin selection
communication
language

### READING TOOL

Compare and contrast the similarities and differences among each type of social interaction. List them in your 🗐 Biology Foundations Workbook.

Outside a seaside restaurant, a young tourist eats a hamburger, unaware that he's being watched—by an iguana. When the boy spots the iguana, he jumps up onto his chair with a shriek. But the iguana, a shy, tree-dwelling vegetarian, ignores the boy. She rushes for some French fries that were knocked to the ground. Iguanas don't normally approach humans. But this one has learned that getting close to humans can provide access to food.

## Behavior and Evolution

The hungry iguana is demonstrating **behavior**, a response to stimuli in the environment. Although many behaviors are triggered by an external stimulus, an individual's response to that stimulus often depends on its internal condition. If the iguana hadn't been hungry, for example, it would probably have kept its distance from the boy and his French fries!

You've learned how physical characteristics, including the nervous system, are shaped by genetic instructions. So, it shouldn't surprise you to learn that some behaviors are also influenced by genes, can be inherited, and can therefore evolve in response to natural selection. For example, genes that code for the behavior of the moth in **Figure 24-24** help the moth escape predators. ⚲ *If a behavior influenced by genes serves as an adaptation that increases an individual's fitness, that behavior will tend to spread through a population.*

How do newly hatched birds know to beg for food moments after hatching? How does a spider know how to spin its web? These innate behaviors, also called instincts, appear in fully functional form the first time they are performed, without any previous experience.

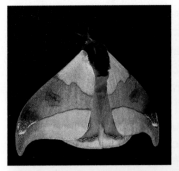

**Figure 24-24**
## Anti-Predatory Display

Moths of the genus *Automeris* normally rest with the front wings over their hind wings. If disturbed, however, the moth will move its front wings to expose a striking circular pattern on its hind wings. This behavior may scare off predators that mistake the moth's hind-wing pattern for the eyes of a predatory owl, such as the great horned owl.

# Learned Behavior

Many complex animals live in unpredictable environments where fitness can depend on behaviors that can be changed as a result of experience, or what we call learning. ✎ *Four major types of learning that scientists have identified are habituation, insight learning, classical conditioning, and operant conditioning.*

**Habituation** The simplest type of learning is habituation, a process by which an animal decreases or stops responding to stimuli that neither rewards nor harms it. Consider the common shore ragworm, which lives in a sandy tube that it leaves to feed. If a shadow passes overhead, the worm will instantly retreat to the safety of its burrow. Yet if repeated shadows pass, the worm will learn that the shadow is neither food nor threat and stop responding. The worm will have become habituated to the stimulus.

**Insight Learning** The most complicated form of learning is insight learning, or reasoning, which occurs when an animal applies something it has already learned to a new situation. For instance, if you are given a new math problem on an exam, you may apply principles you have already learned to solve it. Insight learning is common among humans and some other primates. It may occur in birds and might possibly occur in some octopuses.

**READING TOOL**

As you read about the types of learned behaviors, make a list of examples of your own experiences of learning or of your observations of young children or pets.

▶ **VIDEO**

Learn how turkeys became domesticated.

## Figure 24-25
### Operant Conditioning

After this dog randomly picked up its leash, its owner took it for a walk. This reinforced the behavior. The dog now picks up its leash when it wants to go for a walk—and its owner is similarly trained to attach the leash and take the dog out, lest the dog resort to less positive means of communicating.

**INTERACTIVITY**

Explore the migration patterns of bats.

**Classical Conditioning** One evening, you eat a kind of food you've never tried before. Shortly after eating it, you get sick from a stomach virus. You feel better the next day, but when your parents present you with leftovers of the same food, you feel sick again. From that time on, whenever you smell that particular food, you become nauseated. This is an example of classical conditioning, a form of learning in which a certain stimulus comes to produce a particular response, usually through association with a positive or negative experience. In this case, the stimulus is the smell of that particular food, and the response is nausea. The food didn't make you sick, but you've been conditioned to associate the smell of that food with feeling sick.

**Operant Conditioning** Operant conditioning occurs when an animal learns to behave in a certain way to receive a reward or to avoid punishment. Operant conditioning was first described by the American psychologist B. F. Skinner. Skinner invented a procedure using what is called a "Skinner box," which contains a button or lever that delivers a food reward when pressed. After an animal is rewarded several times, it learns that it gets food whenever it presses the button or lever. At this point, the animal has learned by operant conditioning how to obtain food. In **Figure 24-25**, you can see how a dog can be trained to constructively communicate its desire to go for a walk.

## Behavioral Cycles

Animals, including humans, do not behave in the same way at all times or in all places. We are affected by our environment, which is often changing. *Many animals respond to periodic environmental changes with daily or seasonal behavioral cycles.* Behavioral cycles that occur daily are called circadian rhythms. Other cycles are seasonal. In temperate and polar ecosystems, many species enter a sleeplike state, or hibernation, during winter. This behavioral and physiological adaptation allows organisms to survive periods when food and other resources may not be available.

Another seasonal behavior is migration, the seasonal movement from one environment to another. For example, many songbirds travel to warm tropical regions where food remains available during northern winters. When these birds fly north in the spring, they take advantage of seasonally abundant food and find space to nest and raise their young.

✓**READING CHECK** Compare How do hibernation and migration differ from circadian rhythms?

### The Role of Group Behavior

**Problem** How can group behaviors help animals survive?

In this lab, you will develop and use a model to demonstrate how group behavior can help prey avoid attacks from predators. Then you will use the model to present an explanation for how group behaviors affect an animal's chances to survive and reproduce, and how these behaviors became common in animal populations.

You can find this lab in your digital course.

# Social Behavior

Whenever birds sing, bighorn sheep butt heads, or chimpanzees groom each other, they are engaging in social behavior. Social behaviors include courtship, territoriality, aggression, and the formation of societies. 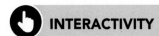 *Social behaviors, such as choosing mates, defending territories or resources, and forming social groups, can increase evolutionary fitness.*

**Courtship** Members of sexually reproducing animal species must locate and mate with other members of their species to reproduce. Courtship is behavior during which members of one sex (usually males) advertise their willingness to mate, and members of the opposite sex (usually females) choose which mate they will accept. Typically, males send out signals that include sounds, visual displays, or chemicals, which attract females. The musical trill of a tree frog, for example, is a breeding call. In some species, courtship involves an elaborate series of behaviors, called rituals, that consist of specific signals and responses that continue until mating occurs. For example, gannets bond by engaging in "beak pointing," or intertwining their necks while pointing their beaks to the sky. Other birds dance for each other, as shown in **Figure 24-26**.

**Territoriality and Aggression** Many animals occupy and defend a specific area, or territory, that contains resources, such as food, water, nesting sites, shelter, and potential mates. If a rival enters a territory, the "owner" attacks in an effort to drive the rival away. While competing for resources, animals often show aggressive, threatening behaviors used to exert dominance. Fights between male sea lions over territory and "harems" of females often leave both rivals bloodied.

> **INTERACTIVITY**
>
> Investigate the social behavior of various animals.

**Figure 24-26**

## Courtship

Male and female cranes perform a dance for each other as a form of courtship.

**INTERACTIVITY**

Figure 24-27

## Animal Societies

As these African wild dog pups play, they reinforce social bonds that grow into mature social behaviors. Honeybees have extremely complex societies, in which worker bees cooperate to perform complex tasks ranging from finding food to building honeycombs.

## BUILD VOCABULARY

**Use Prior Knowledge** The word *society* is used to describe interactions within human communities. Many animal societies involve close interactions and cooperation.

**Animal Societies** A society is a group of animals of the same species that interact closely and often cooperate. Societies can offer a range of advantages that can produce differential reproductive success between group members and individuals. Zebras, for example, are safer from predators when they are part of a group than when they are alone. Societies can also improve animals' ability to hunt, to protect their territory, to guard their young, or to fight with rivals. In wild African dog packs, for instance, adult females take turns guarding all the pups in the pack, while the other adults hunt for prey. Macaque, baboon, and other primate societies hunt together, travel in search of new territory, and interact with neighboring societies.

Members of a society are often related to one another. Elephant herds, for example, consist of mothers, aunts, and their offspring. (Males are kicked out when they reach puberty.) The theory of **kin selection** holds that helping relatives can improve an individual's evolutionary fitness because related individuals share a large proportion of their genes. Helping a relative survive, therefore, increases the chance that the genes an individual shares with that relative will be passed along to offspring.

The most extreme examples of relatedness, and the most complex animal societies (other than human societies), are found among social insects such as ants, bees, and wasps. In social insect colonies, all individuals cooperate to perform extraordinary feats, such as building complex nests. In a bee colony, such as the one in **Figure 24-27**, all workers in the colony are females who are very closely related—which means that they share a large proportion of each others' genes. Worker bees are also sterile. For this reason, it is advantageous for them to cooperate to help their "mother" (the queen) reproduce and raise their "sisters" (other workers). Male bees function only to fertilize the queen.

# Communication

Because social behavior involves more than one individual, it requires **communication**—the passing of information from one individual to another. Communication is an important adaptation among many species. ⚓ *Animals may use a variety of signals to communicate, including visual signals, chemical signals, sound, and language.* See the examples shown in **Figure 24-28**.

**Visual Signals** Many animals use visual signals, and they have eyes that sense shapes and colors. In many species, males and females have different color patterns, and males use color displays to advertise their readiness to mate.

**Chemical Signals** Many animals have well-developed senses of smell, and they communicate with chemical signals. Some animals, including lampreys, bees, and ants, release chemical messengers called pheromones that affect the behavior of other individuals of the same species. Pheromones could be used to mark a territory or signal a readiness to mate.

**Sound Signals** Many species make and detect sounds, and some have evolved elaborate systems of communication. Dolphins communicate using sound signals that travel long distances. Elephants, and some other animals, can send messages through the ground, or through water, that recipients feel rather than hear.

**Language** The most complicated form of communication is **language**—a system that combines sounds, symbols, and gestures according to rules about sequence and meaning, such as grammar and syntax. Many animals, including elephants, primates, and dolphins, have complex communication systems. Some seem to have "words"—calls with specific meanings, such as "lions on the prowl." Many species, including honeybees, convey complex information using various kinds of signals. However, untrained animals don't seem to use the rules of grammar and syntax that we use to define human language.

Visual Signal

Chemical Signal

Sound Signal

Language

**Figure 24-28**
## Communication Signals

Animals use many strategies to send and receive messages.

HS-LS2-8, HS-LS4-4

 **LESSON 24.4 Review**

### ⚓ KEY QUESTIONS

1. How does natural selection affect behavior?

2. Give one example of how humans might learn through classical conditioning.

3. Name two ways in which animal behavior is related to environmental cycles.

4. How does membership in a society increase the evolutionary fitness of individuals in the society?

5. What are the main ways in which animals communicate with one another?

### CRITICAL THINKING

6. **Apply Scientific Reasoning** Explain two ways that an animal's social behavior can influence its evolutionary fitness.

# How are reefs affected by global change?

**As atmospheric carbon dioxide concentrations increase, both air and water temperatures also increase, and the ocean becomes more acidic. What other aspects of global change affect reefs?**

HS-LS2-7, HS-LS4-3, HS-LS4-6, HS-ESS2-4, HS-ESS3-5, CCSS.ELA-LITERACY.RST.9-10.1, CCSS.ELA-LITERACY.RST.9-10.2, CCSS.ELA-LITERACY.WHST.9-10.2, CCSS.ELA-LITERACY.WHST.9-10.7, CCSS.ELA-LITERACY.WHST.9-10.8, CCSS.ELA-LITERACY.WHST.9-10.9

## Make Your Case

Each clade of animals has evolved a range of physical, physiological, and behavioral adaptations that allow them to "make a living" and maintain homeostasis in the environments they inhabit. When environmental conditions change slowly, some populations can adapt. If conditions change too rapidly, species are stressed and can go extinct. And, if a keystone species or group of species such as corals goes extinct, entire ecosystems can collapse.

## Construct an Explanation

1. **Conduct Research** Find out what is happening to coral reefs around the world as oceans warm and become more acidic. Then search for various ways that other forms of human-caused global change are affecting reef ecosystems. Include at least three additional factors.

2. **Defend Your Claim** Compare what we know about the ways corals and coral reefs respond to these changes with what scientists think happened to rudists and their ancient reefs. What other clades of organisms are involved? Propose a hypothesis about the future of coral reefs. Gather further information about global change and its effects to defend your explanation.

A healthy reef is home to a diverse animal community. Bleached coral is all that remains of this reef (inset).

## Careers on the Case

### Work Toward a Solution

People in all sorts of careers are studying climate change and its wide-ranging effects. Some scientists are investigating ways to slow or stop climate change, or even reverse it. Others are working to manage its effects, including those on wildlife.

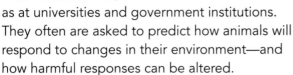

Jane Goodall

### Ethologist

Ethology is the study of animal behavior. Experts in ethology work at zoos and wildlife sanctuaries, as well as at universities and government institutions. They often are asked to predict how animals will respond to changes in their environment—and how harmful responses can be altered.

**▶ VIDEO**

Watch this video to learn about other careers in biology.

hhmi | **BioInteractive**

## Society on the Case

### A Helping Hand to Wildlife

Climate change is arguably the most serious long-term threat to wildlife. It certainly is not the only threat. Human activities that threaten wild animals include cutting down forests, draining wetlands, and letting cities and suburbs expand into wilderness regions. Pollution also takes its toll on wildlife, as does overhunting and overfishing.

The good news is that everyone can take actions to help wildlife. Here are a few simple things you can do that can make a difference.

**Conserve Energy, Fresh Water, and Other Resources** Conserving all resources helps wildlife and people worldwide. The use of fossil fuels contributes to climate change, so reducing their use is a small step in the right direction.

**Eat Sustainable Food** A sustainable practice is able to last for many years. Some animal foods, especially many seafoods, might not be available in the future if their current rates of harvest continue. Begin by learning more about the foods you eat. Try to eat foods raised locally on small farms.

**Visit a Zoo or an Aquarium** Part of your admission fee to these places is used to support wildlife conservation around the world. You also will learn more about wildlife and how you can help wildlife in your community.

**Care for the Animals Near You** Look for easy ways to protect wildlife in your neighborhood. A statue of an eagle or owl can keep birds from crashing into windows. Keeping your cat indoors can protect young birds, snakes, and other prey.

# Lesson Review

Go to your Biology Foundations Workbook for longer versions of these lesson summaries.

## 24.1 Introduction to Animals

Animals are multicellular, heterotrophic, eukaryotic organisms, with cells that lack cell walls. Animals can be grouped into two large groups: invertebrates and chordates. Invertebrates include all animals that lack a backbone, or vertebral column. All chordates exhibit four characteristics during at least one stage of life: a dorsal, hollow nerve cord; a notochord; a tail that extends beyond the anus; and pharyngeal pouches.

Like all organisms, animals must keep their internal environment relatively stable, in a process known as homeostasis. Animals maintain homeostasis by gathering and responding to information, obtaining and distributing oxygen and nutrients, and collecting and eliminating carbon dioxide and other wastes. They must also reproduce.

Each animal phylum has a unique organization of particular body structures that is often referred to as its body plan. Features of animal body plans include levels of organization, body symmetry, formation of body cavities, patterns of embryological development, segmentation, cephalization, and limb formation.

- invertebrate
- chordate
- vertebrate
- feedback inhibition
- radial symmetry
- bilateral symmetry
- zygote
- coelom
- cephalization

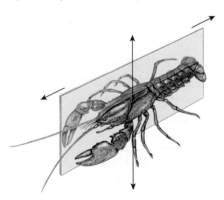

✓**Use Visuals** Discuss how the features of animal body plans relate to this visual.

## 24.2 Animal Evolution and Diversity

Animal clades are typically defined according to adult body plans and patterns of embryological development.

The fossil record indicates that the first animals began evolving long before the Cambrian Explosion. The cladogram of invertebrates presents current hypotheses about evolutionary relationships among major groups of modern invertebrates. It also indicates the sequence in which some important features evolved.

The chordate cladogram presents current hypotheses about evolutionary relationships among chordate groups. It also shows at which points important vertebrate features, such as jaws and limbs, evolved.

- cartilage
- tetrapod

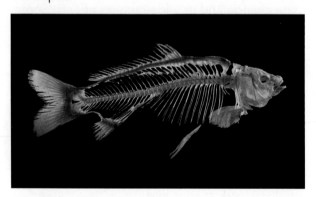

✓**Interpret Photos** What new adaptation led to the success of the bony fishes?

## 24.3 Primate Evolution

In general, a primate is a mammal with relatively long fingers, toes with nails instead of claws, arms that can rotate around shoulder joints, a strong clavicle, binocular vision, and a well-developed cerebrum.

Primates are often divided into two groups. Primates in one group look very little like typical monkeys and include lemurs and lorises. The other group includes tarsiers and the anthropoids. The anthropoids is the group that includes monkeys and apes, including humans.

The skull, neck, spinal column, hip bones, and leg bones of early hominin species changed shape in ways that enabled later species to walk upright.

Many species in our genus existed before our species, *Homo sapiens*, appeared in the fossil record. Furthermore, at least three other *Homo* species existed at the same time as early humans.

- hominoid
- opposable thumb
- bipedal

## 24.4 Social Interactions and Group Behavior

If a behavior influenced by genes serves as an adaptation that increases an individual's fitness, that behavior will tend to spread through a population.

Four types of learning that scientists have identified are habituation, insight learning, classical conditioning, and operant conditioning.

Many animals respond to periodic environmental changes with daily or seasonal behavior cycles.

Social behaviors, such as choosing mates, defending territories or resources, and forming social groups, can increase evolutionary fitness.

Animals may use a variety of signals to communicate.

- behavior
- society
- kin selection
- communication
- language

☑**Construct an Explanation** How do bee colonies increase the chance of survival for the bees that are part of the colony?

Lorises and Lemurs bush babies  Tarsiers  New World monkeys  Old World monkeys  Gibbons  Orangutans  Gorillas  Chimpanzees  Humans

Common primate ancestor

- Lemurs and lorises
- Tarsiers
- Anthropoids

☑**Develop Models** Add nodes to this primate cladogram to represent prehensile tail and bipedal locomotion.

# Organize Information

Complete the table to describe the evolution of these vertebrate groups.

| Group | Sharks and Rays | Bony Fishes | Amphibians | Reptiles | Birds | Mammals |
|---|---|---|---|---|---|---|
| Defining Character | Jaws | 1. | 2. | 3. | 4. | 5. |

# Safe Crossings
## for Wildlife

## Construct a Solution

HS-LS2-7, HS-LS4-6, HS-ETS1-2, HS-ETS1-3, CCSS.ELA-LITERACY.RST.9-10.3, CCSS.ELA-LITERACY.WHST.9-10.2, CCSS.ELA-LITERACY.WHST.9-10.7

**STEM** ▶ Roads and highways pose many threats to wild animals. Roadways cause habitat loss and habitat fragmentation. When wild animals follow or cross the roads to obtain necessary resources in other areas, they put their lives and the lives of motorists at risk. Fatal collisions are not uncommon. All of these factors can lead to a decrease in animal populations and the loss of biological diversity in an area.

In this activity, you will identify the criteria for and constraints on an animal crossing to be built on a new highway planned through your community. The highway will pass through a forest ecosystem, effectively dividing the forest into two parts. You will consider and evaluate competing design solutions that meet the criteria and account for the constraints, and then construct a model to show the design solution that you think is optimal.

1. **Specify Design Criteria** With other members of your group, agree on a list of criteria for and constraints on the animal crossing. Consider each of these properties:

   - The length of the crossing, which corresponds to the total width of the highway at the site of the crossing

   - The size of the forest ecosystem through which the highway passes

   - The types of animals that are predicted to use the crossing

   - The budget for constructing the animal crossing

   - The opinions and concerns of community members

2. **Design a Solution** With members of your group, discuss at least three different design solutions for the animal crossing. Draw simple sketches to illustrate each solution.

**3. Research a Problem** With members of your group, discuss the answers to the questions below. These questions will help you build a model that meets the criteria for and constraints on the animal crossing. Conduct research, if necessary, to help you develop or support your answers.

- What types of animal populations are found in your area?

- What behaviors or activity patterns do these animals have? Evaluate how to best accommodate their need to travel.

- Which design solution will be most likely to keep animals off the highway?

- For which solutions are the construction costs within the budget?

- Do any of the design solutions pose safety hazards, such as insufficient fencing, to animals or motorists? If so, how could the hazards be eliminated?

**4. Develop Models** With member of your group, decide which design is best. Work with group members to sketch your model for the animal crossing.

**5. Refine Your Plan** Revise the sketch of your animal crossing to include important details, such as its length and width; its height above the highway or distance below it; and components such as plantings, fences, and gates.

**6. Construct a Solution** Agree on roles for constructing the model. Different group members can construct each feature of the model, such as the framework for the crossing, the plants covering the crossing, and fences or other details. Or you may choose to work together on the entire model.

**7. Refine Your Plan** As you construct the model, refer to the detailed sketch as necessary. You may need to revise your sketch or your ideas. Or you may need to revise the list of materials you are using to build the model.

**8. Evaluate Your Plan** Evaluate the finished model against the list of criteria and constraints you had identified. If it fails to meet one of the criteria or to consider the constraints, revise your plans or the model.

## 🔍 KEY IDEAS AND TERMS

## 24.1 Introduction to Animals
### HS-LS1-1, HS-LS1-2, HS-LS1-3, HS-LS4-1

1. Which of the following is characteristic of all chordates but not found in invertebrates?
   a. a notochord
   b. four legs
   c. a circulatory system
   d. an exoskeleton

2. Animals that have a backbone, also called a vertebral column, are known as
   a. invertebrates.
   b. prokaryotes.
   c. homeostasis.
   d. vertebrates.

3. A concentration of sense organs and nerve cells in the anterior end of the body is known as
   a. fertilization.
   b. cephalization.
   c. symmetry.
   d. multicellularity.

4. List the characteristics shared by all members of the animal kingdom.

5. Describe how feedback inhibition works.

6. Explain why the term *invertebrate* may be a useful term but is not a true category in the system of classification.

7. The sea star below shows what kind of symmetry?

## 24.2 Animal Evolution and Diversity
### HS-LS4-1

8. The ancestors of many modern animal phyla first appeared during the
   a. Burgess Period.
   b. Precambrian Era.
   c. Cambrian Period.
   d. Ediacaran Period.

9. Most chordates that live on land have
   a. two limbs.
   b. four limbs.
   c. six limbs.
   d. eight limbs.

10. The evolution of jaws and paired fins was an important development during the rise of
    a. tunicates.
    b. lancelets.
    c. fishes.
    d. amphibians.

11. Name two body plan characteristics shared by arthropods and vertebrates.

12. What body plan features did Cambrian animals evolve that made them more likely to become fossils?

13. What is the single most important characteristic that separates birds from other living animals?

14. Which two major groups of fishes evolved from the early jawed fishes and still survive today?

15. Describe how the young of monotremes, marsupials, and placental mammals obtain nourishment.

## 24.3 Primate Evolution
### HS-LS4-1

16. Anthropoids include monkeys and
    a. lemurs.
    b. lorises.
    c. tarsiers.
    d. humans.

17. Which of the following is a characteristic specific to primates?
    a. body hair
    b. rotation at the shoulder joint
    c. notochord
    d. ability to control body temperature

18. How many hominin species exist today?
    a. one
    b. two
    c. nine
    d. twelve

19. What anatomical characteristic allows for the binocular vision that occurs in primates?

20. Describe the adaptations that make some primates successful tree dwellers.

21. List the unique characteristics of hominins. Give an example of a hominin.

## 24.4 Social Interactions and Group Behavior
### HS-LS2-8, HS-LS4-4

22. The way an organism reacts to stimuli in its environment is called
    a. behavior.
    b. learning.
    c. conditioning.
    d. imprinting.

23. Animal behaviors can evolve through natural selection because
    a. what an animal learns is incorporated into its genes.
    b. all behavior is completely the result of genes.
    c. all behavior is completely the result of environmental influences.
    d. genes that influence behavior that increases an individual's fitness can be passed on to the next generation.

24. Which of the following is NOT a type of social behavior?
    a. operant conditioning
    b. territoriality
    c. hunting in a pack
    d. courtship

25. Describe an example of a stimulus and a corresponding response in animal behavior.

26. What is operant conditioning?

27. What is kin selection?

## CRITICAL THINKING
### HS-LS1-2, HS-LS2-8, HS-LS4-1, HS-LS4-2

28. Classify What characteristics distinguish vertebrates from nonvertebrate chordates?

29. Cite Evidence Why is bilateral symmetry an important development in the evolution of animals? Cite evidence from the chapter to support your analysis.

30. Interpret Visuals List three primate characteristics shown by the monkey in the photo.

31. Design a Solution Describe how you could use operant conditioning to train a pet dog to complete a useful task.

32. Organize Data Rank the following developments in the order of their appearance during evolution: tissues, anus-first development, multicellularity, mouth-first development.

33. Form a Hypothesis Animals with radial symmetry, such as sea anemones, lack cephalization, while animals with bilateral symmetry have it. State a hypothesis that would explain this observation.

34. Construct an Explanation Which anatomical characteristics of nonvertebrate chordates suggest that, in terms of evolutionary relationships, these animals are more closely related to vertebrates than to other groups of animals? Draw evidence from the text to support your answer.

35. Synthesize Information Life on Earth began in water. What were some of the major adaptations that animals evolved that allowed them to survive out of water?

36. Infer A baby smiles when her mother comes near. Often, the baby is picked up and cuddled as a result of smiling. Explain what type of learning the baby is showing.

37. Form a Hypothesis Although the members of many animal species derive benefits from living in social groups, members of other species live alone. What might be some of the advantages of solitary living?

38. Construct an Explanation Because a highway has been constructed through a forest, many of the animals that once lived there have had to move to a different wooded area. Is their move an example of migration? Explain your answer.

39. Construct an Explanation Analyze and explain how aggression and territorial behavior are related.

# ☑ASSESSMENT

## CROSSCUTTING CONCEPTS

**40. Structure and Function** In what ways do the digestive and respiratory systems depend on the circulatory system to carry out the functions of obtaining nutrients and eliminating wastes?

**41. Cause and Effect** Describe generally how the nervous and musculoskeletal systems of a rabbit react when it sees a predator such as a coyote.

## MATH CONNECTIONS

## Analyze and Interpret Data

CCSS.MATH.CONTENT.MP2

Mice can learn to run through a maze to find a food reward. As they have more practice runs in the maze, they take fewer wrong turns and reach the food more quickly. Twelve mice are put in a maze once a day for 10 days. The mean of their times to reach the food is calculated and plotted as the red line below. The mice are then kept out of the maze for a month. The blue line shows the results of those later trials. Use the graph to answer questions 42–44.

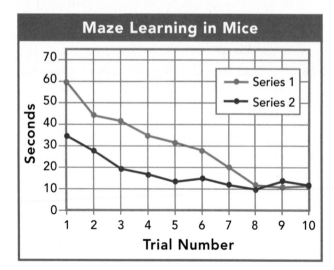

**42. Analyze Graphs** Explain what is happening after trial 8 on both sets of trials.

**43. Ask Questions** After the first set of trials, what kinds of questions might the experimenters have asked that resulted in their performing the second set of trials?

**44. Interpret Data** Explain the difference in the shapes of the graphs of the two trials.

The table shows the estimated numbers of living members of the reptile clade. Use the table to answer questions 45 to 48.

| Reptile Clade Diversity | |
|---|---|
| **Group** | **Estimated Number of Species** |
| Lizards and snakes | 8400 |
| Turtles and tortoises | 310 |
| Crocodilians | 23 |
| Tuataras | 2 |
| Birds | 10,000 |

**45. Graph** Construct a circle graph that presents the data in the table.

**46. Evaluate Information** What was your biggest challenge in representing these data in a circle graph?

**47. Analyze Data** Consider other methods of graphing data. Which type of graph might represent these data in a more helpful way?

**48. Graph** Graph these data using a method you would consider more helpful to a reader, or explain why none would be more helpful.

## LANGUAGE ARTS CONNECTION

## Write About Science

CCSS.ELA-LITERACY.WHST.9-10.2, CCSS.ELA-LITERACY.RST.9-10.7

**49. Write Procedures** Outline the steps of a procedure for classifying a vertebrate as a fish, an amphibian, a reptile, a bird, or a mammal.

**50. Write Technical Processes** Choose one of the cladograms presented in the chapter. Write a paragraph that describes the evolutionary relationships that the cladogram defines.

## Read About Science

CCSS.ELA-LITERACY.RST.9-10.2, CCSS.ELA-LITERACY.RST.9-10.7

**51. Determine Central Ideas** Describe how animals have achieved diversity through segmentation and cephalization.

1. Scientists use cladograms like this one to illustrate evolutionary relationships.

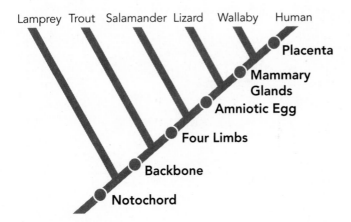

Lamprey Trout Salamander Lizard Wallaby Human

Placenta

Mammary Glands

Amniotic Egg

Four Limbs

Backbone

Notochord

Based on the cladogram, which anatomical feature do modern humans and trout share with a common ancestor?
A. Notochord
B. Placenta
C. Four limbs
D. Amniotic egg
E. Mammary glands

2. Fossil records provide evidence for the scientific theory of evolution. Based on the fossil record, which is the correct order for the appearance of bone, jaws, notochords, and vertebrae in chordate evolution?
A. bone, notochord, jaws, vertebrae
B. bone, notochord, vertebrae, jaws
C. notochord, bone, vertebrae, jaws
D. notochord, vertebrae, jaws, bones
E. vertebrae, notochord, bones, jaws

3. Between 6 and 7 million years ago, the lineage that led to hominins split from the lineage that led to chimpanzees. Which of the following best describes one of the ways hominins evolved?
A. Hominins evolved a smaller skull and smaller brain capable of designing tools.
B. Hominins evolved an opposable thumb that enabled hands to grasp objects.
C. Hominins evolved shoulder bones that enabled them to walk faster on all four limbs.
D. Hominins evolved more chromosomes that enabled them to reason and solve problems.
E. Hominins evolved forward-facing eyes that enabled them to have binocular vision.

4. In a bee colony, all the worker bees are closely related females. They work together to complete complicated tasks such as building nests. What is the evolutionary benefit of this type of behavior?
A. This behavior allows related individuals to compete for resources.
B. This behavior increases the chances that diseases will spread to related individuals.
C. This behavior makes them more attractive to mates and increases genetic diversity.
D. This behavior increases the chances that genes shared by relatives will be passed to offspring.
E. This behavior increases the chances that syntax rules will be communicated to related individuals.

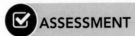 **ASSESSMENT**

For additional assessment practice, go online to access your digital course.

| If You Have Trouble With... | | | | |
|---|---|---|---|---|
| **Question** | 1 | 2 | 3 | 4 |
| **See Lesson** | 24.2 | 24.2 | 24.3 | 24.4 |
| **Performance Expectation** | HS-LS4-1 | HS-LS4-1 | HS-LS4-1 | HS-LS2-8 |

| 25.1 | 25.2 | 25.3 | 25.4 |
|------|------|------|------|
| Feeding and Digestion | Respiration | Circulation | Excretion |

**Go Online to access your digital course.**

- ▶ **VIDEO**
- 🔊 **AUDIO**
- 👆 **INTERACTIVITY**
- 📖 **eTEXT**
- 👁 **ANIMATION**
- 🧪 **VIRTUAL LAB**
- ☑ **ASSESSMENT**

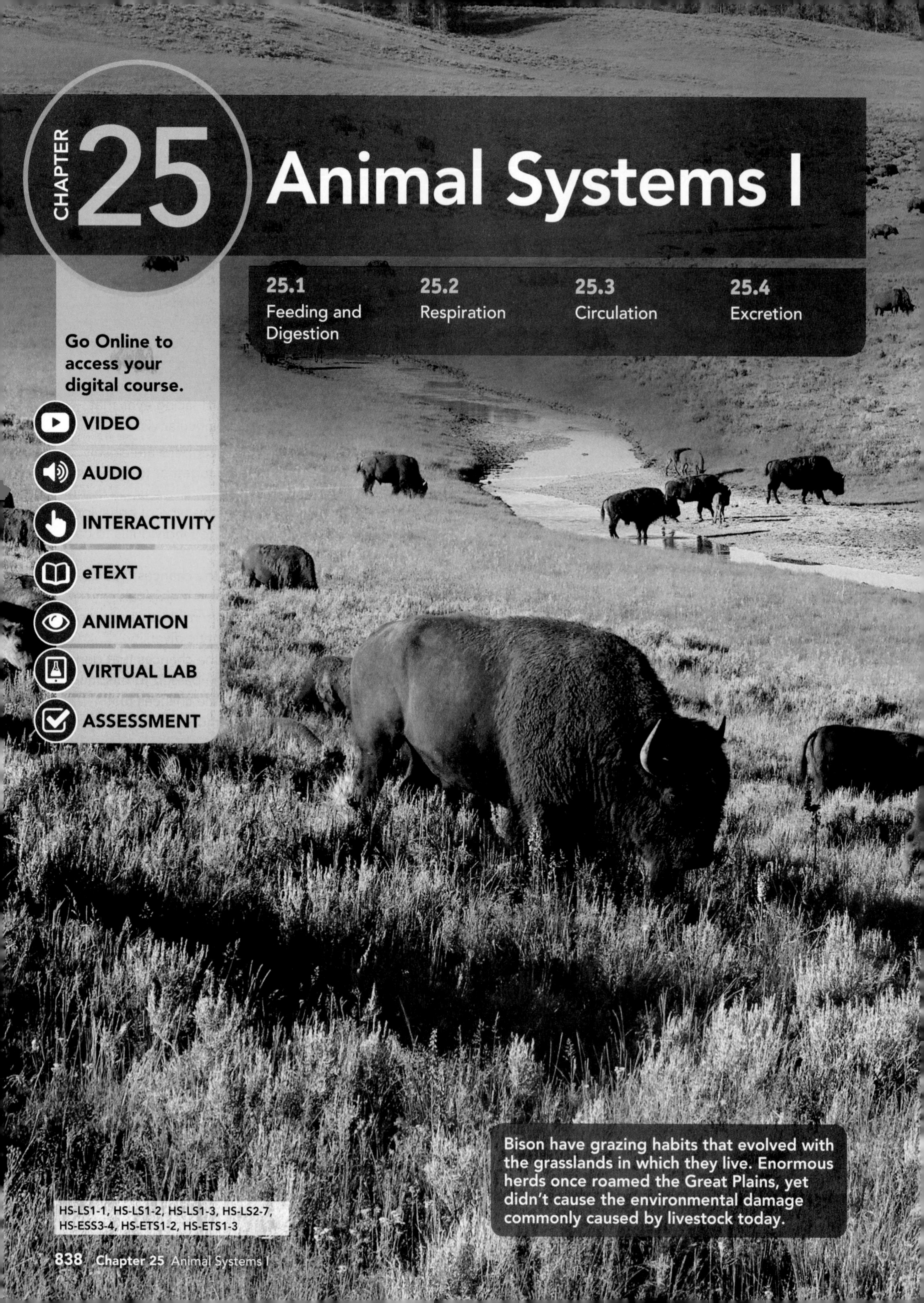

Bison have grazing habits that evolved with the grasslands in which they live. Enormous herds once roamed the Great Plains, yet didn't cause the environmental damage commonly caused by livestock today.

HS-LS1-1, HS-LS1-2, HS-LS1-3, HS-LS2-7, HS-ESS3-4, HS-ETS1-2, HS-ETS1-3

# How do animal processes and human activity affect the environment?

All animals, large and small—including humans—must acquire food, oxygen, and water. All of us must also get rid of waste products, typically including solid wastes, liquid wastes, and carbon dioxide. These processes—feeding, breathing, and excreting—all affect the environment in which animals live. Therefore, there is no such thing as a form of life that has no environmental impact. What does vary among organisms, and among populations of different sizes, are the types of impact, and the size and scale of environmental effects.

Animals in nature interact with each other, with producers, and with their environment. Population sizes rise and fall. Nutrient cycles work differently at different times of year. However natural systems usually, although not always, pass through periods of stability and change without catastrophic effects.

Long before humans entered the scene, enormous herds of bison and other grazing animals roamed over the Great Plains of North America. Huge herds of wildebeest, antelope, zebra, buffalo, and other animals covered the grasslands and savannahs of Africa. The total biomass of these herds is almost unimaginable.

Yet today, when modern society raises beef or pork, environmental side effects seem to be everywhere. Overgrazing does permanent harm to ecosystems, killing plants and damaging soil structure. In feedlots for cattle and pigs, enormous quantities of solid and liquid wastes pollute ground and surface water, and give off a foul stench that spreads for miles. What happened?

Before humans, animal species and evolutionary lineages that survived and reproduced over the ages did so in ways that didn't create toxic conditions for themselves or for other species on which they depended.

The hooves and heavy footsteps of those giant herds buried grass seeds and decomposing organic matter, and churned and aerated the soil. Animals' wastes decomposed, returning nutrients to the soil. Herds were often on the move; so intense grazing was followed by periods of fewer disturbances. The plants of those great grasslands evolved ways to survive this kind of grazing by herbivores.

But when humans started raising livestock in large quantities, they did things differently. They raised large herds in fenced-in pastures, concentrating grazing in the same places for much of the year, including along fragile streambeds. Feedlots concentrate animals in higher numbers and at higher densities than any ecosystem could support naturally. Food and clean water are supplied, and the animals produce wastes in unmanageable quantities.

Does it have to be that way? Are there ways to raise animals for our use and preserve environmental services at the same time? What can we learn from ranchers and farmers who understand their crops and livestock?

**Throughout this chapter, look for connections to the** CASE STUDY **to help you answer these questions.**

# Feeding and Digestion

A whale shark is a vertebrate filter feeder.

## 🔍 KEY QUESTIONS

- *How do animals obtain food?*
- *How does digestion occur in animals?*
- *How are mouthparts adapted for different diets?*

**HS-LS1-1:** Construct an explanation based on evidence for how the structure of DNA determines the structure of proteins which carry out the essential functions of life through systems of specialized cells.

**HS-LS1-2:** Develop and use a model to illustrate the hierarchical organization of interacting systems that provide specific functions within multicellular organisms.

**HS-LS1-3:** Plan and conduct an investigation to provide evidence that feedback mechanisms maintain homeostasis.

## VOCABULARY

**digestive tract**
**rumen**

## READING TOOL

As you read this lesson, complete the table in your 📖 **Biology Foundations Workbook** to explain how different types of animals obtain food.

## ▶ VIDEO

Watch how black bears hibernate all winter without eating.

## BUILD VOCABULARY

**Word Origins** The word part -*vore* comes from the Latin verb *vorare*, which means "to devour."

From mosquitoes that "bite" us to dine on our blood to bison that feed on prairie grasses to giant whale sharks that feed on plankton, all animals are heterotrophs that obtain nutrients and energy from food. The variety of feeding adaptations is a large part of what makes animals interesting.

## Obtaining Food

There's an old saying that "You are what you eat." We can rephrase that as "What you eat and how you eat it determine how you look and act." Evolutionary adaptations for feeding on different foods have shaped the body structures and behaviors of animals, such as those in **Figure 25-1**.

**Filter Feeders** 🔍 *Most filter feeders catch algae and small animals by using modified gills or other structures as nets that filter food items out of water.* Many invertebrate filter feeders are small or colonial organisms, like worms and sponges, that spend their adult lives in a single spot. Some vertebrate filter feeders, such as blue whales, are huge, and feed while swimming.

**Detritivores** Detritus is made up of decaying bits of plant and animal material. 🔍 *Detritivores feed on detritus, often obtaining extra nutrients from bacteria, algae, and other microorganisms that grow on and around it.* Detritivores are essential members of many food webs.

**Herbivores** 🔍 *Herbivores eat plants or parts of plants or algae.* Fruits are often filled with energy-rich compounds, and are easy to digest. (That's why we eat so many of them!) Leaves don't have many calories, are tough to digest, and can contain poisons or hard particles that wear down teeth.

Filter Feeders: Barnacles    Detritivores: Earthworms    Herbivore: Green sea turtle

**Carnivores** 🔍 *Carnivores eat other animals.* Mammalian carnivores, such as wolves, use teeth, claws, and speed or stealthy hunting tactics to capture prey. Many carnivorous invertebrates would be as menacing as tigers if they were larger. Some cnidarians paralyze prey with poison-tipped darts, while some spiders immobilize their victims with venomous fangs.

**Nutritional Symbionts** Recall that a symbiosis is a close relationship between two or more species. Symbionts are the organisms involved in a symbiosis. 🔍 *Many animals rely upon symbiosis for their nutritional needs.*

*Parasitic Symbiosis* Parasites live within or on a host organism, where they feed on tissues or on blood and other body fluids, disrupting the health of their hosts. Some parasites are just nuisances, but many cause serious diseases in humans, livestock, and crop plants. Parasitic flatworms and roundworms harm millions of people, particularly in the tropics.

*Mutualistic Symbiosis* Mutualistic nutritional relationships benefit both participants, and are often important in maintaining the health of organisms. Reef-building corals depend on symbiotic algae that live within their tissues for most of their energy. Those algae capture solar energy, recycle nutrients, and help corals lay down calcium carbonate skeletons. The algae, in turn, obtain nutrients from coral wastes.

Many animals, including humans, have tightly knit relationships with symbiotic microorganisms that live within their digestive tracts. These microbial partners are vital parts of their hosts' microbiomes. Animals that eat wood or plant leaves rely on symbiotic microorganisms to break down cellulose, which no animal can digest on its own. Microorganisms living in our intestines help in digestion and nutrient absorption, manufacture some essential vitamins, and help protect us from other potentially harmful microorganisms. In fact, understanding the importance of the human microbiome is critical to maintaining our health.

✅ **READING CHECK** **Describe** What is the difference between a parasitic symbiosis and a mutualistic symbiosis?

Carnivore: Orca

**CASE STUDY**

Figure 25-1

**Obtaining Food**

All animals take in food from their environment, but they do so in different ways.

 **INTERACTIVITY**

Explore the different methods animals use to obtain food.

**READING TOOL**

Make a table of similarities and differences between carnivores and herbivores and fill it out as you read about them.

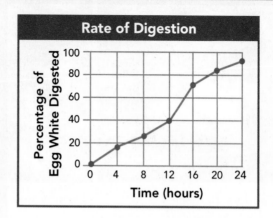
# Processing Food

Obtaining food is just the first step. Food must then be broken down, or digested, and absorbed to make energy and nutrients available to body tissues. 🔍 *The simplest animals, such as sponges, digest food inside specialized cells that pass nutrients to other cells by diffusion. More complex animals break food down outside cells in a digestive cavity and then absorb the nutrients they need.* A variety of digestive systems are shown in **Figure 25-2**.

Some relatively simple invertebrates, such as cnidarians, have a digestive cavity with only one opening through which they both ingest food and expel wastes. Cells lining the cavity secrete enzymes and absorb digested food. Other cells surround food particles and digest them in vacuoles. Nutrients are then transported to cells throughout the body.

Many invertebrates and all vertebrates digest food as it passes through a tube called a **digestive tract**, which has two openings. Food moves in one direction, entering the body through the mouth. Wastes leave through the anus.

### Figure 25-2

### Digesting Food

Animals have different digestive structures with different functions. Ⓐ Sponges filter water as it is drawn through their porous body walls. Ⓑ The cnidarian processes its food in a digestive cavity with only one opening. Ⓒ The bird has a one-way digestive tract with two openings.

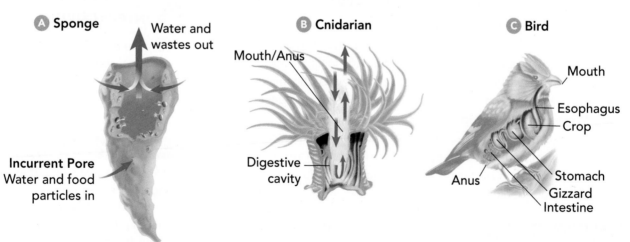

Ⓐ **Sponge**

Water and wastes out

**Incurrent Pore** Water and food particles in

Ⓑ **Cnidarian**

Mouth/Anus

Digestive cavity

Ⓒ **Bird**

Mouth

Esophagus
Crop

Stomach
Gizzard
Intestine

Anus

One-way digestive tracts often have specialized structures, which perform different tasks, as food passes through them. You can think of a digestive tract as a kind of "disassembly line" that breaks down food one step at a time. In some animals, the mouth secretes digestive enzymes that start the chemical digestion of food.

Then, mechanical digestion may occur as specialized mouthparts or a muscular organ called a gizzard breaks down large pieces of food into small pieces. Then, chemical digestion begins or continues in a stomach that secretes digestive enzymes. Chemical breakdown continues in the intestines, sometimes aided by secretions from other organs such as a liver or pancreas. Intestines also absorb the nutrients released by digestion.

No matter how efficiently an animal breaks down food and extracts nutrients, some indigestible material will remain. These solid wastes, or feces, are expelled either through the single digestive opening or through the anus.

✅ **READING CHECK** **Compare and Contrast** How is mechanical digestion different from chemical digestion?

# Specializations for Different Diets

The mouthparts and digestive systems of animals have evolved many adaptations to the physical and chemical characteristics of different foods, as shown in **Figure 25-3**. As a window into these specializations, we'll examine adaptations to two food types that are very different physically and chemically: meat and plant leaves.

**Specialized Mouthparts** Carnivores and leaf-eating herbivores usually have very different mouthparts. These differences are typically related to the different physical characteristics of meat and plant leaves.

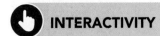
**INTERACTIVITY**

Explore how body systems function and interact, using a frog as a model.

**INTERACTIVITY**

Visual Analogy

**Figure 25-3**

# Mouthparts

The specialized jaws and teeth of animals are well adapted to their diets.

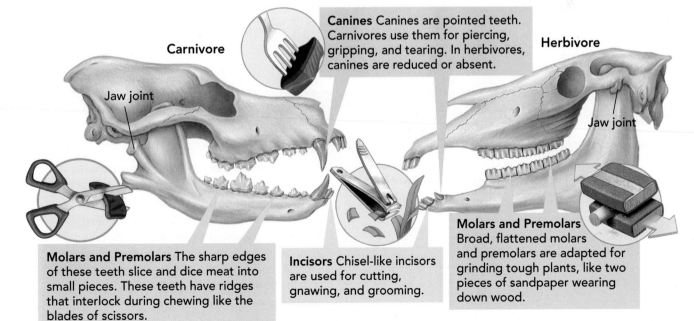

**Canines** Canines are pointed teeth. Carnivores use them for piercing, gripping, and tearing. In herbivores, canines are reduced or absent.

Carnivore

Jaw joint

Herbivore

Jaw joint

**Molars and Premolars** The sharp edges of these teeth slice and dice meat into small pieces. These teeth have ridges that interlock during chewing like the blades of scissors.

**Incisors** Chisel-like incisors are used for cutting, gnawing, and grooming.

**Molars and Premolars** Broad, flattened molars and premolars are adapted for grinding tough plants, like two pieces of sandpaper wearing down wood.

**Figure 25-4**

**Eating Plant Leaves**

The teeth and jaws of herbivores, such as giraffes, are adapted for pulling, rasping, and grinding plant leaves.

**Eating Meat** 🔍 *Carnivores typically have sharp mouthparts or other structures that can capture food, hold it, and "slice and dice" it into small pieces.* Carnivorous mammals, such as wolves, have sharp teeth that grab, tear, and slice food like knives and scissors. The jaw bones and muscles of carnivores are adapted for up-and-down movements that chop meat into small pieces.

**Eating Plant Leaves** 🔍 *Herbivores have mouthparts adapted to rasping or grinding to tear plant cell walls and expose their contents.* Many herbivorous invertebrates, from mollusks to insects, have mouthparts that grind and pulverize plant or algal tissues. Herbivorous mammals, such as the giraffe in **Figure 25-4**, have front teeth and muscular lips adapted to grabbing and pulling leaves, and flattened molars that grind leaves to a pulp. The jawbones and muscles of mammalian herbivores are also adapted for side-to-side "grinding" movements.

## Specialized Digestive Tracts 
Carnivorous invertebrates and vertebrates typically have short digestive tracts that produce fast-acting, meat-digesting enzymes. These enzymes can digest most cell types found in animal tissues.

No animal produces digestive enzymes that can break down the cellulose in plant tissue, however. Some herbivores have very long intestines or specialized pouches in their digestive tracts that harbor the kinds of symbiotic microorganisms discussed earlier.

Animals called ruminants, such as cattle, have a pouchlike extension of their esophagus called a **rumen** (plural: rumina), in which symbiotic bacteria digest cellulose. Ruminants regurgitate food that has been partially digested in the rumen, chew it again, and reswallow it. This process, called "chewing the cud," mechanically breaks down the food and exposes more surfaces to bacterial activity, which helps in digestion.

HS-LS1-1, HS-LS1-2, HS-LS1-3

## ✅ LESSON 25.1 Review

### 🔍 KEY QUESTIONS

1. How might a person be affected if all the microorganisms living in his or her intestines died?

2. Describe how food is digested in a digestive cavity.

3. Describe the adaptations of the mouthparts of leaf eaters and meat eaters.

### CRITICAL THINKING

4. **Use an Analogy** How is a digestive system like a "disassembly line," or an assembly line that acts to take apart a product instead of manufacturing it?

5. **Construct an Argument** The results of a laboratory test show that a type of bacteria called *E. coli* is living in the digestive tract of an animal. Do the results indicate that the animal is suffering a parasitic infection of *E. coli*? Cite evidence to support your argument.

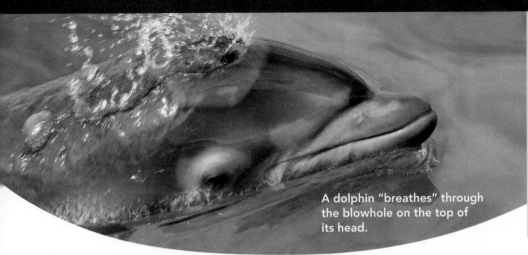

# Respiration

A dolphin "breathes" through the blowhole on the top of its head.

## 🔍 KEY QUESTIONS
- *What characteristics do the respiratory structures of all animals share?*
- *How do aquatic animals breathe?*
- *What respiratory structures enable land animals to breathe?*

**HS-LS1-1:** Construct an explanation based on evidence for how the structure of DNA determines the structure of proteins which carry out the essential functions of life through systems of specialized cells.

**HS-LS1-2:** Develop and use a model to illustrate the hierarchical organization of interacting systems that provide specific functions within multicellular organisms.

## VOCABULARY
gill
lung
alveolus

## READING TOOL

Compare and contrast respiration in different types of animals. Fill in the chart in your 📖 **Biology Foundations Workbook.**

Cellular respiration requires oxygen and produces carbon dioxide as a waste product. So all animals must obtain oxygen from their environment and get rid of carbon dioxide. In other words, all animals need to breathe, or respire. Humans can drown because our lungs are not adapted to absorb sufficient amounts of oxygen from water. Most fishes have the opposite problem; out of water, their breathing structures don't work. How are these different respiratory systems adapted to their different environments?

## Gas Exchange

Despite all the amazing things living cells can do, none can actively pump oxygen or carbon dioxide across membranes. Yet, in order to breathe, all animals must exchange oxygen and carbon dioxide with their surroundings. How do they do it? One way that animals have adapted to different environments is by evolving respiratory structures that promote the movement of these gases by passive diffusion.

**Gas Diffusion and Membranes** Recall that substances diffuse from an area of higher concentration to an area of lower concentration. Gases diffuse most efficiently across a thin, moist membrane that is permeable to those gases. The larger the surface area of that membrane, the more diffusion can take place, just as a bumpy paper towel absorbs more liquid than a smooth one does. These principles of diffusion and absorption create a set of requirements that respiratory systems must meet.

**Requirements for Respiration** Because of the behavior of gases, all respiratory systems share certain basic characteristics. 🔍 *Respiratory structures provide a large surface area of moist, selectively permeable membrane. Respiratory structures maintain a difference in the relative concentrations of oxygen and carbon dioxide on either side of the respiratory membrane, promoting diffusion.*

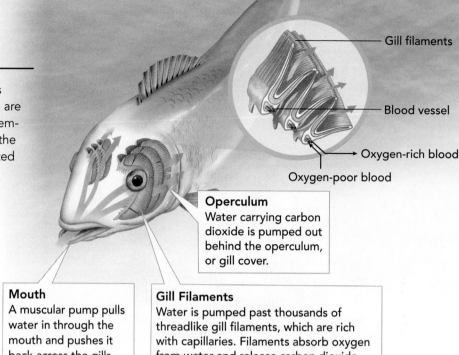

**Figure 25-5**

## Respiration with Gills

Many aquatic animals, such as fishes, respire with gills, which are thin, selectively permeable membranes. As water passes over the gills, gas exchange is completed within the gill capillaries.

Gill filaments

Blood vessel

Oxygen-rich blood

Oxygen-poor blood

**Operculum**
Water carrying carbon dioxide is pumped out behind the operculum, or gill cover.

**Mouth**
A muscular pump pulls water in through the mouth and pushes it back across the gills.

**Gill Filaments**
Water is pumped past thousands of threadlike gill filaments, which are rich with capillaries. Filaments absorb oxygen from water and release carbon dioxide.

**INTERACTIVITY**

Investigate fish respiration and the functioning of gills.

# Respiratory Surfaces of Aquatic Animals

Some aquatic invertebrates, such as cnidarians and some flatworms, are relatively small and have thin-walled bodies whose outer surfaces are always wet. These animals rely on diffusion of oxygen and carbon dioxide through their outer body covering. A few aquatic chordates, including lancelets, some amphibians, and even some sea snakes, rely to varying extents on gas exchange by diffusion across body surfaces.

For large, active animals that consume much larger quantities of oxygen, skin respiration alone is not enough. **✎ Many aquatic invertebrates, fishes, and other animals exchange gases through gills.** As shown in **Figure 25-5**, **gills** are feathery structures that expose a large surface area of thin, selectively permeable membrane to water. Inside the gill membranes is a network of tiny, thin-walled blood vessels called capillaries. Many animals, including aquatic mollusks and fishes, actively pump water over their gills as blood flows through inside. This helps maintain differences in oxygen and carbon dioxide concentrations that promote diffusion.

**✎ Aquatic reptiles and mammals breathe with lungs and must hold their breath underwater.** **Lungs** are organs that exchange oxygen and carbon dioxide between blood and air. Aquatic animals with lungs include sea turtles, whales, dolphins, and manatees. All must come to the water's surface to breathe.

**✓ READING CHECK** **Infer** Why do you think aquatic animals that rely on diffusion for respiration are often small in size?

# Respiratory Surfaces of Terrestrial Animals

Land animals must keep their respiratory membranes moist in dry environments. They must also carry oxygen and carbon dioxide back and forth between those surfaces and the rest of their bodies. Interactions among several body systems are essential for this process.

### Respiratory Surfaces in Invertebrates
The many body plans found among terrestrial invertebrates include many different strategies for respiration. ✎ *Respiratory structures in terrestrial invertebrates include skin, mantle cavities, book lungs, and tracheal tubes.* Some land invertebrates, such as earthworms, live in moist environments and can respire across their skin if it stays moist. Other invertebrates, such as land snails, respire using a mantle cavity lined with moist tissue and blood vessels. Insects and spiders have more complex respiratory systems, as you can see in **Figure 25-6**.

### Lung Structure in Vertebrates
✎ *All terrestrial vertebrates—reptiles, birds, mammals, and the land stages of most amphibians—breathe with lungs.* Although lung structure in these animals varies, the processes of inhaling and exhaling are similar. Inhaling brings oxygen-rich air through the trachea, into the lungs. Inside the lungs, oxygen diffuses into the blood through lung capillaries. At the same time, carbon dioxide diffuses out of capillaries into the lungs. Oxygen-poor (and carbon dioxide-rich) air is then exhaled.

**INTERACTIVITY**

Compare different strategies for respiration.

**Figure 25-6**

### Respiratory Structures of Terrestrial Animals

Terrestrial invertebrates have a wide variety of respiratory structures, including skin, mantle cavities, book lungs, and tracheal tubes. These structures must stay moist even in the driest of conditions in order to function properly.

| Spider | Insect |
|---|---|
| Spiders respire using organs called book lungs, which are made of parallel, sheetlike layers of thin tissues that contain blood vessels. | In most insects, a system of tracheal tubes extends throughout the body. Air enters and leaves the system through openings in the body surface called spiracles. In some insects, oxygen and carbon dioxide diffuse through the tracheal system, and in and out of body fluids. In other insects, body movements help pump air in and out of the tracheal system. |

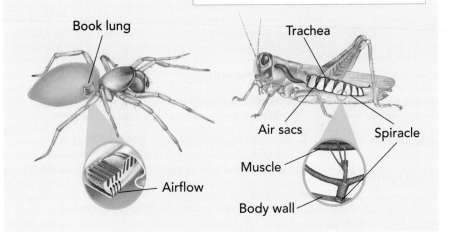

Book lung

Airflow

Trachea

Air sacs

Muscle

Spiracle

Body wall

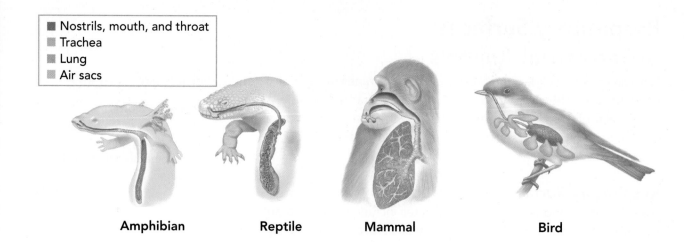

**Amphibian**     **Reptile**     **Mammal**     **Bird**

**Figure 25-7**

**Lungs**

Terrestrial vertebrates breathe with lungs. Lungs with a larger surface area can take in more oxygen and release more carbon dioxide.

**READING TOOL**

Refer to **Figure 25-7** as you read about the lungs of amphibians, reptiles, and mammals. Use the figure to understand the differences in respiration structures between these types of animals.

**Amphibian, Reptilian, and Mammalian Lungs** The internal surface area of lungs increases from amphibians to reptiles to mammals, as shown in **Figure 25-7**. A typical amphibian lung is little more than a sac with ridges. Reptilian lungs are often divided into chambers that increase the surface area for gas exchange. Mammalian lungs branch extensively, and air passages branch and rebranch, ending in bubblelike structures called **alveoli** (singular: alveolus). Alveoli provide an enormous surface area for gas exchange. Alveoli are surrounded by a network of capillaries in which blood picks up oxygen and releases carbon dioxide. Mammalian lung structure helps take in the large amounts of oxygen required by high metabolic rates. When mammals and most other vertebrates breathe, air moves in and out through the same air passages, and some stale, oxygen-poor air remains. In humans, this stale air is typically equivalent to about one third of the air inhaled in a normal breath.

**Bird Lungs** In birds, the lungs are structured so that air flows mostly in only one direction. No stale air gets trapped in the system. A unique system of tubes and air sacs in birds' respiratory systems enables this one-way airflow. Thus, gas exchange surfaces are continuously in contact with fresh air. This highly efficient gas exchange helps birds obtain the oxygen they need to power their flight muscles for long periods of time.

HS-LS1-1, HS-LS1-2

## LESSON 25.2 Review

### KEY QUESTIONS

1. In what ways are the respiratory structures of all animals similar?

2. Compare the functions of gills and lungs in aquatic animals.

3. How do terrestrial invertebrates and terrestrial vertebrates breathe?

### CRITICAL THINKING

4. **Construct an Explanation** Why must whales hold their breath while they are underwater?

5. **Develop Models** To show gas exchange in the gills of a fish, why is it useful to include the mouth of the fish as well? (*Hint:* See **Figure 25-5**.)

6. **Compare and Contrast** How do lungs and airways compare among birds and mammals?

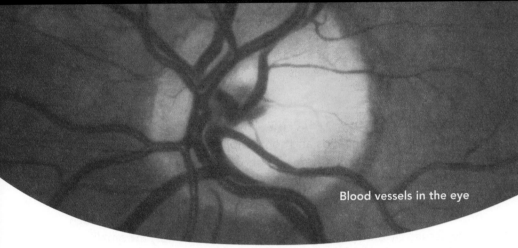

Blood vessels in the eye

## KEY QUESTIONS

- *How do open and closed circulatory systems compare?*
- *How do the patterns of circulation in vertebrates compare?*

HS-LS1-1: Construct an explanation based on evidence for how the structure of DNA determines the structure of proteins which carry out the essential functions of life through systems of specialized cells.

HS-LS1-2: Develop and use a model to illustrate the hierarchical organization of interacting systems that provide specific functions within multicellular organisms.

HS-LS1-3: Plan and conduct an investigation to provide evidence that feedback mechanisms maintain homeostasis.

### VOCABULARY

**heart**
**open circulatory system**
**closed circulatory system**
**atrium**
**ventricle**

### READING TOOL

Compare and contrast the four-chambered heart with the three-chambered heart in the chart in your 📖 **Biology Foundations Workbook.**

When you eat food, your digestive tract breaks it down. But how do energy and nutrients from food get to your cells? How does oxygen from your lungs get to other tissues? How do carbon dioxide and wastes get eliminated? Some aquatic animals with bodies only a few cell layers thick rely on diffusion to transport materials. But in most animals, oxygen, carbon dioxide, nutrients, and wastes are transported through a circulatory system that interacts with other body systems.

## Open and Closed Circulatory Systems

Many animals move blood through their bodies using one or more hearts. A **heart** is a hollow, muscular organ that pumps blood around the body. A heart can be part of any type of circulatory system.

**Open Circulatory Systems** Arthropods and most mollusks have **open circulatory systems**. 🔍 *In open circulatory systems, hearts or heart-like organs pump blood through vessels that empty into a system of sinuses, or spongy cavities.* Blood comes into direct contact with body tissues in those sinuses. Blood then collects in another set of sinuses and eventually makes its way back to the heart, as shown in **Figure 25-8**.

### Figure 25-8

### Open Circulatory System

In an open circulatory system, blood is not entirely contained within blood vessels. Grasshoppers, for example, have open circulatory systems in which blood leaves vessels and moves through sinuses before returning to a heart.

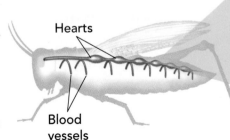
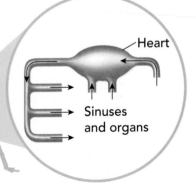

Hearts

Blood vessels

Heart

Sinuses and organs

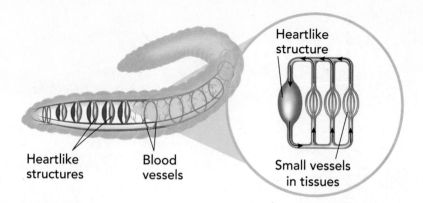

Heartlike structure

Heartlike structures

Blood vessels

Small vessels in tissues

Figure 25-9

**Closed Circulatory System**

Annelids, such as earthworms, and many more complex animals have closed circulatory systems. Blood stays within the vessels of a closed circulatory system.

**Closed Circulatory Systems** Many larger, more active invertebrates, including annelids and some mollusks, and all vertebrates have **closed circulatory systems**, as shown in **Figure 25-9**. 🔍 *In closed circulatory systems, blood circulates entirely within blood vessels that extend throughout the body.* A heart or heart-like organ pumps blood through the vessels. Nutrients and oxygen reach body tissues by diffusing across thin walls of capillaries, the smallest blood vessels. Blood that is completely contained within blood vessels can be pumped under higher pressure, and can be circulated more efficiently, than blood in an open system.

✅ **READING CHECK** **Compare** How are open and closed circulatory systems alike and different?

# Single- and Double-Loop Circulation

As chordates evolved, they evolved more complex organ systems and more efficient channels for internal transport. You can see two main types of circulatory systems of vertebrates in **Figure 25-10**.

👁 **ANIMATION**

Figure 25-10

**Single- and Double-Loop Circulation**

Most vertebrates that use gills for respiration have a single-loop circulatory system that forces blood around the body in one direction. Vertebrates that use lungs have a double-loop system. (Note that in diagrams of animals' circulatory systems, blood vessels carrying oxygen-rich blood are red, while blood vessels carrying oxygen-poor blood are blue.)

**Single-Loop Circulation**

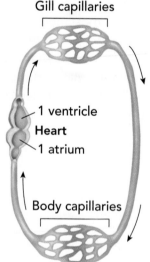

Gill capillaries

1 ventricle
**Heart**
1 atrium

Body capillaries

**Double-Loop Circulation**

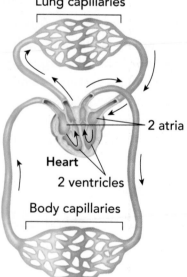

Lung capillaries

2 atria

**Heart**
2 ventricles

Body capillaries

## Single-Loop Circulation

 *Most vertebrates with gills have a single-loop circulatory system with a single pump that forces blood around the body in one direction.* In fishes, for example, the heart consists of two chambers: an atrium and a ventricle. The **atrium** (plural: atria) receives blood from the body. The **ventricle** pumps blood out of the heart and to the gills. Oxygen-rich blood then travels from the gills to the rest of the body, and oxygen-poor blood returns to the atrium.

## Double-Loop Circulation

As terrestrial vertebrates evolved into larger and more active forms, their capillary networks became larger. Using a single pump to force blood through the entire system would have been increasingly difficult and inefficient. *Most vertebrates that breathe with lungs have evolved a double-loop, two-pump circulatory system.* The first loop, powered by one side of the heart, forces oxygen-poor blood from the heart to the lungs. After the blood picks up oxygen and drops off carbon dioxide in the lungs, it returns to the heart. Then the other side of the heart pumps this oxygen-rich blood through the second circulatory loop to the rest of the body. Oxygen-poor blood from the body returns to the heart, and the cycle begins again.

## Heart-Chamber Evolution

Four-chambered hearts like those in modern mammals are actually two separate pumps working next to one another. But where did the second pump come from? During chordate evolution, partitions evolved that divided the original two chambers into four. Those partitions transformed one pump into two parallel pumps that move blood in two different circuits. By looking at the progression of heart partitions over time, we can get an idea of how and why they evolved.

**READING TOOL**

As you read, make an ordered list to show how blood passes through the parts of the circulatory system.

**BUILD VOCABULARY**

**Multiple Meanings** An *atrium* can also be a large open area in a building, and people may gather there. In biology, the **atrium** is a chamber in the heart that receives blood.

**INTERACTIVITY**

Explore open and closed circulatory systems in animals.

## Modeling Lab   Guided Inquiry

### Modeling Vertebrate Hearts

**Problem** How did hearts evolve in vertebrates?

In this lab, you will make models of several different vertebrate hearts. You will use the models to analyze the flow of blood in each of the hearts and identify the strengths and limitations of each heart model. Then you will infer how the heart developed as vertebrates evolved.

You can find this lab in your digital course.

## Figure 25-11

### Reptilian Heart

Under the armor-like hide of this crocodile lies a heart with four chambers, like those of birds and mammals. Although most reptiles have a single ventricle with a partial partition, in crocodiles and their close relatives the ventricle is fully partitioned into two chambers.

▶ **VIDEO**

Compare the blood and circulatory systems of a variety of animals.

**Amphibian Hearts** Amphibian hearts usually have three chambers: two atria and one ventricle. The left atrium receives oxygen-rich blood from the lungs. The right atrium receives oxygen-poor blood from the body. Both atria empty into the ventricle. This undivided ventricle allows blood to be diverted away from the lungs when these animals dive under water. Some mixing of oxygen-rich and oxygen-poor blood in the ventricle occurs. However, the internal structure of the ventricle directs blood flow so that most oxygen-poor blood goes to the lungs, and most oxygen-rich blood goes to the rest of the body.

**Reptilian Hearts** Reptilian hearts typically have three chambers. However, most reptiles have a partial partition in their ventricle, or in some cases a full partition as in the crocodile in **Figure 25-11**. Because of this partition, there is even less mixing of oxygen-rich and oxygen-poor blood than there is in amphibian hearts.

**Mammalian Hearts** Mammals have hearts that are separated into two different circuits. One circuit shuttles blood from the heart to the lungs and back. The other takes oxygenated blood from the heart to rest of the tissues in the body, then back to the heart. Keeping the two circuits separate prevents oxygen-rich blood from mixing with oxygen-poor blood. This gives mammals some of the most efficient circulatory systems on Earth.

HS-LS1-1, HS-LS1-2, HS-LS1-3

## ☑ LESSON 25.3 Review

### ⚘ KEY QUESTIONS

1. How does an open circulatory system differ from a closed circulatory system?

2. Explain the two different patterns of circulation found in vertebrates.

### CRITICAL THINKING

3. **Evaluate Claims** A student observes a blood vessel in a grasshopper. Because the grasshopper has blood vessels, the student claims that it has a closed circulatory system. Evaluate the student's claim.

4. **Construct an Explanation** In closed circulatory systems, how are nutrients and oxygen transported from the blood to body cells? Does this transport occur in all parts of the system? Explain.

5. **Integrate Information** Describe the advantages of a four-chambered heart compared to hearts with two or three chambers.

6. **Develop Models** Make a model to illustrate how respiratory structures interact with double-loop circulatory structures to provide oxygen to body tissues.

# Excretion

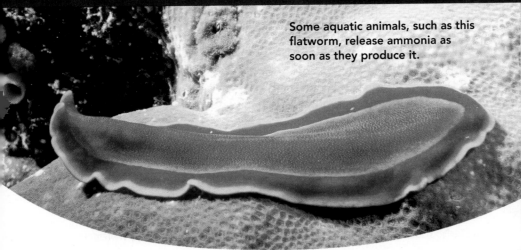

Some aquatic animals, such as this flatworm, release ammonia as soon as they produce it.

### KEY QUESTIONS

- *How do animals manage toxic nitrogenous waste?*
- *How do aquatic animals eliminate wastes?*
- *How do land animals remove wastes while conserving water?*

**HS-LS1-2:** Develop and use a model to illustrate the hierarchical organization of interacting systems that provide specific functions within multicellular organisms.

### VOCABULARY
excretion
kidney
nephridium
Malpighian tubule

### READING TOOL

As you read each section of this lesson, briefly describe the main ideas and key takeaways in the graphic organizer in your 📖 Biology Foundations Workbook.

Cellular metabolism generates several kinds of wastes that are released into body fluids and that must be eliminated from the body. What are these wastes and how do animals get rid of them?

## The Ammonia Problem

When cells break down proteins, they produce a nitrogen-containing waste in a poisonous form: ammonia. Even moderate concentrations of ammonia can kill most cells. Animal systems address this difficulty in one of two ways. ⚲ *Animals either eliminate ammonia from the body quickly or convert it into other compounds that are less toxic.* The elimination of metabolic wastes, such as ammonia, is called **excretion**. Some small animals that live in wet environments, such as the flatworm in **Figure 25-12**, rid their bodies of ammonia by allowing it to diffuse out of their body fluids across their skin. Most larger animals, and even some smaller ones that live in dry environments, have excretory systems that process ammonia and eliminate it from the body.

### Flatworm

Excretory tubules   Flame cells

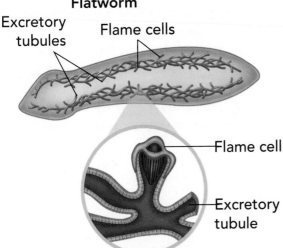

Flame cell

Excretory tubule

**Figure 25-12**

## Eliminating Ammonia

Flatworms excrete ammonia directly into the water and use flame cells to remove excess water.

## Figure 25-13

### Other Nitrogen-Containing Compounds

Large and/or terrestrial animals either convert ammonia to uric acid and excrete it as sticky white guano, as these gulls do, or they convert ammonia into urea and release it, diluted, as urine.

**Storing Wastes That Contain Nitrogen** Animals that cannot dispose of ammonia as it is produced have evolved ways to hold, or "store," nitrogen-containing wastes until they can be eliminated. In most cases, ammonia is too toxic to be stored in body fluids. Insects, reptiles, and birds typically solve this problem by converting ammonia into a sticky white compound called uric acid, which you can see in **Figure 25-13**. Uric acid is much less toxic than ammonia and is also less soluble in water. Mammals and some amphibians, on the other hand, convert ammonia to a different nitrogen-containing compound—urea. Like uric acid, urea is less toxic than ammonia, but unlike uric acid, urea is highly soluble in water.

**Maintaining Water Balance** Getting rid of any type of nitrogen-containing waste involves water. For that reason, excretory systems interact with other systems involved in regulating water balance in blood and body tissues. In some cases, excretory systems eliminate excess water along with nitrogenous wastes. In other cases, excretory systems must eliminate nitrogenous wastes while conserving water.

Many animals use **kidneys** to separate wastes and excess water from blood in a fluid called urine. Kidneys must perform this function despite a serious limitation: No living cell can actively pump water across a membrane! You may recall that cells can pump ions across their membranes. Kidney cells pump ions from dissolved salts in blood in ways that create an osmotic gradient. Water then "follows" those ions passively by osmosis. This process can get rid of nitrogenous wastes and retain water, but leaves kidneys with one weakness: They usually cannot excrete excess salt.

☑ **READING CHECK Summarize** How do kidneys help maintain water balance?

## Excretion in Aquatic Animals

Aquatic animals have an advantage in getting rid of nitrogenous wastes because they are surrounded by water. ✎ *In general, aquatic animals can allow ammonia to diffuse out of their bodies into surrounding water, which dilutes the ammonia and carries it away.* But aquatic animals still face excretory challenges. Many have adaptations that either eliminate water from their bodies or conserve it, depending on whether they live in fresh or saltwater ecosystems, as summarized in **Figure 25-14**.

---

### Quick Lab    Guided Inquiry

#### Water and Nitrogen Excretion

1. Place 2 grams of urea in a test tube. Place 2 grams of uric acid in another test tube. Label the test tubes.

2. Add 15 mL of water to each test tube. Stopper and shake the test tubes for 3 minutes.

3. Observe each test tube. Record your observations.

4. Dispose of all chemicals as instructed by your teacher. Wash your hands with soap and warm water.

#### ANALYZE AND INTERPRET DATA

1. **Observe** Which substance—urea or uric acid—is less soluble in water? Explain how you know.

2. **Construct an Explanation** Reptiles excrete nitrogenous wastes in the form of uric acid. Explain how this adaptation helps reptiles survive on land.

---

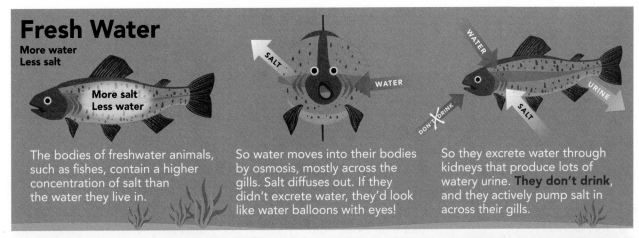

# Fresh Water

**More water**
**Less salt**

**More salt**
**Less water**

The bodies of freshwater animals, such as fishes, contain a higher concentration of salt than the water they live in.

So water moves into their bodies by osmosis, mostly across the gills. Salt diffuses out. If they didn't excrete water, they'd look like water balloons with eyes!

So they excrete water through kidneys that produce lots of watery urine. **They don't drink**, and they actively pump salt in across their gills.

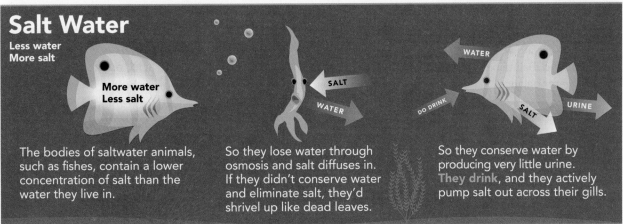

# Salt Water

**Less water**
**More salt**

**More water**
**Less salt**

The bodies of saltwater animals, such as fishes, contain a lower concentration of salt than the water they live in.

So they lose water through osmosis and salt diffuses in. If they didn't conserve water and eliminate salt, they'd shrivel up like dead leaves.

So they conserve water by producing very little urine. They drink, and they actively pump salt out across their gills.

**Freshwater Animals** Many freshwater invertebrates lose ammonia to their environment by simple diffusion across their skin. Many freshwater fishes and amphibians eliminate ammonia by diffusion across the same gill membranes they use for respiration.

But invertebrates and fishes that live in fresh water must excrete wastes while managing an osmotic challenge. The concentration of water surrounding their bodies is higher than the concentration of water in their body fluids. So water moves passively into their bodies by osmosis, and salt leaves by diffusion. Amphibians and freshwater fishes typically excrete excess water in very dilute urine, and pump salt actively inward across their gills.

**Saltwater Animals** Marine invertebrates and vertebrates typically release ammonia by diffusion across their body surfaces or gill membranes. Many marine invertebrates have body fluids with solute concentrations similar to that of the seawater around them. For that reason, these animals have less of a problem with water balance than freshwater invertebrates. Marine fishes, however, tend to lose water to their surroundings because their bodies are less salty than the water they live in. These animals actively excrete salt across their gills. Their kidneys also produce small quantities of urine—an adaptation that conserves water.

**Visual Analogy**

**Figure 25-14**

## Excretion in Aquatic Animals

All animals must rid their bodies of ammonia while maintaining appropriate water balance. Freshwater and saltwater animals face very different challenges in this respect ☑ **Interpret Visuals** What are two ways freshwater fishes avoid looking like "water balloons with eyes"?

# Excretion in Terrestrial Animals

Land animals also face challenges. In dry environments, they can lose large amounts of water from respiratory membranes that must be kept moist. In addition, they must eliminate nitrogenous wastes in ways that require disposing of water—even though they may not have access to water to drink. **Figure 25-15** shows the excretory systems of some terrestrial animals.

**Terrestrial Invertebrates** ☜ *Some terrestrial invertebrates, including annelids and mollusks, produce urine in nephridia.* **Nephridia** (singular: nephridium) are tubelike excretory structures that filter body fluid. Typically, body fluid enters nephridia and becomes more concentrated as it moves through the tubes. Urine leaves the body through excretory pores. ☜ *Other terrestrial invertebrates, such as insects and arachnids, convert ammonia into uric acid.* Nitrogenous wastes, such as uric acid, are absorbed from body fluids by structures called **Malpighian tubules**. Then the wastes are added to digestive wastes traveling through the gut. The wastes lose water, and then crystallize into a thick paste. The paste leaves the body through the anus. This paste contains little water, so these adaptations minimize water loss.

**Terrestrial Vertebrates** In terrestrial vertebrates, excretion is carried out mostly by the kidneys. ☜ *Mammals and land amphibians convert ammonia into urea, which is excreted in urine. In most reptiles and birds, ammonia is converted into uric acid.* Reptiles and birds pass uric acid through ducts into a cavity that also receives digestive wastes from the gut. The walls of this cavity absorb most of the water from the wastes, causing the uric acid to separate out as white crystals. The result is a thick, milky-white paste that you would recognize as "bird droppings."

## Figure 25-15

### Excretion in Terrestrial Animals

Some terrestrial invertebrates, such as annelids, rid their bodies of ammonia by releasing urine created in their nephridia. Some insects and arachnids have Malpighian tubules, which absorb uric acid from body fluids and combine it with digestive wastes. In vertebrates, such as humans, excretion is carried out mostly by the kidneys.

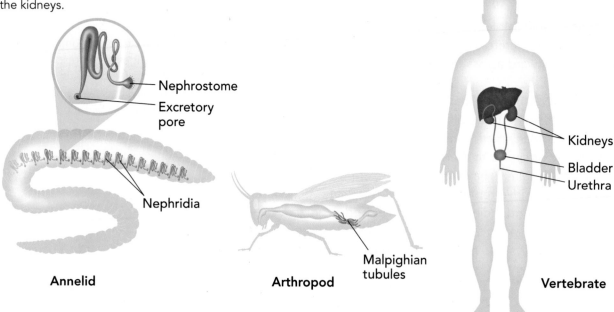

Nephrostome

Excretory pore

Nephridia

**Annelid**

Malpighian tubules

**Arthropod**

Kidneys

Bladder

Urethra

**Vertebrate**

**Adaptations to Extreme Environments** Vertebrate kidneys are remarkable organs, but the way they operate results in some limitations. Most vertebrate kidneys, for example, cannot excrete concentrated salt. That's why most vertebrates cannot survive by drinking seawater. Taking in extra salt would overwhelm the kidneys, and the animal would die of dehydration. Some marine reptiles and birds, such as the petrel in **Figure 25-16**, have evolved adaptations in the form of specialized glands in their heads that excrete very concentrated salt solutions. Another excretory adaptation is found in the kangaroo rats of the American southwest. The kidneys of these desert rodents produce urine that is 25 times more concentrated than their blood! In addition, their intestines are so good at absorbing water that their feces are almost completely dry.

**INTERACTIVITY**

Analyze the ideal conditions needed for clam farming.

**INTERACTIVITY**

**Figure 25-16**

**Excretion Adaptations**

Some terrestrial animals that spend a large amount of time in salt water, such as this petrel, have special adaptations to excrete excess salt. Specialized salt glands produce a concentrated salt solution, which can sometimes be seen dripping out of their elongated nostrils.

HS-LS1-1, HS-LS1-2, HS-LS1-3

# ☑ LESSON 25.4 Review

## ⚲ KEY QUESTIONS

1. Why does the metabolic waste ammonia pose a problem for all animals?

2. How do most aquatic animals remove ammonia?

3. In what form do (a) annelids and mollusks, (b) insects and arachnids, (c) mammals and land amphibians, and (d) reptiles and birds excrete nitrogenous wastes?

## CRITICAL THINKING

4. **Compare and Contrast** How do the differing water balance needs of freshwater animals and saltwater animals explain the difference in their excretion of nitrogenous wastes?

5. **Develop Models** Make a model to illustrate how kidneys interact with other systems to help maintain homeostasis while processing nitrogenous wastes.

6. **Synthesize Information** Why are most terrestrial animals, including humans, not able to survive by drinking salt water?

7. CASE STUDY Predict how the wastes of large, crowded herds of cattle could affect surrounding ecosystems. (*Hint:* Recall what you learned about nutrient limitation.)

# How do animal processes and human activity affect the environment?

**Vast herds of grazing animals once roamed Earth's grasslands. Can we learn from history to raise livestock in ways that make sense both ecologically and economically?**

HS-LS2-7, HS-ESS3-4

## Make Your Case

Ranchers on family farms have close connections to their land, and are learning to move herds around and keep them away from streams to minimize environmental impacts. Conservationists hoping to use management practices to store carbon in soil are learning that properly managed livestock can play an important role.

## Develop a Solution

1. **Conduct Research** Use print or digital resources to research sustainable ranching. Using a variety of reliable sources, make a list of some of the benefits and possible drawbacks of some of the methods.

2. **Evaluate a Solution** Based on your research, how would you evaluate the progress so far in changing ranching practices? Write a short summary of your findings.

## Society on the Case

### Feedlot Frenzy

Around the world, livestock live for at least part of their lives in feedlots and other places where they are packed together under extremely crowded conditions. There, they eat grains (including corn) instead of grass or other kinds of food more like their ancestors' natural diets. The unnaturally crowded conditions create stress for the animals, and the unnatural diets affect their systems in various ways.

Critics argue that these kinds of agricultural practices are not sustainable, meaning that they cannot continue in the future without causing long-term problems. For example, life in feed-lots enables infection-causing bacteria to hop easily from animal to animal. That situation is a threat to public health, and not just because it means the animals themselves can get sick easily. Many feedlot operations add significant amounts of antibiotics to animal feed, in part because those drugs help control infection, and in part because they act as growth stimulants.

But the constant presence of antibiotics in crowded, bacteria-rich conditions is known to drive the evolution of antibiotic resistance. And once antibiotic-resistant bacterial populations evolve, they can spread from livestock to humans in a number of ways. The search for sustainable alternatives to feedlots is underway.

## Careers on the Case

### Work Toward a Solution

Understanding animal body systems is essential in any career that involves animals.

### Animal Nutritionist

Every animal has its own dietary needs. Animal nutritionists study these needs, and they work to develop a cost-effective diet. Many animal nutrition-ists work for companies that make animal food. Others work for universities or government agencies.

 **VIDEO**

Watch this video to learn about other careers in biology.

# STUDY GUIDE

## Lesson Review
Go to your Biology Foundations Workbook for longer versions of these lesson summaries.

### 25.1 Feeding and Digestion

Adaptations for feeding on different foods in different ways have shaped the body structures of animals. Most filter feeders catch algae and small animals by using modified gills or other structures that filter food items out of water. Detritivores feed on detritus. Herbivores eat plants or algae. Carnivores eat other animals. Many animals rely on symbiosis for their nutritional needs.

Food must be digested and absorbed to make energy and nutrients available to body tissues. The simplest animals digest food inside specialized cells that pass nutrients to other cells by diffusion. More complex animals break food down outside cells in a digestive cavity or a digestive tract. Specialized mouthparts are related to the different characteristics of meat and plant leaves. Carnivores have sharp mouthparts that capture food and tear or slice it. Herbivores eat plants or algae. Because cellulose in plant tissues cannot be digested, some herbivores re-chew food after it has been partially digested in the rumen.

- digestive tract
- rumen

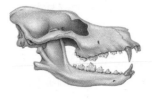 

☑ **Compare and Contrast** Which jaw is that of a carnivore? Which is the herbivore's? Explain how the differences in the structures relate to the types of food eaten by carnivores and herbivores.

### 25.2 Respiration

All animals must exchange oxygen and carbon dioxide with their surroundings. Gases diffuse most efficiently across a thin, moist membrane that is permeable to those gases. Respiratory structures provide a large surface area of moist, selectively permeable membranes. They maintain a difference in the relative concentrations of oxygen and carbon dioxide on either side of the respiratory membranes, promoting diffusion. Some aquatic animals rely on diffusion through their outer body covering. Many aquatic invertebrates exchange gases through gills. Some aquatic reptiles and mammals breathe with lungs and must hold their breath underwater.

Respiratory surfaces in terrestrial invertebrates include skin, mantle cavities, book lungs, and tracheal tubes. All terrestrial vertebrates breathe with lungs. Mammalian lungs branch extensively, with branches ending in alveoli that provide a large surface area for gas exchange. Bird lungs have evolved a system of tubes and air sacs that permit more efficient gas exchange, helping birds obtain the oxygen they need to power flight muscles for long periods of time.

- gill
- lung
- alveolus

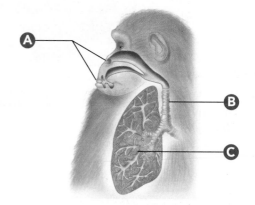

☑ **Identify** What are the structures labeled A, B, and C? What are their functions in respiration?

## 25.3 Circulation

Many animals move blood through their bodies using one or more hearts. A heart is a hollow, muscular organ that pumps blood. Open circulatory systems pump blood through vessels that empty into a system of sinuses or spongy cavities. In closed circulatory systems blood circulates entirely within blood vessels. Nutrients and oxygen reach body tissues by diffusing across thin walls of capillaries.

Most vertebrates with gills have a single-loop circulatory system with a single pump that circulates blood in one direction. Most vertebrates that breathe with lungs have a double-loop, two-pump circulatory system. One side of the heart pumps oxygen-poor blood from the heart to the lungs, where it picks up oxygen and drops off carbon dioxide. It returns to the other side of the heart, which pumps the oxygen-rich blood to the rest of the body.

- heart
- open circulatory system
- closed circulatory system
- atrium
- ventricle

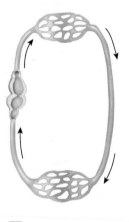 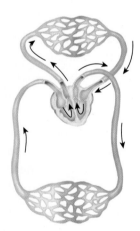

☑ **Compare and Contrast** How are these two circulatory systems alike? How do they differ?

## 25.4 Excretion

When cells break down proteins, they produce ammonia. Ammonia is poisonous, so it must be either excreted quickly or converted to a less harmful form. Insects, reptiles, and birds convert ammonia to a white pasty compound called uric acid. Mammals and some amphibians convert ammonia to urea, which is soluble in water. Many animals use kidneys to separate wastes and excess water from blood in the fluid called urine. Aquatic animals can allow ammonia to diffuse out of their bodies into surrounding water. Saltwater animals must actively maintain their osmotic balance by excreting salt across their gills.

Some terrestrial invertebrates produce urine in tube-like excretory structures called nephridia. Insects and arachnids convert ammonia into uric acid, which is absorbed from body fluids by structures called Malpighian tubules. In many terrestrial vertebrates, kidneys generate urine that is excreted out of the body.

- excretion
- kidney
- nephridium
- Malpighian tubule

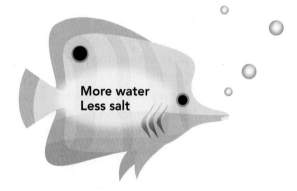

More water
Less salt

☑ **Interpret Visuals** How does this saltwater fish maintain its osmotic balance?

# Organize Information

Describe how each of these organ systems contributes to the maintenance of homeostasis.

| Digestive | Respiratory | Circulatory | Excretory |
|---|---|---|---|
| 1. | 2. | 3. | 4. |

# Design a Zoo Exhibit

## Design a Solution

HS-LS2-7, HS-ETS1-2, HS-ETS1-3, CCSS.ELA-LITERACY.WHST.9-10.7, CCSS.ELA-LITERACY.WHST.9-10.8,
CCSS.ELA-LITERACY.WHST.9-10.9

**STEM** Throughout the 1800s, zoos began opening in cities around the world. The zoos were founded to display wild animals to a curious public. Most animals were kept in cages or simple pens. Some animals were taught tricks to entertain visitors.

Today, zoos are more popular than ever. In the United States, more than 50 million people visit zoos every year. However, the purpose of zoos has grown beyond entertainment. Today, zoos promote the conservation of wildlife. Sometimes they act as a temporary stop for an animal before it is returned to the wild. Zoos may also become the last refuge for endangered animals, such as elephants, tigers, and baboons. The natural habitats of these animals have been disappearing. In the near future, only the artificial habitats in zoos may remain.

In this activity, you will design an animal exhibit for a zoo. This task is complex because the exhibit must meet many criteria. The exhibit should provide for the safety, health, and well-being of the animals it houses.

It must also allow visitors to observe and interact with the animals. Zookeepers must have access to the exhibit so that they can feed and care for the animals when necessary.

To begin, your teacher will assign one of the animals listed in the table. Alternatively, choose one of these animals or another wild animal that interests you. Then follow the steps to design and construct a model of a zoo exhibit.

| Criteria for Animal Exhibits | | |
|---|---|---|
| **Animal** | **Natural Habitat** | **Exhibit Criteria** |
| Penguins | Coastlines of Antarctica, Southern Ocean | • Water and land<br>• Aboveground and underwater viewing stations |
| Giraffes | African savanna | • Tall feeding platforms<br>• Elevated viewing stations |
| Bats (many species) | Caves, forests | • Artificial day/night cycle, so viewers can see nocturnal activity |

1. **Define the Problem** In your own words, describe the problem that your design for a zoo exhibit should solve.

2. **Ask Questions** What questions would help you gather information to design the zoo exhibit? List at least three questions.

3. **Conduct Research** Use the Internet or print reference sources to research answers to the questions you asked. Find out about the animals' natural habitat, and how the animals are displayed in existing zoo or aquarium exhibits. Look for ideas that you could include or adapt in the exhibit you are designing.

4. **Identify Criteria** Review the criteria for a zoo exhibit. Add criteria that apply to the animal that you selected.

5. **Develop Possible Solutions** Discuss your ideas for the exhibit with group members. Draw sketches to illustrate your ideas and to help you revise them. Work as a group to agree on a plan that incorporates all useful ideas and suggestions. Make a sketch or simple blueprint to show the plan for the exhibit.

6. **Revise Solutions** Review the criteria that you listed in step 4. Evaluate your plan to see if it meets all the criteria. Revise your plan if necessary.

7. **Develop Models** Follow the plan you devised to construct a model of the animal exhibit. The model could be a detailed drawing, a virtual model on a computer, or a physical model built from simple materials. Your model should include the following features:

   - an enclosure for the animals

   - viewing stations or platforms for zoo visitors to observe the animals

   - descriptions of any unusual materials needed to construct the exhibit

   - a written explanation of the features of the model and how they meet the criteria

8. **Revise Your Model** Present your model to classmates, and ask them to evaluate and critique it. If appropriate, revise the model to incorporate useful suggestions.

## 🔑 KEY IDEAS AND TERMS

### 25.1 Feeding and Digestion
HS-LS1-1, HS-LS1-2, HS-LS1-3

1. Aquatic animals that strain plants and animals from the water that they live in are
   a. parasites.
   b. herbivores.
   c. detritus feeders.
   d. filter feeders.

2. Look at the teeth in the photograph. The sharp, pointed teeth in the lion's mouth are best suited for

   a. tearing meat.
   b. filtering plankton.
   c. grinding leaves.
   d. cracking seeds.

3. Describe the differences between the canine and molar teeth of herbivorous and carnivorous animals.

4. What is the difference between mechanical and chemical digestion?

5. How do vertebrate filter feeders obtain food?

6. Explain the function of the rumen in digestion. What advantage is provided to animals that have a rumen?

### 25.2 Respiration
HS-LS1-1, HS-LS1-2

7. Which of the following groups of animals has the most efficient gas exchange?
   a. amphibians      c. birds.
   b. reptiles.       d. mammals.

8. Gases diffuse most efficiently across a
   a. thin, moist, selectively permeable membrane.
   b. thin, dry, permeable membrane.
   c. thick, dry, selectively permeable membrane.
   d. thick, moist, impermeable membrane.

9. Why do whales and sea turtles come to the surface regularly to breathe?

10. How are some aquatic animals able to breathe without lungs or gills?

11. What respiratory organ is present in all terrestrial vertebrates?

12. What do skin, mantle cavities, book lungs, and tracheal tubes have in common?

### 25.3 Circulation
HS-LS1-1, HS-LS1-2, HS-LS1-3

13. A closed circulatory system is one in which
    a. blood spreads freely throughout the body's tissues.
    b. blood travels through a system of blood vessels that extend throughout the body.
    c. blood travels through blood vessels into spongy cavities called sinuses.
    d. blood travels through a system of blood vessels and air sacs.

14. Oxygen constantly diffuses from air or water into an animal's bloodstream. For this to happen, the concentration of oxygen in the blood must be
    a. greater than the concentration of oxygen in the air or water.
    b. greater than the concentration of carbon dioxide in the air or water.
    c. lower than the concentration of oxygen in the air or water.
    d. lower than the concentration of carbon dioxide in the air or water.

15. What are the different functions of the atrium and the ventricle?

16. How do the circulatory systems of arthropods and most mollusks differ from those of larger mollusks and all vertebrates?

17. What characteristic of the reptilian heart shows an evolutionary similarity toward the mammalian four-chambered heart?

18. You are dissecting an organism that has a three-chambered heart, but no partition in the ventricle. What type of animal are you likely working with?

## 25.4 Excretion

HS-LS1-1, HS-LS1-2, HS-LS1-3

19. Kidneys that can conserve water are essential to homeostasis because
    a. some animals live in dry or salty environments.
    b. some animals drink water.
    c. urea is not soluble in water.
    d. cells will be unable to convert ammonia into urea if excess water is excreted.

20. Insects convert ammonia to uric acid in their
    a. nephrons.
    b. nephridia.
    c. kidneys.
    d. Malpighian tubules.

21. What do animals do to eliminate ammonia from their bodies?

22. What is the difference in kidney function of fresh-water fishes and saltwater fishes?

23. How do some desert animals overcome the disadvantage of excreting urine?

24. Why can drinking salt water kill an animal?

## CRITICAL THINKING

HS-LS1-2

25. **Construct an Explanation** Why are fruits more commonly used as foods than the leaves of plants?

26. **Integrate Information** How is mutualistic symbiosis essential for human life? Include an example as evidence.

27. **Classify** In a cnidarian, water and food particles flow in and out of an interior space. Is this space classified as a digestive cavity or a digestive tract? Explain your answer.

28. **Ask Questions** Hummingbirds eat high-energy foods such as nectar. Many ducks eat foods that contain less energy, such as plant leaves. What are some research questions you could investigate to discover more about the diet of a bird species and its energy needs?

29. **Infer** A student is studying the skeleton of a large mammal. Which feature of the skeleton is most likely to be useful for classifying the animal as an herbivore or carnivore? Explain.

30. **Interpret Visuals** The diagrams represent two kinds of circulatory systems.

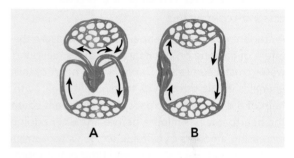

A          B

   a. Which diagram illustrates a heart with blood containing carbon dioxide but little oxygen?
   b. Which diagram shows the type of circulatory system that occurs with a four-chambered heart?

31. **Construct an Explanation** How do a fish's respiratory and circulatory systems work together to maintain homeostasis in the body as a whole?

32. **Critique** The textbook describes ammonia as a problem for organisms to solve. Critique this statement.

33. **Apply Concepts** Of all the nitrogenous wastes that animals generate, uric acid requires the least water to eliminate. Why is the production of uric acid an advantage to animals that live on land?

34. **Infer** How is it useful for tissues of the respiratory system to cover a large surface area?

35. **Evaluate Claims** A classmate claims that with enough time and food, an earthworm could grow as large as an alligator. How do you evaluate this claim? Apply facts about the earthworm's body systems to support your evaluation.

36. **Construct an Explanation** Kidneys are able to vary the concentration of urine they produce. How does this ability help an animal that lives in dry environments on land?

## CROSSCUTTING CONCEPTS

**37. Structure and Function** How do digestive tracts differ between grass-eating herbivores, such as cattle and sheep, and carnivores, such as lions and tigers? Explain this difference.

**38. Systems and System Models** How do the respiratory systems of fishes compare with those of animals that live on land?

## MATH CONNECTIONS

## Analyze and Interpret Data

CCSS.MATH.CONTENT.MP.2

A student conducts an experiment to measure the effect of caffeine on the heart rate of a small pond-water crustacean called *Daphnia*. The heart of this animal is visible through its transparent shell. With the help of a dissecting microscope, the student counts the heartbeats per minute before and after adding increasing amounts of caffeine to the water surrounding the animal. Each data point in the graph represents the mean of five trials. Use the graph to answer questions 39 and 40.

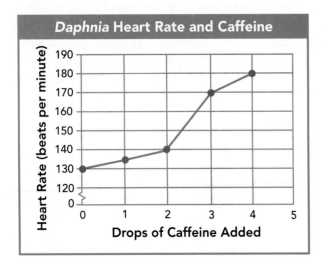

**Daphnia Heart Rate and Caffeine**

**39. Interpret Graphs** Describe the effect of caffeine on the heart rate of *Daphnia*.

**40. Predict** What would be your prediction of the effect of five or more drops of caffeine on the heart rate of *Daphnia*?

A researcher conducted an experiment to see how air temperature affects the speed at which a snake can hunt for food. The experimenter placed the snake a fixed distance away from a piece of food and recorded the air temperature. Then she recorded the time it took for the snake to reach the food. She repeated the experiment four times. Each time, the experimenter changed the air temperature. The data collected are shown in the data table.

| The Effect of Temperature on Snake Hunting Speed | |
|---|---|
| Temperature (°C) | Time (seconds) |
| 4 | 51 |
| 10 | 50 |
| 15 | 43 |
| 21 | 37 |
| 27 | 35 |

**41. Interpret Tables** At what temperature did the snake reach the food the fastest?

**42. Analyze Data** How did the time to reach the food change as the temperature increased?

**43. Draw Conclusions** What conclusions about snake hunting and temperature can you draw from the data?

## LANGUAGE ARTS CONNECTIONS

## Write About Science

CCSS.ELA-LITERACY.WHST.9-10.2, HS-LS1-2

**44. Write Explanatory Texts** Write a paragraph to compare and contrast the structure and function of the fish heart and the mammal heart.

## Read About Science

HS-LS1-2, CCSS.ELA-LITERACY.RST.9-10.1

**45. Cite Textual Evidence** How does a bird's specialized respiratory system provide an adaptation that helps it to fly? Cite evidence from this chapter to support your answer.

1. The illustration below shows models of two different circulatory systems.

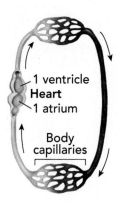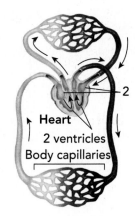

How do these models illustrate two body systems working together?

A. The heart of the circulatory system pumps oxygen-poor blood to the tissues of the excretory system so it can be excreted.

B. The heart of the circulatory system pumps oxygen-poor blood to the tissues of the respiratory system where the blood is oxygenated.

C. The heart of the circulatory system pumps blood to the tissues of the digestive system where the blood is oxygenated during digestion.

D. The ventricles of the respiratory system contract to force blood throughout the tissues of the circulatory system.

E. The ventricles of the respiratory system contract to force oxygenated air through the digestive system.

2. Which of the following is a relationship between the digestive system and another system that allows carnivores to eat meat?

A. The respiratory system has passages where food particles can enter the digestive system.

B. Food is digested inside specialized immune system cells that are in the digestive system.

C. Muscles within the digestive system contract to regurgitate partially digested meat.

D. The jaw bones of the skeletal system are specialized to chop meat and begin the process of digestion.

E. The circulatory system pumps food particles throughout the tissues of the digestive system.

3. Renee is creating a diagram of nitrogen metabolism in animals. How do animals get rid of their nitrogen-containing wastes?

A. they are removed from the blood in the lungs and exhaled

B. they are removed from the blood in the kidneys and excreted

C. they are digested by symbiotic microorganisms in the gut

D. they are converted to amino acids

E. they are converted to nucleic acids

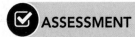 ASSESSMENT

For additional assessment practice, go online to access your digital course.

| If You Have Trouble With... | | | |
| --- | --- | --- | --- |
| Question | 1 | 2 | 3 |
| See Lesson | 25.3 | 25.1 | 25.4 |
| Performance Expectation | HS-LS1-2 | HS-LS1-2 | HS-LS1-2 |

| 26.1 | 26.2 | 26.3 | 26.4 |
| Response | Movement and Support | Reproduction | Homeostasis |

**Go Online to access your digital course.**

▶ VIDEO

🔊 AUDIO

👆 INTERACTIVITY

📖 eTEXT

👁 ANIMATION

🧪 VIRTUAL LAB

☑ ASSESSMENT

The wings of birds, such as this African fish eagle, served as an inspiration for airplanes.

HS-LS1-1, HS-LS1-2, HS-LS1-3, HS-LS1-4, HS-LS4-2, HS-ETS1-1, HS-ETS1-2

# How can engineers learn from animal systems?

Dreams of imitating animals' abilities are as old as the human imagination. More than 2000 years ago, Greek myths told of an inventor who used bird wings as models for artificial wings that could allow him to fly with his son, Icarus. Centuries later, in the real world, artist and inventor Leonardo Da Vinci used birds as inspiration in his efforts to design and build "flying machines." And a little more than 100 years ago, two bicycle mechanics observed how the structure and shape of pigeons' wings enabled them to fly. After testing lots of prototypes, Wilbur and Orville Wright actually did build a successful "flying machine"—their first airplane—in 1903.

Today collaborations between biology and engineering design have a name: biomimicry, or "mimicking life." Translating that concept into engineering solutions that work requires tackling design challenges from two approaches at once.

Approach 1: Engineers identify a human need and create what is called a "design brief" that describes and defines a design challenge.

Approach 2: Biologists search for a living system in which evolution has "solved" that challenge. They ask, "What structures in nature enable organisms to fly? Or run quickly? Or swim through water with minimal drag? Or climb walls?"

Then biologists and engineers combine approaches 1 and 2. First, they work together to identify how those biological structures perform the desired function. Then they figure out how to apply what they've learned in designing an engineering solution.

Natural selection has produced some animal structures we can adapt for our purposes and other structures we can't use so well. So bird wings, for example, have served as useful models for airplane wings. Bee and dragonfly wings, not so much.

But insect wings offer different inspiration for engineers designing more efficient blades for wind turbines. Insect wings are sturdy, yet flexible. Studies of insect flight show that slightly elastic wings can adapt to changing wind conditions in ways that improve performance. Early trials of "insect-wing" prototypes suggest that turbine blades of the right flexibility could generate 35 percent more power than rigid blades!

There are hundreds of examples. Engineers trying to boost the speed of Japan's "bullet trains" hit a challenge. The trains were moving so quickly that when they entered tunnels, they created shock waves strong enough to damage tunnel structures! Solution? Engineers modeled the "nose" of the train after the beaks of kingfishers—birds that nose-dive into water to snag their prey ... and do so with very little splash. Trains with kingfisher-inspired noses create no shock waves, but also run faster, and use less energy!

What else can inventors learn from studying animals? Can you think of a useful design patterned after an animal body part or activity? **Throughout this chapter, look for connections to the** CASE STUDY **to help you answer these questions.**

# Response

Imagine that you are at a favorite place—a beach, a volleyball court ... wherever. Think about how the sun and wind feel on your face. Or how you should judge the distance and location of other players as you prepare for the perfect spike. Now think about the way you experience that place. You gather information about your surroundings through senses such as vision and hearing. Your brain decides how to respond to that information. Then your muscles transform that decision into action. All animals do pretty much these same things, but the sensory world of a dog, cat, or mosquito is different from yours. Let's examine why.

## How Animals Respond

Animals must often respond to events or environmental conditions within seconds, or even fractions of a second. Sometimes they need to catch food. Other times, they need to avoid being caught by other animals that want to make them into food! Most animals have evolved nervous systems that enable them to respond to events around them. Nervous systems are composed of different kinds of nerve cells, or **neurons**. Neurons are connected to one another in ways that enable them to pass information from one cell to the next. In this way, neurons acquire information from their surroundings, interpret that information, and then "decide" what to do about it.

**Detecting Stimuli** Information in the environment that causes an organism to react is called a **stimulus**. Chemicals in air or water can serve as stimuli. Light or heat can also stimulate the nervous system. The sound of your phone buzzing or vibrating on a Friday night is a stimulus that might prompt you to answer it. Animals' ability to detect stimuli depends on specialized cells called **sensory neurons**. Each type of sensory neuron responds to a particular stimulus such as light, heat, or a chemical.

Humans have many types of sensory cells similar to those in other animals. For that reason, many animals react to stimuli that humans notice, too, including light, taste, odor, temperature, sound, water, gravity, and pressure. But many animals have types of sensory cells that humans don't have. That's one reason that some animals respond to stimuli that humans can't detect, such as weak electric currents or Earth's magnetic field.

**Processing Information** Does a particular odor indicate food or danger? Is the immediate environment too hot, too cold, or just right? When sensory neurons detect a stimulus, they pass information about it to other nerve cells. Those neurons, which typically pass information to yet more neurons, are called **interneurons**, shown in **Figure 26-1**. Interneurons process information and determine how an animal responds. The number of interneurons an animal has, and the ways those interneurons process information, determine how flexible and complex an animal's behavior can be.

Some invertebrates, such as cnidarians and worms, have few interneurons. These animals are capable of only simple responses to stimuli. They may swim toward light or toward a chemical stimulus that signals food. Vertebrates, such as this leopard, have more highly developed nervous systems with greater numbers of interneurons, especially in the brain. This is the reason that vertebrate behaviors can be more complex than behaviors of most invertebrates.

**Responding** A specific reaction to a stimulus is called a **response**. For example, waking up when you hear your alarm clock go off is a response. 🔍 *When an animal responds to a stimulus, body systems—including the nervous system and the muscular system—work together to generate the response.* Responses to many stimuli are directed by the nervous system. However, those responses are usually carried out by other types of cells or tissues, such as muscle tissue. Nerve cells called **motor neurons** carry "directions" from interneurons to muscles. Other responses to environmental conditions may be carried out by other body systems, such as respiratory or circulatory systems.

✅ **READING CHECK** **Classify** What type of nerves do animals use when they respond to loud noises?

**BUILD VOCABULARY**

**Prefixes** The prefix *inter-* means "between" or "among." An **interneuron** is located between two other neurons.

**Figure 26-1**

# Neural Circuits

In some neural circuits, sensory neurons connect to motor neurons in ways that enable fast but simple responses. In others, specialized sensory cells connect to sensory neurons, which connect to interneurons, which connect to motor neurons. Mammals, such as the leopard shown, have complex neural circuits, and therefore can process and respond to information in complex ways.

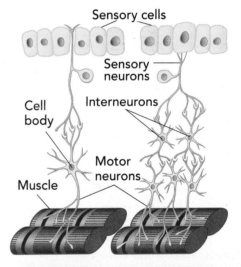

Sensory cells
Sensory neurons
Cell body
Interneurons
Muscle
Motor neurons

# Trends in Nervous System Evolution

Nervous systems vary greatly in organization and complexity across the animal kingdom. ✍ *Animal nervous systems exhibit different degrees of cephalization and specialization.*

**Invertebrates** Invertebrate nervous systems range from simple collections of nerve cells to complex organizations that include many interneurons. You can see some examples in **Figure 26-2**.

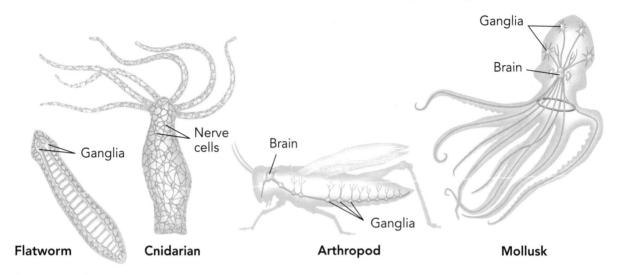

Flatworm     Cnidarian     Arthropod     Mollusk

**Figure 26-2**

## Invertebrate Nervous Systems

Invertebrate nervous systems have different degrees of cephalization and complexity. Flatworms have centralized nervous systems with small ganglia in their heads. Cnidarians have a nerve net that despite its simplicity, enables them to be successful predators. Arthropods and cephalopod mollusks have a brain and specialized sensory organs.

***Nerve Nets, Nerve Cords, and Ganglia*** Cnidarians, such as jellyfishes, have simple nervous systems called nerve nets. As the name implies, nerve nets consist of neurons connected into a net-like arrangement with few specializations. In echinoderms such as sea stars, some interneurons are grouped together into nerves or nerve cords that form a ring around the animals' mouths and stretch out along their appendages. In other invertebrates, interneurons are grouped together into small structures called **ganglia** (singular: ganglion), where interneurons connect with one another.

***"Heads"*** As you learned in Chapter 24, bilaterally symmetric animals often exhibit cephalization, the concentration of sensory neurons and interneurons into a "head." Certain flatworms and roundworms show some cephalization. Some cephalopod mollusks and many arthropods show higher degrees of cephalization. In these animals, interneurons form ganglia in several places. Typically, the largest ganglia are located in the head region and are called cerebral ganglia.

***Brains*** In some species, cerebral ganglia are further organized into a structure called a brain. The brains of some cephalopods, such as octopuses, enable complex behavior, including several kinds of learning. In fact, some cephalopod mollusks, such as this octopus, can be trained to complete tasks such as opening a jar!

**Chordates** Some very simple chordates have nothing you would recognize as a "head" as adults, but still have a cerebral ganglion. Most vertebrates show a high degree of cephalization and have highly developed nervous systems. Vertebrate brains are formed from many interneurons within the skull. These interneurons are connected with each other and with sensory neurons and motor neurons in the head and elsewhere in the body. The human brain contains more than 100 billion nerve cells, each of which sends signals to as many as 1000 other nerve cells and receives signals from up to 10,000 more.

*Parts of the Vertebrate Brain* Regions of the vertebrate brain include the cerebrum, cerebellum, medulla oblongata, optic lobes, and olfactory bulbs. The **cerebrum** is the "thinking" region of the brain. It receives and interprets sensory information and determines a response. The cerebrum is also involved in learning, memory, and conscious thought. The **cerebellum** coordinates movement and controls balance, while the medulla oblongata controls the functioning of many internal organs. Optic lobes are involved in vision, and olfactory bulbs are involved in the sense of smell. Vertebrate brains are connected to the rest of the body by a thick collection of nerves called a spinal cord, which runs through a tube in the vertebral column.

*Vertebrate Brain Evolution* Brain evolution in vertebrates follows a general trend of increasing size and complexity from fishes, through amphibians and reptiles, to birds and mammals. **Figure 26-3** shows how the size and complexity of the cerebrum and cerebellum increase.

✔ **READING CHECK** **Infer** How do the folds of the mammalian cerebellum increase its surface area?

**READING TOOL**

The main idea of this section is that evolution has lead to increasing cephalization and specialization in animal nervous systems. Look for and identify the details that support this idea.

**INTERACTIVITY**

**Figure 26-3**

**Vertebrate Brains**

The cerebrum and cerebellum increase in size from fish to mammal. In fishes, amphibians, and reptiles, the cerebrum, or "thinking" region, is relatively small. In birds and mammals, and especially in primates, the cerebrum is much larger and may contain folds that increase its surface area. The cerebellum is also most highly developed in birds and mammals.

| ▮ Olfactory bulb | ▮ Cerebellum |
| --- | --- |
| ▮ Cerebrum | ▮ Medulla oblongata |
| ▮ Optic lobe | ▮ Spinal cord |

  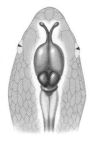  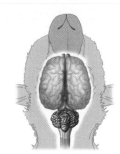

**Bony Fish**　　**Amphibian**　　**Reptile**　　**Bird**　　**Mammal**

👆 **INTERACTIVITY**

Learn how different sense organs are adapted to the their needs.

# Sensory Systems

The more complex an animal's nervous system is, the more developed its sensory systems tend to be. ✎ *Sensory systems range from individual sensory neurons to sense organs that contain both sensory neurons and other cells that help gather information.*

**Invertebrate Sense Organs** Many invertebrates have sense organs that detect light, sound, vibrations, movement, body orientation, and chemicals in air or water. Invertebrate sense organs vary widely in complexity. Flatworms, for example, have simple eyespots that detect only the presence and direction of light. More cephalized invertebrates have specialized sensory tissues and well-developed sense organs. Some cephalopods and arthropods have complex eyes that detect motion and color and form images. **Figure 26-4** shows a variety of invertebrate sensory systems.

**Chordate Sense Organs** The simplest chordates have few specialized sense organs. In tunicates, sensory cells in and on the siphons and other internal surfaces help control the amount of water passing through the pharynx. Lancelets have a cerebral ganglion with a pair of eyespots that detect light.

Most vertebrates have highly evolved sense organs, as you can see in **Figure 26-5**. Many have very sensitive organs of taste, smell, and hearing. Some sharks, for example, can sense 1 drop of blood in 100 liters of water! And although all mammalian ears have the same basic parts, they differ in their ability to detect sound. Bats and dolphins can find objects in their environment using echoes of their own high-frequency sounds. A great many species of fishes, amphibians, reptiles, birds, and mammals have color vision that is as good as, or better than, that of humans.

### Figure 26-4

### Invertebrate Sense Organs

The compound eye of this insect is made up of many lenses that detect minute changes in movement.

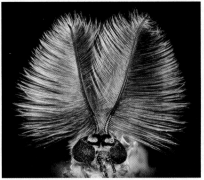

The antennae of this male midge can sense sound waves and air motion.

The garden spider can detect vibrations in its web through its legs.

Some species, including certain fishes and duck-billed platypuses, can detect weak electric currents in water. Some sharks use this "electric sense" to navigate by detecting electric currents in seawater caused by ocean currents moving through Earth's magnetic field. Other "electric fish" create their own electric currents. These fishes use electric pulses to communicate with one another in much the same way that other animals communicate using sound. Many species that can detect electric currents use that ability to track down prey in dark, murky water. Some birds can detect Earth's magnetic field directly, and they use that ability to navigate during their long-distance migrations.

CASE STUDY

Figure 26-5

## Vertebrate Sense Organs

The senses and sense organs of vertebrates can inspire inventors. For example, the ability of bats and dolphins to sense objects through reflected sound inspired naval sonar and medical sonograms. The rattlesnake can detect infrared (heat) radiation from other animals using an organ in its face, similar to motion detectors in alarm systems. The eagle has extremely sharp eyesight. The eye helped inspire the invention of the camera.

**HS-LS1-1, HS-LS1-2**

## ✓ LESSON 26.1 Review

### ⚲ KEY QUESTIONS

1. What is the role of motor neurons in the response to stimuli?

2. Describe three examples of specialization in the nervous systems of animals.

3. Give an example of an animal with a very simple sensory system and an example of one with a complex sensory system.

### CRITICAL THINKING

4. **Construct an Explanation** An eagle sees a mouse on the ground and then swoops down to catch it. Describe the events that occur in the nervous system of the eagle as it completes this activity.

5. **Interpret Visuals** Study the vertebrate brains shown in **Figure 26-3**. Compare the brain of the mammal with other brains. How do brain structures help explain the abilities of mammals?

# Movement and Support

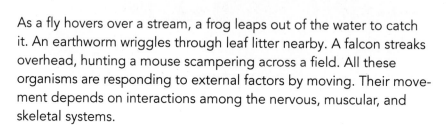

**HS-LS1-2:** Develop and use a model to illustrate the hierarchical organization of interacting systems that provide specific functions within multicellular organisms.

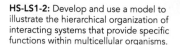

**VOCABULARY**
hydrostatic skeleton
exoskeleton
endoskeleton
joint

**READING TOOL**

As you read through this lesson, take notes on the different types of skeletons that protect and support organisms. Fill in the graphic organizer in your 📖 **Biology Foundations Workbook.**

As a fly hovers over a stream, a frog leaps out of the water to catch it. An earthworm wriggles through leaf litter nearby. A falcon streaks overhead, hunting a mouse scampering across a field. All these organisms are responding to external factors by moving. Their movement depends on interactions among the nervous, muscular, and skeletal systems.

## Types of Skeletons

To move efficiently, all animals must generate physical force and somehow apply that force against air, water, or land in order to push or pull themselves around.

**Skeletal Support** Animals can move most efficiently if they have some kind of rigid body parts. Why? Because rigid body parts help apply the force generated by muscles. Legs push against the ground. Bird wings push against air. Fins or flippers apply force against water. Each of these body parts is rigid because each is supported by some sort of skeleton. 🔍 *Animals have three main kinds of skeletal systems: hydrostatic skeletons, exoskeletons, and endoskeletons.* The three types of skeletons are shown in **Figure 26-6.**

***Hydrostatic Skeletons*** Some invertebrates, such as cnidarians and annelids, have hydrostatic skeletons. The **hydrostatic skeleton** of an earthworm, for example, consists of fluids held in a body cavity that can alter the earthworm's body shape by working with contractile cells in its body wall. Earthworms have two major groups of body muscles. Longitudinal muscles run from the front of the worm to the rear and can contract to make the worm shorter and fatter. Circular muscles wrap around each body segment and can contract to make the worm longer and thinner. The earthworm moves by alternately contracting these two sets of muscles.

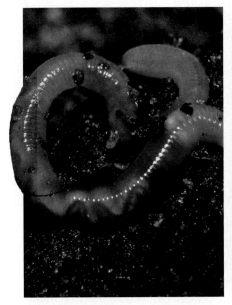

Earthworm: Hydrostatic Skeleton    Cicada: Exoskeleton    Crinoid: Endoskeleton

*Exoskeletons* Many arthropods have **exoskeletons**, or external skeletons, as do most mollusks, such as snails and clams. Arthropod exoskeletons, which typically cover their bodies, are made of a complex carbohydrate called chitin. Most mollusks have hard shells made of calcium carbonate. Arthropods' exoskeletons enable them to swim, fly, burrow, walk, crawl, and leap. They can also provide watertight coverings that enable some species to live in Earth's driest places. An exoskeleton can also provide physical protection from predators—as you know if you have ever tried to crack a crab shell. Mollusks with two-part shells can also close their shells to avoid drying out.

But exoskeletons have disadvantages. An external skeleton poses a problem when the animal it belongs to needs to grow. To increase in size, arthropods break out of their exoskeleton and grow a new one in a process called molting. Exoskeletons are also relatively heavy. The larger arthropods get, the heavier their skeletons become in proportion to their body weight. This is one reason that some science fiction monsters could never exist in the real world. The legs of a spider the size of an elephant would collapse under the spider's weight!

*Endoskeletons* Echinoderms and vertebrates have **endoskeletons**, which are any kind of structural support system that is inside the body. Crinoids and other echinoderms have an endoskeleton made of calcified plates. These skeletal plates support and protect echinoderms, and also give them a bumpy texture.

As an internal skeleton does not surround the body, it cannot protect an animal the way that an exoskeleton can. On the other hand, an internal skeleton can grow as an animal grows, so the animal does not need to molt. Because endoskeletons are lightweight in proportion to the bodies they support, even land-dwelling vertebrates can grow very large.

**Figure 26-6**

**Invertebrate Skeletons**

Some invertebrates, such as this earthworm, have hydrostatic skeletons. Many arthropods, such as cicadas, periodically outgrow their exoskeleton and must literally break out of them, and grow a new exoskeleton, in order to increase in size. Some invertebrates (including this crinoid) and all chordates have an endoskeleton.

**BUILD VOCABULARY**

**Prefixes** The prefix *exo-* means "outside," so an **exoskeleton** is outside the animal. The prefix *endo-* means "within," so an **endoskeleton** is within, or inside, the animal.

 **INTERACTIVITY**

Learn how skeletons, muscles, and joints are all related.

**Joints** If any kind of rigid skeleton were made of one piece, or if its parts were rigidly attached to each other, the animal couldn't move. Arthropods and vertebrates can move because their skeletons are divided into many parts that are connected by **joints**. In vertebrates, bones are connected at joints by strong connective tissues called ligaments.

**READING CHECK** **Describe** What features of an endoskeleton provide support and movement?

## Muscles and Movements

The muscular structure of an animal, such as the sloth shown in **Figure 26-7**, helps determine how it lives and moves. Muscles are specialized tissues that produce physical force by contracting, or shortening, when they are stimulated by the nervous system. Muscles can relax when they aren't being stimulated, but they cannot actively get longer. That presents a problem. Think about the way you move. You walk by swinging your legs forward and then backward, pushing against the ground as you walk. But how do you get your legs to move backward and forward if your muscles can generate force in only one direction? The answer involves interactions between the muscular system and the skeletal system. ⚲ *In many animals, muscles work together in pairs or groups that are attached to different parts of a skeleton.* Muscles are attached to bones around the joints by tough connective tissue called tendons. Tendons are attached in such a way that they pull on bones when muscles contract. Typically, muscles are arranged in groups that pull parts of the skeleton in opposite directions.

**Movement** Arthropod muscles are attached to the inside of the exoskeleton. Vertebrate muscles are attached around the outside of bones. In both cases, different pairs or groups of muscles pull across joints in different directions. As you can see in **Figure 26-8**, when one muscle group contracts and the other is relaxed, it bends the joint. When the first group relaxes and the second group contracts, the joint straightens and the first muscle group is stretched. Muscles can only contract, so they must be stretched back into position by the opposing muscle group.

**READING TOOL**

Refer to **Figure 26-8** as you read about muscles and movement. Use the diagram to explain why muscles generally work in pairs to create movement.

**Figure 26-7**

**Vertebrate Musculoskeletal Systems**

A great variety of bones, muscle groups, and joints have evolved in vertebrates. For instance, a sloth's muscles and bones are well suited for climbing through trees.

**Vertebrate Muscular and Skeletal Systems** An amazing variety of complex combinations of bones, muscle groups, and joints have evolved in vertebrates. In many fishes and snakes, muscles are arranged in blocks on opposite sides of the backbone. These muscle blocks contract in waves that travel down the body, bending it first to one side and then to the other. These waves of movement generate thrust. The limbs of many modern amphibians and reptiles stick out sideways, as though the animals were doing push-ups. Sideways movements of their backbone move their limbs forward and backward.

Most mammals stand with their legs straight under them, whether they walk on two legs or four. The shapes and relative positions of bones, muscles, and joints are linked closely to the functions they perform. Limbs may be specialized for high-speed running, flying, swimming, manipulating objects, or climbing. Paleontologists can reconstruct the habits of extinct animals by studying the joints of fossil bones and the places where tendons and ligaments once attached.

 **ANIMATION**

**Figure 26-8**

## Muscles and Joints

The diagrams show how muscles work with a vertebrate endoskeleton and an arthropod exoskeleton to bend and straighten joints.

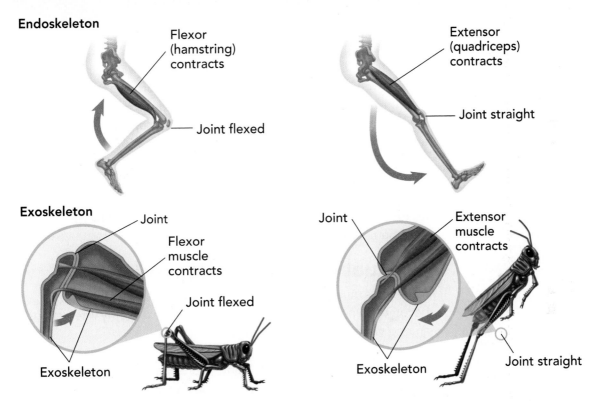

**Endoskeleton**

Flexor (hamstring) contracts

Joint flexed

Extensor (quadriceps) contracts

Joint straight

**Exoskeleton**

Joint

Flexor muscle contracts

Joint flexed

Exoskeleton

Joint

Extensor muscle contracts

Exoskeleton

Joint straight

HS-LS1-2

---

## ✓ LESSON 26.2 Review

### ⚲ KEY QUESTIONS

1. Describe the three main types of skeletons.

2. How does the organization of muscles allow animals a variety of movements?

### CRITICAL THINKING

3. **Predict** When is an animal with an exoskeleton most vulnerable to attack from predators? Explain your prediction.

4. **Construct an Explanation** Why are spiders unable to grow to large sizes, as they are sometimes depicted in science fiction movies?

5. **Use Models** Create a model of a vertebrate or invertebrate joint. Make sure the muscles are attached to the same skeletal structures they would be attached to in a real animal and that the muscles and skeletal structure allow the joint to bend and flex.

# Reproduction

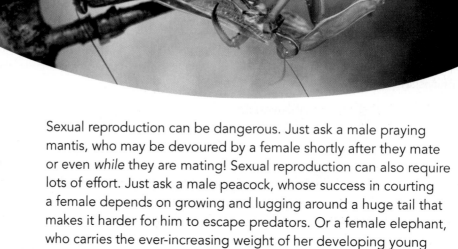

## 🔍 KEY QUESTIONS

- *How do asexual and sexual reproduction in animals compare?*
- *How do internal and external fertilization differ?*
- *Where do embryos develop?*
- *How are terrestrial vertebrates adapted to reproduction on land?*

**HS-LS1-1:** Construct an explanation based on evidence for how the structure of DNA determines the structure of proteins which carry out the essential functions of life through systems of specialized cells.

**HS-LS1-2:** Develop and use a model to illustrate the hierarchical organization of interacting systems that provide specific functions within multicellular organisms.

**HS-LS1-4:** Use a model to illustrate the role of cellular division (mitosis) and differentiation in producing and maintaining complex organisms.

**HS-LS4-2:** Construct an explanation based on evidence that the process of evolution primarily results from four factors: (1) the potential for a species to increase in number, (2) the heritable genetic variation of individuals in a species due to mutation and sexual reproduction, (3) competition for limited resources, and (4) the proliferation of those organisms that are better able to survive and reproduce in the environment.

## VOCABULARY

**placenta**
**metamorphosis**
**amniotic egg**
**mammary gland**

---

### READING TOOL

Keep track of the similarities and differences between sexual and asexual reproduction. Fill in the Venn diagram in your 📕 **Biology Foundations Workbook.**

Sexual reproduction can be dangerous. Just ask a male praying mantis, who may be devoured by a female shortly after they mate or even *while* they are mating! Sexual reproduction can also require lots of effort. Just ask a male peacock, whose success in courting a female depends on growing and lugging around a huge tail that makes it harder for him to escape predators. Or a female elephant, who carries the ever-increasing weight of her developing young for twenty-two months! Yet most animal species engage in sexual reproduction during at least part of their life cycles. Why do they take the risk?

## Asexual and Sexual Reproduction

All animals must reproduce, or their populations and species become extinct. This vital function is made possible by interactions among virtually all body systems.

**Asexual Reproduction** Many invertebrates and a few chordates can reproduce asexually in various ways. Some cnidarians divide in two. Some animals reproduce through budding, which produces new individuals as outgrowths of the body wall. Females of some species can reproduce asexually by producing eggs that develop without being fertilized. This kind of asexual reproduction occurs in some crustaceans and insects but very rarely in vertebrates.

🔍 *Asexual reproduction requires only one parent, so individuals in favorable environmental conditions can reproduce rapidly. Offspring produced asexually carry only a single parent's DNA, so they have less genetic diversity than offspring produced sexually.* Lack of genetic diversity can be a disadvantage to a population if its environment changes.

**Sexual Reproduction** Recall that sexual reproduction in animals involves meiosis, the process that produces haploid reproductive cells, or gametes. Gametes carry half the number of chromosomes found in body cells. Typically, male animals produce small gametes, called sperm, that can "swim" using flagellum. Females produce larger gametes called eggs, which do not swim. When haploid gametes join during fertilization, they produce a zygote that contains the diploid number of chromosomes.

🔍 *Sexual reproduction maintains genetic diversity in a population by creating individuals with new combinations of genes.* Because genetic diversity is the raw material on which natural selection operates, sexually reproducing populations are better able to evolve and adapt to changing environmental conditions. On the other hand, sexual reproduction requires two individuals of different sexes. So the density of a population must be high enough to allow mates to find each other.

In most animal species that reproduce sexually, every individual is either male or female. Among annelids, mollusks, and fishes, however, some species are hermaphrodites (hur MAF roh dyts), which means that some individuals can function as both male and female. Some hermaphrodites, such as the nudibranch in **Figure 26-9**, can produce eggs and sperm at the same time. Usually these animals don't fertilize their own eggs but rather exchange sperm with another individual. Other hermaphroditic species change from one sex to the other as they mature.

 **VIDEO**

Watch some of the different ways that animals are born.

**Figure 26-9**
**Hermaphrodites**

Although nudibranchs are hermaphrodites, they must mate in order to reproduce.

**Reproductive Cycles** A number of invertebrates have life cycles that alternate back and forth between sexual and asexual reproduction. Parasitic worms and cnidarians alternate between forms that reproduce sexually and forms that reproduce asexually.

Parasitic worms, such as blood flukes, mature in the body of an infected person, reproduce sexually, and release embryos that pass out of the body in feces. If the embryos reach fresh water, they develop into larvae and infect snails, in which they reproduce asexually. Then the larvae are released, ready to infect another person.

**Figure 26-10**

## Alternating Reproductive Cycles

The reproductive cycle of *Aurelia*, a jellyfish, alternates between asexual and sexual reproduction.

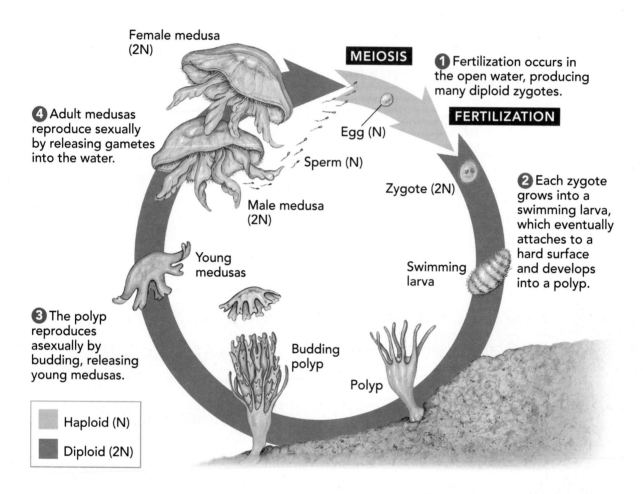

Female medusa (2N)

**MEIOSIS**

**1** Fertilization occurs in the open water, producing many diploid zygotes.

**FERTILIZATION**

**4** Adult medusas reproduce sexually by releasing gametes into the water.

Egg (N)

Sperm (N)

Zygote (2N)

Male medusa (2N)

**2** Each zygote grows into a swimming larva, which eventually attaches to a hard surface and develops into a polyp.

Young medusas

Swimming larva

**3** The polyp reproduces asexually by budding, releasing young medusas.

Budding polyp

Polyp

Haploid (N)

Diploid (2N)

Many cnidarians alternate between two body forms: polyps that grow singly or in colonies, and medusas that swim freely in the water. The life cycle of a common jellyfish, *Aurelia*, is shown in **Figure 26-10**. In these jellyfish, polyps produce medusas asexually by budding. Those medusas then reproduce sexually by producing eggs and sperm they release into the water. After fertilization, the resulting zygote grows into a free-swimming larva that eventually attaches to a hard surface and develops into a polyp.

☑ **READING CHECK** Interpret Diagrams Refer to **Figure 26-10**. Which part of the life cycle includes sexual reproduction?

# Internal and External Fertilization

In sexual reproduction, eggs and sperm may meet either inside or outside the body of the egg-producing individual. These methods are called internal and external fertilization, respectively.

**Internal Fertilization** Many aquatic animals and nearly all terrestrial animals reproduce by internal fertilization. 🔑 *During internal fertilization, eggs are fertilized inside the body of the egg-producing individual.*

*Invertebrates* Many different kinds of invertebrates reproduce by internal fertilization. The eggs of sponges and some other aquatic animals are fertilized by sperm released by others of their species and taken in from the surrounding water. In many arthropod species, males deposit sperm inside the female's body during mating. The crab in **Figure 26-11** carried fertilized eggs until they hatched.

*Chordates* Some fishes and amphibians, and all reptiles, birds, and mammals, reproduce by internal fertilization. In some amphibian species, males deposit "sperm packets" into their environment. Later, females will pick up these packets and put them inside their own body. In many other chordate species, males have an external sexual organ that deposits sperm inside the female during mating.

**External Fertilization** Many aquatic invertebrates and vertebrates reproduce by external fertilization. 🔑 *In external fertilization, eggs are fertilized outside the body of the egg-producing individual.*

*Invertebrates* Invertebrates with external fertilization include corals, worms, and mollusks. These animals release large numbers of eggs and sperm into the water. Gamete release is usually synchronized with tides, phases of the moon, or seasons, so that eggs and sperm are present at the same time. Fertilized eggs develop into free-swimming larvae that typically grow for a time before changing into adult form.

*Chordates* Chordates with external fertilization include most nonvertebrate chordates and many fishes and amphibians. In some fish species, males and females spawn in a school, releasing large numbers of eggs and sperm into the water. Other fishes and many amphibians spawn in pairs. In these cases, the female usually releases eggs onto which the male deposits sperm.

**INTERACTIVITY**

Learn about some of the different reproductive strategies in the animal kingdom.

**Figure 26-11**
## Internal Fertilization

Many female arthropods, like this crab, carry fertilized eggs until they hatch.

# Development and Growth

After eggs are fertilized, the zygote divides through mitosis and the cells undergo differentiation. In this process, the cells develop into the specialized tissues needed for a multicellular organism to function. This development occurs under different circumstances in different species.

**Where Embryos Develop** Embryos develop either inside or outside the body of a parent in various ways. ✎ *Animals may be oviparous, ovoviviparous, or viviparous.*

**Oviparous: Loggerhead sea turtle**

*Oviparous Species* Embryos develop in eggs outside of the parental body in an oviparous (oh VIP uh rus) species. Most invertebrates, many fishes and amphibians, most reptiles, all birds, and a few odd mammals are oviparous.

*Ovoviviparous Species* In species that are ovoviviparous (oh voh vy VIP uh rus), embryos develop within the mother's body, but they depend entirely on the yolk sac of their eggs, and receive no additional nutrients from the mother. The eggs either hatch within the mother's body or are released immediately before hatching. The young swim freely shortly after hatching. Guppies and other fishes in their family, along with some shark species, are ovoviviparous.

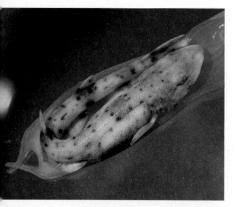

**Ovoviviparous: Cat shark**

*Viviparous Species* Embryos that obtain nutrients from the mother's body during development belong to a viviparous (vy VIP uh rus) species. Viviparity occurs in most mammals and in some insects, sharks, bony fishes, amphibians, and reptiles. In viviparous insects, and in some sharks and amphibians, the young are nourished by secretions produced in the mother's reproductive tract. In placental mammals, the young are nourished by a placenta—a specialized organ that enables exchange of respiratory gases, nutrients, and wastes between the mother and her developing young.

**How Young Develop** Most newborn mammals and newly hatched birds and reptiles look a lot like miniature adults. Infant body proportions are different from those of adults, and newborns have less hair, fur, or feathers than adults have, but it is pretty clear that a newly hatched snake is not going to grow up to be an eagle!

The young of many groups of invertebrates, fishes, and amphibians, however, can look very different from adults. As they develop, they undergo metamorphosis—a developmental process that involves dramatic changes in shape and form.

**Viviparous: Thomson's gazelle**

*Aquatic Invertebrates* Many aquatic invertebrates have a larval stage that looks nothing like an adult. These larvae often swim or drift in open water before undergoing metamorphosis and assuming adult form. Members of some groups, such as cnidarians, have a single larval stage. Other groups, such as crustaceans, may pass through several larval stages before they look like miniature adults.

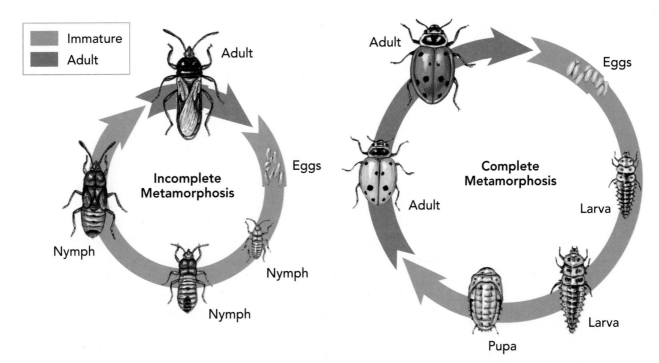

**Terrestrial Invertebrates** Insects may undergo one of two types of metamorphosis, as shown in **Figure 26-12**. Some insects, such as grasshoppers, undergo gradual or incomplete metamorphosis. Immature forms, or nymphs, resemble adults, but lack functional sexual organs and some adult structures such as wings. As they molt several times and grow, nymphs gradually acquire adult structures.

Other insects, such as butterflies, undergo complete metamorphosis. Larvae of these animals look nothing like their parents, and they feed in different ways as well. Larvae molt and grow but change little in appearance. Then they undergo a final molt and change into a pupa (PYOO puh; plural: pupae), the stage in which an insect larva develops into an adult. During the pupal stage, the entire body is remodeled inside and out! The adult that emerges looks like a completely different animal. Don't let your familiarity with caterpillars and butterflies dull your wonder at this change. If land vertebrates underwent this kind of metamorphosis, a larva that looks like a snake could grow up into an eagle.

Hormones control metamorphosis in arthropods. Recall that hormones are chemicals produced in one organ of an organism that affect that organism's other tissues and organs. In insects that undergo complete metamorphosis, high levels of a juvenile hormone keep an insect in its larval form. As the insect matures, its production of juvenile hormone decreases. Eventually, the concentration of juvenile hormone drops below a certain threshold. The next time the insect molts, it becomes a pupa. When no juvenile hormone is produced, the insect undergoes a pupa-to-adult molt.

**Amphibians** Like insects, most amphibians undergo metamorphosis that is controlled by hormones. This metamorphosis changes amphibians from aquatic young into terrestrial adults. Tadpoles are the larvae of a frog or toad.

**INTERACTIVITY**

**Figure 26-12**

**Insect Metamorphosis**

Some insects will undergo metamorphosis during growth. The chinch bug undergoes incomplete metamorphosis, in which the nymphs look similar to adults. The ladybug undergoes complete metamorphosis. The developing larva and the pupa look completely different from the adult.

**INTERACTIVITY**

Explore the commonalities that exist in many species during development.

Relate an animal's reproductive system and strategy to its ability to care for offspring.

**Care of Offspring** Animals' care of their offspring varies from no care at all to years of nurturing. Most aquatic invertebrates and many fishes and amphibians release large numbers of eggs that they completely ignore. This reproductive strategy succeeds in circumstances favoring populations that disperse and grow rapidly.

But other animals care for their offspring. Some amphibians incubate their young in their mouth, on their back, or even in their stomach! Birds and mammals generally care for their young. Maternal care is an important mammalian characteristic. Males of many species also help care for the young. Parental care helps the young survive in crowded, competitive environments. Typically, species that provide intensive or long-term parental care give birth to fewer young than species that offer no parental care.

**✓ READING CHECK Summarize** How is parental care related to the number of offspring that the animal produces?

# Reproductive Diversity in Chordates

Chordates first evolved in water, so early chordate reproduction was suited to aquatic life. The eggs of most modern fishes and amphibians still need to develop in water, or at least in very moist places. As some vertebrate lineages left the water to live on land, they evolved new reproductive strategies. ⚲ *In many terrestrial chordates, reproductive strategies enable the fertilized eggs to develop somewhere other than in a body of water.*

**Figure 26-13**

**Amniotic Egg**

An amniotic egg contains several membranes and an external shell. Although it is waterproof, the eggshell is porous, allowing gases to pass through. The shell of a reptile egg is usually soft and leathery, while the shell of a bird egg is hard and brittle.

**The Amniotic Egg** Reptiles, birds, and a few mammals have evolved amniotic eggs in which an embryo can develop outside its mother's body, and out of water, without drying out. The **amniotic egg** is named after the amnion, one of four membranes that surround the developing embryo. You can learn about the functions of the membranes in **Figure 26-13**. The amniotic egg is one of the most important vertebrate adaptations to life on land.

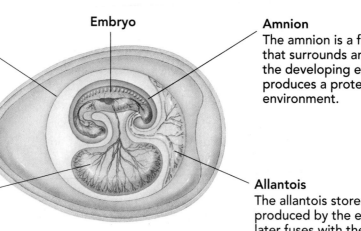

**Chorion**
The chorion regulates the transport of oxygen from the surface of the egg to the embryo and the transport of carbon dioxide, one product of respiration, in the opposite direction.

**Embryo**

**Amnion**
The amnion is a fluid-filled sac that surrounds and cushions the developing embryo. It produces a protected, watery environment.

**Yolk Sac**
This baglike structure contains a yolk that serves as a nutrient-rich food supply for the embryo.

**Allantois**
The allantois stores the waste produced by the embryo. It later fuses with the chorion and serves as a respiratory organ.

## Mammalian Reproductive Strategies

The three groups of mammals—monotremes, marsupials, and placentals—differ greatly in their means of reproduction and development, but all nourish their young with mother's milk.

**Monotremes** Reproduction in monotremes is a bizarre combination of reptilian and mammalian traits. Like a reptile, a female monotreme lays soft-shelled amniotic eggs that are incubated outside her body. The eggs hatch in about ten days. But like other mammals, young monotremes are nourished by milk produced by the mother's **mammary glands**. Female monotremes secrete milk through pores on the surface of the abdomen. The duck-billed platypus and four species of echidna are examples of monotremes.

**Marsupials** Little more than embryos when they emerge, marsupial infants crawl across their mother's fur and attach to a nipple in her pouch. They spend several months drinking milk and completing their development. Kangaroos are marsupial mammals.

**Placentals** Placental mammals are named for the placenta, a specialized organ that transfers nutrients and oxygen to the embryo. It is also the means of removing carbon dioxide and other wastes from the embryo. The placenta allows the embryo to develop for a long time inside the mother and allows the offspring to be born at a fairly advanced stage of development.

### Analyzing Data

## Gestational Period

In placental mammals, the time from fertilization to birth is called the gestational period. The table lists gestational periods and typical weights of several adult female mammals.

| Gestation Time and Weight | | |
|---|---|---|
| Species | Gestation (days) | Female Weight (kg) |
| Mouse | 20 | 0.02 |
| Rabbit | 33 | 1 |
| Goat | 150 | 15 |
| Chimpanzee | 227 | 40 |
| Human | 226 | 50 |
| Bison | 270 | 600 |
| Elephant (African) | 640 | 5000 |

1. **Compare** How does the gestational period of humans compare with that of the other species listed in the table?

2. **Identify Patterns** What trend is shown by the data?

3. **Ask Questions** What questions could you ask, and then investigate, to help explain the trend you identified?

HS-LS1-1, HS-LS1-2, HS-LS1-4, HS-LS4-2

 **LESSON 26.3** Review

### ⚗ KEY QUESTIONS

1. Compare the advantages of sexual reproduction and asexual reproduction.

2. Describe the two main ways that animal eggs are fertilized.

3. Describe the three main ways that animal embryos develop.

4. How did the evolution of the amniotic egg provide an advantage to terrestrial chordates?

### CRITICAL THINKING

5. **Compare and Contrast** How are complete and incomplete metamorphosis alike? How are they different?

6. **Construct an Explanation** How are sperm and egg cells specialized for reproduction? Why is the specialization necessary?

# Homeostasis

A kangaroo rat conserves water so well, it can survive without drinking.

## KEY QUESTIONS

- Why are interactions among body systems essential?
- How do animals control their body temperature?

HS-LS1-2: Develop and use a model to illustrate the hierarchical organization of interacting systems that provide specific functions within multicellular organisms.

HS-LS1-3: Plan and conduct an investigation to provide evidence that feedback mechanisms maintain homeostasis.

## VOCABULARY

endocrine gland
ectotherm
endotherm

## READING TOOL

As you read about ectotherms and endotherms, take notes listing the differences between these types of animals. Fill in the Venn Diagram in your 📖 Biology Foundations Workbook.

A herd of wildebeests plods across Africa's Serengeti Plain. The land is parched, so they move toward greener pastures. They walk slowly, their steps using as little energy as possible. With no food in their guts, their bodies mobilize energy stored in fat deposits, and distribute it to body tissues. Between watering holes, their bodies conserve water by producing as little urine as possible. Survival requires interactions among body systems that perform the functions of regulation, nutrient absorption, reproduction, and defense from injury or illness.

## Interrelationship of Body Systems

Homeostasis, the control of internal conditions, is vital to survival. Kangaroo rats can survive without ever drinking any water, getting all the moisture they need from the other foods they eat. Yet their brain cells, like those of humans, require a stable temperature and a steady stream of glucose for energy—even when the animal is under stress. Brain cells must be bathed in fluid with a constant concentration of water. Metabolic wastes must be eliminated. These conditions must not dramatically change during droughts, floods, famines, heat, or cold. Failure of homeostasis, even for a few minutes, would lead to permanent brain injury or death.

You've learned about the digestive, respiratory, circulatory, excretory, nervous, muscular, and skeletal systems separately. Yet these systems are tightly interconnected. ⚲ **All body systems interact to maintain homeostasis.** In most animals, respiratory and digestive systems would be useless without circulatory systems to distribute oxygen and nutrients. Excretory systems require a circulatory system that collects carbon dioxide and nitrogenous wastes from tissues and delivers them to the lungs and excretory organs. Muscles wouldn't work without a nervous system to direct them and a skeletal system to support them.

In addition to the organ systems you've already learned about, you will now learn about other body systems: those that defend against illness, regulate body temperature, and produce and release hormones that regulate many body systems—all to help ensure homeostasis.

**Fighting Disease** The environment within an animal's body is a comfortable place for disease-causing microorganisms, or pathogens, that may "steal" oxygen and nutrients. If pathogens enter the body and grow, they can disrupt homeostasis in ways that disrupt the health of an organism, causing disease.

Most animals have an immune system that can distinguish between "self" and "other." Once the immune system discovers "others" in the body, it attacks the invaders and works to restore homeostasis. An example is the macrophage attack shown in **Figure 26-14**. You experience this process whenever you catch a cold or fight off other infections. During the process, you may develop a fever and feel other effects of the battle going on within your body.

**Chemical Controls** Most vertebrates and many invertebrates regulate body functions using a system of chemical controls. Endocrine glands are part of that regulatory system. **Endocrine glands** interact with other body systems by releasing hormones into the blood that are carried throughout the body.

In insects, several hormones interact with other body systems to regulate growth, development, and metamorphosis. In vertebrates, several endocrine glands make up an endocrine system that interacts with other body systems. Some endocrine glands receive information about environmental changes from the nervous system. If danger threatens, endocrine glands release hormones that help the body respond rapidly. Other endocrine glands respond to concentrations of water and other molecules in the blood by regulating the amount of water in the body and the amount of calcium in bones.

✅ **READING CHECK** **Summarize** How do endocrine glands help maintain homeostasis?

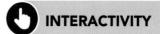

**INTERACTIVITY**

Learn about the various regulatory systems in animals.

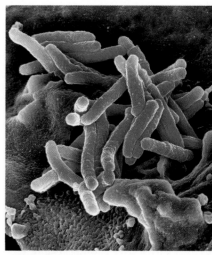

SEM 2600×

**Figure 26-14**

**Macrophages**

The immune system uses white blood cells called macrophages to defend against invaders, such as the tuberculosis bacterium (pink).

HS-LS1-3

🧪 **Modeling Lab**   **Guided Inquiry**

### The Role of Endocrine Glands

**Problem** How do endocrine glands help humans maintain homeostasis?

In this lab, you will use a model to demonstrate the role of the endocrine system in maintaining blood glucose levels. You will use the model to explain the function of the endocrine system and its importance for maintaining homeostasis.

You can find this lab in your digital course.

**INTERACTIVITY**

Explore how endothermic animals are able to maintain their rates of metabolism.

**BUILD VOCABULARY**

**Word Origins** The words **ectotherm** and **endotherm** are both derived from the Greek word *therme*, meaning "heat." The prefix *endo-* is a Greek word meaning "within." Therefore, the word *endotherm* literally means "heat from within."

**Figure 26-15**

## Regulating Body Temperature

This shovel-snouted lizard, an ectotherm, lives in the Namib Desert in Africa, one of the hottest places on Earth. It is regulating its body temperature by stilting—raising its body off the hot sand by performing a sort of push-up. Many endotherms, such as this cheetah, pant when they are very warm. Panting allows air to evaporate some of the moisture in the blood-vessel rich mouth and respiratory tract, cooling the blood.

# Body Temperature Control

Every organism must respond to environmental temperature, because control of body temperature is essential to homeostasis. Why? Many body functions are influenced by temperature. For example, muscles cannot operate if they are too cold or too hot. Cold muscles contract slowly, making an animal slow to react. If muscles get too hot, on the other hand, they may tire easily.

Body temperature control requires three components: a source of heat, a way to conserve heat, and a method of eliminating excess heat. An animal may be described as an ectotherm or endotherm based on the structures and behaviors that enable it to control its body temperature. Two examples are shown in **Figure 26-15**.

**Ectotherms** On cool, sunny mornings, lizards bask in the sun. This doesn't mean that they are lazy! A lizard is an **ectotherm**—an animal whose regulation of body temperature depends mostly on its relationship to sources of heat outside its body. ⚲ *Most reptiles, invertebrates, fishes, and amphibians are ectotherms that regulate body temperature primarily by absorbing heat from, or losing heat to, their environment.*

Ectotherms have relatively low metabolic rates when resting, so their bodies don't generate much heat. When active, their muscles generate heat, just as your muscles do. However, most ectotherms lack effective body insulation, so their body heat is easily lost to the environment. That's why ectotherms warm up by basking in the sun. But they also have to regulate body temperature when it is hot. Ectotherms also often use underground burrows, where there are fewer temperature extremes. On hot, sunny days, they might seek shelter in a burrow that is cooler than the land surface. On chilly nights, those same burrows are warmer than the surface, enabling the animal to conserve some body heat.

**Endotherms** An **endotherm** is an animal that regulates body temperature, at least in part, with the heat that its body generates. ⚲ *Endotherms, such as birds and mammals, have high metabolic rates that generate heat, even when they are resting.* Birds conserve body heat primarily with insulating feathers, such as fluffy down. Mammals use combinations of body fat and hair for insulation. Some birds and most mammals can get rid of excess heat by panting. Humans sweat when overheated. As sweat evaporates, it removes heat from the skin and the blood in capillaries just under the surface of the skin. Thus, as warm blood flows through the cooled capillaries, it loses heat.

## Comparing Ectotherms and Endotherms

Ectothermy and endothermy each have advantages and disadvantages in different situations. Endotherms move around easily during cool nights or in cold weather because they generate and conserve their own body heat. That's how musk oxen live in the tundra and killer whales swim through freezing polar seas. But the high metabolic rate that generates this heat requires a lot of fuel. The amount of food needed to keep a single cow alive would be enough to feed ten cow-sized lizards!

Ectothermic animals need much less food than similarly sized endotherms. In environments where temperatures stay warm and fairly constant, ectothermy is a more energy-efficient strategy. But large ectotherms run into trouble if it gets very cold at night or stays cold for long periods. It takes a long time for a large animal to warm up in the sun after a cold night. That's one reason that most large lizards and amphibians live in tropical or subtropical areas.

**Evolution of Temperature Control** There is little doubt that the first land vertebrates were ectotherms. But questions remain about when and how often endothermy evolved. Although modern reptiles are ectotherms, a great deal of evidence suggests that some dinosaurs were endotherms. Many feathered dinosaur fossils have been discovered recently, suggesting that these animals, like modern birds such as the one in **Figure 26-16**, used feathers for insulation. Current evidence suggests that endothermy has evolved at least twice among vertebrates. Endothermy evolved once along the lineage of ancient reptiles that led to birds, and once along the lineage of ancient reptiles that led to mammals.

**INTERACTIVITY**

Figure 26-16

### Temperature Regulation

Like some of their dinosaur ancestors, modern birds use feathers to stay warm. When a bird gets cold, its dense, fluffy undercoat of down feathers stands up and creates spaces next to the bird's skin in which body heat is trapped.

HS-LS1-2, HS-LS1-3

## LESSON 26.4 Review

### KEY QUESTIONS

1. How does the body maintain homeostasis? Describe an example.

2. Compare how ectotherms and endotherms maintain body temperature.

### CRITICAL THINKING

3. Predict You are touring several ecosystems, including an icy coastline in the Arctic, and a dry desert in the southwest United States. Do you predict that you will observe equal numbers of ectotherms and endotherms in all ecosystems? Explain your prediction.

4. Construct an Explanation Why is maintaining homeostasis important when the body is fighting an infection?

5. Synthesize Information How does a high metabolic rate help a bird or mammal regulate its body temperature?

# How can engineers learn from animal systems?

## Biomimicry informs and inspires engineering design.

HS-ETS1-1, CCSS.ELA-LITERACY.RST.9-10.1, CCSS.ELA-LITERACY.WHST.9-10.1

## Make Your Case

Animals body systems accomplish a range of essential functions—from running, digging, flying, or swimming to maintaining homeostasis. Use your imagination and online research to produce a design brief for a function whose design you think could be inspired by an animal system or structure.

## Produce a Design Brief

1. **Conduct Research** After reviewing the chapter, go online to search for important and potentially useful animal adaptations that could solve the challenge posed by your design brief. Learn more about how this adaptation works for the animal, and describe how you could put that function to use.

2. **Construct an Argument** Describe a way to fulfill the requirements of your design based on the animal adaptation you researched. Investigate some of the challenges and opportunities involved in applying biologically inspired design to your project.

The beak of the kingfisher (inset) inspired the design of the nose of high-speed trains.

# Careers on the Case

## Work Toward a Solution

A successful inventor needs to understand science and engineering, as well as the needs of society for new technology.

### Biomechanical Engineer

This career combines biology and engineering to develop new products. The work of biomechanical engineers has led to powerful artificial limbs, efficient and safe exercise equipment, and plastic bags that break apart in landfills. Biomedical engineers work in manufacturing, hospitals, universities, and research facilities.

▶ **VIDEO**

Watch this video to learn about other careers in biology.

hhmi | **BioInteractive**

# Technology on the Case

## Research and Engineering in Action

What do X-ray movies of kangaroos on treadmills, the design of athletic shoes, and the engineering of artificial knee joints have in common? They involve the way muscles, skeletons, and joints work. And data from studies like those can inform the design of things ranging from artificial knee joints to athletic shoes optimized for running or other sports.

If you've never injured yourself, you may take the way your body works for granted. You don't think about what your knees or ankles do when you walk. But if you have ever pulled a major body muscle or injured a joint, you KNOW how each of those structures affects your ability to function. Knee and ankle joints, in particular, handle lots of stress, and move in several different ways. And ask your family how long it took you to learn to walk!

That complexity makes designing prostheses—artificial body parts—very difficult. Fifty years ago, most prosthetic limbs were very simplistic, and could barely do anything close to natural body function. Biomechanical studies of human and animal muscular and skeletal systems are informing the designs of ever-more-sophisticated prosthetics.

By studying how natural joints react to stress and impact, engineers are learning to design prostheses that may not look much like the body parts they replace, but function in ways that allow their wearers to compete in the Paralympic Games. And, excitingly, engineers and surgeons are learning to connect nerves to prosthetic limbs, in ways that will soon enable wearers to control them.

# Lesson Review

Go to your Biology Foundations Workbook for longer versions of these lesson summaries.

## 26.1 Response

When an animal responds to a stimulus, body systems—including the nervous system and the muscular system—work together to generate a response. The nervous system acts to control body movements and responses to the environment. The system is made up of a variety of nerve cells, or neurons. Sensory neurons detect stimuli, such as an odor, a touch, or a change in temperature. Interneurons help process stimuli. Motor neurons act to move muscles. A muscular movement is often the body's response to a stimulus.

A nerve net is a relatively simple nervous system found in some invertebrates consisting of a few neurons in a netlike arrangement. In other invertebrates, interneurons gather in structures called ganglia. A brain is a complex structure of many ganglia.

Sensory systems range from individual sensory neurons to sense organs that contain both sensory neurons and other cells that help gather information.

- neuron
- stimulus
- sensory neuron
- interneuron
- response
- motor neuron
- ganglion
- cerebrum
- cerebellum

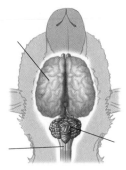

✔**Use Diagrams** Label the cerebrum, the cerebellum, and the medulla oblongata.

## 26.2 Movement and Support

Animals have three main kinds of skeletal systems: hydrostatic skeletons, exoskeletons, and endoskeletons. A hydrostatic skeleton is a skeleton made of fluid-filled body segments that work with muscles to allow the animal to move. An exoskeleton is an external skeleton, and an endoskeleton is an internal skeleton. Exoskeletons are hard outer coverings, and are found in insects and mollusks. Endoskeletons are inside the body and made of bone and cartilage.

In many animals, muscles work together in pairs or groups that are attached to different parts of a skeleton.

- hydrostatic skeleton
- exoskeleton
- endoskeleton
- joint

## 26.3 Reproduction

All animals must reproduce, or their populations and species will become extinct. Asexual reproduction requires only one parent, so individuals in favorable environmental conditions can reproduce rapidly. But since offspring produced asexually carry only a single parent's DNA, they have less genetic diversity than offspring produced sexually. On the other hand, sexual reproduction requires two parents, and maintains genetic diversity in a population by creating individuals with new combinations of genes.

During internal fertilization, eggs are fertilized inside the body of the egg-producing individual. In external fertilization, eggs are fertilized outside the body of the egg-producing individual.

Embryos develop either inside or outside of the body of the parent. The pattern of development may be oviparous, ovoviviparous, or viviparous.

Reptiles, birds, and a few mammals have evolved amniotic eggs in which an embryo can develop outside its mother's body, and out of water, without drying out. The amniotic egg is one of the most important vertebrate adaptations to life on land.

- placenta
- metamorphosis
- amniotic egg
- mammary gland

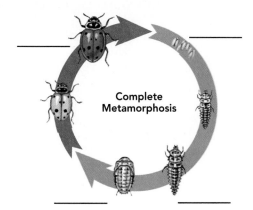

Complete Metamorphosis

☑ **Interpret Diagrams** Add labels to show the stages of complete metamorphosis.

## 26.4 Homeostasis

Homeostasis refers to the control of the internal conditions of the body. Homeostasis allows an organism to withstand changes in environmental conditions, such as a change in temperature, as well as changes in internal conditions, such as a decrease in available energy or an infection.

Processes of homeostasis involve all body systems working together. Endocrine glands help coordinate body systems by releasing hormones. Homeostasis also involves the regulation of growth and development.

Ectotherms, such as fishes and reptiles, lack mechanisms for conserving body heat. Endotherms, which include mammals and birds, are able to keep heat inside their bodies and maintain a constant internal temperature.

- endocrine gland
- ectotherm
- endotherm

☑ **Interpret Visuals** What can you infer about temperature regulation in the bird shown here?

## Organize Information

Complete the chart to show examples of the body systems discussed in this chapter. Some examples are entered for you.

| Purpose | Example (Invertebrate) | Example (Vertebrate) |
|---|---|---|
| Response | Nerve net in jellyfish | 1. |
| Movement and Support | 2. | 3. |
| Reproduction | 4. | 5. |
| Homeostasis | 6. | Endocrine glands |

# Design a model of Interacting Systems

## Design a Solution

HS-LS1-2, HS-ETS1-2, CCSS.ELA-LITERACY.RST.9-10.3

**STEM** As you learned in this chapter, every animal has a group of body systems that work together to perform specific functions for the organism. A nervous system senses the environment and controls movement. A skeletal system supports the body, while the muscular system pulls on the skeleton to move it. The circulatory, digestive, and respiratory systems work together to deliver food and oxygen to cells, and work with the excretory system to remove wastes. Homeostasis is maintained by many systems working together. Perhaps most remarkably of all, a reproductive system allows animals to make more of their own kind.

No one has succeeded in developing an artificial, robotic clone of even the simplest animal. However, engineers have designed and built devices that mimic many animal functions. Robotic arms, for example, can pivot, bend, and grasp, much as a human arm can. Robots now work in factories and assembly lines. Tirelessly and ceaselessly, they perform repetitive tasks without complaint.

You can use ordinary materials to make a very simple model of the bones and muscles at the elbow. Use a brad (stationery fastener) to join two strips of cardboard. The strips should rotate freely about the brad, which represents the elbow joint. Attach strings on either side of the model arm to represent the muscles that bend and flex the elbow.

Construct the model arm. Then follow the steps to develop a model of other interactions between body systems.

1. **Identify Criteria** You will develop and use a model of another interaction between body systems. Your teacher will assign your group one of the interactions shown below.

   - the nervous and muscular systems working together to control movement

   - the circulatory and respiratory systems working together to take in oxygen, and to remove carbon dioxide

   - the circulatory and digestive systems working together to take in food

   - the endocrine system working to control another body system or organ.

2. **Develop Models** With your group members, discuss ways to represent the interaction between body systems. Draw sketches and share your ideas, and conduct research as necessary. Your model could be a physical model, such as the model of the elbow discussed earlier. Or it could be a diagram with labels and captions, or an interactive computer model.

3. **Construct Models** Decide on a plan for your model, and make a detailed diagram to show your plan. With your teacher's approval, follow your plan and diagram to construct the model. You may revise your plan as necessary for the model to be useful and accurate.

4. **Use Models** Show the model to your teacher or a classmate. Use the model to explain how the systems interact to provide a specific function for the organism.

5. **Communicate** Share your plans or completed model with classmates. In your presentation, respond to these questions.

   - What challenges did you face in developing the model? How did you meet these challenges?

   - How does the model illustrate an interaction between body systems? What is the function of this interaction?

   - How do you think you could improve your model, or revise it to illustrate other functions?

# ☑ ASSESSMENT

## ✎ KEY QUESTIONS AND TERMS

### 26.1 Response

HS-LS1-1, HS-LS1-2

1. Information received from the environment that causes an organism to respond is called a
   a. response.
   b. stimulus.
   c. reaction.
   d. trigger.

2. The simplest nervous systems are called
   a. cephalopods.
   b. motor neurons.
   c. nerve nets.
   d. sensory neurons.

3. In vertebrates, the part of the brain that coordinates body movements is the
   a. olfactory lobe.
   b. optic lobe.
   c. cerebrum.
   d. cerebellum.

4. The arrows in this diagram are pointing to which structures?

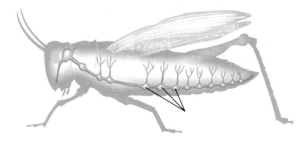

   a. ganglia
   b. brains
   c. nerve nets
   d. motor neurons

5. What two major trends in the evolution of the nervous system do invertebrates exhibit?

6. In general, how do the brains of mammals compare with the brains of other vertebrates? What is the significance of that difference?

7. What kinds of environmental stimuli are some animals capable of sensing that humans cannot?

### 26.2 Movement and Support

HS-LS1-2

8. Which of the following animals uses a hydrostatic skeleton?
   a. arthropod
   b. sponge
   c. fish
   d. annelid

9. Vertebrates have endoskeletons made of
   a. chitin.
   b. calcium carbonate.
   c. cartilage and/or bone.
   d. bone only.

10. Muscles generate force
    a. only when they lengthen.
    b. only when they shorten.
    c. when they lengthen or shorten.
    d. all the time.

11. Describe how a fish uses its muscles to swim.

12. What is the function of joints in a skeleton?

13. Describe how muscles work together to bend and straighten the knee.

### 26.3 Reproduction

HS-LS1-1, HS-LS1-2, HS-LS1-4, HS-LS4-2

14. Which reproductive strategy is rarely used in vertebrates?
    a. internal fertilization
    b. asexual reproduction
    c. budding
    d. amniotic eggs

15. A species that lays eggs that develop outside the mother's body is
    a. oviparous.          c. ovoviviparous.
    b. viviparous.         d. nonviparous.

16. Which structure in female mammals produces milk to nourish young?
    a. kidney              c. mammary gland
    b. pupa                d. placenta

17. Describe the life cycle of a typical cnidarian. Be sure to include the alternation of the polyp form with the medusa form.

18. Compare and contrast internal and external fertilization.

19. What survival advantages does the placenta confer on mammals?

## 26.4 Homeostasis

HS-LS1-2, HS-LS1-3

**20.** Stable internal conditions are called
  **a.** homeostasis.
  **b.** ectothermy.
  **c.** endothermy.
  **d.** reactivity.

**21.** The main source of heat for an ectotherm is
  **a.** its high rate of metabolism.
  **b.** the environment.
  **c.** its own body.
  **d.** its food.

**22.** What do all endotherms do?
  **a.** control body temperature through behavior.
  **b.** control body temperature from within.
  **c.** obtain heat from outside their bodies.
  **d.** maintain relatively low rates of metabolism.

**23.** How do endocrine glands help regulate body activities?

**24.** What is the function of the endocrine system with regards to homeostasis?

**25.** Explain the advantages and disadvantages of ectothermy and endothermy.

**26.** What does current evidence suggest about the evolution of endothermy?

## CRITICAL THINKING

HS-LS1-2, HS-LS1-3, HS-LS4-2

**27. Construct an Explanation** How is it useful for animals to have paired muscles across a joint, instead of only one muscle?

**28. Compare** Describe and compare the three major types of neurons.

**29. Evaluate Reasoning** A pet dog is walking with poor coordination. The veterinarian decides to take a CT scan of the dog's brain. What does the veterinarian suspect might be wrong with the dog? Cite evidence from the chapter to support your answer.

**30. Compare and Contrast** List two advantages and two disadvantages of exoskeletons and endoskeletons.

**31. Compare and Contrast** Describe the differences between a newborn placental mammal and a newborn marsupial.

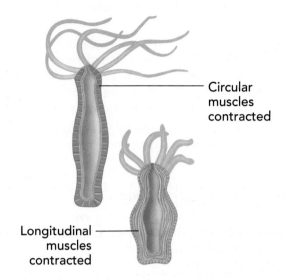

Circular muscles contracted

Longitudinal muscles contracted

**32. Apply Concepts** The diagrams show a type of skeletal system found in invertebrates. What is the name for this type of skeleton? Describe how it functions.

**33. Infer** Many mammals care for their young for extended periods of time. This parental behavior does not help the parent survive. Why might extended parental care have been naturally selected for in these species?

**34. Apply Concepts** What two body systems interact to deliver hormones to the organs they affect? Describe how this interaction takes place.

**35. Form a Hypothesis** Birds and mammals live in both warm and cold biomes, but most reptiles and amphibians live in relatively warm biomes. Form a hypothesis that would explain this difference.

Use the diagram to answer questions 36 and 37.

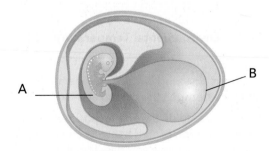

A          B

**36. Interpret Visuals** What is the function of the membrane labeled A?

**37. Infer** What is membrane B? What is the function of the structure it surrounds?

## CROSSCUTTING CONCEPTS

**38. Structure and Function** How does an insect's exoskeleton help the insect survive? What are the drawbacks or limitations of the exoskeleton?

**39. Systems and System Models** The nervous system of an animal can be compared to the network of noncellular telephones and the wires that connect them in a city. Describe how a telephone network acts as a model of the nervous system.

**40. Cause and Effect** Describe an example of a cause-and-effect relationship that involves homeostasis.

## MATH CONNECTIONS

## Analyze and Interpret Data

CCSS.MATH.CONTENT.HSN.Q.A.1

The line graph plots the internal body temperature of various animals against the environmental temperature, or temperature of the air or water outside their bodies. For the alligator and snake, the short lines show the limited temperature range over which the animals survive. Use the graph to answer questions 41 to 43.

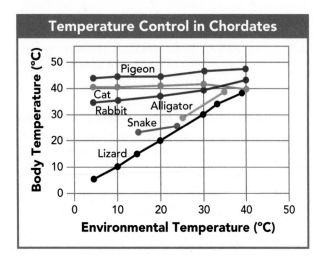

**41. Interpret Graphs** How does temperature control compare between the pigeon and the lizard?

**42. Classify** Based on the line graph, classify the six animals represented as ectotherms or endotherms. Explain how you classified them.

**43. Fit a Function to Data** Write a linear equation to relate the body temperature of the lizard to its environmental temperature. Identify the range at which the equation models the situation.

The table lists the hearing range for several animals. The hearing range is measured in hertz (Hz), where the two numbers indicate the lowest and highest frequency sounds that the animal can hear. Use the table to answer questions 44 and 45.

| Animal | Hearing Range (Hz) |
|---|---|
| Tree frog | 50–4000 |
| Canary | 250–8000 |
| Dog | 67–45,000 |
| Bat | 2000–110,000 |
| Human | 30–23,000 |
| Elephant | 16–12,000 |
| Bottlenose dolphin | 75–150,000 |

**44. Interpret Data** How does human hearing range compare with the ranges of the animals listed in the table?

**45. Infer** Bats and dolphins are two of the few types of animals that navigate by echolocation. In this process they emit sounds and then listen for the echoes. What do the data in the table suggest about echolocation?

## LANGUAGE ARTS CONNECTION

## Write About Science

CCSS.ELA-LITERACY.WHST.9-10.2

**46. Write Procedures** Write a procedure for classifying animals according to their skeletons.

**47. Write Informative Texts** Write a paragraph that describes the advantages and disadvantages offered by the two different types of reproduction.

## Read About Science

CCSS.ELA-LITERACY.RST.9-10.2

**48. Summarize Text** Describe the importance of homeostasis in an animal.

# END-OF-COURSE TEST PRACTICE

1. Vertebrate brain evolution follows a trend of increased size in which part(s) of the brain?

   I. cerebrum
   II. cerebellum
   III. medulla

   A. I only
   B. II only
   C. III only
   D. I and II only
   E. I, II, and III

2. Keshawn is constructing models to show the differences between various animal nervous systems. Which of the following would NOT be in a model of any invertebrate nervous system?

   A. ganglia
   B. interneurons
   C. brain
   D. cerebellum
   E. sensory organs

3. Animal movement is made possible by the interaction of which two systems?

   A. endoskeleton and exoskeleton
   B. nervous and endocrine
   C. skeletal and muscle
   D. cerebrum and cerebellum
   E. cartilage and bone

Use the figure of the reproductive cycle of the *Aurelia* jellyfish to answer question 4.

4. Which process is necessary for a jellyfish zygote to develop into a polyp?

   A. meiosis
   B. fertilization
   C. mitosis
   D. budding
   E. mutation

5. What is an advantage of asexual reproduction?

   A. increased genetic diversity
   B. requires only one parent
   C. one organism can produce both eggs and sperm
   D. fewer mutations
   E. more offspring survived

6. A function of both the immune system and the endocrine system is to

   A. restore homeostasis.
   B. control body temperature.
   C. regulate the amount of water in the body.
   D. stimulate growth and development.
   E. regulate gamete production.

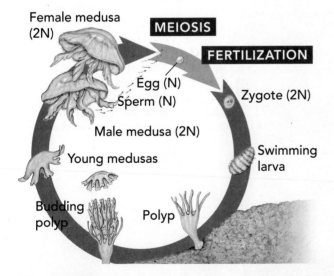

Female medusa (2N)

MEIOSIS

FERTILIZATION

Egg (N)
Sperm (N)
Male medusa (2N)

Zygote (2N)

Swimming larva

Young medusas

Budding polyp

Polyp

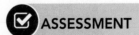

☑ ASSESSMENT

For additional assessment practice, go online to access your digital course.

| If You Have Trouble With... | | | | | | |
| --- | --- | --- | --- | --- | --- | --- |
| Question | 1 | 2 | 3 | 4 | 5 | 6 |
| See Lesson | 26.1 | 26.1 | 26.2 | 26.3 | 26.3 | 26.4 |
| Performance Expectation | HS-LS1-2 | HS-LS1-2 | HS-LS1-2 | HS-LS1-4 | HS-LS4-2 | HS-LS1-3 |

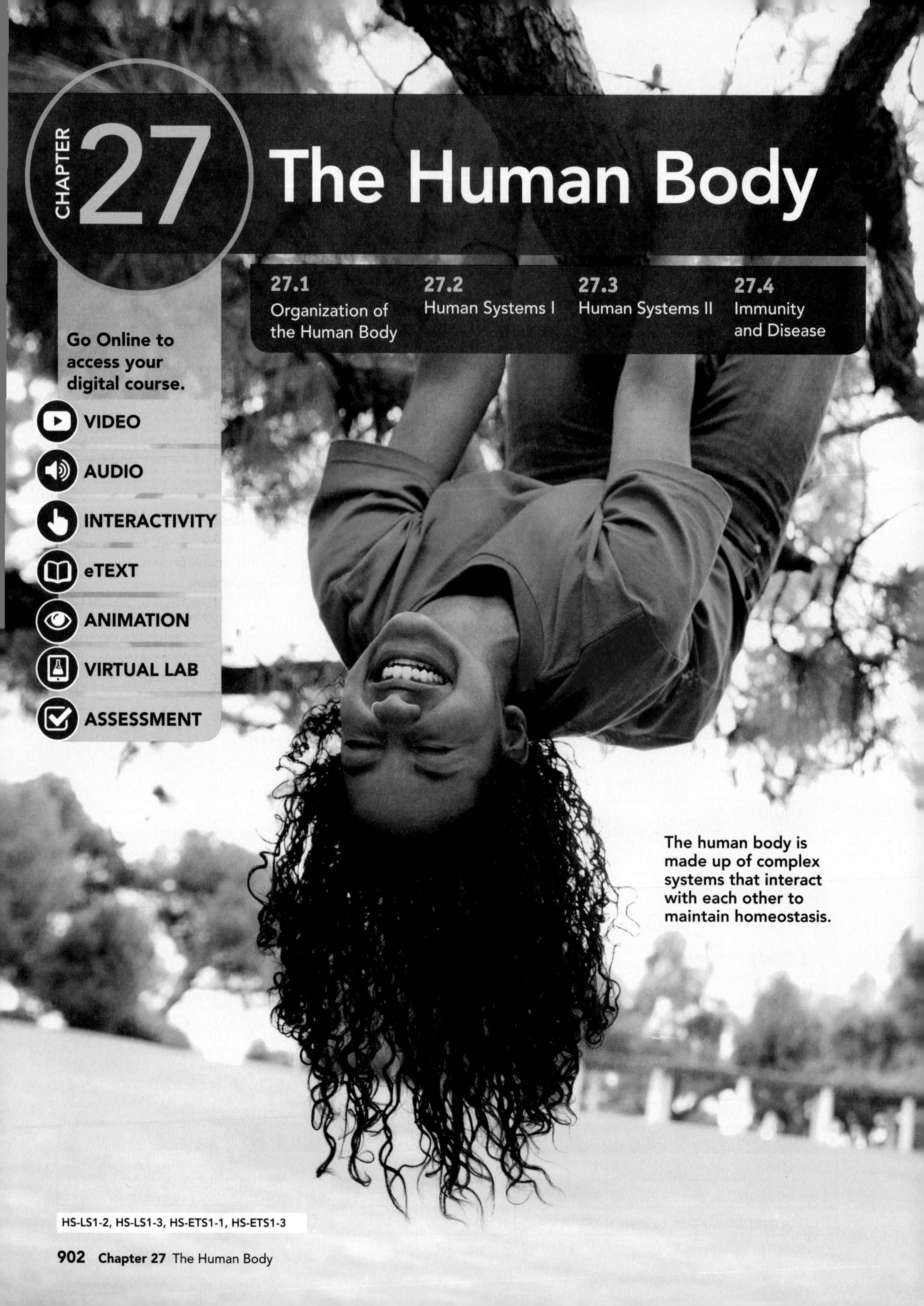

**27.1**
Organization of
the Human Body

**27.2**
Human Systems I

**27.3**
Human Systems II

**27.4**
Immunity
and Disease

Go Online to
access your
digital course.

▶ VIDEO

◀ AUDIO

👆 INTERACTIVITY

📖 eTEXT

👁 ANIMATION

🧪 VIRTUAL LAB

☑ ASSESSMENT

The human body is
made up of complex
systems that interact
with each other to
maintain homeostasis.

HS-LS1-2, HS-LS1-3, HS-ETS1-1, HS-ETS1-3

# What's wrong with the water?

> Public water systems that produce plenty of clean, healthful drinking water have always been one of the hallmarks of progress in developed societies, and America is no exception. Recently, however, many parts of the country have realized that their water systems are no longer as safe as they should be.

In 2014, the people of Flint, Michigan, began to notice disturbing changes in the appearance, the taste, and even the smell of their tap water. The water had become discolored and at times had a rancid odor. Testing revealed that the water had been contaminated by a number of dangerous chemicals, including lead. In one home, the drinking water had a lead level of more than 13,000 ppb (parts per billion). Water with a lead level greater than 5000 ppb is actually classified as hazardous waste!

The likely cause of the contamination was a change in the source of the water pumped into the system. The new water leached lead out of many of the old pipes used in the water supply system. Lead was once commonly used in pipes, as well as in paint, gasoline, and other materials. However, due to lead's negative health effects, especially in young children, it can no longer be used in these products.

Unfortunately, other communities across the country are suffering from similar problems. Water can be polluted from fertilizers and pesticides, from industrial chemicals, and from spilled oil. In some towns in rural Kentucky, the water has been unsafe for decades. When residents take a bath or shower with tap water, their skin burns or develops rashes. Coal mining is a leading cause of the problem. Among the byproducts of mining are metals such as arsenic, lead, and nickel, all of which are harmful to human health.

As these troubles demonstrate, the human body depends on the natural environment to work in peak condition and stay healthy. The body depends on clean air to breathe, clean water to drink, and nutritious food to eat. Polluted air can lead to diseases of the lungs and respiratory system, as can the use of tobacco products. A poor diet can lead to unhealthful weight loss or weight gain, as well as to diabetes and heart disease. When the environment contains toxic materials such as lead, chances are high that the toxins will enter the body, too.

How do the systems of the human body work together to keep the body functioning and healthy? How does the body defend itself from bacteria and other agents that can cause harm? If an illness does strike, how does the body recover from it?

**Throughout this chapter, look for connections to the** CASE STUDY **to help you answer these questions.**

# Organization of the Human Body

The batter slaps a ground ball to the shortstop, who fields it cleanly and throws the ball toward you at first base. In a single motion, you extend your glove hand, catch the ball, and extend your foot to touch the edge of the base. An easy out, a routine play. But think about how many systems of your body worked together to make this "routine" play.

## Organization of the Body

Every cell in the human body is both an independent unit and a part of a larger community—the entire organism. To complete a successful play, a player at first base has to use her eyes to watch the ball and use her brain to figure out how to position her body. With the support of her bones, muscles move her body to first base. Meanwhile, the player's lungs absorb oxygen, which her blood carries to cells for use during cellular respiration. Her brain monitors the location of the ball and sends signals that guide her glove hand to make the catch.

How can so many individual cells and parts work together so efficiently? One way to answer this question is to study the organization of the human body. ✎ *The levels of organization in the body include cells, tissues, organs, and organ systems.* At each level of organization, these parts of the body work together to carry out the major body functions.

**Cells** A cell is the basic unit of structure and function in living things. As you learned earlier, individual cells in multicellular organisms tend to be specialized. Specialized cells, such as bone cells, blood cells, and muscle cells, are uniquely suited to perform a particular function.

**Tissues** A group of cells that perform a single function is called a tissue. **Figure 27-1** shows examples of each of the four basic types of tissues in the human body.

| | Epithelial Tissue | Connective Tissue | Nervous Tissue | Muscle Tissue |
|---|---|---|---|---|
| **FUNCTIONS** | Protection, absorption, and excretion of materials | Binding of epithelial tissue to structures, support, and transport of substances | Receiving and transmitting nerve impulses | Voluntary and involuntary movements |
| **LOCATIONS** | Skin, lining of digestive system, certain glands | Under skin, surrounding organs, blood, bones | Brain, spinal cord, and nerves | Skeletal muscles, muscles surrounding digestive tract and blood vessels, the heart |
| | LM 65× | LM 70× | LM 88× | LM 54× |

*Epithelial Tissue*  The tissue that lines the interior and exterior body surfaces is called **epithelial tissue**. Your skin and the lining of your stomach are both examples of epithelial tissue.

*Connective Tissue*  A type of tissue that provides support for the body and connects its parts is **connective tissue**. This type of tissue includes fat cells, bone cells, and even blood cells. Many connective tissue cells produce collagen, a long, tough fiberlike protein that gives tissues strength and resiliency.

*Nervous Tissue*  Nerve impulses are transmitted throughout the body by **nervous tissue**. Neurons, the cells that carry these impulses, are examples of nervous tissue.

*Muscle Tissue*  Movements of the body are possible because of **muscle tissue**. Some muscles are responsible for the movements you control, such as the muscles that move your arms and legs. Some muscles are responsible for movements you cannot control, such as the tiny muscles that control the size of the pupil in the eye.

**Organs**  A group of different types of tissues that work together to perform a single function or several related functions is called an organ. The eye is an organ made up of epithelial tissue, nervous tissue, muscle tissue, and connective tissue. As different as these tissues are, they all work together for a single function—sight.

**Organ Systems**  An organ system is a group of organs that perform closely related functions. For example, the brain and spinal cord are organs of the nervous system. The organ systems interact to maintain homeostasis in the body as a whole. The organ systems, along with their structures and main functions, are shown on the next page in **Figure 27-2**.

**Figure 27-1**

**Types of Tissues**

The four major types of tissues in the human body are epithelial tissue, connective tissue, nervous tissue, and muscle tissue.

**INTERACTIVITY**

Investigate the organization of the human body.

# Human Body Systems

Although each of the organ systems shown here has a different set of
functions, they all work together, as a whole, to maintain homeostasis.

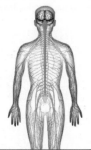  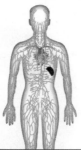 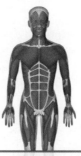 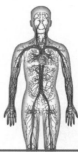 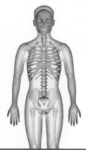

| | Nervous System | Integumentary System | Immune/ Lymphatic Systems | Muscular System | Circulatory System | Skeletal System |
|---|---|---|---|---|---|---|
| **STRUCTURES** | Brain, spinal cord, nerves | Skin, hair, nails, sweat and oil glands | White blood cells, thymus, spleen, lymph nodes, lymph vessels | Skeletal muscle, smooth muscle, cardiac muscle | Heart, blood vessels, blood | Bones, cartilage, ligaments, tendons |
| **FUNCTIONS** | Recognizes and coordinates the body's response to changes in its internal and external environments | Guards against infection and injury and ultraviolet radiation from the sun; helps to regulate body temperature | Helps protect the body from disease; collects fluid lost from blood vessels and returns it to the circulatory system | Works with skeletal system to produce voluntary movement; helps to circulate blood and move food through the digestive system | Transports oxygen, nutrients, and hormones to cells; fights infection; removes cell wastes; helps to regulate body temperature | Supports the body; protects internal organs; allows movement; stores mineral reserves; contains cells that produce blood cells |

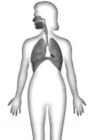 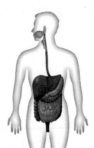 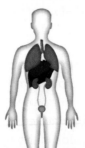 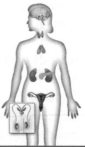 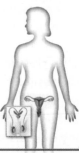

| | Respiratory System | Digestive System | Excretory System | Endocrine System | Reproductive System |
|---|---|---|---|---|---|
| **STRUCTURES** | Nose, pharynx, larynx, trachea, bronchi, bronchioles, lungs | Mouth, pharynx, esophagus, stomach, small and large intestines, rectum | Skin, lungs, liver, kidneys, ureters, urinary bladder, urethra | Hypothalamus, pituitary, thyroid, parathyroids, adrenals, pancreas, ovaries (in females), testes (in males) | Testes, epididymis, vas deferens, urethra, and penis (in males); ovaries, Fallopian tubes, uterus, vagina (in females) |
| **FUNCTIONS** | Brings in oxygen needed for cellular respiration and removes excess carbon dioxide from the body | Breaks down food; absorbs nutrients; eliminates wastes | Eliminates waste products from the body | Controls growth, development, and metabolism; maintains homeostasis | Produces gametes; in females, nurtures and protects developing embryo |

# Homeostasis

Some things about human activity are easy to observe. When you run or swim or write the answer to a test question, you can see your body at work. But behind the scenes, your body works constantly to do something that is difficult to see—maintaining a controlled, stable internal environment. This process is called **homeostasis**, which means "keeping things the same." 🔍 *Homeostasis describes the relatively constant internal conditions that organisms maintain despite changes in internal and external environments.* Homeostasis may not be obvious, but for a living organism, it's a matter of life or death.

**Feedback Inhibition** If you've ever watched someone driving a car down a straight road, you may have noticed the person slightly moving the wheel left and right, adjusting direction to keep the vehicle in the middle of the lane. In a sense, that's how the systems of the body work, keeping internal conditions within a certain range, never allowing them to go too far one way or the other.

***A Nonliving Example*** One way to understand homeostasis is to look at a nonliving system that keeps conditions within a certain range, such as a home heating system. In many homes, heat is supplied by a furnace. When the temperature within the house drops below a set point, a thermostat sensor switches the furnace on. Heat produced by the furnace warms the house. When the temperature rises above the set point, the thermostat switches the furnace off, keeping the temperature within a narrow range.

A system like this example is controlled by feedback inhibition. **Feedback inhibition**, or negative feedback, is the process in which a stimulus produces a response that opposes the original stimulus. **Figure 27-3** summarizes the feedback inhibition process in a home heating system. When the furnace is switched on, it produces a product (heat) that changes the environment of the house by raising the air temperature. This environmental change then "feeds back" to "inhibit" the operation of the furnace. In other words, heat from the furnace eventually raises the temperature high enough to trigger a feedback signal that switches the furnace off. Systems controlled by feedback inhibition are generally very stable.

✅ **READING CHECK** **Apply Concepts** Describe another example of a nonliving system that requires constant adjustment.

**VIDEO**

Learn how feedback inhibition is used to return the body to its normal, homeostatic state.

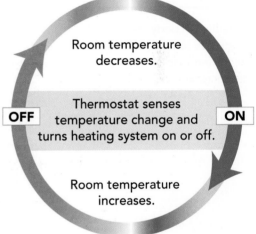

Room temperature decreases.

Thermostat senses temperature change and turns heating system on or off.

**OFF**     **ON**

Room temperature increases.

**Figure 27-3**
## Feedback Inhibition

A home heating system uses a feedback loop to maintain a stable, comfortable environment within a house.

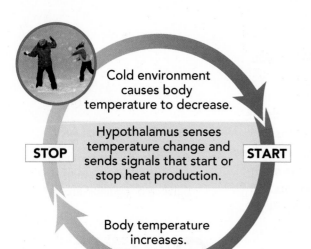

Cold environment causes body temperature to decrease.

**STOP** Hypothalamus senses temperature change and sends signals that start or stop heat production. **START**

Body temperature increases.

Warm environment and exercise cause body temperature to increase.

**STOP** Hypothalamus senses temperature change and sends signals that start or stop cooling mechanisms. **START**

Body temperature decreases.

**INTERACTIVITY**

Figure 27-4

**Body Temperature Control**

In the human body, temperature is controlled through various feedback inhibition mechanisms.

***A Living Example*** Could biological systems achieve homeostasis through feedback inhibition? Absolutely. One example is the maintenance of body temperature. **Figure 27-4** shows how the body regulates temperature in a way similar to that of a home heating system.

A part of the brain called the hypothalamus contains nerve cells that monitor body temperature. If the nerve cells sense that the core temperature has dropped much below 37°C, the hypothalamus produces chemicals that signal cells throughout the body to speed up their activities. Heat produced by this increase in activity, especially cellular respiration, causes a rise in body temperature, which is detected by nerve cells in the hypothalamus.

Have you ever been so cold that you began to shiver? If your body temperature drops well below its normal range, the hypothalamus releases chemicals that signal muscles just below the surface of the skin to contract involuntarily—to "shiver." These muscle contractions release heat, which helps the body temperature to rise.

If body temperature rises too far above 37°C, the hypothalamus slows down cellular activities to reduce heat production. This is one of the reasons you may feel tired and sluggish on a hot day. The body also responds to high temperatures by producing sweat, which helps to cool the body surface by evaporation.

HS-LS1-2

## Quick Lab  Guided Inquiry

### How Do You Respond to an External Stimulus?

1. Have your partner put on safety goggles.
2. Crumple up a sheet of scrap paper into a ball.
3. Watch your partner's eyes carefully as you toss the paper ball toward his or her face.
4. Repeat step 3, three times.
5. Exchange roles and repeat steps 1, 3, and 4.

### ANALYZE AND CONCLUDE

1. **Observe** Describe your partner's reaction to step 3.
2. **Compare and Contrast** Did you see any change in behavior as you repeated step 3? Explain.
3. **Infer** What is the function of the blink reflex?
4. **Develop Models** Draw a model to show how different systems of the body interacted.

**The Liver and Homeostasis** The liver is technically part of the digestive system because it produces bile, which aids in the digestion of fats. However, the liver is one of the body's most important organs for homeostasis.

For example, when proteins are broken down for energy, ammonia, a toxic byproduct, is produced. The liver quickly converts ammonia to urea, which is much less toxic. The kidneys, as you will discover a bit later, then remove urea from the blood. The liver also converts many dangerous substances, including some drugs, into compounds that can be removed from the body safely.

One of the liver's most important roles involves regulating the level of a substance we take almost for granted as something completely harmless—the simple sugar glucose. Glucose is obtained from the foods we eat, and cells take glucose from the blood to serve as a source of energy for their everyday activities. Naturally, right after a meal, as the body absorbs food molecules, the level of glucose in the blood begins to rise. That's where the liver comes in. By taking glucose out of the blood, it keeps the level of glucose from rising too much. As the body uses glucose for energy, the liver releases stored glucose to keep the level of the sugar from dropping too low.

The liver's role in keeping blood glucose levels within a certain range is critical. Too little glucose, and the cells of the nervous system will slow down to the point that you may lose consciousness and pass out. On the other hand, too much glucose gradually damages cells in the eyes, kidneys, heart, and even the immune system. Abnormally high levels of blood glucose are associated with a disease called diabetes. In diabetes, changes occur in either the pancreas or body cells that affect the cells' ability to absorb glucose. Diabetes, one of the fastest-growing health problems in the developed world, is the unfortunate result of the failure of homeostasis with respect to blood glucose levels.

> **READING TOOL**
>
> Draw a diagram or flowchart to show how the liver helps control blood glucose levels, both when blood glucose is too low and when it is too high.

HS-LS1-1, HS-LS1-2, HS-LS1-3

## ☑ LESSON 27.1 Review

### ⚗ KEY QUESTIONS

1. Describe the relationship among cells, tissues, organs, and organ systems in the human body.

2. What is homeostasis? Describe an example of how the body maintains homeostasis.

### CRITICAL THINKING

3. **Infer** After a large meal, blood glucose levels increase only moderately. Describe an action of the body that helps keep glucose levels within tolerable limits.

4. **Construct an Explanation** How does feedback inhibition help the body maintain homeostasis?

5. **Synthesize Information** Describe how a person uses many organ systems to accomplish a simple task such as brushing his or her teeth.

# Human Systems I

**🔑 KEY QUESTION**

- *What are the structures and functions of the digestive system, excretory system, circulatory system, lymphatic system, and respiratory system?*

**HS-LS1-1:** Construct an explanation based on evidence for how the structure of DNA determines the structure of proteins which carry out the essential functions of life through systems of specialized cells.

**HS-LS1-2:** Develop and use a model to illustrate the hierarchical organization of interacting systems that provide specific functions within multicellular organisms.

**HS-LS1-3:** Plan and conduct an investigation to provide evidence that feedback mechanisms maintain homeostasis.

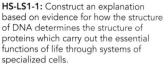

**READING TOOL**

Complete the chart in your 📖 **Biology Foundations Workbook** to show the sequence of events in which food is digested.

**▶ VIDEO**

Learn how geography can be an advantage or a disadvantage for athletes.

Imagine a luscious peach, so perfectly ripe that you can smell its sweetness even as you bring it up to your mouth for the first delicious bite. The fuzz tickles your lips as you sink your teeth into the fruit. You savor the tangy sweetness as you chew and then swallow. It doesn't get much better than this! And you take another bite. What's your favorite food? Whether you're a fan of fruit or pizza, the food you eat becomes fuel and materials for your body.

## The Digestive System

The need for food presents every animal with at least two challenges—how to obtain it and how to convert that food into molecules the body can use. In humans and many other animals, this is the job of the digestive system. 🔑 *The digestive system converts food into small molecules that can be used by the cells of the body.*

**Digestion** The first step in the process is ingestion, the act of putting food into your mouth. Food in the digestive system is broken down in two ways—by mechanical and chemical digestion. Mechanical digestion is the physical breakdown of large pieces of food into smaller pieces. During chemical digestion, enzymes break down food molecules. **Figure 27-5** summarizes the process of digestion.

Mechanical digestion occurs in your mouth as your teeth break up and grind your food. Chemical digestion occurs as enzymes in saliva start to break down carbohydrates. Once you swallow, that clump of food, now called a *bolus*, travels down the esophagus to your stomach, where more mechanical and chemical digestion occur. Muscles in the stomach wall cause a churning motion. Meanwhile, enzymes and hydrochloric acid continue the chemical breakdown of food. Chemical digestion is completed in the small intestine. Now the food is reduced to molecules that can be absorbed.

**Figure 27-5**

# The Digestive System

Food travels through many organs as it is broken down into nutrients your body can use. The time needed for each organ to perform its role varies based on the type of food consumed.

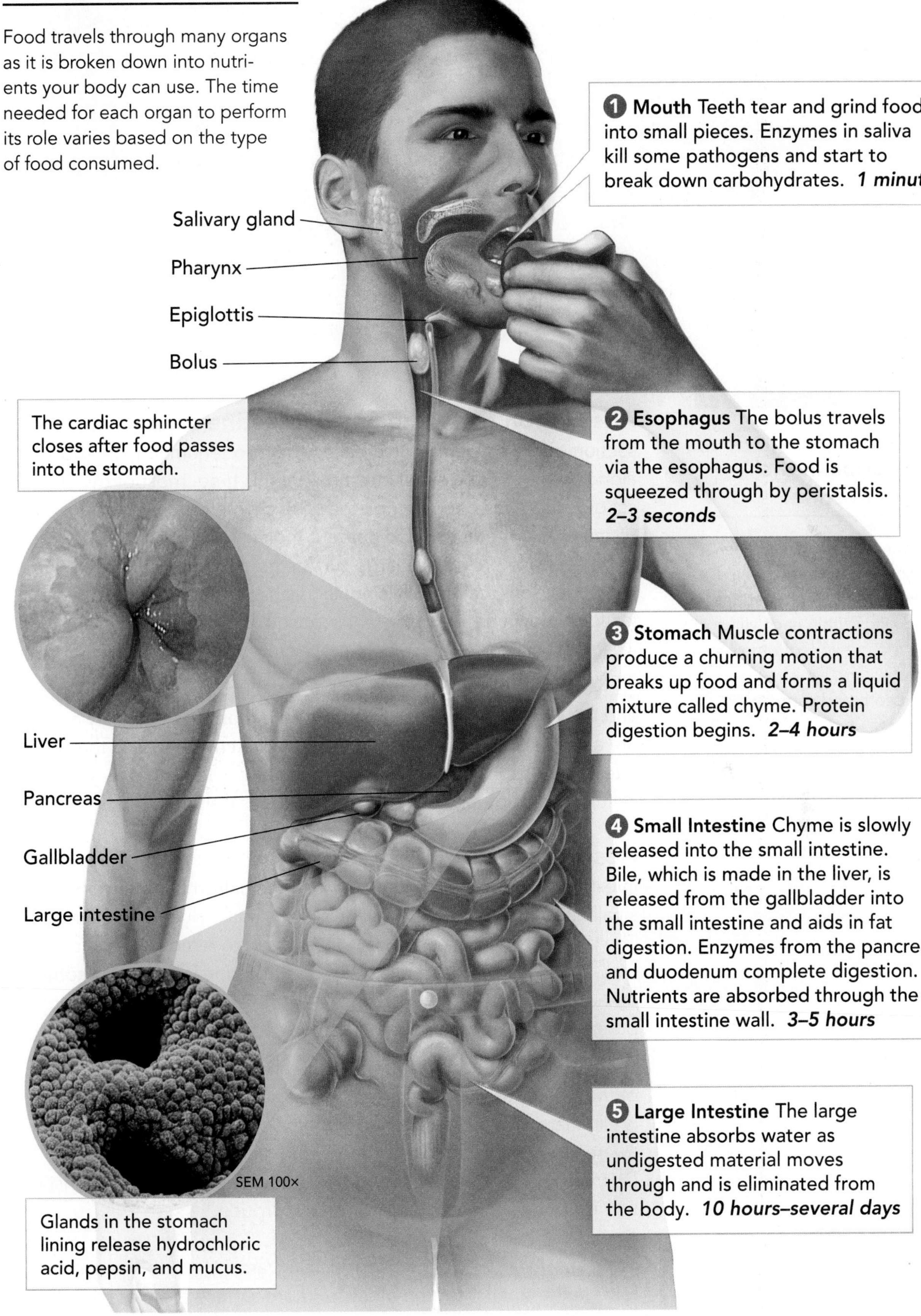

Salivary gland

Pharynx

Epiglottis

Bolus

**❶ Mouth** Teeth tear and grind food into small pieces. Enzymes in saliva kill some pathogens and start to break down carbohydrates. *1 minute*

**❷ Esophagus** The bolus travels from the mouth to the stomach via the esophagus. Food is squeezed through by peristalsis. *2–3 seconds*

The cardiac sphincter closes after food passes into the stomach.

**❸ Stomach** Muscle contractions produce a churning motion that breaks up food and forms a liquid mixture called chyme. Protein digestion begins. *2–4 hours*

Liver

Pancreas

Gallbladder

Large intestine

**❹ Small Intestine** Chyme is slowly released into the small intestine. Bile, which is made in the liver, is released from the gallbladder into the small intestine and aids in fat digestion. Enzymes from the pancreas and duodenum complete digestion. Nutrients are absorbed through the small intestine wall. *3–5 hours*

SEM 100×

Glands in the stomach lining release hydrochloric acid, pepsin, and mucus.

**❺ Large Intestine** The large intestine absorbs water as undigested material moves through and is eliminated from the body. *10 hours–several days*

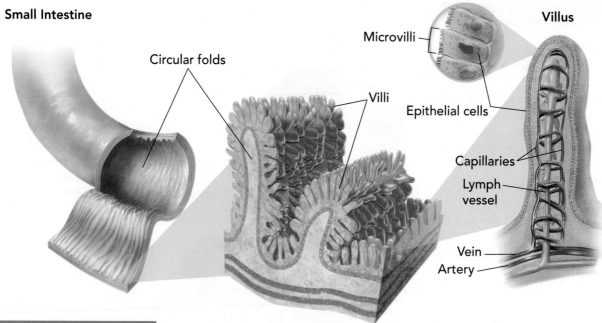

Small Intestine

Circular folds

Villi

Microvilli

Villus

Epithelial cells

Capillaries

Lymph vessel

Vein

Artery

**Figure 27-6**

## Absorption in the Small Intestine

The lining of the small intestine consists of folds that are covered with tiny projections called villi. Within each villus there is a network of blood capillaries and lymph vessels that absorb and carry away nutrients.

## Absorption From the Small Intestine
After leaving the first section of the small intestine, called the duodenum, chyme moves along the rest of the small intestine. By this time, most of the chemical digestion has been completed. The chyme is now a rich mixture of small- and medium-sized nutrient molecules. The small intestine's folded surface provides a large surface area for absorption. Its fingerlike projections, called villi (singular: villus), are covered with tiny projections known as microvilli, which absorb the nutrients. **Figure 27-6** illustrates villi and microvilli.

Nutrient molecules then pass into the circulatory system. Sugars and amino acids go into capillaries, while most fats and fatty acids are absorbed by lymph vessels. By the time chyme leaves the small intestine, most nutrients have been absorbed, leaving only water, cellulose, and other indigestible substances behind.

## Absorption and Elimination
Chyme next enters the large intestine, or colon. The large intestine is actually much shorter than the small intestine. The large intestine gets its name due to its diameter. The primary function of the large intestine is to remove water from the material that is left. Bacteria in the large intestine break down some of the indigestible substances in the chyme and then produce compounds that the body is able to absorb and use, including vitamin K.

The concentrated waste material, called feces, forms after most of the water has been removed. Feces passes into the rectum and is eliminated from the body through the anus. You usually become aware of any problems with water removal in the large intestine. Diarrhea occurs when not enough water is absorbed, while constipation is the result of too much water absorption.

**READING CHECK** **Interpret Diagrams** How do the circular folds in the small intestine allow for more surface area for digestion?

# The Excretory System

The chemistry of the human body is a marvelous thing. However, every living thing produces chemical waste products, some of which are toxic and must be expelled from the system. Ammonia, one of the most toxic of these waste compounds, is produced when amino acids from proteins are used for energy. Ammonia is converted to a less toxic compound called urea, but it, too, must be eliminated from the body. The process by which these metabolic wastes are eliminated is called excretion.

🔍 *The excretory system includes the skin, lungs, liver, and kidneys. This system excretes metabolic wastes from the body.* The ureters, urinary bladder, and urethra are also involved in excretion. **Figure 27-7** shows the major organs of excretion.

**Skin** Many excretory organs are part of other body systems as well. The skin removes excess water, salts, and a small amount of urea in sweat. By releasing sweat in very small amounts, this process eliminates wastes even when you may not think you're sweating.

**Lungs** The blood transports carbon dioxide, a waste product of cellular respiration, from the body cells to the lungs. When you exhale, your lungs excrete carbon dioxide and small amounts of water vapor.

**Liver** The liver plays many important roles in excretion. One of its principal activities is to convert dangerous nitrogen-based wastes into urea, which is a less toxic compound. Urea is then transported through the blood to the kidneys for elimination from the body.

**Kidneys** The major organs of excretion are the kidneys, a pair of fist-sized organs located on either side of the spinal column near the lower back. The kidneys remove excess water, urea, and metabolic wastes from the blood. The kidneys produce and excrete a waste product known as urine. Ureters transport urine from the kidneys to the urinary bladder, where urine is stored until it is released through the urethra.

**BUILD VOCABULARY**

**Prefixes** The Latin prefix *ex-* means "out." The process of moving wastes *out* of the body is <u>ex</u>cretion. When you <u>ex</u>hale, or breathe out, you excrete the waste product carbon dioxide.

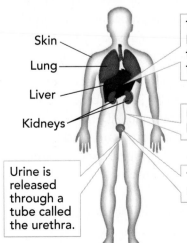

Skin

Lung

Liver

Kidneys

The liver processes and neutralizes toxins. If the quantity of toxins is too great or the toxins are types the liver cannot process, the toxins build up in the body.

Ureters transport urine from each kidney to the urinary bladder.

Urine is released through a tube called the urethra.

The urinary bladder stores urine until it is released from the body.

**CASE STUDY**

**Figure 27-7**

**The Excretory System**

The excretory system removes metabolic wastes and can also neutralize some toxins.

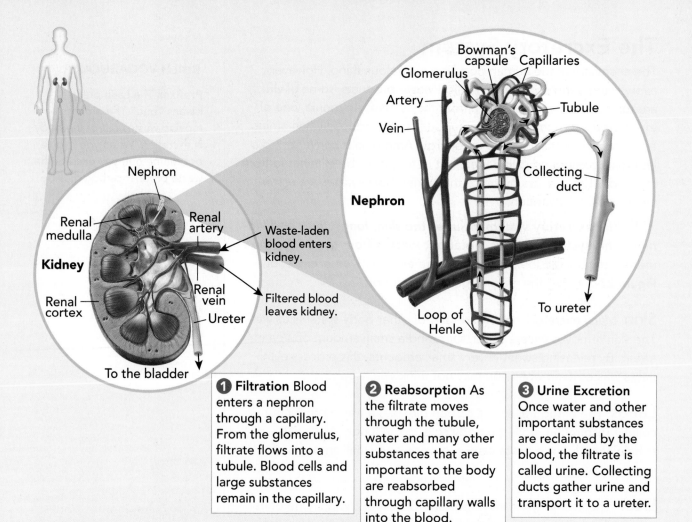

① **Filtration** Blood enters a nephron through a capillary. From the glomerulus, filtrate flows into a tubule. Blood cells and large substances remain in the capillary.

② **Reabsorption** As the filtrate moves through the tubule, water and many other substances that are important to the body are reabsorbed through capillary walls into the blood.

③ **Urine Excretion** Once water and other important substances are reclaimed by the blood, the filtrate is called urine. Collecting ducts gather urine and transport it to a ureter.

**Up Close**

**Figure 27-8**

## Structure and Function of the Kidneys

Kidneys are made up of nephrons. Blood enters a nephron, where impurities are filtered out and emptied into the collecting duct. Purified blood leaves a nephron through a vein.

To a large extent, the activity of the kidneys is controlled by the composition of the blood itself. **Figure 27-8** summarizes how the kidneys function. The kidneys respond directly to the composition of the blood. They are also influenced by the endocrine system. For example, if you eat salty food, the kidneys will respond to the excess salt in your blood by returning less salt to your blood during reabsorption. If the blood is too acidic, then the kidneys excrete more hydrogen ions in the urine. If your blood glucose levels rise past a certain point, the kidneys will even excrete glucose into the urine. This is one of the signs of diabetes, a disease caused by the body's inability to control the concentration of glucose in the blood.

Endocrine glands release hormones that also influence kidney function. For example, if the amount of water in your blood drops, the pituitary gland releases antidiuretic hormone (ADH) into the blood. This causes the kidneys to reabsorb more water and to excrete less water in the urine. If the blood contains excess water, ADH secretion stops and more water is excreted.

☑ **READING CHECK** **Identify** What role do the lungs play in removing waste from the body?

# The Circulatory System

Some animals are so small that all of their cells are in direct contact with the environment. Diffusion and active transport across cell membranes supply their cells with oxygen and nutrients and remove waste products. The human body, however, contains billions of cells that are not in direct contact with the external environment. Because of this, humans need a circulatory system. ⚘ *The circulatory system transports oxygen, nutrients, and other substances throughout the body, and it removes wastes from tissues.*

Blood is pumped through the body by the heart. An adult's heart contracts on average 72 times a minute, pumping about 70 milliliters of blood with each contraction. As **Figure 27-9** shows, the heart is divided into four chambers. A wall called the septum separates the right side of the heart from the left side. The septum prevents oxygen-poor and oxygen-rich blood from mixing. On each side of the septum is an upper and lower chamber. Each upper chamber, or atrium (plural: atria), receives blood from the body. Each lower chamber, or ventricle, pumps blood out of the heart.

**READING TOOL**

Before you read this section, preview the diagrams associated with the circulatory system. Write down any questions that you have.

**Figure 27-9**

## The Heart

Valves located between the atria and ventricles and between the ventricles and vessels leaving the heart prevent blood from flowing backward between heartbeats.

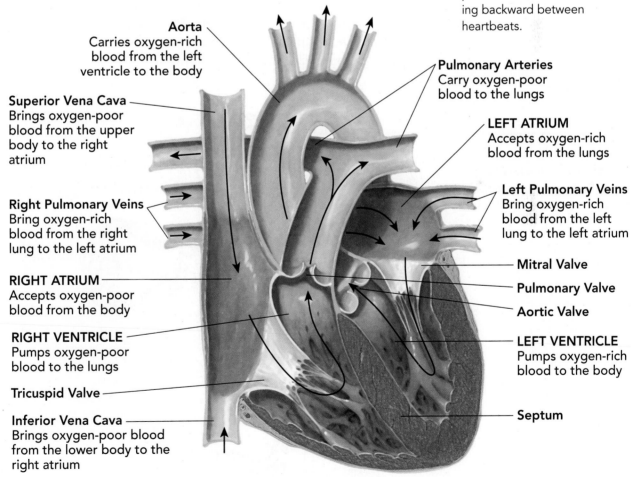

**Aorta**
Carries oxygen-rich blood from the left ventricle to the body

**Superior Vena Cava**
Brings oxygen-poor blood from the upper body to the right atrium

**Right Pulmonary Veins**
Bring oxygen-rich blood from the right lung to the left atrium

**RIGHT ATRIUM**
Accepts oxygen-poor blood from the body

**RIGHT VENTRICLE**
Pumps oxygen-poor blood to the lungs

**Tricuspid Valve**

**Inferior Vena Cava**
Brings oxygen-poor blood from the lower body to the right atrium

**Pulmonary Arteries**
Carry oxygen-poor blood to the lungs

**LEFT ATRIUM**
Accepts oxygen-rich blood from the lungs

**Left Pulmonary Veins**
Bring oxygen-rich blood from the left lung to the left atrium

**Mitral Valve**

**Pulmonary Valve**

**Aortic Valve**

**LEFT VENTRICLE**
Pumps oxygen-rich blood to the body

**Septum**

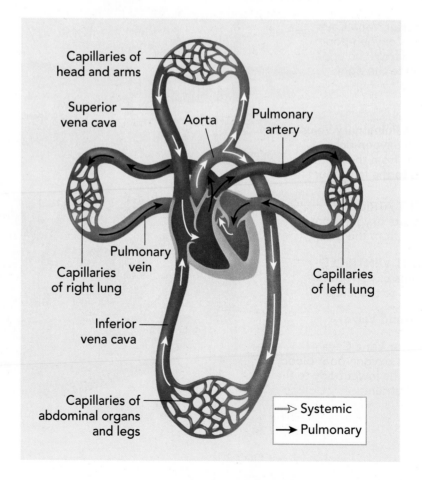
**Circulation** The heart functions as two pumps. As shown in **Figure 27-10**, one pump pushes blood to the lungs, while the other pump pushes blood to the rest of the body.

The right side of the heart pumps oxygen-poor blood from the heart to the lungs through the pulmonary circulation. In the lungs, carbon dioxide diffuses from the blood, and oxygen is absorbed into the blood. Oxygen-rich blood then flows to the left side of the heart.

The left side of the heart pumps oxygen-rich blood to the rest of the body through the systemic circulation. Cells absorb the oxygen that they need and load the blood with carbon dioxide by the time it returns to the heart.

Blood leaves the heart to go to the rest of the body through the aorta, the first of a series of vessels that carries blood through the systemic circulation. As blood flows through the circulatory system, it moves through three types of blood vessels—arteries, capillaries, and veins.

**Arteries** Large vessels, or arteries, carry blood from the heart to the tissues of the body. Except for the pulmonary arteries, all arteries carry oxygen-rich blood. Arteries have thick elastic walls that help them withstand the powerful pressure produced when the heart contracts and pumps blood through them. **Figure 27-11** describes the layers of tissue found in the walls of arteries and veins—connective tissue, smooth muscle, and endothelium.

**Figure 27-10**

## Circulation

Pulmonary circulation carries blood between the heart and lungs. Systemic circulation carries blood between the heart and the rest of the body.

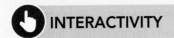

## INTERACTIVITY

### Figure 27-11
### Blood Vessels

The three basic types of blood vessels are arteries, capillaries, and veins. The scanning electron micrograph shows red blood cells and a few white blood cells inside a ruptured venule.

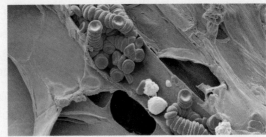

SEM 525x

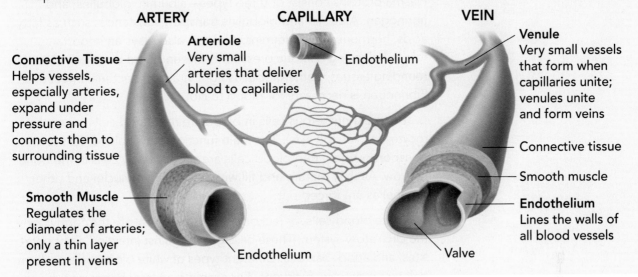

**ARTERY**

**Connective Tissue** Helps vessels, especially arteries, expand under pressure and connects them to surrounding tissue

**Arteriole** Very small arteries that deliver blood to capillaries

**Smooth Muscle** Regulates the diameter of arteries; only a thin layer present in veins

Endothelium

**CAPILLARY**

Endothelium

**VEIN**

**Venule** Very small vessels that form when capillaries unite; venules unite and form veins

Connective tissue

Smooth muscle

**Endothelium** Lines the walls of all blood vessels

Valve

**Capillaries** The smallest blood vessels are the capillaries. Most capillaries are so narrow that blood cells pass through them in a single file. Their thin walls allow oxygen and nutrients to diffuse from blood into tissues and allow carbon dioxide and other waste products to move from tissues into blood.

**Veins** After blood passes through the capillaries, it returns to the heart through veins. Many veins are located near and between skeletal muscles. When you move, the contracting skeletal muscles squeeze the veins. Many veins contain valves, which ensure blood flows in one direction through these vessels toward the heart.

☑ **READING CHECK** **Compare and Contrast** How are arteries and veins alike and different?

HS-LS1-3

 **Exploration Lab** **Open Ended Inquiry**

### Exercise and Heart Rate

**Problem** How does exercise affect heart rate?

Heart rate is the number of times per minute that the heart contracts, or beats, to push blood through the circulatory system. In this lab, you will investigate how the body maintains homeostasis during exercise. You will plan and carry out an investigation to show how exercise affects heart rate, and then construct an explanation for the data that the class obtains.

You can find this lab in your digital course.

**Blood** In addition to serving as the body's transportation system, components of blood also help regulate body temperature, fight infections, and produce clots to minimize the loss of body fluids from wounds.

The human body contains 4 to 6 liters of blood. About 55 percent of total blood volume is a fluid called plasma. Plasma is about 90 percent water and 10 percent dissolved gases, salts, nutrients, enzymes, plasma proteins, cholesterol, and other compounds. Plasma proteins consist of three types—albumin, globulins, and fibrinogen. Albumin and globulins transport substances such as fatty acids, hormones, and vitamins. Albumin also plays an important role in balancing osmotic pressure between blood plasma and surrounding tissues. Some globulins fight viral and bacterial infections. Fibrinogen is necessary for blood to clot.

The most numerous cells in blood are red blood cells, or erythrocytes (eh RITH roh syts). The main function of red blood cells is to transport oxygen. Red blood cells are produced by cells in the bone marrow. As they mature and fill with hemoglobin, nuclei and other organelles are forced out.

White blood cells, or leukocytes (LOO koh syts), are the "army" of the circulatory system. These cells guard against infection, fight parasites, and attack bacteria. Different types of white blood cells perform different protective functions. For example, macrophages engulf pathogens. Lymphocytes are involved in the immune response. B lymphocytes produce antibodies that fight infection and provide immunity. T lymphocytes help fight tumors and viruses. In a healthy person, red blood cells outnumber white blood cells by almost 1000 to 1.

Minor cuts and scrapes bleed for a bit and then stop. Why? Because platelets and plasma proteins cause blood to clot. Platelets are formed when the cytoplasm of particular bone marrow cells breaks apart into tiny membrane-enclosed fragments that then enter the blood. **Figure 27-12** explains the clotting process.

## Figure 27-12
### Blood Clotting

Platelets help blood to clot and thereby seal wounds. As shown in the scanning electron micrograph of a blood clot, filaments of fibrin form a netlike structure that traps blood cells.

**❶ Capillary Wall Breaks** A blood vessel is injured by a cut or scrape.

**❷ Platelets Take Action** Platelets clump at the site and release the clotting factor thromboplastin, which triggers a series of reactions. Thromboplastin converts the protein prothrombin into the enzyme thrombin.

SEM 1100x

**❸ Clot Forms** Thrombin converts the soluble protein fibrinogen into sticky fibrin filaments. These form a clot that seals the break until the capillary wall can regrow and heal.

# The Lymphatic System

The human circulatory system is not a perfect closed system. As blood circulates, some blood cells and plasma leak out through the capillary walls. Each day, about 3 liters of fluid leave the blood in this way. Most of this fluid, known as lymph, is reabsorbed into capillaries, but not all of it. The rest goes into the lymphatic system, which is shown in **Figure 27-13**. ✎ *The lymphatic system is a network of vessels, nodes, and organs that collects the lymph that leaves capillaries, "screens" it for microorganisms, and returns it to the circulatory system.*

**Role in Circulation** Lymph collects in a system of capillaries that slowly conducts it into larger lymph vessels. Pressure on lymph vessels from surrounding skeletal muscles helps move lymph through the system into larger and larger ducts. Like veins, lymph vessels have valves that prevent lymph from flowing backward. These ducts return lymph to the blood through openings in veins just below the shoulders. When injury or disease blocks lymphatic vessels, lymph can accumulate in tissues, causing swelling called edema.

**Role in Immunity** Hundreds of small lymph nodes are scattered along lymph vessels throughout the body. Lymph nodes act as filters, trapping microorganisms, stray cancer cells, and debris. White blood cells inside lymph nodes destroy this cellular "trash." When large numbers of microorganisms are trapped in lymph nodes, the nodes become enlarged. The "swollen glands" that are symptoms of certain kinds of infections are actually swollen lymph nodes.

The thymus and spleen also play important roles in the immune functions of the lymphatic system. T lymphocytes mature in the thymus before they can function in the immune system. The functions of the spleen are similar to those of lymph nodes. However, instead of lymph, blood flows through the spleen, where it is cleansed of microorganisms, damaged cells, and other debris.

**Role in Nutrient Absorption** The lymphatic system also plays an important role in the absorption of nutrients. A system of lymph vessels runs alongside the intestines. The vessels pick up fats and fat-soluble vitamins from the digestive tract and transport these nutrients into the bloodstream.

✅ **READING CHECK** **Summarize** What are three roles of the lymphatic system?

## Figure 27-13
## The Lymphatic System

The lymphatic system is a network of vessels, nodes, and organs that recycles fluids from tissues and plays a role in nutrient absorption and immunity. If the lymphatic system isn't working well, fluid can build up in tissues, causing swelling.

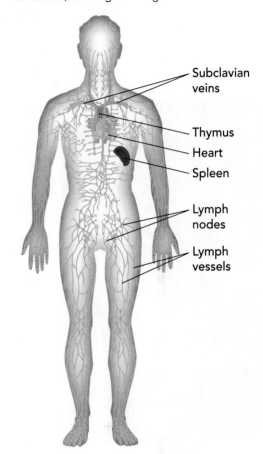

- Subclavian veins
- Thymus
- Heart
- Spleen
- Lymph nodes
- Lymph vessels

# The Respiratory System

Breathing involves two opposite processes: inhaling and exhaling. You might complete both processes without much thought, but the singer shown in **Figure 27-14** should pay close attention to his breathing. Both inhaling and exhaling exchange gases with the environment, which is called respiration. ✎ *The respiratory system picks up oxygen from the air as we inhale and releases carbon dioxide as we exhale.* With each breath, air enters the body through the air passageways and fills the lungs. In the lungs, gas exchange takes place and oxygen enters the circulatory system. As shown in **Figure 27-15**, the respiratory system consists of the nose, pharynx, larynx, trachea, bronchi, and lungs.

**Air Flow** As air enters the respiratory system, it is warmed and filtered in the inner nasal cavity and sinuses. Air then moves from the nose to a cavity at the back of the mouth called the pharynx, or throat, and then into the trachea, or windpipe. A flap of tissue called the epiglottis covers the entrance to the trachea, ensuring that food or liquid goes into the esophagus instead of the trachea. Between the pharynx and the trachea is the larynx, which contains two highly elastic folds of tissue known as the vocal cords. Your ability to speak, shout, and sing comes from these tissues. Mucus produced in the trachea traps inhaled particles, which cilia then sweep away from the lungs toward the pharynx.

From the trachea, air moves into two large tubes called bronchi (singular: bronchus) leading to the lungs. These tubes divide into smaller bronchi, and then into even smaller bronchioles. Bronchi and bronchioles are surrounded by smooth muscles that regulate the size of air passageways. The bronchioles lead to several hundred million tiny air sacs called alveoli (singular: alveolus). A delicate network of capillaries surrounds each alveolus.

**Gas Exchange and Transport** When you inhale, a muscle called the diaphragm contracts and flattens, creating a partial vacuum inside the tightly sealed chest cavity. Atmospheric pressure does the rest, filling the lungs as air rushes into the breathing passages. As air enters the alveoli, oxygen diffuses across thin capillary walls into the blood. Meanwhile, carbon dioxide diffuses in the opposite direction.

Diffusion of oxygen from alveoli into capillaries is a passive process. Oxygen dissolves into the bloodstream, and then becomes bound to hemoglobin in red blood cells. The ability of hemoglobin to bind oxygen increases the blood's oxygen-carrying capacity more than 60 times.

When carbon dioxide diffuses from body tissues to capillaries, most of it enters red blood cells and combines with water, forming carbonic acid and then bicarbonate. The rest of it dissolves in plasma or binds to hemoglobin and proteins in plasma. These processes are reversed in the lungs before the carbon dioxide is exhaled.

**Figure 27-14**

**Breathing and Singing**

Professional singers try to time their breathing to avoid pauses in a song. The vocal cords vibrate and make sounds when air rushes by them during an exhalation.

## Figure 27-15

# The Respiratory System

Air moves through the nose, pharynx, larynx, trachea, and bronchi into the lungs.

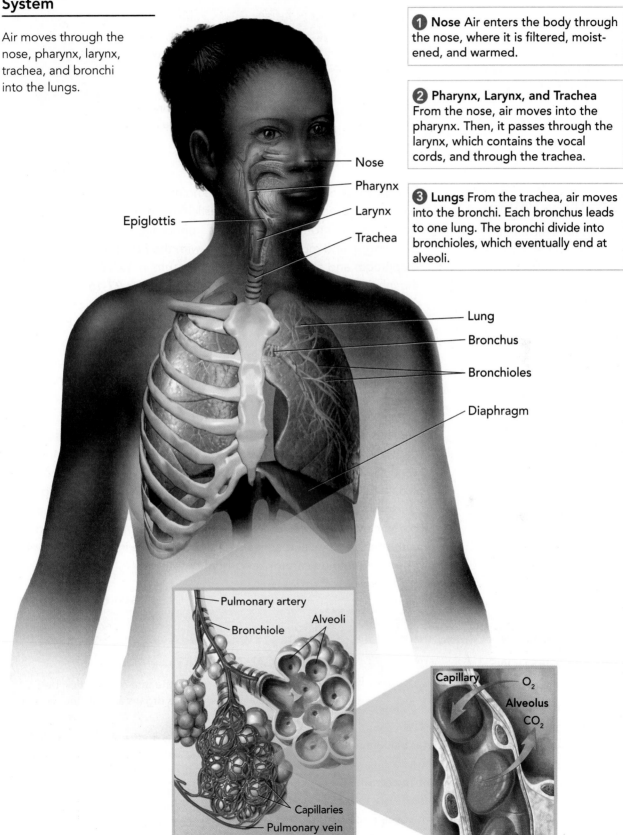

**1** **Nose** Air enters the body through the nose, where it is filtered, moistened, and warmed.

**2** **Pharynx, Larynx, and Trachea** From the nose, air moves into the pharynx. Then, it passes through the larynx, which contains the vocal cords, and through the trachea.

**3** **Lungs** From the trachea, air moves into the bronchi. Each bronchus leads to one lung. The bronchi divide into bronchioles, which eventually end at alveoli.

Nose

Pharynx

Larynx

Epiglottis

Trachea

Lung

Bronchus

Bronchioles

Diaphragm

Pulmonary artery

Bronchiole

Alveoli

Capillaries

Pulmonary vein

Capillary

$O_2$

Alveolus

$CO_2$

## Figure 27-16

## Breathing

During inhalation, the rib cage rises and the diaphragm contracts, increasing the size of the chest cavity. During exhalation, the rib cage lowers and the diaphragm relaxes, decreasing the size of the chest cavity.

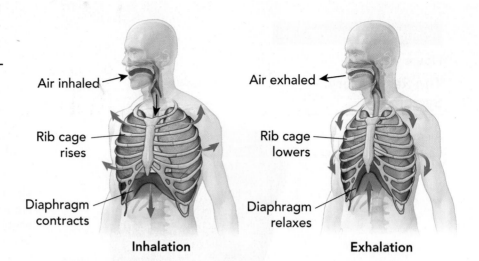

Air inhaled →

Rib cage rises

Diaphragm contracts

**Inhalation**

Air exhaled ←

Rib cage lowers

Diaphragm relaxes

**Exhalation**

 **INTERACTIVITY**

Survey the structures and functions of the digestive, excretory, cardiovascular, lymphatic, and respiratory systems.

**Breathing** Surprisingly, there are no muscles in our lungs or connected directly to them that participate in breathing. The force that drives air into the lungs comes from ordinary air pressure, the diaphragm, and muscles associated with the ribs. Movements of the diaphragm and rib cage change air pressure in the chest cavity during inhalation and exhalation, as shown in **Figure 27-16**.

**Breathing and Homeostasis** You can control your breathing almost any time you want, to blow up a balloon or to play a trumpet. But this doesn't mean that breathing is purely voluntary. Your nervous system has final control of your breathing muscles even when you are unconscious. Breathing is initiated by the breathing center in the part of the brain stem called the medulla oblongata. Sensory neurons in or near the medulla and in some large blood vessels gather information about carbon dioxide levels in the body and send the information to the breathing center. When stimulated, the breathing center sends nerve impulses that cause the diaphragm and chest muscles to contract, bringing air into the lungs. The higher the blood carbon dioxide level, the stronger the impulses. If the blood carbon dioxide level reaches a critical point, the impulses become so powerful that you cannot keep from breathing.

HS-LS1-1, HS-LS1-2, HS-LS1-3

##  LESSON 27.2 Review

### 🔍 KEY QUESTIONS

1. What happens to food after it is ingested?

2. Describe the organs involved in excreting different types of metabolic wastes.

3. Describe how the heart circulates blood through the body.

4. How does the lymphatic system interact with the circulatory system?

5. Describe the pathway of air as it travels into and out of the respiratory system.

### CRITICAL THINKING

6. **Predict** How would the rate of digestion be affected if the various organs and glands did not release enzymes?

7. **Apply Concepts** How do the circulatory and excretory systems work together to eliminate nitrogen-containing wastes?

8. **Construct an Explanation** Muscles are required for all movement within the body. How do muscles move blood through the circulatory system? How do they move air through the respiratory system?

# Human Systems II

🔑 **KEY QUESTION**

• *What are the structures and functions of the nervous system, skeletal system, muscular system, integumentary system, endocrine system, and the male and female reproductive systems?*

HS-LS1-1: Construct an explanation based on evidence for how the structure of DNA determines the structure of proteins which carry out the essential functions of life through systems of specialized cells.

HS-LS1-2: Develop and use a model to illustrate the hierarchical organization of interacting systems that provide specific functions within multicellular organisms.

HS-LS1-3: Plan and conduct an investigation to provide evidence that feedback mechanisms maintain homeostasis.

The billions of messages sent through your body at any given moment may tell you to laugh at a joke or tell you that it's cold outside. These messages enable the organs of the body to act together and also to react to external conditions.

## The Nervous System

The nervous system is our window on the world. 🔑 *The nervous system collects information about the internal and external environment, processes that information, and responds to it.* All of these messages are carried by electrical signals, called impulses, through nerve cells called neurons. A neuron is shown in **Figure 27-17**. The neurons and supporting cells that form the peripheral nervous system collect information about the body's external and internal environments. The brain and spinal cord form the central nervous system, which processes and creates a response to that information. This response is carried to muscles, glands, and other tissues by the peripheral nervous system.

**Neurons** Neurons are classified as one of three types. Sensory neurons carry impulses from sense organs, such as eyes and ears, to the central nervous system. Motor neurons carry impulses from the central nervous system to muscles and glands. Interneurons process information and send commands to other interneurons or motor neurons.

Neurons have certain features in common, including a cell body, multiple dendrites, and an axon. Some axons are covered by a myelin sheath.

**READING TOOL**

As you read, connect to the visuals in this lesson by completing the chart in your 📖 **Biology Foundations Workbook.**

**Figure 27-17**

### Neurons

The basic unit of the nervous system is the neuron, or nerve cell.

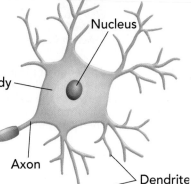

Nucleus

Cell body

Myelin sheath

Axon

Dendrite

Axon terminals

Nodes

## The Nerve Impulse

**The Nerve Impulse** Neurons carry information by using specialized proteins in their cell membranes to create small electrical currents. But nerve cells do *not* carry electric currents the way that telephone wires do. Neurons at rest have an electrical charge of −70 millivolts (mV), called the resting potential, between the inside and outside of their cell membranes. The charge is produced by membrane proteins that pump sodium ions ($Na^+$) out of the cell and potassium ions ($K^+$) into it. Separate potassium channel proteins make it easier for $K^+$ ions than $Na^+$ ions to diffuse back across the membrane. Because the pumps create a higher concentration of $K^+$ ions inside the cell, positively charged $K^+$ ions diffuse out of the cell. The inside of the cell therefore becomes negatively charged compared to the outside.

When a neuron receives a large enough stimulus, this resting potential changes suddenly, producing a nerve impulse called an action potential. The smallest stimulus that can produce an action potential is called a threshold stimulus. Stimuli weaker than the threshold will not produce an action potential.

Nerve impulses are not created by a flow of electrons down the axon. Instead, each action potential is produced by a sudden reversal of the resting potential, as shown in **Figure 27-18**. This charge reversal travels down the axon like ripples passing down the surface of a stream. The impulse travels faster through an axon with a myelin sheath than through an axon with no myelin sheath.

**ANIMATION**

### Figure 27-18

### The Resting Neuron and the Nerve Impulse

In a resting neuron, sodium-potassium pumps use ATP to pump $Na^+$ from the cell and to pump $K^+$ in. Some $K^+$ ions diffuse out of the cell, but gated channels block $Na^+$ from flowing into the resting neuron. Once a nerve impulse begins, it will move through an axon until it reaches the end.

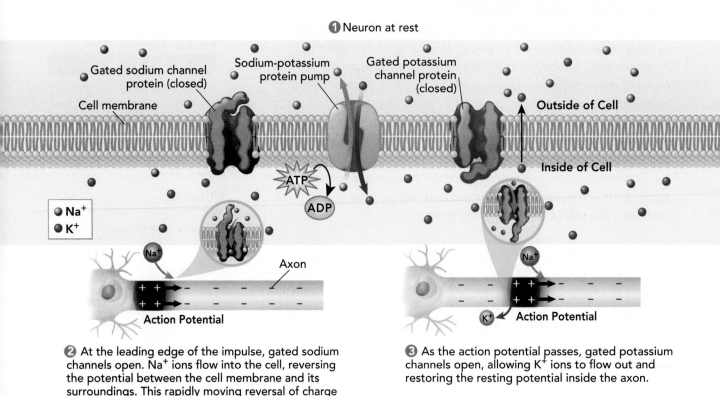

❶ Neuron at rest

❷ At the leading edge of the impulse, gated sodium channels open. $Na^+$ ions flow into the cell, reversing the potential between the cell membrane and its surroundings. This rapidly moving reversal of charge is called an action potential.

❸ As the action potential passes, gated potassium channels open, allowing $K^+$ ions to flow out and restoring the resting potential inside the axon.

**The Central Nervous System** As shown in **Figure 27-19**, the central nervous system, which includes the brain and the spinal cord, is contained almost entirely inside the bony structures of the skull and vertebral column. Sensations from various body areas are "felt" by specific brain regions. Commands to muscles originate in other brain areas. The spinal cord, which contains most neurons that enter and leave the brain, links the brain to the rest of the body.

**The Peripheral Nervous System** The peripheral nervous system contains nerves and associated cells that are not part of the brain or spinal cord. It has two major divisions—sensory and motor. The sensory division consists of receptor cells, which gather information, and sensory neurons, which transmit impulses from sense organs to the central nervous system. The motor division transmits impulses from the central nervous system to the muscles and glands. These messages are relayed through networks called the somatic nervous system and the autonomic nervous system.

*Somatic Nervous System* The somatic nervous system regulates activities such as movement of skeletal muscles. Some somatic nervous system actions are under voluntary control. When you lift your finger or wiggle your toes, impulses originating in the brain are carried through the spinal cord to motor neurons, which stimulate muscles. Other somatic nervous system actions occur automatically. If you step on a tack with your bare foot, your leg may recoil before you are aware of the pain. This rapid response (a reflex) is produced by impulses that travel through a pathway known as a reflex arc. Reflex arcs produce fast responses because the pain signal does not have to travel all the way to the brain. An interneuron in the spinal cord processes the information and sends a response to leg muscles via motor neurons.

*Autonomic Nervous System* The autonomic nervous system regulates activities that are not under conscious control. For instance, when you start to run, the autonomic nervous system speeds up your heart rate and blood flow to skeletal muscles, stimulates sweat glands, and slows down contractions of smooth muscles in the digestive system.

The autonomic nervous system consists of two equally important parts, the sympathetic nervous system and the parasympathetic nervous system, which usually have opposite effects. This division enables precise control of body systems, in the same way that using both the gas pedal and the brake enables a driver to control the speed of a car. In general, the sympathetic system prepares the body for intense activity—often called a "fight or flight" reaction. The parasympathetic system produces the "rest and digest" response.

✔ **READING CHECK** **Classify** In which division of the nervous system would you find an interneuron?

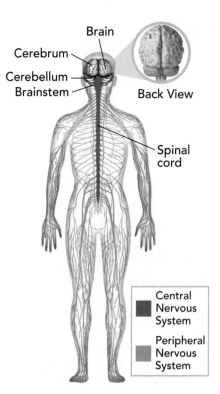

**Figure 27-19**

**The Nervous System**

The nervous system is comprised of the central nervous system and the peripheral nervous system. The central nervous system includes the brain and spinal cord.

**INTERACTIVITY**

Explore the lobes of the brain to discover how the brain functions.

## Figure 27-20

## The Skeleton

The human skeleton is divided into the axial skeleton and the appendicular skeleton. The skeleton consists of living tissue that has many roles in the body. ☑ **Summarize** What are four functions of the skeletal system?

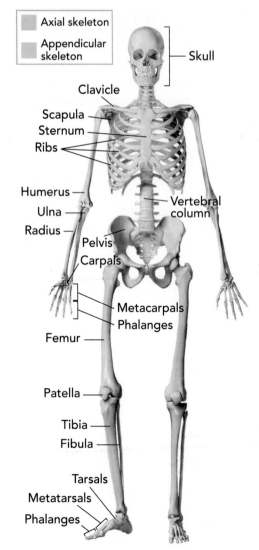

Axial skeleton
Appendicular skeleton

Skull
Clavicle
Scapula
Sternum
Ribs
Humerus
Ulna
Radius
Pelvis
Carpals
Vertebral column
Metacarpals
Phalanges
Femur
Patella
Tibia
Fibula
Tarsals
Metatarsals
Phalanges

# The Skeletal System

The skeletal system, shown in **Figure 27-20**, supports and shapes the body the way an internal wooden frame supports a house. 🔍 *The skeleton supports the body, protects internal organs, assists in movement, stores minerals, and is a site of blood cell formation.* Bones also act as rigid rods on which muscles exert force to produce movement. In addition, bones contain reserves of minerals, such as calcium salts.

The 206 bones in the adult human skeleton form the axial skeleton and the appendicular skeleton. The axial skeleton—the skull, the vertebral column, and the rib cage—supports the body's central axis. The bones of the arms, legs, pelvis, and shoulder area make up the appendicular skeleton.

**Bones** Bones are living tissue made up of a solid network of cells and protein fibers surrounded by deposits of calcium salts. **Figure 27-21** shows the structure of a bone. Bones are surrounded by tough connective tissue called periosteum (pehr ee AHS tee um). Beneath the periosteum is a thick layer of compact bone. Nerves and blood vessels run through compact bone in channels called Haversian canals. A less dense tissue known as spongy bone may be found under the compact bone, especially in the ends of long bones. Despite its name, spongy bone is quite strong.

Near the ends of bones where force is applied, spongy bone forms latticework structures that resemble supporting girders in a bridge. These structures add strength without excess mass.

Inside many bones are cavities containing one of two types of bone marrow. Yellow marrow consists primarily of cells that store fat. Red marrow contains stem cells that produce most types of blood cells.

☑ **READING CHECK** **Use Visuals** Use Figure 27-21 to provide evidence for the statement that bones are living tissue.

| Functions of the Skeleton |
|---|
| **Support** The bones of the skeleton support and give shape to the human body. |
| **Protection** Bones protect the delicate internal organs of the body. For example, the ribs form a basketlike cage around the heart and lungs. |
| **Movement** Bones provide a system of levers on which muscles produce movement. |
| **Mineral Storage** Bones contain reserves of minerals, including calcium, that are important to many body processes. When blood calcium levels are low, some reserves are released from the bones. |
| **Blood Cell Formation** Many types of blood cells are produced in soft tissue that fills the internal cavities of some bones. |

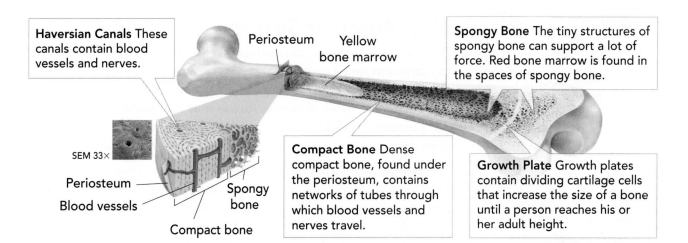

**Haversian Canals** These canals contain blood vessels and nerves.

Periosteum

Yellow bone marrow

**Spongy Bone** The tiny structures of spongy bone can support a lot of force. Red bone marrow is found in the spaces of spongy bone.

SEM 33×

Periosteum

Blood vessels

Spongy bone

Compact bone

**Compact Bone** Dense compact bone, found under the periosteum, contains networks of tubes through which blood vessels and nerves travel.

**Growth Plate** Growth plates contain dividing cartilage cells that increase the size of a bone until a person reaches his or her adult height.

**Joints** A place where two or more bones meet each other is called a joint. Joints contain connective tissue that holds bones together and permits bones to move without damaging each other. Joints can be classified as immovable, slightly movable, or freely movable.

Immovable joints, often called fixed joints, allow no movement. The bones at an immovable joint are interlocked and grow together until they are fused. Most bones in the skull meet at immovable joints.

Slightly movable joints permit a small amount of movement. Unlike the bones of immovable joints, the bones of slightly movable joints are separated from each other. The joints between the two bones of the lower leg and the joints between vertebrae in the spine are examples of slightly movable joints.

Freely movable joints, like the shoulder joint, permit movement in two or more directions. Freely movable joints are grouped according to the shapes of the surfaces of the adjacent bones. Several types of freely movable joints are shown in **Figure 27-22.**

**Up Close**

Figure 27-21

**Structure of a Bone**

A typical long bone, such the femur, contains spongy bone and compact bone. Within compact bone are Haversian canals, which contain blood vessels and nerves.

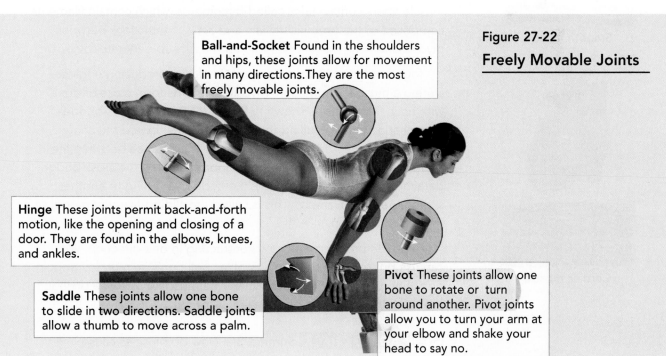

Figure 27-22

**Freely Movable Joints**

**Ball-and-Socket** Found in the shoulders and hips, these joints allow for movement in many directions. They are the most freely movable joints.

**Hinge** These joints permit back-and-forth motion, like the opening and closing of a door. They are found in the elbows, knees, and ankles.

**Saddle** These joints allow one bone to slide in two directions. Saddle joints allow a thumb to move across a palm.

**Pivot** These joints allow one bone to rotate or turn around another. Pivot joints allow you to turn your arm at your elbow and shake your head to say no.

Figure 27-23

## Types of Muscle

Skeletal muscle is striated, and smooth muscle is not. Although cardiac muscle is striated like skeletal muscle, it is not under voluntary control.

**Skeletal muscle**

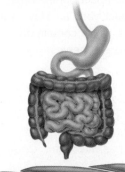

**Smooth muscle**

**Cardiac muscle**

# The Muscular System

Despite the animations you may have likely seen in horror films, a skeleton cannot move by itself. Muscles generate the force needed to power movement—from a leap in the air to the hint of a smile. ✎ *There are three different types of muscle tissues that are specialized for different functions: skeletal, smooth, and cardiac muscle.* The three types of muscles and their locations in the body are shown in **Figure 27-23**.

Skeletal muscles are usually attached to bones. They are responsible for voluntary movements. When viewed under a microscope at high magnification, skeletal muscle appears to have alternating light and dark bands called "striations." For this reason, skeletal muscle is said to be striated. Most skeletal muscle movements are consciously controlled by the central nervous system. Skeletal muscle cells are large, have many nuclei, and vary in length.

Smooth muscle cells are so named because they don't have striations and, therefore, look "smooth" under the microscope. These cells are spindle-shaped and usually have a single nucleus. Smooth muscle movements are usually involuntary. They are found throughout the body and form part of the walls of hollow structures such as the stomach, blood vessels, and intestines. Most smooth muscle cells can function without direct stimulation by the nervous system.

Cardiac muscle is found in just one place in the body—the heart. Cardiac muscle is striated like skeletal muscle, although its cells are smaller and usually have just one or two nuclei. Cardiac muscle is similar to smooth muscle because the cells can contract on their own without stimulation by the nervous system.

**Muscle Contraction and Movement** Muscles produce movements by shortening, or contracting, from end to end. Skeletal muscle fibers contain units called sarcomeres, which contain filaments composed of the proteins myosin and actin. Interactions between myosin and actin make it possible for muscles to generate force.

Together, myosin and actin form tiny force-producing engines. During a muscle contraction, myosin filaments form cross-bridges with actin filaments, as shown in **Figure 27-24**. The cross-bridges then change shape, pulling the actin filaments toward the center of the sarcomere. This action decreases the distance between the ends of the sarcomere, so the fiber shortens. Then the cross-bridge detaches from actin and repeats the cycle by binding to another site on the actin filament. This is called the sliding-filament model of muscle contraction.

A muscle produces force by contracting in one direction. We can use our muscles to push as well as pull because muscles work in opposing pairs around joints. When one muscle in the pair contracts, the other muscle in the pair relaxes.

✓ **READING CHECK** **Summarize** How do muscles cause movement?

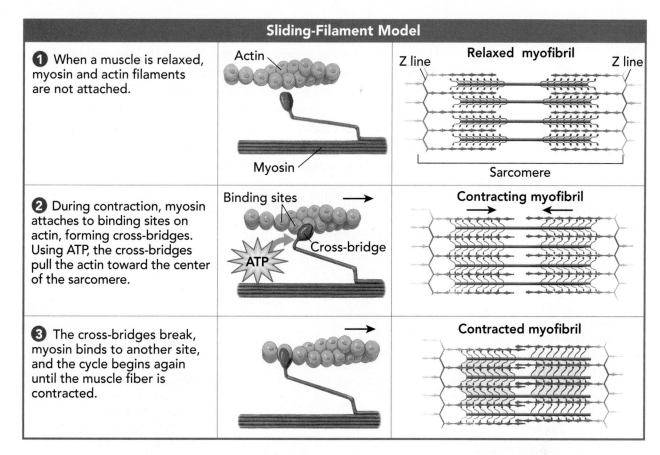

**Sliding-Filament Model**

❶ When a muscle is relaxed, myosin and actin filaments are not attached.

Actin

Myosin

Relaxed myofibril

Z line          Z line

Sarcomere

❷ During contraction, myosin attaches to binding sites on actin, forming cross-bridges. Using ATP, the cross-bridges pull the actin toward the center of the sarcomere.

Binding sites

Cross-bridge

ATP

Contracting myofibril

❸ The cross-bridges break, myosin binds to another site, and the cycle begins again until the muscle fiber is contracted.

Contracted myofibril

**Figure 27-24**

**Sliding-Filament Model**

Myosin ratchets along the actin in a sarcomere, causing a muscle to contract.

# The Integumentary System

🔍 *Skin and its related structures—the hair, nails, and glands— make up the integumentary system.* The integumentary system serves as a barrier against infection and injury, helps to regulate body temperature, removes wastes, gathers sensory information, and produces vitamin D.

The outer layer of the skin is the epidermis, which has two layers. The outer layer is made of dead cells. The inner layer consists of stem cells that divide rapidly and push to the top. These cells eventually lose their organelles and become the tough, dead cells that protect your body from invading pathogens and injuries. Other cells in the epidermis produce melanin, which protects the skin by absorbing ultraviolet radiation from the sun.

The dermis lies below the epidermis. It contains blood vessels, nerve endings, glands, sensory receptors, smooth muscles, and hair follicles. Blood vessels in the dermis narrow when it is cold to conserve heat. The blood vessels widen on warm days to help the body lose heat. Excess heat and wastes are released when sweat glands produce perspiration. Beneath the dermis is a layer of fat and loose connective tissue that helps to insulate the body.

The basic component of human hair and nails is a protein called keratin. Hair on the head protects the scalp from ultraviolet radiation. Hair in the nostrils, around the eyes, and in ear canals prevents dirt from entering the body. Nails protect fingertips and toes from damage.

# The Endocrine System

How are you feeling today? A major influence on your well-being is the endocrine system, which helps to regulate mood and metabolism, tissue function, growth and development, and reproductive processes. The endocrine system produces chemicals called hormones that affect many parts of the body. ⚲ *The glands of the endocrine system release hormones that travel through the blood and control the actions of cells, tissues, and organs.* Most endocrine glands release their hormones directly into the blood. The major endocrine glands are shown in **Figure 27-25.**

✓ **READING CHECK** **Explain** How does the endocrine system depend on the circulatory system?

**Figure 27-25**

**The Endocrine System and Its Organs**

Endocrine glands produce hormones that affect many parts of the body.

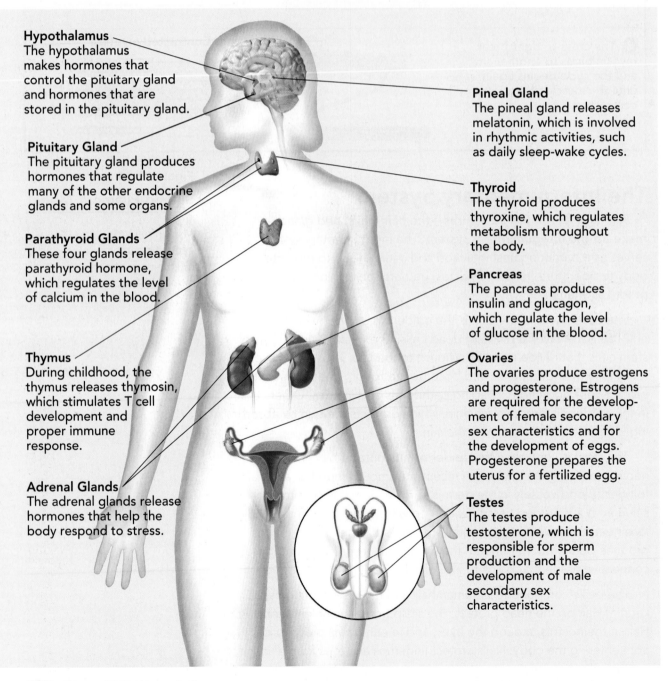

**Hypothalamus**
The hypothalamus makes hormones that control the pituitary gland and hormones that are stored in the pituitary gland.

**Pituitary Gland**
The pituitary gland produces hormones that regulate many of the other endocrine glands and some organs.

**Parathyroid Glands**
These four glands release parathyroid hormone, which regulates the level of calcium in the blood.

**Thymus**
During childhood, the thymus releases thymosin, which stimulates T cell development and proper immune response.

**Adrenal Glands**
The adrenal glands release hormones that help the body respond to stress.

**Pineal Gland**
The pineal gland releases melatonin, which is involved in rhythmic activities, such as daily sleep-wake cycles.

**Thyroid**
The thyroid produces thyroxine, which regulates metabolism throughout the body.

**Pancreas**
The pancreas produces insulin and glucagon, which regulate the level of glucose in the blood.

**Ovaries**
The ovaries produce estrogens and progesterone. Estrogens are required for the development of female secondary sex characteristics and for the development of eggs. Progesterone prepares the uterus for a fertilized egg.

**Testes**
The testes produce testosterone, which is responsible for sperm production and the development of male secondary sex characteristics.

**Hormone Action** Hormones fall into two general groups—steroid hormones and nonsteroid hormones. Steroid and nonsteroid hormones work in different ways, but both affect cells by binding to specific chemical receptors located either on cell membranes or within cells. Cells that have receptors for a particular hormone are called target cells. If a cell does not have receptors for a particular hormone, the hormone has no effect on it. **Figure 27-26** shows how the two types of hormones act upon their target cells.

## Steroid Hormone Action

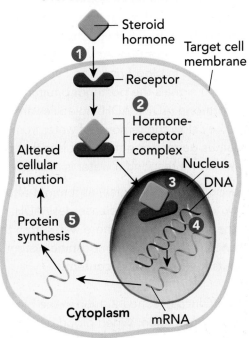

## Nonsteroid Hormone Action

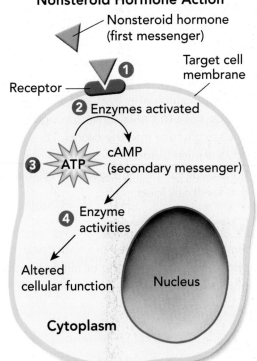

### Figure 27-26

### Hormones

Steroid hormones act by entering the nucleus of a cell and changing the pattern of gene expression. Nonsteroid hormones bind to receptors on a target cell membrane and cause the release of secondary messengers that affect cell activities.

### Steroid Hormones

❶ Because steroid hormones are lipids, they can pass directly across the cell membrane.

❷ Once inside, the hormone binds to a receptor (found only in the hormone's target cells) and forms a hormone-receptor complex.

❸ The hormone-receptor complex enters the nucleus, where it binds to regions of DNA that regulate gene expression.

❹ This binding initiates the transcription of specific genes to messenger RNA (mRNA).

❺ The mRNA moves into the cytoplasm and directs protein synthesis. This ability to alter gene expression makes the effects of many steroid hormones especially powerful and long lasting.

### Nonsteroid Hormones

❶ The binding of the hormone activates enzymes on the inner surface of the cell membrane.

❷ These enzymes release secondary messengers such as calcium ions, nucleotides, and fatty acids to relay the hormone's message within the cell.

❸ One common secondary messenger is cAMP (cyclic AMP), which is produced from ATP.

❹ These secondary messengers can activate or inhibit a wide range of cell activities.

**Control of the Endocrine System** The endocrine system is one of the master control systems of the body. Like most body systems, the endocrine system is regulated by negative feedback mechanisms that function to maintain homeostasis. Recall that negative feedback, also called feedback inhibition, occurs when an increase in a substance "feeds back" in a way that inhibits the system. Concentrations of hormones, and their effects on other body systems, are controlled in similar ways.

*Maintaining Water Balance* Water balance in the body is one example of how the endocrine system maintains homeostasis. When you exercise, you sweat and lose water. If this water loss continued, your body would soon become dehydrated. But your hypothalamus contains cells that monitor blood water content. As you lose water, concentrations of dissolved materials in blood rise. The hypothalamus responds in two ways. First, it signals the posterior pituitary gland to release antidiuretic hormone (ADH). ADH molecules are carried to the kidneys, where they slow the removal of water from blood. Second, the hypothalamus generates nerve impulses that produce a sensation of thirst to which we respond if water is available.

When concentrations of dissolved materials fall, as it might after you drink several glasses of water, the pituitary releases less ADH. As ADH concentrations fall, the kidneys remove more water from the blood, restoring its proper concentration. This homeostatic system sets both upper and lower limits for blood water content.

*Blood Glucose Regulation* Glucose concentration in the bloodstream is controlled by insulin and glucagon. When blood glucose concentration rises, the pancreas releases insulin. Insulin stimulates liver and skeletal muscle cells to convert blood glucose to glycogen, and it stimulates fat cells to convert glucose to lipids. These actions together prevent blood glucose concentrations from rising too rapidly. They also store energy for future use. In between meals, when blood glucose concentration drops, the pancreas releases glucagon. Glucagon stimulates liver and skeletal muscle cells to break down glycogen and release glucose into the blood. These actions raise blood glucose concentrations back to normal. **Figure 27-27** shows this feedback loop.

**Figure 27-27**

**Glucagon and Insulin**

Insulin and glucagon are opposing hormones that ensure that blood glucose levels stay within a normal range.

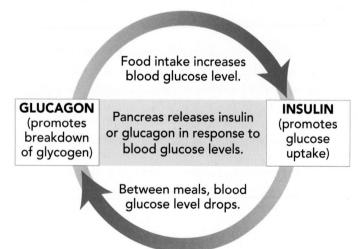

Food intake increases blood glucose level.

**GLUCAGON** (promotes breakdown of glycogen)

Pancreas releases insulin or glucagon in response to blood glucose levels.

**INSULIN** (promotes glucose uptake)

Between meals, blood glucose level drops.

**☑ READING CHECK**

**Summarize** How does the endocrine system respond to rising or falling blood glucose levels?

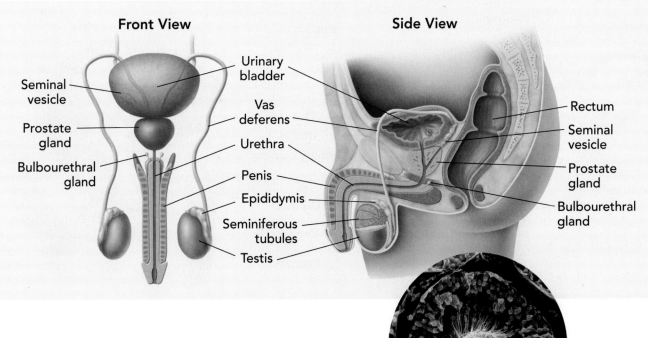

**Front View**

Seminal vesicle

Prostate gland

Bulbourethral gland

Urinary bladder

Vas deferens

Urethra

Penis

Epididymis

Seminiferous tubules

Testis

**Side View**

Rectum

Seminal vesicle

Prostate gland

Bulbourethral gland

SEM 48×

# The Male Reproductive System

As a male approaches puberty, the hypothalamus signals the pituitary to produce two hormones—luteinizing hormone (LH) and follicle stimulating hormone (FSH). LH stimulates the testes to produce testosterone. Testosterone directs the male physical changes associated with puberty and, together with FSH, stimulates sperm development. 🔍 *When puberty is complete, the male reproductive system is fully functional, meaning that it can produce and release active sperm.* The male reproductive system is shown in **Figure 27-28**.

The testes (singular: testis) are located in a sac called the scrotum outside the body cavity, where a slightly lower temperature promotes sperm development. Specialized cells within the testes undergo meiosis to form haploid sperm nuclei. Sperm then move into the epididymis, where they mature and are stored. A mature sperm cell consists of a head, which contains a highly condensed nucleus; a midpiece, packed with mitochondria; and a tail, or flagellum, which propels the cell forward. Some sperm are moved into tubes called vas deferens, which empty into the urethra.

Glands lining the reproductive tract produce nutrient-rich seminal fluid that nourishes the sperm. The combination of sperm and seminal fluid is known as semen. Between 20 million and 150 million sperm are present in 1 milliliter of semen. That's about 3 million sperm per drop! When a male is sexually aroused, the autonomic nervous system stimulates the penis to become erect. Semen is ejected through the urethra by contractions of smooth muscles lining the reproductive tract in a process called ejaculation.

**Figure 27-28**

## Male Reproductive System

The main structures of the male reproductive system produce and deliver sperm. The micrograph shows a cross section of one tiny seminiferous tubule containing developing sperm.

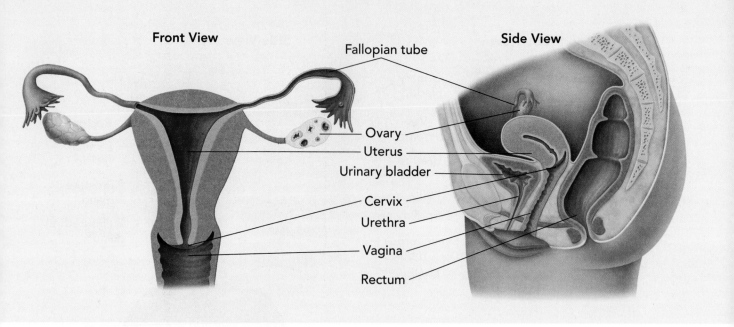

**Front View**

**Side View**

Fallopian tube

Ovary

Uterus

Urinary bladder

Cervix

Urethra

Vagina

Rectum

Figure 27-29

**Female Reproductive System**

The ovaries are the main organs of the female reproductive system.

# The Female Reproductive System

The primary reproductive organs of the female are the ovaries. As in males, puberty in females starts when the hypothalamus signals the pituitary gland to release FSH and LH. FSH stimulates cells within the ovaries to produce increased amounts of estrogens and to start producing egg cells. ✎ *The main functions of the female reproductive system are to produce egg cells, or ova (singular: ovum), and to prepare the body to nourish a developing embryo.* The female reproductive system is shown in **Figure 27-29**.

FSH and LH together stimulate the maturation of clusters of cells within the ovary, known as follicles. Each follicle contains a developing egg cell. Other cells within the follicle respond to these pituitary hormones by producing estrogens.

At puberty each ovary contains about 400,000 follicles. However, a female's ovaries only release about 400 eggs during her lifetime. One ovary releases an egg every 28 days or so. Egg release is part of the menstrual cycle, a regular sequence of events involving the interaction of the reproductive system and the endocrine system. Meanwhile, estrogens stimulate the uterus to grow new blood vessels in preparation for receiving a fertilized egg.

If an egg is not fertilized, or if a fertilized egg fails to attach to the uterine wall, it is discharged. The new blood vessels and the lining of the uterus deteriorate and are also discharged. A new menstrual cycle then begins. If an egg is fertilized, embryonic development begins. If the developing fertilized egg successfully attaches to the wall of the uterus, the menstrual cycle ceases, and tissues from both the developing embryo and the mother's uterus form a new organ called the placenta.

✓ **READING CHECK** **Identify** Which organ in the female reproductive system produces egg cells?

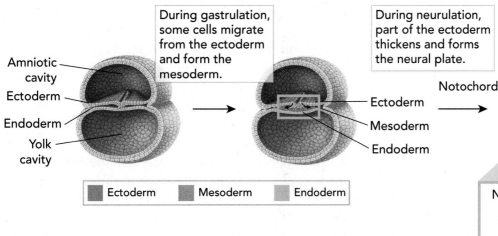

During gastrulation, some cells migrate from the ectoderm and form the mesoderm.

During neurulation, part of the ectoderm thickens and forms the neural plate.

Amniotic cavity
Ectoderm
Endoderm
Yolk cavity

Ectoderm
Mesoderm
Endoderm

Notochord

Ectoderm | Mesoderm | Endoderm

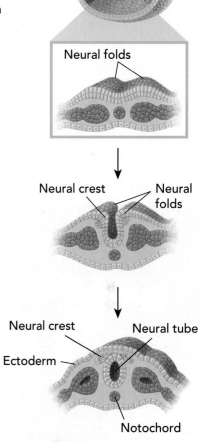

Neural folds

Neural crest
Neural folds

Neural crest
Ectoderm
Neural tube
Notochord

**Figure 27-30**

**Gastrulation and Neurulation**

The cells of human embryos, like those of other animal embryos, go through a series of complex changes during early development.

## Fertilization and Early Development
Human development begins with fertilization, the fusion of sperm and egg. During intercourse, semen containing millions of sperm is released into the vagina. Sperm swim through the uterus into the Fallopian tubes. The outer layer of an egg contains binding sites to which sperm can attach. The haploid (N) sperm nucleus enters the haploid egg, and their two nuclei fuse to form a single diploid (2N) nucleus.

The fertilized egg then undergoes multiple rounds of mitosis. A cavity forms in the center, and the embryo becomes a hollow ball of cells known as a blastocyst. About a week after fertilization, the blastocyst attaches to the wall of the uterus and grows into the mother's tissues. Cells in the blastocyst then begin to differentiate, producing different body tissues. A cluster of cells within the blastocyst cavity develops into the body of the embryo. Other blastocyst cells differentiate into tissues that support and protect the embryo.

### Gastrulation
The result of gastrulation is the formation of three cell layers called the ectoderm, mesoderm, and endoderm. As shown in **Figure 27-30**, the ectoderm and endoderm form first. The ectoderm develops into skin and the nervous system. Mesoderm cells develop into many of the body's internal structures, including bones, muscles, and blood cells. The endoderm forms the lining of organs in the digestive, respiratory, and excretory systems.

### Neurulation
The process of neurulation marks the beginning of the nervous system development. Some mesodermal tissue differentiates into a notochord. Nearby ectoderm thickens and forms the neural plate, neural folds, and neural crest. The neural folds form the neural tube, from which the spinal cord and brain develop. Neural crest cells become nerve cells, skin pigment cells, and other structures, such as the lower jaw.

**READING TOOL**

Record the sequence of events that occur during fertilization and development.

**The Placenta** As the embryo develops, specialized membranes form to protect and nourish the embryo. The amnion, a sac filled with fluid, cushions and protects the developing embryo. Another sac, the chorion, just outside the amnion, makes contact with the uterus. Small fingerlike projections form on the outer surface of the chorion and grow into the uterine lining to form the placenta, the vital connection between mother and embryo. The mother's blood and the embryo's blood flow past each other in the placenta, but they do not mix. Oxygen and nutrients diffuse from the mother's blood to the embryo's blood, and carbon dioxide and metabolic wastes diffuse from the embryo's blood to the mother's blood. The umbilical cord connects the embryo to the placenta.

**Figure 27-31**

**Fetus**

This MRI of a full-term fetus shows the umbilical cord and placenta.

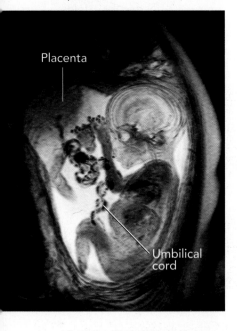

Placenta

Umbilical cord

**Later Development** At about 5 weeks, a week after neurulation is complete, the embryo is about 7 millimeters long. The pharyngeal pouches and tail that characterize chordates are visible. After 8 weeks, the embryo is called a fetus. At this point, it is about 25 millimeters long and has eyes, fingers and toes, ears, and most major organs. Throughout the rest of the first trimester, or first three months of pregnancy, the fetus continues to grow and become more human in appearance.

During the second trimester, the tissues and organs of the fetus become more complex and begin to function. The fetal heart becomes large enough that it can be heard with a stethoscope. Bone continues to replace the cartilage that forms the early skeleton. A layer of soft hair grows over the skin of the fetus, and the eyes, ears, and nose move to their final positions.

During the third trimester, the last three months before birth, the fetus doubles in mass. Fat deposited beneath the skin makes the fetus look less wrinkled and skinny and more like a baby. The soft hair vanishes from the face and then from the rest of the body. The central nervous system and lungs continue developing throughout the third trimester, and complete their development at about 40 weeks, just before birth. A full-term fetus is shown in **Figure 27-31.**

HS-LS1-1, HS-LS1-2, HS-LS1-3

## ☑ LESSON 27.3 Review

### 🔍 KEY QUESTIONS

1. What is the role of neurons in the nervous system?
2. List the different functions of the skeletal system.
3. What are the differences among the three types of muscle tissue?
4. List the functions of the integumentary system.
5. How do endocrine glands send messages to other organs?
6. How does puberty affect the male and female reproductive systems?

### CRITICAL THINKING

7. **Synthesize Information** Describe how the muscular and skeletal systems work together to move the body.
8. **Compare and Contrast** How are the actions of the nervous and endocrine systems alike? How are they different?
9. **Relate Cause and Effect** How do the outcomes of gastrulation and neurulation contribute to human development?

# Immunity and Disease

## KEY QUESTIONS
- *What causes infectious disease?*
- *What are the body's nonspecific defenses against pathogens?*
- *What is the function of the immune system's specific defenses?*
- *What health problems result when the immune system does not function properly?*

**HS-LS1-1:** Construct an explanation based on evidence for how the structure of DNA determines the structure of proteins which carry out the essential functions of life through systems of specialized cells.

**HS-LS1-2:** Develop and use a model to illustrate the hierarchical organization of interacting systems that provide specific functions within multicellular organisms.

## VOCABULARY
infectious disease
pathogen
inflammatory response
antigen
humoral immunity
cell-mediated immunity

## READING TOOL

As you read, complete the table with information about the causes and effects of disease and prevention in your **Biology Foundations Workbook.**

What causes disease? People once believed that diseases were caused by curses, evil spirits, or bad behavior. Today, however, we know the causes of many diseases, and that has made it possible to prevent and cure many of them.

## Classifying Diseases

A disease is an abnormal condition that harms an organism. Throughout most of human history, the causes of most diseases and how they were spread were a baffling mystery. This lack of knowledge led to "cures" that often did more harm than good. In the mid-nineteenth century, French chemist Louis Pasteur and German bacteriologist Robert Koch proposed the germ theory of disease, which is that **infectious diseases** occur when microorganisms disrupt normal body functions. Today, we call such microorganisms **pathogens**, meaning "sickness producers." *Infectious diseases are caused by viruses, bacteria, fungi, "protists", and other pathogens.*

**How Infectious Disease Spreads** Many bacteria and viruses are spread through coughing, sneezing, and physical contact. When pathogens are released into the air, someone else may inhale them. Or the droplets may land on a surface, such as a doorknob. When an uninfected person touches the doorknob, he or she will pick up the pathogen.

Other types of diseases are spread through the exchange of body fluids that occurs during sexual intercourse or through blood transfusions. Donated blood is tested for a range of diseases before it becomes part of the blood supply.

Many pathogens that infect the digestive tract are spread through contaminated water. Contaminated water may be consumed, or it may carry pathogens onto fruit or vegetables that are later eaten.

**Figure 27-32**

## Minamata Disease

Minamata disease, named after the Japanese city in which the condition was first discovered, results from severe mercury poisoning. Unfortunately, Minamata is not the first or last city in which citizens have been injured or killed by industrial pollution.

 **VIDEO**

Learn about the strange actions of the pathogen that causes Lyme disease.

**Disease Caused by Toxins** Another important category of diseases involves toxic chemicals that may be found in food or drinking water. For example, in the 1950s, a chemical plant in Minamata, Japan, released large amounts of methyl mercury into local waters. The mercury contaminated the fish that people ate.

The results were tragic, as shown in **Figure 27-32**. More than 2000 people were affected, suffering convulsions or paralysis. Like many heavy metals, mercury binds to proteins and blocks enzyme activity. In particular, mercury ions attack enzymes in the central nervous system that usually prevent cells from being damaged by oxidation. Eventually, nearly 1800 people in Minamata died from mercury poisoning.

Other chemicals found in water that can damage the body include compounds of arsenic, lead, and chromium. Some of these compounds occur naturally at low levels in streams and groundwater. However, some are released into the environment by mining or industrial activities. Public water systems are vulnerable as well, especially those built many decades ago when water pipes were made with lead.

# Nonspecific Defenses

With pathogens all around us, how do we stay healthy most of the time? The reason is that our bodies have a series of defenses that protect us against infection. Some of these act against a wide range of pathogens and are called nonspecific defenses. *Nonspecific defenses include the skin, tears, and other secretions; the inflammatory response; and fever.*

**First Line of Defense** The most widespread nonspecific defense is the skin, a physical barrier that keeps most pathogens out of the body. Even the openings in the skin are protected. Saliva, mucus, and tears contain lysozyme, an enzyme that breaks down bacterial cell walls, while stomach secretions destroy many pathogens in food or water.

## Second Line of Defense

If pathogens do make it into the body, a second line of defense swings into action. Its mechanisms include the inflammatory response and fever. The **inflammatory response,** which is illustrated in **Figure 27-33,** causes infected areas to become red and painful, or inflamed. The response begins when pathogens stimulate cells called mast cells to release chemicals known as histamines that increase the flow of blood to the affected area. White blood cells then move into infected tissues, engulfing and destroying bacteria.

The immune system also releases chemicals that increase body temperature, producing a fever. Increased body temperature may slow down or stop the growth of some pathogens. Higher body temperature helps to speed up the immune response.

**BUILD VOCABULARY**

**Related Word Forms** The verb *inflame* means "to make sore, red, and swollen."

**Figure 27-33**

## Inflammatory Response

The inflammatory response is a nonspecific defense reaction to tissue damage caused by injury or infection. ☑ **Infer** What part of the inflammatory response leads to redness around a wounded area?

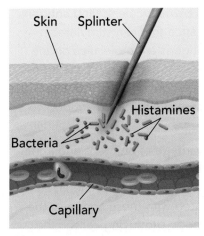

**1** In response to the wound and invading pathogens, mast cells release histamines, which stimulate increased blood flow to the area.

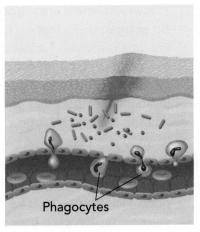

**2** Local blood vessels dilate. Fluid leaves the capillaries and causes swelling. Phagocytes move into the tissue.

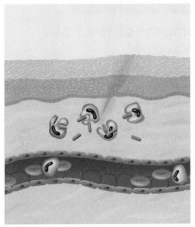

**3** Phagocytes engulf and destroy the bacteria and damaged cells.

# Specific Defenses: The Immune System

The body also has specific defenses, which respond to particular pathogens. 🔍 *The immune system's specific defenses distinguish between "self" and "other," inactivating or killing foreign substances or cells.*

## Recognizing "Self" and "Nonself"

The immune system recognizes cells that belong in the body and treats these as "self." These cells carry chemical markers that act as passwords, saying, "I belong here. Don't attack me!" However, once the immune system recognizes a bacterium or virus as "other," it uses cellular and chemical weapons to attack it. In addition, after encountering an invader, the immune system "remembers" it. This immune "memory" enables a more rapid and effective response if the same pathogen attacks again.

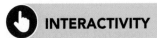

**INTERACTIVITY**

Explore the different responses of the immune system to invading pathogens.

Figure 27-34

## Effectiveness of the Polio Vaccine

The polio vaccine greatly reduced the number of cases of polio in the United States. This in turn decreased the number of people who were paralyzed or died from the disease.

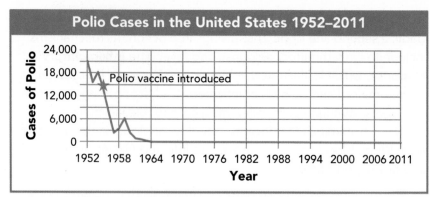

**Polio Cases in the United States 1952–2011**

SOURCE: National Notifiable Disease Surveillance System, CDC

### Analyzing Data

#### Impact of the Polio Vaccine

Polio is an infectious viral disease that spreads from person to person by contact or through contaminated water. It infects the brain and spinal cord and can cause paralysis and death. The graph shows the number of polio cases in the United States over time.

1. **Analyze Graphs** Why might the number of cases have decreased in 1953 and then increased in 1954?

2. **Evaluate a Solution** How effective was the vaccine in eliminating polio in the short and long term?

3. **Construct a Counter-Argument** Some parents choose not to vaccinate their children. These parents claim that vaccines are unnecessary because the diseases they protect against are no longer prevalent in modern society. What might the consequences be if a significant number of people did not receive the vaccine?

How does the immune system recognize "others"? Specific immune defenses are triggered by molecules called antigens. An **antigen** is any foreign substance that can stimulate an immune response. Typically, antigens are molecules on the outer surfaces of bacteria, viruses, or parasites. The immune system responds to antigens by producing cells that attack the invaders directly or that produce proteins called antibodies that tag them for destruction.

Vaccines work by taking advantage of antigens and immunological memory. Vaccines contain the antigens of pathogens that cause diseases, such as smallpox, diphtheria, and polio. When a person is vaccinated with these antigens, the immune system generates antibody-producing cells. If the person comes in contact with this antigen again, the body is ready to fight. As **Figure 27-34** shows, within a few years of its introduction, the polio vaccine virtually eliminated this disease in the United States.

**Fighting Infections** The main working cells of the immune response are B lymphocytes (B cells) and T lymphocytes (T cells). B cells are produced in the bone marrow. T cells are produced in the bone marrow but mature in the thymus. Each B cell and T cell is capable of recognizing one specific antigen. Although both types of cells recognize antigens, they go about it differently.

Both B cells and T cells continually search the body for signs of antigens. The specific immune response has two main styles of action: humoral immunity and cell-mediated immunity. **Humoral immunity** depends on the action of antibodies that circulate in the blood and lymph. **Cell-mediated immunity** defends the body against some viruses, fungi, and single-celled pathogens. The two types of immune response are shown in **Figure 27-35**.

☑ **READING CHECK** **Explain** How do vaccines prevent disease?

## Figure 27-35
## Specific Immune Response

In humoral immunity, antibodies bind to antigens in body fluids and tag them for destruction by other parts of the immune system. In cell-mediated immunity, body cells that contain antigens are destroyed.

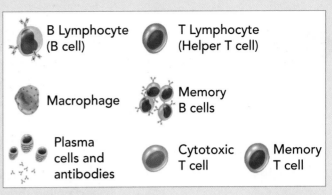

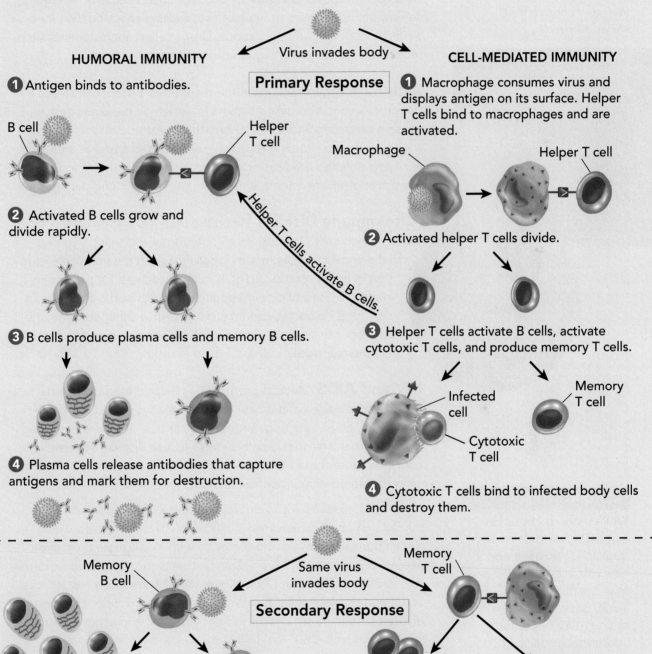

**HUMORAL IMMUNITY**

**Virus invades body**

**Primary Response**

**CELL-MEDIATED IMMUNITY**

❶ Antigen binds to antibodies.

B cell

Helper T cell

Helper T cells activate B cells.

❷ Activated B cells grow and divide rapidly.

❸ B cells produce plasma cells and memory B cells.

❹ Plasma cells release antibodies that capture antigens and mark them for destruction.

❶ Macrophage consumes virus and displays antigen on its surface. Helper T cells bind to macrophages and are activated.

Macrophage

Helper T cell

❷ Activated helper T cells divide.

❸ Helper T cells activate B cells, activate cytotoxic T cells, and produce memory T cells.

Infected cell

Memory T cell

Cytotoxic T cell

❹ Cytotoxic T cells bind to infected body cells and destroy them.

Memory B cell

Same virus invades body

Memory T cell

**Secondary Response**

Helper T cells

❺ Memory B cells respond more quickly than B cells in the primary response.

❺ Memory T cells respond more quickly than helper T cells in the primary response.

**Figure 27-36**
**Allergies**

Ragweed pollen is a well-known allergen.

SEM 306x

# Immune System Disorders

Failure of the immune system to react to pathogens can be life threatening. But the immune system can also cause problems when it overreacts to harmless antigens found in pollen, dust mites, pet dander, and even one's own cells. ⚲ *Problems with immune system function can result in allergies, asthma, autoimmune disease, and AIDS.*

**Allergies** Antigens that cause allergic reactions, such as the ragweed pollen shown in **Figure 27-36,** are called allergens. Allergens can trigger an inflammatory response, causing sneezing, watery eyes, a runny nose, and other irritations. Drugs called antihistamines help relieve allergy symptoms by counteracting these effects.

**Asthma** Allergic reactions in the respiratory system can create a dangerous condition called asthma, in which air passages narrow, causing wheezing and difficulty breathing. Asthma attacks can be triggered by respiratory infections, exercise, and stress as well as by allergens. Inhaled medications can relax smooth muscles around the airways and relieve asthma symptoms, preventing lung damage.

**Autoimmune Disease** When the immune system attacks the body's own cells, it produces an autoimmune disease. Type I diabetes is an autoimmune disease in which the immune system attacks insulin-producing cells in the pancreas. Other autoimmune diseases include rheumatoid arthritis and lupus. People with Type I diabetes can take insulin, while other autoimmune diseases can be treated with medications that suppress the immune response.

**HIV and AIDS** Medical progress has helped eradicate many once-deadly diseases, but new ones can always arise. During the late 1970s, physicians began reporting serious infections produced by microorganisms that didn't normally cause disease. Researchers concluded that these illnesses were symptoms of a new disorder they called acquired immunodeficiency syndrome (AIDS).

In 1983, researchers identified the cause of AIDS, which is the human immunodeficiency virus (HIV). HIV attacks key cells within the immune system, leaving the body with inadequate protection against pathogens. HIV is a retrovirus that carries its genetic information in RNA, rather than DNA. **Figure 27-37** shows how HIV attacks an immune system cell. Over time, HIV destroys T cells, crippling the ability of the immune system to fight HIV itself and other pathogens, which leads to AIDS.

HIV is deadly, but it is not transmitted through coughing, sneezing, sharing clothes, or other forms of casual contact. The four main ways that HIV is transmitted are sexual intercourse with an infected person; sharing needles with an infected person; contact with infected blood or blood products; or transmission from an infected mother to her child during pregnancy, birth, or breast-feeding.

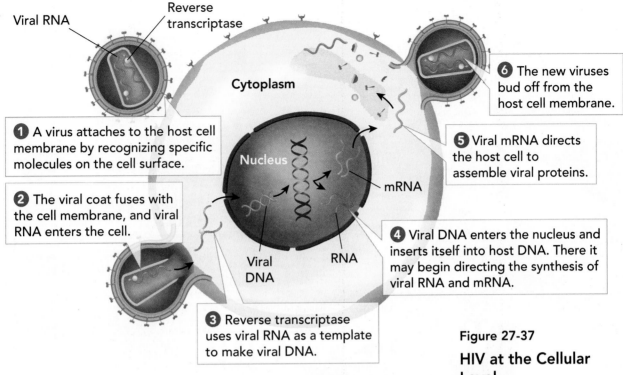

① A virus attaches to the host cell membrane by recognizing specific molecules on the cell surface.

② The viral coat fuses with the cell membrane, and viral RNA enters the cell.

③ Reverse transcriptase uses viral RNA as a template to make viral DNA.

④ Viral DNA enters the nucleus and inserts itself into host DNA. There it may begin directing the synthesis of viral RNA and mRNA.

⑤ Viral mRNA directs the host cell to assemble viral proteins.

⑥ The new viruses bud off from the host cell membrane.

Viral RNA

Reverse transcriptase

Cytoplasm

Nucleus

mRNA

Viral DNA

RNA

**Figure 27-37**

**HIV at the Cellular Level**

HIV travels through the blood, where it binds to receptors on a helper T cell. Inside the cell, the viral DNA directs the cell to produce many new viruses. These new viruses are quickly released back into the blood, where they infect more cells.

You can choose behaviors that reduce your risk of becoming infected with HIV. The best ways to avoid HIV infection are abstinence from sexual activity and avoidance of illegal intravenous drug use. Within a committed relationship, sexual fidelity between two uninfected partners presents the least risk of becoming infected with HIV.

At present, there is neither a cure for nor a reliable vaccine against AIDS. However, a steady stream of new drugs makes it possible to survive HIV infection for years. Unfortunately, these successful drugs have given some people the misconception that HIV is not serious. That idea is dead wrong. Each year in the United States about 40,000 people are diagnosed with HIV, and another 7,000 die from AIDS-related complications.

HS-LS1-1, HS-LS1-2

# ☑ LESSON 27.4 Review

## ⚲ KEY QUESTIONS

1. What are the ways in which infectious diseases are spread?

2. Describe three of the nonspecific defenses against infection.

3. Why is it important for the immune system to distinguish "self" from "other"?

4. How does HIV damage the immune system?

## CRITICAL THINKING

5. **Classify** Why can AIDS be classified as both an infectious disease and an immune system disorder?

6. **Compare and Contrast** How are nonspecific defenses against disease different from the immune system?

7. **Construct an Explanation** How can toxic chemicals cause disease? Cite a specific example.

# What's wrong with the water?

**Fertilizers, pesticides, heavy metals, and a variety of harmful chemicals can all contaminate drinking water. Human health depends on keeping drinking water free of pollution.**

HS-ETS1-1, HS-ETS1-3, CCSS.ELA-LITERACY.RST.9-10.8, CCSS.ELA-LITERACY.WHST.9-10.1, CCSS.ELA-LITERACY.WHST.9-10.7

## Make Your Case

Our need for clean, safe water is one way that the environment and personal health are interrelated. In many communities in the United States and around the world, to drink water from the tap is to risk infection, cancer, or other diseases. When lead from old pipes leaches into drinking water, it causes some very serious health problems.

## Evaluate a Solution

1. **Conduct Research** What is the source of drinking water for your home or community? How is the water treated before it reaches you? Research these questions and any issues that involve the community water supply.

2. **Engage in Argument** Evaluate the system that delivers water in your community. Argue that the system is sufficient for the community or that improvements are needed. Cite evidence from your research and this chapter to support your argument.

Flint River, Flint, Michigan

## Careers on the Case

### Work Toward a Solution

Toxicologists work closely with physicians and other healthcare providers to help prevent and treat the effects of poisons and toxins.

### Toxicologist

This career specializes in the effects of chemicals on humans, wildlife, and ecosystems. Some toxicologists assess the risks to human health from a polluted environment. Others conduct research on potential toxins and poisons, such as new pesticides or industrial chemicals.

▶ **VIDEO**

Learn more about toxicologists and other related careers.

## Technology on the Case

### Get the Lead Out!

In the 1910s, chemist Thomas Midgley wanted to improve engine performance in automobiles. Midgley's solution was to add a compound called tetraethyl lead to the fuel. The lead compound proved to be wonderful for engines. Unfortunately, the lead also caused—and continues to cause—terrible health problems.

Even in Midgley's time, scientists knew that lead was toxic. Nevertheless, lead continued to be used for decades in gasoline, as well as in paints, pipes, and other products. As a result, lead spread throughout the environment. By the late 1970s, almost 90 percent of U.S. children ages 1 to 5 had elevated levels of lead in their blood.

The United States banned leaded gasoline in 1973, and the use of lead in paint and other products was phased out soon after. These actions greatly reduced the threat of lead. Over many years, the average blood levels of lead in children decreased significantly—although not to zero.

Today, lead persists in many homes and in the environment. The Environmental Protection Agency (EPA) has programs to help contractors remove lead paint safely. The EPA also helps homeowners test for lead in drinking water. However, as shown by the water crisis in Flint, Michigan, lead seems likely to cause trouble for years to come. The widespread use of lead in the previous century is a lesson about the side effects of a new technology. The effects can be unintended, harmful—and long lasting.

## Lesson Review
Go to your Biology Foundations Workbook for longer versions of these lesson summaries.

### 27.1 Organization of the Human Body

The human body is an organization of cells, tissues, organs, and organ systems. At each level of organization, these parts work together to carry out the major body functions. The four basic types of tissues in the human body are epithelial, connective, nervous, and muscle.

The human body is constantly undergoing processes to maintain a controlled, stable internal environment called homeostasis. One way the body maintains homeostasis is through feedback inhibition. The liver is one of the body's most important organs for homeostasis.

- epithelial tissue
- connective tissue
- nervous tissue
- muscle tissue
- homeostasis
- feedback inhibition

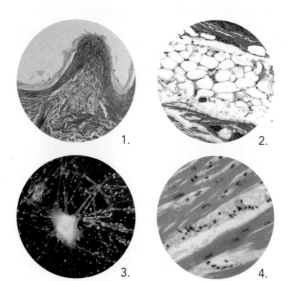

1.   2.

3.   4.

☑ **Compare and Contrast** Identify each type of tissue. What are some of the functions of each type of tissue?

### 27.2 Human Systems I

The digestive system converts food into small molecules that can be used by the cells of the body. The digestive system includes the mouth, esophagus, stomach, small intestine, and large intestine. The pancreas and gallbladder release substances that are involved in digestion.

The excretory system removes metabolic wastes from the body. The excretory system includes the skin, lungs, liver, and kidneys.

The circulatory system uses blood to transport oxygen, nutrients, and other substances throughout the body. Blood also transports wastes from tissues. Blood is pumped through the body by the heart.

The lymphatic system is a network of vessels, nodes, and organs that collects lymph that leaves capillaries, "screens" it for microorganisms, and returns it to the circulatory system. The lymphatic system also plays an important role in the absorption of nutrients, especially fats.

The respiratory system picks up oxygen from the air we inhale and releases carbon dioxide as we exhale. The respiratory system includes the nose, pharynx, larynx, trachea, bronchi, and lungs.

☑ **Identify** Which circulation pathway is indicated by the white arrows? By the black arrows? Briefly describe each pathway.

## 27.3 Human Systems II

The nervous system collects, processes, and responds to information about the internal and external environment. Neurons transmit nervous system signals. The central nervous system consists of the brain and spinal cord. The peripheral nervous system consists of nerves that transmit signals to and from the central nervous system.

The skeletal system supports the body, protects internal organs, assists in movement, stores minerals, and produces blood cells. Bones are a solid network of living cells. Joints permit bones to move without damaging each other.

There are three types of muscle tissue: smooth, skeletal, and cardiac. Skeletal muscles pull on body parts as they contract.

The integumentary system includes the skin, hair, and nails; serves as a barrier against infection and injury; and helps to produce vitamin D.

The endocrine system is made of glands that release hormones into the blood. The endocrine system is regulated by feedback mechanisms. The male and female reproductive systems produce sperm and eggs, respectively. The female reproductive system also prepares the female's body to nourish an embryo. The fusion of egg and sperm is called fertilization. A fertilized egg is a zygote that may develop into an embryo.

☑ **Review** Draw a diagram of the nervous system. Label the spinal cord, cerebrum, brain stem, and peripheral nerves.

## 27.4 Immunity and Disease

Infectious diseases are caused by pathogens. Environmental chemicals can also cause damage to the human body. The body has a series of defenses to protect itself against infection. Nonspecific defenses include the skin, tears, and other secretions; the inflammatory response, and fever. The immune system's specific defenses distinguish between "self" and "other," and they inactivate or kill any foreign substance or cell that enters the body.

- infectious disease
- pathogen
- inflammatory response
- antigen
- humoral immunity
- cell-mediated immunity

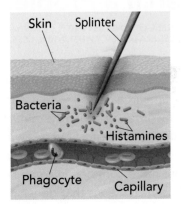

☑ **Interpret Visuals** Develop a description of the process depicted in this diagram. In your description, use all of the labels shown in the diagram.

## Organize Information

Complete the table by describing the function of the organ systems and listing their major organs.

| Organ System | Function | Major Organs |
|---|---|---|
| Circulatory System | 1. | Heart, blood vessels |
| Respiratory System | 2. | 3. |
| Nervous System | 4. | 5. |
| Muscular System | Movement of the body | 6. |
| Endocrine System | 7. | 8. |
| Digestive System | 9. | 10. |
| Reproductive System | 11. | 12. |

# A Tale of Two Diseases
## Lung Cancer and Melanoma

## Research a Problem

HS-ETS1-1, CCSS.ELA-LITERACY.RST.9-10.7, CCSS.ELA-LITERACY.WHST.9-10.4, CCSS.ELA-LITERACY.
WHST.9-10.7, CCSS.ELA-LITERACY.WHST.9-10.8, CCSS.ELA-LITERACY.WHST.9-10.9

**STEM** ▸ Cancer can strike anyone and at any time in a person's life. Cancer also can strike any organ or organ system. However, the risk of developing cancer varies with age, and it varies from person to person. Many types of cancer are more common in some families than others, which means that genes play a role. Other cancers are linked to the environment.

For example, using tobacco products increases a person's risk for developing lung cancer. According to the Centers for Disease Control and Prevention (CDC), cigarette smoking is linked to 80 to 90 percent of lung cancers in the United States. Smokers are up to 30 times more likely than nonsmokers to develop lung cancer—as well as to die from it. Inhaling secondhand smoke, which is tobacco smoke exhaled by someone else, is also a risk factor for lung cancer.

Another cancer linked to the environment is melanoma, which is a dangerous form of skin cancer. Heavy exposure to ultraviolet (UV) rays causes damage to skin cells that can lead to melanoma. UV rays are emitted by the sun and by the artificial lights used in tanning beds.

At the CDC, researchers gather data on all types of cancer and their effects on the population. Their data were used to construct the two graphs displayed here. The graphs show the number of cases of lung cancer and melanoma by year and by sex. Use the graphs, your research skills, and scientific reasoning to answer the questions that follow.

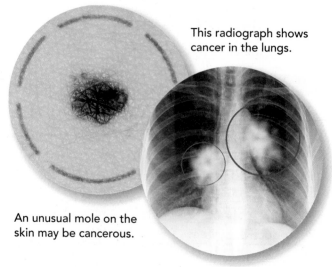

This radiograph shows cancer in the lungs.

An unusual mole on the skin may be cancerous.

## Lung and Bronchial Cancer Incidence Rates* for Males and Females, United States, 1999–2013**

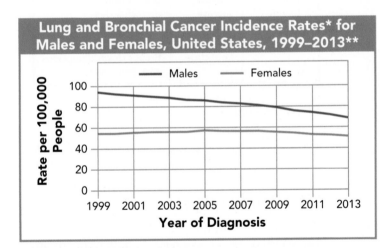

## Melanoma of the Skin Incidence Rates* for Males and Females, United States, 1999–2013**

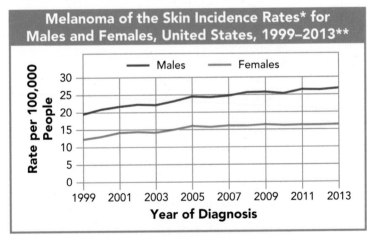

\* Rates are the number of cases per 100,000 persons and are age-adjusted to the 2000 U.S. standard population

\*\* Data are compiled from cancer registries that meet the data quality criteria for all invasive cancer sites combined for all years, 1999–2013 (covering approximately 92% of the U.S. population).

Sources: CDC's National Program of Cancer Registries and National Cancer Institute's Surveillance, Epidemiology, and End Results program

1. **Interpret Graphs** For the time period shown in the graph, what are the trends in lung cancer cases for males and females? What are the trends for cases of melanoma?

2. **Form a Hypothesis** State reasonable hypotheses to explain the trends you identified.

3. **Ask Questions** What questions could you ask, and then investigate, to help you evaluate your hypotheses?

4. **Conduct Research** Choose either lung cancer or melanoma. Find trustworthy sources to research the answers to the questions you asked about the disease. Also research additional information about the risk factors of the disease, its treatments, and likely outcomes.

5. **Evaluate Evidence** Does the information you discovered support your hypothesis? If not, what other explanations can you propose for the trend you identified?

6. **Communicate** Share your findings in a written report, computer presentation, or poster. Include useful advice and the evidence that supports the prevention of the type of cancer you researched.

# ☑ASSESSMENT

## 🔑 KEY IDEAS AND TERMS

## 27.1 Organization of the Human Body

**HS-LS1-1, HS-LS1-2, HS-LS1-3**

1. Which of the following is the correct order, from simplest to most complex, for the levels of organization in the human body?
   a. organ systems, tissues, organs, cells
   b. cells, tissues, organs, organ systems
   c. organ systems, organs, tissues, cells
   d. cells, organs, organ systems, tissues

2. Read the following statements. In maintaining homeostasis, what is the correct order in which these events occur?
   1) The liver removes glucose from the blood.
   2) The body absorbs food molecules after eating.
   3) As the body uses glucose for energy, the liver releases stored glucose into the blood.
   4) The levels of glucose in the blood rise.
   a. 3, 4, 1, 2
   b. 4, 1, 2, 3
   c. 2, 4, 1, 3
   d. 1, 2, 3, 4

3. Why is it important for an organism to maintain homeostasis?

4. Which tissues make voluntary movement possible?

## 27.2 Human Systems I

**HS-LS1-1, HS-LS1-2, HS-LS1-3**

5. Where does mechanical digestion begin?
   a. the esophagus
   b. the mouth
   c. the large intestine
   d. the small intestine

6. What structure removes excess water, urea, and metabolic waste from the blood?
   a. kidney          c. urinary bladder
   b. renal vein      d. ureter

7. What are the components of blood, and what are their functions?

8. What is the main muscle in the respiratory system?

9. What are alveoli, and in which organ system do they function?

10. How does the lymphatic system work?

Use the following table to answer questions 11 and 12.

| Effects of Digestive Enzymes | | |
|---|---|---|
| **Active Site** | **Enzyme** | **Effect on Food** |
| Mouth | Salivary amylase | Breaks down starches into disaccharides |
| Stomach | Pepsin | Breaks down proteins into large peptides |
| Small intestine (released from pancreas) | Pancreatic amylase | Continues the breakdown of starch |
| | Trypsin | Continues the breakdown of protein |
| | Lipase | Breaks down fat |
| Small intestine | Maltase, sucrase, lactase | Breaks down remaining disaccharides into monosaccharides |
| | Peptidase | Breaks down dipeptides into amino acids |

11. Which enzymes are involved in the breakdown of sugar and starch?

12. Suppose you ate a peach. How and where would enzymes break down the proteins in the peach?

## 27.3 Human Systems II

**HS-LS1-1, HS-LS1-2, HS-LS1-3**

13. Which division of the nervous system speeds up your heart rate?
    a. somatic
    b. autonomic
    c. central
    d. brain and spinal cord

14. Which type(s) of muscle can contract without stimulation from the nervous system?
    a. skeletal only
    b. skeletal and smooth
    c. smooth and cardiac
    d. cardiac only

15. What do bones do besides support the body and protect internal organs?

16. What are the functions of the skin?

17. How does a feedback mechanism regulate the activity of the endocrine system?

18. What are the major organs of the human reproductive system in males and females?

## 27.4 Immunity and Disease

HS-LS1-1, HS-LS1-2

19. The body's nonspecific defenses against invading pathogens include
    a. antibodies.
    b. mucus, sweat, and tears.
    c. antibiotics.
    d. cytotoxic T cells.

20. What causes asthma?
    a. Bacteria that are resistant to antibiotics infect the body.
    b. Particular antigens trigger muscle contractions that make it difficult to breathe.
    c. Antibodies and cytotoxic T cells attack cells in the tissues of the lungs.
    d. Mosquito-borne pathogens enter the bloodstream.

21. Which type of immune response involves redness and swelling around damaged cells?
    a. cell-mediated response
    b. humoral response
    c. inflammatory response
    d. autoimmune response

22. Explain the difference between a specific and a nonspecific immune response.

23. How do vaccines prevent disease?

24. What is an antigen, and how is it harmful?

25. What is HIV? What type of disease does it cause?

26. Explain what is happening in this image. Which type of immune response will this lead to—humoral immunity or cell-mediated immunity?

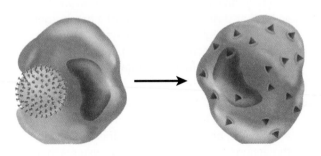

## CRITICAL THINKING

HS-LS1-2, HS-LS1-3

27. **Classify** Is blood classified as a cell, a tissue, an organ, or an organ system? Explain the classification.

28. **Infer** Many people have had their stomachs either partially or completely removed. They survive by eating predigested food. Could a person survive without a small intestine? Explain your inference.

29. **Synthesize Information** How does the lymphatic system interact with the digestive, circulatory, and muscular systems?

30. **Predict** Explain how the removal of someone's lymph nodes can affect his or her ability to fight disease.

31. **Use Analogies** How is transmission of an action potential through a neuron similar to ripples spreading across a pond?

32. **Infer** Disks of cartilage are found between the vertebrae of the spinal column. Cartilage also lines many joints, including the shoulder and knee. What is the likely function of the cartilage?

33. **Use Scientific Reasoning** Tobacco smoke can damage white blood cells in the respiratory tract. These cells help clear airways of debris from the environment. How could this damage contribute to respiratory diseases?

The table shows the percentages of blood that flow through several organs of the human body. Use the table to answer questions 34 to 36.

| Blood Flow Through Human Organs | |
|---|---|
| Organ | Percentage of Total Flow |
| Brain | 14% |
| Heart | 5% |
| Kidneys | 22% |
| Liver | 13% |
| Lungs | 100% |
| Skeletal muscles | 18% |
| Skeletal muscles during exercise | 75% |

34. **Reason Quantitatively** How does exercise affect the flow of blood through skeletal muscles?

35. **Interpret Visuals** Refer to the diagram of the circulatory system in Figure 27-10. How does the diagram help explain the percentage of blood flow to the lungs?

36. **Infer** Which organ receives the lowest percentage of blood flow? Use your knowledge of human systems to suggest an explanation for this low percentage.

# ☑ ASSESSMENT

## CROSSCUTTING CONCEPTS

**37. Stability and Change** Discuss how the body of a developing fetus is an example of both stability and change.

**38. Systems and System Models** The systems of a city are sometimes used to model the organ systems of the human body. Consider these three city systems: roads and vehicles, telephone wires, and sewage systems. How are they useful models of organ systems?

## MATH CONNECTIONS

## Analyze and Interpret Data

CCSS.MATH.CONTENT.MP2, CCSS.MATH.CONTENT.HSS.ID.A.1

The graph shows the relationship between neuron diameter and impulse conduction speed in a typical mammal nerve (myelinated). Use the graph to answer questions 39 and 40.

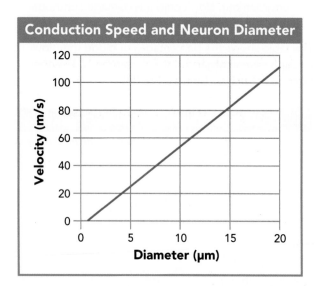

**39. Interpret Graphs** What conclusion about the speed of nerve conduction and the diameter of the neuron is supported by the graph?

**40. Calculate** In a reflex response, your hand touches a hot object and immediately pulls away. During this action, impulses travel a total distance of about 1.5 meters down neurons that are 5 μm in diameter. How much time is needed for the impulse to travel this distance?

The following line graph shows the levels of glucose in the blood of two people during a five-hour period immediately following the ingestion of a typical meal. Use the graph to answer questions 41 and 42.

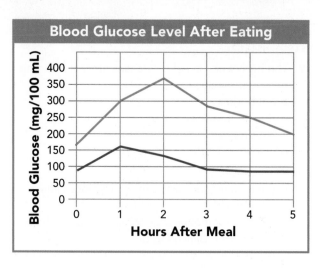

**41. Interpret Graphs** How long does it take the blood glucose level of the person represented by the blue line to return to homeostatic value?

**42. Defend Your Claim** The body of a person with Type 2 diabetes does not use insulin properly. At first, the body makes extra insulin to make up for this. Over time, however, the body cannot make enough insulin to keep blood glucose at normal levels. Based on this information and the diagram of the feedback loop in Figure 27-27, which person probably has Type 2 diabetes? Justify your choice.

## LANGUAGE ARTS CONNECTION

## Write About Science

CCSS.ELA-LITERACY.WHST.9-10.2

**43. Write Explanatory Texts** A children's television workshop wants to explain the process of digestion to young viewers. You are asked to write a script that describes the travels of a hamburger and bun through the digestive system. Write an outline of your script, including information about what happens to food as it moves through the digestive system.

**44. Write Informative Texts** Choose a simple activity from everyday life, such as opening a door, eating a sandwich, or saying hello to a friend. Describe the actions of at least three organ systems that work together to complete this activity.

## Read About Science

CCSS.ELA-LITERACY.RST.9-10.2

**45. Summarize Text** How does blood travel through the circulatory system? Identify the organs that blood passes through and the events that occur in these organs.

**1.** The circulatory system transports substances throughout the body. The diagram shown summarizes blood flow through the circulatory system.

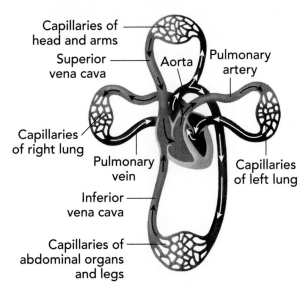

Capillaries of head and arms
Superior vena cava
Aorta
Pulmonary artery
Capillaries of right lung
Pulmonary vein
Capillaries of left lung
Inferior vena cava
Capillaries of abdominal organs and legs

If a clot were to form in the pulmonary artery, how would this affect other systems?

**A.** Blood flow from the heart to the lungs would be reduced.

**B.** Blood flow from the heart to body tissues would be reduced.

**C.** Blood flow from the lungs to body tissues would increase.

**D.** Blood flow from the lungs to the heart would increase.

**E.** Blood flow from the aorta to the arms and legs would increase.

**2.** Ricardo is investigating ways that the human body maintains homeostasis. What is one way that the body can maintain homeostasis?

**A.** When the hypothalamus senses an increase in body temperature it sends signals for the body to produce sweat.

**B.** When the hypothalamus senses an increase in body temperature it sends signals for the body to increase cellular respiration.

**C.** When the hypothalamus senses a decrease in body temperature it sends signals for the kidneys to produce urine.

**D.** When the hypothalamus senses a decrease in body temperature it sends signals for the body to absorb nutrients from food.

**E.** When the hypothalamus senses a decrease in body temperature it sends signals for the liver to release stored glucose.

**3.** How does the immune system depend on other systems to produce an immune response?

**A.** B cells are produced in the bone marrow of the skeletal system.

**B.** Vaccines are produced in the blood vessels of the circulatory system.

**C.** Antigens are secreted by the endocrine system.

**D.** Allergens are secreted in the airways of the respiratory system.

**E.** Fever occurs when muscles in the muscular system contract.

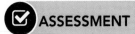 ASSESSMENT

For additional assessment practice, go online to access your digital course.

| If You Have Trouble With... | | | |
|---|---|---|---|
| **Question** | 1 | 2 | 3 |
| **See Lesson** | 27.2 | 27.1 | 27.4 |
| **Performance Expectation** | HS-LS1-2 | HS-LS1-3 | HS-LS1-2 |

# END OF BOOK
# TABLE OF CONTENTS

# A VISUAL GUIDE TO
# The Diversity of Life

You have probably heard this animal called a 'koala bear,' but koalas are not bears, not even close! Koalas are the only remaining species of a family of marsupials, and their closest living relatives are animals called wombats.

The Visual Guide will give you a glimpse of life's great variety and evolutionary history.

# A VISUAL GUIDE TO
# The Diversity of Life

## CONTENTS

# HOW TO USE THIS GUIDE

Use this visual reference tool to explore the classification and characteristics of organisms, including their habitats, ecology, behavior, and other important facts. This guide reflects the latest understandings about phylogenetic relationships within the three domains of life. Divided into six color-coded sections, the Visual Guide begins with a brief survey of the Bacteria and Archaea domains. It next discusses the major groups of protists, fungi, and plants. The final section provides information on nine animal phyla.

**❶** See how the group of organisms relates to others on the tree of life.

**❷** Learn about the general characteristics that all members of the group share.

**❸** Discover the members of the group and learn about their traits.

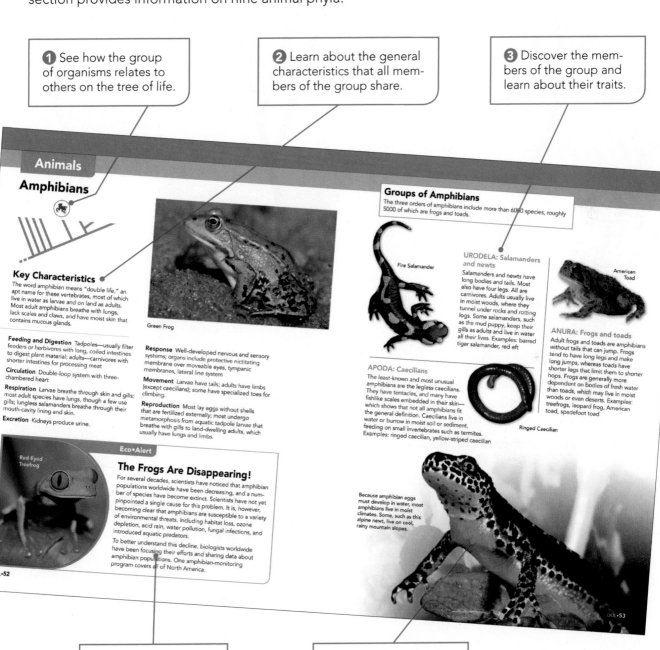

## Animals

### Amphibians

#### Key Characteristics
The word amphibian means "double life," an apt name for these vertebrates, most of which live in water as larvae and on land as adults. Most adult amphibians breathe with lungs, lack scales and claws, and have moist skin that contains mucous glands.

**Feeding and Digestion** Tadpoles—usually filter feeders or herbivores with long, coiled intestines to digest plant material; adults—carnivores with shorter intestines for processing meat

**Circulation** Double-loop system with three-chambered heart

**Respiration** Larvae breathe through skin and gills; most adult species have lungs, though a few use gills; lungless salamanders breathe through their mouth-cavity lining and skin.

**Excretion** Kidneys produce urine.

**Response** Well-developed nervous and sensory systems; organs include protective nictitating membrane over moveable eyes, tympanic membranes, lateral line system

**Movement** Larvae have tails; adults have limbs (except caecilians); some have specialized toes for climbing.

**Reproduction** Most lay eggs without shells that are fertilized externally; most undergo metamorphosis from aquatic tadpole larvae that breathe with gills to land-dwelling adults, which usually have lungs and limbs.

Green Frog

Red-Eyed Treefrog

##### Eco•Alert
**The Frogs Are Disappearing!**
For several decades, scientists have noticed that amphibian populations worldwide have been decreasing, and a number of species have become extinct. Scientists have not yet pinpointed a single cause for this problem. It is, however, becoming clear that amphibians are susceptible to a variety of environmental threats, including habitat loss, ozone depletion, acid rain, water pollution, fungal infections, and introduced aquatic predators.

To better understand this decline, biologists worldwide have been focusing their efforts and sharing data about amphibian populations. One amphibian-monitoring program covers all of North America.

DOL•52

#### Groups of Amphibians
The three orders of amphibians include more than 6000 species, roughly 5000 of which are frogs and toads.

Fire Salamander

**URODELA: Salamanders and newts**
Salamanders and newts have long bodies and tails. Most also have four legs. All are carnivores. Adults usually live in moist woods, where they tunnel under rocks and rotting logs. Some salamanders, such as the mud puppy, keep their gills as adults and live in water all their lives. Examples: barred tiger salamander, red eft

American Toad

**ANURA: Frogs and toads**
Adult frogs and toads are amphibians without tails that can jump. Frogs tend to have long legs and make long jumps, whereas toads have shorter legs that limit them to shorter hops. Frogs are generally more dependent on bodies of fresh water than toads, which may live in moist woods or even deserts. Examples: treefrogs, leopard frog, American toad, spadefoot toad

**APODA: Caecilians**
The least-known and most unusual amphibians are the legless caecilians. They have tentacles, and many have fishlike scales embedded in their skin—which shows that not all amphibians fit the general definition. Caecilians live in water or burrow in moist soil or sediment, feeding on small invertebrates such as termites. Examples: ringed caecilian, yellow-striped caecilian

Ringed Caecilian

Because amphibian eggs must develop in water, most amphibians live in moist climates. Some, such as this alpine newt, live on cool, rainy mountain slopes.

DOL•53

**❹** Investigate current news and interesting facts about the group.

**❺** See photographs of representative animals within each group.

# THE TREE OF LIFE

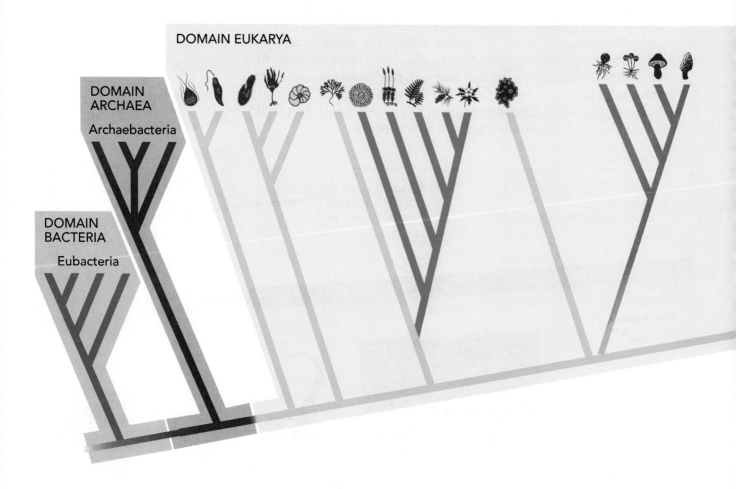

DOMAIN EUKARYA

DOMAIN ARCHAEA

Archaebacteria

DOMAIN BACTERIA

Eubacteria

Before you begin your tour through the kingdoms of life, review this big picture from Chapter 19. The pages that follow will give you a glimpse of the incredible diversity found within each of the branches shown here.

## DOMAIN BACTERIA

Members of the domain Bacteria are unicellular and prokaryotic. The bacteria are ecologically diverse, ranging from free-living soil organisms to deadly parasites. This domain corresponds to the kingdom Eubacteria.

## DOMAIN ARCHAEA

Also unicellular and prokaryotic, members of the domain Archaea live in some of the most extreme environments you can imagine, including volcanic hot springs, brine pools, and black organic mud totally devoid of oxygen. The domain Archaea corresponds to the kingdom Archaebacteria.

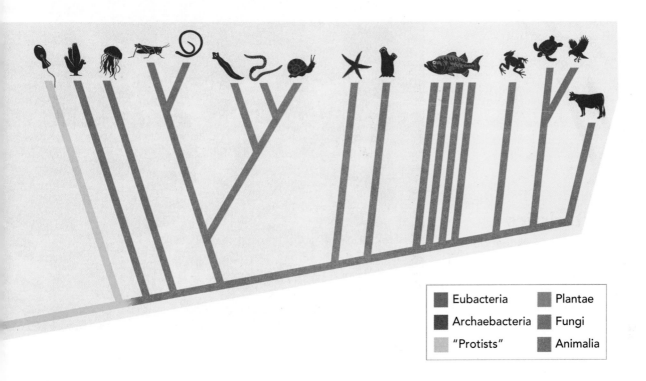

| Eubacteria | Plantae |
| Archaebacteria | Fungi |
| "Protists" | Animalia |

# DOMAIN EUKARYA

The domain Eukarya consists of all organisms that have cells with nuclei. It is organized into the four remaining kingdoms of the six-kingdom system: Protista, Fungi, Plantae, and Animalia.

### THE "PROTISTS"

Notice that the branches for the kingdom Protista are not together in one area, as is the case with the other kingdoms. In fact, recent molecular studies and cladistic analyses have shown that "eukaryotes formerly known as Protista" do not form a single clade. Current cladistic analysis divides these organisms into at least six clades. They cannot, therefore, be properly placed into a single taxon.

### FUNGI

Members of the kingdom Fungi are heterotrophs. Most feed on dead or decaying organic matter. The most recognizable fungi, including mushrooms, are multicellular. Some fungi, such as yeasts, are unicellular.

### PLANTS

Members of the kingdom Plantae are autotrophs that carry out photosynthesis. Plants have cell walls that contain cellulose. Plants are nonmotile—they cannot move from place to place.

### ANIMALS

Members of the kingdom Animalia are multicellular and heterotrophic. Animal cells do not have cell walls. Most animals can move about, at least for some part of their life cycle.

# Bacteria

Actinobacteria
Cyanobacteria
Spirochaetes
Proteobacteria

*Leptospira* is a spirochaete that causes disease. (SEM 22,000×)

## Key Characteristics

Bacteria are prokaryotes—cells that do not enclose their DNA in membranous nuclear envelopes as eukaryotes do. Many details of their molecular genetics differ from those of Archaea and Eukarya.

**Cell Structure** Variety of cell shapes, including spherical, rodlike, and spiral; most have cell walls containing peptidoglycan. Few if any have internal organelles. Some have external flagella for cell movement.

**Genetic Organization** All essential genes are in one large DNA double helix whose ends join to form a closed loop. Smaller loops of DNA (plasmids) may carry nonessential genes. Simultaneous transcription and translation; introns generally not present; histone proteins absent

**Reproduction** By binary fission; no true sexual reproduction; some achieve recombination by conjugation.

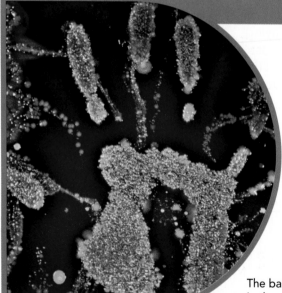

## Did You Know?

# A World of Bacteria
### Putting Bacteria in Proper Perspective

"Planet of the Bacteria" was the title of an essay by the late Stephen Jay Gould. He pointed out that the dominant life forms on planet Earth aren't humans, or animals, or plants. They are bacteria. They were here first, and they inhabit more places on the planet than any other form of life. In fact, bacteria make up roughly 10 percent of our own dry body weight! In terms of biomass and importance to the planet, bacteria truly do rule this planet. They, not we, are number one.

The bacterial colonies shown here are growing in the print of a human hand on agar gel.

# Groups of Bacteria

There is no generally agreed phylogeny for the bacteria. Included here are some of the major groups within the domain.

*Helicobacter pylori* is rod-shaped and has several flagella used for movement. This bacterium infects the stomach lining and causes ulcers in some people. (TEM 7100×)

## PROTEOBACTERIA

This large and diverse clade of bacteria includes *Escherichia* (*E. coli*), *Salmonella, Helicobacter,* and the nitrogen-fixing soil bacterium *Rhizobium.*

The spiral-shaped bacterium that causes syphilis is *Treponema pallidum.* (SEM 10,000×)

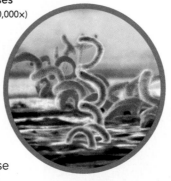

## SPIROCHAETES

The spirochaetes (SPY roh keets) are named for their distinctive spiral shape. They move in a corkscrew-like fashion, twisting along as they are propelled by flagella on both ends of the cell. Most are free-living, but a few cause serious diseases, including syphilis, Lyme disease, and leptospirosis.

## ACTINOBACTERIA

A large number of soil bacteria belong to this group. Some form long filaments. Members include the *Streptomyces* and *Actinomyces,* which are natural producers of many antibiotics, including streptomycin. A related group is the *Firmicutes.* The *Firmicutes* include *Bacillus anthracis* (anthrax), *Clostridia* (tetanus and botulism), and *Bacillus thuringiensis,* which produces a powerful insecticide used for genetic engineering in plants.

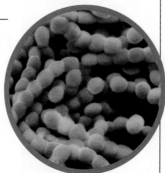

Chains of spores of soil bacteria, genus *Streptomyces* (SEM 3400×)

## CYANOBACTERIA

The cyanobacteria are photosynthetic prokaryotes that were once called "blue-green algae." They are among the oldest organisms on Earth, having been identified in rocks dating to more than 3 billion years ago. They are found in salt water and fresh water, in the soil, and even on the surfaces of damp rocks. They are the only organisms on Earth that are able to fix carbon and nitrogen under anaerobic conditions, and this enables them to play critical roles in the global ecosystem, where they serve as key sources of carbon and nitrogen.

Many cyanobacteria form long filaments of attached cells, like those shown here (genus *Lyngbya,* SEM 540×).

A Closer Look

# The Gram Stain
## A Microbiologist's Quick Diagnostic

The Gram stain, developed by the nineteenth-century Danish physician Hans Christian Gram, allows microbiologists to categorize bacteria quickly into one of two groups based on their cell wall composition. Gram-positive bacteria lack a membrane outside the cell wall and take up the stain easily. Gram-negative bacteria, on the other hand, have an outer membrane of lipids and carbohydrates that prevents them from absorbing the Gram stain. Many Gram-negative bacteria are found among the proteobacteria. On the other hand, actinobacteria are mostly Gram-positive.

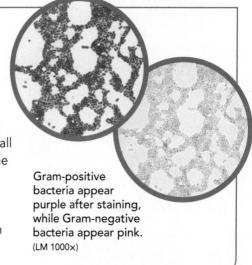

Gram-positive bacteria appear purple after staining, while Gram-negative bacteria appear pink. (LM 1000×)

# Archaea

## Key Characteristics

Archaea are prokaryotes that differ from bacteria in so many details of structure and metabolism that they are viewed as a different domain than bacteria. Genetically, they have more in common with eukaryotes than with bacteria. Their cell walls do not contain peptidoglycan.

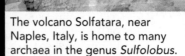

Korarchaeotes  Crenarchaeotes  Euryarchaeotes  Nanoarchaeotes

**Cell Structure** Cells similar to those of bacteria in appearance; many have flagella that are different in structure and biochemical composition from bacterial flagella. Cell membrane lipids are also different from those of bacteria; few internal organelles

**Genetic Organization** As in bacteria, all essential genes are in one large DNA double helix whose ends join to form a closed loop. Proteins responsible for transcription and translation are similar to those of eukaryotes. Also like eukaryotes, most species contain introns, and all species contain DNA-binding histone proteins.

**Reproduction** By binary fission; no true sexual reproduction, but some achieve recombination by conjugation.

These halophilic archaea thrive in salty environments.
(SEM 25,000×)

The volcano Solfatara, near Naples, Italy, is home to many archaea in the genus *Sulfolobus*.

## Did You Know?

# Hot Enough for You?
### The Original Extremists

Long before extreme sports and extreme reality TV shows came the archaea—the original and ultimate extremists. When archaea were first discovered, biologists called them *extremophiles*, a term that literally means "lovers of the extreme." For many archaea, the name still fits. In fact, they have proven especially difficult to grow in the lab, since they require such extreme temperatures and dangerous chemical conditions to thrive. One species will grow only in sulfuric acid! Archaea found in deep-sea ocean vents flourish in temperatures exceeding 100° Celsius, while others enjoy life in the frigid waters of the Arctic.

## Groups of Archaea

To date, four major clades of archaea have been identified. Biologists continue to debate how these clades are related to one another.

### CRENARCHAEOTES

The crenarchaeotes (kren AHR kee ohts) include organisms that live in the hottest and most acidic environments known. Most of the known species have been isolated from thermal vents and hot springs—the prefix *cren-* means "spring." Some species grow using organic compounds as energy sources, but others fix carbon from carbon dioxide, using hydrogen or sulfur to provide chemical energy.

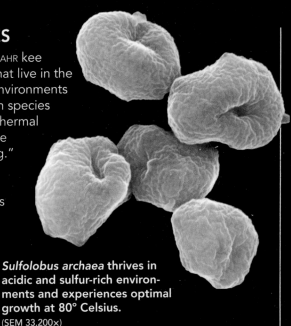

*Sulfolobus archaea* **thrives in acidic and sulfur-rich environments and experiences optimal growth at 80° Celsius.**
(SEM 33,200×)

### NANOARCHAEOTES

Only a single species of this group has been discovered, in 2002, attached to a much larger crenarchaeote! Nanoarchaeotes (na noh AHR kee ohts) grow in hot vents near the coastal regions of the ocean and show definite molecular differences from other archaea. More research is needed to characterize this group, but it is known to have the smallest genome of any organism.

### KORARCHAEOTES

Scientists recently discovered the korarchaeote (kawr AHR kee oht) lineage in Obsidian Pool, Yellowstone National Park, and have since discovered more species in Iceland. Their DNA sequences place them apart from other archaea. The korarchaeotes may in fact be one of the least-evolved lineages of modern life that has been detected in nature so far.

**Archaea live in extreme environments including these geothermal pools in Yellowstone National Park.**

### EURYARCHAEOTES

The euryarchaeotes (yoor ee AHR kee ohts) are a very diverse group of archaea, living in a broad range of habitats. The prefix *eury-* comes from a Greek word meaning "broad." The methanogens are a major group of euryarchaeotes that play essential roles in the environment. They help to break down organic compounds in oxygen-poor environments, releasing methane gas in the process. Another group, the *Halobacteria*, are found in salt ponds, where the concentration of sodium chloride approaches saturation.

**Colony of** *Methanosarcina* **archaea** (SEM 40,000×)

# Protists

## Key Characteristics

A protist is a eukaryote, generally single-celled, that does not fit into any of the other major taxonomic groups. The protists do not make up a true kingdom.

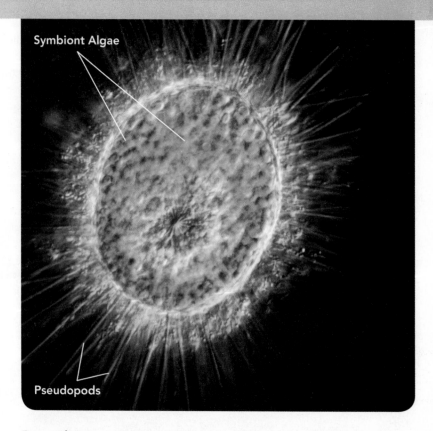

Symbiont Algae

Pseudopods

Biologists are not certain how to classify *Heterophrys*, the freshwater protist shown in this micrograph. It harbors symbiotic photosynthetic algae called zoochorellae. *Heterophrys* is one of many protists called "heliozoans" (literally, "sun animals") because of the thin pseudopods extending from its surface, giving it a sun-like appearance.

**Organization**  Great diversity of cell organelles and organization: some have cell walls, some have chloroplasts, most have mitochondria or organelles related to mitochondria; those that are multicellular have relatively little differentiation into tissues.

**Movement**  Some move by cilia or flagella.

**Reproduction**  Most reproduce by cell division; many have sexual phases to their life cycle; some exchange genetic material by conjugation.

---

## Did You Know?

### The Kingdom That Isn't

#### The Challenges of Classifying Protists

Biologists traditionally classified protists by splitting them into funguslike, plantlike, and animal-like groups. This seemed to work for a while, but when they studied protists more carefully with new research tools, including genome-level molecular analysis, this traditional system simply fell apart.

Biologists now think that protists shouldn't be classified as a kingdom at all. In fact, when scientists look for the deepest and most fundamental divisions among eukaryotes, they find that all of those divisions are within the protists themselves, not between protists and other eukaryotes. Starting over, biologists could simply use those

Plants    Fungi    Animals

divisions to define newer, more accurate "kingdoms," but that might cause new problems. For one thing, it would lump two of the traditional kingdoms (animals and fungi) together, and it would leave a handful of kingdoms that contain only unicellular organisms. There is no perfect solution to this problem. Here, "protists" are considered a kingdom for the sake of convenience, but keep in mind that their differences are really too great for any single kingdom to contain.

# Excavates

## Key Characteristics

Excavates (EKS kuh vayts) have a characteristic feeding groove, usually supported by microtubules. Most have flagella. A few lack mitochondria and are unable to carry out oxidative phosphorylation, although they do possess remnants of the organelle.

### GROUPS OF EXCAVATES

The excavates include a wide diversity of protists, from free-living photosynthesizers to some of humankind's most notorious pathogens.

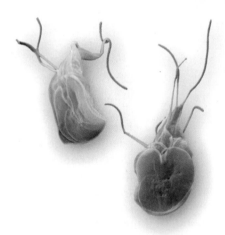

The diplomonad *Giardia* is a dangerous intestinal parasite that frequently contaminates freshwater streams. *Giardia* infections are common in wildlife and pet dogs and cats. (SEM 1800×)

### DIPLOMONADS

These organisms get their name from the fact that they possess two distinct and different nuclei (from Greek, *diplo* = double). The double nuclei probably derived from an ancient symbiotic event in which one species was engulfed by another. Cells contain multiple flagella, usually arranged around the body of the cell. Most species of diplomonads are parasitic.

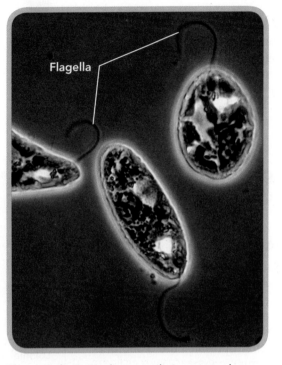

Flagella

Photosynthetic *Euglena gracilis* is commonly found in lakes and ponds. (LM 250×)

### DISCICRISTATES

Discicristates (disk ee KRIS tayts) are named for the disc-shaped cristae present in their mitochondria. Some species are photosynthetic and free-living, such as *Euglena*, while others are dangerous parasites.

The ribbonlike cells of *Trypanosoma brucei* cause African sleeping sickness. The parasitic protist is transmitted by tsetse flies to humans, where it infects the blood, lymph, and spinal fluid. Severe nervous system damage and death are the usual result. (SEM 6700×)

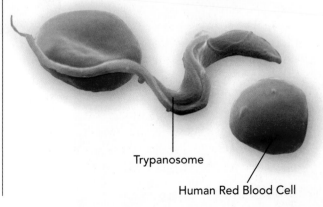

Trypanosome

Human Red Blood Cell

# Chromalveolates

## Key Characteristics

Chromalveolates (krohm AL vee uh layts) get their name from alveoli, flattened vesicles that line the cell membrane. The prefix *chromo-*, meaning "pigment," reflects evidence that members of this clade share a common ancestor that had accessory pigments used in photosynthesis.

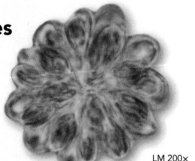

SEM 280x

SEM 1000x

## Groups of Chromalveolates

The chromalveolates are one of the largest and most diverse groups of eukaryotes.

### PHAEOPHYTES: Brown algae

Phaeophytes (FAY uh fyts) are mostly found in salt water. They are some of the most abundant and visible of the algae. Most species contain fucoxanthin, a greenish-brown pigment from which the group gets its common name.

The multicellular brown algae known as giant kelp can grow as large as 60 meters in length.

LM 200x

This species, in genus *Synura*, is a colonial alga.

### CHRYSOPHYTES: Golden algae

Chrysophytes (KRIS oh fyts) are known for colorful accessory pigments in their chloroplasts. Most are found in fresh water and are photosynthetic.

Diatoms often produce intricate shells made from silicon dioxide that persist long after they die.

### DIATOMS

Diatoms are mostly found in salt water. When they die, they sink to the ocean floor, and their shells pile up in large deposits. Diatomaceous earth, as these deposits are known, can be used to screen out small particles, and is often used in swimming pool filters.

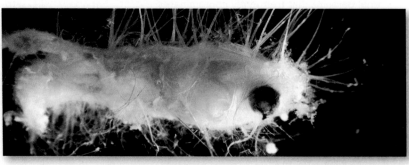

Water molds growing on a dead goldfish

### OOMYCETES: Water molds

These nonphotosynthetic organisms are often confused with fungi. Oomycetes (oh uh MY seed eez) typically produce fuzzy mats of material on dead or decaying animals and plants. Oomycetes are also responsible for a number of serious plant diseases, including potato blight, sudden oak death, and ink disease, which infects the American chestnut tree.

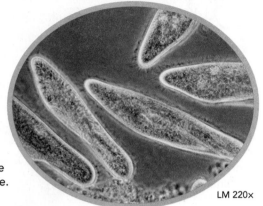

*Paramecium multimicronucleatum* is the largest paramecium, with cells that are visible to the naked eye.

LM 220×

## CILIATES

These common organisms may contain hundreds or even thousands of short cilia extending from the surface of the cell. The cilia propel the ciliate through the water, and may sweep food particles into a gullet. Ciliates are large compared to other protists, with some cells exceeding 1 mm in length.

## DINOFLAGELLATES

Dinoflagellates are photosynthetic protists found in both fresh and salt water. Their name comes from their two distinct flagella, usually oriented at right angles to each other. Roughly half of dinoflagellate species are photosynthetic; the other half live as heterotrophs. Many dinoflagellate species are luminescent, and when agitated by sudden movement in the water, give off light.

SEM 1360×

The two flagella of dinoflagellates originate in grooves within thick plates of cellulose that resemble a cross shape, as shown here (genus *Protoperidinium*).

Human Red Blood Cell

SEM 5000×

Apicomplexans in genus *Plasmodium* are mosquito-borne parasites. Shown in green are the remnants of a red blood cell that burst when plasmodia reproduced inside.

## APICOMPLEXANS

The apicomplexans (AYP ih kum plek sunz) are named for a unique organelle near one end of the cell known as the apical complex. This structure contains vesicles with enzymes that allow apicomplexans to enter other cells and take up residence as parasites.

A red tide containing toxic dinoflagellates

### Eco•Alert

# Toxic Blooms
## Dangerous Dinoflagellates

Great blooms of the dinoflagellates *Gonyaulax* and *Karenia* have occurred in recent years on the East Coast of the United States, although scientists are not sure of the reason. These blooms are known as "red tides." *Gonyaulax* and *Karenia* produce a toxin that can become amplified in the food chain when filter-feeding shellfish such as oysters contentrate it in their tissues. Eating shellfish from water affected by red tide can cause serious illness, paralysis, and even death.

# Cercozoa, Foraminiferans, and Radiolarians

There is no single morphological characteristic that unites this diverse trio, but many have extensions of cytoplasm called pseudopods and many produce protective shells. The grouping together of Cercozoa, Foraminifera, and Radiolaria is based almost entirely on molecular analyses and not on morphology.

## FORAMINIFERANS

Foraminifera (fawr uh min IF uh ra) produce intricate and beautiful shells that differ from species to species. Slender pseudopods that emerge through tiny holes in the shell enable them to capture food, including bacteria. As many as 4000 species exist.

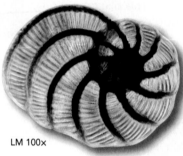

*Peneroplis pertusus* has a spiral-shaped shell.

LM 100x

SEM 175x

Radiolarian shells are composed of silica or strontium sulfate.

## CERCOZOA

Members of this clade are common in soil, where they feed on bacteria as well as decaying organic matter. Many have flagella, and some produce scales made of silica that protect their surfaces.

## RADIOLARIANS

These organisms have an intricate structure in which the nucleus is found in an inner region of the cell known as the endoplasm. The outer portion of the cell, known as the ectoplasm, contains lipid droplets and vacuoles. These organisms sometimes form symbiotic relationships with photosynthetic algae, from which they obtain food.

## A Look Back in Time

# Foraminiferan Fossils
### Ancient Climates Revealed

Abundant fossils of foraminiferans have been found in sediments dating to the Cambrian period (560 million years ago). For decades, oil companies have taken advantage of these ancient fossils to locate the sediments most likely to contain oil, but now there is another use for them—measuring the sea temperature of ancient Earth. Foraminiferans take dissolved oxygen from seawater to make the calcium carbonate ($CaCO_3$) in their shells, and when they do so, they take up two isotopes of oxygen, $^{16}O$ and $^{18}O$. Because water made from $^{16}O$ is less dense, more of it evaporates into the atmosphere when the seas are warm—increasing the

## Foraminiferan Isotope Ratios and Climate Change

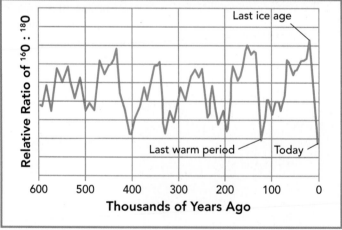

Relative Ratio of $^{16}O : {}^{18}O$

Last ice age

Last warm period

Today

Thousands of Years Ago

amount of $^{18}O$ in the remaining seawater, and in the fossil shells. The ratio between $^{16}O$ and $^{18}O$ in these fossils allows scientists to study the history of seawater temperature, as shown in the graph above.

# Rhodophytes

Also known as the red algae, these organisms get their name (from Greek, *rhodo* = red and *phyte* = plant) from reddish accessory pigments called phycobilins (fy koh BIL inz). These highly efficient pigments enable red algae to grow anywhere from the ocean's surface to depths as great as 268 meters. Most species are multicellular. Rhodophytes are the sister group to kingdom Plantae.

Some things that we call seaweeds, such as this rhodophyte, are actually protists.

# Amoebozoa

Members of the Amoebozoa (uh MEE boh zoh ah) are amoebalike organisms that move by means of cytoplasmic streaming, also called amoeboid movement, using pseudopods.

This solitary amoeba, *Penardia mutabilis*, has very slender pseudopods.

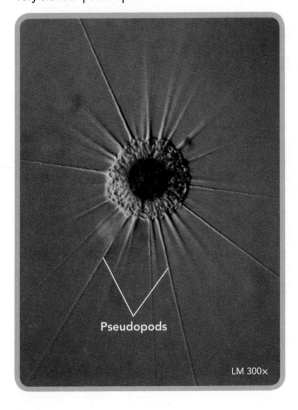

Pseudopods

LM 300×

Slime molds live as single microscopic amoebas in the soil, but aggregate into a colony when conditions are right, forming a multicellular fruiting body. In this image, some of the fruiting bodies have burst, releasing spores.

Fruiting Body

SEM 85×

# Choanozoa

Members of the clade Choanozoa (koh AN uh zoh uh) can be solitary or colonial and are found in aquatic environments around the world. This clade is the sister group to kingdom Animalia.

Choanoflagellates are a major group in the clade Choanozoa. They get their name from a collar of cytoplasm that surrounds their single flagellum (from Greek, *choano* = collar). Many species trap food within the collar and ingest it.

# Fungi

## Key Characteristics

Fungi are heterotrophic eukaryotes with cell walls that contain chitin. Fungi were once thought to be plants that had lost their chloroplasts. It is now clear, however, that they are much more closely related to animals than to plants. More than 100,000 species of fungi are known. Distinctions among the phyla are made on the basis of DNA comparisons, cell structure, reproductive structures, and life cycles.

*Omphalotus olearius* is a poisonous mushroom.

**Organization** Some are unicellular yeasts, but most have a multicellular body called a mycelium that consists of one or more slender, branching cells called hyphae.

**Feeding and Digestion** Obtain food by extracellular digestion and absorption

**Reproduction** Most have sexual phases to their life cycle and are haploid at most points during the cycle. Most produce tough, asexual spores, which are easily dispersed and able to endure harsh environmental conditions. Asexual reproduction by budding and splitting is also common.

Fly agaric (*Amanita muscaria*) is poisonous to humans.

## A Closer Look

# Consumers Beware!
### Edible and Inedible Mushrooms

Many types of fungi have long been considered delicacies, and several different species of mushrooms are cultivated for food. You may have already tasted sliced mushrooms on pizza, feasted on delicious sautéed portobello mushrooms, or eaten shiitake mushrooms. When properly cooked and prepared, domestic mushrooms are tasty and nutritious.

Wild mushrooms are a different story: Although some are edible, many are poisonous. Because many species of poisonous mushrooms look almost identical to edible mushrooms, you should never pick or eat any mushrooms found in the wild. Instead, mushroom gathering should be left to experts who can positively identify each mushroom they collect. The result of eating a poisonous mushroom can be severe illness, or even death.

# Basidiomycetes

The basidiomycetes, or club fungi, are named for the basidium (buh SID ee um; plural: basidia). The basidium is a reproductive cell that resembles a club.

**Life Cycle** Basidiomycetes undergo what is probably the most elaborate life cycle of all the fungi, shown below.

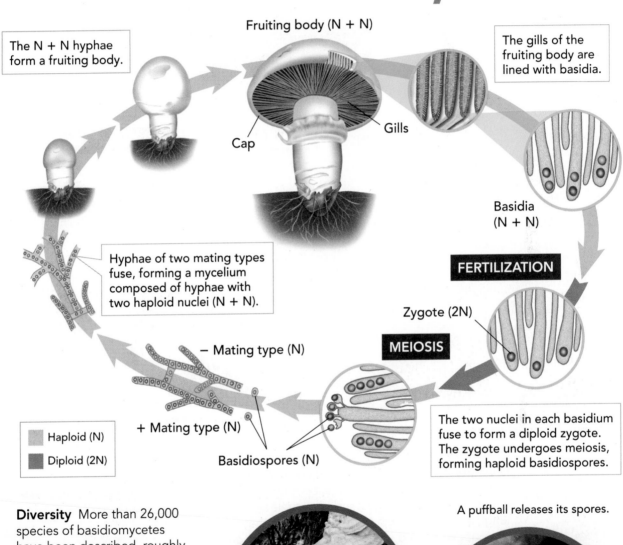

The N + N hyphae form a fruiting body.

Fruiting body (N + N)

The gills of the fruiting body are lined with basidia.

Cap

Gills

Basidia (N + N)

**FERTILIZATION**

Hyphae of two mating types fuse, forming a mycelium composed of hyphae with two haploid nuclei (N + N).

Zygote (2N)

**MEIOSIS**

− Mating type (N)

+ Mating type (N)

Basidiospores (N)

The two nuclei in each basidium fuse to form a diploid zygote. The zygote undergoes meiosis, forming haploid basidiospores.

Haploid (N)

Diploid (2N)

**Diversity** More than 26,000 species of basidiomycetes have been described, roughly a quarter of all known fungal species. Examples include the stinkhorn and fly agaric mushrooms shown on the previous page, and the shelf fungus and puffball at right.

Shelf fungi (Polypore family) often grow on the sides of dead or dying trees.

A puffball releases its spores.

# Ascomycetes

The ascomycetes, or sac fungi, are named for the ascus (AS kus), a saclike reproductive structure that contains spores.

**Life Cycle** The ascomycete life cycle includes an asexual phase, in which haploid spores are released from structures called conidiophores, and a sexual phase.

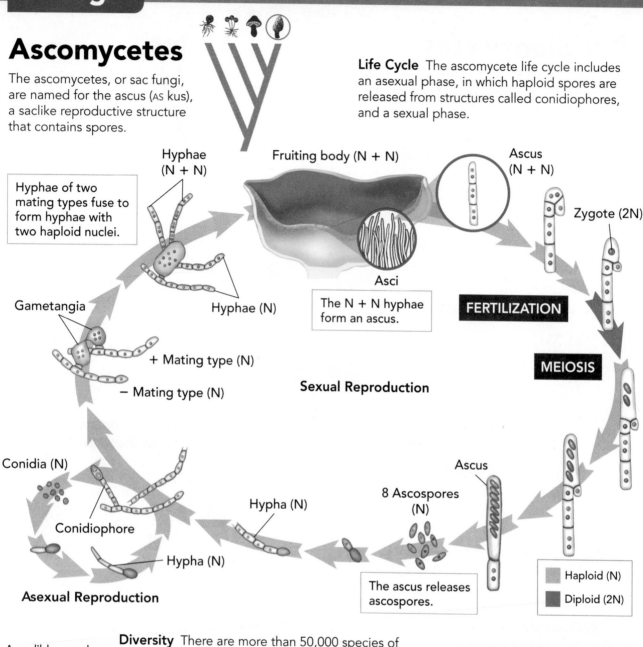

Hyphae (N + N)

Fruiting body (N + N)

Ascus (N + N)

Zygote (2N)

Hyphae of two mating types fuse to form hyphae with two haploid nuclei.

Hyphae (N)

Asci

The N + N hyphae form an ascus.

**FERTILIZATION**

**MEIOSIS**

Gametangia

+ Mating type (N)

− Mating type (N)

**Sexual Reproduction**

Conidia (N)

Ascus

Conidiophore

Hypha (N)

8 Ascospores (N)

Hypha (N)

The ascus releases ascospores.

**Asexual Reproduction**

Haploid (N)

Diploid (2N)

**Diversity** There are more than 50,000 species of ascomycetes, making it the largest phylum of the Fungi. Some ascomycetes, such as morels and cup fungi, are large enough to be visible when they grow above ground. Others, such as the common yeasts used for baking bread, are microscopic.

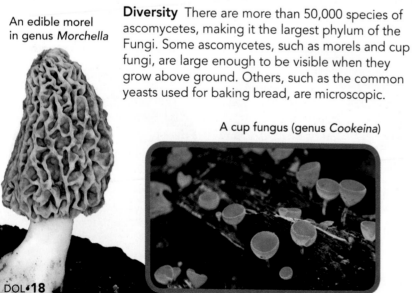

An edible morel in genus *Morchella*

A cup fungus (genus *Cookeina*)

SEM 4900×

*Saccharomyces cerevisiae*, the yeast used to raise bread dough, is a unicellular ascomycete that reproduces asexually by budding.

# Zygomycetes

The hyphae of zygomycetes generally lack cross walls between cells. Zygomycetes get their name from the sexual phase of their reproductive cycle, which involves a structure called a zygosporangium that forms between the hyphae of two different mating types. One group within the zygomycetes, the Glomales, form symbiotic mycorrhizae (my koh RY zee) with plant roots.

The fruiting body of the common black bread mold, *Rhizopus stolonifer* (SEM 450×)

This micrograph shows mycorrhizal fungi in symbiosis with soybean roots. The soybean plant provides nutrient sugars to the fungus, while the fungus provides water and essential minerals to the plant. (SEM 200×)

# Chytrids

Spores of *Synchytrium endobioticum* in potato cells (LM 500×)

Members of this phylum live in water or moist soil. Their reproductive cells have flagella, making them the only fungi known to have a motile stage to their life cycle. Chytrids are especially good at digesting cellulose, the material of plant cell walls—some live in the digestive systems of cows and deer, helping them to digest plant matter. Others are pathogens—certain chytrids have recently been associated with the decline of frog populations around the world. About 1000 species are known, many of them recently discovered.

Lichen-covered Japanese beech

## Look to the Lichens

### Lichens as Bio-Indicators

Lichens are mutualistic associations between a fungus, usually an ascomycete, and a photosynthetic organism, usually an alga. They are incredibly durable, and have even been reported to survive in the vacuum of space. However, they are also incredibly sensitive indicators of the state of the atmosphere. In particular, when sulfur dioxide is released into the atmosphere, it often reacts with water to form acids (including sulfuric acid) that pollute rainfall. Lichens can be severely damaged by acidic rainfall, although the degree of damage depends on the substrate upon which they grow. Lichens disappear first from the bark of pine and fir trees, which are themselves somewhat acidic. Lichens on elms, which have alkaline bark, are the last to go. By carefully monitoring the health of lichen populations of various trees, scientists can use these remarkable organisms as low-tech monitors of the health of the environment.

# Plants

## Key Characteristics

Plants are eukaryotes with cell walls composed of cellulose. Plants carry out photosynthesis using the green pigments chlorophyll *a* and *b*, and they store the products of photosynthesis as starch.

A typical plant life cycle

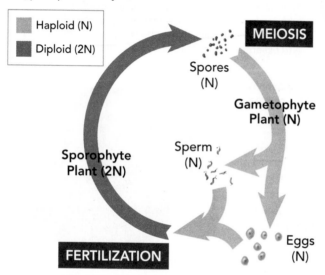

- Haploid (N)
- Diploid (2N)

MEIOSIS

Spores (N)

Gametophyte Plant (N)

Sperm (N)

Sporophyte Plant (2N)

Eggs (N)

FERTILIZATION

A saguaro cactus can live for hundreds of years.

## A Closer Look

## Prokaryotes Within
### The Origins of Chloroplasts

Chloroplasts, which contain their own DNA, are found in all green plants, but where did they come from? In 1905, the Russian botanist Konstantin Mereschkowsky, noticing the similarities between chloroplasts and cyanobacteria, proposed that these organelles originated from a symbiotic relationship formed with the ancestors of today's plants.

This hypothesis still holds up very well today. New DNA studies suggest that all chloroplasts are descended from a single photosynthetic prokaryote, closely related to today's cyanobacteria.

The photosynthetic membranes (shown in green) visible in this thin section of a cyanobacterium resemble the thylakoid membranes of plant cell chloroplasts. (TEM 14,000×)

# Green Algae

## Key Characteristics

The green algae are plants that do not make embryos. All other plants form embryos as part of their life cycle. The green algae include both unicellular and multicellular species, and they are primarily aquatic.

**Organization** Single cells, colonies, and a few truly multicellular species

**Movement** Many swim using whiplike flagella.

**Water Transport** Water diffuses in from the environment.

**Reproduction** Asexual and sexual, with gametes and spores; some species show alternation of generations.

Clumps of *Spirogyra*, a filamentous green alga, are commonly called water silk or mermaid's tresses.

## Groups of Green Algae

The three most diverse groups of green algae are profiled below.

### CHLOROPHYTES: Classic green algae

These algae usually live as single cells, like *Chlamydomonas*, or in colonies, like *Volvox*. They are found in both fresh and salt water, and some species are even known to live in arctic snowbanks.

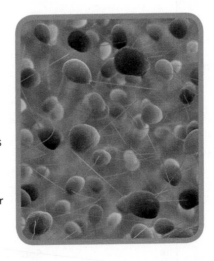

*Chlamydomonas* is a unicellular green alga. Each cell has two flagella, which are used in movement. (SEM 3000×)

### CHAROPHYTES: Stoneworts

Among the green algae, the charophytes (KAHR uh fyts) are the closest relatives of more complicated plants. They are mostly freshwater species. Their branching filaments may be anchored to the substrate by thin rhizoids.

*Chara* with antheridia (sperm-producing structures) visible

Antheridia

### ULVOPHYTES: Sea lettuces

The ulvophytes are large organisms composed of hundreds or thousands of cells. Most form large, flattened green sheets and are often simply called seaweed. They show both haploid and diploid phases in their life cycle, but in many species, such as the common sea lettuce, *Ulva*, it is difficult to tell the two phases apart.

*Ulva lactuca*

# Bryophytes

## Key Characteristics

Bryophytes (BRY oh fyts), found mostly on land, are multicellular plants that lack true vascular tissue. This lack of vascular tissue limits their height to just a few centimeters and restricts them to moist soils.

**Organization** Complex and specialized tissues, including protective external layers and rhizoids

**Movement** Adults stationary; male gametes swim to egg cells using flagella.

**Water Transport** Diffusion from cell to cell; in some mosses, water flows through specialized tissue.

**Reproduction** All reproduce sexually with alternation of generations, producing gametes and spores. Most reproduce asexually, too. The gametophyte stage is dominant, with the sporophyte stage dependent on the gametophyte.

Mosses thrive in shady, damp locations, such as this forest floor.

## Groups of Bryophytes

Although they are listed together here, the three major groups of bryophytes are now considered to have evolved independently from each other.

### MOSSES:
### Classic bryophytes

Mosses are found on damp, well-shaded soil, and occasionally along the sides of tree trunks.

### LIVERWORTS

Liverworts are flat, almost leaflike plants that grow on the damp forest floor. Sporophytes are small and grow on the underside of female gametophytes.

### HORNWORTS

Hornworts get their name from their sporophytes, tiny green structures resembling horns. Like other bryophytes, hornworts are found mostly in damp, well-shaded areas. Only about 100 species are known.

Sporophyte

Mat of gametophytes

Gametophyte

Sporophytes

# Seedless Vascular Plants

## Key Characteristics

This informal grouping lumps together all the plants that have true vascular tissue but lack seeds. Vascular tissue is a key adaptation to life on land. By carrying water and food throughout plant structures, vascular tissue permitted the evolution of roots and tree-size plants, and it allowed plants to spread into dry areas of land.

**Organization** Complex and specialized tissues, including true roots, stems, and leaves

**Movement** Adults stationary; male gametes swim to egg cells using flagella.

**Water Transport** Through vascular tissue

**Reproduction** Alternation of generations, producing spores, eggs, and swimming sperm; the sporophyte stage is dominant, but the sporophyte is not dependent on the gametophyte as it is in bryophytes.

## Groups of Seedless Vascular Plants

Besides the flowering plants, these organisms make up the most diverse collection of land plants, with more than 10,000 known species.

### FERNS

Ferns are common and abundant. Because they need standing water to reproduce, ferns are generally found in areas that are damp at least part of the year. The sporophyte phase of the life cycle is dominant. Spores are produced in prominent clusters known as sori (SOH ry) on the undersides of leaves.

*Polypodium vulgare*

Sori

### CLUB MOSSES

Not really mosses, these vascular plants are also called lycopods (LY koh pahdz). These plants were especially abundant during the Carboniferous Period 360 to 290 million years ago, when they grew as large as trees. Today, their remains make up a large part of coal deposits mined for fuel.

The small club moss known as *Lycopodium* can be found growing on the forest floor throughout the temperate regions of North America. They look like tiny pine trees at first glance, but they are, in fact, small, seedless plants.

### HORSETAILS

Only a single living genus of horsetails is known, *Equisetum* (ek wi SEET um). They get their name due to their resemblance to horses' tails. Today, only 25 species are known, confined to wet areas of soil. But horsetails were once much more diverse, larger in size, and abundant. Abrasive silica, found in many horsetails, was used in colonial times as a scouring powder to help clean pots and pans.

*Equisetum*

# Gymnosperms

## Key Characteristics

Gymnosperms are seed-bearing vascular plants whose seeds are exposed to the environment, rather than being enclosed in a fruit. The seeds are usually located on the scales of cones.

**Organization**  True roots, stems, and leaves

**Movement**  Adults stationary; within pollen grains, male gametophytes drift in air or are carried by animals to female structures, where they release sperm that move to eggs.

**Water Transport**  Through vascular tissue

**Reproduction**  Sexual; alternation of generations; the sporophyte stage is dominant. Female gametophytes live within the parent sporophyte. Because pollen grains carry sperm to eggs, open water is not needed for fertilization.

This sequoia tree is 83 meters tall and over 11 meters in diameter at the base.

The high heat of a forest fire opens the cones of the jack pines, releasing their seeds. In this photograph, jack pine seedlings are growing among the charred remnants of mature trees that burned in a forest fire.

### Did You Know?

## Rising From the Ashes
### Fire's Role in Seed Germination

We generally think of forest fires as being natural disasters, and that's typically true. Some gymnosperm species, however, are so well adapted to the arid conditions of the American West that they actually depend upon such fires to spread their seeds.

The best-known example is the jack pine, *Pinus banksiana*. Its seed cones are thick and heat resistant. When engulfed in a fire, its seeds escape damage. The fire's high heat helps to open the outer coat of the cone, enabling the seeds to pop out afterward. As a result, jack pines are among the very first plants to repopulate a forest that has been damaged by fire.

# Groups of Gymnosperms

There are four groups of gymnosperms, representing about 800 species in total.

## CONIFERS

Conifers are by far the most diverse group of living gymnosperms, represented by nearly 700 species worldwide. They include the common pine, spruce, fir, and redwood trees that make up a large share of the forests in the temperate regions of the world. Conifers have enormous economic importance. Their wood is used for residential building, to manufacture paper, and as a source of heat. Compounds from their resins are used for a variety of industrial purposes.

Most conifers retain their leaves year-round.

## CYCADS

Cycads (SY kads) are beautiful palmlike plants that have large cones. Cycads first appeared in the fossil record during the Triassic Period, 225 million years ago. Huge forests of cycads thrived when dinosaurs roamed Earth. Today, only nine genera of cycads exist. Cycads can be found growing naturally in tropical and subtropical places such as Mexico, the West Indies, Florida, and parts of Asia, Africa, and Australia.

A sago palm, *Cycas revoluta*

Ginkgoes are often planted in urban settings, where their toughness and resistance to air pollution make them popular shade trees.

## GINKGOES

Ginkgoes (GING kohs) were common when dinosaurs were alive, but today the group contains only one species, *Ginkgo biloba*. The living *Ginkgo* species looks similar to its fossil ancestors—in fact, *G. biloba* may be one of the oldest seed plant species alive today.

## GNETOPHYTES

About 70 present-day species of gnetophytes (NET oh fyts) are known, placed in just three genera. The reproductive scales of these plants are clustered in cones.

*Welwitschia mirabilis*, an inhabitant of the Namibian desert in southwestern Africa, is one of the most remarkable gnetophytes. Its huge leathery leaves grow continuously and spread across the ground.

Cones

# Angiosperms

## Key Characteristics

Angiosperms are plants that bear seeds in a closed ovary. The ovary is part of a reproductive organ known as a flower. Seeds are formed in a double fertilization event, which forms a diploid embryo and a triploid endosperm tissue. As seeds mature, ovaries develop into fruits that help to disperse the seeds.

**Organization** True roots, stems, and leaves

**Movement** Adults stationary; within pollen grains, male gametophytes drift in air or are carried by animals to female structures, where they release sperm that move to eggs.

**Water Transport** Through vascular tissue

**Reproduction** Sexual, with alternation of generations; also asexual. The sporophyte stage is dominant. Female gametophytes live within the parent sporophyte. Pollen carries sperm to eggs, so open water is not needed for fertilization.

Flowers in the genus *Passiflora* have a very distinct shape.

## A Closer Look

# Whatever Happened to Monocots and Dicots?

Traditionally, flowering plants have been divided into just two groups, monocots and dicots, based on the number of seed leaves in their embryos. Today, however, molecular studies have shown that the dicots aren't really one group. Some of the most primitive flowering plants (like *Amborella*) are dicots, and so are some of the most advanced flowering plants, while the monocots fall right in between. So, while monocots are indeed a single group, the term *dicots* is now just an informal, though still useful, grouping.

*Amborella*   Water lilies   Monocots   Magnoliids   Eudicots

**Ancestral Angiosperm**

# Groups of Angiosperms

The great majority of plant species—over 260,000—are angiosperms.

Water lilies are aquatic plants that produce flowers and leaves, which float on the surface of the water.

## NYMPHAEACEAE: Water lilies

About 50 species of water lilies are known, and they are of special interest to plant taxonomists. Their DNA and flower structure suggest that they are, along with *Amborella*, one of the earliest groups to have split off from the main line of flowering plant evolution. Examples of water lilies are found throughout the world.

## AMBORELLA

*Amborella* does not represent a group of plants but instead just a single species found only on the island of New Caledonia in the South Pacific Ocean. DNA studies show that *Amborella* is equally separated from all other flowering plants living today, suggesting that it is descended from plants that split off from the main line of flowering plant evolution as long ago as 100 million years.

## MAGNOLIIDS:
## Magnolia trees and others

The most famous genus of these plants is *Magnolia*, which includes nearly 200 species. Laurels and tulip poplars are also magnoliids (mag NOH lee ids). Because of their flower structure, magnoliids were once thought to be nearly as primitive as water lilies. Genetic studies now suggest that they split off from the rest of the angiosperm line after monocots and, therefore, do not represent the earliest flowering plants.

Magnolia trees produce conspicuous flowers, which contain multiple stamens and multiple pistils.

The tulip poplar is a tall, straight tree often used as wood for telephone poles. Its flowers are greenish and shaped like tulips.

## Groups of Angiosperms continued...

### MONOCOTS

The monocots include an estimated 65,000 species, roughly 20 percent of all flowering plants. They get their name from the single seed leaf found in monocot embryos, and they include some of the plants that are most important to human cultures. Monocots grown as crops account for a majority of the food produced by agriculture. These crops include wheat, rice, barley, corn, and sugar cane. Common grasses are monocots, as are onions, bananas, orchids, coconut palms, tulips, and irises.

Many orchid species are grown by enthusiasts for their rare beauty. Notice the aerial roots on this specimen, which grows as an epiphyte in its natural environment.

Aerial roots

This African hillside is dotted with clumps of wild pampas grass.

Onions are just one of many examples of monocot crop species.

After harvest, sugar cane regrows without being planted again for several cycles.

### Eco•Alert

# Coevolution: Losing the Pollinators

The successes of flowering plants are clearly due to coevolution with their insect pollinators. Common honeybees are among the most important of these, because they gather nectar from the flowers of hundreds of plant species and spread pollen from plant to plant as they go.

Unfortunately, beekeepers around the world, including the United States, are facing a serious crisis. "Colony collapse disorder," as beekeepers describe it, causes bees to fly away from the hive and either never return, or return only to weaken and die. The disease threatens to affect scores of important crops, which depend upon bees to produce fruit and seeds. Suspicion has centered on a fungus or a virus that might spread from colony to colony, but at this point there is no definitive cause or cure.

## EUDICOTS: "True Dicots"

Eudicots (YOO dy kahts) account for about 75 percent of all angiosperm species. The name means "true dicots," and these plants are the ones usually given as examples of dicot stem, leaf, and flower structure. Eudicots have distinctive pollen grains with three grooves on their surfaces, and DNA studies strongly support their classification in a single group. They include a number of important subgroups, five of which are described here.

Clusterhead Pinks

### Ranunculales

The ranunculales subgroup (ruh NUNH kyu lay les) includes, and is named after, buttercups (genus *Ranunculus*). Also included in this subgroup are well-known flowers such as columbines, poppies, barberries, and moonseed.

Rocky Mountain Columbine

### Caryophyllales

Cacti are probably the best-known plants in the caryophyllales subgroup (KAR ee oh fy lay les). Pinks and carnations, spinach, rhubarb, and insect-eating plants, such as sundews and pitcher plants, are also members.

Oranges

Peony

### Rosids

The rosids include, as you might expect, the roses. However, this subgroup also includes many popular fruits, such as oranges, raspberries, strawberries, and apples. Some of the best-known trees, including poplars, willows, and maples, are also members.

### Saxifragales

Plants in the saxifragales (SAK suh frij ay les) subgroup include peonies, witch hazel, gooseberries, and coral bells.

### Asterids

The nearly 80,000 asterid species include sunflowers, azaleas, snapdragons, blueberries, tomatoes, and potatoes.

The flower heads in a field of sunflowers all track the sun as it moves across the sky; thus, they all face the same direction.

# Animals

Burchell's Zebras

## Key Characteristics

Animals are multicellular, heterotrophic, eukaryotic organisms whose cells lack cell walls.

A Closer Look

## A Common Ancestor

Recent molecular studies and cladistic analyses recognize the clade Choanozoa to be the true sister group to all Metazoa—multicellular animals. Choanozoa is one group of organisms formerly called "protists" and is named for choanoflagellates, single-celled, colonial organisms that look like certain cells of sponges and flatworms. Evidence suggests that the choanoflagellates alive today are the best living examples of what the last common ancestor of metazoans looked like.

# Porifera (Sponges)

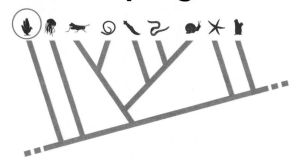

## Key Characteristics

Sponges are the simplest animals. They are classified as animals because they are multicellular and heterotrophic, lack cell walls, and have some specialized cells. They are aquatic, lack true tissues and organs, and have internal skeletons of spongin and/or spicules of calcium carbonate or silica. Sponges have no body symmetry.

**Feeding and Digestion** Filter feeders; intracellular digestion

**Circulation** Via flow of water through body

**Respiration** Oxygen diffuses from water into cells as water flows through body

**Excretion** Wastes diffuse from cells into water as water flows through body

**Response** No nervous system; little capacity to respond to environmental changes

**Movement** Juveniles drift or swim freely; adults are stationary.

**Reproduction** Most—sexual with internal fertilization; water flowing out of sponge disperses sperm, which fertilizes eggs inside sponge(s); may reproduce asexually by budding or producing gemmules

## Groups of Sponges

There are more than 5000 species of sponges; most are marine. Three major groups are described below.

### DEMOSPONGIAE: Typical sponges

More than 90 percent of all living sponge species are in this group, including the few freshwater species. They have skeletons made of spongin, a flexible protein. Some species have silica spicules. Examples: yellow sponge, bath sponges, carnivorous Mediterranean sponge, tube sponges

Orange elephant ear sponge

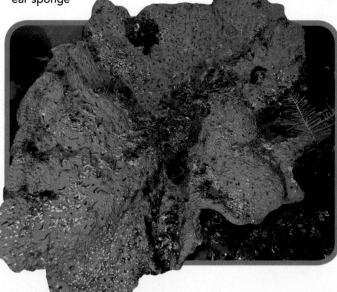

### HEXACTINELLIDA: Glass sponges

Glass sponges live in the deep ocean and are especially abundant in the Antarctic. They are called "glass" sponges because their skeletons are made of glasslike silica spicules. Examples: Venus's flower basket, cloud sponge

Glass Sponge

### CALCAREA: Calcareous sponges

Calcareous sponges live in shallow, tropical marine waters and are the only sponges with calcium carbonate spicules. Example: *Clathrina*

Yellow Tubular Sponge

# Cnidarians

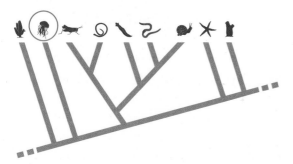

## Key Characteristics

Cnidarians are aquatic, mostly carnivorous, and the simplest animals to have specialized tissues (outer skin and lining of the gastrovascular cavity) and body symmetry (radial). Their tentacles have stinging cells called nematocysts used in feeding.

Sea anemone in a rock pool

**Feeding and Digestion** Predatory, stinging prey with nematocysts; digestion begins extracellularly in gastrovascular cavity and is completed intracellularly; indigestible materials leave body through single opening; many, especially reef-building corals, also depend on symbiotic algae, or zooxanthellae.

**Circulation** No internal transport system; nutrients typically diffuse through body.

**Respiration** Diffusion through body walls

**Excretion** Cellular wastes diffuse through body walls.

**Response** Some specialized sensory cells: nerve cells in nerve net, statocysts that help determine up and down, eyespots (ocelli) made of light-detecting cells

**Movement** Polyps stationary, medusas free-swimming; some, such as sea anemones, can burrow and creep very slowly; others move using muscles that work with a hydrostatic skeleton and water in gastrovascular cavity; medusas such as jellyfish move by jet propulsion generated by muscle contractions.

**Reproduction** Most alternate between sexual (most species by external fertilization) and asexual (polyps produce new polyps or medusae by budding)

The color of this star coral is caused by zooxanthellae algae living within it.

## Eco•Alert

# Coral Symbionts

Reef-building coral animals depend on symbiotic algae called zooxanthellae for certain vital nutritional needs. In many places, reef-building corals live close to the upper end of their temperature tolerance zone. If water temperatures rise too high, the coral-zooxanthellae symbiosis breaks down, and corals turn white in what is called "coral bleaching." If corals don't recover their algae soon, they weaken and die. This is one reason why coral reefs are in grave danger from global warming.

# Groups of Cnidarians

There are more than 9000 species of cnidarians.

## HYDROZOA: Hydras and their relatives

Hydras and their relatives spend most of their time as polyps and are either colonial or solitary. They reproduce asexually (by budding) or sexually, or they alternate between sexual and asexual reproduction. Examples: hydra, Portuguese man-of-war

**A Portuguese man-of-war is actually a colony of polyps.**

Black
Sea
Nettle

## ANTHOZOA: Corals and sea anemones

Corals and sea anemones are colonial or solitary polyps with no medusa stage. The central body is surrounded by tentacles. They reproduce sexually or asexually. Examples: reef corals, sea anemones, sea pens, sea fans

Sea Anemone

## SCYPHOZOA: Jellyfishes

Jellyfishes spend most of their time as medusas; some species bypass the polyp stage. They reproduce sexually and sometimes asexually by budding. Examples: lion's mane jellyfish, moon jelly, sea wasp

*Chrysaora fuscescens* can grow to 45 cm in diameter and over 4 m long.

# Arthropods

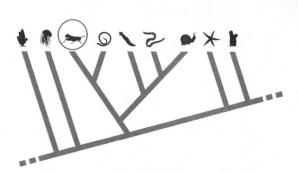

## Key Characteristics

Arthropods are the most diverse of all multicellular organisms. They have segmented bodies and jointed appendages. They are supported by tough exoskeletons made of chitin, which they periodically shed as they grow. Arthropods are coelomate protostomes with bilateral symmetry.

## Eco•Alert

### Beetle Damage

You probably know that some insects can seriously damage crop plants. But insects affect plants in natural habitats, too. One example is the mountain pine beetle, which is dramatically extending its range. Global warming appears to be enabling the beetle to survive farther north, and at higher altitudes, than it used to. The new beetle infestation is causing extensive damage to northern and high-altitude forests in North America. The death of millions of acres of trees has resulted in the release of large amounts of carbon dioxide, a greenhouse gas, into the atmosphere. You can see the sort of damage the beetles cause in the photo at right.

Mountain pine beetle damage to pine trees in White River National Forest, Colorado

**Feeding and Digestion** Extremely diverse: herbivores, carnivores, detritivores, parasites, blood-suckers, scavengers, filter feeders; digestive system with two openings; many feeding specializations in different groups

**Circulation** Open circulatory system with heart and arteries

**Respiration** Terrestrial—tracheal tubes or book lungs; aquatic—gills or book gills (horseshoe crabs)

**Excretion** Terrestrial—Malpighian tubules; aquatic—diffusion into water

**Response** Well-developed nervous system with brain; sophisticated sense organs

**Movement** Muscles attached internally to jointed exoskeletons

**Reproduction** Usually sexual, although some species may reproduce asexually under certain circumstances; many undergo metamorphosis during development

Most animals, including this caterpillar, are arthropods.

# Groups of Arthropods

The phylum Arthropoda contains more known species than any other phylum. Scientists have identified more than 1,000,000 arthropod species, and some scientists expect there are millions yet to be identified. Arthropods are classified based on their number and structure of their body segments and appendages.

## CRUSTACEA: Crustaceans

There are crustacean species in almost every habitat, but most are aquatic, and most of these are marine. They have two or three body sections, two pairs of antennae, and chewing mouthparts called mandibles. Many have a carapace, or "shell," that covers part or all of the body. Examples: crabs, lobsters, crayfish, pill bugs, water fleas, barnacles

Lobster

## CHELICERATA: Chelicerates

Living chelicerates include horseshoe crabs and arachnids. (Their extinct relatives include trilobites and giant "sea-scorpions.") Most living chelicerates are terrestrial. The body is composed of two parts—the cephalothorax and abdomen. The first pair of appendages are specialized feeding structures called chelicerae. Chelicerates have no antennae.

### Merostomata: Horseshoe crabs

The class Merostomata once included many species, but only four species of horseshoe crab survive today. All are marine. They have five pairs of walking legs and a long, spinelike tail.

### Arachnida: Arachnids

The vast majority of arachnids are terrestrial. They have four pairs of walking legs and no tail. Examples: spiders, ticks, mites, scorpions, daddy longlegs

Mexican Fireleg Tarantula

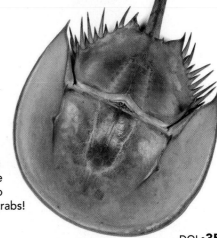

Horseshoe crabs are actually more closely related to spiders than to crabs!

# Animals

## UNIRAMIA: Uniramians

Most uniramians are terrestrial, although some are aquatic for all or part of their lives. They have one pair of antennae, mandibles, and unbranched appendages. Uniramians include at least three fourths of all known animal species!

Uniramians include centipedes, millipedes, and insects—more than three fourths of all known animal species, including this green snaketail dragonfly.

Centipede

## Chilopoda: Centipedes

Centipedes have a long body composed of many segments. Each segment bears one pair of legs. They are carnivorous and have claws that release poisons to capture prey.

## Diplopoda: Millipedes

Millipedes have a long body composed of many segments. Each segment bears two pairs of legs. Most millipedes are herbivorous.

Giant Millipede

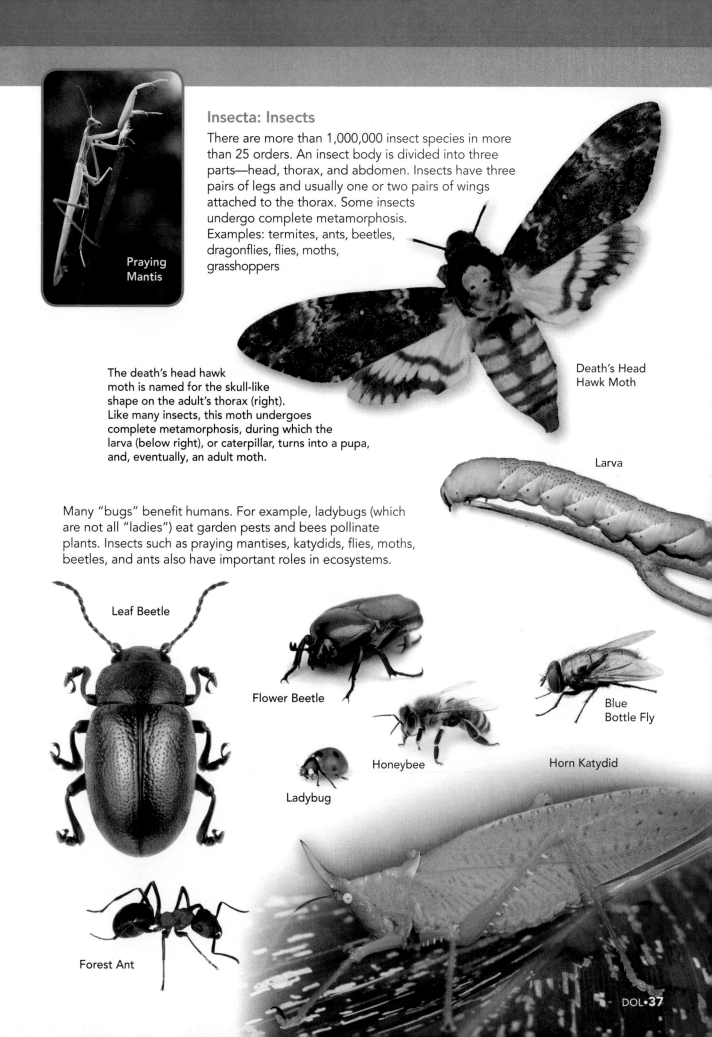

## Insecta: Insects

There are more than 1,000,000 insect species in more than 25 orders. An insect body is divided into three parts—head, thorax, and abdomen. Insects have three pairs of legs and usually one or two pairs of wings attached to the thorax. Some insects undergo complete metamorphosis. Examples: termites, ants, beetles, dragonflies, flies, moths, grasshoppers

Praying Mantis

The death's head hawk moth is named for the skull-like shape on the adult's thorax (right). Like many insects, this moth undergoes complete metamorphosis, during which the larva (below right), or caterpillar, turns into a pupa, and, eventually, an adult moth.

Death's Head Hawk Moth

Larva

Many "bugs" benefit humans. For example, ladybugs (which are not all "ladies") eat garden pests and bees pollinate plants. Insects such as praying mantises, katydids, flies, moths, beetles, and ants also have important roles in ecosystems.

Leaf Beetle

Flower Beetle

Blue Bottle Fly

Honeybee

Ladybug

Horn Katydid

Forest Ant

# Nematodes (Roundworms)

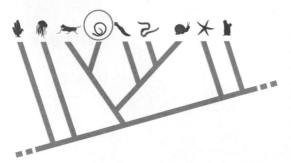

Pinworm (colorized SEM)

Pinworms can infest the intestinal tract of humans. Although anyone can become infected with pinworms, infection is most common in children aged 5 to 10.

## Key Characteristics

Nematodes, or roundworms, are unsegmented worms with a tough outer cuticle, which they shed as they grow. This "molting" is one reason that nematodes are now considered more closely related to arthropods than to other wormlike animals. Nematodes are the simplest animals to have a "one-way" digestive system through which food passes from mouth to anus. They are protostomes and have a pseudocoelom.

**Feeding and Digestion** Some predators, some parasites, and some decomposers; one-way digestive tract with mouth and anus

**Circulation** By diffusion

**Respiration** Gas exchange through body walls

**Excretion** Through body walls

**Response** Simple nervous system consisting of several ganglia, several nerves, and several types of sense organs

**Movement** Muscles work with hydrostatic skeleton, enabling aquatic species to move like water snakes and soil-dwelling species to move by thrashing around.

**Reproduction** Sexual with internal fertilization; separate sexes; parasitic species may lay eggs in several hosts or host organs.

## Groups of Roundworms

There are more than 15,000 known species of roundworms, and there may be half a million species yet to be described. Free-living species live in almost every habitat imaginable, including fresh water, salt water, hot springs, ice, and soil. Parasitic species live on or inside a wide range of organisms, including insects, humans, and many domesticated animals and plants. Examples: *Ascaris lumbricoides*, hookworms, pinworms, *Trichinella*, *C. elegans*

### A Closer Look

## A Model Organism?

*Caenorhabditis elegans* is a small soil nematode. Fifty years ago, this species was selected as a "model organism" for the study of genetics and development. We can now chart the growth and development of *C. elegans*, cell by cell, from fertilization to adult. This information is invaluable in understanding the development of other species—including many other nematodes that cause serious disease.

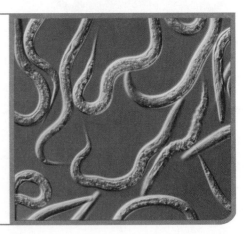

*C. elegans* (LM 64x)

# Platyhelminthes (Flatworms)

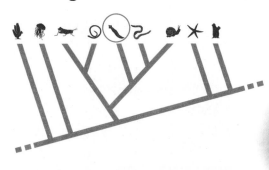

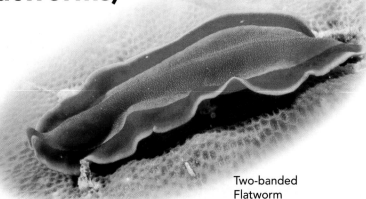

Two-banded Flatworm

## Key Characteristics

Flatworms are soft worms with tissues and internal organ systems. They are the simplest animals to have three embryonic germ layers, bilateral symmetry, and cephalization. They are acoelomates.

**Feeding and Digestion** Free-living—predators or scavengers that suck food in through a pharynx and digest it in a system that has one opening. Parasitic—feed on blood, tissue fluids, or cell pieces of the host, using simpler digestive systems than free-living species have. Tapeworms, which absorb nutrients from food that the host has already digested, have no digestive system.

**Circulation** By diffusion

**Respiration** Gas exchange by diffusion

**Excretion** Some—flame cells remove excess water and may remove metabolic wastes such as ammonia and urea. Many flame cells are connected to tubules that release substances through pores in the skin.

**Response** Free-living—several ganglia connected by nerve cords that run through the body, along with eyespots and other specialized sensory cells; parasitic—simpler nervous system than free-living forms have

**Movement** Free-living—using cilia and muscle cells

**Reproduction** Free-living—most are hermaphrodites that reproduce sexually with internal fertilization; parasitic—commonly reproduce asexually by fission but also often reproduce sexually

## Groups of Flatworms

Flatworms are an amazingly diverse group of worms that include more than 20,000 species. They have historically been placed into three classes, but these taxa now appear not to be true clades, and will probably change.

### TREMATODA: Flukes

Most flukes are parasites that infect internal organs of their hosts, but some infect external parts such as skin or gills. The life cycle typically involves more than one host or organ. Examples: *Schistosoma*, liver fluke

Liver Fluke

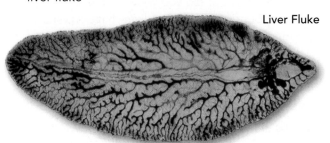

### TURBELLARIA: Turbellarians

Turbellarians are free-living aquatic and terrestrial predators and scavengers. Many are colorful marine species. Examples: *planarians*, polyclad flatworm

### CESTODA: Tapeworms

Tapeworms are very long intestinal parasites that lack a digestive system and absorb nutrients directly through their body walls. The tapeworm body is composed of many repeated sections (proglottids) that contain both male and female reproductive organs.

# Annelids (Segmented Worms)

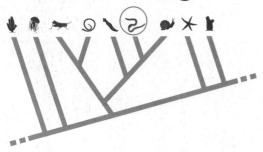

## Key Characteristics

Annelids are coelomate protostome worms whose bodies are composed of segments separated by internal partitions. The annelid digestive system has two openings.

Christmas tree worms are found on coral reefs and use their spirals of plumes for respiration and feeding.

**Feeding and Digestion** Filter feeders, carnivores, or parasites; many obtain food using a muscular pharynx, often equipped with "teeth"; widely varied digestive systems—some, such as earthworms, have complex digestive tracts.

**Circulation** Closed circulatory system with dorsal and ventral blood vessels; dorsal vessel pumps blood like a heart.

**Respiration** Aquatic—gills; terrestrial—skin

**Excretion** Digestive waste exits through anus; nitrogenous wastes eliminated by nephridia

**Response** Nervous system includes a rudimentary brain and several nerve cords; sense organs best-developed in free-living saltwater species

**Movement** Hydrostatic skeleton based on sealed body segments surrounded by longitudinal and circular muscles; many annelids have appendages that enable movement.

**Reproduction** Most—sexual, some through external fertilization with separate sexes, but others are simultaneous hermaphrodites that exchange sperm; most have a trochophore larval stage.

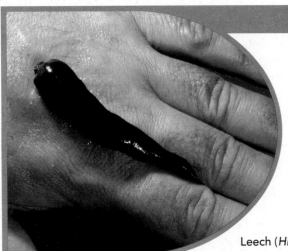

## Did You Know?

# Not-So-Modern Medicine

You may have heard that medieval healers used leeches to remove "excess" blood from patients and to clean wounds after surgery. But did you know that leeches—or at least compounds from leech saliva—have a place in modern medicine? Leech saliva contains the protein hirudin, which prevents blood from clotting. Some surgeons use leeches to relieve pressure caused by blood that pools in tissues after plastic surgery. Hirudin is also used to prevent unwanted blood clots.

Leech (*Hirudo medicinalis*) drawing blood from a hand

**Feather-Duster Worms**

# Groups of Annelids

There are more than 15,000 species of annelids.

### POLYCHAETA: Polychaetes

Polychaetes live in salt water; many move with paddle-like appendages called parapodia tipped with bristle-like setae. Examples: sandworms, bloodworms, fanworms, feather-duster worms

The white, bristle-like structures on the sides of this bearded fireworm are setae.

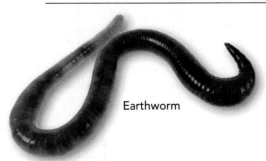

Earthworm

### OLIGOCHAETA: Oligochaetes

Oligochaetes live in soil or fresh water. They lack appendages. Some use setae for movement but have fewer than polychaetes. Examples: *Tubifex*, earthworms

### HIRUDINEA: Leeches

Most leeches live in fresh water. They lack appendages. Leeches may be carnivores or blood-sucking external parasites. Example: medicinal leech (*Hirudo medicinalis*)

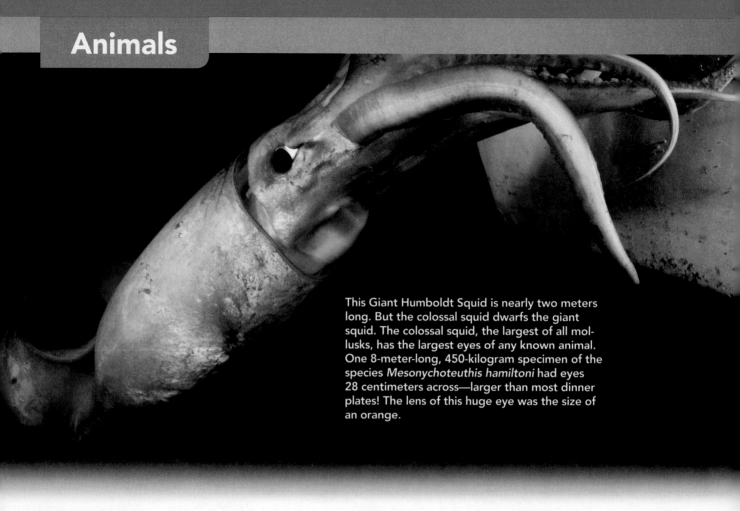

This Giant Humboldt Squid is nearly two meters long. But the colossal squid dwarfs the giant squid. The colossal squid, the largest of all mollusks, has the largest eyes of any known animal. One 8-meter-long, 450-kilogram specimen of the species *Mesonychoteuthis hamiltoni* had eyes 28 centimeters across—larger than most dinner plates! The lens of this huge eye was the size of an orange.

# Mollusks

## Key Characteristics

Mollusks have soft bodies that typically include a muscular foot. Body forms vary greatly. Many mollusks possess a hard shell secreted by the mantle, but in some, the only hard structure is internal. Mollusks are coelomate protostomes with bilateral symmetry.

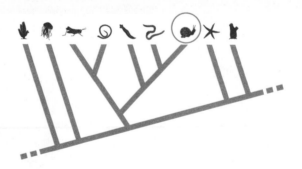

**Feeding and Digestion** Digestive system with two openings; diverse feeding styles—mollusks can be herbivores, carnivores, filter feeders, detritivores, or parasites.

**Circulation** Snails and clams—open circulatory system; octopi and squid—closed circulatory system

**Respiration** Aquatic mollusks—gills inside the mantle cavity; land mollusks—a saclike mantle cavity whose large, moist surface area is lined with blood vessels.

**Excretion** Body cells release ammonia into the blood, which nephridia remove and release outside the body.

**Response** Complexity of nervous system varies greatly; extremely simple in clams, but complex in some octopi

**Movement** Varies greatly, by group; some never move as adults, while others are very fast swimmers.

**Reproduction** Sexual; many aquatic species have a free-swimming trochophore larval stage.

# Groups of Mollusks

Mollusks are traditionally divided into several classes based on characteristics of the foot and the shell; specialists estimate that there are between 50,000 and 200,000 species of mollusks alive today.

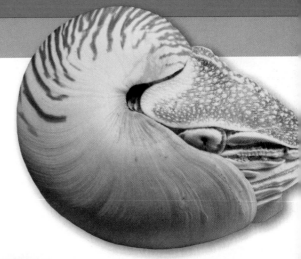

**Chambered Nautilus**

**Giant Clam**

## BIVALVIA: Bivalves

Bivalves are aquatic. They have a two-part hinged shell and a wedge-shaped foot. They are mostly stationary as adults. Some burrow in mud or sand; others attach to rocks. Most are filter feeders that use gill siphons to take in water that carries food. Clams have open circulatory systems. Bivalves have the simplest nervous systems among mollusks. Examples: clams, oysters, scallops, mussels

**Garden Snail**

## GASTROPODA: Gastropods

There are both terrestrial and aquatic gastropods. Most have a single spiral, chambered shell. Gastropods use a broad, muscular foot to move and have a distinct head region. Snails and slugs feed with a structure called a radula that usually works like sandpaper. Some species are predators whose harpoon-shaped radula carries deadly venom. They have open circulatory systems. Many gastropod species are cross-fertilizing hermaphrodites. Examples: snails, slugs, nudibranchs, sea hares

## CEPHALOPODA: Cephalopods

Cephalopods live in salt water. The cephalopod has a highly developed brain and sense organs. The head is attached to a single foot, which is divided into tentacles. They have closed circulatory systems. Octopi use beaklike jaws for feeding; a few are venomous. Cephalopods have the most complex nervous systems among mollusks; octopi have complex behavior and have shown the ability to learn in laboratory settings. Examples: octopi, squids, nautilus, cuttlefish

Nudibranchs, such as this *Hypselodoris* species, are marine gastropods without shells. They breathe through gills (the orange structures) on their backs.

# Echinoderms

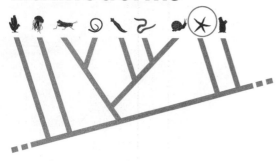

## Key Characteristics

Echinoderms are marine animals that have spiny skin surrounding an endoskeleton. Their unique water vascular system includes tube feet with suction-cuplike ends used in moving and feeding. The water vascular system also plays a role in respiration, circulation, and excretion. Echinoderms are coelomate deuterostomes. Adults exhibit five-part radial symmetry.

## Crinoids Then and Now

Echinoderms have a long fossil record that dates all the way back to the Cambrian Period. Although these animals have been evolving for millions of years, some fossil crinoids look a great deal like living crinoids.

Crinoid fossil, about 400 million years old

Living modern crinoid (feather star)

**Feeding and Digestion**  Method varies by group—echinoderms can be filter feeders, detritivores, herbivores, or carnivores.

**Circulation**  Via fluid in the coelom, a rudimentary system of vessels, and the water vascular system

**Respiration**  Gas exchange is carried out by surfaces of tube feet, and, in many species, by skin gills.

**Excretion**  Digestive wastes released through anus; nitrogenous cellular wastes excreted as ammonia through tube feet and skin gills.

**Response**  Minimal nervous system; nerve ring is connected to body sections by radial nerves; most have scattered sensory cells that detect light, gravity, and chemicals secreted by prey.

**Movement**  In most, tube feet work with endoskeleton to enable locomotion.

**Reproduction**  Sexual, with external fertilization; larvae have bilateral symmetry, unlike adults.

You can't miss the five-part radial symmetry of this brightly colored sea star.

# Groups of Echinoderms

There are more than 7000 species of echinoderms.

## CRINOIDEA: Crinoids

Crinoids are filter feeders; some use tube feet along feathery arms to capture plankton. The mouth and anus are on the upper surface of the body disk. Some are stationary as adults while others can "walk" using short "arms" on the lower body surface. Examples: sea lily, feather star

**Feeding Crinoid**

**Sea Star**

## ASTEROIDEA: Sea stars

Sea stars are bottom dwellers whose star-shaped bodies have flexible joints. They are carnivorous—the stomach pushes through the mouth onto the body tissues of prey and pours out digestive enzymes. The stomach then retracts with the partially digested prey; digestion is completed inside the body. Examples: crown-of-thorns sea star, sunstar

**Basket Star**

**Sea urchins grazing on kelp**

## OPHIUROIDEA: Ophiuroids

Ophiuroids have small body disks, long, armored arms, and flexible joints. Most are filter feeders or detritivores. Examples: brittle star, basket star

## ECHINOIDEA: Echinoids

Echinoids lack arms. Their endoskeletons are rigid and boxlike and covered with movable spines. Most echinoids are herbivores or detritivores that use five-part jawlike structures to scrape algae from rocks. Examples: sea urchin, sand dollar, sea biscuit

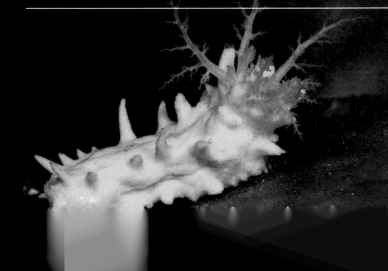

## HOLOTHUROIDEA: Sea cucumbers

Sea cucumbers have a cylindrical, rubbery body with a reduced endoskeleton and no arms. They typically lie on their side and move along the ocean floor by the combined action of tube feet and body-wall muscles. These filter feeders or detritivores use a set of retractable feeding tentacles on one end to take in sand and detritus, from which they glean food

# Nonvertebrate Chordates

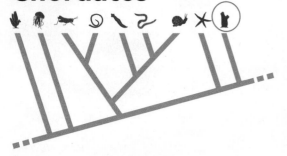

Tunicates are chordates named for the colorful tunic-like covering the adults have. As larvae, tunicates have all the characteristics of chordates, as well as bilateral symmetry, but as adults, they look very, very different.

## Key Characteristics

The nonvertebrate chordates are the only chordates that lack a backbone. Like other chordates, they have a nerve cord, notochord, pharyngeal pouches, and a tail at some point during development. They are coelomate deuterostomes. The two subphyla, tunicates and lancelets, differ significantly.

**Feeding and Digestion** Filter feeders; tunicates—in most, water carrying food particles enters through an incurrent siphon; food is strained out in the pharynx and passed to the digestive system; lancelets—mucus in the pharynx catches food particles carried in by water, which are then carried into digestive tract

**Circulation** Closed; tunicates—heart pumps blood by "wringing out," and flow periodically reverses direction; lancelets—no heart, but blood vessels pump blood through body in one direction

**Respiration** Tunicates—gas exchange occurs in the gills and across other body surfaces; lancelets—through pharynx and body surfaces

**Excretion** Tunicates—most through excurrent siphon; lancelets—flame cells in nephridia release

water and nitrogenous wastes into the atrium and out through an opening called an atriopore.

**Response** Cerebral ganglion, few specialized sensory organs; tunicates—sensory cells in and on the siphons and other internal surfaces help control the amount of water passing through the pharynx; lancelets—a pair of eyespots detects light.

**Movement** Tunicates—free-swimming larvae, but most are stationary as adults; lancelets—no appendages: They move by contracting muscles paired on either side of the body.

**Reproduction** Tunicates—most sexual and hermaphroditic with external fertilization, but some reproduce by budding; most have free-swimming tadpole-like larvae that metamorphose into adults; lancelets—sexual with external fertilization

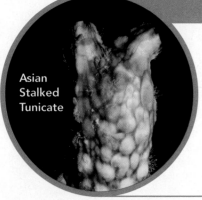

Asian Stalked Tunicate

## Out-of-Control Tunicates

You've never heard of them, but Asian stalked tunicates are disrupting marine ecosystems in Washington State; Prince Edward Island, Canada; and elsewhere. Tunicate larvae are carried in the ballast water of freight ships and discharged wherever the ships make port. There, away from their usual predators, the tunicates grow out of control, smothering shellfish beds and covering boats, docks, and underwater equipment. Researchers are still trying to figure out how to control them.

# Groups of Nonvertebrate Chordates

There are two major groups of nonvertebrate chordates: tunicates and lancelets (sometimes called amphioxus).

## CEPHALOCHORDATA: Lancelets

Lancelets are fishlike animals that have bilateral symmetry and live in salt water. They are filter feeders and have no internal skeleton. Example: *Branchiostoma*

Lancelets live buried in seabeds.

## UROCHORDATA: Tunicates

Tunicates are filter feeders that live in salt water. Most adults have a tough outer covering ("tunic") and no body symmetry; most display chordate features and bilateral symmetry only during larval stages. Many adults are stationary; some are free-swimming. Examples: sea squirts, sea peaches, salps

Pastel Sea Squirt

Sea Squirts

# Fishes

## Key Characteristics

The word *fish* is used informally to describe aquatic vertebrates that look similar even though they belong to several different clades, because all are adapted to life in water. Most vertebrates we call fishes have paired fins, scales, and gills.

**Feeding and Digestion** Varies widely, both within and between groups: herbivores, carnivores, parasites, filter feeders, detritivores; digestive organs often include specialized teeth and jaws, crop, esophagus, stomach, liver, pancreas

**Circulation** Closed, single-loop circulatory system; two-chambered heart

**Respiration** Gills; some have specialized lungs or other adaptations that enable them to obtain oxygen from air.

**Excretion** Diffusion across gill membranes; kidneys

**Response** Brain with many parts; highly developed sense organs, including lateral line system

**Movement** Paired muscles on either side of backbone; many have highly maneuverable fins; the largest groups have two sets of paired fins; some have a gas-filled swim bladder that regulates buoyancy.

**Reproduction** Methods vary within and between groups: external or internal fertilization; oviparous, ovoviviparous, or viviparous

## A Look Back in Time

# Live Birth in Devonian Seas

You might think that live birth is a recent addition to chordate diversity. Guess again. Recent fossil finds of fishes from the Devonian Period show that at least one group of fishes was already bearing live young 380 million years ago. Two incredibly well preserved fossils, including that of the fish *Materpiscis*, show the remains of young with umbilical cords still attached to their mothers' bodies. This is the earliest fossil evidence of viviparity in vertebrates.

This sailfish is herding thousands of smaller fish into a tight pack called a bait ball.

# Groups of Fishes

Fishes are the largest group of vertebrates, including more than 30,000 species. Evolutionary classification of these animals is still a work in progress; many traditional groups are not clades. "Fishes" actually represent several ancient clades, one of which includes tetrapods, or four-limbed vertebrates. Fishes, as we treat them here, include two groups of jawless fishes (hagfishes and lampreys), cartilaginous fishes, and bony fishes.

## "JAWLESS FISHES"

Hagfishes and lampreys make up separate clades, but their bodies share common features that distinguish them from other fishes. They have no jaws, they lack vertebrae, and their skeletons are made of fiber and cartilage.

## PETROMYZONTIDA: Lampreys

Lampreys are mostly filter feeders as larvae and parasites as adults. The head of an adult lamprey is taken up almost completely by a circular, tooth-bearing, sucking disk with a round mouth. Adult lampreys typically attach themselves to fishes. They hold on to their hosts using the teeth in their sucking disk and then scrape away at the skin with a rasping tongue. Lampreys then suck up their host's tissues and body fluids. Because lampreys feed mostly on blood, they are called "vampires of the sea."

Lamprey Mouth

Lamprey

## MYXINI: Hagfishes

Atlantic Hagfish

Hagfishes have pinkish gray, wormlike bodies and four or six short tentacles around their mouths. They retain notochords as adults. Hagfishes lack image-forming eyes, but have light-detecting sensors scattered around their bodies. They feed on dead and dying animals using a rasping tongue that scrapes away layers of flesh.

# Animals

Tiger Shark

## CHONDRICHTHYES: Cartilaginous fishes

Members of this clade are considered "cartilaginous" because they lack true bone; their skeletons are built entirely of cartilage. Most cartilaginous fishes also have tough scales, which make their skin as rough as sandpaper.

## Holocephalans: Chimaeras

Chimaeras have smooth skin that lacks scales. Most have just a few platelike, grinding teeth and a venomous spine located in front of the dorsal fin. Examples: ghostfish, ratfish, rabbitfish

Elephant Fish

## Elasmobranchii: Sharks, skates, and rays

Sharks, skates, and rays are very diverse, but all have skin covered with toothlike scales known as dermal denticles. Elasmobranchii make up the vast majority of living cartilaginous fish species.

Dermal denticles on shark skin reduce drag, helping the shark to swim faster. (SEM 40×)

## Galeomorphi: Sharks

Most of the 350 or so shark species have large, curved asymmetrical tails, torpedo-shaped bodies, and pointed snouts with a mouth underneath. Predatory sharks, such as the great white, have many teeth arranged in rows. As teeth in the front rows are worn out or lost, new teeth replace them. Some sharks go through 20,000 teeth in their lifetime! Other sharks are filter feeders, and some species have flat teeth for crushing mollusk and crustacean shells. Examples: great white shark, whale shark, hammerhead shark

## Squalomorphi: Skates and rays

Skates and rays have diverse feeding habits. Some feed on bottom-dwelling invertebrates by using their mouths as powerful vacuums. Others filter-feed on plankton. When not feeding or swimming, many skates and rays cover themselves with a thin layer of sand and rest on the ocean floor. Example: stingray

Blue-Spotted Stingray

Hammerhead Shark

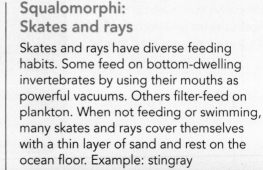

## OSTEICHTHYES: Bony fishes

The skeletons of these vertebrates are made of true bone. This clade includes the ancestors and living members of all "higher" vertebrate groups—including tetrapods.

---

### Actinopterygii: Ray-finned fishes

Almost all living bony fishes, such as these rainbow trout, belong to a huge group called ray-finned fishes. The name ray-finned refers to the slender bony rays that are connected to one another by a layer of skin to form fins.

Rainbow Trout

---

Coelacanth

### Sarcopterygii: Lobe-finned fishes

Seven living species of bony fishes, including lungfishes and coelacanths, are classified as lobe-finned fishes. Lungfishes live in fresh water; coelacanths live in salt water. The fleshy fins of lobe-finned fishes are supported by strong bones rather than rays. Some of these bones are homologous to the limb bones of land vertebrates. Examples: lungfish, coelacanths

This clade includes the ancestors of tetrapods, which means, that all living tetrapods (including us!) are Sarcopterygians. As a result, the bony-fish clade includes almost half of all chordate species.

# Amphibians

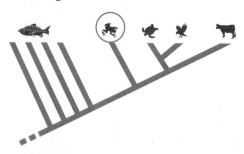

Green Frog

## Key Characteristics

The word *amphibian* means "double life," an apt name for these vertebrates, most of which live in water as larvae and on land as adults. Most adult amphibians breathe with lungs, lack scales and claws, and have moist skin that contains mucous glands.

**Feeding and Digestion** Tadpoles—usually filter feeders or herbivores with long, coiled intestines to digest plant material; adults—carnivores with shorter intestines for processing meat

**Circulation** Double-loop system with three-chambered heart

**Respiration** Larvae breathe through skin and gills; most adult species have lungs, though a few use gills; lungless salamanders breathe through their mouth-cavity lining and skin.

**Excretion** Kidneys produce urine.

**Response** Well-developed nervous and sensory systems; organs include protective nictitating membrane over moveable eyes, tympanic membranes, lateral line system

**Movement** Larvae have tails; adults have limbs (except caecilians); some have specialized toes for climbing.

**Reproduction** Most lay eggs without shells that are fertilized externally; most undergo metamorphosis from aquatic tadpole larvae that breathe with gills to land-dwelling adults, which usually have lungs and limbs.

Red-Eyed Treefrog

## Eco•Alert

# The Frogs Are Disappearing!

For several decades, scientists have noticed that amphibian populations worldwide have been decreasing, and a number of species have become extinct. Scientists have not yet pinpointed a single cause for this problem. It is, however, becoming clear that amphibians are susceptible to a variety of environmental threats, including habitat loss, ozone depletion, acid rain, water pollution, fungal infections, and introduced aquatic predators.

To better understand this decline, biologists worldwide have been focusing their efforts and sharing data about amphibian populations. One amphibian-monitoring program covers all of North America.

# Groups of Amphibians

The three orders of amphibians include more than 6000 species, roughly 5000 of which are frogs and toads.

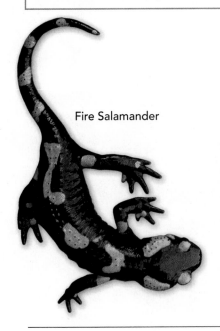

Fire Salamander

## URODELA: Salamanders and newts

Salamanders and newts have long bodies and tails. Most also have four legs. All are carnivores. Adults usually live in moist woods, where they tunnel under rocks and rotting logs. Some salamanders, such as the mud puppy, keep their gills as adults and live in water all their lives. Examples: barred tiger salamander, red eft

American Toad

## ANURA: Frogs and toads

Adult frogs and toads are amphibians without tails that can jump. Frogs tend to have long legs and make long jumps, whereas toads have shorter legs that limit them to shorter hops. Frogs are generally more dependent on bodies of fresh water than toads, which may live in moist woods or even deserts. Examples: treefrogs, leopard frog, American toad, spadefoot toad

## APODA: Caecilians

The least-known and most unusual amphibians are the legless caecilians. They have tentacles, and many have fishlike scales embedded in their skin—which shows that not all amphibians fit the general definition. Caecilians live in water or burrow in moist soil or sediment, feeding on small invertebrates such as termites. Examples: ringed caecilian, yellow-striped caecilian

Ringed Caecilian

Because amphibian eggs must develop in water, most amphibians live in moist climates. Some, such as this alpine newt, live on cool, rainy mountain slopes.

Corn snakes have a variety of patterns and colors.

# Reptiles

## Key Characteristics

Living reptiles, traditionally classified in the class Reptilia, are ectothermic vertebrates with dry, scaly skin; lungs; and amniotic eggs. Modern evolutionary classification now recognizes a larger clade Reptilia that includes living reptiles, extinct dinosaurs, and birds—the living descendants of one dinosaur group.

**Feeding and Digestion** Feeding methods vary by group; digestive systems—herbivores have long digestive systems to break down plant materials; carnivores may swallow prey whole

**Circulation** Two loops; heart with two atria and one or two ventricles

**Respiration** Spongy lungs provide large surface area for gas exchange; lungs operated by muscles and moveable ribs

**Excretion** Kidneys; urine contains ammonia or uric acid

**Response** Brain; well-developed senses including, in some species, infrared detectors that can spot warm-bodied prey in the dark

**Movement** Strong limbs (except snakes)

**Reproduction** Internal fertilization via cloaca; amniotic egg with leathery shell

## Eco•Alert

## Calling Doctor 'Gator!

You might think of alligators mostly as killing machines, but their blood may soon provide medicines that can save lives. An alligator's immune system works quite differently from our own. Proteins in their white blood cells can kill multidrug resistant bacteria, disease-causing yeasts, and even HIV. Remarkably, these proteins work against pathogens to which the animals have never been exposed. Researchers are currently sequencing the genes for these proteins and hope to develop them into human medicines in the near future.

## Groups of Reptiles

There are nearly 9000 species of reptiles (not including birds).

### SQUAMATA: Lizards, snakes, and relatives

There are more than 8000 species of lizards and snakes. Most lizards have legs, clawed toes, and external ears. Some lizards have evolved highly specialized structures, such as glands in the lower jaw that produce venom. Snakes are legless; they have lost both pairs of legs through evolution. Examples: iguanas, milk snake, coral snake

Leopard Gecko

Leopard Tortoise

### TESTUDINE: Turtles and tortoises

Turtles and tortoises have a shell built into their skeleton. Most can pull their heads and legs into the shell for protection. Instead of teeth, these reptiles have hornlike ridges covering their jaws equipped with sharp beaklike tips. Strong limbs can lift their body off the ground when walking or, in the case of sea turtles, can drag their body across a sandy shore to lay eggs. Examples: snapping turtles, green sea turtles, Galápagos tortoise

### SPHENODONTA: Tuataras

The tuatara, found only on a few small islands off the coast of New Zealand, is the only living member of this group. Tuataras resemble lizards in some ways, but they lack external ears and retain primitive scales.

Tuatara

### ARCHOSAURS: Crocodilians; pterosaurs and dinosaurs (extinct); and birds

This clade includes some of the most spectacular animals that have ever lived. The extinct dinosaurs and pterosaurs (flying reptiles), whose adaptive radiations produced some of the largest animals ever to walk Earth or fly above it, are the closest relatives of birds. Living crocodilians are short-legged and have long and typically broad snouts. They are fierce carnivorous predators, but the females are attentive mothers. Crocodilians live only in regions where the climate remains warm year-round. We discuss birds separately. Examples: extinct types: *Tyrannosaurus*, *Pteranodon*; living types: alligators, crocodiles, caimans, and birds (see following pages)

Spectacled Caiman

# Birds

Today, only birds have feathers. These delicate, intricately interlocking and beautiful structures keep birds warm and cool and enable most to fly.

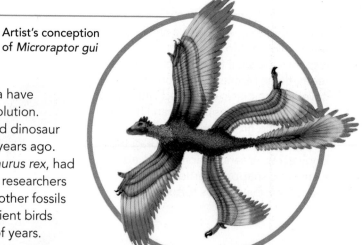

Great Gray Owl

## Key Characteristics

Birds, once placed in a class of their own, are now recognized as endothermic reptiles with feathers and hard-shelled, amniotic eggs that are descended from dinosaurs. Birds have two scaly legs and front limbs modified into wings, which enable most species to fly.

**Feeding and Digestion**  No teeth; bills adapted to widely varied foods, including insects, seeds, fruits, nectar, fish, meat; organs of the digestive system include crop, gizzard, cloaca

**Circulation**  Two loops with four-chambered heart; separation of oxygen-rich and oxygen-poor blood

**Respiration**  Constant, one-way flow of air through lungs and air sacs increases the efficiency of gas exchange and supports high metabolic rate

**Excretion**  Kidneys remove nitrogenous wastes from blood, converting them to uric acid, which is excreted through cloaca.

**Response**  Brain with large optic lobes and enlarged cerebellum; highly evolved sense organs including, in some species, eyes that can see ultraviolet light

**Movement**  Skeleton made up of lightweight, hollow bones with internal struts for strength; powerful muscles; most fly

**Reproduction**  Internal fertilization via cloaca; amniotic egg with hard, brittle shell; depending on species, newly hatched young may be precocial—downy-feathered chicks able to move around and feed themselves, or altricial—bare-skinned and totally dependent on their parents

## A Look Back in Time

Artist's conception of *Microraptor gui*

### Birds of a Feather

Fossils recently discovered in lake beds in China have greatly expanded our understanding of bird evolution. One exciting discovery was that of a four-winged dinosaur named *Microraptor gui* from about 125 million years ago. *Microraptor gui*, which was related to *Tyrannosaurus rex*, had feathers on both its wings and its legs, so some researchers hypothesize that it flew like a biplane! This and other fossils show that several lineages of dinosaurs and ancient birds evolved various kinds of feathers over millions of years.

# Groups of Birds

Evolutionary classification of living birds is still a work in progress, as different techniques and analyses produce different results. There are about 10,000 species. The groups described below illustrate some of the diversity of birds.

Ostrich

## PALEOGNATHAE: Ostriches, emus, kiwis, and relatives

This group represents an early branch of the bird family tree that is separate from all other living birds. This clade includes the largest birds alive today. Ostriches can be 2.5 meters tall and weigh 130 kilograms! Kiwis, however, are only about the size of chickens. Roughly a dozen living species are scattered throughout the Southern Hemisphere. All are flightless, but the larger species can run very fast. They generally eat a variety of plant material, insects, and other small invertebrates. Examples: ostrich, emus, brown kiwi, greater rhea, dwarf cassowary

## SPHENISCIDAE: Penguins

These flightless birds of the Southern Hemisphere are adapted to extreme cold and hunting in water. Though they cannot fly, they use their wings as flippers when they swim. Penguins have more feathers per square centimeter than any other bird; this density allows them to repel water and conserve heat effectively. Some species form large colonies. Examples: emperor penguin, chinstrap penguin, king penguin

King Penguins

Redhead

## ANATIDAE: Ducks, geese, and swans

These birds spend much of their time feeding in bodies of water. Webbed feet enable them to paddle efficiently across the surface of the water. Most fly well, however, and many species migrate thousands of kilometers between breeding and resting locations. Examples: redhead, Ross's goose, trumpeter swan

## FALCONIDAE AND ACCIPITRIDAE:
## Falcons, eagles, and hawks

These fierce predators, often called raptors, typically have powerful hooked bills, large wingspans, and sharp talons. Raptors have powerful flight muscles and keen eyesight, enabling them to see prey at a distance. Examples: Eurasian kestrel, golden eagle, Galápagos hawk

Ferruginous Hawk

## PICIDAE AND RAMPHASTIDAE:
## Woodpeckers and toucans

Woodpeckers are tree-dwelling birds with two toes in front and two in back. (Most birds have three in front and one in back; the two-and-two arrangement makes moving up and down tree trunks easier.) Woodpeckers are typically carnivores that eat insects and their larvae. Toucans usually use their huge, often colorful bills to eat fruit. Examples: black woodpecker, keel-billed toucan

Great-Spotted
Woodpecker

Keel-Billed Toucan

## PASSERIFORMES: Passerines

Also called perching birds, passerines constitute by far the largest and most diverse group of birds, with about 5000 species. Most are songbirds. Examples: flycatchers, mockingbirds, cardinals, crows, chickadees, and finches

Hooded Warbler

Scarlet Tanager

Blue Grosbeak

Lark Sparrow

Great Crested Flycatcher

Mammals provide intensive care to their young. Meerkets are often seen in groups. Multiple families work together to forage for food.

# Mammals

## Key Characteristics

Mammals are endothermic vertebrates with hair and with mammary glands that produce milk to nourish their young.

**Feeding and Digestion** Diet varies with group; foods range from seeds, fruits, and leaves to insects, fish, meat, and even blood; teeth, jaws, and digestive organs are adapted to diet

**Circulation** Two loops; four-chambered heart; separation of oxygen-rich and oxygen-poor blood

**Respiration** Lungs controlled by two sets of muscles

**Excretion** Highly evolved kidneys filter urea from blood and produce urine.

**Response** Most highly evolved brain of all animals; keen senses

**Movement** Flexible backbone; variations in limb bones and muscles enable wide range of movement across groups: from burrowing and crawling to walking, running, hopping, and flying

**Reproduction** Internal fertilization; developmental process varies with group (monotreme, marsupial, placental)

# Groups of Mammals

The three living groups of mammals are the monotremes, the marsupials, and the placentals. There are about 5000 species of mammals, usually divided into about 26 orders, most of which are placentals. There is only one order of monotremes.

Short-Beaked Echidna

## MONOTREMATA: Monotremes

Monotremes—egg-laying mammals—share two important characteristics with reptiles. First, the digestive, reproductive, and urinary systems of monotremes all open into a cloaca similar to that of reptiles. Second, monotreme development is similar to that of reptiles. Like a reptile, a female monotreme lays soft-shelled eggs incubated outside her body. The eggs hatch in about ten days. Unlike reptiles, however, young monotremes are nourished by mother's milk, which they lick from pores on the surface of her abdomen. Only five monotreme species exist today, all in Australia and New Guinea. Examples: duckbill platypus, echidnas

## MARSUPIALIA: Marsupials

Marsupials bear live young at an extremely early stage of development. A fertilized egg develops into an embryo inside the mother's reproductive tract. The embryo is then "born" at what would be an embryonic stage for most other mammals. It crawls across its mother's fur and attaches to a nipple that, in most species, is located in a pouch called the marsupium. The embryo spends several months attached to the nipple. It continues to nurse until it can survive on its own. Examples: kangaroos, wallabies, wombats, opossums

Wombat

Did You Know?

# Platypus: Mix-and-Match Genome

The duckbill platypus has such an odd mix of reptilian and mammalian features that some scientists thought the first specimens were hoaxes produced by sticking parts of different animals together! Recent genome studies have revealed an equally odd mix of reptilian and mammalian genes. Genes for reptile-like vision, the production of egg yolk, and the production of venom link the platypus to reptiles. Genes for the production of milk link it to other mammals. The evidence provides confirmation that this monotreme represents a truly ancient lineage, one from the time close to that at which mammals branched off from reptiles.

# Animals

## PLACENTALIA: Placental Mammals

Placental mammals are the mammals with which you are most familiar. This group gets its name from a structure called the placenta, which is formed when the embryo's tissues join with tissues within the mother's body. Nutrients, gases, and wastes are exchanged between embryo and mother through the placenta. Development may take as little as a few weeks (mice), to as long as two years (elephants). After birth, most placental mammals care for their young and provide them with nourishment by nursing. Examples: mice, cats, dogs, seals, whales, elephants, humans

### Chiroptera: Bats

These are the only mammals capable of true flight. There are more than 900 species of bats! They eat mostly insects or fruit and nectar, although a few species feed on the blood of other vertebrates. Examples: fruit bats, little brown myotis, vampire bat

Lioness attacking Greater Kudu

Epauletted Bat, roosting

### Carnivora: Carnivores

Many members of this group, such as tigers and hyenas, chase or stalk prey by running or pouncing, and then kill with sharp teeth and claws. Dogs, bears, and other members of this group may eat plants as well as meat. Examples: dogs, cats, skunks, seals, bears

### Sirenia: Sirenians

Sirenians are herbivores that live in rivers, bays, and warm coastal waters scattered throughout the world. These large, slow-moving mammals lead fully aquatic lives. Examples: manatees, dugongs

Manatee mother and nursing calf

Four-Toed Hedgehog mother and baby

### Insectivora: Insectivores

These insect eaters have long, narrow snouts and sharp claws that are well suited for digging. Examples: shrews, moles, hedgehogs

## Perissodactyla: Hoofed, odd-toed mammals

This group is made up of hoofed animals with an odd number of toes on each foot. Like artiodactyls, this group contains mostly large, grazing animals. Examples: horses, zebras, rhinoceroses

Tapir hoof

Central American Tapir

## Artiodactyla: Hoofed, even-toed mammals

These large, grazing, hoofed mammals have an even number of toes on each foot. Examples: cattle, sheep, pigs, hippopotami

Giraffe Hoof

Angolan Giraffes

## Rodentia: Rodents

Rodents have a single pair of long, curved incisor teeth in both their upper and lower jaws, used for gnawing wood and other tough plant material. Examples: rats, squirrels, porcupines

Marmot

## Cetacea: Cetaceans

Like sirenians, cetaceans—the group that includes whales and dolphins—are adapted to underwater life, yet must come to the surface to breathe. Most cetaceans live and breed in the ocean. Examples: whales, dolphins

Atlantic Spotted Dolphin

# Animals

European Hare

## Lagomorpha: Rabbit, hares, and pikas

Lagomorphs are entirely herbivorous. They differ from rodents by having two pairs of incisors in the upper jaw. Most lagomorphs have hind legs that are adapted for leaping.

Tamandua

## Xenarthra: Edentates

The word *edentate* means "toothless," which refers to the fact that some members of this group (sloths and anteaters) have simple teeth without enamel or no teeth at all. Armadillos, however, have more teeth than most other mammals! Examples: sloths, anteaters, armadillos

## Proboscidea: Elephants

These are the mammals with trunks. Some time ago, this group went through an extensive adaptive radiation that produced many species, including mastodons and mammoths, which are now extinct. Only two species, the Asian elephant and the African elephant, survive today.

Asian Elephant and calf

## Primates: Lemurs, monkeys, apes, humans, and relatives

Members of this group are closely related to ancient insectivores but have a highly developed cerebrum and complex behaviors.

Sifaka

Tarsier

Langur

Baboon and baby

Orangutan

Gorilla

Chimpanzee

# LAB SKILLS HANDBOOK

## Safety Symbols

These symbols appear in laboratory activities to alert you to possible dangers and to remind you to work carefully.

**Safety Goggles** Always wear safety goggles to protect your eyes during any activity involving chemicals, flames or heating, or the possibility of flying objects, particles, or substances.

**Lab Apron** Wear a laboratory apron to protect your skin and clothing from injury.

**Plastic Gloves** Wear disposable plastic gloves to protect yourself from contact with chemicals or organisms that could be harmful. Keep your hands away from your face, and dispose of the gloves according to your teacher's instructions at the end of the activity.

**Breakage** Handle breakable materials such as thermometers and glassware with care. Do not touch broken glass.

**Heat-Resistant Gloves** Use an oven mitt or other hand protection when handling hot materials. Hot plates, hot water, and glassware can cause burns. Never touch hot objects with your bare hands.

**Heating** Use a clamp or tongs to hold hot objects. Do not touch hot objects with your bare hands.

**Sharp Object** Scissors, scalpels, pins, and knives are sharp. They can cut or puncture your skin. Always direct sharp edges and points away from yourself and others. Use sharp instruments only as directed.

**Electric Shock** Avoid the possibility of electric shock. Never use electrical equipment around water or when the equipment or your hands are wet. Be sure cords are untangled and cannot trip anyone. Disconnect equipment when it is not in use.

**Corrosive Chemical** This symbol indicates the presence of an acid or other corrosive chemical. Avoid getting the chemical on your skin or clothing, or in your eyes. Do not inhale the vapors. Wash your hands when you are finished with the activity.

**Poison** Do not let any poisonous chemical get on your skin, and do not inhale its vapor. Wash your hands when you are finished with the activity.

**Flames** Tie back loose hair and clothing, and put on safety goggles before working with fire. Follow instructions from your teacher about lighting and extinguishing flames.

**No Flames** Flammable materials may be present. Make sure there are no flames, sparks, or exposed sources of heat present.

**Fumes** Poisonous or unpleasant vapors may be produced. Work in a ventilated area or, if available, in a fume hood. Avoid inhaling a vapor directly. Test an odor only when directed to do so by your teacher, using a wafting motion to direct the vapor toward your nose.

**Physical Safety** This activity involves physical movement. Use caution to avoid injuring yourself or others. Follow instructions from your teacher. Alert your teacher if there is any reason that you should not participate in the activity.

**Animal Safety** Treat live animals with care to avoid injuring the animals or yourself. Working with animal parts or preserved animals may also require caution. Wash your hands when you are finished with the activity.

**Plant Safety** Handle plants only as your teacher directs. If you are allergic to any plants used in an activity, tell your teacher before the activity begins. Avoid touching poisonous plants and plants with thorns.

**Disposal** Chemicals and other materials used in the activity must be disposed of safely. Follow the instructions from your teacher.

**Hand Washing** Wash your hands thoroughly when finished with the activity. Use soap and warm water. Lather both sides of your hands and between your fingers. Rinse well.

**General Safety Awareness** You may see this symbol when none of the symbols described earlier applies. In this case, follow the specific instructions provided. You may also see this symbol when you are asked to design your own experiment. Do not start your experiment until your teacher has approved your plan.

# Science Safety Rules

Working in the laboratory can be an exciting experience, but it can also be dangerous if proper safety rules are not followed at all times. To prepare yourself for a safe year in the laboratory, read the following safety rules. Make sure that you understand each rule. Ask your teacher to explain any rules you don't understand.

## Dress Code

1. Many materials in the laboratory can cause eye injury. To protect yourself from possible injury, wear safety goggles whenever you are working with chemicals, burners, or any substance that might get into your eyes. Avoid wearing contact lenses in the laboratory. Tell your teacher if you need to wear contact lenses to see clearly, and ask if there are any safety precautions you should observe.

2. Wear a laboratory apron or coat whenever you are working with chemicals or heated substances.

3. Tie back long hair to keep it away from any chemicals, burners, candles, or other laboratory equipment.

4. Before working in the laboratory, remove or tie back any article of clothing or jewelry that can hang down and touch chemicals and flames.

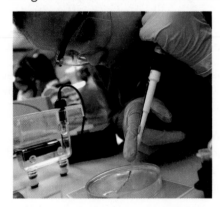

## General Safety Rules and First Aid

5. Read all directions for an experiment several times. Follow the directions exactly as they are written. If you are in doubt about any part of the experiment, ask your teacher for assistance.

6. Never perform investigations your teacher has not authorized. Do not use any equipment unless your teacher is in the lab.

7. Never handle equipment unless you have specific permission.

8. Take care not to spill any material in the laboratory. If spills occur, ask your teacher immediately about the proper cleanup procedure. Never pour chemicals or other substances into the sink or trash container.

9. Never eat or drink in, or bring food into, the laboratory.

10. Immediately report all accidents, no matter how minor, to your teacher.

11. Learn what to do in case of specific accidents, such as getting acid in your eyes or on your skin. (Rinse acids off your body with lots of water.)

12. Be aware of the location of the first-aid kit. Your teacher should administer any required first aid due to injury. Your teacher may send you to the school nurse or call a physician.

13. Know where and how to report an accident or fire. Find out the location of the fire extinguisher, fire alarm, and phone. Report any fires to your teacher at once.

## Heating and Fire Safety

14. Never use a heat source such as a candle or burner without wearing safety goggles.

15. Never heat a chemical you are not instructed to theat. A chemical that is harmless when cool can be dangerous when heated.

16. Maintain a clean work area and keep all materials away from flames. Be sure that there are no open containers of flammable liquids in the laboratory when flames are being used.

17. Never reach across a flame.

18. Make sure you know how to light a Bunsen burner. (Your teacher will demonstrate the proper procedure for lighting a burner.) If the flame leaps out of a burner toward you, turn the gas off immediately. Do not touch the burner. It may be hot. Never leave a lighted burner unattended!

19. When you are heating a test tube or bottle, point the opening away from yourself and others. Chemicals can splash or boil out of a heated test tube.

20. Never heat a closed container. The expanding hot air, vapors, or other gases inside may blow the container apart, causing it to injure you or others.

21. Never pick up a container that has been heated without first holding the back of your hand near it. If you can feel the heat on the back of your hand, the container may be too hot to handle. Use a clamp or tongs when handling hot containers or wear heat-resistant gloves if appropriate.

## Using Chemicals Safely

22. Never mix chemicals for "the fun of it." You might produce a dangerous, possibly explosive substance.

23. Many chemicals are poisonous. Never touch, taste, or smell a chemical that you do not know for certain is harmless. If you are instructed to smell fumes in an experiment, gently wave your hand over the opening of the container and direct the fumes toward your nose. Do not inhale the fumes directly from the container.

24. Use only those chemicals needed in the investigation. Keep all container lids closed when a chemical is not being used. Notify your teacher whenever chemicals are spilled.

25. Dispose of all chemicals as instructed by your teacher. To avoid contamination, never return chemicals to their original containers.

26. Be extra careful when working with acids or bases. Pour such chemicals from one container to another over the sink, not over your work area.

27. When diluting an acid, pour the acid into water. Never pour water into the acid.

28. If any acids or bases get on your skin or clothing, rinse them with water. Immediately notify your teacher of any acid or base spill.

## Using Glassware Safely

29. Never heat glassware that is not thoroughly dry. Use a wire screen to protect glassware from any flame.

30. Keep in mind that hot glassware will not appear hot. Never pick up glassware without first checking to see if it is hot.

31. Never use broken or chipped glassware. If glassware breaks, notify your teacher and dispose of the glassware in the proper trash container.

32. Never eat or drink from laboratory glassware. Thoroughly clean glassware before putting it away.

## Using Sharp Instruments

33. Handle scalpels or razor blades with extreme care. Never cut material toward you; cut away from you.

34. Notify your teacher immediately if you cut yourself in the laboratory.

## Working With Live Organisms

35. No experiments that will cause pain, discomfort, or harm to animals should be performed anywhere.

36. Your teacher will instruct you how to handle each species that is brought into the classroom. Animals should be handled only if necessary. Special handling is required if an animal is excited or frightened, pregnant, feeding, or with its young.

37. Clean your hands thoroughly after handling any organisms or materials, including animals or cages containing animals.

## End-of-Experiment Rules

38. When an experiment is completed, clean up your work area and return all equipment to its proper place.

39. Wash your hands with soap and warm water before and after every experiment.

40. Turn off all burners before leaving the laboratory. Check that the gas line leading to the burner is off as well.

## Use of the Microscope

The microscope used in most biology classes, the compound microscope, contains a combination of lenses. The eyepiece lens is located in the top portion of the microscope. This lens usually has a magnification of 10x. Other lenses, called objective lenses, are at the bottom of the body tube on the revolving nosepiece. By rotating the nosepiece, you can select the objective through which you will view your specimen.

The shortest objective is a low-power magnifier, usually 10x. The longer ones are of high power, usually up to 40x or 43x. The magnification is marked on the objective. To determine the total magnification, multiply the magnifying power of the eyepiece by the magnifying power of the objective. For example, with a 10x eyepiece and a 40x objective, the total magnification is 10 × 40 = 400x.

Learning the name, function, and location of each of the microscope's parts is necessary for proper use. Use the following procedures when working with the microscope.

1. Carry the microscope by placing one hand beneath the base and grasping the arm of the microscope with the other hand.

2. Gently place the microscope on the lab table with the arm facing you. The microscope's base should be resting evenly on the table, approximately 10 cm from the table's edge.

3. Raise the body tube by turning the coarse adjustment knob until the objective lens is about 2 cm above the opening of the stage.

4. Rotate the nosepiece so that the low-power objective (10x) is directly in line with the body tube. A click indicates that the lens is in line with the opening of the stage.

5. Look through the eyepiece and switch on the lamp or adjust the mirror so that a circle of light can be seen. This is the field of view. Moving the lever of the diaphragm permits a greater or smaller amount of light to come through the opening of the stage.

6. Place a prepared slide on the stage so that the specimen is over the center of the opening. Use the stage clips to hold the slide in place.

7. Look at the microscope from the side. Carefully turn the coarse adjustment knob to lower the body tube until the low-power objective almost touches the slide or until the body tube can no longer be moved. Do not allow the objective to touch the slide.

8. Look through the eyepiece and observe the specimen. If the field of view is out of focus, use the coarse adjustment knob to raise the body tube while looking through the eyepiece. **CAUTION:** *To prevent damage to the slide and the objective, do not lower the body tube using the coarse adjustment while looking through the eyepiece.* Focus the image as best you can with the coarse adjustment knob. Then, use the fine adjustment knob to focus the image more sharply. Keep both eyes open when viewing a specimen. This helps prevent eyestrain.

1. **Eyepiece:** Contains a magnifying lens.
2. **Arm:** Supports the body tube.
3. **Low-power objective:** Provides a magnification of 10×.
4. **Stage:** Supports the slide being observed.
5. **Opening of the stage:** Permits light to pass up to the eyepiece.
6. **Fine adjustment knob:** Moves the body tube slightly to adjust the image.
7. **Coarse adjustment knob:** Moves the body tube to focus the image.
8. **Base:** Supports the microscope.
9. **Illuminator:** Produces light or reflects light up toward the eyepiece.
10. **Diaphragm:** Regulates the amount of light passing up toward the eyepiece.
11. **Stageclips:** Hold the slide in place.
12. **High-power objective:** Provides a magnification of 40×.
13. **Nosepiece:** Holds the objectives and can be rotated to change the magnification.
14. **Body tube:** Maintains the proper distance between the eyepiece and the objectives.

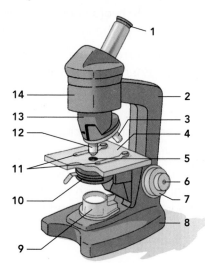

9. Adjust the lever of the diaphragm to allow the right amount of light to enter.

10. To change the magnification, rotate the nosepiece until the desired objective is in line with the body tube and clicks into place.

11. Look through the eyepiece and use the fine adjustment knob to bring the image into focus.

12. After every use, remove the slide. Return the low-power objective into place in line with the body tube. Clean the stage of the microscope and the lenses with lens paper. Do not use other types of paper to clean the lenses; they may scratch the lenses.

## Preparing a Wet-Mount Slide

1. Obtain a clean microscope slide and a coverslip. A coverslip is very thin, permitting the objective lens to be lowered very close to the specimen.

2. Place the specimen in the middle of the microscope slide. The specimen must be thin enough for light to pass through it.

3. Using a dropper pipette, place a drop of water on the specimen.

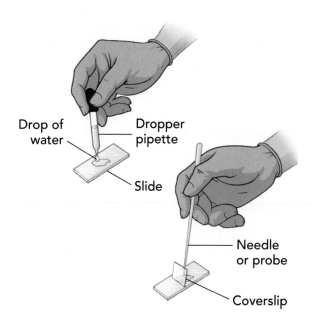

Drop of water — Dropper pipette — Slide — Needle or probe — Coverslip

4. Lower one edge of the coverslip so that it touches the side of the drop of water at about a 45° angle. The water will spread evenly along the edge of the coverslip. Using a dissecting needle or probe, slowly lower the coverslip over the specimen and water as shown in the drawing. Try not to trap any air bubbles under the coverslip. If air bubbles are present, gently tap the surface of the coverslip over the air bubble with a pencil eraser.

5. Remove any excess water around the edge of the coverslip with a paper towel. If the specimen begins to dry out, add a drop of water at the edge of the coverslip.

## Staining Techniques

1. Obtain a clean microscope slide and coverslip.

2. Place the specimen in the middle of the microscope slide.

3. Using a dropper pipette, place a drop of water on the specimen. Place the coverslip so that its edge touches the drop of water at a 45° angle. After the water spreads along the edge of the coverslip, use a dissecting needle or probe to lower the coverslip over the specimen.

4. Add a drop of stain at the edge of the coverslip. Using forceps, touch a small piece of lens paper or paper towel to the opposite edge of the coverslip, as shown in the drawing. The paper causes the stain to be drawn under the coverslip and to stain the cells in the specimen.

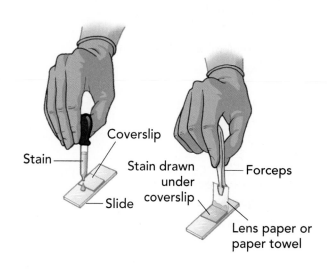

Stain — Coverslip — Slide — Stain drawn under coverslip — Forceps — Lens paper or paper towel

## The Metric System

SI (*Système International d'Unités*) is a revised version of the metric system, which was originally developed in France in 1791. SI units of measurement are used by scientists throughout the world. The system is based on units of 10. Each unit is 10 times larger or 10 times smaller than the next unit. The table lists the prefixes used to name the most common SI units.

## Common SI Prefixes

| Prefix | Symbol | Meaning |
|--------|--------|---------|
| kilo- | k | 1000 |
| hecto- | h | 100 |
| deka- | da | 10 |
| deci- | d | 0.1 (one tenth) |
| centi- | c | 0.01 (one hundredth) |
| milli- | m | 0.001 (one thousandth) |

## Common Metric Units

### Length

For measuring length, or distance from one point to another, the unit of measure is a meter (m). A meter is slightly longer than a yard.

**Useful equivalents:**

1 kilometer (km) = 1000 ($10^3$) meters (m)
1 meter (m) = 100 ($10^2$) centimeters (cm)
1 meter (m) = 1000 millimeters (mm)
1 centimeter (cm) = 0.01 ($10^{-2}$) m
1 millimeter (mm) = 0.001 ($10^{-3}$) meter

**Metric to English conversions:**

1 km = 0.62 miles
1 m = 1.09 yards
1 m = 3.28 feet
1 m = 39.37 inches
1 cm = 0.394 inch
1 mm = 0.039 inch

**English to metric conversions:**

1 mile = 1.61 km
1 yard = 0.914 m
1 foot = 0.305 m
1 foot = 30.5 cm
1 inch = 2.54 cm

### Area

The amount of space inside a boundary of an object is its area.

**Useful equivalents:**

1 square meter ($m^2$) = 10,000 square centimeters
1 square centimeter ($cm^2$) = 100 square millimeters

**Metric to English conversions:**

1 $m^2$ = 1.1960 square yards
1 $m^2$ = 10.764 square feet
1 $cm^2$ = 0.155 square inch

**English to metric conversions:**

1 square yard = 0.8361 $m^2$
1 square foot = 0.0929 $m^2$
1 square inch = 6.4516 $cm^2$

### Volume

For measuring the volume of a liquid, or the amount of space an object takes up, the unit of measure is a liter (L). A liter is slightly more than a quart.

**Useful equivalents:**

1 liter = 1000 milliliters (mL)
1 kiloliter (kL) = 1000 liter
1 mL = 0.001 liter
1 mL = 1 cubic centimeter ($cm^3$)

**Metric to English conversions:**

1 kL = 264.17 gallons
1 L = 0.264 gallons
1 L = 1.057 quarts

**English to metric conversions:**

1 gallon = 3.785 L
1 quart = 0.946 L
1 quart = 946 mL
1 pint = 473 mL
1 fluid ounce = 29.57 mL

## Mass

For measuring the mass, or the amount of matter in an object, the unit of measure is the gram (g). A paper clip has a mass equal to about one gram.

### Useful equivalents:

1 metric ton (t) = 1000 kilograms
1 kilogram (kg) = 1000 grams (g)
1 gram (g) = 1000 milligrams
1 milligram (mg) = 0.001 gram

### Metric to English conversions:

1 t = 1.103 ton
1 kg = 2.205 pounds
1 g = 0.0353 ounce

### English to metric conversions:

1 ton = 0.907 t
1 pound = 0.4536 kg
1 ounce = 28.35 g

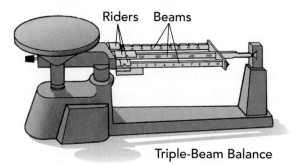

Riders  Beams

Triple-Beam Balance

## Temperature

To measure the hotness or coldness of an item, or its temperature, you use the unit degrees. The freezing point of water is 0°C (Celsius). The boiling point of water is 100°C.

### Metric to English conversion:

$°C = 5/9 (°F - 32)$

### English to metric conversion:

$°F = 9/5°C + 32$

As part of your study of biology, you will carry out many scientific investigations in the laboratory or in the field. The goal of these experiments is not to make startling discoveries, but rather to help you gain an understanding of how knowledge is obtained in science. You will find that there are certain general approaches or steps that are used in most scientific investigations. These steps are sometimes called the scientific method. But there is not just one scientific method. In fact, scientists may use a variety of approaches depending on the type of investigation.

Scientists and engineers use similar processes, although their end goals are a bit different. A scientist generally designs and performs investigations in order to find the answer to a question. An engineer designs and performs investigations in order to solve a problem.

The eight practices described in this handbook are essential to your development as a young scientist or engineer. Each investigation you perform will not require that you use all eight practices, and in some ways many of these practices overlap. Read on to explore and try the following practices:

1. Asking questions (for science) and defining problems (for engineering)

2. Developing and using models

3. Planning and carrying out investigations

4. Analyzing and interpreting data

5. Using mathematics and computational thinking

6. Constructing explanations (for science) and designing solutions (for engineering)

7. Engaging in argument from evidence

8. Obtaining, evaluating, and communicating information

## Asking Questions and Defining Problems

### Asking Questions

Scientific inquiry usually begins with asking a question about an observation. Questions can also arise from experiences and inferences. Your curiosity plays a role, too. To serve as the basis of a scientific investigation, a question must be clearly stated. Because others may have asked similar questions, you should do research to find what information is already known about the topic before you go on with your investigation.

Scientific questions are questions about the natural world. The answers to scientific questions are found by observing, measuring, or investigating. Questions based on an opinion or on personal values are not scientific questions. Scientific questions can often be stated very simply. Consider the question "Why are leaves green?" This is a question that might have occurred to anyone who noticed that, although plants differ in many ways, the leaves are all similar in color. Consider this scenario that sparked an investigation.

*A gardener collected seeds from a favorite plant at the end of the summer, stored them indoors for the winter, and then planted them the following spring. None of the stored seeds developed into plants, yet uncollected seeds from the original plant germinated in the normal way. The gardener wondered: Why didn't the collected seeds germinate?*

An experiment may have its beginning when someone asks a specific question or wants to solve a particular problem. Sometimes the original question leads directly to an experiment, but often researchers must restate the problem before they can design an appropriate experiment. The gardener's question about the seeds, for example, is too broad to be tested by an experiment, because there are so many possible answers. To narrow the topic, the gardener might think about related questions: Were the seeds I collected different from the uncollected seeds? Did I try to germinate them in poor soil or with insufficient light or water? Did storing the seeds indoors ruin them in some way?

## Practice Your Skills

Science is an organized way of gathering and analyzing evidence about the natural world. Often, the first step in a scientific investigation is to ask questions. People ask questions every day, but not every question is a scientific question. Scientific questions must be answerable using scientific methods. These questions are used to generate hypotheses—scientific explanations for observations that can be tested.

Read each of the following questions.

a. What will happen when water is poured into a beaker of strong acid?

b. Which is prettier, a tulip or a rose?

c. What is the effect of varying road surfaces on acceleration?

d. Which is a better good luck charm, a four-leaf clover or a horseshoe?

e. Why won't my car start this morning?

f. How does the composition of concrete affect its strength?

g. What is the meaning of life?

h. What affects whether a person prefers science or English classes?

i. Do reports of ghost sightings increase around Halloween?

j. What causes the red spot on Jupiter?

Use your understanding of science and the limitations of science to answer the following questions.

1. **Define** What is the definition of the word *science*?

2. **Identify Criteria** Using your answer above, explain your criteria for deciding which of the questions are scientific.

3. **Classify** Which of the questions are scientific questions? Which of the questions are not scientific questions?

4. **Construct an Explanation** For any of the questions you classified as unscientific, explain your reasoning.

## Defining Problems

Engineers use scientific and technological knowledge to solve practical problems. Before engineers begin designing a new product or solution, they must first identify the need they are trying to meet or the problem they want to solve. For example, suppose you are a member of a design team in a company that makes model cars. Your team has identified a need: a model car that is inexpensive and easy to assemble.

## Researching the Question or Problem

Before the question can be investigated or the problem solved, you will need to learn a lot about the question or problem. Scientists and engineers often begin by gathering information that will help them with their investigation or design development. This research may include making observations in nature or finding articles in books, in magazines, or on the Internet. It may also include talking to other scientists or engineers who are working on similar subjects. For your model car you could look at model cars that are similar to the one you want to design. You could also test some materials to see whether they would work well in a model car.

## Forming a Hypothesis

In science, after you have asked questions and done some research, you are ready to form a hypothesis. A hypothesis is a proposed explanation of observed facts or events. It is subjected to confirmation by further observation and experimentation. A hypothesis must be testable. In most cases, the vehicle for testing a hypothesis is a scientific investigation. Data from the investigation either will support the hypothesis or will not support it. If the experimental evidence does not support the hypothesis, a scientist is likely to develop and test another hypothesis.

The main purpose of a hypothesis is to express a statement that can be supported or disproved by evidence. After you've made a hypothesis, you can design an experiment to help you determine whether it is supported or not supported. You will need to design a procedure for an experiment. But often you will be asked to do experiments that have been designed for you. A hypothesis is a useful tool even when you are following a predesigned procedure. Making a hypothesis will ensure that you understand the purpose of a lab and why you will be asked to make certain types of observations.

This handbook describes the "full version" of a hypothesis, which tends to be long and full of details. Such detailed statements are essential for a scientist who is doing research. But for most of the labs in this program, it will be acceptable for you to write shorter hypotheses with fewer details.

Most experiments test the relationship between two factors. You change the independent variable. Then you observe whether the dependent variable changes in response. A useful hypothesis should state how you think the variables are related. In the full version, you must also state how the relationship will affect the results of the experiment. The following statement is a fully developed hypothesis.

*If the presence of fertilizer is related to increased algal growth, then algae that are provided with fertilizer will exhibit greater growth than algae that are not provided with fertilizer.*

Is this hypothesis useful? Yes, because it relates the use of fertilizer to the growth of algae. It also describes what results to expect if the hypothesis is correct.

### Practice Your Skills

**5.** Identify the variables in this hypothesis: *If the heart rate of* Daphnia *is related to the concentration of salt in their water, then changing the salt concentration of a Daphnia's water will cause its heart rate to change.*

Dependent variable: _____

Independent variable: _____

**6.** Rewrite this hypothesis so that it is more useful for experimental design: *Bean plants will grow more slowly when exposed to acid rain.*

# Developing and Using Models

## What is a Model?

A model is a mental or physical representation of an object, process, or event. In science, models are usually made to help people understand natural objects and processes. Models can be varied. Common types of models are drawings, maps, diagrams, analogies, three-dimensional physical models, and computer simulations. Engineers often use blueprints and prototypes to model their designs.

Mental models, such as mathematical equations, can represent some kinds of ideas or processes. For example, the equation for the surface area of a sphere can model the surface of Earth, enabling scientists to determine its size.

Before selecting the type of model you will develop or use, you need to consider the purpose of your model. For example, if your teacher asks you to produce a model that shows the structure of a human heart, you could choose to use modeling clay. But what if your teacher also asked that your model could show the function of the human heart? Modeling clay may work well to demonstrate a heart's structure, but not necessarily its function. When planning a model, ask yourself the following questions:

- What is my objective in using this model?
- Who is my audience? Am I using the model to show that I understand a structure or process, or to teach others a concept?
- What information do I need to convey in my model? Will I use words or images, or both? How much space will I need to communicate all of the information I need to communicate?
- Does my model need to be built to scale?
- What are the merits and limitations of this model? Could I overcome any limitations by choosing a different type of model?

Before presenting your model to an audience, test the model to make sure it works as you intended. Implement changes to your model based on the results of your testing.

## Types of Models

**Drawings** Drawings are an example of a two-dimensional (flat) physical model. They help scientists collect and communicate information. For some labs, you will be asked to make a drawing to record your observations or show your experimental design. If you are not used to drawing, you may not know how to begin. The following suggestions may help.

### *Example*

You need to make a drawing of a flower before you dissect it. Start by drawing the general outline of the flower. Use a pencil in case you need to make corrections.

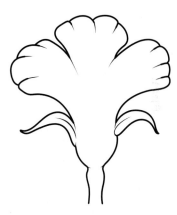

Next, add the different structures. Focus on the general shape and location of each structure.

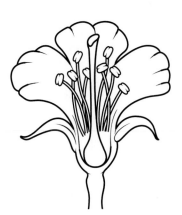

You may choose to use shading to highlight some features of your drawing. The shading in this drawing emphasizes the path that the pollen travels to reach the ovary.

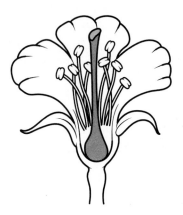

For most drawings, you will need to add labels. Print the labels and position them horizontally. Use a ruler to draw a line between the label and the structure. Avoid having one label line cross over another.

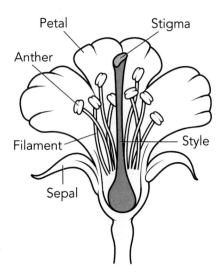

When you draw objects that you view with a microscope, use a circle to represent the field of view. Also include the magnification at which you viewed the object.

**Three-Dimensional Models**  Physical models that have depth are called three-dimensional. Common three-dimensional models include a representation of a DNA molecule and a plastic skeleton of an animal.

Physical models can be made of a huge variety of materials. Physical models can also be made "to scale," which means they are in proportion to the actual object they represent. Something very large, such as an area of land being studied, can be shown at 1/100 of its actual size. A tiny organism can be shown at 100 times its size.

Some cities refuse to approve any new buildings that could cast shadows on other buildings or perhaps a popular outdoor venue. As architects plan buildings in such locations, they use scale models that can show where a proposed building's shadow will fall at any time of day in any season of the year.

**Analogies**  Analogies can also be considered models because they use one process or object to represent another one. For example, comparing organelles in a cell to areas or machines in a factory is another way to recall and understand how a cell works. As with any model, analogies have their strengths and limitations. Discussing the strengths and limitations of an analogy can reveal your understanding of the structure, system, or process that the analogy represents.

**Computer Simulations**  Scientists may use computer simulations to model complex or large systems such as climate or the movements of tectonic plates. Simulations can allow the user to change characteristics of a system or move pieces around and see the outcome quickly rather than the hundreds, or even, millions of years it could take in real time. Or, processes that occur far too quickly for the human eye to see can be slowed and analyzed. Experiments with dangerous chemicals can be performed safely in a virtual environment. Modeling with computer simulations has become a valuable tool for professional scientists in the laboratory and amateur scientists in the classroom.

**Blueprints** During the development process, engineers often need to make technical drawings, or blueprints. With a design solution in mind, engineers will identify the materials and processes needed. They will make a sketch of their proposed solution and then make technical drawings. A technical drawing shows the dimensions of the design product and indicates the materials to be used. It contains all the information needed to build the product.

An engineering drawing is often referred to as a blueprint. The name comes from a printing process that was once used to produce many copies of a hand-drawn technical drawing. Today, engineers use computers to create technical drawings of their designs. Computers have made the job of creating technical drawings much easier. They enable the design team to view their design in three dimensions and make adjustments more quickly.

**Prototypes** A design team may choose to build a prototype of its product design. A prototype is a working model used to test a design. Prototypes are used to test the operation of a product, including how well it works, how long it lasts, and how safe it is to use. Sometimes the prototype is built as a scale model. A scale model has the same proportions as the product but is built to a different scale. Prototype testing allows the design team to identify problems with its design.

### Practice Your Skills

Answer the following questions in your notebook:

1. Find three examples of models in your classroom or in this book. Describe what each model represents and what type of model each example is.

2. Suppose you are given the opportunity to design new lockers for your school. The new lockers must be the same size as your current lockers. Draw a blueprint of your design that shows the dimensions, features, and materials included in your design. Then, describe the design features of your locker, including materials.

## Planning and Carrying Out Investigations

When you have developed a testable hypothesis, you are ready to plan an investigation. A carefully designed experiment can test a hypothesis in a reliable way, ruling out other possible explanations. All of the steps that follow are relevant to the work of scientists and engineers.

### Plan the Procedure

The procedure describes what you plan to do and identifies the data you plan to collect. When writing a procedure, you also need to plan out your variables, materials and equipment, time, and data collection methods. Your procedure needs to be thorough and concise so that others can replicate your experiment.

**Controlling Variables** As researchers design an experiment, they identify the variables, factors that can change. Some common variables include mass, volume, time, temperature, light, and the presence or absence of specific materials. An experiment involves three categories of variables: independent, dependent, and controlled.

The factor that scientists purposely change is called the independent variable. An independent variable is also known as a manipulated variable. The factor that may change because of the independent variable and that scientists want to observe is called the dependent variable. A dependent variable is also known as a responding variable. Factors that scientists purposely keep the same are called controlled variables. In your procedure, you should write a step-by-step description of how you will change the independent variable and observe the effects upon the dependent variable.

By controlling variables, researchers can conclude that the changes in the dependent variable are due exclusively to changes in the independent variable. The gardener who asked questions about why his seeds did not germinate decided to study three groups of seeds: (1) some that would be left outdoors throughout the winter, (2) some that would be brought indoors and kept at room temperature, and (3) some that would be brought indoors and kept cold. The independent variable is whether the seeds were exposed to cold conditions. The dependent variable is whether or not the seeds germinate. Among the variables that must be controlled are whether the seeds remain dry during storage, when the seeds are planted, the amount of water the seeds receive, and the type of soil used.

**Choosing Materials and Equipment** When choosing materials, follow your teacher's instructions. Your teacher may request that you use only materials that are available in the school. Your teacher may allow you to purchase new materials, but within a given budget.

As you plan and carry out investigations for this course, you will need to select appropriate scientific equipment and technology. Appropriate equipment includes safety equipment such as goggles, aprons, and gloves.

Scientific equipment and technology help you perform many different tasks. You will select equipment and technology to measure quantities such as distance, time, mass, volume, and temperature. For example, a triple-beam balance enables you to measure the mass of objects. Electronic probeware can be selected for many kinds of experiments to measure such factors as pH, moisture content, and temperature. Other instruments, such as microscopes or binoculars, help with viewing specimens or organisms in the laboratory or field.

Digital cameras, audio recorders, and video cameras can record data. Computers and calculators can be selected to perform calculations, store data, and display data in graphs, tables, and charts. Global Positioning System (GPS) devices allow you to record, store, and display specific locations on an electronic map.

As you continue with your plan, you may need to revise your materials and equipment lists. Before carrying out an investigation, check your procedure against your materials and equipment list to make sure you have accounted for everything you will need.

**Estimating Time** As you plan the investigation, consider the time you will need to complete it. An investigation that will continue for several weeks may extend past the time that your teacher would like you to devote to this one investigation.

**Collecting Data** Part of your plan should be a description of how and when you will collect data. While planning your investigation, you should consider the intervals at which you need to collect data. For example, if you need to collect data more than once a day, you might plan to do your experiment at home instead of at school. If you are performing a long-term investigation at school that requires daily data collection, consider that missing data from weekends will impact the quality of your data. Before you begin your investigation, set up data tables or spreadsheets so that you will have an organized place to record your data.

## Carrying Out an Investigation

When your plan is complete, you are ready to carry out your investigation. Following is a brief description of the steps you will likely complete during the investigation. You will find more detailed information about each step as you work through the handbook.

**Analyze and Interpret Data** Data are all of the observations and measurements made during an experiment. When the experiment is finished, the data are analyzed. Trends, or patterns, in the data can let you see if the data support your hypothesis. Data tables, charts, and graphs are good ways to record and display data in order to look for trends.

**Construct Explanations** After the data have been collected and analyzed, you need to compare your results to your hypothesis. A conclusion tells what was learned in the experiment. The conclusion tells whether or not the hypothesis was supported by the data. It may take several trials before you can construct an explanation of your results.

### Practice Your Skills

1. Choose a question from the list below as a topic for an experiment. Alternatively, pose a scientific question or identify an engineering problem of your own and obtain your teacher's approval to use that question. Remember, in one of the first steps in planning your investigation, you may need to narrow your original question. Then write a hypothesis and design an experiment to answer the question. Be sure to include all the necessary parts of an experiment, such as naming the dependent and independent variables and identifying the variables you will control. Describe how you will record your data.

a. How are bean seedlings affected by water that is polluted by detergent?

b. Does the presence of plants growing on a hillside affect the amount of soil erosion?

c. How is the germination of bean seeds affected by temperature?

# Analyzing and Interpreting Data

The observations and measurements that are made in an experiment are called data. Scientists usually record data in an orderly way. When an experiment is finished, the researcher analyzes the data for trends or patterns, often by doing calculations or making graphs, to determine whether the results support the hypothesis.

For example, after planting the seeds in the spring, the gardener counted the seeds that germinated and found these results: None of the seeds kept at room temperature germinated, 80 percent of the seeds kept in the freezer germinated, and 85 percent of the seeds left outdoors during the winter germinated. The trend was clear: The gardener's prediction appeared to be supported.

To be sure that the results of an experiment are correct, scientists review their data critically, looking for possible sources of error. Here, error refers to differences between the observed results and the true values. Experimental error can result from human mistakes or problems with equipment. It can also occur when the small group of objects studied does not accurately represent the whole group. For example, if some of the gardener's seeds had been exposed to an herbicide, the data might not reflect the true seed germination pattern.

## Tools to Organize Data

How can you make sense of the data from a science experiment or prototype test? The first step is to organize the data. When you do a lab, you may be asked to record your observations in words or drawings. You may have to make and record measurements. How you organize the data you collect can affect your ability to analyze the data, which is an important part of the experimental process. When you present data in a clear and logical way, you also make it easier for others to interpret and evaluate your results.

**Data Tables** When scientists do experiments, they typically do many trials using the same procedure. After the scientists analyze the results, they may adjust the procedure and do more trials. This process can continue for months or years, resulting in a vast amount of data. Data tables are an excellent way to organize large amounts of data.

### Example

A team of researchers collected venom from ten different species of snakes. They tested the venom to determine how toxic each sample was. They also collected data about the outcomes for people who were bitten by each type of snake. Compare the following description of the data they collected with the same data presented in a data table. In which format are the results easier to analyze?

*For the southern United States copperhead, the death rate was less than 1 percent. For the western diamondback rattlesnake, the death rate was 5–15 percent. The death rate was 5–20 percent for the eastern coral snake and the king cobra. For the Indian krait, the death rate was 77 percent. For the European viper, the death rate was 1–5 percent. The death rate was 100 percent for the bushmaster and 10–20 percent for the fer-de-lance. For both the black-necked cobra and the puff adder, the death rate was 11–40 percent.*

| Death Rates After Snake Bites | |
|---|---|
| **Type of Snake** | **Death Rate (%)** |
| Black-necked cobra | 11–40 |
| Bushmaster | 100 |
| Copperhead | <1 |
| Eastern coral snake | 5–20 |
| European viper | 1–5 |
| Fer-de-lance | 10–20 |
| Indian krait | 77 |
| King cobra | 5–20 |
| Puff adder | 11–40 |
| Rattlesnake | 5–15 |

Each column in a data table should have a head that describes the data in the column. In the table about snake bites, the column heads are the independent variable (Type of Snake) and the dependent variable (Death Rate). When the variable is a measurement, the unit of measurement, such as (cm) for length or (g) for mass, is often included with the head.

The rows in a table may be arranged by trial (Trial 1, Trial 2, and so on) or by the days on which measurements are made (Day 1, Day 3, Day 5, and so on). But sometimes the choice is less obvious.

### Practice Your Skills

Answer the following questions in your notebook:

1. How are the rows organized in the snake bite table?

2. How might you rearrange the rows to make the data easier to analyze?

**Using Data Tables** When you have a completed data table, you can apply another important scientific skill—posing questions. For example, scientists looking at the data on snake bites might wonder about the reliability of the data. They might ask questions such as, "What procedure did the researchers use to gather the data?" "How large were the samples that were used to calculate the percentages?"

Some of the ranges in the snake bite table are very broad, such as the 11–40 percent death rate for the puff adder. Perhaps data from different sources were combined. If so, think of a follow-up question that a scientist might want to ask and write it in your notebook.

## Importance of Organizing Data

Have you ever jotted down notes while working in the lab and been unable to locate the notes later? Have you found the notes but been unable to figure out what the notes referred to? Making a data table in advance helps ensure that the data you collect will not get lost and that all the data will be recorded.

For some labs in this course, a data table is provided for you to fill in. For other labs, you will be asked to construct an appropriate data table. You will need to decide how to best arrange the data in the table. Experiments often require a data table with more than two columns.

### Example

Students who were studying inherited physical traits collected data on hair color from three different classes.

| Class 1 | Class 2 | Class 3 |
|---------|---------|---------|
| Black: 2 | Black: 0 | Black: 4 |
| Blond: 3 | Blond: 7 | Blond: 12 |
| Brown: 20 | Brown: 18 | Brown: 15 |
| Red: 0 | Red: 1 | Red: 0 |

The hair-color data could be arranged in a table as follows. This arrangement draws attention to differences among the classes.

| Distribution of Hair Color by Class | | | |
|---|---|---|---|
| Hair Color | Class 1 | Class 2 | Class 3 |
| Black | 2 | 0 | 4 |
| Blond | 3 | 7 | 12 |
| Brown | 20 | 18 | 15 |
| Red | 0 | 1 | 0 |

Making a table in advance also gives you a chance to evaluate your experimental design before you begin. While constructing a data table for the study on hair color, you might be prompted to think, "How will I decide whether to classify a color as dark brown or as black?" "Will all the hair colors I observe be natural?" "Will I be able to draw any useful conclusions if I survey only three classes?"

### Practice Your Skills

**3.** The table could be constructed to focus more on hair color and less on the individual classes. The rearranged data have been entered in the following table. Copy this table into your notebook and complete the table by filling in the missing heads.

| Hair Color of Students | | | | |
|---|---|---|---|---|
| | 2 | 3 | 20 | 0 |
| | 0 | 7 | 18 | 1 |
| | 4 | 12 | 15 | 0 |
| Total | 6 | 22 | 53 | 1 |

**Using Graphs** A graph is a pictorial representation of data. Graphs are used to show a relationship between two or more factors. Plotting the data you collect on a graph may reveal a pattern that isn't obvious when data are organized in a table. Before you plot your data, you will need to decide which type of graph to use.

**Line Graphs** A line graph has one or more lines connecting a series of data points. A line graph is often the best choice for showing how an independent variable is related to a dependent variable. With a line graph, you are also able to estimate values for points that lie between or beyond the measured data points.

### Example

This line graph relates the length of a tortoise shell to the age of a tortoise. One line shows data for a tortoise that was raised in a zoo. The second line shows data collected from wild tortoises of the same species. Having the two lines on one graph makes it easier to compare the effect of a third variable—the conditions under which growth occurred.

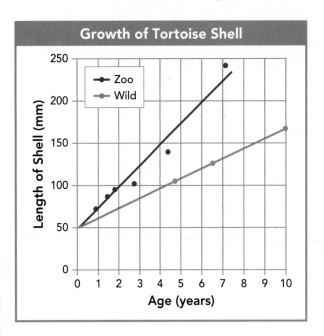

## Practice Your Skills

4. Fish "breathe" by pumping water through their mouths and over their gills, where oxygen is extracted. Use the data in the table and graph paper to make a graph that relates the temperature of the water to the breathing rate of a fish. Decide which variable is the independent variable and place it on the horizontal axis, or *x*-axis. Place the dependent variable on the vertical axis, or *y*-axis. Label the axes. Choose a scale for each axis. Consider the range of data and the number of available squares. If your scale unit is too large, your graph will be too small and difficult to read. If your scale unit is too small, some of your data will not fit on the graph. Units that are multiples of 1, 2, 5, and 10 are easiest to work with.

| Temperature (°C) | Rate (per minute) |
|---|---|
| 10 | 15 |
| 15 | 25 |
| 18 | 30 |
| 20 | 38 |
| 23 | 60 |
| 25 | 57 |
| 27 | 25 |

**Bar Graphs** You can also use a bar graph to compare data. Like a line graph, a bar graph has an *x*-axis and a *y*-axis. But instead of points, a bar graph uses a series of columns, or bars, to display data. Bar graphs are especially useful when the data are not continuous—when you cannot use the graph to estimate values that were not measured. On many bar graphs, the *x*-axis lists categories rather than a numerical scale.

## Example

A driver must be alert and able to react quickly to changing road conditions or to the actions of other drivers. The following bar graph shows how alcohol can affect a driver's ability to react. What is the relationship between the blood alcohol concentration and the reaction time?

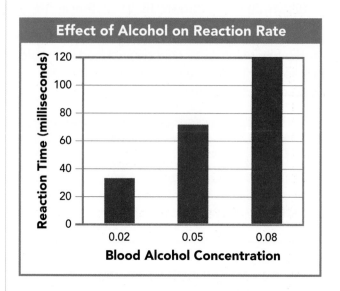

Recall that you can introduce a third variable to a line graph by adding lines. You can do something similar with the bars on a bar graph.

## Example

The following bar graph compares the fat content of butter, margarine, and olive oil. For each source, the data is divided by type of fat—saturated, unsaturated, and trans fat.

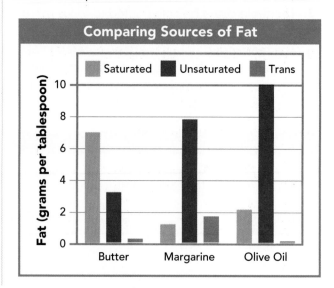

**5.** Use the following table to make a bar graph showing the percentage of students at each grade who take part in vigorous physical activity. Differentiate the male and female bars, and include a legend.

| Grade | Males | Females |
|-------|-------|---------|
| 9th | 74% | 64% |
| 10th | 71% | 58% |
| 11th | 70% | 52% |
| 12th | 63% | 49% |

## Identifying Sources of Error

Part of analyzing and interpreting data is considering sources of error. For example, density is calculated by dividing an object's mass by its volume. An error in the measurement of either mass or volume will result in the calculation of an incorrect density.

### Example

A student measured the mass of an object as 2.5 g and its volume as 2.0 cm$^3$. The actual mass of the object is 3.5 g; the actual volume is 2.0 cm$^3$. What is the effect of the measurement error on the calculation of density?

Follow these steps to determine the effect of a measurement error on calculation.

**1.** Determine the density using the student's measurements.
Density = Mass/Volume
Density = 2.5 g/2.0 cm$^3$
Density = 1.25 g/cm$^3$

**2.** Determine the density using the actual values.
Density = Mass/Volume
Density = 3.5 g/2.0 cm$^3$
Density = 1.75 g/cm$^3$

**3.** Compare the calculated and the actual values. In this case, a measurement of mass that was less than the actual value resulted in a calculated value for the density that was less than the actual density.

**Accuracy** The accuracy of a measurement is its closeness to the actual value. Measurements that are accurate are close to the actual value. Both clocks below show a time of 3:00. Suppose, though, that these clocks had not been changed to reflect Daylight Savings Time. The time shown on the clocks would be inaccurate. On the other hand, if the actual time is 3:00, these clocks would be accurate.

**Precision** Precision describes the exactness of a measurement. The clocks shown below differ in precision. The analog clock measures time to the nearest minute. The digital clock measures time to the nearest second. Time is measured more precisely by the digital clock than by the analog clock.

**Comparing Accuracy and Precision** There is a difference between accuracy and precision. Measurements can be accurate (close to the actual value) but not precise. Measurements can also be precise but not accurate. When scientific measurements are made, both accuracy and precision are important. Accurate and precise measurements result from the careful use of high-quality measuring tools.

### Practice Your Skills

**6.** The temperature at which water boils at sea level is 100°C. You use a thermometer to measure the boiling point of water at sea level five times and receive the following measurements: 97.0°C, 97.1°C, 96.9°C, 97.0°C, 96.9°C. Explain if these measurements are accurate or precise, or both.

# Using Mathematics and Computational Thinking

Scientists use math to organize, analyze, and present data. This handbook will help you review some basic algebra skills you will use in biology.

## Formulas and Equations

Formulas and equations are used in many areas of science. Both formulas and equations show the relationships between quantities. Any numerical sentence that contains at least one variable and at least one mathematical operator is called an equation. A formula is a type of equation that states the relationship between unknown quantities represented by variables. For example,

$$\text{Speed} = \text{Distance} \div \text{Time}$$

is a formula, because no matter what values are inserted, speed is always equal to distance divided by time. The relationship between the variables does not change.

### Example

Follow these steps to convert a temperature measurement of 50°F to Celsius.

1. Determine the formula that shows the relationship between these quantities.
$°F = (9/5 \times °C) + 32°F$

2. Insert values you know into the formula.
$50°F = (9/5 \times °C) + 32°F$

3. Solve the resulting equation.
$50°F - 32°F = (9/5 \times °C)$
$18°F = 9/5 \times °C$
$18°F \times 5/9 = 10°C$

## Applying Formulas and Equations

There are many applications of formulas in science. The following example uses a formula to calculate density.

### Example

Follow these steps to calculate the density of an object that has a mass of 45 g and a volume of 30 cm³.

1. Determine the formula that shows the relationship between these quantities.
Density = Mass/Volume

2. Insert values you know into the formula.
Density = 45 g/30 cm³

3. Solve the resulting equation.
Density = 1.5 g/cm³

## Mean, Median, and Mode

The mean is the average, or the sum of the data divided by the number of data items. The middle number in a set of ordered data is called the median. The mode is the number that appears most often in a set of data.

### Example

A scientist counted the number of distinct songs sung by seven different male birds and collected the following data.

| Male Bird Songs | | | | | | | |
|---|---|---|---|---|---|---|---|
| **Bird** | A | B | C | D | E | F | G |
| **Number of Songs** | 36 | 29 | 40 | 35 | 28 | 36 | 27 |

To determine the mean number of songs, find the sum of the songs sung by all the male birds and divide by the number of male birds.

Mean = 231/7 = 33 songs

To find the median number of songs, arrange the data items in numerical order and identify the number in the middle.

27  28  29  35  36  36  40

The number in the middle is 35, so the median number of songs is 35. When the number of data points is even, the median is the mean of the two middle points.

The mode is the value that appears most frequently. In the data, 36 appears twice, while every other item appears only once. Therefore, 36 is the mode. The mode is useful when you are dealing with categories of data, such as age ranges when studying a population's age distribution.

## Estimation

An estimate is a reasonable approximation of a numerical value. Estimates are made based on careful assumptions and known information. Scientists use estimates in biology for two primary reasons: when an exact count or calculation cannot be made or is impractical to make, and to make reasonable approximations of answers that will be calculated or measured later.

One method for estimation used in biology is sampling. In sampling, the number of organisms in a small area (a sample) is multiplied to estimate the number of organisms in a larger area.

### Example

Follow these steps to use sampling to estimate the total number of birds in the photo.

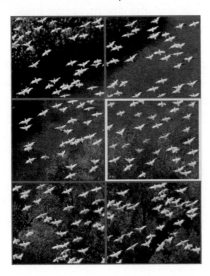

1. Count the birds in the highlighted area of the photo. In the highlighted area of the photo, there are 36 birds.

2. Determine the portion of the entire photo represented by the highlighted area. In this case, the highlighted area is 1/6 of the total area.

3. Calculate your estimate by multiplying the number of birds in the sample area by 6 (because the entire photo is 6 times as large as the sample area). A reasonable estimate of the total number of birds is 36 × 6, or 216 birds.

**HINT:** Estimates and calculated answers are rarely exactly the same. However, a large difference between an estimated answer and a calculated answer indicates there may be a problem with the estimate or calculation.

## Significant Figures

Significant figures are all of the digits that are known in a measurement, plus one additional digit, which is an estimate. In the figure on the next page, the length of a turtle's shell is being measured with a centimeter ruler. The ruler has unnumbered divisions representing millimeters. In this case, two numbers can be determined exactly: the number of centimeters and the number of millimeters. One additional digit can be estimated. So, the measurement of this turtle's shell can be recorded with three significant figures as 8.80 centimeters.

**Rules for Significant Digits** Follow these rules to determine the number of significant figures in a number.

All nonzero numbers are significant.

**Example:** 3217 has four significant digits.

Zeros are significant if
- They are between nonzero digits. Example: 509
- They follow a decimal point and a nonzero digit. Example: 7.00

Zeros are not significant if
- They follow nonzero digits in a number without a decimal. Example: 7000
- They precede nonzero digits in a number with a decimal. Example: 0.0098

**Calculating With Significant Figures** When measurements are added or subtracted, the precision of the result is determined by the precision of the least-precise measurement. The result may need to be rounded so the number of digits after the decimal is the same as the least-precise measurement.

### Example

Follow these steps to determine the correct number of significant figures when 4.51 g, 3.27 g, and 6.0 g are added together.

1. Determine which measurement is reported with the least degree of precision. In this case, the least-precise measurement, 6.0 g, has one digit after the decimal point.

**2.** The result must be rounded so that it also has one digit after the decimal point. After rounding, the result of this calculation is 13.8 g.

When measurements are multiplied or divided, the answer must have the same number of significant figures as the measurement with the fewest number of significant figures.

### *Example*

Follow these steps to determine the correct number of significant figures when 120 m is multiplied by 6.32 m.

**1.** Determine the number of significant figures in each of the measurements. In this case, the measurement 120 m has two significant figures; the measurement 6.32 m has three significant figures.

**2.** The result must be rounded to have only two significant figures. After rounding, the result of this calculation is 760 m$^2$.

## Scientific Notation

In science, measurements are often very large or very small. Using scientific notation makes these large and small numbers easier to work with.

Using scientific notation requires an understanding of exponents and bases. When a number is expressed as a base and an exponent, the base is the number that is used as a factor. The exponent tells how many times the base is multiplied by itself. For example, the number 25 can be expressed as a base and an exponent in the following way:

$$25 = 5 \times 5 = 5^2$$

In the example above, 5 is the base and 2 is the exponent. In scientific notation, the base is always the number 10. The exponent tells how many times the number 10 is multiplied by itself.

A number written in scientific notation is expressed as the product of two factors, a number between 1 and 10 and the number 10 with an exponent. For example, the number 51,000 can be expressed in scientific notation. To find the first factor, move the decimal to obtain a number between 1 and 10. In this case, the number is 5.1. The exponent can be determined by counting the number of places the decimal point was moved. The decimal point was moved four places to the left. So, 51,000 expressed in scientific notation is 5.1 × 10$^4$.

Numbers that are less than one can also be expressed in scientific notation. In the case of numbers less than one, the decimal point must be moved to the right to obtain a number between 1 and 10. For example, in the number 0.000098, the decimal point must move five places to the right to obtain the number 9.8. When the decimal point is moved to the right, the exponent is negative. So, 0.000098 expressed in scientific notation is 9.8 × 10$^{-5}$.

**Calculating With Scientific Notation** Numbers expressed in scientific notation can be used in calculations. When numbers expressed in scientific notation are added or subtracted, the first factors must be rewritten so the exponents are the same.

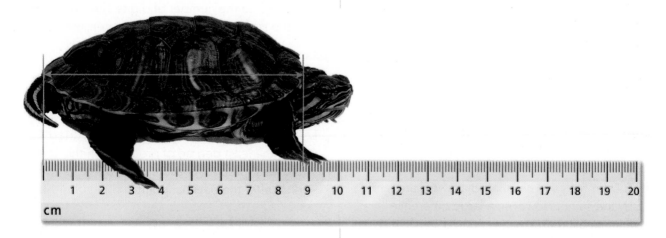

### Example

Follow these steps to add $(4.30 \times 10^4) + (2.1 \times 10^3)$.

1. Move the decimal point in one of the expressions so the exponents are the same.
$(43.0 \times 10^3) + (2.1 \times 10^3)$

2. Add the first factors, keeping the value of the exponents the same.
$(43.0 \times 10^3) + (2.1 \times 10^3) = 45.1 \times 10^3$

3. Move the decimal point so the first factor is expressed as the product of a number between and 1 and 10 and an exponent with base 10.
$45.1 \times 10^3 = 4.51 \times 10^4$

When numbers expressed in scientific notation are multiplied, the exponents are added. When numbers expressed in scientific notation are divided, the exponents are subtracted.

### Example

Use the following steps to determine the area of a rectangular field that has a length of $1.5 \times 10^3$ meters and a width of $3.2 \times 10^2$ meters.

1. Write down the expressions to be multiplied.
$(1.5 \times 10^3 \text{ m})(3.2 \times 10^2 \text{ m})$

2. Multiply the first factors, add the exponents, and multiply any units.
$= (1.5 \times 3.2)(10^{3+2}) \text{ m} \times \text{m}$
$= 4.8 \times 10^5 \text{ m}^2$

## Dimensional Analysis

Scientific problems and calculations often involve unit conversions, or changes from one unit to another. Dimensional analysis is a method of unit conversion.

Suppose you were counting a pile of pennies. If there were 197 pennies in the pile, how many dollars would the pennies be worth? To determine the answer, you need to know the conversion factor between pennies and dollars. A conversion factor simply shows how two units are related. In this case, the conversion factor is 100 pennies = 1 dollar. Determining that 197 pennies is equal to $1.97 is an example of a unit conversion.

In dimensional analysis, the conversion factor is usually expressed as a fraction. Remember that the two values in any conversion factor are equal to one another. So, the two values form a fraction with the value of 1. Look at the example below to see how dimensional analysis can be applied to an everyday problem.

### Example

A student walked 1.5 kilometers as part of a school fitness program. How many meters did the student walk?

1. 1.5 km = ? m

2. 1 km = 1000 m

3. 1000 m/1 km

4. 1.5 km × 1000 m/1 km = 1500 m (cross out "km" in two places); 1.5 km = 1500 m

## Applying Dimensional Analysis

There are many applications of dimensional analysis in science. The example below demonstrates the use of dimensional analysis to convert units.

### Example

The average teenage girl needs about 2200 kilocalories of energy from food each day. How many calories is this equivalent to?

Use the following steps to convert kilocalories to calories.

1. Determine the conversion factor that relates the two units.
1 kilocalorie = 1000 calories

2. Write the conversion factor in the form of a fraction.
1000 calories/1 kilocalorie

3. Multiply the measurement by the conversion factor.
2200 kilocalories ×1000 calories/1 kilocalorie = 2,200,000 calories

### Practice Your Skills

Answer the following questions in your notebook:

1. You are using a 25-mL graduated cylinder to measure the volume of a liquid. The smallest marked unit on the cylinder is a milliliter. The volume is more than 10 mL and less than 15 mL. How many significant figures can you report in your answer? Explain.

2. For adult women, the average number of white blood cells per liter of blood is 5.8 billion. Express this data in scientific notation. Hint: You may want to write out the number with all its zeros first.

3. In a garden, the heights of five sunflowers are 135.0 cm, 162.5 cm, 180.0 cm, 185.0 cm, and 167.5 cm. Calculate the mean and the median for this data set.

4. In a second garden, the heights of five sunflowers are 130.0 cm, 162.5 cm, 165.0 cm, 160.0 cm, and 162.5 cm. For this data set, would you use the mean or the median, and why?

5. What is the mode for the data set in Question 4?

## Constructing Explanations and Designing Solutions

In scientific work, logical reasoning involves drawing valid conclusions or developing valid scientific ideas from scientific evidence. Scientists base their reasoning on empirical evidence, which is evidence based on observation or experience. The reasoning process often, but not always, begins with an observation. The observation triggers questions in the mind of the scientist. The questions lead to the development of one or more hypotheses, investigations, and conclusions.

### Developing Conclusions

If researchers are confident that their data are reliable, they make a final statement explaining and summarizing their results. That explanation, called the conclusion, indicates whether the data support or refute the hypothesis. The gardener's conclusion was this: *Some seeds must undergo a period of freezing in order to germinate.* A conclusion is considered valid if it is a logical interpretation of reliable data.

When an experiment has been completed, one or more events often follow. Researchers may repeat the experiment to verify the results. They may publish the experiment so that others can evaluate and replicate their procedures. They may compare their conclusion with the discoveries made by other scientists. And they may raise new questions that lead to new experiments. For example, are the spores of fungi affected by temperature as these seeds were? Researching other discoveries about seeds would show that some other types of plants in temperate zones require periods of freezing before they germinate. Biologists infer that this pattern makes it less likely the seeds will germinate before winter, thus increasing the chances that the young plants will survive.

## Developing Theories

In science, a theory is a very powerful concept and is the product of logical reasoning. A theory is an explanation of observed relationships and facts that has been supported by many observations or investigations. A theory may also unify a great many observed facts, or even a number of hypotheses. Examples of theories include cell theory, atomic theory, the theory of plate tectonics, and the theory of evolution. Although a theory is based on a large amount of data, it can be modified or even discarded if new scientific evidence refutes part or all of it.

## Designing Solutions

Research gives engineers information that helps them design a product. When engineers design new products, they usually work in teams. After identifying the problem and doing some initial research, the team next brainstorms ideas.

**Brainstorm Ideas** Often, design teams hold brainstorming meetings in which any team member can contribute ideas. Brainstorming is a creative process in which one team member's suggestions can spark ideas in other group members. Brainstorming can lead to new approaches to solving a design problem.

**Document the Process** As the design team works, its members document, or keep a record of, the process. Having access to documentation enables others to repeat, or replicate, the process in the future. Design teams document their research sources, ideas, lists of materials, and so on because any part of the process may be a helpful resource later.

**Identify Constraints** During brainstorming, a design team will often come up with several possible designs. To better focus their ideas, team members consider constraints. Constraints are factors that limit or restrict a product design. Physical characteristics, such as the properties of materials used to make your model car, are constraints. Money and time are also constraints. If the materials in a design cost a lot, or if the product takes a long time to make, the design may be impractical.

**Make Trade-Offs** Design teams usually need to make trade-offs. In a trade-off, engineers give up one benefit of a proposed design in order to obtain another. In designing your model car, you will have to make trade-offs. For example, you might decide to give up the benefit of sturdiness in order to obtain the benefit of lower cost.

**Choose One Solution** After considering the constraints and trade-offs of the possible designs, engineers then select one idea to develop further. That idea represents the solution that the team thinks best meets the need or solves the problem that was identified at the beginning of the process. The decision includes selecting the materials that will be used in the first attempt to build a product.

**Design and Construct a Prototype** After the team has chosen a design plan, the engineers build a prototype of the product. A prototype is a working model used to test a design.

**Test the Prototype** Engineers test the prototype to see whether it meets the goal. They must determine whether it works well, is easy to operate, is safe to use, and holds up to repeated use. Part of the evaluation includes collecting data in the form of measurements. For example, think of your model car. After you decide how to build your prototype, what would you want to know about it? You might want to measure how much baggage it could carry or how its shape affects its speed.

**Communicate Results** After testing the prototype and collecting data, researchers communicate the data to others. Sharing the results allows others to offer feedback that may help with improvements.

**Evaluate and Redesign** After results have been collected and communicated, team members analyze the results and identify any problems. The team then tries to troubleshoot, or fix, the design problems. Troubleshooting allows the team to redesign the prototype to improve on how well the solution meets the need.

### Practice Your Skills

Answer the following questions about designing a new backpack in your notebook.

1. One product that is part of almost every student's life is a backpack. List five qualities you value in a backpack and assign each a relative point value. Indicate if there are any design constraints associated with those qualities. Evaluate your own backpack in terms of functional requirements and design constraints. Rate its overall performance using your scale, indicating how many points it received against the possible total.

2. One recent technological advance in backpack design is the rolling pack. In addition to shoulder straps, a rolling pack has a pair of wheels at its base and a retracting handle so that you can pull the pack. Identify at least two trade-offs with this design.

3. The data table provides dimensions for two models of backpacks. Determine the carrying capacity, or volume, of each (volume = length × width × depth). Both are sold for the same price. What does this information suggest about a design constraint in the manufacturing process?

| Type of Pack | Length (cm) | Width (cm) | Depth (cm) | Volume (cc³) |
|---|---|---|---|---|
| Shoulder pack | 48 | 35 | 25 | |
| Rolling pack | 44 | 24 | 20 | |

4. Assume the average textbook is 28.5 cm × 23.0 cm × 4.5 cm. How many textbooks do you typically carry to school each day? Is each pack capable of carrying all your textbooks? Which value determines this?

5. Are you carrying more than the maximum safety load? How do you know?

6. Apply a risk-benefit analysis to the following situation. Dylan plans to purchase a shoulder pack or a rolling pack. The mass of a backpack should be no more than 15 percent of a person's body mass. Dylan weighs 115 pounds and typically carries five textbooks each day. Calculate the total mass of Dylan's textbooks, assuming an average mass of 1.65 kg each. Determine Dylan's maximum safe load in kilograms and make a recommendation. Hint: To convert weight in pounds to mass in kilograms, multiply the pounds by 0.45 and round up.

# Engaging in Argument from Evidence

Suppose someone asks you to sign a petition to "protect" the Canada geese in your area. He says, "People are trying to keep the geese away from our parks!" A person standing nearby says, "But the geese make an awful mess!" You're confused. You need to learn more about the issue.

## Scientific Literacy

To understand the many issues you encounter in your biology class and in the rest of your world, you need scientific literacy. Scientific literacy refers to understanding scientific terms and principles well enough to ask questions, evaluate information, and make decisions. By increasing your scientific literacy, you can distinguish good sources of scientific information from unreliable ones, evaluate sources for accuracy, and apply the knowledge to relevant issues or questions.

## Evidence and Opinion

To evaluate scientific information, you must first distinguish between evidence and opinion. In science, evidence includes observations and conclusions that have been repeated. Evidence may or may not support a scientific claim. An opinion is an idea that may be formed from evidence but has not been confirmed by evidence.

## Inferring

When you explain or interpret the things you observe, you are inferring, or making inferences. Inferring is not guessing. However, inferences are also not facts; they are just possible interpretations of an observation, based on what you already know. They can also be assumptions that you make about your observations. For example, if you hear your dog barking, you may infer that someone is outside your front door. However, your dog may also be barking because it wants to go for a walk. An inference may turn out to be incorrect even if it is based on accurate observations and logical reasoning. The only way to find out if an inference is correct is to investigate further.

## Evaluating Evidence

For scientific data to be valid, they must be the same regardless of who makes the observation or who performs the experiment. For example, one person might think it is mild enough outdoors to wear a sweater instead of a jacket. Another person might think that it is cold enough to wear both a sweater and a jacket. Both people have made an observation about the temperature but have drawn different conclusions about it. Both people, though, read the same thermometer and obtained the same measurement of the temperature.

## Subjective and Objective Thinking

The choice of a sweater or jacket or both is a subjective measurement of the temperature. A subjective measurement relies on the feelings or opinions of the person making it. The reading of a thermometer is an objective measurement. An objective measurement is the same regardless of the person making the measurement or observation. It is imperative that scientists take into consideration only objective measurements and observations when drawing conclusions.

## Bias

For evidence to be useful to a scientist, it must be free from any kind of bias. Bias is any influence that affects the validity of the data or how the data are interpreted. Bias can come from a number of different sources. Personal bias is based on a scientist's preconceived ideas. For example, personal bias might lead a researcher to conclude that one group of people is more intelligent than another group of people, even though there is no scientific evidence to support this conclusion. Cultural bias is the result of where the observer grew up and what he or she experienced. In some cultures, people might resist being immunized against diseases because they have been led to believe that immunizations can be either harmful or ineffective. This kind of cultural bias might impact the work or thinking of health professionals in the culture. Experimental bias can occur when a scientist expects a certain outcome and unconsciously interprets data so the expected outcome seems valid.

### Defending Your Explanations

When you construct explanations about your own work, you need to present an organized argument that includes data you collected and valid evidence from other sources that support your claim. You need to openly and honestly present the weaknesses of your data and collected evidence and explain how the weaknesses affect your claim. As you refine your explanations and possibly look forward to future investigations, you need to consider the critiques and suggestions from your teacher, lab partners, and other peers.

#### *Practice Your Skills*

1. **Apply Concepts** A pharmaceutical company claims that a study shows that a new pharmaceutical drug helps people lose 30 lbs of extra weight per month without restricting calories. The researchers who conducted the study are employed by the pharmaceutical company that manufactures the drug. What potential biases may have affected the study?

2. **Evaluate** An environmental group issues a press release claiming that a nearby river has been heavily polluted by a local chemical plant. The group reasons that the large number of dead fish found on the banks of the river provides evidence that support the claim. The chemical plant issues a response stating that it has not polluted the river. The officials of the chemical plant claim that the clear water in the river is proof that it is not polluted. Evaluate the claims made by the environmental group by examining all sides of the scientific evidence.

### Obtaining, Evaluating, and Communicating Information

Scientific literacy gives you the tools to obtain, evaluate, and communicate information. Scientific reasoning gives you the process.

#### Evaluating Scientific Claims

You can use scientific reasoning to evaluate scientific claims by looking for bias and errors in the research, by evaluating data, and by identifying faulty reasoning. The promotional material below makes several claims hoping to persuade the reader to order KnowHow.

From the data provided, you might infer that Subject B had a higher test score after using KnowHow. However, you can also use scientific literacy and reasoning to evaluate the claims in the promotional material. One of the first things you might notice about the KnowHow ad is that the research results included just two subjects, whereas a scientific experiment or study should really include a large number of subjects. Another error in the study is that the variables, such as time and the study environment, were not controlled. Without the variables being controlled, it is impossible to determine which variable caused the observed results.

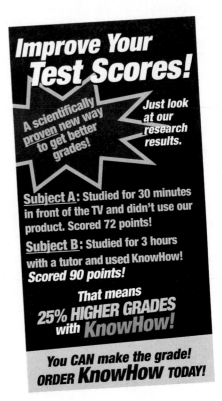

## Evaluating Scientific Explanations

When you evaluate a scientific explanation, you are determining whether the claim is valid. You must evaluate the data to determine whether they are reliable and whether they support the claim that is being made. To evaluate a scientific explanation, you can ask questions such as the following:

- Are there sources of bias in the investigation?
- What are the possible sources of error in the investigation?
- Is the source of the data and explanation reliable? Reliable information originates from a person or organization that is not biased.
- Do the data given support the conclusions?
- Are there alternate explanations for the data?
- Are the data accurate? Were the data collected with precision?

## Evaluating a Solution

After a design team has tested its prototype, it can evaluate a design and determine if the design can be further improved.

The evaluation of a design takes into account three basic criteria.

1. Functional requirements: Does the product do what it's supposed to do?
2. Constraints: Are there any factors that limit the design from functioning as it should?
3. Overall performance: Does the product meet all of its design objectives?

A performance metric is a quantifiable measure of the product's capacity to meet all of its design specifications.

## Communicating and Obtaining Information

No matter how talented the players on a team may be, one player alone cannot ensure victory for the team. Individuals must collaborate, or work together, for the good of the team. Think about volleyball players on the same volleyball team. In volleyball, the person who spikes the ball depends on the person who sets up the ball. Unless the ball is set up properly, the spiker will have limited success. Some sports even recognize the importance of collaboration by keeping track of assists. During a volleyball game, the players also communicate with one another so it is clear who is going to do which task. Strategies that are successful in sports can also work in science. When scientists collaborate and communicate with one another, they increase the likelihood of a successful outcome.

**Collaboration** Scientists choose to collaborate for different reasons. For example, some research problems are so complex that no one person could have all the knowledge, skills, and resources to solve the problem. It is often necessary to bring together individuals from different disciplines. Each scientist will typically bring different knowledge and, perhaps, a different approach to a problem. Just talking with a scientist from another discipline may provide insights that are helpful.

There may be a practical reason for collaboration. For example, an industry may give a university funding for pure research in an area of interest to the industry. Scientists at the university receive the equipment and financing required for the research. In exchange, the scientists share their ideas and expertise. The industry may profit from its investment by using and marketing applications based on the research.

Collaboration isn't always a smooth process. Conflicts can arise about use of resources, amount of work, who is to receive credit, and when and what to publish. In science class, you will likely work in pairs or on in a small group in the laboratory. If so, you may face some challenges. However, you can also experience the benefits of a successful collaboration.

**Communicating Results** Whenever you talk on the phone, text someone, or listen to your teacher at school, you are communicating. Communicating is the process of sharing ideas and information with other people. The way that scientists communicate with each other and with the public has changed over the centuries. In earlier centuries, scientists exchanged ideas through letters. They also formed societies to discuss the latest work of their members. When societies began to publish journals, scientists used the journals to keep up with new discoveries.

Today, many scientists work in teams. They communicate face to face but also exchange ideas with other scientists by e-mail, by phone, and through local and international conferences. Scientists still publish their results in scientific journals, which are the most reliable source of information about new discoveries. Most journals are now published online and are readily accessible. Journal articles are published only after being reviewed by experts in the authors' field. Reviewers may find errors in experimental design or challenge the authors' conclusions. This review process is good for science because it keeps work that is not well founded from being published.

**Obtaining Information** The Internet has become both a means of communication and a major source of information. One advantage of the Internet is that anyone with a computer can access the information. One disadvantage is that anyone can post information on the Internet without first having that information reviewed. To judge the reliability of information you find there, you have to consider the source. This same advice applies to articles in journals, magazines, newspapers, or the news you encounter on television. If a media outlet has a reporter who specializes in science, the chances are better that a report will be accurate.

In science, you need to do research to design an experiment. You may also need to do research to learn more about a particular topic. Therefore, you will need relevant, reliable background information. Relevant information is knowledge that relates to the question. Information qualifies as reliable if it comes from a person or organization that is accurate and not biased. Generally, universities, museums, and government agencies are sources of reliable information. So are many nonfiction books, magazines, and educational Web sites.

## Methods for Organizing Information

When you study or want to communicate facts and ideas, you may find it helpful to organize information visually. Here are some common graphic organizers you can use. Notice that each type of organizer is useful for specific types of information.

**Flowcharts** A flowchart can help you represent the order in which a set of events has occurred or should occur. Flowcharts are useful for outlining the steps in a procedure or stages in a process with a definite beginning and end.

To make a flowchart, list the steps in the process you want to represent and count the steps. Then, create the appropriate number of boxes, starting at the top of a page or on the left. Write a brief description of the first event in the first box, and then fill in the other steps, box by box. Link each box to the next event in the process with an arrow.

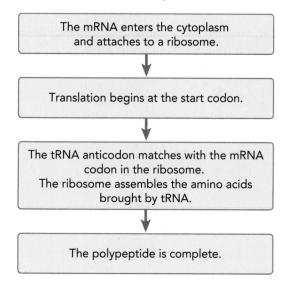

**Concept Maps** Concept maps can help you organize a topic that has many subtopics. A concept map begins with a main idea and shows how it can be broken down into specific topics. It makes the ideas easier to understand by presenting their relationships visually.

You construct a concept map by placing the concept words (usually nouns) in ovals and connecting the ovals with linking words. The most general concept usually is placed at the top of the map or in the center. The content of the other ovals becomes more specific as you move away from the main concept. The linking words, which describe the relationship between the linked concepts, are written on a line between two ovals.

If you follow any string of concepts and linking words down through a map, they should sound almost like a sentence.

Some concept maps may also include linking words that connect a concept in one branch to another branch. Such connections, called cross-linkages, show more complex interrelationships.

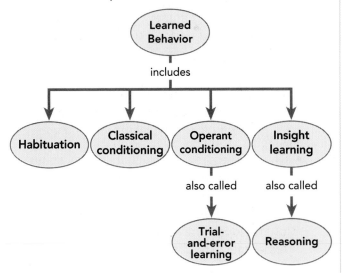

**Compare/Contrast Tables** Compare/contrast tables are useful for showing the similarities and differences between two or more objects or processes. The table provides an organized framework for making comparisons based on specific characteristics. To create a compare/contrast table, list the items to be compared across the top of the table. List the characteristics that will form the basis of your comparison in the column on the left. Complete the table by filling in information for each item.

| Comparing Fermentation and Cellular Respiration | | |
|---|---|---|
| **Characteristic** | **Fermentation** | **Cellular Respiration** |
| Starting reactants | Glucose | Glucose, oxygen |
| Pathways involved | Glycolysis, several others | Glycolysis, Krebs cycle, electron transport |
| End products | $CO_2$ and alcohol or $CO_2$ and lactic acid | $CO_2$, $H_2O$ |
| Number of ATP molecules produced | 2 | 36 |

**Venn Diagrams** Another way to show similarities and differences between items is with a Venn diagram. A Venn diagram consists of two or more ovals that partially overlap. Each oval represents a particular object or idea. Characteristics that the objects share are written in the area of overlap. Differences or unique characteristics are written in the areas that do not overlap.

To create a Venn diagram, draw two overlapping ovals. Label them with the names of the objects or the ideas they represent. Write the unique characteristics in the part of each oval that does not overlap. Write the shared characteristics within the area of overlap.

**Kingdom Plantae**     **Kingdom Fungi**

autotrophs
chloroplasts
cell walls
of cellulose

eukaroyotes
multicellular

heterotrophs
unicellular
cell walls
of chitin

**Cycle Diagrams** A cycle diagram shows a sequence of events that is continuous, or cyclical. A continuous sequence does not have a beginning or an end; instead, each event in the process leads to another event. The diagram shows the order of the events. To create a cycle diagram, list the events in the process and count them. Draw one box for each event, placing the boxes around an imaginary circle. Write one of the events in an oval, and then draw an arrow to the next oval, moving clockwise. Continue to fill in the boxes and link them with arrows until the descriptions form a continuous circle.

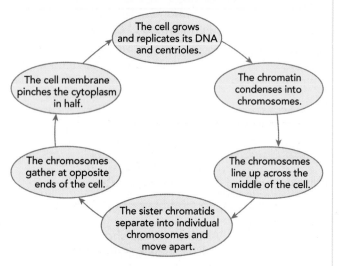

## Methods for Communicating Results

A crucial part of any scientific investigation is reporting the results. Scientists can communicate results by writing in scientific journals or speaking at conferences. Scientists also exchange information through conversations, e-mail, and Web sites. Young scientists often present their research at science fairs.

An engineering team needs to communicate the final design to the people who will manufacture and use the product. To do this, teams may use sketches, detailed drawings, computer simulations, and written descriptions. The team may also present the evidence that was collected when the prototype was tested. This evidence may include mathematical representations, such as graphs and data tables, that support the choice for the final design.

Different scientists may interpret the same data differently. This important notion is the basis for peer review, a process in which scientists examine other scientists' work. Not only do scientists share research with their peers, but they also invite feedback from those peers. Peer review encourages comments, suggestions, questions, and criticism from other scientists. Peer review can also help determine if data were reported accurately and honestly. Based on their peers' responses, the scientists who submitted their work for review can then reevaluate how to best interpret their data. As a student of science, you will also have to communicate your results. There are many methods of doing so.

**Oral Reports** An oral report is a spoken presentation that presents information. Often an oral report will include posters, models, or demonstrations. Usually, the presenter will be asked to answer questions at the end.

**Lab Reports** Writing a lab report helps you define what you are trying to achieve in an experiment. It also helps you organize your data. A lab report should describe an experiment so clearly that another person could perform the experiment using the report as a guide.

- Lab reports have several parts.
- The title tells someone looking at the report what the report is about. The title should be precise.
- The problem, or introduction, clearly states the subject of the experiment. It can also explain why the experiment was chosen and describe other research that has been done on the topic. The important variables of the experiment should be mentioned in this section.
- The hypothesis, or prediction, states what the experiment will test.
- The hypothesis is followed by a list of all materials used in the experiment.
- Next is a detailed description of the way the experiment was set up and the conditions under which it was performed. This is called the procedure.

- The observations section includes a detailed record of all observations made and all data collected during the experiment.

- Because raw data aren't usually enough to explain what happened in an experiment, the data must be analyzed. This is done in the analysis section. This section may contain graphs, sketches, and calculations that explain the data.

- Each lab report ends with a conclusion. The conclusion includes a brief summary of the analysis of the data and an explanation of whether the data support the hypothesis.

**Summaries** A summary is a brief statement or account covering the substance or main points of an experiment. As noted before, the conclusion of a lab report usually includes a summary of the analysis of the data and an explanation of whether the data support the hypothesis. Sometimes you might be asked to provide a summary separate from a lab report.

**Journals** A journal can refer to a scientific journal in which scientists publish their results. But in your case, a journal is usually a composition notebook in which you record everything from notes and worksheet answers to lab reports with data collection, data analysis, and conclusions.

Scientists accumulate vast amounts of data by observing events and taking measurements. Interpreting these data can be a difficult task if they are not organized. A journal allows you to organize your data, which can help you prepare your lab reports. A journal can also be a place where you record the raw data for your experiment. It is important to write down all the data from an experiment, in case another scientist questions your conclusions or you want to reinterpret your own results.

**Technology-Based Reports** A technology-based report is a report that uses technology to help present information. This technology can include audio or video recordings, presentation slides, or Web sites.

## Practice Your Skills

1. **Obtain Information** You are working on a science fair project and need to gather research on your project. List three places you would look for reliable information and three places you would not look.

Use the following information to answer Questions 2–4.

In its promotional materials, a drug company announced that a new drug can improve the memory of mice with brain injuries. Working with 100 mice, scientists at the drug company injected 50 of the mice with the drug. The other 50 mice did not receive any treatment. After three months, the scientists tested the memory of both groups of mice by seeing whether they recognized objects. The group that did not receive the drug remembered the objects 40 percent of the time. In contrast, the group that received the drug remembered the objects about 70 percent of the time.

2. **Identify** What data does the paragraph supply about the results of the experiments?

3. **Infer** What is an inference that can be made on the basis of the data?

4. **Evaluate** In its promotional materials, the drug company claims that this experiment was a major breakthrough in the treatment of brain injuries in humans. Would this claim be justified on the basis of the data? Explain.

5. **Evaluate** A scientist covered one half of a tray with dry paper towels and the other half of the tray with moistened paper towels. The scientist then put five earthworms in the middle of the tray, making certain that half of each earthworm's body rested on the moist paper and half rested on the dry paper. After five minutes, the scientist counted the number of worms that had moved to the moist paper toweling and the number that had moved to the dry paper toweling. The scientist wrote an explanation of the results, with the conclusion that earthworms prefer moist conditions to dry conditions. Analyze, evaluate, and critique the explanation by examining all sides of the scientific evidence that the scientist used.

# A TIPS FOR SUCCESSFUL FIELD TRIPS

Sometimes you may go on field trips outside the classroom to perform investigations. Biology field trips can have different purposes and take place in a variety of environments. The steps you take and the observations you make can vary greatly. However, field trips often involve common elements, such as the way you plan the event and what you do at the site. If you plan well and organize your activities thoughtfully, your field trips will be more productive and enjoyable. Here are some suggestions to consider.

## Planning the Trip

1. Discuss with your teacher and classmates the type of area you will visit, and decide what you are likely to gather. This will help determine the materials needed to collect specimens.

2. When you go on a field trip, you will encounter some living things you can collect and some you cannot.

   - For things you can't collect, such as most animals and large plants or plants on other people's property, take a photograph or make a sketch.

   - For things you can collect, such as water samples, soil samples, small plants, flowers, pine cones, fungi, and insects, take containers such as prelabeled plastic bags and jars with lids. Some jar lids should contain air holes or have cheesecloth covers with rubber bands. You may also need tools for collecting, such as a small trowel or garden spade for soil and an aquarium net for small water organisms.

3. List the materials you will need, including the following items:

   - blank sheets of paper in a firm notebook or on a clipboard

   - a camera

   - marking pens and writing utensils

   - a hand lens

4. Write the steps in your plan. Have your teacher check it for practicality and safety.

## During the Trip

1. Before leaving for the site, make sure you have all the materials listed in your plan.

2. Wear sturdy shoes, long sleeves, and long pants. Depending upon the time of year and the site itself, you should also consider wearing insect repellent and sunscreen.

3. Work in the groups that your teacher has assigned.

4. When you collect samples to bring back to the classroom, make sure you follow these rules:

   - Observe all local laws, and respect other people's property.

   - Avoid contact with poisonous plants and animals. Bright colors and highly contrasting colors may indicate that an animal is dangerous.

   - When turning over logs and stones, use a long stick in case stinging insects or snakes are underneath.

   - Do not collect any animals without the permission of your teacher. All animals collected for study must be returned to their environment unharmed.

   - As soon as possible after you are finished, wash your hands thoroughly with soap and warm water.

## After the Trip

Make sure that the samples you bring back to the classroom for observation are stored under the appropriate conditions. Generally, samples should have access to air (either put holes in the lids of the containers or keep them loosely covered). Do not leave any samples completely uncovered, because they might dry out. Keep the samples cool and do not store in direct sunlight.

## Review

1. **Ask Questions** Think of a scientific question that you would like to answer. Write the question in your notebook, and then write a sentence stating what you could do to find an answer to your question.

2. **Analyze** Is the statement "Plants can respond to human emotions" a testable hypothesis? In your answer, explain why or why not.

3. **Apply Concepts** Why would you select a computer for use in a scientific investigation?

4. **Review** What is a variable?

5. **Compare and Contrast** How are descriptive, comparative, and experimental investigations similar? How are they different?

6. **Observe** Look at the illustration below. In your science notebook, list four observations you can make about this scene.

7. **Ask Questions** In your science notebook, write two scientific questions about the scene in the illustration.

8. **Formulate Hypotheses** Review the questions you wrote in Number 7. Use one question to develop a hypothesis that could be tested.

9. **Plan an Experiment** How could your hypothesis be tested? Write a brief description of an investigation that could test your hypothesis.

10. **Select Equipment and Technology** Describe the equipment and technology that you would select to carry out the investigation described above.

# B TECHNOLOGY AND DESIGN

**STEM** The human body is a complex machine made up of many interconnected parts that work together. But what happens if one of these parts is missing or becomes damaged over time? How can you keep the "machine" running? The mechanics charged with solving this problem include physicians, biologists, chemists, physicists, engineers, inventors, and designers. They collaborate to design solutions that prolong or improve the lives of people with disabilities and chronic illnesses. Various technologies are available to replace a part of the human body or a function that a diseased body is no longer able to do on its own. Some of these technologies are shown below.

This paraplegic woman is able to move and walk due to an "exoskeleton." The battery-driven device is guided by hand movements and can recognize the movement intentions of the user.

## Your Task: Refine the Design

Evaluate a technology modeled on human body systems, and propose a way to improve the design. A useful technology is one that solves a problem. Your task is to research a medical problem and the technology available to solve it. The solution may be mechanical, or it may be a biochemical treatment for a functional problem, such as a hormone deficiency. After studying the nature of the problem and the range of possible solutions, you will suggest an optimized solution. It may be a refinement of an existing solution, or it may be an alternative solution that you design. Use the rubric on the next page to evaluate your work for this task.

**Define the Problem** Discuss with your teacher the technology you wish to focus on. What is the problem or need that the technology was designed to solve? List the strengths and weaknesses of the technology. Make sure to consider the people who use it. What else might they add to your list? Explain why the current solution to the problem is incomplete.

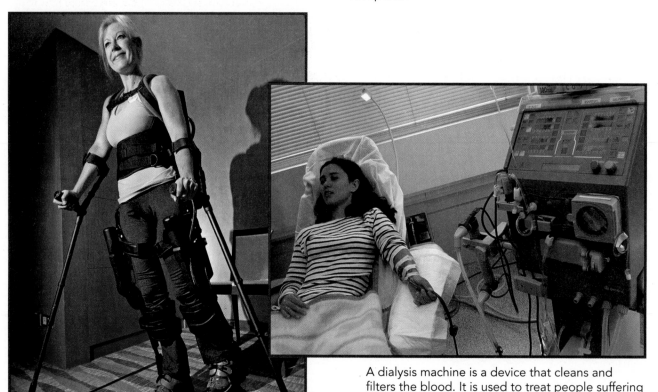

A dialysis machine is a device that cleans and filters the blood. It is used to treat people suffering from kidney failure.

Identify the requirements that must be met in order to solve the problem or need. These requirements are called design criteria. Then list the factors that might limit the success of your design. These factors are called design constraints.

**Design a Solution** Generate ideas for solving the problem. How would you design an improvement or alternative to the solution(s) currently in use? Evaluate your ideas for a solution based on the design criteria and constraints that you have specified. Select one or more of these ideas to develop further.

**Develop Models** Use sketches, physical models, or simulations to help you visualize and test your design. What does the model tell you about the strengths and limitations of your design? Ask your classmates for feedback on your proposed solution,

and revise the design as needed. What feedback might you expect from the people in need of your solution? What flaws might they identify based on your model?

**Obtain, Evaluate, and Communicate Information** Create a Web page or presentation that summarizes your work. With your teacher's help, identify an expert on the problem you are solving, and ask that person to provide feedback on your design. Use the feedback to further improve your design.

## Score Your Work!

The rubric below will help you evaluate your work as you design your solution and communicate your findings.

| SCORE YOUR WORK! | Score your work a ❹ if: | Score your work a ❸ if: | Score your work a ❷ if: | Score your work a ❶ if: |
|---|---|---|---|---|
| **Define the Problem** | Your problem statement is well researched and comprehensive. You have specified design criteria and constraints that have been refined through discussion and feedback. You feel as if you can discuss the problem as an expert. | Your problem statement identifies the problem, who is impacted by it, and why it is important. You have specified design criteria and constraints that your solution must meet. | You have written a statement that identifies the problem, and you have identified some basic design criteria for a solution. | You have identified what you think is a problem but are unsure how to explain or define it. |
| **Design a Solution** | You have generated ideas for solutions, evaluated them, and refined them. You understand that different solutions may be optimized for different design criteria. | You have generated ideas for solutions and evaluated them based on design criteria and constraints. | You have generated ideas for possible solutions, but you are not sure how to compare or evaluate them. | You have brainstormed an idea for a possible solution. |
| **Develop Models** | You have refined your design through iterative rounds of sketching or modeling. You have identified and discussed the strengths and limitations of your design. | You have sketched or modeled your design, analyzed it, and identified strengths and limitations of the design. | You have sketched or modeled a design for a possible solution. | You have identified a possible solution that can be realized through modeling and/or testing. |
| **Obtain, Evaluate, and Communicate Information** | You have presented and discussed your final design solution with an audience beyond your class and/or school. | You have presented your design proposal and have received feedback from students and teachers. | You have organized your documents and findings but have not shared or presented them. | You have compiled notes and materials documenting the design process, but you are unsure how to present them. |

| Cambrian Period | Ordovician Period | Silurian Period |
|---|---|---|

### Cambrian Period

During the Cambrian Period, multicellular life experienced its greatest adaptive radiation in what is called the Cambrian Explosion. Many species were fossilized during this period because many organisms evolved hard body parts, including shells and outer skeletons. Landmasses moved in ways that created vast shallow marine habitats. Jawless fishes first appeared. The Cambrian ended with a large mass extinction in which nearly 30 percent of all animal groups died.

*Elrathia*

### Silurian Period

During the Silurian Period, land areas rose, draining shallow seas and creating moist tropical habitats. Jawless fishes underwent an extensive radiation, and the first fish with true jaws appeared. The first multicellular land plants evolved from aquatic ancestors. Arthropods became the first animals to live on land.

Sea Lily Fossil

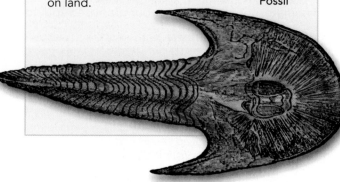

*Cephalaspis* (raylike jawless fish)

*Stenaster* (early sea star)

*Pleurocysities* (early echinoderms)

### Ordovician Period

Oceans flooded large land areas, creating more shallow marine habitats. Animal groups that survived the Cambrian extinction experienced dramatic adaptive radiations. These radiations generated great diversity in major animal phyla. Invertebrates dominated the seas. Early vertebrates evolved bony coverings.

## Devonian Period

During the Devonian Period, invertebrates and vertebrates thrived in the seas. Fishes evolved jaws, bony skeletons, and scales. Sharks began their adaptive radiation. Certain groups of fishes evolved leglike fins, and some of these evolved into the first amphibians. Some land plants, such as ferns, adapted to drier areas. Insects began to radiate on land.

## Permian Period

Crinoid

During the Permian Period, invertebrates, vertebrates, and land plants continued to expand over Earth's continents. Reptiles experienced the first of several major adaptive radiations, which produced the ancestors of modern reptiles, dinosaurs, and mammals. The Permian Period ended with the biggest mass extinction of all time. More than 50 percent of terrestrial animal families and more than 95 percent of marine species became extinct.

Fossil Fern From
Carboniferous Period

## Carboniferous Period

During the Carboniferous Period, mountain building created a wide range of habitats, from swampy lowlands to drier upland areas. Giant ferns, club mosses, and horsetails formed vast swampy forests. Amphibians, insects, and land plants experienced major adaptive radiations. Winged insects evolved into many forms, including huge dragonflies and cockroaches. For early vertebrates, insects were food; for plants, insects were predators. The first reptiles evolved from ancient amphibians.

| Triassic Period | Jurassic Period | Cretaceous Period |
| --- | --- | --- |

### Triassic Period

During the Triassic Period, surviving fishes, insects, reptiles, and cone-bearing plants evolved rapidly. About 225 million years ago, the first dinosaurs evolved. The earliest mammals evolved during the late Triassic. Triassic mammals were very small, about the size of a mouse or shrew.

Living Horsetail        Horsetail Fossil

*T. rex*

### Cretaceous Period

During the Cretaceous Period, *Tyrannosaurus rex* roamed the land, while flying reptiles and birds soared in the sky. Turtles, crocodiles, and other, now-extinct reptiles like plesiosaurs swam among fishes and invertebrates in the seas. Leafy trees, shrubs, and flowering plants emerged and experienced adaptive radiations. The Cretaceous ended with another mass extinction. More than half of all plant and animal groups were wiped out, including all dinosaurs except the ancestors of modern birds.

### Jurassic Period

During the Jurassic Period, dinosaurs became the most diverse land animals. They "ruled" for about 150 million years, but different types lived at different times. One lineage of dinosaurs evolved feathers and ultimately led to modern birds. *Archaeopteryx*, the first feathered fossil to be discovered, evolved during this time.

Pterodactyl Fossil

*Maiasaura* Nest

# CENOZOIC ERA

| Paleogene Period | Neogene Period | Quaternary Period |
|---|---|---|

## Paleogene Period

During the Paleogene Period, climates changed from warm and moist to cool and dry. Flowering plants, grasses, and insects flourished. After the dinosaurs and giant marine reptiles went extinct, mammals underwent a major adaptive radiation. As climates changed, forests were replaced by open woods and grasslands. Large mammals—ancestors of cattle, deer, and sheep and other grazers—evolved and spread across the grasslands. In the sea, the first whales evolved.

Early Mammal

## Neogene Period

During the Neogene Period, colliding continents pushed up modern mountain ranges, including the Alps in Europe and the Rockies, Cascades, and Sierra Nevadas in North America. As mountains rose, ice and snow built up at high elevations and in the Arctic. Falling sea levels and colliding continents created connections between North and South America, and between Africa, Europe, and Asia. Those connections led to great movements of land animals between continents. Climates continued a cooling and drying trend, and grasslands continued to expand. Modern grazing animals continued to coevolve with grasses, evolving specialized digestive tracts to deal with tough, low-nutrient grass tissue.

Neanderthal Skull

## Quaternary Period

During the Quaternary Period, Earth cooled. A series of ice ages saw thick glaciers advance and retreat over parts of Europe and North America. So much water was frozen in glaciers that sea levels fell by more than 100 meters. Then, about 20,000 years ago, Earth's climate began to warm. Over thousands of years, glaciers melted, and sea levels rose. In the oceans, algae, coral, mollusks, fishes, and mammals thrived. Insects and birds shared the skies. Land mammals—among them bats, cats, dogs, cattle, and mammoths—became common. Between 6 and 7 million years ago, one group of mammals began an adaptive radiation that led to the ancestors and close relatives of modern humans.

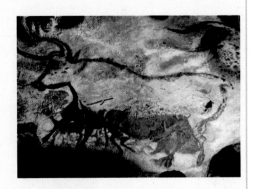

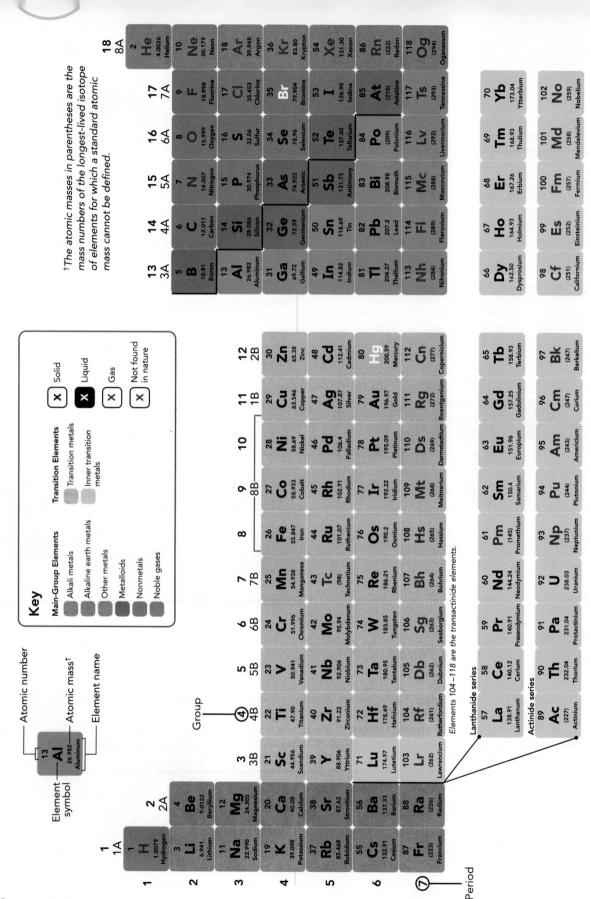

# GLOSSARY

**abiotic factor:** physical, or nonliving, factor that shapes an ecosystem (81)

  **factor abiótico:** factor físico, o inanimado, que da forma a un ecosistema

**acid:** compound that forms hydrogen ions (H⁺) in solution; a solution with a pH of less than 7 (51)

  **ácido:** compuesto que en una solución produce iones hidrógeno (H⁺); una solución con un pH inferior a 7

**activation energy:** energy input that is needed for a reaction to begin (59)

  **energía de activación:** energía necesaria para que comience una reacción

**adaptation:** heritable characteristics that increase an organism's ability to survive and reproduce in an environment (556)

  **adaptación:** características heredables que aumentan la capacidad de un organismo para sobrevivir y reproducirse en un medio ambiente

**adaptive radiation:** process by which a single species or a small group of species evolves into several different forms that live in different ways (657)

  **radiación adaptativa:** proceso mediante el cual una sola especie o un grupo pequeño de especies evoluciona y da lugar a diferentes seres que viven de diversas maneras

**adhesion:** force of attraction between different kinds of molecules (48)

  **adhesión:** fuerza de atracción entre diferentes tipos de moléculas

**aerobic:** process that requires oxygen (312)

  **aeróbico:** proceso que requiere oxígeno

**age structure:** number of males and females of each age in a population (146)

  **estructura etaria:** número de machos y hembras de cada edad en una población

**allele:** one of different forms of a gene (380)

  **alelo:** cada una de las diversas formas de un gen

**allele frequency:** number of times that an allele occurs in a gene pool compared with the number of alleles in that pool for the same gene (581)

  **frecuencia alélica:** número de veces que aparece un alelo en un caudal genético comparado con la cantidad de alelos en ese caudal para el mismo gen

**alternation of generations:** life cycle that has two alternating phases—a haploid (N) phase and a diploid (2N) phase (701, 725)

  **alternancia de generaciones:** ciclo vital con dos fases que se alternan, una fase haploide (N) y una fase diploide (2N)

**alveolus (alveoli):** bubblelike structures at the end of air passages in mammalian lungs (848)

  **alvéolos:** estructuras en forma de burbujas que se encuentran al extremo de las vías respiratorias de los pulmones de los mamíferos

**amino acid:** compound with an amino group on one end and a carboxyl group on the other end (55)

  **aminoácido:** compuesto que contiene un grupo amino en un extremo y un grupo carboxilo en el otro extremo

**amniotic egg:** egg composed of shell and membranes that creates a protected environment in which the embryo can develop out of water (886)

  **huevo amniota:** huevo formado por una cáscara y membranas que crea un ambiente protegido en el cual el embrión puede desarrollarse fuera del agua

**anaerobic:** process that does not require oxygen (312)

  **anaeróbico:** proceso que no requiere oxígeno

**analogous structure:** body parts that share a common function, but not an evolutionary history (564)

  **estructuras análogas:** partes del cuerpo que tienen la misma función, pero no la misma historia evolutiva

**anaphase:** phase of mitosis in which the chromosomes separate and move to opposite ends of the cell (347)

  **anafase:** fase de la mitosis en la cual los cromosomas se separan y se desplazan hacia los extremos opuestos de la célula

**angiosperm:** any of a group of seed plants that bear their seeds within a layer of tissue that protects the seed; also called flowering plant (734)

  **angiospermas:** grupo de plantas con semillas, que están protegidas con una capa de tejido. Se conocen también como plantas que florecen

**antheridium** (pl, antheridia): male reproductive structure in some plants; produces sperm (730)

  **anteridio:** en algunas plantas, estructura reproductora masculina que produce esperma

**anthrome** globally significant ecological region created by long-term interactions between humans and ecosystems (205)

  **antromas o biomas antropogénicos:** regiones de significancia ecológica creadas por las interacciones de largo plazo entre los seres humanos y los ecosistemas

**antibiotic:** group of drugs used to block the growth and reproduction of bacterial pathogens (695)

    **antibiótico:** grupo de medicamentos que se usan para bloquear el crecimiento y la reproducción de patógenos bacterianos

**anticodon:** group of three bases on a tRNA molecule that are complementary to the three bases of a codon of mRNA (447)

    **anticodón:** grupo de tres bases ubicadas en una molécula de ARNt complementarias a las tres bases de un codón de ARNm

**antigen:** any substance that triggers an immune response (940)

    **antígeno:** sustancia que desata una respuesta inmunitaria

**aphotic zone:** dark layer of the oceans below the photic zone where sunlight does not penetrate (98)

    **zona afótica:** zona oscura de los océanos, situada por debajo de la zona fótica, en la que no penetra la luz del sol

**apical dominance:** phenomenon in which the closer a bud is to the stem's tip, the more its growth is inhibited (778)

    **dominancia apical:** fenómeno en el que cuanto más cerca está el brote de la punta del tallo, más se inhibe su crecimiento

**apoptosis:** process of programmed cell death (352)

    **apoptosis:** proceso de muerte celular programada

**aquaporin:** water channel protein in a cell (262)

    **acuaporinas:** proteínas que forman los canales de agua en la célula

**archegonium** (pl, archegonia): structure in plants that produces egg cells (730)

    **arquegonio:** estructura vegetal que produce oosferas

**artificial selection:** selective breeding of plants and animals to promote the occurrence of desirable traits in offspring (554)

    **selección artificial:** reproducción selectiva de plantas y animales para promover la aparición de rasgos deseables en la descendencia

**asexual reproduction:** process of reproduction involving a single parent that results in offspring that are genetically identical to the parent (23, 341)

    **reproducción asexual:** proceso reproductivo que consiste de un solo reproductor que produce individuos que son genéticamente iguales a él

**atmosphere:** thin layer of gases that surround Earth (82)

    **atmósfera:** incluye todos los gases que rodean la Tierra

**atom:** the basic unit of matter (42)

    **átomo:** unidad básica de la materia

**ATP (adenosine triphosphate):** compound used by cells to store and release energy (282)

    **ATP** (adenosín trifosfato o trifosfato de adenosina): compuesto que utilizan las células para almacenar y liberar energía

**ATP synthase:** an enzyme for the synthesis of ATP; consists of a cluster of proteins that span the cell membrane and allow hydrogen ions ($H^+$) to pass (293)

    **síntesis de ATP:** enzima necesaria para la síntesis de ATP; está formada por un grupo de proteínas que atraviesan la membrana celular y permiten el paso de iones hidrógeno ($H^+$)

**atrium (pl, atria):** upper chamber of the heart that receives blood (851)

    **aurícula:** cavidad superior del corazón que recibe la sangre

**autosome:** chromosome that is not a sex chromosome; also called autosomal chromosome (475)

    **autosoma:** cromosoma que no es un cromosoma sexual; también llamado cromosoma somático

**autotroph:** organism that is able to capture energy from sunlight or chemicals and use it to produce its own food from inorganic compounds; also called a producer (114, 285)

    **autótrofo:** organismo capaz de capturar y usar la energía solar o de sustancias químicas para producir su propio alimento a partir de compuestos inorgánicos; también llamado productor

**auxin:** regulatory substance produced in the tip of a growing plant that stimulates cell elongation and the growth of new roots (777)

    **auxina:** sustancia reguladora que se produce en la punta de una planta en crecimiento que estimula la elongación celular y el crecimiento de nuevas raíces

**background extinction:** extinction caused by slow and steady progress of natural selection (654)

    **extinción natural:** extinción causada por el progreso lento y continuo de la selección natural

**bacteriophage:** kind of virus that infects bacteria (414, 685)

    **bacteriófago:** tipo de virus que infecta a las bacterias

**base:** compound that produces hydroxide ions ($OH^-$) in solution; solution with a pH of more than 7 (51)

    **base:** compuesto que, en solución, produce iones hidróxido ($OH^-$); solución con un pH de más de 7

**base pairing:** principle that bonds in DNA can form only between adenine and thymine and between guanine and cytosine (422)

    **apareamiento de bases:** principio que afirma que en el ADN los enlaces se pueden formar solo entre adenina y timina y entre guanina y citosina

**behavior:** manner in which an organism reacts to changes in its internal condition or external environment (822)

    **comportamiento:** manera en la que un organismo reacciona a los cambios en sus condiciones internas o en su medio ambiente externo

**behavioral isolation:** form of reproductive isolation in which two populations develop differences in courtship rituals or other behaviors that prevent them from breeding (593)

    **aislamiento conductual:** forma de aislamiento reproductivo en el que dos poblaciones desarrollan diferentes rituales de cortejo u otros comportamientos que impiden que se apareen entre sí

**bias:** particular preference or point of view that is personal rather than scientific (20)

    **sesgo:** preferencia particular o punto de vista que es personal y no científico

**bilateral symmetry:** body plan in which a single imaginary line can divide the body into left and right sides that are mirror images of each other (803)

    **simetría bilateral:** plano corporal en el que una línea imaginaria divide el cuerpo en dos partes, izquierda y derecha, que son el reflejo la una de la otra

**binary fission:** process in which a cell replicates its DNA and then divides in half to produce two identical cells (692)

    **fisión binaria:** proceso en el cual una célula replica su ADN, se divide por la mitad y produce dos células hijas idénticas

**binomial nomenclature:** classification system in which each species is assigned a two-part scientific name (612)

    **nomenclatura binaria:** sistema de clasificación en el que a cada especie se le asigna un nombre científico específico de dos partes

**biodiversity:** total of the variety of organisms in the biosphere (186)

    **biodiversidad:** todas las variedades de organismos que existen en la biosfera

**biogeochemical cycle:** process in which elements, chemical compounds, and other forms of matter are passed from one part of the biosphere to another (123)

    **ciclo biogeoquímico:** proceso mediante el cual los elementos, los compuestos químicos y otras formas de la materia se transfieren de una parte de la biosfera a otra

**biogeography:** study of past and present distribution of organisms (560)

    **biogeografía:** estudio de la distribución pasada y actual de los organismos

**biological magnification:** increasing concentration of a harmful substance in organisms at higher trophic levels in a food chain or food web (216)

    **magnificación biológica:** proceso de acumulación de una sustancia dañina en los organismos de los niveles tróficos superiores de la cadena o red alimentaria

**biology:** scientific study of life (22)

    **biología:** estudio científico de la vida

**biomass:** total amount of living tissue within a given trophic level (122)

    **biomasa:** cantidad total de tejido vivo dentro de un nivel trófico determinado

**biome:** group of ecosystems that share similar climates and typical organisms (92)

    **bioma:** grupo de ecosistemas que comparten climas similares y organismos típicos

**biosphere:** part of Earth in which life exists, including land, water, and air or atmosphere (25, 78)

    **biósfera:** partes de la Tierra en las que existe la vida, incluyendo la tierra, el agua y el aire o la atmósfera

**biotechnology:** process of manipulating organisms, cells, or molecules to produce specific products (506)

    **biotecnología:** proceso de manipular organismos, células o moléculas para crear productos específicos

**biotic factor:** any living part of the environment with which an organism might interact (81)

    **factor biótico:** cualquier parte viva del medio ambiente con la cual un organismo podría interactuar

**bipedal:** the ability to walk upright (819)

    **biópedo:** capacidad de caminar erguido

**blastocyst:** stage of early development in mammals that consists of a hollow ball of cells (357)

    **blastocisto:** etapa del desarrollo temprano de los mamíferos que consiste en una esfera hueca de células

**bottleneck effect:** a change in allele frequency following a dramatic reduction in the size of a population (588)

    **efecto cuello de botella:** cambio en la frecuencia de los alelos que es consecuencia de una reducción drástica en el tamaño de una población

**bryophyte:** group of plants that have specialized reproductive organs but lack vascular tissue; includes mosses and their relatives (729)

    **briofitas:** grupo de plantas con órganos reproductores especializados que carecen de tejido vascular; incluyen a los musgos y sus análogos

**buffer:** compound that prevents sharp, sudden changes in pH (51)

    **solución amortiguadora:** compuesto que impide cambios bruscos y repentinos en el pH

**calorie:** amount of energy needed to raise the temperature of 1 gram of water by 1 degree Celsius (310)

    **caloría:** cantidad de energía necesaria para elevar 1 °C la temperatura de 1 gramo de agua

**Calvin cycle:** light-dependent reactions of photosynthesis in which energy from ATP and NADPH is used to build high-energy compounds such as sugar (294)

    **ciclo de Calvin:** reacciones de fotosíntesis dependientes de la luz en las cuales se utiliza la energía del ATP y del NADPH para formar compuestos ricos en energía, como por ejemplo, el azúcar

**cancer:** disorder in which some of the body's cells lose the ability to control growth (353)

**cáncer:** enfermedad en la que algunas células del cuerpo pierden la capacidad de controlar su crecimiento

**canopy:** dense covering formed by the leafy tops of tall rain forest trees (93)

**dosel forestal (o canopia):** cubierta densa formada por las copas de los árboles altos del bosque tropical

**capillary action:** tendency of water to rise in a thin tube (774)

**capilaridad:** tendencia del agua a ascender en un tubo delgado

**capsid:** protein coat surrounding a virus (683)

**cápside:** estructura proteica que rodea a un virus

**carbohydrate:** compound made of carbon, hydrogen, and oxygen atoms; types of nutrients that are the major source of energy to the body (53)

**hidratos de carbono:** compuestos formados de átomos de carbono, hidrógeno y oxígeno; tipos de nutrientes que son la fuente principal de energía del cuerpo

**carrying capacity:** largest number of individuals of a particular species that a particular environment can support (151)

**capacidad de carga:** cantidad máxima de individuos de una especie determinada que un ambiente puede mantener

**cartilage:** type of connective tissue that supports the body; is softer and more flexible than bone (810)

**cartílago:** tipo de tejido conector que sustenta el cuerpo, más suave y flexible que el hueso

**Casparian strip:** waterproof strip that surrounds plant endodermal cells and is involved in the one-way passage of materials into the vascular cylinder in plant roots (767)

**banda de Caspary:** banda impermeable que rodea a las células endodérmicas de las plantas y participa en el transporte unidireccional de las sustancias hacia el interior del cilindro vascular de las raíces de las plantas

**catalyst:** substance that speeds up the rate of a chemical reaction (60)

**catalizador:** sustancia que aumenta la velocidad de una reacción química

**cell:** basic unit of all forms of life (243)

**célula:** unidad básica de todas las formas de vida

**cell cycle:** series of events in which a cell grows, prepares for division, and divides to form two daughter cells (345)

**ciclo celular:** serie de sucesos en los que una célula crece, se prepara para dividirse y se divide para formar dos células hijas

**cell division:** process by which a cell divides into two daughter cells (340)

**división celular:** proceso mediante el cual una célula se divide en dos células hijas

**cell-mediated immunity:** immune response that defends the body against viruses, fungi, and abnormal cancer cells (940)

**inmunidad celular:** respuesta inmunitaria que defiende al cuerpo de virus, hongos y células cancerígenas anormales

**cell membrane:** thin, flexible barrier that surrounds all cells; regulates what enters and leaves the cell (246)

**membrana celular:** barrera delgada y flexible alrededor de la célula que controla lo que entra y sale de la célula

**cell theory:** fundamental concept of biology that states that all living things are composed of cells; that cells are the basic units of structure and function in living things; and that new cells are produced from existing cells (243)

**teoría celular:** concepto fundamental de la biología que afirma que todos los seres vivos están compuestos de células, que las células son las unidades básicas de estructura y función de todos los seres vivos y que las células nuevas se producen a partir de las células existentes

**cell wall:** strong, supporting layer around the cell membrane in some cells (256)

**pared celular:** capa fuerte de apoyo alrededor de la membrana celular de algunas células

**cellular respiration:** process that releases energy by breaking down glucose and other food molecules in the presence of oxygen (311)

**respiración celular:** proceso que libera energía al descomponer la glucosa y otras moléculas alimenticias en presencia de oxígeno

**centriole:** structure in an animal cell that helps to organize cell division (346)

**centríolo:** estructura de las células animales que ayuda a organizar la división celular

**centromere:** region of a chromosome in which the two sister chromatids attach (346)

**centrómero:** región de un cromosoma en la que las dos cromátidas hermanas se unen

**cephalization:** concentration of sense organs and nerve cells at the anterior end of an animal (805)

**cefalización:** concentración de los órganos sensoriales y de las células nerviosas en el extremo anterior de un animal

**cerebellum:** part of the brain that coordinates movement and controls balance (873)

**cerebelo:** parte del cerebro que coordina el movimiento y controla el equilibrio

**cerebrum:** part of the brain responsible for voluntary activities of the body; includes the "thinking" regions of the brain (873)

**cerebro:** parte del encéfalo que controla las actividades voluntarias del cuerpo; incluye las regiones del encéfalo en las que se produce el pensamiento

**chemical reaction:** process that changes, or transforms, one set of chemicals into another set of chemicals (58)
**reacción química:** proceso que cambia, o transforma, un conjunto de sustancias químicas en otro conjunto de sustancias químicas

**chemosynthesis:** process in which chemical energy is used to produce carbohydrates (115)
**quimiosíntesis:** proceso en el cual la energía química es utilizada para producir hidratos de carbono

**chitin:** complex carbohydrate that makes up the cell walls of fungi; also found in the external skeletons of arthropods (704)
**quitina:** hidrato de carbono complejo que forma las paredes celulares de los hongos; también se encuentra en los exoesqueletos de los artrópodos

**chlorophyll:** principal pigment of plants and other photosynthetic organisms (286)
**clorofila:** pigmento principal de las plantas y de otros organismos fotosintéticos

**chloroplast:** organelle found in cells of plants and some other organisms that captures the energy from sunlight and converts it into chemical energy (254)
**cloroplasto:** orgánulo de las células vegetales y otros organismos que absorbe energía de la luz solar y la convierte en energía química

**chordate:** animal that has, for at least one stage of its life, a dorsal, hollow nerve cord; a notochord; a tail that extends beyond the anus; and pharyngeal pouches (800)
**cordado:** animal que tiene, al menos en una etapa de su vida, un cordón nervioso dorsal, un notocordio, una cola que se extiende más allá del ano y bolsas faríngeas

**chromatid:** one of two identical "sister" parts of a duplicated chromosome (346)
**cromátida:** una de las dos partes "hermanas" idénticas de un cromosoma duplicado

**chromatin:** substance found in eukaryotic chromosomes that consists of DNA tightly coiled around histones (344)
**cromatina:** sustancia que se encuentra en los cromosomas eucariotas compuesta de ADN fuertemente enrollado alrededor de las histonas

**chromosome:** threadlike structure of DNA and protein that contains genetic information; in eukaryotes, chromosomes are found in the nucleus; in prokaryotes, they are found in the cytoplasm (343)
**cromosoma:** estructura filamentosa de ADN y proteína que contiene información genética; en los eucariotas, los cromosomas se encuentran en el núcleo; en los procariotas se encuentran en el citoplasma

**cilium** (pl, cilia): short hair-like projection that produces movement (700)
**cilios:** diminutas prolongaciones parecidas a pelos que producen movimiento

**clade:** evolutionary branch of a cladogram that includes a single ancestor and all its descendants (619)
**clado:** rama evolutiva de un cladograma que incluye a un único ancestro y a todos sus descendientes

**cladogram:** diagram depicting patterns of shared characteristics among species (620)
**cladograma:** diagrama que representa los patrones de las características compartidas entre las especies

**class:** in classification, a group of closely related orders (615)
**clase:** en la clasificación, grupo de órdenes estrechamente relacionados

**climate:** average year-to-year conditions of temperature and precipitation in an area over a long period of time (85)
**clima:** condiciones promedio anuales de temperatura y precipitación de un área por un periodo largo

**climate change:** measurable long-term changes in averages of temperature, clouds, winds, precipitation, and the frequency of extreme weather events such as floods, major storms, and heat waves (208)
**cambio climático:** cambios mensurables a largo plazo en los promedios de temperatura, nubosidad, vientos, precipitaciones y la frecuencia de eventos climáticos extremos como inundaciones, tormentas fuertes y olas de calor

**clone:** member of a population of genetically identical cells produced from a single cell (515)
**clon:** miembro de una población de células genéticamente iguales producidas a partir de una única célula

**closed circulatory system:** type of circulatory system in which blood circulates entirely within blood vessels that extend throughout the body (850)
**sistema circulatorio cerrado:** tipo de sistema circulatorio en el cual la sangre viaja solo dentro de vasos sanguíneos que se extienden por todo el cuerpo

**codominance:** situation in which the phenotypes produced by both alleles are completely expressed (390)
**codominancia:** situación en la que los fenotipos que producen ambos alelos se manifiestan por completo

**codon:** group of three nucleotide bases in mRNA that specify a particular amino acid to be incorporated into a protein (445)
**codón:** grupo de tres bases nucleótidas del ARNm que especifican qué aminoácido en particular se va a incorporar a una proteína

**coelom:** body cavity lined with mesoderm (804)
**celoma:** cavidad corporal alineada con el mesodermo

**coevolution:** process by which two species evolve in response to changes in each other over time (658)
**coevolución:** proceso mediante el cual dos especies evolucionan en respuesta a los cambios de la otra en el transcurso del tiempo

**cohesion:** attraction between molecules of the same substance (48)

  **cohesión:** atracción entre moléculas de la misma sustancia

**commensalism:** symbiotic relationship in which one organism benefits and the other is neither helped nor harmed (181)

  **comensalismo:** relación simbiótica en la cual un organismo se beneficia y el otro ni se beneficia ni sufre daño

**communication:** passing information from one organism to another (827)

  **comunicación:** transmitir información de un organismo a otro

**community:** assemblage of different populations that live together in a defined area (79)

  **comunidad:** concurrencia de diferentes poblaciones que habitan juntas en un área específica

**competitive exclusion principle:** principle that states that no two species can occupy the same niche in the same habitat at the same time (178)

  **principio de exclusión competitiva:** principio que establece que dos especies no pueden ocupar el mismo nicho en el mismo hábitat al mismo tiempo

**compound:** substance formed by the chemical combination of two or more elements in definite proportions (44)

  **compuesto:** sustancia formada por la combinación química de dos o más elementos en proporciones definidas

**conjugation:** process in which paramecia and some prokaryotes exchange genetic information (692)

  **conjugación:** proceso mediante el cual los paramecios y algunos procariotas intercambian información genética

**connective tissue:** type of tissue that provides support for the body and connects its parts (905)

  **tejido conector:** tipo de tejido que proporciona soporte al cuerpo y une sus partes

**consumer:** organism that relies on other organisms for its energy and food supply; also called a heterotroph (116)

  **consumidor:** organismo que depende de otros organismos para conseguir su energía y aporte alimenticio; también llamados heterótrofos

**control group:** group in an experiment that is exposed to the same conditions as the experimental group except for one independent variable (12)

  **grupo de control:** en un experimento, grupo expuesto a las mismas condiciones que el grupo experimental excepto por una variable independiente

**controlled experiment:** experiment in which only one variable is changed (12)

  **experimento controlado:** experimento en el cual solo se cambia una variable

**convergent evolution:** process by which unrelated organisms independently evolve similarities when adapting to similar environments (657)

  **evolución convergente:** proceso mediante el cual organismos no relacionados desarrollan semejanzas de manera independiente cuando se adaptan a ambientes semejantes

**cotyledon:** first leaf or first pair of leaves produced by the embryo of a seed plant (737, 749)

  **cotiledón:** primera hoja o primer par de hojas producidas por el embrión de una planta con semillas

**covalent bond:** type of bond between atoms in which the electrons are shared (45)

  **enlace covalente:** tipo de enlace entre átomos en el cual se comparten los electrones

**crossing-over:** process in which homologous chromosomes exchange portions of their chromatids during meiosis (394)

  **entrecruzamiento cromosómico:** proceso mediante el cual los cromosomas homólogos intercambian partes de sus cromátidas durante la meiosis

**cyclin:** one of a family of proteins that regulates the cell cycle in eukaryotic cells (352)

  **ciclina:** perteneciente a una familia de proteínas que regula el ciclo celular en las células eucariotas

**cytokinesis:** division of the cytoplasm to form two separate daughter cells (346)

  **citocinesis:** división del citoplasma para formar dos células hijas independientes

**cytoplasm:** in eukaryotic cells, all cellular contents outside the nucleus; in prokaryotic cells, all of the cells' contents (248)

  **citoplasma:** en las células eucariotas, todos los contenidos celulares que se encuentran fuera del núcleo; en las células procariotas, todo el contenido de las células

**cytoskeleton:** network of protein filaments in a eukaryotic cell that gives the cell its shape and internal organization and is involved in movement (253)

  **citoesqueleto:** red de filamentos proteicos en las células eucariotas que da a la célula su forma y organización interna e interviene en el movimiento

**data:** evidence; information gathered from observation (12)

  **datos:** evidencia; información reunida por medio de la observación

**deforestation:** the cutting down of forests (210)

  **deforestación:** tala indiscriminada de los bosques

**demographic transition:** change in a population from high birth and death rates to low birth and death rates (160)

    **transición demográfica:** cambio en una población de tasas altas de nacimiento y mortalidad a tasas bajas de nacimiento y mortalidad

**demography:** scientific study of human populations (160)

    **demografía:** ciencia que estudia las poblaciones humanas

**denitrification:** process by which bacteria convert nitrates into nitrogen gas (129)

    **desnitrificación:** proceso mediante el cual las bacterias convierten los nitratos en gas nitrógeno

**density-dependent limiting factor:** a limiting factor that depends on population density (153)

    **factor limitante dependiente de la densidad:** factor limitante que depende de la densidad de población

**density-independent limiting factor:** limiting factor that affects all populations in similar ways, regardless of the population density (156)

    **factor limitante independiente de la densidad:** factor limitante que afecta a todas las poblaciones de manera similar, sin importar la densidad de población

**dependent variable:** variable that is observed and that changes in response to the independent variable; also called the responding variable (12)

    **variable dependiente:** variable que se observa y que cambia en respuesta a la variable independiente; también llamada variable de respuesta

**derived character:** trait that appears in recent parts of a lineage, but not in its older members (621)

    **carácter derivado:** rasgo que aparece en miembros recientes de un linaje, pero no en los miembros más antiguos

**detritus:** material made up of decaying bits of plant and animal material (116)

    **detrito:** material formado a partir de elementos vegetales y animales en descomposición

**dicot:** angiosperm with two seed leaves in its ovary (737)

    **dicotiledónea:** angiosperma que tiene dos semillas en su ovario

**differentiation:** process by which cells become specialized in structure and function (356, 454)

    **diferenciación:** proceso por el cual las células se especializan en su estructura y función

**diffusion:** process by which particles tend to move from an area where they are more concentrated to an area where they are less concentrated (260)

    **difusión:** proceso mediante el cual las partículas tienden a moverse de un área donde están más concentradas a otra donde están menos concentradas

**digestive tract:** tube that begins at the mouth and ends at the anus (842)

    **tracto digestivo:** tubo que comienza en la boca y termina en el ano

**diploid:** term used to refer to a cell that contains two sets of homologous chromosomes (393)

    **diploide:** término usado para referirse a una célula que contiene dos grupos de cromosomas homólogos

**directional selection:** form of natural selection in which individuals at one end of a distribution curve have higher fitness than individuals in the middle or at the other end of the curve (587)

    **selección direccional:** forma de selección natural en la cual los individuos de un extremo de una curva de distribución tienen mayor aptitud que los individuos que se encuentran en la mitad o en el otro extremo de la curva

**disruptive selection:** natural selection in which individuals at the upper and lower ends of the curve have higher fitness than individuals near the middle of the curve (587)

    **selección disruptiva:** forma de selección natural en la cual los individuos que se encuentran en los extremos superior e inferior de la curva tienen mayor aptitud que los individuos que se encuentran cerca de la mitad de la curva

**DNA (deoxyribonucleic acid):** genetic material that organisms inherit from their parents (23)

    **ADN (ácido desoxirribonucleico):** material genético que los organismos heredan de sus padres

**DNA fingerprinting:** tool used by biologists that analyzes an individual's unique collection of DNA restriction fragments; used to determine whether two samples of genetic material are from the same person (521)

    **huella genética:** herramienta utilizada por los biólogos para analizar una colección única de fragmentos de restricción de ADN de un individuo; se utiliza para determinar si dos muestras de material genético pertenecen al mismo individuo

**DNA microarray:** glass slide or silicon clip that carries thousands of different kinds of single-stranded DNA fragments arranged in a grid. A DNA microarray is used to detect and measure the expression of thousands of genes at one time (520)

    **chip de ADN:** placa de vidrio o clip de silicona que lleva miles de tipos diferentes de fragmentos de hebras sencillas de ADN ordenados en una matriz. Un chip de ADN se utiliza para detectar y medir la expresión de miles de genes simultáneamente

**DNA polymerase:** principal enzyme involved in DNA replication (425)

    **ADN polimerasa:** enzima principal de la replicación del ADN

**domain:** larger, more inclusive taxonomic category than a kingdom (618)

    **dominio:** categoría taxonómica más grande e inclusiva que un reino

**dormancy:** period of time during which a plant embryo is alive but not growing (749)

**latencia:** período de tiempo durante el cual el embrión de una planta está vivo pero no crece

**double fertilization:** process of fertilization in angiosperms in which the first event produces the zygote, and the second produces the endosperm within the seed (744)

**doble fecundación:** proceso de fecundación en las angiospermas mediante el cual el primer evento produce el cigoto y el segundo produce el endosperma dentro de la semilla

**ecological footprint:** the total amount of functioning ecosystem needed both to provide the resources that a human population uses and to absorb the wastes that the population generates (202)

**espacio ecológico:** cantidad total de ecosistema funcional necesario tanto para proporcionar los recursos que utiliza una población humana como para absorber los desechos que la población genera

**ecological pyramid:** model of the relative amounts of energy or matter contained within each trophic level in a given food chain or food web (121)

**pirámide ecológica:** modelo de las cantidades relativas de energía o materia contenida dentro de un nivel trófico en una cadena o red alimentaria dada

**ecological succession:** series of gradual changes that occur in a community following a disturbance (182)

**sucesión ecológica:** serie de cambios graduales que ocurren en una comunidad después de una perturbación

**ecology:** scientific study of interactions among organisms and between organisms and their environment (78)

**ecología:** ciencia que estudia las interacciones entre los organismos y entre estos y su medio ambiente

**ecosystem:** all the organisms that live in a place, together with their nonliving environment (79)

**ecosistema:** todos los organismos que viven en un lugar, junto con su medio ambiente no vivo

**ecosystem diversity:** variety of habitats, communities, and ecological processes in the biosphere (186)

**diversidad de ecosistemas:** variedad de hábitats, comunidades y procesos ecológicos de la biósfera

**ecosystem services:** the benefits for humans that are provided by healthy ecosystems (188)

**servicios de los ecosistemas:** beneficios que los ecosistemas brindan a los seres humanos

**ectotherm:** animal whose body temperature is determined by the temperature of its environment (890)

**ectotermo:** animal cuya temperatura corporal está determinada por la temperatura de su medio ambiente

**electron:** negatively charged particle; located in the space surrounding the nucleus (42)

**electrón:** partícula de carga negativa; se ubica en el espacio que rodea al núcleo

**electron transport chain:** series of electron carrier proteins that shuttle high-energy electrons during ATP-generating reactions (292)

**cadena de transporte de electrones:** serie de proteínas portadoras de electrones que trasladan electrones de gran energía durante las reacciones generadoras de ATP

**element:** pure substance that consists entirely of one type of atom (43)

**elemento:** sustancia pura formada en su totalidad por un único tipo de átomo

**embryo:** developing stage of a multicellular organism (355)

**embrión:** etapa de desarrollo de un organismo multicelular

**embryo sac:** female gametophyte within the ovule of a flowering plant (743)

**saco embrionario:** gametofito femenino que se encuentra en el interior del óvulo de una planta con flores

**emigration:** movement of individuals out of an area (148)

**emigración:** movimiento de individuos fuera de un área

**endocrine gland:** gland that releases its secretions (hormones) directly into the blood, which transports the secretions to other areas of the body (889)

**glándula endocrina:** glándula que libera sus secreciones (hormonas) directamente en la sangre, la cual las transporta a otras zonas del cuerpo

**endoplasmic reticulum:** internal membrane system found in eukaryotic cells; place where lipid components of the cell membrane are assembled (250)

**retículo endoplasmático:** sistema interno de membranas que se encuentra en las células eucariotas; se ubica donde se juntan los componentes lípidos de la membrana celular

**endoskeleton:** internal skeleton; structural support system within the body of an animal (877)

**endoesqueleto:** esqueleto interno; sistema estructural de soporte ubicado dentro del cuerpo de un animal

**endosperm:** food-rich tissue that nourishes a seedling as it grows (744)

**endosperma:** tejido rico en nutrientes que alimenta a la semilla mientras crece

**endospore:** structure produced by prokaryotes in unfavorable conditions; thick internal wall that encloses the DNA and a portion of the cytoplasm (692)

**endospora:** estructura producida por los procariotas en condiciones poco favorables; gruesa pared interna que rodea al ADN y a una parte del citoplasma

**endosymbiotic theory:** theory that proposes that eukaryotic cells formed from a symbiotic relationship among several different prokaryotic cells (663)

**teoría endosimbiótica:** teoría que propone que las células eucariotas se forman a partir de una relación simbiótica entre diferentes células procariotas

**endotherm:** animal whose body temperature is regulated, at least in part, using heat generated within its body (890)

**endotermo:** animal cuya temperatura corporal es regulada, al menos en parte, usando calor generado dentro de su cuerpo

**enzyme:** protein catalyst that speeds up the rate of specific biological reactions (60)

**enzima:** proteína catalizadora que acelera la velocidad de reacciones biológicas específicas

**epidermis:** in plants, single layer of cells that makes up dermal tissue (763)

**epidermis:** en las plantas, única capa de células que forma el tejido dérmico

**epithelial tissue:** type of tissue that lines the interior and exterior of the body surfaces (905)

**tejido epitelial:** tipo de tejido que recubre el interior y el exterior de las superficies corporales

**era:** major division of geologic time; usually divided into two or more periods (646)

**era:** gran división del tiempo geológico; por lo general, se divide en dos o más períodos

**estuary:** kind of wetland formed where a river meets the ocean (101)

**estuario:** tipo de pantanal que se forma donde un río se junta con el océano

**eukaryote:** organism whose cells contain a nucleus (246)

**eucariota:** organismo cuyas células contienen un núcleo

**evolve:** change over time (24)

**evolucionar:** cambiar en el transcurso del tiempo

**evolution:** change over time; the process by which modern organisms have descended from ancient organisms (544)

**evolución:** cambios a través del tiempo; proceso mediante el cual los organismos modernos han descendido de los organismos antiguos

**excretion:** process by which metabolic wastes are eliminated from the body (853)

**excreción:** proceso mediante el cual se eliminan los desechos metabólicos del cuerpo

**exon:** expressed sequence of DNA; codes for a protein (444)

**exón:** secuencia expresada del ADN; códigos de una proteína

**exoskeleton:** external skeleton; tough external covering that protects and supports the body of many invertebrates (877)

**exoesqueleto:** esqueleto externo; cubierta externa dura que protege y sostiene el cuerpo de muchos invertebrados

**exponential growth:** growth pattern in which the individuals in a population reproduce at a constant rate (148)

**crecimiento exponencial:** patrón de crecimiento en el cual los individuos de una población se reproducen a una tasa constante

**extinct:** term used to refer to a species that has died out and has no living members (642)

**extinto:** término usado para referirse a una especie que ha muerto y de la cual no queda miembro vivo

**facilitated diffusion:** process of diffusion in which molecules pass across the membrane through cell membrane channels (261)

**difusión facilitada:** proceso de difusión mediante el cual las moléculas atraviesan la membrana a través de canales de la membrana celular

**family:** in classification, a group of similar genera (614)

**familia:** en la clasificación, un grupo de géneros similares

**feedback inhibition:** process in which a stimulus produces a response that opposes the original stimulus; also called negative feedback (801, 907)

**inhibición de retroalimentación:** proceso mediante el cual un estímulo produce una respuesta que es opuesta al estímulo original; también llamada inhibición negativa

**fermentation:** process by which cells release energy in the absence of oxygen (321)

**fermentación:** proceso mediante el cual las células liberan energía en ausencia de oxígeno

**fertilization:** process in sexual reproduction in which male and female reproductive cells join to form a new cell (379)

**fecundación:** proceso de la reproducción sexual en el que las células reproductoras masculinas y femeninas se unen para formar una nueva célula

**fitness:** how well an organism can survive and reproduce in its environment (556)

**aptitud:** capacidad de un organismo para sobrevivir y reproducirse en su medio ambiente

**fibrous roots:** part of a root system in which roots branch to such an extent that no single root grows larger than the rest (765)

**raíz fibrosa:** raíces ramificadas que crecen desde la base del tallo y que ayudan a muchas plantas a fijar el suelo en su lugar

**flagellum** (pl, flagella): structure used by protists for movement; produces movement in a wavelike motion (700)

**flagelo:** estructura utilizada por los protistas para moverse; produce un movimiento ondulado

**food chain:** series of steps in an ecosystem in which organisms transfer energy by eating and being eaten (118)
   **cadena alimentaria:** serie de sucesos en un ecosistema por medio de los cuales los organismos transfieren energía al comer o al ser comidos por otros

**food web:** network of complex interactions formed by the feeding relationships among the various organisms in an ecosystem (118)
   **red alimentaria:** red de las complejas interacciones que se forma por las relaciones de alimentación entre los diversos organismos de un ecosistema

**forensics:** scientific study of crime scene evidence (522)
   **forense:** ciencia que estudia la evidencia de la escena de un crimen

**fossil:** preserved remains of, or traces of, ancient organisms (547)
   **fósil:** restos o vestigios conservados de organismos antiguos

**founder effect:** change in allele frequencies as a result of the migration of a small subgroup of a population (589)
   **efecto fundador:** cambios que se producen en las frecuencias de los alelos como resultado de la migración de un pequeño subgrupo de una población

**frameshift mutation:** mutation that shifts the "reading frame" of the genetic message by inserting or deleting a nucleotide (458)
   **mutación con desplazamiento del marco de lectura:** mutación que cambia el "marco de lectura" del mensaje genético al insertar o eliminar un nucleótido

**fruit:** structure in angiosperms that contains one or more matured ovaries (737)
   **fruto:** estructura de las angiospermas que contiene uno o más ovarios maduros

**fruiting body:** reproductive structure of a fungus that grows from the mycelium (705)
   **órgano fructífero:** estructura reproductora de un hongo que crece a partir del micelio

**gamete:** sex cell (381)
   **gameto:** célula sexual

**gametophyte:** gamete-producing plant; multicellular haploid phase of a plant life cycle (725)
   **gametofito:** planta productora de gametos; fase haploide multicelular del ciclo vital de una planta

**ganglion** (pl, ganglia): group of interneurons (872)
   **ganglio:** grupo de interneuronas

**gel electrophoresis:** procedure used to separate and analyze DNA fragments by replacing a mixture of DNA fragments at one end of a porous gel and applying an electrical voltage to the gel (486)
   **electroforesis en gel:** procedimiento utilizado para separar y analizar fragmentos de ADN al reemplazar una mezcla de fragmentos de ADN en un extremo de un gel poroso y aplicar un voltaje eléctrico al gel

**gene:** sequence of DNA that codes for a protein and thus determines a trait; factor that is passed from the parent to offspring (380)
   **gen:** secuencia de ADN que codifica una proteína y, por ende, determina un rasgo; factor que se transmite del progenitor a la descendencia

**gene flow:** the movement of genes into or out of a population (591)
   **flujo genético:** movimiento de genes dentro o fuera de una población

**gene pool:** all the genes, including all the different alleles for each gene, that are present in a population at any one time (581)
   **patrimonio genético:** todos los genes, incluyendo todos los alelos diferentes de cada gen, que están presentes en una población en cualquier momento

**gene therapy:** process of changing a gene to treat a medical disease or disorder; an absent or faulty gene is replaced by a normal working gene (518)
   **terapia genética:** proceso que consiste en cambiar un gen para tratar una enfermedad o un trastorno médico; el gen ausente o defectuoso se cambia por un gen con función normal

**genetic code:** collection of codons of mRNA, each of which directs the incorporation of a particular amino acid into a protein during protein synthesis (445)
   **código genético:** colección de codones de ARNm, cada uno de los cuales dirige la incorporación de un aminoácido particular en una proteína durante la síntesis de proteínas

**genetic diversity:** sum total of all the different forms of genetic information carried by a particular species or by all organisms on Earth (186)
   **diversidad genética:** total de todas las diferentes formas de información genética que porta una especie en particular o todos los organismos de la Tierra

**genetic drift:** sum total of all the different forms of genetic information carried by a particular species, or by all organisms on Earth (588)
   **deriva genética:** suma total de todas las distintas formas de información genética portadas por una especie en particular, o por todos los organismos de la Tierra

**genetic equilibrium:** situation in which allele frequencies in a population remain the same (589)

**equilibrio genético:** situación en la cual las frecuencias de los alelos de una población permanecen sin cambios

**genetic marker:** alleles that produce detectable phenotypic differences useful in genetic analysis (512)

**marcador genético:** alelos que producen diferencias fenotípicas detectables que resultan útiles en el análisis genético

**genetics:** scientific study of heredity (378)

**genética:** ciencia que estudia la herencia

**genome:** entire set of genetic information that an organism carries in its DNA (474)

**genoma:** toda la información genética que un organismo lleva en su ADN

**genomic imprinting:** process in which epigenetic chemical marks can be passed from one generation to the next in a sex-specific way (492)

**impronta genética:** proceso mediante el cual las marcas químicas epigenéticas se pueden transmitir de una generación a la siguiente de una manera sexual específica

**genotype:** genetic makeup of an organism (385)

**genotipo:** composición genética de un organismo

**genus:** groups of closely related species; the first part of the scientific name in binomial nomenclature (613)

**género:** grupos de especies estrechamente relacionadas; la primera parte del nombre científico de la nomenclatura binaria

**geographic isolation:** form of reproductive isolation in which two populations are separated by geographic barriers such as rivers, mountains, or bodies of water, leading to the formation of two separate subspecies (593)

**aislamiento geográfico:** forma de aislamiento reproductivo en la cual dos poblaciones son separadas por barreras geográficas como ríos, montañas o cuerpos de agua, lo que lleva a la formación de dos subespecies distintas

**geologic time scale:** timeline used to represent Earth's history (646)

**escala de tiempo geológico:** línea cronológica utilizada para representar la historia de la Tierra

**geosphere:** all of the rock at and below Earth's surface (82)

**geósfera:** materiales sólidos de la Tierra, así como los materiales líquidos que se encuentran en su interior; incluye rocas, continentes y el suelo oceánico

**germination:** resumption of growth of the plant embryo following dormancy (749)

**germinación:** reanudación del crecimiento del embrión de una planta después de la latencia

**gill:** feathery structure specialized for the exchange of gases with water (846)

**branquia:** estructura filamentosa especializada en el intercambio de gases con agua

**global warming:** increase in the average temperatures on Earth (208)

**calentamiento global:** aumento en las temperaturas promedio de la Tierra

**glycolysis:** first set of reactions in cellular respiration in which a molecule of glucose is broken into two molecules of pyruvic acid (314)

**glucólisis:** primer conjunto de reacciones de la respiración celular en el cual una molécula de glucosa se descompone en dos moléculas de ácido pirúvico

**Golgi apparatus:** organelle in cells that modifies, sorts, and packages proteins and other material from the endoplasmic reticulum for storage in the cell or release outside the cell (251)

**aparato de Golgi:** orgánulo de la célula que modifica, clasifica y empaqueta proteínas y otras sustancias del retículo endoplasmático para su almacenamiento en la célula o para liberarlos fuera de esta

**gradualism:** the evolution of a species by gradual accumulation of small genetic changes over long periods of time (655)

**gradualismo:** evolución de una especie debido a la acumulación gradual de pequeños cambios genéticos que ocurren durante largos períodos de tiempo

**gravitropism:** response of a plant to the force of gravity (780)

**gravitropismo:** respuesta de las plantas a la fuerza de la gravedad

**greenhouse effect:** process in which certain gases (carbon dioxide, methane, and water vapor) trap sunlight energy in Earth's atmosphere as heat (86)

**efecto invernadero:** proceso mediante el cual ciertos gases (dióxido de carbono, metano y vapor de agua) atrapan la energía de la luz solar en la atmósfera de la Tierra en forma de calor

**growth factor:** one of a group of external regulatory proteins that stimulate the growth and division of cells (351)

**factor de crecimiento:** uno de un grupo de proteínas reguladoras externas que estimulan el crecimiento y la división de las células

**guard cell:** specialized cell in the epidermis of plants that controls the opening and closing of the stomata (772)

**célula de guarda (o célula oclusiva):** célula especializada de la epidermis vegetal que controla la abertura y el cierre de los estomas

**gymnosperm:** group of seed plants that bear their seeds directly on the scales of cones (734)

**gimnospermas:** grupo de plantas con semillas, que tienen sus semillas directamente sobre las escamas de los conos

**habitat:** area in which an organism lives, including the biotic and abiotic factors that affect it (174)

**hábitat:** área en la cual vive un organismo, incluyendo los factores bióticos y abióticos que lo afectan

**half-life:** length of time required for half of the radioactive atoms in a sample to decay (644)

**vida media:** período de tiempo requerido para que se desintegre la mitad de los átomos radiactivos de una muestra

**haploid:** term used to refer to a cell that contains only a single set of genes (394)

**haploide:** término que se usa para referirse a una célula que posee un solo juego de genes

**Hardy-Weinberg principle:** principle that states that allele frequencies in a population remain constant unless one or more factors cause those frequencies to change (590)

**principio de Hardy-Weinberg:** principio que afirma que las frecuencias alélicas de una población permanecen constantes a menos que uno o más factores ocasionen que esas frecuencias cambien

**heart:** hollow muscular organ that pumps blood throughout the body (849)

**corazón:** órgano muscular hueco que bombea la sangre a todo el cuerpo

**heterotroph:** organism that obtains food by consuming other living things; also called consumers (116, 285)

**heterótrofo:** organismo que obtiene su alimento consumiendo otros seres vivos; también llamado consumidor

**heterozygous:** having two different alleles for a particular gene (384)

**heterocigota:** que tiene dos alelos diferentes para un gen dado

**homeobox gene:** a DNA sequence of approximately 130 base pairs, found in many homeotic genes that regulate development. They code for transcription factors and proteins that bind to DNA, which regulate the expression of other genes (454)

**gen homeobox:** secuencia de ADN de aproximadamente 130 pares de bases que se encuentra en muchos genes homeóticos que regulan el desarrollo. Codifica los factores de transcripción y las proteínas que se unen al ADN, las cuales regulan la expresión de otros genes

**homeostasis:** relatively constant internal physical and chemical conditions that organisms maintain (24, 260, 907)

**homeostasis:** las condiciones físicas y químicas internas, relativamente constantes que mantienen los organismos

**homeotic gene:** a class of regulatory genes that determine the identity of body parts and regions in an embryo; mutations in these genes can transform one body part into another (454)

**gen homeótico:** tipo de genes reguladores que determinan la identidad de las partes y regiones del cuerpo en un embrión; las mutaciones de esos genes pueden transformar una parte del cuerpo en otra

**hominoid:** group of anthropoids that include gibbons, orangutans, gorillas, chimpanzees, and humans (817)

**homínido:** grupo de antropoides que incluye a los gibones, orangutanes, gorilas, chimpancés y seres humanos

**homologous:** term used to refer to chromosomes in which one set comes from the male parent and one set comes from the female parent (393)

**homólogos:** término utilizado para referirse a los cromosomas en los que un juego proviene del progenitor masculino y un juego proviene del progenitor femenino

**homologous structures:** structures that are similar in different species of common ancestors (562)

**estructuras homólogas:** estructuras que son similares en distintas especies que tienen ancestros en común

**homozygous:** having two identical alleles for a particular gene (384)

**homocigota:** que tiene dos alelos idénticos para un gen dado

**hormone:** chemical produced in one part of an organism that affects another part of the same organism (776)

**hormona:** sustancia química producida en una parte de un organismo que afecta a otra parte del mismo organismo

**Hox gene:** a group of homeotic genes clustered together to determine the head to tail identity of body parts in animals; all Hox genes contain the homeobox DNA sequence (454, 597)

**gen Hox:** grupo de genes homeóticos agrupados en un conjunto que determinan la identidad posicional de las partes del cuerpo de los animales; todos los genes Hox contienen la secuencia de ADN homeobox

**humoral immunity:** immunity against antigens in the body fluids, such as blood and lymph (940)

**inmunidad humoral:** inmunidad contra los antígenos presentes en los fluidos corporales, como la sangre y la linfa

**humus:** material formed from decaying leaves and other organic matter (95)

**humus:** material formado a partir de hojas en descomposición y otra materia orgánica

**hybrid:** offspring of crosses between parents with different traits (379)

**híbrido:** descendencia del cruce entre progenitores que tienen rasgos diferentes

**hybridization:** breeding technique that involves crossing dissimilar individuals to bring together the best traits of both organisms (507)

**hibridación:** técnica de cría que consiste en cruzar individuos diferentes para reunir los mejores rasgos de ambos organismos

**hydrogen bond:** weak attraction between a hydrogen atom and another atom (47)

**enlace de hidrógeno:** atracción débil entre un átomo de hidrógeno y otro átomo

**hydrosphere:** all of the water—salt water and fresh water, in the form of liquid, ice, or vapor—above and below Earth's surface and in the atmosphere (82)

**hidrósfera:** compuesta por toda el agua dulce y salada de la Tierra, incluyendo el vapor de agua, la lluvia de la atmósfera y las aguas subterráneas

**hydrostatic skeleton:** skeleton made of fluid-filled body segments that work with muscles to allow the animal to move (876)

**esqueleto hidrostático:** esqueleto constituido por segmentos corporales llenos de fluido que trabajan con los músculos para permitir el movimiento del animal

**hypertonic:** when comparing two solutions, the solution with the greater concentration of solutes (262)

**hipertónica:** al comparar dos soluciones, la solución que tiene la mayor concentración de solutos

**hypha** (pl, hyphae): one of many long, slender filaments that make up the body of a fungus (705)

**hifa:** uno de muchos filamentos largos y delgados que componen el cuerpo de un hongo

**hypothesis:** possible explanation for a set of observations or possible answers to a scientific question (12)

**hipótesis:** explicación posible para un conjunto de observaciones o respuestas posibles a una pregunta científica

**hypotonic:** when comparing two solutions, the solution with the lesser concentration of solutes (262)

**hipotónica:** al comparar dos soluciones, la solución que tiene la menor concentración de solutos

**immigration:** movement of individuals into an area occupied by an existing population (148)

**inmigración:** desplazamiento de individuos a un área ocupada por una población ya existente

**inbreeding:** continued breeding of individuals with similar characteristics to maintain the derived characteristics of a kind of organism (507)

**endogamia:** la cría continua de individuos con características semejantes para mantener las características derivadas de un tipo de organismo

**incomplete dominance:** situation in which one allele is not completely dominant over another allele (389)

**dominancia incompleta:** situación en la cual un alelo no es completamente dominante sobre otro alelo

**independent assortment:** one of Mendel's principles that states that genes for different traits can segregate independently during the formation of gametes (387)

**distribución independiente:** uno de los principios de Mendel que establece que los genes para rasgos diferentes pueden segregarse independientemente durante la formación de los gametos

**independent variable:** factor in a controlled experiment that is deliberately changed; also called manipulated variable (12)

**variable independiente:** en un experimento controlado, el factor que se modifica a propósito; también llamada variable manipulada

**index fossil:** distinctive fossil that is used to compare the relative ages of fossils (644)

**fósil guía:** fósil distintivo usado para comparar las edades relativas de los fósiles

**infectious disease:** disease caused by a microorganism that disrupts normal body function (937)

**enfermedad infecciosa:** enfermedad causada por un microorganismo que altera las funciones normales del cuerpo

**inference:** a logical interpretation based on prior knowledge and experience (12)

**inferencia:** interpretación lógica basada en la experiencia y en conocimientos previos

**inflammatory response:** nonspecific defense reaction to tissue damage caused by injury or infection (939)

**respuesta inflamatoria:** reacción defensiva no específica al daño causado a los tejidos por una herida o una infección

**interneuron:** type of neuron that processes information and may relay information to motor neurons (871)

**interneurona:** tipo de neurona que procesa información y la puede transmitir para estimular las neuronas

**interphase:** period of the cell cycle between cell divisions (345)

**interfase:** período del ciclo celular entre las divisiones celulares

**intron:** sequence of DNA that is not involved in coding for a protein (444)

    **intrón:** secuencia de ADN que no participa en la codificación de una proteína

**invasive species:** non-native species whose introduction causes, or is likely to cause, economic harm, environmental harm, or harm to human health (214)

    **especie invasive:** especie no nativa cuya introducción causa, o puede causar, daños a la economía, al medio ambiente o a la salud humana

**invertebrate:** animal that lacks a backbone, or vertebral column (800)

    **invertebrado:** animal que carece de columna vertebral

**ion:** atom that has a positive or negative charge (45)

    **ion:** átomo que tiene una carga positiva o negativa

**ionic bond:** chemical bond formed when one or more electrons are transferred from one atom to another (45)

    **enlace iónico:** enlace químico que se forma cuando uno o más electrones se transfieren de un átomo a otro

**isotonic:** when the concentration of two solutions is the same (262)

    **isotónica:** cuando la concentración de dos soluciones es la misma

**isotope:** one of several forms of a single element, which contains the same number of protons but different number of neutrons (43)

    **isótopo:** cada una de las diferentes formas de un único elemento, que contiene la misma cantidad de protones pero cantidades distintas de neutrones

**joint:** place where one bone attaches to another bone (878)

    **articulación:** sitio donde un hueso se une a otro hueso

**karyotype:** micrograph of the complete diploid set of chromosomes grouped together in pairs, arranged in order of decreasing size (474)

    **cariotipo:** micrografía de la totalidad del conjunto diploide de cromosomas agrupados en pares, ordenados por tamaño decreciente

**keystone species:** single species that is not usually abundant in a community yet exerts strong control on the structure of a community (180)

    **especie clave:** especie que habitualmente no es abundante en una comunidad y sin embargo ejerce un fuerte control sobre la estructura de esa comunidad

**kidney:** an organ of excretion that separates wastes and excess water from the blood (854)

    **riñón:** órgano excretor que separa los residuos y el exceso de agua de la sangre

**kingdom:** largest and most inclusive group in Linnaean classification (615)

    **reino:** grupo más grande e inclusivo del sistema de clasificación de Linneo

**kin selection:** theory that states that helping relatives can improve an individual's evolutionary fitness because related individuals share a large portion of their genes (826)

    **selección de parentesco (o familiar):** teoría que establece que ayudar a los parientes puede mejorar la aptitud evolutiva de un individuo porque los individuos relacionados comparten una gran parte de sus genes

**Krebs cycle:** second stage of cellular respiration, in which pyruvic acid is broken down into carbon dioxide in a series of energy-extracting reactions (316)

    **ciclo de Krebs:** segunda fase de la respiración celular en la cual el ácido pirúvico se descompone en dióxido de carbono en una serie de reacciones que liberan energía

**language:** system of communication that combines sounds, symbols, and gestures according to a set of rules about sequence and meaning, such as grammar and syntax (827)

    **lenguaje:** sistema de comunicación que combina sonidos, símbolos y gestos según un conjunto de reglas sobre la secuencia y el significado, como la gramática y la sintaxis

**lichen:** symbiotic association between a fungus and a photosynthetic organism (708)

    **liquen:** asociación simbiótica entre un hongo y un organismo fotosintético

**light-dependent reaction:** set of reactions in photosynthesis that use energy from light to produce ATP and NADPH (289)

    **reacciones dependientes de la luz:** en la fotosíntesis, conjunto de reacciones que emplean la energía proveniente de la luz para producir ATP y NADPH

**light-independent reaction:** set of reactions in photosynthesis that do not require light; energy from ATP and NADPH is used to build high-energy compounds such as sugar; also called the Calvin cycle (290)

    **reacciones independientes de la luz:** en la fotosíntesis, conjunto de reacciones que no necesitan luz; la energía proveniente del ATP y del NADPH se emplea para construir compuestos con gran contenido energético, como el azúcar; también llamado ciclo de Calvin

**limiting factor:** factor that causes population growth to decrease (152)

    **factor limitante:** factor que provoca que el crecimiento de una población disminuya

**limiting nutrient:** single essential nutrient that limits productivity in an ecosystem (130)

    **nutriente limitante:** un solo nutriente esencia que limita la productividad de un ecosistema

**lipid:** macromolecule made mostly from carbon and hydrogen atoms; includes fats, oils, and waxes (54)

    **lípido:** macromolécula compuesta principalmente por átomos de carbono e hidrógeno; incluye las grasas, los aceites y las ceras

**lipid bilayer:** flexible double-layered sheet that makes up the cell membrane and forms a barrier between the cell and its surroundings (256)

    **bicapa lipídica:** lámina flexible de dos capas que constituye la membrana celular y forma una barrera entre la célula y su entorno

**logistic growth:** growth pattern in which a population's growth slows and then stops following a period of exponential growth (150)

    **crecimiento logístico:** patrón de crecimiento en el cual el desarrollo de una población se reduce y luego se detiene después de un período de crecimiento exponencial

**lung:** respiratory organ; place where gases are exchanged between blood and inhaled air (846)

    **pulmón:** órgano respiratorio; lugar donde se intercambian los gases entre la sangre y el aire inhalado

**lysogenic infection:** type of infection in which a virus embeds its DNA into the DNA of the host cell and is replicated along with the host cell's DNA (685)

    **infección lisogénica:** tipo de infección en la cual un virus inserta su ADN en el ADN de la célula huésped y se replica junto con el ADN de dicha célula huésped

**lysosome:** cell organelle that breaks down lipids, carbohydrates, and proteins into small molecules that can be used by the rest of the cell (252)

    **lisosoma:** orgánulo celular que descompone los lípidos, los hidratos de carbono y las proteínas en moléculas pequeñas que pueden ser utilizadas por el resto de la célula

**lytic infection:** type of infection in which the virus enters a cell, makes a copy of itself, and causes the cell to burst (685)

    **infección lítica:** tipo de infección en la cual un virus penetra una célula, hace copias de sí mismo y provoca la muerte celular

**macroevolutionary pattern:** changes in anatomy, phylogeny, ecology, and behavior that take place in clades larger than a single species (652)

    **patrones de macroevolución:** cambios que ocurren en la anatomía, filogenia, ecología y comportamiento de clados que abarcan a más de una especie

**Malpighian tubule:** structure in most terrestrial arthropods that concentrates the uric acid and adds it to digestive wastes (856)

    **túbulo de Malpighi:** estructura de la mayoría de los artrópodos terrestres que concentra el ácido úrico y lo incorpora a los residuos digestivos

**mammary gland:** gland in female mammals that produces milk to nourish the young (887)

    **glándula mamaria:** glándula de las hembras de los mamíferos que produce leche para alimentar a las crías

**mass extinction:** event during which many species become extinct during a relatively short period of time (654)

    **extinción masiva:** suceso durante el cual se extinguen muchas especies durante un período de tiempo relativamente corto

**matrix:** innermost compartment of the mitochondrion (316)

    **matriz:** compartimento más interno de la mitocondria

**meiosis:** process in which the number of chromosomes per cell is cut in half through the separation of homologous chromosomes in a diploid cell (394)

    **meiosis:** proceso por el cual el número de cromosomas por célula se reduce a la mitad mediante la separación de los cromosomas homólogos de una célula diploide

**meristem:** region of specialized cells responsible for continuing growth throughout a plant's lifetime (764)

    **meristemos:** regiones de células especializadas responsables del crecimiento continuo de una planta durante su vida

**mesophyll:** specialized ground tissue found in leaves; performs most of a plant's photosynthesis (770)

    **mesófilo:** tejido fundamental especializado que se halla en las hojas; realiza la mayor parte de la fotosíntesis de una planta

**messenger RNA** (mRNA): type of RNA that carries copies of instructions for the assembly of amino acids into proteins from DNA to the rest of the cell (442)

    **ARN mensajero (ARNm):** tipo de ARN que transporta copias de las instrucciones para el ensamblaje de los aminoácidos en proteínas, desde el ADN al resto de la célula

**metabolism:** the combination of chemical reactions through which an organism builds up or breaks down materials (24)

**metabolismo:** la combinación de reacciones químicas a través de las cuales un organismo acumula o descompone sustancias

**metamorphosis:** a developmental process that involves dramatic changes in shape and form (884)

**metamorfosis:** proceso de desarrollo que implica cambios drásticos en la forma

**metaphase:** phase of mitosis in which the chromosomes line up across the center of the cell (347)

**metafase:** fase de la mitosis en la cual los cromosomas se alinean a través del centro de la célula

**mitochondrion** (pl, mitochondria): cell organelle that converts the chemical energy stored in food into compounds that are more convenient for the cell to use (254)

**mitocondria:** orgánulo celular que convierte la energía química almacenada en los alimentos en compuestos más apropiados para que la célula los use

**mitosis:** part of eukaryotic cell division during which the cell nucleus divides (346)

**mitosis:** fase de la división de las células eucariotas durante la cual se divide el núcleo celular

**mixture:** material composed of two or more elements or compounds that are physically mixed together but not chemically combined (49)

**mezcla:** material compuesto por dos o más elementos o compuestos que están mezclados físicamente pero no están combinados químicamente

**molecule:** smallest unit of most compounds that displays all the properties of that compound (45)

**molécula:** la unidad más pequeña de la mayoría de los compuestos que exhibe todas las propiedades de ese compuesto

**monocot:** angiosperm with one seed leaf in its ovary (737)

**monocotiledónea:** angiosperma con una hoja embrionaria en su ovario

**monoculture:** farming strategy of planting a single highly productive crop year after year (211)

**monocultivo:** estrategia agrícola que consiste en plantar año tras año un único cultivo altamente productivo

**monomer:** small chemical unit that makes up a polymer (53)

**monómero:** pequeña unidad química que forma un polímero

**motor neuron:** type of nerve cell that carries directions from interneurons to either muscle cells or glands (871)

**neurona motora:** tipo de célula nerviosa que lleva las instrucciones provenientes de las interneuronas a las células musculares o las glándulas

**multiple alleles:** gene that has more than two alleles (390)

**alelos múltiples:** gen que tiene más de dos alelos

**multipotent:** cell with limited potential to develop into many types of differentiated cells (357)

**multipotentes:** células con potencial limitado para generar muchos tipos de células diferenciadas

**muscle tissue:** type of tissue that makes movements of the body possible (905)

**tejido muscular:** tipo de tejido que hace posibles los movimientos del cuerpo

**mutagen:** chemical or physical agents in the environment that interact with DNA and may cause a mutation (460)

**mutágeno:** agentes físicos o químicos del medio ambiente que interaccionan con el ADN y pueden causar una mutación

**mutation:** change in the genetic material of a cell (457)

**mutación:** cambio en el material genético de una célula

**mutualism:** symbiotic relationship in which both species benefit from the relationship (181)

**mutualismo:** relación simbiótica en la cual ambas especies se benefician

**mycelium** (pl, mycelia): densely branched network of the hyphae of a fungus (705)

**micelio:** red de filamentos muy ramificados de las hifas de un hongo

**mycorrhiza** (pl, mycorrhizae): symbiotic association of plant roots and fungi (709)

**micorriza:** asociación simbiótica entre las raíces de las plantas y los hongos

**NAD⁺** (nicotinamide adenine dinucleotide): electron carrier involved in glycolysis (315)

**NAD⁺** (dinucleótido de nicotinamida adenina): transportador de electrones que participa en la glucólisis

**NADP⁺** (nicotinamide adenine dinucleotide phosphate): carrier molecule that transfers high-energy electrons from chlorophyll to other molecules (288)

**NADP⁺** (fosfato de dinucleótido de nicotinamida adenina): molécula transportadora de electrones que transfiere electrones de alta energía desde la clorofila a otras moléculas

**natural selection:** process by which organisms that are most suited to their environment survive and reproduce most successfully; also called survival of the fittest (557)

**selección natural:** proceso por el cual los organismos más adaptados a su medioambiente sobreviven y se reproducen más exitosamente; también llamada supervivencia del más apto

**nephridium** (pl, nephridia): excretory structure of the annelid that filters body fluid (856)
   **nefridio:** estructura excretora de los anélidos que filtra el fluido corporal

**nervous tissue:** type of tissue that transmits nerve impulses throughout the body (905)
   **tejido nervioso:** tipo de tejido que transmite los impulsos nerviosos por el cuerpo

**neuron:** nerve cell; specialized for carrying messages throughout the nervous system (870)
   **neurona:** célula nerviosa; especializada en conducir mensajes a través del sistema nervioso

**niche:** full range of physical and biological conditions in which an organism lives and the way in which the organism uses those conditions (177)
   **nicho:** toda la variedad de condiciones físicas y biológicas en las que vive un organismo y la manera en la que dicho organismo utiliza esas condiciones

**nitrogen fixation:** process of converting nitrogen gas into nitrogen compounds that plants can absorb and use (129)
   **fijación de nitrógeno:** el proceso mediante el cual el gas nitrógeno se convierte en los compuestos nitrogenados que las plantas pueden absorber y utilizar

**node:** part on a growing stem where a leaf is attached (768)
   **nudo:** parte de un tallo en crecimiento donde está adherida una hoja

**nondisjunction:** error in meiosis in which the homologous chromosomes fail to separate properly (480)
   **no disyunción:** error que ocurre durante la meiosis, en el que cromosomas homólogos no logran separarse adecuadamente

**nonrenewable resource:** resources that cannot be replenished by a natural process within a reasonable amount of time (225)
   **recurso no renovable:** recurso que no se puede reponer mediante un proceso natural dentro de un período de tiempo razonable

**nucleic acid:** macromolecules containing hydrogen, oxygen, nitrogen, carbon, and phosphorous (55)
   **ácido nucleico:** macromoléculas que contienen hidrógeno, oxígeno, nitrógeno, carbono y fósforo

**nucleotide:** subunit of which nucleic acids are composed; made up of a 5-carbon sugar, a phosphate group, and a nitrogenous base (55)
   **nucleótido:** subunidad que constituye los ácidos nucleicos; compuesta de un azúcar de 5 carbonos, un grupo fosfato y una base nitrogenada

**nucleus:** the center of an atom, which contains the protons and neutrons (42); in cells, the structure that contains the cell's genetic material in the form of DNA (246)
   **núcleo:** el centro de un átomo, el cual contiene los protones y los neutrones; en las células, la estructura que contiene el material genético de la célula en forma de ADN

**nutrient:** chemical substance that an organism needs to sustain life (126)
   **nutriente:** sustancia química que un organismo necesita para continuar con vida

**observation:** process of noticing and describing events or processes in a careful, orderly way (12)
   **observación:** método de percibir y describir sucesos o procesos de manera atenta y ordenada

**open circulatory system:** type of circulatory system in which blood is only partially contained within a system of blood vessels as it travels through the body (849)
   **sistema circulatorio abierto:** tipo de sistema circulatorio en el cual la sangre está solo parcialmente contenida dentro de un sistema de vasos sanguíneos

**operator:** short DNA region, adjacent to the promoter of prokaryotic operon, that binds repressor proteins responsible for controlling the rate of transcription of the operon (452)
   **operador:** pequeña región de ADN, adyacente al promotor del operón de una procariota, que une las proteínas represoras responsables de controlar la tasa de transcripción del operón

**operon:** in prokaryotes, a group of adjacent genes that share a common operator and promoter and are transcribed into a single mRNA (451)
   **operón:** en las procariotas, grupo de genes adyacentes que comparten un operador y un promotor en común y que son transcritas a un solo ARN mensajero

**opposable thumb:** thumb that enables the grasping of objects and the utilization of tools (818)
   **pulgar oponible o prensible:** pulgar que permite aferrar objetos y utilizar herramientas

**order:** in classification, a group of closely related families (614)
   **orden:** en la clasificación, un grupo de familias relacionadas estrechamente

**organ:** group of tissues that work together to perform closely related functions (268)
   **órgano:** grupo de tejidos que trabajan juntos para realizar funciones estrechamente relacionadas

**organ system:** groups of organs that work together to perform a specific function (268)
   **sistema de órganos:** grupo de órganos que realizan juntos una función específica

**organelle:** specialized structure that performs important cellular functions within a cell (248)
   **orgánulo:** estructura especializada que realiza funciones celulares importantes dentro de una célula

**osmosis:** diffusion of water through a selectively permeable membrane (262)

**ósmosis:** difusión de agua a través de una membrana de permeabilidad selectiva

**osmotic pressure:** pressure that must be applied to prevent osmotic movement across a selectively permeable membrane (263)

**presión osmótica:** presión que debe aplicarse para evitar el movimiento osmótico a través de una membrana de permeabilidad selectiva

**ovary:** in plants, the structure that surrounds and protects seeds (737)

**ovario:** en las plantas, la estructura que rodea a las semillas y las protege

**ovule:** structure in seed cones in which female gametophytes develop (735)

**óvulo:** estructura de las semillas coníferas donde se desarrollan los gametos femeninos

**ozone layer:** atmospheric layer in which ozone gas is relatively concentrated; protects life on Earth from harmful ultraviolet rays in sunlight (215)

**capa de ozono:** capa atmosférica en la cual el gas ozono se encuentra relativamente concentrado; protege a los seres vivos de la Tierra de los perjudiciales rayos ultravioletas de la luz solar

**parasitism:** relationship in which one organism lives inside or on another organism and harms it (181)

**parasitismo:** relación en la cual un organismo vive sobre otro organismo o en su interior y lo perjudica

**pathogen:** disease-causing agent (694, 937)

**patógeno:** agente que causa una enfermedad

**pedigree:** chart that shows the presence or absence of a trait according to the relationships within a family across several generations (478)

**árbol genealógico:** diagrama que muestra la presencia o ausencia de un rasgo de acuerdo con las relaciones intrafamiliares a través de varias generaciones

**period:** division of geologic time into which eras are subdivided (646)

**período:** división del tiempo geológico en la que se subdividen las eras

**permafrost:** layer of permanently frozen subsoil found in the tundra (96)

**permacongelamiento:** permafrost capa de subsuelo congelado en forma permanente que se halla en la tundra

**pH scale:** scale with values from 0 to 14, used to measure the concentration of H⁺ ions in a solution; a pH of 0 to 7 is acidic, a pH of 7 is neutral, and a pH of 7 to 14 is basic (50)

**escala del pH:** escala con valores de 0 a 14, utilizada para medir la concentración de iones H⁺ en una solución; un pH de 0 a 7 es ácido, un pH de 7 es neutro y un pH de 7 a 14 es básico

**phenotype:** physical characteristics of an organism (385)

**fenotipo:** características físicas de un organismo

**phloem:** vascular tissue that transports solutions of nutrients and carbohydrates produced by photosynthesis through the plant (731)

**floema:** tejido vascular que transporta por toda la planta las soluciones de nutrientes e hidratos de carbono producidos en la fotosíntesis

**photic zone:** sunlight region near the surface of water (98)

**zona fótica:** región cerca de la superficie del mar en la que penetra la luz solar

**photoperiodism:** plant response to the relative lengths of light and darkness (782)

**fotoperiodismo:** la respuesta de una planta a los tiempos relativos de luz y oscuridad

**photosynthesis:** process used by plants and other autotrophs to capture light energy and use it to power chemical reactions that convert carbon dioxide and water into oxygen and energy-rich carbohydrates such as sugars and starches (114, 285)

**fotosíntesis:** proceso empleado por las plantas y otros organismos autótrofos para captar la energía luminosa y utilizarla para impulsar reacciones químicas que convierten el dióxido de carbono y el agua en oxígeno e hidratos de carbono de gran contenido energético, como azúcares y almidones

**photosystem:** cluster of chlorophyll and proteins found in the thylakoids (291)

**fotosistema:** conjunto de clorofila y proteínas que se hallan en los tilacoides

**phototropism:** tendency of a plant to grow toward a light source (780)

**fototropismo:** tendencia de una planta a crecer hacia una fuente de luz

**phylogeny:** the evolutionary history of lineage (619)

**filogenia:** historia evolutiva del linaje

**phylum** (pl, phyla): in classification, a group of closely related classes (615)

**filo:** en la clasificación, un grupo de clases estrechamente relacionadas

**phytoplankton:** photosynthetic algae found near the surface of the ocean (118)

> **fitoplancton:** algas fotosintéticas que se hallan cerca de la superficie del océano

**pigment:** light-absorbing molecule used by plants to gather the sun's energy (286)

> **pigmento:** moléculas que absorben la luz, empleadas por las plantas para recolectar la energía solar

**pioneer species:** the first species to populate an area during succession (182)

> **especies pioneras:** las primeras especies en poblar un área durante la sucesión

**placenta:** specialized organ that enables exchange of respiratory gases, nutrients, and wastes between the mother and her developing young (884)

> **placenta:** órgano especializado que permite intercambiar los gases respiratorios, los nutrientes y los residuos entre la madre y su cría en desarrollo

**plankton:** microscopic organisms that live in aquatic environments; includes both phytoplankton and zooplankton (98)

> **plancton:** organismos microscópicos que viven en medios ambientes acuáticos; incluye el fitoplancton y el zooplancton

**plasmid:** small, circular piece of DNA located in the cytoplasm of many bacteria (511)

> **plásmido:** pequeña porción circular de ADN ubicada en el citoplasma de muchas bacterias

**plate tectonics:** geologic processes, such as continental drift, volcanoes, and earthquakes, resulting from plate movement (649)

> **tectónica de placas:** procesos geológicos, como la deriva continental, los volcanes y los terremotos, que son consecuencia de los movimientos de las placas

**pluripotent:** cells that are capable of developing into most, but not all, of the body's cell types (357)

> **pluripotentes:** células capaces de convertirse en la mayoría de las células del cuerpo, pero no en todas

**point mutation:** gene mutation in which a single base pair in DNA has been changed (457)

> **mutación puntual:** mutación genética en la cual se ha modificado un único par de bases en el ADN

**pollination:** transfer of pollen from the male reproductive structure to the female reproductive structure (735)

> **polinización:** transferencia de polen desde la estructura reproductora masculina hacia la estructura reproductora femenina

**pollutant:** any harmful material created as a result of human activity and released into the environment (214)

> **contaminante:** material nocivo producto de la actividad humana y liberado en el medio ambiente

**polygenic trait:** trait controlled by two or more genes (391, 584)

> **rasgo poligénico:** rasgo controlado por dos o más genes

**polymerase chain reaction** (PCR): the technique used by biologists to make many copies of a particular gene (510)

> **reacción en cadena de la polimerasa (PCR):** técnica usada por los biólogos para hacer muchas copias de un gen específico

**polymer:** molecule composed of many monomers; makes up macromolecules (53)

> **polímero:** molécula compuesta por muchos monómeros; forma macromoléculas

**polypeptide:** long chain of amino acids that make proteins (445)

> **polipéptido:** cadena larga de aminoácidos que forma las proteínas

**polyploidy:** condition in which an organism has extra sets of chromosomes (461)

> **poliploidía:** condición en la cual un organismo tiene grupos adicionales de cromosomas

**population:** groups of individuals of the same species that live in the same area (79)

> **población:** grupo de individuos de la misma especie que viven en la misma área

**population density:** number of individuals per unit area (146)

> **densidad de población:** número de individuos que viven por unidad de superficie

**population distribution:** the way individuals are spaced out across their range (146)

> **distribución de población:** la forma en que los individuos se sitúan en su espacio

**primary growth:** pattern of growth that takes place at the tips and shoots of a plant (769)

> **crecimiento primario:** patrón de crecimiento que tiene lugar en las puntas y en los brotes de una planta

**primary producer:** first producer of energy-rich compounds that are later used by other organisms (114)

> **productores primarios:** los primeros productores de compuestos ricos en energía que luego son utilizados por otros organismos

**primary succession:** succession that occurs in an area in which no trace of a previous community is present (182)

  **sucesión primaria:** sucesión que ocurre en un área en la cual no hay rastros de la presencia de una comunidad anterior

**principle of dominance:** Mendel's second conclusion, which states that some alleles are dominant and others are recessive (380)

  **principio de dominancia:** segunda conclusión de Mendel, que establece que algunos alelos son dominantes y otros son recesivos

**probability:** likelihood that a particular event will occur (383)

  **probabilidad:** posibilidad de que ocurra un suceso dado

**product:** elements or compounds produced by chemical reactions (58)

  **producto:** elemento o compuesto producido por una reacción química

**prokaryote:** unicellular organism that lacks a nucleus (246, 689)

  **procariota:** organismo unicelular que carece de núcleo

**promoter:** specific region of a gene where RNA polymerase can bind and begin transcription (443)

  **promotor:** región específica de un gen en donde la ARN polimerasa puede unirse e iniciar la transcripción

**prophage:** bacteriophage DNA that is embedded in the bacterial host's DNA (685)

  **profago:** ADN del bacteriófago que está alojado en el interior del ADN del huésped bacteriano

**prophase:** first and longest phase of mitosis in which the genetic material inside the nucleus condenses and the chromosomes become visible (346)

  **profase:** primera y más prolongada fase de la mitosis, en la cual el material genético dentro del interior del núcleo se condensa y los cromosomas se hacen visibles

**protein:** macromolecule that contains carbon, hydrogen, oxygen, and nitrogen; needed by the body for growth and repair (55)

  **proteína:** macromolécula que contiene carbono, hidrógeno, oxígeno y nitrógeno; necesaria para el crecimiento y reparación del cuerpo

**punctuated equilibrium:** pattern of evolution in which long stable periods are interrupted by brief periods of more rapid change (655)

  **equilibrio interrumpido:** patrón de evolución en el cual largos periodos de estabilidad se ven interrumpidos por breves periodos de cambio más rápido

**Punnett square:** diagram that can be used to predict the genotype and phenotype combinations of a genetic cross (385)

  **cuadro de Punnett:** un diagrama que puede utilizarse para predecir las combinaciones de genotipos y fenotipos en un cruce genético

**radial symmetry:** body plan in which any number of imaginary planes drawn through the center of the body could divide it into equal halves (803)

  **simetría radial:** diseño corporal en el cual cualquier número de ejes imaginarios dibujados a través del centro del cuerpo lo dividirá en mitades iguales

**radiometric dating:** method for determining the age of a sample from the amount of a radioactive isotope to the nonradioactive isotope of the same element in a sample (644)

  **datación radiométrica:** método para determinar la edad de una muestra a partir de la cantidad de un isótopo radioactivo en relación a la del isótopo no radiactivo del mismo elemento en dicha muestra

**reactant:** elements or compounds that enter into a chemical reaction (58)

  **reactante:** elemento o compuesto que participa en una reacción química

**receptor:** on or in a cell, a specific protein to whose shape fits a specific molecular messenger, such as a hormone (269, 776)

  **receptor:** proteína específica que puede encontrarse en la membrana celular o dentro de la célula, cuya forma se corresponde con la de un mensajero molecular específico, por ejemplo una hormona

**recombinant DNA:** DNA produced by combining DNA from different sources (511)

  **ADN recombinante:** ADN producido por la combinación de ADN de orígenes diferentes

**relative dating:** method of determining the age of a fossil by comparing its placement with that of fossils in other rock layers (644)

  **datación relativa:** método para determinar la edad de un fósil comparando su ubicación con la de los fósiles hallados en otras capas de roca

**renewable resource:** resource that can be produced or replaced by a healthy ecosystem (224)

  **recurso renovable:** recurso que se puede producir o reemplazar mediante un ecosistema saludable

**replication:** process of copying DNA prior to cell division (424)

  **replicación:** proceso de copia de ADN previo a la división celular

**reproductive isolation:** separation of a species or population so that they no longer interbreed and evolve into separate species (592)

  **aislamiento reproductor:** separación de una especie o de una población de tal manera que ya no pueden aparearse y evolucionan hasta formar dos especies separadas

**resilience:** describes the ability to recover after a disturbance; the ability to deal with change and move on (187, 225)

    **resiliencia:** describe la capacidad de recuperación después de una perturbación; capacidad de lidiar con el cambio y seguir adelante

**resource:** any necessity of life, such as water, nutrients, light, food, or space (177)

    **recurso:** todo lo necesario para la vida, como agua, nutrientes, luz, alimento o espacio

**response:** specific reaction to a stimulus (871)

    **respuesta:** reacción específica a un estímulo

**restriction enzyme:** enzyme that cuts DNA at a sequence of nucleotides (485)

    **enzima restrictiva:** enzima que corta el ADN en una secuencia de nucleótidos

**retrovirus:** RNA virus that contains RNA as its genetic information (686)

    **retrovirus:** ARN viral cuya información genética está contenida en el ARN

**ribosomal RNA** (rRNA): type of RNA that combines with proteins to form ribosomes (442)

    **ARN ribosomal:** tipo de ARN que se combina con proteínas para formar los ribosomas

**ribosome:** cell organelle consisting of RNA and protein found throughout the cytoplasm in a cell; the site of protein synthesis (250)

    **ribosoma:** orgánulo celular formado por ARN y proteína que se halla en el citoplasma de una célula; lugar donde se sintetizan las proteínas

**RNA** (ribonucleic acid): single-stranded nucleic acid that contains the sugar ribose (440)

    **ácido ribonucleico (ARN):** ácido nucleico de una única hebra que contiene el azúcar ribosa

**RNA polymerase:** enzyme that links together the growing chain of RNA nucleotides during transcription using a DNA strand as a template (443)

    **ARN polimerasa:** enzima que enlaza los nucleótidos de la cadena de ARN en crecimiento durante la transcripción, usando una hebra de ADN como patrón o molde

**rumen:** stomach chamber in cows and related animals in which symbiotic bacteria digest cellulose (844)

    **panza:** cavidad del estómago de las vacas y otros rumiantes en la cual bacterias simbióticas digieren la celulosa

**secondary growth:** type of growth in dicots in which the stems increase in thickness (769)

    **crecimiento secundario:** tipo de crecimiento de las dicotiledóneas en el cual los tallos aumentan su grosor

**secondary succession:** type of succession that occurs in an area that was only partially destroyed by disturbances (183)

    **sucesión secundaria:** tipo de sucesión que ocurre en un área destruida sólo parcialmente por alteraciones

**seed:** plant embryo and a food supply encased in a protective covering (733)

    **semilla:** embrión vegetal y fuente de alimento encerrada en una cubierta protectora

**segregation:** separation of alleles during gamete formation (381)

    **segregación:** separación de los alelos durante la formación de los gametos

**selective breeding:** method of breeding that allows only those organisms with desired characteristics to produce the next generation (506)

    **reproducción selectiva o selección artificial:** método de reproducción que solo permite la producción de una nueva generación a aquellos organismos con características deseadas

**selectively permeable:** property of biological membranes that allows some substances to pass across it while others cannot; also called semipermeable membrane (257)

    **permeabilidad selectiva:** propiedad de las membranas biológicas que permite que algunas sustancias pasen a través de ellas mientras que otras no pueden hacerlo; también llamada membrana semipermeable

**sensory neuron:** type of nerve cell that receives information from sensory receptors and conveys signals to the central nervous system (870)

    **neurona sensorial:** tipo de célula nerviosa que recibe información de los receptores sensoriales y transmite señales al sistema nervioso central

**sex chromosome:** one of two chromosomes that determines an individual's sex (475)

    **cromosoma sexual:** uno de los dos cromosomas que determinan el sexo de un individuo

**sex-linked gene:** gene located on a sex chromosome (477)

    **gen ligado al sexo:** gen situado en un cromosoma sexual

**sexual reproduction:** type of reproduction in which cells from two parents unite to form the first cell of a new organism (23, 341)

    **reproducción sexual:** tipo de reproducción en la cual las células de dos progenitores se unen para formar la primera célula de un nuevo organismo

**sexual selection:** the selection of mates based on heritable traits (590)

    **selección sexual:** selección de pareja con base en sus rasgos heredables

**single-gene trait:** trait controlled by one gene that has two alleles (583)

    **rasgo de un único gen (monogénico):** rasgo controlado por un gen que tiene dos alelos

**smog:** gray-brown haze formed by a mixture of chemicals (215)

**esmog:** neblina marrón grisácea formada por una mezcla de compuestos químicos

**society:** group of closely related animals of the same species that work together for the benefit of the group (826)

**sociedad:** grupo de animales de la misma especie, estrechamente relacionados, que actúan juntos para el beneficio del grupo

**solute:** substance that is dissolved in a solution (49)

**soluto:** sustancia que está disuelta en una solución

**solution:** type of mixture in which all the components are evenly distributed (49)

**solución:** tipo de mezcla en la cual todos los compuestos están distribuidos de forma homogénea

**solvent:** dissolving substance in a solution (49)

**solvente:** sustancia que disuelve una solución

**speciation:** formation of a new species (592)

**especiación:** formación de una nueva especie

**species:** group of similar organisms that can breed and produce fertile offspring (79)

**especie:** un grupo de organismos similares que pueden reproducirse y producir una descendencia fértil

**species diversity:** number of different species that make up a particular area (186)

**diversidad de especies:** número de especies diferentes que forman un área determinada

**sporangium:** spore capsule in which haploid spores are produced by meiosis (730)

**esporangio:** cápsula en la cual se producen las esporas haploides mediante meiosis

**sporophyte:** spore-producing plant; the multicellular diploid phase of a plant life cycle (725)

**esporofito:** planta productora de esporas; la fase diploide multicelular del ciclo vital de una planta

**stabilizing selection:** form of natural selection in which individuals near the center of a distribution curve have higher fitness than individuals at either end of the curve (587)

**selección estabilizadora:** forma de selección natural en la cual los individuos situados cerca del centro de una curva de distribución tienen mayor aptitud que los individuos que se hallan en cualquiera de los extremos de la curva

**stem cell:** unspecialized cell that can give rise to one or more types of specialized cells (357)

**célula troncal:** célula no especializada que puede originar uno o más tipos de células especializadas

**stimulus** (pl, stimuli): signal to which an organism responds (24, 870)

**estímulo:** señal a la cual responde un organismo

**stoma** (pl, stomata): small opening in the epidermis of a plant that allows carbon dioxide, water, and oxygen to diffuse into and out of the leaf (771)

**estoma:** pequeña abertura en la epidermis de una planta que permite que el dióxido de carbono, el agua y el oxígeno entren y salgan de la hoja

**stroma:** fluid portion of the chloroplast; outside of the thylakoids (287)

**estroma:** parte fluida del cloroplasto; en el exterior de los tilacoides

**substrate:** reactant of an enzyme-catalyzed reaction (60)

**sustrato:** reactante de una reacción catalizada por enzimas

**suspension:** mixture of water and non-dissolved material (49)

**suspensión:** mezcla de agua y material no disuelto

**sustainable development:** using resources in ways that preserve ecosystem services (223)

**desarrollo sostenible:** uso de los recursos de forma que conserve los ecosistemas

**symbiosis:** relationship in which two species live close together (181)

**simbiosis:** relación en la que dos especies viven en estrecha asociación

**systematics:** study of the diversity of life and the evolutionary relationships between organisms (613)

**sistemática:** estudio de la diversidad de la vida y de las relaciones evolutivas entre los organismos

**taiga:** biome with long cold winters and a few months of warm weather; dominated by coniferous vergreens; also called boreal forest (96)

**taiga:** bioma con inviernos largos y fríos y pocos meses de tiempo cálido; dominado por coníferas de hojas perennes; también llamada bosque boreal

**taproot:** the primary root found in some plants that grows longer and thicker than the other roots (765)

**raíz primaria:** en las plantas, la gran raíz principal

**target cell:** cell that has a receptor for a particular hormone (776)

**célula diana o célula blanco:** célula que posee un receptor para una hormona determinada

**taxon** (pl. taxa): group or level of organization into which organisms are classified (613)

**taxón:** grupo o nivel de organización en que se clasifican los organismos

**taxonomy:** system of naming and classifying organisms based on shared characteristics and universal rules (612)

    **taxonomía:** sistema de clasificación y nomenclatura de los organismos con base en características compartidas y reglas universales

**telomere:** repetitive DNA at the end of a eukaryotic chromosome (426)

    **telómero:** ADN repetitivo situado al extremo de un cromosoma eucariota

**telophase:** phase of mitosis in which the distinct individual chromosomes begin to spread out into a tangle of chromatin (347)

    **telofase:** fase de la mitosis en la cual los distintos cromosomas individuales comienzan a separarse en una maraña de cromatina

**temporal isolation:** form of reproductive isolation in which two or more species reproduce at different times (593)

    **aislamiento temporal:** forma de aislamiento reproductivo en la cual dos o más especies se reproducen en épocas diferentes

**tetrad:** structure containing four chromatids that forms during meiosis (394)

    **tétrada:** estructura con cuatro cromátidas que se forma durante la meiosis

**tetrapod:** vertebrate with four limbs (812)

    **tetrápode:** vertebrado con cuatro extremidades

**thylakoid:** saclike photosynthetic membranes found in chloroplasts (287)

    **tilacoide:** membranas fotosintéticas con forma de bolsa situadas en los cloroplastos

**theory:** well-tested explanation that unifies a broad range of observations and hypotheses, enabling scientists to make accurate predictions about new situations (14)

    **teoría:** explicación bien probada que unifica un amplio rango de observaciones e hipótesis y permite a los científicos hacer predicciones precisas sobre nuevas situaciones

**thigmotropism:** response of plant to touch (780)

    **tigmotropismo:** respuesta de una planta al tacto

**tissue:** group of similar cells that perform a particular function (268)

    **tejido:** grupo de células similares que realizan una función en particular

**tolerance:** ability of an organism to survive and reproduce under circumstances that differ from its optimal conditions (174)

    **tolerancia:** capacidad de un organismo de sobrevivir y reproducirse en circunstancias que difieren de sus condiciones óptimas

**totipotent:** cells that are able to develop into any type of cell found in the body (including the cells that make up the extra-embryonic membranes and placenta) (357)

    **totipotentes:** células capaces de convertirse en cualquier tipo de célula del cuerpo (incluidas las células que forman las membranas situadas fuera del embrión y la placenta)

**tracheid:** hollow plant cell in xylem with thick cell walls strengthened by lignin (731)

    **traqueida:** célula vegetal ahuecada del xilema con paredes celulares gruesas, fortalecida por la lignina

**tracheophyte:** vascular plant (731)

    **traqueófita:** planta vascular

**trait:** specific characteristic of an individual (379)

    **rasgo:** característica específica de un individuo

**transcription:** synthesis of an RNA molecule from a DNA template (443)

    **transcripción:** síntesis de una molécula de ARN a partir de un patrón o molde de ADN

**transfer RNA** (tRNA): type of RNA that carries each amino acid to a ribosome during protein synthesis (442)

    **ARN de transferencia:** tipo de ARN que transporta a cada aminoácido hasta un ribosoma durante la síntesis de proteínas

**transformation:** process in which one strain of bacteria is changed by a gene or genes from another strain of bacteria (413)

    **transformación:** proceso en el cual una cepa de bacterias es transformada por uno o más genes provenientes de otra cepa de bacterias

**transgenic:** term used to refer to an organism that contains genes from other organisms (514)

    **transgénico:** término utilizado para referirse a un organismo que contiene genes provenientes de otros organismos

**translation:** process by which the sequence of bases of mRNA is converted into the sequence of amino acids of a protein (447)

    **traducción (genética):** proceso por el cual la secuencia de bases de un ARN mensajero se convierte en la secuencia de aminoácidos de una proteína

**transpiration:** loss of water from a plant through its leaves (771)

    **transpiración:** pérdida del agua de una planta a través de sus hojas

**trophic level:** each step in a food chain or food web (121)

    **nivel trófico:** cada paso en una cadena o red alimenticia

**tropism:** movement of a plant toward or away from stimuli (780)

    **tropismo:** movimiento de una planta hacia los estímulos o en dirección opuesta a ellos

**tumor:** mass of rapidly dividing cells that can damage surrounding tissue (353)

**tumor:** masa de células que se dividen rápidamente y pueden dañar al tejido circundante

**understory:** layer in a rain forest found underneath the canopy; formed by shorter trees and vines (93)

**sotobosque:** en un bosque tropical, la capa de vegetación que se halla bajo el dosel forestal, formada por árboles más bajos y enredaderas

**vaccine:** preparation of weakened or killed pathogens used to produce immunity to a disease (695)

**vacuna:** preparación hecha con organismos patógenos debilitados o muertos que se utiliza para producir inmunidad a una enfermedad

**vacuole:** cell organelle that stores materials such as water, salts, protein, and carbohydrates (252)

**vacuola:** orgánulo celular que almacena sustancias como agua, sales, proteínas e hidratos de carbono

**van der Waals force:** slight attraction that develops between oppositely charged regions of nearby molecules (46)

**fuerza de van der Waals:** atracción leve que se desarrolla entre las regiones con cargas opuestas de moléculas cercanas

**vascular bundle:** cluster of xylem and phloem tissue in stems (768)

**hacecillo vascular:** manojo de tejidos del xilema y del floema en los tallos

**vascular tissue:** specialized tissue in plants that carries water and nutrients (729)

**tejido vascular:** tejido especializado de las plantas que transporta agua y nutrientes

**vegetative reproduction:** method of asexual reproduction in plants, that enables a single plant to produce offspring that are genetically identical to itself (746)

**reproducción vegetativa:** método de reproducción asexual de las plantas que permite que una única planta produzca descendencia genéticamente idéntica a sí misma

**ventricle:** lower chamber of the heart that pumps blood out of the heart to the rest of the body (851)

**ventrículo:** cavidad inferior del corazón que bombea la sangre fuera del corazón hacia el resto del cuerpo

**vertebrate:** animal that has a backbone (800)

**vertebrado:** animal que posee una columna vertebral

**vestigial structure:** structure that is inherited from ancestors but which has lost much or all of its original function (564)

**estructura vestigial:** estructura heredada de los ancestros que ha perdido gran parte o por completo su función original

**virus:** particle made of protein, nucleic acids, and sometimes lipids that can replicate only by infecting living cells (682)

**virus:** partícula compuesta por proteínas, ácidos nucleicos y, a veces, lípidos, que puede replicarse sólo infectando células vivas

**weather:** day-to-day conditions of the atmosphere, including temperature, precipitation, and other factors (85)

**tiempo:** condiciones diarias de la atmósfera, entre las que se incluyen la temperatura, la precipitación y otros factores

**wetland:** ecosystem in which water either covers the soil or is present at or near the surface at least part of the year (100)

**humedal:** ecosistema en el cual el agua cubre el suelo o está presente cerca de la superficie durante al menos una parte del año

**xylem:** vascular tissue that carries water upward from the roots to every part of a plant (731)

**xilema:** tejido vascular que transporta el agua hacia arriba, desde las raíces a cada parte de una planta

**zygote:** fertilized egg (804)

**cigoto:** huevo fertilizado

# INDEX

*Note:* Page numbers in **bold** refer to definitions.

# INDEX

# INDEX

# INDEX

# INDEX

# INDEX

External fertilization, 883
External regulatory proteins, 351
Extinction
    adaptation and, 652–653
    atmospheric oxygen and, 662
    background, 654
    climate change and, 91
    hunting and, 214
    from invasive species, 214
    at the K-T boundary, 670–671
    limiting factors and, 157
    mass extinctions, 91, 654, 656, 670–671
    patterns of, 654
    Permian, 656
Extinct species, **642**–643, 652–654
Eyes, 816, 874–875

# F

$F_1$ crosses, 381–382, 384–387
$F_2$ crosses, 387
Facilitated diffusion, **261**–263
FAD/FADH$_2$, 316–319
Fallopian tube, 934
Family, in classification, **614**
Farmers, 529
Fats, 310, 912, 919
Fatty acids, 55
Feathers, 814, 891
Feces, 843, 857, 910, 912
Feedback inhibition, **801, 907**–908, 932
Female reproductive system, 934–936
Fermentation, **321**–325, 327, 330–331, 694
Ferns, 726, 731–733
Fertilization, **379**
    in animals, 882–883
    cyclin and, 352
    double, 744–745
    in humans, 935
    in plants, 379, 725, 732, 735–736, 744–745
    runoff, as pollution, 230
Fertilizers, 130–133, 136–137, 743, 751, 786
Fetus, 936
Fibrinogen, 918
Fibrous roots, **765**
Fight or flight reaction, 925
Filter feeders, 840, 841

Fingers, 816
Fins, 811
"Fishapod," 813
Fishes
    bony, 812–813, 884
    care of offspring, 886
    circulatory systems, 850, 851
    cladogram of, 810
    as ectotherms, 890
    excretion, 854–855
    jawless, 811
    mercury pollution and, 217
    reproduction, 881, 883, 884
    respiration, 846, 884
    sense organs, 875
Fishing, 214, 227
Fitness, **556**–557
Fixed joints, 927
Flagella (singular: flagellum), 253, 664–665, 691, **700,** 881
Flatworms, 803, 808–809, 846, 872, 874
Fleming, Alexander, 579
Flint, Michigan drinking water, 903, 945
Flooding, ocean, 201
Floral meristems, 764
Flowcharts, as models, 20
Flowering plants. *See* Angiosperms
Flowers, 658, 737, 739, 740–742, 765
Fluid mosaic model, 257
Fluorescence, 510, 526–527
Fluorescence imaging, 253
Fluorescent dyes, 244
Flu virus, 683, 687, 697
Follicles, 934
Follicle stimulating hormone (FSH), 933, 934
Food
    carbohydrates, 53, 126, 257, 320
    chemical energy in, 310–311, 320
    composition of, 311
    eating locally, 789
    fats, 310, 912, 919
    fermentation of, 322–323, 326–327, 330–331
    flammability of, 314
    genetically modified, 505, 516, 518, 525–526, 528–529
    proteins, 842
    from rooftop gardens, 792–793
    sustainably produced, 829

Food chains, **118,** 120
Food safety inspectors, 429
Food scientists, 63
Food webs, **118**–120
"Foolish seedling" disease, 779
Forensics, **522**
Forensics Lab, 416, 523
Forests, 94, 96, 126, 210–211
Fossil fuels, 208–209, 216, 217, 225
Fossil preparators, 667
Fossil record, 642–651
    biological forces and, 651
    dating Earth's history, 561, 644–645
    evidence of ancient life, 642–643
    extinct organisms in, 547, 670–671
    gaps in, 561
    geologic time scale, 646–648
    on hominine evolution, 818–820
    plant evolution, 723, 726, 727, 731, 733–734
    plate tectonics and, 649–650
    rates of evolution, 655–656
    speciation and extinction, 652–654
    trace fossils, 807
Fossils, **547,** 642–644, 667, 670
Fossil series, 561–562
Founder effect, **589,** 594, 656
Frameshift mutations, **458**
Franklin, Rosalind, 420, 423
Freely movable joints, 927
Frogs, 81
Fronds, 732
Fruiting body, **705**
Fruits, 747–748
FSH (follicle stimulating hormone), 933, 934
Fukushima radioactive material release, 63
Fuller, Buckminster, 204
Fungi (singular: fungus), 704–709
    animal diseases from, 707
    in bioremediation, 274–275
    characteristics of, 704–705
    diversity of, 706
    in the environment, 707
    human uses of, 709
    in lichens, 708
    mutualism by, 709
    in mycorrhizae, 709
    parasitism in, 707–708

# INDEX

# INDEX

# INDEX

# INDEX

# INDEX

# INDEX

## INFOGRAPHIC

**82, 84, 85, 87, 88, 90, 91, 104, 109, 124, 125, 127, 129, 135, 140, 145, 153, 159, 169, 193, 207, 208, 213, 214, 219, 229, 233:** Adapted from the *Understanding Global Change* Infographic, © University of California Museum of Paleontology, Berkeley.

## TEXT

### Chapter 01

*"Community Analysis and Feedback"*—Adapted from Understanding Evolution, University of California Museum of Paleontology. Reprinted by permission.

*"Benefits and Outcomes"*—Adapted from Understanding Evolution, University of California Museum of Paleontology. Reprinted by permission.

*"Community Analysis and Feedback Detail"*—Adapted from Understanding Evolution, University of California Museum of Paleontology. Reprinted by permission.

*"Exploration and Discovery"*—Adapted from Understanding Evolution, University of California Museum of Paleontology. Reprinted by permission.

*"The Process of Science"*— Adapted from Understanding Evolution, University of California Museum of Paleontology. Reprinted by permission.

*"Benefits and Outcomes Detail"*— Adapted from Understanding Evolution, University of California Museum of Paleontology. Reprinted by permission.

### Chapter 06

*"AS6 Primary Succession Graph"* by Mark Harmon, Ph.D. Andrews Experimental Forest. Oregon State University. Reprinted by permission.

### Chapter 17

*"Evolution in Action"*: Data Analysis. Copyright © by HHMI BioInteractive. Reprinted by permission.

### Unit 1

*"Solar Still Made of Bubble Wrap Could Purify Water for the Poor"*. Copyright © AAAS. Reprinted with permission.

### Unit 2

*"To Tame a 'Wave' of Invasive Bugs, Park Service Introduces Predator Beetles"*. Copyright © 2016 National Public Radio, Inc. Excerpts from NPR news report "To Tame A 'Wave' Of Invasive Bugs, Park Service Introduces Predator Beetles" as originally broadcast on NPR's Morning Edition on June 2, 2016 and is used with the permission of NPR. Any unauthorized duplication is strictly prohibited.

### Unit 3

*"Gold rush for algae"* by Amanda Leigh Mascarelli. Reprinted by permission from Macmillan Publishers Ltd: Nature Vol. 461, pp. **460–461**. Copyright © 2009.

### Unit 4

Perelman School of Medicine at the University of Pennsylvania. *"Genes essential to life found in mouse mutants are related to many human disease genes." ScienceDaily.* ScienceDaily, 16 September 2016.

### Unit 5

*"Tiktaalik's Internal Anatomy explains evolutionary shift from water to land"*. Copyright © 2008 by The University of Chicago Chronicle. Reprinted by permission.

### Unit 6

*"Walnut trees may not be able to withstand climate change"*. Copyright © by Purdue University. Reprinted with permission.

### Photographs

Photo locators denoted as follows: Top (T), Center (C), Bottom (B), Left (L), Right (R), Background (Bkgd)

### Covers

**Front Cover**: Honeybee and yellow flower: Anatolii/Fotolia
**Background**: ftotti1984/Fotolia
**Back Cover**: Western honeybee: Daniel Prudek/Shutterstock
**Spine**: Western honeybee: Daniel Prudek/Shutterstock

### Front Matter

**iii** (T) Kenneth Miller; **iii** (B) Joe Levine; **xiii** T Science Source; **xiii** B Bence Mate/Nature Picture Library; **xiv** T Bernard Friel/Danita Delimont Photography/Newscom; **xiv** B Andy Rouse/Nature Picture Library; **xv** T Visual China Group/Getty Images; **xv** C Chase Dekker Wild-Life Images/Moment/Getty Images; **xv** B Joe Raedle/Staff/Getty Images; **xvi** T Steve Gschmeissner/Science Source; **xvi** B Soner Bakir/Alamy Stock Photo; **xvii** T Professor Pietro M. Motta/Science Source; **xvii** B Eric Cohen/Science Source; **xviii** T Zuzule/iStock/Getty Images; **xviii** B Brian J. Skerry/National Geographic/Getty Images; **xix** T Image Broker/Alamy Stock Photo; **xix** C Franckreporter/E+/Getty Images; **xix** B Roger Bacon/Reuters/Alamy Stock Photo; **xx** T Buddy Mays/Corbis Documentary/Getty Images; **xx** B SPL/Science Source; **xxi** T RosaIreneBetancourt 10/Alamy Stock Photo; **xxi** B Science History Images/Alamy Stock Photo; **xxii** T Humeau Guy/Alamy Stock Photo; **xxii** B Michele and Tom Grimm/Alamy Stock Photo; **xxiii** T Ozgurdonmaz/Istock/Getty Images; **xxiii** C Pascal Kobeh/Nature Picture Library; **xxiii** B JREden/iStock/Getty Images; **xxiv** T Education Images/UIG/Getty Images; **xxiv** B Hero images/Getty images; **xxvi** Aiseeeit/E+/Getty Images; **xxvii–xxix** Bkgd Jon Bilous/Alamy Stock Photo; **xxx** Bkgd Mliberra/Shutterstock, Maksim Kabakou/Shutterstock, T Irin-k/Shutterstock, BL Slavko Sereda, BR Kenneth Miller; **001** Bkgd Mliberra/Shutterstock, Maksim Kabakou/Shutterstock, T Kokhanchikov/Shutterstock, B Joe Levine

### Chapter 01

**006–007** Science Source; **008** John Cancalosi/Nature Picture Library; **009TL** Michael Nichols/National Geographic/Getty Images; **009TR** Mark Edward Atkinson/Tracey Lee/Blend Images/Getty Images; **009B** Pete Mcbride/National Geographic Creative/Alamy Stock Photo; **010–011** Claude Balcaen/Biosphoto/Getty Images; **012** Steve Woods Photography/Cultura RM/Alamy Stock Photo; **013** Kjersti/Fotolia; **015** Kristopher Grunert/Corbis/VCG/Getty Images; **016** Stockbroker/MBI/Alamy Stock Photo; **017** Iakov Filimonov/Shutterstock; **018T** Skynesher/E+/Getty Images; **018B** Lauree Feldman/Photolibrary/Getty Images; **019** Monkey Business Images/iStock/Getty Images; **021T** Will&Deni Mcintyre/Science Source/Getty Images; **021C** Science Photo Library—PASIEKA/Brand X Pictures/Getty Images; **021B** 3drenderings/Shutterstock; **022** NIBSC/Science Source; **023** Stanley45/E+/Getty Images; **024T** Igor Stevanovic/Alamy Stock Photo; **024B** Jonathan Larsen/Diadem Images/Alamy Stock Photo; **025T** Aaali/Fotolia; **025C** Andersphoto/Fotolia; **025B** M88/Fotolia; **027CL** Andrew Brookes/Cultura/Getty Images; **027CR** Mediaphotos/IStock/Getty Images; **027L** Suzanne Long/Alamy Stock Photo; **027R** TEK Image/SPL/Getty Images; **028** Oli Scarff/Getty Images; **029T** Raul Gonzalez Perez/Science Source; **029B** ERproductions Ltd/Blend Images/Alamy Stock Photo; **030** Sabza/Shutterstock; **030–031** NorGal/Shutterstock; **031T** YinYang/iStock/Getty Images; **031B** Goodluz/Panther Media GmbH/Alamy Stock Photo; **034–035** Tim Masters/Shutterstock; **036** Oli Scarff/Getty Images;

### Chapter 02

**040–041** Bence Mate/Nature Picture Library; **042** Oliveromg/Shutterstock; **044T** Alfred Pasieka/Science Source; **044B(a)** Gareth Boden/Savvas Learning Company; **044B(b)** By Ian Miles-Flashpoint Pictures/Alamy Stock Photo; **044B(c)** Levent Konuk/Shutterstock; **046L** Andrew Syred/Science Source; **046C** Natural Visions/Alamy Stock Photo; **046R** Martin Harvey/Corbis Documentary/Getty Images; **047** Kristina Vackova/Shutterstock; **048T** Blickwinkel/Derder/Alamy Stock Photo; **048C(a)** Chip Clark/Fundamental Photographs; **48C(b)** Kavram/Shutterstock; **048B** Raisa Kanareva/Shutterstock; **050T(a)** Nano/iStock/Getty Images; **050T(b)** Milosluz/iStock/Getty Images; **050T(d)** Noam Armonn/iStock/Getty Images; **050(c)** S-F/Shutterstock; **050B** Kesu/Shutterstock; **052** Biophoto Associates/Science Source; **053** Stevecuk/Fotolia; **054** Valentyn Volkov/Shutterstock; **056** Nastenok/Shutterstock; **058** Alexey Stiop/Shutterstock; **059** Yeko Photo Studio/Shutterstock; **061** Javier Larrea/Pixtal/Age Fotostock; **062–063** Mark Waugh/Alamy Stock Photo; **063T** Kyodo/AP Images; **063B** Monika Wisniewska/123RF; **066–067** Gabriella Kemeny/EyeEm/Getty Images;

### Chapter 03

**076–077** Bernard Friel/Danita Delimont Photography/Newscom; **078** JSC/NASA; **079{a}** Tim Graham/Getty Images; **079{b}** Efimova Anna/Shutterstock; **079{c}** Nik Wheeler/Alamy Stock Photo; **079{d}** Dmitri Kessel/The LIFE Picture Collection/Getty Images; **079{e}** Planetary Visions Ltd/Science Source; **079{f}** NASA; **080** David Hay Jones/Science Source; **082TL** Pakhnyushchy/Shutterstock; **082TR** Szefei/Shutterstock; **082BL** Irabel8/Shutterstock; **082BR** Jim Lopes/Shutterstock; **083** Swedewah/E+/Getty Images; **085** DeepDesertPhoto/RooM/Getty Images; **090T** Xingmin07/E+/Getty Images; **090B** Pakhnyushchy/Shutterstock; **092** Eric Gevaert/Shutterstock; **093** Gary Yim/Shutterstock; **094T** Stefan Auth/ImageBROKER/Alamy Stock Photo; **094C** Sam Dcruz/Shutterstock; **094B** Irina Mos/Shutterstock; **095T** Turtix/Shutterstock; **095C** Chris Wallace/Alamy Stock Photo; **095B** Sehit/Fotolia; **096T** Candice Cusack/E+/Getty Images; **096C** Bill Brooks/Alamy Stock Photo; **096B** Ron Niebrugge/Alamy Stock Photo; **097** Sergey Uryadnikov/Shutterstock; **099** Rich Carey/Shutterstock; **100T** Mishella/Shutterstock; **100C** Clement Philippe/Arterra Picture Library/Alamy Stock Photo; **100B** Maximilian Weinzierl/Alamy Stock Photo; **101** Shannon Matteson/Shutterstock; **102–103** Ian Dagnall/Alamy Stock Photo; **103T** Khlongwangchao/iStock/Getty Images; **103B** Andrey Popov/Fotolia; **106–107** Tim Roberts Photography/Shutterstock; **108TL** Szefei/Shutterstock; **108TR** Pakhnyushchy/Shutterstock; **108BL** Irabel8/Shutterstock; **108BR** Jim Lopes/Shutterstock;

### Chapter 04

**112–113** Andy Rouse/Nature Picture Library; **114** Hero Images/Getty Images; **115L** Photo_master2000/Shutterstock; **115R** Dr Ken Macdonald/Science Photo Library/Getty Images; **116BCGRD** Will & Deni McIntyre/The Image Bank/Getty Images; **116TL** Kevin Schafer/Photolibrary/Getty Images; **116TR** Anna Yu/Alamy Stock Photo; **116C** Roy Toft/National Geographic/Getty Images; **116CL** Carol Farneti-Foster/Oxford Scientific/Getty Images; **116CR** Courtesy of Project Amazonas(www.projectamazonas.org); **116B** MJ

Prototype/Shutterstock; **118** Bill Draker/Rolf Nussbaumer Photography/Alamy Stock Photo; **121** Mimagephotography/Shutterstock; **123** Polarpx/Shutterstock; **128** NASA; **132** John Walsh/Science Source; **124{A}** Joel Sartore/National Geographic/Getty Images; **124{B}** Image Source/Getty Images; **124{C}** Francesco Ruggeri/Photographer's Choice/Getty Images; **124{D}** NASA; **124{E}** EpicStockMedia/Shutterstock; **124{F}** Derrick Neill/Fotolia; **124{G}** Stephen Mcsweeny/Shutterstock; **124{H}** Keith Wood/Corbis/Getty Images; **126** AustralianCamera/iStock/Getty Images; **132–133** EPA European Pressphoto Agency b.v./Alamy Stock Photo; **133T** Michael Layefsky/Moment/Getty Images; **133B** AdShooter/E+/Getty Images; **134TL** Kevin Schafer/Photolibrary/Getty Images; **134TR** Photo_master2000/Shutterstock; **134BL** Anna Yu/Alamy Stock Photo; **134BR** MJ Prototype/Shutterstock; **136–137** Biophoto Associates/Science Source;

**Chapter 05**
**142–143** Visual China Group/Getty Images; **144** Superjoseph/Fotolia; **146L** Wouter Pattyn/Buiten-Beeld/Alamy Stock Photo; **146C** Juniors Bildarchiv GmbH/Alamy Stock Photo; **146R** Reinhard Dirscherl/Alamy Stock Photo; **148** Vitchanan Photography/Shutterstock; **149T** SCIMAT/Science Source; **149B** Csharrard/iStock/Getty Images; **151** Daryl Balfour/Gallo Images/Alamy Stock Photo; **152** 1084712/Shutterstock; **153T** Mircea Costina/Alamy Stock Photo; **153B** Tewan Banditrukkanka/Shutterstock; **154** ZUMA Press Inc/Alamy Stock; **155** Layne Kennedy/Corbis Documentary/Getty Images; **156** Ashley Cooper pics/Alamy Stock Photo; **157** Popperfoto/Getty Images; **158** Luciano Mortula/Shutterstock; **162–163** Top Photo Corporation/Alamy Stock Photo; **163T** Pictorial Press Ltd/Alamy Stock Photo; **163B** Rocketclips/Fotolia; **164T** Ashley Cooper pics/Alamy Stock Photo; **164BL** Mircea Costina/Alamy Stock Photo; **164BR** Tewan Banditrukkanka/Shutterstock; **166–167** Chris Titze/123RF;

**Chapter 06**
**172–173** Chase Dekker Wild-Life Images/Moment/Getty Images; **174** Brian Lasenby/Fotolia; **179** Tom & Pat Leeson/a/Mary Evans Picture Library Ltd/Age Fotostock; **181** Magnusdeepbelow/Shutterstock; **182** Mike Lyvers/Moment Open/Getty images; **184** Adam Crowley/Blend Images/Alamy Stock Photo; **185** Ulet Ifansasti/Stringer/Getty Images; **186** Vlad61/Shutterstock; **187** Epa European Pressphoto Agency b.v./Alamy Stock Photo; **188** Clement Philippe/Arterra Picture Library/Alamy Stock Photo; **189{A}** Joe Vogan/Alamy Stock Photo; **189{B}** Robert67/iStock/Getty Images; **189{C}** Burnyipotok/iStock/Getty Images; **189{D}** David Tipling/Stockbyte/Getty Images; **189{E}** Gerard Soury/Photodisc/Getty Images; **189{F}** Gary Crabbe/Alamy Stock Photo; **189{G}** Thailand Wildlife/Alamy Stock Photo; **190–191** Jason Maehl/Moment Open/Getty Images; **191T** Martin Grosnick/ardea/Mary Evans Picture Library Ltd/Age Fotostock; **191B** ImageBROKER/Alamy Stock Photo; **192** Michael S. Nolan/Age fotostock; **194–195** Robert C. Paulson/Alamy Stock Photo; **196T** A/Fotolia; **196TC** Eduard Kyslynskyy/Shutterstock; **196B** Richard A McMillin/Shutterstock; **196BC** 123RF; **197** Joe Restuccia III/Danita Delimont/Alamy Stock Photo;

**Chapter 07**
**200–201** Joe Raedle/Staff/Getty Images; **202** Diego Mariottini/EyeEm/Getty Images; **203** Hero Images/Getty Images; **206** Jjwithers/iStock Unreleased/Getty Images; **208** Joop Hoek/Fotolia; **209BCGRD** Fred Bahurlet/EyeEm/Getty Images; **209T** Haveseen/Fotolia; **209BL** Iceink/Shutterstock; **209BR** Alexander Semenov/Science Source; **211** Chris Patterson; **212T** NOAA photo courtesy Vera Trainer; **212B** Diego Mariottini/EyeEm/Getty Images; **213** Sue Cunningham Photographic/Alamy Stock Photo; **214T** Tom Stoddart/Reportage Archive/Getty Images; **214B** Gaertner/Alamy Stock Photo; **215T** Greg Shirah/NASA Goddard Spac/NASA; **215B** Kyodo/AP Images; **218** Ragnar Th Sigurdsson/Arctic Images/Alamy Stock Photo; **219** Thatree Thitivongvaroon/Moment/Getty Images; **220** Ondřej Prosický/123RF; **221** Adam Burton/Robertharding/Getty Images; **222** Tier Und Naturfotografie J und C Sohns/Photographer's Choice/Getty Images; **223T** Hero Images/Getty Images; **223B{A}** 4Max/Shutterstock; **223B{B}** Larry Lilac/Alamy Stock Photo; **223B{C}** Mariusz Blach/Fotolia; **224** Xinhua/Alamy Stock Photo; **225** Lalomartinez/iStock/Getty Images; **226–227** JodiJacobson/iStock/Getty Images; **227T** Haitao Zhang/Moment/Getty Images; **227B** Christian Science Monitor/Contributor/Getty Images; **230** NPS Photo/Alamy Stock Photo; **230–231** Beth Gao/Shutterstock; **231B** Florida Images/Alamy Stock Photo; **233** Gaertner/Alamy Stock Photo;

**Chapter 08**
**240–241** Steve Gschmeissner/Science Source; **242** The Print Collector/Alamy Stock Phot; **243TL** Akg-images/Newscom; **243TR** World History Archive/Alamy Stock Photo; **243C** Grafissimo/E+/Getty Images; **243B** Biophoto Associates/Science Source; **244** Vshyukova/Fotolia; **245L** Michael Abbey/Science Source; **245C** Dr. Gopal Murti/Science Source; **245R** Scimat/Science Source; **248** Vladimir Salman/Shutterstock; **252L** Mary Martin/Biophoto Associates/Science Source; **252R** Eric Grave/Science Source; **253T** Dr. Torsten Wittmann/Science Source; **253B** Peter Satir/Science Source; **254** Biophoto Associates/Science Source; **255** Nancy R. Schiff/Getty Images; **256** Steve Gschmeissner/Science Source; **257** Sololos/iStock/Getty Images; **260** Big Face/Fotolia; **265** Biophoto Associates/Science Source; **266** Steve Gschmeissner/SPL/Getty Images; **267T** Jose Luis Calvo/Shutterstock; **270–271** Degree/eStock Photo/Alamy Stock Photo; **271T** Nevodka/123RF; **271B** Greenshoots Communications/NCP Images/Alamy Stock Photo; **267B** Biophoto Associates/Science Source; **269** David M. Phillips/Science Source; **274–275** Danny E Hooks/Shutterstock; **275** Eye of Science/Science Source; **276** Scimat/Science Source;

**Chapter 09**
**280–281** Soner Bakir/Alamy Stock Photo; **282** Birdiegal/Shutterstock; **284** Wavebreak Media ltd/Alamy Stock Photo; **285** Brian E. Kushner/Moment/Getty Images; **286** Tawee Wongdee/Shutterstock; **287T** Atoss/Fotolia; **287B** Alanphillips/E+/Getty Images; **289** Andrew Lambert Photography/Science Source; **291** Shihina/123RF; **292** Artens/Shutterstock; **296** Arto Hakola/Alamy Stock Photo; **297** You Touch Pix of EuToch/Shutterstock; **298–299** Bo Valentino/Alamy Stock Photo; **299T** Deanne Fitzmaurice/National Geographic Creative; **299B** Kali9/E+/Getty Images; **301** You Touch Pix of EuToch/Shutterstock; **302–303** Yuriy Kulik/Shutterstock; **302B** Cathleen A Clapper/Shutterstock; **304** Science Source/Getty Images; **306** MattoMatteo/iStock/Getty Images;

**Chapter 10**
**308–309** Professor Pietro M. Motta/Science Source; **310** Sumos/Fotolia; **314** Steve Muscatello/The Journal of New Ulm/AP Images; **321** Danita Delimont/Gallo Images/Getty Images; **323T** Marek/Fotolia; **323B** D. Winters/Science Source; **324** Tim Tadder/Corbis/Getty Images; **325** Bjanka Kadic/Alamy Stock Photo; **326** Mediscan/Alamy Stock Photo; **326–327BKGD** AlexPro9500/iStock/Getty Images; **327T** Hank Morgan/RGB Ventures/SuperStock/Alamy Stock Photo; **327B** WavebreakmediaMicro/Fotolia; **330–331** Wavebreak Media Ltd/123Rf; **331** Givaga/Alamy Stock Photo;

**Chapter 11**
**336–337** Eric Cohen/Science Source; **338** BirdImages/E+/Getty Images; **339** Poelzer Wolfgang/Alamy Stock Photo; **341L** Dr. Tony Brain/Science Source; **341C** M. I. Walker/Science Source; **341R** Warayoo/Fotolia; **342** NHPA/Superstock; **343** Carolina K. Smith MD/Shutterstock; **348L** Dr. Gopal Murti/Science Source; **348R** Ed Reschke/Oxford Scientific/Getty Images; **349BC** Ed Reschke/Photolibrary/Getty Images; **349TC** Ed Reschke/Photolibrary/Getty Images; **349TL** Ed Reschke/Photolibrary/Getty Images; **349TR** Ed Reschke/Photolibrary/Getty Images; **349BL** Ed Reschke/Photolibrary/Getty Images; **349BR** Ed Reschke/Photolibrary/Getty Images; **350** Ryan A. Denu/Univ. of Wisconsin Carbone Cancer Center/National Cancer Institute; **351L** Jim Craigmyle/First Light/Getty Images; **351R** Scott Camazine/Science Source; **354L** Sebastian Gauert/Shutterstock; **354R** Moredun Animal Health Ltd/Science Photo Library/Newscom; **355T** D.P. Wilson/FLPA/Science Source; **355BC** M. I. Walker/Science Source; **355BL** Last Refuge/Robertharding/Alamy Stock Photo; **355BR** Garry DeLong/Science Source; **357** Choksawatdikorn/Shutterstock; **358L** Steve Gschmeissner/Science Photo Library/Getty Images; **358CL** Steve Gschmeissner/Science Source; **358CR** Steve Gschmeissner/Science Photo Library/Getty Images; **358R** Steve Gschmeissner/Science Source; **360** Rick Wood/Rapport Press/Newscom; **362** Milkovasa/Fotolia; **362–363** Dr Jan Schmoranzer/Science Photo Library/Getty Images; **363T** John Chadwick/AP Images; **363B** National Park Service; **364** Ed Reschke/Oxford Scientific/Getty Images; **366–367** Inga Spence/Alamy Stock Photo;

**Chapter 12**
**376–377** Zuzule/iStock/Getty Images; **378L** FloralImages/Alamy Stock Photo; **378R** Photo Researchers, Inc/Alamy Stock Photo; **383** Peppi/Panther Media GmbH/Alamy Stock Photo; **385** Flowerphotos/Alamy Stock Photo; **388** Studiotouch/Shutterstock; **389** Mb-fotos/Stock/Getty Images; **390CL** Petro Perutskyi/Alamy Stock Photo; **390CR** Michaela Rehle/Reuters/Alamy Stock Photo; **392L** Robert Shantz/Alamy Stock Photo; **390BL** Huetter, C./Picture alliance/Arco Images G/Newscom; **390BR** Arco/G. Lacz/Arco Images GmbH/Alamy Stock Photo; **392R** Alvin E. Staffan/Science Source; **393** Stargazer/Shutterstock; **396** Thomas Barwick/Lconica/Getty Images; **398L** J Kottmann/Blickwinkel/Age Fotostock; **398TC** Solvin Zankl/Nature Picture Library; **398TR** Hermann Eisenbeiss/Science Source; **398BC** Alfred Schauhuber/ImageBROKER/Alamy Stock Photo; **398BR** Steve Hopkin/Ardea/Mary Evans Picture Library Ltd/Age Fotostock; **400** Alexander Raths/Shutterstock; **400–401** Jessie M Niedens; **401T** SPL/Science Source; **401B** Fernando Salazar/MCT/Newscom; **404–405** Leon Rafael/Shutterstock; **407** RyersonClark/iStock/Getty Images;

**Chapter 13**
**410–411** Brian J. Skerry/National Geographic/Getty Images; **412** Rudmer Zwerver/Shutterstock; **414** Eye of Science/Science Source; **415** Pictures From History/Newscom; **416** Jim Weber/The Commercial Appeal/AP Images; **418** lukasx/Fotolia; **420L** Jewish Chronicle/Heritage Image Partnership Ltd/Alamy Stock Photo; **420R** Omikron/Science Source; **421L** A. Barrington Brown/Science Source; **421C** Photo Researchers, Inc/Alamy Stock Photo; **424** Philippe Garo/Science Source; **425** Dr. Gopal Murti/Science Photo Library/Getty Images; **426T** Los Alamos National Laboratory/The LIFE Images Collection/Getty Images; **426B** Moodboard/Alamy Stock Photo; **428–429** Vlada Z/Fotolia; **429T** Houin/BSIP SA / Alamy Stock Photo; **429B** Michael J. Ermarth/ZUMA Press/Newscom; **432–433** Razvan Ionut Dragomirescu/Alamy Stock Photo; **434** Science Source;

**Chapter 14**
**438–439** Image Broker/Alamy Stock Photo; **440** Bilgesu Korkmaz/EyeEm/Getty Images; **442** FatCamera/E+/Getty Images; **445** Ronstik/iStock/Getty Images; **442** Blend Images/Hill Street Studios/Getty Images; **450** Micheline Pelletier/Corbis/Getty Images; **451T** Joseph Shields/Photographer's Choice/Getty Images; **451B** Steve Gschmeissner/Science Source; **455** Stanley45/E+/Getty Images; **457** Einar Muoni/Alamy Stock Photo; **459** Stockbroker/MBI/Alamy Stock Photo; **460** Paul Bradbury/OJO Images Ltd/Alamy Stock Photo; **461L** Ian Thraves/Alamy Stock Photo; **461R** Serge Vero/Alamy Stock Photo; **462** Gilaxia/

E+/Getty Images; **462–463** Glowimages/Getty Images; **463T** Steve Gschmeissner/Science Source; **463B** BreatheFitness/E+/Getty Images;

**Chapter 15**
**472–473** Franckreporter/E+/Getty Images; **474** Caiaimage/Robert Daly/OJO+/Getty Images; **475** Biophoto Associates/Science Source/Getty Images; **476** Bartomeu Amengual/Pixtal/AGE Fotostock; **477L** Ewelina Kowalska/Alamy Stock Photo; **477R** Hans Reinhard/Science Source; **478** Tim Macpherson/Cultura Creative (RF)/Alamy Stock Photo; **480** Science Source; **481** Leonard Lessin/Science Source; **483** SPL/Science Source; **485** Tek Image/Science Source; **489** Philippe Garo/Science Source; **490BCGRND** Blickwinkel/Hartl/Alamy Stock Photo; **490{A}** Blickwinkel/Hartl/Alamy Stock Photo; **490{B}** CloseImages/iStock/Getty Images; **490{C}** Bartomeu Amengual/Pixtal/AGE Fotostock; **490{D}** R. Richter/Tierfotoagentur/Alamy Stock Photo; **490{E}** Charlotta Fredriksson/Alamy Stock Photo; **490{F}** WaterFrame_mza/WaterFrame/Alamy Stock Photo; **490{G}** Vladimir Wrangel/Shutterstock; **490{H}** Dr Jeremy Burgess/Science Photo Library/Getty Images; **490{I}** Mediscan/Alamy Stock Photo; **492L** Madiz/iStock/Getty Images; **492R** Science Source; **494–495** Stockbroker/MBI/Alamy Stock Photo; **494** Alfred Pasieka/Science Source; **495T** Tek Image/Science Source; **495B** Viktor Cap/Alamy Stock Photo; **496** Leonard Lessin/Science Source; **498–499** David Bank/Moment/Getty Images; **499** Bob Thomas/Popperfoto/Getty Images;

**Chapter 16**
**504–505** Roger Bacon/Reuters/Alamy Stock Photo; **506** Cynoclub/Shutterstock; **507** Stevecuk/Fotolia; **508** Ian 2010/Fotolia; **509** Science Photo Library—Tek Image/Brand X Pictures/Getty Images; **516** Nigel Cattlin/Alamy Stock Photo; **517** Reuters/Alamy Stock Photo; **518** Erik De Castro/Reuters/Alamy Stock Photo; **519L** Victor Moriyama/Stringer/Getty Images; **519R** Sinclair Stammers/Science Source; **520** Deco/Alamy Stock Photo; **522** Monica Wells/Alamy Stock Photo; **523** Martin Shields/Alamy Stock Photo; **524** Chutima Chaochaiya/Shutterstock; **526** FoodPhotography/Alamy Stock Photo; **527** Ted Kinsman/Science Source; **528–529** ImagineGolf/E+/Getty Images; **528** ZUMA Press Inc/Alamy Stock Photo; **529T** AKG images/Newscom; **529B** Dusan Kostic/Fotolia; **532L** Marcy Nighswander/AP Images; **532R** Alfred Pasieka/Science Source; **533L** Courtesy of Migdalia Q. Gelsinger; **533R** Patrick Kovarik/Staff/AFP/Getty Images;

**Chapter 17**
**542–543** Buddy Mays/Corbis Documentary/Getty Images; **544L** Science Source; **544R** Science Source; **545** Jess Kraft/Shutterstock; **546L** AfriPics/Alamy Stock Photo; **546R** Robybenzi/Shutterstock; **547T** Jele/Shutterstock; **547B** CarolineTolsma/Shutterstock; **548** The Natural History Museum/Alamy Stock Photo; **549T** Pia Marina Meerstedt/EyeEm/Getty Images; **549B** The Natural History Museum/Alamy Stock Photo; **551T** Roger Ressmeyer/Corbis/VCG/Getty Images; **551C** Larry Geddis/Alamy Stock Photo; **551B** Eachat/iStock/Getty Images; **552** Westend61/Getty Images; **553T** Snark/Art Resource, NY; **553B** Rilueda/iStock/Getty Images Plus; **554T** Portrait of Pouter Pigeon (coloured engraving), Wolsenholme, D. (fl.1862)/Down House, Kent, UK/Bridgeman Images; **554BL** Portrait of a Carrier Pigeon (coloured engraving), Wolsenholme, D. (fl.1862)/Down House, Kent, UK/Bridgeman Images; **554BR** Portrait of a Beard Pigeon (coloured engraving), Wolsenholme, D. (fl.1862)/Down House, Kent, UK/Bridgeman Images; **555** Joe Petersburger/National Geographic Creative/Alamy Stock Photo; **558L** Jack Jeffrey/Photo Resource Hawaii/Alamy Stock Photo; **558R** Jack Jeffrey/Photo Resource Hawaii/Alamy Stock Photo; **559** LETZ/SIPA/Newscom; **560** Peter Scoones/The Image Bank/Getty Images; **561** Juergen Ritterbach/Alamy Stock Photo; **564** Auscape/Universal Images Group/Getty Images; **565** Tom Stewart/Corbis/Getty Images; **568–569** JH Pete Carmichael/The Image Bank/Getty Images; **569T** Piumatti Sergio/Prisma Bildagentur AG/Alamy Stock Photo; **569B** Barry Lewis/Alamy Stock Photo; **570L** AfriPics/Alamy Stock Photo; **570R** Portrait of Pouter Pigeon (coloured engraving), Wolsenholme, D. (fl.1862)/Down House, Kent, UK/Bridgeman Images; **572–573** Angela Drake/Alamy Stock Photo; **574** Westend61/Getty Images;

**Chapter 18**
**578–579** SPL/Science Source; **580** Blickwinkel/Bellmann/Alamy Stock Photo; **582T** Michael Charles/Alamy Stock Photo; **582C** Science Source; **582B** Jalala/iStock/Getty Images; **583** Premaphotos/Alamy Stock Photo; **584** Rare Book Division or Print Collection/New York Public Library; **585** B Brown/Shutterstock; **586** Robert Shantz/Alamy Stock Photo; **588** B. Von Hoffmann/ClassicStock/Alamy Stock Photo; **590L** Jack Nevitt/Shutterstock; **590R** Arco Images GmbH/Alamy Stock Photo; **591** Nature and Science/Alamy Stock Photo; **592** Prasit_Chansareekorn/iStock/Getty Images; **593** Adrian Warren/ardea/Mary Evans Picture Library Ltd/Age Fotostock; **596** Michel Boks/EyeEm/Getty Images; **600–601** Ian Cuming/Alamy Stock Photo; **601T** Don Despain/Alamy Stock Photo; **601B** Sigrid Gombert/MITO Images/Getty Images; **604–605** Bill Barksdale/Design Pics/Getty Images;

**Chapter 19**
**610–611** RosalreneBetancourt 10/Alamy Stock Photo; **612** Don Johnston/Alamy Stock Photo; **613TL** Alexey/Fotolia; **613TC** Ger Bosma/Alamy Stock Photo; **613TR** Peter Turner Photography/Shutterstock; **613BL** Anette Holmberg/Shutterstock; **613BC** Monkey Business/Alamy Stock Photo; **613BR** Jamsedel/Shutterstock; **615L** Richard Waters/Shutterstock; **615C** Flpa/Alamy Stock Photo; **615R** Taveart/Shutterstock; **616L** Balashova Ekaterina/Shutterstock; **616C** SKY2015/Shutterstock; **616R** Matthew Ward/Dorling Kindersley/Getty Images; **617TL** Scimat/Science Source; **617TC** Blickwinkel/Fox/Alamy Stock Photo; **617TR** David C. Phillips/Garden Photo World/Alloy/Getty Images; **617BL** Eye of Science/Science Source; **617BC** Aleksas Kvedoras/Fotolia; **617BR** Sergey Skleznev/Fotolia; **619** McPhoto/Blickwinkel/Age Fotostock; **621TL** Audrey Snider-Bell/Shutterstock; **621TC** Martin Harvey/Alamy Stock Photo; **621BR** Blickwinkel/Layer/Alamy Stock Photo; **623T** Unspotdesign Fotografia Digital/Age Fotostock; **623B** Gaertner/Alamy Stock Photo; **624TL** Nic van Oudtshoorn/Alamy Stock Photo; **624TR** Birds and Dragons/Shutterstock; **624B** Joël Behr/Fotolia; **625TL** Amadeusamse/iStock /Getty Images Plus/Getty Images; **625TR** Anette Holmberg/Shutterstock; **625CL** Iourii/Fotolia; **625CR** W. Layer/McPHOTO/Blickwinkel/Age Fotostock; **628** MBI/Alamy Stock Photo; **629** Figure courtesy of David M. Hillis, Derrick Zwickl, and Robin Gutell, University of Texas at Austin.; **630–631BKGD** Dave Watts/naturepl/Alamy Stock Photo; **631T** Laguna Design/Science Photo Library/Getty Images; **631B** Blend Images/Superstock; **632TL** Martin Harvey/Alamy Stock Photo; **632TR** Blickwinkel/Layer/Alamy Stock Photo; **632BR** Audrey Snider-Bell/Shutterstock; **634–635** Tomas Kotouc/Shutterstock; **636TL** David C. Phillips/Garden Photo World/Alloy/Getty Images; **636TR** Aleksas Kvedoras/Fotolia; **636BL** Blickwinkel/Fox/Alamy Stock Photo; **636BR** Sergey Skleznev/Fotolia; **637** Justin Lewis/DigitalVision/Getty Images;

**Chapter 20**
**640–641** Science History Images/Alamy Stock Photo; **642** John Cancalosi/Alamy Stock Photo; **643** Jason Edwards/National Geographic/Getty Images; **646** Chase Studio/Science Source; **650T** Homebrew Films Company/Gallo Images/Getty Images; **650BL** Norbert Probst/imageBROKER/Alamy Stock Photo; **650BC** Homebrew Films Company/Gallo Images/Getty Images; **650BR** Homebrew Films Company/Gallo Images/Getty Images; **651** Sinclair Stammers/Science Source; **652** Global_Pics/iStock/Getty Images; **653** Pascal Goetgheluck/Science Source; **656{A}** David Steele/Shutterstock; **656{B}** Johner Images/Alamy Stock Photo; **656{C}** Ondrej Prosicky/Shutterstock; **656{D}** Berndt Fischer/Age Fotostock/Alamy Stock Photo; **656{E}** Duncan Noakes/Fotolia; **656{F}** Nicolas Larento/Fotolia; **656{G}** Anne/Fotolia; **657TL** Kajornyot/iStock/Getty Images; **657TR** Richard & Susan Day/DanitaDelimont/Alamy Stock Photo; **657BL** James Laurie./Shutterstock; **657BR** Age Fotostock/Superstock; **658** Scott Camazine/Science Source; **659** Ammit/Alamy Stock Photo; **662** Xenomanes/Fotolia; **664** Science Photo Library—Heather Davies/Brand X Pictures/Getty Images; **665** Ammit/Alamy Stock Photo; **666** Ralf-Finn Hestoft/Corbis/Getty Images; **666–667** Corbin17/Alamy Stock Photo; **667T** D. Roberts/Science Source; **667B** Dirk Wiersma/Science Source; **668** Martin Shields/Alamy Stock Photo; **669** Xenomanes/Fotolia; **670–671** Ted Soqui/Corbis/Getty Images; **672** Gabrielle & Michel Therin-Weise/Robertharding/Alamy Stock Photo;

**Chapter 21**
**680–681** Humeau Guy/Alamy Stock Photo; **680A** Humeau Guy/Alamy Stock Photo; **682** Nigel Cattlin/Alamy Stock Photo; **683** Biozentrum, University of Basel/Science Source; **683C** Science Source; **683R** James Cavallini/Science Source; **689** Ca-ssis/iStock/Getty Images; **690** Lynn Y/Shutterstock; **691** Juergen Berger/Science Source; **691C** S. Lowry/Univ Ulster/The Image Bank/Getty Images; **691L** Eye of Science/Science Source; **692C** CNRI/Science Source; **692L** CNRI/Science Source; **692R** Dr. L. Caro/Science Source; **693B** Dan Guravich/Science Source; **693T** Claire Ting/Science Source; **698** Imagine China/Newscom; **702B** Steven Trainoff Ph.D./Moment Open/Getty Images; **702C** Martin Strmiska/Alamy Stock Photo; **702T** Richard Mittleman/Gon2Foto/Alamy Stock Photo; **703B** Eye of Science/Science Source; **703L** CDC/JANICE Carr/BSIP SA/Alamy Stock Photo; **703R** Eye of Science/Science Source; **704B** Blickwinkel/Hecker/Alamy Stock Photo; **704T** Iarigan - Patricia Hamilton/Moment Open/Getty Images; **705** John Swithinbank/Alamy Stock Photo; **706** Premierlight Images/Alamy Stock Photo; **708L** Inga Spence/Science Source; **708R** John Watney/Photo Researchers, Inc/Alamy Stock Photo; **709** Albertus Engbers/123RF; **710** Cynthia Goldsmith/CDC; **710–711** Khlungcenter/Shutterstock; **711B** David Dobbs/Alamy Stock Photo; **711T** Staff/MCT/Newscom; **712** CNRI/Science Source; **714–15** Dieu Nalio Chery/AP Images

**Chapter 22**
**720-721** Michele and Tom Grimm/Alamy Stock Photo; **720A** Michele and Tom Grimm/Alamy Stock Photo; **722** Adventure_Photo/iStock/Getty Images; **723L** The Natural History Museum/Alamy Stock Photo; **723R** Universal Images Group North America LLC/DeAgostini/Alamy Stock Photo; **724–725** Bill Wight/Photolibrary/Getty Images; **724a** Blickwinkel/Guenther/Alamy Stock Photo; **724b** Freedom Man/Shutterstock; **724c** StuartDuncanSmith/E+/Getty Images; **724d** Srekap/Shutterstock; **724e** Claudio Divizia/Zoonar/Alamy Stock Photo; **726** LeoPatrizi/E+/Getty Images; **727BL** Chase Studio/Science Source; **727BR** Chase Studio/Science Source; **727T** Yattiworld/Moment/Getty Images; **729L** Perennou Nuridsany/Science Source; **729R** Roland Birke/Photolibrary/Getty Images; **731** Mark Bolton Photography/Alamy Stock Photo; **732** Blickwinkel/Jagel/Alamy Stock Photo; **733** Photocrea/Shutterstock; **734a** Radka Palenikova/Shutterstock; **734b** Kristian Peetz/Age Fotostock; **734c** Naturefolio/Alamy Stock Photo; **734d** Manfred Dietsch/CHROMORANGE/Alamy Stock Photo; **734e** Susumu Nishinaga/Science Source; **734f** Peter Chadwick/Dorling Kindersley Limited; **734g** Cheryl Power/Science Source; **734h** Chushkin/Stock/Getty Images; **734i** Brian Ormerod Photographer/Alamy Stock Photo; **735** Rvo233/Stock/Getty Images; **737** Olga Lipatova/Zoonar/Alamy Stock Photo; **738a** Custom Life Science Images/Alamy Stock Photo; **738b** Blickwinkel/Baesemann/Alamy Stock Photo; **738c** Alesikka/Shutterstock; **738d** Nick Kurzenko/Alamy Stock Photo; **738e** G_Hanke/ImageBROKER/Alamy Stock Photo; **739C** Paulfjs/iStock/Getty Images; **739L** Island Images/Alamy Stock Photo; **739R** Mama_mia/Shutterstock; **741** Biophoto Associates/Science Source; **742** Solarisys/Shutterstock; **742BL** Giancesare Guidi/EyeEm/Getty Images; **742BR** Blickwinkel/Fieber/Alamy Stock Photo; **742TC** Simon Marlow/EyeEm/Getty Images; **742TR** Labrador Photo Video/Shutterstock; **744TL** Blickwinkel/Kottmann/Alamy Stock Photo; **744TR** Darlyne A. Murawski/National Geographic/Getty Images; **746** Charles Harker/Moment Open/Getty Images; **746BL** Inacio Pires/Shutterstock; **746BR** Wacharaphong/iStock/Getty Images; **746TC** P&R Fotos/Age fotostock/Alamy Stock Photo; **746TL** Dorling Kindersley Universal Images

Group/Newscom; **746TR** Peter Van Rhijn/All Canada Photos/Alamy Stock Photo; **747BL** Bergamont/Shutterstock; **747BR** Deenida/Shutterstock; **747C** Anna Kucherova/Shutterstock; **747TL** Rolf Klebsattel/Shutterstock; **747TR** Leonid Nyshko/Alamy Stock Photo; **748BL** Jhorrocks/iStock/Getty Images; **748BR** IanRedding/Shutterstock; **748TL** John Devries/Science Source; **748TR** BrianAJackson/iStock/Getty Images Plus; **750** Baxternator/iStock/Getty Images; **750–751** James P. Blair/National Geographic/Getty Images; **751B** PeopleImages/DigitalVision/Getty Images; **751T** Chelovek/iStock/Getty Images; **754–755** Soru Epotok/Shutterstock; **754B** Protasov AN/Shutterstock; **756a** Blickwinkel/Guenther/Alamy Stock Photo; **756b** Freedom Man/Shutterstock; **756c** StuartDuncanSmith/E+/Getty Images; **756d** Srekap/Shutterstock; **756e** Claudio Divizia/Zoonar/Alamy Stock Photo; **757** Domnicky/iStock/Getty Images

**Chapter 23**
**760–761** Ozgurdonmaz/Istock/Getty Images; **762** Jeep2499/Shutterstock; **762A** Ozgurdonmaz/Istock/Getty Images; **763** Dr. Keith Wheeler/Science Source; **764B** Biology Pics/Science Source; **764T** Ed Reschke/Photolibrary/Getty Images; **765L** Richard Griffin/123RF; **765R** Tim Gainey/Alamy Stock Photo; **768** Science Stock Photography/Science Source; **771** Igor Zh/Shutterstock; **772** Ed Reschke/Photolibrary/Getty Images; **773** Itsik Marom/Alamy Stock Photo; **774** Savvas Learning Company; **776** Igor Stevanovic/Alamy Stock Photo; **778L** Adam Gryko/Shutterstock; **778R** Anastasia_Panait/Shutterstock; **779** Photo Researchers, Inc/Alamy Stock Photo; **781B** Francesco Tomasinelli/Science Source; **781T** Bill Lea/Dembinsky Photo Associates/Alamy Stock Photo; **783B** Argument/iStock/Getty Images; **783T** Mina Doroudi Photography/Moment/Getty Images; **784** Iakov Filimonov/Shutterstock; **785** Ingram Publishing/Newscom; **786** Science Photo/Shutterstock; **786B** Science Photo/Shutterstock; **786T** Oli Scarff/Staff/Getty Images; **787C** Arts Vector/Shutterstock; **787L** Hill Street Studios/Blend Images/Alamy Stock Photo; **787R** Dean Drobot/Shutterstock; **788** Pkanchana/iStock/Getty Images; **788–789** Antpkr/iStock/Getty Images; **789B** Moodboard/Brand X Pictures/Getty Images; **789T** Valentinrussanov/E+/Getty Images; **792–793** Michel Setboun/Corbis Documentary/Getty Images

**Chapter 24**
**798–799** Pascal Kobeh/Nature Picture Library; **798A** Pascal Kobeh/Nature Picture Library; **800** Mohd Zaidi Razak/Alamy Stock Photo; **801** Kant Liang/EyeEm/Getty Images; **802** Besjunior/iStock/Getty Images; **804** Tcareob72/Shutterstock; **805** Sam Yue/Alamy Stock Photo; **806** Oleg Znamenskiy/Shutterstock; **809a** Seaphotoart/Shutterstock; **809b** Ksenija Ok/Shutterstock; **809c** Vivek Gour-Broome/Ephotocorp/Alamy Stock Photo; **809d** Scott Camazine/Science Source; **809e** CK Ma/Shutterstock; **809f** Reinhard Dirscherl/WaterFrame/Getty Images; **809g** Andrey Nekrasov/Alamy Stock Photo; **809h** Seaphotoart/Shutterstock; **811B** Sergey Uryadnikov/Shutterstock; **811CL** KINA/Bertus Webbink/Newscom; **811CR** Todelete/Blickwinkel/Alamy Stock Photo; **811T** Mark Conlin/Alamy Stock Photo; **812BL** Peter Scoones/Science Source; **812BR** Michael Patrick O'Neill/Alamy Stock Photo; **812T** London Taxidermy/Alamy Stock Photo; **813BL** Education Images/Universal Images Group/Getty Images; **813BR** Danté Fenolio/Science Source; **813T** Christina Rollo/Alamy Stock Photo; **815C** Tier Und Naturfotografie J und C Sohns/Photographer's Choice RF/Getty Images; **815L** Frank Lukasseck/Photographer's Choice/Getty Images; **815R** Frank Sommariva/ImageBroker/Alamy Stock Photo; **816** Per-Andre Hoffmann/Look/Age Fotostock; **819L** Euan Denholm/Reuters/Alamy Stock Photo; **819R** Sabena Jane Blackbird/Alamy Stock Photo; **822** Poul Riishede/Shutterstock; **823B** Joel Zatz/Alamy Stock Photo; **823TL** Natalia Zakhartseva/Alamy Stock Photo; **823TR** Millard H Sharp/Science Source/Getty Images; **824B** Marie Read/Science Source; **824T** GK Hart/Vikki Hart/Stone/Getty Images; **825B** Bickwinkel/McPhoto/W. Rolfes/Alamy Stock Photo; **825T** Steve Jones/Stocktrek Images/Getty Images; **826L** The Africa Image Library/Alamy Stock Photo; **826R** Lehrer/Shutterstock; **827** Lehrer/Shutterstock; **827a** Norbert Probst/ImageBroker/Alamy Stock Photo; **827b** Allgord/Istock/Getty Images; **827c** Morley Read/Alamy Stock Photo; **827d** Milles Studio/Shutterstock; **828–829** Andrew Thirlwell/Alamy Stock Photo; **828–829** Rainer von Brandis/iStock/Getty Images; **828TL** Rainer von Brandis/iStock/Getty Images; **829B** Apic/Hulton Archive/Getty Images; **829T** Maskot/Getty Images; **832–833** Skyward Kick Productions/Shutterstock; **834** LiiS Pesur/Foap/Getty Images; **835** Joe Vogan/Alamy Stock Photo

**Chapter 25**
**838–839** JREden/iStock/Getty Images; **838A** JREden/iStock/Getty Images; **840** Reinhard Dirscherl/Alamy Stock Photo; **841** Laura Dinraths/Shutterstock; **841** Patila/Shutterstock; **841B** Theo Allofs/Corbis Documentary/Getty Images; **841TL** Tim Rock/WaterFrame/Age Fotostock; **844** Tina Gadiot/EyeEm/Getty Images; **845** Barry Brown/Danita Delimont/Alamy Stock Photo; **849** Steve Allen/Science Photo Library/Getty Images; **851** Asiseeit/E+/Getty Images; **852** Darlyne A. Murawski/National Geographic Magazines/Getty Images; **852** Vusta/E+/Getty Images; **853** Agency Animal Picture/Photographer's Choice RF/Getty Images; **857** Patagonian Stock AE/Shutterstock; **858–859** QiuJu Song/Shutterstock; **859B** 123ducu/iStock/Getty Images; **859T** Peter Noyce Gens/Alamy Stock Photo; **862–863** John Coletti/The Image Bank/Getty Images; **864** Pal Teravagimov Photography/Moment/Getty Images

**Chapter 26**
**868–869** Education Images/UIG/Getty Images; **868A** Education Images/UIG/Getty Images; **870** Petra Wallner/Image Broker/Alamy Stock Photo; **871** Aditya Singh/Moment/Getty Images; **872** Jorgen Jessen/Epa/Newscom; **874C** Scenics & Science/Alamy Stock Photo; **874L** iStock/Getty Images; **874R** kavcicm/iStock/Getty Images; **875BL** Karine Aigner/National Geographic/Getty Images; **875BR** Simon Marlow/EyeEm/Getty images; **875T** Owen Newman/Nature Photographers Ltd/Alamy Stock Photo; **876** F. Rauschenbach/F1online digitale Bildagentur GmbH/Alamy Stock Photo; **877** George Grall/National Geographic Creative/Alamy Stock Photo; **877** Images & Stories/Alamy Stock Photo; **877** Vinicius Tupinamba/Shutterstock; **878** Oyvind Martinsen Wildlife Collection/Alamy Stock Photo; **880** Lorraine Bennery/Nature Picture Library; **881** WaterFrame/Alamy Stock Photo; **883** Reinhard Dirscherl/Alamy Stock Photo; **884B** Arco Images GmbH/G. Lacz/Alamy Stock Photo; **884C** Paulo Oliveira/Alamy Stock Photo; **884T** Nature Picture Library/Jose B. Ruiz/Alamy Stock Photo; **888** Rick & Nora Bowers/Alamy Stock Photo; **889** Darknesss/Shutterstock; **889B** Ian Shaw/Alamy Stock Photo; **889T** SPL/Science Source; **890L** Martin Harvey/Alamy Stock Photo; **890R** David Cantrille/Alamy Stock Photo; **892** Blickwinkel/Eckstein/Alamy Stock Photo; **892–893** STR/AFP/Getty Images; **893B** Hero Images Inc./Alamy Stock Photo; **893T** Michael Svoboda/Vetta/Getty Images; **895** Darknesss/Shutterstock; **896–897** Jagadeesh NV/EPA/Newscom

**Chapter 27**
**902–903** Hero Images/Getty images; **902A** Hero Images/Getty images; **904** Dennis MacDonald/PhotoEdit; **905CL** Kateryna Kon/Shutterstock; **905CR** Steve Gschmeissner/Science Source; **905L** Image Source/Getty Images; **905R** Steve Gschmeissner/Science Photo Library/Getty Images; **908** CLS Digital Arts/Shutterstock; **908** Greg Ceo/The Image Bank/Getty Images; **910** Image Source/Dreampictures/Alamy Stock Photo; **911B** Steve Gschmeissner/Science Source; **911T** Gastrolab/Science Source; **917B** TongRo Images/Alamy Stock Photo; **917T** Steve Gschmeissner/Science Photo Library/Getty Images; **918** David M. Phillips/Science Source; **920** Stockyimages/123RF; **923** Rolfo/Moment/Getty Images; **927** Dominique Douieb/PhotoAlto/Alamy Stock Photo; **933** Dr Clifford Barnes, University of Ulster/Science Source; **936** Du Cane Medical Imaging Ltd/Science Photo Library/Getty Images; **937** KidStock/Blend Images/Getty Images; **938** Kyodo News/Getty Images; **942B** Mediscan/Alamy Stock Photo; **942T** Barabasa/Shutterstock; **944** Christina Kennedy/Alamy Stock Photo; **944–945** DenisTangneyJr/iStock/Getty Images; **945B** Microgen/Shutterstock; **945T** Asiseeit/E+/Getty Images; **946BL** Steve Gschmeissner/Science Source; **946BR** Steve Gschmeissner/Science Photo Library/Getty Images; **946TL** Image Source/Getty Images; **946TR** Kateryna Kon/Shutterstock; **948–949** Corey Jenkins/Image Source/Alamy Stock Photo; **948B** Muratart/Shutterstock; **948C** Jamesbenet/E+/Getty Images

**End Matter**
**DOL-001**, **DOL-002** Marcella Miriello/Fotolia; **DOL-003TL** Igor Gorelchenkov/Shutterstock; **DOL-003TC** Fotografik/Fotolia; **DOL-003TR** Kevin Snair/Superstock; **DOL-003C** Alessandro Mancini/Alamy Stock Photo; **DOL-003BL** Hjfotos/Fotolia; **DOL-003BR** Juniors Bildarchiv/F300/Alamy Stock Photo; **DOL-050TR** Kelvin Aitken/V&W/Image Quest Marine; **DOL-006T** CNRI/Science Source; **DOL-006B** Science Pictures Ltd./Science Source; **DOL-007TL** Science Source; **DOL-007TR** A. Barry Dowsett/CAMR/Science Source; **DOL-007CL** Microfield Scientific Ltd/Science Source; **DOL-007CR** Microfield Scientific Ltd/Science Source; **DOL-007BL** Michael Abbey/Science Source; **DOL-007BR** Michael Abbey/Science Source; **DOL-008T** Stephen & Donna O'Meara/Science Source; **DOL-008B** Eye of Science/Science Source; **DOL-009T** Eye of Science/Science Source; **DOL-009C** LaiQuocAnh/Shutterstock; **DOL-009B** Eye of Science/Science Source; **DOL-010** M. I. Walker/Science Source; **DOL-011T** Roland Birke/Photolibrary/Getty Images; **DOL-011C** Eye of Science/Science Source; **DOL-011B** Eye of Science/Science Source; **DOL-012CR** Steve Gschmeissner/Science Source; **DOL-012T** Steve Gschmeissner/Science Source; **DOL-012CL** M. I. Walker/Science Source; **DOL-012BL** Joseph Belanger/123RF; **DOL-012BR** Noble Proctor/Science Source; **DOL-013TL** Michael Abbey/Science Source; **DOL-013TR** Eye of Science/Science Source; **DOL-013C** Biophoto Associates/Science Source; **DOL-013B** Pete Atkinson/Balance/Photoshot./Newscom; **DOL-014L** Eric V. Grave/Science Source; **DOL-014R** Eye of Science/Science Source; **DOL-015T** Jennifermazzucco/Stockimo/Alamy Stock Photo; **DOL-015R** Eye of Science/Science Source; **DOL-015L** M. I. Walker/Science Source; **DOL-016T** Mildenmi/Shutterstock; **DOL-016B** Thomas Northcut/Photodisc/Getty Images; **DOL-017L** NorthScape/Alamy Stock Photo; **DOL-017R** FLPA/Alamy Stock Photo; **DOL-018L** Scott Camazine/Science Source; **DOL-018C** I Viewfinder/Shutterstock; **DOL-018R** Thomas Deerinck/NCMIR/Science Source; **DOL-019TR** Biophoto Associates/Science Source; **DOL-019TL** Eye of Science/Science Source; **DOL-019C** Biophoto Associates/Science Source; **DOL-019B** Shunsuke Yamamoto Photography/Photodisc/Getty Images; **DOL-020T** Nelson Sirlin/Shutterstock; **DOL-020B** A. Barry Dowsett/Science Source; **DOL-021T** Dr Jeremy Burgess/Science Source; **DOL-021C** Andrew Syred/Science Source; **DOL-021BL** Paulo Oliveira/Alamy Stock Photo; **DOL-021BR** Nick Upton/Nature Picture Library; **DOL-022T** Olandsfokus/Fotolia; **DOL-022BL** Roger Provins/Alamy Stock Photo; **DOL-022BC** Blickwinkel/Stenner/Alamy Stock Photo; **DOL-022BR** Daniel Vega/AGE Fotostock; **DOL-023L** Slavko Sereda/Shutterstock; **DOL-023(Inset)** Custom Life Science Images/Alamy Stock Photo; **DOL-023C** Dieter Hopf/ImageBroker/Alamy Stock Photo; **DOL-023R** Robert Henno/Alamy Stock Photo; **DOL-024T 123RF**; **DOL-024B** Mike Grandmaison/All Canada Photos/Alamy Stock Photo; **DOL-025T** Tromp Willem van Urk/Alamy Stock Photo; **DOL-025CR** Saruri/Fotolia; **DOL-025CL** Alan and Linda Detrick/Science Source; **DOL-025B** Hoberman Collection/UIG/Getty Images; **DOL-.026** st1909/Fotolia; **DOL-027T** Pavelmidi/iStock/Getty Images; **DOL-027C** Vincent noel/Shutterstock; **DOL-027B** Stefy Morelli/Shutterstock; **DOL-028T** boroda003/iStock/Getty Images Plus; **DOL-028CL** Anne Kitzman/Shutterstock.; **DOL-028C** Mafuta/iStock/Getty Images; **DOL-028CR** Margouillat photo/Shutterstock; **DOL-028B** KirsanovV/iStock/Getty Images Plus; **DOL-029TR** Martin Siepmann/Age Fotostock; **DOL-029TL** Laura Gangi Pond/Shutterstock; **DOL-029CL** Valeriya/iStock/Getty Images Plus; **DOL-029CR** Anton Burakov/Shutterstock; **DOL-029B** Pongsak.pilasjit/Shutterstock; **DOL-030** Jean-Marc Strydom/Fotolia; **DOL_031T** Jez Tryner/Image Quest Marine; **DOL_031BL** Masa Ushioda/Image Quest Marine; **DOL-031BR** Daniel L. Geiger/SNAP/Alamy Stock Photo; **DOL-032T** Alta Oosthuizen/Fotolia; **DOL-032B** Andrew J. Martinez/Science Source; **DOL-033TL** Peter

Parks/Image Quest Marine; **DOL-033TR** Kippy Spilker/Shutterstock; **DOL-033C** Geophoto/Natalia Chervyakova/ImageBROKER/Alamy Stock Photo; **DOL-033B** Pavlo Vakhrushev/Fotolia; **DOL-034T** R_Koopmans/iStock/Getty Images; **DOL-034B** Wildscotphotos/Alamy Stock Photo; **DOL-035T** JustineG/ E+/Getty Images; **DOL-035BR** Andrewburgess/iStock/Getty Images; **DOL-035BL** Blickwinkel/Alamy Stock Photo; **DOL-036T** Hintau Aliaksei/Shutterstock; **036C** Fivespots/Shutterstock; **DOL-036B** GlobalP/iStock/Getty Images; **DOL-037[a]** Juanma Aparicio/Alamy Stock Photo; **DOL-037[b]** Jewo55/Fotolia; **DOL-037[c]** Florian Andronache/Shutterstock; **DOL-DOL-037[d]** Alslutsky/Shutterstock; **DOL-037[e]** Eric Isselee/Shutterstock; **DOL-037[f]** Alex Staroseltsev/Shutterstock; **DOL-037[h]** Vladimirdavydov/Fotolia; **DOL-037[g]** Dani Vincek/Shutterstock; **DOL-037[i]** Potapov Alexander/Shutterstock.; **DOL-037[j]** Luis Louro/Alamy Stock Photo; **DOL-038T** Steve Gschmeissner/Science Source; **DOL-038B** Sinclair Stammers/Science Source; **DOL-039T** RiverNorthPhotography/iStock/Getty Images; **DOL-039B** Volker Steger/Science Source; **DOL-040T** Daniela Dirscherl/WaterFrame/Getty Images; **DOL-040B** Leslie Newman & Andrew Flowers/Science Source; **DOL-041T** Carlos Villoch/Image Quest Marine; **DOL-041C** John Anderson/Fotolia; **DOL-041B** Kuttelvaserova Stuchelova/Shutterstock; **DOL-042** Amanda Cotton/Alamy Stock Photo; **DOL-043TL** Ingvars Birznieks/Shutterstock; **DOL-043TC** Alexander Makarov/123RF; **DOL-043TR** Ernest Manewal/SuperStock/Alamy Stock Photo; **DOL-043B** Roger Steene/Image Quest Marine; **DOL-044TL** Kaj R. Svensson/Science Source; **DOL-044TR** Jez Tryner/Image Quest Marine; **DOL-044B** Andrey Nekrasov/Alamy Stock Photo; **DOL-045TL** Jez Tryner/Image Quest Marine; **DOL-045TR** Michelle Pacitto/Shutterstock.; **DOL-045CL** WaterFrame/Alamy Stock Photo; **DOL-045CR** Joe Dovala/WaterFrame/Getty Images; **DOL-045B** WaterFrame_fur/Alamy Stock Photo; **DOL-046T** Helmut Corneli/ImageBROKER/Alamy Stock Photo; **DOL-046B** Age Fotostock/Superstock; **DOL-047T** Heather Angel/Natural Visions/Alamy Stock Photo; **DOL-047C** WaterFrame_eda/Alamy Stock Photo; **DOL-047B** Levent Konuk/Shutterstock; **DOL-048** Alexander Safonov/Moment Select/Getty Images; **DOL-049T** Peter Batson/Image Quest Marine; **DOL-049C** blickwinkel/Hecker/Alamy Stock photo; **DOL-049B** Blickwinkel/Koenig/Alamy Stock Photo; **DOL-050TL** James Watt/Image Quest Marine; **DOL-050TR** Kelvin Aitken/V&W/Image Quest Marine; **DOL-050C** Eye of Science/Science Source; **DOL-050BL** Mark Doherty/Shutterstock; **DOL-050BR** Filip Nowicki/Fotolia; **DOL-051T** Evok20/Shutterstock; **DOL-051B** Tom McHugh/Science Source; **DOL-052T** Igor Gorelchenkov/Shutterstock; **DOL-052B** Hjfotos/Fotolia; **DOL-053TL** Fotografik/Fotolia; **DOL-053TR** Kevin Snair/Superstock; **DOL-053C** Alessandro Mancini/Alamy Stock Photo; **DOL-053B** Juniors Bildarchiv/F300/Alamy Stock Photo; **DOL-054** Sasint/Fotolia; **DOL-055TR** Karl Shone/DK Images; **DOL-055TL** Erllre/Fotolia; **DOL-055C** Fivespots/Shutterstock; **DOL-055B** Itinerant Lens/Shutterstock; **DOL-056T** Wild Wonders of Europe/Cairns/Nature Picture Library/Alamy Stock Photo; **DOL-056B** Spencer Sutton/Science Source/Getty Images; **DOL-057T** Age Fotostock/Superstock; **DOL-057BL** Blickwinkel/McPHOTO/WEY/Alamy Stock Photo; **DOL-057BR** Bernd Zoller/ImageBroker/Alamy Stock Photo; **DOL-058T** Stephen Mcsweeny/Shutterstock; **DOL-058BL** FomaA/Fotolia; **DOL-058BR** Edurivero/iStock/Getty Images; **DOL-059TL** Stubblefield Photography/Shutterstock.; **DOL-059TR** Cal Vornberger/Alamy Stock Photo; **DOL-059C** G. Mill/Shutterstock; **DOL-059BL** Martha Marks/Shutterstock; **DOL-059BR** Glenn Bartley/Glow Images; **DOL-060** Arco Images/Delpho, M./Alamy Stock Photo; **DOL-061T** Steven David Miller/Nature Picture Library; **DOL-061C** Timothy Craig Lubcke/Shutterstock.; **DOL-061B** Dave Watts/Nature Picture Library; **DOL-062TR** Martin Harvey/Alamy Stock Photo; **DOL-062BL** Liquid Productions, LLC/Shutterstock; **DOL-062BR** Eric Isselee/Shutterstock; **DOL-063TL(Inset)** Jim Clare/Nature Picture Library; **DOL-063TL** Roland Seitre/Nature Picture Library; **DOL-063TR(Inset)** Sean Tilden/Alamy Stock Photo; **DOL-063TR(Inset)** Mogens Trolle/Shutterstock; **DOL-063C** Top-Pics TBK/Alamy Stock Photo; **DOL-063B** Reinhard Dirscherl/Age Fotostock; **DOL-064TL** Matthijs Wetterauw/Shutterstock; **DOL-064TR** Karel Gallas/Shutterstock; **DOL-064C** Lockwood & Dattatri/Nature Picture Library; **DOL-064B(a)** Bob Ascott/Shutterstock.; **DOL-064B(b)** BlueOrange Studio/Shutterstock; **DOL-064B(c)** Stephane Bidouze/Shutterstock; **DOL-064B(d)** Iv Nikolny/Shutterstock; **DOL-064B(e)** Kjersti Joergensen/Shutterstock; **DOL-064B(f)** Prisma/Superstock; **DOL-064B(g)** Steve Bloom Images/Alamy Stock Photo;

## Unit Material

**002–003** Sarmdy/iStock/Getty Images; **003T** Science Source; **003B** Bence Mate/Nature Picture Library; **004** Scott London/Alamy Stock Photo; **004T** Marcus Harrison—outdoors/Alamy Stock Photo; **004B** Fizkes/Shutterstock; **005T** George Ni; **005B** Focal Point/Shutterstock; **072–073BKGD** Carlton Ward/National Geographic/Getty Image; **073(a)** Bernard Friel/ Danita Delimont Photography/Newscom; **073(b)** Andy Rouse/Nature Picture Library; **073(c)** Visual China Group/Getty Images; **073(d)** Chase Dekker Wild-Life Images/Moment/Getty Images; **073(e)** Billy Hustace/Iconica/Getty Images; **074T** Ian Waldie/Staff/Getty Images; **074B** Lunatic67/Fotolia; **075T** Maryann Frazier/Science Source; **075B** Paul Efird/ZUMA Press/Newscom; **236–237BKGD** Biophoto Associates/Science Source; **237(a)** Steve Gschmeissner/Science Source; **237(b)** Soner Bakir/Alamy Stock Photo; **237(c)** Professor Pietro M. Motta/Science Source; **237(d)** Eric Cohen/Science Source; **238** M. I. Walker/Science Source; **238T** DPA Picture Alliance Archive/Alamy Stock Photo; **239TL** Mintra Chumpoosueb/Shutterstock; **239** D.P. Wilson/FLPA/Science Source; **239TR** Michael Abbey/Science Source; **372–373BKGD** Enot-poloskun/E+/Getty Images; **373(a)** Zuzule/iStock/Getty Images; **373(b)** Brian J. Skerry/National Geographic/Getty Images; **373(c)** Image Broker/Alamy Stock Photo; **373(d)** Franckreporter/E+/Getty Images; **373(e)** Roger Bacon/Reuters/Alamy Stock Photo; **374** Miguel Schincariol/AFP/Getty Images; **374T** Luis Domingo/AGE Fotostock/Alamy Stock Photo; **374B** Magdalena Rehova/Alamy Stock Photo; **375** Agencja Fotograficzna Caro/Alamy Stock Photo; **375** Mark Wilson/Getty Images; **375T** Oneo/Shutterstock; **375C** Chuyuss/Shutterstock; **538–539BKGD** Danita Delimont/Gallo Images/Getty Images; **539(a)** Buddy Mays/Corbis Documentary/Getty Images; **539(b)** SPL/Science Source; **539(c)** RosalreneBetancourt 10/Alamy Stock Photo; **540T** Microgen/Shutterstock; **540B** David Herraez/Alamy Stock Photo; **541TL** Sabena Jane Blackbird/Alamy Stock Photo; **541TR** Scigelova/Shutterstock; **541BL** I love photo/Shutterstock; **541BR** Peter Casolino/Alamy Stock Photo; **676–677** Cordier Sylvain/Hemis.fr/Getty Images; **678TR** Accent Alaska.com/Alamy Stock Photo; **678BL** Tom Walker/Alamy Stock Photo; **679CL** Anthony Souffle/NewsTribune/AP Images; **679CR** Paul Kennedy/Alamy Stock Photo; **679TR** Chris Mattison/Alamy Stock Photo;

## Appendix

**A-01** Ammit/Alamy Stock Photo; **A-02** Peter Casolino/Alamy Stock Photo; **A-08** Goodluz/Fotolia; **A-22** Richard Haynes/Savvas Learning Company; **A-36L** Beranger/BSIP SA/Alamy Stock Photo; **A-36R** Kneffel Peter/DPA/ABACA/Newscom; **A-38** Colin Keates/Dorling Kindersley Ltd.; **A-38** Colin Keates/Dorling Kindersley Ltd.; **A-38** Colin Keates/Dorling Kindersley Ltd.; **A-38** Chase Studio/Science Source; **A-38** Dorling Kindersley Ltd.; **A-38** Colin Keates/Dorling Kindersley Ltd.; **A-39** John Cancalosi/Alamy Stock Photo; **A-39** Dorling Kindersley Ltd.; **A-39** Laurie O'Keefe/Science Source; **A-39** Kevin Schafer/Corbis Documentary/Getty Images; **A-39** Jerry LoFaro/Stocktrek Images, Inc./Alamy Stock Photo; **A-39** Christian Jegou/Publiphoto/Science Source; **A-40** John Cancalosi/Photolibrary/Getty Images; **A-40** Kurt Miller/Stocktrek Images/Getty Images; **A-40** Dorling Kindersley Universal Images Group/Newscom; **A-40** John Cancalosi/Photolibrary/Getty Images; **A-40** Blickwinkel/Alamy Stock Photo; **A-40** DEA PICTURE LIBRARY/De Agostini Picture Library/Getty Images; **A-40** The Natural History Museum/Alamy Stock Photo; **A-40** Dimair/Shutterstock; **A-41** Dorling Kindersley Universal Images Group/Newscom; **A-41** Dozier Marc/Hemis/Alamy Stock Photo; **A-41** Dorling Kindersley Ltd.; **A-41** Robert Marien/Corbis/Getty Images; **A-41** Millard H. Sharp/Science Source.